THE BLACKWELL DICTIONARY OF
TWENTIETH-CENTURY
SOCIAL THOUGHT

THE BLACKWELL DICTIONARY OF

TWENTIETH-CENTURY SOCIAL THOUGHT

Editors
WILLIAM OUTHWAITE
TOM BOTTOMORE

Advisory Editors
Ernest Gellner
Robert Nisbet
Alain Touraine

BLACKWELL
Reference

First published 1993

Blackwell Publishers
108 Cowley Road, Oxford OX4 1JF, UK

238 Main Street
Suite 501
Cambridge, Massachusetts 02142, USA

Library of Congress Cataloging in Publication Data
The Blackwell dictionary of twentieth-century social thought/edited by William Outhwaite, Tom Bottomore.
ISBN 0-631-15262-8
1. Social sciences—History—20th century—Encyclopedias.
2. Philosophy—History—20th century—Encyclopedias.
3. Civilization, Modern—20th century—Encyclopedias.
I. Outhwaite, William.   II. Bottomore, T. B.
H41.B53   1992
300′.3—dc20   92-20837   CIP

British Library Cataloguing in Publication Data
A CIP catalogue record for this book is available from the British Library.

Typeset in 9 on 11 pt Ehrhardt
by The Alden Press, Oxford
Printed in Great Britain by The Alden Press, Oxford

This book is printed on acid-free paper.

CONTENTS

PREFACE

A dictionary of twentieth-century social thought must necessarily range very widely, from the social sciences to philosophy, political theories and doctrines, cultural ideas and movements, and to the influence of the natural sciences. In compiling the present work we have tried to encompass this vast field by commissioning entries on three themes: first, the major concepts which figure in social thought; second, the principal schools and movements of thought; and third, those institutions and organizations which have either been important objects of social analysis, or have themselves engendered significant doctrines and ideas.

Much of the dictionary is devoted to particular bodies of thought that have been influential in this century: individual social sciences, philosophical schools, political doctrines, distinctive styles of art and literature. In each of these cases a long general entry is supplemented by other entries which elaborate specific aspects of the ideas and theories involved; thus, for example, the entry on economics is further developed in entries on the diverse schools and concepts which have emerged in economic thought, and similarly the entry on Marxism is complemented by entries on various forms that this body of theory and doctrine has assumed. Indeed, all the major spheres of social thought have developed and proliferated historically, and we have aimed to incorporate this historical aspect, reaching back in many cases to the ideas of earlier centuries.

We have excluded from the main body of the dictionary biographical accounts of individual thinkers because these would often cover much the same ground as other entries on concepts and theories, but we have appended a section of short biographical notes on those people who have made a major contribution to, or had a lasting influence on, social thought. In addition there is a general index providing easy reference to concepts, schools and individual thinkers.

Each entry is followed by a short list of further reading, and there is also a general bibliography at the end of the dictionary which lists all books and articles referred to in the text. The author–date citations in the text generally refer to first editions or first appearances of the works; dates of subsequent editions are given in brackets where applicable.

While each entry is intended to be complete within itself, cross-references to other entries which would illuminate or extend the subject under discussion are signalled by the use of small capitals in the text.

Contributors

Philip Abbott
Wayne State University

Nicholas Abercrombie
Lancaster University

Hugh G. J. Aitken
Amherst College

Martin Albrow
Roehampton Institute, London

David E. Apter
Yale University

Anthony Arblaster
University of Sheffield

David Armstrong
Guy's Hospital, University of London

Giovanni Arrighi
State University of New York at Binghamton

Michael Bacharach
Christ Church, Oxford

Peter Baehr
Memorial University of Newfoundland

Paul Bailey
University of Edinburgh

E. Digby Baltzell
University of Pennsylvania

Lorraine F. Barić
*Information Technology Institute,
University of Salford*

Clive Barker
University of Warwick

Rodney Barker
London School of Economics

Alan Barnard
University of Edinburgh

Michèle Barrett
City University, London

D. J. Bartholomew
London School of Economics

Kaushik Basu
Delhi School of Economics

Patrick Bateson
University of Cambridge

James A. Beckford
University of Warwick

Leonard Beeghley
University of Florida

Reinhard Bendix

Geoffrey Bennington
*School of European Studies,
University of Sussex*

Ted Benton
University of Essex

Henry Bernstein
*Institute for Development Policy and
Management,
University of Manchester*

Christopher J. Berry
University of Glasgow

Roy Bhaskar
Linacre College, Oxford

Michael Billig
Loughborough University

Ken Binmore
University of Michigan

Mildred Blaxter
*School of Economic and Social Studies,
University of East Anglia*

Josef Bleicher
Queen's University, Glasgow

J. Blondel
European University Institute, Florence

Stephan Boehm
University of Graz

Peter J. Boettke
New York University

Tom Bottomore
Professor Emeritus, University of Sussex

Gerhard Botz
Institut für Geschichte,
Universität Salzburg

Raymond Boudon
Groupe d'Etude des Méthodes de l'Analyse
Sociologique, Université de Paris-Sorbonne

Margaret M. Braungart
State University of New York

Richard G. Braungart
Syracuse University

E. A. Brett
Institute of Development Studies,
University of Sussex

Asa Briggs
Sussex

George W. Brown
Royal Holloway and Bedford New College

Rogers Brubaker
University of California, Los Angeles

Hauke Brunkhorst
Institut für Grundlagen der Politik,
Freie Universität Berlin

W. Brus
Wolfson College, Oxford

Alan Bryman
Loughborough University

Tom Burden
Leeds Polytechnic

Colin Campbell
University of York

Tom D. Campbell
Australian National University

Julius Carlebach
Hochschule für Jüdische Studien,
Heidelberg

Allan C. Carlson
Rockford Institute, Illinois

Elwood Carlson
University of South Carolina

Terrell Carver
University of Bristol

Alan Cawson
School of Social Sciences,
University of Sussex

Gérard Chaliand
Paris

Simon Clarke
University of Warwick

Ira J. Cohen
Rutgers University

Selma Jeanne Cohen
New York

David E. Cooper
University of Durham

Lewis A. Coser
Cambridge, Massachusetts

Bernard Crick
Birkbeck College,
University of London

Roger Crisp
St Anne's College,
Oxford

Ian Crowther
Literary Editor,
The Salisbury Review

Fred D'Agostino
University of New England

R. W. Davies
Centre for Russian and East European
Studies, University of Birmingham

Meghnad J. Desai
London School of Economics

Torcuato S. Di Tella
Buenos Aires

Marco Diani
Centre d'Analyse et d'Intervention
Sociologiques, Paris

James Donald
Media Studies,
University of Sussex

François Dubet
Ecole des Hautes Etudes en Science Sociale,
Paris

Bohdan Dziemidok
University of Gdansk

Andrew Edgar
College of Cardiff, University of Wales

S. Eilon
Imperial College of Science and Technology,
London

Peter P. Ekeh
University of Buffalo

Pascal Engel
Centre de Recherche
en Epistémologie, Paris

Helen Fein
Institute for the Study of Genocide,
New York

Joseph V. Femia
School of Politics and Communication Studies,
University of Liverpool

Zsuzsa Ferge
Institute of Sociology and Social Policy,
Eötvos Loránd University, Budapest

Rubem César Fernandes
Instituto de Estudos da Religiao,
Rio de Janeiro

Robert A. Foley
University of Cambridge

Tom Forester
School of Computing and Information
Technology,
Griffith University, Queensland

Murray F. Foss
American Enterprise Institute for Public
Policy Research,
Washington DC

Lawrence Freedman
King's College, London

Christopher Freeman
Science Policy Research Unit,
University of Sussex

R. G. Frey
Bowling Green State University

Diego Gambetta
University of Oxford

David Garland
University of Edinburgh

Ernest Gellner
University of Cambridge

Norman Geras
University of Manchester

Naomi R. Gerstel
Department of Sociology, and Social and
Demographic Research Unit,
University of Amherst

Margaret Gilbert
University of Connecticut, Storrs

Hannes H. Gissurarson
University of Reykjavik

Peter E. Glasner
University of the West of England

Frank Gloversmith
University of Sussex

Jack A. Goldstone
Center for Comparative Research in History,
Society and Culture,
University of California, Davis

Stanislaw Gomulka
London School of Economics

Peter Goodrich
Birkbeck College,
University of London

Robert Grant
University of Glasgow

S. J. D. Green
School of History,
University of Leeds

Roger Griffin
Brooke University, Oxford

David B. Grusky
Stanford University

Anne-Marie Guillemard
Université de Paris IV (Panthéon-Sorbonne)

Peter Gurney
University of Glamorgan

Peter Halfpenny
University of Manchester

John A. Hall
McGill University, Montreal

Charles Hallisey
Committee on the Study of Religion,
Harvard University

Norman Hampson
Emeritus Professor, University of York

Shaun P. Hargreaves Heap
University of East Anglia

Gwyn Harries-Jenkins
University of Hull

Laurence Harris
School of Oriental and African Studies,
University of London

David M. Heer
University of Southern California

Arnold Heertje
Universiteit van Amsterdam

András Hegedüs
Budapest

Adrian Henri
Liverpool

John Heritage
University of California,
Los Angeles

J. H. Hexter
John M. Olin Professor Emeritus of the
History of Freedom, Washington University

Susan Himmelweit
Open University

Barry Hindess
Australian National University

Paul Quentin Hirst
Birkbeck College,
University of London

Barry Holden
University of Reading

Martin Hollis
University of East Anglia

Axel Honneth
Universität Konstanz

Leo Howe
University of Cambridge

T. W. Hutchison
Professor Emeritus,
University of Birmingham

Richard Hyman
Industrial Relations Research Unit,
University of Warwick

Marie Jahoda
Sussex

Hans Joas
John F. Kennedy Institut,
Freie Universität Berlin

Terry Johnson
University of Leicester

Kay Junge
Institute of Sociology,
Justus-Liebig-Universität Giessen

Mary Kaldor
Graduate Institute for Contemporary
European Studies,
University of Sussex

Haider Ali Khan
Graduate School of International Studies,
University of Denver

V. G. Kiernan
Professor Emeritus, University of Edinburgh

Richard Kilminster
University of Leeds

Alden S. Klovdahl
Australian National University

I. S. Kon
Institute of Ethnography and Anthropology,
Academy of Russia, Moscow

Krishan Kumar
University of Kent at Canterbury

Jorge Larrain
University of Birmingham

Gerhard Lenski
University of North Carolina

Charles T. Lindholm
Boston University

Alain Lipietz
Centre d'Etudes Prospectives d'Economie Mathématique Appliquées à la Planification, Paris

Peter Lloyd
University of Sussex

Eero Loone
University of Tartu, Estonia

Alfred Louch
Claremont Graduate School, California

Terry Lovell
University of Warwick

Steven Lukes
European University Institute, Florence

Francis P. McHugh
St Edmund's College, University of Cambridge

John Spencer Madden
The Countess of Chester Hospital, Chester

Michel Maffesoli
Université de Paris V (René Descartes)

Peter T. Manicas
University of Hawaii at Manoa

Patrice Mann
University of Bordeaux

Peter Marsh
MCM Research

David A. Martin
London School of Economics

Ali A. Mazrui
State University of New York at Binghamton

Ulrike Meinhof
University of Manchester

Volker Meja
Memorial University of Newfoundland

J. G. Merquior

Ian Miles
Programme of Policy Research in Engineering, Science and Technology, University of Manchester

David Miller
Nuffield College, Oxford

Enzo Mingione
University of Messina, Milan

Kenneth R. Minogue
London School of Economics

Simon Mohun
Queen Mary and Westfield College, University of London

Maxine Molyneux
Birkbeck College, University of London

Raymond A. Morrow
University of Alberta

Michael Mulkay
University of York

Eleanor M. Nesbitt
Religious Education and Community Project, University of Warwick

Robert Nisbet
Albert Schweitzer Professor Emeritus, Columbia University

Peter Nolan
School of Business and Economic Studies, University of Leeds

Roderick C. Ogley
Emeritus Reader, University of Sussex

John O'Neill
School of Social Sciences, University of Sussex

Geoffrey Ostergaard

William Outhwaite
School of European Studies, University of Sussex

John E. Owens
School of Social and Policy Sciences, University of Westminster

Trevor Pateman
Institute of Continuing and Professional Education, University of Sussex

Geoff Payne
University of Plymouth

Donald Peterson
Cognitive Science,
University of Birmingham

Tony Pinkney
University of Lancaster

Jennifer Platt
School of Social Sciences,
University of Sussex

Ken Plummer
University of Essex

Jonathan Powis
Balliol College, Oxford

Vernon Pratt
School of Independent Studies,
Lancaster University

Allan Pred
University of California

David L. Prychitko
State University of New York, Oswego

Derek Pugh
School of Management,
The Open University

Terence H. Qualter
University of Waterloo, Ontario

Ali Rattansi
City University, London

L. J. Ray
Lancaster University

Gavin C. Reid
University of St Andrews

Karin Renon
Centre d'Analyse et d'Intervention
Sociologiques, Paris

John Rex
Professor Emeritus, University of Warwick

Adrian D. Rifkin
University of Leeds

Paul Rock
London School of Economics

C. A. Rootes
University of Kent at Canterbury

Steven P. R. Rose
The Open University

W. D. Rubinstein
School of Social Sciences,
Deakin University

Anne Showstack Sassoon
School of Social Science,
Kingston University

Werner Sauer
Institute of Philosophy,
Karl-Franzens-Universität Graz

Johann F. Schneider
Universität des Saarlandes

John Scott
University of Leicester

Teodor Shanin
University of Manchester

A. M. Sharakiya
State University of New York at Binghamton

Andrew Sherratt
Ashmolean Museum,
University of Oxford

Cris Shore
Goldsmiths' College,
University of London

Kazimierz M. Slomczynski
Institute of Sociology,
University of Warsaw

Peter Sluglett
University of Durham

Andrew Spencer
University of Essex

Patricia M. Springborg
University of Sydney

Nico Stehr
University of Alberta

Herbert Stein
American Enterprise Institute for Public
Policy Research,
Washington DC

Rudi Supek
Zagreb

György Széll
Fachbereich Sozialwissenschaften,
Universität Osnabrück

Steve Taylor
London School of Economics

John B. Thompson
Jesus College, Cambridge

J. K. J. Thomson
School of Social Sciences,
University of Sussex

Alan Tomlinson
University of Brighton

Alain Touraine
Centre d'Analyse et d'Intervention
Sociologiques, Paris

Peter Townsend
University of Bristol

Keith Tribe
Keele University

Sylvaine Trinh
Centre d'Analyse et d'Intervention
Sociologiques, Paris

Bryan S. Turner
University of Essex

Jonathan H. Turner
University of California, Riverside

Ernest Tuveson
University of California, Berkeley

John Urry
Lancaster University

Ivan Varga
Kingston, Ontario

Loic J. D. Wacquant
Society of Fellows,
Harvard University

Sylvia Walby
London School of Economics

Nigel Walker
Professor Emeritus, Institute of Criminology,
University of Cambridge

Immanuel Wallerstein
State University of New York at
Binghamton,
and Maison des Sciences de l'Homme, Paris

J. W. N. Watkins
London School of Economics

Carolyn Webber
Survey Research Center,
University of California, Berkeley

Wlodzimierz Wesolowski
Institute of Philosophy and Sociology,
Polish Academy of Sciences, Warsaw

Michel Wievorka
Centre d'Analyse et d'Intervention
Sociologiques, Paris

Aaron Wildavsky
Survey Research Center,
University of California, Berkeley

R. A. Wilford
The Queen's University of Belfast

Robin M. Williams Jr.
Cornell University

Christopher Wilson
London School of Economics

Charles R. M. Wilson
Portsmouth Polytechnic

H. T. Wilson
York University, Toronto

Peter Worsley
London

Dennis H. Wrong
New York University

Lucia Zedner
London School of Economics

Sami Zubaida
Birkbeck College,
University of London

INTRODUCTION

At the end of the nineteenth century the term 'social' was still a relatively new one, as was for the most part the concept of distinct 'social sciences'. The first professional associations and journals were just beginning to be established and some new social sciences, such as sociology, were gaining recognition, while economics as an older discipline was developing rapidly in the neoclassical form given to it by Carl Menger, Léon Walras, Alfred Marshall and others, or with quite a different emphasis in the work of the German historical school. All the social sciences could look back on distinguished precursors in the eighteenth and nineteenth centuries, or earlier still in the case of political science and history, and the ideas of some of these precursors have remained influential. But in the twentieth century the social sciences have become more distinctly constituted and differentiated, and they have had a stronger impact on social thought as a whole. Political doctrines generally, and social criticism in particular, became more dependent on theories of society, and many nineteenth–century ideas came to find an institutional embodiment. Positivism established itself in a rather different form from its original Comtean one, as a philosophy of science particularly influential among social scientists. Evolutionism survived all kinds of attacks and retained its place in social thought, assuming new forms after World War II in conceptions of modernization, underdevelopment and development, and more recently in theories of the development of moral reasoning and human thought as a whole. The influence of Marxism, as a critique of political economy, a theory of society and a political doctrine, grew steadily during most of the century, though in increasingly diversified ways that were reflected, after the Russian Revolution and still more after 1945, in the sharp division between Marxism-Leninism and what came to be called Western Marxism, the latter being itself extremely diverse. The dramatic events of 1989 put an end to the communist dictatorships in Eastern Europe and to the world influence of Leninism, but although Marxism and to some extent socialism are at present in eclipse in post–communist Europe this is not so evidently the case elsewhere.

Everywhere, however, there is much rethinking of the social and political doctrines which had their origins in the eighteenth and nineteenth centuries, and flowered in the present century against the background of massive and rapid changes in the structure and culture of human societies. The Industrial Revolution and the political revolutions in France and America had initiated this transformation, giving birth to the democratic movement and later to socialism, as well as to the counter–doctrines of conservatism and liberalism, but the new industrial capitalist societies were also characterized by nationalism and imperialist expansion. As a result the twentieth century, contrary to the expectations of Auguste Comte and Herbert Spencer, came to be one of the most violent in human history, with two immensely destructive and savage world wars and innumerable, equally savage, lesser conflicts, as well as persecution and genocide on a large scale. New forms of aggressive expansionism emerged with the fascist regimes in Europe, which also established totalitarian dictatorships of a new kind (though these had a parallel, or even precursor, in Stalinist Russia), and in a different, more militaristic style in Japan.

Underlying the destructiveness of modern warfare has been the unprecedented advance during the past century of natural science and technology, which has transformed the conditions and modes of social life. Incessant technological innovation in the industrial countries has been a major factor in economic growth, and an important factor in the emergence of giant corporations, among them, notably in the past four decades, multinational corporations, which increasingly dominate the world economy. At the same time innovation and growth have a disruptive effect, not proceeding steadily and smoothly, but in a cycle of boom and depression, marked by periods of large-scale unemployment, as in the 1930s and again in the 1980s. Hence there has been much debate about ways of regulating the economy for social ends, a debate which until 1989 often involved contrasting (relatively) free market capitalist economies with the centrally planned economies, and still raises questions about the role of partial, indicative planning in the management of the economic system.

Economic growth itself has raised new issues for social thinkers; first, the contrast between the growing wealth of the industrial countries, within which there remain however substantial impoverished sectors, and the widespread poverty—in some cases increasing, as in large parts of Africa—of much of the Third World, and secondly, the environmental impact of growth itself. In relation to the first issue there have been many attempts to formulate models of development for the poorer countries, and to work out practical policies for overcoming this North/South divide, but the policies actually implemented have not so far been notably successful and by the end of the 1980s the transfer of resources from rich to poor countries, through aid programmes and other means, had turned, as a result of accumulated debt, into a reverse flow from the poor to the wealthy. In consequence a critical debate about what is to be understood by development in a world context, or by the idea of a 'new international economic order', which so far remains largely a catchphrase, has engaged an increasing number of social thinkers, and the debate has expanded into an additional area of concern with the human environment. Indeed it is with this issue, and with the burgeoning ecology movements, that much social thought has been engaged in recent decades. The pollution and destruction of the human habitat through industrial production and the apparently insatiable demand for raw materials, has affected not only the industrial societies themselves but also the countries of the Third World, where it is often even more devastating, sometimes compounded by the effects of rapid population growth.

It is against the background of the upheavals, conflicts, discontinuities and new problems of the present century that social thought, whether produced by social and political activists themselves or by the growing army of professional scholars, must be understood. Yet many of its central themes remain much as they were in the 1900s: the nature of work, the role of the nation-state, the relation between individual and society, the effect of money on social relations, the contrast between *Gemeinschaft* (community) and *Gesellschaft* (society/association), stratification and equality, the tension between partisanship and value-freedom in the social sciences, even such labels as *fin de siècle* itself. The latest diagnoses of postmodernity or postindustrialism look remarkably like early accounts of modernity and industrialism, and modern futurology, despite the availability of computer models, not unlike the predictions of nineteenth- and early twentieth-century social thinkers.

These earlier themes, however, have in many cases acquired a new content. The nature and meaning of work has now to be examined in the context of a radically changing occupational structure, the reduction of working hours, and the expansion of time available for freely chosen activities. The state has become more obviously the provider of vital social services and of the essential economic infrastructure, but the experience of fascism and Stalinism has shown that its power can be used in some circumstances to establish a totalitarian system. Democracy, which at the beginning of the century was a relatively new and limited growth, in only a small minority of countries, and was subsequently destroyed again in some of them, has become (in theory at least) an almost universal political value, though its eventual scope is still vigorously debated between advocates of liberal or participatory democracy, and in the context of recent discussions of the meaning of citizenship. Stratification and equality, which have had a central place in the political conflicts between left and right throughout this century, have become more complex issues in recent decades as other kinds of inequality—of gender, race and nationality—have been more strongly emphasized by new social movements, and as the claims of communist societies to have eliminated class inequalities were more vigorously disputed by internal and external critics of their strongly hierarchical structures.

This dictionary aims to provide a reliable and comprehensive overview of the main themes of social thought, broadly conceived, and of its development from the beginning of the century (or earlier) to near its end, against the background of the vast and shifting panorama of social life in this turbulent era. It will prove, we hope, a valuable source of reference for all those who, in different ways, are concerned with the prospects for the future development of human society as we prepare to enter a new century and a new millennium.

WILLIAM OUTHWAITE

TOM BOTTOMORE

A

---

action and agency Someone performs an action when what he or she does can be described as intentional (see Davidson, 1977). Actions are practical conclusions drawn from intentions and beliefs; 'action' and 'rationality' are interrelated. Sociological action theories from the time of Max Weber build on this relation in analysing action into components and types. Social actions are always part of larger systems and of processes of intersubjective understanding, and this raises the question of the role of the acting subject ('human agency') in the processes by which actions are coordinated.

Rationality of action
Aristotle, in his *Nichomachean Ethics*, saw the rationality of an action as lying in the conclusion which leads from intentions or norms and from assessments of the situation and of the available means to immediate consequences in terms of action. Action is rational in so far as it follows premises which ground and justify its performance. A minimal rationality must therefore be presupposed in any action, in any bodily movement falling under this definition. Aristotle emphasized that even undisciplined actions which escape rational control, such as the excessive consumption of sweet things, can be formally at least fitted into the model of rational justification (cf. Davidson, 1980; Wright, 1971).

Will formation
A simple example of purposive-rational will formation is provided by Kant's technical imperative, the 'imperative of capability', in which intentions are extended from ends to means (cf. Wright, 1971). Someone who wants something and knows how it is to be obtained must want to obtain it by these means. Even the complex process of social will formation, coming to a decision as a consequence of collective deliberation, can be described as a process of practical inference. This involves a union of many (at least two and at most all) actors concerned with a common purpose or problem. If this union is not brought about through force, threat or propaganda, it must be through the free compulsion of argumentative inference, that is through convincing reasons (cf. Habermas, 1971; Apel, 1973, 1979). Practical discourses are not concerned with the extension of intentions from ends to means, explaining to the actor why it is rational for *him or her* to take certain decisions, but rather with whether it is possible to generalize the ends and make clear to all why *they* should follow particular norms (see Norm). In what Hegel (*Logic*) called the 'conclusion of the good', in which means and end are identical and the act is good in itself, it is a question of what is legitimate and justifiable in the light of shared and freely accepted principles (Wellmer, 1979, pp. 25ff.).

Consequences of actions
The conclusion of a practical inference is an action. From the observer's perspective, the choice of available means to given ends *explains* the action. Such an explanation also has prognostic relevance, since institutional and normative contexts ensure that intentions and beliefs remain stable and are regularly reproduced (cf. Wright, 1971). But since one can never exclude the possibility of actors changing their intentions, forgetting the best way to do things or unexpectedly finding new ways to solve a problem, the link between intentions and beliefs and future behaviour is a contingent one. But we can only identify a given behaviour *as* a specific action if we succeed in interpreting it, in the perspective of a participant, as the consequence of rationally understandable intentions and beliefs. 'To interpret behaviour as intentional action is to understand it in the light of an intention' (Wellmer, 1979, p. 13).

The participant's perspective, and only that perspective, opens up a similar logical-semantic relation between intentions and actions. For the actor, the practical conclusion *means* an obligation to perform a future action. It is not empirically guaranteed that someone who promises to come on time will in fact do so, but someone who has given that undertaking will need to offer an apology if he or she is not punctual. The expectation that in normal circumstances someone who has promised to be on time very probably will be is not only inductively supported by observed behavioural regularities; this expectation is based even more on the fact that we can usually rely on one another. The Other will probably be on time because the agreement has reciprocal validity (cf. Apel, 1979). This is not an empirical and contingent relation between intentions and activities but a logical-pragmatic one. We recognize the seriousness of the intention by its consequences for action; we call someone who does not do what he or she wants to do and can do, inconsistent. This is not unlike the case of someone who asserts that snow is all white *and* all black. Just as we suspect weakness of will as the cause of inconsistent action, we may infer that someone who unintentionally utters contradictions is weak in the head. Like evidently contradictory statements, evidently inconsistent action has 'something essentially irrational' about it, so that such actors might find it hard to recognize themselves in their actions (cf. Davidson, 1980).

Types of action
Disturbances of action through such massive inconsistencies that we cannot understand our own action ('I don't know how I could have done it') bring us up against the internal connection between action and self-understanding. Max Weber and Sigmund Freud drew opposite conclusions from this relation. Whereas Freud is interested in the unconscious causes of self-deception, Weber bases his sociology on an IDEAL TYPE of meaningfully oriented action intelligible to the actor; his well-known typology of action is founded on this relation of self-evidence.

Social action is 'behaviour which is meaningfully oriented to the behaviour of others' (Weber, 1921-2). One limiting case of social action is the completely self-evident, conventional, habitual and almost mechanical course of traditional action based on 'internalized habit'. This 'dully habitual everyday action', quietly adapted to the normative background of the life-world, is pushed into an affectual or emotional reaction when the conventionally meaningful background of everyday action suddenly collapses and confronts the actor with unfamiliar and exceptional demands, problems and conflicts. This is the other limit case of social action.

To speak of *action* which is governed by 'present affects and emotions' means that, even in uninhibited reaction to an exceptional stimulus, the actor retains scope to decide how to react, or whether not to react at all and to swallow his or her rage. But Weber reserves the description 'rationally intelligible' for social behaviour which is fully conscious and based only on reasons which the actor considers to be valid and conclusive; this corresponds to the ideal types of purposive-rational and value-rational action. With this distinction Weber looks back, via NEO-KANTIANISM, to the Aristotelian theory of action. Whereas value-rational action follows what Hegel called the 'conclusion of the good' and identifies means and ends in 'the unconditioned value in itself of a specific behaviour', in purposive-rational action all that counts is the effectiveness of means to a given end. In Weber's conception, only this type of action can be fully rationalized; it is therefore the true ideal type of meaningfully oriented behaviour that expresses Hegel's 'conclusion of action'. Only here can one say 'that *if* someone were to act in a strictly purposive-rational manner, they could *only* do it this way and no other way' (Weber, 1921-2).

For Weber, the rational understanding (see VERSTEHEN) of action advances methodically from this universal and counterfactual rationality assumption. This makes it possible to explain actual actions as a deviation from an ideal standard. Freud's interest in explaining irrational action is therefore complementary to Weber's interest in understanding the rationality of consistent action. In a world shaped by causal reasoning, rational action of this kind is only possible when the actor's reasons for a particular action are causally effective *as intentions*, and *cause* the action (cf. Davidson, 1980). If a real action is to be understood as the consequence of a rational inference (for example, rational argumentation), the reasons must have a causal, that is, rationally motivating, force as causes of the action-event. The causal force which a grounded will, transforming reasons into intentions, gives to our actions is of course, as Davidson (1980) and Apel (1979, p. 189) have shown in their criticisms of C.G. Hempel, a causality without causal laws. What Kant called the 'causality of freedom', in which the will or the intention which causes the action counts as a valid justification for it, involves not causal laws, but normative-universal principles of rationality (Apel, 1979). The case of unconscious self-deception with which Freud is concerned is one in which an action or speech-act is caused as an event without being justified by its causes (cf. Löw-Beer, 1990). In this case the action or speech-act is not rationally motivated, by a valid sequence of symbols, but only empirically, by way of 'split-off symbols' (cf. Habermas, 1968, pp. 246ff.; 1981, pp. 8ff.). But because this explanation in terms of merely empirically effective motives presupposes the possibility of rational action, Freud can combine his methodological interest with a therapeutic interest in emancipation and the critique of action which is not brought about by reasons.

This interest does not of course come near to satisfying Weber's criterion of ideal purposive rationality. The irrational action with which Freud is concerned is caused by the latent force of distorted, compulsively integrated communication. To explain it as action which is no longer intelligible to the actor it is not enough to postulate an ideal type of purposive-rational action and to measure its divergence. What must be presupposed is rather an ideal criterion of *undistorted communication* (cf. Habermas, 1968; Apel, 1979). What the actor who needs the help of a therapist finds unintelligible about his or her own action is the breaks in the system of reasons which would appear acceptable to a community of autonomous subjects. The motives which cause the action and speech of the neurotic, without justifying and grounding it, are causes which cannot count as reasons because a free communication community could not accept them as reasons.

Action, system and subject
Weber's theory of action appears inadequate in another quite different respect. It underestimates from the start the complexity of the *double contingency* (cf. Parsons and Shils, 1951, pp. 14ff.) in the meaningfully oriented reciprocal perspectives of ego and alter, as well as the hypercomplexity of any meaningful orientation. The improbability of a meaningfully guided act, related to an unlimited and inconceivable multiplicity of alternative possibilities which might have been realized, is further increased by the improbability in *social* action that everyone knows that everyone can act or not act as expected. Without mechanisms for the reduction of this monstrous and in principle ungraspable complexity of meaningfully oriented action, mechanisms which functionally integrate the individual actions independently of the will and consciousness

of the subjects, social order seems impossible (cf. Luhmann, 1970–90, vol. 2, pp. 204ff.; 1981, pp. 195ff.). The question is then whether social order can be envisaged entirely without collective will formation and whether actions can be separated from a notion of agency produced by subjects themselves by means of acceptable reasons.

Reading
Brubaker, Rogers 1984: *The Limits of Rationality: An Essay on the Social and Moral Thought of Max Weber.*
Davidson, D. 1980: *Essays on Actions and Events.*
Parsons, T. 1937: *The Structure of Social Action.*
                                HAUKE BRUNKHORST

addiction   The state of undue attachment or reliance usually refers to a drug such as alcohol or heroin, though the concept has been extended to addictive behaviours such as gambling and overeating. An alternative description often preferred is 'dependence'. The World Health Organization (1981) proposed the following features of drug addiction:

– subjective compulsion to take a drug;
– desire to cease consumption although intake continues;
– a stereotyped, inflexible pattern of intake;
– adaptation of nerve systems affected by the drug, leading to tolerance to its effects and withdrawal symptoms when the drug is stopped;
– priority of drug-seeking behaviour over other activities;
– rapid reinstatement of the syndrome when a period of abstinence is broken.

Not every feature is shown by each drug or each affected person.

With respect to causation, inheritance is a minor culprit for alcohol dependence. The most powerful causative forces are potentially the most open to remedy: socioeconomic factors which determine the acceptability and availability of psychoactive compounds. Such influences, including the cost of alcohol, explain the differences in addiction prevalences between countries, races, religions, sexes and eras. The dependence-producing interactions between drugs and the brain are best understood for opiates, which exert similar effects to the innate endorphin-like neurotransmitters. Dependence is further promoted by learned reactions of responding to external and internal stimuli by craving and drug intake.

The most common – and the most lethal – addiction is to tobacco. The addiction, which is maintained by the nicotine content, is declining among the richer and better informed nations but increasing in poorer states. Alcohol dependence (alcoholism) has entered a cycle of decrease in the more prosperous countries, but with the growth in international marketing of alcohol beverages it has been expanding in less affluent regions. Illicit drug usage, particularly of heroin, cocaine and amphetamines, gives growing concern for its social, criminal and health implications. The use of tobacco is more frequent in low income strata, and the use of illegal drugs in deprived urban areas.

The social consequences of addiction arise in part from intoxication – with disturbed interpersonal relationships, accidents, declining work performance – and sometimes from illicit activities to fund drug consumption (see also CRIME AND DEVIANCE). Physical harms are most prominent from tobacco (lung cancer, obstructive lung disease, cardiovascular disorders) and from alcohol (including brain and liver damage). Contaminated drug injections lead to infections, notably with the organisms of viral hepatitis and Aids. Psychological complications of addiction include depression with suicidal risk, anxiety and transient psychoses.

The view that addiction represents a moral failing has battled across the centuries with the disease concept (see also MEDICINE). The medical model took over from the 1930s, and is in turn challenged by the tenet that addiction is a learned state amenable to psychological techniques of unlearning. The arguments are in part semantic (what is a disease?), in part determined by power struggles between professions. Biology, medicine, psychology, sociology, anthropology, economics and religion all contribute to an understanding of addictive behaviour, and often of its treatment and prevention.

The addictions possess a spontaneous proportion of remissions so evaluation difficulties lead to debate over the merits of particular therapies. Brief counselling can help persons with early alcohol dependence, and assists enough people with tobacco addiction to make intervention by their doctors worthwhile. Other persons require more prolonged help. Voluntary organizations are increasingly prominent. Alcoholics Anonymous, founded in 1936, is the paradigm for self-help groups in the addictive behaviours and in other areas of distress.

Preventive means are divided between reduction of supply and reduction of demand for drugs. Supply reduction involves legal controls over the production and distribution of licit and illicit psychoactive substances. Opponents of law enforcement point to its failure to prevent illegal drug trafficking. Adherents note that national and international restrictions limit drug misuse and dependence, and can refer to successes from legal measures.

Demand reduction includes early recognition and treatment of addicts, the less tangible area of improvement in social conditions, and education. Although methods of education, and even its value, are disputed, the reduction of tobacco and alcohol addiction and harm in several countries has followed an enhancement of public awareness.

Reading
Ghodse, H. and Maxwell, G. eds 1990: *Substance Abuse and Dependence: An Introduction for the Caring Professions.*
Jellinek, E.M. 1960: *The Disease Concept of Alcoholism.*
Marlatt, A. and Gordon, J. 1985: *Relapse Prevention.*
Orford, J. 1985: *Excessive Appetites: A Psychological View of Addiction.*
Royal College of Psychiatrists 1986: *Alcohol: Our Favourite Drug.*
—— 1987: *Drug Scenes.*

JOHN SPENCER MADDEN

aesthetics   In its modern meaning aesthetics is most frequently understood as a philosophical discipline which is either a philosophy of aesthetic phenomena (objects, qualities, experiences and values), or a philosophy of art (of creativity, of artwork, and its perception) or a philosophy of art criticism taken broadly (metacriticism), or, finally, a discipline which is concerned philosophically with all three realms jointly.

Aesthetic reflection is much older than the term itself. The history of Western aesthetics begins usually with Plato, whose writings contain a systematic reflection on art and a speculative theory of beauty. Neither Plato nor his great disciple Aristotle, however, treated these two great themes of aesthetics in conjunction.

The term 'aesthetics' was introduced to philosophy as late as the mid-eighteenth century by a German philosopher, Alexander Gottlieb Baumgarten (1714–1762). Baumgarten, a disciple of Leibniz's follower Christian Wolff (1679–1754), concluded that the system of philosophical disciplines was incomplete and required a science parallel to logic which was a science of clear and distinct cognition achieved by the intellect. The new science should be aesthetics, a science of clear and confused cognition realized by the senses. This view was expressed for the first time by Baumgarten in his dissertation *Meditationes philosophicae de nonnullis ad poema pertinentibus* (of 1735) and in a completed form 15 years later in his *Aesthetica*.

Contrary to the expectations which the etymology of the word aesthetica might suggest (Greek *aistheticos*=perceptive), this work did not concern itself with the theory of sensory cognition but dealt with the theory of poetry (and indirectly of all the arts) as a form of sensory cognition for which the main object of perception is beauty. The combination of the two – the reflection on art and the reflection on beauty – defined the subsequent development of the newly emerged branch of philosophy, but this has become the source of both its accomplishments and never-ending theoretical and methodological difficulties. Without doubt it was an event of historical significance, marking the beginning of a new period in the development of the philosophy of art, particularly in that it coincided with a summing up of the longlasting search for the common denominator of all the arts which was achieved by a French theorist of art Charles Batteux in his *Traité des beaux arts réduit à un même principe* (in 1746). Batteux recognized that the common feature of the fine arts is the beauty proper to them all, and therefore they may be termed *beaux arts*.

The name aesthetics took some time to be accepted. Immanuel Kant (1724–1804) began with a criticism of Baumgarten for his lack of consistency, and in his *Critique of Pure Reason* (of 1781 and 1787) used the term transcendental aesthetics to mean a philosophical science of sensory perception. However, in his *Critique of Judgment* (of 1790) he used the term aesthetics to define the reflection on beauty and judgements of taste. The traditional meaning of aesthetics became popular in the nineteenth century through the influence of Hegel (1770–1831), whose lectures on the philosophy of the fine arts in 1820–9 were posthumously published as *Vorlesungen über die Ästhetik* (in 1835).

Kant, Schelling and Hegel were the first prominent philosophers for whom aesthetics constituted an inherent part of their philosophical systems. For Kant aesthetics was first and foremost the theory of beauty, of the sublime and of aesthetic judgements.

For Hegel aesthetics was mainly the philosophy of the fine arts. The two models of moulding aesthetics either as a philosophy of beauty (and later of aesthetic values) and of aesthetic experience, or as a philosophy of art become dominant in the aesthetics of nineteenth century and at the beginning of the twentieth century. Most frequently, the two variants were joined together and the results were varied.

In the course of years, however, the idea of aesthetics as philosophy of art appeared to be more popular. In the nineteenth century there was the first attempt to go beyond philosophy in aesthetic considerations and to create a scientific aesthetics. In his *Vorschule der Aesthetik* of 1876, the German psychologist Gustav Theodor Fechner attempted to create an experimental aesthetics on the basis of psychology, and the twentieth century also witnessed attempts to create a psychological aesthetics by the representatives of gestalt psychology (Rudolf Arnheim and Leonard Meyer) and of depth psychology (Ernst Kris and Simon Lesser). Other developments have included mathematical aesthetics (George Birkhoff and Max Bense), informatics aesthetics (Abraham Moles), semiotic and semiological aesthetics (Charles Morris, Umberto Eco, Yuri Lotman), and sociological aesthetics (J.M. Guyau, P. Francastel, Pierre Bourdieu, Janet Wolff). In the philosophical domain the project of creating a scientific aesthetics was attempted by Etienne Souriau and Thomas Munro. Aesthetics, however, has not ceased to be a branch of philosophy.

Since the turn of the century there has been a growing interest in the methodological difficulties of aesthetics, which began to take into account doubts and arguments directed against the scientific status of aesthetics and the very sense of creating aesthetics theories. Of particular relevance here are the still popular ideas of Max Dessoir (1906) and Emil Utitz (1914–20). These thinkers introduced a distinction between aesthetics and a general science of art and emphasized that the two disciplines cross but do not overlap: the functions of art cannot be reduced to aesthetic functions only, whereas aesthetic merits are to be found in objects which are not works of art at all, such as natural phenomena and extra-artistic man made products. They also claimed that the general science of art differs methodologically from aesthetics and should evolve into an independent branch outside philosophy. Aesthetics, too, should go beyond the borders of philosophy and make much greater use of the results produced by other sciences, in particular psychology and sociology (see also SOCIOLOGY OF ART).

The first aesthetician who not only systemized the objections against aesthetics but also attempted to overcome them was Edward Bullough, in his lectures of 1907 on '*the modern conception of aesthetics*' (in Bullough, 1957). He ordered the objections raised against aesthetics into two groups: popular and theoretical, both kinds being reducible to assertions that:

1   Attempts to create a theory of such specific, relative, subjective and mutable phenomena as beauty, aesthetic effects and the pleasure and displeasure connected with them are futile. These phenomena cannot be rationalized and verbalized, they can be only experienced.

2   The definitions of beauty and other aesthetic phenomena are too abstract and general and thus are completely useless and practically unnecessary. They do not help anyone to enjoy beauty and art.

3   Both the artists and the enthusiasts of art are worried and annoyed by the fact that the rules of creation and reception are defined and imposed on artists and the public, and presented moreover with absurd and insolent pedantry.

Bullough's work was the first self-examination which summed up the actual internal methodological difficulties of aesthetics, and the objections raised from outside, which, if not always fully justified, were not without reason.

According to Stefan Morawski (1987), Bullough's work began the third period in the history of aesthetics, the period of critical self-knowledge of its research status, and of the development of its methodological self-reflection. This process reached its peak in 1954 with the publication of W. Elton's famous anthology *Aesthetics and Language*, and the equally famous papers by M. Weitz 'The role of theory in aesthetics' (1956) and W.E. Kennick 'Does traditional aesthetics rest on a mistake?' (1958), which continued and developed the ideas set out in Elton's collection. These three works were inspired by the ideas in Wittgenstein's *Philosophical Investigations* (1953), and they criticized traditional philosophical aesthetics sharply and thoroughly for its lack of linguistic precision, conceptual vagueness and mistaken theoretical and

methodological assumptions which were most apparent in the unsuccessful attempts to create a philosophical theory of art. Wrong assumptions led naturally to the failure of the hitherto proposed philosophical theories of art.

The first mistaken assumption identified was the essentialist claim that art possesses a universal nature, or an absolute essence, which it is the task of aesthetics to dig out and define. Art, it was now claimed, is an incessantly mutable phenomenon, lacking any universal essence, and the notions 'art', 'work of art', 'aesthetic experience', and so on are therefore open concepts (Weitz, 1959) and cannot be defined. Secondly, the representatives of traditional aesthetics missed another basic truth that every work of art is valued for its uniqueness and unrepeatable originality, and therefore there is no place for any general rules of creation and evaluation of such work. The aestheticians, however, were persistent in their attempts to discover or make such general rules, even though any generalizations about art are unjustified and dubious. The aestheticians' arguments were analogical to those in ethics, but any analogies appeared to be misleading. Generalizations in ethics are possible and necessary, whereas in aesthetics the situation is quite different. 'When in aesthetics one moves from the particular to the general, one is travelling in the wrong direction' (S. Hampshire in Elton, 1954). Thirdly, aesthetics followed philosophy in its mistaken assumption that facts can be disclosed and interpreted, whereas in fact its proper task is not disclosing facts but clarifying the meanings of words. Words, concepts and expressions are used in a number of ways which are not always proper. A solution of philosophical problems consists in recognizing how given words are properly used. The basic problem of aesthetics is not answering the question 'What is art?' but 'What kind of concept is "art"?' (Weitz).

The criticism of aesthetics by analytical philosophy, however, did not result either in the death of aesthetics or in a lasting victory of cognitive minimalism, and the abandonment of new attempts to create a theory of art. One might even defend the view that anti-essentialist criticism of aesthetics resulted in its recovery and revival in the 1970s and the 1980s. At the same time, however, aesthetics continued to be criticized from outside and the aestheticians continued their methodological self-reflection which in part answered the external criticism and in part resulted from aesthetics' inherent needs. Nonetheless, the aestheticians rejected all the basic objections articulated by the analytical philosophers. Aesthetics should and indeed can be practised with a greater logical and linguistic precision, but at the same time it cannot be reduced to the analysis of concepts and the ways they are used. In this respect the situation of aesthetics does not differ substantially from the other branches of the humanities. It is a misunderstanding if one applies to aesthetics the requirements applied to science or mathematics. Moreover, even in natural sciences there is no single and universal paradigm of scientific exactness.

One has to realize that any generalizations concerning such diverse and mutable phenomena as art and the aesthetic experience are very risky but there is no need to abandon such generalizations altogether. Avoiding essentialist and anti-historical definitions of traditional aesthetics does not mean abandoning attempts to create a theory of art and of aesthetic phenomena. Normative considerations which jeopardize the freedom of creation and which are notoriously ascribed to aesthetics are by no means characteristic of aesthetics and occur much more frequently in art criticism. It is true, however, that the majority of aesthetic theories do contain elements of evaluation. But then again, axiological aspects are typical of any discipline and form an organic part of cognition, they cannot be, and do not have to be, eliminated from science. At the same time it is possible to create purely descriptive theories of art (Dickie, 1971).

Rejecting far-reaching criticism of aesthetics by analytical philosophers, aestheticians themselves periodically take note of criticisms and reservations directed against their discipline, and express their own doubts as to its research status. In most cases, however, they defend its value, though some would like to pursue it in a fully or partly modified form. At least three attempts to balance the arguments pro and contra made by aestheticians themselves in the last three decades are worth noting.

The first was made in 1960 by Jerome Stolnitz in *Aesthetics and Philosophy of Art Criticism* (pp. 7–19). The second was made by Stefan Morawski in two works published in Polish (1973, 1987). Morawski's conclusions differ in the two works, however; in the first he defends the significance of aesthetics, while in the other he abandons this defence and argues that it is now in decline. The third author who listed the objections raised, and defended aesthetics against them, is Göran Her-

meren, who devoted the final chapter of his *Aspects of Aesthetics* (1983, pp. 224–60) to this question.

A considerable number of the doubts and reservations about aesthetics repeat themselves. There are also new criticisms which have arisen in the course of development of modern culture and in particular of avant-garde art, mass media and mass culture. Recent criticism has two main aspects. In the first place, the main reservations still concern the status of aesthetics as a field of research. The critics assert that aesthetics is cognitively futile, anachronistic and inadequate, its methods old-fashioned and based on mistaken methodological principles. Consequently, even if it did make some sense in the past, it appears to be completely helpless when faced with the latest avant-garde in art and the most significant phenomena of mass culture. So it ignores them (a disqualifying attitude) or tries to describe them, interpret them and evaluate them using its traditional methods and traditional, quite irrelevant categories, which leads to its failure and humiliation.

This mode of criticism is to be found in the papers by T. Binkley, in Michael Kirby's *The Art of Time* (1969), and in the latest works by Stefan Morawski. Kirby holds that traditional philosophical aesthetics should be rejected in favour of historical or situational aesthetics. Binkley claims that aesthetics could survive if it reduced the scope of its interest to a reflection on aesthetic phenomena and abandoned creating theories of art, since aesthetics cannot explain avant-garde art, which as such rejects the aesthetic paradigm of art, if it keeps assuming that the nature of art is aesthetic. Morawski claims that aesthetics is declining not only because of avant-garde art but also because art 'has lost part of its significance and its further existence is jeopardized'. Aesthetics, then, should give the floor either to 'poietics' as the theory of creativity or to anti-aesthetics understood in terms of 'a critical reflection on the crisis of the culture and art of our times' (1987, p. 77). It is not the methodology that is responsible for the decline of aesthetics; it is the disintegration of its main object: art.

Aesthetics however, is criticized not only for its helplessness in the face of avant-garde art, but also because of its *a*historical attitudes, 'aspirations for totality' (Werckmeister, 1971), essentialism and making abstract rules irrespective of the fact that 'art is a dynamic syndrome' (Adorno, 1984), and that art itself and its reception are produced by a historical process (Bourdieu, 1979). If aesthetics wishes to survive it has to transform itself and become a dialectical aesthetics (Adorno) or a sociological aesthetics (Bourdieu).

The other kind of argument against aesthetics consists in suggesting that no one really needs it. Aesthetics does not help ordinary recipients of modern art to find their way about in the chaos of the latest artistic phenomena. Someone with a serious interest in aesthetics would do better to refer to works on the history and theory of particular realms of art, or on the psychology of art, sociology of art, philosophy of CULTURE, the theory of mass communication, semiotics, and so on.

It is hard to foresee the future of aesthetics. The theses about its death or decline, however, are just as weak as the theses about the death or decline of art. But aesthetics has to change, taking account of the transformations of its subject and the achievements of other disciplines concerned with art and aesthetics phenomena. Perhaps one should come back to the idea of two disciplines, in the vein of Dessoir and Utitz: the philosophy of art and the philosophy of aesthetic values and experiences. There is no doubt, however, that the development of psychology, sociology, semiotics and other disciplines concerned with art does not eradicate strictly philosophical (axiological, methodological, cognitive and ontological) problems of art and of aesthetic phenomena. This is the unquestionable *raison d'être* of aesthetics.

See also ART, SOCIOLOGY OF; LINGUISTIC PHILOSOPHY; MODERNISM AND POSTMODERNISM.

Reading

Adorno, Theodor 1984: *Aesthetic Theory*, trans. C. Lenhardt.
Barrett, Cyril ed. 1965: *Collected papers on Aesthetics*.
Beardsley, Monroe 1958: *Aesthetics: Problems in the Philosophy of Criticism*.
Elton, William ed. 1954: *Aesthetics and Language*.
Ingarden, Roman 1985: *Selected Papers in Aesthetics*.
Margolis, Joseph ed. 1987: *Philosophy Looks at the Arts*.
Shusterman, Richard ed. 1989: *Analytic Aesthetics*.
Sparshott, Francis 1963: *The Structure of Aesthetics*.
Tatarkiewicz, Władysław 1970–4: *History of Aesthetics, 3 vols.*
Werckmeister, Otto 1971: *Ende der Ästhetik*.
Wolff, Janet 1983: *Aesthetics and the Sociology of Art*.

BOHDAN DZIEMIDOK

affluent society   A society in which there is sufficient wealth to ensure the continued satisfaction of the privately serviced basic needs of the majority of the population (such as food and clothing) with the result that individuals employ their disposable incomes to gratify ephemeral and insatiable wants, while insufficient funds may be directed to the satisfaction of publicly serviced needs (such as health care and education).

The term was made famous by Kenneth Galbraith in his book *The Affluent Society*, first published in 1958. This is a powerful critique of the pattern of resource allocation then prevailing in the United States (and, by extension, in some individual national economies of Western Europe) and involves three main claims. First, that increases in productive capacity and efficiency have resulted in an economy capable of providing a great and unprecedented affluence for the majority of people. As Galbraith observes, in the contemporary United States many goods are 'comparatively abundant', a point which he illustrates by pointing to the fact that more people die each year from eating too much food than from eating too little (p. 102).

Secondly, he argues that conventional economic wisdom has failed to take this development into account, continuing to embody the earlier and anachronistic assumption that further annual increases in production are necessarily to be desired. What, in particular, is outdated is the priority accorded to the ever-increasing production of goods in the private sector, which leads to a situation where 'private affluence' is matched by 'public squalor'. The 'great and comprehensive contrast between the care and encouragement which is lavished on the production of private goods and the severe restraint which it imposes on those that must emerge from the public sector' is for Galbraith 'the most singular feature of the affluent society' (p. 155).

Thirdly and lastly, the stimulation of artificial wants through advertising coupled with an excessive provision of credit is required in order to maintain a high level of demand, now that there are no longer any urgent needs to be satisfied.

The term Galbraith introduced is still widely encountered, having entered into popular use. The critique of conventional economic thought is usually missing from this usage, however, as too is the implied contrast between private affluence and public squalor, while the harsher economic climate of the 1980s also resulted in the phrase being used in a more ironic manner than Galbraith ever intended. The kernel of meaning which therefore remains is the suggestion that citizens of such a society experience a state of widespread and unprecedented abundance with the consequence that economic resources are predominantly employed in the wasteful gratification of trivial wants rather than in the necessary satisfaction of fundamental needs.

Galbraith's claims have been extensively criticized. His third thesis in particular has been fiercely attacked on the grounds that he denigrates consumer choice, fails to distinguish between the general cultural conditioning of wants and the specific influence exerted by producers, and ignores the empirical evidence concerning the effects of advertising (Hayek, 1967; Riesman, 1980). His famous contrast between private affluence and public squalor has also been criticized, largely on the grounds that his approach involves a misunderstanding of the declining marginal utility of goods while underestimating the natural profligacy of governments (Rothbard, 1970). Despite this, even his fiercest critics tend to accept that it is accurate to describe modern North American and Western European countries as affluent societies (Friedman, 1977, p. 13). Hence Galbraith's central thesis can be said to have found widespread acceptance and to have exerted a major influence on modern social and economic thought. In this respect it is particularly important to note that his exposure of the taken-for-granted nature of the wisdom of striving for ever-increasing levels of production and his attack on the conventional view that supremacy should be accorded to market values has undoubtedly assisted the subsequent emergence of environmental and anti-growth critiques of modern society.

See also CONSUMER SOCIETY; ECONOMIC GROWTH.

Reading
Beckerman, W. 1974: *In Defence of Economic Growth.*
Hession, C.H. 1972: *John Kenneth Galbraith and his Critics.*
Riesman, David 1980: *Galbraith and Market Capitalism.*
Sharpe, Myron, E. 1973: *John Kenneth Galbraith and the Lower Economics.*

COLIN CAMPBELL

age   *See* OLD AGE

agency   *See* ACTION AND AGENCY

aggression   While almost all current theories of aggression have been developed in the twentieth century, the underlying conceptual issues and major debates have much earlier roots. Recent arguments concerning the extent to which aggression is biologically rooted in human nature revive themes from Thomas Hobbes's *Leviathan* and the liberal philosophies of Jean-Jacques Rousseau. Freud (1920), for example, recasts many of Hobbes's original ideas on the inherent brutality of man towards his fellows in a psychoanalytical framework, providing a model subsequently emulated in the very different field of ethology by Konrad Lorenz (1966) and the neo-Darwinists.

Such approaches, focusing on rather simplistic assumptions of instinctual mechanisms, while still reviewed extensively in the major text books, are now seen as largely excluded from current accounts of aggression. The aspect of Freud's work which focuses on aggression is viewed, with the benefit of hindsight, as a rather hurried attempt to patch up apparent weaknesses in his theoretical approach, which relied heavily on the *pleasure principle* to explain psychological processes and human behaviour. The bloody catastrophe of World War I required some quite different model, and so *thanatos*, or the death instinct, appeared: 'As a result of a little speculation, we have come to suppose that this instinct is at work within every living creature and is striving to bring it to ruin and reduce life to its original condition of inanimate matter.'

A particular difficulty with these early instinct theories was the central notion of 'spontaneity'. Not only was aggression genetically preprogrammed, and therefore ineradicable, it took the form of a drive which must be consummated, channelled or displaced. Expressions of aggression, whether in the form of interpersonal VIOLENCE or in some less direct form, were thus inevitable. Emphasis was placed on the need to direct this hydraulic force, rather than on ways of reducing it. Energetic sports and physical competition were seen as essential ingredients in the control of 'natural' male aggression, providing much of the rationale of the British public school system.

While such views, like aspects of many early psychological theories, have been incorporated into lay 'social representations' of aggression and violence, modern accounts of aggression in the social sciences eschew virtually all notions of genetic factors and biological substrates. The vast majority of published works since the 1950s lay emphasis on the role of learning, social conditions and depriva-tion. The essential assumption is that aggression is a form of *behaviour*, rather than a primary psycho-logical force, and that, like any other behaviour, it can be modified, controlled and even eradicated. This is equally evident in the laboratory-based work of psychologists such as Bandura (1973) and in the sociological approaches of writers as varied as Wolfgang and Weiner (1982) and Downes and Rock (1979). We find a similar emphasis on 'liberal' understandings of aggression in postwar social anthropology with much effort being devoted to finding totally peaceful societies in which aggres-sion does not, or did not, exist – thus firmly nailing the false assumption of a genetic determinant. Such attempts were, by and large, unconvincing. Indeed, as Fox (1968) has pointed out, naive views of the Kalahari Bushmen as a people free from aggression were a little wide of the mark since evidence existed to show that they had a homicide rate higher than that in Chicago.

To some extent the rejection of biological theories of aggression is due not only to the manifest inadequacies of those theories but also to the gradual introduction of 'political correctness' into academic debates in the social sciences. People cannot be said to be naturally aggressive because that would mean that violence and destruction could never be eradicated, and that, unlike in the early decades of the century, does not fit at all with the contemporary intellectual Zeitgeist.

This new polarization, and the heated nature–nurture debate which has occupied most of the century, has probably detracted more than any-thing else from a 'sensible' understanding of aggression. Marsh (1978, 1982) has argued that whether aggression has a biological root or whether it is learned is a largely irrelevant argument since (a) it is undoubtedly both, and (b) the prognoses for the modification of behaviour are not much differ-ent in either case. An analogy can be made here with sexual behaviour. It would be foolish to assume that human sexuality does not have genetic, biological and hormonal bases. But sexual behaviour is largely controlled through cultural and social rule frame-works. People do not, in the main, consummate their sexual drives in random and spontaneous fashion – they are obliged to follow social conven-tions and observe ritual requirements. All cultures develop 'solutions' which maximize the advantages of sexuality and inhibit its potentially negative consequences.

It has become increasingly unfashionable in the social sciences to suggest that aggression has any positive value. Indeed, many current definitions of aggression exclude such a possibility. In psycho-logy the most dominant definition is 'Intentional behaviour intended to harm another person who is motivated to avoid it.' In other social science fields it is most frequently viewed as 'maladaptive' behaviour or an unfortunate response to pathologi-cal social conditions (see also CRIME AND DEVIANCE). Only in fields such as Marxist sociology do we find the view that aggression is a rational and justified form of conduct.

In everyday discourse, however, it.is clear that aggression is seen as having positive as well as pejorative connotations. In the world of sports we regularly praise the athlete for running an aggres-sive race, or hold in esteem the gutsy and aggressive quarter-back. In these arenas aggression is not only permissible, it is an essential ingredient of excel-lence. Similarly, aggression in the business world is the hallmark of the valued entrepreneur, without whom both post-Thatcherite Britain and the twen-tieth-century American Way would wither and die.

It is no wonder that writers such as Bandura (1973) have called the field of aggression a 'semantic jungle'. With several hundred definitions of aggres-sion extant in the social sciences, it is inevitable that confusions reign and unnecessary arguments domi-nate the debate. The more promising approaches are those which have left the nature–nurture debate behind and focus on the understanding of specific forms of aggressive behaviour and the factors which influence them. Analysis of social frameworks which encourage or inhibit displays of aggression has also proved fruitful in explaining social phe-nomena such as football hooliganism (Marsh, 1978), female violence (Campbell, 1982), extreme political violence (Billig, 1978), etc. Work con-cerned with the role of specific physiological mechanisms (such as Brain, 1986) has also contri-buted to a more rational debate in which there are fewer obstacles to examining the complex interplay between biological and social factors. Whether we view aggression as an avoidable pathology or as an inevitable component of the human condition, our understanding of the phenomena will only increase if the focus is on why certain individuals in certain social contexts display extreme antipathy towards each other in order to achieve specific goals, whether these goals be the injury of others or the development of social prestige and status.

Reading

Berkowitz, L. 1962: *Aggression: A Social Psychological Analysis.*

Fromm, Erich 1973: *The Anatomy of Human Destructiveness.*

Geen, R.G. and Donnerstein, E.I. eds 1983: *Aggression: Theoretical and Empirical Reviews*, vol. 2: *Issues in research.*

Sian, G. 1985: *Accounting for Aggression.*

PETER MARSH

AI   *See* ARTIFICIAL INTELLIGENCE

alienation   In the writings of Marx, this is the historical process whereby human beings have become successively estranged from Nature and from the products of their activity (commodities and capital, social institutions and culture) which then come to confront subsequent generations as an independent, objectified force, that is, as an alienated reality. He focused in particular on the deleterious effects of alienated labour in capitalist industrial production (see LABOUR PROCESS). Secondly, it refers to a sense of estrangement from society, group, culture or the individual self that people commonly experience living in complex industrial societies, particularly in large cities. Alienation evokes experiences such as depersonalization in the face of bureaucracy; feelings of powerlessness to affect social events and processes; and a sense of lack of cohesion in people's lives. That alienation in this general sense constitutes a recurring problem in contemporary societies such as our own is a prominent theme in the sociology of the modern urban experience (see MASS SOCIETY; URBANISM; ANOMIE).

In Europe between the wars the predicament of humankind in modern secular societies was widely discussed by existentialist philosophers, psychoanalysts, theologians and Marxists as the problem of alienation. The debate was further fuelled by the publication in 1932 of Marx's analysis of alienation in his *Economic and Philosophic (Paris) Manuscripts* (1844). The term is often linked with REIFICATION, which was not used by Marx but by the Marxist writer György Lukács in his influential *History and Class Consciousness* (1923), which anticipated the theme of human 'objectification' discussed in the *Manuscripts*. For Lukács, reification is the extremity of the alienation of humans from their products which arises from COMMODITY FETISHISM in developed capitalist societies.

In Britain, the concept of alienation came into currency in sociology and adjacent fields in the 1960s and 1970s via Marxism. A controversy subsequently raged about the significance of Marx's early writings on this subject for our understanding of his work as a whole. Some Marxists, for example Louis Althusser (1965), argued that Marx abandoned the humanistic concept of alienation in his early writings in favour of a scientific analysis of modes of production, while others, such as István Mészáros (1970) and David McLellan (1980) argued that the concept was integral to all his works, both early and late.

In Marx, the historical process of alienation has transformed human beings increasingly from creative subjects into passive objects of social processes. Hegel had already described, in a metaphysical framework, such a process, but Marx insisted that the end of alienation had to be achieved in practice by real people and not apparently solely in the realm of consciousness or self-awareness, as in Hegel (see PRAXIS). Marx's secular humanism relied heavily on Ludwig Feuerbach's materialist theory of religion in which he claimed that human beings have projected their own essence and potentialities into God, who then confronts them in an alienated form. In the *Manuscripts* Marx claimed that religious alienation was only one aspect of the propensity of human beings to alienate themselves in their own products, which could all be explained as aspects of economic alienation.

This analysis was then fused with the politics of communism, into which future society Marx projected the 'complete return of man himself as a *social* (i.e. human) being – a return become conscious, and accomplished within the entire wealth of previous development' (Marx, 1844). History is thus the simultaneous loss of human beings in their own products and their subsequent recovery of themselves, a real process that Hegel had simply perceived in a mystified manner. In Marx's theory of history the developing forces of production (content) progressively outgrow their relations (forms) in a series of historical modes of production as the realization of this process. With the social formation of capitalism 'the pre-history of human society accordingly closes' (Marx, 1859). Marx's social-scientific theory of the historical genesis of alienation and its overcoming in practice was thus burdened with the same teleology as that of the metaphysical theory it was trying to supplant.

In common with Feuerbach and with echoes of

Jean-Jacques Rousseau, Marx assumes that the essence or 'species being' of humankind is – unlike that of animals – inherently sociable and cooperative. Also, that labour too should have a communal character as the productive and creative life of the species as a whole in their necessary appropriation of Nature. Labour not only creates wealth, but is also its own reward and the means by which humankind has raised itself above the animal world and created human history. For Marx, therefore, the organization of large-scale commodity production and the individualistic wage labour contract of the early capitalist factories of his time constituted a travesty of the species character that labour should have if it were to be organized in a way truly congruent with the assumed nature of man. Alienation is thus a 'critical' concept, used as a measuring rod calibrating the human costs of capitalist civilization.

Alienated labour alienated workers from (1) their product, which did not belong to them; (2) work itself, because it was only a means of survival, something forced on them in order to live; (3) from themselves because their activity was not their own, resulting in feelings of self-estrangement; (4) from other people in the factory because each was there individually selling their labour power as a commodity. For Marx, human egoism was a product of alienated labour, as was private property, which was not founded on a collective relation of humans to Nature. Hence neither represented enduring characteristics of human beings and their lives together, but were a product only of class societies in the capitalist phase. The abolition of alienated labour would mean that labour would acquire its true species character.

Two problem areas have dominated discussions of alienation. Firstly, the status of the model of human beings at the heart of the theory. In today's terminology, Marx's analysis is an example of philosophical anthropology because he posits, *a priori*, a timeless picture of HUMAN NATURE. His model of *homo laborans* takes labour from the dominant experience of factory work of his time and instates it as the universal defining human characteristic. Around this idea are then hung a number of further assumptions about human sociability, freedom and control, self-realization and collective labour as its own reward. Like all models of its kind, it is open to the charge of arbitrariness.

Secondly, controversy has continued about the feasibility of de-alienation. Existentialists have suggested that while alienation may be exacerbated under capitalist production, it is basically symptomatic of something perennial in the human social-natural condition. Marx thought that economic alienation was the basis of all other aspects, so the supersession of private property would mark the end of expropriation by the capitalists and hence all alienations. But, as Axelos says, 'Marx was unable to recognize the will to power' (1976, p. 305), so did not foresee the emergence of new forms of expropriation and the exploitation of people by each other and, hence, further alienation. The existence of powerful communist establishments in the socialist societies of Eastern Europe and the former Soviet Union, where private property was effectively abolished, would seem to bear this out. Also, eliminating alienation at the point of production by workers' self-management (as in the former Yugoslavia) leaves the spheres of distribution and exchange untouched as further sources of alienation.

The issue of the extent to which alienation can be eliminated ultimately turns on whether it is feasible to abolish the DIVISION OF LABOUR in a complex society. In the *German Ideology* Marx anticipates its utopian abolition under communism, which also dissolves the distinction between mental and physical labour. Thus would arise the universal human being who is able to 'hunt in the morning, fish in the afternoon, rear cattle in the evening, criticise after dinner . . . without ever becoming hunter, fisherman, shepherd or critic' (Marx and Engels, 1845–6). Whereas later, in the *Grundrisse* and in *Capital*, he more cautiously says that in any society, even a socialist one, nature as a 'realm of necessity' cannot be eliminated nor can the superintendence, coordination and regulation of work, in short some kind of division of labour and, hence, alienation.

For Emile Durkheim (1858–1917) in the *Division of Labour* and other writings, the negative, alienating aspects of the division of labour are counterbalanced to some degree by the increased opportunities for individual self-realization made possible by its extension. He advocated developing occupational associations to promote solidarity and a new morality that acknowledges people's increasing dependence on each other that also accompanies it. Robert Blauner (1964) broke the concept of alienation down into the four testable dimensions of powerlessness, meaninglessness, isolation and self-estrangement in the workplace. In a study of various industrial settings in the USA he found that alienation and freedom were unevenly distributed in the modern productive process. Alienation was at its greatest in mass production and at its least in craft production. Some have argued that this kind of empirical approach misses the critical-philosophical intention of Marx's concept, whereas others have said that it is the only way to give any kind of precision to a concept which is quasi-metaphysical and inherently indeterminate. Interest in the concept as used by Marx has waned in recent years.

Reading
Althusser, Louis 1965 (*1969*): *For Marx*.
Axelos, Kostas 1976: *Alienation, Praxis and Techne in the Thought of Karl Marx*.
Blauner, Robert 1964: *Alienation and Freedom*.
Durkheim, Emile 1893 (*1984*): *The Division of Labour in Society*.
Lukács, György 1923 (*1971*): *History and Class Consciousness*.
McLellan, David 1980: *The Thought of Karl Marx*, 2nd edn.
Mészáros, István 1970: *Marx's Theory of Alienation*.
RICHARD KILMINSTER

analytical philosophy   *See* LINGUISTIC PHILOSOPHY; PHILOSOPHY

anarchism   Repudiation of rulers is at the core of anarchism. In developing this negative notion, modern anarchists, broadly classifiable as either individualist or socialist, reject the state, hold that social order is possible in its absence and advocate moving directly towards 'society without a state'. The first to elaborate a theory of anarchism was Godwin (1793) but Proudhon (1840) was the first to call himself, defiantly, an anarchist. As a social movement, anarchism, in a revolutionary form, crystallized in opposition to Marxism in the period of the First International 1864–72, partly over the issue of whether socialists should seek the immediate 'abolition of the state'. In the twentieth century, as socialism became increasingly statist, the anarchist movement has declined but its ideas have influenced other movements and contributed to the critique of statist theories and practices. Anarchism also remains of interest because it raises issues fundamental to social and political theory.

One such relates to authority. 'Philosophical anarchism', a component especially of the individualist variety, rejects the idea of legitimate authority in the sense of the right of anyone (state official or not) to command the obedience of another.

Individual autonomy, conceived morally, as by Godwin and by Wolff (1970), requires individuals to act according to their own judgements. Conceived egoistically, as by Stirner (1845), it implies that 'the unique one' who truly 'owns himself' recognizes no duties to others; within the limit of his might, he does what is right *for him*.

Since 'philosophical anarchism' makes cooperation and formal organization problematical, anarchists are often less radical. Although generally suspicious of authority, they may recognize the rational authority of experts within their fields of competence and the moral authority of basic social norms, such as 'contracts should be kept.' And in the sense in which 'politics' occurs in all organized groups when unanimity is lacking, they may recognize even political (but not state) authority. Thus, decisions taken participatorily by members of a commune or workers' cooperative may be deemed morally binding. But they reject authority backed by coercive power – the kind institutionalized, preeminently but not exclusively, in the STATE.

Anarchists reject the modern state because, within its territory, it divides people into rulers and the ruled, monopolizes the major means of physical coercion, claims sovereignty over all persons and property, promulgates laws held to override all other laws and customs, punishes those who break its laws, and forcibly appropriates through taxation and in other ways the property of its subjects. Further, with other states, it divides human society against itself into national societies, and periodically wages war, thereby authorizing mass murder. For anarchists, even a democratic state lacks legitimacy since it is not based on consent in any strict sense and the ruler–ruled relationship is merely masked. Anarchists may admit that sometimes the state performs useful functions, such as protecting – as well as also violating – human rights, but argue these could and should be carried out by voluntary organizations.

In rejecting the state, anarchists deny the widely held view, classically expressed by Thomas Hobbes (1651), that in its absence there is no society and life is solitary, poor, nasty, brutish and short. Humans, they believe, are naturally social, not asocial; and until the first states developed some five thousand years ago all humans lived in stateless societies. Anarchists take John Locke's view that 'the natural condition of mankind', in which all are free and equal, no one having the right to command obedience of others, does constitute a society. They do not accept Locke's justification in terms of consent of the limited state, an agency for protecting natural rights, especially the right to property – the nightwatchman view of the state associated with *laissez-faire* liberalism, which reappears in the libertarian work of Nozick (1974). But they endorse Locke's view, later vividly expressed by Paine (1791–2, pt 2, ch. 1) and recently restated by Hayek (1973, ch. 2), that social order exists independently of the state – an order spontaneously generated, a product of human sociability. What distinguishes anarchists from such liberals is their belief that this natural order does not need supplementing by order imposed from above. In the language of rational choice theory, although social order is a 'public good', a good characterized by indivisibility and non-excludability, people – under conditions envisaged by anarchists – will cooperate voluntarily to provide it themselves (Taylor, 1982). For anarchists, unlike classical liberals, the state is not a 'necessary' but a 'positive' evil – a major source, as in war, of disorder in human society. They champion, therefore, the idea of 'natural society', a self-regulated, pluralistic society in which power and authority are radically decentralized.

In distinguishing sharply between society and state, both individualist and socialist anarchism build on liberal foundations. The former may be seen as liberalism taken to an extreme, or logical, conclusion. The individual is the basic unit, 'society' is a collective term for aggregations of individuals, FREEDOM is defined negatively as absence of coercion, and the aim is to maximize individual liberty in ways compatible with the equal liberty of others. Against the state's claim to sovereignty is pitted the principle of 'the sovereignty of the individual'. On the economic side, individualists have usually insisted on the importance of private property or possession, favoured individual production, condemned all monopolies, and praised the free market. In the belief that their proposals would secure to persons the fruits of their own labour and not lead to accumulation of possessions through the exploitation of the labour of others, nineteenth-century individualists sometimes thought of themselves as socialists. But their successors today, such as Murray Rothbard (1973), having abandoned the labour theory of value, describe themselves as 'anarcho-capitalists'. Their programme amounts to complete privatization. They argue that the free market can supply all goods and services, including protection of persons and property, now allegedly provided by the political monopoly called the state.

Socialist anarchism may be seen as a fusion of liberalism with socialism. High value is placed on individual liberty but freedom is defined not only negatively but also as the capacity to satisfy needs. Insisting on social and economic equality as a necessary condition for the maximum liberty of all, it rejects capitalist private property along with the state. Social solidarity, expressed in acts of mutual aid, is emphasized. Society is thought of as a network of voluntary associations but, more importantly, as composed of local communities. Communal individuality is the ideal.

Socialist anarchism was largely shaped by Proudhon's ideas: liberty is the mother, not the daughter, of order; all political parties are varieties of despotism; the power of the state and of capital are synonymous; the proletariat, therefore, cannot emancipate itself by the use of state power but only by (peaceful) direct action; and society should be organized as autonomous local communities and producer associations, linked by 'the federal principle'. However, his successors, Michael A. Bakunin and Peter A. Kropotkin in Russia, substituted for his 'mutualism' first 'collectivism' and then 'communism' – the latter implying 'everything belongs to everyone' and distribution according to needs.

Also, under Bakunin's inspiration, anarchists adopted the strategy of encouraging popular insurrections in the course of which, it was envisaged, capitalist and landed property would be expropriated and collectivized, and the state abolished. In its place would emerge autonomous, but federally linked, communes: a socialist society organized from below upwards, not from above downwards. To foster the spirit of revolt among the oppressed, anarchists adopted the tactic of 'propaganda by the deed' in the form of, first, exemplary local insurrections and, then, acts of assassination and terrorism. Faced with the consequent repression of their movement, other anarchists adopted an alternative strategy associated with SYNDICALISM. The idea was to turn trade unions into revolutionary instruments of class struggle and to make them, rather than communes, the basic units of a new society. It was through syndicalism that anarchists exercised their greatest influence on socialist movements in the period 1895–1920. The influence lasted longer in Spain where, during the civil war of 1936–9, anarcho-syndicalists, with some shortlived success, attempted to carry through their conception of revolution.

In Spain, as earlier in revolutionary Russia, anarchism continued its quarrel with Marxism, even though anarchists often accepted much of Marx's economic analysis, while Marxists agreed that the coming classless, communist society would be stateless. The differences were in part about means to this end. Anarchists opposed the Marxist idea that workers should organize themselves into a distinct political party to win concessions from the bourgeois state as a prelude to its overthrow. And they opposed the idea of a workers' state – 'the dictatorship of the proletariat' – which, supposedly, would 'wither away' as capitalist property relations were abolished. Anarchists argued that the first would lead to the degeneration of the workers' movement and its co-option by the bourgeois state, and that, even if it did not, the second would lead to a dictatorship *over* the proletariat and hence to a new form of class rule. But underlying these differences, there are others, notably about the nature of the state. While anarchists agree that dominant economic classes use the state to maintain their dominance, they see the state as embodying political power which cannot be reduced, even 'in the last analysis', to economic power. Because political power has independent roots, the state is an organization with its own dynamics and 'logic'. Unless resisted, that logic leads to the complete domination of society by the state: TOTALITARIANISM.

Sharply contrasting with revolutionary anarchism in its methods but not in its vision of a new socialist society is anarchism that derives from the pacifist tradition (see PACIFISM). 'The law of love', expressed in the Sermon on the Mount, led Leo Tolstoy, the Russian novelist, to denounce the state as 'organized violence' and to call on people to disobey its immoral demands. The call influenced Gandhi in developing his philosophy of non-violence in India. He popularized the technique of mass non-violent resistance and originated the key notion of anarcho-pacifism: 'non-violent revolution', described as a progamme not for the seizure of power but the transformation of relationships. For him, national independence was only the first step in such a revolution which Vinoba Bhave, campaigning for voluntary villagization of land, continued in an effort to realize Gandhi's dream of an India of self-sufficient, self-governing village republics (Ostergaard, 1982).

In a century that has witnessed everywhere a vast increase in the power of the state, its further militarization and its general acceptance as the normal political organization of national societies, anarchism has clearly been 'against the current'. But it survives and shows a notable ability to outlive specific anarchist movements. A generation after the eclipse of ANARCHO-SYNDICALISM, anarchist ideas reemerged, sometimes spectacularly, in the context of the New Left movements of the 1960s. Their influence is still discernible today, notably in movements for peace, feminism, lesbian and gay liberation, radical social ecology, animal liberation and workers' self-management. Direct action, the classical anarchist alternative to conventional political action, has also become popular. At the other end of the political spectrum, individualist anarchism, reborn as anarcho-capitalism, is a significant tendency in the libertarian New Right.

The anarchism that survives and fertilizes other movements does not call, as Bakunin did, for the immediate abolition of the state. It calls, rather, for 'anarchy in action' here and now and for changes that promote the 'anarchization', not the 'statization' of human society. Beyond that, it survives as a permanent protest against all coercive power relationships, however disguised, and all theories that deny the fundamental insight of liberalism: human beings are naturally free and equal.

See also LIBERTARIANISM.

Reading
Apter, D.E. and Joll, J. eds 1971: *Anarchism Today*.
Bookchin, M. 1982: *The Ecology of Freedom*.
Guérin, D. 1970: *Anarchism*.
Miller, D. 1984: *Anarchism*.
Pennock, J.R. and Chapman, J.W. eds 1978: *Anarchism*.
Ritter, A. 1980: *Anarchism*.
Ward, C. 1982: *Anarchy in Action*.
Woodcock, G. 1963 *(1986)*: *Anarchism*, 2nd edn.

GEOFFREY OSTERGAARD

anarcho-syndicalism   As the prefix suggests, this is the anarchist variety of syndicalism – *revolutionary* trade unionism. The core idea of the latter is that the organizations developed by workers to defend their interests *vis-à-vis* employers should become the instruments to overthrow capitalism and then constitute the basic units of socialist society. Through 'direct action' in the form, principally, of strikes culminating in the social general strike, the unions would take control of the means of production and all other necessary social functions, dispossess capitalist owners and displace all bourgeois institutions, thereby establishing genuine 'working-class socialism'. In the French labour movement, where these ideas gained wide currency in the period 1895–1914, anarchists, notably Fernand Pelloutier (1867–1901), pioneered their propagation. But in France, as in other countries such as Italy, Russia, the USA, the UK, Sweden and Argentina, where syndicalism became a lively tendency in labour movements, not all syndicalists accepted anarchist ideas – the abolition of the state and radically decentralized organization based on 'the federal principle'. 'Pure' syndicalists regarded their movement as sufficient unto itself, saw anarchism as one of several competing political ideologies and left open the question of whether a syndicalist society would be organized as a political entity. On the other hand, anarchists adopted one of three attitudes towards syndicalism. Some regarded its ideas as too limited or mistaken, and therefore remained aloof. Others, seeing syndicalism as essentially a *means* to achieve an anarchist society, encouraged participation in the movement but warned against identifying anarchism with it. Yet others – the anarcho-syndicalists – took the view that syndicalism was essentially the expression of mature anarchism in contemporary capitalist society. It was in Spain with its strong anarchist tradition that anarcho-syndicalism became a significant force in the shape of the CNT (Confederación Nacional de Trabajo), an organization embracing by 1936 one million members, in which militants of the FAI (Federación Anarquista Ibérica) exercised a preponderant influence. It was in Spain, too, in the region of Catalonia, that anarcho-syndicalists during the early months of the civil war, 1936–9, attempted with some initial but shortlived success to establish a system of 'workers' control' of industry.

Except in Spain, syndicalist tendencies in Western labour movements were weakened by the nationalist fervour unleashed at the outbreak of war in 1914. They were further seriously weakened following the success of the Bolsheviks in Russia in 1917 which led many syndicalists to abandon their conception of revolution centred on the unions in favour of the Leninist model with its emphasis on the 'vanguard' role of communist parties. Those syndicalist unions and groups which refused to follow the communist path then formed in 1922 the International Working Men's Association, in which the Spanish CNT until 1939 was the largest

national section. Later retitled the International Workers' Association, its 14 national sections (including a revived but weak and divided CNT) remained into the 1990s the vehicles for promoting anarcho-syndicalist ideas – but voiced now only in the margins of labour movements that are overwhelmingly reformist.

See also ANARCHISM and SYNDICALISM.

Reading
Brenan, G. 1950: *The Spanish Labyrinth*, 2nd edn.
Richards, V. 1983: *Lessons of the Spanish Revolution*, 3rd edn.
Rocker, R. 1989: *Anarcho-Syndicalism*.

GEOFFREY OSTERGAARD

Annales school   This 'school' of historiography, if school it may be called, may justly lay claim to being the most distinctively twentieth-century contribution to historical writing. Its origins are usually traced to the founding of the *Revue de synthèse historique* by Henri Berr in 1900. It arose out of discomfort with, indeed protest against, the idiographic thrust that had come to dominate European historiography since the Rankean 'revolution' – the call to write history empirically 'as it really happened', based on primary sources – and in particular had become institutionalized in France at the Sorbonne and in the *Revue historique* (founded in the 1870s). Much later, in 1953, Lucien Febvre would suggest that this French historiography, as exemplified by such figures as Gabriel Monod and Emile Bourgeois, was 'history as written by those defeated in 1870'. He argued that their emphasis on diplomatic history was sustained by a kind of subtext that read: 'Ah, if we had studied it more carefully, we should not be where we are today' (Febvre, 1953, p.vii).

It was not that there was objection to the search for empirical data in so-called primary sources. It was the sense that there was no history worth writing that was not 'synthetic' – hence the title of Berr's journal – or in Febvre's later formulation that was not *histoire pensée* or *histoire-problème* as opposed to being *histoire historisante*.

Henri Berr sought to break the narrow confines of a presumed 'discipline' by opening his journal to other 'disciplines', especially the new social sciences. This tradition was renewed, reemphasized and deepened when, in 1929, Lucien Febvre and Marc Bloch joined together in founding the journal which gave this group its name. There are two main things to be noted about the journal. First of all, there is its name. It was called *Annales d'histoire économique et sociale*, which was a direct (and deliberate) translation of the title of the German review which incarnated the Schmoller school of 'institutional' history, the *Vierteljahrschrift für Sozial- und Wirtschaftsgeschichte*. (See also METHODENSTREIT.) The title was not merely a means of identification with a parallel anti-idiographic current in Germany; it was also a programme. It said that the journal would emphasize the economic and the social, implicitly because they were more enduring, more important and more fundamental than the political and the diplomatic, the normal focus of most historical writing.

The second thing to notice about the review is its locus, and that of its authors and readers. The journal was located not in Paris, but in Strasbourg where Febvre and Bloch were then teaching. This was symbolic of their institutional marginality, which continued even when Febvre was appointed to the Collège de France and Bloch to the Sorbonne. The number of subscribers was small, only several hundred. But the authors and readers were international from the beginning, as were the themes of the journal. In particular, there were strong links with Italy and Spain.

After World War II, the influence of the *Annales* movement grew dramatically, with an important institutional expansion. Bloch had been killed by the Nazis, but Febvre continued to lead the movement until his death in 1956. Febvre associated to himself, however, a younger historian, Fernand Braudel, who would come to symbolize the so-called 'second generation' of the *Annales* movement. Febvre would lavish praise on Braudel's great work, published in 1949, *La Méditerranée et le monde méditerranéen à l'époque de Philippe II*. He called it the 'image of history' as *Annales* had been calling for it, marking 'the dawn of a new era' (Febvre, 1950, p. 224).

Although Braudel was refused an appointment at the Sorbonne, he received one at the Collège de France, as had Febvre, which in the politics of the French university system was honorific but lacking real power. Febvre and Braudel were determined to create an alternative power base and, with the aid of a senior civil servant, Gaston Berger, were able to implement an idea from the 1870s, the creation of a VIe Section (for economic and social sciences) of the École Pratique des Hautes Études. The École was a peculiar institution, invented in the nine-

teenth century to offer 'adult education' outside the university system. But, very quickly, Febvre and Braudel were able to transform the VIe Section into a vibrant locus of graduate studies and scholarly research in history and the social sciences. The journal too was revitalized in 1946 under a new name, *Annales: Economies, Sociétés, Civilisations*.

It was Braudel who developed most explicitly and most theoretically the position of the *Annales* movement on the social construction of time and temporalities. He divided his book on the Mediterranean into three parts corresponding with what he considered the three social times of *structure*, *conjoncture*, and *événement*. In *The Mediterranean*, he cast his famous *boutade*, 'Events are dust' (Braudel, 1949, vol. 1, p. 901). In 1958, he published what is probably the theoretical centrepiece of the *Annales* movement, 'History and the social sciences'. It was in this article that the case is made for the third great theme which has distinguished the *Annales* movement. In addition to 'synthesis' and to 'economic and social history', there is the emphasis on the *longue durée*, the time of the slow-moving structures of social life. Braudel is however careful to spell out in this essay that the *longue durée* is not the eternal and the unchanging universal. He calls this latter time the 'very *longue durée*' and says of it: 'if it exists, [it] can only be the time of the wise men . . .' (Braudel, 1958).

Suddenly, that is between 1945 and 1970, the epoch of the second generation, the *Annales* movement moved from the wings to centrestage, and not only in France. By the time the VIe Section was rechristened the École des Hautes Études en Sciences Sociales in 1975, it had become more prestigious to have an appointment there than in the now multiple Paris universities. *Annales E.S.C.* had become one of the world's major scholarly journals. It seemed that almost everyone, or at least very many scholars, were proclaiming themselves *Annalistes*.

For the *Annales* movement, as for so many other currents of thought, 1968 was a breakpoint. It was only after 1968 that the influence of the *Annales* movement moved beyond what might be called the 'extended' French cultural zone – Latin Europe, Quebec, Poland, Hungary and Turkey. (For an analysis of this phenomenon see the special issue of *Review*, 1978, which also includes articles explaining why Great Britain showed a certain early receptivity as well.) It began to have an important influence in zones that had been hitherto resistant –

the United States, Germany, and finally the USSR. (For many years, the official Soviet position was one condemning the *Annales* movement. There were nonetheless many closet *Annalistes* in the USSR. It was only in 1989, with *glasnost*, that the Institute of Universal History of the Academy of Sciences could sponsor an international colloquium on 'Les Annales – hier et aujourd'hui'.)

In 1972, Braudel retired both as editor of *Annales E.S.C.*, and as president of the VIe Section, to be replaced by the so-called 'third generation'. The year 1970 marked the official launching of the last great institutional construction of the *Annales* movement, the Maison des Sciences de l'Homme, of which Braudel would remain the administrator until his death in 1985. The Maison has as its *raison d'être* the intellectual collaboration of French scholars with scholars everywhere else in the world, pursuing the same hope of synthesis that had inspired Henri Berr in 1900.

The events of 1968 opened up new intellectual horizons everywhere. In some parts of the world, it made scholars (and students) receptive for the first time to the *via media* of *Annales*, struggling simultaneously against IDIOGRAPHIC history and universalizing social science. On the other hand, it was precisely in those parts of the world where *Annales* influence had already been strong that the scholarly community was entering into a 'post-Marxist' mood, and was hence somewhat suspicious of the great emphasis on economic history of the 'second generation'.

The 'third generation' shifted the emphasis noticeably from the economic to the social (even including in the latter political culture). This translated itself into a renewed concern with *mentalités*, an extraordinary expansion of empirical research on a wide range of sociocultural phenomena, and an important blending of interest with those anthropologists who were themselves putting new emphasis on the symbolic sphere.

The *Annales* movement in its 'third generation' has pursued the spirit of 'inclusiveness', of studying any and all aspects of social reality, that was a central part of the *Annales* ethos from the beginning. The third generation has used the social to expand the economic in the same way as the previous generations had used the economic to expand the political. But while it is clear that they have been more 'inclusive', it is less sure that they have been as holistic, as 'synthetic'.

The third generation has tried to bring back the importance of the political arena by seeing it as a central part of *mentalités*. In doing so, they have had to come closer to a consideration of 'events', even if under the guise of symbolic occurrences.

As the 'third generation' has come to occupy more and more place in the world of knowledge – in the double sense of being more numerous and concerning themselves with more empirical issues – they have inevitably begun to lose the sense of being a movement. Most *Annalistes* refuse today outright the expression, 'the *Annales* school'.

Is there then a spirit of *Annales* which remains? It seems so, in the sense that the extremes of idiographic narrative and ahistorical generalizing are still rejected. What might be said is that whereas, for the first and second generations, the *via media* was a very narrow passageway between two highly menacing and very large schools of Scylla and Charybdis, for the third generation, the *via media* has become a wide highway between two highly diminished extremist positions. It is the difference between having a self-image of David versus Goliath and having the sense that what one does is not merely normal and respectable, but thought of as such.

Will there really be a 'fourth generation' of the *Annales* movement? The question is open.

Reading
Braudel, Fernand 1958 (*1972*): History and the social sciences. In *Economy and Society in Early Modern Europe*, ed. Peter Burke.
Review 1978: The *Annales* school and the social sciences. Special issue, 1.3–4 (Winter–Spring).
Wallerstein, Immanuel 1991: Beyond *Annales*? *Radical History Review* 49, 7–15.

IMMANUEL WALLERSTEIN

anomie   The term derives from the Greek *anomia*, meaning: without law and connoting iniquity, impiety, injustice and disorder (Orru, 1987). It reappeared in English in the sixteenth century and was used in the seventeenth to mean disregard of divine law. It reappeared in French in the writings of Jean-Marie Guyau (1854–1888) who gave it a positive connotation. An anti-Kantian, Guyau looked forward to an ideal future of *moral anomie* – that is, the absence of absolute, fixed and universal rules – and *religious anomie*, freeing individual judgement from all dogmatic faith.

Anomie's sociological career began with Emile Durkheim, who criticized Guyau's ideas but appropriated the term, giving it once more a negative connotation, first in *The Division of Labour in Society* (1893) and then in *Suicide* (1897). It was subsequently taken up by Robert Merton in the 1930s, after which it achieved its greatest diffusion in the 1950s and 1960s among American sociologists studying SUICIDE, delinquency and deviance (see CRIME AND DEVIANCE). Thereafter anomie came to signify a personality trait or set of attitudes (increasingly indistinguishable from ALIENATION) for the measurement of which various scales were devised. Subsequently its meaning became increasingly indeterminate as its use spread more widely among sociologists and extended to psychologists. In this process, anomie became 'psychologized' and detached from any wider theory of society. The story of its transmutation from Durkheim's initial usage to those of Merton and his successors is interesting. As Besnard observes, anomie which, with Durkheim, 'characterized a state of the social system was later applied to the situation of the individual actor, or even to his attitudes or state of mind'. Furthermore, Durkheim's 'concept critical of industrial society was transformed into a conservative notion designating maladaption to the social order' (Besnard, 1987, p. 13).

In Durkheim's *Division of Labour* the 'anomic form' of the division of labour is 'abnormal'. This consisted in the absence of a body of rules governing the relations between social functions; it was to be seen in industrial and commercial crises and the conflict between labour and capital; and its chief cause lay in the rapidity with which INDUSTRIALIZATION occurred, such that 'the conflicting interests have not had time to strike an equilibrium.' As the market extends and large-scale industry appears, the effect is to 'transform the relationship between employers and workers'. Urbanization caused 'the needs of workers to increase'. With mechanization and the replacement of small workshops by manufacturing, 'the worker is regimented' and removed both from his family and his employer. Finally, work is made less meaningful, reducing the worker to 'the role of a machine' unaware 'of where the operations required of him are leading' (Durkheim, 1893, pp. 305–6).

In *Suicide* anomie constitutes one of the social causes of suicide, a state of the social environment as a function of which suicide rates rise. It is a state of deregulation leaving 'individual passions . . . without a curb to regulate them'. He distinguished two kinds of anomie, economic and conjugal. The former consisted in the breakdown of an accepted normative framework that stabilized expectations; it was manifested in economic crises, whether booms or slumps. But he also thought such anomie was chronic in contemporary societies in the industrial and commercial world, resulting from the decline of religious, political and occupational controls, and the growth of the market and of ideologies celebrating acquisitiveness, a malady of infinite aspiration, 'daily preached as a mark of moral distinction', elevating 'to a rule the lack of rule from which [its victims] suffer' (Durkheim, 1897, pp. 258, 256, 257). Conjugal anomie, he thought, was also chronic, consisting in a 'weakening of matrimonial regulation' of an accepted normative framework that reined in desire and controlled passions, of which divorce was both an expression and a powerful contributory cause (ibid, p. 271).

Robert Merton's anomie shares neither Durkheim's view of human nature nor his project of diagnosing the social and hence personal ills of a rapidly industrializing capitalism. For him anomie was conceived 'as a breakdown in the cultural structure, occurring particularly when there is an acute disjunction between the cultural norms and goals and the socially structured capacities of members of the group to act in accord with them' (1949, p. 162). Merton thought that aspirations to 'succeed' (mainly though not wholly in material terms) were universally prescribed in contemporary US society. Socially structured strain, or anomie, resulted where institutionally permitted means to succeed were unavailable. There were four ways of adapting to this strain, apart from conformity to both goals and institutionalized means – all of them forms of deviance:

Innovators (e.g. professional thieves, white-collar criminals, cheaters in examinations) adhere to the goals but reject the normatively prescribed means. Ritualists (e.g. bureaucrats who slavishly follow the rules without regard for the ends for which they were designed) make a virtue of over-conformity to the institutionalised norms at the price of underconformity to the culturally prescribed goals. Retreatists (e.g. tramps, chronic drunkards, and drug addicts) withdraw from 'the rat race' by abandoning both goals and means. Rebels (e.g. members of revolutionary movements) withdraw allegiance to a cultural and social system they deem unjust and seek to reconstitute the society anew, with a new set of goals and prescriptions for attaining them. (Cohen, 1966, p. 77)

This focus on shared cultural norms and goals and on blocked possibilities of legitimately realizing them set an agenda for deviance research which lasted several decades. Yet, as Besnard has observed, it was, in effect, an inversion of the Durkheimian notion, for 'where Durkheim described individuals uncertain of what they must do as the horizon of possibilities expands, Merton proposes actors sure of the objectives to be attained, but whose aspirations are blocked by a situation of closure with respect to the possibilities of success' (1987, p. 262).

Reading

Besnard, P. 1987: *L'Anomie: ses usages et ses fonctions dans la discipline sociologique depuis Durkheim.*
Durkheim, E. 1897 (*1951*): *Suicide*, trans. J.A. Spaulding and G. Simpson.
Merton, R.K. 1949 (*1968*): *Social Theory and Social Structure*, revised edn, chs 4 and 5.

STEVEN LUKES

anthropology Broadly considered to be the scientific study of man, this orthodox definition highlights a number of problems that help to illustrate both the diversity of anthropology today and its unifying features. First among these is that while the origins of anthropology as a coherent discipline lie in the Darwinian revolution of the middle of the nineteenth century, and hence were part of the general interest in EVOLUTION, much of its subsequent development has been a reaction against evolutionary and in particular progressionist notions of human society and behaviour. The fragmentation of anthropology into distinctly *social* and *biological* branches reflects not only different responses to the development of evolutionary ideas, but also a rejection by much of social anthropology in particular of the feasibility of a purely scientific approach to the problems of the study of humans. Secondly, the rise of feminist critiques has led to caution about, if not an outright rejection of, the use of the term 'man' to designate the human species as a whole. Although it is possible to see the term 'man' as an all-embracing reference to the species as a whole, it is at least a reminder that much of the reconstruction of human evolution and diversity has historically been seen largely from a male perspective.

Given this fragmentation into social and biological elements, not to mention yet further subdivisions, it is questionable whether there remains any coherence to the term anthropology at all, and furthermore, whether the growth of a whole range of life, human and social sciences, not to mention more humanistic approaches, has not led to a redundancy in which there is no clear niche for anthropology nor a distinctive character to an anthropological approach. A positive answer can be provided by considering what is unique or predominant in anthropological investigations. More than any other part of the human or social sciences, anthropology is characterized by an emphasis on comparative approaches, on variation rather than norms in behaviour and societies, and a rejection of Western societies or populations as a model for humanity. This comparative framework is of paramount importance. Traditionally social anthropologists have focused on non-Western societies, and although there has been an increasing interest in applying similar methods and concepts to societies that lie within the European sphere, what has always been the case is that the human social experience is best viewed as a range of variations, each with their own cultural logic, and in particular that Western society does not provide a yardstick against which these other cultures should be assessed. The range of cultural variations provides this distinctly comparative framework for social anthropologists.

Equally, biological anthropologists, or physical anthropologists as they have previously been known, use biological principles and methods to provide another comparative framework. This may be an explicitly evolutionary one, comparing humans with other primates, or it may be the examination of the extent and nature of human biological variation today. If, following American usage of the term anthropology, archaeology is included, then the comparative framework is provided by time – the way in which human societies have varied through prehistory and history. Underpinning all the branches of anthropology is this concern with mapping human variation – biological, behavioural and cultural – and attempting to explain, interpret and understand the patterns in ways that do not make any unwarranted assumptions about directions of development or human uniqueness. The anthropological project is ultimately characterized by these global perspectives.

This comparative framework has provided the

basis for anthropology's impact on twentieth-century thought.

Primitive societies

The discovery by Europeans of the enormous variation in human societies occurred primarily during the period 1500 to 1900, and brought with it the need to understand how and why this diversity occurred. The adoption of evolutionary (although not necessarily Darwinian) perspectives during the late nineteenth century provided the first coherent basis for such a perspective. Evolution was viewed by many thinkers who were influenced by Darwin, such as Herbert Spencer, as a progressive ladder of change, from primitive organisms through to humans (see SOCIAL DARWINISM). Other species represented cases of arrested development in a *scala naturae*. In similar vein, human societies could be ranked on a ladder of progress, from the primitive to the advanced. European, and particularly industrial, society stood on the top rung. Primitive societies could therefore be seen as both the stages through which humans and their societies had passed, and examples of a lack of evolutionary progress. The first anthropological syntheses, such as those developed by E.B. Tylor and L.H. Morgan, provided such a model, with various stages of development identified – primeval hordes, barbarism, civilization, for example, or matrilineal and patrilineal, or through economic concepts such as hunting and farming.

Although this evolutionary paradigm provided the basis for modern anthropology, the primary contribution of anthropologists to the ideas of the twentieth century have paradoxically derived from the rejection of this view. For a number of reasons ranging from the pursuit of exotica to the need to administer empires, anthropology paved the way for direct observation and interaction between European observers and the societies involved. It was direct and intimate contact, leading to the development of the methods of participant observation, by anthropologists such as B. Malinowski, A.R. Radcliffe-Brown and E.E. Evans-Pritchard that overturned the evolutionary perspective and led to a rejection of notions of progress in human societies. Experience of the detailed workings of non-European societies showed first that they were far from simple and could not be neatly classified in evolutionary terms. For example, although economically simple, Australian aboriginal societies possessed among the most complex kinship systems

and cosmologies known among humans. Furthermore, by replacing evolutionary concepts with functional ones, it became clear that non-European societies were not primitive attempts at economic organization and social structure, but instead functioned well as integrated systems in particular social and environmental settings. For example, the acephalous society of the Nuer of the Southern Sudan studied by Evans-Pritchard, far from being a primitive and anarchic system, was a multilayered society where the institutions of kinship lineages, marriage patterns and livestock herding dovetailed neatly together.

Although many of the tenets of FUNCTIONALISM have since been abandoned, the notion that the variety of human social and economic organization should be seen in terms of specific ecological circumstances, cultural traditions and alternative responses to unique conditions has remained of central importance, and beyond anthropology has led to the abandonment of a sense of evolutionary hierarchy among human societies. In its place has come a greater sense of independent cultural traditions and alternative social strategies. This has had practical consequences for attitudes towards development, with less willingness to impose change for change's sake and an awareness of the dangers of economic change independent of cultural considerations. It has also revolutionized attitudes towards aesthetics and art, apparent in the interchange of icons between Western and other art forms.

Culture

The central anthropological concept that underpinned these changes was that of CULTURE. This term is multilayered and has itself changed meaning over the years. At one level it refers to those characteristics of behaviour that are unique to humans, relative to other species. It also carries with it the notion of behaviour that is learned and taught, rather than instinctive. Developments in ETHOLOGY have somewhat undermined this aspect as it has become clear that the learned/instinctive dichotomy in animal behaviour is invalid and that other species share characteristics that were formerly thought to be uniquely human (such as tool-making). Another level is that of the human capacity to generate behaviour. Although specific behaviours may not be unique to humans, nonetheless the human mind's ability to generate an almost infinite flexibility of response through its symbolic and linguistic potential sets humans apart. Recent interpretations of culture stress the cognitive source of human behaviour. At another level is the view that such behaviour is deeply imbedded in social relations and other social characteristics. And finally, the outcome of these processes is the empirically observable phenomenon of human cultures – the separate identities of distinct human societies, characterized by specific cultural traditions.

The recognition of the diversity of human cultures and subcultures is a major conceptual step that has arisen out of the practice of social anthropology – the detailed study of specific societies (ethnography). Principal among the implications of studies of peoples in cultural units and contexts is the recognition that they are bound together not by genetic or biological identity but by social traditions, and that ETHNICITY is a major factor in relationships between people and societies.

Furthermore, culture is not just the accretion of social traditions, but is deeply enmeshed with the entire cognitive system such that a person's view of the world is constructed and constrained by cultural experience. Given the independence of cultural traditions this has enormous implications for the intercommunicability of concepts and values between societies.

Cultural relativism

The problem of translation across cultures has led in one direction to cultural relativism. In one sense this is an extreme reaction to the progressive notions of evolutionary approaches, which held that societies and cultures could be ranked from primitive to advanced. Cultural relativism has developed within social anthropology as a means of emphasizing both the difficulty of making comparisons between cultures and the absence of any independent criteria for making judgements about the relative merits of different social traditions. At its most extreme, cultural relativism espouses the view that a culture can only be considered within the context of its own cultural traditions and logic. At a practical level this has had important and positive consequences for the way in which racial and ethnic problems have been considered, and has led also to a much deeper understanding of values, knowledge systems and cosmologies around the world. More negative effects have been the abandonment of the comparative approaches that

underpin anthropology, a tendency towards historical particularism, and an ambiguity about the universality of human rights.

Unity of the human species

While social anthropology has rejected evolutionary approaches that are based on a progressive view of human society, a rather different trend can be found in biological anthropology. Recent work on the history of Darwinism have shown that while many of Darwin's followers were keen to see a progressive element, he himself was aware that this was not the case and that his strongly selectionist arguments (see NATURAL SELECTION) predicted adaptational diversity rather than unilinear change. Indeed, it was for that reason that most evolutionists in the late nineteenth and early twentieth century abandoned selection theory while maintaining an evolutionary perspective. However, Darwin's key evolutionary concept – descent with modification – did provide a simple solution to a major problem, that of monogenesis or polygenesis. The discovery of diverse peoples in the Americas and other parts of the world raised the question for pre-Darwinian scientists of whether these peoples all had a single origin or creation, or whether they were the product of several different acts of creation. Monogenesis implied a unity of all humans, polygenesis opened up the possibility that some human forms were not really part of the specifically human creation of biblical history. The establishment of the fact of evolution, regardless of the mechanism of change, meant that anthropologists were able to show that all humans are descended from a single common ancestor, and that all humans belong to a single species. Subsequent biological work showed the inter-fertility of all humans. Thus biological approaches to anthropology paved the way to the predominant view of this century that humankind is unified, united by a biological heritage that is far greater than any of the differences. The acceptance of the unity of the human species is now a fundamental consensus that forms the basis for many ideas that go beyond the strictly biological.

Human diversity

In the same way that social anthropologists have focused on the diversity of human cultural forms, so too have biological anthropologists looked at biological diversity. An implication of the tree-like structure of the evolutionary process when looking at humans was that human populations could be divided up into discrete units, representing either geographical isolates or evolutionary stages. The apparent diversity of humans, particularly in features such as skin colour and face shape, lent credence to this view, and became the basis for the analysis of human variation in terms of RACE. For most of the late nineteenth and early twentieth century race was the central concept in the study of human biological diversity. Most anthropologists took the view that human races represented ancient divisions within mankind, that they could be viewed also as stages of development, and that biological race was linked to the other social and cultural characteristics. Races provided both a horizontal (i.e. geographical) and a vertical (i.e. through time) categorization of humans. A principal aim was therefore to document this process historically through the study of archaeological and fossil samples. Furthermore race was also used as an explanation for the differences in patterns of development. In the early part of this century physical anthropology lent a biological foundation to more widespread ideas about race and an underpinning to theories of EUGENICS and NATIONAL SOCIALISM. Until World War II race was the central concept in the study of human biology from an anthropological and evolutionary perspective.

This situation was completely transformed after the war, and even before, biologists such as A. C. Haddon and Julian Huxley were highly critical. In recent anthropology, race has been completely rejected as a useful biological and analytical concept. Part of the reason for this was no doubt a reaction against the way in which biology had been used to justify political action. Equally important was the development of NEO-DARWINISM which showed that there was no biological basis for treating variation within a species either as evolutionary stages or as discrete categories. Moreover, the increasingly direct study of genetic rather than physical variation showed that the geographical variation was continuous and extremely complex, thus demonstrating that selective features such as pigmentation did not provide the criteria for distinguishing races. As a result recent work in biological anthropology has shown that race is not a useful biological concept. Biological anthropologists turned instead to elucidating the functional and adaptive basis (disease, climate, ecology) of human variation.

Human evolution

The development of modern genetics has shown above all that the human species is an extremely young one, that all modern humans share a recent common ancestor, and therefore that any geographical patterns that can be seen do not signify deep divisions among humans but the recent and superficial product of migration and local adaptation. The contribution of anthropology to the ideas of this century thus do return to its original concerns with evolution, but with a rather different emphasis. Evolution does not show a ladder of progress but a source of diversity, and instead of tracing humans further and further back in time it emphasizes how young our species is, and thus the unity of human populations. Against this background, though, specialists in human evolution have also documented the antiquity (more than five million years) and complexity of the diverse lineages that have led to modern humans appearing in the last 100,000 years.

Modern anthropology

With the growth of anthropology during the century and the shift away from a programme of documenting historical patterns, anthropologists have turned to questions that range far more widely and have increasingly practical applications. Among social anthropologists there has been a greater focus on the links between cultural processes and economic, political and sociological ones, leading to an increasing emphasis on cultural aspects of cognition. Furthermore, the marked changes in the traditional societies that anthropologists have studied has led them to become deeply involved in the problems of their development and survival, and anthropology has contributed to a much greater awareness of the indivisible links between culture and other aspects of development. Equally, biological anthropologists have worked increasingly with the problems of disease and nutrition in the Third World, providing especially a greater understanding of the populational aspects of the ecological probems that face vast portions of the human population.

Reading
Bowler, P.J. 1987: *Theories of Human Evolution: A Century of Debate.*
Harris, M. 1968: *The Rise of Anthropological Theory: A History of Theories of Culture.*
Harrison, G.A., Tanner, J.M., Pilbeam, D.R. and Baker,

P.T. 1988: *Human Biology: An Introduction to Human Evolution, Variation, Growth and Adaptability.*
Kuper, A. 1982: *Anthropology and Anthropologists.*
Leach, E. 1982: *Social Anthropology.*
Spencer, F. ed. 1982: *A History of American Physical Anthropology.*

ROBERT A. FOLEY

anti-Semitism   Originally a term popularized by political movements in Germany in the 1870s and 1880s which were campaigning for the reversal of the newly achieved social and political emancipation of the Jews, the term is, strictly speaking, inaccurate because it does not concern itself with opposition to 'Semites' but is confined to all forms of hostility to Jews. As such it has a long history going back to the pre-Christian era when Jewish monotheism and exclusiveness led to suspicion and mistrust. With the advent of Christianity, the Jews became a 'problem' in that their continued existence seemed to belie Christian concepts of a 'new covenant' and the rejection of the Jews by God. Throughout the history of Europe, as Christianity spread, Jews were segregated, forcibly converted or expelled. In the course of time they were also increasingly restricted to commercial and money-lending activities, which added the fear of the usurer to the already well-established images of deicide and other offences against Christianity. As the power of the 'Christian state' declined, the economic hostility to Jews became the greater concern and was, with the rise of German idealist philosophy, linked to the 'essence' (*Wesen*) of Judaism, which was said to be inimical to the interests of European states. It was but a short step from the concept of an 'essence' to the notion of the Jews as a 'race'. While Christian Wilhelm Dohm opened the debate (in 1781) on the emancipation of the Jews by arguing that their 'bad' characteristics were the result of persecution, his contemporaries took the view that it was more likely to be the other way round, that Jewish characteristics were the 'cause' of their persecution. Neither Dohm nor the philosophers approved of the persecution of Jews, but their conceptualizations laid the foundations for a debate on, and for the most part against, the Jews, which focused on the *reasons* for hostility to Jews, thus elevating it into a rational issue. This led to the identification of different forms of anti-Semitism – social, economic, religious and racial, according to the perceptions of the initiators. All are united, however, on the basic foundations of anti-Semitism which propounds 'theories' of a Jewish quest for world domination and the collective guilt of the Jews.

The unrestrained expressions of hostility towards the Jews which marked the early decades of this century led to a deliberate or apathetic acceptance of the racial doctrines of NATIONAL SOCIALISM in Germany and culminated in the systematic destruction of six million Jews during World War II. The 'holocaust' was followed by a considerable reduction in 'Jew-baiting' but has been itself drawn into the debate about Jews by those who wish to minimize the extent of the crime or those who deny that it ever took place. The strongest issue of the postwar period, however, has been the emergence of the state of Israel and with it the 'anti-Zionist' lobby, which insists on a sharp division between anti-Semitism and anti-Zionism. Nevertheless, the real divide in the anti-Zionist camp, like that in the anti-Semitic camp, is between those who oppose the Jews and the state of Israel *per se* and those who object to specific acts and policies of some Jews and some Israeli politicians. The literature on anti-Semitism is extensive and continues to grow, with the holocaust and the state of Israel developing their own very substantial literatures. A useful starting point would be the bibliography in the *Encyclopedia Judaica* (1971, col. 160). For a detailed historical survey see Leon Poliakov (1965–85). A conceptual history is offered by Jacob Katz (1980) and a political analysis by Paul W. Massing (1967). Two recent studies are *Antisemitism in the Contemporary World* (Curtis 1986) and *Because they were Jews* (Weinberg, 1986).

See also JUDAISM.

Reading
Curtis, Michael ed. 1986: *Antisemitism in the Contemporary World.*
Encyclopedia Judaica, 1971.
Katz, Jacob 1980: *From Prejudice to Destruction: Antisemitism 1700–1933.*
Massing, Paul W. 1967: *Rehearsal for Destruction.*
Poliakov, Leon 1965–85: *History of Antisemitism,* 4 vols.
Weinberg, Meyer 1986: *Because they were Jews: A History of Antisemitism.*
Wistrich, Robert 1991: *Antisemitism: The Longest Hatred.*

JULIUS CARLEBACH

archaeology and prehistory   Both these disciplines – the study of the human past through its material remains, and the part of the subject concerned with the period before written records – are relatively recent. The term 'archaeology' came into use in the eighteenth century to describe the study of the material culture of the ancient world, especially that of Greece and Rome. It denoted a form of art-historical scholarship which was closely associated with connoisseurship and collecting, and largely dependent on the existence of textual evidence for explanation. The timescale of biblical chronology allowed little scope for an extended period before written records. Although Enlightenment philosophers discussed broader questions about the remote past, such as the origins of farming and civilization, they did so largely on the basis of comparative ethnography and without reference to archaeology. It was only with the Romantic movement that the remains of preliterate cultures came to be of interest in their own right, often in the context of nationalistic concerns for the origins of the northern European nations. The accumulation of material evidence allowed Scandinavian antiquarians to postulate a succession of technological stages characterized by the use of tools of stone, bronze and iron; although these 'three ages' were believed to be largely contemporary with the literate civilizations of the Mediterranean.

The scope of archaeology became evident in the later nineteenth century with the development of geology and the rejection of a biblical chronology, and the respectability of evolutionary ideas in biology (see EVOLUTION). The idea of prehistory is thus a relatively recent development, closely related to the growth of ANTHROPOLOGY. Classical archaeology continued as a largely separate discipline, although excavations in Greece and Turkey (at sites such as Mycenae and Troy, famous in ancient mythology) revealed the existence of Bronze Age predecessors to the classical civilizations there. The Stone Age was recognized to be a period of considerable length, corresponding to the earlier phases of human evolution during which humanity had been dependent on hunting (the Palaeolithic or Old Stone Age), and to the early stages of farming (Neolithic or New Stone Age). Comparative ethnography could now be related to the material record, and the new subject was called (somewhat unhappily) 'prehistory', with equivalent terms in other European languages (préhistoire; Vorgeschichte). Its methods were potentially global in application, but the subject was dominated by European evidence.

The liberal scientific and evolutionary interpretation of early human history, however, gave way in the earlier twentieth century to a renewed national-

istic emphasis which was accompanied by a divorce of archaeological from anthropological thought. Prehistory (in Germany often termed Urgeschichte, to stress its continuity with historical peoples) was interpreted either in terms of the migrations of particular peoples, or the diffusion of culture from centres such as Egypt. Anthropology turned from historical reconstruction to firsthand observation and description, with an interest in functionalist interpretations. Although the archaeological exploration of other continents produced a wealth of new evidence, the study of each individual area tended to develop as an introverted specialism. One of the few archaeologists to maintain a broader view was the prehistorian V. Gordon Childe (1892–1957), whose studies of European and Near Eastern prehistory were motivated by a desire to escape from the nationalistic emphasis of much contemporary German scholarship through the exploration of Marxist models. He revived the nineteenth-century (and, indeed, Enlightenment) interest in the origins of farming and civilization, which he saw as economic revolutions comparable in importance with the Industrial Revolution, and termed the Neolithic and the Urban Revolution respectively. These ideas were expounded in two classic works, *Man Makes Himself* (in 1936) and *What Happened in History?* (in 1941), which were among the few books which succeeded in bringing archaeological evidence to the attention of social theorists outside the subject at this time.

Despite Childe's political espousal of Marxism and his emphasis on historical materialism, his theories differed from those of contemporary British Marxist historians in their consensual rather than conflictual interpretation of these events. Childe saw a managerial role for early secular elites, with religion as a major force impeding technological progress. He combined a Hegelian vision of the successive roles of Oriental, classical and Western civilization with a diffusionist view of the history of technology, to produce a sophisticated social model in which the innovations that produced early urban societies were stifled by political centralization there, but nevertheless provided the basis for further development in societies which acquired these techniques without paying the social cost. This model (which was influenced by more recent examples such as the industrialization of Japan) explained for him the unique characteristics of West European societies, and set the divergence of 'Western' from 'Oriental' culture back into the

Bronze Age. Although many aspects of these ideas have a rather nineteenth-century flavour, they nevertheless marked a great advance on the inherently metaphysical explanations of national or racial genius which abounded in contemporary archaeological discourse; and they were a remarkable achievement by the subject's lone intellectual.

One factor inhibiting archaeology from exploiting the potential of its evidence to contribute to wider bodies of social theory was its marginal position in the universities. Most practitioners of the subject in the first half of the century were either attached to museums and bodies concerned with ancient monuments, or freelance excavators raising money for their expeditions. The expansion in higher education since World War II therefore had a major effect on the nature of archaeological discourse, which for the first time included a substantial methodological and theoretical component as well as excavation reports and discussions of primary material. Since the archaeology of those areas and periods where textual evidence was available was largely conducted from departments of history and classical or Oriental studies, the major impetus to comparative analysis came initially from prehistory, which was often (and in the United States almost entirely) conducted under the aegis of anthropology. The movement in the later 1960s which came to be known as the 'new archaeology' was thus largely a North American and British phenomenon, echoed in other parts of the English-speaking world and northern Europe, though conspicuously absent in Germany (and Japan) where intellectual adventurism was inhibited by wartime experience; and it was scarcely reflected for at least a decade in classical archaeology. Some similar innovations occurred in the USSR, although constrained by the changing needs of political orthodoxy; and comparable new thinking in France took a rather different form which was initially less sympathetic to the wider movement.

The new archaeology was characterized by an opening up of the subject to a broader range of interests from neighbouring disciplines, and an eagerness to participate in their debates. While it was associated with some important methodological advances (often from areas of new technology quite outside the subject, as with radiocarbon dating from nuclear physics), it tended to absorb and reproduce theories rather than generate its own; and it shared many of its enthusiasms with contemporary movements in history and economics – for instance its concern with ECOLOGY and DEMOGRAPHY. Computers and SYSTEM THEORY provided its *lingua franca*. Like Braudelian history (see ANNALES SCHOOL), it concentrated on process rather than event – hence its alternative name of processual archaeology. Avoiding the unique and the particular (and especially the production of 'pseudo-history'), it claimed that more rigorous – and especially quantitative – methods could reconstruct social as well as simply technological or stylistic information about prehistory. Among its methodological and conceptual innovations were the ideas of numerical taxonomy for the classification of artefacts, spatial sampling to reconstruct settlement patterns from field survey of surface scatters of material, the reconstruction of environment and diet from animal and plant remains, trade patterns from the identification of raw materials, and social structures from the different kinds of artefacts deposited in graves.

While each of these endeavours produced copious new information, its interpretation was often naive, and strongly constrained by the prevailing paradigms of neo-evolutionary anthropology which owed much to Herbert Spencer (1820–1903). Explanations typically stressed population pressure and agriculture intensification (echoing Esther Boserup's ideas in development economics), settlement colonization and expansion, economic specialization and the formation of social hierarchies, and the emergence of central places (echoing themes in the 'new geography' – see also HUMAN GEOGRAPHY). These common themes were found to underlie the emergence of farming and cities, and the general development of human societies worldwide – an evolutionary succession from bands to tribes, chiefdoms and states.

Despite their high technology, novel statistical sophistication and wealth of new information, these interpretations show a great similarity to the views of Enlightenment writers such as Adam Smith (who knew no archaeology at all). In espousing a comparative model, based on the idea of evolution, such work produced a series of case studies which assumed an autonomy of local development and were insensitive to larger structures of the kind postulated by Gordon Childe. Diffusionism was effectively outlawed by this framework, since it was both hard to quantify and had no place in the paradigm. In this respect new archaeology resembled much of 1960s development economics; and during the 1970s such work was criticized in a way similar to that in which modernization theory was challenged by Marxist theories of underdevelopment and world-systems, associated with the names of Andre Gunder Frank and Immanuel Wallerstein (see DEVELOPMENT AND UNDERDEVELOPMENT). Although the concept of underdevelopment proved inapplicable to earlier contexts, the idea of core and periphery gave new life to the study of relationships between urban populations and their illiterate hinterlands, and especially to the asymmetrical trading relationships between them – for instance the Roman wine trade with their Celtic neighbours. The very concept of 'prehistory' was seen as misleading for the later metal ages, since 'civilized' and 'barbarian' societies formed parts of the same economic system. Chiefdoms, even tribes, might be contact phenomena rather than evolutionary stages.

More fundamentally, material culture itself came to be seen during the 1980s as important in its own right, rather than simply reflecting underlying ecological differences and abstract social structures. The desire to possess goods can be as powerful a motivation of change as population pressure or soil deterioration. The 'prestige goods' of European origin which circulated in sub-Saharan Africa were an active component of the power of native chiefs who monopolized their supply and used them to legitimate their authority. So, too, perhaps the intensification of agrarian production in later prehistoric Europe might have been stimulated by the availability of Mediterranean trade goods. Far from being benevolent providers or economic managers, chiefs could be seen as exploiters and monopolizers; and not just in contact situations, but in the genesis of crafts such as metallurgy which involve the supply of rare and costly materials. But if social structures are not abstract hierarchies, and instead consist in various kinds of illusions which minorities succeed in persuading their followers to accept, how is comparative study possible? Surely each social 'structure' is unique, both in its relationships, symbols and materials? If interpretations are so volatile and contextually dependent, what certainty is possible? Do archaeological theories say more about the present than the past? In this way archaeology has tracked the cycle of the social sciences, from the confident comparativism and determinism of the 60s to the relativism and deconstructed postmodernist introversion of the later 1980s (see MODERNISM AND POSTMODERNISM).

Such *angst* is by no means universal. All across the world, men and women sit in trenches recording stratigraphies and recovering artifacts and environmental evidence for laboratory examination, refining datings, noticing correlations, having ideas that help to make sense of what they find. Some of these ideas are new, some of them are old: classical archaeologists have now discovered central place theory, and are playing the games that prehistorians played in the 1960s. If there can be no final understanding of the present, there can certainly be none about the past; but we have yet to know less in one decade than we knew in the one before.

Reading
Binford, L.R. 1983: *In Pursuit of the Past.*
Daniel, G. and Renfrew, A.C. 1988: *The Idea of Prehistory.*
Hodder, I. 1990: *Reading the Past.*
Scarre, C. ed. 1988: *Past Worlds: the Times Atlas of World Archaeology.*
Sherratt, A.G. ed. 1980: *The Cambridge Encyclopedia of Archaeology.*
Wenke, R. 1989: *Pattern of the Past.*

ANDREW G. SHERRATT

aristocracy In its oldest sense, aristocracy denoted a political system. The ancient Greeks took the term to mean a regime where power and merit went together; this usage predominated in the West during two millennia. But at the time of the French revolution, aristocracy, and the new coining 'aristocrat', moved into the realm of social analysis (and polemic). Now the focus was on aristocracy as an elite within the community: an elite in which accumulations of wealth and political authority were concentrated, marked out by privilege, and passed on by hereditary transmission. These are the terms in which 'aristocracy' is now most likely to be invoked by social scientists or historians.

Study of a wide range of contexts and problems has led essentially to a more precise understanding of these characteristic features of aristocracy. The *hereditary transmission* of aristocratic rank has rarely meant anything approaching the total exclusion of newcomers: not least because of the hazards of natural extinction. The scale and character of recruitment into aristocratic status may themselves provide insights into the values and material conditions of a society. In traditional societies, aristocratic *wealth* was likely to be based on a dominant share of landed resources, and Marxist analysts in particular have linked the transition from an agrarian economy to concomitant weakening of aristocratic power. But the source of wealth may have been less important than the leisure it afforded for the exercise of general preeminence in the community. There may indeed be circumstances where new forms of wealth creation proliferate so rapidly that a hereditary elite loses its capacity for decisive economic influence. Students of Europe's commercial or industrial development have nevertheless provided striking evidence for aristocratic adaptability alongside emerging business or manufacturing classes: an adaptability often eased by financial (and family) links between new wealth and old. In traditional societies, again, the *political* role of aristocracy made it more or less co-extensive with the ruling class, or at any rate the class from which civil and military leaders were more or less exclusively drawn. More complex and impersonal systems did something to displace this relationship between public authority and a hereditary ruling elite, with power increasingly exercised in the name of king, state or people. But here again aristocratic adaptation proved striking, and strikingly longlasting: whether as royal ministers, or parliamentary managers, or local bosses.

Some social scientists have seen elites in the contemporary world as displaying yet further stages in the evolution of these aristocratic characteristics: the *nomenklatura* of Eastern Europe, for instance, or the Bostonian notables of New England. Here power and family interests are certainly to be found in concentrated and revealing fashion: privilege flourishes. But the privilege of traditional aristocracies was defined and proclaimed in terms of a distinctive, often formally 'noble', status; and those claims were in some sense accorded recognition by the community at large. Where we can translate 'privilege' merely as 'advantage', there we might say aristocracy no longer exists.

See also ELITE THEORY; SOCIAL DIFFERENTIATION.

Reading
Bottomore, T. 1964 (*1966*): *Elites and Society*.
Bush, Michael 1983: *Noble Privilege*.
——1988: *Rich Noble, Poor Noble*.
Powis, Jonathan 1984: *Aristocracy*.

JONATHAN POWIS

art, sociology of   This attempts to understand the production and consumption of art as the effect, reflection or representation of a general social process. Without being a clearly defined discipline or having a unitary methodology, the sociology of art is best seen as either dispersed among or as the tool of a number of disciplines and areas of enquiry. These may include historical writing as well as art history, social anthropology or the study of subcultures, the historical and sociological study of social classes and groups, the SOCIOLOGY OF KNOWLEDGE, linguistics and art criticism. Although such a linkage may be considered contentious (Wolff, 1981), the sociology and the history of art practised as a form of social history will here be grouped together. Indeed one of the undisputed pioneers of both, Pierre Francastel, did this in the 1940s. He also argued (Francastel, 1965, p. 16) that the subject in itself is characteristic of the modern period of self-conscious historicist thinking, and pleaded for it not to be developed as little more than a 'function of exhausted values'.

The expression 'sociology of art' articulates two terms with completely separate histories. If the word 'sociology' emerged in the last century as the name for various methods of enquiry into human society, 'art', on the contrary, has been in use since antiquity. Over this period it has denoted or qualified a range of phenomena from practical, conceptual or erotic skills to easel painting, from 'gallery art' to lifestyle. The modern, commonsense definition of 'art' as being painting, sculpture, print, etc. accepts art as being a non-artisanal form of production combining manual work with ethical and aesthetic value, and performed by a specially endowed kind of person (Wittkower and Wittkower, 1963).

This category 'art', as it is consolidated and reproduced through the practices of connoisseurship, curating and art history among others, functions retrodictively. It groups together for sale, display or formal criticism materials from origins that are both temporally, geographically or socially disparate and discontinuous. Major national galleries or collections of the type configured in the last century or since, such as the Louvre in Paris, include under the rubric of art many objects which were not recognized as such either at the time or in the place of their production. By implication, then, the sociology of art is liable to be dealing with an object of knowledge that needs constantly to be problematized in the light of a complex series of historical specificities. Such a sociology tends to be in principle opposed to accepting a Kantian ideal of art as the object of any disinterested and categorical aesthetic judgement, just as it is committed to explain rather than to agree the idea of artistic creativity and personality as transcending social conditions. Both must be seen as specific manifestations of the social, which is why, as Pierre Bourdieu (1980, p. 207) has put it, 'Sociology and art make a bad household.'

It is useful, then, to think in terms of a line of development that leads from Marx and Engels's (1845–6) reflections on the political economy of culture to Bourdieu's systematic critique of Kantian judgement, the feminist deconstruction of creativity as a historically gendered category, or the post-colonial rejection of 'Western' artistic values (Bourdieu, 1979; Nochlin, 1989; Pollock, 1988; Said, 1978; Tickner, 1988). An important aspect of the sociology of art has been its oppositional relationship to what it sees as conservative AESTHETICS, whether they be articulated through philosophical rationalism or the demands of the art market. Working from a complex and highly differentiated political terrain, sociology of art is committed to showing that 'art' as a category is always and in many ways overdetermined. At the same time it has continued to be concerned with or reserve the problem of the specificity of art and the questions that this presents for any totalizing explanation of art's meanings (Wolff, 1981; Francastel, 1965; Duvignaud, 1967; Raphael, 1968).

The fractured character of the subject is further emphasized if art is taken to include MUSIC and LITERATURE. Now the paradigmatic basis for the sociology of art is seen to be inseparable from the more general problematic of how to theorize the ensemble of modern cultural forms. Commentaries on and theories of modern cultural formation from the poet Charles Baudelaire in the nineteenth century to the writings of Kracauer (1937), Bloch (1985) and Adorno (1963) have focused on musical form as a model of artistic discourse. The work of Lukács (1970) and Goldmann (1967) has provided methods for the contextual framing and analysis of literature from which the sociology of art has derived many of its basic principles. Thus an art historian like T.J. Clark (1973) who, in his influential work on Manet and Courbet, has put critical theory at the top of the art-historical agenda, draws on a theoretical field in which the visual arts have been largely marginal.

The conception of 'art' is also stratified by such notions as 'popular art', 'art for the people', 'traditional art' or 'ethnic art', not to mention 'political art' or 'women's art'. Understanding all or any of these and the relations between them may call for a variety of methods of enquiry that might combine ethnology, psychology or psychoanalysis with different aspects of sociological method. 'Art' as a ritual element in peasant labour, or of longue durée religious practices, in the work of social historians is a different object of analysis from the 'art' that forms the point of accession to or exclusion from social values in the group sociology of Bourdieu (1979) and Moulin (1967). Indeed it is difficult enough to conceive of a traditional art form such as the ex-voto (an image offered in gratitude) of the eighteenth century in France (Cousin, 1980) as belonging to the same cultural formation as its contemporary salon art let alone to think of it in the same terms as modern, avant-garde painting. Significantly, however, we must assume that the sociological study of any of these will treat aesthetic value as part of the system of beliefs that frame the individual work.

In the work of the social art historians Antal (1948) and Klingender (1968) understanding art has required a radical and subtle differentiation of public, patronage and conditions of production for different works or types of art. Antal's Florentine Painting and Klingender's Art and the Industrial Revolution suggest as much a new form of social history as a history of art – one in which art is to play a role as a signifier rather than as an illustration. The practices of art in fourteenth-century Florence or nineteenth-century Britain become primary evidence of processes of social formation and representation.

With Baxandall (1980), in his work on fifteenth-century German sculpture, even the author function comes to be seen as an effect of the complex and uneven conditions of production and the contention of interests between artist and patron to which they give rise. The sculptor signs the work to establish his position in an unequal relationship with a patron who owns the means of production. The signature signifies an attempted appropriation of power rather than the locus of creativity. Baxandall's work thus suggests ways in which the theoretical propositions of Foucault (1969) can be rethought through a long-term historical process. Yet it also suggests that historical and sociological critique of the idea of the 'artist' requires a variety of carefully inflected techniques of enquiry. A fifteenth-century sculptor cannot be framed in the same terms as a late ninteenth-century 'mad genius' such as Vincent van Gogh. Even if both come to be framed within a modern system of beliefs about art, the specificities of their history, as of this system itself, need to be carefully differentiated.

It may also be argued that a broadly sociological concern with art precedes the emergence of the word sociology and the modern idea of the artist. This prehistory can be exemplified in the discussions of the French Royal Academy where, in the eighteenth century, it was common to explain the supremacy of ancient Greek art by the representation of Athens as a healthy and successful society. Academic arguments that had recourse to extra-aesthetic categories, such as climate, the coherence of social order and the wisdom of patronage, to explain and define artistic quality flourished alongside cultural relativism and materialism in Montesquieu or Diderot. At the end of the century the theocratic apologist Louis de Bonald was also able to suggest an explanation of artistic change that was in its turn appropriate to the justification of a need for social continuity (Reedy, 1986).

In the 1840s, when the idea of the individual, expressive artist was on its way to becoming current, single works of art came to be read as socially symptomatic, whether redemptive or critical. Proudhon, with his *Du Principe de l'art et de sa destination sociale* (1865), was pre-eminent in constructing a history of modern art in which his interpretation of the work of artists such as Jacques-Louis David and Gustave Courbet articulated a general political and social theory. By the mid-century in both France and England one can commonly read histories of art, art criticism or essays on folk art, as well as discussions about industrial progress or Universal Exhibitions, that deploy some system of social reference in understanding art as a sign of its times. It is arguable that a concept of art as inherently social was, in effect, thoroughly diffused by the 1850s. As Thoré-Burger put it in his review of the Parisian Salon of 1855, 'Do not the arts themselves represent the historical traditions, the real life of the peoples?'

However it should be emphasized that many texts which explain art in broadly sociological terms do not have the elaboration of a sociology of art as a primary or even as a conscious objective. Thus the work of Champfleury (1869) on French folk art or of Wagner (1849) on the origins of artistic feeling and expression are focused around the problem of defining a national CULTURE. A preoccupation with art as part of the formation of national consciousness emerges once again on both sides of the

political camp in the 1920s and 1930s. In Italy Gramsci (*1985*) understood the popular consumption of detective comics and opera as indicating a weakness in proletarian class formation, while in Germany the idea of modern art as a symptom of decadence was elaborated. At any point in its development the sociology of art is overdetermined by a variety of discourses on the sociability of art.

A potentially systematic sociology of art is generally understood to emerge in the writing of Marx and Engels and with Hyppolite Taine's histories of art and literature. While Taine became notorious for his deterministic formula 'environment, race and moment' (Taine, 1853), with its echoes of the previous century, its influence in professional sociology or in social history has been less significant than that of Marxism. In the *German Ideology* Marx and Engels attempt to explain the power and significance of a Renaissance artist such as Raphael in terms of a complex historical process which alone made his painting possible:

> Raphael as much as any other artist was determined by the technical advances in art made before him, by the organisation of society and the division of labour in his locality, and, finally, by the division of labour in all the countries with which his locality had intercourse.

Marx and Engels were here arguing against the idea of a 'unique' individual as propounded by Max Stirner, but in so doing they begin to map out a frame of reference made up of social and economic relations that form part of the conceptual structures of the sociology of art up to our own time.

They also attempt to define art as specific to its mode of production, pointing to the sales pitch of the capitalist press of the 1830s and 1840s as the condition for the emergence of the serial novel. In *Theories of Surplus Value*, where this discussion is developed, they laid out two further lasting parameters. One of these is the concern with the artist as a particular type of worker who is essentially an 'unproductive labourer'. The other is the preoccupation with the 'commodification' of art itself and its conversion by capitalism from its previous historical statuses into no more than an item of exchange value, whether this notion is construed as monetary or ideological (Marx and Engels, *1976*). Here again is a starting point for discussions on the relation of art and society as distinct as those of György Lukács, Theodor Adorno, Walter Benjamin or Pierre Bourdieu. The sociology of art may turn out to be at the centre of twentieth-century Marxism. But the concept of alienation will fuel both Benjamin's willingness to accept the popular and Adorno's definition of art as necessarily the negation of the social forces that produce it.

Recently, in the writing of Jacques Rancière, Adorno's negativity has been used to revalue the Kantian aesthetic. If the transcendent and the negative can be read through each other, then the desire for art must be understood in terms of the negation of the social structure (Rancière, 1983). From this point of view, Bourdieu's elaboration of the production and consumption of art as the confirmation and reproduction of social status turns out to be a wholly inadequate framing of the complexities of social identity, the sociology of art a hollow enterprise. Analogously both feminist and post-colonial discourses frame the social in such a way as to suggest that much of what has been taken as adequate sociology, and by implication, sociology of art, needs to be radically rethought. The construction of art as either a form of domination or as a means of accession to social value is polymorphous and inexhaustible, ever constrained and continuously reworked in historically specific conditions.

In his essay of 1923, 'On the interpretation of *Weltanschauung*', Karl Mannheim presciently outlined these problematics in a sociology of culture (in Mannheim, 1952). Rejecting a reductive procedure of cultural analysis derived from the model of natural science, he tried to demonstrate how an understanding of the 'objective', 'expressive' and 'documentary' meanings of a cultural object would lead to a complex mapping of the parallel, but not necessarily causal, relations of a sociocultural totality. Arguably the flow and interweaving of methods in Mannheim's disclosure of a cultural whole requires the same kinds of skill as do the iconological analyses of the Warburg school of Art History. The study of a painting by Botticelli (Wind, 1958), for example, calls for a knowledge of the sociability of different levels of culture from banal and everyday phenomena to humanist commentaries on classical texts. The exceptional artwork becomes one point at which disparate forms of knowledge and cultural practice find a relatively total articulation.

But despite the value of approaches that either deduce the meaning of a work of art from social data or induce the fabric of the social from the reading of the artwork, the notion of cultural objects as expressive of totality or as 'total social facts' has fallen into disrepute. The work of art may belong to any one or more than one of a series of knowledges. Thus the construction of the public for a painting may be as one of the psychoanalytic category of voyeur, implicated in the modes of scopophilia, without a primary regard for social stratification. Or it may be as a social group with access to the art market and an eye to figuring its own prestige through purchase. Two contemporaneous paintings may share a position in a commonly accepted, historical language of visual signs and yet belong to quite different sites in the development of art education and the systems of production and distribution. Art criticism may as well be read in terms of its relation to literary and political discourse as in terms of its declared object of attention. The future development and configuration of the social history and sociology of art alike will necessarily depend on the recognition of this diversity as of the problems that it presents. To be truly fruitful, interdisciplinary work may well have to accept that difference is more structuring than totality.

Reading

Adorno, Theodor 1963: *Quasi una Fantasia.*

Bourdieu, Pierre 1979 (*1984*): *Distinction: A Social Critique of the Judgement of Taste.*

Clark, T.J. 1973: *The Absolute Bourgeois: Artists and Politics in France 1848–1851.*

Duvignaud, Jean 1967 (*1972*): *The Sociology of Art.*

Francastel, Pierre 1965: Oeuvres 11, *La Réalité figurative, éléments structurels de sociologie de l'art.*

Hauser, Arnold 1959: *The Philosophy of Art History.*

Mannheim, Karl 1952: *Essays on the Sociology of Knowledge,* ed. Paul Kecskemeti.

Marx, Karl and Engels, Friedrich 1845–6 (*1970*): *The German Ideology.*

Moulin, Raymonde 1967: *Le Marché de la peinture en France.*

Proudhon, Pierre-Joseph 1865: *Du Principe de l'art et de sa destination sociale.*

Wolff, Janet 1981: *The Social Production of Art.*

ADRIAN D. RIFKIN

artificial intelligence The term describes what is shown by a machine when it emulates cognitively sophisticated human performances. Mechanical calculators (beginning with the 'calculating clocks' of the seventeenth century) and even mechanical robots of the eighteenth and nineteenth centuries could be seen as early vehicles, but it is in the programming of computers in the twentieth century that artificial intelligence began to be identified as a field of study (Pratt, 1987).

The term came into currency following its use in the title of a conference convened in 1956 at Dartmouth College, New Hampshire, by John McCarthy (MacCorduck, 1979). It served to define a collection of projects which attempted to exploit the potential of the electronic computer, which had been born in World War II and, in the early 1950s, was emerging into the civilian world.

Leading projects at that time included attempts to get the machines to play draughts and chess, to solve geometry and logic problems, to recognize patterns and to 'understand' ordinary English (Feigenbaum and Feldman, 1963). These reflected two types of interest which came together in the formation of the new field, and which have persisted to the present day. One is an interest in human psychological processes, the other in getting the machine to do ever more sophisticated (and therefore to human users, more convenient) things. Some of the earliest Artificial Intelligence (AI) programs, for example ones that generated proofs in logic, were devised as a way of studying human decision-making. Others, programs playing chess and draughts particularly, were conceived as studies in learning. Latterly, the perspective that looks on the brain as an 'information processor' has created *cognitive psychology* (not so much a new branch of an old subject as a proposal to replace it), and from this point of view trying to achieve emulation of human behaviour or performance by programming the machine is a powerful research technique (Anderson, 1980).

Pattern recognition studies began with the other motivation – with programmers wanting to equip their machine with the capacity to read typescript, so that programs could be fed into it using that medium. They discovered that, for example, a letter of the alphabet is not to be defined by a coordinate–definable configuration of dots, but that an indefinite number of such configurations can be identified by the human eye as the *same* letter; what the computer had to be got to pick out was the *pattern* the different configurations all fall under. This particular project has since come to fruition (in optical character-recognition devices of great human significance), but the problem of pattern recognition in a variety of other domains remains significant and taxing (Fischler and Firscheim, 1987).

The project of teaching the computer English (that is, natural language) similarly began its long and as yet uncrowned career as an attempt to make the machine more user friendly to the programmer. It is one that has gained in perceived significance even as its difficulty has been borne in upon those who have worked at it (Allen, 1987; Gazdar and Mellish, 1989). There is a view that visual perception is mediated through the concepts of natural language, and it is also quite possible that knowledge is articulated and memorized using linguistic structures (Winograd, 1983).

To a striking degree most of these foundation projects have continued to absorb interest and defy complete solution. New ones have also been embraced. During the second decade of AI's existence great attention was focused on robots, with the attempt to equip mechanical devices with refined motor controls and with the ability to use visual data obtained from the surroundings to enable them to move about or manipulate objects or both. This work issued in the automated assembly lines that have now become commonplace (Engelberger, 1980).

Latterly, the great preoccupation of AI has been with understanding how human knowledge might be stored in the machine, in such a form as to make that knowledge, and any implications it might have for the solution of everyday problems, easily accessible. This is the effort to construct 'expert systems' which would take the place of or at least assist human experts of various kinds (teachers, solicitors, financial consultants).

The future will probably see a developing revival of interest in the learning potential of 'nerve nets', a plurality of processors linked multiply together (Hinton and Anderson, 1981). Breaking with the structure that has become the norm for a computer, which funnels all the action through a single processor, the 'nerve-net' alternative attempts to get closer to the structure of organic nervous tissue (an idea pursued without success by a forerunner of AI, cybernetics, in the 1950s). The present hope is that the new structures may be got to provide guidance as to the future behaviour of complex systems, not by working out the various laws which together govern it but by getting the net to pick up the pattern of past behaviour and project it into the future. 'Connection science' is sometimes used as a label for this perspective (Rumelhart et al., 1986; Zeidenberg, 1989).

The notion of a 'heuristic', originally applied in the realm of seeking mathematical proofs, is one important idea that has been developed in the course of a number of AI projects. Solutions to certain problems can be discovered in principle by going through a finite list of possibilities. For example, in a game like chess there are at any point a finite number of moves open to a player, and moreover each possible sequence of moves will issue at some point in one of three endings: a win for one or other of the two players, or a draw. One approach theoretically therefore would be to work through a complete set of 'what if' conjectures. Unfortunately (or fortunately – chess is a nice game), even a machine taking no more than a millionth of a second to calculate each possible position in a 40-move game, would require 10^{95} years to work out a first move (Shannon, 1954).

Needed for a practical chess-playing program are ways of improving on the systematic but blind generation of candidate moves, ways of ruling out without consideration unlikely possibilities if not of positively picking out likely ones. One might, for example, ignore all moves to unprotected squares. The merit of generating all possibilities systematically is that if you carry on long enough, you cover them all. It is this merit that such short-cuts, or 'heuristics', sacrifice: in place of certainty in the long run you have something less than certainty within a more acceptable timespan.

Even with the help of heuristics, AI problem-solving frequently involves checking through large numbers of possibilities, and has thus highlighted the need to store information in such a way as to maximize the efficiency of searching through it. A branching 'tree' structure has been one influential outcome here. Another technique, not exactly new with AI, but receiving in AI work the precise articulation that programming demands, is to resolve the problem that has to be solved into component simpler problems, and those problems into even simpler ones – and so on until a level is reached where solutions can be found (Newell and Simon, 1972).

AI has also given, particularly in its early years, substantial sponsorship to the idea that concepts and propositions are to be treated as lists of symbols, the members of which could be got at and manipulated. A computer language, LISP (LISt Processor) was invented to facilitate the carrying out of such processes on the machine, and has turned out to be so generally useful for the projects pursued by the AI community that the use of it almost serves to define the field (McCarthy, 1963).

From the earliest days AI workers have seen the relevance of LOGIC to their concerns. Being able to reason seems to be an aspect of possessing intelligence, and one way of thinking of logic is as the attempt to articulate the rules of valid reasoning, the rules which allow us to conclude, from a list of things we know to be established, that certain other things must also be true. If the machine could be got to manipulate propositions according to these rules (supposing we knew what they were) it would not only eliminate the role of the human logician and mathematician (for their occupation is showing that such and such a proposition can be proved) but represent a considerable aid in all kinds of human endeavour where reasoning from established knowledge plays a part.

For a certain type of reasoning, as a result of the labours of logicians down the centuries, the rules have been worked out (Prior, 1962). They are straightforward to represent on the computer, and so representing them was one of AI's earliest projects. Applied to the particular domain of medical expertise, for example, the computer implementation of this part of logic yielded a program which offered a diagnosis of medical conditions. Medical knowledge is incorporated into the program in the form of rules which express the known links between symptoms and possible illnesses. The patient is prompted to add in the symptoms they are actually suffering from and the program then uses the rules of logic it has been given to work out what diagnosis is implied (Shortliffe, 1976).

Systems of this kind are not without practical value, though the fact that they can emulate only a restricted type of reasoning is a severe limitation. It is the type formulated in what is known as the *propositional calculus*, and the limitation is that it cannot represent reasoning that hangs on the *internal structure* of propositions. For example, the propositional calculus treats the doctor's reasoning 'If Tom has a high temperature, he must be ill' as having the form 'If p then q', where p stands for the proposition 'Tom has a high temperature' and q for 'he must be ill'. But a great deal of reasoning does hang on the internal structure of propositions (for example: 'If every number has a successor, then there is no number such that it is larger than every other number').

Logicians have, however, been successful with these other types of reasoning too, inspired by the work of Gottlob Frege towards the end of the nineteenth century, developing what is known as the *predicate calculus* (Kneale and Kneale, 1962). For reasons uncovered in famous mathematical work by Kurt Gödel and others (Davis, 1965), there can be no certainty in advance that a mechanical representation of the predicate calculus will issue in a determination of every legitimate enquiry put to it. In completing, the machine is giving the answer 'Yes' to the enquiry put (essentially, does such and such a proposition of the predicate calculus follow from the information available?). But *before* it has completed the user doesn't know whether this is because the answer is 'No', or because the answer will never be determined. This creates an unwelcome degree of uncertainty, but ways of coping with the limitation have been devised which leave predicate calculus machines nevertheless with a good deal of utilitarian potential (Shepherdson, 1983).

One fruit of this work has been the construction of a computer language called PROLOG (from 'programming in logic') which applies the rules of the predicate calculus to work out what propositions follow from the facts put into the system, considered in conjunction with the 'knowledge base' it has previously been provided with (Kowalski, 1979).

Another has been the construction of a new generation of expert system programs, the promise of which at the present time still however outstrips accomplishment.

See also COGNITIVE SCIENCE.

Reading
Beardon, C. 1989: *Artificial Intelligence Terminology.*
Boden, M.A. 1986: *Artificial Intelligence and Natural Man*, 2nd edn.
Michie, D. 1974: *On Machine Intelligence.*
Minsky, M. 1967: *Computation: Finite and Infinite Machines.*
O'Shea, T. and Eisenstadt, M. eds. 1984: *Artificial Intelligence.*
Shapiro, S., Eckroth, D. and Vallasi, G. 1987: *Encyclopaedia of Artificial Intelligence.*
Sharples, M., Hogg, D., Hutchison, C., Torrance, S. and Young, D. 1989: *Computers and Thought.*
Simon, H.A. 1970: *The Sciences of the Artificial.*
Turing, A.M. 1954: Can a machine think? In *The World of Mathematics*, vol. 3, ed. J.R. Newman.

                                        VERNON PRATT

Austrian economics   The label connotes a distinct mode of economic reasoning or research agenda. During the 1970s and 1980s Austrian economics came to the fore as one among several contending schools of economic thought suspicious of mainstream economics (see POST-KEYNESIANISM). It is called 'Austrian' because it traces its pedigree to the original triumvirate of Carl Menger, Eugen Böhm von Bawerk and Friedrich von Wieser, who taught in the University of Vienna during the twilight of the Habsburg Empire.

The Austrian or Viennese school constituted one important strand – along with the British (Marshallian) and Lausanne (Walrasian) traditions – of what became subsequently known as neoclassical (as opposed to classical political economy) or MARGINALIST ECONOMICS. While in broad agreement with these other streams of thought in regard to general outlook, the Austrians distinguished themselves from the outset by a more relentless elaboration of the subjectivist viewpoint in economics. The Austrian theory of value is a case in point: in contrast to classical notions, 'value' was not something that could be objectively measured like the length of a table; it did not turn on some physical quantity inherent in goods, but rather it was seen to be at the heart of a relationship between appraising decision-makers and the object of their appraisal. Conceiving of value as a subjectivist concept paved the way for a redirection in the focus of economics. In line with a general shift of attention away from problems of production (technology), i.e. wealth creation, to demand issues, the choosing (economizing) individual began to occupy centre-stage in economic analysis. The move entailed a concern with (a) individual decision processes enveloped in the vagaries of time and ignorance; and (b) linking those decisions up with an explanation of the emergence of a complex web of interconnected exchange relationships constituting the market order.

The identity of the Austrian contribution came into sharper focus as a result of several fierce controversies: with the German historical school in the so-called METHODENSTREIT; with the theorists of AUSTRO-MARXISM; in the debate over SOCIALIST CALCULATION with the champions of market socialism; and with the adherents of the new KEYNESIANISM.

By the early 1940s the intellectual and political ascendancy of the Keynesian revolution, in particular, had discredited Austrian economics to such an extent that it seemed as if it had become a closed chapter in the history of thought. Apart from Ludwig von Mises and Ludwig Lachmann there was hardly anyone who espoused an explicit Austrian position (F. A. Hayek had deserted economic theory for social philosophy). The situation changed drastically, however, when the widely felt dissatisfaction with the general drift of economics which had begun to assert itself in the late 1960s and early 1970s encouraged a lot of soul-searching among economists and the resurgence of once discredited ideas and traditions. The revival of Austrian economics began gradually as a very small genre in the USA; it then spread to parts of the UK and the continent, and even to South America. Today it is in the vanguard of ideas on economic reform in Eastern European countries such as Poland.

Those who are committed to Austrian economics profess allegiance to methodological and political INDIVIDUALISM; their central concern is with the nature of entrepreneurially driven, rivalrous market processes rather than with the analysis of equilibrium states devoid of these processes (see COMPETITION and ENTREPRENEURSHIP); they emphasize the discovery aspects of markets; and they subscribe to a theory of the emergence of economic, political and cultural institutions as spontaneously evolved, undesigned outcomes of individual pursuits not guided by 'the common good'.

Reading
Kirzner, Israel M. 1973: *Competition and Entrepreneurship.*
Lachmann, Ludwig M. 1986: *The Market as an Economic Process.*
Lavoie, Don 1985: *Rivalry and Central Planning: The Socialist Calculation Debate Reconsidered.*
Littlechild, Stephen ed. 1990: *Austrian Economics*, 3 vols.
O'Driscoll, Gerald P. Jr and Rizzo, Mario J. 1985: *The Economics of Time and Ignorance.*

STEPHAN BOEHM

Austro-Marxism   One of the earliest distinct schools of Marxist thought, which developed from the work of a group of thinkers in Vienna at the end of the nineteenth century, the most prominent among them being Max Adler, Otto Bauer, Rudolf Hilferding and Karl Renner. This new form of MARXISM, according to Bauer (1927), was a response to new philosophical doctrines (neo-Kantianism and positivism), to developments in economic theory (Austrian marginalism) and to the issues raised by the problem of nationalities in the multinational Habsburg Empire; but it was also influenced by the revisionist controversy in Germany (see REVISIONISM) and by the remarkable flowering of Viennese cultural and intellectual life at the turn of the century, as a result of which it was innovative in many different fields.

The first public manifestation of a new school of thought was the creation in 1904 of the *Marx-Studien*, a collection of monographs edited by Adler and Hilferding and published irregularly until 1923, and this was followed by the publication, from 1907, of a theoretical journal, *Der Kampf*, which soon came to rival Kautsky's *Die Neue Zeit* as the leading European Marxist review. The Austro-Marxists were all active in the leadership of the growing Social Democratic Party (SPÖ), and they devoted themselves particularly to the promotion of workers' education.

The philosophical and theoretical foundations of Austro-Marxism were developed mainly by Adler, who conceived Marxism as 'a system of sociological knowledge . . . the science of the laws of social life and its causal development' (1925, p. 136). In his first major work (1904) he analysed the relation between causality and teleology, emphasizing that there are diverse forms of causality and that the causal relation in social life is not a mechanical one, but is mediated by consciousness; this was a view which he later expressed by saying that even 'economic phenomena themselves are never "material" in the materialist sense, but have precisely a "mental" character' (1930, p. 118). Adler regarded as the basic concept in Marx's theory of society, 'socialized humanity' or 'social association', and treated this in neo-Kantian fashion as being 'transcendentally given as a category of knowledge' (1925), that is, as a concept furnished by reason, not derived from experience, which is a precondition of an empirical science.

This conception of Marxism as a sociological system provided the framework of ideas which directed the studies of the whole Austro-Marxist school, as is particularly clear in Hilferding's economic analyses. In his criticism of marginalist economic theory (1904) Hilferding opposed to the individualist 'psychological school of political economy' Marx's theory of value, which is based on a conception of 'society' and 'social relations', while the Marxist theory as a whole 'aims to disclose the social determinism of economic phenomena', its starting point being 'society and not the individual'. Elsewhere, in the preface to *Finance Capital* (1910), he referred directly to Adler in asserting that 'the sole aim of any [Marxist] enquiry – even into matters of policy – is the discovery of causal relationships', and went on to investigate the major causal factors in the most recent stage of capitalist development, concluding with an analysis of imperialism which was the basis of later studies by Bukharin and Lenin.

Another major field for sociological investigation was that of nationality and nationalism. Bauer's classic study (1907) set out to provide a comprehensive theoretical and historical analysis, from which he concluded:

> For me, history no longer reflects the struggles of nations; instead the nation itself appears as the reflection of historical struggles. For the nation is only manifested in the national character, in the nationality of the individual . . . [which] . . . is only one aspect of his determination by the history of society, by the development of the conditions and techniques of labour.

From a different perspective, concentrating on the legal and constitutional problems of the different nationalities in the Habsburg Empire, Renner (1899, 1902) also contributed important studies, in the course of which he advanced the idea – original in its time and not without relevance to the present development of Europe – of a transformation of the empire into a 'state of nationalities' which might become a model for the socialist organization of a future world community.

Renner is best known, however, for his pioneering contribution to a Marxist sociology of law. In his study (1904) of the social functions of law he set out to show how the existing legal norms change their functions in response to changes in society and more particularly to changes in its economic structure, and then raised as major problems for a sociology of law questions about how the legal norms themselves change and the fundamental causes of such changes. In this discussion, as in other writings, it is clear that Renner attributes an active role to law in maintaining or modifying social relations and by no means treats it simply as an ideology reflecting economic conditions, citing as consonant with this view Marx's comments on law in the introduction to the *Grundrisse*. Another important contribution to formulating the principles of a Marxist sociology of law was made by Adler (1922) who, in the course of his critique of Hans Kelsen's 'pure theory of law', which excludes any enquiry into either the ethical basis of law or its

social context, examined in detail the differences between a formal and a sociological theory of law.

The Austro-Marxists also undertook major studies in other fields. They were among the first Marxists to examine systematically the increasing involvement in the economy of the 'interventionist state'. Renner (1916), writing on the effects of prewar capitalist development and the 'war economy', noted 'the penetration of the private economy down to its elementary cells by the state: not the nationalization of a few factories, but the control of the whole private sector of the economy by willed and conscious regulation', and he continued: 'state power and the economy begin to merge . . . the national economy is perceived as a means of state power, state power as a means to strengthen the national economy . . . It is the epoch of imperialism.' Similarly, in essays published between 1915 and 1924, Hilferding developed, on the basis of his analysis in *Finance Capital*, a theory of 'organized capitalism' in which the action of the state begins to assume the character of a conscious, rational structuring of society as a whole (see SOCIALIZATION OF THE ECONOMY). From this situation two lines of development were possible: towards socialism if the working class were to gain state power, or towards a corporate state if the capitalist monopolies maintained their political dominance. In Italy and Germany the latter possibility was realized in the form of FASCISM, and Bauer (1936) provided one of the most systematic Marxist accounts of the economic and social conditions in which the fascist movements were able to emerge and triumph. Subsequently, Hilferding (1941) began a radical revision of the Marxist theory of history, in which he attributed to the modern nation state a more independent role in the formation of society, arguing that in the twentieth century there had been a profound 'change in the relation of the state to society, brought about by the subordination of the economy to the coercive power of the state', and that 'the state becomes a totalitarian state to the extent that this subordination takes place' (see TOTALITARIANISM).

The changing class structure, and its political consequences, were other subjects to which the Austro-Marxists devoted much attention. Bauer made an important contribution in his comparative account of the situation of workers and peasants in the Russian and German revolutions, in his detailed analysis (1923) of the Austrian revolution, and in his critical writings on the emergence of a new dominant class in the USSR as the dictatorship of the proletariat was transformed into the dictatorship of an all-powerful party apparatus (see especially Bauer, 1936). Adler (1933), writing in the context of the defeat and destruction of the working class movement in Germany, analysed the changes in the composition of the working class in capitalist society; while noting that 'already in Marx's work the concept of the proletariat displays a certain differentiation', he argued that more recent changes had been so extensive as to produce a 'new phenomenon', so that 'it is doubtful whether we can speak of a single class.' In this new proletariat there were several distinct strata which had given rise to three basic, often conflicting, political orientations: that of the labour aristocracy, comprising skilled workers and office employees; that of the organized workers in town and country; and that of the permanent or long-term unemployed. But even among the main body of workers, he argued (in a manner reminiscent of Roberto Michels's account of OLIGARCHY), the development of party and trade union organizations had created a fatal division between the growing stratum of salaried officials and representatives, and the largely passive membership. The weakness of the working class in face of fascist movements was largely due, he concluded, to this differentiation of socioeconomic conditions and political attitudes (see WORKING CLASS). After World War II, as the class structure continued to change even more rapidly, Renner (1953) focused his attention on the growth of new social strata – public officials and private employees – which he referred to collectively as a 'service class' of salaried employees whose contracts of employment did not create 'a relationship of wage labour'. Many Marxists, he considered, had adopted a superficial approach to 'the real study of class formation in society, and above all the continuous restructuring of the classes'. In particular, they had failed to recognize that 'the working class as it appears (and scientifically was bound to appear) in Marx's *Capital* no longer exists.'

The 'golden age' of Austro-Marxism was the period from the end of the nineteenth century to 1914, when the seminal writings of these thinkers were published and the work of the school as a whole had a wide influence in the European socialist movement. After the Russian revolution, however, it was overshadowed first by Leninist and then by Stalinist versions of Marxism; the course it

followed, 'between reformism and Bolshevism', in expounding an undogmatic Marxism open to revision and development in response to new historical experience and to critical questions posed by other approaches to social analysis had little international influence. But in Vienna, where the SPÖ was continuously in power from 1918 to 1934, Austro-Marxism still provided a coherent framework of ideas for an ambitious and effective policy of social reform, until it was finally overwhelmed by the rise of Austrian fascism and the incorporation of Austria into the Third Reich. Since the late 1960s there has been a notable renewal of interest in the Austro-Marxists, not only in Austria where their ideas still have a significant influence on the development of socialism, but in other European countries. In the conditions created by the disintegration of 'official Marxism' throughout Eastern Europe, it may be that these ideas, and further elaborations of them, will have an even greater impact on the organization of the economy, the construction of democratic institutions, and attitudes to the persisting problem of nationalities, in a new European system.

Reading
Bottomore, Tom 1989: Austro-Marxist conceptions of the transition from capitalism to socialism. *International Journal of Comparative Sociology* 30. 1–2.
Bottomore, Tom and Goode, Patrick eds 1978: *Austro-Marxism*.
Kolakowski, Leszek 1978: *Main Currents of Marxism*, vol. 2, ch. 12.
Leser, Norbert 1966: Austro-Marxism: a reappraisal. *Journal of Contemporary History* 1. 2.
——1968 (*1985*): *Zwischen Reformismus und Bolschewismus. Der Austromarxismus als Theorie und Praxis*, 2nd abridged edn.
Mozetič, Gerald 1987: *Die Gesellschaftstheorie des Austromarxismus*.

TOM BOTTOMORE

authority   Although authority can conveniently be defined as the right, most often by mutual recognition, to require and receive submission, there is endemic disagreement among social theorists about its nature. This is not surprising, since different conceptions of authority tend to reflect different social and political theories and worldviews. However, the various conceptions of authority seem to have two components in common. One is the non-exercise of private judgement; the other is the identification of the authorities to be recognized.

This leads to some useful distinctions. If somebody submits to the judgement of authorities by reference to a set of rules prevalent in a society, we speak of a *de jure* authority. However, if somebody submits to the judgement of others because he or she accepts their claims to be the rightful authorities, it is an instance of a *de facto* authority. Parents typically have both *de jure* and *de facto* authority over their children. It is conceivable, however, that they have the former kind of authority without having the latter, and vice versa. If authority is identified and recognized over belief, we speak of *an* authority (such as a doctor advising a patient). If it is, on the other hand, identified and recognized over conduct, then it is a case of somebody being *in* authority (such as a policeman directing traffic).

Perhaps the best way to elucidate the concept of authority is to describe different solutions to three problems about it.

In the first place, why is there a need for the concept? While Hannah Arendt and Bertrand de Jouvenel give different accounts of authority, they agree (with most other social theorists) that the cohesion and continuity of social life cannot be adequately explained in terms of coercion, LEADERSHIP or rational discussion. Arendt (1960) believes that authority implies an obedience in which people retain their freedom. She distinguishes it from POWER, force and violence, and also from persuasion, because in persuasion people are equal. The rise of totalitarianism in the twentieth century was preceded by the loss of authority, she believes: the lonely crowd seeks comfort in political mass movements and feels a need for leaders.

According to Jouvenel (1957), authority is the ability of somebody to get his or her proposals accepted. It is different from power, because it is exercised only over those who voluntarily accept it. However, the people in authority, or the rulers, may have authority only over a part of their subjects, but over a sufficient number that they may coerce the rest; this would be power over all by means of authority over a part, or an authoritarian state. It is a mistake, Jouvenel believes, to oppose authority to liberty, because authority ends where voluntary assent ends: the dissolution of human aggregates is the worst of all evils, he says, and police regimes come in when prestiges go out.

Secondly, how do people in authority come to have it? Max Weber (1921–2) distinguished between three types of authority, or 'legitimate domination'. Legal authority rested on a belief in the legality of enacted rules and the right of those elevated to authority under such rules to issue commands. Police officers are obeyed because the authority conferred upon them by the legal and political order is accepted. Traditional authority rested on an established belief in the sanctity of immemorial traditions and the legitimacy of those exercising authority under them. This kind of authority is also defined in terms of a set of rules, but the rules are mostly expressed in traditions and customs. Finally, charismatic authority rested on devotion to the exceptional sanctity, heroism or exemplary character of an individual person, and of the normative patterns or order revealed or ordained by him (see CHARISMA). The best example is Jesus who spoke 'with authority' in the Temple, though only 12 years of age, and whose utterances were of the form, 'It is written, . . . but I say unto you.'

According to Weber, these three types of authority are 'ideal types'. They almost always exist in a mixed form. Peter Winch (1967) has pointed out that, in the final analysis, all three rest on tradition. Even charismatic authority presupposes tradition, since the charismatic leader always reforms an existing tradition and his actions are unintelligible apart from it: indeed Jesus said that he had not come to break the law, but to fulfil it. It should also be pointed out that the difference between legal and traditional authority on the one hand and charismatic authority on the other, in Weber's theory, is somewhat similar to the difference between Jouvenel's arbitrator of existing and conflicting claims and aims, *rex*, and his leader or originator of new policies, *dux*.

The third question is why people should defer to authority. Radical political thinkers, notably anarchists and Marxists, believe that they should not. Marxists contend that authority is asymmetric, masking the class nature of the capitalist state and the imposition of a legitimating ideology. Jürgen Habermas (1973) believes, for example, that the state in 'late capitalism' faces a legitimation crisis. Modern anarchists, like Robert Paul Wolff (1970), fasten their eyes on the alleged conflict of individual autonomy and authority. According to them authority necessarily implies the private surrender of judgement.

Conservatives and liberals reply that an extensive intellectual division of labour is necessary in today's complex social order. They also point out that a certain kind of law structures rather than restricts individual liberty, and that it therefore serves as a condition, not a constraint, of autonomy.

Modern liberals typically distinguish between the authority of the law, which they regard as necessary for facilitating social cooperation, and the power of individuals, which they tend to distrust. They differ, however, on how they derive the authority of the law. For John Rawls (1971) and James M. Buchanan (1975), it derives from a SOCIAL CONTRACT. People defer to authority, because it is in their interest; they would choose (a certain kind of) authority if provided with the relevant information or if placed in the appropriate setting. For Friedrich A. Hayek (1979), authority emerges from a long historical process of the mutual adaptation of individuals, as expressed in statutes, traditions, conventions and customs: except where the political unit is created by conquest, he argues, people submit to authority not to enable it to do what it likes, but because they trust somebody to act in conformity with certain common conceptions of what is just. For Robert Nozick (1974) the authority of the state rests on its non-violation of individual rights.

On the other hand, some modern thinkers, Michael Oakeshott (1962), Hannah Arendt and others, taking their lead from Aristotle, Rousseau and Hegel, do not refer to interests or rights, but to social identities. They replace the unencumbered (and to them enervated) selves of liberal theory by situated selves, partly constituted by their social roles, practices, places and times. The reason we accept authority, these 'communitarian' theorists contend, is that it expresses our common will or that it reflects our common identity, our shared values and beliefs. While some communitarian arguments against liberalism are similar to those put forward by conservatives (especially British Tories) in the early nineteenth century, they usually lead to more egalitarian policies. But when the selves are situated in an individualist culture, communitarians can become quite libertarian, Oakeshott being one example.

Finally, political 'realists' believe that authority does not come into existence by shared beliefs or by convention, but by imposition. Vilfredo Pareto described politics as the competition among elites trying to pursue their own aims by the manipulation of mass support: 'All governments use force and all assert that they are founded on reason' (Pareto, 1916–19, sect. 2183). According to Gaetano Mosca (1896), the governing class dominated the unorganized majority, legitimating its power by a 'political formula'. Marxists and anarchists agree to some extent with the political realists about the nature of authority, although the two groups, unlike the realists, find it unacceptable and want to replace it by something else about whose nature, however, they do not agree. But most political philosophers and political sociologists alike believe that authority is an inevitable and ineradicable feature of social life.

Reading

Arendt, Hannah 1960: What is authority? In *Between Past and Future: Eight Exercises in Political Thought*.
de Jouvenel, Bertrand (*1957*): *Sovereignty: An Inquiry into the Political Good*, trans. J.F. Huntington.
Lukes, S. 1978: Power and authority. In *A History of Sociological Analysis*, ed. T. Bottomore and R. Nisbet.
Peters, R. 1967: Authority. In *Political Philosophy*, ed. A. Quinton.
Weber, Max 1921–2 (*1978*): *Economy and Society: An Outline of Interpretative Sociology*, ed. Günther Roth and Claus Wittich.
Winch, P. 1967: Authority. In *Political Philosophy*, ed. A. Quinton.

HANNES H. GISSURARSON

automation   In describing a system in which machines are used to control processes and perform sequences of tasks that previously required human attention, activity and intervention, the term does not refer merely to using machines to carry out single tasks (mechanization), a capability humans have long possessed, but to the method of harnessing electronic sensing and control devices in order to model and replace human senses, minds and hands in a repeated operation.

All automated systems have distinguishable aspects:

1   action, for instance, drilling, heating, spraying, treating with chemicals;

2   positioning, which may involve moving, turning, aligning, transferring, conveying from one place to another;

3   control, referring to the means of carrying out decisions, e.g. a valve that can be made to open and close;

4   a computer program, with instruction for carrying out a process, as in (1) to (3) above;

5   a computer program in command of the whole operation, that is, of the sequence of processes;

6   a means of sensing (identifying and measuring) and reporting the qualities of what is being

processed, such as size, optical properties, weight and heat;

7   decision-making elements, which compare reported information with a required state and make appropriate corrections of deviations.

These aspects working together form a feedback system capable of operating with minimal human intervention.

Automation is adopted to increase production and productivity, standardize products, improve efficiency, relieve humans of unpleasant or hazardous tasks, reduce operating costs and carry out procedures that are beyond human capabilities.

The first practical automated industrial systems began to emerge in the 1950s. In the 1960s and 1970s, anticipation of the spread of automation led to much speculation about the likely economic, social and cultural consequences for societies in general and the nature of industrial work in particular. Some conclusions about trends were derived from the precursor of automation in industrial production – the mechanization of production lines – in which the production process was split into sub-processes, each aided by a machine. Since workers were treated as adjuncts of the machine, the effect was to degrade and limit workers' skills. At the level of the individual production worker, deskilling, involving a reduction of craft knowledge and a loss of freedom, was foreseen as a major direct consequence of automation. At the level of the organization, it was anticipated that workers with new skills would emerge, such as design engineers, toolmakers and machine builders, maintenance engineers and new types of machine operators and supervisors. Industrial organizations, as they grew greater in size and complexity, would require new management skills, stressing information and control. At the level of society and economy, inequality and unemployment were expected to grow, and overall a shift was predicted away from industrial production and towards service industries.

Two factors have made it difficult to foretell consequences with any accuracy: the lack of a tight causal relationship between technology and the nature of societies or organizations; and the fact that automation is not only a more complex process than mechanization but is qualitatively different.

The notion of deskilling is too crude to apply to automation, making the assumption that individuals have specific fixed skills, whereas the recognition of skills is socially and culturally determined, and responsive to changing situations. Furthermore, the substitutability between workers thought to accompany deskilling has been of minor importance in automation, since managing automated systems usually requires more skill and training, not less.

Automation's impact on the shift from manufacturing to service industries has also not been clear-cut. Two things are implied: a shift in measures of production and/or a shift in the proportion of the labour force employed in manufacturing. Manufacturing production has expanded enormously in those countries with highly automated industries. Even in countries with an apparent decline, manufacturing, linked as it is to growth in service industries as well as export demand, fluctuates, so that the link between the manufacturing/services shift and automation is not demonstrated. In any case, the shift was established before automation took its modern form. Furthermore, although automation first affected manufacturing industries, it is having widespread impacts on all activities, including office management, communications, transport, distribution, clerical and administrative work, banks and financial services, retail trade, printing and publishing, health and public services, design, and the information technology industry itself. As the use of 'intelligent' knowledge-based systems spreads in professional activity, automation will affect work and decision making in almost every non-manufacturing occupation.

The relationship between automation and unemployment is similarly complex. Common-sense arguments which saw the obvious effects of replacing workers by robots led to simple conclusions about the disappearance of jobs in general and industrial jobs in particular. Despite evident destruction of traditional jobs, devastating to old industrial communities, there has been an increase in new types of non-repetitive, skilled jobs. Whether trends in unemployment are due to automation as such, or whether they reflect the dislocation of changing labour markets in a changing world economy, is open to question.

Currently, the term 'automation' is less used in manufacturing industry than some more precise terms, such as CIM (computer-integrated manufacturing), AMT (advanced manufacturing technology), and CADCAM (computer-aided design, computer-aided manufacture). The term 'robotics' refers to the increasingly sophisticated study of complex automated machines able to sense, decide and manipulate in a recognizably human-like way.

See also INFORMATION TECHNOLOGY AND THEORY; TECHNOLOGICAL CHANGE; WORK.

Reading
Adler, F. et al. eds 1986: *Automation and Industrial Workers: A Fifteen Nation Study*, vol. 2.
Braverman, H. 1974: *Labor and Monopoly Capital: The Degradation of Work in the Twentieth Century*.
Forester, T. ed. 1985: *The Information Technology Revolution*.
Forslin, J., Sarapata, A. and Whitehill, A.M. eds 1979: *Automation and Industrial Workers: A Fifteen Nation Study*, vol. 1.
Granovetter, M. and Tilly, C. 1988: Inequality and the labor process. In *Handbook of Sociology*, ed. N. Smelser.
Handy, C.B. 1984: *The Future of Work: A Guide to Changing Society*.
Hyman, R. and Streeck, W. eds 1988: *New Technology and Industrial Relations*.

LORRAINE F. BARIĆ

avant-garde This French term literally means no more than its English contraction 'vanguard', that is the advance guard or foremost part of an army. Its metaphorical uses date roughly from the beginning of the twentieth century, though the idea, that of political or cultural LEADERSHIP on the part of an enlightened, self-appointed elite, is in one sense at least a century older, and in another, as old as the human race. In Anglo-American usage the English term is generally reserved for political leadership (such as the 'vanguard party', in Leninism) and the French term for cultural and artistic leadership (our concern here).

The expression 'avant-garde' presupposes or implies the following:

1   A condition of permanent cultural or aesthetic revolution, to be initiated, articulated or directed by an 'advanced' minority, usually in accordance with some allegedly immanent historical process (cf. PROGRESS);
2   Reluctance on the part of the 'led' (variously the proletarian 'masses' or the bourgeois 'philistines') to be so 'led' (see MASS CULTURE);
3   A non-mandated right on the part of the avant-garde to 'lead' them, or at least to goad, insult or irritate them by offering to do so;

4   This right to be justified, if at all, by the avant-garde's claims willy-nilly to represent the inner, unacknowledged aspirations of those excluded from it (cf. the Marxist doctrine of 'false consciousness', to the effect that under imperfect social arrangements the unenlightened are kept ignorant of their 'real' needs and desires, which only the 'vanguard' can perceive).

An avant-garde is constituted not by conventional status determinants such as wealth, birth or administrative function, but solely by personal merit or aesthetic talent (as assessed by itself). It stands to the surrounding culture in the ambiguous relation of simultaneous dependence and ALIENATION.

Though they have both ENLIGHTENMENT and Romantic roots (cf. Shelley's view of poets as 'unacknowledged legislators'), avant-gardes are essentially a modernist phenomenon, one which to a great extent overlaps with another, that of INTELLECTUALS. Even when culturally and politically conservative (as in the case of T.S. Eliot and many other modernists), avant-gardes are radical in their expressive techniques, which will be self-consciously obscure, mannered, ironic, erudite, allusive, or even (as in the Dadaist movement of Tristan Tzara and others in the early twentieth century) deliberately meaningless.

Like modernism generally, avant-gardes are in part a reaction to bourgeois democracy, an aristocratism of the déclassé. Hence they have often depended on the traditional aristocracy for their support. However, their chief clientele nowadays (especially in London and New York) is the status-seeking bourgeoisie, a fact which is proving fatal to their credibility. At the moment of writing, indeed, avant-gardes seem everywhere to be in decline, while post-modernism and a revived traditionalism flourish, above all in the most public of the arts, architecture (see MODERNISM AND POSTMODERNISM).

Reading
Butler, Christopher 1980: *After the Wake: The Contemporary Avant-Garde*.
Kermode, Frank 1971: *Modern Essays*.
Ortega y Gasset, José 1964: *The Dehumanization of Art and Other Writings on Art and Culture*.
Poggioli, Renato 1968: *The Theory of the Avant-Garde*.

ROBERT GRANT

B

base and superstructure These are Marxist metaphors to describe the relations between the economy (production relations) and government, politics and ideology. Marx and Engels never developed their ideas about the base and superstructure in a specific treatise and in a systematic manner, but it is possible to discern at least three basic characteristics of their thought on the subject: compatibility, feedback, and non-reductionism.

1 A society can exist if there is a compatibility between its government (politics, laws), its ideas and its economic structures. Everything is not possible: if the economy changes, the government and the ideas will have to change. Marx probably thought that there could be one and only one type of superstructure compatible with a given base. G. V. Plekhanov, Lenin and Stalin certainly assumed this view. Compatibility has also been interpreted as the inevitability of change in the superstructure following the change of the base. This is the strong interpretation of compatibility. According to the weak interpretation, the number of compatible superstructures has to be smaller than the number of all (possible) superstructures; the correspondence is one-to-many. Thus statements about the superstructure can still be explained by recourse to statements about the base but the description of the superstructure cannot be inferred from the description of the base. The inevitability thesis can also be weakened into a compound thesis that (a) if a base changes then either the superstructure changes to restore compatibility, or the base returns to the former type, or the society is destroyed by an internal conflict; and (b) if a superstructure changes then either the base changes to restore compatibility or the superstructure returns to the former type or the society is destroyed.

2 There is a feedback relationship between base and superstructure. The term 'feedback' was first systematically used in this context by an East German philosopher, Georg Klaus, after 1960. The idea is implicit in the writings of Marx and explicit in those of Engels. Feedback explains the appearance of the functionality of a superstructure towards its base. Statements about the functions of government or ideas can be translated into conditional sentences acceptable within the scientific mode of explanation. The feedback thesis is compatible with both the strong and the weak interpretation of the compatibility thesis.

3 All properties of the superstructure are not dependent on some properties of the base. There are entities in, and properties of government and thought that cannot be explained by recourse to statements about the base (or their descriptions cannot be reducd to the descriptions of the base). A superstructure develops from a preceding one, and results from a free choice or chance actions within the structural restraints imposed by the compatibility and feedback conditions. Superstructure is deemed a necessary component part of any human society; it is not purely a servant or slave of the base.

Feedback and non-reductionism are covered by the composite label 'relative autonomy of the superstructure'. The concept of base and superstructure thus becomes a concept of restraints and enabling conditions of human actions and activities. No general method of stating *ante factum* which properties and entities within some superstructural institutions are dependent on the base, and which are not, is available in Marxist writings. Thus we do not have a general sociological theory, although we do have a useful theory-sketch pointing to some important relationships within a society that can be used as the core of a research programme in history, sociology, social anthropology, law and political science.

The expression 'base and superstructure' is widely applied to the relationships between societal institutions. It is also applicable to the relations between levels within the compound institutions (families, hunter-gatherer bands, ethnic units, and so forth).

The words 'base and superstructure' were introduced by Marx (1859). He claimed that state, politics and ideological forms made up a super-structure built on the base of production relations, the latter being compatible with a definite level of the means of production. Thus the superstructure was not described by Marx as directly dependent on technology. The dependence was mediated by the economic structures. As early as 1844, Marx wrote in his Paris manuscripts that some human values were dependent on economic conditions (in particular, alienated attitudes towards work and freedom were described as being dependent on the presence of alienation in the economy). The claim that thought and government are based on the MODE OF PRODUCTION is pervasive in the *German Ideology* (Marx and Engels, 1845–6). Engels discussed the relations between the base and super-structure in a number of letters written between 1890 and 1895. He introduced the feedback description of the relationships between the base and superstructure, pointing out that the institutions belonging to the superstructure have some characteristics not determined by their base. Sometimes he used the term *base* rather loosely, to include the natural environment and the whole mode of production (Engels, 1894).

In the 1920s some Soviet writers began making distinctions between the technological base (part of the means of production) and the economic base. The latter consisted of the relations of production, exchange and distribution. Western economic writings since 1870 were practically unknown to Soviet philosophers and economists; thus there are no detailed investigations of production relations by the majority of Marxists. Nevertheless, the expression 'base' (or 'economic base') is not used by Soviet authors to denote the whole mode of production. They also treat superstructure as being outside the mode of production and based on the mode. Their majority view came to be that although production relations are the major determining factor for the superstructure, there can also exist direct determining relations from the means of production towards the superstructure. A socioeconomic formation is said to combine a mode of production and a superstructure. This Soviet (and East European) use differs from that of some Western writers influenced by a French Marxist tradition according to which the word 'base' is used to denote both the means and relations of production. The standard Soviet usage agreed well with Marx (1859) and seemed exegetically to be closer to the whole corpus of Marx's and Engels's writings. J. Plamenatz has argued that Marx interpreted production relations as legal ownership relations. This view has been rejected by G. A. Cohen, who has also provided analyses of the microfoundations of the base–superstructure relations. Cohen's views are based on good textual evidence (Marx, 1859).

There is a tendency in modern Western writings about MARXISM to treat the ideas about the base and superstructure as explanatory principles. G. A. Cohen insists that relations between superstructure and base are functional and that functional explanation is a valid form of explanation. This has led to a controversy in analytical studies of Marxism over the nature of functional relations and the role of functional explanations. In nineteenth-century social science, EXPLANATION had not yet become a fashionable word. Marx and Engels were essentially interested in finding out what they thought were real relationships between real entities. Although they developed concepts and terminology for the purposes of understanding and explanation, their interest was not centred on the concepts but on social reality and revolutionizing that reality.

The simplistic non-metaphorical use of the concepts 'base and superstructure' by some Marxists and anti-Marxists is essentially a twentieth-century development. Marxism was made into a close, all-embracing and non-falsifiable theoretical system by some Second International thinkers, by Lenin, and by the Stalinist interpreters of Marx.

Reading
Cohen, G.A. 1978: *Karl Marx's Theory of History.*
Collins, H. 1982: *Marxism and Law.*
Elster, J. 1985: *Making Sense of Marx.*
Newman, K.S. 1983: *Law and Economic Organization: A Comparative Study of Preindustrial Societies.*
Plamenatz, J. 1954: *German Marxism and Russian Communism.*
Plekhanov, G.V. 1895 (*1975*): The development of the monist view of history. In *Selected Philosophical Works in Five Volumes*, vol. 1.
Therborn, G. 1980: *What Does the Ruling Class Do When It Rules? State Apparatuses and State Power under Feudalism, Capitalism and Socialism.*

EERO LOONE

behaviourism This has been the dominant school of thought in academic PSYCHOLOGY since the publication of J. B. Watson's classic work *Behaviourism* in 1924. Few psychologists since his time would accept his theory without reservations. Most, however, would subscribe to the general features of his position. He claims:

1 mental events cannot constitute the data of a reputable science, the proper object of psychological study being behaviour, not thought or feeling;
2 all behaviour is the effect of reinforcement, that is the response to a stimulus is the consequence of the repeated coincidence of the response with a reward (or punishment);
3 experimental techniques in psychology allow us to manipulate behaviour towards socially approved ends. Since all behaviour is conditioned anyway, the objection to conditioning as opposed to rational persuasion fails.

The school of behaviourism first arose in protest against the unsatisfactory state of psychology at the turn of the century. Wilhelm Wundt, Edward Titchener and William James supposed that psychology studied mental events by means of introspection. This process was notoriously unreliable, lacking any way of replicating reported findings. It was anathema to a generation guided by a conception of science drawn from Ernst Mach and envious of scientists widely celebrated for their successes in predicting events in the physical world. Bodily movements, in contrast, seemed to satisfy the scientific demand for reliable data. The assumption that behaviour is always a response to reinforced stimuli provided the conditions for controlled experiment. So far then, behaviourism is the point of view of experimental psychology itself.

Watson, however, went further. At Chicago he had been a student of Jacques Loeb, who was celebrated for his claim to have created life in a testtube, and who thought of science as a means to control and change nature. Watson shared this view, and with his pupil B. F. Skinner (1938; 1959; 1971), made popular an image of behaviourism as a recipe for solving individual anxieties and the world's ills. Where psychologists like Clark L. Hull and E. C. Tolman thought of stimulus–response (S–R) as a technique to refine our conception of the mental or physiological apparatus which they supposed must mediate between a stimulus and a response, Skinner looks upon reinforcement as a device used by the experimenter to induce behaviour.

This view might be called ideological behaviourism, since it entails a conception of behaviour shaped by favoured ends of action. It requires the language of successful and failed performance, not merely the neutral description of bodily movements, which is normally thought to be the scientific bedrock of psychological theory. Defining behaviour to meet the data requirement is a problem for behaviourism generally. The classic maze experiment is constructed on the assumption that the subject will be gratified to come upon the reward, and will then solve the maze more quickly on further trials. The subject's behaviour is not described more exactly by analysing it into its units. Experimental strategy already assumes the subject is seeking the reward. But it is then not clear why we can't say straightaway that the subject *wants* the reward and *knows* how to find it.

Much of the energy devoted to maze experiments has had the less ambitious objective of arriving at numbers recording, for example, the rate of learning. Whether these results have important implications for our understanding of the behaviour and the structure of organisms may itself be questioned. Rate of learning experiments neither entail nor exclude inner events. Neither do they require description in terms of bodily movements. Learning is an achievement; it is experimental data. Behaviour in that context is what organisms *do*, not merely how they *move*. Skinner's large claims to efficacy in changing behaviour by employing methods sanitized of mental content appear at odds with his equally large claim that, given sufficient control over an organism, we can get it to do pretty much anything we *want*. Dogs walking on their hind legs, dolphins leaping through hoops of fire, soldiers marching into battle testify to the possibility of control. But a description of the methods of conditioning appears to entail some reference to ends, intentions and motives, at least of the experimenter. If so they entail as well a description of organisms as acting, not merely exhibiting physical movements.

Many of Skinner's critics have objected to his views on moral and political grounds. He reduces human motivation, they say, to the most simplistic form of hedonism. He advocates positive reinforcement (rewards rather than punishments), not because it is better to be kind but because, in his view, it is a more efficacious method of manipulation. His claims to efficacy are moreover overstated. Responses fade over time (extinction), and thus require frequent bouts of retraining. Fading habits may of course be explained theoretically, but as a method of social policy, conditioning would burden society with staggering costs.

Criticisms of this kind are important, though they focus, perhaps too exclusively, on Skinner's polemical work. Nonetheless they bring out the ends-oriented aim of much of experimental psychology, which vitiates the claim to have described behaviour without recourse to the language of motive, purpose and action.

Purging psychological language of purposive and mentalistic language was as we have seen a reaction to the unverifiable claims of introspectionists. This reaction took two forms. Radical behaviourists like Watson and Skinner denied the existence, or at least the significance, of events discovered through introspection. Assuming that any use of purposive or mental talk implicated the speaker in the discredited process of introspection, they were led to deny that anything intervenes between the stimulus and response. All references to drives, motives or awareness are reducible to the S–R language. Skinner is thus led to exclude physiological explanation which, since the time of Pavlov (1927), provided an important impetus to the development of behaviouristic methods. The work of Hebb (1949) is an instructive example. Physiologists require refined ways of describing bodily movement in order to draw inferences about the structure and function of the nervous system.

Other psychologists, like Hull (1943) and Tolman (1958), supposed the precise identification of stimulus and response was necessary to get at the interior processes which introspectionists imperfectly observed. Their views received encouragement from the prevailing view that in science one posits 'hypothetical constructs' or 'intervening variables', from which experimental evidence follows logically and by which further events can be predicted. For some the models do not refer to real events or structures, but are merely heuristic devices for making predictions; for others exact description of the learning process was warranted on the grounds that it can give us more accurate maps of the mind (for instance, Tolman). The concept of drive plays a central role in all theories of this type. Drive strength is alleged to facilitate prediction. (Skinner, of course, would argue that there is no difference between the drive and the summary of responses.) It also supports claims about interior processes, whose nature nonetheless remains problematical.

It is no longer as clear as it may have seemed around 1950 that psychological behaviourism has contributed much to our understanding of the behaviour of organisms. Some of the grounds for scepticism have been noted. The most far-reaching criticism is based on the work of Wittgenstein (1953) and Ryle (1949), who have themselves been described as behaviourists, because they agree that introspection is not the appropriate means of access to the mind. Wittgenstein argues that we cannot be sure we correctly apply a term to private experiences. Thus our talk about thoughts and feelings cannot logically be reports of private data. Ryle attacks the conception of the mind as a place where mental events take place. We do not observe our thoughts and report them; our thoughts are our speech. We do not describe our feelings so much as we express them. Mental activity, or much of it, is what we do.

But in Wittgenstein and Ryle the externalization of the mind is not motivated by the attempt to define behaviour in scientific terms. Their inquiry leads instead back to ordinary life and the everyday language we use to facilitate it. In this setting, it is inappropriate to speak of the movements of organisms as the basis for inferences about thoughts, intentions, feelings and goals. Our ground-floor descriptions of behaviour consist of talk about successful and failed action, not movements.

The implications of philosophical 'behaviourism' for empirical psychology are momentous. If its arguments are sound, the bloated mental universe of the introspectionist is purged without leaving a vacuum to be filled by scientific research. We have seen how far experimental design in psychology is implicated in the point of view of daily life. The maze is built with a view to discovering how quickly the subject *solves* it. The food pellet is called a *reward* and hours of food deprivation a stimulus or drive-excitation, language which is hard to distinguish conceptually from remarks about the subject's hunger, its preferences, its strategies and discoveries. This is language in which an understanding of behaviour is implicit. 'In psychology', Wittgenstein says, 'there is experimental method and *conceptual confusion*' (*Philosophical Investigations*, II, p. xiv). The behaviourist's reduction of action to movement is successful if it focuses attention on psychological problems; otherwise it seeks its justification not in the puzzles about what we do, but in positivist recipes for doing science.

There has been a marked falling off in recent years in behaviourist theory, though this has been accompanied by new defences of the S–R model by epistemologists and philosophers of LANGUAGE. Quine's *Word and Object* (1960) is a good example. But in psychology, conceived as an autonomous scientific discipline, little has been done since Spence's (1956) attempts to carry forward the work of Hull. During the past 15 years the idea that the experimental study of the responses of organisms under controlled conditions could lead to a science of behaviour has come increasingly under attack from those who believe that no legitimate account of behaviour is possible except in the context of a biological and evolutionary understanding of organisms. Classical behaviourists look at what organisms do strictly within the perspective provided by explicit rewards or aversive stimuli. They are thus incapable of recognizing the significance of altruistic behaviour. This is a response, sociobiologists say, only explainable on the assumption that altruism maximizes the chance of genetic material passing on to the next generation. The development of SOCIOBIOLOGY has marked similarities to psychological behaviourism, and has been criticized in much the same way. It is of interest here because it draws attention to what is fundamental to behaviourist strategy, and its deficiencies. Behaviourism is best seen as an attempt to mark off psychology as a science from other disciplines.

Reading

Austin, John 1961 (*1970*): A plea for excuses. In *Philosophical Papers*.
Chomsky, Noam 1959: Review of B.F. Skinner's *Verbal Behaviour*. *Language* 35.
Hebb, D.O. 1949: *The Organization of Behaviour*.
Hull, Clark L. 1943: *Principles of Behaviour*.
MacCorquodale, K. and Meehl, P.E. 1948: On a distinction between hypothetical constructs and intervening variables. *Psychological Review* 85, 95–107.
Melden, A.I. 1961: *Free Action*.
Pavlov, Ivan 1927: *Conditioned Reflexes*.
Peters, R.S. 1958: *The Concept of Motivation*.
Ryle, Gilbert 1949 (*1963*): *Concept of Mind*.
Scriven, Michael 1958: A study of radical behaviourism. In *Minnesota Studies in the Philosophy of Science*, ed. H. Feigl and M. Scriven.
Skinner, B.F. 1938: *The Behaviour of Organisms*.
—— 1959: *Verbal Behaviour*.
—— 1971: *Beyond Freedom and Dignity*.
Spence, Kenneth 1956: *Behaviour Theory and Conditioning*.
Tolman, E.C. 1958: *Behaviour and Psychological Man*.
Watson, J.B. 1924: *Behaviourism*.
Wilson, E.O. 1975: *Sociobiology*.
Wittgenstein, L. 1953 (*1967*): *Philosophical Investigations*.

ALFRED LOUCH

Bloomsbury group   This expression has long been used to denote an informal nexus of aesthetes and INTELLECTUALS influential, or at least conspicuous, in the first half of this century, and still, on account of their unconventional opinions and (especially) sex lives, of apparently inexhaustible interest to popular biographers. The name derives from the removal, on the death of the Victorian man of letters and first editor of the *Dictionary of National Biography* Sir Leslie Stephen (1832–1904), of his four children, who included the painter Vanessa (Bell) and the novelist Virginia (Woolf), from Hyde Park Gate to 46, Gordon Square, in the then highly unfashionable Bloomsbury district of central London. Here they and their friends met for regular soirées and discussions, and a nucleus of like-minded people evolved which long survived the break-up of the original household.

The group never had any official identity, though many of its members had belonged to Cambridge University's elite Society of Apostles. The Bloomsbury group, in fact, was almost exclusively Cambridge-educated and (later) Cambridge-based: it included the philosophers G. E. Moore and (peripherally) Bertrand Russell (both Trinity College), the historian G. Lowes Dickinson, the art critic Roger Fry, the biographer and literary critic Lytton Strachey, the novelist E. M. Forster, and the economist J. M. Keynes (all graduates or Fellows of King's College). Lesser lights were the critic Clive Bell (husband of Vanessa), the painter Duncan Grant, and the colonial administrator and Fabian thinker Leonard Woolf (husband of Virginia, and also founder, with her, of the Hogarth Press). The group's influence persisted well into the 1950s and beyond, in part through their children but also through such younger recruits as the Sunday newspaper critic Raymond Mortimer (said to be the model for the depraved Prince Daniyal in the most powerful of all satires on Bloomsbury, L. H. Myers's novel *The Root and the Flower* (1935)).

Bloomsbury was essentially the bohemian offspring of enlightened, upper-middle-class, late Victorian Cambridge. From Cambridge it took its rationalism, scepticism and religious agnosticism, but rejected its elders' UTILITARIANISM, puritanism and public spirit (typified by the Stephen and Strachey clans, which boasted, as well as early Evangelical connections, a number of distinguished legal, military and administrative figures among their number). The Bloomsbury outlook was Epicurean, hedonistic, pacifist, subjectivist and (except where art and 'personal relations' were concerned) somewhat monotonously irreverent. 'Nothing mattered,' Keynes noted in a famous *Memoir* (1949), 'except states of mind, our own and other people's, of course, but chiefly our own . . . We repudiated entirely customary morals, convention, and traditional wisdom.'

Bloomsbury's sole debt to Oxford was in AESTHETICS. Here it took its cue from Fry, who had been influenced by the FORMALISM and aversion to NATURALISM of the Aesthetic movement as typified by Walter Pater and Oscar Wilde. For Fry, as for J. A. McNeill Whistler, the value of a painting was located in the abstract, disinterested 'aesthetic states' supposedly induced in the sensitive spectator by its form, texture and colour alone, irrespective of representational content. He found these qualities of Significant Form (as Bell called it) preeminently exemplified in the work of Paul Cézanne, whom he introduced to the Anglo-Saxon world through two 'post-impressionist' exhibitions he organized in London in 1910 and 1912.

This idea – in itself far from novel – that value was essentially *sui generis* was substantially echoed, if not actually prompted, by G. E. Moore's view of the moral life as set forth in his *Principia Ethica* (1903), which has been called 'the Bloomsbury bible'. For the Good, too, was irreducible, except to the subjective 'states of mind' provoked by aesthetic stimuli on the one hand and friendship (or 'personal relations') on the other.

Moore's metaphysics, as he himself said, were those of 'common sense'. Things had a real existence independent of our perception of them, a view contemptuously dismissed by the earlier generation of Idealists against whom Moore had reacted. Nevertheless, the Bloomsbury outlook made few concessions to any objective or external world in the vulgar sense. It was essentially 'ivory tower'. Values might theoretically be 'objective', but in practice the individual was free to make up his own, since, being embodied only in ineffable private sensations, they were opaque to public inspection or criticism. (In this, oddly enough, they resembled the despised Puritan 'conscience'.) They amounted in the end to little more than tastes or preferences for which no apology was thought necessary beyond the traditional liberal appeal to the sovereignty of the individual (see LIBERALISM; INDIVIDUALISM).

Accordingly most critics of the Bloomsbury group (including one of the fiercest, the writer D. H. Lawrence, himself notably eccentric) have accused them of an amoral trivial-mindedness, made possible only by the financial independence to which most of them were born, and which enabled them to insulate themselves from the quotidian pressures which work and ordinary unsought social life impose on the less fortunate.

There is some truth in these strictures. In most Bloomsbury thinking there is indeed a pervasive 'thinness', even a certain self-congratulatory, clique-ish complacency. But it is surely extravagant, and a darkening of counsel, to lay (as has been done) the inflationary crises of the economically Keynesian 1970s at the door of Keynes's homosexuality and Bloomsbury *mores* generally. The supposed link is that Keynesian economics (as exemplified by demand management and deficit finance), homosexuality and the pursuit of mere aesthetic 'sensation' alike look only to the 'short run'; but it is now known that (by his own account) Keynes was prescribing mainly for the peculiar conditions of the 1930s, even if he also said, incontrovertibly enough, that 'in the long run we are all dead.'

Doubtless second- or third-raters such as Strachey and Bell have survived only because the Bloomsbury group as a whole has caught the public imagination (though Strachey's early *Landmarks in French Literature* and his posthumous *Books and Characters* are still worth any educated person's attention, unlike Bell's snobbish and pretentious *Civilization*). But people such as Keynes, Russell and even Moore would surely have been outstanding in any period or milieu, while writers such as Forster and (above all) Virginia Woolf display not only a technical inventiveness, but a fragile, precious and genuine spirituality that no age could or can afford to dispense with.

Reading
Bell, Quentin 1972: *Virginia Woolf: A Biography*, 2 vols.
Forster, E.M. 1947: *Howards End*.
Fry, Roger 1920: *Vision and Design*.
Harrod, R.F. 1951: *The Life of John Maynard Keynes*.
Johnstone, J.K. 1954: *The Bloomsbury Group*.
Keynes, J.M. 1949: *Two Memoirs*.
Moore, G.E. 1903: *Principia Ethica*.
Myers, L.H. 1935 (*1984*): *The Root and the Flower*.
Strachey, G. Lytton 1948: *Eminent Victorians*.
Woolf, Virginia 1966: *Collected Essays*, 4 vols.
——1927 (*1977*): *To the Lighthouse*.

ROBERT GRANT

body, sociology of the   In a short article on jeans Umberto Eco demonstrates the dialectic between depth and surface which essentially dictates the lifestyle of a given moment in history. Summarizing his argument: worn as a type of armour, clothes have influenced the behaviour, hence the external morality, of civilization (Eco, 1983). Moreover the examples he quotes show that morality *per se*, in other words customs, are determined by how the body covers itself.

Let us dwell on two major points of Eco's analysis. 'Epidermic self-consciousness' on the one hand (see also IDENTITY), and the concept of the body as a 'communication machine' on the other. This is not the place to go into the crucial role Eco attributes to the aggregation factor, that is, the way diverse types of uniforms come to be adopted by people living in an urban civilization. What is certain is that the anthropological structure constituted by the body is both cause and effect of the intensification of social activity.

The concern with body image which is expressed in fashion, body-building and so on is not simply a gratuitous or superficial display, but is part of a vast symbolic game and expresses the ways in which we can touch one another, form relationships and 'socialize', that is, create society. This is the lesson which the sociology of the body draws from dress fashion and from the various ways of endowing the body with value and significance. Together they create the 'social body' and constitute, in the simplest sense of the term, its specific economy. They show how figure, form and image, despite their static connotations, also play an important role in social evolution.

Thus the 'frivolous' (fashion, design, style, everything which expresses the ambient 'corporeality') proves on closer inspection to have unsuspected depths, for in the act of display the body is always both cause and effect of dynamic sociality. At the same time it is clearly a pre-eminent manifestation of aesthetics in the etymological sense of the word: that of sharing the same emotions, the same environment, the same values, so that individuals can finally lose themselves in an all-embracing theatricality.

At the heart of this approach to the topic lies a banal fact which it is still important not to lose sight of, namely that 'the psycho-physical unity' which forms our individuality is also a body. It is like an envelope which in turn is enveloped within the external world. Many philosophical, psychological and sociological analyses insist quite rightly on the profound epistemological consequences of this platitude. It amounts to saying that the body cannot be identified unless it has been delimited and situated. One thing is certain: this situational approach and, to coin a term, the 'envelopmentalism' which is its correlative, allow us to evaluate the profusion of *body-centred practices* observed by today's sociologists (body-building, body-care, dietetics, cosmetics, theatricality . . .). In particular, 'corporealism' allows us to understand that all the various types of appearance belong to a vast symbolic system where social effects are far from negligible. One is even tempted to suggest that the increasingly dominant role played by COMMUNICATION in contemporary society is nothing but today's version of that symbolic system. This insight could cast a new light on all those periods in history generally thought of as naive but which lived out intensely the symbolic–communicational charge of the 'envelopmentalism' specific to the body itself or to the social body. One could add that the concern and the care for the body which are so conspicuous today, the masks and dress fashions which form an anthropological constant can be analysed as yet another way human beings situate themselves in relation to others. Seen in this context, the body becomes both cause and effect of communication, in other words, of society itself.

See also EVERYDAY LIFE.

Reading

Berthelot, J.M. 1985: Les Sociologies et le corps. *Current Sociology* 33.2.
Eco, Umberto 1983 (*1986*): *Faith in Fakes.*
Guyau, M. 1911: *Les Problèmes de l'esthétique contemporaine.*
Maffesoli, M. 1982 (*1985*): *L'Ombre de Dionysos*, 2nd edn.
Mauss, M. 1935 (*1973*): Les Techniques du corps. Trans. in *Economy and Society* 2.1, pp. 70–88.
Turner, J.H. 1986: *The Body and Society.*

MICHEL MAFFESOLI

Bolshevism   *See* LENINISM

Bonapartism   A type of rule, epitomized by the regimes of Napoleon I and III, in which CIVIL SOCIETY and representative political institutions are subordinated to military-police power. The Bonapartist regime is installed through *coup d'état*, a consequence of the prior disintegration of republican institutions and of social turmoil. The leader at its head claims to express directly the indivisible will of the sovereign People, and attempts, but is unable, to establish a dynasty. Exceptional measures are legitimated by mass plebiscite. This bald definition, however, fails to convey the term's range of inflections, and also the conceptual sophistication it has on occasion received, particularly in Marxist thought.

The term Bonapartism was already in use by 1815–16 (*OED*, 1971, p.245; Robert, 1966, p.510), but its familiarity in educated European circles was largely a phenomenon of the 1850s and 1860s. In this period the word described, criticized or praised the rule of Louis Bonaparte. His governance, first as President, then as Emperor (1852–70) of France, was felt to enshrine a novel political mutation: simultaneously populist (see POPULISM), authoritarian, patriotic and militarily adventurist. The word was often used as a synonym for CAESARISM, though some writers polemicized against that equation, accusing it of anachronism (Marx, 1852; Mommsen, 1901, p.325) or even irreverence (Mommsen, pp.326–7).

Twentieth-century usage can be roughly divided into two overlapping categories. The first offers a sociopolitical, Marxist account of Bonapartism and seeks to apply the term to 'modern' conditions. According to Marx and Engels's many-sided analyses (not always consistent: see Rubel, 1960; Wippermann, 1983), Napoleon III's regime was made possible both by the pervasive bureaucratization of French society and by a specific conjuncture: the balance of class forces which lent the executive arm substantial room for political manoeuvre. Bonapartism's historical significance lay in its ability to promote vigorous capitalist development in conditions where the bourgeoisie required massive state intervention on their behalf (Marx, 1852 and 1871; Engels, 1871).

Marx himself rarely employed the term Bonapartism, probably because he was reluctant to elevate the Napoleonic experience into a general political category – something which the 'ism' suffix, from the Greek *ismos*, evolved to convey (Koebner and Schmidt, 1965, p.xiv). Later Marxists proved less cautious. Accordingly Bonapartism was alleged to be evident in Kerensky's Provisional Government (Lenin, 'The beginning of Bonapartism' and 'They do not see the wood for the trees', in *Collected Works*, vol. 25; Trotsky, 1932, pp.663–8), 'the Stalin regime' (Trotsky, 1937, pp.277–9); and the pre-Nazi administrations of Brüning and Hindenburg–Papen–Schleicher (Trotsky, 1932; see also Kitchen (1974) on Thalheimer). In these cases, Bonapartism takes on varying shades of meaning, but the idea of relative state autonomy, arising from social class equilibrium or stalemate, remains fundamental, as does the opprobrium that accompanies the term. More recent Marxist discussions of Bonapartism have re-emphasized its military character (Hobsbawm, 1977, pp.177–91), its similarities to, and differences from, FASCISM (Kitchen, 1976, pp.71–82), its existence as one form of regime (others include Bismarckism, fascism, military juntas) which the 'exceptional capitalist state' is capable of assuming (Poulantzas, 1974, pp.313–30; cf. Engels, 1884).

The second usage of the concept locates it squarely in its own time: 'Bonapartism' becomes a means of interpreting and reconstructing elements of nineteenth-century European history. Often this itself has proceeded within a Marxist-influenced framework: for instance, depicting the 'Bonapartism' of the French Second Empire as a 'modernizing dictatorship' (Magraw, 1983, pp.159–205), or as an 'authoritarian bureaucratic' regime (Perez-Diaz, 1978), or expanding the concept to embrace Bismarck's 'revolution from above' in nineteenth-century Prussia (Wehler, 1970, and 1985, pp.55–62; but see also Mitchell, 1977, and Eley, 1984, pp.149–53). Yet non-Marxist writers have also found work for the concept. Some have employed it to indicate the parallels and contrasts between the regimes of Napoleon I and III (for instance, Fisher, 1928). Others have used the term to map the historical complexity of the phenomena it denotes: for instance the evolutionary quality of Napoleon III's rule, the uneven geographical distribution of its mass base, its links to Orleanism – the political movement which supported the idea and institution of constitutional monarchy – and republicanism, its relation to the rural and urban populace, the origins and varieties of its right-wing support – say, from notables and clerics (Zeldin, 1979, pp.140–205; Rémond, 1966, pp.125–65, 366–84, who also compares Gaullism in twentieth-century France to Bonapartism; Bluché, 1980). Finally, Bonapartism has prompted interest as a term in nineteenth-century political discourse, and has been studied as one of a family of concepts – which includes despotism, tyranny, usurpation, DICATATORSHIP and CAESARISM – denoting changing forms of 'illegitimate domination' (Richter, 1982 and 1988).

Reading
Draper, H. 1977: *Karl Marx's Theory of Revolution*, 2 vols. Vol. 1, *State and Bureaucracy*.
Groh, D. 1972: Cäsarismus, Napoleonismus, Bonapartismus, Führer, Chef, Imperialismus. In *Geschichtliche Grundbegriffe*, 7 vols. Vol. 1, ed. O. Brunner, W. Conze, and R. Koselleck, pp. 726–71.
Hammer, K., and Hartmann, P.C. 1977: *Der Bonapartismus: Historisches Phänomen und politischer Mythos.*
Wehler, H-U. 1985: *The German Empire 1871–1918.*
Zeldin, T. 1958: *The Political System of Napoleon III.*
—— 1979: *France 1848–1945: Politics and Anger.*

PETER BAEHR

bourgeoisie   A term dating from the thirteenth century which (like such equivalents as burghers, Bürgertum) originally denoted a category of town dwellers in medieval Europe, particularly merchants and artisans, who enjoyed a special status and rights within feudal society. But with the development of capitalism, and especially from the eighteenth century, the meaning of the term gradually changed and it came to refer more specifically to wealthy employers who were active in manufacture, commerce and finance – a usage which is partly reflected in Hegel's conception of *bürgerliche Gesellschaft* (civil society) as the sphere of private economic interests. Marx, who was mainly responsible for giving the term its wide currency in later social thought, started out from Hegel's distinction between the bourgeois and the citizen but soon developed, from his critical study of Hegel's philosophy and still more from his voracious reading of political economy, an entirely different conception of the bourgeoisie as the dominant class in a specific (capitalist) mode of production. As Engels (1847) summarized this view, the bourgeoisie 'is the class of the great capitalists who, in all developed countries, are now almost exclusively in possession of all the means of consumption, and of the raw materials and instruments (machines, factories) necessary for their production'; and later (1888) 'the class of modern capitalists, owners of the means of social production and employers of wage labour'.

Marx's conception (and that of later Marxists) had several distinctive features. It formed part of a general theory of history as the succession of modes of production and forms of society, each characterized by a determinate level of development of the forces of production (primarily technology) and a particular class structure (or relations of production) within which there is endemic conflict. In capitalist society, which emerged, according to the Marxist view, from the growth of new productive powers and the class struggle of the bourgeoisie against the feudal system, historical change is more rapid than ever before: 'The bourgeoisie, during its rule of scarce one hundred years, has created more massive and more colossal productive forces than all preceding generations together' (Marx and Engels, 1848); but at the same time it brought into existence a new class, the proletariat, which engages in ever more widespread and intense conflict with it.

Two distinct processes, therefore, go on in capitalist society. The bourgeoisie continues to revolutionize the system of production, one effect of which is an increasing centralization of capital in large corporations, facilitated by the expansion of credit money provided by the banks (Hilferding, 1910), and, in the twentieth century particularly, a massive internationalization of capital (Mandel, 1975). But bourgeois dominance is also increasingly challenged by the industrial proletariat (see WORKING CLASS), whose struggle, according to Marx, would eventually give rise to a new, socialist and classless, society. Marx's expectations depended in part on his view that society would be increasingly polarized between the two major classes, a small bourgeoisie formed as a result of the 'expropriation of many capitalists by few', and a large proletariat constituting the 'immense majority' of the population; though he also recognized that there were significant intermediate strata, including the petty bourgeoisie made up of small independent producers, traders and professional people, and even expected the middle class as a whole to increase in size (to judge from two passages in the manuscripts of *Theories of Surplus Value*).

Later Marxists, in the twentieth century, have had to deal with more complex problems arising from the rapid growth of the 'new middle class' of clerical workers, technical and professional employees and service personnel of all kinds (see MIDDLE CLASS), higher living standards and more extensive social welfare, which have almost everywhere diminished the intensity of class conflict in recent times. The bourgeoisie of the present day, still immensely wealthy and controlling giant corporations, is nevertheless more constrained in various respects than its nineteenth-century predecessor, by varying degrees of public ownership and economic planning and by a limited redistribution of wealth and income, so that its lifestyle and social prestige is no longer perhaps in quite such blatant contrast with that of a substantial part of the rest of society.

Many social thinkers had always emphasized other aspects of the social role of the bourgeoisie, and these features have become more prominent in recent debates. Max Weber (1904–5) associated the capitalist spirit with the Protestant ethic, and saw the bourgeoisie as being animated by ideas of rationality and enterprise, individual liberty and responsibility, which equipped them for the leadership required to maintain a dynamic and democratic society. J. A. Schumpeter (1942) similarly emphasized the importance of entrepreneurship and connected the development of modern democracy with the rise of capitalism, but unlike Weber he saw in socialism a continuation of the bourgeois outlook: 'The ideology of classical socialism is the offspring of bourgeois ideology. In particular it shares the latter's rationalist and utilitarian background and many of the ideas and ideals that entered the classical doctrine of democracy' (pp. 298–9). A historian, Henri Pirenne, also saw the bourgeoisie (or middle class as he sometimes calls it) in medieval towns as 'spreading the idea of liberty far and wide' (1925, p. 154), though many late medieval towns were in fact dominated by a small number of patrician families (Holton, 1986, pp. 79–83). Most recently, in the writings of Hayek (1973–9) and some thinkers of the NEW RIGHT, the existence of a free and democratic society is rigorously connected with private ownership of productive resources (though the concept of a bourgeoisie is not generally used) and with free markets, which together are also considered to achieve a high level of efficiency in the economy.

Reading

Bottomore, Tom, and Brym, Robert J. eds 1989: *The Capitalist Class: An International Study.*

Holton, R.J. 1986: *Cities, Capitalism and Civilization.*

Pirenne, Henri 1925: *Medieval Cities.*

Riedel, M. 1975: Bürger, Staatsbürger, Bürgertum. In *Geschichtliche Grundbegriffe*, ed. O. Brunner et al., vol. 1.

Sombart, Werner 1913 (*1967*): *Der Bourgeois*, trans. as *The Quintessence of Capitalism.*

TOM BOTTOMORE

Buddhism Over the course of 25 centuries, Buddhism has developed into a distinctive pan-Asian religious tradition and civilization, but at the same time it has always readily accommodated local variation. This has been especially the case with the forms of social life accepted by Buddhists; Buddhist social life in China has had more in common with Confucian values (see CONFUCIANISM) than with those affirmed by South Asian Buddhists who shared many of their social values with Hindus (see HINDUISM AND HINDU SOCIAL THEORY). As a result, the social configurations and practices of the Buddhist tradition have historically been extraordinarily diverse, so much so that the first Western observers of Buddhism found it difficult to recognize that the religion they encountered in Japan was related to that found in Thailand. At the same time, Buddhist thinkers generally expended little effort in attempts to make sense of this diversity by defining the nature of the ideal society, especially in comparison to intellectuals in other religious traditions, such as Islam and Hinduism. This has changed in the twentieth century, and an interest in articulating social knowledge and values that are distinctively Buddhist is a striking feature of contemporary Buddhism around the world.

Traditionally, normative Buddhist thought was quite ambivalent about social life. For example, the *Aggañña Sutta*, a canonical myth about the origins of community, portrays the emergence of the basic elements of social life, such as the family, as a response to immorality and greed. Moreover, institutionalized social structures were portrayed as inherently compromised and morally suspect because they often accommodated and sometimes abetted the propensities towards evil found among humans. Other authoritative accounts portray social life as an inevitable source of suffering because of the natural impermanence and commonplace duplicity of relations among humans. Actual social life provided abundant confirmation of this dark vision. In contrast, the ideal Buddhist life was meant to root out the inclination to evil and to end suffering. It was often portrayed as highly individualized, free of social responsibilities, with social interaction limited to consensual relations among beings differentiated only by spiritual attainment. This ideal was institutionalized in the Buddhist monastic order (*sangha*), in which the patterns of dependence and hierarchy typical of all human communities were rejected. In short, Buddhist thinkers commonly saw life in society as irredeemable, and concluded that the best that an individual might do is to cease to participate in its concerns and expectations. This negative attitude towards social life was a source of criticism and scorn directed against Buddhism by thinkers in rival communities in India and China.

Although traditional Buddhist thought saw little possibility of truly reforming human society, certain social virtues were recommended as ways of minimizing the commonplace cruelties of social life. These included filial piety, generosity, gratitude, patience, and a sense of proportion. The exact definition of such virtues and the specification of other social virtues varied from society to society in the Buddhist world. Similarly, traditional Buddhist teaching recommended kingship as an acceptable political structure; in traditional Buddhist political theory, it was a king's responsibility to enforce law and to promote general well-being, but again there was no agreement across the Buddhist world about what constitutes law or the good society which a king should promote.

Some aspects of Buddhist thought were frequently used for legitimizing existing social structures. A central feature of Buddhist thought is the doctrine of karma which provides an explanation of how certain aspects of one's present existence are the result of previous acts, especially actions in a previous life. In traditional Buddhist thought, the effects of karma were correlated with the existential hierarchy found in Buddhist cosmology, which included a range of heavens and hells as well as humans, animals and ghosts; one's future birth in one of these realms would be determined by the good or evil that one did now, just as one's current circumstances were the result of previous actions. The existing social hierarchy among humans in a given community was located within this cosmic hierarchy and social inequalities were thus justified as the fair consequences of moral or immoral action. The basic thrust of this religious world-view was conservative; individuals might be able to change their own position within the social and cosmic hierarchy, but the hierarchy itself was fixed.

In the twentieth century, cosmology, rebirth and karma are generally no longer at the centre of Buddhist thought, largely because such ideas often appear suspect in the light of modern scientific knowledge. Other aspects of Buddhist thought have consequently received more emphasis than has traditionally been the case, although this rethinking has generally been in the guise of a return to the original teachings of the Buddha, the fifth century BCE Indian teacher who was the founder of Buddhism. In this rethinking, the individual, rather than the community, still occupies centre-stage, but in place of the traditional account of karma, special emphasis is given to the human capacity for critical thought, for mental and moral self-discipline, for change in the light of better understanding of human nature and the natural world. This rethinking also suggested the possibility of reforming, if not changing, the structures of society in the light of improved knowledge, instead of accepting them as a cosmological given.

The possibility of social change has inspired Buddhists to reconsider the resources of their tradition in search of new models for better societies. Some Buddhists have seen the idealized portrayal of the monastic order in Buddhist scriptures as an inspirational model for a perfect society. This voluntary society is based in spirit on the rejection of basic evils such as self-gratification and greed, as indicated by the prohibition on the use of money by monks and the affirmation of such virtues as humility and discipline, which check the dangers of individualism. Its governing structures give preference to consensus, which is seen by contemporary Buddhists as a perfect form of democracy, while its economic orientation would be socialist, with resources shared in common according to an ethic of sufficiency. It is organized around a common interest in promoting spiritual advancement, according to the schema of Buddhist soteriology, and all members of the society benefit from participation. There have been some preliminary steps towards actually implementing this model, such as U Nu's programme for Buddhist Socialism in Burma, but these attempts have hardly proved promising.

Another important trend in contemporary Buddhism has been the emergence of a new emphasis on social activism. When it first appeared earlier in this century, this new orientation was generally not motivated directly by the social or ethical values found in the Buddhist tradition, but rather was an attempt to ensure that Buddhism would not become irrelevant in the modern world and thus disappear. The emphasis on social activism did inspire a reconsideration of the ethical resources of the Buddhist tradition in a search for distinctively Buddhist warrants for such behaviour. These activities are thus now encouraged as effective ways of cultivating and expressing traditional Buddhist virtues such as compassion and generosity. Monks are now commonly encouraged to supplement, if not actually replace, their traditional forms of practice with social services as a way of addressing the suffering caused by the rapid changes typical of modern life globally. Similarly, lay people throughout the Buddhist world have supported the establishment of schools, hospitals, and other charities. Given the magnitude of the problems which these activities address, Buddhists have frequently discovered themselves to be part of a community that transcends the individual groups in which they normally participate.

In searching for a systematic basis for distinctively Buddhist social thought, many Buddhist thinkers have turned to the core doctrine of 'co-dependent origination' (*paticca samuppada*) which articulates the fundamental interconnection of all reality. This doctrine defines the world as a place where nothing can exist independently; each existent necessarily occurring in a causal relationship with other existents. The doctrine of interdependence displays the connection of an individual with the entire human race and lays a foundation for moral responsibility towards others. This moral responsibility exists at both a personal and a social level and obligates each individual and group to work towards the solution of global problems, such as nuclear disarmament and the environmental crisis. Of course, this move to a more inclusive common good does not stop with humanity but also embraces the natural world, since humans and the natural world are not distinguishable within the doctrine of co-dependent origination. Thus, ironically, another kind of ambivalence about society has emerged in twentieth-century Buddhist thought. Even as modern Buddhist thinkers have been more concerned with specifying the nature of a good society, and contemporary Buddhists have attempted to improve social conditions and bring into being more moral societies, the aspects of Buddhist thought to which they have turned to justify their concerns and actions have tended to undermine the legitimacy of dividing humanity into distinct societies, with particular structures, or even of thinking about human community in isolation from the larger, interdependent world.

Reading

Dharmasiri, Gunapala 1989: *Fundamentals of Buddhist Ethics*.

Dumoulin, Heinrich ed. 1976: *Buddhism in the Modern World*.

Keyes, Charles F. 1989: Buddhist politics and their revolutionary origins in Thailand. *International Political Science Review* 10, 121–42.

Swearer, Donald K. 1981: *Buddhism and Society in Southeast Asia*.

Welch, Holmes 1968: *The Buddhist Revival in China*.

CHARLES HALLISEY

bureaucracy One of the central categories of modern social science, it refers to a type of administration in which the power to make decisions is invested in an office or function rather than a particular individual. In the course of history bureaucracy appears in widely different social and economic formations, but at the same time it displays several common features, the most important of them being the following.

Bureaucracy separates itself from society, both from the ruling class and the masses. It is organized within a particular institutional system in which a special ideology, an ethos and various formal procedures develop. All this appears as a kind of subculture. The source of its power lies in the fact that guidance and control functions have emerged which society's basic classes cannot fulfil. Usually, however, it attaches new tasks to the historically necessary functions (for instance, irrigation in ancient societies) which ensures the growth of its power over society.

It is a characteristic feature of bureaucracy that administration is carried out not by lay persons but by specialists who regard this work as their life career rather than as a temporary activity performed for certain periods of time. In the bureaucratic institutional system a standardized set of requirements comes into existence, such as the examinations for old-style Chinese state officials, and those in all modern states, which is one of the bases for the stability of bureaucratic power and at the same time involves some exclusivity.

Bureaucracy as defined in the social sciences differs from everyday usage. In many languages the latter merges with the so-called bureaucratism of incompetent clerks whose work is characterized by ineffective, soulless, slow and often irrational formalism. In contrast to this, bureaucratic administration, as Max Weber (1921–2, part 3, ch. 6) argued, proved more effective, rapid and competent than alternative historical forms of administration. This explains why in modern societies bureaucratic administration is expanding, not only in state organizations but in almost every field of social life. The phenomenon is especially conspicuous in the economic arena where the management of medium and large enterprises is being totally bureaucratized (see the comments by Schumpeter, 1942, pp.205–7). Confronted with this tendency, many social scientists (such as W. Mommsen, 1974) refer to the total bureaucratization of life.

Different schools of social science have various approaches to the problem of bureaucracy. The theoretical approach of the Marxist classics is incoherent in many respects. In Marx's early work a definitely anti-bureaucratic stance is apparent. His experience of the Moselle district hunger crisis made him understand that besides the ruling class and the subordinated social groups there existed a state bureaucracy with its own particular interests represented by these apparatuses as general social or state interests. The special spirit of bureaucracy is the secrecy and mystery which protect the particular interests of this group against the external society and interpret every internal matter as a state secret. But in the later works of Marx and Engels the problem of bureaucracy was relegated to the background and the struggle between workers and capitalists came to the fore. They failed to foresee two circumstances. The first was the expansion of bureaucracy to the economy and other areas of society. They did not foresee that the leadership of industry and of the economy in general would pass into the hands of certain bodies distinct from the owners who exercised power over the workers directly, although with their existence continuing to depend on the proprietors who, as shareholders or as family owners, expected them to work efficiently and increase the profit. In this case, too, the bureaucratic system of institutions strives to extend its power, and thus profit becomes a secondary motivation in their decisions.

At the time of classic capitalism the bureaucratization of the economy was still *in statu nascendi*. The management of the enterprises was still largely carried out by the owners themselves. In this respect a major change came at the turn of the century, as was analysed with greater clarity by several thinkers and notably by Max Weber, whose works demonstrate his specific anti-bureaucratic attitude and his specific scientific approach – the latter in the spirit of a *verstehende* (interpretive) sociology.

From the beginning of the century economic life and other areas of society were increasingly bureaucratized, and a particularly important feature has been the bureaucratization of political parties,

with an ever increasing influence over the entire society because of the emergence of Western democratic parliamentarianism, a process analysed by Roberto Michels (1911).

The trade unions, whose formation was dominated by anti-capitalist tendencies, encountered a new 'enemy' – industrial bureaucracy – and at the same time they also produced their own bureaucratic organs. The conflict of interests between workers and capitalists came to appear as a confrontation and consensus between industrial and trade union bureaucracies, a development described by Sidney and Beatrice Webb.

In Western societies the process of bureaucratization has continued into the post-capitalist and postindustrial period, with several of its characteristic features altered. In the economy, an ever-growing role is played by state apparatuses but they do not control economic life in an independent way, as in the period of late feudalism and early capitalism, but in association with the industrial, finance and trade union bureaucracies. This has produced a highly intricate texture of economic power, called the techno-structure by J. K. Galbraith (see also TECHNOCRACY). Chiefly in the economy but also in other areas, bureaucracies in Western countries go beyond national boundaries and assume an international character, and in certain respects this makes the fight for independence which characterizes national states illusory. It may be argued that the significance of anti-capitalism was exaggerated by Marx and Engels to the detriment of anti-bureaucracy. In today's practice it is apparent that the emancipation of humanity in the modern world requires anti-bureaucratism rather than anti-capitalism.

The second error of the classical Marxist authors is that in their socialist vision they failed to see the danger of the bureaucratization of society. They postulated the rapid 'withering away' of the state and the socialization of all types of administration. But the experiences of the former Soviet Union and the East European countries have shown that a whole range of interwoven bureaucratic institutions comes into existence to perform the administrative functions, and at the centre of this institutional network was the monolithically dominant one-party system and its leading organs. These played an integrative function among various bureaucratic institutions (industrial, economic, military, cultural) and exercised control over the mass organizations (trade unions, youth and official peace movements and so on) and over the mass media organized from above. Strict party control over bureaucratic institutions debilitated the forms of existence of CIVIL SOCIETY, including political and cultural movements and ethnic and religious organizations. This bureaucratized world did not only characterize state-management socialism, so-called Stalinism, but also the Yugoslav self-management system where in practice various bureaucratic organs preserved their dominant role. Social activity, however, increasingly asserted itself against the bureaucratization of administration, and aspirations developed for a world in which bureaucracy as such no longer exists and power is directly in the hands of the people.

The modern world cannot do without bureaucratic institutions, and a realistic anti-bureaucratic goal can only be control over the bureaucratic power by civil society. That underlines the importance of the reforms of political institutional systems in Eastern Europe and the former USSR, precisely for the following reasons. As a result of the reforms the monolithic system has been transformed into a pluralistic one and this has destroyed the hegemony of bureaucracy dominated by the one-party system. In the course of the reforms civil society has been revived. Political parties, organizations and movements have emerged over which bureaucracy no longer has any control, while the main aim of civil society is to control this very bureaucracy.

Reform socialism (or SOCIAL DEMOCRACY), in contrast to the state-management system, is a socio-economic formation in which, though various bureaucratic institutions survive, their monolithic domination ceases to exist and they operate under effective control by civil society. Thus anti-bureaucratic movements can also be observed in Western societies, which may be termed alternative movements. Especially significant among them is the working out and introduction of a so-called alternative enterprise structure which is not dominated by a hierarchical bureaucracy but by cooperation between various associations of workers (see COOPERATIVE MOVEMENT; SOCIAL MOVEMENT). It is another question whether the anti-bureaucratic movements may also produce their own bureaucracies, as historical experiences have revealed. In spite of this, the world of bureaucratic phenomena and the struggle against it are some of the most important features of our age.

See also DIVISION OF LABOUR.

Reading
Galbraith, J.K. 1967: *The New Industrial State*.
Hegedüs, A. 1976: *Socialism and Bureaucracy*.
Michels, Roberto 1911 (*1962*): *Political Parties*.
Mommsen, W. 1974: *The Age of Bureaucracy*.
Mouzelis, N.P. 1967: *Organisation and Bureaucracy*.
Rizzi, B. 1985: *The Bureaucratization of the World*.
Webb, Sidney and Webb, Beatrice 1897: *Industrial Democracy*.
Weber, Max 1921–2 (*1967, 1978*): *Economy and Society*, part 3, ch. 6. Also in Gerth, H. H. and Mills, C. Wright eds 1946: *From Max Weber*.

ANDRÁS HEGEDÜS

business cycle   As recurrent fluctuations in the economic activity of industrial economies, business cycles can be observed statistically when one examines the historical record of a nation's overall economic performance – say, annual statistics of gross national product corrected for price change (real GNP). Typically what is apparent is a pattern of long-term growth marked by alternations of expansion and contraction. These recurrent alternations above and below the long-term trend are business cycles. The word cycle suggests fixed and perhaps symmetrical timing patterns but economists have long rejected that notion. Although some economists now prefer to describe these phenomena as 'economic fluctuations', the term business cycle remains in common use.

Cyclical movements in an economy are pervasive. When real GNP rises (or falls), so do employment, real income, profits and other broad aspects of activity. Relatively few industries depart from the overall pattern, although industries producing durable goods are subject to greater than average fluctuations. Furthermore the movements, first in one direction and then in another, tend to persist for extended periods of time – unlike seasonal fluctuations, for example, which occur within the compass of a year. In business cycle parlance, rising activity or the expansion culminates in a peak, and then gives way to a recession (also referred to as a downturn or contraction), whose low point is designated as a trough. This is followed by the recovery, or upturn, which is the initial phase of the expansion. In the United States the half-century since 1949 has witnessed eight expansions ranging in length from one year to about nine, with a median duration of about 3·5 years. Contractions, much less variable, have averaged a little less than a year. Both expansions and contractions have shown great variability in intensity. The Great Depression of the 1930s had a profound effect on subsequent economic policies of governments but its severity and length were unique in twentieth-century business cycle records (see also ECONOMIC DEPRESSION).

Theories of the business cycle have abounded although interest on the part of economists has itself been subject to its ups and downs. Interest in the 1920s, stimulated by Britain's economic problems, was greatly intensified in the next decade because of the Great Depression. Keynes's (1936) *General Theory of Employment, Interest and Money* was not primarily concerned with the traditional core of business cycle theory – explaining the recurrent fluctuations in overall economic activity – but not long after the *General Theory* appeared the belief became fairly common that government stabilization policies could make the business cycle a thing of the past. Economists shifted their attention to the new field of macroeconomics, which became the dominant field of interest for those concerned with overall activity. The prosperity of the decade or two after the end of World War II encouraged the view that the business cycle was outmoded. An international conference of business cycle specialists in the late 1960s produced a volume entitled *Is the Business Cycle Obsolete?* (Bronfenbrenner, 1969). Most economists did not think that was so, but any doubts about whether the cycle might have disappeared were dispelled in the 1970s and 1980s, which witnessed severe business downturns and high rates of both unemployment and inflation. The 1970s also saw the emergence of new theoretical developments and a renewed interest by economists in the business cycle, which persisted through the 1980s.

In seeking causes of the business cycle economists have distinguished between factors outside the economic system and those within the system itself. Wars, major inventions or changing government fiscal and monetary policies are examples of outside causes and have been variously referred to as 'disturbances', 'shocks', 'impulses' or 'exogenous' factors. These are different from the internal working of the economy itself and its tendency to fluctuate over extended periods. These are 'endogenous' rather than exogenous factors or 'propagation mechanisms' as distinct from shocks, disturbances or impulses. Writers recognized these distinctions before World War II, but they usually put the greater emphasis on the working of the economic system itself, that is, the tendency of the economy towards instability even in the absence of outside disturbances.

In his renowned 1937 League of Nations study *Prosperity and Depression*, Gottfried Haberler's analysis of modern business cycle theories led him to group theories into several broad classes although he noted that differences among classes were chiefly a matter of emphasis. He pointed out that most modern theories viewed the business cycle as the result not of any single factor but of several, many of which were common to different theories, and that the factors giving rise to a cycle in one period were not necessarily the same as those causing a cycle in another. These judgements of a half-century ago remain valid. However, these early theories, unlike those after World War II, tended to emphasize endogenous factors rather than outside influences as causes of the business cycle. Among the more important categories in Haberler's classification of theories are: those he describes as purely monetary; overinvestment; underconsumption; psychological; and those attributing cycles to price–cost maladjustments.

Several theories are embraced under the rubric of overinvestment theories, which stress the key role of business spending on new buildings and durable equipment. Because these investment goods are long-lasting and are bought with an eye to the future it is not difficult intuitively to see how errors in businessmen's judgements can give rise to excesses in investment and their inevitable corrections. F. A. Hayek was one of several writers who gave a monetary explanation of overinvestment (see also MONETARISM). Non-monetary explanations were given by economists such as Joseph Schumpeter, who stressed the special role of innovations, the opening of new markets and their subsequent shrinkage. An important variant of the overinvestment theory assigned a crucial role to the 'acceleration' principle, according to which a mere decline in the rate of increase in business sales, say, to consumers, could give rise to an absolute decline in the production of investment goods. These stand in contrast to underconsumption theories, put forth by writers such as J. A. Hobson, which held that as the expansion proceeds consumers tended to 'oversave', as a result of which consumer demand declined.

A number of theories are classified as psychological. The distinctive feature of these, in Haberler's words, is that the response of total investment to objective factors is stronger than rational economic considerations would suggest (Haberler, 1937, p. 147). During the boom businessmen are subject to 'errors of optimism', which lead to errors in the opposite direction once businessmen see that their anticipations cannot be realized. Keynes's theory of the business cycle (a chapter in the *General Theory*, pp. 313–32) placed major stress on businessmen's anticipations and the key role they played in business decisions to invest (see KEYNESIANISM).

The flagging of interest in business cycle theory in the two decades or so after the end of World War II was not only due to Keynes and the general prosperity. Several factors fostered interest in empirical research: the development of national income and product statistics, advances in econometric model building and the appearance of electronic computers for the solution of large complex models. Model building proliferated and some models seemed to 'work', that is, given certain assumptions about policy they tracked the behaviour of the economy fairly closely. Thus they seemed to validate the economic principles on which they were based. This period witnessed a shift in emphasis away from endogenous models to models in which exogenous influences were dominant, notably government spending and tax policies, and private business investment. In these essentially Keynesian models monetary policy did not appear to be very important. In addition, they embodied a trade-off between the rate of inflation and the rate of unemployment in the short run.

In his presidential address before the American Economic Association, Milton Friedman (1968) made a monetarist counterattack on the Keynesian system and models based on it. Unlike Keynes, Friedman saw the private economy as fundamentally stable; like R. G. Hawtrey early in the century, Friedman attributed instability in the economy to changing monetary policy. Changes in monetary policy by the central bank – to stimulate or slow down the economy – constituted the chief outside shocks to the economic system, and it was for this reason that Friedman advocated that the Federal Reserve pursue a policy in which the money supply would grow at a stable rate. The early 1970s saw the beginnings of a new theory, attributable to Robert Lucas (1977), Thomas Sargent and others, which rekindled academic interest in the business cycle. This was the rational expectations-equilibrium theory of macroeconomics, which was mainly a critique of the Keynesian macroeconomic view of the world but which has also had business cycle applications. (See RATIONAL EXPECTATIONS HYPOTHESIS.)

Since the appearance of Keynes's *General Theory* the dominant macroeconomic view has held that prices and wages are either rigid or very sluggish in responding to changes in overall demand and thus fail to perform their traditional market-clearing functions. In the Keynesian view increases or decreases in overall demand in the short run, such as occur in a business cycle expansion or contraction, are reflected mainly in changes in the real economy, that is, in production and employment. However, proponents of the rational expectations-equilibrium theory maintain that supply and demand even at the level of the overall economy are constantly being balanced by adjustments in prices and wages. According to these newer views, which hark back to pre-Keynesian economists, the real economy is not fundamentally unstable. How then account for the pronounced fluctuations in economic activity so readily apparent? One answer (and several have been put forth, tested and found wanting) is that workers and businessmen, although rational about the markets in which they themselves operate, are ignorant about every other market and consequently are prone to make mistakes – about how much to produce or how much labour to supply in response to a change in demand. Making these errors and then correcting them give rise to cyclical movements. A more recent theory in the equilibrium genre is that of the real business cycle, which attributes fluctuations to 'productivity shocks', the responses to which by business and labour occur with a pronounced lag. If these theories have not been entirely convincing (Okun, 1980; Gordon, 1986, pp. 8–9), their persistence in varying forms thus far must be due in large part to the breakdown of Keynesian macroeconomic models in the 1970s, when the inflation–unemployment trade-off in the short run vanished and high rates of inflation existed side by side with high rates of unemployment. In addition, the new theory of rational expectations emphasizes a long-established tenet central to economic analysis, namely, that economic agents are rational optimizing individuals.

Another strand of the business cycle worthy of note is the empirical approach associated with Wesley Mitchell early in the century and later with his colleagues at the National Bureau of Economic Research. They examined thousands of economic time series, seeking recurring patterns and regularities from which might be derived generalizations that would describe and ultimately explain the cyclical behaviour of the economy. This started the work, which has continued to the present, of measuring expansions and contractions, dating turning points (peaks and troughs), classifying particular statistical series as leading or lagging at business cycle turning points, and the like. Although *Measuring Business Cycles* (Burns and Mitchell, 1946) was greeted with disdain by mainstream economists for its failure to bow in the direction of the new Keynesian macroeconomics (Koopmans, 1947) the approach has shown a certain hardiness partly because business cycles have persisted and partly because the leading indicators have become transformed into a forecasting device.

Where do we stand today on the business cycle, which is so much a part of modern economic life? It is very likely that economists and governments have learned enough to prevent a repetition of the Great Depression but beyond this there is no single dominating theory to which most economists would subscribe, as Victor Zarnowitz made clear in his comprehensive review article of 1985. Probably most would agree that the business cycle has many causes, some coming from outside the economic system and some a reflection of the way in which the system itself works. Either source can be real or monetary in nature. It may be that the business cycle itself is of such complexity in a modern industrial economy that much of its essential nature can never be captured by an econometric model of whatever sophistication or novelty. It is perhaps a commentary on the unsatisfactory state of affairs that exists today with model forecasts that empirical forecasting tools find a ready market.

Forecasting goes hand in hand with the business cycle. It is a burgeoning activity in most large market-oriented industrialized countries, engaged in by businesses, governments and international organizations, and has itself given rise to a substantial forecasting industry. Gauged by the US experience, economists have had a fair degree of success in forecasting economic activity (real GNP) about a year ahead, with a notable lack of success in forecasting turning points (McNees, 1988). They do distinctly better than 'naive models' which predict that the change in next year's real GNP will be the same as the past year's; by this standard they do less well, however, in predicting the rate of inflation. Some of this success, such as it is, can be attributed to what economists have learned about macroeconomics, although how much is an uncertain quantity.

See also LONG WAVES.

Reading
Bronfenbrenner, M. ed. 1969: *Is the Business Cycle Obsolete?*

Gordon, R.J. ed. 1986: *The American Business Cycle.*

Haberler, G. 1937 (*1958*): *Prosperity and Depression.*

Moore, G.H. 1983: *Business Cycles, Inflation and Forecasting*, 2nd edn.

Sheffrin, S.M. 1983: Inflation and unemployment. In *Rational Expectations*, pp. 27–70.

Zarnowitz, V. 1985: Recent work on business cycles in historical perspective: a review of theories and evidence. *Journal of Economic Literature* 23, 523–80.

MURRAY F. FOSS

C

Caesarism   A term denoting a form of dictatorship loosely modelled on the career of Julius Caesar (100–44 BC), the populist general and autocrat who seized power from the Roman senatorial oligarchy in 49 BC, and whose regime accelerated the collapse of the Roman Republic. However, this definition requires immediate qualification. For not only has the term been employed to include figures who *predate* Julius – like the Athenians Pisistratus (*c*.600–527 BC) and Pericles (*c*.495–429 BC) and the Spartan Cleomenes III (*c*.260–219 BC) (Neumann, 1957, pp. 237–8; Weber, 1921–2); it is also the case that Augustus Caesar (63 BC to AD 14), not Julius, has sometimes been credited as the exemplar of Caesarism (Riencourt, 1958). Moreover, though many twentieth-century usages seek analogy with ancient Rome, others do not, so that today Caesarism is a concept in the utmost confusion.

Coined probably by J. F. Böhmer in 1845 (Böhmer, 1868, pp. 277–9), the word received its first sustained treatment from the Frenchman A. Romieu (1850). Thereafter Caesarism became widely employed in European educated circles – particularly in France and Germany – to describe the regime of Napoleon III (from 1851 to 1870) and its implications for modern politics (Momigliano, 1956, 1962; Groh, 1972; Richter, 1981, 1982; Gollwitzer, 1987). By 1920 the term was no longer in popular currency and has survived only as a tool of academic analysis.

Broadly speaking, three camps are evident in twentieth-century thinking on the subject. The first continues the tradition of explicitly linking Caesarism to the BONAPARTISM of Napoleon III, and also Napoleon I. Here Caesarism is depicted as a highly personalized, militaristic form of leadership, born of illegality (such as a *coup d'état*), characterized by populist rhetoric (the leader claims to embody and defend 'the people' *en bloc*, against the narrow, divisive interest of elites or classes), contemptuous of established representative political institutions (the Caesarist ruler governs by diktat, employing police measures to stifle opposition), and legitimated by direct appeals to the masses, through the medium of plebiscites. This kind of usage is discernible, with modifications, in Thody (1989), and Namier (1958), where the Caesarist pantheon is extended to include figures such as Pétain and de Gaulle, Mussolini and Hitler.

In contrast, the second camp of thinking about Caesarism develops the notion much more haphazardly, and with only the most cursory reference to the two Napoleons. Thus, Caesarism is employed to designate: the electoral manipulations, awesome stature and 'illegitimacy' of Bismarck (Weber, 1921–2; Baehr, 1988); the leader-dominated nature of modern British politics (Ostrogorski, 1902, pp. 607–8; Tönnies, 1917, pp. 49–53; Weber, 'Politics as a vocation', in Weber, ed. Gerth and Mills, *1970*, p. 106–7, and 1978, p. 1452); a cyclical return to 'formlessness' and 'primitivism' (Spengler, 1918–22, vol. 1); a theocratic-militaristic type of 'oriental despotism', exemplified by the Diocletian empire of the Romans (Gerth and Mills, 1954, p. 210; a 'populist' or 'democratic' DICTATORSHIP, comparable to, or manifested in, Peronism in South America, among other regimes (respectively Canovan, 1981, p. 137; Neumann, 1957, pp. 236–43); the accretion of power evident in the American presidential system (Riencourt, 1958).

Finally, a usage of Caesarism exists which both draws on the Napoleonic example and also departs from it in fundamental ways. Of Marxist provenance, this position relates Caesarism to BONAPARTISM (Gramsci, 1929–35, pp. 215, 219); distinguishes between 'progressive' and 'reactionary' Caesarism, depending on whether it aids or hinders revolutionary class struggle (Gramsci, p. 219); and augments the notion to describe coalition, centrist political alliances or governments whose presence marks an interim stage between a social crisis and its resolution (Gramsci, p. 220; Hall, 1983, pp. 309–21; Schwarz, 1985, pp. 33–62).

In the majority of academic usages, it must be said, 'Caesarism' bears little resemblance to the career and biography of its most famous namesake (see Gelzer, 1969). Arguably, only the military and populist aspects attributed to Caesarism are historically compelling. For Julius Caesar was both a brilliant strategist (and inspirational field commander) and was also called by his class contemporaries, in derisive tones, a *popularis*, that is, a demagogue, or champion of the people (Croix, 1981, pp. 352–5, 362; Taylor, 1949, p. 15; cf. Cicero, *Pro Sestio and In Vatinium*, trans. Gardner, *1958*, pp. 167–79).

Reading

Baehr, P. 1987: Accounting for Caesarism. *Economy and Society* 16, 341–56.
Brantlinger, P. 1983: *Bread and Circuses: Theories of Mass Culture as Social Decay.*
Mosse, George L. 1971: Caesarism, circuses and monuments. *Journal of Contemporary History* 6, 167–82.
Thody, P. 1989: *French Caesarism: From Napoleon I to Charles de Gaulle .*
Yavetz, Z. 1983: *Julius Caesar and his Public Image.*

PETER BAEHR

capitalism A type of economy and society which, in its developed form, emerged from the Industrial Revolution of the eighteenth century in Western Europe, capitalism was subsequently conceptualized in a variety of ways by economists, historians and sociologists (the term itself only came to be widely used in the later nineteenth century, particularly by Marxist thinkers). Marx (*Capital*, 1867, vol. 1) defined it as a 'commodity-producing society' in which the principal means of production are owned by a particular class, the BOURGEOISIE, and labour power also becomes a commodity that is bought and sold. This conception was elaborated in the framework of Marx's theory of history – his 'economic interpretation' – and capitalism was regarded as the most recent stage in a long process of evolution of human modes of production and forms of society. Its distinctive features, according to Marx, were its capacity for self-expansion through ceaseless accumulation (the centralization and concentration of capital), its continual revolutionizing of the methods of production (strongly emphasized in the *Communist Manifesto*), intimately connected with the advance of science and technology as a major productive force, the cyclical character of its process of development, marked by phases of prosperity and depression, and a more clearly articulated division,

along with increasing conflict, between two major classes (see CLASS) – bourgeoisie and proletariat (see WORKING CLASS).

Marxist theory had a profound influence on most later studies. Max Weber, while rejecting Marx's theory as a whole and constructing quite a different model or 'ideal type' of capitalism, nevertheless incorporated in it important elements derived from Marxist thought. In particular, he specified among the basic conditions of a capitalist economy the 'appropriation of all physical means of production . . . as disposable property of autonomous private industrial enterprises' and the existence of 'free labour', that is, of persons 'who are not only legally in the position, but are also economically compelled, to sell their labour on the market without restriction'. At the same time he introduced other elements; the 'method of enterprise' as a basic characteristic, and such further preconditions as 'freedom of the market', 'rational capital accounting', 'rational technology . . . which implies mechanization', 'calculable law', and the 'commercialization of economic life' (1923, pp. 207–9).

Weber's interest as a historian, however, was directed more to the question of the origins of capitalism, which he explained by sociological as well as economic factors – the influence of a new religious ethic (Weber, 1904–5), the growth of cities, and the formation of a 'national citizen class' in the modern nation-state (Weber, 1923, p. 249) – than to the dynamic features of capitalism and its continuing development, which preoccupy Marxist thinkers and also Schumpeter. The latter devoted his major writings to expounding a theory of economic development (Schumpeter, 1911), analysing the fluctuations of the capitalist economy in the business cycle (1939), and examining those tendencies in the development of capitalism which he considered would lead to the supersession of the capitalist social order by SOCIALISM (1942). In the first of these books he emphasized the role of the entrepreneur, as the innovator who continually drives the economy in new directions in a turbulent process of change and expansion. The second book analysed in detail the phases of economic growth and subsequent recession in this process, giving particular prominence to the LONG WAVES of approximately 50 years' duration. Finally, in discussing capitalism and socialism he attributed a fundamental importance to the SOCIALIZATION OF THE ECONOMY, whereby large corporations came to dominate the economic system in a new period of 'trustified' capitalism which he contrasted with an earlier 'competitive' capitalism.

Much of Schumpeter's argument is very close to that of later Marxist theorists, and in particular the Austro-Marxists (see AUSTRO-MARXISM), who also distinguished a new phase of capitalism that had emerged clearly by the beginning of the twentieth century, characterized by the formation of trusts and cartels, protectionism, and imperialist expansion (see IMPERIALISM). At the same time they emphasized the role of the banks in the formation of large corporations and cartels (Hilferding, 1910), and this conception too was incorporated, though in a narrower form, into Schumpeter's later definition of capitalism (1946) as involving not only private ownership of means of production and production for private profit, but also the provision of bank credit as an essential feature. The Austro-Marxists, and notably Hilferding (Bottomore, 1985, pp. 66–7), went on, however, to distinguish a further stage of 'organized capitalism' after World War I, characterized by a continued growth of large corporations, and in addition by increased state intervention in the economy and the introduction of 'partial planning'.

These conceptions are important in analysing the more recent development of capitalism since 1945. In this postwar period the structure of capitalist society again changed significantly, with a further growth of giant corporations, increasingly transnational in their operations, and still greater state involvement in the economy (particularly in Western Europe) through the extension of welfare services, public ownership of some sectors of the economy, and an enhanced role for economic and social planning, so that public expenditure reached new levels of some 40 per cent, or even higher in a few countries, of the gross domestic product (GDP). This new type of capitalism was conceptualized by orthodox Marxist-Leninists as MONOPOLY CAPITALISM, and subsequently as 'state monopoly capitalism', but Hilferding's discussion of 'organized capitalism' remains more illuminating, and it has affinities not only with Schumpeter's (1950) idea of a 'halfway house' between capitalism and socialism, but also with more recent analyses, by some Western social theorists, of welfare capitalism, the mixed economy, the social market economy, and CORPORATISM. A major contribution to the conception of welfare capitalism was made earlier by Keynes (1936) who, while not undertaking an analysis of the capitalist system as a whole,

rejected the view of the mainstream neoclassical economists that capitalism, through the operation of MARKET mechanisms, tended spontaneously towards equilibrium and sustained growth. On the contrary, writing during the depression of the 1930s, he argued that specific government policies in various fields – taxation, money supply, interest rates, public works, budget deficits – were essential in order to achieve full employment and economic growth. The work of Keynes and his followers thus encouraged government intervention in, and regulation of, the economy, if not economic planning in a wider sense, and it had a significant influence on economic policy-making for three decades after the war.

The economic changes were accompanied by important social changes, notably in the occupational and class structure, with the decline of traditional manufacturing, the expansion of clerical, technical and service occupations, and more generally the movement towards a knowledge-based economy in which information technology plays an increasingly important role (see INFORMATION TECHNOLOGY AND THEORY). A significant change in social attitudes has also taken place compared with the prewar period, evident in the broadly diffused commitment to the social policies of the welfare state and to public ownership in the sphere of basic infrastructural services, although there are major differences between countries in these respects.

However, this halfway house, or welfare capitalism, does not seem to have the long-term stability that was attributed to it by some social theorists in the 1960s and 1970s. In the first place it was still predominantly capitalist, and hence subject to the fluctuations of the business cycle, notwithstanding government anti-cyclical policies, as became clear with the onset of recession in the mid-1970s, and after a modest recovery, a renewed and deeper recession in the late 1980s. Much lower rates of economic growth, rising unemployment and ageing populations then created fiscal problems for the welfare state and generated increasing social tensions. At the same time economic growth itself, in some of its major aspects, has come to be more widely questioned in terms of its effects on the global environment, and this has stimulated discussion of an 'alternative economy'.

One response to the problems encountered by welfare capitalism has been a revival of neoclassical economics in its Austrian version (see AUSTRIAN

ECONOMICS). From this standpoint the welfare state is criticized for creating a 'dependency culture' as against a 'culture of enterprise', and the virtues and achievements of a more laissez-faire type of capitalism, defined as a free market and free enterprise system (see ENTREPRENEURSHIP), are strongly reasserted. In some countries, including some former Communist countries in Eastern Europe, such ideas have been translated into government policies of privatization of publicly owned enterprises, a curtailment of planning and regulation, and so far as possible reduced spending on public services.

The future development of capitalism is uncertain. In so far as Austrian neoclassical policies are pursued, a renewal of economic growth would seem to depend on an upturn in the long wave, and this, if we follow Schumpeter's analysis, requires a new burst of innovation like those which produced in the past a 'railroadization', a 'motorization', or a 'computerization' of the world. But there is little indication at present of such new entrepreneurial opportunities, and in addition there are fresh constraints imposed by environmental concerns, as well as problems resulting from the shift in economic power from the USA to Japan and to the European Community (led economically by Germany), and from the growing rivalry between these three centres. Furthermore, the long-term success of capitalism in promoting economic growth has had as its dark side economic instability, social injustice, unemployment and poverty, so that as a social, and not simply an economic, system it has been continuously criticized by thinkers and social movements advocating an alternative type of society.

It should be observed further, in this context, that the most successful period of capitalist economic development, in the 1950s and 1960s, was associated with a great expansion of the economic activities of the state, involving in many countries an extension of public ownership and economic planning, designed to mitigate the harmful consequences – both economic and social – of an inadequately regulated free enterprise, free market economy. The experience of recession in the 1990s may therefore lead eventually to an abandonment of those economic and social policies associated with the NEW RIGHT, and a revival of more interventionist policy-making. In that sense, the opposition between capitalism and socialism which has been a focal point of ideological and political confrontation throughout the twentieth century seems likely to persist. But it will do so in new circumstances, of much greater complexity, in which the principles and basic elements of an alternative economic and social system are more difficult to specify precisely; and any movement towards this alternative society appears most likely to involve a continuing gradual modification of capitalism, of the kind that has been taking place over the past century, rather than any abrupt changes.

Reading
Bottomore, Tom 1985: *Theories of Modern Capitalism*.
Braudel, Fernand 1981–4: *Civilization and Capitalism*, 3 vols.
Maddison, Angus 1991: *Dynamic Forces in Capitalist Development*.
Mandel, Ernest 1975: *Late Capitalism*.
Schumpeter, J.A. 1942 (*1987*): *Capitalism, Socialism and Democracy*.
Weber, Max 1923 (*1961*): *General Economic History*, part 4.

TOM BOTTOMORE

capitalism, monopoly *See* MONOPOLY CAPITALISM

caste The term denotes a hereditary, endogamous group associated with a traditional occupation and ranked accordingly on a scale of ritual purity. Despite changes and much criticism, caste survives as a structure and ideology in the twentieth century.

The Portuguese used the word *casta*, derived from the Latin *castus* (pure) to mean the distinct communities which they encountered in India. Although SOCIAL STRATIFICATION is a universal human phenomenon and the term 'caste' is used loosely for groupings elsewhere, this entry focuses on caste in the context of Hinduism in South Asia – particularly India – and of Hindu diaspora communities worldwide (see also HINDUISM AND HINDU SOCIAL THEORY).

In scholarly discourse on South Asian communities, caste means 'jati' (a word with the root meaning of birth), a hereditary endogamous group. Each jati consists of exogamous lineages (gotra). Complex marriage rules dictate into which gotras a particular person may acceptably marry.

The total number of jatis runs into thousands and each region of India has its specific hierarchy. However, Hindus locate their own jati and other people's on a scale of four varnas (classes), recognized throughout the Hindu world. There is often a discrepancy between the varna to which members of a jati claim to belong and the lower varna to which others ascribe them.

The four classes are respectively the brahmin, kshatriya, vaishya and shudra varna. In the Rig Veda, a sacred text composed about 1,000 BCE, Purusha, the cosmic person, an image for society, is dismembered. His mouth is equated with the brahmin (priest), his arms with the kshatriya (warrior), his thighs with the vaishya (trader) and his feet with the shudra (serf or menial). The men of the first three of these classes came to be regarded as twice-born, as their investiture with the sacred thread signifies rebirth into Hindu society. In the approximately 2,000-year-old Lawbook of Manu (Manu-smriti or Manava dharma shastra) the behaviour permitted for each varna is clearly set out together with penalties for deviation.

In the Bhagavad Gita, a favourite Hindu scripture, Krishna, the incarnation of Vishnu (a major deity), exhorts the reluctant prince, Arjun, to fight because this is his dharma (sacred duty) as a kshatriya.

Over many centuries every jati evolved an unwritten code of practice. Members were not to marry or dine with members of another jati, although both rules, particularly the latter, have, in some contexts, been considerably relaxed. Details of domestic custom and religious ceremony distinguish one jati from another in the same locality.

In traditional village society, prior to the dominance of money as a medium of exchange, members of all castes provided other villagers with caste-specific services on a reciprocal basis. This system is known as jajmani. The castes that were lowest on the scale of purity received least in return for their work. Aspects of this interdependency survive, as when a brahmin performs a ritual and receives clothes or other gifts from his patrons. In each village one or more castes would wield power over the others. Economic power neeed not correspond with high varna.

The caste system is organic and constantly adapting to changing circumstances. Twentieth-century anthropologists have conceptualized the underlying processes in various ways. M. N. Srinivas (1967) postulated Sanskritization, a process whereby members of a low caste change their customs, ritual, ideology, and way of life in the direction of a higher caste (for instance by adopting a strictly vegetarian diet appropriate to brahmins).

By refusing to give their daughters in marriage to families which have not so adapted they create in effect a new jati. The term kshatriyization refers to emulation of wealth and status rather than ritual purity. During the twentieth century the less advantaged castes have tended to strive for power and wealth via education. They have also mobilized as religious movements, giving new meaning to ancient myth and symbol, and building self-respect (Juergensmeyer, 1982).

Among non-Hindus of South Asian origin, caste often persists as a factor in social interaction even when a community's religious teachers inveigh against caste. So, for example, local Christians may worship in separate congregations which happen to be of high and low caste origin respectively. The Sikhs have continued to marry within caste although their Gurus stressed the equality of all and the irrelevance of one's caste to the reunion of the individual soul with God.

With Western-style education, increasing social mobility and industrialization, the link between hereditary occupation and jati has weakened in the twentieth century, although the association persists in people's minds. By working as a pilot, schoolteacher or computer programmer one cannot alter or escape the connotations of one's jati.

Some shudra occupations, such as removing nightsoil or tanning hides, were regarded as highly polluting to all with whom members of those jatis came into contact. As a result these jatis were segregated from the rest of society. In addition to the prohibitions on intermarriage and interdining, they were forbidden to enter many schools and temples or to draw water from the same well as others. They lived, as many still live, outside the village. If the shadow of an 'untouchable' fell upon a brahmin the latter would return home to purify himself.

Largely because of the degradation of the untouchables, reformers in the nineteenth and twentieth centuries have attacked the inequities of the caste system. Swami Dayananda Saraswati (1824–1883) preached that, according to the Veda, society should be divided not into innumerable castes but into four varnas, of which membership should depend on merit rather than birth. Mohandas Karamchand Gandhi (Mahatma Gandhi 1869–1948) valued some aspects of the caste system for building a harmonious society, but he passionately advocated the view that: 'Untouchability is not a sanction of religion, it is a device of Satan' (Gandhi,

1951). By victims of caste discrimination Gandhi's approach is now regarded as paternalistic. They reject the term 'harijans' (children of God) which he popularized, preferring the use of 'Scheduled Castes' – the official designation in India since 1935 – and 'dalit' (oppressed). Their hero is Dr Babasaheb Ambedkar (1891–1956), the lawyer who rose from an untouchable family to frame India's constitution. This was promulgated in 1950 and recognizes not castes but equal citizens. Ambedkar argued that caste was an ideology which could only be abolished if the Hindu religious sanctions for it were removed. He exhorted his followers to abandon Hinduism for Buddhism.

There are currently in India some 120 million people (one-seventh of the population) bearing the stigma of untouchability. Despite legislation, notably the Untouchability (Offences) Act of 1955, as well as policies of positive discrimination in education and in the reservation of certain jobs, prejudice persists. Indeed, with the implementation of such policies the tolerance of higher castes sometimes hardens into hostility.

Like the advent of the train in the nineteenth century, the increased provision of education, rapid urbanization and industrialization have brought members of different castes into contact as never before. These developments, coupled with modern sanitation and piped water supply, have benefited the Scheduled Castes by removing some causes for obvious discrimination. Some members of low castes have become wealthy or achieved high office. However, the caste system has not been replaced by a class structure of the Western type. Features of both systems interact. The democratic political system enables caste to exert a powerful influence as casteism. Candidates play on caste sensibilities to gain support. Many politicians depend on castes as vote-banks.

Caste survives in Hindu communities outside India although the history of specific societies has given each a distinct character. In Bali, Indonesia, a distinction survives between the shudra majority and the brahmin, kshatriya and vaishya classes. The Hindu communities of Fiji, Mauritius, Trinidad and Surinam date back to the mid-nineteenth century when indentured labourers arrived with little hope of return to India. In these countries caste distinctions have largely disappeared except that only brahmins exercise priestly functions. In East Africa, however, where indentured labourers came from India at the beginning of the twentieth century, contact with India was maintained, castes remained endogamous and caste associations were set up.

In Britain, Hindu and Sikh marriages are still usually between members of the same caste. Many public places of worship are run by members of particular castes, such as Ramgarhia, Bhatra and Ravidasi gurdwaras (Sikh places of worship). Hindus of Gujarati origin have caste organizations which arrange social and religious events, especially during the festival of Navaratri.

Reading
Dumont, L. 1970: *Homo Hierarchicus*.
Juergensmeyer, M. 1982: *Religion as Social Vision*.
Mahar, J.M. ed. 1972: *The Untouchables in Contemporary India*.
Nesbitt, E.M. 1991: *'My Dad's Hindu, My Mum's Side are Sikhs': Issues in Religious Identity*.
Schwartz, B.M. ed. 1967: *Caste in Overseas Indian Communities*.
Srinivas, M.N. 1962: *Caste in Modern India*.

ELEANOR M. NESBITT

causality   In Hume's memorable words, causality is 'the cement of the universe', the relation through which one event is bound to another, through which one type of occurrence brings about another. It is a notion which plays a central role in our explanations of the world around us (see EXPLANATION), for example when we respond to 'why' questions with sentences beginning 'because' that identify the antecedents by virtue of which the thing to be explained occurred.

The concept of causality has proved difficult to analyse, however. The problem is how to understand the cement that binds cause to effect, the necessity with which we think of effects following their causes. Twentieth-century accounts usually begin with Hume's empiricist analysis. (EMPIRICISM is the view that all knowledge must be based on experience.) According to Hume, causal connections are not necessary in the sense of being logical relations, for, he argues on the basis of his empiricism, the description of one event does not entail (logically necessitate) the occurrence of any other events. Nor is the binding of an effect to its cause a relation that exists in the world, for we do not have any experience of such a necessary tie between one event (a cause) and another (its effect), only of the two events themselves. Consequently, in Hume's view, even though we may through habit come to *think* of causality as encapsulating necessity, *in the world*, causal connections are no more than constant conjunctions of contiguous and consecutive but logically and materially independent events. As it is nowadays usually accepted that causes can act at a distance and that causes and effects can occur simultaneously, what remains of the Humean view is that causality is embodied in regularities that express constant conjunctions between types of events.

The notion of constant conjunction can be elaborated in terms of necessary and sufficient conditions. (This is a different sense of necessary to that in the discussion above.) A necessary condition for an event is one which always occurs whenever the event occurs, while a sufficient condition is one which whenever it occurs the event occurs too. This enables complications to be taken into account: for example, that an effect might be connected with a conjunction of causes or with different independent causes, and might occur only if certain countervailing causes are absent. These complications are brought together in constant conjunctions of the form 'all LM$\bar{\text{N}}$ or PQ$\bar{\text{R}}$ or ST$\bar{\text{W}}$ are followed by event E', where $\bar{\text{N}}$ symbolizes the absence of a condition of type N and where each letter represents an 'inus' condition for E, that is, an *in*sufficient but *non*-redundant part of a joint condition (e.g. LM$\bar{\text{N}}$) which is itself *un*necessary but *suf*ficient for the result E (Mackie, 1965). An example is a theory of revolution that combines ideas from Marxism and from relative deprivation theory and argues that revolutionary activity (E) follows *either* from the joint occurrence of the polarization of capitalist society into two classes, the bourgeoisie and the proletariat (L), the immiseration of the proletariat (M), and the absence of proletarian false consciousness ($\bar{\text{N}}$) *or* the joint occurrence of the division of society into a hierarchy of groups (P), conformity of the members of one group to the norms of another, higher group (Q) and the absence of legitimate routes of mobility from the lower to the higher group ($\bar{\text{R}}$). Other theories of revolution can be added as extra sets of inus conditions (e.g. ST$\bar{\text{W}}$).

Even this elaborated version of the Humean account seems to suffer from the problem that, like simpler versions, it fails to distinguish causal regularities from what philosophers call accidental generalizations, and what social researchers call spurious or co-symptomatic relations. Examples are day following night, and the cost of damage increasing with the number of firefighters attending a fire, which are constant conjunctions but without the binding cement of causality connecting the antecedent occurrence to the consequent one. Humeans have sought to solve this problem by adding logical or epistemic criteria to differentiate causal laws from accidental generalizations, but critics maintain that all such attempts fail. The difficulties in producing an adequate Humean analysis of causality have led some empiricist philosophers to suggest that causality has no place in the mature sciences (Russell, 1917).

Non-Humean analyses of causality extend beyond the restriction of empiricism. One of the most interesting, the realist view, maintains that the necessity that characterizes causality is physical necessity (see REALISM). Cause and effect events are not independent, as the Humeans insist, but intrinsically related. Causes have the power to bring about their effects, there being a real relation between them, a generative mechanism physically linking cause to effect, even though this link is often beyond our experience. According to this view, constant conjunction might be evidence for a causal connection, but does not exhaust its meaning, which derives from the natural mechanism connecting cause and effect. Indeed, real causal connections might not manifest themselves as regularities, for countervailing causes can intervene between the operation of a cause and the appearance of its effect. For example, pressing a light switch might not have the effect of illuminating the room if a fuse blows and prevents the light bulb from glowing. The failure on this occasion – the refutation of a constant conjunction – does not lead us to reject as causal the real connection between pressing the switch and the bulb lighting through the underlying mechanism of a flow of electrical current. The difficulty with this realist view is that having violated Humean empiricism by granting existence to imputed mechanisms and invisible powers beyond the epistemic control of experience, what restrictions are there upon the mechanisms that can be invoked as causal explanations? If viruses are to be admitted, why not demons or witches' spells?

Given that there are problems with all attempts to analyse causality, some have argued that it is an unanalysable primitive (Anscombe, 1971). Even if it were possible to arrive at a satisfactory analysis of causality in the natural world, questions remain about its place in the social world: are human actions caused, and if so, is free will an illusion? (See DETERMINISM.)

Reading

Davidson, D. 1980: *Essays on Actions and Events.*
Harré, R. and Madden, E.H. 1975: *Causal Powers: A Theory of Natural Necessity.*
Hume, David 1748 (*1975*): *An Enquiry Concerning Human Understanding*, ed. L.A. Selby Bigge.
Mackie, J.L. 1974: *The Cement of the Universe.*
Sosa, E., ed. 1975: *Causation and Conditionals.*
Wright, G.H. von 1971: *Explanation and Understanding.*

PETER HALFPENNY

change, social *See* SOCIAL CHANGE

change, technological *See* TECHNOLOGICAL CHANGE

charisma Today mostly employed to describe a heroic or extraordinary quality of an individual person, the term's history is curious and complex. From obscure beginnings in early Christian usage, where it meant 'the gift of grace', charisma is now a popular catchword among journalists and lay people alike. Its twentieth-century connotations, and the debate it has occasioned, are inseparable from the thought of Max Weber (1864–1920).

Weber adapted the term from the theologian Rudolph Sohm, who had employed it to interpret the development of the early Christian church (see Bendix, 1966, p. 325). Extended to encompass secular as well as religious phenomena, the concept became pivotal to Weber's analysis of history and domination (see especially Weber, 1904–5 (*1930*), p. 178; 1951, pp. 30–42, 119–29; Weber, 1921–2, vol. 1, pp. 241–71, and vol. 2, pp. 1111–57).

In Weber's analysis, charisma denotes an exceptional quality (real or imagined) possessed by a single individual who is able thereby to exercise influence and LEADERSHIP over a group of admirers. The devotees of the charismatic leader see it as their duty to obey him or her, and this they do voluntarily and with rapturous commitment. Charisma is capable of assuming a variety of guises corresponding to the spheres of its influence (military, political, ethical, religious, artistic) but in all cases its consequence is to affect spectacularly the lives of those it touches. Charisma is an inwardly revolutionary force with the power thereby to mobilize human effort and transform the ossified material world it confronts. In Weber's terminology, charisma is a particular form of 'domination' or authority.

Weber contrasts this unorthodox, emotionally highly charged and revolutionary form of domination with two others: traditional (where obedience is based on custom and revered precedent: typical of preindustrial societies) and rational–legal (characteristic of the modern world where conformity to legally established, and bureaucratically executed, rules and procedures is the norm, and where compliance is typically owed to position rather than person). Traditional and rational–legal modes of domination are markedly different in many respects. Yet they both share the same lacklustre quality of being stable, routine and relatively predictable structures of everyday life. Charisma, on the other hand, is explosive – it openly challenges traditional ways, mocks the rigid soullessness of impersonal legality – and in its pure form is mercurial and transient.

Four additional features of Weber's discussion are worth noting. First, the charismatic leader's ethical qualities are irrelevant to the concept. It is their dynamism as individuals which is crucial. Second, charisma is a contingent phenomenon. Though it has a tendency to arise in certain propitious circumstances, notably conditions of excitement, enthusiasm or distress, there is no suggestion in Weber's writings that its appearance is socially destined to occur. Third, the existence and duration of charisma's enchantment depends, above all, on the response of others. To retain its spell over hearts and minds, a person's charisma must be continually displayed and proved in, for instance, miracles (Jesus) or brilliant military campaigns (Napoleon). When devotion turns to indifference, charisma's magic vaporizes. Finally, charisma in its pristine form only ever exists transiently. Because of its personalized character, charisma faces difficulty of transmission when, for instance, its bearer dies. There are various solutions to this problem. But in all cases charisma is either extinguished or becomes 'routinized', that is, it becomes channelled into traditionally or legally oriented institutions, thereby losing its quintessentially heroic quality and becoming instead an attribute of, say, heredity (for instance, a monarch) or office (for instance, the premiership or presidency).

While Weber's analysis of charisma is widely regarded as seminal, it has also attracted criticism or qualification. Some have maintained that his focus on personal leadership lacks a coherent explanation of *why* people regard such leadership as inspiring or compelling, and underestimates 'the social significance of the leader as symbol, catalyst and message bearer' (Worsley, 1957, p. 293). For if charisma depends on social recognition, as Weber insists it does, then the culture and sensibilities of those who come to validate it require greater specification (Baehr, 1990). Moreover, Weber's discussion of charisma's aura tends to leave it in somewhat of a mystical condition. In contrast, recent sociological studies of political oratory and body language (notably by Atkinson, 1984, for example), have shown that what often passes for charisma is in good measure a *technique* – a series of skills, practices and messages learnt and orchestrated by politicians.

Charisma's contribution to social stability, as distinct from revolution, is another area that Weber may have underplayed (though he did not overlook it: see the earlier discussion of routinization). Shils, for instance, writes about a 'charismatic propensity' that can be found in all societies, revealed in the 'awe and reverence' with which certain objects are regarded. Accordingly, charisma is not solely something that is possessed by exemplary leaders, but can inhere in 'ordinary secular roles, institutions, symbols, and strata or aggregates' (Shils, 1965, p. 200). Objects and persons who are deemed by society to possess charisma do so because they embody the society's core values and therefore relate to the ultimate questions with which it is concerned, so that charisma is about the need for social coherence. Thus, in Shils's hands, charisma is changed into a force which is instrumental in maintaining the social order, whereas Weber emphasized its revolutionary attributes.

More recently, social scientists have made use of the concept of charisma in a number of spheres. First, and most obviously, it has been employed in relation to religious sects and cults, whose leaders are able to attract a devoutly committed following (for example, Wallis, 1982). Second, it has been used to describe and account for the appeal of many political leaders (Apter, 1968; Schweitzer, 1984; Willner, 1984). Among these we find leaders of countries who were able to develop a mission which both promised freedom from colonial domination and overcame the conservative implications of allegiance to traditional authority (Gandhi, Nkrumah); revolutionary Marxist leaders (Lenin, Castro); leaders of modern dictatorships (Hitler, Mussolini); and leaders who achieved power in the context of modern democracies (F.D. Roosevelt). Third, there is increasing use of the term to describe some leaders of business organizations (see, for example, Conger, 1989), whose legendary efforts produce a radical transformation of the fortunes of an organization in dire straits (for example, Iacocca of Chrysler) or whose leadership results in the founding of new and vital organizations (for example, Burr of People Express).

Though it is tempting to try to identify types of charisma, such attempts run the risk of generating excessively long lists: Schweitzer (1984), for example, catalogues over 50 types! Two basic dichotomies, however, tend to be employed with some frequency in the literature. First there is the distinction between original and routinized charisma. Here research shows that charismatic leaders sometimes develop elaborate strategies to resist the incursions of routinization, as in the case of David 'Mo' Berg and the Children of God (Wallis, 1982). On the other hand, routinization is not always successful: thus Trice and Beyer's (1986) study of two organizations concerned with alcoholism shows how routinization of the founder's charisma can be frustrated by inappropriate structures or by unexpected events.

A second distinction that is sometimes offered is between real and manufactured charisma (or pseudocharisma). This pairing contrasts the genuine appeal of a truly charismatic individual with the stagecraft and media massaging that often go into the generation of modern charisma (Bensman and Givant, 1975). Arguably, however, this distinction is itself problematic for it fails to recognize that all charisma is in a sense manufactured, that is, dependent on presenting an image appealing enough to enlist a band of followers who will in turn act as emissaries of the cause or mission at stake.

See also MESSIANISM.

Reading
Bendix, R. 1971: Charismatic leadership. In *Scholarship and Partisanship: Essays on Max Weber*, ed. R. Bendix and G. Roth, pp. 170–87.
Berger, P. 1963: Charisma and religious innovation: the social location of Israelite prophecy. *American Sociological Review* 28, 940–50.
Conger, J.A. and Kanungo, R.N. eds 1988: *Charismatic Leadership: The Elusive Factor in Organisational Effectiveness*.

Friedland, W.H. 1964: For a sociological concept of charisma. *Social Forces* 43, 18–26.

Haley, P. 1980: Rudolph Sohm on charisma. *Journal of Religion* 60, 185–97.

Lindholm, C. 1990: *Charisma*.

Roth, G. 1979: Charisma and the counterculture. In *Max Weber's Vision of History. Ethics and Methods*, ed. G. Roth and W. Schluchter, pp. 119–43.

Schram, S.R., 1967: Mao Tse-tung as a charismatic leader. *Asian Survey* 7, 383–8.

Spencer, M.E. 1973: What is charisma? *British Journal of Sociology* 24, 341–54.

Tucker, R.C. 1968: The theory of charismatic leadership. *Daedalus* 97, 731–56.

Weber, Max 1921–2 *(1978)*: *Economy and Society*, ed. G. Roth and C. Wittich (2-vol. edn).

Willner, A.R. 1984: *The Spellbinders: Charismatic Political Leadership*.

ALAN BRYMAN and PETER BAEHR

Chicago economics   This is a distinctive way of looking at economics and economic policy – strongly emphasizing free markets as description and prescription – that has been associated with the University of Chicago at least since the 1930s. Not every economist connected with the University of Chicago has been a member of the 'Chicago school'. Not every member of the school is connected with the University of Chicago. But Chicago is undoubtedly the Mother Church of a way of thinking whose founders taught at Chicago and whose subsequent high priests studied or taught there or both.

The doctrine has not been constant over time and at any one time all members have not been equally orthodox. However, the common tenets as of 1989 may be summarized as follows:

1   Economics is about the behaviour of fully informed individuals seeking to maximize their utility in competitive exchange markets (see also MARKET). Other explanations of human behaviour are not 'economics'. Also, there probably is no other useful, general theory.

2   If the world were organized in the way economics pictures it, certain important beneficial results would follow. In such a world each individual would get as much out of his resources as he could get without forcibly depriving others.

3   The real world operates to a reasonably satisfactory approximation according to the economists' MODEL and realizes the benefits that the model predicts.

4   Government decisions, like decisions made in the private economy, are made by individuals seeking to maximize their own gains. Therefore the government cannot be counted on to achieve any particular objectives – such as efficiency or equity – other than the objectives of the officials involved.

5   The quantity of money is the key factor influencing the behaviour of the level of prices and the stability of aggregate output (see also MONETARISM).

The founders of the Chicago school in the 1930s were Professors Frank H. Knight, Lloyd Mints, Henry C. Simons and Jacob Viner – although Viner denied that he was a member of it. From their teaching, students acquired great respect for the free market as a method of economic organization. Teaching of economics in the 1930s did, however, give much attention to respects in which the real world might differ from the model and would not be ideal even if it conformed to the model. The 1930s was scarcely a time for thinking that the economic system as it existed was yielding ideal results.

The policy implications of the gap between the well-functioning model and the clearly visible world were spelled out chiefly in the writings of Henry Simons. Three points were critical:

1   An adequately competitive market with well-informed participants might not exist and could not be counted upon to come into being spontaneously. The government had a role, therefore, in promoting competition and the flow of information.

2   The private market might generate an unacceptable degree of inequality in the distribution of income, and the government had a proper role in correcting that.

3   Private markets did not guarantee stability of aggregate demand, meaning basically stability of the price level. It was the responsibility of the government to use its fiscal and monetary policies to stabilize the economy.

Thus, as of, say, 1940, 'Chicago' thinking left considerable but limited room for government action.

After World War II leadership of Chicago economics passed to a new generation, of which Milton Friedman and George Stigler were most prominent and in which Aaron Director and Ronald Coase were also highly important. By the 1970s a third generation could be identified, with Gary Becker and Robert Lucas among its leaders.

After World War II, Chicago economics evolved in three main ways. First, like economics in most places, it became more empirical and quantitative, relying less on logical deductions from self-evident propositions and commonplace observations and more on systematically collected historical and statistical data. Second, it became 'purer'. It found that many of the qualifications to the efficiency of free markets that had been previously conceded were invalid or unimportant. The number of competitors needed to achieve the beneficial results of competition was determined to be small. What had previously been regarded as inefficiencies due to inadequate information were seen as efficient adaptations to the cost of obtaining information. The market failures alleged to exist in cases where private actors had no incentive to take account of effects on others were found to be correctable by contracting among the parties.

A process of purification also went on in the approach to macroeconomics. The private market was found to be less inherently unstable than had been thought in the 1930s. The positive role for government in stabilizing the economy was refined from an *ad hoc* combination of fiscal and monetary measures into the maintenance of a constant rate of growth of the money supply. The possible beneficial effects even of monetary policy on real output and employment were thought to be very temporary and in some versions non-existent.

In the third place, Chicago economics became, in George Stigler's term, 'imperialistic'. It reached out to apply its hypotheses and methods to sociology, law and political science. The application to law and political science particularly tended to support the case for free markets by showing that correct interpretation of legal rights would enhance the efficiency of markets and by showing the unreliability of the political process as a corrective to market failures if they existed.

Probably only a small minority of American economists ever considered themselves to be Chicagoans. But the Chicago influence on economic thought was profound. Even economists who did not go as far as the Chicagoans felt the need for a more open-minded and subtle analysis of the market model as explanation and prescription than they had previously done. Similarly, economists who were not 'monetarists' came to agree on the importance of money and on the need to seek better strategies for managing it.

Some members of the Chicago school are debarred from claiming any influence on public policy, because they believe that policy is made by self-interested individuals or groups who have all the information they want. But in a less restrictive view one could see an important influence of Chicago thinking, during the 1970s and 1980s, in reduction of government regulation, in the floating of the dollar, in new directions of antitrust policy and in monetary policy.

Reading
Friedman, M. 1953: *Essays in Positive Economics.*
Knight, F.H. 1935: *The Ethics of Competition.*
Patinkin, D. 1981: *Essays on and in the Chicago Tradition.*
Reder, M.W. 1987: Chicago School. In *The New Palgrave Dictionary of Economics*, ed. J. Eatwell, M. Milgate and P. Newman, vol. 1, pp. 413–18.
Simons, H.C. 1948: *Economic Policy for a Free Society.*
Stigler, G.J. 1988: *Memories of an Unregulated Economist.*

HERBERT STEIN

Chicago sociology Laying foundations on which much of American sociology was built in the twentieth century, the department of sociology at the University of Chicago was created by Albion W. Small, a historian and sociologist who had previously been the president of a small college in Maine. The new University of Chicago, largely financed by John D. Rockefeller, saw it as its mission to compete with the older universities on the eastern seaboard of the USA and to demonstrate that the Middle West was capable of nourishing and fostering a seat of learning that was second to none. The department of sociology shared the university's ambitions and Small built a first-rate department.

The Chicago department was not the first to provide instruction in sociology – there were courses already offered at Brown University, at Yale and at Columbia, but it was the first initiative whose course offerings and research programme did not reflect the personal vision of a central figure but was rather a collective enterprise. The most prominent members of the department, before World War I and after, in addition to Albion Small, the chairperson, were W. I. Thomas, Robert Park and Ernest Burgess. The new department also had close relations with the department of philosophy in which John Dewey and George Herbert Mead developed a pragmatic philosophy with a reformist bent that was congenial to members of the department of sociology and allowed its students easy access to pragmatic philosophy in general and social psychology in particular.

As Martin Blumer has noted, 'The Chicago school presented the first successful American program of collective sociological research' (1984, p. XV).

In the early years, the department of sociology still presented course offerings and accepted doctoral theses that were inspired by Christian reformist social thought or the more secular impulses of reformers such as Jane Addams. In these early years dissertations such as Cecil North's *The Influence of Modern Social Relations upon Ethical Concepts* were by no means atypical. But immediately before World War I, and again after, the department shed some of its reformist zeal and under the guidance of W. I. Thomas, and later under Robert Park, turned to empirical investigations in urban settings. It regarded the city of Chicago as its laboratory.

It has often been charged that the Chicago department neglected sociological theory and stood for a mindless empiricism. This was not the case. Men like Thomas and Park had studied in Germany under some of the country's renowned scholars. Park wrote his dissertation under the guidance of the prominent neo-Kantian philosopher Wilhelm Windelband. But it is a fact that the Chicago sociologists, in contrast to most of their colleagues elsewhere, stressed that sociology could only develop in America if it addressed itself to the study of the many social problems that confronted urban America in the rapid wave of urbanization, industrialization and capitalist expansion after the Civil War. The members of the department studied taxi dance halls, waitresses, hobos, Chicago land values, juvenile delinquents, thieves and Chicago race relations. Chicago students were expected to deal with concrete social problems and issues not only in their dissertations but also in their subsequent careers. And as former students began to dominate new departments of sociology in the Middle West and elsewhere, they gave their distinctive Chicago colour to them.

The Chicago orientation dominated American sociology into the 1930s. The Chicago department published the *American Journal of Sociology*, which long had a monopoly position among sociological publications, and it colonized newer departments much as ancient Athens in the classical age had colonized new cities in the eastern Mediterranean. The Chicago dominance was overthrown in the 1930s when Harvard, Columbia and other eastern universities began to institutionalize sociology, but it had dominated for so long that even afterwards it was often still seen as the very epitome of American empirical sociological research.

Reading
Blumer, Martin 1984: *The Chicago School of Sociology: Institutionalization, Diversity, and the Rise of Sociological Research.*
Faris, Robert E.L. 1967: *Chicago Sociology: 1920–1932.*
Kurtz, Lester R. 1984: *Evaluating Chicago Sociology. A Guide to the Literature with an Annotated Bibliography.*
Matthews, Fred H. 1977: *Quest for an American Sociology: Robert E. Park and the Chicago School.*

LEWIS A. COSER

choice, public   *See* PUBLIC CHOICE

choice, social   *See* SOCIAL CHOICE

Christian social theory   Such theory embraces systematic statements or bodies of knowledge about the relationship of Christianity to society. At one level, these systematic statements are 'theories' in the strict sense of 'overview of the nature of society', paralleling, that is, secular 'social theory' and 'political theory', but including a transcendent perspective. At another level, Christian social theory can be viewed as a 'praxis', in the Aristotelian sense of a study of society with an end, namely, that of facilitating the flourishing of a good and just life in the polis.

The distinctive perspective referred to may be termed 'personalism', which is used to indicate that 'the foundation, cause and purpose of all social institutions are individual human beings, people, that is, who are social by nature and are raised to an order of things which surpasses and subdues nature' (Pope John XXIII, *Mother and teacher*, no. 219). Social systems, in other words, have no purposes, reasons or needs; strictly speaking, only individual human persons do. In Christian social theory, then, voluntarism and the purposive character of human conduct are stressed, as well as the capability of actors to choose between different goals and projects. This does not exclude the analysis and discussion of structures, but it means that Christian social theory is primarily a theory of action.

The feature, appearing in different forms, which

has characterized Christian social theory throughout the history of the subject has been tension. Perhaps only in Old Testament social teaching has this not been the case. In the Old Testament, which is a foundation source for Christian social theory, Hebrew thought retained inseparable ethical and theological links between creation and salvation. There was no separation of this-worldly and other-worldly activities. This sense of the unity of God's acts of creation and salvation, and of our response to these areas, can be observed in the broad range of meanings of the words for 'righteousness', 'justification' and 'faith', as well as in the importance of the Hebrew notion of *tiqqun ha-olam*, restoration of the world. The context of these words is usually social and political.

In the New Testament, however, and especially in the writings of St Paul, 'salvation' is most frequently linked with the 'justification' of the individual who comes to faith in Jesus. Thus the Christian words which reflect the Hebrew 'justice' words moved away from their social context and from the order and harmony in nature and in the whole cosmos of God's creation. This too-anthropocentric a view of creation and salvation in early Christian thinking narrowed the vision of God's grace in the world and restricted the development in Christian social theory of an ethic of responsible stewardship over creation and of duties to ecology, environment and other creatures.

The tension between the demands of the other-world and of this-world, which entered Christian thinking with the New Testament and the development of systematic THEOLOGY, came to have a strong influence on Christian social theory in the Patristic period, which spanned the first eight centuries of Christianity. Even if it can be shown that at times, especially after the conversion of the Emperor Constantine, some of the Fathers engaged in more worldly-minded discourse, it is safe to claim that 'other-worldliness' was a dominant and fundamental element in their thinking.

As the Christian church grew in numbers, wealth and political power, and as the state itself finally became Christian in the first quarter of the fourth century, tension grew between the vital concern for the life after death and the demands of life here on earth. In the economic sphere, the main concern of the Fathers was for the glaring gap between rich and poor, to which their solution was almsgiving. It was not the function of alms to eliminate poverty, but only to relieve extreme distress. In this sense,

there is no economic solution in the corpus of patristic writings. They accepted the right to private property, though attributing its origin to original sin, and arguing that, in the beginning of human society, all things were held in common. In terms of developing Christian social theory, it can be pointed out that Augustine was opposed to individualism, even to that possessive individualism which became the characteristic of modern liberalism. In consequence of this understanding of the common destination of human goods, the Fathers emphasized the obligations of the rich to share, and they held out the common use of riches as an ideal. Many modern writers have commented on this 'socialistic' aspect of patristic teaching, and it is certain that there has been a continuing tension in Christian social theory between the defence of private property and the ideal of social ownership.

In their general presentation of social teaching, the scholastics of the medieval period remained faithful to the earlier emphasis placed by the New Testament and patristic doctrine on the primacy of the 'spiritual' over the 'temporal'. In this form, Christian social theory remained, rather, as a radically theological social doctrine. The influence of Stoic and Aristotelian thought, however, brought developments which made Christian social teaching, as a whole, a philosophical science with certain 'additions' of a theological kind. This new tension between moral-philosophical or theological foundations has remained a feature of Christian social theory right up to the modern period. The Roman Catholic and Anglo-Catholic traditions have retained the long-reflected style of moral philosophy, whereas Reformed traditions have adopted radically theological approaches. In Catholic social theory, a foundation on 'natural law' (an almost instinctive apprehension of a rule of reasonable behaviour appropriate to rational human beings) assisted the development of the 'common good' (a coincidence, driven by justice, of individual good and the good of the community), 'distributive justice' (proportionality of the status of members to the community), the 'principle of subsidiary function' (that state power must be used not to displace initiative but to enable lesser communities and individuals to be themselves) and 'the right to private property'.

The elaboration of Christian social theory in this philosophical form, while taking the motives for action from theology, has had the practical advantage of making this teaching accessible to those not sharing Christian beliefs, which has proved appropriate in present-day pluralist society. This accounts for the insistence in recent papal social teaching that the writings are for all people and not just Catholic believers.

While the unifying principle of natural law made it possible, in the Catholic style of Christian social theory, to mediate between the world of religion and the sociopolitical arena, it also led to confusion in which the ecclesiastical authorities, in the name of the church, became earthly rulers, while secular powers claimed authority in matters spiritual. Luther's solution was to propose, after the style of St Augustine's *Two Cities*, a doctrine of the Two Kingdoms, which became the first Protestant understanding of a political ethic. The two kingdoms are Church and State, the latter being made necessary only because of unbelief. This is a different social theory from the older Catholic one, which acknowledged the need for *potestas coactiva* (political power) as a consequence of original sin, while accepting the need for *potestas directiva* (an administrative state), even before the Fall. In this whole matter, Luther argued that whatever the quality of secular rule, good or bad, the two kingdoms should never be confused, a principle picked up by Karl Barth who insisted that 'the divine must not be politicized and the political must not be divinised.'

The dualism of 'private' and 'public' responsibilities which was derived from Luther's Two Kingdom doctrine, came to be used to justify the absolute claims of political power. The particular form of his Christian social theory prepared the way (quite unintentionally) for this interpretation. Each Kingdom was ruled vertically, but separately, by God, but there was no obvious way in which the Gospel could penetrate, horizontally, the secular kingdom.

In the modern period

In Christendom there had been no secular, only a single community of priesthood and kingdom. But once the secular as a domain was instituted by scientific rationality and political pretension, and then recognized by the Christian religion, the sacred became privatized and spiritualized. In relation to Christian social theory, SECULARIZATION created the conditions in which Grotius, Hobbes and Spinoza established autonomous social theory; independent, that is, of theological grounds.

The challenge was a serious one, since (as John Milbank says) Christian social theory must be either an application of a theology or social ethic which, as a meta-discourse, positions secular disciplines; or else it is positioned, itself, by secular reason. In the face of this challenge, Christian social theory has tended to accept that social sciences carry out fundamental readings of reality, which may be handed on to theology or social ethics. The agenda is set by secular reason. Ernst Troeltsch, in his monumental work, *The Social Teaching of the Christian Churches* (1911) argued that this experience should be accepted and that Christian social theory should seek to establish some coherence with secular rationality. In the conclusion to his work he pointed out that the application of the Gospel's spiritual ideal 'cannot be realized within this world apart from compromise'. He went on to conclude that,

> Nowhere does there exist an absolute Christian ethics, which only awaits discovery; all that we can do is to learn to control the world-situation in the successive phases just as the earlier Christian ethic did in its own way. There is no absolute ethical transformation of material nature or of human nature; all that does exist is a constant wrestling with the problems which they raise.

Christian social theory's terms of compromise, in the case of challenge from secular political theory, was to accept the autonomy of politics; and, in the case of political economy, to acknowledge a rational market. The consequences for Christian social theory have been, in the first instance, to incorporate a tame political theory which accepted a balance of power between autonomous orders; and, in the second, to embrace a benign consensus about the free market as some final economic form.

Two recent forms of Christian social theory have been developed in an attempt to break with received styles of political and economic thought. 'Political theology', which may be defined as a critical corrective to the tendency of contemporary theology to concentrate on the private individual, has challenged the political tendency of modernity to erect a direct relationship between the sovereign state and the 'private' individual, which thus cuts out all middle associations. The communitarian elements in Christian social theory, presented in the form of subsidiarity (in Catholic social teaching) and in 'sphere sovereignty' (in the Reformed tradition) argues for the devolution of power to appropriate intermediary levels. The second contemporary form is LIBERATION THEOLOGY, which has tried to recover the social meaning of the Gospel for Third World countries engaged in the struggle for justice. It has drawn selectively on Marxist analysis, but many commentators are doubtful if this analysis can be used without also accepting the materialist interpretation of history. In general, it may be said of political and liberation theologies that they have, after the restricted style commended by Troeltsch, to appropriate some existing form of social theory (from Marx, say, or Habermas), along with the secularization which these usually entail, and then, in their social ethics or social theology, they limit themselves to interpretations of the remainder.

A radical challenge to all existing forms of Christian social theory has recently been posed by John Milbank (1990), who argues that theology itself is a sociology. Christian social theory, he maintains, has put itself in a weak position by making itself dependent on scarcely validated secular theories and by abandoning its own strength as a specific social theory. It may legitimately claim to be a sociology in the sense that it is a description of the entire PRAXIS (content, narrative, practice and doctrine) of a particular community, and in that it provides a specific account of the final causes at work in human history. In respect of methodology, this theory should pay more attention to 'insider' understandings of the social implications of Christian praxis, and be less dependent on 'outsider' perceptions. This is not to exclude the importance of outsider understandings, but only to emphasize that Christian social theory cannot be reduced to any exact reading off of the historical and social context, but must include a 'speculative moment' (as Milbank calls it) which apprehends doctrinal elements and consequent propositions of a distinctive sociotheological nature.

In conclusion, Christian social theory, from one point of view, must be in continuity with certain aspects of antique ethics. From another point of view, it must go beyond antique ethics by reason of the need for a content of specific virtues and of its being a theory about a distinctive community with a particular praxis.

Reading
Bonino, J.M. 1983: *Towards a Christian Political Ethics.*
Boswell, J. 1990: *Community and the Economy: A Theory of Public Co-operation.*
Milbank, J. 1990: *Theology and Social Theory: Beyond Secular Reason.*

Phan, P.C. 1984: *Social Thought: Message of the Fathers of the Church.*
Troeltsch, E. 1911 *(1981)*: *The Social Teaching of the Christian Churches.*
Viner, J. 1978: *Religious Thought and Economic Society.*

FRANCIS P. MCHUGH

cinema   This refers to the technologies and institutionalized practices through which films, and especially fictional narrative films, are produced, distributed, exhibited and consumed. Although techniques for producing the illusion of moving images have long been known, cinema as such only just pre-dates the twentieth century. Thomas Edison took out patents on the Kinetograph and the Kinetoscope in 1891, and it was in the mid-1890s that companies like Mutoscope in the USA and Lumière Brothers in France began to put on film shows for audiences in vaudeville theatres and other public spaces.

In the early years of the new century, cinema began to emerge as a mass medium in the USA as storefront exhibition theatres – the nickelodeons – provided cheap entertainment for a proletarian, urban, and largely immigrant audience. In 1908, ten leading film producers and manufacturers of cameras and projectors formed a cartel, the Motion Picture Patents Company, to milk the young industry for profit by exploiting their patents on the technologies of cameras, printers and projectors. They succeeded in convincing bankers to invest in cinema, and in creating a nationwide distribution market. Nevertheless, they failed to withstand the challenge of independent producers who, far from the Trust's New York base, were making films around Los Angeles, especially in Hollywood.

These producers, the architects of the studio system, exploited the advantages of the West Coast: cheap land, a temperate climate, varied landscapes for use as locations, and non-unionized labour. Rather than selling film by the metre, they offered for rent longer narratives featuring familiar fictional figures and then, increasingly, named star performers. They also gained control of film distribution domestically and – thanks to the devastation of the European industry by World War I – globally.

It was also during the second decade of the century that the norms of the classical Hollywood style were established. Techniques were developed to reproduce the conventions of character motivation and narrative development familiar from existing popular forms. Editing, lighting, the framing of shots and use of close-ups were all used to produce a coherent and plausible story for the spectator, an illusion of actions unfolding within a unified space over continuous time.

This style of film-making lent itself to industrial efficiency, with one producer overseeing the most economic deployment of labour, sets and equipment across several films simultaneously. This Taylorized system was little affected by the coming of recorded sound and dialogue in the late 1920s. By then, the five major Hollywood studios (Paramount, MGM, Fox, Warner Bros and RKO) had achieved a remarkable degree of vertical integration across production, distribution and exhibition. This was only broken, partially at least, by the combined impact of antitrust legislation and the arrival of television after World War II. From then on, Hollywood has been in a state of economic flux.

To compete with Hollywood's global hegemony, other cinema industries have had either to ape its output or to offer alternative genres and styles. The Expressionism of directors like Fritz Lang, Georg Wilhelm Pabst and Friedrich Murnau in the 1920s was in part an attempt by German studios to identify a niche in the international market. And even while Sergei Eisenstein, Lev Kuleshov and Dziga Vertov were undertaking their radical innovations, the great majority of films actually being screened in the Soviet Union were Hollywood imports. Still, the idea of a 'national cinema', the authentic voice through which a country supposedly speaks itself, has often had a greater cultural significance than the marginal box-office success of the films produced would indicate. Other examples would include the British documentary movement of the 1930s, the neo-Realist cinema which attempted to articulate a new Italian identity in the wake of Fascism and defeat, and, increasingly in recent years, a variety of Third World cinemas. (See also SOCIOLOGY OF ART.) There have also always been forms of film-making less concerned with box-office popularity than with film's potential as a medium for avant-garde experimentation or as a tool of radical politics.

Theories about the aesthetic possibilities of film and the social functions of cinema began to appear within a couple of decades of the first commercial exhibition of movies. In 1916, for example, the poet Vachel Lindsay proposed a Whitmanesque sociology of cinema as an element in an emerging 'hieroglyphic' American democracy, and the Har-vard philosopher Hugo Münsterberg offered the first account of the mental dynamics of film spectatorship. Ever since then, theorists have attempted to define the unique nature of film as an aesthetic medium and also to specify its actual and potential social functions. Often the two aspects have been linked, as by the Soviet theorists and film-makers in the 1920s. Against Eisenstein's theories of montage as the key to the cinematic experience, André Bazin constructed a widely influential ontology of film. He argued that film is (or should be) above all an art of reality, a medium with a unique capacity for reproducing the experience of an innately ambiguous reality.

In the 1960s and 1970s, cinema became the focus of an extremely lively set of debates that drew on SEMIOTICS, structuralism and poststructuralism, Althusserian Marxism and Lacanian psychoanalysis. Cinema was theorized as an apparatus: that is, as technologies deployed to cultural and ideological ends, and at the same time as a specific disposition of semiotic techniques that address the dynamics of desire and fantasy. Cinematic spectatorship was seen as both a determinant and a consequence of that apparatus. Theorists like Jean-Louis Comolli, Jean-Louis Baudry, Christian Metz, Stephen Heath and Laura Mulvey attempted to demonstrate how the symbolic codes of dominant cinema simultaneously deploy and mask strategies of spectator positioning. Hollywood's 'invisible' narrative techniques, they held, offer the spectator a position of imaginary coherence and omnipotence, the illusion of a unified, transcendental subjectivity. That is why cinema can be seen as a paradigm for the mechanisms of IDEOLOGY, particularly as they relate to questions of sexual identification and difference. That model has since been challenged, on both historical and theoretical grounds. Nevertheless, it did successfully identify the dual importance of cinema. It has been a key global industry. Above all, though, through its mass dissemination of fantasy scenarios, it has been the decisive architect of popular imagination in the twentieth century.

See also MASS CULTURE; MASS MEDIA.

Reading
Andrew, J.D. 1976: *The Major Film Theories.*
Bordwell, D., Staiger, J. and Thompson, K. 1985: *The Classical Hollywood Cinema.*
Hansen, M. 1991: *Babel and Babylon: Spectatorship in American Silent Film.*
Penley, C. ed. 1988: *Feminism and Film Theory.*

Rosen, P. ed. 1986: *Narrative, Apparatus, Ideology*.
Sitney, P.A. 1974: *Visionary Film: The American Avant-Garde Film*.

JAMES DONALD

citizenship Ideas of citizenship have flourished in several historical periods – in ancient Greece and Rome, in the towns of medieval Europe, in the Renaissance cities – but modern citizenship, though influenced by such earlier conceptions, has a distinctive character. First, *formal* citizenship is now almost universally defined as membership of a nation-state. Secondly, however, *substantive* citizenship, defined as the possession of a body of civil, political and especially social RIGHTS, has become increasingly important.

In both these aspects there has been a process of development during the twentieth century, and most markedly since World War II, which poses some new questions. Formal citizenship became a more central issue following the massive postwar immigration to Western Europe and North America, which resulted in a new politics of citizenship (Brubaker, 1992). At the same time there has been a growth of 'dual citizenship', in spite of international efforts to diminish it, where immigrants retain citizenship in their country of origin (Hammar, in Brubaker, 1989), and in a different form in the European Community where citizens of member states will eventually have a second citizenship in the EC.

The development of substantive citizenship was analysed in a classic study by T. H. Marshall in 1950 (reprinted in Marshall, 1992), which depicted a sequence of the extension of civil, political and social rights to the whole population of a nation. In Western Europe after 1945 it was the growth of social rights – the creation of a WELFARE STATE – which produced the greatest changes, establishing more collectivist and egalitarian principles and policies which counteracted to some extent the inegalitarian tendencies of the capitalist economy. The situation was different, however, in Eastern Europe where the communist dictatorships severely curtailed civil and political rights at the same time as they provided a considerable range of important social rights. The opposition movements which finally brought about the collapse of these regimes did in fact emphasize very strongly the idea of citizenship as embodying basic civil and political rights, and also the related conception of a necessary independence of the institutions of CIVIL SOCIETY from the state.

Another general question concerns the relation between the rights and the duties of citizens. The revival of ideas of citizenship in the European Renaissance drew largely upon the example of Roman citizenship, emphasizing self-discipline, patriotism and concern for the common good; and such conceptions are clearly still important for the further development of citizenship in the twentieth century, with 'patriotism' perhaps transmuted into the idea of greater popular participation in the business of government, not only of a national community but also of wider regional associations. Participation of this kind, however, depends crucially on the growth of social rights to provide a sufficient general level of economic well-being, leisure and education, and no doubt also on new formulations of what is the 'common good' (see ETHICS).

Reading
Brubaker, W. Rogers ed. 1989: *Immigration and the Politics of Citizenship in Europe and North America*.
——1992: *Citizenship and Nationhood in France and Germany*.
King, D. 1987: *The New Right: Politics, Markets and Citizenship*.
Marshall, T.H. and Bottomore, Tom 1992: *Citizenship and Social Class*.
Turner, Bryan S. 1986: *Citizenship and Capitalism*.

TOM BOTTOMORE

civil society This is an old term, common in European political thought up to the eighteenth century. In this traditional usage, it was a more or less literal translation of the Roman *societas civilis* and, behind that, the Greek *koinōnia politiké*. It was synonymous, that is, with the state or 'political society'. When Locke spoke of 'civil government', or Kant of *bürgerliche Gesellschaft*, or Rousseau of *état civil*, they all meant simply the state, seen as encompassing – like the Greek polis – the whole realm of the political. Civil society was the arena of the politically active citizen. It also carried the sense of a 'civilized' society, one that ordered its relations according to a system of laws rather than the autocratic whim of a despot.

The connection of CITIZENSHIP with civil society was never entirely lost. It forms part of the association that lends its appeal to more recent revivals of the concept. But there was a decisive innovation in the second half of the eighteenth century that broke the historic equation of civil society and the STATE. British social thought was especially influential in this. In the writings of John Locke and Tom Paine, Adam Smith and Adam Ferguson, there was elaborated the idea of a sphere of society distinct from the state and with forms and principles of its own. The growth of the new science of political economy – again largely a British achievement – was particularly important in establishing this decision. Most of these writers continued to use the term civil society in its classical sense, as in Adam Ferguson's *Essay on the History of Civil Society* (1767); but what they were in fact doing was making the analytical distinction that was soon to transform the meaning of the concept.

It is to Hegel that we owe the modern meaning of the concept of civil society. In the *Philosophy of Right* (1821), civil society is the sphere of ethical life interposed between the family and the state. Following the British economists, Hegel sees the content of civil society as largely determined by the free play of economic forces and individual self-seeking. But civil society also includes social and civic institutions that inhibit and regulate economic life, leading by an ineluctable process of education to the rational life of the state. So the particularity of civil society passes over into the universality of the state.

Marx, though acknowledging his debt to Hegel, narrowed the concept of civil society to make it equivalent simply to the autonomous realm of private property and market relations. 'The anatomy of civil society', he said, 'is to be sought in political economy.' This restriction threatened its usefulness. What need was there for the concept of civil society when the economy or simply 'society' – seen as the effective content of the state and political life generally – supplied its principal terms? In his later writings Marx himself dropped the term, preferring instead the simple dichotomy 'society-state'. Other writers too, and not only those influenced by Marx, found less and less reason to retain the concept of civil society. The 'political society' of Alexis de Tocqueville's *Democracy in America* (1835–40) recalled the earlier sense of civil society as education for citizenship; but Tocqueville's example did little to revive the fortunes of what was increasingly regarded as an outmoded term. In the second half of the nineteenth century 'civil society' fell into disuse.

It was left to Antonio Gramsci, in the writings gathered together as the *Prison Notebooks* (1929–

35), to rescue the concept in the early part of this century. Gramsci, while retaining a basic Marxist orientation, went back to Hegel to revitalize the concept. Indeed he went further than Hegel in detaching civil society from the economy and allocating it instead to the state. Civil society is that part of the state concerned not with coercion or formal rule but with the manufacture of consent. It is the sphere of 'cultural politics'. The institutions of civil society are the church, schools, trade unions, and other organizations through which the ruling class exercises 'hegemony' over society. By the same token it is also the arena where that hegemony is challengeable. In the radical decades of the 1960s and 1970s, it was Gramsci's concept of civil society that found favour with those who attempted to oppose the ruling structures of society not by direct political confrontation but by waging a kind of cultural guerrilla warfare. Culture and education were the spheres where hegemony would be contested, and ended.

New life was also breathed into the concept by the swift-moving changes in Central and Eastern Europe in the late 1970s and 1980s. Dissidents in the region turned to the concept of civil society as a weapon against the all-encompassing claims of the totalitarian state. The example of the Solidarity movement in Poland suggested a model of opposition and regeneration that avoided suicidal confrontation with the state by building up the institutions of civil society as a 'parallel society'. In the wake of the successful revolutions of 1989 throughout the region, the concept of civil society gained immensely in popularity. To many intellectuals it carried the promise of a privileged route to the post-communist, pluralist society (see PLURALISM), though they were vague about the details. Western intellectuals, too, were enthused anew with the concept. For them it suggested a new perspective on old questions of democracy and participation in societies where these practices seemed to have become moribund.

Civil society, it is clear, has renewed its appeal. As in the eighteenth century, we seem to feel once more the need to define and distinguish a sphere of society that is separate from the state. Citizenship appears to depend for its exercise on active participation in non-state institutions, as the necessary basis for participation in formal political institutions. This was Tocqueville's point about American democracy; it is a lesson that the rest of the world now seems very anxious to take to heart.

Reading

Arato, Andrew and Cohen, Jean 1992: *Civil Society and Democratic Theory*.

Gellner, Ernest 1991: Civil society in historical context. *International Social Science Journal* 43, 495–510.

Gouldner, Alvin 1980: Civil society in capitalism and socialism. In *The Two Marxisms*.

Keane, John ed. 1988: *Civil Society and the State: New European Perspectives*.

Lewis, Paul ed. 1992: *Democracy and Civil Society in Eastern Europe*.

Riedel, Manfred 1984: 'State' and 'civil society': linguistic context and historical origin. In *Between Tradition and Revolution: The Hegelian Transformation of Political Philosophy*.

KRISHAN KUMAR

civilization From the Latin *civis*, city, the term civilization explicitly concerns the CULTURE of cities, something of which Karl Marx reminded us when he stated that the seat of ancient civilization was the city (*Grundrisse*, 1857–8), and that what Aristotle meant by *zoon politikon* was simply that man is a town dweller (*Capital*, vol. 1). Max Weber, following up Marx's insight, analysed the city under four aspects: the city as a geographical or spatial entity or locale; the city as a market, or merchant city for *producers*; the garrison city; and the consumer city, which lives off the court. The ancient city of the hoplite soldier was characterized by civil rights granted as the quid pro quo for military service, but the medieval city enjoyed what rights to self-regulation of the city and its trade it enjoyed precisely by virtue of immunity from garrison duty (Weber, 1921–2, chapter on 'The city).

Ancient civilization literally controlled the hinterland from the city; the ancient cities of Mesopotamia, for instance, actually enclosed date plantations and fields, which were farmed by urban entrepreneurs with venture capital and slaves, within the city walls, which is why they were so extensive. This situation was reversed only in the European Middle Ages when, as Max Weber tells us, the seat of landed property coincided with the locus of power – in the countryside – and towns existed mainly as markets for the exchange of the surplus produced by nobles on their large estates.

Weber's distinction between the ancient economy and the bourgeois mode of production, like Marx's, rests then on a distinction as much regional as chronological, between the densely settled urban, entrepreneurial littoral or riverine cultures of the Mediterranean basin and the decentralized,

agrarian life of the Germanic and Celtic tribes organized in patriarchal families. The first was city-based *political* civilization in the literal meaning of the term, as founded on the *polis*, or city; the second economic in the literal sense, from *oikos* or family, the economy of extended households. The Weberian distinction between economic and political man, made in this way, is assumed by the political philosopher Hannah Arendt, who unfavourably compares modern society based on the economy of collective housekeeping with the ideal of the classical citizen, and by Gunnar Myrdal (1953), who made a study of the development of the economy of collective housekeeping.

A tradition of post-modern criticism flourished in Germany from the late nineteenth century, including works on the decline of the West by Oswald Spengler (who had a British counterpart in Arnold Toynbee) and, later, members of the Frankfurt school, especially Theodor Adorno, Max Horkheimer and Herbert Marcuse. Sigmund Freud's *Civilization and its Discontents* (1930) may also be read more specifically as a work about urban culture or civilization in the literal sense, his notion that civilization lives off repression, channelling sublimated sexual energy into cultural projects, being exemplified in the great artistic monuments and the elaborately constructed cultures of the city ancient and modern. In some respects Freud's critique of civilization – in terms of the costs to individual gratification, the unequal division of the economic surplus, the psychoses and neuroses produced by the propensity to compare and the economic and social competition to which civilization gives rise – builds on a long tradition of the critique of civilization that we find in the 'four stages' theory of civilization. It has its roots in Stoic thought and was developed in the Enlightenment by Rousseau, Diderot and members of the Scottish Enlightenment, Adam Smith and Adam Ferguson.

Across several disciplines now scholars have observed certain shortcomings in the received historical canon which posits an evolutionary schema from primitivism to *polis* to modern (Western) civilization, the states of the East constituting a residual category. Studies in Assyriology, Iranology, Egyptology, among area specialities, disclose highly developed ancient civilizations which exhibited considerable technological competence. More disquieting still is the fact that economic and technical competencies were accompanied by the full array of social and cultural traits that we associate with 'development' as it is currently conceived (see also DEVELOPMENT AND UNDERDEVELOPMENT). The capacity of the 'irrigation societies', so called, of ancient Sumeria, Mesopotamia more generally, Egypt and China to make the transition from city-state to empire, a transition that the Greek *polis*, for instance, never made (Mann, 1986), was a function precisely of the following developmental competencies:

1   impersonal government administered by a bureaucracy;
2   the conception of man as citizen;
3   forms of political representation;
4   the creation of an economic surplus;
5   a monetarized economy, accompanied by the institutions of credit, commercial law, trade treaties and international laws of contract;
6   a standing army, equipped with advanced military technologies;
7   social stratification along functional lines, comprising classes of farmers, artisans, merchants, an administrative elite and priestly caste;
8   the concept of nature as governed by rational laws;
9   institutions for the acquisition, organization and dissemination of knowledge;
10 the development of writing and basic sciences of mathematics, geometry, astronomy, navigation, architecture, engineering and highly developed skills in construction, metalworking, pottery, textiles, sculpture and painting. (Drucker, 1979; Mann, 1986)

Much reinterpretation of this sort has taken place in the twentieth century. To take the case of Sumeria, scholars (Diakonoff, 1974; Jacobsen, 1976; Kramer, 1963; Oppenheim, 1969) now suggest that city-states like those of Lagash were administered by parallel temple and palace bureaucracies, agents of each required to countersign shipments in and out of the state granaries, for instance (Oppenheim, 1969, pp. 7ff.). The considerable lands of the city comprised palace and temple complexes and their holdings; noble estates and the lands of commoners were organized in 'patriarchal clans and town communities', whose property could be bought and sold by chosen family representatives in transactions for which, around 2400 BC, we already have documentary evidence (Kramer, 1963, pp. 75–7). Corresponding to these, now classic, property divisions was a surprisingly

conventional division of political power. By 2300 BC evidence exists for a bicameral assembly in Lagash, the upper house of which was controlled by the nobility, the lower house confined to commoners, access being granted on property qualifications. Magistracies, appointed on an annual basis, were rotated among an isonomous elite constituted by the judicial, administrative and merchant classes (Oppenheim, 1969). Lagash has the honour of recording in its annals the first known use of the word 'freedom' (Kramer, 1963, p. 79), celebrated in the Urukagina Reform Document of around 2350 BC in terms strikingly reminiscent of Solon's *seisachtheia* nearly 1,800 years later. Freedom meant precisely protection against the predations of the palace tax collector, as well as redress of administrative abuses by the 'ubiquitous and obnoxious bureaucracy' of the temple, Urukagina (like Solon later) promising release of those imprisoned for debt bondage.

Some of the best evidence we have for government by an impersonal bureaucracy is yielded by the third millennium Mesopotamian site of Ebla, in the form of some 20,000 clay tablets. A prosperous city of some 260,000 people, Ebla was ruled by a king, a council of elders and some 11,700 bureaucrats whose ledgers, daybooks and inventories account for some 13,000 clay tablets (Bermant and Weitzman, 1979; Matthiae, 1980). Further evidence for bureaucratically administered rule of LAW is to be found in the provisions of a series of codifications of the common law of the area, from the Ur-Nammu Code of 2050 BC up to and including the famous Hammurabi Code. The code of Ur-Nammu upheld the rights of orphans, widows and small landholders against powerful 'grabbers of property'. It undertook regulation of the marketplace by the introduction of standard weights and measures, instituting a schedule of fines for infringement against the laws of fair trade, in line with other codes for the area, including the Hittite. Court proceedings for the period record litigation regarding 'marriage contracts, divorces, inheritance, slaves, hiring of boats, claims of all sorts, pledges and such miscellaneous items as pretrial investigations, subpoenas, theft, damage to property, and malfeasance in office' (Kramer, 1963, pp. 84–5).

In ancient Egypt, too, although it was perhaps a less litigious society, property transactions were a document-ridden affair, asset dossiers comprising every piece of paper associated with a given piece of property (Lloyd, 1983, p. 314; Pestman, 1983). Ancient Egypt is often painted as the archetypal centralized state, based, according to the Marxist theory of 'the Asiatic mode of production' or later theories of 'oriental despotism', for instance, on the control of water. But, contary to these assumptions, ancient Egypt was in its early history also characterized by independent city-development (Bietak, 1979; Trigger, 1983, pp. 40, 48), private and noble patronage systems (Kemp, 1983, pp. 83–5), and a high level of individualism as attested by the personal signatures of artists to works as early as the Pyramids of Giza (Drucker, 1979, p. 44).

It is not necessary to list in detail the technological accomplishments of ancient Mesopotamia and Egypt. It is worth pointing out, however, that each of the instances Max Weber gives in his preface to *The Protestant Ethic and the Spirit of Capitalism* (1904–5) for the administrative, scientific and technical superiority of the West over the East is erroneous. So ubiquitous are assumptions of Western development and Eastern underdevelopment that a thinker who spent a good deal of his life writing about Eastern systems felt no need to check his facts. He claims that Babylonian astronomy lacked a mathematical basis, neglecting to mention also the invention of geometry as Egyptian (cf. King, 1978, 1980); he claims that Eastern legal traditions lacked the systematic quality of Roman and canonical law – whereas, in fact, Roman Law is derived from the law-codes of the Eastern provinces, codified by those Easterners, Papinian and Ulpian from the Beirut school of law (cf. Cumont, 1911; Driver and Miles, 1952–5). Weber (1904–5) further claims that 'though the technical basis of our architecture came from the Orient . . . the Orient lacked the solution to the problems of the dome' – quite the contrary, the Orient provided the solution not only to the problem of the dome, but also of the arch. On the subject of the compilation and dissemination of knowledge, Weber claims that Western universities are superior to those of China and Islam, 'superficially similar', but lacking 'the rational, systematic and specialized pursuit of sciences with trained and specialized personnel' – he neglects to point out that Islamic universities like al-Azhar were older than those of the West, which did not begin life as scientific institutes either. Evidence for the early existence of medical and law schools, to which women were also admitted, dates in fact to the third-millennium Ebla site, which also furnishes lists of precious metals, minerals and other scientific information (Bermant and Weitzman, 1979, pp. 153–5). Weber goes on to claim, rather surprisingly since this is his special subject, that it is an accomplishment of the West to staff its bureaucracies with a specially trained *organization* of officials. More startling still is his claim that the organization of labour based on freedom to contract is a triumph of the West. But stipulations regarding freedom to contract are to be found in the earliest known Mesopotamian law codes, the Hammurabi Code, for instance, including extensive treatment of both agricultural and commercial labour contracts regarding rates of hire, offences and liabilities involving oxen, husbandmen, agricultural implements, graziers, shepherds, wagons and seasonal workers and wages and rates of hire for craftsmen (Driver and Miles, 1952–5).

If the division and specialization of labour are indices of the level of development of civilizations, premodern societies rated high, ancient Rome recording some 150 professional corporations, medieval Cairo some 265 manual occupations, 90 types of banking and commerce specializations, and around the same number of different 'professionals, officials, religious functionaries and educators' (Goitein, 1967, p. 99). By 1801 Cairo had 278 occupational corporations and by 1901 Damascus had 435 recorded recognized occupations.

Such evidence calls into question evolutionary and developmental assumptions about economic PROGRESS and the sequence of modes of production underlying nineteenth- and twentieth-century macrohistorical schemas, including those of Marx and Weber.

An interest in the phenomenon of civilization and its dynamics is not confined to the West, and, indeed, the first great premodern analyst, Ibn Khaldun (1332–1406), described not only the endogamous life-cycles of civilizations, but the exogamous cross-fertilization of nomadic desert cultures and the sedentary civilizations of the ancient cities. Study of the city and the full array of characteristics we associate with URBANISM – concentrated settlement; internal differentiation into quarters corresponding to occupational divisions; specialized division of labour; functions as industrial and market centres; defence and religious functions – has emerged in the twentieth century as one of the great subjects of sociological and historical enquiry, with the work of the Frenchmen Henri Pirenne, Henri Lefebvre, Gabriel Baer and

Fernand Braudel. The relation between civilization and manners and the court, to take a different tack, has been the subject of a fascinating study by Norbert Elias (1939).

Reading

Braudel, Fernand 1979 (*1983*): *The Wheels of Commerce: Civilization and Capitalism.*
Elias, Norbert 1939 (*1978–82*): *The Civilizing Process*, 2 vols. Vol. 1: *The History of Manners*; vol. 2: *Power and Civility.*
Mann, Michael 1986: *The Sources of Social Power*, vol. 1: *A History of Power from the Beginning to AD 1760.*
Oppenheim, Adolf, L. 1969: Mesopotamia – land of many cities. In *Middle Eastern Cities: A Symposium on Ancient Islamic and Contemporary Middle Eastern Urbanism*, ed. Ira M. Lapidus.
Trigger, Brian J. 1983: The rise of Egyptian civilization. In *Ancient Egypt: A Social History*, ed. B.J. Trigger and B. Kemp.
Weber, Max 1921–2: *Economy and Society: An Outline of Interpretive Sociology*, chapter on 'The city'.

PATRICIA SPRINGBORG

class   In its social sense the term denotes large groups among which unequal distribution of economic goods and/or preferential division of political prerogatives and/or discriminatory differentiation of cultural values result from economic exploitation, political oppression and cultural domination, respectively; all of these potentially lead to social conflict over the control of scarce resources. In the tradition of social thought, social class is a generic concept utilized in studying the dynamics of the societal system in terms of *relational* rather than *distributional* aspects of social structure. In this sense, classes are considered as not merely aggregates of individuals but as real *social groups* with their own history and identifiable place in the organization of society. However, the idea that social classes can be equated with aggregates of individuals distinguished on the basis of similar level of education, income or other characteristics of social inequality still persists and leads to confusion of this concept with SOCIAL STRATIFICATION. Therefore, the meanings attached to the term social class vary and refer to different types of societal STRUCTURATION. In theoretical and historical sociology various types of structuration appear in substantive discussions of economic classes, political classes and cultural classes.

Economic classes

In his general theory of societal evolution Karl Marx distinguished pairs of antagonistic classes specific to each period: slaves and masters in ancient societies, serfs and feudal lords in feudalism, capitalists and workers in capitalism. He elaborated in detail the concept of economic EXPLOITATION of workers by capitalists, expressed in terms of surplus value. In his view, the relations of economic exploitation form the basis for the 'superstructure' of the society, namely political and ideological order: 'The executive of the modern state is but a committee for managing the common affairs of the whole bourgeoisie.' The IDEOLOGY that rules in capitalist society justifies and sanctifies the totality of social relations which have emerged on the foundation of economic exploitation and is functional for reproducing them. Marx believed that classes are collections of individuals who, by acquiring the consciousness of common social position and common fate, are transformed into real social groupings, active in the political arena. He expected that economic exploitation would lead workers to political revolution, overthrowing capitalist society and clearing the ground for a new, socialist society without classes.

Max Weber suggested a distinction, at least analytically, between two separate orders of economic classes: property classes and commercial classes. In the first, owners-rentiers are the 'positively privileged class' and debtors – 'déclassé' people without property, in general – are the 'negatively privileged class'. In the second, industrialists belong to the positively privileged class while workers belong to the negatively privileged class. Weber assumed that the capitalist economic system forms the most favourable background for the existence of 'commercial classes'. He defines the individual's 'class situation' as determined by the opportunities to sell commodities and professional skills. Although he does not state it explicitly, his approach to the structuration of commercial classes allows investigators to construct various aggregations of individuals into groupings with the same opportunities. In this sense the boundaries among them seem arbitrary.

The general ideas of Marx and Weber have been continuously elaborated, extended and modified. Bottomore (1965) suggested the lasting validity of the fundamental premises of the Marxian theory of classes while Dahrendorf (1957) postulated its critical revision. Roemer (1982) proposed an extension of Marx's concept of economic exploitation, which was utilized by Wright (1985) to construct a new scheme of classes in capitalist society. Poulantzas (1974) and Wesołowski (1966) presented integrated theories of 'class domination'. Giddens (1973) and Parkin (1979) suggested several elaborations and extensions of Weber's approach to class; Lockwood (1958), Goldthorpe (1980) and Runciman (1972) conducted empirical research informed by Weber's ideas.

Political classes

Gaetano Mosca (1896) formulated a theory of 'ruling' and 'ruled' classes as groups emerging in any society which reached a level above the primitive. Unequal distribution of power prerogatives is a functional requirement and structural necessity. The existence of the state causes the existence of the ruling class. That class is composed of all of those who play an important role in politics and fulfil state functions. People who actually rule come from a milieu in each historical period that has the resources appropriate to acquiring the expertise to rule. Mosca took for granted that, in his society, wealth was essential for a political career.

Normally, in addition to the ruling class there exists a second, 'lower' segment of society on which efficient rule depends. This segment may be a middle class or BUREAUCRACY. Moreover, within a modern political structure several 'social forces' emerge. Mosca writes that the military segment wishes to rule as well as intellectuals, lawyers, teachers, businessmen and workers. He expresses the opinion that good government should incorporate all of them into the process of ruling.

Parallel with Mosca, Pareto (1916–19) presented his concept of the 'elite' which can be interpreted in class terms. According to him, the 'governing elite' is composed of those who have proven themselves best able to rule – that is to capture power and hold it. 'Circulation' of governing elites is a process of changing the composition of political classes either by force or by peaceful infiltration and cooptation (see ELITE THEORY).

The concept of ruling class appears less frequently in discussions of contemporary Western societies with their democratic political systems than in discussions of contemporary societies with authoritarian rule. In the first case, it appears in the theories of new trends in societal development and new strategic groups considered as the agents of those trends. In these theories it is expected that new classes will deprive the democratic system of its real functions by taking the lead and controlling the society. These classes may be composed of

managers (Burnham, 1941; Gurvitch, 1949), government bureaucrats (Geiger, 1949), or certain professionals – like planners, organizers, scientists – who form alliances with politicians and old-type businessmen (Bell, 1974).

Theories of totalitarian and post-totalitarian rule in the former USSR and Eastern Europe (cf. TOTALITARIANISM) invoke the concept of ruling class in relation to the top leaders of the communist party and high officials of the government who were assigned to their posts by the party and held monopolistic, unlimited and arbitrary power (Djilas, 1957; Hegedüs, 1976). Since both the party and the government were organized according to bureaucratic principles, the rule can be called bureaucratic, monoparty rule. In the totalitarian system, the power structure controls and directs economic and cultural institutions. Many authors argue that bureaucratic and administrative control of economic processes serve as tools for the exploitation of workers by political rulers.

Cultural classes

Jan Wacław Machajski (1904) outlined a theory of future society in which the 'educated class' or 'intelligentsia' of bourgeois society gives rise to a new class that dominates manual workers. Writing from an anarchist perspective, he said that the elimination of capitalists is not enough to change society. Reading Marx's *Capital* (1867, 1885, 1894) he finds the thesis that work which is more skilled, hence requiring more education, should be better paid than work requiring less education. Machajski emphasizes that the Marxist and social democratic programmes for the future socialist society imply the survival of educational inequality and, consequently, economic inequality.

Max Weber indirectly influenced the formation of the concept of cultural class. He proposed that we investigate 'status groups' which have developed a specific style of life. Some status groups clearly do not belong to class-type phenomena, but some do, emerging on the basis of common economic situations or common position within the power structure, or both (such as feudal lords): 'Status groups are often created by property classes.' From Weber's writing one can infer that social classes show an affinity to status groups because both develop their own culture or style of life. Weber considered the bourgeoisie of rising modern towns a 'social class' and attributed to it three characteristics: property, citizen's rights and 'culture'. In the Weberian perspective, culture may be seen as an active, integrative force in class-formation processes.

Alvin Gouldner (1979), inspired directly by Machajski, formulated a theory according to which the 'new class' of humanistic intellectuals and technical intelligentsia, the class of the bearers of knowledge, is on the way to social domination. Members of the new class are owners of 'cultural capital' which exists primarily in the form of higher education. They have begun to replace the 'old moneyed class' in the process of social development as well as in the functioning of the postindustrial societal system. According to Gouldner, the future belongs to them, not to the 'working class' as Marx supposed. Members of the new class will guard their own material and non-material interests – higher income and higher prestige for those with knowledge – but simultaneously, they will represent and promote the interests of the society as a whole, to a much higher degree than any other class hitherto known in history. The new class subverts the old-type hierarchy and promotes the culture of critical discourse, but at the same time introduces a new social hierarchy of knowledge. Since it is both emancipatory and elitist, he says, it is a 'flawed universal class'.

Integrative versus analytical approach
Economic classes, political classes and cultural classes may be conceived of as separate class orders or as one integrated order comprising three aspects. If a theorist views class structure as an integrated order, then the important problem for him/her is how the three aspects produce an integrated whole. Marx suggested the causal chain from the base, that is economic relations, to the 'superstructure' of political and ideological relations. Thus the economic class produces other aspects of class. He did not ignore the feedback influence of the political and cultural aspects on the base; nonetheless, economic structure 'in the last resort' determines all class aspects (see DETERMINISM).

Mosca seems to be less concerned with causal relations among the three aspects of class than with the problem of the significance of the power aspect for the totality of social relations. Division into rulers and ruled is the critical phenomenon in all civilized, non-primitive, differentiated societies; therefore, it explains more of the global societal system. Among contemporary approaches, Lenski

(1966) follows Mosca's tradition, although he does not ignore Marx. For Lenski there are two main forms of power: political power and the power of property. What he emphasizes is that in the whole history of civilization, political power exerts a formative influence on the distributive system, that is, on the distribution of economic privileges and prestige.

Bourdieu (1987; Bourdieu and Passeron, 1970) aims at an integrative approach by suggesting multicausality and interactions in the formation of 'social power' as the globalized characteristic of class. This power is a trajectory of financial, cultural and social capital possessed by individuals. The interaction among these three forms is not predetermined by any petrified weight of each capital or a stable relation between forms of capital. Recently he has elaborated the concept of 'symbolic capital' which integrates all other capitals and reinforces the social power of the dominant class in the public arena.

The analytical approach stresses the autonomy of economic class, political class and cultural class. The premise on which this approach has been founded is that there are autonomous spheres of life – economy, politics and culture – within which emerging groupings do not overlap. It is also argued that an analytical approach is more appropriate than an integrative one for studying modern, as contrasted with premodern society. This approach has its roots in Weber's ideas, although some impact on its formulation was also exerted by Sorokin's (1927) suggestions on autonomous channels of social mobility. Among contemporary authors, Lipset and Zetterberg (1966) argued for this approach and suggested separate study of occupational class, consumption class, social class and power class. However this approach, as well as the analytical approach, has been criticized and their concept of class contested on theoretical grounds (Calvert, 1982).

Social class in empirical sociology
A 'class paradigm' is one of the best established approaches for analysing data on social structure. Within this paradigm, research focuses on detecting differences among social classes with respect to (a) their share of unequally distributed goods; (b) various attitudes and opinions; (c) political behaviour and common group-actions; and (d) the patterns of social mobility. In research practice,

class schemes based on sets of criteria involving control over the means of production and labour power are treated as independent, explanatory variables. The class paradigm proves its usefulness if an application of a class scheme to a particular population leads to the conclusion that *inter*class differences with respect to specified variables are significantly larger than *intra*class differences.

If social class and social stratification are considered autonomous categorizations of social structure, one of the empirical questions is the degree of their interdependence. Are social classes consistently ordered with respect to the formal education, occupational rank and total income of their members? Descriptive statistics for various countries demonstrate the validity of the argument of class theoreticians that, although social class and social stratification have much in common, they are *far from identical*. In Western industrialized countries the association of the social class of individuals with the components of their social stratification position – education, occupation and income – is strong, albeit leaving substantial room for non-class determinants of social inequalities. Moreover, the order of social classes on various dimensions of social inequality is not the same. Owners of the means of production are certainly at the top on the economic dimension, while intellectuals rank highest on the educational dimension. In the middle of the hierarchy, white-collar workers usually have higher prestige from their jobs than small commodity producers have. These kinds of rank shifts confirm that social classes represent *discrete categories* rather than categories consistently arranged along a multidimensional stratificational continuum (Wright, 1978 and 1985).

The interest in the social consciousness of classes stems from the traditional Marxist distinction between *Klasse an sich* (class-in-itself, that is, without a common consciousness) and *Klasse für sich* (class-for-itself, that is with a common consciousness). For many years it has been observed that members of privileged classes tend to be more openminded, more intellectually flexible and more self-directed in their values than members of deprived classes. Class differences are substantial not only with regard to the content of economic and political issues but also with regard to the ways in which people think, in terms of level of abstraction. Kohn (1969; Kohn et al., 1990) advanced a hypothesis that these class differences can be attributed to the conditions of life, especially in the work

situation. Those who are more advantageously located in the class structure have greater opportunity to exercise occupational self-direction; their experience in the work situation becomes generalized to other realms of their life, psychological functioning included. Essentially, class differences in psychological functioning are explained by the learning-generalization mechanism. It should be noted, however, that this interpretation, although psychological in its essence, is far from a so-called 'subjective interpretation of classes'. In the latter case the assumption that people in similar economic circumstances develop a similar sense of reality leads to the concept of social classes 'as psychologically or subjectively based groupings defined by the allegiance of their members' (Centers, 1949, p. 210). In the former case, psychological variables are treated only as *correlates of classes*. However, independent of the interpretation, the differences in the 'psychology of class' support the differences in the 'behaviour of class', political behaviour in particular.

The relationship between social class and political behaviour focuses on differentiated class interests defined with respect to the material situation. In practice, political parties in Western democracies appeal to certain segments of society and seek their support. Studies of voting behaviour have routinely found a correlation between the social class position of voters and the party they typically vote for. Persons belonging to the ownership and managerial classes are more likely to vote for a party which stands for protection of business interests and little welfare legislation than are persons belonging to the working class. Historically, political parties have come to represent specific coalitions of class interests. However, there is some evidence that in Western democracies class voting has decreased substantially in recent decades (Franklin, 1985).

Strikes and revolts are certainly more class-based than voting behaviour in both Western industrialized countries and non-socialist developing countries. In the countries of Eastern Europe, some aspects of the political revolts of 1953 (East Germany), 1956 (Hungary and Poland), 1968 (Czechoslovakia), 1970 and 1980 (Poland) and those of 1989 may be interpreted in terms of *class conflicts* not only between the economically deprived and the economically privileged but also between the ruled and the rulers. Since in these countries, economic and political power overlapped to a great extent, class conflicts became very generalized and involved issues from wage claims to freedom of speech (Touraine et al., 1982; Staniszkis, 1981). In its extreme formulation, class conflicts in these countries have been described as those between owners (those who decide on the use of the means of production), rulers (those who control the means of administration and coercion) and ideologues (those who control the means of interpretation and inculcation of values) on the one hand and the masses on the other. Because of these generalized class conflicts, Nowak (1983) calls socialism a *supraclass formation*.

From a theoretical point of view, the degree of intergenerational SOCIAL MOBILITY is of central importance for class formation since it influences both the composition of classes and the continuity or change of life experience. For these reasons, among neo-Marxists (Westergaard and Resler, 1975; Bottomore, 1965) and neo-Weberians (Parkin, 1979; Giddens, 1973) serious efforts have been made to give the idea of mobility a major role in class theory. Goldthorpe and his associates (1980) have examined and partly rejected three theses pertaining to class mobility: (1) the closure thesis, according to which in order to maintain their advantageous location in social structure, privileged classes apply strategies of social closure/ exclusion against inferior classes; (2) the buffer zone thesis proposing the division between manual and non-manual occupations as a fundamental line of cleavage within class structure; and (3) the counterbalance thesis which claims that worklife mobility – in comparison with social origin – is becoming less probable because access to the middle and higher positions depends more and more on formal education and less and less on training on the job. The critique of these theoretically advanced theses led sociologists to seek complex patterns of class mobility on the basis of data from various countries. They found that the pattern of class mobility is essentially the same in all Western industrialized countries. Moreover, the pattern of class endogamy – that is, the degree to which people tend to choose spouses from social classes similar to their own – shows little intercountry variation. Class mobility and class endogamy – as well as friendship networks – reveal the same pattern of class barriers in the economic, political and cultural dimensions of social structure.

Reading

Bottomore, T.B. 1965 (*1991*): *Classes in Modern Society*.
Calvert, P. 1982: *The Concept of Class*.
Giddens, A. 1973: *The Class Structure of the Advanced Societies*.
Marshall, G. et al. 1988: *Social Class in Modern Britain*.
Ossowski, S. 1957: (*1963*): *Class Structure in the Social Consciousness*.
Wright, E.O. 1985: *Classes*.

WŁODZIMIERZ WESOŁOWSKI and
KAZIMIERZ M. SŁOMCZYŃSKI

coercion Whenever one party controls the behaviour of another by the threat, or actual imposition, of intolerable pain, damage or loss, there is coercion. One way to understand coercion, therefore, is through the analysis of threats.

A threat can be defined as the creation or maintenance, by one party (the 'source'), of a negative incentive for some other party (the 'target') to behave as the source wishes. As Schelling (1960) indicated, against a 'rational' target, a threat, to be successful, must be both adequate (the threatened consequences of non-compliance must be serious enough to outweigh, for the target, the gains in prospect from it) and credible (the target must have good reason to believe that in the event of non-compliance, the threatened consequences will ensue). The point is illustrated in the game theory matrices in the figure.

In each matrix one player, Row, chooses between Top (T) and Bottom (B) rows and the other, Column, between Left (L) and Right (R) columns. For each 'outcome' (combination of choices), Row's payoffs are as in the bottom left-hand corner of the box, and Column's in the top right. The order of play is that first Row can 'threaten', then Column must choose, and finally Row must choose. Both players are assumed to have full knowledge of the facts set out in the matrix.

In G1, if Column can be induced to choose L, Row can gain 3 units by choosing T. A threat by Row to choose B if Column chose R would be both adequate (since Column's payoff for BR is lower than that for TL) and credible (since Row's payoff for BR is higher than that for TR). Schelling calls this a 'warning'. In G2, however, though Row's threat is still adequate (Column is still better off at TL than at BR), its credibility is in doubt, since Row now does better not to

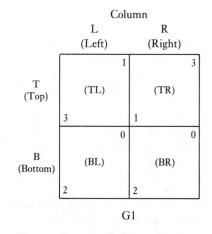

Column

L   R
(Left)   (Right)

	L (Left)	R (Right)
T (Top)	1 (TL) 3	3 (TR) 1
B (Bottom)	0 (BL) 2	0 (BR) 2

Row

G1

Column

L   R
(Left)   (Right)

	L (Left)	R (Right)
T (Top)	1 (TL) 3	3 (TR) 1
B (Bottom)	0 (BL) 0	0 (BR) 0

Row

G2

implement (at TR) than to implement (at BR).

Schelling suggests three devices whereby, in a G2 situation, a source might hope to establish a threat's credibility: putting implementation outside its control (for instance, 'threatening' burglars with bodily harm by installing a ferocious guard dog); cultivating a reputation for recklessness ('the rationality of irrationality') or for always carrying out its threats regardless; and reducing its own payoff for non-implementation (in this case, Row's for TR from 1 to say − 1), either by entering into a legally binding commitment to pay a sum to a third party in that case, or by maximizing the loss of face that would result.

The price of such credibility, however, is rigidity. Row is now less able to adjust to unforeseen circumstances. In real life, as Lieberman (1964) has pointed out, a threat may be both adequate and credible, and yet not advisable, for two kinds of reasons. First, targets of threats may fail to respond rationally through stress, avoidance of information, or bureaucratic incompetence, and the fact of coercion may breed resentment or make forbidden fruit more attractive.

Secondly, while power can be seen, with Deutsch (1963, p. 111) as 'the ability to afford not to learn', coercion, from the source's point of view, is the refusal to learn. By imposing the entire burden of adjustment and goal changing on the target, the coercing source may thus deny itself information which, by revealing how it needs to adjust its policies or goals, may ultimately be essential to its survival. Thus as Gurr (1970), on the basis of a major study of rebellions, concludes, increases in political VIOLENCE are not usually attributable to weakening coercive control. Moreover, even if the ruthless suppression of dissidence does keep rebellion at bay, a government may thereby lose its legitimacy and with it the ability to mobilize its subjects' communal spirit.

According to recent game-theoretical studies by Robert Axelrod (1984) and Michael Taylor (1987), coercion may not be necessary to keep the peace and ensure the minimum cooperation among members of a social group, even assuming that they are, and remain, wholly self-interested. Were these studies confirmed, the domestic coercive apparatus on which practically all states to some extent rely could, in principle, be abolished.

See also POWER.

Reading
Gurr, T.R 1970: *Why Men Rebel.*
Lieberman, E.J. 1964: Threat and assurance in the conduct of conflict. In *International Conflict and Behavioural Science*, ed. R. Fisher.
Pennock, J.R. and Chapman, J.W. eds 1972: *Coercion.*
Schelling, T.C. 1960: *The Strategy of Conflict.*
Taylor, M. 1987: *The Possibility of Cooperation.*

RODERICK C. OGLEY

cognitive science   A newly formed, interdisciplinary investigation of cognition and knowledge, this area of science draws principally on cognitive psychology, artificial intelligence, philosophy of mind, linguistics and neuroscience.

The computer plays a vital and twofold role in this endeavour. On one hand, the belief that cognition has a computational, information-processing character, bearing important similarities to the activities of a computer, constitutes the conceptual centre of cognitive science. On the other hand, the building and investigation of computer programs intended as working models of cognitive processes provides a central method of enquiry.

The influence and character of the computational view of the mind can be seen in the terminology of 'algorithms', 'data', 'information', 'mechanisms', 'modules', 'processes', 'representations', 'syntax' and so on which pervades the literature of cognitive science.

The computational approach to cognition emerged in the mid-1950s, the Harvard Center for Cognitive Studies was opened in 1960, the journal *Cognitive Science* appeared in 1977 and the Cognitive Science Society was founded in 1979. The 1980s saw university courses in cognitive science springing up in the United States and in Europe, and among many publications, a full history of the field in Gardner (1985), the first student textbook in Stillings et al. (1987), a layperson's introduction in Johnson-Laird (1988) and an important collection of papers in Posner (1989).

The variety of work done in the field is considerable, but much of it falls under two general paradigms. During the early phase of development, the predominant paradigm has been a symbol-processing view of mind, which has come to be known as the 'physical symbol system hypothesis' (Newell and Simon, 1976) or 'classical cognitivism' (Clark, 1989). On this view, cognition consists in the manipulation, by algorithms or rules, of data which are symbolic, explicit, precise, static and passive in character.

An alternative, connectionist paradigm stems originally from work with computer simulations of neural networks. The 'knowledge' of a connectionist network on a computer consists not in symbolic data and instructions for its manipulation, but in the pattern of 'activation values' of the individual units which make up the network, and the 'weights' or strengths of connection between them. The capacities of these networks for learning, graceful degradation (gradual degradation in performance given inaccurate input), generalization and completion of partial information are thought to indicate fidelity to natural cognitive processes (Rumelhart and McClelland et al., 1986; Smolensky, 1988; Clark, 1989). The associated view of cognition is of a non-rule-based activity in which data are represented in a dynamic, and in some cases a distributed, implicit and imprecise way. It is also relevant that a hardware implementation of a connectionist network runs in parallel, and so is thought to emulate the activity of the brain better than the usual sequential, von Neumann computer architecture.

The differences and oppositions between these two general approaches to cognitive modelling can, however, be exaggerated, and some recent work has claimed that they are in fact complementary, and has attempted to combine them in hybrid systems.

In the philosophy of mind, considerable attention has been given to the plausibility of the computational view of the mind, and to such associated issues as the 'language of thought hypothesis', 'folk psychology' and the 'functionalist' answer to the mind–body problem (Lycan, 1990; Said et al., 1990).

In its short history, the 'mind's new science' has produced a substantive body of work, and in addition a lively interaction between its component disciplines. Cognitive science at present has a distinctly mechanistic and 'rationalistic' character (Winograd and Flores, 1986), and is not primarily concerned with such factors as subjectivity, feeling or culture. However, the attribution of a particular computational nature to *some* aspects of the mind does not imply that *all* mental activity is of this type, and the future of cognitive science may confirm a plurality of approaches to the mind's many mansions.

See also ARTIFICIAL INTELLIGENCE, LINGUISTICS.

Reading

Clark, A. 1989: *Microcognition: Philosophy, Cognitive Science, and Parallel Distributed Processing.*
Gardner, H. 1985: *The Mind's New Science.*
Johnson-Laird, P.N. 1988: *The Computer and the Mind.*
Posner, M. 1989: *Foundations of Cognitive Science.*
Rumelhart, D.E., McClelland, J.L. and the PDP Research Group 1986: *Parallel Distributed Processing: Explorations in the Microstructure of Cognition*, 2 vols.
Smolensky, P. 1988: On the proper treatment of connectionism. *Behavioural and Brain Sciences* 11, 1–74.
Stillings, N.A. et al. 1987: *Cognitive Science: An Introduction.*

DONALD PETERSON

collective action   The literature has been concerned to establish under what conditions separate individuals will engage in concerted action to strengthen or defend their situation. Although many social scientists have discussed this question, especially Karl Marx and Max Weber, the key text in the modern debate is that of Olson (1965) and the concept of the 'free rider'. In relation to this work a number of other contributions have examined how suboptimal outcomes may result from individuals pursuing their own interests and not what would be in their collective interest.

Olson employs the prisoner's dilemma game in order to analyse the nature of collective action. The contradiction of the game is that if each prisoner pursues his/her individual self-interest then they end up with a result that is less satisfactory than if they had been able to cooperate and to sacrifice such individual interests. Olson generalizes from this situation to every organization that attempts to mobilize large numbers of self-interested individuals. Where the group to be organized is large and where the benefits are collective or public and cannot be confined to specific individuals, then individuals will not join or cooperate unless non-collective benefits are provided. Without such selective benefits individuals can 'free ride', gaining the collective advantages of the organization if any should materialize, but not incurring any of the costs of membership or commitment.

Large groups, such as TRADE UNIONS or political parties, are most likely to suffer from the problem of the 'free rider'. In such cases each individual's contribution will make little difference to the outcome and there will be an absence of intense small group pressures likely to induce commitment. Olson argues that members of a social class are particularly likely to 'free ride' since individuals will gain the benefits of class actions whether or not they actually participate. It is rational to defect from such actions according to Olson.

Various refinements and amendments have been added to Olson's rather simple claims. First, many actual organizations are of an altruistic sort and are not based on such obvious self-interest at all. Second, it is doubtful if 'selective benefits', such as those provided by trade unions to individual members, could explain the enormous diversity and scale of voluntarily joined organizations in most industrialized societies. Third, social life should be seen as iterative. As a result individuals who should rationally defect may come to learn that there are collective benefits which will result from the pursuit of what may appear to be individually non-rational solutions. Through continued interaction in certain contexts people may become con-

cerned and informed about each other and this transforms their pattern of preference. Fourth, attention needs to be paid to the ideologies present within different societies or parts of a society. Where these emphasize INDIVIDUALISM, as in the USA, the 'free rider' problem is likely to be more acute. Fifth, analysis needs to be provided of how different structural positions such as capital and wage labour, have different possibilities of collective action in a sense built into them. The social world does not merely comprise separate individuals but also structures and resources, languages and discourses, and these are also relevant to the possibilities of collective action, offsetting or transcending the 'free rider' problem.

Reading
Barry, B. and Hardin, R. eds 1982: *Rational Man and Irrational Society*.
Elster, J. 1978: *Logic and Society*.
Lash, S. and Urry, J. 1984: The new Marxism of collective action: a critical analysis. *Sociology* 18, 33–50.
Offe, C. and Wiesenthal, H. 1980: Two logics of collective action: theoretical notes on social class and organizational form. *Political Power and Social Theory* 1, 67–115.
Olson, M. 1965: *The Logic of Collective Action*.

JOHN URRY

colonial liberation movement Colonial rule nowhere brought about any radical social reconstruction. Those at the bottom of the pile were apt to sink deeper, while the benefits of the new dispensation went to those already better off. Universities were set up, holding out opportunities to those who could enter them, but little was done in the way of primary education. In all colonies illiteracy remained the common lot; women continued to be very much the 'second sex'. New elites coming to the front largely derived from older ones, though – as in modernizing Japan – not from their highest and most fossilized layers.

There was, all the same, real change, affecting all classes. Novel means of travel and communication quickened the spread of ideas. Western education opened many windows, if at first only for a few; colonial peoples were drawn into closer contact with one another, as well as with Europe. New kinds of business activity made their appearance; new professions, like Western-style law, medicine, journalism, gave rise to a modern intelligentsia. Within its ranks national consciousness could be born, and inspire interest in a nation's history, language, culture. India quickly displayed a genius for legal thinking, a demonstration of how much mental capacity had been lying unused in Asia, with its refined cultures and semi-barbarous political life. Lawyers were to play an immense part in national movements of the more pacific kind. In India Gandhi, Nehru, Jinnah were all learned in the law.

The national idea originated in Western Europe, and from then on there were always – as there still are – Europeans striving for national independence. When patriots in distant lands began to look round their world they found a ready-made ideology to take over, and heroes to emulate like William Tell or Garibaldi. Some of their countries inherited at least an inchoate sense of nationhood, as Vietnam did with its tenacious memories of Chinese attacks repelled long years ago. Others, like India and many in Africa, had little or no such consciousness, though the British occupation of India had stiff regional resistance to overcome. Western rule generated discontents on one hand, ambitions on the other. Both could lead to a conviction that what was necessary was for a people to form itself into a nation, and move towards freedom.

Such an idea could only dawn first in minds with access to foreign education and example; to gather force it had to expand much wider. Would-be leaders had to convince their people that the plight of most of them was due to foreign injustice. What was known in Indian nationalist circles early in this century as the 'drain theory' (it was originated partly by British sympathizers) taught that India was poor because of tribute carried off year by year to Britain. This argument and its many parallels elsewhere had an underlying basis of fact, as well as some exaggerations; they disguised what was equally true, that a great many Indians and others were exploited by their own countrymen. If of course these fellow-countrymen sided with the foreigner when it came to a tug of war, their social misconduct as well as their unpatriotic attitude could be given due emphasis.

Grievances took many specific forms; they were all heightened by the psychological impact of foreign rule, the arrogance of the white man and his unconcealed belief in the inferiority of those under his sometimes harsh authority. Too many of those with modern qualifications, higher or lower, had to compete for government posts which were always too few, for want of other employment. The more highly qualified wanted better positions, civil and

military, to be opened to them instead of reserved for white men. They desired a share in government, modest enough at first. They could find allies among businessmen of the newer sort, learning the ways of foreign traders and millowners and then aspiring to rival them, as they were doing by the 1920s in the jute industry in Bengal. It was a growing complaint that native industry was not protected by tariffs, as it was in industrializing nations in the West.

Lower down, and frequently breaking out in small local revolts or riots, usually quite separate from any organized national movement, were protests against land taxes paid by peasants, or in some African colonies poll taxes; erosion of customary rights on waste lands or in forests; compulsory labour, and in some empires, especially the French, conscription into the armies that all empires raised in their colonies and often made use of abroad, even, during both world wars, in Europe.

Resolve to modify and eventually terminate colonial rule could either follow a mainly peaceful, 'constitutional' path, or resort to force. Which course was taken depended both on a country's history and social structure and culture, and on the attitude of the ruling power. Gandhi's tactics, with their emotionally religious colouring, were peculiar to Hindu India; they could only be practicable under a regime as comparatively liberal and restrained as the British. A French or German viceroy at Delhi would have given the Mahatma a much shorter answer. British officialdom had to harmonize, allowing for some time-lag, with the trend of opinion at home. There had been grave lapses earlier: in Ireland in 1798, in India in 1857–8 during the Mutiny, in Jamaica in 1865. Britons were infected, it must be added, more than most Europeans with racial prejudice. Still, after 1858 it was only once, in the Punjab in an end-of-war hysteria in 1919, that the British in India ran amok. The French temper was more militaristic. French authority in Indochina rested too heavily on the Foreign Legion; in North Africa it lay, notoriously, more with the army of occupation than with the government in Paris. Serious opposition could take only one form, insurrection.

The 1857 explosion belonged to an old India more than a new, and failed to spread outside the Ganges valley. It did bring Muslims and Hindus together, and in this century has been looked back on as the starting point of Indian nationalism. Most provinces however were quiescent for long periods after their conquest, so that British rule could take on an aspect of naturalness and permanence. A generation after the Mutiny feeling of a new political sort was stirring, at first within an English-educated elite nourished on English historical annals, from Hampden to Gladstone. In 1885 the Indian National Congress was launched, with some British encouragement. It was at first no more than an association of public-spirited members of the small professional elite, with English education and ideas, meeting annually to discuss the country's needs; little by little it learned to mobilize broad popular support for its proposals, and grew into a regular political party, India's first and biggest. Provision of cautious safety valves was the official response. One was a newspaper press, tolerated though carefully watched. Local government bodies elected on a narrow franchise were set up, and subsequently given greater scope; they gave politicians, many of them lawyers, their first foothold. In a non-committal way ministers let it be understood that India was being trained for self-government in some unspecified future.

This moderate reformism, respected on both sides, on the Indian side was accompanied by loud and not insincere professions of loyalty to the British connection. Impatience was growing, none the less. All Britain's colonies of white settlement had been granted self-government: it was a parallel process to the extension of voting rights at home, and the American revolution had been a warning against delay. But Indians could not help asking why preference over them in this respect should be given to Afrikaners, a very few years after the Boer War when they had been denounced as worse than barbarians. Bengal, the oldest British province, was the first to begin erupting, in the years before 1914, with a boycott of British goods and some limited terrorist activity. Here Ireland was the model. During the 1914–18 years the National Congress both expanded and took on a more radical complexion. This reflected wartime pressures on India. Economically there was a boom, which strengthened the commercial and industrial sectors, while high prices and shortages inflicted painful hardships on the public. Politically, there was much talk in the Allied camp of this being a war for freedom and progress; the setting up at its end of the League of Nations was supposed by nationalists in many lands, as far away as Korea, to herald a new age.

Gandhi was now the moving spirit in the Congress, with his tactics of mass mobilization combined with non-violence and 'civil disobedience'. They appealed most to the middle classes; workers and peasants were organizing on different lines, with partly communist leadership, and the critical points in their struggles did not coincide with those of the national movement. This was a weakness for it, but at the same time, preserved Congress from internal class division or socialist infection. Wealthy businessmen, always averse to left-wing nationalism, were therefore ready with financial support. They had much to hope from independence. Another Congress defect was that, remaining in many ways a socially conservative body, it had a solidly Hindu and anti-Muslim right wing. Jawaharlal Nehru, with his socialist sympathies, wanted it to draw in the Muslim masses, by taking up their social and economic complaints; Congress could not do so, because these complaints were directed against the wealthier Hindus as well as against the British. From the later 1930s Muslim communalists preaching separation were gaining ground. During the war years the Muslim League headed by Jinnah was at liberty to push its propaganda, while Congress was in opposition and its leaders, after the defeat of the 'August rising' of 1942, were in prison.

After the war independence was inevitable, if only because Britain was tired, and could no longer rely on the loyalty of the now very large Indian armed forces. The Labour government elected in 1945 was sensible enough to recognize this, and independence came in 1947; but so did partition, and communal massacres on a horrific scale, the plunge into bloodshed that Gandhian politics had been designed to prevent. With India given up, Burma and Ceylon necessarily followed. Labour ministers were slow to realize that Africa was waking up, but by 1960, when Nigeria was set free, British Tories also agreed that there was no alternative. They made an exception of colonies where white settlement had taken place. In West Africa climate and disease had prevented this from happening. In Kenya and Rhodesia guerrilla struggles were fought.

Everywhere in the colonial world the slump years around 1930 had been a calamitous time, and intensified dislike of Western rule. In Indonesia and Indochina there were attempts at armed risings. After 1945 the Dutch fought in vain to recover control of Indonesia, where the nationalist party had expanded, as in Burma, under Japanese patronage. Discredited by France's collapse early in the war, the French empire could not be set right either by massacres in Algeria and Madagascar or by the unveiling of a 'French Union' in 1946 which differed from the empire only in name. In Vietnam there were many causes of discontent, among them the seizure of land to be turned into plantations by French settlers, and ill-treatment of labour on them. Restoration of French power was at once resisted. In the north the lead was quickly taken by Ho Chi Minh and the communists, who as in Malaya had been fighting the Japanese (while the French submitted to them). They were recruited mainly from the peasantry, but as in many countries were joined by students, and more gradually by a good part of the old-fashioned, largely rural, intelligentsia. Guerrilla operations led by stages to the creation of the field army which in 1954 defeated and captured a French army at Dienbienphu.

The French gave up and withdrew, but their place was soon taken by the Americans, who persisted in a dreadfully destructive attempt to crush the national movement until 1972. In the meantime, a few months after Dienbienphu the Algerian revolt led by the FLN (National Liberation Front) broke out. Algerians too had been deprived of much of their land to make way for French or cosmopolitan planters. Algeria was in theory, or legal fiction, a part of France, not a colony, and the settlers, backed by the army, vetoed any withdrawal. In 1958 the postwar Fourth Republic fell, and De Gaulle returned to power. In 1961 he in turn was almost overthrown by the army, but in 1962 he was strong enough, as well as rational enough, to abandon the conflict. Fighting had not risen above the guerrilla level, but it had inflicted enormous damage on the Algerian people.

In 1919 the Third or Communist International was set up at Moscow, with a programme of activity in the colonies as well as in the West. Socialism, usually in its communist form, became a factor in nationalist agitation nearly everywhere, and especially when fighting was involved. It could come to the front either because, as in Vietnam and China, middle-class parties failed to show the necessary qualities, or because no such classes or parties existed, as in Portuguese Africa. Within various nationalist movements there was chronic controversy as to whether communist membership or collaboration should be accepted, and within communist parties as to whether they ought to cooperate with 'bourgeois nationalists' or stand apart and organize the working class and peasantry separately. In India communists were always viewed with suspicion by Congress conservatives and their capitalist allies, as well as by the religious zealots, and themselves viewed Congress, and Gandhi personally, as timidly reformist and compromising. They kept out of the 1942 rising, when Congress came closest to adopting revolutionary tactics like their own, because it was damaging to the war effort, and consequently to the USSR. Thereby they forfeited much public respect.

Much of the value of colonial liberation movements lay in their effect on archaic social structures, shaking them up more thoroughly than colonial rule – in some ways petrifying – had done. Women, for instance, took a considerable part in both political and military activities. Armed struggle required popular energies to be fully enlisted. Where it triumphed, native collaborators of the colonial regime were swept away with it; though a war as devastating as Vietnam's might leave a country too exhausted for any rapid recovery. On the other hand, the slighter the effort the more likely was imperial rule to be exchanged only for neo-colonial. Colonies turned adrift without any preparation, as those in sub-Saharan Africa were by De Gaulle, or the Congo by Belgium, were left stagnating, or in chaos. Malaya has been somnolent ever since the British, after defeating a rising by guerrillas from the Chinese half of the population, entrusted power to the native Malays and their safely conservative chiefs.

When India became free the British-trained civil service, which had been loyal to the last to its old masters, was taken over unchanged by their successors; but its inertia was counteracted by the radical outlook of Nehru and the more progressive Congress wing. India remained faithful to the British model of parliamentary government. After armed conflict as in China or Cuba, the outcome was likely to be some form of left-wing dictatorship. Where there was no meaningful popular struggle, as in the Philippines or Pakistan or the Congo, it was a dictatorship of the Right.

See also COLONIALISM.

Reading
Betts, Raymond F. 1985: *Uncertain Dimensions: Western Overseas Empires in the Twentieth Century.*
Davidson, Basil 1955: *The African Awakening.*
Fanon, Frantz 1961 (*1983*): *The Wretched of the Earth.*
Gupta, Partha Sarathi 1975: *Imperialism and the British Labour Movement, 1914–1964.*

Hodgkin, Thomas 1981: *Vietnam: The Revolutionary Path*.

Kiernan, V.G. 1982: *From Conquest to Collapse: European Empires from 1815 to 1960*.

Mansfield, Peter 1971: *The British in Egypt*.

Sarkar, Sunit 1989: *Modern India, 1885–1947*.

Seal, Anil 1968: *The Emergence of Indian Nationalism*.

Wolf, Eric R. 1971: *Peasant Wars of the Twentieth Century*.

V.G. KIERNAN

colonialism This term has come to stand for forcible, long-term occupation by a metropolitan country of territory outside Europe (or the USA).

Territorial conquest, inspired by a great variety of motives, seems to have run all through history, wherever there have been peoples above the most unsophisticated level. It was carried furthest by modern Europeans. By the mid-nineteenth century their ownership of most of the New World had been shaken off, but it had been imposed on much of Asia: above all on India, the grandest of colonies; and, in the second rank, on the Philippines by Spain, on Indonesia by Holland, and on Siberia by Russia.

The period from the 1870s to 1914 has often been called the 'age of imperialism', when the hunt for colonies reached its climax; a prominent feature of it was 'the scramble for Africa', on lines agreed on at the Berlin Conference in 1884. Among the old treasure-hunters, Britain occupied Malaya and what was left of Burma, and much of Africa; zest for empire reached its hysterical height in the Boer War of 1899–1902. French power expanded in northern Africa and Indochina. Portuguese expeditions were pushing inland from their old coastal settlements in Angola and Mozambique. Newcomers were Germany, active in Africa and the Pacific, and Italy in eastern and northern Africa. Japanese modernization was accompanied by a precocious emulation of Western colonialism; in 1894–5 China was defeated and Taiwan annexed. The United States, swollen by continual wars against Amerindians and seizure of large territories from Mexico, in 1899 picked a quarrel with Spain and entered the world arena by annexing the Philippines and Puerto Rico, and turning Cuba into a protectorate.

Competition for colonies had been the cause of many wars of the seventeenth and eighteenth centuries, and it began again to intensify dangerously. In 1904–5 Japan defeated Russia in a war over Manchuria. Italy's seizure of Libya in 1911 led to war with Turkey. In 1914 World War I was set off in part by colonial ambitions. It brought fresh gains to the winners, who took over the German and Turkish possessions, nominally as 'mandates' to be supervised by the new League of Nations. In the 1930s Italy overran Ethiopia, and Japan, having occupied Manchuria, launched its massive attempt to subjugate all the rest of China.

Many theories were put forward, at the time and later, to explain why industrialized nations were seeking colonies so feverishly. Most celebrated was one advanced by Lenin during World War I. A good deal of this was taken over from the English liberal economist J. A. Hobson, writing under the fresh impression of the Boer War; and much else from the Austrian economist Rudolf Hilferding's book *Finance Capital*, published in 1910. According to these men's thinking, at this late stage in capitalist evolution control of capital was coming to be concentrated more and more in a few hands, which left too little purchasing power in the home market for the commodities that could be produced. Because of this underconsumption, capital was being exported instead of invested at home, and in undeveloped regions, which might contain valuable raw materials, it needed the protection of a colonial government. In fact, however, most capital, even in the case of the biggest exporter, Britain, was going not to colonies but to other industrial countries, above all the USA.

There can in reality be no single explanation. In particular cases much of the expansionism may be traced to the desire of frontier officials or army men to distinguish themselves, or to special business interests. Governments could always count on colonial successes to impress both foreigners and their own voters. Territory was often considered worth having for strategic reasons; here the British, with their worldwide possessions and 'spheres of interest', came first. They wanted Egypt partly to protect their route to India, Afghanistan to close a door into India against the Russians. Military costs might be high, but once in occupation invaders could expand their manpower cheaply by recruiting native soldiers, from suitable classes or ethnic groups, and employing them on policing or for further acquisitions. The large Indian army, commanded by British officers, was made use of in a great deal of campaigning outside India, at the expense of the Indian taxpayer. Some colonial governments resorted, unlike the British, to conscription of native troops. For the French indeed, acutely conscious after 1870 of their numerical inferiority to the Germans, a reservoir of colonial manpower to draw on could be thought of as one of the prime rewards of empire.

At bottom the motives of colonialism were economic. Raw materials were wanted for manufactures, and markets for the products. Trade swelled chiefly between industrial countries, but there was stiffening competition as industrialism spread, and protective tariffs threatened to close many outlets. In its own colonies a British company could expect a favoured position, a French company a monopolistic one. Most colonies must have meant a net loss to national economies, but there were always some who profited. Britain's huge empire undoubtedly yielded huge gains, largely of a parasitic sort which may have had the bad effect of tilting the economy away from productive activity. Indian exports of opium, tea and jute gave Britain a favourable trade balance instead of a deficit.

In Britain as elsewhere profits went chiefly to the stock exchange, business, the civil and military services. It was another contention of Lenin's that some 'crumbs' from the feast found their way to the more privileged strata of the working classes, and by raising their standard of living reconciled them to capitalist rule. What may have been more important was the employers' ability to tell workers that they were living better because they had colonies, not because they had trade unions. Britain's empire besides was unique (apart from Siberia) in containing vast areas, such as Canada and Australia, suited to white settlement. They offered a better life to poor emigrants, and this was certainly a weighty reason for the empire's popularity. Few ordinary folk cared much about India or black Africa. Italian propaganda made much of the opportunities for settlement by poor peasants that Ethiopia could provide.

Until well into this century Europe's social structure, and Britain's in particular, made available numbers of men to whom colonial administration was congenial. They came especially from among younger sons of the landed gentry, a class which could claim a natural gift for ruling natives because it had always been accustomed to ruling its own peasantry. England entered the twentieth century with its countryside still surprisingly feudal, though economically capitalist. There was no analogous class in the USA, and less wish for direct colonial rule. From the same sources were drawn the officers of the European armies which con-

quered and garrisoned the colonies. In countries like India with a fair degree of literacy it was as easy to find the assistants indispensable for running the administration as it was to recruit soldiers.

A great deal was heard of the white man's 'civilizing mission', and there was some fitful determination to make a clean sweep of bad old ways and modernize everything. Before long this was giving way to a preference for 'indirect rule', through indigenous institutions and methods familiar to the people. Too much innovation could be judged unsettling and risky. In India the 'Mutiny' of 1857 could plausibly be attributed to this, and after it the ousting of native rulers was abandoned: instead they were treated as junior partners, subject to the minimum of inspection. A quarter of the population was left under their usually unenlightened sway. Relations with the semi-feudal landowning classes surviving from before British rule, or in some provinces created by it, grew increasingly cordial, to the detriment of the hard-pressed tillers of the soil. In Java the Dutch likewise entered into partnership with the heirs of the old aristocracy. In the Philippines the Americans did much the same. A French champion of similar methods was Marshal L. H. Lyautey, Resident-General from 1912 to 1925 in Morocco; a Catholic conservative, he could appreciate the convenience of Islamic conservatism, and the hazards of disturbing it. In Morocco, Indochina, Russian Central Asia, old monarchies were propped up and kept as figureheads. In Africa all European regimes made use of tribal 'chiefs', many of them, with no real claim to such rank, set up by district officials to play an appropriate part.

This strategy was unwelcome to intelligent Africans and Asians, who wanted modernization instead, and to Europeans who had expected beneficial change. One of these was Karl Marx. He held that seizure of colonies sprang from nothing better than brutal greed, but might give a necessary though painful shock to societies long sunk in torpor, and jerk them forward. Nationalist feeling leads many in Asia and Africa nowadays to deny any such necessity, and to argue – questionably – that their countries had been quite capable of making progress on their own, with some borrowing from Europe, just as Japan did. A later offshoot of Marxism, 'dependency theory', goes much further, asserting (still less convincingly) that Afro-Asian countries only became 'backward' and poor when they were reduced to colonies; it was by plundering them that Europe was able to accumulate capital, industrialize, and forge ahead.

Except at moments of excitement, usually when a campaign was going on, few Europeans took any lively interest in colonial affairs, and officials and businessmen were left with a free hand. Catholics and socialists combined at one time to bring about some improvements in Germany's African colonies. An international protest against the atrocities perpetrated in King Leopold's private colony of the Congo led to its taking over in 1908 by the Belgian government. In general political terms imperialism was firmly supported by right-wing parties, and less ardently by liberals. Communists were strongly against it; other socialists wavered, and, like the Labour Party in Britain, criticized it lukewarmly if at all.

Effects of colonialism varied with local circumstances and historical backgrounds. It ended the turmoil which had sometimes prevailed, and took pride in its guardianship of order. Order might often mean nothing better than police rule, especially for poorer people exposed to it, and Western laws might be ill suited to the societies they were imposed on. Still, the principle of impartial justice, an impersonal rule of law, was a valuable innovation. So (if not in all respects) was the advent, for the first time in history outside Europe, of a body of professional lawyers, willing and able to take up cases against the government.

Economic development was oftener than not neglected; predictably in the case of Britain, whose government felt equally little responsibility for it at home. In India (and in Egypt) its best achievement lay in irrigation, where it had a stake of its own because land revenue was for long its mainstay. It built a considerable infrastructure of roads, railways and communications. It did enough for health to begin the reduction of epidemics which formerly kept population increase within bounds. It only very belatedly organized any effective system of famine relief. It could be accused by nationalists of impoverishing the peasantry, and of hindering instead of fostering industry, for the benefit of British exports. Manufactured imports could also be blamed for crippling native handicrafts and spreading unemployment.

World War II gave a mortal blow to colonialism. Italy and Japan were knocked out. Britain was left overstrained, and its people in no humour to go on fighting. With foolish obstinacy Holland, France and Portugal went on for years trying to hold on to their possessions, under the specious Cold War pretext of a fight against communism. So far as real economic interests were concerned, white soldiers and officials had become superfluous. Colonial peoples, or at any rate the elites which had been emerging, were accustomed to their new place in a world mostly belonging to a single complex, and wanted to make the best of it. Decolonization was the rational choice, and was warmly favoured by the USA. Ever since entering the world market as an industrial exporter, in the 1890s, America had preached 'open door' ideas; now it felt that the time had come for empires and their barriers and restrictions to be dismantled, leaving all markets to be captured by the strongest competitor – itself.

Decolonization left true independence still a distant goal. In the world economy into which ex-colonies were sucked, most of them could have only a weak and vulnerable position. Imperial rule was replaced by a 'neo-colonialism' which subjected the weaker to the stronger through unequal economic relations. Such relations had always existed, side by side with direct political and military control. Much of Latin America in the nineteenth century had been financially dominated by Europe, whose 'informal empire' there was now being taken over by the USA. China was only the biggest of a good many countries often referred to as 'semi-colonies', until the communist revolution put an end to its subservience to the West. Semi-colonies – Persia for one – sometimes fared worse than colonies, in the opinion of many observers.

Few of the countries now nominally free had respectable leadership; many fell before long under dictators, easily manipulated from outside. World capitalism on the contrary was more powerfully organized, with the rise of the 'multinational corporations' and the American hegemony, than in its divided past. All the new countries, though they might, like Indonesia, be rich in resources, needed loans, investments, help of all kinds. 'Aid', direct or through institutions like the World Bank and the International Monetary Fund, could be made use of to dictate economic policies. Governments unwilling to fall into line could as a rule be got rid of, or in the official American term 'destabilized', without much difficulty. Examples were that of Mossadeq in Persia in 1953, and that of Allende in Chile in 1974. Both these leaders paid for their recalcitrance with their lives. In the USA's Caribbean 'backyard' what had been entitled 'gun boat diplomacy' continued.

In a few countries, notably South Korea and Taiwan, and for some years Brazil, foreign investments and technology, combined with rule by American-backed dictators, brought about remarkable industrial growth, though the workers' share in the profits has been small. Everywhere Western banks have been making loans on a prodigious scale to 'developing' countries; most of the borrowers have found it hard, some impossible, to keep up their interest payments, and some loans have had to be written off. The gap between advanced and retarded countries is widening instead of narrowing. Neo-colonialism harms poor countries: whether it benefits rich ones in any real way must be doubted. It is not long since empires were thought vital to their owners' prosperity, yet Europe, having lost them, is more prosperous than ever.

See also COLONIAL LIBERATION MOVEMENT.

Reading

Bull, Hedley and Watson, Adam eds 1984: *The Expansion of International Society*.
Etherington, Norman 1984: *Theories of Imperialism: War, Conquest and Capital*.
Fieldhouse, D.K. 1966: *The Colonial Empires: A Comparative Survey from the Eighteenth Century*.
Gopal, S. 1965: *British Policy in India 1858–1905*.
Hobsbawm, E.J. 1987: *The Age of Empire 1875–1914*.
Hobson, J.A. 1902 (*1968*): *Imperialism: A Study*.
Magnus, Philip 1958 (*1968*): *Kitchener, Portrait of an Imperialist*.
Mommsen, Wolfgang J. and Osterhammel, Jürgen eds 1986: *Imperialism and After: Continuities and Discontinuities*.
Pomeroy, William J. 1970: *American Neo-Colonialism: Its Emergence in the Philippines and Asia*.
Thornton, A.P. 1978: *Imperialism in the Twentieth Century*.

V. G. KIERNAN

commodity fetishism   A characteristic of capitalist society first identified by Marx. In a society based on private property in which market relations predominate, processes of production are independent of one another, separated and private. Only in the market are the labours performed in such processes commensurated one with another through reduction to the common standard of money – in this way private labour is rendered social. But the relation between private and social labour appears as an objective property of the commodity output itself, as in a phrase like 'this commodity is worth ten pounds'. The social relations established in historically specific processes of producing things disappear from view and appear instead as something different, as relations between acquisitive ahistorical individuals and the commodities they seek to acquire as consumers. Production relations are dissolved into market relations, class relations are dissolved into an individualism of utility maximization, and the inanimate products of labour appear to possess the animate properties of their producers and to exercise domination over them. Marx interpreted this as an inversion of subject into object, produced by the alienation, or separation, of the producers from the products of their labour in capitalist society, and he considered any analysis which replicated that inversion by personifying things and objectifying people as necessarily supportive of capitalism rather than critical of it.

That the social world of capitalism is constituted by a set of appearances which are different from the underlying reality is obviously the foundation for any theory of IDEOLOGY. Consequently, that appearance or form is different from essence or substance implied for Marx a scientific endeavour (via a process of abstraction) to uncover the latter from the sense impressions yielded by the former. Finally, he considered that when production relations were socialized so that there was no private property in the means of production, the contrast between essence and appearance would disappear; social relations would no longer be mediated through market relations but would be immediately transparent in the democratic and conscious coordination of labouring activity.

The twentieth century has seen this questioned in three different ways. First, positivists have denied the existence of any meaningful distinction between essence and appearance. The appearances of reality are just what reality is, and the only illusions or delusions that exist are either inventions of misguided social theorists or psychological misperceptions of the social observer. However, being based on different premises, this criticism fails to engage with the philosophical realism of Marxism and hence the notion of systemic rather than just perceptual difference between essence and appearance.

A second approach also questions whether reality is constituted by a set of appearances which must be peeled away to reveal its inner essence, but from a rationalist standpoint which insists on the distinction between the object of knowledge and the real object, and the cognitive appropriation of the latter by the former through practice. But simultaneously the individuals who on one level are just the bearers of systemic structures also subjectively experience and relate to their conditions of existence; they do this by a system of representations and this process transforms them into subjects. The contrast between essence and appearance is thus denied and in its place is substituted a contrast between systemic and experiential existence. However, this latter must be a property of any society, in contrast to the former's restriction to capitalist society.

A rather different approach arises out of reflection on Soviet experience. First, as a matter of fact, while market phenomena there have different forms and different functions from their counterparts in capitalist society, several generations of post-1917 Soviet experience do not seem to have eradicated the ALIENATION characteristic of commodity fetishism. Second, as a matter of theory, in reforming centralized planning towards some variant of market socialism, one issue is whether commodity fetishism would necessarily emerge as an outcome of greater reliance on market forces. In part this turns on whether market relations can be detached from private property relations, whether, that is, a socialized market makes either conceptual or practical sense. This has obvious implications for any theorization of what socialism might mean as the twentieth century draws to a close.

Reading

Geras, N. 1971: Essence and appearance: aspects of fetishism in Marx's *Capital*. *New Left Review* 65, 69–86.
Marx, K. 1867 (*1976*): *Capital*, vol. 1, especially chs 1, 6, 19, 23, 24.
Rubin, I.I. 1928 (*1973*): *Essays on Marx's Theory of Value*.

SIMON MOHUN

communication   As well as the specific communicative processes studied in linguistics, SOCIOLINGUISTICS and social psychology, a broader concept of communication has been a major theme of social thought. Aristotle saw the state as a community involving communication between a multiplicity of individual perspectives. Whereas this concerns individual purposive action in the political sphere, Aquinas introduced into medieval Christian thought a broader theoretical conception in which God's nature is communicated in the creation of his creatures. This model led to the generalization of the concept of communication to all human beings and at the same time to a differentiation, which became central for modernity, between the particular (political) and the universal (social) communication community.

This idealizing extension of the concept of communication to all human beings, and its simultaneous differentiation into political and social communication, made it a favoured point of reference for modern sociology and social philosophy. Marx, in the *Grundrisse*, uses the differentiation between political and social communication to turn Aristotle's *zoon politikon* into a 'society' of individuals 'acting and speaking together'. C.S. Peirce analyses the scientific community from the perspective of an (idealized) communication community, and G.H. Mead brings the social processes of individualization by means of socialization into the framework of a 'universal discourse'. The point of this theoretical universalization of the communication community is the claim that, as Jürgen Habermas (1981, p. 105) puts it, 'the social life-process has an inbuilt relation to truth.' This *universalization*, along with the *socialization* (including 'depoliticization' or internal differentiation) of the concept of communication is a characteristic feature of the postmetaphysical thought of MODERNITY, marking a radical break between social scientific thought and the political thought of the ancient world and the classics of political philosophy.

One can understand communication as a means of solving the 'Hobbesian' problem of social order. How can the action plans of several actors be coordinated with one another? If one follows Talcott Parsons in the analysis of situations of *double contingency*, one is struck by the extreme improbability of ordered interaction sequences and communicative agreements. Even in a very simplified laboratory situation with two actors and three possible orientations (for example 'selfish', 'generous' and 'hostile'), reciprocal expectations of expectations yield 9^7 possible combinations. Hence all communication is based on complexity-reducing mechanisms such as 'mutual trust', normality expectations, etc. The actors can maintain or modify this *stabilized* communicative order by the exercise of external *influence* on the *effects* of the actions of the others, or they can re-produce and re-construct it by means of an internal *agreement* on generalizable grounds.

Communication, then, must be seen as a form of action. Whereas the classical concept of action is based on the differentiation between subject and object and between means and ends, the more recent social scientific concept of communication is based on that between ego and alter. Communicative action in Habermas's theory aims ultimately at a rational agreement between ego and alter. Whereas purposive-rational or even value-rational actions form a system by latching on to *other actions*, communicative actions form a social system by attaching themselves to the actions *of others*. To this distinction correspond different conceptions of RATIONALITY AND REASON. Whereas classical Aristotelian theories of action, right down to Max Weber, link the means–ends framework with the concept of purposive or success-oriented rationality, Habermas's theory of social or intersubjective action, which he also calls 'action oriented to mutual understanding', is based on the concept of *communicative rationality*. This pragmatic-communicative concept of rationality going back to Peirce, Mead and Hans-Georg Gadamer's hermeneutics not only sets limits to the generalizability of the means–ends schema, but also goes beyond the limitations of traditional European thought to a reflexive metaphysics of subject and object (compare Rorty, 1980).

Further differentiation of the concept of communication opens up a wide variety of theoretical and empirical perspectives. The differentiation between verbal and non-verbal communication shows that communication between those present is unavoidable (Watzlawick et al., 1967). Corresponding to the distinction between direct and indirect communication is the important difference between simple social systems involving face-to-face communication and complex ones based on mediated communication between physically distant participants (see Luhmann, 1972). The opposition between symmetry and asymmetry is central not just to role theory but also to theories of the ideal conditions of communication (see Habermas, 1971). The differentiation between symmetrical and asymmetrical conditions of communication is important for distinguishing between distorted or disturbed and undistorted communication. This distinction in turn is basic to various theories of communication pathologies (Watzlawick et al., 1967; Habermas, 1988), and of the reconstruction and critique of ideologies (Apel, 1973).

See also DISCOURSE; MASS MEDIA.

Reading
Apel, K.O. 1973 (*1980*): *Towards a Transformation of Philosophy*.
Cashdan, A. and Jordan, M. 1987: *Studies in Communication*.
Habermas, Jürgen 1981 (*1984*): *The Theory of Communicative Action*, vol. 1.
Mellor, D.H. ed. 1990: *Ways of Communicating*.
Rorty, R. 1980: *Philosophy and the Mirror of Nature*.

HAUKE BRUNKHORST

communism A term covering a family of closely related concepts designating (1) a type of human society, (2) theories describing and justifying a communist society, (3) political movements trying to create a communist society. The term 'primitive communism' is used by many Marxists to designate the early stages of human society. Soviet and East European authors, however, generally prefer expressions such as 'primitive society', 'primitive communalist society' or 'tribal society'.

A minimal list of properties necessary for a society to be called *communist* includes common ownership of the means of production (but not neccessarily the means of consumption), self-government in all areas of life, and freedom. Communist theories claim that these properties also provide the neccessary conditions for human happiness (although they might not be sufficient for securing everybody's happiness). Theories of communism usually stress the absence under communism of some characteristics of contemporary societies, like class exploitation (Lenin allowed for exploitation of weak-willed persons by strong-willed ones), money, commodities, permanent government officials and standing armies.

Engels used the terms 'private ownership' and 'common ownership' to denote ownership by one person and ownership by more than one person respectively. A cooperative or a shareholding company were cases of common ownership. A distinction is sometimes made between capitalist common ownership (the shareholders of the firm are not the employees of the same firm) and communist common ownership (the shareholders are the employees of the same firm). Lenin claimed that under capitalism any form of ownership is capitalistic. He considered cooperatives to be capitalist enterprises under capitalism and communist ones under a communist system.

Communist theories usually contrast communism with capitalism, a society with private ownership, production of commodities for sale on free markets, and with free labour and capital markets. For the early writers (T. More, T. Campanella), communism was probably an alternative to capitalism; later it became treated as a post-capitalist society. Some viewed it as a natural state of society, while other writers (Saint-Simon, Fourier, Marx) placed it within a necessary sequence of societal types, to come immediately after capitalism. It was generally implicit in the writings of the nineteenth-century authors that there is only a single sequence of possible societal types. This view was accepted by Russian Bolsheviks and their followers. For the majority of theorists, communism was the final stage of development; Marx supported this eschatological view in his 1844 Paris Manuscripts (Marx, 1844). After 1845, Marx and Engels abandoned eschatology, accepted the idea of other societal types following communism, but claimed that speculation about further developments was meaningless because the necessary evidence would be present only when the later stages of communism had been reached. This view was rejected by the majority of Soviet writers in the 1960s, but came to be accepted by a number of them.

It has never been proven beyond reasonable doubt that societies satisfying the conditions of applicability of the term 'communist' have actually existed. With no democracy in the USSR, the claim that its people owned the means of production is certainly false. Mass slavery, feudal serfdom for the peasants, and totalitarian dictatorship in Stalin's USSR, had no relation to anything called 'communist' in the traditional nineteenth-century sense. After 1953, a dual ownership of the means of production emerged, consisting of a higher-level collective owner (the hierarchically organized Politbureau at the summit of the Communist Party of the Soviet Union) and two parallel lower-level collective owners (the party and the government hierarchies). The employees were definitely not the owners of their respective enterprises. The Chinese and most East European systems were basically similar to that of the USSR.

The prevailing early form of communist theories was a blueprint of a future society designed for general happiness that sometimes used utopian fiction as a literary device. A penetrating critique of the contemporary society was usually added. In the Paris Manuscripts of 1844 Marx provided a philosophical justification of communism. The latter was seen as the means to realize an essential value (humanism, achieved by overcoming the ALIENA-

TION of labour). After 1845, Marx and Engels began to oppose blueprint theories, claiming that it was impossible to provide a full design for future free and creative activity. Thus, they declined to develop a systematic treatment or description of the properties of communist society. They justified communism now as the means of overcoming the basic conflicts within capitalism, liberating the working class and ensuring human progress. Communism was to be possible only after all the available options for the development of the means of production within capitalism were exhausted. Marx never provided an analysis of the level of productive forces that he deemed to be incompatible with the future existence of capitalism. In the 1840s he thought that capitalism had already reached saturation point, but he later admitted having made a mistake. Marx (1867) seems to think that the point of change from capitalism to communism will arrive when the overwhelming majority of mankind will become wage-earners (or working class). Lenin in his later works claimed that a working-class government can use political power to build up the forces of production to the level necessary for the survival of communism but he did not provide any articulated description of that level.

The twentieth-century communist literature deals primarily with the transition from capitalism to communism and avoids detailed discussion of the concept itself. A. Nove has argued that Marx's (and, by implication, Lenin's) communism is not feasible. Thus, Marx was as utopian as were his predecessors. M. Cornforth rejected the idea that communism is a developmental stage (or a mode of production) and claims that it is a moral and political way of life which is based on rights of individuals in their all-round development and freedom.

Lenin insisted in 1917 that Marx used 'socialism' to refer to the first stage of communism, which is characterized by the common ownership of the means of production, retention of the state, absence of economic classes, but also the absence of an ability to satisfy fully the (material) needs of the people. Socialism was to be preceded by the dictatorship of the proletariat (Lenin, 1917). Some writers have treated SOCIALISM as a separate stage which is possibly parallel to communism.

Marx used the term 'communist' to designate the political movement accepting his ideas, or any working-class movement intended to create the communist society. He certainly supported violent revolution and the dictatorship of the proletariat, but he presupposed that under capitalism a non-democratic government, combined with permanent officialdom and a professional army, would in any case use violence to oppose the majority decision to introduce communism and he thought it would be a case of a large (probably 80–95 per cent) majority coercing a small minority. Working-class parties at the end of the nineteenth century usually called themselves socialist or social democratic. After 1917, the term 'communist' was used to describe the parties that accepted violent revolution and the dictatorship of the proletariat as the means of transition to communism, and 'socialism' described those who rejected it. Lenin insisted that only a Marxist party was to be called 'communist' and that government by a single communist party was an essential trait of the dictatorship of the proletariat. He abandoned the requirement for a predominantly working-class society as a starting point of a transition to communism. (Later he admitted that the dictatorship of the proletariat in Russia had degenerated into a dictatorship of the Communist Party and the Red Army over all classes of society.) Western communist parties accepted Soviet claims about the nature of Soviet society in most cases until the end of the 1960s. They are now abandoning the idea of the dictatorship of the proletariat and even the description 'communist'.

Reading

Cornforth, M. 1980: *Communism and Philosophy: Contemporary Dogmas and Revisions of Marxism.*
Marx, K. and Engels, F. 1848 (*1967*): *The Communist Manifesto.*
Moore, S. 1980: *Marx on the Choice between Socialism and Communism.*
Nove, A. 1977: *The Soviet Economic System.*
—— 1983: *The Economics of Feasible Socialism.*
Roemer, J. ed. 1986: *Analytical Marxism.*

EERO LOONE

community   One of the most vague and elusive concepts in social science, community continues to defy precise definition. Part of the problem stems from the diversity of meanings attributed to the term and the emotive overtones it usually conjures up. It has become an omnibus word used to describe social units varying from villages, housing estates and local neighbourhoods to ethnic groups, nations and international organizations. At a minimum, community usually denotes a group of people within a bounded geographical area who interact within shared institutions, and who possess a common sense of interdependence and belonging. However, collections of individuals living or interacting within the same territory do not in themselves constitute communities – particularly if those individuals do not perceive themselves as such. What binds a community is not its structure but a state of mind; a *feeling* of community. This subjective dimension renders community problematic as a tool for sociological analysis because the boundaries of any self-identifying group, from the insiders' perspective, are usually fluid and intangible rather than fixed and finite.

Empirical studies of community often confuse description with the sociologist's preconceived assumptions of what community *should be* (Bell and Newby, 1971, p. 21). Another confusion arises from the conflation of community as a social unit or collectivity (club, hamlet, suburb, town) with community as a type of social relationship (based on ties of sentiment or economics). This confusion can be traced to Tönnies (1887) and his seminal concept of *Gemeinschaft*, which represented the integrated, preindustrial, small-scale community based on kinship, friendship and neighbourhood, where social relations are intimate, enduring and multistranded. In Tönnies' formulation, community was contrasted with its obverse, non-community, or *Gesellschaft* ('association') – symbolizing the impersonal, anonymous, contractual and amoral ties characteristic of modern industrial society.

Following Weber and Tönnies, American sociologists, particularly Talcott Parsons, Robert E. Park, Louis Wirth and Robert Redfield, continued to use community as an ideal type on a continuum between two poles such as tradition–modernity, rural–urban and sacred–secular. Implicit in this approach was a nostalgic and romantic view of the past: the assumed emotional cohesion and 'good life' of the traditional community was used to make invidious comparisons with the anonymity, isolation and alienation of modern MASS SOCIETY.

Despite the proliferation of community studies in sociology this empirical approach 'has remained almost entirely sterile at the theoretical level' (Elias, 1974, p. xvi). In the 1960s attempts were made, notably in the work of Clyde Mitchell and Jeremy Boissevain, to develop a more dynamic approach, with the shift of emphasis towards social networks, cliques, factions and non-groups. However, recent anthropological approaches, exemplified by Cohen (1985), have sidestepped the definitional problem of trying to formulate a structural model of community by concentrating instead on *meaning*. For Cohen community is a symbolic entity with no fixed parameters because it exists only in relation and opposition to other perceived communities; a system of VALUES and moral codes which provide its members with a sense of IDENTITY. The idea of community as an 'imagined' entity and symbolic 'idea-force', has also been successfully used in Anderson's (1983) work on the origins of modern NATIONALISM. With its associations of fellowship and communal living, community has long been a key concept in political and religious thought. It is given special emphasis in the socialist and anarchist tradition. The community–association dichotomy can be linked to contrasting political conceptions of society – as a loose association of competing individuals (liberal/Hobbesian view); or as a collective that is more than the sum of its parts, a moralizing agency through which true citizenship can be realized (socialist/Rousseauian view).

As an analytical concept community has little value, despite its continuing importance as a reality in most people's lives. It has become a shibboleth laden with emotive associations of wholeness, cohesion, communion, the public interest and all things good. As Raymond Williams observed (1976, p. 76), 'unlike all other terms of social organisation (state, nation, society, etc.) it seems never to be used unfavourably.' As a result community appears as an adjunct to a host of institutions whenever deep, horizontal and natural comradeship is implied (community care, community centre, the local community, the European Community), however tenuous the links. It has also been appropriated by politicians, planners and architects to legitimize policies in the name of the public interest, however implausible the reality.

Reading
Anderson, Benedict 1983: *Imagined Communities*.
Bell, Colin and Newby, Howard 1971: *Community Studies*.
Cohen, Anthony 1985: *The Symbolic Construction of Community*.
Elias, Norbert 1974: Towards a theory of communities. In *The Sociology of Community*, ed. C. Bell and H. Newby.
Williams, Raymond 1976: *Keywords*.

CRIS SHORE

comparative sociology The adjective 'comparative' has been added before almost all the social sciences (or closely allied fields): anthropology, (study of) civilizations, history, law, linguistics, politics, psychology, sociology. Yet it has always played a minor role within the organization of knowledge. One has to wonder why.

There is one simple reason, often observed. All social research necessarily involves a comparison among cases of some variables, either explicitly or implicitly. Hence all social research is comparative, at which point the adjective becomes redundant. Yet repeatedly, despite this obvious truism, various scholars have advocated the use of the 'comparative' method in social research. But whenever groups of scholars have seemed to band together in furtherance of the 'comparative' method in particular fields of work, they have repeatedly abandoned the term 'comparative' after some time on the grounds that their work was really in some sense a contribution to 'general' theorizing about the field.

The explanation for this seeming anomaly is that the concept of comparative social research as a special subfield is not intrinsic to the logic of the social sciences but is a heuristic device to overcome organizational problems within the social sciences. Comparative sociology (as comparative anthropology, and so on) tends to refer to the study of the differences in structures and processes among *macro*-level units however defined. That is to say, often when particular scholars become suspicious of hypotheses drawn from empirical work on the grounds that the locus of the empirical work was one particular spatiocultural zone, they argue that looking at the relationship of x and y in the contexts of macro units a and b would provide evidence on whether the perceived correlation of x and y is in fact 'universal' or is particular to the macro unit within which it was originally observed. This becomes a call to 'compare' the macro units.

The organizational problem which the periodic demand for comparative study reflects is the fact that most empirical social research from the middle of the nineteenth century to the middle of the twentieth – with, to be sure, some notable (and oft-noted) exceptions – was done by scholars within the framework of a single macro unit. Those who worked in the so-called nomothetic disciplines – economics, sociology, political science (law) – tended to do their empirical work within the boundaries of their own country. This was justified largely on the grounds of universalism. The relations of variables should hold 'universally' and therefore it was not urgent to vary the loci in which they were collected. In practice these were a few countries of Western Europe and the USA. From time to time sceptics advocated the comparative study of these countries.

Those scholars who called themselves historians tended to work on these same countries and on their own country. This was justified, however, on the opposite grounds of particularism. Since each historical situation was particular and complex, its study required total devotion on the part of the scholar, who did well to attain the necessary knowledge of one country and was scarcely able to master the study of two countries. Of course, some scholars studied the history of countries other than their own (as with an English scholar of German history) but they, too, tended to restrict their work to one other country. Calls for 'comparative history' (such as those made by Marc Bloch) fell on even deafer ears than calls for 'comparative sociology'.

Scholars who were orientalists were equally caught up in the belief in particularism and the difficulty of acquiring scholarly expertise, and were thus resistant to the comparative study of 'civilizations'. No doubt there were audacities such as those of outsiders like Max Weber as well as insiders like Max Müller, particularly in the comparison of world-religions, but most orientalists stuck to a narrower last.

The anthropologists were the most torn on the issue. In so far as they were pushed in an ethnographic, that is idiographic, direction, they tended to specialize in one 'tribe' for the same reasons historians specialized in one (Western) nation: the difficulties of acquiring expertise. But in so far as they had nomothetic pretensions, they could not make the logical leap of an economist using data drawn from his own (Western) country, that the data represented a fair sample of the universe. The anthropologists could only validate their nomothetic claims by what came to be called 'cross-cultural' studies.

It is striking nonetheless how rare this kind of comparison of macro-level units was, prior to the mid-twentieth century. The post-1945 era gave an important stimulus however to 'comparative' work, particularly in sociology and political science. The cause was the entry into public consciousness and scholarly awareness of what came to be called the Third World. One institutional response was the growth of area studies, which minimally led to the comparative study of different countries in the same area (such as Latin America, the Middle East)

and maximally led to the 'comparative study of new nations'. After the Twentieth Party Congress of the Communist Party of the Soviet Union in 1956, the subsequent process of 'desatellization' in what had been previously considered in Western countries a monolithic bloc led to the 'comparative study of communism'. Most of this work was done within the framework of MODERNIZATION theory which presumed parallel stages of development for nation-states and hence the possibility of a systematic comparison.

In the post-1968 era, modernization theory went into an eclipse as part of the general undermining of the legitimacy of what had been mainstream social science in the post-1945 years. One of the major criticisms of modernization theory was that it had been 'ahistorical'. The 1970s saw a considerable flourishing consequently of 'historical sociology'. Since, however, this work purported to be 'sociology' and not merely 'historical', it was not at all idiographic in outlook. Thus, implicitly and very often quite explicitly, the 'historical' work was simultaneously 'comparative'. Indeed within sociology the two terms were often combined in the 1980s as 'historical/comparative sociology'.

Comparative sociology has thus always represented a number of vectors simultaneously: antiethnocentrism (see also WORLD-SYSTEM), interest in the macro levels and in complex structures, hence interest in historical detail. Comparative sociology is not a field, but a critique of whatever seems narrow and reductionist in sociology. The disappearance of the term will mean either the great success or the great failure of this critique.

IMMANUEL WALLERSTEIN

competition   The phrase 'to compete' connotes rivalrous activity between two or more individuals or groups. To compete means to try to outdo the other, as in a sporting event.

In economic terminology, however, competition is not so unambiguously defined. The mainstream body of economic thought in the twentieth century came to define competition not as an activity, but as a state of affairs existing in an idealized market – the model of perfect competition. On the other hand, there have existed throughout the twentieth century dissenting voices (spanning the ideological spectrum) that were (are) dissatisfied with this static and idealized definition and seek to explore the actual processes of dynamic competition that occur in the market place.

Scarcity and rationing

Competition is an inevitable result of scarcity. This was not well understood in the history of ideas because the concept of scarcity was confused with material abundance or wealth by most nineteenth-century thinkers. Scarcity does mean simply the lack of an adequate supply of a good, but also something more fundamental. Scarcity is a logical concept, unrelated to wealth, that concerns the passage of time and the necessity of choice. We cannot do everything at once, so we must choose. Economic analysis is about the consequences of those choices.

As a result of scarcity, individuals must establish priorities and ration their time accordingly to achieve them. Similarly, the social system of production and distribution must be premised on some rationing device to cope with the inexorable scarcity that confronts us, be that prices, voting, beauty, or other, and to aid in the allocation of resources. Competition cannot be eliminated, it can only be transformed.

Competition in a pure market economy coordinates economic decisions through price rationing. A price that is too high for the current market leads to unwanted inventories and downward pressure on the price, while a price that is too low produces a queue and an upward pressure on the price. The active bidding up of price when demand exceeds supply and down when supply exceeds demand serves to allocate resources in an effective manner by clearing markets. Price competition brings into coordination the most willing suppliers and the most willing demanders of a good.

Prices coordinate the multitude of individual plans that make up the market by informing economic actors about the state of existing market conditions and the success or failure of their previous plans. Prices perform this task by providing incentives and knowledge to market participants. The price of any good is a reflection of the relative scarcity of that good in relation to other goods. If the price is high, this signals to market participants that the particular good in question is relatively scarce and should be economized. On the other hand, the low price of a good suggests its relative abundance. In this manner, economic decision-makers receive information about current market conditions from price signals and this aids them in their choices.

Prices also provide information about the economic justification of past decisions. Buying cheap and selling dear is rewarded, while buying dear and selling cheap is penalized. The profit and loss system is a learning device by which systematic error can be eliminated. In addition to these functions, prices also serve as the backdrop against which individuals discover ways to shuffle or reshuffle resources in more effective ways for the satisfaction of ends. The discrepancy between the current array of prices and the imagined future array of prices spurs the entrepreneurial quest for pure profit.

These insights into the workings of the competitive market process were obscured in twentieth-century economics with the development of the concept of perfect competition and general equilibrium.

Perfect competition

Neoclassical economists, enamoured with the methods of physics, developed a highly refined model of idealized competition termed perfect competition. The crucial assumptions of this 'frictionless' model of competition include: an infinite number of buyers and sellers (so that no one buyer or seller possesses any significant degree of market power), complete information about alternative uses, costless mobility of resources and a homogeneous product. The consequence of such a state of affairs would be: the price of any good is treated as given and not a variable of decision by producers (price taking); the price would fully reflect the opportunity cost of production (marginal cost pricing); and zero economic profits (produce a level of output that minimizes average costs of production). Under these conditions and with these results, it was argued, the allocation of resources could be termed optimal, that is, allocative efficiency would be achieved. No one party could be made any better off without simultaneously making someone else worse off. In other words, all the gains to be had from exchange would be exhausted in a competitive equilibrium.

This model led to the development of the structure–conduct–performance paradigm in industrial economics. Market structure was presumed to be either perfectly competitive or monopolistic. Whether a firm was in a competitive situation or a monopolistic one could be measured by market share since under perfect competition no firm would possess any significant market power. Concentration ratios could be used to measure the extent of market power. A firm possessing too large a share of the market could be assumed to be monopolistic.

The pricing conduct of the firm, moreover, could be deduced from the market structure. In a competitive industry a firm would be forced by the logic of the model to set price equal to marginal cost. On the other hand, in a monopolistic situation the firm would be able to restrict output and raise price above marginal cost. The consequence being that under the competitive situation the performance of the industry could be termed optimal, while under monopolistic conditions performance would be suboptimal. This paradigm of industrial economics justified much of the government economic regulation of industry, such as antitrust law, in the twentieth century.

The dominant paradigm, however, suffered from serious drawbacks. From basic confusions of defining the relevant market (national or international) to serious analytical difficulties in explaining the workings of the competitive market process, the standard structure–conduct–performance paradigm was found wanting. For example, if everyone treated price as a parameter how do prices change to clear the market? Moreover, the model contained the serious dilemma that in a situation of perfect knowledge a profit opportunity known to everyone is actually known to no one so that nobody would have any inducement to pursue profit opportunities – thus the logic of the model of market clearing disappears. The basic model of competitive equilibrium, it was discovered, could not even explain the existence of firms or the use of money, let alone shed light on such phenomena as advertising, product differentiation, brand name loyalty, contracting practices, and so on. As a positive analytical device for explicating the workings of a pure market economy, the model of general competitive equilibrium was not very helpful.

This model of perfect competition, at best, could only serve as an imaginary construction which, by the method of contrast, could aid us in illuminating the real world of uncertainty and time. In other words, by studying a world without change we may be able to understand the difficulties change introduces into economic life. Unfortunately, the main-

stream of economic thinking viewed the model in a much more concrete and descriptive manner.

The Counter-Revolution

The development of the model of monopolistic competition provided the first immanent criticism of the model of perfect competition. The model of perfect competition could not explain the existence of product differentiation found in actual markets. The model of monopolistic competition did. But other questions persisted, such as the role of property rights and institutions of contract. Economists began to recognize that the key problem with monopoly was not the ability to price above marginal cost, but the barrier to entry that afforded such artificially restrictive practices. Economists do not possess a positive theory of monopoly, but rather a normative theory of property rights.

The development of a property rights approach to industrial economics has moved the focus of analysis away from the conditions of competitive equilibrium and back to the classical economists' discussion of the dynamic market process within different institutional contexts. As a result the rivalrous behaviour of individuals and firms within economic processes has once again received attention. Competition, rather than being a state of affairs measured by market share and supposed equilibrium conditions, is an active process of learning how better to arrange and rearrange resources to satisfy more effectively the ends sought.

Competition, within an institutional environment of private property, is a discovery procedure which generates both incentives and knowledge for the effective allocation of resources. Perhaps the most important property of the competitive market process is its ability to reveal error and provide the incentive and knowledge for individuals to correct past mistakes. This error detection and correction property of the competitive market is the vital characteristic of the system for the promotion of economic prosperity.

See also SOCIALIST CALCULATION, ENTREPRENEURSHIP, CONSUMER SOCIETY, CHICAGO ECONOMICS and AUSTRIAN ECONOMICS.

Reading

Armentano, D.T. 1982: *Antitrust and Monopoly*.
Brozen, Y. 1982: *Concentration, Mergers and Public Policy*.
Demsetz, H. 1982: Barriers to entry. *American Economic Review* 72, 47–57.

Hayek, F.A. 1948: The meaning of competition. In *Individualism and Economic Order*.

—— 1978: Competition as a discovery procedure. In *New Studies in Philosophy, Politics, Economics and the History of Ideas*.

Kirzner, I. 1973: *Competition and Entrepreneurship*.

McNaulty, P. 1967: A note on the history of perfect competition. *Journal of Political Economy* 75, 395–9.

—— 1968: Economic theory and the meaning of competition. *Quarterly Journal of Economics* 82, 639–56.

Stigler, G. 1965: *Essays in the History of Economics*.

—— 1968: *The Organization of Industry*.

PETER J. BOETTKE

computing *See* ARTIFICIAL INTELLIGENCE

conflict Defined as a struggle over values or claims to status, power and scarce resources, in which the aims of the conflicting parties are not only to gain desired values but also to neutralize, injure or eliminate their rivals, conflicts may take place between individuals or between collectivities. These intergroup as well as intragroup conflicts are perennial features of social life; they are essential components of social interaction in any society. Conflicts are by no means always 'negative factors' undermining collective life. They often contribute to the maintenance and growth of groups and collectivities as well as to the strengthening of interpersonal relations.

Conflict and COMPETITION are related but distinct social phenomena. Competition focuses on gaining specific goals in the face of competing actors whereas conflict is always aimed not just at the gaining of desired values but at hurting or eliminating actors who stand in the way. Competition may be conceived as akin to a race, whereas conflict may be seen as analogous to a boxing match.

Social philosophers and social scientists have been divided on the assessment of conflict ever since antiquity. In modern times, views about the functions, causes and effects of conflicts in social structures have been divided into roughly two camps: those who maintain that conflicts should be viewed as pathological phenomena, as symptoms of sickness in the social body; and those who argue that conflicts are normal forms of social interaction which may contribute to the maintenance, development, change and overall stability of social entities. In modern sociology, the first view is represented by, among others, Emile Durkheim and Talcott Parsons, the second can be found in Hegelian and Marxist thought, but also in SOCIAL DARWINISM and among elite theorists such as Vilfredo Pareto and Gaetano Mosca.

Today in sociology – although this has not always been the case – there is a tendency for conservative thought to emphasize the negative functions of conflict and for radicals to celebrate conflict as a vehicle for social change.

Conflict and social structure

The impact of conflicts on social structures varies with the character of such structures. In open, pluralistic societies conflicts are likely to have stabilizing consequences. If there are viable channels for the expression of rival claims, conflicts in flexible and open societies may lead to new and stable forms of interaction between component actors and allow novel adjustments. In rigid structures, by contrast, conflicts tend to be suppressed but are likely to be highly disruptive if and when they occur.

In open and flexible societies, multiple conflicts are likely to criss-cross each other, thereby preventing cleavages along one axis. In such societies there arise a variety of conflicts in different spheres. Hence multiple involvement of individuals in various conflicts knits society together by fostering different alliances for different issues. Actors who are antagonists in one conflict may be allies in another. This prevents the polarization characteristic of a rigid society where all conflict tends to fall along one axis.

Ever since classical Greek thought a distinction has been made between conflicts that proceed on the basis of societal CONSENSUS and conflicts that, on the contrary, involve dissensus over the basic values on which a society rests. There are conflicts within the rules of the game and conflicts about the rules of the game. The first type of conflict may lead to new adjustments and reform, whereas the second is likely to lead to breakdown or revolutionary change.

Any society contains elements of strain and potential sources of conflict. In flexible structures such conflicts provide the dynamics of social change. Elements that evade and resist the patterned structures of values and norms and the habitual balance of power and interests in such structures can be considered harbingers of alternative patterns. In flexible structures conflicts prevent ossification and decrease the likelihood of purely routine types of action. Change in general and innovation and creativity in particular counter-act habitual adjustments that freeze social life into rigid moulds.

The clash of values and interests, the tensions between what is and what some groups or indi-viduals think ought to be, the conflict between vested interests and new demands for access to wealth, power or status are far from being patho-logical phenomena – they are stimulants of social vitality in societies that are flexible enough to allow or even encourage the unhampered expression of conflicting interests and values.

Conflict theory assessed

Social peace and social feuds, conflict and order, are correlative phenomena. The cementing as well as the breaking of the cake of custom and the dominant systems of wont and use are part of the built-in dialectics of social life. It is hence ill-advised to distinguish a sociology of order and a sociology of conflict or to see a contradiction between a harmony model of society and a con-flict model. Conflict theories or integration theor-ies should not be viewed as rival explanatory systems such as, say, Ptolemaic astronomy versus Copernican, but should be viewed as partial rather than global components of general socio-logy theory. In the last analysis there can only be one overall sociological theory even though it may consist of sets of partial theories of the middle range. Just as modern political theory has aban-doned the fruitless discussion of whether coercion or persuasion is the *real* basis of political struc-tures, and just as most modern psychology has abandoned the vain quest to decide whether either nature or nurture is at the root of personality, so sociological theory should guard itself from encouraging similar fruitless dichotomizing. Whenever analysts encounter what appear to be temporary equilibria they should pay attention to the conflicting forces that led to their establish-ment in the first place. Conversely, the analyst should be sensitized to the likelihood that where there is conflict and disjunction there will also be forces that press towards the establishment of new types of equilibria. Preponderant concern with one or another set of phenomena stands in the way of the overall analysis of social structures and processes. The sociology of conflict aims at explaining variables neglected by other theoretical approaches; it cannot supplant the analysis of other social processes.

Objective and subjective factors

The objective basis of conflicts over scarce values and goods such as income, status or power need to be distinguished from subjective dispositions and attitudes such as hostility, aggressivity and the like. Conflicts and hostile sentiments are different phe-nomena and may not always coincide. Discrimina-tory behaviour, for example, may not always be associated with prejudiced attitudes. Hostile atti-tudes need not necessarily result in conflict beha-viour.

Nor need we expect that objective discrepancies in power, status, class position or income will necessarily lead to the outbreak of conflict, although they should be conceived of as potential sources of conflict. The way people define a situation rather than the objective features of a situation must be the focus of analytical attention. Potential contenders for a change in status, defer-ence or power and wealth may refrain from resorting to conflict either because of a realistic appraisal of their chances of success, or because they consider the existing distribution of valued entities to be legitimate. When, as in the traditional Indian caste system, unequal distributions of valued items are considered legitimate not only by the privileged but by the underprivileged as well, conflicts between the haves and the have-nots will not threaten the system. Only when the underprivi-leged deny legitimacy to an ideology by losing faith in it, as when the relations between their needs and the privileges of the higher ranked become trans-parent to them, can one expect conflict between the haves and the have-nots to break out.

Realistic and non-realistic conflict

The distinction between realistic and non-realistic types of conflicts has of late shown some valuable results in concrete analysis. Realistic conflict arises when individuals or groups clash in the pursuit of rival claims and the expectation of economic gain, power or status. Participants perceive that conflict might be abandoned or replaced by other means if these appear to be more effective. On the other hand, in non-realistic conflicts, which usually arise from hostile feelings only, the means to conduct the conflict are not replaceable because what is at stake is the aggression itself. Scapegoating provides a good example. What is replaceable in this case is not the means but the object. In such conflicts the target is secondary to the dispositional need for attack. Thus in non-realistic conflict there are alternatives as to the target, whereas in realistic conflict there are alternatives to the means used. In scapegoating, for example, the attacked object may be victimized because of ethnic group, beliefs or sex, or other characteristics, depending on the specific situation. In realistic conflict, in contrast, a party in industrial relations may decide that arbitration rather than strike action is more likely to bring results.

Conflict, self-worth and collective strength
Feelings of personal worth, strength and dignity among heretofore despised and underprivileged persons or strata are likely to be enhanced and strengthened if the underprivileged have shown their mettle in contentions with those who have hitherto repressed and oppressed them. The civil rights struggles in the American South, for example, so enhanced the sense of empowerment and worth among the black population that it could now triumphantly proclaim that Black is Beautiful. The working class in all Western industrial countries was slowly transformed from an object to a subject in history, to a class *for* itself, with a sense of power to transform its pariah status. The modern feminist movement has transformed millions of women from largely passive sexual objects to self-conscious actors on the public scene in their quest for full gender equality with men.

Conflict between antagonistic actors may not only enhance the sense of worth, power and dignity of one or both of them, it may also lead to a strengthening of their bonds with each other. Be it in race relations or in marriage, conflicts may allow the emergence of stronger ties rather than the destruction of such ties. Marriage bonds may be reinforced or race relations improved after the relevant actors have gained self-confident strength, after they have clashed in pursuit of their initially divergent interests.

Channelling conflicts
The quest for the elimination of conflict in human society is bound to fail. Conflict is an ineradicable part of human living together; it is as fundamental a component of human association as is cooperation. What is feasible, however, is to transform specific types of conflict behaviour when it is perceived as dysfunctional or noxious. Duelling, once a major component of aristocratic lifestyles, has all but disappeared. The vendetta survives only in isolated remnants of Western societies. The violent strikes

in the labour–management conflicts of the nineteenth and early twentieth century are a thing of the past in all but a few instances. As these few examples show, it is possible to decrease the violence or intensity of conflict by chanelling antagonistic encounters in such a way as to minimize human suffering and costs. If today nuclear warfare has become unthinkable so tomorrow other obnoxious forms of warfare, even though not all warfare, may no longer claim human lives.

See also AGGRESSION; VIOLENCE.

Reading
Collins, Randall 1975: *Conflict Sociology: Toward an Explanatory Science*.
Coser, Lewis A. 1956: *The Functions of Social Conflict*.
—— 1967: *Continuities in the Study of Social Conflict*.
Dahrendorf, Ralf 1957 (*1959*): *Class and Class Conflict in Industrial Society*.
Gluckman, Max 1956: *Custom and Conflict in Africa*.
Himes, Joseph S. 1980: *Conflict and Conflict Management*.
Kriesberg, Louis 1982: *Social Conflicts*, 2nd edn.
Rex, John 1961: *Key Problems of Sociological Theory*.
Simmel, Georg 1908 (*1955*): *Conflict and the Web of Group Affiliations*.

LEWIS A. COSER

Confucianism As an intellectual and ethical tradition, Confucianism is more than 25 centuries old. Its basic values were embraced not only in China proper, but in Japan, Korea and Vietnam as well, and helped to shape East Asia's self-consciousness as a distinct cultural region. As might be expected, there is no essential Confucianism which endured throughout this long history. Rather, the Confucian tradition, like other intellectual and religious traditions of comparable age and significance, evolved and changed, even as some real continuities were maintained. This diverse cultural heritage has provided rich resources for twentieth-century East Asians to reflect on contemporary social life, although Confucianism has also had to face numerous challenges concerning its compatibility with new social knowledge and values.

The Western name 'Confucianism' might suggest that Confucius (a Latinized form of *K'ung Fu-Tzu* – Master K'ung), a Chinese philosopher and teacher who lived in the sixth century BCE, was the founder of this intellectual and ethical tradition. In fact, he saw himself only as a transmitter of a heritage which had taken shape centuries before his time, and generally 'Confucianism' has been known in East Asia as the 'Scholarly Tradition'. Confucius lived in a period of great political and cultural disorder. His concern to restore order and harmony to society and to cultivate individual MORALITY within a social order defined by tradition became values which motivated and guided the subsequent development of Confucian social thought. As a way of life, Confucianism became noted for its concern for personal well-being, social harmony and solidarity, political stability and universal peace, all of which are to be pursued within structures of meaning inherited from the past. (See also TRADITION AND TRADITIONALISM.)

Confucian social thought has generally been corporativist, assuming that the ideal society is a hierarchically differentiated order and that ritually structured human relationships are essential to this ideal. This emphasis on human relationships was expressed in a linked interest in distinguishing between individuals and differentiating the kinds of relations possible among them. Traditionally, Confucians acknowledged the possibility of many kinds of relations between individuals but gave special emphasis to 'five cardinal relations' as fundamental to a proper social order: those between parent and child, those between ruler and subject, between husband and wife, between older brother and younger brother, and between friends. The Confucian concern with those relations within the family, especially those between parents and children, have led some observers to describe Confucian social theory as restrictively group oriented, but the Confucian concern with the possibility and significance of voluntarily constructed relationships, such as those between friends, should not be underestimated. Each of these cardinal relationships fixes roles as well as responsibilities; duty thus corresponds to title. All of these various reciprocal relationships are best established and cultivated through formalized etiquette and ritual (*li*) which have been received from the past.

Proper behaviour within these traditionally defined relationships is not only crucial to the establishment of an ordered society, but is essential to the necessary development of an individual, for in the Confucian view of things persons only become *human* through a lifelong process of cultural and ethical learning. 'To become fully human, the self must enter into continuous dialogue with others within the structures of human relationships' (Tu, 1984, p. 5).

The Confucian tradition was institutionalized in patterns of family life, in a sophisticated educational system, and in government. The Confucian educational system, in principle, was open to anyone, and is one of the few examples of an aspiration to universal education in the premodern world. In the past, Confucian social thought gave a special place to the role of the ruler in establishing the ideal society and encouraging moral perfection in individuals. Some of Confucius' own teachings, collected in the *Analects*, advocated government by exemplary behaviour, rather than by coercion and punishment. He advised rulers to lead the people according to the proper rites (*li*), which would motivate others to fulfil their own roles within society; according to Confucian political theory, a ruler will not be able to govern effectively without proper personal conduct. The elite community of Confucian scholars often aspired to play a role in government as advisors to the ruler. Confucius and his successors urged rulers to give positions of authority to 'people of virtue and ability', that is, those who were successful in Confucian education, and the Confucian tradition generally preferred a meritocracy to any system of government which privileged birthright.

In the twentieth century, many of the core values of Confucian social thought have been subject to extensive criticism and outright rejection. This is particularly the case with the political dimensions of Confucian thought, since few rulers attained the moral status necessary to rule according to the instructions of Confucian political theory. At the turn of the century, Confucianism was identified quite realistically with authoritarianism and political corruption, since its ideals could easily be manipulated to enhance the power of particular individuals or groups. This internal critique of Confucianism in practice, which had many precedents in Chinese history, was accompanied by the challenge of alternative social ideals learned from contact with the West in the nineteenth century. Increasingly, Confucian values and institutions were perceived as incompatible with democratic or socialist ideals, or just with MODERNITY in general. Much of Confucian social thought in the twentieth century has thus been necessarily defensive, attempting to show that Confucian tradition either has values analogous to the new challengers or can promote the attainment of the new ideals.

More recently, there has been a revival of Confucian values throughout East Asia as part of ongoing reconsiderations of cultural identity in the modern world. This revival has emphasized the traditional Confucian insistence that social life should be shaped by the moral and symbolic resources of the past. While it has been critical of the Confucian tradition which it has inherited, this revival has also begun to rethink whether modernity must necessarily be defined with an emphasis on the autonomy of the individual. The example of industrial East Asia suggests that the Confucian values of respect for authority, social solidarity based on familism, and a preference for consensus rather than independent thought can make positive contributions to a modern society.

Reading
King, Ambrose Yeo-Chi 1991: Kuan-hsi and network building: a sociological interpretation. In *The Living Tree: The Changing Meaning of Being Chinese Today*, special issue of *Daedalus*, 120, 63–84.
Levenson, Joseph R. 1958–65: *Confucian China and its Modern Fate*, 3 vols.
Rozman, Gilbert ed. 1991: *The East Asian Region: Confucian Heritage and its Modern Adaptation.*
Tu Wei-ming 1984: *Confucian Ethics Today: The Singapore Challenge.*
—— 1985: *Confucian Thought: Selfhood as Creative Transformation.*
—— 1991: The search for roots in industrial East Asia: the case of the Confucian revival. In *Fundamentalisms Observed*, ed. Martin E. Marty and R. Scott Appleby.
CHARLES HALLISEY

consensus   As a term for general agreement between individuals or groups, not only in thought but also in feeling, the word does not only refer to national agreements but also implies common sentiments – sensing together. Consensus exists when a large proportion of the adult members of a society or of its subgroups, particularly a large proportion of decision makers, are in general agreement as to what decisions are required and what issues have to be addressed. Persons or groups who act in consensus have a sense of affinity with each other and are united by affective ties and common concerns or interests. This definition applies, of course, only to an ideal type. In any concrete situation consensus among some will be accompanied by dissensus or apathetic withdrawal among others. Consensus and dissensus are correlative (see DISSENT).

The term consensus was introduced into the language of the social sciences by Auguste Comte in the nineteenth century; he conceived it as the indispensable cement on which any social structure must rest. He believed that if society was not to collapse into a sandheap of individuals it had to be based on the consensus of a moral community of like-minded and like-feeling individuals. Later social scientists tended to follow in Comte's footsteps while attempting to make his analytical rigidity more flexible. They have stressed, for example, that in no society, however consensual, will such consensus be equally shared by all component members. Nor can it be expected that all members of a group or society will actually wish to participate in decision making. Nor, on the other hand, are all groups or individuals always able to make their voices heard in the public arena. It may turn out that what parades as general consensus is only the consensus of those allowed to play the political game.

Consensus has to be distinguished from COERCION, that is, the forceful imposition of norms of behaviour on the population at large by the political overlords and decision makers. Unreflective conformity and the habitual acceptance of social commands cannot be taken as the equivalent of consensus either. The latter generally implies a process through which agreement between participant actors is brought about. It is to be conceived as an active process and must hence be distinguished from acquiescence, resigned acceptance or simple conformism. The Nazi regime in Germany, for example, could probably count on the consensus of large parts of Germany's political actors in the first years of the regime, but towards the end of the Nazi era most citizens seem to have been motivated by passive conformity to the injunctions of the Nazi leaders.

Rules of the game, as we have just seen, may be coercively imposed by powerful superiors on powerless subordinates. Yet, as political theorists have argued ever since the great Greek philosophers, coercion alone cannot provide a sufficient foundation for a social order. If it is true that policemen can hold a club over potential violators of an imposed order such an order cannot solve the problem of who polices and holds a club over the policemen. A measure of consensus, even if it may involve only a fraction of the population, must inspire some actors to follow the directions of the decision makers for motives other than fear of reprisal.

Consensus does not involve clinging forever to fixed standards that guide conduct. On the contrary, historical reflection will show that what was part of the consensus at one time will no longer govern behaviour at another time. Political parties, at least in modern democratic politics, are continually involved in conflicts that aim at transforming partial consensus into partial dissensus or partial dissensus into partial consensus. For example, beliefs about the need for a measure of social security during periods of unemployment or in old age are now taken for granted and at least grudgingly accepted by defenders of the free market, whereas they were seen in an earlier period as utopian fantasies. Quite often, the crackpots of one generation become the venerated innovators of the next.

Not only may a given consensus be here today but gone tomorrow because of historical flux and change, but the actors who develop consensus and consent may also change over time depending on the relative openness or closure of access to the political arena. Consensus is brought about through a process in which even some originally recalcitrant actors, be they individuals or groups, become motivated, at least in some contexts, to forego egocentric patterns of behaviour through being welded together by a collective 'we'. In such situations, initial disagreements may become part of consensual common beliefs even as newly emerging areas of dissensus already begin to point to another turn of the screw.

Reading
Comte, Auguste *1974: The Essential Comte*, ed. Stanislav Andreski.
Key, V.O. Jr 1961: *Public Opinion and American Democracy*.
Lipset, Seymour 1960: *Political Man: The Social Bases of Politics*.
Shils, Edward 1975: *'Consensus' in Center and Periphery: Essays in Macrosociology*.

LEWIS A. COSER

conservatism   This is a political perspective which is universal in a way that the great modern ideologies of LIBERALISM and SOCIALISM and FASCISM are not. An instinctive aversion to change, and a corresponding attachment to things as they are, these are sentiments from which few human beings have ever been wholly exempt. And sentiments are all that conservatism has amounted to for much of human history. In advanced no less than in primitive societies any other disposition but the conservative has generally seemed aberrant. Unchanging customs, rituals and manners governed human behaviour from generation to generation. Conservatism only awakes from its instinctive

torpor when incited to do so by the onset of rapid and unsettling change. And even then it finds it hard to give voice to instincts which for so long it has taken for granted, and which (quite literally) it has had no *reason* to define or defend. For every Edmund Burke, who was 'alarmed into reflection' by the French revolution, there were a thousand tongue-tied aristocrats and peasants who knew what they loved, but not why.

Hence the 'alarm' which is felt by conservatives in the face of change more often lends itself to, than leads to, 'reflection'. It is nevertheless correct to look for the nativity of conservative thought in conservative sentiment. The feeling for the concrete and the immediate which is so characteristic of the former has its origin in the latter. It can be traced back, more specifically, to the premodern ties and practices of the old Europe upon which the *philosophes* of the eighteenth-century ENLIGHTENMENT heaped so much scorn. Against their drive to reorganize society along 'rational' lines, and to prize individuals loose from the web of attachments in which they had been enmeshed, conservative traditionalists rallied to the defence of their own kind (see RATIONALITY AND REASON). They slowly raised to the level of reflection their experience of institutions and customs as inseparable from the ends of human life. This was in stark contrast to the then emerging liberal emphasis on wholly individual ends and interests, to which institutions and forms of life stand in a merely instrumental relationship. As for long-established institutions, to the liberal individualist they have always seemed to be crutches which people 'come of age' can live perfectly well without (see INDIVIDUALISM). The conservative is altogether less sanguine: people left to their own devices, conservative thinking goes, are people left to their own vices. Society, as the conservative pictures it, is not a sandheap of individual, unconnected atoms. It is rather a *communitas communitatum*, in which the socially detached individual – Shakespeare's 'unaccommodated man' – is the exception and not the rule.

What began as an instinctive opposition to modernizing ideas burgeoned into a full-blown 'counter-enlightenment' when it dawned on conservatives that bourgeois radicals wanted to rationalize and atomize the whole of society. To the extent that the latter succeeded in their aims, some of the conservative opposition to abstract modes of thought was depoliticized, as it lost touch with the world as it was coming to be and took refuge in that internalized experience we recognize as romanticism. But a more durable element in the conservative camp emerged as HISTORICISM. The historical school reacted to the dissolution of the traditional, static world by reinterpreting the conservative attachment to the concrete as an attachment to the organic, that is, that which is living and always evolving. The place which had been occupied in earlier conservative thought by the estate and the local community was filled instead by the organic community of the 'people' (*Volk*).

Change, however, may be so vertiginous that a historicist response to it ends not in adaptation but capitulation. Both history and experience then become treacherous grounds on which to mount an effective opposition to radical change, for the simple reason that – to borrow the language of MARXISM – they are on the side of change. This is why in the twentieth century many conservatives have felt the need for a more discriminating mode of thought: appealing less to tradition itself than to the truths which a healthy tradition embodies. It was a mark of the Judeo–Christian tradition that all members of society accepted it as binding upon themselves. But modern Western man has lost any sense of an objective moral order. The 'privatization' of moral values, which is inevitable and good from the liberal point of view, from the conservative is identical with the affluent nihilism of contemporary society. If values rest on nothing more solid than our arbitrary choice, as RELATIVISM would have it, we can have no good reason to believe in them. The conservative critique of liberal individualism here acquires a cultural and metaphysical – and not just a social and political – perspective. Society and its obligations are not founded on the shifting wills and desires of individuals, but ultimately on the nature of human beings. In other words, prior to the deals we make with one another, in pursuit of our interests, we possess certain duties and rights which are, so to speak, non-negotiable or 'given', because inscribed in our very natures.

The limits placed on change or 'progress' by the twin ideas of human nature and natural law are obviously very considerable. Liberals and radicals, in varying degrees, assume the infinite plasticity of human nature. Natural law conservatives assert to the contrary that it manifests unchangeable features, which in turn implies unchangeable norms. Some have seen this view as pointing to a possible incoherence in conservative theory: how is the belief in a universal natural law – which is by definition applicable to all human beings in all places and at all times – consistent with an attachment to particular and local traditions and customs? Not all conservatives, of course, adhere to both these views; but those who do are usually forced to admit that an existing or traditional culture may indeed fall far short of certain universal moral principles, in which case the former must submit to the judgement of the latter.

It remains true that ever since the Enlightenment used its own idea of human nature to demonstrate the irrationality of all existing societies, many conservatives have shunned the very idea itself as being altogether too abstract. But it is important to understand the great gulf which separates the conservative idea of human nature – as only becoming what essentially it is, as only finding completion, in society – from the modern liberal idea of it as essentially asocial. British and American conservatives have sometimes come close to embracing this liberal view by their enthusiastic espousal of CAPITALISM. However in practice they normally retain some vestige of the older conservative belief that freedom, including economic freedom, is at once inoperable and intolerable outside a strong social and moral framework. It remains to be seen how far conservatism, in anything more than name, can survive in a society which is more inclined to conflate, than connect, freedom with virtue.

Reading
Burke, E. 1790 (*1968*): *Reflections on the Revolution in France.*
Eliot, T.S. 1939: *The Idea of a Christian Society.*
—— 1948: *Notes Towards the Definition of Culture.*
Kirk, R. 1954 (*1986*): *The Conservative Mind*, 7th edn.
Nisbet, R.A. 1966: *The Sociological Tradition.*
Oakeshott, M. 1962: *Rationalism in Politics.*
Scruton, R. 1980: *The Meaning of Conservatism.*
—— ed. 1988: *Conservative Thinkers.*
—— ed. 1988: *Conservative Thoughts.*
Strauss, L. 1949: *Natural Right and History.*
Voegelin, E. 1952: *The New Science of Politics.*

IAN CROWTHER

consumer society Denoting a society organized around the consumption rather than the production of goods and services, this term has come into general use over the past decade. It is commonly employed to designate an interrelated set of socio-economic and cultural tendencies deemed characteristic of the advanced industrial societies of North

America, Western Europe and the Pacific Rim and is seen to distinguish them both from earlier nineteenth-century 'productionist' societies and from the developing societies of the Third World. Popular usage frequently contains the implication that members of such societies identify high levels of consumption with social success and personal happiness and hence choose consuming as their overriding life goal. As such the phrase is often linked to a critique of the status-seeking, materialism and hedonism which are assumed to comprise the dominant values in such societies. Academic usage has increasingly attempted to eschew such evaluative overtones while retaining the insight that the key to understanding modernity lies in recognizing the centrality of the activities of consumption and its associated attitudes and values. The term 'consumer society' is employed to encapsulate this view and usually implies an economy which is geared to satisfying the novel wants rather than merely the recurrent needs of consumers.

The idea that the social and cultural changes occurring in the more advanced economies of North America and Western Europe should be understood as primarily associated with a shift from a focus on production to one on consumption was first advanced in the 1950s by David Riesman, Nathan Glazer and Reuel Denny in *The Lonely Crowd* (1950) and has since been taken up by other, more recent interpreters of modern society, such as Daniel Bell (1976), Bernice Martin (1981) and Colin Campbell (1987). In these works the transition from a production to a consumer society is not viewed as simply consisting of the emergence of a mass market for luxury goods but is equated with a fundamental shift in values and beliefs. Hence discussion of the nature and origin of the consumer society is linked to attempts to explain the decline of the Protestant work ethic and its displacement by an 'expressive', 'hedonistic' or 'romantic' ethos (see PROTESTANT ETHIC THESIS). This concern with the analysis of cultural change has meant that discussion of the consumer society intersects with other debates over the nature of contemporary society (see MASS MEDIA: MODERNISM AND POSTMODERNISM).

However, the assumption that there is a clear watershed in the recent past separating societies shaped by the forces of production from those determined by the forces of consumption has been increasingly questioned by both historians and sociologists. Fernand Braudel (1973) has argued that an understanding of the development of modernity in the West requires an appreciation of how changes in consumer behaviour in the premodern period led to an increased demand for goods, while McKendrick, Brewer and Plumb (1982) identify the 'consumer revolution' which heralded the arrival of the consumer society as occurring in England in the second half of the eighteenth century. Other writers have sought its origins in fifteenth and sixteenth-century Europe (Mukerji, 1983) and mid-nineteenth century France (M. B. Miller, 1981; Williams, 1982).

Such research has given fresh impetus to the debate over how the activity of consumption should best be understood. In this context both the neglect of consumption within neoclassical economics and the 'productionist bias' manifest in the writings of Karl Marx and Max Weber are frequently noted as a marked deficiency within Western social thought. Thorstein Veblen's theory of conspicuous consumption (1899) is that most commonly invoked in an effort to fill this vacuum, although Pierre Bourdieu's (1979) reworking of the traditional Veblenesque themes of taste and social snobbery is increasingly cited as a major source of theoretical inspiration. Other recent attempts to develop a distinctive theory of consumption which could serve as a basis for a theory of consumer society would include those of Appadurai (1986), Campbell (1987) and Daniel Miller (1987).

See also AFFLUENT SOCIETY.

Reading
Campbell, Colin 1987: *The Romantic Ethic and the Spirit of Modern Consumerism*.
McCracken, Grant 1988: *Culture and Consumption: New Approaches to the Symbolic Character of Consumer Goods and Activities*.
McKendrick, Neil, Brewer, John and Plumb, J.H. 1982: *The Birth of a Consumer Society: The Commercialization of Eighteenth-century England*.

COLIN CAMPBELL

contradiction   *See* DIALECTICS

conversation analysis   Sometimes referred to as CA, this field of sociology is concerned with the organization of social interaction in everyday contexts and more specialized institutional environments. Originating in the research of Harvey Sacks and his collaborators Emanuel Schegloff and Gail Jefferson, the field emerged as a product of the influences of ETHNOMETHODOLOGY and the interactional analysis of Erving Goffman. From its inception in privately circulated lectures by Sacks (1964–72), CA has grown into a field of research that is practised worldwide.

The primary research objective of CA is to describe and analyse the social competencies underlying the production and recognition of ordinary social actions. Many of these competencies have a normative dimension. CA shares the ethnomethodological view that a common body of normative practices inform both the production and the interpretation of action and that they are implemented in a dynamic social context that is altered, to a greater or lesser extent, with each successive contribution to interaction. Analysis of these practices is made possible by the fact that, during the course of interaction, each party (whether consciously or not) displays an understanding and analysis of the other's conduct through the production of a next action in a sequence. CA embodies an analytic framework that is based on this fact. Thus rather than focusing on speakers and their individual intentions, CA begins with the normative practices that shape sequences of interaction between speakers and the design of particular actions or utterances within these sequences. Using this approach has resulted in a very large range of findings about the organization of action, of mutual understanding within interaction and, increasingly, of the extent to which findings deriving from interactional data from a particular culture are universal or culturally specific.

The empirical approach of CA is observational and naturalistic rather than experimental. It is based on data that are collected from natural settings of interaction by audiotape or videotape or film recording. Much of this data is taken from casual conversations between friends and acquaintances. This sort of conversation represents the most basic form of interaction in most, if not all, cultures. It is, as Schegloff has observed, a primordial site of human sociality and it is of fundamental significance in the study of social action and practical reasoning. Moreover ordinary conversation is a form of interaction to which humans are first exposed during the course of SOCIALIZATION and through which socialization itself proceeds. Analysis of its underlying organization is providing a baseline against which the conduct that is characteristic of more specialized forms of interaction, for example in courts, news interviews, medical consultation and so on, can be documented and analysed.

CA research and findings embody an innovative fusion of sociological approaches to the nature of social action and interaction with analytic outlooks associated with linguistic pragmatics. The detail and cumulativeness of these findings is creating new opportunities for precisely focused studies of the workings of specific social institutions and is exerting a significant impact in the adjacent disciplines of anthropology, linguistics, social psychology and cognitive science.

Reading
Atkinson, J.M. and Drew, P. 1979: *Order in Court: The Organisation of Verbal Interaction in Judicial Settings.*
Atkinson, J.M. and Heritage, J.C. eds 1984: *Structures of Social Action: Studies in Conversation Analysis.*
Drew, P. and Heritage, J. eds 1991: *Talk at Work.*
Goodwin, C. 1981: *Conversational Organisation: Interaction between Speakers and Hearers.*
Levinson, S.C. 1983: *Pragmatics.*
Sacks, H. 1964–72 (*1992*): *Lectures on Conversation*, ed. G. Jefferson, 2 vols.

JOHN HERITAGE

cooperative movement Associations of people working together for the production and distribution of goods, cooperatives have taken a variety of forms in different national contexts. The International Co-operative Alliance, representing almost 600 million individual members worldwide, has singled out six essential principles: voluntary and open membership, democratic control, limited return on capital, surplus earnings belong to members, education and cooperation among cooperatives (ICA Commission, 1967). Democratic control is the key difference between capitalist and cooperative forms of property. Unlike the joint-stock company each member has the same voting rights regardless of the number of shares held; PARTICIPATION is power, rather than individual ownership of other people's ossified abstract labour.

An ethical, idealist impulse has been a common feature. From its inception, cooperation was seen as a way of building an alternative to capitalism from the bottom up, replacing bourgeois INDIVIDUALISM with a society based on mutuality and social solidarity. An English cooperator defined the ideal thus in 1907: 'By means of mutual association to eliminate the present industrial system, and to substitute mutual Co-operation for the common good as the basis of all human society' (Webb, 1904, p. 2).

The movement originated in Britain during the development of industrial capitalism in the late eighteenth century; cooperative mills were established from the 1790s, evidence of the contest between the 'moral economy' of the labouring poor and laissez-faire ideology and practice (Thompson, 1991). The early nineteenth century was punctuated by waves of cooperative experiment; short-lived worker co-ops were set up during the Luddite agitation in 1811–13; Owenite and Chartist stores were founded from the late 1820s through the 1830s. Although the utopian socialist Robert Owen has often been regarded as the 'father' of the cooperative movement, these ventures were neither inspired nor wholeheartedly supported by the paternalistic Owen who preferred modes of social transformation imposed from above (Taylor, 1983, p. 120).

In 1844 Owenite-inspired weavers formed the Rochdale Society of Equitable Pioneers. This society redistributed the trading surplus among members according to the value of their purchases, the so-called 'dividend', although the ultimate goal was still the establishment of 'a self-supporting home colony of united interests' (Webb, 1904, p. 69). The society expanded at a phenomenal pace and demonstrated the usefulness of this form of working-class association at a time when direct confrontation with the capitalist state was becoming less feasible. Working-class women had a large measure of control over consumption strategies and were consequently highly visible within the movement from its inception and throughout its subsequent history.

The 'essentially contestable' nature of cooperation was apparent from this early phase. Until about 1848 'cooperation', 'communism' and 'socialism' were interchangeable and carried similar anti-capitalist emphases (Bestor, 1948). These concepts have been sites of complex and protracted struggles over the last two centuries. Bourgeois reformers throughout Western Europe attempted to separate 'cooperation' from what were perceived to be more 'revolutionary' modes of social change, especially after the 1848 revolutions. Middle-class Christian Socialists like E. V. Neale and J. M. Ludlow were fervent advocates of producer co-ops

and profit-sharing and believed that these forms would 'humanize' the worker and harmonize capital/labour relations (Backstrom, 1974). Ludlow drafted the Industrial and Provident Societies Act of 1852 which regulated (in the sense of protection and constraint) relations between the state and cooperatives. This attempt to appropriate the meaning of cooperation was effectively countered by the English and Scottish CWS (established in 1863 and 1868) which articulated a neo-Owenite ambition based on the principle of consumer cooperation (Yeo, 1987, p. 231). This strategy, theorized by Charles Gide in France, contained its own contradictions and the constant tension between the rights and duties of producers and consumers has marked subsequent cooperative ideology and practice, in Britain and elsewhere.

By 1914 cooperation had become deeply ingrained within working-class communities, particularly in the north of England. A counter-culture, comprising a wide repertoire of educational and recreational forms, grew up around the movement; here was the equivalent of the cultural construction which characterized the German SPD before World War I (Gurney, 1989). The 'unmaking' of this culture is part of the unwritten social history of the twentieth century. The movement had to struggle not only with its own project but also against powerful outside forces ranged against it. Changes in the capitalist mode of consumption (Aglietta, 1976), particularly the development of 'consumer capitalism' in the widest sense, has checked cooperative advance in Britain and the West generally. The capitalist state has frequently been hostile and there have been repeated attempts to tax cooperative 'surplus' (profits to critics); in 1933 mutual associations were assimilated to joint-stock companies and cooperative reserves taxed in the same way as capitalist firms (Killingback, 1988). This hostility has been apparent even when the custodian of political power has been the Labour Party; antagonism between different wings of the labour movement has been a constant disabling factor, a result of the fractured identities of workers as producers/consumers, men/women, voluntarists/statists.

The British movement inspired cooperative development throughout Europe and North America. Vigorous national movements grew up in France, Germany, Austria, Sweden, Denmark, Belgium and Italy, each with their own peculiarities. Credit unions played an important role in the

German movement and their founder, Schulze-Delitsch, considered cooperation an antidote for Marxist social democracy. The French movement, influenced by the ideas of the utopian socialist Charles Fourier and later by the anarchism of Pierre Proudhon and the moderate socialism of Louis Blanc, was shaped by the revolutionary experience of 1848 and 1871. Agricultural cooperatives were dominant in Russia and played a vital role in the Russian Revolution of 1917 prior to collectivization under Stalin (Carr, 1952).

Today over 100 million people belong to cooperatives in Europe and North America. The most promising experiment since World War II is the Mondragon complex in the Basque region of Northern Spain. Founded in 1958 by Arizmendi, a socialist priest, it now consists of over a hundred cooperatives employing 19,000 worker-owners, and supplies banking, housing, education, social welfare and consumer goods; a living, albeit isolated, example of the effectiveness of a 'culture of cooperation'. This has led some commentators to describe Mondragon as 'a new phenomenon in cooperative history' (Thomas and Logan, 1982, p. 76).

The principles of voluntary membership and democratic control serve largely to disqualify forms of collective enterprise developed by socialist and communist states from inclusion in this discussion. Their overall lack of success points to the incompatibility between cooperation and statist forms of social transformation. This is well illustrated by the Russian *kolkhoz* or collective farm which spectacularly failed to solve the problems of agricultural production in the old Soviet Union. The same can be said of the Ujamaa Village in Tanzania imposed from above by Julius Nyerere in the 1960s. However, this rule has not been inviolate: workers' SELF-MANAGEMENT initiatives in the former Yugoslavia and the Chinese Commune can be viewed in a more favourable light. Communes, formed in both rural and urban districts after 'the great leap forward' in 1958, organized and regulated production, consumption, defence and education. Some commentators have regarded them as the partial realization of a communist utopia (Melnyk, 1985, p. 43). The positive gains represented by these experiments are in danger of being lost as Eastern Europe and China pursue Western modes of capitalist modernization.

Two of the most promising present-day movements are found in India and Japan. Cooperatives exist in almost every village in India. Over a quarter of a million societies with 140 million members have achieved great success, particularly in dairy farming, sugar and fertilizer production. Initially established by the British and used to buttress colonial power in the countryside, the movement continues to suffer from the legacy of corruption. Political parties have frequently interfered in cooperative affairs and appointed leaders against the wishes of the membership. The result has been to alienate the movement from the members (Sharma, 1989). By contrast, the Japanese movement, which originated in the late nineteenth century, has developed a strong democratic structure based around the 'Han' or community group. Established in the late 1950s, the Han is a small group of consumers (10 to 12 families) which makes contracts with suppliers through the local consumers' cooperative and regulates quality and distribution. This form has ensured high member participation and, coupled with the economic boom after World War II, helps account for the movement's growth; Japan now has the world's largest consumer cooperative organization with over 11 million members and a turnover of nearly 13 million US dollars in 1986 (Hasselman, 1989).

Many advocates of cooperation continue to regard it as a viable alternative to both state socialism and monopoly capitalism; hence the importance assigned to a regenerated Russian movement by President Gorbachev in the late 1980s (Gorbachev, 1988). The sector was consequently reborn during *perestroika*, but following the failure of this initiative it is unlikely that the movement will perform the transformative role once envisaged. In the longer term the problems which now confront the world economic system generally may serve to underline anew the relevance of cooperative social and economic forms.

Reading
Bonner, A. 1961: *British Co-operation.*
Cole, G.D.H. 1945: *A Century of Co-operation.*
Desroche, H. 1964: *Coopération et développement: mouvements coopératifs et stratégie du développement.*
Furlough, E. and Strikwerda, C. eds forthcoming: *Consumer Co-operation in Europe and America.*
Jones, B. 1894: *Co-operative Production.*
Laidlaw, A.F. 1981: *Co-operation in the Year 2000.*
Sapelli, G. ed. 1981: *Il Movimento Co-operativo in Italia.*
Watkins, W.H. 1970: *The International Co-operative Alliance, 1895–1970.*
Webb, C. 1927: *The Woman with the Basket.*

PETER GURNEY

corporatism In recent usage in the social sciences, the concept of corporatism has shrugged off its earlier association with authoritarian and fascist regimes, and has come to be deployed as a means for analysing the role of organized interests in present-day liberal democracies. Corporatism has also passed into common political usage as a shorthand for the involvement of trade unions, together with organizations representing the interests of capital in bargaining with governments over economic policies. In public debate corporatism has come to be seen as the antithesis of neoliberalism, in which governments seek to use competition rather than negotiation as the dynamic of policy-making.

Much of the earlier normative writing on corporatism reflected Catholic social doctrine, and the search for an ideological alternative to liberalism and socialism. Corporatist writers espoused organic theories of society, and argued for functional groupings or corporations based on a common set of interests which transcended class divisions. This idea of corporatism as a blueprint for an ideal social system based on the harmonious accommodation of different social groups was nowhere realized in practice, although some of its elements found expression in the projected corporate STATE in Mussolini's Italy.

Among contemporary academic writers, corporatism is usually seen as the antithesis of PLURALISM, and indeed the leading exponent of corporatist theory in the 1970s, Philippe Schmitter (1974), offered corporatism as a critique of what he saw as the dominant pluralist orthodoxy in POLITICAL SOCIOLOGY. Pluralists interpreted the extraordinary range and diversity of interest organizations in modern societies as evidence for the openness of democratic governments to a wide range of influences, and offered a benign view of INTEREST GROUP politics as a supplement to electoral mechanisms for ensuring democratic accountability. By contrast, corporatist theory stressed the limited number of politically influential organizations, and the tendency for such groups to achieve a monopolistic position in representing interests within particular social categories. Such developments tended to supplant rather than supplement parliamentary processes. Governments tended to favour the development of interest monopolies because it made it easier and less time-consuming to bring group interests in line with public policies. By

conferring a privileged public status on those groups whose cooperation was considered important for realizing public policy objectives, governments effectively excluded from the bargaining table a rather larger number of less powerful groups (Offe in Berger, 1981).

There has been a lively debate about what should be the focus of corporatist theory, which has led some critics to doubt its distinctive character. The most widespread modern usage of the term identifies the heart of corporatism as the role of interest organizations as intermediating between the state and CIVIL SOCIETY. Pluralist theory stressed the role of groups as representing the interests of their members and seeking to influence the direction of public policy implemented through the institutions of the state. Corporatist theory laid an equal stress on the delegation of public functions to groups, and their responsibility for the implementation of public policy. Thus groups did not simply represent interests, but carried out a double role which fused together interest representation and policy implementation. The key test for the effectiveness of a corporatist group was thus argued to be its capacity for disciplining its membership to accept and implement bargained agreements with the state. Relatively stable relationships of this kind have also been termed 'private interest government' (Streeck and Schmitter, 1985).

The difference between advanced capitalist societies where corporatism develops incrementally as a consequence of the growing monopoly power of interest organizations, and those where a corporatist design is imposed by the state, is captured in the distinction between societal (or liberal) corporatism and state corporatism (Schmitter, 1974). Societal corporatism develops where the state recognizes the accretion of autonomous power by organizations representing the interests of social categories, and enters into a process of political exchange with them. Societal corporatism has become most strongly institutionalized in countries such as Austria or Sweden where a powerful labour movement has become a 'social partner' with the peak employers' association and the state in negotiating economic and social policies. State corporatism, by contrast, occurs in societies with relatively weakly organized group interests, where states seek to legitimate their rule and accomplish their objectives by mobilizing the population within subordinated organizations. State corporatism tends to be associated with peripheral or dependent capitalist regimes, such as those in Latin America (Malloy, 1977).

The development of corporatism in liberal democracies is often associated with a reduction of the range of decisions which are subject to determination through electoral and parliamentary processes. Many early accounts assumed an evolutionary process of corporatist development with warnings that parliamentary democracies were increasingly becoming 'corporate states'. But with the increasing sophistication of corporatist theory, the appearance of empirical studies of corporatist processes and the conscious rejection of corporatist practices in some countries has come an appreciation of the limits of corporatism and its coexistence with parliamentary and pluralist processes. This has led to the development of a 'dual state' or 'dual politics' thesis which suggests that corporatism is limited to intermediation with respect to a range of issues concerned with production and involving producer interests, and will always coexist with a competitive or pluralistic political process for the determination of consumption issues involving individuals and consumer interest organizations (Cawson and Saunders, 1983).

Where corporatism has become strongly entrenched at the macro level, economic and social policies have been determined on the basis of tripartite negotiation. It has been argued that the ability of some countries to withstand economic recession without resorting to deflation and the creation of unemployment can be explained by the extent to which corporatism facilitates bargaining between capital and labour over the distribution of the social product (Goldthorpe, 1984). In such cases corporatist processes involve class collaboration, and for this reason many Marxist critics (see Panitch in Schmitter and Lehmbruch, 1979) have argued that corporatism can be understood as a strategy which is adopted by capitalist states in order to maintain the subordination of the working class. Related to corporatism as a process of macroeconomic policy-making is recent work by Scandinavian scholars, which has introduced the idea of the 'negotiated economy' as a means of describing economic policy-making regulated by a series of bargains between autonomous institutions (Nielsen and Pedersen, 1988).

An important part of the early writing on liberal corporatism concentrated on the comparative analysis of nation-states, and several attempts were made to rank countries according to the extent to which they conformed to an ideal type of corporatism. Most authors seemed to agree that the country which scored most highly was Austria, that the United States was the least corporatist country, and that in Britain corporatism has been relatively weak. Some attempts (discussed in Cawson, 1986) have been made to measure corporatism and correlate its incidence with other features of national political systems. The results are suggestive rather than conclusive, but there are indications that corporatism is linked to low levels of backlash against high taxation and public spending. Other studies have suggested that the more 'governable' countries are the strongly corporatist ones, and they tend also to have lower unemployment.

Most students of corporatism agree that the prototypical case of macro-corporatism is Austria, followed by the Scandinavian countries, and especially Sweden. Austria has a system of compulsory membership in chambers of commerce, labour, agriculture and the professions, and every working citizen is a member of at least one of these. Each is a highly centralized organization, in which the national leadership maintains effective control over sectoral and territorial subdivisions. The peak trade union organization monopolizes the representation of labour, and individual unions are subunits which depend on the centre for their financial resources. Parity of representation is guaranteed by the state in bargaining over price control and economic planning, and collective socioeconomic bargaining is focused on a highly informal non-bureaucratic agency, the Parity Commission. Thus the Austrian example demonstrates the effective institutionalization of the preconditions of macro-corporatism: monopolistic and centralized interest organizations, parity in class representation, and informal adjustment processes. All of these preconditions have emerged over a considerable historical period, and while none is unique to Austria, the combination of them certainly is (Marin in Grant, 1985).

Less stable and successful examples of corporatist institutions can be found in a number of other countries. For some two decades after World War II the Dutch Social and Economic Council effectively produced an interclass consensus on economic policy, but its influence waned from the 1960s as interest organizations became more fragmented and the formalized system of functional representation failed to adapt. In other cases, such as West Germany, corporatist institutions have come under pressure as a consequence of economic crisis, when employers and sometimes individual unions have sought to circumvent centralized bargaining procedures. In general the resurgence of neoliberal economic strategies since the 1970s has tended to undermine the preconditions for corporatism at the macro level (Goldthorpe, 1984).

Modern usage suggests the following as a concise definition of the concept: Corporatism is a specific sociopolitical process in which organizations representing monopolistic functional interests engage in political exchange with state agencies over public policy outputs, which involves those organizations in a role which combines interest representation and policy implementation through delegated self-enforcement.

Three key features of corporatism distinguish it from pluralistic processes of interest group politics. The first is the monopoly role played by corporatist bodies; the second is the fusion of the representative role with that of implementation; and the third is the presence of the state both in licensing monopoly representation and in co-determining policy. Whereas in pluralist theory interests are identified as prior to organization and political mobilization, in corporatist theory the state is identified as a crucial agent in shaping interests and affecting the outcome of group processes (Cawson, 1986).

The interest organizations which are most likely to achieve monopoly status and enter into a corporatist exchange with state agencies are those which represent producer rather than consumer interests, and which command resources of information or compliance which are necessary for the implementation of state policies. Empirical studies suggest that employers' and trade associations, trade unions and professional bodies are the most common interlocutors. The form that corporatism takes is bargaining, with a high degree of delegation of public authority to nominally private bodies. As a policy mode, corporatism may be contrasted with legal-bureaucratic and market forms of regulation which involve a markedly different form of relationship between the state and interest organizations.

In addition to the macro level, which involves peak associations in bargaining over public policies, corporatism can be identified at a sectoral or meso level in the relationship between state agencies and organizations which have achieved monopoly representation of particular sectoral interest categories. Even in countries such as the United States or Canada, which are weakly corporatist using national-level indicators, in particular policy areas such as agriculture strongly entrenched forms of corporatist intermediation can be found.

Corporatist theory has mounted a strong challenge to pluralism as a model of interest group politics, but as empirical evidence feeds into successive refinements of the theory, it is becoming clear that corporatism and pluralism should not be seen as alternative paradigms for studying interest politics but as end points on a continuum according to the extent to which monopolistic and interdependent relationships between interest organizations and the state have become established (Cawson, 1986).

Reading
Cawson, A. 1986: *Corporatism and Political Theory.*
—— ed. 1985: *Organized Interests and the State: Studies in Meso-Corporatism.*
Grant, W. ed. 1985: *The Political Economy of Corporatism.*
Malloy, J. ed. 1977: *Authoritarianism and Corporatism in Latin America.*
Schmitter, P.C. and Lehmbruch, G. eds 1979: *Trends toward Corporatist Intermediation.*
Williamson, P. 1989: *Corporatism in Perspective.*

ALAN CAWSON

council, democracy   *See* WORKERS' COUNCIL

counterculture   A minority culture marked by a set of values, norms and behaviour patterns which directly contradict those of the dominant society. According to the Oxford English Dictionary, the word was added to the English language in the late 1960s and early 1970s, referring to the values and behaviour of the American younger generation of the 'sixties' who were revolting against the dominant cultural institutions of their largely affluent parents (see AFFLUENT SOCIETY). Although the word entered the language in response to this particular generational conflict in America, the idea is as old as the Judaeo-Christian history of the West; Christianity itself was a counterculture in Jewish Jerusalem and later in pagan Rome. Both J. Milton Yinger, a leading American sociologist of countercultures (1982), and Christopher Hill, a leading British historian of the English revolution (1975), refer to the Bible in their books on countercultures:

> These men who have turned
> The world upside down
> Have come here also.
>
> Acts 17:6

The driving force of Christianity has been built on the dialectical tension between the Old and New Testaments, between law and Gospel, between the Ten Commandments and the Sermon on the Mount. Perfectionists in every generation have usually appealed to the universal Gospel of love as against the culturally rooted laws symbolized by the Ten Commandments. Thus among the multitude of seekers spawned by the English revolution of the 1640s and 1650s, the followers of such sects as 'The Family of Love' were not unlike the flower people and hippies of the 'Love Generation' in the American 'sixties'.

Sectarian and countercultural movements have usually had two aspects, radical activists who seek politically to revolutionize society and bohemians who withdraw from society to live in isolation. Thus John Lillburne, the most popular man in Cromwellian England, led his Levellers in political revolt, but eventually withdrew from political activism and became a Quaker; so Staughton Lynd, a guru of the student New Left who went to Hanoi, showing his solidarity with the enemy when America was still fighting the Vietnam war, also became a Quaker. Theodore Roszak, in an excellent, early book on the counterculture (1969), includes both 'the mind-blown bohemianism of the beats and hippies' and the 'hard-headed political activism of the student New Left' within counterculture.

At the close of World War II, Americans were confident and proud of their institutions which were rooted in Calvinist cultural values. These included faith in reason, science and technology, a Puritan ethic of hard work and self-improvement, representative democracy limited by law and Constitution, and finally, a mildly patriarchal family where divorce was still relatively taboo, parental authority assumed, and family church attendance higher than in any other Western nation. Order and authority in this confident society were shaped by a hierarchical, yet increasingly open and opportunitarian, class system led by elites drawn from, or being assimilated into, a secure and hegemonic WASP ('white Anglo-Saxon Protestant') establishment.

This optimistic society launched the longest economic boom in American history, which produced an unprecedented baby boom lasting well into the 1960s. These baby-boomers went to college and on to graduate and professional schools in increasing numbers. Meanwhile, a prophetic minority (Newfield, 1967) of them became disenchanted with the materialistic values of white America and attempted to turn them upside down in the 1960s, the most anti-authoritarian, anti-elitist and disestablishmentarian decade in American history. In the course of the decade, the hegemony of a WASP establishment over an open class system was replaced by a governmental bureaucracy, bent on levelling downward rather than upward, creating a classless society of ranks based on credentials (such as advanced degrees at prestigious institutions) rather than native ability and drive.

Coming of age in the shadow of the Holocaust and Hiroshima, and faced with the dehumanizing aspects of ever more rationalized and impersonal institutions such as multiversities at Berkeley and Michigan, many members of this generation found all forms of racism and ethnic prejudice as well as war unacceptable; reason, scientism and technology-worship were major parts of the problem rather than any solution; hard work and social mobility became the 'rat race' to be avoided at all cost (better an independent and honest carpenter or plumber than a conforming and conniving bureaucrat); self-improvement through self-denial gave way to the *Playboy* ethic of self-indulgence, love-making courtship rituals were dropped in favour of 'having sex'; husbands and wives were replaced by more or less permanent 'significant others' (lasting relationships were honestly feared); synagogue and church attendance, as well as nineteenth-hole rituals at the suburban golf club, were left to uptight parents while their children fled in search of meaningful lives in the student civil rights movement in the South, New Left politics on the very best campuses of the nation and escape through drugs and various Eastern religious cults in the urban bohemian scenes like the East Village in New York, or Haight-Ashbury in San Francisco, as well as the bohemian fringes of their favourite campuses from Berkeley to Harvard Yard. The Quakers (once called the antinomian Anabaptists of the English revolution who still believe in participatory democracy) went through a slow, steady decline in postwar America and then boomed in the 1960s as new Meetings were founded round campus communities. The largest meeting in Massachusetts was right off Harvard Square.

One important thing about the counterculture was its loss of faith in representative democracy in favour of participatory or demonstration democracy; the student New Left, led by Tom Hayden and other founders of Students for a Democratic Society (SDS), was determined to move political decision-making out of the halls of the legislature to the crowd-filled streets; the ballot was replaced by the bull-horn, the privacy of the voting booth by lonely crowds chanting simplistic solutions to complex political problems. The effectiveness of crowd politics depended on television which soon sent vivid audiovisual images round the 'Global Village' world, dramatizing the crowd behaviour of 3,000 students gathered (for the Free Speech Movement) on Sproul Plaza, at the Berkeley campus of the University of California, in 1964; the crowd of 20,000 in the march on Washington against the Vietnam war, in 1965; of 25,000 hippies and New Leftists marching on the Pentagon, in 1967, and finally, the angry, frightened student crowds battling the 'pigs' (policemen) in Grant Park and on the streets around the Democratic Convention in Chicago, in the summer of 1968, which demoralized the liberals (despised enemies of SDS). James Miller (1987, p. 304) described the end of that day in Chicago as follows:

> The sun set. Klieg lights were switched on. Television cameras recorded the action . . . Suddenly, without warning, the police attacked . . . Fused by panic, rage and pride, the crowd began to chant: 'The Whole World is Watching! The Whole World is Watching! The Whole World is Watching!'

After Chicago the SDS fell apart, leaving a small remnant called the Weathermen who were now dedicated to violence. Their end was symbolized by two events in 1970; in May a splendid town house in New York City on 11th Street, right off Fifth Avenue, in the Village, was accidentally blown up, killing three Weathermen; the survivors, including the owner's daughter, went underground; in May, National Guardsmen opened fire on demonstrating students, killing four.

The rise and fall of the drug culture paralleled that of the student activists. The year following the Free Speech Movement in Berkeley, two hippies opened a psychedelic shop in the Haight-Ashbury district of San Francisco. By the 'Summer of Love' in 1967, the Haight became the Mecca of hippie tribes from all over the nation who had tuned in, dropped out and been turned on by the drug religion of Timothy Leary, a defrocked Harvard professor, and Ken Kesey, the let-it-all-hang-out novelist who wrote *One Flew over the Cuckoo's Nest*, which became a cult novel and film of the sixties generation. In this sad summer, 'love had fixed itself in a place of excrement' (Wolfe, 1968, p. xviii). These love children, who had left homes of stifling comfort and affluence, had no idea how to take care of themselves. Barefooted, longhaired, dressed in rags from thrift shops and grandmothers' attics, they lived on drugs and junk food, suffered from bad teeth, bad digestion and lack of sleep, and were constantly stepping on rusty nails and broken glass; venereal disease flourished alongside sexual freedom. A free medical clinic treated some 3,000 patients a month that summer.

The greatest happening in the history of the counterculture was the Woodstock Festival of Life when some 500,000 youths, left activists, drop-outs and the just plain curious, found their way to a gigantic rock concert held in the middle of a muddy farm in upstate New York, in August 1968, just a month following the tragedy of the Democratic Convention in Chicago. For three days the stripped down, happily stoned crowd were orderly and friendly, even impressing the police and local farmers. If Woodstock was a success, the Let it Bleed festival of Angels and Death, run by Mick Jagger's Rolling Stones, 'the world's greatest rock and roll band', at the Altemont Raceway near San Francisco, in December, was a disaster. The Stones, to save money, hired a band of Hell's Angels (for 500 dollars worth of beer) to keep order (O'Neill, 1971, p. 261). The crowd of some 300,000 was far more stoned than at Woodstock. *Rolling Stone* magazine, leading authority on rock music, photographed Mick Jagger watching the Angels beating a young Negro from Berkeley to death on stage, in front of the freaked-out crowd. Todd Gitlin, obsessed with the stench of death in the stoned crowd, asked himself: 'Who could any longer harbor the illusion that these hundreds of thousands of spoiled, star-hungry children of the Lonely Crowd were harbingers of a good society?' (1987, p. 407).

See also STUDENT MOVEMENT, YOUTH CULTURE.

Reading

Feuer, Lewis S. 1969: *The Conflict of Generations: The Character and Significance of Student Movements.*
Fraser, Ronald 1988: *1968: A Student Generation in Revolt.*
Kennan, George F. 1968: *Democracy and the Student Left.*
Mailer, Norman 1968: *Miami and the Siege of Chicago.*
Rothman, Stanley and Lichter, S. Robert 1982: *Roots of Radicalism: Jews, Christians and the New Left.*
Wolfe, Tom 1968: *The Purple Decade: A Reader.*

                                    E. DIGBY BATZELL

counter-revolution   *See* REVOLUTION

coup d'état   Defined restrictively by Henry R. Spencer as 'a change of government effected by the holders of governmental power in defiance of the state's legal constitution' (1963, p. 508), the concept of a coup d'état would thus tend to cover only the category of executive coups. As underlined by M. N. Hagopian (1975, p. 6), the disadvantage of such a definition is that it excludes those coups fomented by groups not belonging to the power elite (paramilitary coups) or which, despite being part of the state apparatus, do not necessarily hold political power (military coups).

Unlike revolutions or militarized insurrections which also aim at a change of government (see REVOLUTION), a coup d'état in no way calls on the masses to mobilize. This prime characteristic does not exclude 'an eventual empirical interdependence of phenomena', a coup that may well occur 'at the beginning of a revolution, or during it' (Chazel, 1985, p. 637). The second characteristic lies in its manner of execution: prepared and carried out by a small number of people, a coup d'état requires above all secrecy and quick action. In this way there occurs 'the infiltration of a small but critical segment of the state's apparatus which is used to displace the government from the control of the remainder' (Luttwak, 1969, p. 12). The accent placed on limited institutional change is not always a pertinent factor. What is true for traditional societies, where coups are generally centred on personal rivalries – these are not so much executive coups but rather palace revolutions – is not necessarily so for other societies: the coup d'état in Chile in 1973 was accompanied by a significant narrowing of the political arena. Elsewhere, even though the strategic skill (secrecy and quick action) of the factious is crucial in unseating the holders of power, it is not sufficient in itself to guarantee the success of the coup d'état; the Kapp putsch in Germany in 1920 failed as a result of a general strike. However, the link between coups d'état and the civilian capacity to mobilize remains quite a complex one, since it is not rare for military coups to curb violent situations imputable, in developing countries, to a sudden upsurge in the participation of the masses. In this case, the ideology and organization of the military are often contrasted with the low level of institutionalization of political regimes characterizing praetorian societies – because of the absence or weakness of effective political institutions, social forces confront each other nakedly and each employs means which reflect its capabilities: 'the wealthy bribe; students riot; workers strike; mobs demonstrate; and *the military coup*' (Huntington, 1968, p. 196). Yet it would be an exaggeration to say that military coups lead only to authoritarian regimes: the coup in Portugal in 1974 bears witness to the fact that a putsch may sometimes open the way to democracy.

Reading

Chazel, F. 1985: Les ruptures révolutionnaires. In *Traité de Science Politique*, ed. J. Leca and M. Grawitz.
Hagopian, M.N. 1975: *The Phenomenon of Revolution.*
Huntington, S.P. 1968: *Political Order in Changing Societies.*
Luttwak, E. 1969: *Coup d'État: A Practical Handbook.*
Spencer, H.R. 1963: Coup d'État. In *Encyclopaedia of the Social Sciences*, ed. Edwin R.A. Seligman and Alvin Johnson, vol. 3–4, pp. 508–10.
Touraine, A. 1988: *La Parole et le sang.*

                                    PATRICE MANN

crime and deviance   The briefest conventional definition of crime would describe it rather tautologically as a breach of the criminal LAW. More generous definitions would probably add that the breach is considered harmful to the public good and is punishable by the state. Some, like the criminologist Paul Tappan, would further add a reference to a guilty mind, but intention is not a requirement in law. A classic definition of crime was produced by William Blackstone in 1778: 'public wrongs, or crimes and misdemeanours are a breach and violation of the public rights and duties due to the whole community, in its social aggregate capacity ... treason, murder, and robbery are properly ranked among crimes; since besides the injury done the individual, they strike at the very being of society.'

The conventional definition is not universally

liked. For example, a small number of positivist criminologists once declared that entrusting the determination of crime to lawyers and legislators produces a system of classification that is culturally relative, difficult to generalize and scientifically unmanageable. (See CRIMINOLOGY.) Instead of 'crime', Sellin (1938) proposed 'conduct norm' as a more rigorous and fruitful term. 'Conduct norms' are coherent and consistent crime-like things to be studied by criminology. However, they did not find much favour within the discipline.

Again, a small group of radical criminologists attached particular importance to the politics entailed in the identification of crime and criminals. In 1976, Chambliss and Mankoff stated simply that 'acts are defined as criminal because it is in the interests of the ruling class to so define them . . .' So profound were the political, social and moral implications of the word 'crime' thought to be that members of that group were reluctant to allow its definition to remain under the control of a state or class with which they disagreed. 'Crime' would then be allowed to become elastic and metaphorical, a wrong whose meaning was independent of what lawyers, laws and states might say, not very different in use from the condemnation intended in the interchangeable phrases 'it's a shame', 'it's a sin' and 'it's a crime.' Criminology itself would be transformed to study problems set by a radical view of the world. Schwendinger and Schwendinger (1975), for instance, deplored the annexation of the term 'crime' by capitalist states and preferred to exercise their independence by describing such problems as racism, imperialism and sexism as crimes instead. The very title of 'crime', they claimed, is part of a hegemonic system, wrapped up in a politics of naming and condemning which should be resisted.

The vast bulk of criminologists and social thinkers occupied with crime have not been swayed by Sellin or the Schwendingers. They have preferred either to avoid interrogating legal and legislative processes or to accept what those processes engender as solid and indisputable social facts. They have retained some version of the conventional definition. But it is a definition that encounters difficulty unless crime is treated as a special attribute of only a very limited number of contemporary Western societies.

There is the problem posed by the requirement that crime should be regarded as a breach of law punishable by the state. The state does not exist everywhere and certainly not always in a form familiar to Western criminal lawyers and criminologists. In the past, it could be but one of a number of interrelated powers armed with legitimate force and the capacity to penalize. Sharpe (1988), a social historian, has pointed to conceptual difficulties posed by the many offences tried in local manorial and ecclesiastical courts before the nineteenth century. Social anthropologists have pointed to the many preliterate societies possessing arrangements that do most of the work of a criminal justice system but which lack some of its formal structures. Thus, Llewellyn and Hoebel (1941) described policing among the Cheyenne, and Gluckman (1965) wrote about the Barotse system of jurisprudence. Malinowski was quite content to entitle one of his studies of Melanesia, *Crime and Custom in Savage Society* (1932). Something very close to crime can exist in communities which have no written laws or a formal state. Indeed, Reckless proposed an accommodating definition of crime in 1940: 'in the so-called primitive or preliterate societies which do not possess a written or legislated body of criminal law, a crime is a violation of the precious customs and the mores.' It is a definition that introduces a very major qualification.

There is a second problem. There are structurally elaborate states without a neat, predictable and precise criminal law. Ancient Egypt had no written laws because legislation would have encroached on the absolute freedom of the Pharaoh to declare his will. In a not dissimilar instance, totalitarian societies retain crimes by analogy. Crime ceases solely to be a specific breach of a code but can on occasion be behaviour that is deemed reasonably similar to such a breach. Article 79 of the Criminal Code of the People's Republic of China, for instance, states: 'a crime not specifically proscribed under the special provisions of the present law may be confirmed a crime and sentence rendered in light of the most analogous article under the special provisions of the present law.' Nazi Germany and Soviet Russia have had similar stipulations. Crime becomes what the ruling authorities want it to be at any time. In such a case, the appeal of another version of the minimal definition becomes apparent. Clinard (1963), for instance, represented crime merely as 'any act punishable by the state'.

The identification of crime may be eased in states such as Canada where there is a criminal code under periodic scrutiny from lawyers seeking consistency and rationality. Many states lack such a code and crimes there are not a simple and distinct class of events. Thus the legal system of England and Wales contains such an abundance of laws affecting so many areas of political, social and economic life that it has become ever more difficult to discern a simple coherent principle underlying the definition or application of ideas of crime. There are 'crimes' that do not conform to any conventional notion of the criminal. There are acts, particularly in the region of public welfare offences, that do social harm but are not criminalized. In 1980, a committee of Justice, the British section of the International Commission of Jurists, reported in *Breaking the Rules* that it was unable to discover how many different crimes there were in English law and what it was that made some offences crimes rather than 'mere' contraventions of law. There are now many criminal acts that were not formerly so. Clarke argued in *Fallen Idols* (1981) that the rise of financial and business fraud is due in some large part to the sheer expansion of regulation, and Tench argued in *Towards a Middle System of Law* (1981) that 'nowadays practically anything can be a crime.'

It might be added that practically anybody can be a criminal. According to the *Home Office Statistical Bulletin 7/85*, by the time they are 28, some 30 per cent of men in England and Wales will have appeared before the courts, and 40 per cent will have done so by the end of their lives.

One consequence of the proliferation of laws, crimes and criminals is that the meanings of crime seem to have become bifurcated in everyday life. On the one hand, there are many breaches of criminal law whose significance has become somewhat diluted: they are, as it were 'mere crimes'. Criminality has been incorporated into areas of society: 'ducking and diving' and 'wheeling and dealing' are routine and, indeed, admired features of large parts of the East End and South London. Handling stolen goods or 'fiddling' are normal and expected. Crime may indeed constitute a stable support of much organized society.

On the other hand, there is a second meaning of 'crime' that still embodies sentiments of outrage about the harm done to a community, and it is sometimes distinguished from the diluted version by being called 'real crime'. 'Real crime' has become something of a metonym, detached from its strict definition in law and much dependent on customary morality. It tends typically to be regarded as unacceptable, the acts of outsiders or of

oneself in moments when not fully responsible and accountable.

These two meanings are continually played off against one another, shaping the limits of the tolerated and permissible in any situation. Indeed, the precise character and relations of those meanings are of great political and moral importance. They pose questions about the legitimacy of legislators, legislation, police, acts, offenders and victims. It was for that reason, in part, that radical criminologists tried unsuccessfully to gain control over their usage.

What is quite clear is that crime and POWER are inseparable. W. Tallack, S. Schafer, N. Christie and others have chosen to attach special importance to the historical association between the idea of crime and the rise of a central organization capable of making and executing law. They point to the way in which the state organizes the roles and relations of victims, offenders and society. The appearance of crime is itself treated as tantamount to the appropriation of personal conflicts by a usurping government. They argue that, in what has been called the 'golden age of the victim', before the presence of a criminalizing state, people enjoyed some control over their own disputes. Conflict was personal: it engendered recognizable victims and offenders whose quarrels could be mediated and whose losses could be compensated. As the power to intervene in disputes became concentrated in fewer and fewer hands; as victims, offenders and conflicts became detached from one another, and as the state acquired a discrete corporate identity, so personal victims and their relatives and friends began to fade in significance. They lost 'property' in their conflicts: the idea of a victim became increasingly metaphysical, no longer demanding a visible hurt or a tangible person. There was, instead, an abstract entity, the commonwealth or society in what Blackstone called its social aggregate capacity, which required protection: it was not a particular individual's peace but the Queen's Peace that was broken. There even arose the possibility of what Edwin Schur described as 'crimes without victims', crimes involving drugs, prostitution, gambling, homosexuality, abortion and other practices, that produced no victim other than a representation of the affronted state or abstract community.

To be sure, it could also be argued that the golden age may not have been at all golden for the lone, unpopular or weak victim confronting a powerful assailant. There are some conflicts which the victim might well have wished to relinquish and, as Georg Simmel once observed, a third party can do much to defuse a dispute that would otherwise linger on interminably.

Deviance was a neologism introduced to social thought in the early 1960s and chiefly as a response to ideas excited by the publication of Howard Becker's *Outsiders* in 1963. It is one of the most recent of a string of terms devised by those who wished to move beyond the study of crime to embrace a wider area of problems that are not distinctively regulated by the criminal justice system. 'Social disorganization', 'social problems' and 'social pathology' came first, and they were discarded because they were thought either not quite capable of capturing the special character of that wider area or because they no longer resonated with the intellectual discourse fashionable at the time. 'Deviance' was adopted partly because it was thought to permit a useful enlargement of focus: new, interesting and hitherto ignored phenomena could be brought into view for purposes of exploration and comparison. Law and the criminal justice system could themselves be inspected from without and with new eyes.

Above all, a change of term signified an intellectual transition. The deployment of the word 'deviance' symbolized a departure from a preoccupation with crime and criminology which was considered by some to be intellectually cramping. In the USA, the transition was linked with the emergence of the Society for the Study of Social Problems. In Britain, a little later, it was linked with the York Deviancy Symposium. It was celebrated in Lemert's *Social Pathology*, and Becker's *Outsiders* and Cohen's *Images of Deviance*. The word 'deviance' is not only denotative but connotative. It marks the adoption of a discrete method as much as a special subject, being used characteristically by the then 'new' symbolic interactionist and phenomenological sociologists interested in the meanings which people give to their behaviour, in the interactive and dialectical quality of social life, and in the detail of small, embedded and observable scenes. The 'deviance approach' has often been stretched and applied to unconventional problems because social thinkers have found it illuminating, not because the events or people studied are themselves indubitably deviant. E. Freidson, for instance, employed it in the exploration of medicine and health.

'Deviance' includes crime (and it is most often crime that sociologists of deviance actually study) but it is evidently intended to extend to any other sanctionable straying from the path of convention. It has been applied very liberally to a great range of people and activities. Analysed as deviant have been stutterers, giants, dwarfs, prostitutes, the ill, robbers, embezzlers, the stupid, homosexuals and drug takers. Those like A. Liazos, who disparage the failings of such an ill-assorted field, have talked about deviants as being 'nuts, sluts and perverts'.

Deviance is probably not a very good word. It is not a legal or clinical term. Neither is it commonly employed in everyday life. It is peculiarly sociological, its meaning refracting the changing concerns of those who use it, and there is no great accord about its exact definition. Some have described it as statistically infrequent activity but it is apparent that there is frequent behaviour that could otherwise be usefully regarded as deviation: traffic violations and lying are instances. Talcott Parsons took deviance to be a fracturing or incomplete articulation of relations between people or institutions in change, although that description does not accommodate the stable deviance which seems to be built into much social life. Lofland (1969), Duster (1970) and others understand deviance to be the discredited or devalued standing of losers in the competitive politics of moral imputation. E. Erikson, Daniel Bell (1961) and Robert Merton (1949) portrayed deviance as the dark face of society which gives unwitting support to social order: prostitution buttressing marriage; bastardy securing primogeniture; and evil producing good. Theirs is an old and intriguing idea but it does rely on a troubling teleology and an unseen hand, and demonstration is not easy.

Deviance is perhaps most commonly and loosely described as a sanctionable violation of social rules, norms or expectations. There tends to be little hesitation in defining and recognizing its florid core forms. Moreover, Newman (1976) has shown that there appears to be wide agreement within and across societies about the principal rules of conduct. But 'deviance' is intended importantly also to encompass those less spectacular violations which seem to blur ambiguously into the activities around them. It is the very marginality of much deviance that is supposed to have enlarged and improved the intellectual reach of sociology. And marginality and ambiguity are pronounced. In a heterogeneous society, there is such a great scatter of contradictory rules that the pettier kinds of deviance are themselves correspondingly diverse and prolific. They are situated and time-bound, tied to persons, places and occasions. It may not always be possible for insiders or observers to ascertain what rules obtain in a particular setting, how coherent or systematic they are, how they are to be matched with other rules, whether they should be applied, by whom, to whom, and in what measure. Hargreaves's *Deviance in Classrooms* is a long and revealing essay on the tangled problems of rule observance and enforcement in one site, schools: every rule, it seems, has secondary and tertiary rules governing its application, every rule can be overruled in certain instances, and exquisite judgement must be exercised by pupils and teachers in the management of their everyday affairs. Deviants themselves often have a considerable stake in compounding confusion, in misrepresenting and concealing what they do, in passing as normal, and in misleading the observer. In Matza's words, deviants often become devious. So muddling are the phenomena of rules and rule-breaking that Matza (1969) and Douglas and Scott (1972) have represented contradictoriness and absurdity as constitutive of the very character of deviance. Deviance has a power to excite a recognizable sense of confusion and unease.

Because deviance abounds, because it is confusing and because so much is quite insignificant, 'mere' rule-breaking – what Lemert called 'primary deviation' that entails no reappraisal of a self or its actions – intellectual attention has been deflected on to the social reactions elicited by deviance. There is no conceptual bar to the study of primary deviation: Becker (1963) did so in the case of marihuana users. But it is those reactions, and reactions to reactions, that confer greater order, consequence, interest and visibility. The significance of acts and actors can be transformed, sometimes being joined to other putative meanings, graded, classified and appraised. Deviance ceases to be private and becomes a social phenomenon more readily susceptible of analysis. Such a process of symbolic reorganization was called 'secondary deviation' by Lemert. It is part of the work of LABELLING, work that invited sociologists to turn their gaze on institutions and practices of social control that had formerly been overlooked. Large portions of the sociology of deviance have some-what unhappily been entitled 'labelling theory' in consequence.

Reading

Becker, H. 1963: *Outsiders.*
Chambliss, W. and Mankoff, M. 1976: *Whose Law? What Order?*
Cohen, S. ed. 1971: *Images of Deviance.*
Downes, D. and Rock, P. 1988: *Understanding Deviance.*
Justice 1980: *Breaking the Rules.*
Lemert, E. 1951: *Social Pathology.*
Schwendinger, H. and Schwendinger, J. 1975: Defenders of order or guardians of human rights. In *Critical Criminology*, ed. I. Taylor et al.
Sellin, T. 1938: *Culture, Conflict and Crime.*
Sharpe, J. 1988: The history of crime in England. In *A History of British Criminology*, ed. P. Rock.
Sutherland, E. and Cressey, D. 1974: *Principles of Criminology.*

PAUL ROCK

criminology   This is a generic name for a group of closely allied subjects: the study and explanation of lawbreaking; formal and informal ways in which societies deal with it (penology); and the nature and needs of its victims (victimology). The popular use of the term by novelists and journalists to denote the finding and examination of evidence which may inculpate or exonerate suspects (forensic science or criminalistics) is a solecism.

The study of criminals and their behaviour is nowadays the province of psychologists and sociologists. In the past psychiatrists such as Cesare Lombroso and Henry Maudsley, and psychoanalysts such as Edward Glover, wrote about antisocial behaviour as if it were always or usually attributable to abnormalities of personality, constitutional or acquired. Today the wise psychiatrist confines his or her generalizations to offenders who suffer from disorders with unmistakable symptoms. They are a minority, even if 'anti-social personality disorders' are included.

Natural history

Early attempts to explain lawbreaking suffered from ignorance of its 'natural history' – of the facts of criminal life. Some nineteenth-century observers, notably Henry Mayhew (1851–62), described the violence and dishonesties of the urban poor with realism: but the anti-social behaviour of the better-off was left to novelists and court reporters. It was not until well into the twentieth century that criminologists, notably Sutherland

(1937), achieved more detailed descriptions of criminals' lifestyles, and that publishers discovered a middle-class market for the memoirs of literate offenders (for a modern example see Curtis, 1973). These accounts were not without bias, but put some genuine flesh on statistics which recorded little more than ages, previous convictions and sometimes official occupations.

Explanation

The result was a more sophisticated approach to explanation. The ubiquity and diversity of law-breaking began to be appreciated. A few sociologists and psychoanalysts clung to 'general theories' which purported to account for all or most crime, and even deviance as well (see also CRIME AND DEVIANCE); but the natural historians saw that this was no more sensible than offering a single explanation of 'disease'. Even quite specific types of offence such as shoplifting or infanticide are committed by people of quite different personalities, ways of life, and above all motivation. It was also realized that it is one thing to try to explain why this or that country, or culture, district or school, has a particularly high (or low) prevalence of certain kinds of offending behaviour, and quite another to explain why this or that individual is prone to it. Again, explaining an individual's proneness is logically and scientifically distinguishable from accounting for a single, unrepeated, lawbreaking, for which a 'narrative explanation' may be much more plausible (see Walker, 1977).

The contribution of POSITIVISM, however, has been voluminous and valuable, if sometimes in a negative way. Researchers have found statistical associations between lawbreaking (or, more precisely, a history of dishonest or violent offences) and a host of variables: gender, age, parental offending, parental disharmony, housing conditions and locations, intelligence, educational attainment, truancy, unemployment, nature of employment, religious and ethnic affiliations, body build ('somatotype'), abuse of alcohol or other drugs, gang membership, and even, in the case of violence, hot weather. Some of these variables, however, such as poor education and truancy, may well be effects rather than causes. In any case, the associations are seldom very marked (gender being the only exception). Even when mathematically combined the most they offer is a means of discriminating between categories in respect of the probability that a given member engages in lawbreaking (specific or non-specific).

For example, a girl from a harmonious home, with a good education and a white-collar job, is much less likely to be a lawbreaker than a boy with separated parents, minimal education and no steady job. From the explanatory point of view this is a jigsaw with pieces missing. There are too many individuals who fulfil the conditions but whose law-abiding lives can be accounted for only by more personal histories.

Some criminologists prefer the 'situational' approach. The main determinant is seen as being situations which offer opportunities that tempt, or stimuli that provoke. It is assumed that the vast majority of people will take advantage of opportunities – say for theft – if they are sure of impunity. People differ in what tempts them, and in their confidence about their chances of being convicted; but where there is an attractive 'target' sooner or later it will be hit. The existence of people with strong moral inhibitions cannot be denied, but is relatively unimportant so far as the prevalence of dishonest offences is concerned. Like most new contributions to the subject this overstates; but it is of value, as we shall see in the section on prevention (see, for example, Laycock and Heal, 1986).

Penology

This branch of the subject is chiefly concerned with the offical ways in which identified offenders are dealt with: capital punishment, deportation, incarceration, fining, probation and other non-custodial expedients; but some penologists interest themselves in societies' unofficial reactions, such as stigma and ostracism. Among the achievements of penological research have been evidence that the death penalty deters no more murderers than does 'life' (that is, long and indeterminate imprisonment); that general deterrents are not very effective when detection rates are low; that offenders who are amenable to reformative measures are in a minority, and not easily identified at the sentencing stage; and that many offenders detained for long periods in prisons or hospitals for the protection of others would not in fact be dangerous if released under supervision. Penologists have also concerned themselves with the unwanted effects of measures such as incarceration, and have corrected some exaggerations, for example about its psychological effects. Debate about justifications for punishment, or the proper scope of the criminal law, belongs to moral philosophy rather than penology, but familiarity with penology is essential for those who take part in such debates.

Prevention

Although deterrence is, strictly speaking, one sort of attempt to prevent crime (and is so classified by continental criminologists), 'prevention' in Anglo-American criminology tends to mean measures which focus on potential targets rather than potential offenders, who are less easily identified when at large. The situational approach described earlier, and the somewhat discouraging findings about the efficacy of measures aimed at offenders, suggest that more resources should be devoted to vulnerable targets. They may be individuals or property, or even 'the environment'. Individuals can be made less vulnerable by making them aware of the dangers of frequenting certain places at certain times, and wary of strangers who accost them. Women can be advised not to carry handbags. In some countries citizens are able to arm themselves with hand-guns, although the result is probably more casualties than would otherwise occur. Property can be made slightly safer by security devices and identification marks. Burglars and muggers can be made more visible by better street lighting, fewer covered passageways (for instance under streets) and thoughtful architecture. Neighbourhoods are increasingly willing to organize 'neighbourhood watches' and even 'vigilante groups', although the latter are frowned on by law enforcement authorities because their activities are apt to overstep the limits of what is acceptable (see POLICE). These are 'focused measures'. Claims have also been made for unfocused policies such as the improvement of housing, schooling and employment prospects. Evidence that these have worthwhile effects on crime rates is scant, and not easy to interpret with confidence; but such policies have other merits to recommend them.

Victimology

Preventive thinking gets some assistance from victimology. Early in this century natural historians of crime realized that it does not strike entirely at random and that certain occupations, activities and behaviour carry heightened risks of becoming a victim. Prostitutes, cab drivers, security guards and, nowadays, schoolteachers and social workers are well aware of this. In the 1950s a study of homicides by Marvin Wolfgang (1958) drew attention to the ways in which many of them had been provoked or invited by the victim's conduct, and he coined the term 'victim-precipitation'. Most violence against women is committed by husbands or lovers; most child abuse is committed by parents or members of the household. There may even, it has been suggested, be personality types which, especially among the young, invite violence or sexual improprieties. The victims of frauds and confidence tricks are often people whose greed blinded them to the implausibility of what they were being offered. In the case of fights it is often hard for the police, or the courts, to be sure who was victim and who was aggressor.

Victims may not always be blameless; but that does not lessen their needs. Victims of violence need medical attention but they also need humanity in interrogation, especially if the offence was sexual. Confrontation with attackers in court can add to the trauma, especially in the case of children. Special procedures have been devised for obtaining and presenting children's evidence. Many jurisdictions now permit adult as well as juvenile victims of sexual offences to be anonymous so far as the news media are concerned. 'Rape crisis centres' offer free counselling and psychiatric help. There have even been experiments which bring together the perpetrators and victims of crimes such as burglary and rape in the hope of some sort of benefit to both parties. The results have not proved easy to assess.

Reparation

A more material need of many victims is reparation, especially if they are poor. In many Western countries victims can claim financial compensation in the criminal court, instead of facing the daunting prospect of a civil suit. This does not, however, deal with the basic problem – the inability of many offenders to pay more than a fraction of what courts award, especially if they also have to serve a custodial sentence. State schemes of compensation are confined to a limited range of offences, usually those involving violent injury or psychological harm. No country has yet instituted a scheme of compulsory insurance against property crime. This is a problem which has been only partially tackled (see for example Hodgson, 1984).

Victim surveys

A valuable development of recent decades has been the 'victim survey', in which representative samples of the public have been questioned about offences from which they or their children may have suffered within the last year (or other specified period). These surveys have minor defects. Some categories of victim are too busy, vagrant or mentally disordered to be easily accessible to interviewers. Young males, who experience a good deal of violence, are often out drinking or otherwise exposing themselves to violence, instead of being interviewed about it. Some types of offence do not have specific victims and are unlikely to be reported: illegal pollution is an example.

The value of such surveys, however, is that they correct the serious underestimation of crime rates which result from 'under-reporting' and 'under-recording'. Many offences are not reported to the police (or other responsible authority) because those who could report them are too frightened or embarrassed (as in the case of sexual offences), or consider the offence too trivial, or unlikely to be the subject of any effective action. Some prefer to deal with offenders in their own ways, especially when the offenders are juveniles. Even if reported, some offences are not recorded, at least for statistical purposes. Those who report them may not be believed, for example because they may be thought to be acting from malice. The incident may sound too trivial. Too many recordings of unsolved crimes make a police force look inefficient. The net result of under-reporting and under-recording is serious underestimation, which victim surveys to some extent correct. It is conceivable that they will eventually replace police-generated statistics so far as common crimes such as burglary, theft and minor assaults are concerned (see Mayhew et al., 1989).

Penal reform

In theory the criminologist is a scientist, not a penal or social reformer, and confines himself or herself to providing and interpreting the findings of research, which campaigners may publicize if it suits them to do so. In practice the distinction is often blurred. The criminologist's choice of subject for research – say the psychological ill-effects of incarceration – is often dictated by the objectives of the agency which funds it, and even when the choice is with the researcher it probably owes something to his or her own ideology. Fortunately there are criminologists whose integrity compels them to report unexpected or inconvenient findings – for example where they have found that the ill-effects of incarceration have been exaggerated by penal reformers (see Bottoms and Light, 1987, ch. 8).

Reading
Bottomley, K. and Pease, K. 1986: *Crime and Punishment: Interpreting the Data.*
Box, S. 1981: *Deviance, Reality and Society.*
Freeman, J. and Sebba, L. eds 1989: *International Review of Victimology*, vol. 1.
Morris, A. 1987: *Women, Crime and Criminal Justice.*
Radzinowicz, Leon and Hood, R.G. 1986: *The Emergence of Penal Policy.*
Rutter, M. and Giller, H. 1983: *Juvenile Delinquency.*
Ten, C.L. 1988: *Crime, Guilt and Punishment.*
Tonry, M. and Morris, N. 1979–: *Crime and Justice* (annual collections of 'state of the art' papers).
Walker, N. 1988: *Crime and Criminology.*
Wilson, J.Q. and Herrnstein, R.J. 1985: *Crime and Human Nature.*

NIGEL WALKER

crisis   We speak of 'crises' in relation to subjects, a life or a form of life, a system or a 'sphere' of action. Crises decide whether or not something continues. The paradigm case of crisis is the life crisis, in which, at the limit, it is a matter of life and death. In every crisis those concerned are confronted with Hamlet's question: to be or not to be. Crises often have objective causes, but they must also be able to be *experienced* as crises by the subjects or social entities concerned. They always also affect the self-understanding and self-definition of actors, systems or spheres, since they always affect their 'identity', that is, a life or a life situation *as a whole*.

The history of the word is important and illuminating here. The Greek *krisis* does not distinguish between crisis and critique, covering 'difference and conflict, but also decision, in the sense of a definitive outcome, a judicial decision or indeed any judgement – something which today would come within the sphere of criticism' (Koselleck, 1973: p. 197). This original connection between the subjective and objective aspects of crisis remains when criticizing becomes fashionable in modernity. In the age of Enlightenment these two usages diverge, while continuing to overlap. With this separation, however, the terms critique and crisis, primarily used in the Middle Ages in its medical sense, become massively politicized. Sir B. Rudyard applied the medical concept of crisis to the political body: 'This is the Chrysis of Parliaments: We shall know by this if Parliaments live or die.' Even later than the eighteenth century, however, 'Crisis' is a common title for critical and polemical writings. Thomas Paine gave the name *The Crisis* to the journal in which he commented on the events of the American revolution. Here the Greek sense of crisis as judgement remains dominant in a polemical concept of crisis. The judgemental meaning of 'crisis', referring back to a judicial decision, and the medical, diagnostic meaning are combined when we speak, even now, of a *critical situation*.

In ancient Athens, it was the activities of judging (*krisis*) and ruling (*kratein*) that made one into a citizen (Aristotle). Law is a product of the crisis and division of ethical life. When it is given effective expression in a judgement, the end of the division or CONFLICT is brought about. (The German word *Ent-scheidung* indicates this process.) The Aristotelian link between legal judgement and crisis and the status of political citizen is itself the result of a division, separation or differentiation of the spheres of *oikos* and *polis* – a division in which law plays a fundamental role. The separation of the political (and thereby the status of citizen) goes along with the overcoming and replacement of the old legal system (family justice, blood revenge, *oikos* or house-justice) in favour of a bourgeois-political judicial system (see Meier, 1983). Hegel still has in mind this connection between law and crisis in his theory of tragedy. He describes the downfall of the hero in the crisis of the tragic conflict as a 'rational fate' which is played out in the name of a new, tragic and urbane justice, which replaces the 'old, epic justice' now seen as a pre-legal 'blind fate'.

From the Enlightenment to Marx, the present epoch is understood as a crisis and the crisis as practical, revolutionary criticism, as a case brought by the new bourgeois society against the old state or by the classes excluded from bourgeois society against those inside. But Marx is also at the beginning of social scientific theories of crisis; as these develop, the separation of theory and critique is brought out more sharply than in Marx's own philosophy of history. But what has been separated in theory is still combined in political practice: there can be no crisis without a diagnosis of crisis. A crisis diagnosis makes a strong explanatory claim. It does not aim for an end of history, but hypothetically constructs *a* history which could operate as a justification for political action for those who experience the crisis. In this sense Kant's was already a philosophy of history with a practical purpose, presupposing that the court of critical reason tries arguments and not people. From now on crisis and critique fall into different categories. Although criticism can make people aware of a crisis, and a crisis can provoke criticism or turn

criticism itself into crisis, the crisis decides other questions than those of criticism. Whereas the crisis concerns whether a form of social life is to be or not to be, the critique is concerned only with the validity of arguments; whether they are 'true or false', 'accurate or inaccurate'. This distinction (*krisis*) is notoriously ignored by the conservative metacritique of the Enlightenment. This fundamental critique, from Nietzsche and Carl Schmitt to Michel Foucault, conceives argumentation and criticism as war (*polemos*), as a struggle for existence and power. Like the philosophy of history it criticizes, it conflates critique and crisis and thus sees in criticism the real crisis of modern times. 'The crisis is concealed in criticism' (Kosellek, 1973).

The social scientific concept of crisis has deep roots in the philosophy of history, but in the twentieth century it has sunk new, post-metaphysical roots. The concept of crisis grounded in the philosophy of history has developed into an evolutionary one, in the light of which the philosophy of history is itself relegated to the status of a 'missing link' in the transition from the ancient to the modern concept of crisis. The most important connection is undoubtedly its temporalization in Christianity. This makes judicial decision into the final crisis of the Last Judgement. The whole of history is thus dominated by the contradiction that the final decision already occurred with the incarnation of the Messiah, but must still be left open to be ratified in the Last Judgement. This extends the crisis to the whole process between the Revelation or Christ's life and the End of Time; the permanent crisis makes, as Hegel put it, world history into a world court. 'Thus modernity sees the rise of a processual model of crisis which has impregnated numerous philosophies of history' (Kosellek, 1976: p. 1236).

A characteristic feature of the philosophy of history's crisis diagnosis is the way the epoch is treated as a whole. The crisis is always the crisis of a historical totality. The social scientific concept of crisis, by contrast, is always based only on a partial sphere or aspect of a life totality, for example the economic system, research programmes, developmental stages or organizational principles. Statements can no longer be made about ultimate crises or about progress and regress in relation to the Good and the happiness of the Whole. The philosophy of history's perspective on the totality of a 'form of life' (Hegel) remains constitutive for the subjective and intersubjective experience of crisis by those affected by them, but this becomes a mere subjective component of social scientific analysis. What remains from the philosophy of history is a discourse of self-understanding typical of crises – often with therapeutic characteristics. This concerns the identity problems of individuals or collectives. The global discourses of the philosophy of history have their place only *within* these discourses, in which those concerned must make clear who they want or do not want to be (cf. Tugendhat, 1979). But they no longer have a prognostic significance. Conversely, social scientific theories of crisis no longer produce knowledge about the outcome and the consequences of crises. In the crisis it is open how the dice will fall. 'Every crisis evades the planning... based on the belief in progress' (Kosellek, 1973). Books such as Lukács's *History and Class Consciousness* (1923) or Spengler's *Decline of the West* (1918–22) represent one side of the distinction between a concept of crisis based on the philosophy of history and a social scientific conception of crisis: Habermas's *Legitimation Crisis* (1973) or Daniel Bell's *The Cultural Contradictions of Capitalism* (1976) mark the other side. Another example of a social scientific concept of crisis is Thomas Kuhn's *The Structure of Scientific Revolutions* (1962) (see SOCIOLOGY OF SCIENCE). Here too it is a matter of the life of a particular, concrete community of researchers as a whole, attached to a holistic paradigm, but not of the fate of *the* European sciences, as in Husserl's well-known diagnosis (1937), which has not yet left the paths of a metaphysical philosophy of history poised between Fall and Salvation.

At the centre of the social scientific conception of crisis is the concept of system crisis to which Marx first gave clear expression, linking up both with the theories of circulation in classical economics and the French Enlightenment and with Hegel's concept of a *contradiction* between spheres which cannot be resolved inside a closed system. Hegel's theory of tragedy develops the model of crisis which returns in system crises and in conflicts which tear apart the social life-world or an image of the world. The overarching validity of mutually exclusive legal claims is what differentiates crises from wars, and also from revolutions or civil wars. In Greek legend, Creon and Antigone do not relate to one another as friend and enemy in war; they carry *in themselves* the opposition that tears their world apart.

The social scientific significance of this crisis model goes far beyond its interpretation in the philosophies of history of Hegel and Marx (cf. Kojève, 1947). Marx had already combined this model of a crisis oriented to the validity claims of antagonistic social groups (classes) with that of the *objective* system crisis identifiable in steering problems and the imperatives of system maintenance. But even in the diagnoses of the times which modernity has been offering since at least the time of Max Weber, the tragic model of an ethical sphere divided against itself has remained central. It stretches from the 'world of disintegration' of the early Lukács to Weber's diagnosis of the crushing of freedom and meaning in the irresoluble conflict of the mutually estranged value spheres of modern rationalism, through to Jürgen Habermas's theory of the 'pathologies of the life-world' and similar diagnoses offered by neocommunitarian thinkers. Robert N. Bellah and his collaborators (1985), following Alasdair MacIntyre (1981), see American culture stretched between the poles of instrumental and expressive individualism. Michael Walzer (1983) perceptively describes how justified and generally accepted ('justly' divided) spheres of modern life develop critical, indeed life-threatening tendencies to overwhelm and 'dominate' one another. Charles Taylor (1989) locates the inner contradiction of modern times among equally constitutive goods: universalism and pluralism, scientism (instrumentalism) and romanticism, moralism and deconstructive scepticism. The social scientific heirs of the Hegelian and Marxist crisis model have not only dissolved its unhappy link with the philosophy of history, but also replaced the paradigm of reflection by that of language and dissolved the unified perspective into a plurality of crisis tendencies. The contradictions which give rise to crises and open them up to experience no longer have to be understood on the lines of logical antinomies, produced by the rise of Spirit through endless stages of reflection, but can be brought back to their place in language, the contradictions between statements and above all in dialogue.

Crises of maturity and crises of cognitive and moral development, like other crises, are generally sparked off by contingent external circumstances, but they also have an inner, rational aspect. This is expressed, *inter alia*, in actors' attempts to reconcile their experiences with their image of the world. Experiences which conflict with one's image of the world may provide a rational motive to look for coherent solutions. Crises occur when conflicting experiences accumulate and can in the end no longer be integrated, as occurs with the 'anomalies' suffered by Kuhn's 'normal scientists'. Suffering often inspires the search for new and radical solutions, giving rise to a higher-level image of the world which brings old and new experiences into an intelligible and coherent relation. Communicative contradictions occur when diverse and incompatible world-images overlap and compete in the interpretation of the same or similar experiences. When actors with differing or competing world-images are required to dispute and to come to agreement, they must use the common language of everyday life to articulate their various perspectives and world-images. The articulation of their own world-image, with its always egocentric perspective, in ordinary language and with an orientation towards mutual understanding, pushes the actors into a decentring of their egocentrism. Learning processes which lead to the decentring of perspectives on the world can then be explained by the contradictions between idiosyncratic world-views and their articulation in a common language. These contradictions require the actors to transcend their own horizon and to 'fuse' it with that of other actors, in the common language of mutual understanding (see Gadamer, 1960). It thus becomes possible to experience the conflict between world-views or 'value spheres' as a conflict between contradictory articulations of one's own world-view or value sphere. A crisis, if it occurs, will decide whether these are productive or destructive antinomies (see Kesselring, 1981; 1984). Whether they are productive and a source of rational motivation may depend in practice on the institutional possibilities for objective discussion and resolution of conflicts. This holds for both individual and social evolution, for the outcome of individual crises of adolescence as well as for the self-enlightenment of social groups (see Döbert and Nunner-Winkler, 1978; Eder, 1985).

What is decided in a crisis generally depends on a whole constellation of complex and overlapping crisis tendencies. The conjuncture of identity crises and system crises produces critical thresholds, but the expectation of a systematic link between the two types of crisis which inspired Marx and Marxism has been shown to be too speculative. In practice we seem rather to be experiencing a dissociation or decoupling of the most varied cultural, economic, ecological, scientific, administrative and other crisis phenomena. An attempt to systematize possible crisis tendencies can therefore be related to the process of differentiation and centring of social subsystems; one can observe a rough trend away from socioeconomic crises and towards crises of motivation, legitimation and culture. The high degree of interdependence and the growing interpretation of subsystems, however, and above all the changeability and reversibility of evolutionary trends, make firm assertions almost impossible.

Reading
Habermas, J. 1973 (*1976*): *Legitimation Crisis*.
Husserl, E. 1937 (*1970*): *The Crisis of the European Sciences and Transcendental Phenomenology*.
O'Connor, J. 1973: *The Fiscal Crisis of the State*.

HAUKE BRUNKHORST

critical theory *See* FRANKFURT SCHOOL

culture The most striking single fact about the history of humankind is the extraordinary diversity of social forms produced by beings of either the same or very nearly the same genetic type. Differently put, whereas most species have a form of social organization built into their genes, the human animal seems to be programmed instead to pay attention to culture. Diversity is possible because human beings learn through cultural means. Living in accordance with nature is an attractive idea, but in the human case it actually means living with culture.

Social science has pointed to two central roles that culture fulfils for social life. First, culture provides meaning – for most of human history by means of organized religion. If Marx can loosely be seen as insisting that food production is basic to human life, Max Weber insisted quite as strongly that the central problem faced by human societies was that of theodicy, that is, the necessity to offer explanation for birth, suffering and death. This formulation is unhappy in so far as it suggests that there is a natural fit between human needs and social meaning. Rather, organized social life depends on repressing many of our genetically encoded drives, notably, as Freud rightly stressed, those concerned with sexuality. Secondly, culture provides rules of social action without which it would be impossible for human beings within a society to understand each other at all. It is extremely important to note that the world religions, very much in contrast to their supposed 'otherwordliness', are, naturally and inevitably, in large part compendiums of rules for managing daily life. Even a quick glance at Max Weber's studies of the world religions shows that he worked in this spirit, trying as much to explain the creation, content, spread and maintenance of belief systems as to analyse the ways in which they then influence the social order of which they are a part – the insignificance of the impact of Buddhism interestingly being ascribed to its pure otherworldliness, that is, its failure to provide a marriage service until the twentieth century.

The inevitable interpenetration of belief and circumstance – the fact that they tend not to have, to use David Hume's expression, 'distinct existences' – creates tremendous difficulties for social scientists. Powerful theory depends on being able to distinguish the moments at which one source of social power influences another, and it is accordingly of vital import to discover those moments when power sources can be differentiated. Much modern social thought has *not* been high-powered since it has followed a false trail; this is described first, as a preliminary to specifying the three ways in which ideas can be said to have an autonomous impact on society.

Either/or

Much modern social thought has been utterly bifurcated in its approach to culture. 'Idealist' thinkers from Antonio Gramsci to Clifford Geertz and from Talcott Parsons to Louis Althusser have insisted that a society is held together because norms are shared (see NORM). This position tends to relativism, that is, to the doctrine that, in Pascal's phrase, 'truth is different on the other side of the Pyrenees.' This leads a rigorous thinker such as Peter Winch to insist that the pretensions of social science to create universal laws are nonsensical. We may dislike magic but it 'works' for the Azande of East Africa, just as science works for us: all that social investigation can do is to translate and mediate between separate but equal worlds. In stark contrast, 'materialists' see ideologies as veils or masks for interested groups; still more importantly, they tend to believe that most actors are knowledgeable about their own interests, and accordingly unlikely to swallow beliefs that the powerful try to foist on them. Social order in this view depends either on naked power or on a natural harmony of interests between rational, self-interested actors – Marxism being an example of the former, and neoclassical economics of the latter.

Neither of these positions makes much sense. Materialists implausibly imply that history would have run the same course even had paganism, world religions and Marxism never been invented. Moreover, this begs the question as to why anyone *bothers* to invent belief. In the case of Marxism, either the productive forces are irresistible, in which case there is no need to justify them: or they need to be justified, in which case they are not irresistible. Still more important is the actual softness that hides behind the view of individuals seeking to calculate their 'real' material interests. This becomes apparent when we think of trying to 'calculate' whether to marry someone. We need a *coup de foudre* for this sort of life event, for the simple reason that our identities are involved: calculation presumes a solidary and single self, and it is all but useless when a decision involves what we are or may become – as Dostoevsky's novels brilliantly demonstrate. Most of us are not 'unmanned', as was Hamlet, by too much thought because we possess values which give us a sense of IDENTITY; differently put, it is impossible to specify interests which do not contain cultural components. To say this, however, does not entail accepting idealism wholesale. Specifically, there is everything to be said against the slide between saying that humans have values (perfectly true) to accepting the view that societies are held together/constrained by a set of values (very largely false): we may, in other words, learn through culture, but this does not mean that culture is the sole force accounting for change or cohesion in society. A rather large amount of empirical evidence is now available to show that dangerous or lower classes rarely share the values of official culture (see also COUNTERCULTURE). Such evidence should not of course be taken to mean that 'real' and 'material' interests are the sole concern of social actors. What is really at issue is the nature of ideology. For no-holds-barred idealism to make sense, it is necessary that ideologies be clear and consistent, that is, capable of directing social life. Most ideologies are simply not like that: they are rag-bags, replete with different options usable by different groups at will. Medieval villagers felt themselves opposed to church hierarchy, but in the name of the poverty of Christ. If it is true that we have values, it remains the case that we are more than mere concept fodder. And if a thinker like Winch is absolutely right to stress the reality of magic to the Azande, it is the merest intellectual conceit to pretend that magic is on the same level as the cognitive practices of modern science. Crucially, social science depends on those cognitive practices: at the least we bracket local belief (ignoring, for instance, the claim that Islam spread because it was true, so as to investigate the conditions to which it responded), while at most we investigate matters – such as the ability of a belief system such as magic to maintain itself in the face of contradiction – precisely because we know local practices to be mistaken.

The impact of ideas

Freedom from the false antithesis between idealism and materialism allows us to see three ways in which ideas have on occasion had an autonomous impact on society. These three ways can best be described by bearing in mind Max Weber's concern with the 'rationalization' of the West. If some of his insights remain valid, contemporary scholars have usefully complemented his insights as well.

Weber is best known for his *The Protestant Ethic and the Spirit of Capitalism* (1904–5). That book did not say that capitalism emerged simply as the result of Protestantism; to the contrary and in line with his notion of 'elective affinities', Weber insisted that new ideas made sense of the life of the orderly members of the uniquely autonomous cities of north-west Europe. The fact that circumstance is so involved with culture means that the first way in which ideas have an impact is the least autonomous of the three. Nonetheless, there is everything to be said for specifying this as a distinctive social force. What is really at issue here is *morale*. If a Marxist would be able to accept Weber's account, it remains the case that Marxism imagines, effectively in the spirit of B. F. Skinner, that there is a virtual correspondence between circumstance and idea such that the stimulus of circumstance will *automatically* bring forth an ideological response. There is no reason why we should accept this. A class or group needs to believe in its moral destiny if it is to be capable of great collective acts. By and large, the working class has lacked precisely this sort of force. And it was a Marxist, Lucien Goldmann, who showed how an elite grouping could be damaged by its lack of morale. In the late seventeenth and early eighteenth century, the French *noblesse de robe*'s lack of confidence was much exacerbated by the tortuous and tragic mental world created by Pascal and Racine, their ideological representatives.

Idealists are mistaken, as noted, to imagine that most ideologies are so inflexible that we are trapped within the terms of their discourses. Christianity was able, to take an obvious example, to accommodate itself to empire, to its absence and to a system of states, and equally it managed first to endorse and then to oppose slavery. Nonetheless, there are occasions when *discourse* does autonomously affect the historical record. There may indeed be an elective affinity between idea and circumstance, but the repertory of options within a particular ideology, in terms of which circumstance can be understood and justified, may on occasion be limited. This viewpoint probably helps us understand the rise of the West, albeit not in traditional ways. The development of modern science – as John Milton, very much in the spirit of Weber, has pointed out – does seem to depend on the particular terms of discourse embedded in the Western legacy. The fundamental concept of 'law of nature' rests on the combination of Greek investigation of nature and a Judaic conception of a hidden, austere and orderly deity which reveals neither its designs nor the order of things but forces humanity to interpret the surface appearance of things as clues to its grand design. The poverty of Muslim science may well be explicable by the very different terms in which the deity was conceived: as all-powerful as the deity of the West but differing from it in being prone to interfere on an occasionalistic basis with the workings of the world. More generally, what is noticeable about Islam is its intransigence, its difficulty in adapting to new circumstances given that 'the gates of interpretation' were held to have finally closed soon after the death of Muhammad.

The third and final way in which ideas can have an impact on society is the most important. What is at issue is something rather stronger than Weber's contention that ideas can determine the tracks along which interest sends action. This is of little help in some circumstances in so far as it suggests that the tracks have been laid, that a social order is already in place. For the greatest moments of ideological power have been those in which intellectuals have served – to make use of Michael Mann's improvement on Weber – as 'tracklayers', that is, as the makers of society. Ideological power can lead to the *creation* of society. The same point can be further illustrated if we think of Durkheim. If we accept the view that the presence of norms defines a society, then the society of north-west Europe between, say, 800 and 1100 AD was Latin

Christendom. Now to say this is in fact to improve on Durkheim. Quite as much as crude Marxism, Durkheim viewed belief as a reflection of other social processes. But in the early Middle Ages, Christianity was not the reflection of society. It was society. For it was the church that issued rules about external warfare and internal peace. But if we inquire into the genesis of this ideological power, we are forced to recognize that in another way Durkheim still has much to tell us about belief. Christian society was initially created in the Roman Empire by the sending of messages, the epistles, between communities of urban dwellers – craftsmen, women, freed slaves – who could have no part in official culture yet stood above the minimal world of the peasantry. We can best understand the birth of this world religion if we remember that religion, according to Durkheim, is 'society worshipping itself'. Christianity made people, otherwise marginalized, into a community. If the power of ideas sometimes depends on their actual content, what can matter still more is the ability to link people together into a community.

The higher things
Up to this point the emphasis has been on the most important meaning of culture, that is, the anthropological sense of culture as a way of life. But culture can also refer to art – about which two points deserve to be made.

Many modern thinkers believe that art either holds society together or pulls it apart: Daniel Bell manages to combine these positions in asserting that bourgeois art supported capitalism while the demands of modernist art for instant gratification are a threat to the modern world (see also ART, SOCIOLOGY OF). One doubts the descriptive accuracy of this picture: the disenchantment and alienation seen by modernism as characteristic of the modern world probably says more about the position of artists, caught in the interstices of the market, than it does about the feelings of whole sections of the population. But what is most noticeable about this view of art is its idealism: the functioning of society is naively held once again to depend *solely* on the ideological factor.

If the relation of art to social order/disorder has much concerned modern social thought, so too has the relation between 'high' and 'low' culture. These terms can be put to good use: the extent to which official culture is shared throughout society, in history and in contemporary circumstances, is a matter fit for empirical investigation – an approach which allows us to recognize that the consensual categories of a Parsons are not without merit in the analysis of the United States, the set of categories being, of course, a reflection of that extraordinarily Durkheimian social formation. A similar approach could usefully be adopted to a related debate – as to whether artistic standards are 'diluted' by popular art. At times, popular art has enriched 'high' art, as was certainly true for the Shakespearean moment; but equally the organization of mass media – which differs so greatly from nation-state to nation-state – may be such as to homogenize and limit. In the field of culture, there is much to be said for getting away from presuppositions about higher things so as to investigate instead the social workings of art worlds.

Reading
Abercrombie, Nicholas, Hill, Stephen and Turner, Bryan 1980: *The Dominant Ideology Thesis.*
Bell, Daniel 1976 (*1979*): *The Cultural Contradictions of Capitalism.*
Crone, Patricia 1989: *Pre-industrial societies.*
Elster, Jon 1989: *The Cement of Society.*
Gellner, Ernest 1973: *Cause and Meaning in the Social Sciences.*
Goldmann, Lucien 1956: *The Hidden God.*
Mann, Michael 1986: *Sources of Social Power.* Vol. 1: *A History of Power from the Beginning to A.D. 1760.*
Milton, John 1981: The origin and development of the concept 'law of nature'. *European Journal of Sociology* 23.
Weber, Max 1904–5 (*1976*): *The Protestant Ethic and the Spirit of Capitalism.*
Winch, Peter 1958 (*1976*): *The Idea of a Social Science.*
JOHN A. HALL

culture, counter-   *See* COUNTERCULTURE

culture, mass   *See* MASS CULTURE

culture, political   *See* POLITICAL CULTURE

culture, youth   *See* YOUTH CULTURE

D

dance   The belief that dance is a trivial art, suited only for amusement and entertainment, was common at the end of the nineteenth century. At the beginning of the twentieth century, the pioneers of modern dance started their revolt against what they considered the decadence of contemporary ballet. What they urged was a return of dance to its original function in society, that of an instrument to strengthen the sense of community. The instrument could work either to reiterate traditional beliefs, urging their continuing relevance, or it could stir thoughts of protest against existing values. The former direction has generally characterized the genre of folk dance. Theatrical dance has tended toward the latter, though abstract ballets rather than dances of social significance have predominated in the course of this century.

With few exceptions, writers on dance have also concentrated their efforts on analysing the formal structures of dance, rather than seeking out its social content. The nature of dance itself has led this way. Movement can, indeed, be expressive, but what can be best expressed by movements of the body are feelings, emotions, not intellectual ideas. When a traditional society uses dance either to enhance its beliefs or to demonstrate its rebellion against them, it creates an image. A group moves together, affirming its solidarity. Or it chooses a narrative format, conveying its message with an example of the tragic misuse of power or the glorified triumph of good.

Though dances of social significance have not dominated the theatrical dance scene in this century, some outstanding exceptions can be noted. Among the early modern dancers, Ruth St Denis and Ted Shawn turned to the mysticism of the Orient, to the timeless values of ancient myths and legends in works like *Radha* (of 1906) and *White Jade* (of 1926). Isadora Duncan embraced the ideas of the newly established Soviet Union in *Marche Slav*, which depicted the oppression of the masses and the final triumphant breaking of their chains.

A landmark in the history of twentieth-century dance was *The Green Table* (of 1932), by the German Kurt Jooss. Its call for peace began and ended with scenes of the diplomats arguing from their respective sides of the negotiating table. Between these, Jooss set tragic portrayals of the ravages of war on the lives of parents, lovers and friends.

The characters of *The Green Table* are generalized abstractions of types. Social thought in the Soviet Union, however, has used narratives involving specific characters, often with incidents drawn from history. An early work, *The Red Poppy* (of 1927), told of a brave Soviet captain who is threatened by a Chinese conspirator but saved by the sacrifice of a Chinese dancer. More recently Yuri Grivorovich of Moscow's Bolshoi Ballet condemned the cruelty of Tsarist Russia in *Ivan the Terrible*, in 1975, and praised the workers of Siberia in *Angara*, in 1976.

In the United States, explicit social thought has played an insistent, though usually minor, role. During the Depression years of the early 1930s, the Workers' Dance League sponsored concerts promoting social protest. Their dances bore titles like 'Eviction', 'Hunger', 'Unemployment'. In 1955, Anna Sokolow bemoaned the emptiness of city life in *Rooms*, where people live physically together but emotionally isolated. In 1984, Liz Lerman's *Nine Short Pieces about the Defense Budget and Other Military Matters* took a more specifically political stand.

Celebration of the Black heritage began with the work of Katherine Dunham and Pearl Primus, followed by the great success of the company of Alvin Ailey whose 1960 *Revelations*, set to Negro spirituals, became a tremendous popular success. In that decade, too, young choreographers began to work with improvization and individual expression. Anna Halprin formed her San Francisco Dancers' Workshop, a multi-ethnic group, devoted to racial harmony and the well-being of the earth.

In Germany, Pina Bausch exposed problems that people face in contemporary society. The characters in her dance-theatre works perform ingrained rituals as if by rote; their behaviour lacks feeling, lacks motivation. In *1980*, the dancers waver between aggressive exhibitionism and helpless loneliness; between lethargy and hysteria.

In China a rice-planting song 'yang-ko' became the victory theme of the communists in 1949. Dancers used work movements, along with pacing, hand-clapping and body swaying, to accompany the melody. Political narratives followed. In *The White-Haired Girl* (of 1964) the heroine suffers under a cruel landlord until her black hair turns white, but she is eventually freed by the Eighth Red Army when it liberates her village.

In Japan the treatment has been more abstract. Begun as a protest against the horrors of war, the genre known as Butoh has featured dancers with shaven heads and white-painted bodies inhabiting a landscape of despair. Slow paced, with movements that barely move, Butoh shows its audience a troubled world, the consequence of global brutality.

At present, non-theatrical dance faces critical problems. Dances that grew out of the shared experience and needs of a community are now vanishing, along with the way of life that generated them. With the move from rural into urban areas, young people spend much of their leisure time watching television. When they do dance, they prefer forms that offer them opportunities for individual expression rather than those that reflect collective values. Remaining traditionalists find it difficult to interest them in the dances of their forebears. Small groups are trying, however, and some avid European educators are teaching folk dances to eager learners in the primary grades. In some African villages efforts are made to maintain festivals with native dances that restate the values and customs of the community.

Another kind of solution is presented by the theatrical folk dance company, which takes the basic spirit and leitmotifs of indigenous genres, and choreographs them for skilled performers to present in theatrical settings. While many argue that these dances no longer truly represent their native sources, others argue that they still serve to promote feelings of ethnic identity and pride. The success of such groups as the Moisseyev Folk Dance Ensemble of the Soviet Union and the National Dance Company of Senegal certainly serve this purpose.

But at times a social crisis can provoke a revival of interest in community dance. When Nelson Mandela was released from prison in 1990, South African youngsters took to the streets to dance the Toyi-Toyi as an expression of their joy.

The claim has often been made that dance is a universal language. As this century nears its close, that claim is being substantiated. Teachers are working in the schools of various countries to familiarize young dancers with different techniques and styles. More and more often, choreographers are setting their works on dance companies in other nations. Exchanges are underway. As these moves contribute to international understanding, the dance world hopes that nations will also continue to respect and perform the dances that symbolize their own identity.

See also ART, SOCIOLOGY OF; THEATRE.

Reading
Boaz, Franziska ed. 1972: *The Function of Dance in Human Society*.
Brinson, Peter 1983: Scholastic tasks of a sociology of dance. *Dance Research Journal*, no. 1, 100–7; no. 2, 59–68.
Katz, Ruth 1973: The egalitarian waltz. *Comparative Studies in Society and History* 15.3.
Rust, Frances 1969: *Dance in Society*.
Spencer, Paul ed. 1985: *Society and the Dance*.

SELMA JEANNE COHEN

Darwinism   *See* EVOLUTION

Darwinism, neo-   *See* NEO-DARWINISM

Darwinism, social   *See* SOCIAL DARWINISM

decadence   The periods in history which have been described as 'decadent' share the conviction that 'life begins again and again'. This cyclical vision of things is the cornerstone of two vast complexes of themes, the first of which relates to 'correspondences' with the external world, with our immediate environment, with nature and so on, while the other embraces the varied elements of EVERYDAY LIFE, hedonism, scepticism, in short, the valorization of lived experience. The basic premise of both variants is the recognition of social life as it actually is, rather than as it 'should be'. It involves coming to terms with the fact that, whether we like it or not, there is an acceptance of existence which expresses itself in countless forms of repetitions.

This is certainly the hallmark of decadence. Such repetition, which is almost obsessional, is a way of both affirming and denying the passing of time. And in this sense cyclical repetition is an efficient defence mechanism. The appearance of the 'comic strip' can thus be considered an extraordinary symptom of a form of narrative which cannot be encapsulated within linear time.

What one can observe in stereotyped conversation or in the gratuitous send-ups which are basic features of the 'comic strip' is that, perhaps without intending it or at the very least not explicitly, they assert through their intrinsic criticism of dogmatic discourses a certain invariable quality of man and society, and a return of 'the same'. Whether in a playful or in a more sardonic manner, they provide a reservoir for a kind of agnostic anomie which implies that nothing new ever happens in human history. Whether its target is the church or the state, repetition reminds us of the fact that only the present, which is unfailingly identical with itself, deserves our attention. In this sense 'decadence' denotes an 'ethics of the moment' which is not concerned with a heavenly paradise or some future utopia, but obstinately intends *all the same* to live out this existence which, for all the many trials and tribulations it brings, is still captivating despite them or maybe because of them.

One element which throws into relief the importance of cyclical and decadent RELATIVISM in the collective consciousness is the attitude to politics. Once again everyday conversations can teach us a lot; it would require specialized research in this area to analyse all the nuances of suspicion about politics they imply. It would be more precise to say that they show that politics is the focus of intense interest, but is generally regarded as an art, an art with its own rules. In Mediterranean countries for instance, political discourse is meant, in the manner of 'bel canto', to stir passions, to appeal to the heart rather than the head. In the light of the concept of decadence we become aware of just how much social thought owes to this cyclical world-view, according to which 'nothing is new under the sun'. In the last analysis *the imposition* of power is an immutable constant of life, something that people know well, at least intuitively. 'Princes' may come and go, but their actions will always be imposed from outside and thus remain 'abstract', and even when they intend to speak and act on behalf of the least privileged, it is always to demand submission or conformity to the rule.

Decadence not only manifests itself in this popular form of relativism, but also in more erudite expressions. First of all, from a Weberian point of view it is clear that the acknowledgement of antinomic value systems within different societies, as well as within each society – simplified in the expression 'war of the gods' – leads us, if not to an absolute 'axiological neutrality' at least to a certain scepticism about the concept of Truth itself (Weber, 1904). In a deliberately paradoxical fashion, Max Weber tries to think rigorously and to generalize, while at the same time recognizing the fickleness and ephemerality of human passions. One thing is for sure, namely that several of his analyses take place against a background of decadence. The 'antinomy of values' will never be resolved and, in the last analysis, it is because of this antinomy that societies last. Putting it somewhat flippantly we might say that 'so long as the gods are at war with each other, men are at peace.'

A similar perspective is to be found in the sociology of Vilfredo Pareto. Just as Claude Lévi-Strauss argued that 'man has always been able to think equally well,' Pareto was convinced that 'man is always the same.' Evidence of this conviction can be found in his *Treatise on General Sociology* (1915–19). Several of his analyses are informed by this scepticism, which may stem from all the disappointments which marked his career. The conscientious economist, who later became a somewhat disenchanted professor of sociology, was aware of the 'vanity of action' which derives from the sense that eternal return and repetition dominate the history of human societies. In this respect one could say that he is imbued by the tragic sense of existence. A good observer of contemporary politics, he was well aware of the fact that it is not based on rational arguments, whatever its myth about itself, and he sets out to draw from this realization all the necessary conclusions. It is in fact characteristic of decadence to show that reason in the realm of politics, but *a fortiori* even in human activities which do not claim to be a manifestation of it, is no more than what Pareto calls 'derivation', a legitimation which masks all the inconsistencies, ravings and vested interests of passion. Here one cannot help but think of Machiavelli and his *Florentine Histories*, in which he throws into such stark relief the ambiguity and the ambivalence of human action.

In other words, whenever the future predominates, the collective consciousness is wholly turned towards it. When instead the present prevails, a cyclical and decadent vision of the world will reemerge. But why? Perhaps because of the 'saturation' mechanism so well described by Pitirim Sorokin, which causes values, as well as things, to become worn out and exhausted. This would also explain the saturation of a linear conception of time and the desire to recuperate the 'here and now' which permeates everyday life. And the present is never grasped better than when one compares it to some great moments in the past. This is well expressed by Proust's metaphor of time being 'einsteinized'. Cyclical life takes us back to the time of passion which overrules all rationalizing constructions. One certainly cannot talk about decadence without referring, or at least alluding, to the spin-off effect it has on the ways we understand reality. As soon as the 'pro-ject' stops being the driving force of society, the sociologist has to resort to a different mode of evaluating social life. The relativistic acceptance of *what is*, this affirmation of life in all its contingency, is the recognition that all beings and all situations are marked by incompleteness. And this is something which the logic of the 'must be' cannot tolerate.

In defiance of those intellectuals who confuse the erosion of certain VALUES with the tragic and melancholic death of all things, and of those who think that the end of *a* world means the end of *the* world, decadence reminds us that analysing the role of repetition in everyday life and recognizing the hedonistic pleasure to be derived from unleashing the senses opens up a wide field of inquiry. On the basis of this deeply rooted conviction we can dispute the pronouncements of the apologists of the future or of those nostalgic for things past, by arguing that decadence allows us to glimpse the serenity of the Greek 'Kairos', in other words the moments of opportunity offered within the flux of everyday life.

See also PROGRESS.

Reading
Durand, G. 1979: *Figures mythiques et visages de l'oeuvre*.
Freund, J. 1984: *La décadence*.
Maffesoli, M. 1979: *La Conquête du Présent: pour une sociologie de la vie quotidienne*.
Pareto, V. 1915–19 (*1963*): *The Mind and Society: A Treatise on General Sociology*.
Spengler, O. 1918–22 (*1926–8*): *The Decline of the West*, 2 vols.
Weber, M. 1904 (*1949*): *The Methodology of the Social Sciences*.

MICHEL MAFFESOLI

decision theory   Decision theory is the study of how rational agents choose to act given their aims, their options, and their beliefs about the effects of their options on their aims. Even given all this, deciding what to do may be deeply problematic, either because of the sheer complexity of the calculations that are needed (as in the decision problems studied in operations analysis) or because the beliefs are uncertain. This besetting uncertainty may be about the state of 'nature', as in utility theory, or about the choices of other agents whose choice problems interlock with theirs, as in the theory of games.

Decision theory has been developed in its classical form as an axiomatic theory, the axioms laying down *a priori* principles of rational choice. Because the central core of everyday psychological explanation is that action is rationally related to the agent's beliefs and aims, decision theory may be seen as providing, among other things, a formal model of that core (see Lewis, 1983). For a series of defined situations, classical decision theory aspires to deduce the agents' decisions from the *a priori* principles alone. It is thus an idealizing theory, which depicts the agent as never violating the *a priori* principles, and always acting as they logically dictate however demanding this may be to compute. But round this classical, idealizing core of theory there has also been much work concerned with testing empirically human subjects' conformity with the axioms and, in recent years, with developing theories which collect, explain, and study the consequences of observed departures from them.

The two major theoretical achievements of decision theory have been *utility theory* and the *theory of games*. GAME THEORY is the decision theory of the individual in social settings. It is so called because Von Neumann and Morgenstern took parlour games to be isomorphic with, and paradigms for, the economic and other social interactions to which the theory was addressed. It concerns, and attempts to deal in axiomatic style with, the decision problems which two or more persons face when the outcomes of the actions of each one – and so their desirability – depend on the actions of the others. Each is assumed to know the options and desires of all; and moreover that the others have this knowledge. Most of the literature concerns *non-cooperative* games, in which the players cannot learn the intentions of others by communicating with them, but must infer them from knowledge only of their situation (their options, desires and knowledge) and their rationality.

Utility theory concerns the problem of an individual agent who must choose between two or more actions which give rise to 'risky prospects'. A risky prospect for an agent is a set of alternative outcomes together with a probability for each outcome, attached to it by the agent; I, for example, face the risky prospect (£25 with probability one-tenth; minus £1 with probability nine-tenths) if I bet £1 on a horse at odds of 25 to 1 against to whose winning I attach probability of 1 in 10.

Utility theory had its beginnings in Daniel Bernoulli's 1738 paper reporting the 'St Petersburg' curiosum, the fact that no one is willing to pay more than a few pounds to play a certain game of chance, though the *expected value* of a player's winnings is infinite. (The 'expected value' of a risky monetary prospect is the weighted average of the different possible gains, the weights being their probabilities.) In explanation Bernoulli conjectured that the rational gambler is a maximizer of the expected value not of income but of its utility. Von Neumann and Morgenstern (1944) axiomatize this 'expected utility hypothesis'. They show that if a person ranks risky prospects in a manner that meets certain obvious canons of rationality, expressed in the axioms of the theory, then there is a numerical magnitude associated with each outcome, called its *utility*, such that he or she ranks a risky prospect above another just if it gives a greater expected value of this magnitude. For example, I will prefer to make the above bet if and only if $(1/10)u(£25)+(9/10)u(£-1) \geq 0$, where $u(£x)$ denotes the utility of winning £x. Some of the axioms are uncontroversially true of rational preference: for example the Monotonicity Axiom, which says, roughly, that given two outcomes, one (A) preferred to another (B), raising the probability of A gives a preferable prospect. Others are more controversial, notably the Independence Axiom, which says: if an outcome A is at least as well liked as an outcome B, then a given chance at A is at least as well liked as the same chance at B.

Both game theory and utility theory concern rational decisions taken in conditions of uncertainty, but the uncertainty is of radically different kinds in the two theories. In utility theory it is 'risk' – uncertainty representable by probabilities. These attach, in classical utility theory, to the 'state of nature'. In game theory, however, the uncertainty is about the decisions of other rational agents,

who are assumed to derive these decisions by pure reason from the data of their problems. This is not a chancy business, and it is hard to see what basis the first player could have for ascribing probabilities to them. (Decision theory has also concerned itself with uncertainty which resists probabilization for another reason – because the agent is in 'complete ignorance' about which possibility is or will be realized.)

What sort of things are the agent's probabilities in a decision under 'risk'? Von Neumann and Morgenstern supposed them to be objective chances, like those in games of chance, known to the agent. But this is not the only possibility. Within decision theory there has developed the view of probabilities as subjective 'degrees of belief' revealed in 'preparedness to bet'. It is clear that an agent who prefers a lottery which gives a prize if state S transpires and a penalty if not-S does to one that gives the prize if not-S and the penalty if S in some sense believes more strongly in S than in not-S. Just as Von Neumann and Morgenstern 'construct' utilities out of the pattern of the agent's choices among lotteries, when these obey certain axioms, so Ramsey (1926), Savage (1954) and other subjectivists construct numerical degrees of belief out of this pattern. They succeed in showing, for agents obeying their axioms, both that these magnitudes are (mathematically) probabilities, and that the agents choose as if maximizing expected utility reckoned according to them. These results have led to the so-called Bayesian view that all uncertainties that agents face are probabilities and that the expected utility hypothesis provides a comprehensive theory of rational decision-making.

The expected utility hypothesis has been repeatedly disconfirmed in laboratory studies. The most famous experimental violation is the so-called Allais paradox. Another is the 'common ratio effect' demonstrated by Kahneman and Tversky (1979): if a person prefers a moderate prize M to a 50 per cent chance at a large prize L, according to the theory he or she must also prefer a 10 per cent chance at M to a 5 per cent chance at L; but subjects standardly display the first preference and the reverse of the second. Such findings have provoked diverse reactions: some, who regard utility theory as normative and find its axioms entirely compelling, conclude that subjects are in error, and in need of instruction! Others, however, feel that normative theory should reflect the strength of the intuitive judgements that provoke such 'reversals', or else regard utility theory as primarily explanatory or predictive. These attitudes have led to the development of 'non-expected utility' theories, somewhat more complex and/or weaker than utility theory, which are consistent with the recalcitrant observations.

In spite of its empirical rough edges, utility theory has been widely used in explanatory and predictive work in the social sciences, and with considerable success. In political science it has spawned RATIONAL CHOICE THEORY; in economics it is ubiquitous, providing a simple and powerful way of extending to uncertain settings the discipline's central assumption of the efficient pursuit of self-interest. It has a key role in explaining such diverse phenomena as insurance, gambling, the holding of money, and the stickiness of wages in recessions. In many of these cases it is conjoined with the empirical hypothesis that economic agents are *risk averse*, that is, prefer a sum $£x$ for sure to a risky prospect whose expected value is $£x$.

Decision theory has completed a brilliant half-century in which it has contributed powerful and illuminating tools of thought to the social sciences. Yet it remains in a not wholly satisfying state. As a theory of rational human choice it is, in its classical form, both too strong and too weak: too strong in that its axioms – sometimes because they set impossible standards, sometimes because they fail to capture the subtleties of human concerns – are consistently violated by intelligent subjects. Too weak because it ignores constraints on what count as rational beliefs, desires and actions in the specific cultural settings to which it is to be applied. It remains to be seen how far these shortcomings can be repaired without damage to the power and the luminousness of the classical theory.

Reading
Bacharach, M.O.L. and Hurley, S.L. eds 1991: *Foundations of Decision Theory: Issues and Advances*.
Gardenförs, P. and Sahlin, N.-E. eds 1988: *Decision, Probability and Utility*.
Jeffrey, R.C. 1965 (*1983*): *The Logic of Decision*, 2nd edn.
Luce, R.D. and Raiffa, H. 1957: *Games and Decisions: Introduction and Critical Survey*.
Nozick, R. 1969: Newcomb's problem and two principles of choice. In *Essays in Honor of Carl Hempel*, ed. N. Rescher.
Reznik, M. 1987: *Choices: An Introduction to Decision Theory*.

MICHAEL BACHARACH

deconstruction   This has become the word most currently used to describe the work of the French philosopher Jacques Derrida (born 1930) and those who describe themselves as, or are perceived to be, his followers (despite Derrida's own reservations about the term), and 'deconstructionism' is used exclusively by critics of this work. In fact there is no unified 'school' or institution of Derridean thought, although it has inspired a good deal of work, especially in literary theory and philosophy. Deconstruction is still a violently disputed area of thought, and Derrida has been involved in a number of polemical exchanges, notably with Michel Foucault, Hans-Georg Gadamer, Jürgen Habermas, Jacques Lacan and John Searle.

Much of the critical material written about Derrida can be shown to rely on inadequate understanding, but his work is difficult enough to inspire very basic disagreements of interpretation even among supposed experts. It is fashionable and convenient to suggest that there are two opposed receptions of Derrida, whether these be favourable or critical: one as essentially a philosopher who may incidentally have some things to say about literary studies (Jonathan Culler, Rodolphe Gasché, Christopher Norris), the other as almost an anti-philosopher attacking philosophy from the standpoint of something like literature (Habermas, Geoffrey Hartman, Richard Rorty); this type of characterisation can be shown to be fundamentally misguided (Bennington), if only because it relies on a binarist presentation (see below) in a context where binarism is perhaps the primary object of suspicion.

Derrida takes as his object no less than the totality of what he refers to, in the wake of Heidegger, as Western metaphysics or onto-theology. His claim, still following Heidegger, is that this tradition, at least since Plato, has attempted to determine being as *presence*, but that such a determination is dogmatic, relying on an 'ethico-theoretical decision' rather than any theoretical demonstration, and can always be shown to fail in a variety of ways. In Derrida's view, Western thought has habitually proceeded in an oppositional way, proposing binary pairs of concepts (of which some of the most pervasive and general are perhaps inside/outside; good/bad; pure/impure; presence/absence). While presenting these pairs as neutral and descriptive, it in fact determines one of these terms as primary or privileged, and the other as secondary or derived or inferior or parasitic with respect to it. Derrida's early work attempts to show this, improbably, by following the guiding thread provided by the traditional construal of the relationship between speech and writing (in Husserl, Plato, Rousseau, Saussure, Hegel among others). Derrida shows, in a first, exegetical moment, how speech is traditionally valorized above writing by accruing to itself all the values of presence, while writing is (dis)qualified as embodying exteriority, materiality, death and absence. In a second moment, Derrida argues that, even on their own terms, the authors in question cannot fail to show, in spite of their most apparent arguments, that the predicates habitually used in the description of writing are in fact essential predicates of language in general, and therefore of speech as well. Philosophers seem to want to show that speech is primary and writing derivative: they end up showing, in spite of themselves, that speech is itself really a sort of 'writing'.

The core of the argument is as follows: writing is traditionally described as involving the repeatable functioning of a sign in the absence of my animating intention (for example after my death); but without the possibility (the *essential* possibility) of decontextualized repetition (if necessary after my death) even of those things I *speak* and fully intend to say, then language would not function at all. The possibility of repetition (as the *same*, but repeated and to that extent not *identical*) is definitive of language as a whole, and cannot be confined to writing. The deconstruction of the classical opposition (here speech/writing) involves the polemical retention of the previously devalorized term (here writing) to name a more general structure which includes the previously valorized term (here speech). This term (writing) has undergone a displacement (or 'reinscription') in the process, and has disrupted the binary opposition in which it was traditionally defined. This displacement immediately disqualifies a whole range of 'textualist' responses to Derrida (whether supportive or critical), which assume that the term retains its old sense. Further, the displaced concept of 'writing' thus elaborated functions at one and the same time as the condition of possibility of LANGUAGE, and as the condition of impossibility of its ever achieving its traditional *telos* of self-effacement in the interests of thought.

This 'example' of deconstruction immediately suggests a number of important 'methodological' consequences:

1   Texts (even philosophical texts) are not simple and unified, but habitually involve, alongside the most obviously proposed content or doctrine, more or less obvious resources which work against that content or doctrine;

2   The working of these resources can be demonstrated independently of any claim as to what the author intended;

3   The deconstruction is not essentially a critical activity brought to bear by the reader from outside the text, but is in a certain sense already 'in' the text;

4   In so far as texts escape the control of any internally proposed reading (point 1 above), then they do not simply 'deconstruct themselves' either (this again disqualifies a range of responses to Derrida, both laudatory and critical). Deconstruction happens somewhere 'between', say, Derrida and Plato, but cannot be located within the historical schemes of any history of philosophy or ideas.

These consequences would perhaps be of only limited importance (affecting, for example, the historian or reader of philosophy but not the 'doer' of philosophy) were it not for a further claim drawn from this description of how language in general can work. Deconstruction tends to show how any attempt to define concepts or meanings as self-sufficient is incoherent, and how any attempt to determine the consequent relationships between concepts as oppositional (or, by extension, dialectical) breaks down. One of deconstruction's most significant claims is that binary and dialectical accounts still work towards an undifferentiated unity (the 'presence' of metaphysics, precisely). On a deconstructive construal, this relationship must be thought of as *differential* but not *oppositional*, or as involving a difference which (contra Hegel) need not become opposition (see DIALECTIC). Meanings, or effects thereof (for Derrida believes in 'meanings' as little as do Quine or Wittgenstein) result from the multiply differential network in which terms are defined *solely* by their interrelationships. This network is intrinsically *historical* in so far as terms are 'present' only through their repeatability as the same (but non-identical), and is thereby inherently *traditionalistic*. The only means for thought are inherited with this network, and it is naive to expect to be able to think without recourse to it. In the field of philosophical conceptuality, this historicity of the network implies that *any* use of a philosophical concept (and in fact of any concept at all) involves an at least implicit 'reading' of the tradition, which thus cannot be ignored.

This inevitable ambivalent indebtedness to the tradition is also why Derrida retains the name of the old concept (here 'writing') rather than attempting simply to introduce a new one for what he is attempting to think. Elsewhere, the logic of this argument translates into Derrida's habit of borrowing the operators of his arguments from the texts under discussion, thus denying the possibility of any clear demarcation of object-language and metalanguage. This refusal of the traditional philosophical fantasy of achieving a vantage point outside the field of investigation does not, however, commit Derrida to a position of pure immanence: certain terms (*pharmakon*, supplement, *parergon*, and even the notorious neologism 'différance' (an attempt to name the becoming-different of the differential network; see STRUCTURALISM) by a playful modification of the key notion of difference) gain an always limited purchase on the texts in which they remain nonetheless embedded: this 'quasi-transcendental' status (as formalized especially by Rodolphe Gasché) implies an intermediary status between the immanent and the transcendent which perhaps best captures the deconstructive position.

One of the consequences of this situation, which is no longer philosophical in the traditional sense of the term, is that there is nothing outside the thus radically historical network of multilayered interrelated differences, or, in what became a notorious formulation, that 'there is nothing outside the text'. *Différance* means that differences are never absolute (a common misreading of Derrida involves the assimilation of his *différance* to Hegel's absolute difference, in an attempt to show how it must revert to absolute identity), and neither, therefore, are identities. This radically non-teleological situation is one offensive to Rationalism (see RATIONALITY AND REASON), but does not mean that deconstruction is thereby irrationalist or nihilistic: reasons must be given, and Derrida writes much that is recognizable within the norms of philosophical argumentation (*pace* Habermas), but their purchase is never established. Deconstruction does not say that everything is of equal value, but that establishing values as equal or unequal remains always a question; it does not say that there is an infinite number of interpretations or meanings, but that there is not *one* interpretation or meaning (see

HERMENEUTICS). Unlike binary thinking, deconstruction thus opens to a radical multiplicity or 'dissemination' which will always remain relatively disorganized or chaotic. This multiplicity implies that deconstruction attempts to allow events a singularity they are denied in metaphysical philosophy. Because of this multiplicity, events in their singularity are *undecidable* (never quite classifiable in the classical binary way), and therefore, according to Derrida, demand ungrounded decisions which are of the order of what is traditionally thought of as politics. But if traditional political philosophy attempts to domesticate this undecidable dimension, deconstruction affirms it, and to that extent cannot be annexed to recognizable political theories or programmes. Undecidability makes the taking of responsible decisions possible (without it ethics and politics would be reduced to administration and bureaucracy), but makes impossible their secure theoretical or doctrinal gounding. To that extent it is both the resource and the despair of politics in general.

Reading
Bennington, Geoffrey and Derrida, Jacques 1991: *Jacques Derrida*.
Culler, Jonathan 1982: *On Deconstruction: Theory and Criticism after Structuralism*.
Derrida, Jacques 1967 (*1976*): *Of Grammatology*.
—— 1967 (*1978*): *Writing and Difference*.
—— 1972 (*1981*): *Positions*.
Gasché, Rodolphe 1986: *The Tain of the Mirror: Deconstruction and the Philosophy of Reflection*.
                                    GEOFFREY BENNINGTON

definition Social theorists have tended to assume that the stipulative or verbal definition of terms ('By x I mean abc') is an unproblematic and desirable practice, requiring nothing more than clarity and consistency of usage. This view, expressed in the late nineteenth and early twentieth centuries by Emile Durkheim (1895) and Ferdinand Tönnies (1899–1900), is still accepted as a commonplace by most social scientists (see POSITIVISM).

A more complex view can be found in Max Weber's assertion that, for example, a definition of religion can come only at the *end* of an investigation and not at the beginning. Here Weber seems to be following Nietzsche's maxim that concepts which express a whole historical process resist definition. This view, vigorously upheld by Theodor Adorno (see FRANKFURT SCHOOL), tends to go with a stress on the hermeneutic complexity of social phenomena and their intimate relation to VALUES. This in turn was reinforced from the middle of the century in the English-speaking world by Wittgenstein's critique of positivism, giving rise in the work of Winch (1958) and others to an alternative model of social sciences (see VERSTEHEN). The normative relevance of definition was further brought out by Gallie's notion of 'essentially contested concepts' in social and political thought (Gallie, 1955–6).

The decline of positivism into conventionalism, and consequent anxieties over RELATIVISM, have prompted supporters of rationalism and REALISM to revive the notion of 'real definition', in which definitions are intended to express the essential nature of an entity – as in the definition of chemical substances by their molecular structure. How far this is possible for social objects remains controversial, but it is clear that the more sophisticated conception of the nature of social–scientific theory which has come to predominate in recent decades has brought with it a greater sensitivity to the problems of the formation of social–scientific concepts.

Reading

Durkheim, Emile 1895 (1982): *The Rules of Sociological Method.*

Gallie, Duncan 1955–6: Essentially contested concepts. *Proceedings of the Aristotelian Society*, NS, 56.

Hollis, Martin 1977: *Models of Man.*

Outhwaite, William 1983: *Concept Formation in Social Science.*

Tönnies, Ferdinand 1899–1900: Philosophical terminology. *Mind* 8 and 9.

Winch, Peter 1958: *The Idea of a Social Science and its Relation to Philosophy.*

WILLIAM OUTHWAITE

de-industrialization   Referring to the contraction of output and/or employment in the manufacturing sector of the economy, the phenomenon has received particular attention in the United Kingdom since the late 1970s, although a more recent debate in the United States addresses the same issues. It is insufficiently appreciated that a rather different literature exists on the de-industrializing effects of incorporation inside the great European empires of the nineteeth and twentieth centuries. Leaving that aside, the principal characteristic of the recent discussion of de-industrializa-

tion has been generalized confusion. This results from two meanings being carelessly superimposed on each other.

On the one hand, de-industrialization is seen as a natural consequence in the move from early to late (or perhaps to post) industrial society (see POST-INDUSTRIAL SOCIETY). The tertiary sector must grow if the advanced economies wish to retain their competitive edge by moving their industries up the product cycle, that is, moving towards ever higher technology goods. There is nothing 'wrong' with such a move. The smaller share of Gross Domestic Product provided by manufacturing industry represents a relative rather than an absolute decline; that is, de-industrialization does not mean a loss of affluence. Similarly, there is no reason in principle why diminished employment in the secondary sector cannot be taken up in the tertiary sector.

On the other hand, de-industrialization refers to economies which are doing less well than they might for various structural reasons. The British economy suffered an absolute decline in manufacturing from 1979 to 1987, and there is ample evidence to show that its relative decline is due to factors other than successful industrialization elsewhere. If Britain had to decline, the question then becomes whether it had to decline so far below the level of France, Germany and Italy; similar questions are now being asked about the United States. A combination of factors is usually held to account for such poor performance: sometimes the creation of comparative advantage by action of the state elsewhere is blamed; more often attention is paid to internal social rigidities of various types. It is probably no accident that decline in Britain and America has been so steep: both have an Anglo-Saxon dislike of industrial policy, and both tend to favour finance above industry.

The political left has been particularly concerned with de-industrialization. This is scarcely surprising: either form identified here diminishes the importance of the manual working class on whose activities progressive hopes tend to rest. Most plans to reverse de-industrialization, however, are made defective by not distinguishing between the two senses highlighted here – that is, plans are often made to restore manufacturing industry to its full former glory, in unawareness of the fact that some de-industrialization is inevitable, perhaps indeed desirable.

See also TECHNOLOGICAL CHANGE.

Reading
Bell, D. 1974: *The Coming of Post-Industrial Society.*
Blackaby, F. ed. 1979: *De-industrialisation.*
Gershuny, J. 1978: *After Industrial Society.*
Martin, R. and Rowthorn, R. eds 1986: *The Geography of De-industrialisation.*
Singh, A. 1977: UK industry and the world economy: a case of de-industrialisation? *Cambridge Journal of Economics* 1. 2, 113-16.

JOHN A. HALL

democracy   The meaning of the word 'democracy' is 'rule by the people'. It was first used in the fifth century BC by the Greek historian Herodotus, combining the Greek words *demos*, meaning 'the people', and *kratein*, meaning 'to rule'. Abraham Lincoln's famous definition was 'government of the people, by the people, for the people'. By elaborating on the notion of government or rule the meaning can be given more precisely: a democracy is a political system in which the whole people make, and are entitled to make, the basic determining decisions on important matters of public policy. The notion of being 'entitled to make' the basic decisions distinguishes democracy from other systems in which such decisions are in effect determined by the people – for example, where a weak or ailing dictator gives way to the people's wishes because of the threat of riot or insurrection. In a democracy it is *because of* their entitlement to do so that the people can make the decisions; the entitlement derives from a system of basic rules such as a constitution.

The idea of the people making decisions raises the difficulty of how *many different* individual decisions can be combined into *one* collective decision. A common response is to conceive of democracy as majority rule. The idea here is that where unanimity is lacking, that is where the preferences expressed by individuals' decisions are divided, it is the greater rather than the lesser number of preferences which should prevail. The greater number is nearer to being the whole: the majority's decision should be *counted as* the decision of the whole people. There are, however, many difficulties with such an idea. A decision by the *whole* people amounts to something more than a decision by the majority and must involve compromise and consensus; and democracy cannot be properly equated with majority rule (Holden, 1988; Spitz, 1984).

The primary meaning of 'democracy' has just been indicated, but there is also a secondary meaning which stems from the closeness of the connection between the ideas of democracy and equality (see EQUALITY AND INEQUALITY). There is this connection because, apart from anything else, the idea of the whole people making a decision involves the notion – summed up in the slogan 'one man, one vote' – of each individual having an equal say. Without this there would be a decision by some, rather than all, of the people. But so close is the connection that equality sometimes becomes central to democracy's very meaning: this gives us the secondary sense where 'democracy' means, roughly speaking, 'a society in which equality exists'. This subsidiary meaning can also become involved in conceptions such as 'social democracy' and 'economic democracy' where the idea of a system characterized by social and/or economic equality is central (for a different sense of 'economic democracy' see below).

The meaning of 'democracy' is reasonably clear, but this fact tends to be obscured due to the diversity of systems that have been called democracies. Indeed, it might sometimes seem that the only common feature in such diversity is the expression of approval. As approval for democracy is now almost universally expressed, that at least is clearly signified by the use of the term, even if exactly *what* is being approved is not so clear. Indeed, for some it appears that 'democracy' is merely a 'hurrah! word' emptied of all descriptive content, meaning no more than 'hurrah! for this political system'. However, confusion of this sort can be avoided by attending to the distinctions between the *agreed meaning* of 'democracy' – 'rule by the people' – and *differing judgements about what is necessary for such rule to exist*, and hence which political systems actually exemplify it. Thus disagreement about the application of the word 'democracy' – disagreement about where there is rule by the people – does not, in fact, imply that the word merely signifies approval and that it lacks an agreed meaning (Holden, 1974, 1988).

This near universality of approval is a salient feature of democracy today. The other key feature is that modern democracies are *indirect* or *representative* rather than *direct*. They are also now predominantly *liberal* democracies. This, however, is a very recent development (see below), before which there were important disagreements, of the sort just mentioned, concerning the application of 'democracy' to different types of political system.

Although so important today, historically

democracy has been relatively unimportant. For many centuries it did not exist. 'Both as an idea and as a practice, thoughout recorded history hierarchy has been the rule, democracy the exception' (Dahl, 1989, p. 52) – although this state of affairs is now, perhaps, being reversed. For a period in classical Greece democracy was important, notably in Athens in the fifth and fourth centuries BC. After that, though, it was not until the late eighteenth and the nineteenth century that the idea became important again; and not until the twentieth century that it became properly established in practice. And it was only after World War I that a general *dis*approval of democracy was replaced by widespread approval.

The democracy of ancient Greece was *direct* democracy: the people ruled by actually assembling together and directly making the basic political decisions (Held, 1987; Sinclair, 1988). This, most thoroughgoing, form of democracy has continued to have a hold on democratic thought; indeed, until the late eighteenth century 'democracy' only referred to this direct form. However, the Greek *polis*, or city-state, was much smaller than a modern state where it is not possible to assemble the people (in Athens there were 30,000 to 40,000 citizens, and the quorum for the Assembly was 6,000). The increase in size and complexity of states has, then, meant that in the modern world democracy must be *indirect*. Here the people only make a few very basic decisions directly, at elections, the rest being made by their elected representatives: indirect democracy is *representative* democracy. There are differing ideas about the nature and role of representatives in a democracy (Pitkin, 1967; Holden, 1988). However, the basic notion is that representatives make decisions for, or on behalf of, the people who elect them, but that in doing so they are, ultimately at least, subordinate to the people's own decisions expressed at the elections. Voting at elections is thus the key democratic process, and it is necessary for virtually all adults to have the vote for a system to be a democracy. (See also POLITICAL PARTICIPATION.)

The dominant form of democracy today is *liberal democracy*. Those who support liberal democracy believe it to be the only kind of democracy possible; but, until very recently at least, it was held that there were rival forms (see below). The term 'liberal' applied to governmental systems usually implies a concern with protecting individual freedoms by limiting the power of the government (see LIBERALISM). The typical idea is that the power of a government should be limited by subjecting it to regulation by a constitution or bill of rights. In a liberal democracy, then, the elected government expresses the will of the people, but its power is nonetheless limited. Hence it is, to an extent, a qualified form of democracy in which the power of the people – as expressed through their government – is limited. On the other hand, supporters of liberal democracy maintain that key liberal freedoms are necessary for democracy to exist at all. Without freedom of speech, association and so on, the people could not be offered the choices at elections which enable them to make the basic political decisions. In short, free elections are seen as a necessary condition for – and liberal democracy as the only possible form of – democracy.

The notion of liberal democracy is usually associated with important ideas about the further kinds of political structures and processes that are necessary for limiting governmental power and providing electoral choice. Prominent amongst these is the concept of a multiparty system and the associated idea of parties whose function is to oppose the government. These can be seen as components in the overall idea of PLURALISM. This centres on the concept of a plurality of political groups (see INTEREST GROUP), as well as parties, as being important both for providing sources of power alternative to and limiting that of the government, and for creating choice for the electorate.

Until very recently liberal democracy was challenged by alternative types of system that were said by their supporters to have a superior claim to be forms of democracy. These were the one-party systems of the communist world and of many Third World countries: the 'communist variant' and the 'underdeveloped variant' of 'non-liberal democracy' (Macpherson, 1966). The former were referred to as *people's democracies*, and to some extent acted as a model for the latter. The claim to be democratic rested on the idea that the single governing party expressed the *real* will of the people better than they could do themselves. This had similarities with the idea of the 'general will' formulated by Jean-Jacques Rousseau (1712–1778), the famous French political philosopher. Also involved, in the case of people's democracies, was Lenin's notion of the vanguard communist party discerning the real class interest – and hence eliciting the real will – of the proletariat (see LENINISM). Part of the claim on behalf of people's democracies was the contention that in the liberal 'democracies' the power of the people was vitiated by the workings of capitalism.

After World War II one-party democracy provided a powerful challenge to liberal democracy until the dramatic events of 1989–90. Then, the overthrow of communist systems in Eastern Europe involved the general rejection of the idea of one-party democracy in favour of liberal democracy. And Third World one-party democracies are being affected too: they are now being widely rejected in theory, and quite often in practice. This is particularly noticeable in Africa where one-party democracy was widely embraced in the post-colonial period. It is true that some old-style one-party regimes still exist – most notably in China – and that it is as unclear what will happen in the former Soviet Union. However it is pretty clear that the theory of one-party democracy has suffered a mortal blow and that, for the time being at least, liberal democracy has emerged as the only recognized form of democracy.

Theories of liberal democracy were developed in the late eighteenth and in the nineteenth centuries, though they were much influenced by the political philosophy of John Locke (1632–1704). These theories are often lumped together and referred to as 'traditional democratic theory', though there are in fact some important differences among them. We can use a key set of such differences to distinguish two main types of traditional theory: 'conventional' and 'radical democratic theory'. In the type of system endorsed by the former the people have a passive role and merely choose 'negatively' from what candidates have to offer. And the representatives once elected have a large amount of discretion; though the requirements of subsequent elections mean that they are ultimately subordinate to the voters. The most important conventional democratic theorists were James Madison (1751–1836) in America and John Stuart Mill (1806–1873) in Britain. By contrast, in radical democratic theory's model of democracy the people have a positive, initiating role: candidates respond to policy initiatives from the people rather than vice versa. Moreover, elected representatives are not expected to use their discretion but merely to carry out the instructions of their electors; in a word, they are but *delegates*. Key radical democratic theorists were Tom Paine (1737–1809) and Thomas Jefferson (1743–1826) and the English utilitarians (see UTILITARIANISM) Jeremy Bentham (1748–1832) and James Mill (1773–1836). Rousseau also has an important place, though he was the theorist of 'continental' democratic theory rather than mainstream liberal democratic theory (Holden, 1988).

In this century it has been contended that traditional (or, more precisely, radical) theory should be superseded by more realistic, modern, theories of democracy which recognize the complexity of modern political systems and the voters' lack of knowledge and interest. 'Elitist democratic theory', incorporating aspects of ELITE THEORY, is prominent here. Also important is 'pluralist democratic theory'; and in some of the work of the best known modern theorist, Robert Dahl, the two are combined (for example, Dahl, 1956, 1961). However, elitist democratic theorists have, themselves, been subject to criticism by *participatory theorists*, who maintain that the former are not really democratic theorists at all and that what is needed for democracy to exist is extensive PARTICIPATION by the whole people (Pateman, 1970). There are, clearly, echoes of radical democratic theory here, but there is the additional dimension of a belief in INDUSTRIAL DEMOCRACY: mass participation should extend beyond the political system, as usually conceived, into the workplace and into the economy generally. Even Robert Dahl now advocates such 'economic democracy' (1985).

Whether there can be a rational grounding for the judgement – now so widely endorsed – that democracy is the best system of government is a matter of controversy; nonetheless what many regard as cogent arguments have traditionally been offered in its support (Holden, 1988; Dahl 1989). And today democracy is being more widely established in practice as well as approved in theory; there remain very many non-democratic systems in the world, but the recent resurgence of democracy seems to have outdated Dahl's statement about its being the exception throughout recorded history.

Reading
Dahl, R.A. 1989: *Democracy and its Critics.*
Gould, C.C. 1988: *Rethinking Democracy.*
Held, D. 1987: *Models of Democracy.*
Holden, B. 1988: *Understanding Liberal Democracy.*
Macpherson, C.B. 1977: *The Life and Times of Liberal Democracy.*
Pennock, J.R. 1979: *Democratic Political Theory.*
Sartori, G. 1987: *The Theory of Democracy Revisited.*

BARRY HOLDEN

democracy, industrial   *See* INDUSTRIAL DEMOC-
RACY

democracy, social   *See* SOCIAL DEMOCRACY

demography   Describing the study of human
populations, the term embraces a vast array of
work, but at its core are three central concerns:

1   The size and make-up of populations according
to diverse criteria (age, sex, marital status,
educational attainment, and so on). In short,
cross-sectional pictures of a population at a
fixed moment in time.
2   The different processes which directly
influence the composition of populations (fertility, mortality, nuptiality, MIGRATION, and so
on).
3   The relationship between these static and
dynamic elements and the social, economic and
cultural environment within which they exist.

Although there is no strict division, a contrast is
frequently made between formal or technical
demography on the one hand, and social demography or population studies on the other. The former
is concerned mainly with the collection and analysis
of data, while the latter implies a wider frame of
reference drawing in work from related fields.

From its origins in actuarial studies, demography has been pushed forward by a variety of
motivations. Much of the research carried out in
the early twentieth century had close links to
EUGENICS as scholars sought to discover the quantitative dimensions of social and racial differentiation. Following World War II and the abuse of
eugenic research by Nazism, the motivation waned.
However, the rise of SOCIOBIOLOGY in the 1970s led
to a resurgence of interest in demographic studies
of human biology.

During the 1930s fertility in many developed
societies fell to unprecedented levels. This inspired
both technical analytic developments, such as the
calculation of gross and net reproduction rates
aiming accurately to quantify the scale of the
fertility decline, and attempts at a more complete
understanding of the phenomenon, such as the
British Royal Commission on Population in the
1940s (Glass, 1956). Fears of depopulation in
Western countries became obsolete in the 1950s,

however, when fertility rose substantially during
the so-called 'baby boom'.

From the 1950s on the attention of demographers switched to population in the Third World
where rapid mortality improvement and persistent
high fertility produced extremely high rates of
population growth. Concern with rapid population
growth and in particular a desire to promote
reduced fertility in developing countries has been a
major undercurrent of demographic research in the
second half of the century. Controversy has often
reigned between competing theorists of social and
demographic change as they battled for the ear of
governments and funding agencies (Hodgson,
1988).

The baby boom was shortlived and in the
developed world attention has again been focused
on the issue of low fertility following rapid falls in
childbearing since the later 1960s. Concern has
been particularly focused on the phenomenon of
population ageing as societies grapple with the
growth of old age populations.

Both formal and social demography have developed a number of key ideas or models in the course
of the twentieth century. In formal demography
one central notion has been the pursuit of analysis
in terms of cohorts rather than periods. Cohort
analysis, which considers the experience of individuals over time, has many theoretical advantages
over the analysis of events occurring in a given
period. This is particularly so where the events in
question are largely under individual control, as
with fertility and nuptiality, and where past experience plays a role in determining current behaviour
(Ryder, 1968).

Undoubtedly the main contribution of demography to quantitative social science has been the life
table, a detailed description of the mortality of a
population, giving the probability of dying and
various other statistics at each age. The life table is a
powerful tool for the analysis of mortality or any
other phenomenon which cannot recur. It has
found widespread applications in many areas of
social science as well as in the natural sciences and
statistics (Shryock and Siegel, 1976).

The statistical techniques employed by demographers are relatively few in number and generally
straightforward, though with the advent of computers more statistically sophisticated methods
have come into use. For most demographers the
heart of the subject lies in the analysis of mortality,

fertility and nuptiality, with migration regarded as a separate subdiscipline. This is partly attributable to differences in source material and partly to the much greater role of geographers in any form of spatial analysis.

Mathematical demography has been an active sub-branch of the discipline, developing several models which combine formal elegance with considerable practical utility. The most important of these is the theory of stable populations. First formulated in the eighteenth century by Leonard Euler, the theory of the stable population was reinvented and popularized by the American demographer Alfred Lotka (1939). The theory enables the population age-structure consonant with any given combination of mortality and fertility to be calculated, a feature invaluable for the understanding of population dynamics. For example, it has been possible to demonstrate that demographic ageing is principally the result of low fertility rather than of longer individual survival (Coale, 1972).

The most influential concept in social demography is the demographic transition. As Demeny (1972) puts it, 'In traditional societies, mortality and fertility are high. In modern societies fertility and mortality are low. In between there is the demographic transition.' Demographic transition theory was first developed by American demographers in the years around World War II and was a form of the more general modernization theories then current (Notestein, 1945; Davis, 1945). The theory can be broadly divided into three parts:

1   a description of changes over time in fertility and mortality;
2   the construction of theoretical causal models explaining these changes;
3   predictions for future trends, especially in the Third World.

Attention has been especially focused on the factors responsible for fertility decline with different theorists advocating different causal mechanisms. Early work stressed urbanization and industrialization as prime movers, but this has been questioned following the discovery that changes in these factors were not closely correlated with fertility change in historical European populations. Moreover, many Asian and Latin American countries have experienced significant fertility falls with only limited concurrent socioeconomic development (Freedman, 1982). As a result, recent work

has tended to stress cultural factors as playing a crucial role (Cleland and Wilson, 1987).

Many other areas of social thinking have been influenced by demographic ideas. Research on the FAMILY has to take into account the demographic constraints within which all family and kinship relations take place, while analysis of marriage and divorce rely on demography for their quantitative basis. Historical demography has been very influential in the development of social and economic history, and the use of demographic methods in ANTHROPOLOGY has grown rapidly in recent years.

Reading
Pressat, R. 1985: *The Dictionary of Demography*, ed. C. Wilson.
Ross, J.A. ed. 1982: *International Encyclopaedia of Population*.
Woods, R. 1979: *Population Analysis in Geography*.
                                    CHRISTOPHER WILSON

dependency Dependency theory is a body of neo-Marxist thought which arose in Latin American social science in the late 1960s. According to T. dos Santos (1970), 'a relationship of interdependence . . . becomes a dependent relationship when some countries can expand through self-impulsion while others . . . can only expand as a reflection of the expansion of the dominant countries.' Though the term can be found in Marxist writings before Lenin (as in Otto Bauer), it was given prominence by Lenin, especially after his 1916 pamphlet on imperialism as 'the last stage of capitalism'. Indeed dependency theory is basically a revival of Lenin's concept of imperialism, shifting the focus to its effects (to which Lenin paid scant attention) on underdeveloped economies. Kwame Nkrumah, the Ghanaian leader, consciously echoed Lenin when he said '*neo-colonialism* is the last stage of capitalism.'

The idea of dependency was born as a reaction against *dualist* interpretations of Latin American backwardness. Stemming from MODERNIZATION theory, dualism used to distinguish between a modern, progressive sector of the economy and society and stagnant, traditional branches or regions, which were labelled pre-capitalist. Dependency theorists, by contrast, saw DEVELOPMENT AND UNDERDEVELOPMENT as functional positions within the world economy rather than stages along an evolutionary ladder. Previously, Latin American economic thought had been dominated by an outlook identified with ECLA (UN Economic

Commission for Latin America). Its mentor, the Argentinian economist Raul Prebisch, believed that Latin America's underdevelopment reflected its peripheral place in the world economy and resulted from the adoption of free trade policies as the region's commodity exports suffered from a secular decline in their prices. Third World primary producers, unlike grain producers in nineteenth-century areas of white settlement, were not in the long run reaping big profits from free trade. Dependency theory agreed with Prebisch's diagnosis but rejected his Keynesian prescription: protectionist, state-fostered 'import substitution industrialization' (ISI), which became the prevalent development ideology. The early work of an ECLA economist, the Brazilian Celso Furtado (1964), provided a conceptual transition from Prebisch by stressing that in underdeveloped countries the small size of the domestic market restricts capital formation, and by envisaging the state as a means of combating structural bottlenecks. A heavy blow to dualist pieties and nationalist reformism was struck when a Mexican sociologist, Rodolfo Stavenhagen, denouncing several 'mistaken theses about Latin America' (1968), attacked the 'trickle-down' idea that industrialization spreads overall progress, claiming that on the contrary what progress there was had taken place at the expense of backward areas, and denied (a) that national bourgeoisies were inimical to landowners, (b) that workers shared interests with peasants, and (c) that the middle classes were enterprising and progressive.

Dependency theory also changed Latin American views on imperialism. Up to the interwar period (as in the thought of Haya de la Torre) the dominant anti-imperialist stance south of the USA blamed underdevelopment on foreign exploitation *but not on capitalism* as such. But dependency theory chose to follow Lenin's momentous reversal of the Marxist conception of capitalism. While Marx had seen it as a fundamentally progressive (however doomed) historical trend, Lenin came to regard capitalism in its imperialist stage as a decadent, parasitic process which had become an *obstacle* to economic and social progress. This view was shared by 'hard' dependency theorists like A.G. Frank (1969), Dos Santos, Rui M. Marini and Samir Amin (1970). A 'softer', Gramsci-like approach was soon developed by the São Paulo sociologist F.H. Cardoso, with a milder reformist, structuralist line led by Furtado and the Chilean economist Osvaldo Sunkel.

Gunder Frank initiated the dependency school proper in 1967 by taking up Paul Baran's thesis in *The Political Economy of Growth* (1957) that exploitation of the Third World not only went on unabated after the end of colonial rule but became far more efficient, underdevelopment being the result of the economic capture of backward areas by advanced metropolitan capitalism. Frank provided a catchy prase for this process: 'The development of underdevelopment.' For him, development and underdevelopment are not just relative and quantitative but 'relational and qualitative' because 'structurally different'; the same capitalist mechanisms generate both development at the centre and underdevelopment of the periphery. 'Feudal' areas, in the dualist jargon, are just those which have suffered most in the process. Thus the most 'archaic' parts of Latin America, such as highland Peru or the Brazilian north-east, were previously the centre of the economic and commercial dynamics of the region.

Frank's analysis was quickly challenged. E. Laclau (1977) chastised him for defining modes of production, like Paul Sweezy and the dualists, in terms of their relation to the market instead of sticking to the classical Marxist stress on class structure and social relations. The same point was later made by Robert Brenner (1977) in his critique of Immanuel Wallerstein, a neo-Marxist historian of capitalism who skilfully blended Frank's outlook with Fernand Braudel's geographically-minded account of 'world economics' shaped by early modern capital (see Wallerstein, 1974). Frank and Wallerstein became the best-known sources of dependency theorizing. (See also WORLD-SYSTEM.)

Dependency theory in political science (see O'Donnell, 1973) tried to relate the rise of authoritarianism to the exhaustion of ISI. While early ISI concentrated on light, labour-intensive industry, with a low level of technology and investment costs, and production aiming at low-income consumers, *late* ISI produces capital goods or expensive durable consumer goods requiring high technology and costly investment. Consequently consumption growth becomes geared to the upper middle classes and political repression is called on to prevent the lower classes from imposing a more distributivist pattern via the ballot. Dependency entered the picture by means of the multinational companies, the main providers of capital and technology under later ISI. The work of Cardoso and Faletto (1969) was chiefly a seminal typology of bourgeoisies, classified according to their degree of autonomy *vis-à-vis* the export economy and the multinationals in several national contexts. Cardoso strongly qualified Frank's original tenets, stressing the dialectic between market forces, class structures and national political traditions. But the end result of his insightful revamping of dependency theory has been to blur its outlines as a causal hypothesis; what was gained in sense of context was lost in explanatory power. (cf. Jaguaribe, 1973).

The big unanswered question of dependency theory is, how is it that some 'dependent' countries can be so affluent? The Canadian economy is as dependent on trade with the USA, and far more permeated by American capital, than Mexico, yet Canada is a developed country and Mexico a plodding developing one. To be sure, the foreign debt quagmire has cast many developing nations into the throes of acute *financial* dependency. Nevertheless, while the proximate cause of the debt was the soaring interest rates of the era of the Reagan presidency in the USA, its root cause was massive free borrowing dictated by the decision to keep developing economies such as Brazil and Mexico as nearly autarkic as possible (since the alternative route of attracting more foreign investments could have kept their foreign debts at a significantly lower level). To a certain extent, therefore, the current debt predicament, far from reflecting an original situation of dependence, may be deemed a nemesis of the will to autarky.

Reading

Amin, Samir 1970 (*1974*): *Accumulation on a World Scale.*
Cardoso, Fernando Henrique and Faletto, Enzo 1969 (*1979*): *Dependency and Development in Latin America.*
Dos Santos, Theotonio 1970: The structure of dependence. *American Economic Review* 60, May.
Frank, André Gunder 1969 (*1971*): *Capitalism and Underdevelopment in Latin America: Historical Studies of Chile and Brazil.*
Furtado, Celso 1964: *Development and Underdevelopment.*
Larrain, Jorge 1989: *Theories of Development.*

J. G. MERQUIOR

depression, clinical A diagnosis of this condition involves more than a depressed mood, however persistent and severe: a certain number of characteristic symptoms must be present, such as loss of interest, feelings of guilt, sleep and appetite disturbance, suicidal plans, slowing in movement and anhedonia (the inability to feel pleasure). But depression is not a unitary phenomenon. Manic

depression (or bipolar condition), for example, is distinguishable by genetic involvement, clinical recurrence (often involving manic episodes) and responses to specific treatments. However, further diagnostic divisions have proved more difficult to make, and terms such as 'reactive' and 'neurotic' in contrast to 'endogenous' or 'psychotic' are confusing if taken literally. It is now clear, for example, that 'endogenous' conditions (defined by what are thought to be characteristic symptoms and thought by some to arise spontaneously within the individual) can, in fact, be provoked by crises such as a miscarriage or marital separation.

Biological explanations have recently been prominent – especially variations on formulations concerning deficits in neurotransmitter amines in the brain. It is also clear that psychosocial stressors, particularly concerning loss and disappointment, appear to be frequently involved in provoking all forms of depression (leaving aside the relatively rare bipolar condition) and factors such as social support offer some protection. On present evidence, if the broad range of depressive conditions are taken, including those not seen by a psychiatrist and not diagnosed by a general practitioner, psychosocial factors probably play a major role in onset and course, and go far to explain the large social class differences often present in urban settings. Moreover, certain kinds of early adverse experience, particularly involving rejection and abuse by a parent, can also lead to a higher risk of depression in adulthood. Fortunately there is nothing inevitable about such effects since subsequent 'positive' experience, particularly in terms of a supportive marriage or a new opportunity, can greatly lower risk.

Psychiatrists see relatively few of those in the general population who experience a depressive episode, and the task of coming to terms intellectually with what they do see is complicated in several ways. A good deal of the undoubted biological dysfunction present once a person is depressed could be a consequence of external events, although there can be little doubt that some depression is essentially biological in origin. Understandably they quite often see patients who are particularly profoundly depressed. In addition patients very often have more than a straightforward depression. Those with 'acting out' behaviour such as suicide gestures are more likely to be referred to psychiatrists, as well as those with alcoholism, substance abuse and physical illness, as well as instances where the patient has helped to bring about the crisis immediately responsible for his or her depression. Indeed, with the increasing use of anti-depressant drugs in general medicine, psychiatrists may well see relatively few 'ordinary' depressions. Given the selected nature of the depression seen by psychiatrists a certain scepticism on their part is understandable in response to simple aetiological explanations. At the same time, it behoves them to recognize the possibility that the depressive phenomenon as a whole may not prove to be as complex in its origins as it would appear from the perspective of psychiatric practice.

See also PSYCHIATRY AND MENTAL ILLNESS.

Reading

Goldberg, D. and Huxley, P. 1992: *Common Mental Disorders: A Biosocial Model.*
Herbst, K. and Paykel, E. 1989: *Depression: An Integrative Approach.*

GEORGE W. BROWN

depression, economic That the fluctuations in economic activity in capitalist economies are cyclical in character has long been recognized, but the explanations offered for economic cycles, as opposed to their description, remain areas of much controversy. The term 'economic depression' is correspondingly inexact, generally referring to the trough of those cycles that for some reason are more severe and international in scope, as opposed to 'economic recessions', which are more localized, less severe and of shorter duration. Another common usage distinguishes a recession, in which the growth rate falls below trend but remains positive, from a depression, in which the growth rate falls below zero giving a fall in real output.

Economic cycles in capitalist economies are all qualitatively similar but quantitatively different. The former feature suggests the possibility of a general theory, with no restriction to particular time or place, and with no need to rely on particular political or institutional characteristics; the latter, that any theory must be able to account for unique historical events. Explanations divide over what to emphasize: whether economic depressions should be incorporated into a theory of the long-run cycle, or whether they are the contingent outcome of unique and random events. They also divide over the emphasis placed on real versus monetary causes of depression.

In an empirical investigation in the 1920s, N. D. Kondratiev suggested the possibility of long cycles of some 50 years in duration, in which he situated the depressions of around 1815 to 1850, and the 1870s to the 1890s. While he drew attention to the poor quality of the data prior to 1850, and to the small number of cycles, he cautiously suggested an endogenous explanation in terms of the provision of very costly and long-lived fixed capital whose replacement and expansion was bunched and discontinuous. His suggestions were incorporated into an account by J. A. Schumpeter in the late 1930s, but Schumpeter's causality ran in the opposite direction: a focus on the role of exogenous technological innovation which he considered occurred in clusters determined by entrepreneurial assessments of risk and return. Clusters of innovation raise investment which accelerates growth, and depressions occur when growth decelerates through a lack of investment due to the exhaustion of a burst of innovation. Examples of investment due to bursts of innovation at various times include the establishment of the railway, steel and electricity industries. With the long post-war boom, cycle theory fell out of fashion, but the idea of long cycles reemerged in the international recession beginning in the early 1970s; some also pointed to a fresh wave of innovation in microelectronics which would, they predicted, lay the basis for an investment boom and an upturn in the long cycle towards the end of the twentieth century, although the employment implications of microelectronic technology remain controversial.

However, many deny that long cycles exist at all. The empirical evidence is at best only suggestive, and the causal linkages in the theoretical accounts are rather loosely specified. In the light of such inexactitude, economic depressions are, for some, not part of some endogenous pattern of capitalist development, but merely the result of chance events. An extreme is the weight given by the US economists Milton Friedman and A. Schwartz to the fortuitous death of Benjamin Strong of the Federal Reserve Bank of New York in 1928, to whose absence the policy mistakes of the Fed. between 1929 and 1933 could perhaps be attributed. There is also an issue of whether the term 'depression' is meaningful. For example, the period 1933–7 in the USA was the longest peacetime expansion recorded until the 1960s; incomes of the employed rose steadily, so it was hardly a depression; but unemployment was always above 14 per cent, so it was hardly a boom. A similar story could be told of the UK in the 1980s.

It is difficult for theories founded on a notion of economic equilibrium to assimilate economic fluctuations, other than seeing those fluctuations as part of the equilibrium process itself. (See NEO-CLASSICAL ECONOMICS.) On the other hand there are varieties of Marxist theory, all of which stress the endogeneity and functionality of cycles to capitalist development. (See for example REGULATION.) For both the challenge remains: to explain theoretically how the downturn of a cycle sometimes leads into an economic depression, but only sometimes.

See also LONG WAVES.

Reading
Bernstein, M.A. 1987: *The Great Depression: Delayed Recovery and Economic Change in America, 1929–1939.*
Brunner, K. ed. 1981: *The Great Depression Revisited.*
Day, R.D. 1976: The theory of long waves: Kondratiev, Trotsky, Mandel. *New Left Review* 99, 67–82.
Fearon, P. 1987: *War, Prosperity and Depression: The US Economy 1917–45.*
Mandel, E. 1980: *Long Waves of Capitalist Development: The Marxist Interpretation.*
Rosenberg, N. and Frischtak, C.R. 1984: Technological innovation and long waves. *Cambridge Journal of Economics* 8, 7–24.

SIMON MOHUN

deprivation, relative   *See* RELATIVE DEPRIVATION

despotism, oriental   *See* ORIENTAL DESPOTISM

determinism   This is normally understood as the thesis that for everything that happens there are conditions such that, given them, nothing else could have happened. In the influential philosophical form articulated by David Hume and J.S. Mill it appears as *regularity determinism*, viz. that for every event x there is a set of events $y_1 \ldots y_n$ such that they are regularly conjoined under some set of descriptions. This has generally been assumed to hold true in nature this century, at least until very recently, with the exception of quantum mechanics (where it appears impossible to determine simultaneously the position and momentum of elementary particles). However, reservations were expressed about it in the 1960s by P.T. Geach and G.E.M. Anscombe; and in the 1970s more systematically by R. Bhaskar. He argued that reflection on the conditions under which deterministic outcomes are actually possible (from which determinism as a metaphysical thesis derives its plausibility) suggests that apart from a few special – experimentally established or naturally occurring – closed contexts, laws set limits, impose constraints or operate as tendencies rather than prescribe uniquely fixed results. In particular they have a normic and non-empirical character; and they are consistent with situations of dual and multiple control, multiple and plural determination, complexity, emergence and human agency (for instance, in experimental activity). From this perspective laws are not actual or contingent but necessary and real – properties of mechanisms, not conjunctions of events. And the only sense in which science presupposes determinism is the (non-Humean, non-Laplacean) sense of *ubiquity determinism*, that is, the ubiquity of real (but perhaps not necessarily intelligible) causes, including causes for differences, and hence the (however remote) possibility of stratified explanations. 'Determinism', as normally understood, can then be seen to rest on a naive actualist ontology of laws, and in particular on the error of supposing that because an event was caused to happen, it was bound to happen before it was caused (a confusion of (ontological) determination and (epistemological) predetermination). Nor is it the case that relations of natural generation are (logically) transitive. Thus it is not the case that because S_1 produced S_2 and S_2 produced S_3 that S_1 produced S_3 – if, for instance, either S_2 possesses emergent powers or the system in which S_3 is formed is open or the process is stochastic. The development of catastrophe and chaos theory has dealt another blow to regularity determinism, illustrating that non-linear dynamic systems can yield highly irregular (chaotic and unpredictable) results (see also PREDICTION).

The relative rarity of deterministic outcomes and the complexity of agents has implications for the issue of free will. The dominant position in the first half of the century was the 'compatibilist' one that free will presupposes determinism. Under the influence of Gilbert Ryle, John Austin, the later Wittgenstein, F. Waismann, P. Strawson and S. Hampshire, the commonsense view that determinism places our normal concepts of agency (see ACTION AND AGENCY), choice and responsibility in jeopardy was most usually reconciled with a continued commitment to determinism at the physical level in the doctrine that the former concepts operated at or in a different logical level, language stratum or language game. But once actualism is jettisoned, the possibility of a naturalistic revindication of human agency, of the CAUSALITY of reasons and the potential applicability of the predicate 'free' to agents, their actions and their situations is once more opened up.

There has been much controversy in the twentieth century about whether Marxism is a deterministic theory in the sense that it holds outcomes to be (a) inevitable and/or (b) predictable and/or (c) fated. This cannot be discussed here (see entry on 'determinism' in Bottomore et al., 1983) – save to remark that there are good philosophical and historical reasons for not treating the Marxist research programme as deterministic in any of these senses.

Reading
Anscombe, G.E.M. 1971: *Causality and Determination*.
Bhaskar, Roy 1975 (*1978*): *A Realist Theory of Science*, 2nd edn.
Kamminga, H. 1990: Understanding chaos. *New Left Review 181*.
Melden, A. 1961: *Free Action*.
Polanyi, M. 1967: *The Tacit Dimension*.

ROY BHASKAR

development and underdevelopment This denotes the achievement of economic and social progress (development) by transforming conditions of underdevelopment (low productivity, stagnation, poverty) in countries variously designated as 'poor', 'underdeveloped', 'less developed' or 'developing'. ECONOMIC GROWTH is a necessary if not sufficient condition of social progress, charted in the satisfaction of such basic needs as adequate nutrition, health and shelter (overcoming absolute poverty), to which can be added further conditions of a full human existence such as universal access to education, civil freedoms and political participation (overcoming relative poverty or deprivation).

After 1945 the international map was redrawn by anti-colonial movements and the end of colonial empire, by US hegemony in the capitalist world and its rivalry with the USSR to win allies among the independent states of Asia and Africa. In this global context, development in the transformational and transitive sense outlined became a major goal of governments and of international bodies like the United Nations and International Bank for Reconstruction and Development (the World Bank), and

emerged as a field of specialization in the social sciences.

Intense controversy continues to surround the causes of underdevelopment and ways of achieving development, reflecting radically different views of the nature of Western and Japanese (industrial capitalist) development, of the international economy it created and how it conditions the prospects of development in the THIRD WORLD, and of the competing claims of capitalist, socialist and nationalist solutions to problems of development. Social theory concerning development and underdevelopment is thus 'world historical' in its scope and complexity, but several central themes run through the many debates it has generated.

Societal and global factors
One pervasive set of issues is the nature and weighting of internal (societal) and external (global) factors in explaining stagnation and change. In the MODERNIZATION theories of American social scientists in particular, 'traditional' society or culture is, in effect, synonymous with underdevelopment (see also TRADITION AND TRADITIONALISM). Abstractly, tradition and modernity are delineated by the 'pattern variables' of Talcott Parsons (1951), which depict modernization as the evolution of social systems with a high degree of functional and structural differentiation and corresponding mechanisms of integration. Differentiation encompasses a complex social division of labour and a rationality productive of innovation and growth, while integration and its normative system secure social stability.

Underdeveloped countries are characterized by a dual structure of traditional and modern social sectors, beliefs and practices. The motor of transformation is psychocultural – a 'revolution of rising expectations' promoting the diffusion of modernity from developed to underdeveloped countries, and within the latter from modern to traditional sectors. The underlying message is 'follow in the footsteps of the West', and 'we will help you' through foreign aid and investment, transfer of technology, and so on. Problems arise when socioeconomic change fails to satisfy rising expectations, giving way to rising frustrations that require strong 'modernizing elites' which can simultaneously induce accelerated development and maintain order.

Modernization theories thus formulate development as a process of diffusion, adoption and adaptation from a benign external environment, and explain underdevelopment by the barriers of tradition internal to poor countries. The assumptions and prescriptions of modernization – ethnocentric, sometimes implicitly racist, often explicitly anti-communist – have been vigorously challenged by positions that emphasize global factors in explaining underdevelopment.

A historic slogan of this challenge was 'the development of underdevelopment' coined by André Gunder Frank (1969) to argue that underdevelopment is not an original or residual condition (tradition), but was actively created by the incorporation of the Third World in the world economy formed by European expansion from the late fifteenth century.

This capitalist world economy consists of a chain of 'metropole-satellite' relationships between countries, and regions within them, through which dominant metropoles appropriate the economic surplus of subordinate satellites, enriching the former and impoverishing the latter, thereby creating and reproducing their underdevelopment. Apparently traditional or precapitalist social forms in satellite countries and regions are thus really capitalist in consequence of their world market integration. The principal mechanisms of 'surplus drain' are unequal exchange in international trade, expatriation of profits from foreign investment, and of interest on foreign loans, within an international division of labour that systematically favours the metropoles.

This picture of a global system generating development and underdevelopment as two sides of the same coin has been enormously influential. It has also been challenged and modified in various ways, as has Frank's principal prescription of autarchy for Third World countries, their 'disengagement' from the world economy, as a necessary condition of development.

Transcending Frank's stagnationist model, the possibilities and constraints of 'dependent development' were formulated by Latin American intellectuals (Cardoso and Faletto, 1969) and then generalized to the whole of the Third World. As with many terms associated with development, 'dependency' is an elastic notion, but it acknowledges the possibility of rapid economic growth whose patterns and limits are still mainly determined by external dependence, notably on multinational corporations for technology, and on international banks for finance, dramatized in the current Third World debt crisis.

Another approach to theorizing the relationship of internal and external factors is the 'articulation of modes of production'. The key idea here is that rather than destroying other modes of production, capitalism often conserves (or even creates) them by articulating or combining them with its own functioning to obtain 'cheap' commodities to sustain accumulation. These commodities comprise both goods from peasant and artisanal production and labour power, which are cheap because their exchange value is 'subsidized' by unpaid subsistence production. Contemporary pre- or noncapitalist social forms, therefore, neither represent a residual tradition nor are they rendered 'capitalist' simply by their world economy linkages (Frank).

This theoretical approach was developed most systematically by French anthropologists working in Africa, notably Rey (1976) amd Meillassoux (1981), although independent 'modes of production' debates, with somewhat different agendas focused on the agrarian question, also occurred in Latin America (Bartra et al., 1976) and India (Patnaik, 1990). Formulated within a Marxist analysis of capitalism, particularly as interpreted in Rosa Luxemburg's theory of imperialism (1913), articulation explains underdevelopment through the necessary reproduction within global capitalism of pre-capitalist forms supporting a reserve army of labour in impoverished areas and classes.

This idea also features in the eclectic 'world system' project of Wallerstein (1979), which also owes much to Frank and even to Parsons, according to critics of Wallerstein's functionalist account of 'system'. Unlike Frank, Wallerstein explicitly counters Marxism with the argument that proletarianization, central to its account of capitalist development, has been exceptional rather than universal in the modern world system which harnesses a variety of forms of labour, neither fully commoditized nor 'free', to the imperatives of capital accumulation. Additionally, Wallerstein replaces the static dualism of Frank's metropole-satellite structure with a hierarchy of core, semi-peripheral and peripheral locations in the world system, suggesting that countries can shift their location in particular moments of change in the INTERNATIONAL DIVISION OF LABOUR.

Another response to rapid economic growth in parts of Latin American and the NICs ('newly industrialized countries') of East Asia, was to turn the arguments of radical global approaches upside down in the name of reviving an 'orthodox' Marxism. In a major polemic, Bill Warren (1980) maintained that capitalism does develop the post-colonial Third World except where inhibited by socialist, nationalist or populist policies derived from misconceived notions of imperialism (stemming from Lenin, 1916) and dependency. Warren returned full circle to an internal explanation of poor economic performance, suggesting that world market integration is to be encouraged rather than resisted, and that socialist construction is 'premature' until the stage of capitalist transformation is complete.

States, plans, markets
Warren's position partly converges with current neo-liberalism, which highlights another pervasive set of issues: those concerning states, plans and markets in promoting development. Capitalist development and economically active states are clearly compatible; Gerschenkron (1962) suggested that for relative 'latecomers' to development the state has a central role in establishing the conditions of capital accumulation, or undertaking it in strategic sectors, recalling the 'infant industry' thesis of the nineteenth-century German 'national economist' Friedrich List (1841).

Certainly postwar economic development was viewed as the responsibility of states, influenced by the comprehensive planning pioneered in the USSR, and Western wartime economic management followed by European reconstruction under the Marshall Plan and policies influenced by KEYNESIANISM. J.M. Keynes himself participated in establishing the Bretton Woods system of institutions to regulate the international economy, including the World Bank which was centrally involved in promoting planning (Waterston, 1965) until its conversion to an equally ambitious neo-liberal strategy of structural 'reform' in the 1980s.

The extent and nature of the state's role in investment, economic management and social provision, and its relations with the activities of private capital, national and international, is a large and complex subject in itself, manifested in the very mixed record of state-led development in both capitalist and socialist Third World countries. The complexities of these different experiences, and of the demands of analysing them, have been short-circuited by the ideological (if not practical) successes of the neo-liberal doctrine of 'rolling back the state'. This combines a selective core of ideas from

neoclassical economics with an aggressive politics, including a rejection of the discipline of 'development economics' on the grounds of its intrinsic Keynesianism and statism (Lal, 1983). Moreover, neo-liberalism has partly appropriated the ground of widespread popular discontent with state economic inefficiency, inability to meet basic needs, corruption and authoritarianism in many Third World countries, and acquired further impetus with the dramatic collapse of East European state socialism as a perceived alternative to capitalism.

Current conditions and prospects as well as economic history cast doubt on the simplistic account of virtuous markets and vicious states given by neo-liberalism. Even if planning is diminished, state enterprises and functions privatized and deregulated, and external and internal trade liberalized, the 'leaner' state prescribed has to be much more efficient as both technocracy and agency of social control than hitherto in the Third World. This raises issues about the constitution and capacities of states in relation to the deep divisions of class, gender, region and culture of the societies whose development they attempt to direct, as well as in relation to the powerful 'external' forces of the world system.

Nation, class and civil society
A third set of pervasive issues, then, concerns the social and political processes of nation, class and civil society which have critical effects for how the standard macroeconomic variables of development policy work in practice, whether exchange rate and foreign trade regimes, savings rates, sectoral investment priorities or the role of the public sector.

The initial reasons in the Third World for the primacy of the state in development were the experience of colonialism and the fear of 'neocolonial' domination after independence. 'State' and 'nation' were virtually coterminous in the profoundly national(ist) moment of decolonization. Creating a cohesive nation or 'nation building' was seen to be as vital a task for the state as promoting development, or inseparable from it.

As the inherited contradictions of underdevelopment persisted beyond the triumphal moment of independence, and new contradictions of uneven development emerged, class analysis became more central, often conceiving class structure in peripheral capitalism by its deviations from 'classic' or core capitalism: dependent or bureaucratic rather than 'national' bourgeoisies; semi-proletarianized or marginal masses rather than working classes. Other approaches aim to transcend this somewhat mechanistic conception, addressing the historical specificities and complexities of class formation, and how it is enmeshed with other divisions of civil society, notably those of gender.

Feminism has had a substantial impact on the analysis of development and underdevelopment, investigating and demonstrating the ways in which their constituent processes – including class formation and reproduction – are gendered (Agarwal, 1988). It has also contributed to a general rethinking by some scholars of the agenda of development theory and practice, provoked *inter alia* by the convergent critique of the state from left and right. The emerging agenda focuses on questions of social agency that transcend the conventional dualism of (discredited) state direction and the neo-liberal alternative of market individualism, to explore forms of empowerment and 'public action' that express and develop the capacities of oppressed classes and groups. Thus there are indications of a quest for new solutions to persistent problems of development and underdevelopment rooted in the manifestly unequal structures of the capitalist world economy and of the different kinds of societies it encompasses.

Reading
Drèze, J. and Sen, A. 1989: *Hunger and Public Action*.
Edwards, C. 1985: *The Fragmented World*.
Elson, D. ed. 1991: *Male Bias in the Development Process*.
Kay, C. 1989: *Latin American Theories of Development and Underdevelopment*.
Patnaik, P. ed. 1986: *Lenin and Imperialism*.
Post, K. and Wright, P. 1989: *Socialism and Underdevelopment*.
Sklair, L. 1991: *Sociology of the Global System*.
Toye, J. 1987: *Dilemmas of Development: Reflections on the Counter-revolution in Development Theory and Policy*.
Wolpe, H. ed. 1980: *The Articulation of Modes of Production*.

HENRY BERNSTEIN

deviance   *See* CRIME AND DEVIANCE

dialectic   In its most general sense, dialectic has come to signify any more or less intricate process of conceptual or social conflict, interconnection and change, in which the generation, interpenetration and clash of oppositions, leading to their transcendence in a fuller or more adequate mode of thought or form of life, plays a key role. But dialectic is one of the oldest, most complex and contested concepts in philosophical and social thought. Controversy in the twentieth century has, however, revolved around the nineteenth-century figures of Hegel and Marx.

There are two inflections of the dialectic in Hegel: (a) as a logical process; (b) more narrowly, as the dynamo of this process.

(a) In Hegel the principle of idealism, the speculative understanding of reality as (absolute) spirit, unites two ancient strands of dialectic, the Eleatic idea of dialectic as *reason* and the Ionian idea of dialectic as *process*, in the notion of dialectic as a self-generating, self-differentiating and self-particularizing *process of reason*. This actualizes itself by alienating itself, and restores its self-unity by recognizing this alienation as nothing other than its own free expression or manifestation – a process which is recapitulated and completed in the Hegelian System itself.

(b) The motor of this process is dialectic more narrowly conceived, the second, essentially negative, moment of 'actual thought', which Hegel calls 'the grasping of opposites in their unity or of the positive in the negative'. This is the method which enables the dialectical commentator to observe the process by which categories, notions or forms of consciousness arise out of each other to form ever more inclusive totalities, until the system as a whole is completed. For Hegel truth is the whole and error lies in one-sidedness, incompleteness and abstraction: its symptom is the contradictions it generates and its cure their incorporation into fuller, richer, more concrete and highly mediated conceptual forms. In the course of this process the famous principle of *sublation* is observed: as the dialectic unfolds no partial insight is ever lost. In fact the Hegelian dialectic progresses in two basic modes: by bringing out what is implicit, but not explicitly articulated, in some notion; or by repairing some want, lack or inadequacy in it. 'Dialectical', in contrast to 'reflective' (or analytical), thought grasps conceptual forms in their systematic interconnections, not just their determinate differences, and conceives each development as the product of a previous, less developed phase, whose necessary truth or fulfilment it is; so that there is always some tension, latent irony or incipient surprise between any form and what it is in the process of becoming.

At the beginning of the century the absolute idealisms of F.H. Bradley and J. McTaggart in Britain and J. Royce in the USA were influential.

Benedetto Croce developed a form of Hegelianism in Italy during the interwar years. The humanistic readings of A. Kojève and Jean Hyppolite, especially of Hegel's *Phenomenology of Spirit*, in the 1930s helped to form a whole generation of, in particular French, intellectuals, including Jean-Paul Sartre. J. Findlay in the 1950s and Charles Taylor in the 1970s were important in preparing the ground for a re-reception of Hegel in the heyday and aftermath of the positivist philosophical hegemony in the Anglophone world.

Four main issues have dominated intellectual controversy about dialectic in the Marxist tradition: (1) the difference between the Marxian (materialist) and Hegelian dialectics; (2) the role of the dialectic within Marx's work, and more broadly in any Marxist social science; (3) the compatibility of dialectics with formal LOGIC, materialism, scientific practice and rationality generally; and (4) the status of Engels's attempt to extend Marx's dialectic from the social realm to encompass nature and the whole of being generally.

The three most common emphases of the concept in the Marxist tradition are as: (a) the method, most usually scientific method, instancing *epistemological* dialectics; (b) a set of laws or principles, governing some sector or the whole of reality, *ontological* dialectics; and (c) the movement of history, *relational* dialectics. All these are to be found in Marx. But their paradigms are Marx's methodological comments in *Capital*, the philosophy of nature expounded by Engels in *Anti-Dühring*, and the 'out-Hegeling Hegelianism' of the early György Lukács in *History and Class Consciousness* – texts which may be regarded as the founding documents of Marxist social science, DIALECTICAL MATERIALISM and Western Marxism respectively.

There is a remarkable consistency in Marx's criticisms of Hegel from 1843 to 1873. These turn, formally, on Hegel's subject–predicate 'inversions', his principle of identity (involving the reduction of being to thought) and his logical mysticism (involving the reduction of science to PHILOSOPHY); and, substantively, on Hegel's failure to sustain the autonomy of nature and the historicity of social forms. But a definite positive reevaluation of Hegelian dialectic occurs from the time of the *Grundrisse* (1857–8) on. Unfortunately Marx never realized his wish 'to make accessible to the ordinary human intelligence, in two or three printers' sheets, what is *rational* in the method which Hegel

discovered and at the same time mystified'. The evidence, however, seems to indicate that Marx thought it possible to extract *part* of the Hegelian dialectic without being compromised by Hegel's idealism – against both the neo-Fichtean view of the Young Hegelians and Engels that a complete extraction of method from system is viable, and the position of positivistically minded critics from Eduard Bernstein to Lucio Colletti that the dialectic is inseparable from idealism.

Marx understood his dialectic as *scientific*, because it set out to explain the contradictions in thought and the crises of socioeconomic life in terms of the particular contradictory essential relations generating them; as *historical*, because it was both rooted in, and (conditionally) an agent of, the changes in the very relations and circumstances it described; as *critical*, because it demonstrated the historical conditions of validity and limits of adequacy of the categories, doctrines and practices it explained; and as *systematic*, because it sought to trace the various historical tendencies and contradictions of capitalism back to certain structurally constitutive contradictions of its mode of production. The most important of these are the contradictions between the use-value and value of the commodity, and between the concrete useful and abstract social aspects of the labour it embodies. These contradictions, together with the other structural and historical contradictions they ground, are both (a) *real inclusive oppositions*, in that the terms or poles of the contradictions existentially presuppose each other, and (b) *internally related* to a mystifying form of *appearance*. Such *dialectical contradictions* do not violate the principle of non-contradiction, for they may be *consistently described*; nor are they scientifically absurd, for the notion of a real inverted – or otherwise mystifying – misrepresentation of a real object, generated by the object concerned, is readily accommodated within a non-empiricist, *stratified*, ontology, in which thought is included within reality, not hypostatized.

The three most common positions on the dialectic are that it is unintelligible nonsense, that it is universally applicable and that it is applicable to the conceptual and/or social, but not the natural domain. Engels stamped his authority on the second, universalist position. There is no problem about this for Hegel for whom reality is thought, and dialectical logic onto-logic. But it would seem that any such equation must be problematic for a realist committed to the notion of the existence of nature independently of thought and for a materialist committed to the notion of its causal primacy. Yet Engels, underwriting both commitments, nevertheless took dialectic in its essentially Hegelian sense and sought to apply it to being as a whole. While Marx never repudiated Engels's cosmology, his own critique of political economy neither presupposes nor entails a dialectics of nature, and his critique of a priorism implies the a posteriori and subject-specific character of claims about the existence of dialectical, as other types of, processes in reality.

The very supposition of a dialectics of nature has appeared to a line of critics from Lukács to Sartre as categorically mistaken, inasmuch as it involves anthropomorphically (and hence idealistically) retrojecting on to nature categories, such as contradiction and negation, which only make sense in the human realm. Such critics do not deny that *natural science*, as part of the socio-historical world, may be dialectical; what is at stake is whether there can be a dialectic of *nature* per se. Obviously there are differences between the natural and social spheres. But are these specific differences more or less important than their generic similarities? In effect the problem of the dialectics of nature reduces to a variant of the general problem of NATURALISM, with the way it is resolved depending on whether dialectics is conceived sufficiently broadly and the human world sufficiently naturalistically to make its extension to nature plausible. Even then one should not necessarily expect a unitary answer – there may be dialectical polarities and inclusive oppositions in nature, but not dialectical intelligibility or reason.

In both Engels and Lukács 'history' was effectively emptied of substance – in Engels, by being 'objectivistically' interpreted in terms of the categories of a universal process; in Lukács, by being 'subjectivistically' conceived as so many mediations or moments of a finalizing unconditioned act of self-realization, which was its logical ground. Despite these original flaws, both the dialectical materialist and the Western Marxist traditions in the twentieth century have produced some notable dialectical figures. Within Western Marxism, besides Lukács's own dialectic of historical self-consciousness or subject–object dialectics, there are Antonio Gramsci's theory/practice, Herbert Marcuse's essence/existence and Colletti's appearance/reality contradictions, all of more or less directly Hegelian provenance. In Walter Benjamin dialectic

represents the discontinuance and catastrophic aspect of history; in Marc Bloch it is conceived as objective fantasy; in Sartre it is rooted in the intelligibility of the individual's own totalizing activity; in Henri Lefebvre it signifies the goal of de-alienated humanity. Among the more anti-Hegelian Western Marxists (including Colletti), the Della Volpean dialectic consists essentially in non-rigid, non-hypostatized thinking, while the Althusserian dialectic stands for the complexity, preformation and overdetermination of wholes. Poised between the two camps, Theodor Adorno emphasizes, on the one hand, the immanence of all criticism and, on the other, non-identity thinking.

Meanwhile, within the dialectical materialist tradition, Engels's third law (the negation of the negation) was unceremoniously dropped by Stalin from the official ideology of the USSR and the first law (the transformation of quantity into quality and vice versa) relegated by Mao Zedong in China to a special case of the second (the interpenetration of opposites), which from Lenin onwards increasingly discharged most of the burden of the dialectic. Certainly there were good materialist credentials (as well as political motives) for these moves. The negation of the negation is the means whereby Hegel dissolves determinate being into infinity. On the other hand, as Maurice Godelier pointed out, dialectical materialists rarely appreciated the differences between the Marxian *unity* and the Hegelian *identity* of opposites. Within this tradition Mao is noteworthy for a potentially fruitful series of distinctions – between antagonistic and non-antagonistic contradictions, principal and secondary contradictions, the principal and secondary aspects of a contradiction and so on – and stressing, like Lenin and Trotsky, the 'combined and uneven' nature of their development.

Throughout its long and complex history, five basic strands of meaning in dialectic stand out, all occupying the foreground at different times in the twentieth century:

1 *dialectical contradictions*, involving inclusive oppositions or forces of non-independent origins;
2 *dialectical argumentation*, oriented to the pursuit of groundable ideals;
3 *dialectical reason*, which encompasses a spread of connotations ranging from that imaginative and conceptually flexible thinking which, under the discipline of empirical, logical and contex-

tual constraints, plays such a crucial role in scientific development, through enlightenment and demystification to the depth rationality of emancipatory PRAXIS;

4 *dialectical process*, involving a scheme of original unity, historical diremption and eventual return, which is a recurrent and deeprooted motif in Western thought;

5 *dialectical intelligibility*, comprehending both the teleologically (in Hegel) or causally (in Marx) generated presentation of social and cultural forms (including beliefs) and their explanatory critique.

Reading
Adorno, Theodor 1966 (*1973*): *Negative Dialectics*.
Althusser, Louis 1965 (*1969*): *For Marx*.
Anderson, Perry 1976: *Considerations on Western Marxism*.
Bhaskar, Roy 1992: *Dialectic*.
Colletti, Lucio 1975: Marxism and the dialectic. *New Left Review 93*.
Lukács, György 1923 (*1971*): *History and Class Consciousness*.
Rosen, Michael 1982: *Hegel's Dialectic and its Criticism*.
Stedman Jones, Gareth 1973: Engels and the end of classic German philosophy. *New Left Review 79*.
Taylor, Charles 1975: *Hegel*.

ROY BHASKAR

dialectical materialism First developed by G. Plekhanov and Lenin in the context of the revolutionary struggle in Russia to denote Marxist philosophy, the term is also used to designate those parts of Marxist philosophy dealing with ontology, metaphysics and theory of knowledge but excluding 'historical materialism' (social philosophy), aesthetics and ethics. There was a further ritualistic use of the term, as a seal affixed to writing approved by or claiming approval from the authorities in the USSR, the Chinese People's Republic and East European 'socialist' countries (what was 'approved' or 'official' varied from country to country and over time). The basic tenets of dialectical materialism are philosophical materialism, possibility of knowledge, acceptance of development (and, thus, the acceptance of emergent properties and the irreducibility of some differences).

'Materialism' assumes that matter or body has 'primacy' with respect to mind or spirit. 'Primacy' means that minds are not able to exist without bodies while bodies can exist without being continuously dependent on minds as a sufficient condition for their existence. Marx assigned thinking to the category of bodily activities (thinking being the activity of brain, while walking involves some other parts of the body). The terms 'matter' and 'objective reality' are fully interchangeable. Feedback relationships between bodies and ideas are accepted. Materialism is taken to be a basic assumption of modern science and the success of technological uses of the natural sciences is considered to provide practical grounds for supporting materialism. Acceptance of the primacy of matter over mind is seen not only as a result of proof but also as a result of personal choice that logically precedes philosophic reasoning.

Marxists use the words 'agnosticism' and 'scepticism' to denote philosophies that deny the possibility of knowledge. Many Western Marxists described their own position as a variety of realism, while Soviet philosophers did not apply any label to describe their own position within the THEORY OF KNOWLEDGE. The majority position was that everything can be known in principle provided evidence is available, but absolute knowledge is unattainable by particular individuals. The proof of this proposition is seen to be obtainable outside the realm of thought. Human ability to use a theory to produce something predicted by that theory means that some aspects of that theory constitute knowledge of its objects.

'Development' is often understood with the help of dialectical concepts (named 'categories of dialectics'): difference, opposition, conflict, contradiction, quality and quantity, essence and apearance, condition and cause, actual and possible, and so on. The set of categories is an open one. Usually, concepts discussed by Aristotle and Hegel are included, but philosophers are constantly trying to add new ones. The categories are seen as corresponding to some aspects of reality; thus one speaks of objective dialectics (development in the real world), subjective dialectics (development of ideas) and dialectics as a 'theory' (a mode of understanding development). The word 'metaphysics' is sometimes used as a name for modes of thought that reduce development to change, or do not accept change at all, or do not accept that the distinctions drawn by human thought between objects of thought are at once relative and real. The concept of development is not necessarily applied to the world as a whole and there is no need to accept a unilinear story of development.

Nobody has actually succeeded in producing a specific and systematic theory which non-trivially marries dialectics and materialism. György Lukács, Della Volpe and many philosophers in the USSR produced Hegelian reasons for such a theory. M. Cornforth interpreted dialectical materialism as a research programme or a set of paradigmatic constraints and enabling conditions. Some British and Soviet Marxists opposed 'dialectics of nature' and sometimes restricted dialectical materialism to social philosophy. These positions imply that philosophies can be dialectical and materialist, but that there cannot be a dialectical materialism. Thus, some analytical philosophies can be labelled as dialectical and materialist while other analytical writings can be dialectical and idealist (apart from borderline cases and eclecticism). Many Soviet treatises about dialectics confined themselves to giving examples of application for some dialectical concept, although this use is publicly condemned even by its practitioners.

Karl Marx tried to substitute a materialist philosophy for Hegelian idealism in 1843–4. From about 1845 or 1846, he began to assign philosophy to 'ideology', that is, a form of thought used to discuss real issues as issues within that form of thought (the substitution is made unconsciously). Ideological forms were the only ones available to humanity before capitalism. Marx now claimed that ideology had to be replaced by empirical science. Neither Marx nor his principal collaborator Engels were interested in building up a systematic theory of knowledge and they did not think that to be an important part of philosophy.

It was Russian writers of the late nineteenth and early twentieth century (Plekhanov, A.M. Deborin, Lenin) who developed dialectical materialism, and after the Bolshevik revolution, paid positions for philosophers accepting dialectical materialism came into existence and their writings became more numerous. Between 1930 and 1955, philosophical discussions among Marxists were stifled, the publication of books and articles became virtually nonexistent, and the teaching of philosophy in the USSR was greatly reduced. Soviet philosophy reemerged from obscurity between 1955 and 1970. The theory of knowledge became a major part of philosophy and developed into a kind of pragmatic realism, dealing with modern science. Other major subjects were the ontological status of the mind, mind–body relationships, and the meaning and scope of dialectics. The most influential Soviet writers were Kedrov, Kopnin, Lektorski, Ilienkov. Polish and East German philosophers played a major part in these developments; Schaff and G. Klaus have been the most notable among East European philosophers. Italian, French and English-language writings have developed since 1945 (with some exceptions, they were scarcely known in the USSR or Eastern Europe). British and US writers have tried to produce a dialectical materialist and analytical theory of knowledge (M.W. Wartofsky, R. Bhaskar, A. Callinicos).

Hegelianism was strong in the USSR, while Bachelard and Michel Foucault are popular among those who have outgrown the view that Hegel provides the ideal paradigm of how one should philosophize. In the USSR and Poland, the theory of knowledge was often analytical, using logic as a major tool. There were numerous critiques of non-Marxist philosophers. For philosophers in 'socialist' countries, these critiques often provided a ritualistic way of substituting the philosophy supposedly under criticism for dialectical materialism. Western analytical Marxism has been a major development since the 1970s. It has discarded dialectical essentialism and reliance on the traditional concepts of dialectics. It is dialectical only in the wide sense in which all modern analytical philosophy is dialectical.

Reading

Callinicos, A. 1983: *Marxism and Philosophy*.
Cornforth, M. 1980: *Communism and Philosophy: Contemporary Dogmas and Revisions of Marxism*.
Della Volpe, G. 1950 (*1980*): *Logic as a Positive Science*, trans. J. Rothschild.
Graham, L.R. 1987: *Science, Philosophy, and Human Behavior in the Soviet Union*.
Scanlan, J.P. 1985: *Marxism in the USSR: A Critical Study of Current Soviet Thought*.
Wartofsky, M.W. 1979: *Models: Representation and the Scientific Understanding*.

EERO LOONE

dictatorship This is today commonly understood to be a highly oppressive and arbitrary form of rule, established by force or intimidation, which enables a person or group to monopolize political power to the detriment of society at large. However, this very general, almost colloquial definition, captures only one of the term's key meanings. True, 'dictatorship' resonates with ideas of illegality, domination, the rule of the MILITARY and totalitarianism. But it has also often been employed in 'democratic' settings to characterize, for instance, the ascendancy and might of the executive arm, and the inability of parliament to control it. For this twin meaning to be understood, it is necessary to examine the term's historical roots and context.

In the constitution of the Roman Republic (c. 509–31 BC), a dictatorship was not arrogated by someone, but was conferred on him as an extraordinary, albeit perfectly legal, office (Jolowicz, 1967, pp. 53–5). The dictatorship was a magistracy whose incumbent (usually an ex-Consul) was appointed by the Senate for purposes of crisis management – particularly in times of foreign war or civil strife, when decisive action was required and when the rule of one person was felt to be better adapted to deal with the emergency than the more cumbersome collegiate governmental system (cf. Machiavelli, 1531 (1965), pp. 189–90). The dictator was temporarily empowered with wide-ranging civil and military prerogatives (Rossiter, 1948, pp. 15–28). For instance, he was freed from the restraints of the tribunician veto; could raise on his own authority more than four legions – a right denied, in normal times, to a military commander without the express permission of the Senate; and was generally possessed of formidable rights of arrest and execution.

However, the powers vested in the dictatorship were never absolute or unqualified. The dictator's *imperium* – military and jurisdictional authority with a broad discretionary remit (Brunt and Moore, 1967, pp. 83–5) – was normally limited to a period of six months' duration; he had no authority to interfere in civil cases, declare war or tamper with the constitution; while, by 300 BC, the dictator's powers had become subject to *provocatio* – the right of a citizen 'to appeal against a capital sentence' (*Oxford Classical Dictionary*, 1970, pp. 892–3).

The constitutional legality of the Roman dictatorship, together with its circumscribed timespan and jurisdiction, has prompted some writers to be wary about applying the concept to twentieth-century conditions. Roy Medvedev (1981, p. 41) has thus remarked that the

various regimes of Mussolini, Hitler, Salazar, Franco, Somoza, Duvalier and Stroessner are referred to not by the name of tyranny, despotism or fascism but as 'dictatorships'. All of these, incidentally, avoided any time limit. Some of them were transferable by heredity from father to son, and, although the dictatorships of Hitler, Mussolini, Salazar-Caetano and Somoza did not go on forever, they came to an end not because

the dictator himself abdicated 'on the expiry of the specified period' but because he was overthrown by war or revolution.

However, as Medvedev also goes on to say, the conflation of these terms (tyranny, despotism, fascism, dictatorship) is unsurprising given the violence and exceptional powers that attended Roman dictatorial rule. Equally, it is important to recall that by 202 BC the dictatorship in its original form was effectively dead (Jolowicz, 1967, p. 55). Later figures – like Sulla (c. 138–78 BC) and Caesar (100–44 BC) – may have assumed the title of dictator for reasons of legitimation or expediency, but they ruled as *de facto* autocrats. By the twilight years of the Republic, the office of dictatorship was a constitutional sham, employed to mask the bloated ambition, and sanction the virtual omnipotence, of military overlords. (It is sobering to note that, according to the Elder Pliny (cited by Gelzer, 1969, p. 284), 1,192,000 people died in the wars Caesar prosecuted – and that this figure *excludes* the number of Roman citizens who fell.)

This historical background allows us to locate, and render comprehensible, the two main (and somewhat entangled) strands of twentieth-century usage, one drawing on the usurpatory, coercive, militaristic dimension of dictatorship, as found, for instance, in Caesar's almost unbroken occupancy of the office from 49 BC till his murder in 44 BC; the other referring to the older sense and substance of dictatorship implying legality or legitimacy, even if combined with the exercise of powers deemed in some manner extraordinary in their range and intensity.

The first usage is evident in those currents of social thought which *contrast* dictatorship with democracy, and which strongly associate dictatorship with militarism, the politicization of CIVIL SOCIETY, the extirpation of the rule of law and the subordination of the individual to the leadership principle. From this perspective, dictatorship may be studied as one of the historical routes to modernity manifested in, say, German and Japanese FASCISM (Barrington Moore, 1967, esp. pp. 433–52); or the concept may be applied to the post-World War II military regimes of the 'parliamentary semi-periphery', emergent in Argentina (in 1966), Greece (in 1967) and Chile (in 1973) (Mouzelis, 1986, esp. p. 97; see also Poulantzas, 1976). Soviet-type societies have also received the label of dictatorship or, in conjunction with fascism/Nazism, that of 'totalitarian dictatorship' (Neumann, 1957, pp. 243–56; cf. Arendt, 1958, and Shapiro, 1972). However, both designations are controversial (see TOTALITARIAN-ISM), and were so even prior to Gorbachev's liberalization programme and the revolutions of 1989 in Eastern Central Europe. Thus a number of writers have insisted that Soviet-type societies must be seen as a mode of domination unique in human history: for instance, as a 'dictatorship over needs' (Fehér, Heller and Márkus, 1983), or as a 'post-totalitarian' system – conformist, ato-mized, mechanical, manipulative and built on systematic self-deception and bad faith – which the classical notion of dictatorship is far too weak to convey (Havel, 1987).

In the second main strand of thinking on our subject, dictatorship is portrayed as *compatible* with democracy (defined in various contested ways), even to be an integral part or necessary condition of it. This variant has itself at least four permutations. One is apparent in descrip-tions of Bonapartist and Caesarist regimes, which, while repressive in certain respects, none-theless claim to derive their authority directly from the sovereign People, and seek the latter's acclamation through mass plebiscites (see BONA-PARTISM, CAESARISM, POPULISM; also Weber on 'plebiscitary democracy', 1978, p. 268). Another is the Leninist reading of Marx's notion of the 'dictatorship of the proletariat' – with the twist that the concept of democracy, important for Marx, tends to be collapsed into that of (class) dictatorship rendering the very distinction illu-sory (Marx, 1850, p. 123; Marx's letter to Wey-demeyer in Marx and Engels, *Selected Correspon-dence*, 1975, p. 64; Lenin, 1918, pp. 44–67; also Medvedev, 1981.)

A third permutation on the democracy–dictator-ship theme, closest to the classical Roman sense, arises from the analysis of 'constitutional dic-tatorships' (Rossiter, 1948). While the 'dictator-ship of the proletariat' – whether Marxist or Leninist in conception – was always envisaged as the instrument of revolutionary transformation, this third sense of dictatorship focuses on the potentially restorative, reparatory attributes of particular crisis regimes. In this usage, 'constitu-tional dictatorships' emerge during periods of rebellion, war and economic depression to pilot the legitimate social and political order through the emergency. The drastic powers assumed by

these regimes to deal with the extremity are mostly relinquished once the crisis has passed. (Cf. Schmitt's contrast between 'sovereign' and 'commissionary' dictatorships, in Schmitt, 1928, esp. pp. 2, 137–9.)

The three previous usages of dictatorship in a 'democratic' context share a notable feature: they all depict societies which are confronting excep-tional circumstances. In contrast, our fourth and final sense of dictatorship refers to the more normal, everyday workings of 'democratic' government. Nowhere has this usage been more evident than in descriptions of British 'cabinet autocracy' (Hobson, 1909, p. 12), with the Prime Minister's office at its apex. The premier's exten-sive powers of patronage, ability to reduce Parlia-ment to a rubber stamp of policy decided else-where, and plebiscitary relation to the masses via the party 'machine', have often in our century been identified as 'dictatorial'. Indeed, that epithet links the political thought of early twen-tieth-century writers such as Low (1904, pp. 156–8), Hintze (1975, p. 266) and Weber ('Poli-tics as a vocation', in Weber, ed. Gerth and Mills, *1970*, pp. 106–7) to the more recent com-mentary on 'elective dictatorship' (Hailsham, 1976; cf. Ash, 1989, p. 288, and Hirst, 1989, p. 82).

Corresponding to the two main diverging analy-tical treatments of dictatorship outlined above is also a difference in the locutionary force carried by the term. In the former, 'dictatorship' is usually uttered with loathing and horror. In the latter, the tone may be condemnatory, yet is just as often resigned or approving.

Reading

Baehr, P. 1989: Weber and Weimar: the 'Reich President' proposals. *Politics* 9, 20–5.

Birch, A.H. 1964: *Representative and Responsible Govern-ment: An Essay on the British Constitution.*

Bobbio, N. 1989: *Democracy and Dictatorship: The Nature and Limits of State Power*, trans. P. Kennealy.

Bracher, K.D. 1971: *The German Dictatorship: The Origins, Structure and Effects of National Socialism*, trans. Jean Steinburg.

Cobban, A. 1939: *Dictatorship: Its History and Theory.*

Conquest, R. 1971: *The Great Terror: Stalin's Purge of the Thirties.*

Crossman, R.H.S. 1963: Introduction. In W. Bagehot, *The English Constitution*, pp. 1–57.

Keane, J. 1988: Dictatorship and the decline of parlia-ment. Carl Schmitt's theory of political sovereignty. In *Democracy and Civil Society*, pp. 153–89.

Medvedev, R. 1981: The dictatorship of the proletariat.

In *Leninism and Western Socialism*, trans. A.D.P. Briggs, pp. 29–93.

Neumann, F. 1957: Notes on the theory of dictatorship. In *The Democratic and the Authoritarian State*, ed. H. Marcuse, pp. 233–56.

Schmitt, C. 1928: *Die Diktatur*.

PETER BAEHR

discourse   The concept is most usually equated with language 'in use', taking account of actually occurring text/texts in a genuine communicative context. Discourse has thus played a role in a number of disciplines, and various subdisciplines of LINGUISTICS: in textlinguistics, as a way of describing the way propositions are linked together to form a cohesive linguistic unit larger than a sentence (see Beaugrande and Dressler, 1981; Halliday and Hasan, 1976); in systemic linguistics (see SEMIOTICS), as a way of linking the linguistic organization of discourse to particular systematic components of situation types; in psycholinguistics, to account for the cognitive strategies which language users employ in COMMUNICATION, including the activation of world knowledge (see Van Dijk and Kintsch, 1983). Since discourse is concerned with the meaning of the 'utterance' rather than the 'sentence', it is related to pragmatics, though linguistic pragmatics cannot account for all aspects of discourse in its fullest sense. Concepts of discourse thus range from the most narrow text-linguistic description, where discourse is simply 'a continuous stretch of... language larger than the sentence' (Crystal, 1985, p. 96), which may be spoken or written, or both, single authored or dialogic, to macroconcepts which attempt to define theoretically ideological clusters or 'discursive formations' which systematically organize knowledge and experience, and repress alternatives through their dominance (see Foucault, 1969). In this context questions arise as to how discourses can be challenged from within and alternative discourses emerge. Such debates continue in many fields, including feminism and poststructuralism.

Discourse has become one of the most widely and often confusingly used terms in recent theories in the arts and social sciences, without a clearly definable single unifying concept. Discourse and text are often used interchangeably. Where a distinction is made, it is sometimes one of methodological perspective (text=material product; discourse=communicative process) or to account for the interlinking of texts in dialogue. Beaugrande and Dressler (1981) make text coterminous with discourse for as long as it has a single producer, but refer equally to discourse as the sum of interlinking texts. To define text as communicative occurrence, they propose seven standards of textuality. Cohesion and coherence are so-called 'text-centred' criteria. They refer both to grammatical forms marking the connections between sentences inside a text, and to the conceptual links through connected propositions, which do not necessarily appear in specific grammatical forms. In addition there are 'user-centred' criteria: intentionality, acceptability, informativity, situationality and intertextuality. Together these seven standards are constitutive of textual communication. 'User-centred' standards have to account for the fact that the 'meaning' of discourse is not contained within the linguistic forms as such, but that readers or listeners have actively to construct meaning by inferences.

Levinson (1983, ch. 6) limits discourse analysis to the formulation of rules for discourse structure, as expressed in text grammars (see Van Dijk, 1972) and speech-act based theories (Labov and Fanshel, 1977; Coulthard and Montgomery, 1979), and opposes this to conversation analysis practised by ethnomethodologists in a strictly empirical fashion (Sacks et al., 1974; Schenkein, 1978). A more broadly based discourse concept would, however, subsume CONVERSATION ANALYSIS and other sociological approaches to communicative interaction as one of the methods for approaching discourse (see Gumperz, 1982).

In literary theory the concept of discourse signals a way of breaking up the divisions between literary and non-literary texts. The special status of the poetic text is replaced by a continuum of linguistic practices which are more or less context dependent. The difference between 'discourse in life and discourse in poetry' (Vološinov, 1926) thus becomes a matter of degree, not an absolute. According to Vološinov, discourse is ideological in that it arises between socially organized individuals, and cannot be understood outside its context. 'Discourse, taken... as a phenomenon of cultural intercourse... cannot be understood independently of the social situation which engendered it' (ibid., p. 8). The ideological nature of discourse is most transparent in

> authoritative discourse [which] demands our unconditional allegiance. Therefore authoritative discourse permits no play with the context

framing it... It is indissolubly fused with its authority – with political power, an institution, a person – and it stands and falls together with that authority. (Bakhtin, 1934–5, p. 343)

The concept of discourse of Vološinov, Bakhtin, and other writers of the Bakhtin circle, and related concepts in recent writing in social semiotics, thus provide a link to macroversions of discourse found in Bourdieu's definition of 'linguistic capital' (1977), and especially to Foucault's 'discursive formations' (1969).

Reading

Beaugrande, R. de and Dressler, W. 1981: *Introduction to Textlinguistics*.
Foucault, M. 1969 (*1974*): *The Archaeology of Knowledge*.
Gumperz, J.J. 1982: *Discourse Strategies*.
Halliday, M. and Hasan, R. 1976: *Cohesion in English*.
Schenkein, J. ed. 1978: *Studies in the Organisation of Conversational Interaction*.
Van Dijk, T. and Kintsch, W. 1983: *Strategies of Discourse Comprehension*.
Vološinov, V.N. 1926 (*1983*): Discourse in life and discourse in poetry. In *Bakhtin School Papers: Russian Poetics in Translation*, vol. 10, ed. Ann Shukman.

ULRIKE MEINHOF

dissent   The verb 'to dissent' refers to activities that differ from or disagree with the majority in belief and opinion. The noun dissenter refers to a person who engages in such behaviour and holds dissenting views.

The verb and the noun were used originally to refer to religious organizations and their adherents who differed from the doctrine and the teachings of the Church of England. Baptists, Methodists, Quakers and similar Protestant sects and denominations outside the Church of England were historically discriminated against after the Restoration of 1660 and refused access to key positions in Britain. Most of these restrictions were abolished in the nineteenth century, but the long history of discrimination has led members of dissenting sects to take unpopular positions in non-religious fields as well as in the specifically religious domain. It is in this vein that Edmund Burke referred to the American colonists on the eve of the revolution as the Protestants of Protestantism, the dissenters of dissent.

The other major context in which the term dissent appears frequently is the law, especially the common law. Here it refers to those members of a jury or those judges in a law case who dissent from

the view of their colleagues. Since dissenting opinions are frequently formulated with great care and exhibit a high degree of legal sophistication, they are often consulted by lawyers or judges in later cases and their influence on subsequent judicial decisions may be as great as or greater than the majority decision against which they were initially directed. Yesterday's dissents may well become today's established verities. (See also CON-SENSUS.)

Except in the religious or legal context, the term is used infrequently in the social sciences; but near synonyms make a frequent appearance. Robert K. Merton, for example, distinguishes between deviant behaviour engaged in for personal gain, which he terms 'aberrant behaviour', and 'nonconforming behaviour', which is engaged in by individuals or groups that reject prevailing norms and values in the name of alternative guides to conduct for enhancing the quality of life and the common good. He argues that the frequent lack of differentiation among those categories of activities, all of them simply classed as 'deviant', leads to the incapacity to distinguish analytically between a common highway robber and Jesus Christ (Merton and Nisbet, 1961, ch. 1).

While conservative analysts tend to consider dissent a sickness of the body social, liberals and radicals are more likely to conceive of it as a prime engine of social change. They argue that social structures that depend on precedent and habit are bound to ossify and to be unable to respond to the challenge of novelty. Without the virtues of dissent, they argue, modern bureaucratic societies are likely to go the way of ancient Egypt and imperial China.

Reading

Coser, Lewis A. 1988: The functions of dissent. In *A Handful of Thistles: Collected Papers in Moral Conviction*.
Erikson, Kai T. 1966: *Wayward Puritans: A Study in the Sociology of Deviance*.
Merton, Robert K. and Nisbet, Robert eds 1961 (*1976*): *Contemporary Social Problems*, 4th edn.
Morison, Samuel Eliot et al. 1970: *Dissent in Three American Wars*.

LEWIS A. COSER

division of labour   Basically the term refers to the differentiation of tasks involved in the production of goods and services and the allocation of individuals and groups to them. A commonly employed distinction is between the technical and the social division of labour, the former referring to specialized tasks in the production process, the latter to differentiation in society as a whole.

Throughout the twentieth century there has been particular concern in social thought with analysing the impact of increasing specialization on

1 the working experience and responses of manual workers confined to repetitive tasks lacking the need for skill and denuded of the opportunity for knowledge and control related to the labour process, a theme usually referred to as the ALIENATION of the worker;

2 the forms in which divided labour and especially the development of professionalization relate to the social distribution of knowledge and so contribute to relations of power and domination (see PROFESSIONS);

3 the class structure, especially by way of the growing significance of the separation between 'mental' and 'manual' labour (Sohn-Rethel, 1978) and the growth of a 'new middle class' of white collar, professional and managerial workers (see CLASS);

4 the growing bureaucratization of economic and political administration, a process emerging partly from the need to coordinate and manage societies and organizations characterized by increased complexity and interdependence (see BUREAUCRACY);

5 the possibilities of self-management and workers' control over the production process (see WORKERS' COUNCIL);

6 the sexual division of labour and relations of domination and subordination between men and women (see GENDER).

In Britain in the period since World War II there has been an increasing focus on the processes whereby racist exclusionary practices against migrant and second generation ethnic minority workers have led to a racialization of the division of labour (see RACISM) and the formation of a distinct 'underclass' and racialized 'fractions' of other classes (Miles, 1982); the issue of the specific impact of racialization on ethic minority women workers has also been addressed (Phizacklea, 1983) and debates continue on how these processes relate to the articulation between 'race', class and gender (Anthias and Yuval-Davis, 1983). Latterly, important debates have focused on the recomposition of the working class in a 'postindustrial' phase of capitalism, the possibilities for a new division of

labour based on minimizing time spent on work in a 'postindustrial' socialism (Gorz, 1982; Hyman, 1983), and new forms of the INTERNATIONAL DIVISION OF LABOUR.

However, there is confusion in usage because the term variously conflates divided tasks, specialized workers, hierarchies of authority in the workplace, differentiated sectors of the economy and general structural complexity in industrial societies. This is overlain by disagreements about the extent to which the subdivision of tasks and the differentiation of related control structures is primarily an outcome of 'neutral' processes of technological development (or biological characteristics, in the case of the sexual division of labour) and the extent to which they result from the design of work processes to perpetuate relations of social and political domination that are amenable to transformation, especially under conditions of socialist production.

The major twentieth-century contributions to the understanding of the division of labour are related in complex ways to the writings of the ancient Greeks, the writers of the eighteenth-century Scottish Enlightenment, especially Adam Smith and Adam Ferguson, and the nineteenth-century figures Karl Marx and Auguste Comte (Rattansi, 1982). In this century the main contributions have come from (1) Marxism; (2) Emile Durkheim; (3) functionalist sociology; (4) feminism.

Marxism

The concept of division of labour is central in Marxism because of the importance given to labour as a category, underlining the significance of nature-transforming productive activity as the foundation on which rests the creation of wealth, the existence of social classes and the state, the operation of ideologies and the future promise of the abolition of scarcity. Divided labour increases productivity, which is said to give rise to surpluses which are appropriated by a dominant class which owns and controls the means of production. However, stemming in part from differences between Marx's own earlier and later writings on the subject (Rattansi, 1982) and also from the structural development of capitalist and state socialist societies, Marxist social thought has been characterized by significant divisions of view on the effects of the development of the division of labour. Some see it primarily in terms of a tendency to polarize the class structure of capitalism between a mass of largely unskilled manual workers and a small class of owners and the way in which the capitalist transformation of the division of labour gives rise to a more or less permanent new middle class (Carter, 1985); others see it primarily as the outcome of technological development rather than processes of class domination, the more technologically deterministic view surfacing for example in Lenin's attempt in Russia in the 1920s to import what he regarded as class-neutral techniques of 'scientific management' to boost productivity, while a contrary view is contained in Braverman's influential analysis (1974), building on insights in Marx's *Capital*, that scientific management epitomizes the tendency of the capitalist class to structure work processes in a manner which denies most workers any capacity for exercising control or intellectual skills (see LABOUR PROCESS). Marxists also disagree about the extent to which it is possible to abolish the division of labour, confusion about the various meanings of the term becoming particularly evident here (Rattansi, 1982). Nevertheless, Western Marxism in particular has been unified by a concern to challenge the loss of workers' control that is endemic in the design and operation of fragmented work processes dominated by small groups of technical and managerial workers, whether in capitalist or state socialist societies. In common with most non-feminist modes of social thought Marxist theorizing has been especially weak in grasping the significance of male domination in the division of labour, although various attempts have been made to provide Marxist-feminist accounts of the sexual division of labour (Barrett, 1988).

Emile Durkheim (1858–1917)
Durkheim's first book, *De la division du travail social*, translated as *The Division of Labour in Society* (1893), which drew on themes in the work of Comte, remained central to his thinking and has been an influential source for the sociological analysis of the division of labour, especially functionalist analyses of structural differentiation (see DURKHEIM SCHOOL). He deployed the term to include all forms of specialization of social function, thus extending its meaning well beyond the economic sphere. Durkheim saw forms of division of labour as intrinsically connected with types of social order or 'solidarity'. He contrasted 'mechanical solidarity', based on the simple division of

labour of more elementary societies, with the 'organic solidarity' of industrial societies, based on individualism and ties of dependence and exchange created by complex functional differentiation in which a great many specialized economic, political and cultural institutions were involved. Population growth and intersocial contact were identified as the main motors of change towards more complex forms. Durkheim continually wrestled with the problem of what he called 'abnormal' forms of the division of labour, connected with lack of solidarity and moral regulation to govern behaviour. Especially, he wrote of the 'anomic' and 'forced' divisions of labour, transitional states consequent on rapid industrialization in which, because of the absence of appropriate economic, political, and moral regulation for the division of labour and exchange relations, the economy became subject to fluctuations, class conflict intensified, specialization and inequalities were unrelated to natural talents and workers engaged in specialized tasks were unable to understand how their work was essential to the maintenance of society as a whole. Durkheim prescribed state intervention in the economy and the abolition of inherited privileges in access to positions in the division of labour, or what would now be referred to as equality of opportunity. Increasingly, he emphasized the role of 'corporations' or professional associations in mediating between the individual and the state and in creating the types of economic and moral regulation required by a complex technical and social division of labour. However, there is disagreement about the extent to which Durkheim envisaged the possibility of a fundamental transformation of the division of labour in some form of socialist society. Gane (1984) and Pearce (1989) have emphasized the potential radicalism of his political vision while others (Gouldner, 1962) have interpreted his views as only allowing for limited possibilities.

Functionalist sociology
Following Comte, Durkheim and others, the emphasis in this sociological tradition is on division of labour as SOCIAL DIFFERENTIATION linked to the evolutionary specialization of function, especially as a consequence of industrialization. A limited number of functions required for the reproduction of society – such as socialization and the production of goods and services – are said to be performed by an increasing range of specialized institutions, while formerly multifunctional insti-

tutions such as the family, which in preindustrial societies performed both socialization and economic production functions, become confined to the socialization of children. A major weakness of functionalist accounts of the division of labour has been their technological determinism, allied to a neglect of the relations between the division of labour, class domination and women's subordination.

Feminism

A key contention here is that much social thought, by concentrating on the public domain and by defining 'work' as paid employment, has taken sexual inequalities in the division of labour for granted (Stacey, 1981), failing to analyse women's DOMESTIC LABOUR in the home and its relation to women's subordination in the economic and political order. Some feminist analyses see male domination as rooted primarily in family relations, while others argue that male exclusionary practices in the workplace provide the key to understanding the sexual division of labour (Walby, 1986). Other debates have focused on the benefits accruing to private capital accumulation, to the state and to individual men of women's childcaring and labour-reproducing work in the home and their segregation into part-time, low-paid employment, and the extent to which the sexual division of labour is an effect of relations of class domination and therefore requires the abolition of social classes before enabling a major transformation of sexual inequalities. Biological reductionisms, feminist and non-feminist, which portray the sexual division of labour as a 'natural' outgrowth of male–female differences have been an important target within the majority of feminisms which have maintained that male domination within the sexual division of labour is primarily the outcome of *social* relations of male control over women's fertility and labour power.

Reading

Abercrombie, N. and Urry, J. 1983: *Capital, Labour and the Middle Classes.*
Beechey, V. 1987: *Unequal Work.*
Giddens, A. and Mackenzie, G. eds 1982: *Social Class and the Division of Labour.*
Gorz, A. ed. 1973 (*1976*): *The Division of Labour: The Labour Process and Class Struggle in Modern Capitalism.*
Horton, J. 1964: The dehumanization of alienation and anomie: a problem in the ideology of sociology. *British Journal of Sociology* 15, 283–300.
Larson, M.S. 1977: *The Rise of Professionalism.*
Littler, C. and Salaman, G. 1984: *Class at Work: The Design, Allocation and Control of Jobs.*
Lukes, S. 1967: Alienation and anomie. In *Philosophy, Politics and Society*, ed. P. Laslett and W.G. Runciman.
——1973: *Emile Durkheim.*
Rueschemeyer, D. 1986: *Power and the Division of Labour.*
Westwood, S. and Bhachu, P. eds 1988: *Enterprising Women: Ethnicity, Economy and Gender Relations.*
Wilson, W. 1980: *The Declining Significance of Race: Blacks and Changing American Institutions*, 2nd edn.

ALI RATTANSI

division of labour, international   At this scale, the principles of the DIVISION OF LABOUR are extended from the national to the global level. The development of international communications cuts the cost of exchange and allows many activities to be controlled from a single centre. This means growing interdependence, first between local communities to create nation-states, subsequently between nation-states to create international systems.

In societies based on the division of labour, goods and services are produced and distributed through specialization and exchange. In societies based on self-sufficiency, however, they are produced within the family, so that specialization is very limited. The differences between such societies are of fundamental importance in explaining basic aspects of social structure and economic and political capability.

Thus many theorists have associated the emergence of economic and social systems based on the division of labour with the process of modernization itself. 'Traditional' societies were seen as highly self-sufficient, so that each individual or family produced their own food, clothing and housing, educated their own children and took part directly in the political, cultural and other processes involved in community life. In such societies complex economic activities are impossible, while the degree of interaction and cooperation between individuals can only be very limited.

Modern societies are then said to be based on a complex and extended division of labour in which individuals perform increasingly specialized roles, and differentiated institutions emerge to perform the functions required to sustain social cooperation. Thus in the economic sphere individuals specialize in the production of particular commodities and exchange them for all of the other necessities of life; many individuals can then be brought together to produce each commodity, with each being responsible for only a single aspect of the production process. Thus differentiation of function and specialization of task go hand in hand with the necessity for higher and higher levels of exchange and more and more complex forms of organization.

In such communities the principle is applied not only to economic processes, but also to all others. Political, cultural, religious and other sorts of organizations are created and run by specialists who devote their working lives to performing the necessary tasks on behalf of the rest of the community, who then come to depend on them for the satisfaction of their social needs. Thus societies based on the division of labour require higher levels of skill, autonomy and cooperation than those based on subsistence and self-sufficiency.

At the international level, the term is most often applied to the economic sphere, to describe the process through which producers in particular countries choose, or may be constrained, to specialize in the production of particular commodities for which their environment or resources are particularly suited – those in which they have a 'comparative advantage'. Thus some countries are mainly involved in the export of manufactured goods, others of primary products, while the most developed countries are now coming to specialize in the exchange of services of various kinds.

This process involves the exchange of goods and services across national boundaries by independent producers, but it has also involved an increasing tendency for actual producers to be organized as global companies and to operate on an international scale. The largest all operate across national boundaries with subsidiaries in many countries. They have a powerful impact on levels of economic activity in host countries, and are often able to dominate foreign markets and suppress domestic competitors. Associated with this is a GLOBALIZATION of technological processes and possibilities. In an increasingly unified world market, all producers must adopt the most efficient new technology in order to survive, while the largest producers are able to promote their products internationally, leading to homogenization of patterns of consumption as well as of production processes.

The economic side of the division of labour is dominant at the international level because of the ease with which goods and money can be moved across borders, but it is also associated with the development of specialized cultural and political

agencies at that level. The beginnings of capitalism were associated with a global extension of political control by the leading countries which produced the imperial system. More recently political authority has been returned to former dependencies, but there has been a proliferation of specialized international agencies designed to allow the increasingly dense and interdependent system of global exchange to be managed.

The existence of a division of labour can be identified in the earliest accounts of humankind's social interaction, but it is especially associated with the rapid expansion in production and trade induced by the capitalist revolution from the sixteenth century. This has led to great inequality at the global level (the richest dozen countries control more than 80 per cent of the world's trade) and intense competition between companies, countries and regions. This has produced strong local resistance to external economic and political penetration and attempts by nation-states to limit freedom of trade and assert sovereign rights as against those of other countries or international agencies.

It also produced a political revolt against the dominant capitalist form assumed by the international division of labour manifested in the development of the socialist bloc beginning with the Russian revolution in 1917 and covering Eastern Europe, China and several less developed countries. But international exchange continued between both blocs so this limited and altered the tendency, but did not block it altogether. These countries have been unable to produce goods of comparable quality to those produced in the West, or to generate equivalent levels of output and consumption. This failure played a major part in the recent collapse of these statist systems, and of the current attempt to integrate these economies fully into the international division of labour.

Thus, despite these countervailing tendencies, the postwar period has witnessed an immense growth in global interdependence, an extension of the influence of international organizations like the International Monetary Fund, the World Bank and the European Community, and a corresponding weakening of the capacity of particular countries or communities to insulate themselves from the powerful impact of the international division of labour.

See also INTERNATIONAL RELATIONS; DEVELOPMENT AND UNDERDEVELOPMENT.

Reading
Brett, E.A. 1985: *The World Economy since the War*.
Mill, J.S. 1900: *Principles of Political Economy*, book 3, ch. 17.
Grubel, H.G. 1981: *International Economics*.

E.A. BRETT

divorce As one of a number of different ways in which MARRIAGE can end, divorce differs from its alternatives – abandonment and death – in that it is the legal dissolution of marital bonds: as in annulment, neither party has obligations, other than perhaps financial, to the adult left behind. Although divorce has been permitted at various times and places, it is only in the twentieth century that it has become the common way to dissolve a marriage in most of the West (Ireland is an exception; it still does not permit divorce). In contrast, Murdock (1950) found in his classic study of non-Western societies – most of them preliterate and small – divorce rates have historically exceeded those in the West. In the majority of preindustrial settings, divorce is equally available to women and men (Whyte, 1978). In many tribal communities in India, divorce is common and accomplished simply by an individual publicly walking up to a man or woman other than her or his spouse. Today, in Muslim societies, where divorce rates have been extremely high, a man can divorce one of his wives simply by repeating 'I divorce you' three times before credible witnesses (Islamic law does not give women the same right to divorce). But even in many settings outside the USA or Western Europe, whether Bangladesh or Indonesia, Colombia or Mexico, the former USSR or China, divorce is on the rise.

For the first time in the history of the West, during the mid-1970s in the USA and England, the number of marriages ending in divorce exceeded those ending in widowhood. While spouses have always lived apart, only recently have they legitimated that separation through the legal apparatus of divorce. Divorce, unlike separation, means that those who obtain it can legally take another spouse. Today, that has become easy in most parts of the world. Andrew Cherlin (1982), a demographer of the family in the USA, estimates that if recent trends persist, about half the people getting married today will see those marriages end in divorce. Lawrence Stone (1977), a historian of the family, estimates that in England over a third of current marriages will 'end in the divorce courts rather than

in the funeral parlor'. (England and the United States have the highest divorce rates in the Western world, apart from Scandinavia.) Beginning in the 1970s, in the United States spouses could attribute 'no-fault' in the court and in doing so end their spousal (though not family) ties.

Many argue that these new 'no-fault' rationales not only made divorce easier but produced greater difficulties for the women left behind. Those husbands who left them now had their innocence declared by the state, in whose eyes the absence of moral wrongdoing was associated with the absence of financial obligation. Divorcing husbands could now seek a new wife with no financial obligations to their old one. This left many women poor, contributing to what some have called a new 'feminization of poverty'. By creating so much immiseration of women and children, divorce highlighted the remaining economic basis of marriage that many believed had lost its force.

This state of affairs has led a number of commentators to argue that, in effect, marriage has finally become a voluntary contract to be abandoned at the will of either spouse. In turn, they argue, divorce is no longer stigmatized, but rather a commonplace experience that shares much with the act of marriage itself. However, divorce is still stigmatized if by 'stigmatization' we mean that its participants may be excluded from community activities and made to feel blamed for living apart. Moreover, like death, divorce still often brings psychological trauma. This trauma is all the more intense for those who divorce because it is so often unexpected and private rather than anticipated and social. Unlike death, divorce has no ritual, no community event to confirm it. It takes places in the courts and participants' minds rather than in the wider arena of social life. Both ex-husband and ex-wife seek an account – a story – to explain to themselves and others what happened and why. In doing so, they tend to discover that what is often thought of as a private set of troubles turns out to be a public issue.

The experience of divorce, like that of marriage itself, is shaped by gender as well as race. Just as there is a 'his' and a 'hers' in marriage, so, too, there is a his and hers in divorce. White women tend to suffer economically when they lose a spouse; black women less so if only because they can depend on husbands less for a family wage. But white and black men alike suffer socially and emotionally. While women who lose a husband often lose a breadwinner who made their material way of life possible, men who lose a wife lose not only a partner in a division of labour but a companion and confidante who ties them to other kin and friends.

With the upswing in divorce, some now argue that marriage is coming to an end, that individuals no longer seek the support of the church to validate their personal ties, that we are finally seeing the demise of the FAMILY – at least as we have known it. To be sure, the family and marriage are different from what they were during the previous century. In fact, these institutions are changing more rapidly than any had predicted. The question remains: are they disappearing? At least for now, few would answer in the affirmative. Instead, demographers, sociologists, psychologists and economists – albeit for very different reasons – suggest that individuals no longer necessarily seek the support of the church to validate their personal commitments, obligations or ties. But they do, and must, seek the support of the state. No state support, no marriage; no marriage, no divorce. And divorce, like marriage, is still very much with us. It is, in the words of one critic: 'For better or worse, here to stay.'

Reading
Cherlin, Andrew 1982: *Marriage, Divorce, Remarriage.*
Murdock, George 1950: Family stability in non-European cultures. *Annals of the American Academy of Political and Social Science* 5.227, 195–201.
Stone, Lawrence 1977: *The Family, Sex and Marriage.*
Whyte, Martin Kin 1978: *The Status of Women in Preindustrial Societies.*

                                   NAOMI R. GERSTEL

domestic labour   It was modern feminism and the development of gender studies which made the human activity of housework visible within social thought. It was initially brought into prominence by Marxists influenced by feminism who wished to uncover the material base of women's oppression under capitalism. Previous Marxist analysis of gender divisions, or the Woman Question as it had been known, had tended to locate the oppression of women purely in their disadvantaged place in the labour market, which could be explained by women's primary responsibilities in the home. However, such domestic relations tended to be seen as superstructural with mainly ideological effects and not therefore as fundamental as class relations which derived from the mode of production and

thus formed part of the economic base (see MODE OF PRODUCTION; MATERIALISM).

By analysing domestic labour as a set of production relations located within the economic base, it was hoped to give the oppression of women a comparable status within Marxism to class exploitation. Much of the debate turned on which of Marx's categories used for the analysis of wage labour also applied to domestic labour. Thus, for example, some protagonists argued that domestic labour was another form of commodity production because its output was the commodity labour power. Others argued however that it did not produce any commodity; its products were use values that never reached the market and entered directly into the household's consumption, only indirectly aiding the reproduction of labour power.

All sides agreed that domestic labour was not subject to the same relations of production as commodity production. In particular, the forms of control of domestic labour were different; instead of the law of value, which applies to capitalist commodity production, whereby similar commodities have to be made in comparable times for the firms producing them to remain profitable, standards and amount of time spent in domestic labour could vary widely. The form of control is more indirect, housewives are in day-to-day control of their own labour process but have to arrange their work to fit in with the needs of other members of their household and the demands of other social institutions, to standards which are disseminated in a variety of indirect ways, through familial ideology, for example. Similarly, the contractual situation is different; rather than by a specified wage-labour contract that is relatively easily terminated, the allocation of labour within the home is regulated by customary gender roles and although the marriage contract is no longer seen as binding for life it is relatively difficult to change. This applies to the form of remuneration too: for wage-earners a previously specified wage is paid, whereas for domestic labour no wage is given and housewives have to find their own subsistence out of the monetary income provided for the household as a whole, by their own or other members' wage labour. This also has effects on the timing of work: while a wage-worker works for clearly specified periods of time and usually in a place distinct from his or her place of leisure, a housewife's work is quite literally 'never done' and she has no physical or temporal separation between work and leisure time. Further, unlike capitalist commodity production, housework tends to be done in isolation, with little or no specialization or cooperation.

Another area of debate concerned the role domestic labour played in the reproduction of capitalist production relations. Did it produce its own surplus value to be appropriated either by a housewive's husband or by his employer? Or did it contribute to the production of surplus value indirectly by lowering the wage that members of the household needed to be paid to maintain a customary standard of living? Or was its role in the reproduction of capitalist relations more indirect still, providing the home comforts which made work under capitalist conditions bearable, and absorbing those areas of use-value production, such as childcare, that could for some reason not be taken into capitalist production? Did domestic labour form a separate mode of production articulated with the capitalist mode or should the definition of the capitalist mode of production be expanded to include the relations of domestic production? (Himmelweit and Mohun, 1977, surveys these debates.)

Side by side with these debates within Marxism, a number of empirical studies of housewives and housework were carried out (see, for instance, Oakley, 1974). Historical studies were done of the development of domestic labour and domestic technology, which compared time budgets to show that although the content of domestic labour had changed significantly over the last century, the advent of labour-saving devices had barely reduced the amount of time spent on it, suggesting that the less economistic Marxist explanations of its persistence might have more in them than those which saw its role purely in terms of its contribution to the production of surplus value (see Bose, 1979).

As part of the Marxist theoretical project of explaining the material base of women's oppression, the domestic labour debate must be considered a failure. The specific production relations of domestic labour were analysed through the debate and this together with subsequent empirical work made domestic and other informal work not only more visible within social science, but more recognized within society too; for example, insurance companies now quantify the value of a housewife's work in assessing the value of her productive life. However, the debate failed to explain why it was largely women who work under these particular production relations. In other words it recognized that capitalist society depends on a division of labour between waged commodity production and unwaged domestic labour, but failed to explain why that division coincided with a sexual division of labour. This was not surprising given the failure to incorporate into the analysis concepts other than those developed by Marx for the analysis of wage labour, which were inherently sex-blind. Although extensions have subsequently been suggested which incorporate notions of patriarchy, this is just to add on another structure which in itself needs explanation. Without recognizing that domestic labour is more than just another form of work, but has a specific connection to human reproduction, where, of course, the differences between the sexes are crucial, the study of domestic labour can never provide a complete analysis of sexual oppression.

Reading
Fox, B. ed. 1980: *Hidden in the Household: Women's Domestic Labour under Capitalism.*
Himmelweit, S. and Mohun, S. 1977: Domestic labour and capital. *Cambridge Journal of Economics*, 1.
Molyneux, M. 1979: Beyond the domestic labour debate. *New Left Review*, no. 116, 3–28.
Oakley, A. 1974: *The Sociology of Housework.*
Seccombe, W. 1974: The housewife and her labour under capitalism, *New Left Review*, no. 83, 3–24.

SUSAN F. HIMMELWEIT

domination   *See* AUTHORITY

drama   *See* THEATRE

Durkheim school   This is the name given to the collaborators and disciples of Emile Durkheim, who flourished in France between the late 1890s and World War II. They began as a remarkably effective research team, applying, refining, developing and sometimes modifying Durkheim's ideas across a wide variety of disciplines. They were organized around the remarkable journal, the *Année sociologique*, 12 volumes of which appeared between 1898 and 1913. It published reviews, monographs and editorial notes across a very wide range, written for the most part by the Durkheimians, but not exclusively: the *Année* also published Georg Simmel. As Marcel Mauss recalled,

A good laboratory depends not only on the person in charge but also on the existence of reliable participants, i.e. new and old friends with a lot of ideas, extensive knowledge and working hypotheses, and who, most importantly, are ready to share these with one another, to join in the work of the longer standing members and to launch the works of the newcomers. We were such a team. (In Besnard, 1983, p. 140)

The *Année sociologique* established what came to be called 'the French school of sociology'. After World War I, which decimated the Durkheimians, and Durkheim's own death in 1917, the survivors continued to produce many significant individual works, though no longer as a working group (though the *Année* appeared twice in the 1920s and the *Annales sociologiques* briefly in the 1930s). They came to occupy important positions in French higher education – at the Sorbonne (Célestin Bouglé, Paul Fauconnet, Maurice Halbwachs, Georges Davy), at the Collège de France (Mauss, François Simiand, Halbwachs), at the École normale supérieure (Bouglé) and at the Académie de Paris (Paul Lapie). They influenced a whole generation of specialists in several disciplines, and for a time they achieved some influence over the training of secondary school teachers throughout France. In 1920, Paul Lapie, an editor of and contributor to the *Année* and the director of primary education in France, introduced as part of a new programme for the Écoles normales primaires, a course entitled 'sociology applied to morality and education'. Its goal was to introduce teachers to 'the objective study of social facts' which, Lapie argued, 'suggests an appreciation of their value, and consequently, far from leading to a form of indifference, it ends by solidly justifying our moral practices' (quoted in Besnard, 1983, p. 121). But the course was much attacked and its content was diluted. By 1930 the ideology of the Durkheimians was already outmoded. Moreover, as a 'school' they did not survive. Other, incompatible, intellectual influences such as Marxism, phenomenology and existentialism prevailed after World War II in France (though there was a marked continuity within social anthropology), while Durkheimian ideas were taken up elsewhere, notably in Anglo-Saxon social anthropology and SOCIOLOGY.

Durkheim's driving preoccupation was to study social life as an objective reality, in all its aspects, currently divided up into academic disciplines, yet all amenable, he thought, to the sociological mode of inquiry. This required a comparative method, involving the classification of societies into types, and an insistence on seeking social (as opposed to individual or pyschological or material) causes, even, indeed perhaps especially, for what might seem least amenable to such explanation: hence his famous study of suicide, and his interest in the sociology of religion, knowledge and morals. It also involved a focus on what he called *représentations collectives* – collective beliefs and sentiments that prevail in a given social milieu. Accordingly, the second volume of the *Année* states in its preface the general principle that religious, juridical, moral and economic phenomena must always be related to a particular social milieu, and that their causes must always be sought in the constitutive features of the type of society to which that milieu belongs (Durkheim, 1858–1917, p. 348).

The Durkheimians pursued this imperialistic programme, across the disciplines of the social sciences, including history, 'incorporating', as Marcel Mauss put it, 'facts within a sociological framework, and simultaneously organising them and dissecting the raw data provided by the descriptive branches of our sciences' (in Besnard, 1983, p. 143), but always through an intense engagement with current scholarship and often in combat with prevailing academic traditions. Their goal was to dissolve arbitrary barriers between academic fields and establish a new perspective on their subject matter. Who, Durkheim asked, would until quite recently have supposed 'that there are relationships between economic and religious phenomena, between demographic adaptations and moral ideas, between geographic forms and collective manifestations, and so on?' (Durkheim, 1858–1917, p 348). They were rationalists and positivists: they believed in the explanatory power of clear and distinct ideas methodically applied through the division of academic labour. They stood for an Enlightenment-inspired vision of the reorganization of all the various specialized branches of scientifically established knowledge which would then furnish a solid basis for social progress, which they interpreted to mean movement towards a planned industrial social order anchored in common beliefs and sentiments enlightened by social science.

Most were socialists (sympathetic to Jean Jaurès, not revolutionaries and certainly not Marxists) but they drew a sharp line between their scientific and their political work. Like the Comteans and the Saint-Simonians before them, the Durkheimians thought of religions as offering a mystifying account of the social world, which social science would render clearly, but they saw themselves neither as the priests of a new secular religion nor as the practical entrepreneurs of a new industrialism. Rather they were, above all, practising social scientists who sought, through their research and teaching, to strengthen the secular and reformist ideology of the French Third Republic. Like Durkheim himself, they were, for the most part, evolutionary optimists, relatively blind to those elements in social life that Weberians and Marxists stressed – above all mechanisms of domination and conflicts of interests. Nor were they alive to the demonic, irrational forces a modern society could harbour and which erupted in Nazi Germany.

Three central figures contributed most to the *Année sociologique*, as both editors and contributors: Durkheim, Marcel Mauss and Henri Hubert. Mauss was Durkheim's nephew and the closest to him, and contributed importantly to the latter's *Suicide* (1887) and *The Elementary Forms of the Religious Life* (1912). A specialist in ethnology and the history of religions, he edited, with Hubert, the section on 'relingous sociology' and wrote major studies of primitive classificatory systems (with Durkheim: Durkheim and Mauss, 1903), of sacrifice and of magic (with Hubert: Hubert and Mauss, 1899; Mauss and Hubert, 1904), a remarkable study of prayer, of reciprocity and gift-giving (Mauss, 1925) and of the very notion of the person or 'self' (in 1938: see Carrithers et al., 1985). Of all the Durkheimians, Mauss was undoubtably the most important and influential figure. His work has stood the test of time and remains fundamental – above all, *The Gift*. Moreover, he was an inspirational teacher of whom it was said that out of his ideas others wrote theses and books. He devoted much of his volatile energy to collaboration and to the publication of work by colleagues lost in World War I. Tragically, after World War II, he lost his reason.

Hubert, apart from his collaboration with Mauss, published an important study of the representation of time in relingon and magic, and also wrote on the theory of folk relingon and on historical archaeology. Hubert's Polish pupil Stefan Czarnowski also made important contributions to the sociology of folk religions, notably his study of Saint Patrick and the cult of heroes in Celtic legends. Robert Hertz wrote brilliant studies of the collective conception of death in primitive societies

(1907) and of the symbolic dualism of right and left (1909) that have had considerable subsequent influence, but he also investigated the Alpine cult of Saint-Besse (in a work that is of all these Durkheimian studies the closest to ethnographic field work) and folklore gathered from infantrymen in World War I (which claimed his life). Maurice Halbwachs not only extended Durkheim's theory of suicide in very interesting ways, he also investigated the social framework of memory (Halbwachs, 1980) and explored the social determinants of differential standards of living and varying definitions of 'needs' in relation to social class, and of budgets and consumption patterns.

Célestin Bouglé was in charge of the section of 'general sociology' and was particularly interested in the place of psychology in the study of social phenomena. He also studied the social preconditions of the growth of egalitarian ideas, the evolution of values and the Indian caste system (Bouglé, 1908). Paul Fauconnet (who with Durkheim edited the sections on 'criminal sociology and moral statistics' and 'the study of moral and legal rules') examined forms of responsibility as socially determined, analysing its conditions, nature and functions. The brothers Hubert and Georges Bourgin edited the section on 'economic sociology'. François Simiand, the group's economist, investigated the determinants of wages and prices, of economic fluctuations and of the value of money, and the origin, evolution and role of money, as well as writing extensively about the methodology of the social sciences. Henri Beuchat, who worked in American archaeology and philology, also collaborated with Mauss in their important study of the impact of 'social morphology' or structure on the seasonally varying legal, moral, domestic and religious life of the Eskimos (Mauss and Beuchat, 1906), Georges Davy studied the rise and evolution of contract and, with the Egyptologist Alexandre Moret, published a study of the origins of Egyptian civilization 'from clans to empires'. There were also Gaston Richard, whose early work was on the social origins of the idea of law but who eventually became a sharp critic of Durkheimian sociology, and Paul Lapie, whose work in educational sociology, and in particular on the determinants of educational success, on schooling and delinquency and on education and social mobility, was pathbreaking and far ahead of his time (see Besnard, 1983).

Ater the group's effective dissolution, individuals within and close to the Durkheimian circle carried its influence into their respective fields. Among them were the great comparative linguist Antoine Meillet, the eminent sinologist Marcel Granet (Granet, 1922), the jurists Emmanuel Lévy and Paul Huvelin, and the pioneering scholar of Ancient Greek law Louis Gernet, the arabist Eduard Doutté, the historians Georges Bourgin, Georges Lefebvre, Albert Mathiez, Marc Bloch and Lucien Febvre (through Bloch and Febvre the Durkheimians powerfully influenced the *Annales* school of historians – see ANNALES SCHOOL), the psychologists Charles Blondel, Georges Dumas and Henri Wallon, the economic and social geographer Albert Demangeon, the philosopher-sociologist Lucien Lévy-Bruhl, and a whole generation of French ethnologists trained or influenced by Mar-

cel Mauss, notably Claude Lévi-Strauss and Louis Dumont.

Reading
Besnard, P. ed. 1983: *The Sociological Domain: The Durkheimians and the Founding of French Sociology.*
Durkheim, Emile 1858–1917 (*1960*): *Emile Durkheim 1858–1917: A Collection of Essays, with Translations and a Bibliography*, ed. K. Wolf.
Durkheim, E. and Mauss, M. 1903 (*1963*): *Primitive Classification*, trans. and ed. R. Needham.
Hertz, R. 1907 (*1960*) Contribution à une étude sur la réprésentation collective de la mort. Trans. R. Needham and C. Needham in *Death and The Right Hand*.
Hubert, H. and Mauss, M. 1899 (*1964*): *Sacrifice: Its Nature and Function*, trans. W.D. Hall.
Mauss, M. 1925: (*1954*) *The Gift*, trans. I. Cunnison.
Mauss, M. and Hubert H. 1904 (*1972*): *A General Theory of Magic*, trans. R. Brain.

STEVEN LUKES

E

ecology Etymologically derived, like the word 'economic', from the Greek *oikos* or 'household', the modern use of the term 'ecology' is generally credited to the nineteenth-century German evolutionist, Ernst Haeckel. However, the concept was already present in the eighteenth-century idea of an 'economy of nature'. According to this view, each living species was assigned its own proper place in nature; its own specific type of food, geographical range, and population, within a harmonious pattern of interdependence between the different species. Recognition of the widespread phenomenon of extinction led to a weakening of the idea of providential design and rational harmony in the nineteenth century, while Darwin's concept of natural selection relied on the assumption of a competitive struggle for existence both among organisms and between them and their physical conditions of life. Nevertheless, the idea of a harmonious economy of nature is not entirely lost in Darwin, since the mechanism of natural selection has as its outcome an ever closer fit, or adaptation, between organisms and their conditions of life. Although Darwin and other evolutionary biologists of the nineteenth century did carry out detailed studies of associations between interdependent species (Darwin's own studies of the pollination of orchids by insects are a famous example), there were few attempts to integrate such studies systematically into a disciplinary specialism until the 1890s.

The pioneering work of E. Warming, A. Schimper and others in synthesizing plant geography with physiology led to a focus on the ecology of plant communities and their succession through time. Notable early work on plant ecology included the studies of prairie ecology by groups at Nebraska and Chicago in the USA and the botanical ecology of A.G. Tansley in Britain. Despite the early (1881) establishment of physiological animal ecology by the German K.C. Semper, and the still earlier focus on insect pollination, the general development of animal ecology proceeded more slowly than plant ecology. The recognition, as a central insight of ecology, of more or less stable patterns of association between populations of different species of animals and plants, together with geological, topographical and climatic conditions, necessitated a holistic approach to both field studies and theoretical explanation. F.E. Clements's controversial concept of an ecosystem as a 'superorganism' is not now defended within scientific ecology, but various forms of holistic 'systems' approaches are retained. Modern ecology is centrally concerned with the cycling of nutrients through ecosystems, and with patterns of energy flow and interchange. The economic metaphor by which the 'functions' of different groups of organisms within an ecosystem are classified – 'producers' (mainly green plants), consumers (herbivores and their predators) and decomposers (mainly micro-organisms) – carries a clear resonance of the earlier notion of an 'economy of nature'. Increasingly there has developed a recognition that the different ecosystems are themselves interrelated. Of fundamental importance for contemporary social thought about human ecology has been the synthesis (Cole, 1958) of the concept of the biosphere (the totality of all living things on the earth) with that of an ecosystem to yield the concept of the 'ecosphere': the planet considered as an immensely complex global system of ecosystems. This concept provides the basis for a study of human social and economic activity from the standpoint of its global ecological conditions and impacts.

Recognizably ecological influences on European social and political thought were licensed by the emphasis in the eighteenth and nineteenth centuries on human malleability and 'perfectibility'. Montesquieu attributed a significant role to geographical and climatic factors in the shaping of social and cultural diversity and the variety of forms of government, while Malthus used the idea of a shortage of means of subsistence relative to the 'power' of population growth as a weapon against proposals for radical social change. Western industrialism of the nineteenth and early twentieth centuries gave rise to successive waves of romantic nostalgia for a lost harmony with nature, and many socialist writers saw a transformed relationship with nature as central to the post-capitalist future.

The dominant traditions of Western social thought in the twentieth century have been founded on a dualistic opposition between nature and society or culture. But in seeking to resist SOCIAL DARWINISM and other forms of biological determinism, these traditions of thought also cut themselves off from a potentially productive encounter with newer developments in the life sciences, especially ecology. An important early exception to this was the sociology of the Chicago school in the 1920s and 1930s. The work of R.E. Park and E.W. Burgess, especially, was premised on an opposition between those forces which operate in and on social life independently of the consciousness and agency of social actors, and the significance assigned to these forces and processes by the actors involved. Explicity drawing on the work of Warming and Clements in plant ecology and the pioneering animal ecologist, C. Elton, Park and Burgess referred to the former class of social forces as an 'ecological' order. This analogy between plant and animal ecology and the unwilled dimension of human social life was most fully developed and applied in the field of urban sociology, where Park and Burgess analysed the effects of competition for scarce resources between individuals and groups, and the resulting 'selective' pressures, adaptive responses and diversions of labour. In these terms could be understood the shifting distributions and patterns of temporal 'succession' of ethnic groups, subcultures, specialized activities and so on as between geographically defined natural areas or 'zones' in the city.

The shift from metaphorical to direct, literal application of ecological concepts to human social life was established only in the 1960s, following the globalization of the ecological perspective in the form of the concept of the 'ecosphere'. The dramatic 'doomwatch' warnings of Paul Ehrlich, Edward Goldsmith, the authors of *Limits to Growth* and others writing at the end of the 1960s and early 1970s resulted from attempts to extrapolate current global trends in population, pollution and resource depletion into the future, setting them against the ecological recognition of a finite global 'carrying capacity'.

The first wave of 'ecological politics', often designated, somewhat misleadingly, as 'neo-Malthusianism', soon gave way to a multiplicity of attempts to incorporate an ecological perspective into social and political theory. B. Commoner, A. Gorz and others attempted to reconstruct the Marxian critique of capitalism in terms of its ecologically destructive consequences, while feminists, such as C. Merchant, linked together modern science, patriarchy and ecological destruction in a distinctive tradition of 'ecofeminism'. In environmental social philosophy, a distinction is drawn between 'shallow' and 'deep' ecology (Naess, 1989). In the former case, concern for the environment is based on an enlightened recognition of its importance for human well-being, whereas in the latter intrinsic value is attributed to the environment, quite independently of specifically human interests. Allegedly reactionary and misanthropic social movements may be associated with deep ecology.

See also ENVIRONMENTALISM; GREEN MOVEMENT.

Reading

Bahro, R. 1982: *Socialism and Survival.*
Bramwell, A. 1989: *Ecology in the Twentieth Century: A History.*
Enzenberger, H.M. 1988: A critique of political ecology. In *Dreamers of the Absolute.*
Gorz, A. 1980: *Ecology as Politics.*
Lowe, P.D. and Rudig, W. 1986: Political ecology and the social sciences: the state of the art. *British Journal of Political Science* 16, 513–50.
Matthew, F.H. 1977: *Quest for an American Sociology: Robert E. Park and the Chicago School.*
Meadows, D.H. et al. 1972: *The Limits to Growth.*
Merchant, C. 1980: *The Death of Nature: Women, Ecology and the Scientific Revolution.*
Ryle, M. 1988: *Ecology and Socialism.*

TED BENTON

econometrics Normally regarded as the application of statistical techniques to economic data in order to investigate economic problems, econometrics more inclusively defined would encompass the entire array of measurement problems in economics. Such a definition could include problems of operationalizing a concept, testing a theory, gathering data and building specific models (see MODEL). Though the term was first used in the twentieth century by early practitioners like Ragner Frisch, the tradition of a statistical–mathematical approach to social phenomena goes back to seventeenth-century political arithmetic. The origin of econometrics in this century is tied up with efforts to resolve the theoretical disputes between the marginalists and their critics by resorting to empirical testing of the marginal productivity theory of distribution by economists such as H.L. Moore. Moore tried to demonstrate the validity of J.B. Clark's theory of wages by using the methods of correlation.

From such crude beginnings econometrics developed into a rigorous discipline through the efforts of pioneers such as R. Frisch and J. Tinbergen in Europe and researchers in the USA at the Cowles Foundation. After World War II the field expanded rapidly with the invention of the high-speed computer. Today it is more appropriate to speak of the various branches of econometrics than of econometrics as a single field.

Theoretical econometrics has traditionally focused on building statistical models germane to the testing of economic theories. The classical linear regression model has been extended by investigating the violation of various assumptions regarding the error term. A distinct contribution by econometricians has been the development of simultaneous equation models. More recently work on qualitative dependent variables, distributed lags, dynamic models and a number of other topics has enlarged the repertoire of theoretical econometrics.

Using these continuously developing tools, many theoretical propositions in all areas of ECONOMICS have been subjected to empirical tests. These range from consumer demand theory and efficient market hypothesis in microeconomics to the testing of exchange rate determination theories in international economics.

Another important area in the development of econometrics has been the formulation and validation of macroeconometric models. Starting with early work by Elmer Working on identification of the demand and supply curves from economic data, the work of Frisch and Tinbergen in Europe advanced the frontier of econometrics considerably. Later work at the Cowles Foundation led by J. Marschak and T.C. Koopmans produced a solid analytical foundation for estimating simultaneous equation models. The actual estimation of such models for a real economy was pioneered by Klein and Goldberger (1955) and continues in ever more sophisticated forms with large numbers of equations in many countries. Internationally, this approach resulted in the LINK project, an international, cooperative study group started in 1968 in order to create a system of models. LINK models consist of national, regional and world trade models.

Recently R.E. Lucas has pointed out that the parameters of such models will change as a result of policy announcements. Theoretically, the point is quite valid though its relevance for a macroeconometric model in practice remains an empirical issue. Many recent models embody the assumption of rational expectations introduced by J.F. Muth and R.E. Lucas. A different approach advocated by C.A. Sims is to use empiricist techniques such as vector autoregression methods.

In a different way English econometricians such as D.F. Hendry recognize the problems of exogeneity assumptions in solving the identification problems of macroeconometric models. However, Hendry still recognizes the value of econometrics for testing economic theories. His work in this area falls within the rubric of model selection procedures.

In the area of model selection and in the approach to econometrics in general the Bayesian approach has been a contender with the classical approaches described above. In contrast with the classical frequentist approach, the Bayesian approach is concerned with how new information modifies a researcher's beliefs about parameter values. It also eschews the need for justifying the estimating procedure by appealing to the awkward classical concept of the performance of the estimator in hypothetical repeated samples. However, philosophically the acceptance of the Bayesian approach commits one to a subjectivist view of probability that clashes with the objectivist view of probability as emerging from features of the world independent of the observer. Therefore, classical and Bayesian approaches have distinct and opposed ontological commitments.

Given the diversity of contributions and viewpoints in modern econometrics, any summary view is apt to be misleading. At the moment several new developments have begun to recognize the need for more data generation, diagnostic tests, inclusion of degrees of belief and the use of models which recognize data limitations. At the same time more emphasis is being placed on non-linear and dynamic model building.

Reading
Aigner, D. and Zellner, A. eds 1988: Causality. *Journal of Econometrics* 39. 1–2.

Hendry, D.F. 1987: Econometrics methodology: a personal perspective. In *Advances in Econometrics, Fifth World Congress*, vol. 2, ed. T.F. Bewley.

Klein, L. and Goldberger, A. 1955: *An Econometric Model of the United States: 1929–1952.*

Leamer, E.E. 1987: Econometric metaphors. In *Advances in Econometrics, Fifth World Congress*, vol. 2, ed. T.F. Bewley.

Pesaran, M.H. 1987: *The Limits to Rational Expectations.*

Sims, C.A. 1987: Making economics credible. In *Advances in Econometrics, Fifth World Congress*, vol. 2, ed. T.F. Bewley.

Tinbergen, J. 1939: *Statistical Testing of Business Cycle Theories*, 2 vols.

Zellner, A. 1983: Statistical theory and econometrics. In *Handbook of Econometrics*, Z. Griliches and M.D. Intriligator.

HAIDER ALI KHAN

economic depression   *See* DEPRESSION, ECONOMIC

economic growth   The experience and the prospect of economic growth have profoundly shaped twentieth-century discourse; their effect on culture and reasoning has been quite different from the effects in other epochs although periods of extraordinary growth have been experienced previously. From 1820 to 1980 the total product of today's 16 leading capitalist economies grew 60-fold; their output per capita grew 13-fold. One outstanding period, from 1950 to 1973, is regarded as a Golden Age, since the rate of growth of their output then was more than twice as high as in previous decades. In the twentieth century, the state-directed socialist system of the Soviet Union also experienced high rates of output growth, as did some Third World countries, especially after 1960. In the course of that experience, ideas concerning economic growth and ideas shaped by it have had a key role in modern conceptual structures. They may be summarized in five, non-exhaustive categories – growth conceptualized in relation to: national politics; social transformation; expansion of output; Third World development; and its environmental or other costs.

National politics
The European system of national politics constructed in the nineteenth century developed an expansionist dynamic at an early stage. This political expansionism derived in part from the adoption of economic growth as a characteristic of nationhood. It was marked by external expansion in the form of imperialism with its national rivalries, and by ideals of expanding domestic production and wealth to strengthen the nation-state and underpin 'great power' ambitions; Bismarckian Germany exhibited both characteristics most clearly, but not uniquely.

The political ideas germinating then have, a century later, become a universal feature of official politics in capitalist and socialist states. In the discourse of Western democracies, the principal measure of national strength is the country's relative rate of growth. The absolute level of its wealth is treated as having little significance compared to the dynamism of output growth (or lack of dynamism). Although the United States is the world's richest major country, its political identity and direction has been shaped in recent years by doubts over its rate of growth (compared to Japan's in particular), and party political contests in European democracies have been informed by comparisons of economic growth under different governments.

The Soviet Union's political ambitions were defined partly in relation to economic growth since Lenin's day. In modern times, the role of economic growth in superpower rivalry was represented most sharply by Khrushchev's claim that Soviet growth would enable his country to win the Cold War by overtaking US income levels in two decades (Halliday, 1983); while, on the other hand, the political crisis that actually overtook the Soviet system in the 1980s is widely conceived as the result of a slowdown in the rate of growth (rather than absolute poverty).

Growth as social transformation
Associated with the political salience of economic growth is a conception of it as more than a quantitative category, or growth of output. In the twentieth century, social scientists and social historians have established economic growth as a leading object of enquiry; and from that perspective economic growth is conceived as a process of fundamental social transformation. Modern views of growth as a continual process of social transformation were, effectively, initiated by Karl Marx's analyses of the genesis and progress of capitalism, and the ideas derived from his work have shaped debates over both capitalist growth and socialist growth.

Capitalist growth   The twentieth century understanding of capitalist growth, or accumulation, from this perspective has revolved around three central problems: the nature of the transformation from feudalism to capitalist growth; the role of crises in capitalist growth; and the historical transformations of the capitalist system itself. Marxist analysis of the historical transformation from feudalism to capitalism in England has been the basis for important analyses of modern economic growth in the specific circumstances of two capitalist societies: Japan and Britain. In Japan, debates since the 1920s focused on whether growth since the 1868 Meiji restoration was capitalist or whether the full transition from feudalism occurred later, even as late as the land reform imposed in the 1940s. At issue was an understanding of the specific character of capitalist growth in Japan, and, in that respect, the debate is similar to that initiated by Anderson (1964) who sought to explain the specific character of Britain's growth over recent centuries by the character of the transition from feudalism.

Economic growth under capitalism has been characterized by regular crises, which Marx claimed to explain. The economic crisis identified with the 1930s has entered consciousness as the exemplar, one which stimulated divergent analyses of the character of capitalist growth. A widespread view was that it was an indication that capitalism had exhausted its potential for economic growth and was doomed to stagnation or a social upheaval that would install socialism (Strachey, 1935); another, which became dominant, was the Keynesian view that the crises hitherto endemic to capitalism could be eliminated by changed social and political structures (see KEYNESIANISM). A third interpretation, promulgated by Joseph Schumpeter, was that crises are a 'process of creative destruction', a process of transformation which, instead of heralding stagnation, was the precondition for renewed economic growth under capitalism (Schumpeter, 1942). This line of reasoning had parallels with Marx's theory of the relation between growth and crises, for the devaluation of capital it entailed can lay the conditions for renewed accumulation notwithstanding Marx's view that capitalist accumulation had its eventual limits. There is no doubt that the Marxist and Schumpeterian view, that global crises are adjustments which are generally functional for capitalist economic growth, is supported by experience; it is now embedded in the prevalent view that, however deep a recession, it will be followed by a boom.

The idea that crises are a period of adjustment in the growth process is linked to the idea that economic growth under capitalism is marked by transformations of capitalism – distinct phases, in each of which a different social-economic structure dominates (for example, a *laissez-faire* stage, a monopoly capital stage, and a stage of state monopoly capitalism) (Fine and Harris, 1979; Mandel, 1975; Uno, 1980). Kondratiev originated the idea, taken up by Schumpeter, that economic growth under capitalism proceeds in a succession of LONG WAVES each of which can be seen as a distinct 'age'; in its subsequent development the theory emphasizes the role of technological innovations in growth and the role of crises in promoting them, and it achieved renewed prominence during the instability and slowdown of growth in the West after 1973. As a theory it reflects the widespread general view that growth is a reflection of scientific and technical development, although in most versions it locates those within definite social conditions (Kondratiev, 1926; Kondratiev, 1935; van Duijn, 1983).

The instability of the last quarter of the twentieth century also stimulated the development of a new Marxist perspective on the stages of capitalist growth. Within the general framework of this 'regulation school', writers have concentrated on the analysis of the transformation of capitalism in the late twentieth century from a 'Fordist' to a 'post-Fordist' regime of accumulation. The instability marks a crisis of Fordist accumulation, and the bases for post-Fordist renewed capitalist growth are to be located in changes in the international division of labour and the capitalist labour process itself (Aglietta, 1979; Lipietz, 1987).

Socialist growth   The idea that growth is a process of social transformation received its greatest prominence in the seminal debate over planning growth in the socialist society of the Soviet Union, the great INDUSTRIALIZATION debate of the 1920s. The social transformation considered necessary was to be industrialization, the building of a dynamic industrial sector under state ownership and regulated by central planning. However, different routes to industrialization were promoted, with corresponding differences in the character of social change; especially at issue was the pace and character of rural transformation, relations between the state and other sectors, and, indirectly, the political measures appropriate to industrialization.

The leading arguments of N. Bukharin and E. Preobrazhensky differed on the pace of industrialization and on the degree of imbalances in the development of agriculture, light industry, and heavy industry. In terms of the balance of output, the arguments concerned the allocation of resources to the production of consumption goods and capital goods respectively. They also differed on the mechanisms through which the state sector should relate to the others, and the extent to which resources should be forcibly transferred from other sectors to finance state industrialization (Bukharin, *Selected Writings, 1982*; Preobrazhensky, 1926). This debate has had enormous influence on twentieth-century thought, partly because of its importance for understanding the genesis of Stalinism, but also because it influenced the conception of economic growth implemented in China and other centrally planned economies in the 1950s. (See also NATIONAL ECONOMIC PLANNING.)

Growth as expansion of output
Writers on economic growth as a process of social transformation have not been in the mainstream of Western economic theory. Since the seminal essays of Roy Harrod (1939) and Evsey Domar (1946) a profusion of articles on the pure economic theory of growth have been concerned with a number of questions related to the problem of whether stable economic growth is possible. The models used abstract from social structures, conceiving economic agents as undifferentiated individuals and treating growth simply as the expansion of output of commodities. The Harrod–Domar model is best known for its concern with whether capitalist economies can achieve a rate of growth at which the growth of demand for output matches the expansion of productive capacity. The question turns on the balance between aggregate saving and aggregate investment in a growing economy, and on the difference between the rate of growth warranted by that balance and the rate of growth of productive capacity. The model engendered pessimism on the possibility of stable full employment growth being achieved automatically, and acted as a stimulus to the adoption of Keynesian ideas about the necessity for state intervention to promote investment.

The Harrod–Domar model was based on special simplifying assumptions: that saving is a constant proportion of income and that the ratio of capital to output is also constant. Substituting those two axioms with alternative assumptions led to two directly opposed schools: neoclassical and Cambridge.

Neoclassical models, following Solow's and Swan's simplified presentations (Solow, 1956; Swan, 1956), have shown that by changing the assumption of a fixed capital–output ratio – by postulating that, with a given level of technology, the economy can smoothly move towards more capital intensive or more labour intensive techniques of production – and assuming that saving is equal to investment, the capitalist economy will be on a stable equilibrium growth path. Unless technological change occurs, output will grow at the same rate as the labour force. This basic neoclassical model has been expanded in a number of directions to deal with the puzzles its simplifications leave unanswered. One is the problem of how technical innovation can be introduced into the model: which types of technical progress are consistent with an equilibrium growth path and how does technical change (learning) occur? Another simplification in the Solow–Swan model, that it is a one-sector model which does not distinguish between the sector producing consumer goods and the capital goods producing sector, has been addressed by the development of two-sector growth models, especially following Uzawa's (1961) contribution. (See also NEOCLASSICAL ECONOMICS.)

Writers of the Cambridge school replace the Harrod–Domar assumption of a fixed savings ratio with the assumption that changes in the distribution of total income between wages and profits cause changes in society's saving ratio since capitalist and workers have different saving ratios (Kaldor, 1955–6; Pasinetti, 1961–2). Consequently, the rate of economic growth is directly connected to the balance between wages and profits and the model thereby addresses one of the key problems of growth in actual economies. This model's analysis of income distribution is in sharp contrast to that of the neoclassical model, and the debate over this difference involved a substantial critique of the logical basis of the concept of the aggregate capital stock used in one-sector models such as Solow's (Robinson, 1956).

Third World Development
The problem of achieving high rates of economic growth in Third World countries, in order to overcome absolute poverty and close the gap between them and industrialized countries, is firmly rooted in late twentieth-century discourse. The concepts designed to analyse growth in capita-

list or centrally planned economies do not directly address the problem of achieving high rates of growth in Third World economies which have a 'mixed economy' approach to policy and an economic base with different technological and social conditions in different sectors. The exception is the Harrod–Domar model which provided the basis for (largely unrealized) national development plans of the newly independent nations in the wake of the mid-century wave of decolonization, and on the basis of which techniques for estimating foreign aid requirements were developed. A number of 'development economics' models have been formulated to address the problem of growth in the special circumstances of the Third World. The most influential theoretical innovation has been the surplus labour model of W. Arthur Lewis (1954). Lewis described a simple dual economy characterized by a traditional and modern sector, and, in a classical tradition derived from Ricardo, demonstrated the centrality for development of the disposition of the economic surplus. (See also DEVELOPMENT AND UNDERDEVELOPMENT.)

Costs of growth

The twentieth century's dominant concept of economic growth is benign, but an undercurrent of thought has articulated the negative side of growth and stimulated an anti-growth sentiment (or at least a sentiment for more modest and less capital intensive growth) with considerable popular appeal. One strand is the argument that the growth of material output involves major social costs not fully borne by the individual producer or consumer. In an essentially conservative argument against high growth Mishan (1967) demonstrated the power that external diseconomies such as congestion have to undermine the claim that output growth is welfare enhancing. A second strand is the view that economic growth involves unsustainable depletion of the earth's resources which, apart from producing external costs (such as the effects deforestation has on rainfall and soil erosion), will quickly produce an insuperable limit to growth as those resources become exhausted (Meadows, 1972).

However, proponents of the view that markets can provide the wellspring of growth, which has become hegemonic in the last quarter of the twentieth century, have countered those anti-growth views with the argument that price adjustments (or policies to make market signals work

better) can ensure a growth path which optimally takes those costs into account (Pearce and Turner, 1990).

A more intractable and unacceptable cost of economic growth may be human rights. In its sharpest form a debate over whether economic growth 'requires' acute suppression of human rights at certain stages has focused on the question 'Was Stalin necessary?' (Nove, 1964). More generally, the suppression of human rights under both capitalist-oriented and socialist-oriented growth regimes has underpinned social movements that reject economic growth.

Reading
Maddison, A. 1982: *Phases of Capitalist Development.*
Schumpeter, J.A. 1942 *(1987): Capitalism, Socialism and Democracy.*
Sen, A. 1970: *Growth Economics.*

LAURENCE HARRIS

economic history Described by one of its earliest practitioners as 'not so much the study of a special class of facts as the study of all the facts of a nation's history from a special point of view' (W.J. Cunningham), economic history does not have rigidly defined frontiers but spills over into social and political history as well as into economics. Its principal concerns, though, are the analysis of economic growth and decline, and the relating of economic change to social welfare.

Origins

The subject has its roots in the period in which the importance of the economic factor for the political strength of nations was first fully realized – that of 'mercantilism'. The new preoccupation engendered its own literature, by the so-called 'political arithmeticians', of which the best-known English example was Gregory King's *Natural and Political Observations on the State and Condition of England* of 1688.

The Enlightenment, with its belief in systems and in human affairs following rules of nature, gave rise to a more theoretical approach. In this development the writings of the 'physiocrats' (literally 'rule of nature') in France and of participants in the 'Scottish Enlightenment' stand out in particular. The former gave priority to agriculture in their theory, arguing that it was the only source of 'net product', and categorizing industry as a 'sterile art'. Their leading figures were François Quesnay

(1694–1774) and A.R.J. Turgot (1727–1781). Quesnay's *Tableau économique*, published in 1758, was instrumental in diffusing the physiocratic idea that the economy functioned according to natural rules. Turgot combined the role of economic theorist and politician, writing a work *On Universal History* in 1750–1 which introduced a new basis for the periodization of history in terms of economic stages, and attaining the position of Controller General in 1774, from which he attempted unsuccessfully to remodel the French economy on physiocratic principles.

John Millar (1735–1801) and Adam Smith (1723–90) were the two participants in the Scottish Enlightenment whose work had most significance for the development of the subject. Smith, in his *Wealth of Nations* (1776), reacted against the excessive deductivism and the agricultural bias of the physiocrats. Like them he believed that there was a natural and ideal pattern according to which an economy developed and in which agriculture had primacy, but his knowledge of history, and his observations in Scotland itself and on his travels, had shown him that it was rarely conformed to.

Although distinct national traditions have been detected in the Enlightenment, its overriding characteristic was an exceptional international unity in the priority which it attributed to reason and in its optimism concerning the future. The substantial divisions in national intellectual traditions are best seen, therefore, as having their sources in the two revolutions of the 1780–1815 period. These were to mark economic history as they did other academic disciplines. First, the Industrial Revolution destroyed some of the basic assumptions of Smith's theory of economic growth, and in particular his belief that there was a natural ceiling to the process set by a society's natural resources. It also gave rise in the short term to an increase in economic inequality – with Britain achieving an extraordinary lead over the rest of the world by 1850 – which made the attainment of international consensus on economic theory and history much more difficult to achieve.

Curiously it was in the country whose economic history was most interesting that the subject received its most severe setback. England's very economic success, combined with the fact that history had become (in the face of the challenge of the rationalism of the French revolution) the arm of conservatism, contributed to the development and acceptance of the deductive, ahistorical economics

of David Ricardo (1772–1823) (Burrow, 1966, pp. 59–64). The historical approach had a reverse experience in France. The extent of social and political disruption generated reflection on history and a concern to establish a new basis for social consensus. This was the task which positivism set itself, aiming to reconcile the scientific approach with the requirements of social order. Economic history had a part in this – Saint-Simon (1760–1825) developed the insights of Turgot and Condorcet (1743–1794) into a materialist theory of history, incorporating a revolutionary element and anticipating Marx – but its role was a subordinate one. Saint-Simon's purpose, unlike Smith's, was not primarily to provide a model for economic growth, but rather political, to induce acceptance of a new type of society dominated by industrialists and scientists.

The turning point was less marked in Germany, where Herder's (1744–1803) emphasis on 'national character' already contrasted with the ahistorical universalism of Enlightenment writers, but it clearly reinforced the existing tendency; Ranke's (1795–1886) emphasis on seeing the past from the inside, in its own terms, is judged to have provided a basis for a 'Berlin revolution in historical studies' (Marwick, 1970, pp. 34–40). The combination of this historical tradition with the fact of Germany's relative backwardness and political division, which caused it to have difficulties achieving an early industrialization from a free-trading situation, gave rise to the emergence of a school of 'historical economics', with an emphasis on relating the study of economics to the development of economic systems.

National contexts were not totally impervious but they did become the predominating influences on the development of economic history until after 1945. Various trajectories for the subject need therefore to be traced before the impact of the recent, more intense intellectual exchange is described.

The German tradition
The precursor of German 'historical economics' was Friedrich List (1789–1846), a campaigner for German national unity and author of *The National System of Political Economy* of 1841, which put forward an infant-industry argument against free-trading theory. Its earliest practitioners were Bruno Hildebrand (1812–1878), Wilhelm Roscher (1817–1894) and Karl Knies (1821–1898); it can be said to

have emerged as a distinct 'school' under the influence of Gustav von Schmoller (1838–1917) and his disciples, who included Werner Sombart (1863–1941) and Max Weber (1864–1920). It was distinguished by the political commitment of its members to social reform and it rejected both the French Comtean tradition and the English commitment to laissez-faire. Its political position was one of social conservatism. Its methods were eclectic – drawing on the whole range of social sciences – and it promoted extensive historical research, particularly in political archives. In so far as it developed an economic theory, it was one of a predominantly pragmatic kind based on the analysis of historical examples. Although Schmoller was to publish a theoretical work of synthesis, it was the relative weakness of this theoretical side of the school's work which was the ground for the METHODENSTREIT during the 1880s. The dispute, though, did little to shake its hegemony – Schmoller had developed an unchallengeable institutional position, directing Germany's principal publication series in the social sciences, and intervening in most professoral appointments in economics. This held back the development of economic theory in Germany, but also, in the long run, it tainted economic history; following World War I there was a backlash and the subject was neglected for many years, history limiting itself to the study of the political (J.A. Schumpeter, 1954, pp. 501–10).

The French tradition

The French tradition developed later than the German, lasted longer and was to exercise great influence. Its origin lay in a reaction against the conservatism of history, in terms of its concentration purely on political events and its penetration by German historicist attitudes, as it was studied in France during the Third Republic. The main intellectual influence on it was positivism – the thought of Auguste Comte, with its emphasis on the similarity of the human to the natural sciences, and hence on the possibility of generalization and explanation; and above all that of Emile Durkheim, with its rejection of psychological explanations for social change in favour of the study of 'social facts', and his belief that objectivity was achievable by the treatment of these as 'things'. It was not so much economic history which was being established but a new definition of history as a subject, in which the economic in conjunction with the social and cultural was given particular importance and the political event demoted.

In 1900 the *Revue de Synthèse Historique* was founded and it was in its pages that Lucien Febvre (1878–1956) and Marc Bloch (1886–1944), the principal promoters of the new history, found an early outlet for their ideas. Lucien Febvre's thesis *Philippe II et le Franche-Comté* of 1912 provided an early example of one aspect of the approach – it is a move towards a 'total history' in which the social, cultural and economic as well as political life of a region is revealed. Marc Bloch's *Les Caractères originaux de l'histoire rurale française* of 1931 is even more clearly Durkheimian, using the most concrete of evidence, field patterns drawn from old cadastral surveys, as well as aerial photography, as its principal source. In 1929 the journal *Annales d'Histoire économique et sociale* was founded which was to provide a name for the new approach – the ANNALES SCHOOL. The journal was renamed *Annales: Economies, Sociétés, Civilisations* in 1946, and the school, whose origins had been in provincial universities, acquired a power base in 1947 with the establishment of the Sixth Section of the Ecole Pratique des Hautes Etudes, an interdisciplinary centre for teaching and research in the social sciences. Leadership of this section, and thus of the 'school', was assumed on Febvre's death in 1956 by Fernand Braudel (1902–85). Braudel's thesis, *The Mediterranean and the Mediterranean World in the Age of Philip II* (1949) was influential in promoting a form of geographical determinism, in the way it distinguished between different concepts of time and in its dismissive attitude to events. The best practitioners of the Annales approach have been Emmanuel Le Roy Ladurie and Pierre Goubert, both of whose backgrounds as historians, like so many Annalistes, lie in regional history, that of the Languedoc and that of the Beauvaisis. More recently it has attracted criticism, particularly from François Furet, for its lack of theory and neglect of politics (Iggers, 1975, pp. 43–79).

The British tradition

The strength of the reaction against the historical approach had been such that its reintroduction from the Continent was necessary. The main agents for this were John Stuart Mill (1806–1873) and H.S. Maine (1822–1888), who were influenced respectively by Comte's progressive view of the historical process, and German philology (Collini et al., 1983, pp. 210–11). It was the establishment of history as a university subject which provided the first openings for economic history. It was taught and examined as part of the new History tripos at Oxford, initially in conjunction with political economy and later on its own. It received an additional boost as historians themselves broadened their approach to include economic, legal and social questions (Harte, 1971, pp. xviii–xix; Kadish, 1989, pp. 3–13). Once established, its progress was rapid. It could benefit from a tradition of industrial histories and the compiling of statistical data which had never been interrupted, and soon was to experience a growing popular demand for its wares from a public in need of professional qualifications for which the study of economic history proved particularly apt. It was clearly a practical activity and a relevant one, too, in a country whose history had been so heavily marked by the economic . This popular identification with the subject was to remain a principal mainstay (Harte, 1971, pp. xxiii–xxiv).

The subject emerged to prominence as a consequence of a British 'methodenstreit', one in which situations were the reverse of those in Germany, with theoretical economics the established approach, and historical economics the challenger. Its principal advocates were Arnold Toynbee (1852–1883), W.J. Ashley (1860–1927) and W.J. Cunningham (1849–1919). All were influenced by the German school, using its technique of carrying out historical studies of different epochs in order to undermine the pretensions of classical economics to universality. The attack was ultimately unsuccessful, principally because Alfred Marshall (1842–1924) had brilliantly reformulated economic theory in his *Principles of Economics* (1890), broadening its definition to include much of what concerned historical economists (Collini et al., 1983, pp. 267–71). Failure with respect to its major ambition, however, effectively favoured the development of economic history as a discipline, since its study had been given sufficient momentum to ensure that it obtained a foothold as an independent university subject. The teaching of economic history was prominent in the London School of Economics (founded 1895). Its first director, W.A.S. Hewins (1865–1931), was an economic historian and the first lectureship specific to economic history was created there in 1904. The first chair in the subject was at Manchester in 1910. Others followed at London in 1921, Cambridge in 1928 and Oxford in 1931. Further landmarks were the establishment of

the Economic History Society and the journal *The Economic History Review* in 1926 (Harte, 1971, pp. xxiv–xxx; Coleman, 1987, p. 94).

Character of the subject

A fourth and major tradition in the subject is the Marxist one. Marx's belief that inherited economic structures were the determining influence on all levels of human existence, and that competition between social classes was the motor of history, clearly gave priority to the study of the economic. Marx's theory, though, was the only approach in which economic history was given the status of a matrix subject. In the others, as emphasized above, its status was effectively a subordinate one, its development being a by-product of larger intellectual or political forces, and its character was marked by this. Thus in Germany the subject's subordination to the desire for a historical economics, and the connection of this with nationalism, caused an emphasis in particular on different forms of economic system. In France its development within a positivist current – opposing the role of individuals and political events – while giving it the status of possibly the most important causal layer in a 'total' historical process, made it neglect the problem of economic development in favour of an emphasis on continuities – not surprisingly the best *Annales* studies have been on the preindustrial economy. Finally, the focus of the English approach initially tended to be predominantly partisan, addressed to highlighting what it regarded as the particular abuses of laissez-faire capitalism. In the USA, too, where the subject had emerged towards the end of the nineteenth century, it was deployed in connection with issues of particular national relevance – Frederick Jackson Turner (1861–1932) developed the frontier thesis as an explanation of specific characteristics of American society, and Charles A. Beard (1874–1948) argued for the decisiveness of economic interests for the character of the American constitution and nineteenth-century politics.

From the 1930s, economic history in the USA and Britain has made greater use of economic theory. In the British case, J.H. Clapham (1873–1946) and T.S. Ashton (1889–1968) were the principal architects of the change. From the mid-1950s the links have become yet closer with the development of 'new economic history' or 'cliometrics' in the United States, where economic history tended to be taught in economics departments, and they campaigned for a more explicit use of economic theory and of quantitative methods in the subject. This approach spread to England in the 1960s and more widely afterwards (McCloskey, 1987, pp. 77–84).

With increased concern with economic growth since 1945, as well as a general expansion in higher education and the study of the social sciences, the subject has grown rapidly in recent years. By the 1970s there were some 24 professors of economic history and nearly as many economic history departments in British universities, and membership of the Economic History Society had risen to over 5,000. The American Economic History Association experienced a similar rate of growth after 1945, attaining 3,600 subscribers in the mid-1970s (Harte, 1971, pp. xxiv–xxx; Coleman, 1987, p. 94). In addition, the subject has spread internationally with a *Scandinavian Economic History Review* being founded in 1953, an Australian in 1967, and particularly rapid development in Japan. Japan's unique industrialization pattern and its concern with catching up caused an early interest in the subject – there were nearly 1,000 scholars specializing in it by the mid-1980s (Sin-Ichi Yonekawa, 1985, p. 107).

The foundation of the International Economic History Association in 1960 created an organization specifically committed to the spread of the subject. It has organized international conferences at four-yearly intervals, and these, as well as the general intensification in international, intellectual contacts, and the common stimulus of a greater resort to economics, have resulted in a growing interaction between the different national approaches to the subject. Examples of this are Fernand Braudel's collaboration with Immanuel Wallerstein, a development economist who switched to working on the economic history of the early modern period. This influenced Braudel's approach in his *Civilization and Capitalism 15th–18th Centuries* (3 vols, 1967, 1979, 1981–4) and gave rise to the foundation of the Fernand Braudel Center for the Study of Economies, Historical Systems, and Civilizations at Binghamton University in 1977. It also influenced the introduction into England of French techniques of demographic research, with the foundation of the Cambridge Group for the Study of Population and Social Structure in the 1960s. In addition various path-breaking publications in the subject have contributed to eroding frontiers. Among these are W.W. Rostow's *Stages of Economic Growth* (1960), a provocative rival theory of

history to Marx's which, though judged erroneous, gave rise to the general diffusion of terms such as 'take-off' and 'age of high mass consumption' as well as to imitative studies; A. Gerschenkron's *Economic Backwardness in Historical Perspective* (1962) which launched comparative economic history by developing a model accounting systematically for the contrasting character of industrialization in different countries, and Sidney Pollard's *Peaceful Conquest: The Industrialization of Europe, 1760–1960* (1981) which undermined the very foundations of the national approach by arguing that European industrialization was an international process in which the dynamic of growth took place at the regional level. It is the extension of this comparative approach which will ensure that the achievements of economic history within national frameworks are consolidated and built on, and that the subject will be of service in a world more than ever in need of a historical viewpoint.

Reading
Blaug, M. 1986: *Economic History and the History of Economics.*

Burke, P. 1990: *The French Historical Revolution: The Annales School 1929–89.*

Cannadine, D. 1984: The past and the present in the English industrial revolution, 1880–1980. *Past and Present* 103, 131–72.

Coleman, D.C. 1987: *History and the Economic Past: An Account of the Rise and Decline of Economic History in Britain.*

Harte N. ed. 1971: *The Study of Economic History: Collected Inaugural Lectures, 1893–1970.*

Iggers, G. 1975: *New Directions in European Historiography.*

Koot, G.H. 1987: *English Historical Economics, 1870–1926: The Rise of Economic History and Neomercantilism.*

Schumpeter, J.A. 1954: *History of Economic Analysis.*

Tribe, K. 1988: *Governing Economy: The Reformation of German Economic Discourse 1750–1840.*

Tuma, E.H. 1971: *Economic History and the Social Sciences: Problems of Methodology.*

J.K.J. THOMSON

economic planning   *See* NATIONAL ECONOMIC PLANNING

economics   Described as a social science concerned with the production and allocation of goods and services and with their consequent impact on the material well-being of human beings, economics is, as ought to be expected with a one-line definition, that and more. Further, its contours are continuously expanding in response to new research and our changing concerns.

In the twentieth century the progress of economics has been phenomenal. It has stepped out of the groves of academe into the world of law, national policy making and international organization.

John Maynard Keynes, one of the most influential economists of this century, once suggested that economics would become redundant in the long run because it would solve the major problems confronting the economy. That has not happened; its success has not been so spectacular. There were others who felt that economics, the dismal science, would wither away because its failures would be too marked. That did not happen either. Fortunately for economics, and more so, I suppose, for economists, the performance of the subject was somewhere in between the two predictions; and with the increasing complexity of the world – international debt crises, currency unions and more – economics is here to stay. There are still reasons for introspection and criticism, but advances in this century have established economics as an indispensable discipline with an immense intellectual lure.

The next few pages briefly traverse the chronology of the subject through this century, describe the major achievements, and argue that the marginalist mode of analysis is in the process of being replaced by what may be described as 'strategic analysis'. This is a difficult terrain because for marginalist analysis we could borrow techniques from the natural sciences, whereas for strategic analysis there are no precursors; the route of intellectual pilferage is unfortunately not open.

Looking back over the years, it appears that an important achievement of economics has been its internal intellectual coherence. Abstract logical exercises in economic theory (and I am distinguishing this from mathematical economics, which has often shown a tendency to get mired down in technicalities) are today conducted at a level of excellence comparable to any other discipline. Its most major failures have been on the practical side.

Antecedents

Economists at the turn of the century had inherited a new technique: marginalist analysis (see AUSTRIAN ECONOMICS; MARGINALIST ECONOMICS). This would soon become their *leitmotif*, the mark distinguishing 'economics' from its ancestor, 'political economy'. The founding work on marginalism was done by, among others, Leon Walras (1834–1910), Stanley Jevons (1835–1882) and Carl Menger (1840–1921). If one had to choose a founding date for this new approach, which, as the cornerstone of 'neoclassical economics', would be immensely influential, one would probably have to settle for 19 February 1860 on the basis of a euphoric entry in Jevons's diary (La Nauze, 1953). The central idea that struck Jevons was that the value of a good is not the amount of resource that goes into its production. The value is the price that people are willing to pay for it. Of course, this would *depend* on the resources needed to produce the good but it would also depend on demand and utility. Thus for the same good, say silk shirts, the value would rise if, for some reason, its supply fell, or fashion went in its favour, because that would ensure that the utility to consumers from each silk shirt would be greater. This would be true even if the resource content of each silk shirt remained unchanged.

With this discovery, Jevons's research got (somewhat disproportionately) focused on consumer theory. The heart of it was the law of diminishing marginal utility, which asserts that as a consumer gets more and more of a good the utility from the last unit becomes less and less. The law of diminishing marginal utility and its counterpart in production analysis, the law of diminishing marginal productivity, with their focus on what happens to utility or output as, respectively, consumption or input increases by a tiny amount, made economics extremely amenable to the use of calculus and, in particular, differentiation. Physicists were already using a great deal of calculus. This seemed a boon and a lot of early economic theory grew by imitating the methods of the physical sciences.

Early concerns

Attention having shifted to prices, it was natural to ask: how is price determined? Whereas for each good considered in isolation, the answer may be easy, it turned out that if we wanted to know how prices of all goods get determined in a system where the outcome in the market for one good influences that for another, the problem is much harder and requires very different methods. This was the heart of *general equilibrium* analysis, begun by Walras. Walras's work raised questions that were sufficiently hard and important to be a major theme of research in the twentieth century.

In a nutshell the problem was as follows. It had been known for a long time that the price of a good depends on its demand and supply. Thus if the demand for gas were to exceed its supply, we would expect the price in equilibrium to be higher. But this may cause a problem elsewhere. If the price of gas rises, it is natural to expect the demand for kerosene (or any other gas substitute, for that matter) to rise. Hence, it is possible that as the price of gas moves towards its equilibrium level, the petrol market will get thrown into disequilibrium. A price configuration such that in all markets demand equals supply is known as a *general equilibrium*. But under what circumstances will a general equilibrium exist? What are its properties? These questions were investigated by Walras but definitive answers would not be possible till well into the twentieth century because of the want of a mathematical instrument – the fixed point theorem. The fixed point theorems of Brouwer and Kakutani, which would subsequently become ubiquitous in several areas of economics, were used by Kenneth Arrow and Gerard Debreu to demonstrate the conditions under which general equilibrium would exist (see Debreu, 1959).

But as the refinement of abstract theory grew, so did the economist's ambition to solve the problems of the world. The scope of marginalist analysis for addressing practical questions of taxation, industrial policy and land tenure was highlighted in the works of several economists, such as Alfred Marshall (1842–1924) and Francis Edgeworth (1845–1926). In particular, Marshall's *Principles*, which first appeared in 1890 and went into several editions (see Marshall, 1890), bolstered the confidence of economists in facing the world. Indeed, Marshall, who was openly dismissive of abstraction like that of the Walrasian system, was consciously trying to harness economics to the needs of the world. But, unwittingly, having exhibited the full strength of economic analysis, Marshall was opening up a new theoretical agenda. One grouse which many observers had against neoclassical economics, and which was the cause of some discomfiture even among some mainstream economists, was that many of its theorems hinged on the ability to measure numerically phenomena that were not amenable to such quantification. Utility and welfare were obvious candidates. But was the quantification of utility essential? The answer turned out to be no. John Hicks (1905–1989) drawing on the earlier work of Vilfredo Pareto (1848–1923) set out to show that the theorems of economics were based on fewer assumptions (and, therefore, were more

robust) than appeared under Marshall's scheme (see Blaug, 1962).

In fact, an agenda got set for basing economics – not just consumer theory – on fewer and fewer assumptions. The laws of the margin were getting replaced by requirements of convexity; cardinal utility was being deposed by ordinality; and finally Paul Samuelson's influential work led to utility itself being replaced by preference relations and axioms of consistency.

Around the same time that all this was happening a more dramatic revolution was occurring which would wrench economics out of its quietude into the world of public affairs and policy. I am referring to the work of John Maynard Keynes (1883–1946).

The Keynesian revolution

Keynes's work has been analysed, diagnosed and developed more than that of any other economist in this century; but no one could do a better job of advertising it than Keynes himself. Using literary panache, his immense intellectual reputation, which was established well before the appearance of the *General Theory*, and even a certain amount of obfuscation, Keynes thrust his economics beyond the ivory tower. He was helped by the times. By the late 1920s the Great Depression had set in. With industrial production stagnating, unemployment soared. In 1931 in Germany 5 million out of a labour force of 21 million were unemployed; in the USA unemployment was 25 per cent; and these countries were no exceptions. In 1932 the volume of industrial output in the US was just a little above 50 per cent of the level in 1929 (Routh, 1975, pp. 263–4).

The initial governmental reaction to this was the natural one, encouraging people to save as one should in bad times and to practise thrift. But, according to Keynes, that was exactly the opposite of the right prescription. If all individuals practise thrift, then everybody can become worse off because effective demand in the economy would fall and this would cause a shrinkage in total production, and that would cause an even smaller demand and so on. This was the 'paradox of thrift'. It meant that a cure to the problem lay in boosting effective demand. The government could achieve this through a larger fiscal deficit. This, reversing the above argument, would have several rounds of expansionary impacts – the so-called 'multiplier effect'.

It is true that the 'right policies' had been

effected even before Keynes's economics had been ingested. But unlike the *ad hoc* policies devised hurriedly by bureaucrats and politicians, Keynes had provided a whole framework, a framework of planned intervention by the government to keep the free market well oiled. Keynes's economics ensured that we would not have such a deep depression again – at least not of the same kind.

Keynes was not a theorist; and, I believe, his work would not have had as large an effect on theory if it were not for some of the subsequent elucidators of Keynes. The most influential work was a classic article of John Hicks (Hicks, 1937). This gave birth to the famous IS–LM curves and via these to modern macroeconomics, and macroeconometric modelling. The latter is a staple instrument nowadays for most governments to plan their policies and forecast the future.

Reassessing the Invisible Hand
The old discovery, attributed to Adam Smith (1723–1790), that individual selfish behaviour, acting through the 'invisible hand' of the market mechanism, can result in the social good acquired some special significance in the light of Keynes's work. The latter was an analysis of market failure, something which individual rationality had failed to prevent. What brought the law of the invisible hand under closer scrutiny was, also, the newly emerging models of imperfect competition, on the one hand, and research on the welfare properties of general equilibrium, on the other. Under what conditions would individual rationality result in social optimality? To answer this, economists used Pareto's definition of optimality (see WELFARE ECONOMICS) and gave us the precise relation between a free-market equilibrium and optimality. This was economic theory at its best. It had summed up in two neat theorems – known as the fundamental theorems of welfare economics – a relation which had been the source of debate and speculation since Smith (1776). The first theorem stated that, *given certain conditions* (such as continuity and no externality), a competitive market equilibrium would indeed be Pareto optimal. The second theorem asserted that *given certain conditions*, every Pareto optimal state can be attained as a competitive market equilibrium if a suitable redistribution of the initial endowments of agents could be effected.

These must be the most misused theorems in economics. Unabashed believers in the free market

ignored the proviso 'given certain conditions', and treated the theorem as a verdict for zero intervention. Hardened interventionists saw little else but the conditions. In reality the theorems showed that the goodness of the market can neither be ignored nor presupposed.

The macroeconomic concerns of Keynes and some subsequent writers and the microeconomic theorems of general equilibrium were on a convergent route. It was all but inevitable that these two researches would meet and we would begin to lay the foundations of macroeconomics on rigorous microtheory. This happened most clearly in the fix-price models of the 'French school' that tried to categorize Keynesian and classical descriptions of the economy as different kinds of fix-price (and, in that sense, non-Walrasian) equilibria.

Concurrent themes
If it is true that in all subjects theoretical advances move ahead of empirical work, in economics this was surely being practised as high art. While the use of anecdotal evidence and piecemeal data was common, econometrics, that is, the systematic statistical analysis of data, was lagging behind. This was not surprising because some of the leading lights of the day, including Keynes, were pessimistic about the value of econometrics. But if economics was to take its place in the pantheon of scientific disciplines, it needed formally to test its laws. Given the great importance of econometrics today the subject must have grown faster than the rest of economics.

Econometrics took the message of economics to the outside world. Along with input–output analysis, it became the major vehicle for large corporations and national governments to forecast changes in variables and plan their activities. Econometrics had to face major intellectual challenges because this was the first time that highly sophisticated statistical methods were being used in the study of society. Among other things this meant that if we wanted to know how x had influenced y we did not generate the relevant data through experiments designed to find this out. Instead we had to use whatever data arose naturally through time and sift out the relation between x and y from a morass of available evidence (see ECONOMETRICS).

Another very different kind of 'practical concern' also reared its head in the late 1940s and 1950s. As nations in the Third World emerged from the shadows of colonialism, economists became aware that a majority of human beings were chronically living in conditions which, if the industrialized nations had to suffer them for a few months, would be considered a crisis. Chronic conditions do not make news and are therefore likely to be overlooked. Moreover, for scientists to get interested in a problem it is not enough for the problem to be serious. It is essential that the problem poses an intellectual challenge.

But the plight of nations in Asia, Africa, Latin America and even parts of Europe did pose a puzzle. These nations were tucked away deep inside their production possibility frontiers, that is, within what would be feasible through a full utilization of resources. If the Walrasian market system broke down in the developed countries in the 1930s, it had never taken off in more than half the world. Why? This question was at the heart of enquiries by, among several others, Ragnar Nurkse (1907–1959), Maurice Dobb (1900–1976) and Arthur Lewis (1915–1991).

The enquiry linked up with experiments being actually conducted and written about in the Third World. India had begun experimenting with planning, and Prasanta Mahalanobis (1893–1972) and others were writing about it. From Latin America was emerging a literature on inflation and the terms of trade, with Raul Prebisch (1901–1986) being its main courier to the industrialized world. In recent decades, development economics, which had got left by the wayside during the heyday of the neoclassical revolution, has been drawn into mainstream theoretical and econometric research.

Another concurrent research which occurred in the 1950s resulted in what is, in my view, the most momentous single paper (it was published as a booklet) that has emerged from economics. It had tremendous consequences for political scientists, welfare economists and decision theorists. This was Arrow's impossibility theorem published in 1951; and it provoked a large literature and the new subdiscipline of welfare economics (see also SOCIAL CHOICE.

Current developments

It is arguable that we are living in the midst of a paradigm shift as dramatic as the one which occurred in the late nineteenth century. Ever since its inception, marginalist analysis has been the subject of attack from many sides. Some of the more compelling critiques came from Marxist or neo-Keynesian economists like Piero Sraffa (1898–

1983) and Joan Robinson (1903–1983). The analysis of how output is distributed, for instance, among entrepreneurs, landlords and workers, was always a weak point of mainstream economics, and the 'Cambridge' critique was directed mainly against this. The measurability of capital as a factor of production was challenged, and critical questions were raised about the foundations of marginal productivity theory. What Sraffa's work tried to show was, in Joan Robinson's somewhat unrestrained words (1961, p. 13), 'that the marginal productivity theory of distribution is all bosh'. In response, marginalist theory had to abandon some of its claims to realism; but by refining its theorems and creating a more sparse framework it held its ground in terms of abstract consistency.

In more recent times, however, marginalism has been beginning to give way, but as a consequence of what is best described as inhouse research. It is being replaced by strategic analysis, based on the methods of GAME THEORY. Though game theory had its beginning in the 1940s (Von Neumann and Morgenstern, 1944), its impact on economics was for many years marginal. This has changed sharply over the last two decades. Even though pure game theory may yet fall into the chasm between the abstract elegance of mathematics and the practical concerns of the social sciences, the game-theoretic *mode* of analysis will be with us for some time to come.

One of the reasons for the long gap between the birth of game theory and its applications is that the theory of *extensive-form* games (that is, games played over time) was lagging behind. In industrial organization theory, where the application of game theory has been the largest, strategic interactions do not occur in the twinkling of an eye. These are 'games' played out over long stretches of time and it may be worthwhile for 'players' to sacrifice immediate profit for reputation. For this we need extensive-form games. Though the origin of extensive-form games goes back to the work of Harold Kuhn in the early 1950s, it was only in the 1960s and 1970s that the analysis of extensive-form games emerged as a full-blown subject.

There is a risk that research will get caught up in the labyrinth of minor mathematical and technical discoveries, while the larger conceptual problems that confront us are left to languish. But such tendencies have appeared in the past and invariably, in the long run, the works dealing with larger social concerns, blending logic with economic realism, have survived and dominated. With the rise of strategic analysis, economics is armed to resurrect some of the larger issues of political economy which have been raised throughout its long history but have had to be abandoned for want of more appropriate tools of analysis. Social and political norms, for instance, play critical roles in the functioning of economies. But where do norms come from and how exactly do they interact with our economic functioning? We are at a stage where we can seriously attempt to answer such questions. And this, in turn, could enrich our understanding of the role of the state, the *raison d'être* of firms and the nature of international economic relations.

Reading
Arrow, K.J. 1951: *Social Choice and Individual Values.*
Hicks, J.R. 1939: *Value and Capital.*
Keynes, J.M. 1936: *The General Theory of Employment, Interest and Money.*
Samuelson, P.A. 1947: *Foundations of Economic Analysis.*
Schumpeter, J.A. 1954: *A History of Economic Analysis.*
Sraffa, P. 1960: *Production of Commodities by Means of Commodities.*

KAUSHIK BASU

economics, Austrian   *See* AUSTRIAN ECONOMICS

economics, Chicago   *See* CHICAGO ECONOMICS

economics, Keynesian   *See* KEYNESIANISM

economics, marginalist   *See* MARGINALIST ECONOMICS

economics, neoclassical   *See* NEOCLASSICAL ECONOMICS

economics, new classical   *See* NEW CLASSICAL ECONOMICS

economics, socialist   *See* SOCIALIST ECONOMICS

economy, evolutionary processes in the   *See* EVOLUTIONARY PROCESSES IN THE ECONOMY

economy, socialization of the   *See* SOCIALIZATION OF THE ECONOMY

education and social theory   If one takes SOCIALIZATION to refer to the sum of practices by which new individuals are made into members of existing societies, then 'education' is that subset of practices which have as their intended outcome particular kinds of more or less reflected-upon shaping. More narrowly still, 'education' is used as a synonym for schooling, specific institutional provision for the transmission of knowledge and skills, the development of competences and beliefs.

There is a pervasive background assumption in twentieth-century social thought that socialization *is* the right way to characterize what transpires between new individuals and their societies, and that individuals are plastic to an indefinite number of kinds of shaping. Against this background, sociologists appear to have the straightforward descriptive task of characterising *how* different societies socialize individuals, and *what* they socialize them into. But if there are failures of socialization, as there are, it becomes hard(er) to sustain the idea of plasticity (cf. Hollis, 1977; Wrong 1977). For example, if individuals do differ biologically in intelligence this will limit the possible success of any schooling system which provides equality of treatment in the expectation that this will produce equality of achievement.

Political commitments to achieving equality of opportunity, treatment and/or outcomes have inspired (and funded) innumerable research programmes and projects in twentieth-century sociology (see also EQUALITY AND INEQUALITY). For example, in the context of a commitment to the view that schooling ought to enable social mobility by identifying talent and/or effort independently of social origins – thus making talent and effort available (as 'merit') as identifiable discriminators for occupational selection – there have been a large number of studies of why origins and destinations remain obstinately linked, despite at least formal meritocratic commitments. Three kinds of resultant explanation may be distinguished, which can be labelled determinist, demystifying and voluntarist. The explanations are not mutually exclusive, though often presented as such.

Determinist explanations   There are two kinds of determinists. First, those who argue that individuals differ biologically in intelligence and/or that groups (blacks, females, as against whites, males) differ on average in biologically determined intelligence and this explains outcome differences. The literature on this kind of determinism is both vast and vastly overrated, since very few if any policy conclusions are clearly derivable from it, whatever the truth of the matter is. For example, suppose some children just are cleverer than others. What follows about their education and the education of those who are less clever? Absolutely nothing, since the most obvious consequent question is this: should those who are cleverer get more/better education (to benefit the rest indirectly) or less (since they don't need it)? And nothing in the mere fact of differences helps settle this question. Most educational systems tacitly acknowledge difference and spend more *both* on those who are cleverer *and* on those who are notably handicapped and identified as having special educational needs.

The second kind of determinist argues from society, rather than biology, showing how children come to school advantaged or burdened by their social (class, educational, status) background. Consequently, relative success and failure in school is determined by the assets or burdens children bring with them, and schooling itself cannot compensate for society – the school is a causally less powerful agent than home or community (see Halsey et al., 1980).

The actual mechanisms of social determination are many and various. If at home there are no books, nowhere to study, no wordprocessor facility to produce elegant coursework, mum and dad are always arguing, the baby doesn't sleep, and your mates are always knocking on the door for a game of football – well, what chance a good exam result in history? (See also RELATIVE DEPRIVATION.)

Demystifying explanations   Schools are themselves social institutions, staffed by teachers whose precise social class or status has been the subject of considerable debate (see Ozga and Lawn, 1981). The reality of schools may, and in fact does, diverge from their rhetoric. So, for example, a formal commitment to equality of opportunity does not guarantee that a teacher treats girls and boys in such ways that both have equal chances of succeeding in that teacher's classroom. Indeed, the evidence is, overwhelmingly, that teachers – male and female – discriminate in their treatment of boys and girls in educationally significant ways (Stanworth, 1983). In addition, schools are shaped as institutions by the formal requirements of national and local governments, and informally shaped by the pressures exerted by parents, governors and local commerce or industry. The conjunction of formal requirements and informal pressures actually conspires to ensure that the recognition and reward of individual merit is only one of several conflicting goals which schools pursue. Schools also have a 'hidden curriculum' (Snyder, 1971) which recognizes and rewards conformity to its norms of good behaviour and acceptable self-presentation (see Ball, 1990). These norms are not neutral as between groups, but instead systematically discriminate by class and gender. So, to take a less than obvious example, at secondary school level the norm of neat handwriting would seem systematically to favour girls, though the 'reward' is actually acceptability for work which has low rewards, and moderate status, such as clerical and secretarial employment. No girl in her right mind should allow herself to have neat handwriting.

In general, says the demystifying sociologist, schools are not 'neutral' social locations, helpless in the face of 'external' social determinations. Their own institutionally embedded practices shape outcomes differentiated by class, gender and other irrelevant discriminators, such as ethnicity.

Voluntarist explanations   Both the determinist and the demystifier are, in effect, assuming not only the plasticity but also the passivity of the school pupil. But it may be that children are themselves active in shaping their own destinies, and from an early age. They have their own perceptions of their origins and aspirations towards social distinction: they want to be doctors, nurses and pop stars. They do or do not want to follow dad down the pit. In this context, teachers may or may not represent a status or set of values with which pupils can identify or to which they can aspire. And this is important because it can shape an orientation to the whole business of learning. In an influential study, Paul Willis (1977) has argued that part of the explanation for the fact that working-class kids get working-class jobs is simply that they *want* such jobs; they positively reject the more 'white-collar' CULTURE of the school, which is not that of their families of origin. The way teachers behave and live (a subject of some fascination to most pupils) does not strike them as something to be copied or sought after.

Whatever mix of explanations is the right one, working-class kids get working-class jobs and girls end up doing women's work. Social and sexual mobility is always much less than anyone committed to equality of opportunity can be satisfied with. Detailed sociological work on the reproduction of a stratified labour force is offered within the British tradition by Halsey et al. (1980) and from an American Marxist perspective in Bowles and Gintis (1976).

Some have sought to ensure that schooling becomes a more powerful influence than origin, for example by lengthening the period of compulsory schooling, by ensuring that each school takes in some pupils at every level of ability, and by downgrading the culture of 'useless' knowledge (Latin and Greek, for example), the main motive for the acquisition of which is, or would be, the desire to mark social distinction (see Bourdieu, 1979).

Others have become critical of the institution of schooling itself. From the NEW LEFT, Ivan Illich argued in the very influential *Deschooling Society* (1971) that schools privilege certification over actual competence, unreasonably restrict the domain of what counts as worth learning, and prescribe restrictive and unhelpful modes of learning – as I write that last phrase, it occurs to me that tomorrow my daughter will put on a new collar and tie without which she will not be allowed to learn anything. It is her first day at an ordinary English comprehensive school.

The NEW RIGHT has adapted to its own purposes some of the themes of the New Left critique of schooling, expressed as the idea of producer-capture: teachers have set their own agendas for schools when it should be parents who set agendas for teachers. The New Right then argues for breaking up schooling monopolies and for enfranchizing the consumer.

Both New Left and New Right thinking is at odds with those central, social democratic and liberal democratic conceptions – such as John Dewey's (1966) – which see schooling as a leading institution in the creation of a just, democratic and unified society. And within the Marxist tradition, Antonio Gramsci expresses positive approval of the kind of traditional schooling system of which he was an individual beneficiary (Entwistle, 1979). Gramsci's case should also serve to make us aware that while sociologists have generally occupied themselves with explaining why children fail at school, there is also another interesting research question which asks why certain children who ought by all sociological accounts to fail actually succeed in the most unlikely circumstances. There

are very few schooling systems which cannot boast their poor boys made good, and a biographical approach to the study of their success may highlight factors overlooked in macrosociological approaches to the study of education. (For rather different uses of a biographical approach, see Hoggart, 1957, and Lacey, 1970.)

Reading
Bowles, Samuel and Gintis, Herbert 1976: *Schooling in Capitalist America*.
Halsey, A.H., Heath, A. and Ridge, J.M. 1980: *Origins and Destinations: Family, Class and Education in Modern Britain*.
Illich, Ivan 1971: *Deschooling Society*.
Willis, Paul 1977: *Learning to Labour*.

TREVOR PATEMAN

elite theory   The word *élite* was used in France in the seventeenth century to describe goods of particular excellence, and somewhat later was applied to superior social groups of various kinds, but it was not widely employed in social and political thought until the end of the nineteenth century, when it began to be diffused through the sociological theories of elites propounded by Vilfredo Pareto (1916–19) and, in a somewhat different form, by Gaetano Mosca (1896). Pareto began with a very general definition of the elite as those people who have the highest indices of ability in their branch of activity, whatever its nature, but then concentrated his attention on what he called the 'governing elite', contrasted with the non-governing masses. This conception owed something to Mosca – the first to attempt the construction of a new science of politics based on the distinction between elite and masses – who summarized his general conception by saying that in all societies one obvious fact stands out; namely, that 'two classes of people appear – a class that rules and a class that is ruled.'

The elite theories were directed against socialism (especially Marxist socialism) and to some extent, notably in the case of Pareto, against democratic ideas. They contested the Marxist concept of a 'ruling class' whose political power was based on the ownership of the means of production, by arguing that ruling groups were characterized by superior abilities and by being 'organized minorities' whose 'dominion ... over the unorganized majority is inevitable' (Mosca, 1896, p. 50). The argument was pursued further by denying that a 'classless society' as envisaged by most socialists, or democracy in the sense of 'government *by* the people', could ever be attained. Mosca, however, eventually developed a more complex theory in which he recognized the importance of property ownership in constituting the organized minority (or 'political class'); the influence on government of diverse 'social forces', representing different interests in society; the importance for political stability of a subelite comprising, in effect, the 'new middle class'; and the possibility in a parliamentary democracy for the unorganized majority, through its representatives, to have some control over government policy.

The works of Pareto and Mosca had a pervasive influence. Max Weber, in a similar way, rejected the idea of government *by* the people and redefined democracy as 'competition for political leadership', in which he was later followed by J.A. Schumpeter (1942); and in his arguments against socialism he emphasized the relative independence of political power, asserting that a socialist revolution was more likely to establish the dictatorship of officials than the dictatorship of the proletariat (Weber, 1918). From another aspect, Weber's close associate Roberto Michels, in his study of political parties, argued that all of them (including socialist parties) inevitably developed an oligarchical structure, resulting in domination by the leading officials. Both Weber and Michels attributed primary importance in political leadership to elites as well as 'charismatic' individuals (Beetham, 1981; Mommsen, 1981), and their ideas had a considerable influence on later social thought. Raymond Aron (1950) attempted a synthesis of 'class' theory and 'elite' theory through an analysis of the relation between SOCIAL DIFFERENTIATION and political hierarchy in modern societies, and followed Weber in arguing that 'inequality in political power is in no way eliminated or diminished by the abolition of classes, for it is quite impossible for the government of a society to be in the hands of any but a few.' In this text and elsewhere (Aron, 1964) he also used the elite concept to make a distinction between the 'plurality of elites' in democratic capitalist societies and the 'unified elite' in 'classless' societies (and more specifically in the USSR); and these writings were a major contribution to the controversies about the emergence of a new ruling class or dominant elite in the socialist countries. C. Wright Mills (1956), much influenced by Weber, also used the term 'power elite' in preference to 'ruling class', which he thought assumed too easily that an economic class rules politically, but unlike Aron he conceived this elite as unifying three separate groups in American society (the heads of business corporations, political leaders and military chiefs) and his analysis seemed to lead to a reassertion, in a qualified form, of the ultimate determining force of property ownership.

Much of the extensive research on elites since World War II has been concerned with the recruitment and the social role of particular elite groups – political leaders, company executives (especially in large corporations), high-ranking officials, military chiefs, and intellectuals – in different societies, and it has been an important element in studies of social mobility (Heath, 1981). More generally, elite theories have been at the centre of controversies about the relation between elites and democracy. Karl Mannheim, who had originally connected the elite theories with fascism and with anti-intellectualist doctrines of 'direct action', later argued that democracy and elites were not necessarily incompatible: in a democratic society there would be 'a new mode of elite selection and a new self-interpretation of the elite', together with a reduction of the distance between the elite and the rank-and-file (Mannheim, 1956, p. 200). In the 1960s, however, the left-wing radical movements renewed the attack on elitism in their advocacy of 'participatory democracy', and although some of these movements have declined during the past decade their criticisms of elite rule are still influential in the green parties and among the advocates of self-management.

In postwar social thought the theory of elites has become less an alternative to the theory of classes than a complement to it, especially in analysing the nature of political domination in socialist countries (themselves involved since the end of the 1980s in a process of radical change in which both classes and elites play a part). What now seems most important is the relation of elites to democracy, and the new issues posed by more recent versions of elite theory for conceptions of the further evolution of democracy in the advanced industrial societies (Albertoni, 1987, part 2).

Reading

Albertoni, Ettore A. 1987: *Mosca and the Theory of Elitism*.
Aron, Raymond 1950 (*1988*): Social structure and the ruling class. In Aron, *Power, Modernity and Sociology*.
Bottomore, Tom 1964 (*1966*): *Elites and Society*.
Mannheim, Karl 1956: *Essays on the Sociology of Culture*.

Michels, Roberto 1911 (*1962*): *Political Parties.*

Mills, C. Wright: 1956 *The Power Elite.*

Mosca, Gaetano 1896 (*1939*): *Elementi di scienza politica* (2nd revised and enlarged edn 1923). The English version edited by Arthur Livingston under the title *The Ruling Class* conflates these two editions.

Pareto, Vilfredo 1916–19 (*1963*): *A Treatise on General Sociology*, 2 vols.

Schumpeter, Joseph A. 1942 (*1987*): *Capitalism, Socialism and Democracy*, 6th edn.

TOM BOTTOMORE

emancipation Used in the nineteenth century to refer to the freeing from legal restrictions of European Jews, Russian serfs and American slaves, the terms 'emancipation' and 'liberation' have retained links with the imagery of slavery. Along with motifs from the French revolution and the workers' movements, these formed the rhetoric of anti-colonial 'national liberation movements' (see Fanon, 1961).

Mary Wollstonecraft (1792) had pointed to the similarities between the condition of women and that of slaves, and women's movements have traditionally used the terms emancipation and liberation. (Outside these movements, too, the 'emancipated' woman was associated with an unconventional lifestyle.) (See also WOMEN'S MOVEMENT.)

In other areas of radical thought, these terms are often used as alternative or complementary to a vocabulary of social revolution, notably in critical theory (see FRANKFURT SCHOOL). Herbert Marcuse's *Essay on Liberation* (1969) extended traditional socialist conceptions of liberation to incorporate ideas from the student and hippy movements, and from women's and gay liberation.

Jürgen Habermas's more austere concept of a 'knowledge-guiding interest' in emancipation characterizing 'critical' sciences such as psychoanalysis and the Marxist critique of ideology was also extremely influential as an alternative to the ideal of value freedom (see VALUES). In Habermas's model, emancipatory sciences combine the study of causal processes to be found in empirical science with the transformation of our understanding of ourselves to be obtained from HERMENEUTICS; they involve the identification and removal of causal obstacles to understanding such as psychological blocks and dominant social ideologies. The existing links between science and domination and the possible contribution of science (including social science) to human emancipation have been an important theme in critical theories of science.

See also FREEDOM.

Reading

Bhaskar, Roy 1986: *Scientific Realism and Human Emancipation.*

Marcuse, Herbert 1969: *An Essay on Liberation.*

WILLIAM OUTHWAITE

embourgeoisement This term refers to the alleged process by which sections of the working class are incorporated into the middle classes (or bourgeoisie). Embourgeoisement really represents a collection of ideas and may be assessed by comparing the situations of the working class with that of the lower middle class along the following three dimensions:

1 Market situation. How do rates of pay, hours of work, promotion prospects and pension and holiday entitlements compare?

2 Work situation. For example, do manual workers have a similar degree of autonomy to that enjoyed by, say, clerical workers?

3 Aspirations, status, politics and mores. Are members of the working class adopting middle-class values, for instance?

Historically, the last of these dimensions has commanded most interest. Engels, for example, referred to the way that English workers craved respectability and thought politically in the same way as the bourgeoisie. Later on in the 1930s, Max Adler bemoaned the presence of petit bourgeois ideals which made workers abandon the prospect of revolutionary transformation in favour of gradual social improvement. Theodor Geiger similarly argued that the class structure of the twentieth century was changing as workers became more petit bourgeois in their habits.

More recently the notion of embourgeoisement was extensively discussed in British sociology in the period after World War II, chiefly under the influence of the important study, *The Affluent Worker* (Goldthorpe, Lockwood, Bechhofer and Platt, 1969). Goldthorpe and his colleagues set out to test the claim that as the living standards of many manual workers were rising, so they adopted many middle-class habits and lifestyles. Broadly, the authors did not find this but discovered instead important areas of common social experience which were distinctively working class. However, the study also pointed towards a process of normative convergence between certain manual and non-manual groups, which meant for the former a shift away from a community oriented form of social life towards the importance of the conjugal family, a definition of work in terms of material reward, and a certain lessening in class consciousness.

Although the concept of embourgeoisement refers specifically to the erosion of the boundary between the upper reaches of the working class and lower elements of the middle class, it is also clearly part of a wider debate about the significance of class boundaries and class struggle in advanced societies. So the debate about embourgeoisement is related to the parallel argument concerning the alleged proletarianization of certain middle-class occupations, such as clerical and retail work. Ironically some Marxist sociologists, in arguing that the position of clerical workers is becoming more like that of the working class, are effectively saying that class boundaries are becoming less well defined.

See also CLASS.

Reading
Goldthorpe, J.H., Lockwood, D., Bechhofer, F. and Platt, J. 1969: *The Affluent Worker in the Class Structure.*
Marshall, G., Newby, H., Rose, D. and Vogler, C. 1988: *Social Class in Modern Britain.*
Wright, E.O. 1985: *Classes.*

NICHOLAS ABERCROMBIE

empiricism · An ensemble of theories of explanation, definition and justification of our concepts and/or knowledge is denoted here, to the effect that they are derived from and/or to be explicated (and/or justified) in terms of sense-experience (or introspection). Typically empiricists have assumed knowledge to be established by induction from (or tested by adversion to) incorrigible, or at least uninferred, observation statements. This has always raised problems about the status of mathematical propositions (argued by J.S. Mill and, in the late twentieth century, David Bloor, to be empirical), apparently synthetic a priori principles, such as the uniformity of nature (conceded by Bertrand Russell to be a limit to empiricism) and of empiricism itself (is it analytic, and therefore in John Locke's phrase 'trifling', as Wittgenstein was prepared to concede; or merely empirical, and therefore subject to inductive doubt?). Moreover in its canonical Humean form, empiricism readily leads to scepticism about the existence of (a) objects

independently of our perception of them and (b) natural necessity (that is, necessary connections in nature – and thence to a problem about the status of laws). Characteristic of POSITIVISM generally, empiricism has been the dominant epistemology and theory of science for most of this century; but it has also extended its influence into ethics (as emotivism), linguistics and psychology (as behaviourism) and social science generally. In its perhaps most influential phase it assumed the shape of the logical empiricism of the Vienna circle of the 1920s and 1930s, which initially married Ernst Mach's sensationalist epistemology with Russell and Wittgenstein's logical atomism, and whose leading members were M. Schlick, R. Carnap and Otto Neurath.

The structure of empiricist epistemology in the twentieth century is squarely based on:

P_1, the principle of *empirical-invariance*, viz. that laws are or depend upon empirical regularities; and P_2, the principle of *instance-confirmation* (or falsification), viz. that laws are confirmed (or falsified) by their instances.

The definition of the instances may be ostensive or operational (P.W. Bridgman); and if ostensive, either physicalist (Neurath) or phenomenalist – the dominant response to problem (a), on which objects were analysed as actual or possible sense-data, but which came under damaging criticism from Wittgensteinians and the Oxford school of LINGUISTIC PHILOSOPHY led by John Austin and Gilbert Ryle after mid-century. P_1 is susceptible of descriptivist and instrumentalist (Ryle) interpretations; and of transcendental idealist as well as strictly empiricist ones. P_2 is susceptible of inductivist (Carnap) and falsificationist (Karl Popper) interpretations; and of conventionalist as well as positivist ones. Flowing from P_1 and P_2 are theories of the explanation of events, laws, theories and sciences – deductivism – of the symmetry of explanation and prediction, and of the development of science as monistic, and of confirmation or corroboration and falsification, and of scientific rationality (see Bhaskar, 1975, appdx to ch. 2). Philosophy of science during the third quarter of the century called into question the sufficiency of P_1 and P_2; while in the final quarter of the century the work of Bhaskar questioned the necessity of P_1 and P_2 as well, replacing the underlying ontology of empirical realism with the stratified and differentiated ontology of transcendental realism and providing a realist counter to empiricist problem (b) in a defence of the idea of the necessity and universality (analysed as non-empirical transfactuality) of laws. Transcendental realism made possible a non-Kantian sublation of empiricism and rationalism, in which it was shown how, in the development of science, we could come to have knowledge of natural necessity a posteriori.

It is worth going into the demise of twentieth-century empiricism in some detail. To some extent logical empiricism collapsed under the weight of its own internal aporiai (see THEORY OF KNOWLEDGE). N.R. Campbell in the 1920s had already argued against the sufficiency of the deductivist theory of explanation, maintaining that models were indispensable to intelligibility in science. His legacy was taken up by philosophers such as Scriven, who launched a major assault on the idea of the symmetry of explanation and prediction, S.E. Toulmin, M.B. Hesse and especially Rom Harré, who argued that models could denote generative mechanisms and causal structures which could come to be empirically established – either by a direct perceptual or an indirect causal criterion – as real, a surmise readily supported by the history of sciences such as physics and chemistry. At the same time the work of Popper, Thomas Kuhn, I. Lakatos and P. Feyerabend undermined the credibility of the associated monistic theory of scientific development, registering the magnitude of the scientific changes which had occurred in the twentieth century. The reductionism and atomism implicit in the entailed theory of scientific language came under fire from W.V.O. Quine, W. Sellars, N.R. Hanson and others. They argued that observational predicates were attached to the object world in a much more complicated, non-isomorphic and theory-dependent way than empiricists had typically assumed.

Meanwhile the champions of hermeneutics – most notably perhaps H.-G. Gadamer and P. Winch – had questioned the applicability of the empiricist model to the social domain. Both the theory and practice of empiricist social science have been criticized by anti-naturalist and anti-empiricist naturalist writers concerned to stress the specificity of the human sciences. Particularly influential here was Jürgen Habermas's argument that positivism, in its preoccupation with the observable and manipulable, reflected a form of technical–instrumental practice embodying only one limited human interest. At the same time critical naturalists such as Bhaskar argued that the empiricist model had led hermeneuticists and dualists (such as Habermas) to exaggerate the differences between the social and natural sciences. Particular attention was paid to the limits to measurement and quantitative investigations in the social sciences and to the effects of empiricism (for instance, in generating interactionist and reductionist regresses in the search for closure) in the social sciences. Behaviourist psychology came under a fusillade from a variety of quarters, including Erving Goffman, Harold Garfinkel's ethnomethodology, and social psychology formed in a Wittgensteinian and Vygotskian mould. The empiricist model of language learning, associated particularly with B.F. Skinner, and language generally, came under heavy attack from Noam Chomsky's rationalist and deep structuralist linguistics. The international reception in the 1970s of the ideas of Vološinov and Bakhtin (first formulated in the 1920s) and the development of structuralism from Ferdinand de Saussure through Claude Lévi-Strauss led to the emergence of semiotics – or a structural science of signs – in the hands of practitioners as varied as Roland Barthes and M. Pêcheux. All this was perceived as involving a critique of the subject–object identity, isomorphism or correspondence assumed by empiricism.

In the 1980s there was a partial resurgence of empiricism in the work of writers such as B. van Fraassen and N. Cartwright. More usually, empiricism tended to mutate (Outhwaite, 1987a, ch. 2) into some form of conventionalism, pragmatism such as represented by Richard Rorty, or even super-idealism as in the varieties of poststructuralism and postmodernism generally, on which criteria of objectivity, truth and human need tended to get altogether lost. Meanwhile a spin-off of the critical realist critique of empiricism was a reassessment of Marx's work as anti-empiricist but not (contrary to the characteristic Western Marxist interpretation) anti-empirical and of dialectical materialism as itself involving a form of objectivistic empiricism. As the century draws to a close, among the topics under investigation are the conditions of the possibility and effects of empiricism itself (with its reification of facts and tacit personification (humanization) of things); the breakdown of the fact–value and theory–practice distinctions (at least in the social domain) with which empiricism has characteristically been associated; and the renewed possibility of realism in ethics.

Reading

Bhaskar, Roy 1975 (*1978*): *A Realist Theory of Science*, 2nd edn.

Bloor, David 1976: *Knowledge and Social Imagery*.

Chomsky, Noam 1959: Review of B.F. Skinner's *Verbal Behaviour*. *Language 35*.

Habermas, Jürgen 1968 (*1971*): *Knowledge and Human Interests*.

Harré, R. and Madden, E. 1975: *Causal Powers: A Theory of Natural Necessity*.

Lovibond, Sabina 1983: *Realism and Imagination in Ethics*.

Scriven, M. 1962: Explanation, prediction and laws. In *Minnesota Studies in the Philosophy of Science* vol. 3, ed. H. Feigl and G. Maxwell.

Vološinov, V.N. 1929 (*1973*): *Marxism and the Philosophy of Language*.

ROY BHASKAR

Enlightenment The Enlightenment was more a way of thinking than a movement. Broadly speaking, it was a consequence of the 'scientific revolution' of the late seventeenth century that had transformed most educated people's conception of the world they inhabited. In the first place, Nature was thought to be regulated by an interlocking system of universal laws, of which gravitation was a prime example. Hitherto it had been regarded as a collection of unrelated phenomena, often the product of divine intervention, and hence as a source of moral lessons to 'Man'. Secondly, Man, despite possession of an immortal soul, which most of the writers of the Enlightenment continued to believe, was in all other respects a part of Nature. Human society was therefore regulated by general laws – such as those of economics or sociology – which corresponded to the scientific laws that controlled the material universe. Man's understanding of himself and of society could only be achieved by the scientific methods of observation and deduction that enabled him to grasp the principles that governed the behaviour of matter. He was admittedly exceptional in his possession of a highly developed intelligence that enabled him to engage in abstract thought and even to think about thinking, but, as John Locke claimed to have demonstrated, ideas were not the product of a special sense or of divine inspiration. They were induced by Man's capacity to process the information that he received through his senses.

The Enlightenment was therefore both liberating and restricting. It offered the prospect of the indefinite expansion of knowledge while at the same time denying metaphysics. What could not be observed scientifically could only be the subject of speculation and conjecture. A final assumption of the Enlightenment was that the universe had been created by a beneficent Providence, that scientific laws had been designed with a view to human happiness. Rational action therefore meant conformity to a system that was morally self-validating. The 'invisible hand' of Providence ensured that the individual's pursuit of enlightened self-interest would always be conducive to the welfare of society as a whole (See also UTILITARIANISM). The science that underpinned these beliefs was mainly physics; in other words, the study of forces acting in a timeless present. Biology, with its emphasis on growth and change, did not begin to make substantial progress until the second half of the eighteenth century. The thought of the Enlightenment consequently tended to be somewhat static, in its preoccupation with how things worked, rather than with how they had become what they were. Alexander Pope's *Essay on Man*, of 1733, offers a convenient summary of the collection of attitudes to which most of the men of the Enlightenment subscribed.

These common assumptions took different forms when Enlightened thinkers addressed themselves to the problems of the specific societies in which they lived and in which they were welcomed or proscribed. This is particularly evident in the matter of religion. Whatever else it might imply, the Enlightenment stood for religious toleration and the assumption that whatever was conducive to human happiness was also in accordance with the will of God. On the whole, the Protestant churches assimilated themselves to what then tended to become a new orthodoxy. In the process the conception of God and of Man's place in the world held by the clergy evolved in ways that tended to reduce the distance between the secular and the spiritual. This was broadly true of Lutheran Germany and of Anglican England. In Scotland the Enlightened attitudes of the educated – and Anglicized – laity had a harder fight against Calvinist doctrine. In Catholic Europe on the other hand, the Enlightenment fell foul of a more dogmatic church and of political regimes that were more inclined to equate political stability with intellectual and religious uniformity.

Although Enlightened attitudes pointed towards some general conclusions, for example, to economic liberalism and the belief that the type of government best suited to a particular state was determined by its size, economic structure and geographical situation, the proponents of the Enlightenment were sometimes welcomed by their governments and sometimes seen as threatening them. This in turn affected the political conclusions that they drew from their theories. Montesquieu and Burke had a great deal in common but the former was one of the oracles of the French Revolution and the latter one of its leading intellectual opponents.

Belief that economic matters were best left to the beneficent operation of Providential laws inspired an almost universal conviction that economic liberalism was a scientific law. Where politics was concerned there was no such consensus. To some extent this was due to divergent views of human nature that emphasized either the rationality of people or the extent to which they were conditioned by the society in which they grew up. The Enlightenment could opt for either autocratic rule by a government dedicated to the pursuit of scientific policies, which was assumed to be the case in the Prussia of Frederick II, or for making political power reflect the opinions and beliefs of the population as a whole, or at least of its propertyowners, as allegedly happened in Great Britain.

During the second half of the eighteenth century the Enlightenment was challenged by a revulsion against what was seen as a mechanistic conception of the universe, a denial of the truths of insight and emotion and an evasion of the conflict between inclination and duty. Jean-Jacques Rousseau in particular, although he shared some of the assumptions of the Enlightenment, based his theory of popular sovereignty on a concept of the moral regeneration of the individual by society that derived its dynamism from conscience and an intuitive morality. Although the Enlightenment was nowhere identified with a programme of political revolution, it contributed to the belief that all political problems admitted of rational solutions. The men who found themselves in control of France in 1789, in their overwhelming majority, shared its assumptions. The subsequent history of the French Revolution, culminating in the Reign of Terror, was widely, if not altogether logically, assumed by its opponents to be the punishment for human presumption. As a prevailing orthodoxy the Enlightenment expired during the Revolutionary and Napoleonic period, giving way to more collectivist conceptions of society, whether socialist or idealist, to a Romantic movement that substituted

the truths of emotion for those of reason, and to a revival of traditional religion.

See also RATIONALITY AND REASON.

Reading
Becker, C.L. 1932: *The Heavenly City of the Eighteenth-century Philosophers.*
Cassirer, E. 1951: *The Philosophy of the Enlightenment.*
Gay, P. 1967–9: *The Enlightenment, An Interpretation*, 2 vols.
Hampson, N. 1968: *The Enlightenment.*
Hazard, P. 1935 (*1953*): *The European Mind*, trans. J. Lewis May.
——— 1946 (*1954*): *European Thought in the Eighteenth Century*, trans. J. Lewis May.
Yolton, John W. et al., eds 1991: *Blackwell Companion to the Enlightenment.*

NORMAN HAMPSON

entrepreneurship   Alertness to opportunities for pure profit is the essence of the entrepreneurial function. In speaking about entrepreneurship we are not talking about specific individuals, that is, entrepreneurs, but rather the function of entrepreneurship and its analytical importance in understanding the nature of the competitive market process.

Economic man and homo agens

Human action consists of the continuous attempt to substitute an imagined better future state of affairs for the current unsatisfactory state. Human beings must arrange and rearrange their means to obtain the ends sought in a more effective manner. The notion of economizing, that is, the allocation of scarce means among competing ends, captures only a small aspect of human action. There is an element of human action which cannot be analysed within the economizing and maximizing mode and eludes our understanding if we try. That element is the entrepreneurial aspect of all human action.

Within the standard model of economic behaviour, rational economic man (*homo oeconomicus*) maximizes his utility in a framework of given ends and means. Such mechanical instrumental rationality, however, limits the analysis to the allocation problem that follows from the juxtaposition of scarce means and competing ends. Within this perspective, the choice-making process is simply a problem of applied mathematics. Human action, though, encompasses much more than the computation of a solution to a maximizing problem. It also encompasses the perception of the ends and means framework within which economizing activity is to transpire. *Homo agens* (the 'human actor') not only possesses the propensity to pursue goals effectively, once ends and means are clearly identified, but also possesses the alertness to identify which ends are to be sought and what means are available.

Only within an open-ended framework of means and ends can we begin to understand the nature of the entrepreneurial element evident in all human action and the entrepreneurial market process that follows. On the other hand, if we simply view human choices within a given framework of means and ends, as much of neoclassical economics in the twentieth century has tended to do, then the entrepreneurial role is not so much misunderstood as simply ignored and the vision of the market is one of a static equilibrium state and not the dynamic market process we sought to understand and explain in the first place. In competitive general equilibrium there is no role for entrepreneurship by definition.

As long as economists focus their attention on the mechanical allocation of scarce means among competing ends within a given framework, the dynamic nature of market activity will elude their understanding. The entrepreneurial role only becomes important to our understanding of economic life in a world of uncertainty and continuous change, a world outside of equilibrium.

Two views of entrepreneurship

There are basically two views of the function of entrepreneurship in economic activity. One view, associated with Joseph Schumpeter, maintains that entrepreneurship is the catalyst for innovation in economic life. The innovative entrepreneur disturbs the existing equilibrium, initiates change and creates new opportunities. Although the system settles into a new equilibrium after each burst of entrepreneurial innovation, the Schumpeterian entrepreneur is fundamentally a *disequilibrating* force in economic activity. Thus, in Schumpeter's analysis, the entrepreneur is introduced as an exogenous force of change to prod the economy from one equilibrium to another.

The other view, associated with Ludwig von Mises and his student Israel Kirzner, emphasizes the *equilibrating* role of the entrepreneur in economic life. The real world of pervasive ignorance, uncertainty and change is incapable of settling into an equilibrium position. Any analysis of market competition should not assume what it sets out to

explain – namely the tendency toward equilibrium. Standard economic analysis of competitive equilibrium, however, does just that by postulating an equilibrium state that an adequate explanation of the competitive process ought to explain as a consequence of this process. If, on the other hand, we study the dynamic market as a competitive process of learning and discovery, then the crucial role of entrepreneurship in economic coordination can be understood. The entrepreneur responds to the current disequilibrium situation, characterized by missed opportunities, in a manner which prods the system towards the mutual adjustment and coordination of previously discordant elements. In this manner, the entrepreneur exercises alertness to opportunities for pure profit and in so doing moves the system towards the hypothetical state of equilibrium. Of course, before the system attains this equilibrium state, changes in the underlying economic reality reveal new inefficiencies. But, only by recognizing the human propensity to learn from experience in the market and to adjust expectations and alter plans accordingly, can we begin to answer the crucial questions concerning the forces that bring about changes in the buying, selling, producing and consuming decisions that compel the multitude of individuals within economic society to act in concert with one another.

The very existence of current inefficiencies motivates the entrepreneurial market process. By being alert to possible opportunities to arrange better or rearrange resources for the satisfaction of ends, the entrepreneur coordinates economic activity. The entrepreneur is an endogenous force within the market which eliminates inefficiency. The discrepancy between the existing array of inefficient prices and the imagined future array motivates alert economic actors, in search of pure profit, to discover better and more effective ways to satisfy consumers (or achieve ends). The competitive market process is a process of learning and discovery and its logic depends crucially on understanding the coordinating role of entrepreneurship.

See also SOCIALIST CALCULATION; COMPETITION; AUSTRIAN ECONOMICS.

Reading

Baumol, W.J. 1968: Entrepreneurship in economic theory. *American Economic Review* 58.
Buchanan, J.M. 1979: *What Should Economists Do?*
Kirzner, I. 1973: *Competition and Entrepreneurship*.
—— 1979: *Perception, Opportunity and Profit*.
—— 1985: *Discovery and the Capitalist Process*.

Schumpeter, J. 1911 (*1961*): *The Theory of Economic Development*.
—— 1942: *Capitalism, Socialism and Democracy*.
von Mises, L. 1966: *Human Action: A Treatise on Economics*, 3rd rev. edn.

PETER J. BOETTKE

environmentalism In its broadest sense this may be defined as any perspective which emphasizes or values the role of external conditions and forces, as against inner structures and processes, in shaping the growth and development, capacities and activities of beings – especially human beings. Biological theories of evolution, for example, can be divided into those which represent the historical emergence of new species as an unfolding of potentials already present in the earliest forms of life, as against those (such as Darwin's) which explain the formation of new species as an effect of external conditions of life on populations of organisms. The history of embryology has been marked by a related opposition between preformationist and epigenetic theories. The post-Darwinian concern with the mechanism of biological inheritance led, in the decades around the turn of the present century, to an intense dispute between advocates of 'nature' as against 'nurture' in the formation of individual human attributes. Hereditarian views, advocated by Francis Galton and Karl Pearson in Britain and by C.B. Davenport in the USA were strengthened by the emergence of the modern genetic theory of inheritance and were quickly transformed into popular movements for eugenic programmes of 'race improvement'. Controversial economic and social inequalities were explained and implicitly justified in terms of the biological inferiority of the lower classes, women, and non-European races, while the talents and genius of prevailing elites were likewise attributed to hereditary superiority. Measures to increase the reproductive rates of the better human stock and diminish the inferior, together with outright support for genocide, were advocated by many of these early twentieth-century hereditarians.

More or less simultaneous environmentalist manifestos appeared in anthropology, psychology, and philosophy, in the shape of the cultural anthropology of Franz Boas, G.H. Mead, R.H. Lowie and A.L. Kroeber, the behaviourism of W.B. Watson and the pragmatist philosophy of John Dewey. Dewey's philosophy was continuous, in its emphasis on human malleability, with the broad Western tradition stemming from the Enlightenment. Watson and the behaviourists concentrated their fire against the concept of the 'instincts', vigorously asserting the role of learning and the environment in individual development, while the cultural anthropologists selected specifically sociocultural processes as the pertinent environmental focus in the shaping of beliefs, values and personality.

Though these controversies have persisted throughout our century, the term 'environmentalism' has acquired more specific connotations since World War II. In this sense, 'environmentalism' covers a range of social and political movements and value perspectives which share a concern to protect or improve the quality of the rural, urban, domestic or working contexts of modern social life. Modern anxiety about environmental deterioration can be linked to the historical processes of industrialization and urbanization, and in particular to successive waves of romantic cultural repugnance at their effects. It is commonly argued that the ebb and flow of popular support for environmental movements is linked closely to patterns of economic expansion. With relatively high levels of material affluence, attention is turned to issues – such as the preservation of wilderness, the aesthetic appeal of the countryside and the physical squalor of the urban environment – which reflect our interest in the quality of life. This hierarchy of policy priorities, according to which material affluence, national security and so on must be assured before relatively low-priority questions of environmental policy can enter the public agenda, is itself closely connected with a widespread view of human needs as also hierarchically ordered. Only when physical and then emotional or relational needs are met is self-actualization through aesthetic and spiritual experience sought.

An aesthetic and spiritual valuation of nature and a preference for an arcadian rural life in harmony with the countryside has informed much of the environmentalism of the twentieth century. Until the 1960s at least, this established a deep gulf between environmental conservationists, on the one hand, and a wide spectrum of 'progressive' opinion which favoured technological advance, economic growth and development and a scientific-rational approach to policy, on the other. Environmentalism was seen by many as an attempt to protect both a privileged style of life and an elite set of cultural values. But against that one-sided view has to be set the contribution of a 'progressive' environmentalism which had, since the nineteenth century, denounced the environmental degradation of working-class residential districts, pointed out the links between environmental pollution, poverty and ill health, and argued for environmentally informed approaches to architecture and urban planning.

Since the 1960s the terms of debate concerning the environment have been radically transformed by two principal developments: the integration of scientific ECOLOGY into social and political thought, and the recognition of survival-threatening global impacts of human social and economic activity. Several highly influential texts of the early 1970s put both of these issues high on the agenda of public debate. Currently prevailing rates of resource depletion, pollution impacts and population growth were shown to be unsustainable in the long run, given a finite global 'carrying capacity'; worldwide economic and population 'overshoot', and consequent catastrophe was, sooner or later, inevitable unless radical changes were urgently implemented. 'Environmentalism' had come to mean, not just concern at the loss of hedgerows or of rural tranquillity, but widespread panic at the prospect of global annihilation.

Despite methodological criticism of this wave of environmental tracts, and a certain reassertion of an optimistic faith in technological 'fixes' for the environmental side-effects of continued global economic growth, environmental issues have not been far from the headlines since the early 1970s, and environmental protest and pressure groups have continued to grow in size, influence and diversity throughout the world.

As an organized social force, environmentalism has taken three main forms: as 'ginger groups' or tendencies pressing for environmental reform within one or other of the dominant political parties; as political parties in their own right, giving a central place to environmental regulation and sustainability across the whole range of policy issues; and as politically non-aligned pressure groups. These latter are very diverse, some concentrating on high-profile actions to raise awareness and mobilize opposition to environmental abuses, some seeking 'insider' status as authoritative 'expert' advisers in official planning processes, some attempting to bring an environmental perspective to the whole range of policy fields such as agriculture, food, health, energy, transport and industrial development, and some having a 'single-issue' focus on such questions as countryside access, wildlife preservation or environmental health.

This continued presence of environmentalism on the political agenda has been sustained by three main conditions. First, a series of very high-profile specific environmental disasters – at the Bhopal and Seveso plants and the 3-Mile Island and Chernobyl nuclear reactors, and the Exxon Valdez oil tanker spillage – together with an increasingly environmentalist understanding of 'natural' disasters such as famine and flooding linked to desertification and deforestation. Second, the effect on the quality of life experienced by influential, educated and articulate sectors of the population in the Western societies from the impact of rapid and unregulated industrial and agricultural development (industrialization and urbanization of the 'rural idyll'; adulteration, infection and chemical poisoning of food; noise, pollution and congestion from generalized use of the private car; and so on). The spatial and social distribution of these costs is such that they cannot easily be evaded by the affluent or influential as could the by-products of earlier phases of economic development. Third, increasingly well-publicized evidence of global environmental impacts of actual or forseeable human activity – the 'nuclear winter', ozone depletion, global warming and acid rain. These are, generally, not directly experienced, but are increasingly *intelligible* to educated publics.

A link may be made between all these forms of environmentalism in their common recognition of the dependence of humans for their personal fulfilment, physical, moral, intellectual and aesthetic development, as well as mere survival, upon a complex web of interconnected social, economic and biophysical conditions and processes. Environmentalists in the more specific, recent sense of the term have concentrated on the need consciously to regulate human activity with a view to the sustainability of the conditions for it, especially the biophysical conditions. Depending on the other moral and political perspectives with which environmentalism is combined, the perception of this need may be related to an analysis of the conditions for mere survival, to the aim of living a fulfilled, emancipated and convivial communal life, or to a 'deep ecological' commitment to the well-being of the biosphere as a value in its own right.

See also GREEN MOVEMENT.

Reading

Carson, R. 1972: *Silent Spring*.

Cotgrove, S. 1982: *Catastrophe or Cornucopia: The Environment, Politics and the Future*.

Meadows, D.H. et al. 1972: *The Limits to Growth*.

O'Riordan, T. 1981: *Environmentalism*, 2nd edn.

Passmore, J. 1974: *Man's Responsibility for Nature*.

Pepper, D. 1986: *The Roots of Modern Environmentalism*.

Rose, S., Kumin, L.J. and Lewontin R.C. 1984: *Not in Our Genes*.

Stocking, G.W. 1968: *Race, Culture and Evolution*.

TED BENTON

equality and inequality The belief that societies should aspire to treat their members more equally, in both a formal and a material sense, has a central place in twentieth-century thought. The idea that human beings are fundamentally equal to one another is, in contrast, a very old one. But for centuries this idea found expression primarily in religious belief, in the notion that everyone is equal in the eyes of God. It was only when the relatively rigid social hierarchies of the *ancien régime* broke down, and mobile and fluid societies centred on the market economy emerged in their place, that equality became a social ideal with practical force. In the eighteenth and nineteenth centuries the ideal manifested itself in demands for equal rights before the law, and equal rights to participate in politics. In the twentieth century, equality of these kinds has been taken for granted (in theory if not always in practice) in all advanced societies, and attention has been focused on a new demand: for social equality.

By social equality is meant the idea that people should be treated as equals in all the institutional spheres that affect their life-chances: in their education, in their work, in their consumption opportunities, in their access to social services, in their domestic relations, and so forth. But what does it mean to be treated equally? Broadly speaking there have been two answers to this highly controversial question, which we may label *equality of opportunity* and *equality of outcome* respectively.

Equality of opportunity holds that everyone should have an equal chance to achieve the various benefits and rewards that a society makes available, that there should be no artificial barriers holding some people back, and no special privileges giving others an unfair advantage. The place that a person gets to in a society – the job he or she holds, the income he or she earns, the partner he or she marries – should depend only on that person's efforts, abilities and free choice. This immediately rules out formal discrimination such as the barring of people of a particular sex, race or religion from careers or public offices. But many have thought that equal formal access is not enough to secure genuine equality of opportunity. People must be given an equal start, especially through a common education system which gives each child an equal chance to develop his or her talents. Furthermore barriers can take the form of unspoken prejudices and psychological expectations which deter people who belong to a particular category from, for instance, applying for university places or entering careers. A fiercely debated issue is whether affirmative action policies that seek to encourage women and racial minorities to take such opportunities (and in some cases weight the entry requirements in their favour) are inconsistent with equality of opportunity, or are the best means of achieving it. Equality of opportunity says nothing directly about how wide or narrow the range of outcomes that people may achieve should be, although radicals like R.H. Tawney have argued that it cannot be properly realized without greater equality of condition (Tawney, 1931).

Turning now to equality of outcome, there are three aspects that need to be considered. The first is 'equality of what?' – if people are to be made materially equal, in what respects should their condition be equalized? The second is the issue of measurement: how should we judge how egalitarian or inegalitarian a particular distribution of benefits is? The third is the ethical issue: should we value equality of outcome, and if so why? Most empirical research on equality has focused on equality of income and wealth and equality of access to social services (see, for instance, Atkinson, 1983; Le Grand, 1982). The aim has been to compare different societies in these respects, and in particular to see how far government policies have succeeded in bringing about greater material equality (see SOCIAL WELFARE). From a more theoretical perspective, however, this focus is open to criticism: two people may enjoy the same income, but if one has special needs or responsibilities that the other lacks, are they really equal in the sense that counts? This suggests that we should look behind external resources to see whether people enjoy equal welfare or well-being. But, apart from the serious practical problems involved in making interpersonal comparisons of welfare, this also seems open to objection: equality of welfare would require us to give those who have cultivated expensive tastes extra resources to satisfy those tastes (for a discussion see Dworkin, 1981a, 1981b; Miller, 1990). A third suggestion is that people should enjoy equal basic capabilities: resources should be distributed in such a way that each person is able to exercise the same set of capacities (for instance, is physically mobile, can feed and clothe himself or herself) (Sen, 1982). This proposal has the advantage that it is sensitive to differences in individuals' needs but not to their tastes; but it fails to offer a comprehensive conception of equality in the sense that it sets a minimum standard that everyone should achieve rather than identifying an overall distribution.

It appears that there is no agreed answer to the question 'In what respect should people be judged more or less equal?' The same applies to the question of measurement. Suppose we have to decide which of two income distributions is the more egalitarian: what criterion should we use? Should we consider the range, the dispersion from the mean, etc? (For a discussion, see Sen, 1973.) In particular, how far, if at all, should our measure reflect our concern about the welfare implications of inequality: should we give greater weight to inequalities at the bottom end of the distribution than to those at the top, on the grounds that the former matter more than the latter? This shows that the measurement issue is not merely a technical one, but reflects disagreement about the precise idea of equality that any proposed measure ought to capture.

Whereas equality of opportunity is a widely shared ideal in twentieth-century thought – differences occurring less over the ideal itself than over the policies that are required to achieve it – equality of outcome, in any of its versions, is inherently controversial. Conservative critics allege that the pursuit of equality is incompatible with FREEDOM, that it destroys the incentives on which the market economy relies, and that it is ultimately futile since new forms of inequality will inevitably emerge to replace those that have been suppressed (see Flew, 1981; Letwin, 1983). Liberals give greatest weight to equality of opportunity, and generally endorse equality of outcome only in the form of a minimal level of provision to which each person is entitled (though there may be different views of ways of setting this minimum, see POVERTY and RELATIVE DEPRIVATION). It is only within the socialist tradition that equality of outcome has become a fundamental value. But even here we must be cautious. Many socialists have argued for *greater* equality of

material condition, rather few for *complete* equality. Indeed the latter idea is part and parcel of COMMUNISM.

In their full-blown form, communist ideas have been practised in the twentieth century only within small communities, and never at the level of the nation-state. The best-known examples are the kibbutz settlements in Israel, whose internal arrangements are strongly egalitarian: income is distributed equally, and members are provided with a range of goods and services in common. In contrast, even those societies formally committed to communism as a long-term goal, including the former Soviet Union and its satellites, never sought either in practice or in theory to eliminate all material inequality. Although their income distributions did not mirror exactly those found in Western capitalist societies – different types of work attracted the highest pay – the overall extent of income inequality was roughly the same. The justification that was offered for this was that a socialist society should reward people according to the value of their labour; Stalin, for example, famously dismissed equality as a 'petty-bourgeois' idea.

Socialists in the Western democracies have also been somewhat guarded in their advocacy of equality: their aim has been to narrow the distribution of income and wealth rather than to flatten it completely. It may be most fruitful to see this modest egalitarianism as stemming from two sources. On the one hand, it arises from a concern with JUSTICE and the avoidance of EXPLOITATION: socialists would claim that unreformed capitalism throws up a set of inequalities that cannot be justified in terms of people's differing efforts and abilities. On the other hand, it arises from a concern with community or fraternity: a society marked by large disparities in standards of living is inevitably also a society in which people are divided from one another by barriers of class and prevented from understanding and sympathizing with each other's predicament. On this reading, strict equality of outcome is not a fundamental value even for those who are most egalitarian in outlook. They may instead be committed to an ideal of social equality which has the following elements: the differential rewards people receive should correspond to real differences in effort and ability; no one's standard of living should fall below a prescribed minimum; and the range of inequality should not be so great as to give rise to class divisions.

There remains the question whether even a moderate idea of equality of this kind is feasible for an advanced industrial society. Assuming that the market continues to play a central role in the production and distribution of goods and services, it seems inevitable that substantial inequalities will continue to arise from people's relative success and failure in market competition, and such inequalities are very difficult to control directly. The most viable strategy may be that suggested by Michael Walzer's notion of 'complex equality'. Walzer (1983) argues that a modern society incorporates a number of spheres of distribution in which different goods are allocated each by its own independent criterion. Provided the boundaries between spheres are respected, one person's pre-eminence in, say, the sphere of money may be offset by another's higher social prestige and a third's success in holding political office. In this way social pluralism may lead to a kind of equality in which no one decisively outranks anyone else. The practical problem here is one of containing the influence of economic position, which in present-day societies has a marked influence on a person's ability to obtain the other goods in Walzer's catalogue, such as reputation, political power, education, and health care (see SOCIAL STRATIFICATION). But if we follow Walzer's suggestion, the cause of social equality may now be best promoted not by attacking market-based economic inequalities directly but by strengthening those institutions, public and private, which allocate goods on a different basis.

Reading

Baker, J. 1987: *Arguing for Equality*.
Berlin, I. 1978: Equality. In *Concepts and Categories*.
Gutmann, A. 1980: *Liberal Equality*.
Le Grand, J. 1982: *The Strategy of Equality: Redistribution and the Social Services*.
Letwin, W. ed. 1983: *Against Equality*.
Lukes, S. 1974: Socialism and equality. In *The Socialist Idea*, ed. L. Kolakowski and S. Hampshire.
Miller, D. 1990: Equality. In *Philosophy and Politics*, ed. G.M.K. Hunt.
Phelps Brown, H. 1988: *Egalitarianism and the Generation of Inequality*.
Weale, A. 1979: *Equality and Social Policy*.

DAVID MILLER

ethics   In its broadest sense, ethics refers to the normative appraisal of the actions and character of individuals and social groups. It is often used interchangeably with MORALITY to refer to obliga-

tions and duties that govern individual action. However, there are grounds for holding that morality in this sense is a peculiarly modern institution, and that the term 'ethics' should be understood more widely (Williams, 1985). Ethics can appear in social theory at three different levels: (1) different systems of ethical belief and conduct can form the object of study of social theory; (2) social theories can make *meta-ethical* claims about the logic and epistemological status of ethical utterances; and (3) social theories can commit themselves to substantive ethical standpoints. (See VALUES.)

Meta-ethical debates in social theory have focused on the relationship between ethical and descriptive claims. Defenders of value freedom argue that descriptive and ethical claims are logically independent, and commit themselves to the value position that while doing social science the social theorist ought to make no ethical claims (Weber, 1904). Critics of value freedom either reject this value position (Gouldner, 1964) or deny the logical independence of fact and value (Strauss, 1953).

Substantive ethical argument within social theory has been dominated by two broad ethical perspectives: utilitarian ethics (Glover, 1990; Sen and Williams, 1972; Smart and Williams, 1973); and RIGHTS based ethics with Kantian or contractarian foundations.

Classical utilitarianism has two components: consequentialism – the rightness of an action is to be judged by its consequences; and hedonism – the only thing good in itself is happiness conceived of as pleasure and the absence of pain. The best action is that the consequences of which maximize happiness. Some later varieties of utilitarianism have rejected the hedonistic component of the classical doctrine. The most influential variety is preference utilitarianism according to which the best action is that which maximizes preference satisfaction of affected parties. This ethical principle appears in the guise of an efficiency principle in modern WELFARE ECONOMICS. In both neoclassical economics and Austrian economics values are treated as expressions of subjective preferences (see VALUE). In cost–benefit analysis the weights of such preferences are taken to be measurable by a person's willingness to pay for their satisfaction. The standard efficiency criterion it employs is the *potential* Pareto improvement criterion: a proposal is efficient if preference satisfaction is greater than preference dissatisfaction, so that gainers would be in a position to compensate losers and still be better off (Kaldor, 1939; Hicks, 1939). This 'efficiency' criterion embodies a substantive ethical position, preference utilitarianism: the most 'efficient' of a group of proposals is that which maximizes preference satisfaction over dissatisfaction. However, it is claimed that it is compatible with a central doctrine of much of recent liberal political theory – that the state should be neutral between different conceptions of the good. Since it takes values to be expressions of preferences and takes these as given, it remains neutral between different values.

While utilitarianism remains central to liberal economic theory, within political theory liberalism has tended to be of a deontological variety. To hold a deontological ethic is to deny consequentialism and to claim that moral reasons are grounded in certain duties, such as a duty not to torture. Where the utilitarian allows the welfare of an individual to be overridden if this leads to the maximization of happiness or preference satisfaction, the deontological liberal argues that individuals have rights which embody moral claims that cannot be thus overridden. Individual rights are trumps in ethical and political argument (Dworkin, 1977, p. xi). Rights based ethics give primacy to principles of JUSTICE which utilitarianism, as an aggregative principle, treats as derivative. The conflict between utilitarian and rights based ethical perspectives dominates both theoretical and policy debates. (For a good example of the latter see Glover et al., 1989.)

Rights based ethics appeal for their foundation either to a Kantian conception of respect for persons, according to which persons should be treated 'always as ends in themselves and never merely as a means', or to a contractarian account of ethical principles according to which defensible ethical principles are those to which self-interested individuals would agree in ideal conditions, or, as is the case with John Rawls, to both. For Rawls (1971), defensible principles of justice are those to which self-interested individuals would agree in conditions of ignorance concerning their particular social position, characteristics, capabilities and conceptions of the good. Agents under a veil of ignorance would arrive at two basic principles; the Equality principle according to which each has equal rights to basic liberties, and the Difference principle according to which social and economic inequalities are justified only if the worst off are better off than they would be in conditions of

equality. The first principle has priority over the second. Another influential proponent of rights based liberalism is Nozick (1974) who simply starts from the assumption that individuals have certain rights, and proceeds to defend a minimalist state within a free-market economy. (See also Gauthier, 1986.)

An account of ethics which makes no use of the idea of a contract, but shares with Rawls a Kantian heritage and a commitment to principles of justice neutral between different conceptions of the good, is that of Jürgen Habermas (1986, p. 170). Habermas attempts to found ethics in 'communicative reason'. In performing a *speech act* a speaker commits herself to the meaningfulness of her utterance, and to the claims that it is true, that she is sincere and that she has rights to speak as she does. While particular speech acts often fail to meet the claims they implicitly make, these claims must be in principle justifiable or 'redeemable'. They invoke, Habermas argues, an 'ideal speech situation', characterized as one in which individuals arrive at consensus without force or deception, and where each has the means and opportunity to participate in the dialogue through which the consensus is achieved. The normative principles presupposed by communicative acts provide for Habermas the basis of a reconstituted Kantian ethic. (See Habermas, 1981 and 1983; Benhabib and Dallmayr, 1990.)

Both utilitarians and Kantians share a common assumption that ethical appraisal is founded on principles that are universal, that is, they apply to all, and impartial, that is, they are based on the prescription that individuals or their interests are to be given equal respect. This assumption has been questioned by particularist conceptions of ethics which argue that such principles are unable to account for ethical appraisal that takes place in the context of particular relations to others. This point lies at the heart of the *communitarian* criticism of liberalism that liberalism presupposes a view of the self as unencumbered by particular commitments to other individuals, traditions, practices and conceptions of the good. Against this view the communitarian asserts that an agent's identity is constituted by such specific commitments which form the starting point for ethical appraisal and debate (MacIntyre, 1981; Sandel, 1982; Taylor, 1975, pt 4). A similar criticism has emerged from a different direction in Gilligan's work on a *female ethic* (Gilligan, 1982; Kitay and Meyers, 1987). Gilligan's work stems from a critique of Lawrence Kohlberg's Piagetian account of moral development which conceives of the child as moving towards a 'post-conventional' stage of moral maturity characterized in Kantian terms. Moral maturity is understood in terms of a 'justice perspective' in which morality consists in the application of universal, impartial and abstract principles. Gilligan argues that Kohlberg's work describes a specifically 'male' path of ethical development, and she suggests that there is a distinctive 'female' pattern of development in which moral maturity is understood in terms of 'a care perspective' in which ethics consists of care for specific individuals to whom the agent stands in particular relations, for instance as friend, child, parent.

Some defenders of a particularist conception of ethics, most notably MacIntyre, have also rejected a second assumption shared by both utilitarians and Kantians, that ethics is primarily concerned with the *actions* of agents and answers the question, 'How ought I to act?' Against this assumption proponents of a *virtues ethic* have revived the classical Aristotelian view of ethics according to which ethical appraisal is primarily concerned with the *character* of agents and answers the question 'what sort of person should I be?' Virtues, understood as dispositions of character which are necessary conditions of the good life for individuals, replace duties as the central evaluative concepts of ethical vocabulary. The issue of what it is to lead a good or flourishing life, which in much liberal discourse is treated as a matter of personal preference, regains centre-stage in ethical debate.

Similar points are to be found in recent work in Marxist ethics. This addresses a central paradox in Marx's writings on morality – that on the one hand he condemns morality as ideological and illusory and states that communists preach no morality, while on the other his work abounds with ethical criticism of capitalism. The most promising resolution to this paradox is the argument that when Marx criticizes morality he is not rejecting all ethical claims about human life, but, rather, a distinctive form of ethical argument and appraisal which appeals to the quasi-legal moral concepts of rights and duties. His own ethical arguments against capitalism, notably of the alienation and exploitation it involves, appeal to a set of non-moral goods which are necessary for individuals to lead a flourishing human life. (Different versions of this claim are defended by Lukes, 1985; Miller, 1984; Skillen, 1977; see also Nielsen and Patten, 1981; Geras, 1985.)

Recent work on *environmental* ethics has provided another challenge to utilitarian, Kantian and contractarian views of ethics. Each of these perspectives presupposes a particular account of the boundary to the class of being to which direct ethical consideration is due. Kantians and contractarians extend ethical considerability to persons. Classical utilitarianism extends it further to all capable of feeling pain and pleasure and hence includes in its ethical constituency non-human sentient animals (Singer, 1977). Proponents of an environmental ethic maintain that non-human beings have intrinsic value, and have extended the boundaries of ethical considerability to include for example non-sentient living things and ecosystems (Goodpaster, 1978; Naess, 1973; Routley and Routley, 1979). Such an extension of the constituency of ethical concern would require a radical revision of existing ethical theory.

Reading
Gilligan, C. 1982: *In a Different Voice*.
Goodpaster, K. 1978: On being morally considerable. *Journal of Philosophy* 75.
Gouldner, A. 1964: Anti-Minotaur: the myth of value-free sociology. In *The New Sociology*, ed. I. Horowitz.
Habermas, J. 1981 (*1984, 1989*): *The Theory of Communicative Action*, vol. 1.
Hicks, J.R. 1939: The foundations of welfare economics. *Economic Journal* 49.
Kaldor, N. 1939: Welfare comparisons of economics and interpersonal comparisons of utility. *Economic Journal* 49.
Lukes, S. 1985: *Marxism and Morality*.
MacIntyre, A. 1981 (*1985*): *After Virtue*, 2nd edn.
Naess, A. 1973: The shallow and the deep, long-range ecology movement: a summary. *Inquiry* 16.
Nielsen, K. and Patten, S. eds 1981: *Marx and Morality*. Suppl. to *Canadian Journal of Philosophy* 7.
Rawls, J. 1971: *A Theory of Justice*.
Smart, J. and Williams, B. 1973: *Utilitarianism: For and Against*.
Taylor, C. 1975: *Hegel*.
Weber, M. 1904 (*1949*): *The Methodology of the Social Sciences*.
Williams, B. 1985: *Ethics and the Limits of Philosophy*.

JOHN O'NEILL

ethnicity   This is one of the principal socially relevant characteristics of human beings. To understand it we must show how it is to be distinguished from RACE, class, status (see SOCIAL STRATIFICATION), and estate, but also how it interacts with them in the formation of groups and social systems.

It is important to distinguish ethnicity from racial differentiation. Whereas the latter is in terms of physical differences thought to be biologically inherited, ethnic differentiation is in terms of cultural differences which have to be learned. The distinction is confused in non-scientific racist theory which assumes that cultural behaviour as well as physical characteristics are biologically inherited. One of the characteristics of ethnicity and the ethnic groups to whose formation it contributes is, however, that ethnic characteristics are shared by those who are biological kin. The learning process through which culture is acquired takes place between biological parents and children, and not surprisingly, therefore, races and ethnic groups sometimes overlap. A race may also be an ethnic group and an ethnic group may consist exclusively of individuals of the same race. Nonetheless races are much wider groups, and ethnic groups involve subtle differentiations of behaviour so that within any of the major races or subraces of the world there may be a great deal of internal ethnic differentiation. It is also possible for individuals of different race to become members of the same ethnic group in so far as the cultural behaviour of an ethnic group may in principle be learned and is not dependent on biological inheritance. The Jews in Germany were wrongly represented by Nazi ideologists as being a race, whereas in fact they were an ethnic group with a distinctive religiously based culture.

Social classes are collectivities the individual members of which are united in the first place by shared interests. In this respect they are distinct from ethnic groups for whom shared interest is not a basic defining characteristic. For classes to become collective actors, however, it is necessary that they should become united by bonds of a shared organization, shared culture and shared consciousness. It may be the case, that a 'class' which can rely on ethnic bonding will be stronger and more capable of collective action than one which develops a new organization and consciousness around shared interest. On the other hand ethnic groups might be transformed by their interaction with a system of interests. Very often the bonds of ethnicity lie latent and may not even lead to group formation unless the individuals become activated by the sharing of common interests.

Status groups like ethnic groups are based on the shared cultural characteristics of their members. Unlike ethnic groups, however, it is in the nature of status groups that the cultural characteristics which define the group are based on invidious distinction between one group and another. As Weber says in *Economy and Society*, status groupings are based on the 'differential apportionment of honour'. A single status group cannot exist on its own; it must form part of a hierarchical system of groups. While ethnic groups may become status groups when individuals compare and evaluate their own cultural characteristics as against those of other groups and while ethnicity may be one of the evaluated characteristics in a status system, this type of status ordering is not of the essence of ethnicity. In practice what we often find, however, is the combined operation of an ethnic and status order. It should also be noted that both ethnicity and status may be transmitted in kin groups from parents to children. Neither, however, are as strongly determined by inheritance as are racial groups. It is possible for individuals of diverse parentage to be united by ethnicity and, in a status system, mobility is possible from one status group to another.

An estate system is a more complex form of social organization, and one with which ethnicity may become involved. Like a status system it involves a differential apportionment of honour, but has the additional features of functional specialization by the different estates and legal and political inequality between the estates, as in the classical estate system of medieval Europe and in colonial societies. In the colonial case, the groups which are differentially incorporated may well be ethnic groups. Societies of this kind, characterized by the differential incorporation of different ethnic groups are what sociologists call plural societies (Smith, 1963 and 1974). According to the terminology adopted here a plural society is a society in which diverse ethnic groups are organized into an estate system.

Ethnicity and ethnic grouping, it would seem, rest on the cultural differentiation of individuals and on the creation of social bonds between those who share a common CULTURE. In an ideal typical sense it is possible to posit a society which consists of such groups and of such groups only. In practice, however, ethnicity becomes involved in and is apparent through the interaction of races, of classes, of status groups and estates. Not surprisingly, therefore, when attempts have been made to define ethnicity reference has been made not to the characteristics of ethnicity in itself but to the structural differentiation and grouping within which ethnicity is expressed.

Classical attempts by anthropologists to define ethnicity have divided into 'primordial' theories associated with the name of Clifford Geertz (1963) and 'situational' theories associated with the name of Frederick Barth (1969). According to Geertz, ethnicity and ethnic grouping are 'primordial' factors in the sense that they are given in the very conditions of human existence. These givens include what he calls 'contiguity' and 'live connection' (that is, connections deriving from territorial proximity or kinship) but beyond these 'the givenness that stems from being born into a particular religious community, speaking a particular language or even a dialect of a language and following particular social practices'. Geertz continues:

> These continuities of blood, speech, custom and so on have an ineffable and sometimes overpowering consequence in and of themselves. One is bound to one's kinsman, one's neighbour, one's fellow-believer ipso facto as a result not merely of personal attraction, tactical necessity, common interest of incurred moral obligation, but at least in great part by virtue of some unaccountable absolute import attributed to the very tie itself. (1963, p. 109)

Here Geertz develops an ideal type of ethnicity in itself. He distinguishes it very clearly from class and class-like groupings which are based on 'tactical necessity' and 'common interest'; from the liking and disliking and perhaps honouring and dishonouring characteristic of status systems; and from the intergroup obligations which perhaps characterize estate systems. He does, however, include biological relatedness in his list of primordial factors and would seem at first to be confusing race and ethnicity. It might be argued, however, that physical features come to be evaluated along with purely cultural ones and so become a part of culture. What is most interesting about Geertz's definition, however, and what adds something to what has been said above is that certain evaluated features of human appearance and behaviour are evaluated not as a matter of arbitrary choice but as part of the very conditions of existence.

Situational theories of ethnicity relate it closely to the pursuit of interests. The primordial factors which Geertz refers to are seen as remaining latent unless the situation makes them relevant to the attainment of ends. In this case they may be resources which are important for the cooperation necessary to attain ends. On the other hand, the various factors involved in ethnicity might constitute a stigma and a liability in relation to the attainment of ends. Here it would seem the situational theorists are drawing attention to the tactical necessities and shared interests which Geertz excludes. I have also excluded them from the ideal type of ethnicity, although noting that in the real world ethnic groups become deeply intertwined with social class formations. At the same time, the notion of stigma draws attention to the development of invidious distinctions as a system of ethnic groups becomes intertwined with the status order.

All in all, we can see that ethnicity, understood as primordial in Geertz's sense, is one factor among several involved in the basic ordering and structure of human society. Stated in another way we may say that pure ethnicity is an ideal type, an analytic abstraction of the social scientists. Such ideal types, however, are essential to social science and there is no way in which a complete account of social structure can be given which ignores the element of ethnicity.

Reading

Barth, Frederick 1969: *Ethnic Groups and Boundaries.*
Geertz, Clifford 1963: *Old Societies and New States: The Quest for Modernity in Asia and Africa.*
Smith, Michael Garfield 1963: *The Plural Society in the British West Indies.*
—— 1974: *Corporations and Society.*
Warner, W. Lloyd 1936: American class and caste. *American Journal of Sociology*, 42 (Sept.).
Weber, Max 1921–2 (*1967*): *Economy and Society*, vol. 2, ch. 9.

JOHN REX

ethnomethodology This field of sociology investigates the functioning of commonsense knowledge and practical reasoning in social contexts. In contrast to perspectives that view human behaviour in terms of external causal factors or internalized motivations, ethnomethodology stresses the active, reasoned and knowledgeable character of human conduct. Its founder and leading theorist, Harold Garfinkel, argued that a theory of social action and organization would be incomplete without an analysis of how social actors use shared commonsense knowledge and reasoning in the conduct of their joint affairs. For without such an analysis it would be impossible to show how members of the social world engage in realistic, concerted courses of action. His central innovation was to establish an account of the properties of commonsense knowledge, shared understandings and ordinary social action that could be developed into a coherent programme of empirical research.

Ethnomethodology developed in the 1960s from the phenomenological writings of Alfred Schutz (1962–6) who argued that commonsense knowledge is patchy and incomplete, is held in a form that is typified, approximate and revisable and that shared understandings between persons are contingent achievements based on this knowledge. Using a series of quasi-experimental procedures (known as 'breaching experiments') to create basic departures from taken-for-granted social expectations, Garfinkel (1967) was able to demonstrate the significance of these ideas. The experimental departures engendered deep confusion and moral indignation in their subjects. They indicated that shared understandings, social actions and, ultimately, social institutions are underpinned by a complex body of presuppositions, tacit assumptions and methods of inference – in short, a body of methods or methodology – that informs the production of culturally meaningful objects and actions and that also informs understandings of them. It is these methods of commonsense reasoning and their properties that are the subject matter of ethnomethodology.

Methods of commonsense reasoning are fundamentally adapted to the recognition and understanding of events-in-context. In Garfinkel's analysis, ordinary understandings are the product of a circular process in which an event and its background are dynamically adjusted to one another to form a coherent 'gestalt'. Garfinkel described this process, following Karl Mannheim, as 'the documentary method of interpretation' and argued that it is a ubiquitous feature of the recognition of all objects and events from the most mundane features of everyday existence to the most recondite of scientific or artistic achievements. In this process, linkages are assembled between an event and its physical and social background using a variegated array of presuppositions and inferential procedures. The documentary method embodies the property of reflexivity: changes in an understanding of an event's context will evoke some shift or elaboration of a person's grasp of the focal event and vice versa. When it is employed in a temporally dynamic context, which is a characteristic of all situations of social action and interaction, it forms the basis for temporally updated shared understandings of actions and events among the participants.

The inherent contextuality of the documentary method is associated with other properties of practical reasoning and practical action. A central proposition of ethnomethodology is that all objects and products of practical reasoning – concepts, descriptions, actions and so on – have *indexical* properties. This means that the sense of these objects is elaborated and particularized by the contexts in which they appear. Although this property is a recognized obstacle to the formal analysis of language and action (and is so treated in the literature of logic from which the term 'indexical' derives), it is not an obstacle to the conduct of practical action. In fact, social actors regularly design their conduct so as to use local contexts to elaborate and particularize the sense of their talk and actions. They thus exploit the indexical properties of action and practical reasoning. Conversely, however, these particularities cannot be sustained out of context. There is an inherently approximate fit between particular events and their more general representations in descriptions and mathematical formulations and this fit can only be achieved through a range of approximating interpretive activities which Garfinkel terms 'ad hoc practices'. These practices are thus crucial to the processes through which social actors sustain the coherence, normality and reasonableness of their everyday circumstances and activities.

The ethnomethodological programme of research is based on these basic observations. Its central dynamic arises from the view that shared understandings of all aspects of the social world rest on a highly complex body of tacit methods of reasoning which are socially shared and procedural in character. Just as these methods of reasoning are used to *recognize* objects, events, persons and to understand descriptions of all of these, so they are equally relied upon to *produce* features of the social world that are recognizable and describable or, to use Garfinkel's term – *accountable*. The fact that the same set of reasoning procedures is employed both to recognize social events and produce them is the underlying basis on which the members of a culture can come to inhabit a fundamentally shared social world.

Garfinkel's fundamental theorizing has been

employed in a diverse body of empirical sociological studies. Important among these have been a range of investigations into the symbolic and practical construction of particular, circumscribed social worlds (Wieder, 1974) and into the underlying reasoning through which persons' joint sense of a shared reality is managed and sustained (Pollner, 1987). Other studies have taken up the theme of the approximate fit between descriptions and real world events. Most notable in this context have been investigations of the organizational creation of the statistical data that many sociological studies rely on. Here, it has been argued – particularly in relation to statistics of crime, deviance, suicide and so on, that the practical reasoning of organizational personnel has built theoretical assumptions about the causes of these phenomena so deeply into statistical data that the results are unusable for sociological research (Cicourel, 1968; Atkinson, 1978). Other significant products of the ethnomethodological programme have embraced studies of social interaction (most prominently CONVERSATION ANALYSIS) and major initiatives in the sociology of science (Lynch, 1985).

During the course of its development, ethnomethodology has alternated between 'constructive' and 'deconstructive' tendencies. In the process, new fields of research in sociology and related disciplines have been created and new perspectives on traditional problem areas have emerged. Over and above the specific areas in which ethnomethodology has been an important source of innovation, however, it is clear that it has also had a major and continuing impact both on basic sociological theory and on the ways in which many types of empirical research problems are addressed. This influence has extended into the adjacent fields of SOCIAL PSYCHOLOGY, LINGUISTICS and ARTIFICIAL INTELLIGENCE. In all of these ways, it is a dynamic force in contemporary social thought.

Reading

Atkinson, J.M. 1978: *Discovering Suicide: Studies in the Social Organization of Sudden Death*.
Cicourel, A.V. 1968: *The Social Organization of Juvenile Justice*.
Garfinkel, H. 1967: *Studies in Ethnomethodology*.
Heritage, J. 1984: *Garfinkel and Ethnomethodology*.
Lynch, M. 1985: *Art and Artifact in Laboratory Science*.
Pollner, M. 1987: *Mundane Reason: Reality in Everyday and Sociological Discourse*.
Schutz, A. 1962–6: *Collected Papers*, 3 vols.
Wieder, D.L. 1974: *Language and Social Reality*.

JOHN HERITAGE

ethology   Konrad Lorenz and Niko Tinbergen are commonly regarded as the founders of modern ethology, the biological approach to the study of behaviour. For their pioneering achievements, they shared the Nobel prize with Karl von Frisch in 1973. Lorenz and Tinbergen treated behaviour in the same way as any other aspect of an animal in the sense that behaviour patterns often have a regularity and consistency that relates to obvious needs of the animal. Moreover, the behaviour of one species often differs markedly from that of another. This insight was a crucial step in bringing the study of behaviour into the Darwinian synthesis that was being forged in the 1930s. Impregnated as their thinking has been with the Darwinian theory of evolution, ethologists repeatedly speculated on the adaptive significance of the differences between species.

The interest in biological function has led to many excellent studies of animals in natural conditions. A captive animal is usually too constrained by its artificial environment to provide a complete understanding of the functions of the great variety of activities which most animals are capable of performing. Studies in unconstrained conditions of animals, and increasingly of humans, have been an important feature of ethology and played a major role in developing the distinctive and powerful methods for observing and measuring behaviour. Even so, it would be a mistake to represent ethologists as non-experimental and merely concerned with description.

Tinbergen was a master of elegant field experiments and the fine tradition he established has continued to the present day. Tape recordings of predators or conspecifics (such as offspring or potential mates) are played to free-living animals in order to discover how they respond. Dummies of different designs have similarly been used to gauge responsiveness to a particular shape or colour, such as the pecking of gull chicks at different objects more or less resembling the bills of their parents. These and many other examples make the point that even mainstream ethology involves a great deal more than passive observation. Moreover, a great many ethologists have devoted much of their professional lives to laboratory studies of the control and development of behaviour. Indeed, some of the most striking ethological discoveries, such as imprinting in birds, have been made in artificial conditions and have markedly influenced how behaviour has been interpreted.

When observed in handreared birds, the elaborate sequence involved in building a nest is not easily explained in terms of a series of learned actions each triggered by a particular stimulus from the environment. None the less, the readiness to consider what a particular behaviour pattern might be for in the natural environment has been distinctive of the subject. When this approach was coupled with comparisons between animals, the easy assumption that all animals solve the same problem in the same way was quickly shown to be false. The comparative approach continues to be an important characteristic of broad ethology.

Tinbergen pointed to four broad but separate problems raised by the biological study of behaviour. The issue of how a behaviour pattern is controlled deals with the internal and external factors that regulate its occurrence and the way in which the underlying processes work. Study of the development of behaviour is concerned with the genetic and environmental influences on the assembly of a behaviour pattern in the lifetime of the individual and with how the developmental processes work. The problem of behavioural function is about the way a behaviour pattern helps to keep the animal alive and propagate its genes into the next generation. Finally, evolutionary studies of behaviour are concerned with the ancestral history and with the ways in which a behaviour pattern evolved. These four areas of research are distinct. However, the ethological stance is that they should not be too strongly divorced from each other. By placing a particular question in a broader conceptual context, greater understanding is achieved, whatever the central question may have been. The functional approach has certainly helped those who are interested in the study of mechanism and the study of the development and integration of behaviour has provided important insights into the pressures and constraints which have operated in the course of evolution.

Certain key concepts and theories were associated with ethology at one time. They no longer form such a central part of ethological thought, although they were important in its development. Two basic concepts were the 'sign stimulus' and the 'fixed action pattern'. The notion of the sign stimulus, such as the red breast of a robin releasing an attack from an opponent, was productive in leading to the analysis of stimulus characters that selectively elicit particular bits of behaviour. Fixed action patterns (or modal action patterns as they are perhaps better called) provided useful units for description and comparison between species. Behavioural characters were used in taxonomy and the zoological concern with evolution led to attempts to formulate principles for the derivation and ritualization of signal movements.

Both the concept of sign stimulus or releaser and that of the fixed action pattern played important roles in the early ethological attempts to develop systems models of behaviour. Lorenz's lavatory cistern model was a flow diagram in more than one sense and provided a generation of ethologists with a way of integrating their thinking about the multiple causation of behaviour, both from within and without. However, the model was seriously misleading and in some systems of behaviour, notably aggression, performance of behaviour makes repetition *more* likely, not less as the model predicts. Another systems model has stood the test of time rather better. It was developed by Tinbergen and was concerned with the hierarchical organization of behaviour. Here again, though, its major role lay not so much in its predictive power but in helping ethologists to bring together evidence that would otherwise have seemed unrelated.

A classic ethological concern was with the inborn character of much behaviour and the subject was strongly associated with the development of a theory of instinct. However, even the founders of the subject did not deny the importance of learning. On the contrary, they gave great prominence to developmental processes like imprinting, which specifies what an animal treats as its mother or its mate, and song learning that specifies the way a male bird sings a different dialect from another male of its own species. Even so, Lorenz saw adult behaviour as involving the intercalation of separate and recognizable 'learned' and 'instinctive' elements. Few people share this view any longer and the work by the developmentally minded ethologists has been important in illustrating how the processes of development involve an interplay between internal and external factors. After the early abortive attempts to classify behaviour in terms of instincts, attention has increasingly focused on faculties or properties of behaviour that bridge the conventional functional categories such as feeding, courtship, caring for young and so forth. Consequently, more and more emphasis is being placed on shared mechanisms of perception, storage of information and control of output. As this happens, the interests of many ethologists are coinciding to a greater and greater extent with the traditional concerns of PSYCHOLOGY.

Modern work has also eroded another belief of the classical ethologists that all members of the same species of the same age and sex will behave in the same way. The days are over when a field worker could confidently suppose that good description of a species obtained from one habitat could be generalized to the same species in another set of environmental conditions. The variations in behaviour within a species may, of course, reflect the pervasiveness of learning processes. However, some alternative modes of behaviour are probably triggered rather than instructed by prevailing environmental conditions. In the gelada baboon, for instance, many adult males are much bigger than females and once they have taken over a group of females, defend them from the attentions of other males. Other males are the same size as a female and sneak copulations when a big male is not looking. The offsetting benefit for the small males is that they have much longer reproductive lives than the big ones. It seems likely that any male can go either way and the particular way in which it develops depends on conditions. Examples such as this are leading to a growing interest in alternative tactics, their functional significance and the nature of the developmental principles involved.

Modern ethology abuts so many different disciplines that it defies simple definition in terms of a common problem or a shared literature. It overlaps extensively with the fields known as behavioural ecology and SOCIOBIOLOGY. Moreover, those who call themselves ethologists are now to be found working alongside neurobiologists, social and developmental psychologists, anthropologists and psychiatrists, among many others. Ethologists are accustomed to think in ways that reflect their experience with free-running systems that both influence and are affected by many things about them. These skills have enabled them to understand the dynamics of behavioural processes and are prized by those people with whom they collaborate. At one time ethology looked as though it might succumb to its sister disciplines. However, it has reemerged as an important subject that will continue to play an important integrative role in the drive to understand what behaviour patterns are for, how they evolved, how they developed and how they are controlled.

Reading
Alcock, J. 1989: *Animal Behavior*, 4th edn.
Hinde, R.A. 1982: *Ethology*.
Immelmann, K. and Beer, C. 1989: *A Dictionary of Ethology*.
Jaynes, J. 1969: The historical origins of 'ethology' and 'comparative psychology'. *Animal Behaviour* 17, 601–6.
McFarland, D. 1985: *Animal Behaviour*.
Manning, A. and Dawkins, M. 1992: *An Introduction to Animal Behaviour*.
Martin, P. and Bateson, P. 1986: *Measuring Behaviour*.
Slater, P.J.B. 1985: *An Introduction to Ethology*.
Slater, P.J.B. ed. 1986: *The Collins Encyclopedia of Animal Behaviour*.

PATRICK BATESON

eugenics Describing an applied science that seeks to improve the genetic heritage of the human race, the term also refers to a social movement that seeks to popularize the principles and practices of the science. The word was adapted from the Greek in the late nineteenth century by the English scientist, Francis Galton (1883, p. 17).

Prior to its advocacy by the Nazis in the 1930s, the idea of eugenics enjoyed widespread support in liberal as well as conservative circles in many countries. This reflected a complex mix of influences and concerns. In part, it reflected the growth of rationalist thought and the growing interest in social engineering. It also reflected an awareness that certain forms of social disability had a hereditary basis. And, finally, it reflected the influence of racialist theories (see RACISM).

In the early decades of the century, proponents of eugenics focused their concern on the costs to society of mental retardation and illness and moral degeneracy. This led to the advocacy of sterilization as a means of preventing the carriers of such traits from transmitting them to future generations. In the United States, more than 60,000 individuals were sterilized under state laws providing for compulsory sterilization of the mentally ill and retarded. In Nazi Germany, a system of special eugenics health courts ordered the sterilization of more than half a million individuals who were judged to be suffering from physical deformities, mental retardation, schizophrenia, epilepsy and other illnesses. Because the science of genetics was barely in its infancy at the time, and because racialist theories seemed self-evidently true to many advocates of eugenics, racial and ethnic minorities were disproportionately targeted for sterilization.

Following revelations of the enormity of the crimes committed under the influence of Nazi ideology, racialist theories were repudiated by most Western intellectuals, and the eugenics movement, because of its association with those theories, went into eclipse. Compulsory sterilization laws were repealed and efforts to improve the human race by application of the principle of selective breeding all but abandoned. Such laws are operative today only in a few isolated areas, as, for example, in parts of China.

Despite the demise of the eugenics movement in its original form, efforts to improve the genetic heritage of the human race have begun anew in a radically different form. During the second half of the twentieth century, the science of genetics has made extraordinary advances, and one consequence of this is that many serious human diseases have been shown to be genetically transmitted (for instance, diabetes and sickle cell anaemia). Couples at risk are now encouraged to undergo genetic screening and to consider the possibility of remaining childless or to abort a foetus diagnosed as having a serious genetic defect.

Comparing the older and newer phases of the eugenics movement, one sees a shift from involuntary to voluntary actions by the individuals affected, and from a concern with poorly understood mental disabilities to a limited set of clearly understood physical disabilities. Because of these changes, public support for the new eugenics movement has increased in recent years, but many remain cautious, and some are actively hostile to all efforts to alter the genetic heritage of our species.

See also SOCIAL DARWINISM.

Reading

Haller, M. 1963: *Eugenics: Hereditarian Attitudes in American Thought.*
Kevles, D.J. 1985: *In the Name of Eugenics: Genetics and the Use of Human Heredity.*
Ludmerer, K.M. 1972: *Genetics and American Society: A Historical Appraisal.*
Osborn, F. 1951: *Preface to Eugenics.*
Pickens, D.K. 1968: *Eugenics and the Progressives.*
Searle, G.R. 1976: *Eugenics and Politics in Britain 1900–1914.*

GERHARD LENSKI

everyday life   In the attempt, which we inherited from the nineteenth century, to subordinate everything to reason and to find a reason for everything, we seem to have forgotten, in Silesius' beautiful expression, that 'the rose does not have a reason.' Epistemologically speaking, by insisting so much on what is 'said' in social relations, we have forgotten that they also depend on what is 'not said' – a vacant space overflowing with possibilities. Exploring daily life in this way can bring us to the very formulation of a concrete form of sociality which has a consistency of its own and must not be seen simply as the reflection of our ideas. This is a piece of basic common sense (one which the discursive intellect finds hard to acknowledge, partly because it feels relativized by it) which regularly returns both in everyday life and in intellectual debate. One could even say that if there is a general disaffection with overarching and abstruse ideologies, it is because we are witnessing the emergence of a multiplicity of new ideologies lived out day by day and based on familiar values. This feeling for the concreteness of existence can therefore be interpreted as the expression of a healthy, robust vitality. This vitalism engenders an organic way of thinking, with all the characteristics of this type of thought, namely an insistence on intuitive insight as a way of perceiving things from within, on understanding as an all-embracing, holistic grasp of the different elements of situations, and on experience as something which, lived through in common with others, is felt to constitute empirical knowledge.

Some authors, albeit very few, have insisted on the primacy of this organic way of thinking: W. Dilthey of course, but also the thinkers inspired by Nietzsche who prioritize everyday life and its tactile, emotional, collective, unifying aspects. G.E. Moore's 'Defence of common-sense' (1925) also stresses the truths concealed in everyday life; Moore elegantly noted that 'most philosophers . . . go against the very common-sense which they also share in their everyday life.' Other authors similarly concentrate on topics which are close to hand, for instance sociological phenomenologists such as Alfred Schütz, Peter Berger and Thomas Luckmann, who discussed a range of major epistemological issues from this perspective (see PHENOMENOLOGY). In fact what we may call vitalism and this 'common-sensology' are closely related, and combining them allows us to emphasize the intrinsic quality of the 'here and now', the value of living in the present, a 'presentism' whose full potential has yet to be explored.

Social existence is never one-dimensional; it is in many respects monstrous, fragmented, and never where one thinks it has been pinned down. It is animated by a pluralism which it must be the task of the sociology of everyday life to uncover and examine. Beyond the rationalizations and legitimations to which we have become accustomed, social existence is shaped by ill-defined feelings and emotions, by those 'unclear moments' which we cannot ignore and whose impact on our lives is palpably growing.

One must bear in mind that it is above all what we take for granted (as A. Schütz has pointed out), what is self-evident, which underpins all intellectual constructions. As an example one only has to think of popular sayings and proverbs, which Emile Durkheim saw as 'the condensed expression of a collective idea or feeling' (Durkheim, 1893), or everyday conversation, which sometimes contains a more elaborate philosophy of life and a greater sense of the problems which the future holds in store than many academic discussions. They are quintessential cultural phenomena in that they are what society is built upon. It follows that everyday life is an epistemological issue which lies at the forefront of sociological debate.

Reading
Heller, A. 1970 (*1984*): *Everyday Life.*
Lefebvre, H. 1968: *La Vie quotidienne dans le monde moderne.*
Maffesoli, M. 1979: *La Conquête du Présent: pour une sociologie de la vie quotidienne.*
—— 1985: *La Connaissance ordinaire: précis de sociologie compréhensive.*
—— 1989: The sociology of everyday life. *Current Sociology* 37.1.
Moore, G.E. 1925 (*1959*): A defence of common-sense. In *Contemporary British Philosophical Papers*, ed. J.H. Muirhead.

                                    MICHEL MAFFESOLI

evolution   In the most general sense evolution is an extended process of change or transformation of populations or systems in which later states of an entity develop by degrees out of earlier states. Social and cultural evolution, therefore, are special cases of a much more general phenomenon. In all its various manifestations, evolution is usually conceived of as an irreversible process, though rare exceptions may occur.

The concept of evolution today is the basis of important paradigms in sciences ranging from astrophysics to zoology and is applied to entities ranging from the cosmos itself to populations of microscopic organisms. The astrophysicist, I.D. Novikov (1983, p. xiii), for example, defines cosmology as 'the study of the structure and evolution of the Universe'.

In pre-Darwinian usage, evolution meant an unfolding or developmental process whereby the successive states of an entity were predetermined by inherent attributes or potentialities, as when a flower unfolds or an organism develops from foetus to adulthood. Biologists today, however, refer to such processes as development, reserving the term evolution for processes involving populations of organisms in which the outcome is the product of interaction between a population and its environment, as in intergenerational transformations of plant and animal populations. In the social sciences, however, the terms evolution and development are often used interchangeably. The former tends to be used when referring to changes over centuries or millennia that involve the entire human population, the latter to changes over shorter periods that involve individual societies.

Although the concept of evolution refers primarily to a process of change, it incorporates a recognition of the fact of continuity. This is because it is predicated on the assumption that the entities that change are populations or systems made up of multiple components. Thus, although such entities may be drastically altered in the long run (thus mammals are descendants of single-celled organisms), many components persist unchanged for extended periods (for instance, the genetic codes of all species have apparently employed pairs of the same four nucleotides for billions of years). In the shorter run, moreover, continuity is usually far more evident than change. This ability to synthesize two such fundamental but seemingly contradictory features of the empirical world is obviously one of the great attractions of the evolutionary concept in the various sciences.

The evolutionary concept is also attractive because it directs attention to the important linkages between past, present and future. René Dubos (1968, p. 270), a noted biologist, expressed this well when he wrote, 'The past is not dead history; it is living material out of which man makes himself and builds the future.'

Despite its attractions, the concept of evolution has not been without critics. These have included not only creationists, who reject evolutionism on theological grounds, but also many social scientists.

Social scientists have advanced at least four reasons to justify their rejection of evolutionism. First, many assume that the concept implies a belief in moral progress and an inevitable betterment of the human condition. Second, many reject the idea of evolution on the grounds that it implies some form of biological reductionism. Third, social scientists with a humanistic bent reject all generalizing explanations of human history and insist on the importance of contingent factors in shaping the outcome of every event. Finally, many reject evolutionism because of its sometime association with SOCIAL DARWINISM.

Although there has been substantial justification for these objections in the past, newer evolutionary thought has generally responded to the problems raised. Thus, the newer evolutionism explicitly denies both the inevitability or universality of moral progress and betterment in the human condition (Lenski and Lenski, 1987, pp. 399–406). Progress (or directionality) is seen in human history only in morally neutral matters, such as growth in the store of useful cultural information, in the scale of organization, in inter- and intra-organizational differentiation, and in the power of humans to manipulate the biophysical environment. Even in these matters, progress is evident only in the human population considered as a whole, not in each and every individual society.

Second, the newer evolutionism explicitly rejects biological determinism, identifying culture as the dynamic mechanism in social change. Although the new evolutionism asserts that all cultures reflect the genetic heritage of our species, it sees this heritage as explaining only the most basic characteristics of the evolutionary process (such as the universal use of symbol systems), not its specifics. This is very different from the simplistic reductionism of some of the older evolutionism and of much contemporary sociobiology.

Third, newer evolutionary theories are formulated in probabilistic terms, not in the deterministic mode to which humanistic critics object. Their aim is to define and describe the nature of the field of forces that influence the actions of individuals and societies under specified conditions, and thereby provide a basis for estimates of the probability of various outcomes – not predictions or explanations of outcomes in individual cases.

Finally, despite the association of evolutionary thought with social Darwinism, the link seems largely fortuitous. One need only recall Marx's great appreciation of Darwin's work, or Engels's graveside eulogy for his friend, to appreciate the diverse nature of the political implications of evolutionism (Berlin, 1939, pp. 247–8; Harris, 1968, p. 68). One would suppose that its critics will eventually come to see that social evolutionism does not provide firm undergirding for any single political agenda.

See also EVOLUTIONARY PROCESSES IN THE ECONOMY; EVOLUTIONARY PROCESSES IN SOCIETY; NATURAL SELECTION; NEO-DARWINISM.

Reading
Calvin, M. 1969: *Chemical Evolution: Molecular Evolution Towards the Origin of Living Systems on the Earth.*
Dobzhansky, T. 1962: *Mankind Evolving: The Evolution of the Human Species.*
Harris, M. 1968: *The Rise of Anthropological Theory.*
Holland, H. 1984: *The Chemical Evolution of the Atmosphere and Oceans.*
Laszlo, E. 1987: *Evolution: The Grand Synthesis.*
Lenski, G. and Lenski, J. 1987: *Human Societies: An Introduction to Macrosociology*, 5th edn.
Lewontin, R.C. 1968: The concept of evolution. In *International Encyclopedia of the Social Sciences*, ed. D.L. Sills, vol. 5, pp. 202–10.
Mayr, E. 1982: *The Growth of Biological Thought.*
Novikov, I.D. 1983: *Evolution of the Universe*, trans. from Russian by M.M. Basko.
Simpson, G.G. 1949: *The Meaning of Evolution: A Study of the History of Life and of its Significance for Man.*
Tax, S., ed. 1960: *Evolution After Darwin: The University of Chicago Centennial*, vol. 1: *The Evolution of Life*; vol. 2: *The Evolution of Man.*
Tax, S. and Callender C. eds 1960: *Evolution After Darwin: The University of Chicago Centennial*, vol. 3: *Issues in Evolution.*

GERHARD LENSKI

evolutionary processes in society These are changes within the social structure which are brought about by a selective retention of deviant random variations. The explanation of evolutionary processes has become an all-encompassing interdisciplinary endeavour of modern science. In the social sciences is has only lately freed itself from a providentialist, unilinear notion of human history which dominated nineteenth-century social thought (Auguste Comte, Karl Marx, Herbert Spencer). This kind of evolutionism had the sometimes open ambition of becoming a new form of secular religion. Even today the term 'evolution' is still, although less often, used in its pre-Darwinian sense as a synonym for development and progress and almost all critics think of such approaches as their target (Nisbet, 1986). To avoid such criticism the more recent post-Darwinian attempts conceive of an evolutionary process in a more limited and operationally specified way (Toulmin, 1972, pp. 319–56). To observe an evolutionary process one has to distinguish between a mechanism of blind variation and a mechanism of selective retention. Only this distinction allows us to recognize a social process as being evolutionary and not merely some kind of self-unfolding development.

Most sociologists today restrict themselves to meaning-systems and their communicative realization. They are most cautious about the possible wider interplay between biological and social evolution and regard those matters as irrelevant for the analysis of society. However, this was certainly different during the earliest stages of human evolution and a number of biologists and anthropologists have started to focus more closely on the co-evolution and structural coupling between genetic and cultural inheritance systems or levels of selection (Boyd and Richerson, 1985).

Evolutionary processes, to a certain – but often underestimated – degree, cannot be calculated in advance. Any sociological theory trying to observe them can at best estimate their range of future possibilities and types of potential breakthroughs, while the definite outcome will necessarily be a matter of chance. By perpetuating random variations evolutionary processes give chance a chance. They may create a new temporarily stable order based on the selection of such random variations, while this new order again changes and perhaps enhances the probability for the selection of events, which before that order came into being had to be considered altogether impossible. Every selection of a new variation conditions the range of admissible future possibilities. An evolutionary process is not necessarily directional and is never unidirectional. Evolution does not imply the inevitable selection of the more complex (Axelrod, 1984) nor does it tend towards environmental adaptation. There is no control of standards against which it would be evaluated in advance although such standards may exist in the eye of the beholder or be superimposed on the data after the fact (Weick, 1979; Luhmann, 1982).

The accelerating evolution of modern world society can be estimated by considering the increasing differentiation among the basic mechanisms of evolution itself, that is the separation of variation, selection and retention (Luhmann, 1982). This evolution of evolution within society, that is within a system of communication, cannot be adequately understood by looking for people (see SOCIAL DARWINISM) or ideas as the elements of selection. A variation within the process of communication must be a difference that makes a difference in the context of further communications. It can be identified as a deviant communication, that is, one that does not conform to the prevailing pattern of expectations. These acts can be characterized as blind or random because their justification always comes only after they have been generated and tested (Weick, 1979, p. 123). Usually such acts will be punished, but the experience of deviant acts of communication might also cause a change within the structure of expectations and eventually be incorporated into it.

Every communication can be negated, and a deviant communication especially runs the risk of being rejected. The acceptability of deviant communications, that is their selection into the general pattern of expectations, is highly improbable within a social structure that is bound by the constraints of face-to-face interaction. These limitations dissolved historically with the expansion of communicative possibilities beyond the range of such interaction, as a result of the invention of writing, of phonetic writing systems or their equivalents, the printing press, and to a not yet observable degree the invention of electronic media. These facilities made possible a decoupling of the evolutionary mechanism of variation and stimulated the evolution of symbolically generalized media of communication as new mechanisms for selection. These media, for example, money, symbolic power, scientific truth, or romantic love, make deviant communication acceptable as long as it sticks to the specific standards of behaviour defined by one of the different codes of these media. If so, then it can be expected that for example the monetary code will succeed in spite of local customs and moral warnings, political power will set up its own ethical standards apart from religious concerns, scientific truth will free itself from immediate political influence, love will be successful in spite of status obligations and so on. Such media codes facilitate the autonomy of specific subsystems of society by enforcing their recursive reproduction. These subsystems gain new degrees of freedom which were not open to them before this process of evolutionary decoupling had taken place. The differentiation of society into several more or less autonomous subsystems stabilizes the selective procedures of their different media and thereby provides them with a mechanism of retention.

Since their evolutionary take-off the several subsytems of modern world society have become more and more autonomous and unpredictable, not only for one another but even for themselves. The evolutionary processes in society differentiate and accelerate and with this evolution of evolution modern society becomes centreless and less and less conservative. What a theory of social evolution has to offer is a better understanding of those evolutionary processes which make up the modern world society. It can demonstrate the improbability of its evolutionary drift, and reflect the several risks of different distinctions which might operate as guidelines for the self-description of society. However, evolution will continue as an undirectable process.

See also EVOLUTION; HISTORICISM; OPEN SOCIETY; SOCIAL DIFFERENTIATION.

Reading
Luhmann, Niklas 1982: The differentiation of society. In *The Differentiation of Society*, pp. 229–54.
Schmid, Michael and Wuketits, Franz, eds. 1987: *Evolutionary Theory in Social Science*.

KAY JUNGE

evolutionary processes in the economy   The emergence and destruction of economic relations can be described as evolutionary if they are due to the selective retention of innovations. Evolutionary models taken from biology started to attract the attention of economists as a viable alternative to the unrealistic abstractions of equilibrium models. The latter claim that at a certain price supply and demand will balance, but they cannot explain how equilibrium prices actually come about. The possibility of equilibrium prices depends on several and often only implicitly made assumptions: all participants in the economy must have perfect knowledge and complete foresight, they have to maximize profits and utility, and there has to be unlimited competition. When equilibrium models were set on a rigorous mathematical foundation and these implicit assumptions became explicit, the application of such models to actual economic systems turned out to be less enlightening than most economists had expected (Hahn, 1981). The rather unlikely preconditions for the existence of an economic equilibrium impose severe constraints on a meaningful application of equilibrium models.

By reversing the whole theoretical framework evolutionary models tackle the basic problem of economic order anew. They incorporate incomplete information and uncertain foresight as axioms and dispense with the classical idea of economic man as the profit and utility maximizing agent. In a pioneering article (1950) A.A. Alchian outlined the basic principles of an evolutionary model. He identifies the economic counterparts of the biological mechanisms of evolution – mutation, natural selection and genetic heredity – as innovation, the making of positive profits and imitation. Alchian focuses on the selective mechanism of the economy as a social system where individual motivations are no longer essential. Whatever individual motivation might be like and even if economic decisions were completely random, only those participants realizing positive profits would continue in the economic process. As long as such economic behaviour is taken as random or as trial and error it cannot account for more than blind variation. Which variation finally turns out to be an innovation, be it consciously pursued or not, can be discovered only when it has actually been successful. Innovations can only be identified *a posteriori*, after they have been selected. Into this model, working with variation and selection, Alchian incorporated a further mechanism to account for the observed uniformity among the selected and successful variations in the actual economy. This mechanism can be taken as a mechanism for retention. It works on the basis of imitation. The imitation of those patterns of action associated with past successes seems to serve as a good strategy for actors facing an uncertain and too complex environment.

In a similar vein H.C. White (1981) has suggested that the differentiation of markets can be understood in terms of the observation and imitation of successful behaviour. This kind of orientation generates self-reproducing cliques of firms. A market then is no longer understood as being defined by a set of buyers, but can be seen as a historically shaped structure of roles among a stable set of producer firms, or as an 'ecology of niches among a crowd of competing organisms' (White, 1981, p. 526). Any innovation within such a context will at least partly destroy the existing ecology of niches and give it a new shape. Innovations become successful through an evolutionary process of 'creative destruction' (Schumpeter, 1942). Evolutionary processes in the economy are processes of drifting that gather a history of their own by selecting random variations. There can be no advance assurance that some of them will not end up in disaster. However, although they are built up on the unreliable grounds of randomness these processes nevertheless supply temporarily stable and reliable structures which can orientate economic behaviour.

To observe the economy as a system structured by evolutionary processes has the advantage of grasping more of the crucial aspects of economic life than most of the other equilibrium models could handle. Until recently this advantage could only be had at the price of verbal vagueness, but this is now compensated to an increasing degree by the building and testing of computer models aiming to simulate the stochastic processes of economic evolution.

See also DIVISION OF LABOUR; ECONOMIC GROWTH; EVOLUTION; RATIONAL CHOICE THEORY.

Reading
Nelson, Richard R. and Winter, Sidney G. 1981: *An Evolutionary Theory of Economic Change.*

KAY JUNGE

exchange theory   *See* SOCIAL EXCHANGE THEORY

existentialism   An influential twentieth-century European philosophy, deriving from PHENOMENOLOGY, existentialism's distinctive doctrine is one of radical human freedom. The term was coined during World War II as a name for the emerging ideas of Jean-Paul Sartre and Simone de Beauvoir. The label was extended first to such friends of theirs as Maurice Merleau-Ponty, and it was then applied to the work of other philosophers, notably Martin Heidegger and Karl Jaspers, who had influenced Sartre. Few of those labelled 'existentialist' appreciated this, being understandably concerned at too close an association with Sartre's particular views. Existentialism as a philosophy should be distinguished from the cult among Parisian youth in the 1940s and 1950s which borrowed the title. This 'café existentialism' may well have been an expression of postwar 'spiritual dishevelment' (in the phrase of the *Oxford Companion to French Literature*, 1959, p. 261), whereas the philosophical claims are of perennial relevance.

Existentialism is a fusion of two themes: the idea, traceable to Kierkegaard, that human existence is of a unique kind; and the central insights of phenomenology. Human existence is distinguished, first, by the unique capacity of people for self-awareness and self-concern. Human being is an 'issue' for itself (Heidegger, 1927, p. 67); it is being 'For-itself', as against the being 'In-itself' of mere things (Sartre, 1943, p. lxiii). Second, and relatedly, what a person becomes cannot be explained by any given constitution or essential characteristics, but only by the choices he or she makes in resolving the 'issue' of his or her life. Thus a person's 'existence precedes [his or her] essence' (Sartre, 1946, p. 28); or, as Ortega puts it, 'existence is the process of realizing the aspirations we are' (1941, p. 113).

A main insight inherited from phenomenology was into the priority of what Edmund Husserl called the *Lebenswelt*, 'the world for all of us', over the specialized 'worlds' abstracted by scientists. We relate to the world, fundamentally, not as natural objects causally interacting with others, but 'intentionally' – that is, by encountering it as a network of meaning and significance, through which alone things can stand out for us. Existentialists crucially depart from Husserl, however, in insisting that we are not pure, disembodied egos, but active 'beings-in-the-world' who experience that world as 'equipment' (Heidegger, 1927, p. 97), as a 'world of tasks' and 'projects' (Sartre, 1943, p. 199).

The two themes are intimately connected. It is because we are always 'on the way' to realizing aspirations that the world is revealed as a field of meanings – as obstacles and opportunities, say. And it is because we relate to things 'intentionally', and are not 'in' the world in the natural manner of stones or fish, that we must recognize ourselves as creatures to whom things matter, ones whose existence can become an 'issue'.

These themes converge to produce Sartre's radical account of FREEDOM, which is at once a metaphysical and a moral concept. It denotes, first, the absolute independence of choice from causal constraint; a freedom directly experienced, allegedly, in the mood of *Angst*. My character, motives and situation cannot compel my choices, since they are partly constituted by choices and interpretations. My fatigue, for example, is a motive for stopping rather than for pressing on with extra effort only in the light of ambitions I have or have not adopted. Since the values I use to justify my actions are also 'projected' through my aspirations, and are furnished neither by Nature nor by God, then my freedom is a moral one too. My decisions allow for no final, objective 'foundations'; hence the sense of 'absurdity' to which Sartre refers (1943, p. 479). Freedom, in these aspects, means that a person is totally responsible for his actions. He cannot excuse them by pleading compulsion, or palm off the values which inform his choices as anything but his own commitments. There remains, however, a moral imperative of *authenticity*: the full, lived recognition of one's responsibility, whose antithesis is the 'bad faith' indulged in by most of us for most of the time, as when, for example, we put our failings down to some inexorable force called 'character'.

Existentialism impinges on social thought at several places. For one thing, it provides an important version of the view that, *pace* FUNCTIONALISM, social behaviour is intelligible only in terms of people's own perception and understanding of their situations. Second, it engages with issues of ALIENATION. People's sense of an alien, 'disenchanted' world is primarily due to a failaure to appreciate the phenomenological insight that ours is a 'human world', from which the neutral universe of the scientist is an artificial abstraction. Existentialists are acutely aware, however, that the emphasis on the freedom to 'choose and refuse' threatens to alienate the individual from his fellows: for, as Jaspers says, I can and should put up 'inner resistance' to the 'social I imposed upon me' (1932, vol. 2, p. 30). This leads, third, into discussions of relations with 'the Other', which are regarded by most existentialists as potentially inimical to the attainment of authenticity. For Heidegger, the anonymous 'They' (*Das Man*) seduces or 'tranquillizes' the individual into passive acceptance of 'Their' 'average' ways and opinions (1927, p. 222), while for Sartre the danger comes from 'the Look' (*le regard*) of the Other, his power to categorize and reify me (1943, p. 263; cf. de Beauvoir's account in *The Second Sex*, 1949, of how the Other, in the shape of men, manages to constitute women's understanding of themselves). 'Hell is other people,' writes Sartre – not because they are evil, but because they can dispossess me of a sense of my freedom (1947, p. 182). Personal relations inherently tend, therefore, towards the agonistic, with each person attempting to reduce the freedom of the other by way of a preemptive strike against the threat which this poses. In his more optimistic moments, however, Sartre envisages a community in which people appreciate that 'the oppressor oppresses himself', and that the only route to authentic self-understanding is via a firm recognition of the reciprocal character of freedom among human beings (1983, p. 443). His *Critique of Dialectical Reason* (1960, 1986) also engages fundamentally with Marxism in developing a theory of political action.

Reading

Baldwin, Thomas 1986: Sartre, *Existentialism and Humanism*. In *Philosophers Ancient and Modern*, ed. G. Vesey, pp. 287–307.

Cooper, David E. 1990: *Existentialism: A Reconstruction*.

Heidegger, Martin 1927 (*1962, 1970*): *Being and Time*, trans. J. Robinson and E. Robinson.

Jaspers, Karl 1932 (*1969, 1970, 1971*): *Philosophy*, trans. E.B. Ashton, 3 vols.

Merleau-Ponty, Maurice 1945 (*1962*): *Phenomenology of Perception*, trans. C. Smith.

Sartre, Jean-Paul 1943 (*1957*): *Being and Nothingness: An Essay on Phenomenological Ontology*, trans. H. Barnes.

——— 1946 (*1966*): *Existentialism and Humanism*, trans. P. Mairet.

——— 1983: *Cahiers pour une morale*.

Sprigge, T.L.S. 1984: *Theories of Existence*.

Warnock, Mary 1970: *Existentialism*.

DAVID E. COOPER

explanation This involves relating what is to be explained (the *explanandum*) to something other (the *explanans*) – but it is unlikely that even such a general definition as this can embrace the wide variety of explanations we find acceptable in our everyday and scientific pursuits. In part, the variety arises from alternative views about the nature of the explanans and the nature of the relation linking the explanans and explanandum.

Views about the explanans fall broadly into two types. First, some articulate psychological requirements, for example that the explanans be known or familiar or previously assented to by the recipient of the explanation. What is common here is that the explanans is selected so as to remove perplexity in the explanation's audience: explanatory success is relative to its recipients, who must see the explanation before they can be considered to have it. Second, there are views about the explanans that stress logical requirements, for example that the explanans includes an axiom or a self-evident truth or an empirically true description of an invariable sequence of events. Here, the emphasis is on the formal conditions for explanatory success and consequently recipients can be considered to have an explanation even if they cannot see it.

Views about the relation linking the explanans and explanandum also include some that stress formal requirements, for example, that the relation be one of entailment, where it would be self-contradictory to accept the truth of the explanans but reject the truth of the explanandum. Others insist that the relation be causal; this introduces further diversity into the notion of explanation because of the variety of characterizations of causal connection (see CAUSALITY).

Twentieth-century attempts to analyse explanation have largely focused on the formal conditions to be attached to the explanans and linking relation, especially when considering explanations in the natural sciences, which have commanded attention because they seem especially authoritative. Hempel and Oppenheim's (1948) deductive-nomological or covering law model has been particularly influential. According to this, a phenomenon is explained when its description is deduced from an explanans which contains the statement of a set of initial conditions together with a law or laws (*nomos* being Greek for law). To use one of Hempel's (1965) examples, why the underwater part of a straight oar appears bent upwards is explained by reference to the laws of refraction and the initial condition that water is optically denser than air.

The deductive-nomological schema faces considerable criticism, of three types. First, internal difficulties; for example, the laws in the explanans must be universal if they are to guarantee the explanation, yet there are both practical and logical difficulties in establishing universal empirical truths. Second, arguments that the schema cannot account for all types of explanation in the natural sciences; for example, statistical explanations, where there is only a probability and not certainty that the event described in the explanandum will occur, such as the likelihood that a very heavy smoker will get lung cancer, and realist explanations where occurrences are explained by identifying the underlying workings that are causally responsible for them, such as the movement of the hands around the face of a clock being explained by revealing the spring and cogs that drive them (see REALISM). Third, criticisms that the schema cannot be extended to the social sciences and beyond, where intentional explanations, which explain actions by appeal to the intentions, reasons, motives and so on of the actors involved, are often more appropriate and where functional explanations, which explain actions and institutions by identify-

ing the part they play in maintaining the whole society, are also important. Whether realist explanations can be extended from the natural to the social sciences, and whether intentional and functionalist explanations are distinct from causal explanations continue to be matters of dispute in the PHILOSOPHY OF SOCIAL SCIENCE. Whether the deductive-nomological schema can embrace causal, including realist, explanations continues to be a matter of debate in the PHILOSOPHY OF SCIENCE.

Reading

Halfpenny, P. 1982: *Positivism and Sociology: Explaining Social Life.*
Harré, R. 1970: *The Principles of Scientific Thinking.*
Taylor, C. 1964: *The Explanation of Behaviour.*
Van Parijs, P. 1981: *Evolutionary Explanation in the Social Sciences.*
Wright, G.H. von 1971: *Explanation and Understanding.*

                                        PETER HALFPENNY

exploitation   Although it can also refer to the way people make use of natural resources, political situations or moral arguments, 'exploitation' is a term most frequently applied to relations between people or groups of people in which one group or individual is structurally in a position enabling them to take advantage of others. Exploitation always has some connotation of unfairness; however schools of thought vary as to what constitutes such an unfair advantage and under what structural conditions it occurs.

For Marxism, exploitation is a relation between classes. In any society where not all available labour time is needed to provide for the direct consumption needs of the population, classes develop around the production and control of surplus labour time. One class is 'exploited' because it produces more than it consumes, whereas another 'exploiting' or ruling class maintains its power through its control of that surplus product. Different modes of production and the classes within them are defined by the specific way in which exploitation takes place. Thus for Marxism exploitation is the basic relation of any historical epoch around which classes themselves are defined (see MODE OF PRODUCTION).

Under capitalism, exploitation is hidden by the apparent freedom and equality of the exchange process in which workers freely sell their ability to labour, their labour power, for a wage of equivalent value (Marx, 1867). Nevertheless, workers are exploited because the working day is longer than that necessary to produce their wages and the remainder of their day is spent producing a surplus as profit for their capitalist employer. This occurs because the freedom of exchange is double-edged; since workers have no other access to the means of production they have only the choice between the freedom to sell their labour power to some employer or the freedom to starve. However, it is not the exchange relation which is exploitative under capitalism, for workers are paid the value of their labour power, but the fact that having purchased it employers can then use that labour power to produce more than they had to pay for it. Indeed that is the motive for their employment, for without exploitation employers would make no profits. Thus for Marx exploitation occurs in production and is the common condition of all workers employed by capitalist firms.

By contrast, in NEOCLASSICAL ECONOMICS exploitation occurs only if workers are paid less by their employer than their marginal revenue product, the marginal addition in profits their employment makes possible. A profit-maximizing firm will employ workers up to the point at which the marginal cost of their employment equals their marginal revenue product. A firm facing a competitive labour market will not be able to influence wage levels, so its marginal cost of employing an extra worker will just equal the wage, and profit maximization simply involves ensuring that workers produce a marginal revenue product equal to their wage. Exploitation in the neoclassical sense is therefore an impossibility for a fully competitive firm (see, for instance, Gravelle and Rees, 1981, p. 382).

However a firm with monopsony buying powers in the labour market will be able to influence wage levels; its profit maximizing level of employment will therefore be one at which workers are hired at wages lower than their marginal revenue product, resulting in their exploitation. So for neoclassical economics, exploitation is not the common condition of the whole working class, but a specific characteristic of some individual workers, those that work for firms with monopsony buying powers

in the labour market. Further, instead of being a characteristic of capitalist production relations it is an attribute of particular market conditions.

More recently, the school of analytical Marxism has used some of the methods of neoclassical economics to explore further the conditions under which exploitation can occur. Roemer (1988) shows that 'Marxist' exploitation is a result of unequal distribution of productive resources rather than the specific relations of production. For him this means that Marxism should see inequality rather than exploitation as its basic critique of capitalism. His critics (see, for instance, Lebowitz, 1988), however, use this result instead to demonstrate how his methods fail to capture the essential differences between Marxist and neoclassical approaches: that for the former exploitation depends on production relations and is intimately bound up with the existence of the two main classes of capitalism, while for the latter it is a contingent relation between individuals dependent on specific market conditions.

Exploitation has also been used in various radical social critiques to refer to the relations between other groups in society. For example, some feminists describe relations between men and women as exploitative. This can be either, by direct analogy with the Marxist concept, that husbands, their employers or even the capitalist system as a whole benefit from women doing more work than is required to provide for their own consumption or, in a more nebulous sense, it may be sexual or reproductive practices which are seen as exploitative.

Reading

Braverman, H. 1974: *Labor and Monopoly Capital: The Degradation of Work in the Twentieth Century.*
Lebowitz, M. 1988: Analytical Marxism. *Science and Society* 52.2.
Marglin, S.A. 1974–5: What do bosses do? The origins and function of hierarchy in capitalist production. *Review of Radical Political Economics* 6,2, 60–112; 7,1, 20–37.
Marx, K. 1867 (*1976*): *Capital*, vol. 1.
Roemer, J. 1988: *Free to Lose; An Introduction to Marxist Economic Philosophy.*

SUSAN F. HIMMELWEIT

F

Fabianism This term identifies an argument not so much for the moral desirability of socialism, as for its status as the logical and historical continuation of the principles already visible in the existing direction of government and politics. Socialism was to be an extension of democracy from the political into the social and economic sphere, and was thus summed up in the term SOCIAL DEMOCRACY. This view of socialism was developed by the Fabian Society, and in particular by its three leading members, Beatrice Webb, Sidney Webb and George Bernard Shaw, between 1884 and the outbreak of World War II.

Society was to be collectively organized for the general good by the state, nationally and locally, acting on behalf of an enfranchised people. The characteristic Fabian method and expectation were summed up in the phrase, 'the inevitability of gradualness'. Critics of Fabianism have picked up the second part of the phrase, but the first part was equally important. Hard work, persuasion, and research rather than class war would slowly but inevitably continue the movement of society in a socialist direction. In the ideal Fabian state, trained intelligence would play a central part, and its recognition and use in a meritocratic public service would be one of the features that would mark off socialism from capitalism. Far from the hierarchies of capitalism being replaced by equality of power, they would be refined by a system of democratically accountable elites, staffed by the most capable, whereas capitalism's elites had been staffed only by the most fortunate. There was often a high moral tone here, praising the ascetic dedication of the professional, and being dismissively patronizing about the 'average sensual man'. The high responsibility given to trained intelligence in national politics was exported in Fabianism to become an advocacy of the right and duty of the advanced industrial nations of Western Europe to administer the less developed parts of the world and bring them up to the same socialist heights that were to be attained at home.

Fabianism saw democracy as the exercise of the political function of the people as a whole, in their universal category of consumers. Within this structure, individuals would participate in their various roles as citizens, workers and so on, contributing by their efforts to the common good from which they would benefit. Forms of direct popular power such as referendums or legislative initiatives were condemned as promoting discontinuity and irrationality, and what was considered as the sectional and potentially selfish self-government of groups organized on the basis of production in various forms of workers' control was opposed as inconsistent with democracy. Fabianism's stress on the collective and the public led it to ignore problems such as the nature of work or divisions of gender.

Reading
McBriar, A.M. 1966: *Fabian Socialism and English Politics 1884–1914*.
McKenzie, N. and McKenzie, J. 1977: *The First Fabians*.
Pimlott, B. ed. 1984: *Fabian Essays in Socialist Thought*.
Shaw, G.B. ed. 1889 (*1931, 1962*): *Fabian Essays*.
Webb, S. and Webb, B. 1920: *A Constitution for the Socialist Commonwealth of Great Britain*.

RODNEY BARKER

family Although many historians and anthropologists have for some time pointed to remarkable variation among family forms, others have nonetheless sought to identify the universal characteristics of the family. In 1949, anthropologist George Murdock ventured such a universal definition (based on his analysis of some 500 societies) and argued that 'the family' was 'a social group characterized by common residence, economic cooperation and reproduction. It includes adults of both sexes, at least two of whom maintain a socially approved sexual relationship, and one or more children, own or adopted, of the sexually cohabiting adults' (Murdock, 1949, p. 1). For many years, Murdock's definition was the standard definition – cited in numerous textbooks and scholarly essays – applauded for its applicability to developing countries as well as to the modern West. Ironically, that definition can no longer be applied accurately even to the West.

Nowadays, though Murdock is still widely cited, new evidence – on both family norms and household forms – is available to challenge him on each criterion that he advanced. At least since the 1960s in much of the modern West and in the developing world, Murdock's family form accounts for only a minority of households. The family, Murdock's critics claim, often consists of a sole parent (typically mother) and child or cohabiting adults with no child. (See also DIVORCE.) Or couples voluntarily forego parenting, often to pursue other ends. They are, in the lingo of the day, 'childfree'.

To be sure, for women, men and children alike, the family has remained an institution based on economic dependence. Despite the worldwide and unprecedented entry of wives into the labour force, most women continue to depend financially on their husbands. Despite the apparent financial independence of husbands, most depend on wives not only for 'invisible' and unpaid household work but also for the income provided by their wife's paycheque. Despite children's growing assertion of independence, most offspring still depend on their parents for current and future class position just as they increasingly take jobs in the expanding service and informal sectors of the economy and share their income at home. However, although a division of labour links husband with wife and children with parents, ideologies transmute and mystify the economic significance of these exchanges, casting them in terms of love and companionship. In this ideology, economic cooperation has become voluntary, the division of labour trivialized. Thus, the economic glue of which Murdock wrote appears to be in the process of dissolution.

Others suggest that, by applying his definition, we apply a distinctly biased ideology that characterizes neither the function of modern families nor their structure. A large body of research in the USA and Britain, in the late 1950s and 1960s, showed that even the middle class typically lived in 'modified extended families' (Litwak, 1965) rather than the isolated nuclear family that Talcott Parsons had proposed (Parsons and Bales, 1955). Modern individuals around the world, by and large, keep in touch with kin, even those who live at some distance from them. Modern technology provides them with the opportunity to do so. Often, because of their independent careers, some

spouses – whether in the United States, Japan or China – even spend much of their time in separate residences instead of sharing a single home. They forfeit claims not only to a residentially intact 'family' but to the geographic proximity of a shared 'community' and 'neighbourhood'. Yet even then they avail themselves of the new technologies that make possible new definitions and understandings of family. Geographically proximate spouses are no longer the *sina qua non* of family life.

Just as geographically non-proximate middle-class spouses transform our notions of family, so, too, do the urban poor. Both Liebow and Stack describe how poor blacks in the USA turn friends into 'fictive kin' because family is supposed to be more reliable than friendship (see also KINSHIP). Friends become kin because they can be counted on to exchange money, goods and services, not simply love. From her ethnographic research in a large US city, Stack develops a new definition of family:

Ultimately, I defined family as the smallest, organized, durable network of kin and non-kin who interact daily, providing domestic needs of children and assuring their survival. The family network is diffused over several kin-based households . . . An arbitrary imposition of widely accepted definitions of the family, the nuclear family, or the matrilocal family blocks the way to understanding how people in the Flats describe and order their world. (Stack, 1974, p. 31)

Here, family becomes local network – not household or neighbourhood. More important, family becomes subjective: it is the unit that permits survival and orders one's world (Gerstel and Gross, 1987). Overall, then, the economic bonds of black families, at least among the poor, differ from those of white families, at least among the middle class. Disadvantaged black men are, for whatever reasons, unable to provide women with economic security (Wilson, 1988). Yet, this is not to say that economic ties among black families disappear altogether. Rather, they are reconstituted along different lines, emphasizing extended and fictive kin rather than conjugal ties. These patterns of extending family ties have much in common with strategies for survival outside the modern West. As Pine (1982) finds of urban Ghana, the members of low income couples tend far more than the upper and middle class to live separately, often with kin, and to be involved in day-to-day reciprocal relationships with those kin. As she writes of West Africa:

> It may well be argued that in many complex societies with uneven economic development, the nuclear family, as an economic and domestic unit in which the members are interdependent is a viable or at least desirable alternative primarily for the middle and upper classes . . . For women, especially those with children, a sporadically employed or unemployed male may be more of a liability than an asset, while female kin can offer each other mutual aid, companionship and labor . . . In terms of family and kinship, it is more useful to look at the wider kinship relationships between the urban poor than to concentrate upon variations on, or lack of, conjugal units. (p. 401)

Thus, as Rapp has suggested, the debate about the value and future of the family is based on experiences that vary by race and class. The Third World feminist who defends the family and the middle-class feminist who thinks it ought to be abolished 'aren't talking about the same families' (Rapp, 1978, p. 278).

To be sure, a politically powerful right wing in many advanced industrial societies seeks to restore the hegemony of the heterosexual couple, permanently wed, in which the husband is the primary (or better yet, sole) breadwinner and household head, the wife a housekeeper and mother (see also DOMESTIC LABOUR), and the children (there are always some) subject to parental (especially paternal) control. But the right's programme is little more than reactive; it neither represents the majority view nor addresses the predominant and worldwide structural trends in family life.

Changing empirical and political realities, however, have not been the only challenge to the monolithic concept of the family. Equally important, feminist scholars have challenged the belief that 'any specific family arrangement is natural, biological or functional in a timeless way' (Thorne and Yalom, 1982, p. 2). More important, recent scholarship suggests that the search for a universal 'family' hides historical change as it sets in place an ideology of 'the family' that obscures the diversity and reality of family experience in any particular time and place.

For example, in colonial America, family membership was defined in terms of productive contribution and household membership. Thus, servants who lived and worked in one household, but were not related by blood, were often viewed and treated as family members by those with whom they shared that home. They provided labour as they were taught productive skills, religious doctrine and moral values. They were family members because they shared a household and were subject to the authority of its head, not because they were treated with nurturance, affection or love. Conversely, as one recent critic put it, as late as the end of the Middle Ages, the German language had no word for the private groups of parents and children that we currently understand as family (Mitterauer and Sieder, 1982). Many scholars argue that the defining characteristic of the 'modern family' in the West (with its roots in the nineteenth century) are altogether different: this modern family is formed on the basis of affection and love; it operates on behalf of the personality to provide psychological security and tension management; and its spouses are companions as its parents (especially mothers) are nurturant and self-sacrificing. Moreover, whereas the colonial family (a little commonwealth) was all but indistinguishable from the community, scholars suggest the modern family has become increasingly privatized, quiet and secluded. Relations within the family become more intimate and valued as relations outside of it become more remote, specialized and tenuous. As one recent analyst writes:

> Indeed, it has become increasingly clear that 'family' and related 'domestic' concepts as we know them are relatively recent developments. Many of the distinguishing features of contemporary family discourse – in particular the notions of privacy and sentiment – were either absent from or unimportant to the discourse of primary social relations prior to the last few centuries. (Gubrum and Holstein, 1990, p. 17)

Some well respected scholars even suggest that it is only from the fifteenth century that we can find a rise of a new concept: the concept of the family. The arrangement was present, Aries contended in his ground-breaking work, but: 'the family existed in silence; it did not awaken feelings strong enough to inspire poet or artist. We must recognize the importance of this silence: not much value was placed on the family' (1962, p. 364).

Given these new meanings, many now lay claim to the title Family. Lesbians and gay men, for example, demand that the state and church legitimize their union because they, too, share these modern emotional ties. Single parents argue that they and their children are 'family' because they are tied together not only by blood but, more important, by emotion. Cohabiting couples, with and without children, demand the rights of marriage because they share the emotions of spouses. At the same time, right-wing rhetoric plays on the nurturant, intimate bonds we have come to associate with 'family'. But these groups – whether on the left or the right – obscure the actual conditions of modern families. They assert that family is about love. While the modern West has come to emphasize the family's emotional significance, we may have changed the conditions that could sustain such an emphasis. The very concept – the family – then, cannot capture the range and diversity of experience that many now define as their own. A family – really many different families – are 'here to stay'. The family is an ideological and social construct. Any attempts to define it, as a bounded institution with characteristics universal across place or time, will necessarily fail.

Reading

Ariès, Philippe 1960 (*1962*): *Centuries of Childhood.*
Gerstel, Naomi and Gross, Harriet eds 1987: *Families and Work.*
Gubrum, Jaber F. and Holstein, James A. 1990: *What is Family?*
Litwak, Eugene 1965: Extended family relations in an industrial society. In *Social Structure and the Family: Generational Relations,* ed. E. Shanas and G. Strieb.
Mitterauer, Michael and Sieder, Reinhard 1982: *The European Family.*
Murdock, George 1967: *Ethnographic Atlas.*
Parsons, Talcott and Bales, R. 1955: *Family Socialization and Interaction Patterns.*
Pine, Frances 1982: Family structure and the division of labor: female roles in urban Ghana. In *Introduction to the Sociology of Developing Societies,* ed. Hamza Alavi and Teodor Shanin.
Rapp, Rayna 1978: Family and class in contemporary America: notes toward an understanding of ideology. *Science and Society* 5.42, 278–300.
Stack, Carol 1974: *All Our Kin.*
Thorne, Barrie and Yalom, Marilyn eds 1982: *Rethinking the Family.*
Wilson, William 1988: *The Truly Disadvantaged.*

NAOMI R. GERSTEL

fascism   Used generically, fascism is a term for a singularly protean genus of modern politics inspired by the conviction that a process of national rebirth (palingenesis) has become essential to bring to an end a protracted period of social and cultural

DECADENCE, and expressing itself ideologically in a revolutionary form of integral NATIONALISM (ultranationalism). Confined to publicistic writings and groups of activists on the margins of political life prior to the outbreak of World War I and since the end of World War II, fascism provided the rationale for the formations and political parties of the ultra-right which surfaced to combat liberalism, socialism and conservatism in practically every European country between 1918 and 1945. Notable fascist movements appeared in Austria, Belgium, Britain, Finland, France, Germany, Hungary, Italy, Romania and Spain, as well as further afield in South Africa and Brazil. Though some of these temporarily broke through to become the nucleus of popular movements, or to play a part in collaborationist regimes under NATIONAL SOCIALISM, only in Italy and Germany did particular conjunctures of events enable fascism to seize power autonomously through a combination of legality with violence, giving rise to Mussolini's Fascist State (1925–43) and Hitler's Third Reich (1933–45).

These two regimes exhibited the marked contrasts both in surface ideology and in potential for ruthless brutality in the pursuit of domestic and foreign policy which distinguish different permutations of fascism. However, their drive to regenerate the whole nation through a popular reawakening set both apart generically from the many contemporary authoritarian states of the ultra-right which, though adopting many of the trappings of fascist Italy and Germany, were essentially opposed to the social revolution envisaged by fascism and hence are best seen as 'fascistized' or 'para-fascist' regimes (for example, Dolfuss's Christian Social Austria or Salazar's *Estado Novo* in Portugal). The anti-conservative dimension of fascism is partly obscured by the extensive collusion with traditional power elites (such as the army, the church, industry) which both Fascism (best spelt with a capital to distinguish it from generic fascism) and Nazism were forced to make on pragmatic grounds (see Blinkhorn, 1990). Similarly, the genuine populism intrinsic to their ideology is easily lost from view because of the extensive social engineering (involving intensive propaganda and state terror) necessitated in practice by the bid to turn the utopia of a homogeneous and revitalized national community into a reality. Any fascist revolution is doomed to fail since it is the outstanding example of a palingenetic or regenerationist modern political movement with a small natural constituency seeking to operate as the exclusive truth system for the whole of a pluralistic society. When such an ideology becomes the basis of a regime it leads inevitably to systematic inhumanity and TOTALITARIANISM.

This definition of fascism is inevitably contentious since it is an IDEAL TYPE which has so far resisted attempts by academics to turn it into a social scientific category about which a workable consensus prevails (compare the definitions in the companion volumes to this one: Bottomore, 1983; Sternhell, 1987; Wilkinson, 1987). What distinguishes the present approach is that it locates the 'fascist minimum' in a core myth of the reborn nation which can express itself in a wide range of rationalizations and permutations. Historically there has been a high level of agreement among different fascists on which forces threaten the health of the nation, namely Marxism-Leninism, materialism, internationalism, liberalism, individualism, but considerable variation in what forces are advocated as their remedy and the degree of imperialist and racist violence envisaged in order to impose it. Being ultra-nationalist in inspiration, each fascism will inevitably draw on the history and culture of the country in which it arises so as to legitimize its assault on the status quo, as exemplified in the Nazi vision of Germany as an Aryanized Third Reich or the Fascist claim that Italy was renewing its Roman heritage. In the past fascisms have incorporated elements of militarism, technocracy, ruralism, imperialism, neoclassicism, avant-garde art, syndicalism, national socialism, neo-romanticism, politicized Christianity, paganism, occultism, biological racism, ANTI-SEMITISM, voluntarism, SOCIAL DARWINISM, or more recently elements of 'alternative culture' (for instance of 'New Ageism' and the green movement). In the 1980s a convention of Italian neo-fascists was held at Camp Hobbit, and a British neo-fascist stood as a 'green-wave' candidate.

Though the rampant eclecticism of fascism makes generalizations about its specific ideological contents hazardous, the general tenor of all its permutations places it in the tradition of the late nineteenth-century revolt against liberalism and positivism which impart to it a strong emphasis on the primacy of vitalism and action over intellect and theory. Consistent with the ideological complexity of fascism, the social basis of individual movements is highly heterogeneous, and by no means restricted to the lower middle or capitalist classes (see Mühlberger, 1987), despite a persistent assumption to the contrary. Fascism also draws on the tradition of ELITE THEORY, though the self-appointed activist and paramilitary vanguards of its interwar variants were convinced of their mission to revolutionize society not just 'from above', but from below through a mass movement capable of transforming the alleged chaos and degeneracy of modern society into a coordinated and healthy national COMMUNITY.

Since the war nearly every Westernized country has seen the appearance of small and often ephemeral groups modelling themselves on Nazism or Fascism to agitate for crude versions of racism and chauvinism in what might be called 'mimetic' fascism. More significantly, perhaps, a number of parties have arisen which, even when officially dissociated from interwar fascism, campaign for a palingenetic version of ultra-nationalism adapted to postwar conditions, as for example Italy's MSI (Movimento Sociale Italiano) and the German Republicans. In France Le Pen's spectacularly successful Front National has some fascist followers, but its official platform is a racist perversion of conservative liberalism rather than a revolutionary creed. In terms of its direct impact on mainstream politics, perhaps the most significant fascist formation in the early 1990s was the Afrikaner Weerstandsbeweging in South Africa.

The postwar period has also seen the emergence of new rationalizations of palingenetic ultra-nationalism. The most influential of these are the post-Nietzschean vision of a 'conservative revolution' preached by De Benoist on behalf of the French 'New Right' (to be distinguished from Anglo-American neoliberalism) and Julius Evola's 'Traditionalist' fusion of Hindu and occultist pseudo-science adopted by many currents of the Italian 'Radical Right' (see Sheehan, 1981), both of which have influenced contemporary neo-fascism in Britain (see for example the periodical *Scorpion*). Characteristic of much European neo-fascism is the theme of a new Europe made up of a league of regenerated nations acting as a bastion against the twin decadent powers, America and (till 1990) Russia, a theme already explored by some elements of interwar fascism. The tenaciousness of illiberal nationalism even in the most stable liberal democracies (see Ó Maoláin, 1987, and current issues of *Searchlight*) makes it likely that fascism and neo-fascism will be a perennial ingredient of modern politics, and it was to be expected that after the autumn of 1989 minute neo-Nazi and neo-fascist movements surfaced in several of the 'new democracies' (for example Pamyat in Russia). However, the conjuncture of structural forces that allowed Fascism and Nazism to conquer state power no longer obtain, and it is condemned to leading a highly marginalized existence for the foreseeable future (see Cheles, 1991).

In terms of fascism's contribution to social thought, some of its theorists, notably in Germany, Italy and France, produced relatively elaborate theories on such themes as the organic concept of the state, the leader principle, economics, corporatism, aesthetics, law, education, technology, race, history, morality and the role of the church. Though they all neglect fundamental liberal (and Marxist) methodological principles, they offer important case studies in the application of nationalist and irrationalist myth to academic discourses as a contribution to the legitimation and normalization of revolutionary politics. As for the light thrown on fascism by orthodox social thought, the Durkheimian concept of ANOMIE, the Weberian concept of charismatic politics and leadership, research in sociology, social anthropology and social psychology on the complex dynamics of revolutions, personal dictatorships, youth movements and authoritarianism, all have a bearing on fascism. So do studies which investigate the mythic dimension of nationalism and the utopian component in all revolutionary ideologies without confusing them with religious millenarianism.

Reading
Griffin, R.D. 1991: *The Nature of Fascism*.
Laqueur, W. ed. 1979: *Fascism: A Reader's Guide*.
Mosse, G.L. ed. 1979: *International Fascism: New Thoughts and Approaches*.
Payne, S.G. 1980: *Fascism: Comparison and Definition*.
ROGER GRIFFIN

federalism   This denotes a division of powers within a legal framework between central and subsidiary governments, and in such a way that, unlike under devolution, the centre cannot change the division without special and difficult procedures. All modern political thinkers face the dilemma that if a state is too strong, it will threaten the liberties of its people; but if weak, it may not be able to help and protect them. Jean-Jacques Rousseau (1762) argued that sovereign power could only

be exercised justly in a small state, 'But if it is very small, will it not be subjugated? No, I shall show later how the external strength of a large people may be combined with the free government and good order of a small state.' And a footnote promised a sequel (which he never wrote) on 'the subject of confederations. This subject is entirely new, and its principles have yet to be established.'

The American federal constitution of 1787 established such principles, clearly expounded in reasoned polemics for its adoption, *The Federalist Papers* (Hamilton and Madison, 1787–8). The federal government was a new central government set up above 13 existing states, former royal colonies, all with constitutions; but the powers of this central body were limited by law and subject to judicial review. English Tories at the time mocked any such proposals as inherently unstable, so deeply did they believe that a fully sovereign state was essential to political order. But the young Jeremy Bentham mocked back, 'Do you not think that the Switzers have government?' (1776).

Federal governments are now common. Even the Stalin constitution proclaimed the USSR a federation, although the national elements seemed only a facade. But with the collapse of Communist power in the 1980s, a reality of divided powers was revealed. And it must be remembered that the American colonies had enjoyed a considerable degree of self-government before federation. There are no examples in the world of a unitary state choosing to turn itself into a federation; the highly successful federalism of postwar West Germany, for example, was imposed by conquest.

Behind these different institutional arrangements lie profound differences of political theory. Modern thinkers as different as Lenin, Sidney and Beatrice Webb and apologists for the sovereignty of parliament in Britain line up behind Thomas Hobbes in believing that without a central, sovereign state, inefficiency, at the best, is rampant and, at the worst, civil war is latent. Look what happened with the collapse of Soviet power! But others challenge the concept of sovereignty itself. To John Adams (1774) 'sovereignty is very tyranny.' And modern pluralist thinkers hold that the very concept of sovereignty is a dangerous illusion: all power rests on consent of some kind and has different limitations arising from the sociology, culture and tradition of different societies (see PLURALISM). Then federalism becomes a general theory of complex societies, not simply a preferred set of institutions. Harold Laski once said 'all power is federal' (1925).

See also REGIONALISM.

Reading
Forsyth, M. 1989: *Federalism and Nationalism.*
King, P. 1982: *Federalism and Federation.*
Vile, M.J.C. 1967: *Constitutionalism and the Separation of Powers.*

BERNARD CRICK

feminism This can be defined as the advocacy of equal rights for women and men, accompanied by a commitment to improve the position of women in society. It thus presupposes an underlying condition of inequality, be this conceived as male domination, PATRIARCHY, gender inequality or the social effects of sexual difference. In 1938 Virginia Woolf provocatively described 'feminist' as 'a vicious and corrupt word that has done much harm in its day and is now obsolete': an extreme statement that illustrates the disagreements about politics that occur even among those who support the cause of women.

In Britain and the USA the longest feminist tradition is that of democratic, liberal feminism directed towards obtaining equal rights and opportunities for women. The founding texts of this tradition are Mary Wollstonecraft's *A Vindication of the Rights of Women* in 1792 and John Stuart Mill's essay *The Subjection of Women* in 1869. A useful modern discussion of this tradition can be found in Phillips (1987). In the nineteenth century much of this work was focused on removing educational and professional barriers, and the impetus behind these reforming campaigns was often quite militant. The culmination of this 'equal rights' militancy came with the violent struggles of the early twentieth-century suffragettes in their fight for the vote, documented in the British context by Ray Strachey in *The Cause* (1928). More recent areas of contestation in the North American and European contexts have been employment rights, equal pay and equality in social benefits, taxation and so on.

Western societies since the late 1960s have seen the rise (and decline) of feminist movements with a more radical edge, proposing some sort of revolutionary political shake-up of society rather than a redistribution of rights and resources, and insisting that the oppression of women is embedded in deep psychic and cultural processes and that feminist objectives hence require fundamental rather than superficial change. A particular focus of these campaigns has been the fight for women's control over their own bodies – notably on the issue of a woman's right to choose about abortion – and the network of groups and refuges organized to protect women and their children from violent men. Although the rise of this so-called 'second wave' feminism is often linked to the politics emerging from the American Civil Rights movement of the 1960s, the roots of these more radical ideas lie more obviously in indigenous European political traditions: utopian socialism, anarchism, libertarianism, Marxism and so on. Other important sources of ideas were Frantz Fanon's work on the internalization of colonialism and Mao Zedong's approach to political consciousness. During the 1980s and the 1990s this type of feminism – directed at broad cultural change – has been active around issues connecting masculinity and war (for example the Greenham Common peace campaign in Britain against nuclear weapons) and the flourishing 'eco-feminism' that links women to a particular concern with the preservation of the planet. Founding texts of this Western 'second wave' feminism are Simone de Beauvoir's *The Second Sex* (1949), Virginia Woolf's *Three Guineas* (1938), and Kate Millett's *Sexual Politics*, Shulamith Firestone's *The Dialectic of Sex* and Germaine Greer's *The Female Eunuch* (all 1970). In the British context one would add Sheila Rowbotham's *Hidden From History* (1975) and Juliet Mitchell's *Women: The Longest Revolution* (1974).

Western second-wave feminism has posed many issues for discussion and it may help, in locating its context in social and political thought in the twentieth century, to take up two of these: (1) the question of feminist 'separatism', and (2) the relationship of feminism to socialist thought and politics.

(1) Feminist utopias have often depicted communities of women where the violent, militaristic, hierarchical and authoritarian characteristics attributed to men are mercifully absent. This strand of feminist thought inclines to pessimism on the question of ameliorating male brutality and advises the establishment of female communities and the strengthening of women's ties to each other. Historically this tradition tended to involve a sentimentalization of women's relationships, rather than an eroticization. In second-wave feminism the political articulation of lesbianism as an option has

been marked, although not by any means necessarily as a separatist one. The Western Women's Liberation Movement of the 1970s and 1980s at some points linked with a more general liberationist politics around sexuality, particularly in defence of gay rights.

(2) The relationship of feminism to socialist ideas and politics has been the subject of much discussion (see Barrett, 1988). With the collapse of the Soviet bloc, and the decline of Marxism as an intellectual force in the West, this relationship is likely to be eroded. It is worth noting that societies attempting to implement a transition to socialism have, however they may have failed in general, attached considerable weight to the emancipation of women. Hence, for example, the reunification of Germany (in 1991) has involved a loss of rights and resources for women in the erstwhile DDR. Similarly one might note that state socialist regimes have offered women opportunities that are infinitely superior to those of regimes inspired by Islamic or other fundamentalist religious programmes.

It can be argued that feminism in the West, both in its nineteenth- and twentieth-century forms, has tended to oscillate around the issue of whether to press for equality and hence perhaps a 'sameness' of women and men (androgyny), or whether to start from the position that women and men are essentially 'different' from each other (whether understood biologically, culturally or socially) and hence to press for a re-evaluation of women's distinctive contribution. Certainly there is a tension in Western feminist thought and politics on this question, which has arisen in many specific contexts. The 'protective legislation' of the nineteenth century, barring women from certain conditions of work (such as mining underground, or night shifts) can, for example, be interpreted from a 'difference' position as a proper protection of the reproduction of the species or from an 'equality' position as a cynical move to exclude women from advantageous positions in the workforce. Decisions as to whether to fight for the repeal of such legislation or to leave it in force involved taking up a position on this 'equality or difference' debate. Similar dilemmas arise with regard to maternity provision, affirmative action policies, arrangements for maintenance and custody of children after divorce, not to mention more contentious issues of surrogate motherhood or new reproductive technologies. Policy debates on these issues in Britain, the USA and Australia are discussed in Bacchi (1990). More

profoundly, it has also been argued (Scott, 1990) that the traditional binary opposition between 'equality' and 'difference' is a disabling one that contemporary feminism should refuse rather than continue to work with. Equality need not involve the elimination of difference.

The characteristic theoretical assumptions of second-wave Western feminism, from a high point of influence in the 1970s, have now given way to a more dispersed and heterogeneous set of ideas. What one might call '1970s feminism' assumed that one could specify a 'cause' of women's oppression, however much feminists differed as to what that cause might be (male control of women's fertility, capitalism's need for a docile labour force and so on). In the taxonomies beloved of this period, there were various packages of answers ('liberal', 'socialist' or 'radical' feminist) to these questions; with hindsight, the diversity of these answers can be seen to have concealed a high degree of consensus on what were the right questions to be posed. It was assumed, too, that all women were oppressed or subordinated, and that the dynamic of this oppression lay at the level of determining social structures. Arguments stressing the importance of biology, nature, hormones or genetics were all dispatched with confidence as 'biologism' and the social and cultural causes of sexist attitudes affirmed. Sexual difference, and the salience of childbearing and rearing for the lives of both women and men, were largely ignored.

The breaking up of this consensus could be attributed to three main sources: (1) the critique of Western feminism for attempting to universalize the experience of white (often middle-class) women in advanced capitalist countries; (2) a collapse of confidence in the sociological model of GENDER implied in the approach and a concomitant reassertion of 'sexual difference' as an important psychic and cultural phenomenon; and (3) the incorporation of unsettling ideas of poststructuralist and postmodernist provenance.

(1) Here it is important to note that black feminists delivered an eloquent critique of the failure of white feminism to engage with questions of racism and ethnocentrism. While this point was made 'on the doorstep' of Western feminism, it was also argued that the high profile of Western feminism had itself dwarfed awareness of women's struggles elsewhere in the world (see WOMEN'S MOVEMENT). Certainly, it is true to say that political priorities vary significantly and that the feminist

agenda is very different in non-Western societies. Attempts by Western feminists to address these issues in a comparative context (for example, Robin Morgan's *Sisterhood is Global* (1984) have understandably been criticized for reproducing these underlying differences of power.

(2) Sexual difference came to be viewed as more intransigent, but also more positive, than had been allowed at the high point of second-wave feminism, which had tended to echo the view of de Beauvoir (1949) that femininity was not only a cultural 'achievement' but also a lessening, or distortion, of woman's human potential. This shift was signalled in the growing interest in psychoanalytic explorations of sexual difference and identity, an influential text being Juliet Mitchell's *Psychoanalysis and Feminism* (1975), and in the analysis of mothering, massively developed after the publication in 1978 of Nancy Chodorow's *The Reproduction of Mothering*. An important aspect of this process was a reappropriation by feminism of the identity of woman, and a realization that the impulse towards 'androgyny' or 'equality' was yet another capitulation to a masculine norm of denying the salience of sex and gender.

(3) The relationship of feminist thought to the theoretical currents of poststructuralism and postmodernism is complex, necessarily so if the historical roots of feminism as a liberal humanist doctrine are considered. Various writers on this theme (Hekman, 1990; Pollock, 1992; Barrett, 1992) conclude that feminism straddles the modernity/postmodernity divide (see MODERNISM AND POSTMODERNISM). It is thus difficult to link feminism as a historical political movement in any obvious way with poststructuralist positions, although many attempts to do so have been made (for example Weedon, 1987). Riley (1988) explores the problematic implications for feminism of a poststructuralist 'deconstruction' of the category of 'woman'. Feminist theory in Europe, North America and Australia is currently exercised by the implications of poststructuralist ideas for conceptualization of any feminist project and hence the possibilities for feminist politics.

A final point might be made concerning the idea of 'post-feminism', currently enjoying some popularity in the West. Many young people in advanced Western societies appear to have a more progressive and open view of the life choices open to women than the generation of their parents, and to some extent this can rightly be attributed to the work of the active feminist movement of the 1970s and 1980s. Nevertheless, the idea that feminism is now obsolete and that a 'post-feminist' culture of choice prevails is, quite simply, not borne out by any sociological or political investigation of gendered inequality and power in contemporary societies.

Reading
Bacchi, Carol Lee 1990: *Same Difference: Feminism and Sexual Difference*.
Barrett, M. and Phillips, A. eds 1992: *Destabilizing Theory: Contemporary Feminist Debates*.
Beauvoir, Simone de 1949 (*1974*): *The Second Sex*.
Hirsch, M. and Keller, Evelyn Fox eds 1990: *Conflicts in Feminism*.
Millett, Kate 1970: *Sexual Politics*.
Morgan, Robin 1984: *Sisterhood is Global: The International Women's Movement Anthology*.
Phillips, Anne ed. 1987: *Women and Equality*.
Rowbotham, Sheila 1975: *Hidden from History*.
Woolf, Virginia 1938: *Three Guineas*.

MICHÈLE BARRETT

feudalism Modern interest in this early system of social organization does not occur only for its own sake. The combination of individualism and hierarchy found in European feudalism were sources of political liberty, capitalism and science – all based on competition, whether of rulers, resources or ideas. Two conditions of competition, absence of central coercive capacity and independence of participants, provide clues to the context and content of feudalism.

Non-centralized governments are found throughout history: in ancient Mesopotamia during the Kassite period; Egypt during the Middle Kingdom; Byzantium between the tenth and twelfth centuries; China during the Chou, late Han and late Tang dynasties; Japan between the ninth and eighteenth centuries; and more. Over time, governmental authority has been fragmented among local jurisdictions more often and for longer periods than it has been centralized. Only in medieval Europe, however, did a non-centralized economy and society generate competitive elements sufficiently strong to survive recentralization.

An eclectic system of governance and economic organization emerged there during the tenth century AD, largely from mutual need for defence against invaders from Scandinavia. Under European feudalism, the collectivism (subordination of individual interest to group interests) associated with ancient hierarchical polities combined with rudiments of political individualism stemming from relationships among Germanic tribal leaders and their followers between the sixth and ninth centuries.

By the sixth century AD, when all traces of western Roman imperial administration had disappeared in northern Europe, such limited government as still existed had become privatized. Common defence and maintenance of law and order devolved on local bishops and landowners who were descendants of Germanic invaders.

The warriors (vassals) in local chieftains' defence forces gave volunteer service for nothing more than daily camaraderie and lifetime subsistence in their master's house. Weak Merovingian and Carolingian kings who were these chieftains' descendants rewarded their vassals with extensive land grants (fiefs) in exchange for 40 days' armed service each year; and, with unsettled conditions following the ninth century invasions, vassalage acquired a political function. A relationship among near equals arising from mutual obligation evolved into a hierarchy adapted to local governance and military defence.

In the vacuum created by the collapse of the Carolingian monarchy in the ninth century, each vassal assumed authority to govern all who lived on his fiefdom. He administered justice, collected taxes, built roads and bridges and mobilized a private army from its residents. He could claim labour service from peasants and was entitled to all agricultural produce. Thus, with virtually no distinction between private and public authority, management of public services and facilities was indistinguishable from private estate management.

However independent each vassal might in fact have been, the traditional obligation to provide defence forces sustained symbolic ties with the grantor. By the tenth century, when land titles and the political power and social status corresponding to scale of ownership could be inherited, the mutual defensive obligations of successive landowning generations were being formalized in a feudal contract. Heirs to the largest fiefdoms stood near the apex of a social pyramid, superiors in an emerging feudal nobility.

In a ceremony administered by the church, the vassal pledged fealty to his master, promising to supply armed knights for a defence force in wartime, and to garrison the master's castle in peacetime. (The master, in turn, would adjudicate disputes among vassals and provide military aid if a vassal's lands were attacked.) To meet his obliga-

tion to supply armed knights, a vassal with large holdings would divide them, giving over use of the land to lower ranking associates, and these men would further subdivide their estates until, after a succession of partitions, the smallest holding belonged to one knight. With sub-infeudation, as this process is now called, each level of the hierarchy pledged fealty, promising to supply armed knights to the magnate directly above him, until at the highest levels the chief vassals owed feudal dues to the crown.

Sub-infeudation stabilized the feudal relationship: a principal vassal might hesitate to violate his feudal contract with the king because his actions would set an unfavourable example to the men who owed him feudal service.

Emerging feudal customary law further stabilized hierarchical relationships by protecting the master's rights in intergenerational transfers. The rule of primogeniture (inheritance by the eldest son) ensured that land, titles and rank in feudal society passed intact to heirs. If the vassal's heir was incompetent, the lord's power of escheat permitted him to reclaim a fief and reassign it. By exercising the power of wardship when a child inherited a fiefdom, a magnate could assert control until the child was old enough to take the oath of fealty. The magnate had rights to approve a widow's remarriage and to approve mates for his vassals' daughters. Finally, the open-ended power of entail permitted a grantor to recover a fiefdom if its holder failed to meet his demands. Perhaps these powers indicate ways vassals tried to evade their obligations.

Individual power under feudalism was limited in two important respects. No local governing notable could control all or most of the others, nor could any one magnate maintain his authority without resources provided by subordinates, each of whom ruled independently over land within the higher magnate's domain.

Although hierarchical social and economic relations persisted within each individual domain, where land might be worked by slaves and tied tenants (serfs) completely dependent on the landowner for survival, a few peasant families, especially on the continent, held land in freehold tenure and were exempt from feudal dues. By the twelfth century, as slavery disappeared and serfs bought their freedom and moved into towns, rules of hierarchy controlled fewer areas of life.

No strong temporal authority existed throughout the Middle Ages; late medieval feudal monarchs ruled over decentralized kingdoms. By the late Middle Ages, however, elements of interdependence permeated relationships among feudal masters. As coalitions among near-equals formed, were dissolved and reinitiated to attain mutual advantage, the bargaining that went on weakened collectivism. Bargaining, in which self-regulation substitutes for authority, is characteristic of the individualism commonly associated with capitalism.

Slowly, as weak feudal monarchs took over local notables' authority to administer justice and defence, they negotiated a workable combination of individualism and collectivism. Eventually hierarchy came to dominate the polity. Yet its formal structure coexisted with elements of individualism, and over time these elements grew ever stronger.

See also STATE.

Reading
Bloch, Marc 1940 (*1961*): *Feudal Society*.
——1974: The rise of dependent cultivation and seignorial institutions. In *Cambridge Economic History of Europe*, vol. 1, ch. 4.
Duby, Georges 1974: *The Early Growth of the European Economy: Warriors and Peasants from the Seventh to the Twelfth Century*.
Lyon, Bruce 1972: *The Origins of the Middle Ages: Pirenne's Challenge to Gibbon*.
Stephenson, Carl 1969: *Medieval Feudalism*, chs 1, 2 and 5.
Strayer, Joseph R. 1971: The two levels of feudalism. In *Medieval Statecraft and the Perspectives of History*.
Webber, Carolyn and Wildavsky, Aaron 1986: Finance in private governments of medieval Europe: poor kings. In *A History of Taxation and Expenditure in the Western World*.

CAROLYN WEBBER AND AARON WILDAVSKY

film   *See* CINEMA

Fordism and post-Fordism   The term Fordism was coined in the 1930s by the Italian Marxist Antonio Gramsci and by the Belgian socialist Henri de Man to refer to an interpretation of the writings of the car manufacturer Henry Ford as formulating the premises for a major change in capitalist civilization. In the 1960s, the term was rediscovered by a number of Italian Marxists (R. Panzieri, M. Tronti, A. Negri) and then by the French regulation school (M. Aglietta, R. Boyer, B. Coriat, A. Lipietz) as a name for the model of economic

development *actually* established in advanced capitalist countries after World War II. Ford had insisted on two major points. First he emphasized the industrial paradigm that he had implemented in his factory, where he not only developed the principles of 'scientific management' first proposed by F. Taylor – a systematization, by the design of methods, of the one best way to perform each elementary productive act, a sharp division between these elementary tasks, and a specialization of each job in one standardized way – but added a search for automation through an ever more intense mechanization (see also RATIONALIZATION). The other aspect of Ford's 'Fordism' was an advocacy of higher wages (5 dollars a day), for which he advanced two reasons. High wages were a reward for the discipline and stability of the workforce in a rationally organized firm. But it would also (should this practice be generalized) provide the necessary outlets for mass production. In both cases, the working class was invited to benefit from its own submission to management authority within the firm. Gramsci emphasized the 'microcorporatist' aspect of this compromise (within each firm), while Henri de Man concentrated on the possibility of a 'macrocorporatism' at the level of society (see also CORPORATISM).

This was the time of the Great Depression, when fascists, social democrats and communists were criticizing the 'anarchy of the capitalist market', or, as Karl Polányi said, 'the domination of a self-regulating market over society'. Macrocorporatism was on the agenda of all these anti-liberal tendencies, and in fact Henri de Man ended as a fascist. But after World War II, the 'social democratic solution' and the 'American way of life' became hegemonic in the West under the sway of President Roosevelt's liberating armies. Through the New Deal in the USA, the Front Populaire in France, the implementation of the Beveridge report in Britain, the successes of social democracy in Scandinavia, macrocorporatism was stabilized by the formalization of the Fordist compromise between management and the trade unions, under the auspices of the state. Social legislation was systematized, the welfare state extended, collective bargaining generalized. This compromise resulted in a 20-year boom in productivity, investment and purchasing power.

Fordism is thus a kind of 'hierarchical holism'. Society secures for everyone participation in collective work, and shares the benefits among all. But this 'society' is organized by private or civil 'managers' constructing the world according to their 'science'. In this respect, Fordism is connected with 'modernity', as a bureaucratic style in governance and as a rationalist style in urbanism. However, contrary to Stalinism or fascism, the glory of Fordism lies not in its collective achievements but in a general access to mass private consumption. Hence it paved the way to the AFFLUENT SOCIETY, a form of generalized individualism controlled by advertisement and regulation.

In the 1970s, the economic crises of Fordism proceeded both from its 'Taylorian' aspect and from its 'regulated' aspect. Taylorian principles proved less effective with new information technologies, and the internationalization of the economy made state regulation more difficult. Hence, in the 1980s, the search for a 'post-Fordism', which was conceived at first as an inversion of Fordism: craft specialization instead of Taylorism and mass production, flexibility instead of strict regulation. This is the 'flexible specialization' (Piore and Sabel, 1984) conception of post-Fordism, which inspires some left-wing thinkers in the Anglo-Saxon world, and also the 'postmodernist' styles and ideologies (see also MODERNISM AND POSTMODERNISM). But it is strongly criticized as abandoning the rights that labour had gained under Fordism. On the European continent, it is emphasized that 'specialized skills' imply rigidity of the wage contract, and that 'flexibility' fosters deskilling. Thus, there exist opposed conceptions of the way out of the crisis of Fordism, several 'post-Fordisms'. History is still open at the end of the twentieth century, but the more 'flexible' capitalist countries (Britain, USA) seem to be industrially dominated by the more 'organized' and 'skilled' ones (Japan, Germany).

See also CAPITALISM.

Reading
Hall, S. and Jacques, M. eds 1991: *The Changing Face of Politics in the 1990s.*
Harvey, D. 1989: *The Condition of Postmodernity: An Enquiry into the Origins of Cultural Change.*
Lipietz, A. 1987: *Mirages and Miracles: The Crises of Global Fordism.*
——1991: *Choosing Audacity: An Alternative for the Twenty-first Century.*
Piore, M. and Sabel, C. 1984: *The Second Industrial Divide: Possibilities for Prosperity.*
Polányi, K. 1944: *The Great Transformation: The Political and Economic Origins of our Time.*

ALAIN LIPIETZ

formalism The groups of young progressive Russian writers, artists, and critics who started to challenge the cultural values and aesthetic theories of traditional Realists and Romantics became known, pejoratively, as Formalists. The Moscow Linguistic Circle was formed in 1915, and included Roman Jakobson, Osip Brik, and Boris Tomashevsky. The complementary Petersburg group, which founded the Society for the Study of Poetic Language (Opoiyaz) in 1916, had among its members Viktor Shklovsky, Boris Eichenbaum, and Vladimir Mayakovsky. The Formalist groups shared the major project of establishing a strictly scientific poetics, beginning with the demolition of some standard critical principles and approaches. There could be no further place for the concept of the artist-as-genius, for notions of authorial control, expressiveness, or intuitive presence. The biographical and psychological studies, along with the philosophical and the impressionistic, became irrelevant. Works could not be identified in terms of ideas, thoughts, propositions or themes.

The task the Formalists set themselves was to specify, by detailed analysis, exactly what was to constitute a 'literary fact', distinguishing literature from any spoken or non-literary language, seen as automatized, cliché-ridden, blunt, rigidified. They proposed no one single position or fixed doctrine, but all shared this founding assumption about poetic language. It is quite other than 'natural' language, everyday speech, and not to be taken as some mere variation. It is a complete, self-contained system on its own, with its own forms, codes, and self-regulating laws. One exceptional characteristic quality is its self-referentiality, its power to draw attention to itself. All the components of poetic writing, its units, patterns, forms and techniques, are directed towards this play of language, a self-delighting awareness of expression to which all other features are subordinate. The aesthetic function is not identifiable with the communicative, but prior and superior to it. (Jakobson's commentary on Shakespeare's Sonnet 129 brilliantly exemplifies this approach.)

The research into 'literariness' had produced handsome results with poetry. Formulating a stylistics from this work, the Moscow and Petersburg critics boldly went on to apply its principles to prose. Shklovsky's *Theory of Prose* of 1929 was the manifesto. The thrust of all the critique of language had, of course, been directed against mimesis, against all notions of representation, of language as transparent, as directly mediating an external reality. The application of Formalist principles to narrative prose is seen in the work of Eichenbaum and Shklovsky. Gogol's tales, such as *The Overcoat*, are treated as a sophisticated play of discrepant styles, a baring of the devices operating in the artistic process. The extended analyses of Laurence Sterne's *Tristram Shandy* and Cervantes' *Don Quixote* by Viktor Shklovsky take Eichenbaum's method to its limits. Paradoxically, Sterne is said to have composed 'the most typical novel in world literature', since 'literature without subject-matter' is the Formalists' definition of what qualifies as literature. Similarly, the humour, the character contrasts, the entertaining events, the pathos and resolutions of Cervantes' novel have to be seen as almost inadvertently produced, incidental to the parodic exposure of chivalric romance.

The Formalists' account of literary evolution attributes change to development tendencies within LITERATURE itself, and to the passage of time. On this account, the succession is not particularly causal, since older, earlier forms could return with the same effect in disturbing the settled or canonical forms. As in the evolution of the genre, so in the internal formal shaping of the particular text. There emerges, from the processes of defamiliarization, the peculiar and uniquely fresh awareness that breaks stock responses and habits of perception. Texts effecting this shock of the new have the quality of 'literariness'. Shklovsky concludes: 'Art is a means of re-experiencing the making of objects, but objects already made have no importance for art.' The elusiveness of the 'object' (thing, content or subject) in Formalist explications is akin to the elusiveness of the non-object, 'literariness', the ultimate quality that is to be defined. In so far as the conventions and literary forms are the target, then the concept tends to be aestheticized (see AESTHETICS), confined to literary constructions. In so far as it is ideas, attitudes and values, then extraliterary objects, ideologies, understanding itself are targets; content returns with a vengeance, and form is returned to the social, to the cultural, to the historical and the immediately contemporary. Defamiliarization, even when confined to literary codes and conventions, proves to have similar paradoxes. In so far as literary norms and canons have necessarily to be subverted, then the concept itself is essentially relative to what is to be 'made strange'. As the new production becomes in turn the accepted norm, then there is no set or range of

stable forms in historical equilibrium, from which the qualities that define 'literariness' can be inferred and articulated. The ultimate goal recedes, and the process is self-cancelling.

Reading
Bann, S. and Boult, J.E. eds 1973: *Russian Formalism.*
Bennett, Tony 1979: *Formalism and Marxism.*
Jameson, Fredric 1972: *The Prison-House of Language: A Critical Account of Structuralism and Russian Formalism.*
Lemon, L.T. and Reis, M.J. eds 1965: *Russian Formalist Criticism: Four Essays.*
Matejka, L. and Pomorska, K. eds 1971: *Readings in Russian Poetics: Formalist and Structuralist Views.*
Pike, Chris ed. 1979: *The Futurists, the Formalists and the Marxist Critique.*

FRANK GLOVERSMITH

Frankfurt school   Among the attempts made during the period between the two world wars to develop Marxist thought, the critical theory of the Frankfurt school occupies a prominent place. What initially distinguished it was not so much its theoretical principles, but its methodological objectives, which were the result of an unreserved acknowledgement of the empirical sciences. One of its primary goals was the systematic incorporation of all social scientific *research* disciplines into a materialistic theory of society, thus facilitating a cross-fertilization of academic social science and Marxist theory.

The idea of an interdisciplinary extension of Marxism had matured during the 1920s in the thinking of Max Horkheimer, who recognized the value of the empirical sciences (Korthals, 1985). When he succeeded Carl Grünberg as Director of the Frankfurt Institute of Social Research in 1930, he used his inaugural address to introduce publicly the programme of a critical theory of society (Horkheimer, ed. Brede, *1972*). In the following years, he elaborated this approach, together with Herbert Marcuse, in the *Zeitschrift für Sozialforschung*, the journal which was established in 1932 and which formed the intellectual focus of the Institute's work until 1941. The fundamental idea of critical theory was to bridge the gap between substantive research and philosophy, fusing these two branches of knowledge into a single form of reflection modelled on the Hegelian philosophy of history. In order to accomplish this it was of course necessary to have a theory of history capable of determining the effective powers of reason which lie in the historical process itself. The basic assumptions of such a conception of the philosophy of history were derived by both Horkheimer and Herbert Marcuse from the tradition of Marxist thought (see MARXISM).

As late as the 1930s, Horkheimer and Marcuse were still defending the classical version of the Marxist theory of history, according to which the development of the productive forces is assumed to be the central mechanism of social progress (Horkheimer, 1932) and critical theory was now to be incorporated into this historical succession of events as a measure of society's knowledge of itself. As Marcuse, drawing on Horkheimer, put it, critical theory was to make apparent 'the possibilities to which the historical situation itself has matured' (1937, p. 647). At the same time, however, Horkheimer and Marcuse no longer believed that the rationality embodied in the forces of production in contemporary society was also expressed in the revolutionary consciousness of the proletariat. Their works were permeated by an awareness of the fact that, owing to the increasing integration of the working class into the late capitalist system, a theory based on Marx had lost its social target group. For Horkheimer, the point of reference for all the Institute's research activity was the question of 'how the psychic mechanisms come about which make it possible for tensions between social classes, which are forced to become conflicts because of the economic situation, to remain latent' (1932, p. 136). Horkheimer's particular achievement was to establish the research programme of the Institute by expressing the overarching question of capitalism's new forms of integration in terms of its specific relevance to the empirical disciplines. The programme which guided the Institute's work was based on a nexus of three disciplines: an *economic analysis* of the post-liberal phase of capitalism (undertaken by Friedrich Pollock); a *sociopsychological investigation* of the integration of individuals through socialization (by Erich Fromm); and a *cultural analysis* of the effects of mass culture, which came to concentrate on the newly emerging culture industry (by Theodor W. Adorno and Leo Lowenthal).

However, the idea of interdisciplinary social research only exerted a vital, formative influence at the institute until the early 1940s. The signs of an overall shift in orientation were already manifest in the essays which Horkheimer contributed to the final volume of the *Zeitschrift für Sozialforschung* (Horkheimer, 1941a and 1941b). This change affected not only the premises of critical theory based on the philosophy of history, but also its perception of its own political role and objectives. During the 1930s, despite resignation in the face of fascism, the Institute retained the hope for progress inherent in the Marxist conception of history, and even though the idea of a necessarily revolutionary proletariat had long since been abandoned, the idea of revolution continued to provide a vague background for critical theory's political understanding of its role and its goals (Dubiel, 1978 (*1985*), A.1). Horkheimer still conceived the Institute's research work as an intellectual form of reflection related to the labour movement, because he clung to a positive conception of the mastery over nature as a condition for emancipation, allowing the forces of production to be liberated from the capitalistic form of their organization. At the end of the 1930s, this ideational world finally and definitively collapsed: in terms of practical politics through the experience of fascism, Stalinism and capitalist mass culture joining forces to form a totalitarian whole; and in terms of theory through a shift from a positive to a negative model of social labour. The productivistic view of progress gave way to a critique of reason that was critical of progress, and called into question the very possibility of changing social relations by means of a political revolution.

It was Theodor Adorno, however, who was the foremost representative of this new conception of critical theory. His thought was profoundly marked by the historical experience of fascism as a catastrophic product of civilization, which had from the beginning made him sceptical of the historical-materialist ideas of progress. Moreover, his intellectual development had been so strongly shaped by artistic interests that he was bound to have doubts about the narrow rationalism of the Marxist theoretical tradition, and under the influence of Walter Benjamin he made his first attempts to render aesthetic methods of interpretation fruitful for the materialist philosophy of history (Buck-Morss, 1977, pp. 43–80). *The Dialectic of Enlightenment*, which he wrote with Horkheimer in the early 1940s (Horkheimer and Adorno, 1947), is an expression of this new intellectual motif in a negative philosophy of history. Totalitarianism could not be explained as an outcome of the conflict between forces of production and relations of production, but was conceived as arising from the internal dynamic of the formation of human consciousness. Horkheimer and Adorno departed from the framework given by the theory of capitalism and now presupposed the process of civilization as a whole as the system of reference underpinning their argument. In this context fascism appeared as the final historical stage of a 'logic of decay' which is inherent in the original form of existence of the species itself. The process of civilization took the form of a spiral of increasing REIFICATION which was set in motion by the original acts of subjugating nature and reached its logical conclusion in fascism. One conclusion which *The Dialectic of Enlightenment* forces us to draw (Habermas, 1985, ch. 5) is the denial of any dimension of progress in civilization other than that which is manifested in an intensification of the forces of production. A second conclusion is that every form of political praxis is control-oriented action, so that they had to exclude it in principle from the range of positive alternatives. The Institute's innermost circle of researchers were thus deprived once and for all of the possibility of situating their own research activity in real politics.

An alternative to such negativistic theoretical models would have been the approach of Franz Neumann and Otto Kirchheimer, who belonged, together with Walter Benjamin and later also Erich Fromm, to a group who were only temporarily or indirectly associated with the Institute. This might have called into question that image of a 'totally administered society', which necessarily led to the cul-de-sac of political abstentionism. During their period of exile in New York, Neumann and Kirchheimer contributed to the Institute's work by conducting research into legal theory and theories of the state, and they put forward an analysis of fascism whose explanatory power was superior to the theory of state capitalism (Wilson, 1982). They recognized that social integration does not simply take place via the persistently unconscious fulfilment of the functional imperatives of society, but rather via political communication between social groups. Their active participation in the class conflicts which characterized the Weimar republic led them to a realistic assessment of the 'ratio of power of social interests'; they saw that the power potential which evolves from private capitalist control over the means of production could not be overestimated. Finally, their acquaintance with AUSTRO-MARXISM made them aware that social orders as a whole are characterized by compromise. The institutional structures of a society are to be understood as momentary fixations of agreements reached within society by the various interest groups in accordance with their respective power potentials. All of this formed a model of society at the centre of which stood the overarching process of communication between the social groups.

When the Institute was reopened in Frankfurt in 1950, it resumed its research activity without any direct continuation of the social-philosophical outlook of the 1930s and 1940s (Wiggershaus, 1986, pp. 479–520). This was the point at which critical theory ceased to be a unified, philosophically homogeneous school of thought. However, the idea of a 'totally administered world' did initially still represent a reference point for its work in social philosophy. This idea runs like a leitmotif through the critique of civilization in the studies of Horkheimer, Adorno and Marcuse. There was no departure from the philosophical premises of this diagnosis of contemporary society until a new approach was formulated by Jürgen Habermas who, although he was a product of the Institute, had a very different theoretical background and orientation. In the development of Habermas's thought, philosophical anthropology, HERMENEUTICS, PRAGMATISM and finally linguistic analysis brought theoretical currents to the fore which had always been regarded as alien, indeed hostile, by the older generation surrounding Adorno and Horkheimer. Nevertheless, Habermas's works gradually led to the formation of a theory which was unmistakably motivated by the original objectives of critical theory, and is founded on an insight into the linguistic intersubjectivity of social action. Habermas arrived at this central premise through his concern with hermeneutic philosophy and Wittgenstein's analysis of language, from which he learned that human subjects have always been bound to one another by the medium of reaching understanding through language. This is therefore a fundamental, inescapable prerequisite for the reproduction of social life.

It was via this route that he also arrived at a critique of Marxism, the result of which was a conception of history that had been expanded to include the dimension of a theory of action. If the life-form of the human being is distinguished by the medium of reaching understanding through language, then social reproduction cannot be reduced to the single dimension of labour, as Marx had reduced it in his theoretical writings. Rather, in addition to the activity of dominating nature, the practice of linguistically mediated interaction must be regarded as an equally fundamental dimension of historical development (Habermas, 1968).

However, the decisive step which led to Habermas's own theory of society was not taken until the two action concepts of 'labour' and 'interaction' were associated with different categories of rationality. In the subsystems of purposive-rational action into which the tasks of social labour and political administration are organized, the species evolves through the accumulation of technical and strategic knowledge; while within the institutional framework in which the socially integrating norms are reproduced, the species evolves through liberation from all constraints which inhibit communication (Habermas, 1968). All the extensions to his theory which Habermas undertook in the course of the 1970s follow the lines of this model of society, in which action systems organized according to purposive-rational criteria are distinguished from a sphere of communicative everyday practice. In the *Theory of Communicative Action* (1981) this programme was presented in systematic form for the first time. The fruits of the various studies are here consolidated into a single theory in which the rationality of communicative action is reconstructed in the framework of a theory of the speech act, further developed into the basis for a theory of society by reviewing the history of sociological theory from Max Weber to Talcott Parsons, and finally made into the point of reference for a critical diagnosis of contemporary society. The results of the discussion which this work has provoked will decide the future of critical theory (Honneth and Joas, 1991).

Reading
Arato, A. and Gebhardt, E. eds 1978: *The Essential Frankfurt School Reader.*
Benhabib, Seyla 1986: *Critique, Norm and Utopia.*
Bottomore, Tom 1984: *The Frankfurt School.*
Buck-Morss, S. 1977: *The Origin of Negative Dialectics.*
Held, David 1980: *Introduction to Critical Theory.*
Horkheimer, Max 1968 (*1972*): *Critical Theory.*
Jay, Martin 1973: *The Dialectical Imagination: A History of the Frankfurt School and the Institute of Social Research 1923–50.*
Wellmer, Albrecht 1969 (*1974*): *Critical Theory of Society.*
AXEL HONNETH

freedom   A concept which has been interpreted in diverse ways in very varied social doctrines. An initial distinction may be made between what have been called 'negative' and 'positive' conceptions of individual freedom. In its negative sense freedom

signifies the absence of 'unnecessary or hurtful restraint' (Lewis, 1832, p.154), or more broadly, of 'the deliberate interference of other human beings within the area in which I could otherwise act' (Berlin, 1958, p.122), and from this it follows that freedom is greater where there is less restraint or interference. This is the primary sense in which freedom (above all *vis à vis* governments) was understood by liberal thinkers such as J. S. Mill and Alexis de Tocqueville in the nineteenth century, and by their successors in the twentieth century. All of them recognized, however, that some restrictions, established mainly by law, are necessary in the interests of social cohesion, justice and other values, though they differed greatly in their views of how much restraint is required or is tolerable, and present-day libertarians (such as Hayek, 1973–9) argue strongly for a severe curtailment of restrictive legislation and the activities of government.

The positive sense of freedom was defined by Lewis (pp.151–2) as signifying the possession of 'rights the enjoyment of which is beneficial to the possessor of them', and this formulation has a very modern ring, for recent discussions of positive freedom have frequently invoked the notion of CITIZENSHIP, involving the establishment of a wide range of civil, political and social rights. The growth of freedom is then conceived as a development of citizenship. Underlying such a conception is the view that if freedom is not to be merely an abstract and empty notion, then conditions must exist in which individuals can actually exercise their freedom in order to achieve the maximum degree of self-realization and self-direction of which they are capable.

In relation to these issues there is a further distinction to be made between individual freedom and what may be termed collective freedom. National liberation or independence movements, class movements, women's movements and others aim to secure greater freedom, in a specific sense, for whole categories of people, though this is of course related to the achievement of certain kinds of individual freedom. Such phenomena make evident the fact that freedom in its most universal sense depends on a complex of social institutions which constitute a particular type of social order. Human beings are not 'born free'; they are born into a pre-existing network of social relationships, as subjects of an empire, or members of a tribe or nation, of a caste or class, a gender, a religious community; and the limits of their freedom are conditioned by these circumstances. But they are not wholly determined thereby, for individuals and groups can and do struggle for greater freedom, all the more successfully as human productive powers and the wealth of society increase. In modern societies, and particularly in the twentieth century, there has undoubtedly been, in spite of numerous retrograde movements, a considerable enlargement of freedom as a result of the acquisition of civil, political and social rights on a much broader scale. These gains are the outcome of many collective struggles, for universal suffrage, the economic and social rights of women, liberation from colonial rule and from various forms of political dictatorship.

But it may also be argued that the extension of social rights in particular, in modern democratic welfare states, has been attained at the cost of greatly increased government intervention and regulation, and a growth of bureaucracy, which themselves constitute new limitations on the freedom of the individual. One principal source of such views is Max Weber's exposition of the processes of rationalization and bureaucratization of life in modern industrial societies, which he argued tend to undermine the autonomy and integrity of the individual (see Löwith, 1932; Mommsen, 1974). These are not, however, the only issues which arise in considering how social changes that are intended to promote freedom may, while initially accomplishing their aims in one sphere, create new restrictions in others. Revolutions and radical reforms, conceived as emancipatory, have frequently led to dictatorial regimes, while in democratic societies the danger always exists of that tyranny of the majority which Mill analysed.

More generally, it is evident that the liberty of individuals or groups always involves, or is likely to involve, some limitation of the liberty of others – the most extreme statement of this idea being Jean-Paul Sartre's dictum that 'hell is other people.' Human life is necessarily social, and liberty can best be conceived as a continually changing balance between the competing claims of individuals and groups within an inclusive society, the boundaries of which may also expand as human rights are asserted on a global scale. Hence a conceptual analysis of freedom needs to be undertaken in the framework of broader social theories, where both the negative sense of freedom, concerned with those forces which restrict individuals, in different ways and degrees according to their social position, and its positive sense, of the possibilities for self-realization and self-direction, likewise varying with social circumstances, are critically examined.

Reading
Berlin, Isaiah 1958 (*1969*): Two concepts of liberty. In *Four Essays on Liberty*.
Hayek, F.A. 1973–9 (*1982*): *Law, Legislation and Liberty*.
Mill, J.S. 1859 (*1991*): *On Liberty*. In *On Liberty and Other Essays*.
Ryan, A. ed. 1979: *The Idea of Freedom*.

TOM BOTTOMORE

functionalism This brand of analysis in the social sciences refers to a methodological and theoretical orientation in which the consequences of a given set of empirical phenomena, rather than its causes, are the focus of analytical attention. The term has been applied to a variety of divergent approaches, but the common element they share is a focus on the relations of one part of society to another, and perhaps more frequently to the whole society. Causal and functional analysis are two distinct approaches that need not be in competition with each other.

Functional analysis emerged from the attempt to use in social analysis notions first developed in the biological realm. This mode of methodological reasoning was pioneered by Emile Durkheim in France and by Herbert Spencer in Britain. The Durkheimian strain was further developed by the anthropologists A. R. Radcliffe-Brown and Bronislaw Malinowski in Britain, and by Talcott Parsons, Robert K. Merton and their disciples in the United States. Functionalism dominated American sociology from the war years to the middle of the 1960s but has since been subject to a variety of attacks that led to loss of its former dominance, and it never assumed major importance in Europe.

A few examples will show the nature of this approach. If one wishes to analyse marital patterns in Western society, one may try to account for them through an analysis of, say, Christian ideas of marriage as they developed from the days of Saint Paul to the pronouncements of the current Pope. But one may also raise a different sort of question. For example: why have monogamous marriage systems been dominant in the Western world for a very long time? In this case a satisfying answer must not only focus attention on the history of the modern Western family system but needs, in addition, to account for its persistence over a very long stretch of Western history. This is best addressed by comparing such a family system with other family systems and investigating its consequences for the wider framework of Western society and for specific elements within it.

Systematic search for the social consequences of a given set of phenomena should be distinguished from another 'forward-looking' notion in the social sciences: that of purpose. While the latter refers to conscious motivations of one or more actors, the former is used to investigate consequences of which the actor may not be conscious. Such a distinction was first formulated by Robert K. Merton when he introduced a distinction between manifest and latent (that is unconscious) functions, as in the following examples. All societies have rules of inheritance which determine who is to inherit what. Functional analysis is not interested in the historical development of such rules, but rather turns the focus of inquiry to a consideration of the differential societal impact of different systems of inheritance. It investigates, for example, the salient consequences of systems of primogeniture and of systems that favour an equal partition among sons and daughters; or of systems that provide for succession through the father's line, or the mother's, or the will of the testator. Each one of these different systems of inheritance has strong structural consequences in as far as it leads, for example, to concentration or dispersal of family wealth. The concept of latent function extends attention beyond the question of whether behaviour attains the purpose of the actors, and directs attention to ranges of consequences of behaviour of which the actors are unaware and which they did not anticipate. In particular, behaviours that strike the observer as irrational and senseless may turn out, in the light of functional analysis, to have important consequences. While rain dances are not likely to change the weather, they may well contribute to the raising of the morale of a group that is demoralized by an extended period of drought.

Many social scientists, in particular anthropologists, have focused their major attention on the consequences of a particular social fact for the wider structure in which it is embedded. It would seem, however, that an equally fruitful analytical strategy would be to trace the consequences of a given item for another such item within a larger whole. This perspective suggests, for example, that it is likely to be fruitful to analyse the impact of a depression on the birthrate, or the consequences of drug use for the mobility patterns of a particular minority.

There has been an unfortunate tendency among some functional analysts to assume that any item that contributes to the maintenance of a larger whole is therefore a positive factor. But only those with a conservative bias assume that what exists is necessarily desirable. Such conservative bias can be avoided if it is pointed out that it is possible to focus on alternatives which may have positive functions for a given item and yet are not tied to a set of undesirable consequences. Thus, while magic may give actors a sense of security in an environment that is unpredictable, it is also true that insurance policies may have the same consequences as one moves from a tribal to a modern society. Attention to *alternative functions* prevents analysis being tied to conservative ideology.

Another conservative bias may be introduced into functional analysis if analytical attention is limited to positive functions. Merton distinguishes between functions and dysfunctions. He shows moreover that given items under analysis may have functional or dysfunctional consequences for different parts of a social system. For example, patterns of individual mobility in an industrial society might be strengthened by giving financial assistance to promising lower-class youngsters, allowing them to attend superior high schools or college. But such 'creaming off' of promising lower-class students is likely to deplete the pool of able leaders for a labour party or trade union. When the dysfunction of a particular item becomes obvious, this may encourage reform-minded social scientists and laymen to envisage alternative modes of organization.

As is often the case in the history of science when a new approach, method or theory has been published, those introduced to it seem to feel that it would explain everything under the sun. The early Freudians tended to see sexual symbolism in Zeppelins or Havana cigars, and the early functional analysts believed that everything must necessarily have a function. This simple faith retains few worshippers today. Just as medicine is aware that there are parts of the anatomy, such as the appendix, that have no discernible functions, so most functionalists now know that there are parts of the body social that seem no longer to have a function, or may never have had a function.

Another approach to functional analysis, the notion of functional prerequisites, enjoyed a good deal of attention a decade or two ago but seems since to have been rather neglected. The notion of prerequisites suggests that any social system needs to meet certain indispensable functions if it is to survive. The focus of attention here is on the preconditions and functional prerequisites for a society. This seems a valuable notion. Unfortunately, however, this unobjectionable proposition has often been followed up by the idea that a particular existing item is a functional prerequisite, and this is a highly questionable notion. Not only is attention turned away from the alternative structures, but it is also argued that specific cultural items must be operative if the system is to survive. So, for example, religion has been said to be a functional requirement for the maintenance of solidarity in a society. Such a proposition can only be maintained by arguing either that formally non-religious cultural institutions are actually of a religious character (for instance, that communism is really a religion) or that religion is indeed an indispensable and irreplaceable institution, which has not been shown to be the case. Analysts arguing along these lines have never convincingly established that religion is the irreplaceable cement to glue society together. Moreover, many lists that have been compiled by authors upholding this point of view turn out on inspection to be not much more than lists of items, such as food production and sexual regulation, that are indeed part of society by definition. It seems of limited value to insist that people must indeed have something to eat if the society is to survive.

Functional analysis is at present very much on the defensive in the United States and also in Europe. Yet it is also a fact that much sociological writing continues to use functional logic and reasoning but without doing so explicitly. Molière's character M. Jourdain did not know that he had always been talking prose, and many members of the sociological guild do not know, or do not want their readers to know, that they are really using functional analysis.

Only the future will show whether functional analysis is indeed a requisite of a sophisticated sociology.

See also STRUCTURALISM; TELEOLOGY.

Reading
Davis, Kingsley 1949: *Human Society*.
Demerath, N.J. and Peterson, R.A. eds 1967: *System, Change and Conflict*.
Durkheim, E. 1895 (*1938*): *The Rules of Sociological Method*.
Giddens, A. 1977: Functionalism: après la lutte. In *Studies in Social and Political Theory*.
Kluckhohn, Clyde 1944: *Navaho Witchcraft*.
Malinowski, B. 1944: The functional theory. In *A Scientific Theory of Culture and other Essays*.
Merton, Robert K. 1949 (*1968*): *Social Theory and Social Structure*, enlarged edn.
Parsons, Talcott 1951: *The Social System*.
Radcliffe-Brown, A.R. 1952: On the concept of function in social science. In *Structure and Function in Primitive Society*.
Stinchcombe, Arthur 1968: *Constructing Social Theories*.

LEWIS A. COSER

fundamentalism Beginning its life with reference to a variety of conservative Protestantism, more particularly in the United States, the term in its contemporary use is loosely extended to include varieties of conservative Islam and conservative Judaism, and ought to include the kind of militant and dogmatic Catholicism found in the Opus Dei movement.

Christian fundamentalism had originally to do with specifically designated fundamentals of belief, which included the inerrancy of the Bible as well as the Virgin Birth and the Atonement. As a movement fundamentalism represents one major response to liberal Protestantism. Liberal Protestants accepted a higher critical approach to the Bible and adopted a flexible hermeneutic, with all that implies with respect to modernization and relativization. From the liberal viewpoint, Christianity had ceased to be a unique and final revelation delivered to mankind in the Bible, but was rather an evolving awareness of the divine existing alongside other spiritual resources generated by other faiths. Liberalism in this mode was necessarily on the move, usually in a direction further away from orthodoxy, whereas fundamentalism saw itself as standing by 'the faith once-for-all delivered to the saints'.

Typically fundamentalists held to the literal truth and precise historicity of the Bible, and to the Mosaic authorship of the Pentateuch as somehow bound up in literalism. They rejected Darwin along with modern scientific accounts of the origins of the cosmos and the usual understandings of the fossil record. Much of English Protestantism, even of a conservative kind, absorbed evolution and modern cosmology, even though there were some intellectual tragedies, for example the distinguished marine biologist Philip Gosse, who had to circumvent his own evidence. But in the United States there developed a closer interpenetration, especially in the South, of moral conservatism, fundamentalism and cultural defence. Perhaps this was in part because there is more room in the United States for the creation of networks of institutions outside the educational heartlands controlled by the liberal intelligentsia (and their allies in the liberal clergy). So though the fundamentalist cause was set back in 1925 by the adverse publicity attending the trial of John Scopes for illegally teaching evolution, it managed to reinforce its institutional defences and has reemerged a generation or so later in alliance with several varieties of moral, theological, cultural and political conservatism. In some areas fundamentalists acquired enough clout to ensure that 'creationism' was taught in schools alongside other accounts. (Creationism is itself very varied, ranging from the standard view of God as Creator to a periodization based on the Book of Genesis to a strict adherence to the narratives in Genesis 1 and 2). It is worth emphasizing that the public profile and internal cohesiveness of fundamentalism has been strengthened by religious television and radio, and by 'Christian' schools which help create an all-encompassing 'plausibility structure'. Such clout as fundamentalists achieved through participation in the Moral Majority involved novel alliances with conservatives of other faiths.

Many commentators see fundamentalism just as a reaction and as a case of what Steve Bruce has called 'cultural short trousers' (1990). However, this view is too biased towards the liberal understanding of the matter. Religious conservatives may be engaged in a form of cultural defence but they exist easily in the commercial and technical world without their neighbours noting any marked oddity or backwardness. In any case, the main conservative denomination, the Southern Baptists, is expanding where most liberal denominations are contracting, and Pentecostalism is part of a world-wide movement making astonishing progress in Latin America (compare, here, LIBERATION THEO-LOGY), the Caribbean, parts of Africa, South Korea, and the Pacific rim. It is interesting that Pentecostalism is only incidentally fundamentalist rather than taking off from the fundamentalist premise. Pentecostals treat the Bible in a conservative manner, but their *raison d'être* turns on the gifts of the Spirit, and on healing and exorcism.

Fundamentalism in Europe also seems only incidental, whether it is part of Pentecostalism or older forms of pietism, evangelicalism and reviva-lism. That is to say there are layers of religious conservatism in, for instance, western Norway, north-east Holland, northern Jutland, northern Scotland, Northern Ireland, which do not place fundamentalism in the front line of their cultural defence. An intellectual centre with international ramifications exists at the Free University of Amsterdam; and there are minor political parties in much of northern Europe devoted to traditional religious MORALITY. Parallel movements of religious conservatism have arisen of recent years inside most of the established churches, and some of these are charismatic in emphasis. But again, their conservatism is more linked to devotional attitude and moral discipline than to strictly fundamentalist views of the Bible.

Clearly, Christian fundamentalism is just one element in a massive shift towards conservative and evangelical versions of the faith. It runs parallel to a comparable shift in the Islamic world, more particularly among Shi'ites. In one sense ISLAM is inherently fundamentalist given the emphasis on the perfect Word of God finally embodied in the Qur'an. Alongside this, as one of the 'fundamentals' of Islam, is the promotion of Islam and Islamic law as a complete way of life encompassing the state wherever power and numbers allow. The theocratic ambitions of Islam are in sharp contrast to the modest pressure group activity of conservative Protestants. In contemporary usage, a 'fundamentalist' Muslim is either linked to one of the conservative movements or else simply characterized by militancy and fanaticism. Certainly this kind of militancy is part of a reaction to the freeing of many Christian societies from Muslim (mainly Ottoman) colonialism and the advance of Western culture and colonialism, including in that advance secularity and pluralism, into the Islamic world.

Reading
Bruce, Steve 1990: *A House Divided: Protestantism, Schism and Secularization*.
Marsden, George 1982: *Fundamentalism and American culture: The Shaping of Twentieth-century Evangelicalism, 1870–1925*.
Martin, David A. 1990: *Tongues of Fire: The Explosion of Conservative Protestantism in Latin America*.

DAVID A. MARTIN

futurology   Early in the twentieth century it was apparent that rapid change in human capabilities and ways of life was likely to continue. A number of influential commentators urged that efforts be made to systematize our thinking about the future. Notably H.G. Wells, who had used science fiction as much to provoke questions about social prospects as to provide a platform for exposition of popular science, called for the establishment of a new academic discipline with these efforts at its core.

These calls met with little immediate response, and much of the speculation about the future in the first decades of the century can now be seen as rehearsing World War I, and as being aimed at alerting leaders and populations to the supposed threat posed by other world powers. The period between the two world wars did witness important developments, such as a series of books published by Kegan Paul in the UK, which invited well-known intellectuals to speculate about the future. In the United States, William F. Ogburn's reports on social trends and their consequences laid much of the foundation for later work on trend extrapolation, social indicators and technology assessment – all associated with more recent studies of the future. But it was not until the 1960s that a concerted body of work began to appear.

Much of this work derived from the studies undertaken in a number of US 'think tanks'. Almost as soon as World War II had concluded, the US army established a series of long-range technological forecasts, which led to multidisciplinary organizations like the RAND Corporation becoming centres where academics could share ideas with members of the military-industrial complex. Efforts at assessing military and geopolitical contingencies led to the development of a number of influential approaches to forecasting – such as the Delphi method and cross-impact analysis, more sophisticated methods of trend extrapolation, group brainstorming, and scenario analysis. (Probably the only substantial addition, since the 1960s, to this armoury of methods is computer simulation.) These approaches were found to be useful to large corporations and, indeed, a wide range of other bodies concerned with the uncertain future environments in which they might be operating. They were also popularized through widely read books by the controversial Herman Kahn and other researchers. More academic echoes were to be found in the work of Daniel Bell and other writers on POSTINDUSTRIAL SOCIETY. (Indeed, scanning the future through futurological methods, and applying planning tools such as systems analysis, was seen as being one of the ways in which postindus-

trial societies would guide their own progress and avoid the economic and political crises of earlier social formations.)

In Europe this period was similarly marked by efforts to consolidate thinking about the future, with a number of new bodies being founded and major reports being prepared. In contrast to the mainstream US work, the European 'futures movement' was rather more questioning about the form that the future might take – for example, European writers on postindustrial society tended to be far less confident as to the absence of socioeconomic conflict and the end of ideology. The term 'futurology' itself was introduced by Ossip Flechtheim, a German researcher who was concerned with creating visions of a future other than those represented by American capitalism and Soviet socialism. Ironically, the futurological studies emanating from the former Soviet Union are in many respects mirror images of those of the 1960s US, sharing their social and technological optimism, but with superpowers' roles as progressive and reactionary forces being reversed. East European studies, by contrast, tended to be more guardedly critical.

The term 'futurology' was widely used to describe the pioneering efforts to think systematically about the long-term future, and it is the term that has entered the public consciousness. Other terms are 'futures studies' and 'futures research', and in the French traditions 'futuribles' and 'prospective studies' are often used, while the German literature often refers to 'prognostics'. The term 'futurology', despite being the best known of the contenders to the general public, is often rejected by those working in this field. It is seen as making spurious claims to scientific understanding of the future – terms like 'futures studies' in contrast give more of a sense of there being alternative futures, of matters not being already cut and dried and merely awaiting discovery by rational or technical means, of a field that is open to non-scientists. Perhaps, too, futurology is seen as being too closely associated with the 1960s American researchers who established the field. It is noteworthy that the two main professional bodies in the field – the World Futures Society and the World Futures Studies Federation – do not use the term 'futurology'; the main journals are *Futures*, *Futures Research Quarterly* and *Futuribles*, together with the more popular *The Futurist*.

Whatever label is applied to them, however, a distinction is commonly drawn between such approaches and more conventional forecasting. Forecasting is seen as typically being short term, concerned with the extrapolation of trends and other 'surprise-free' developments, as trying to predict or plan some feature of the future. Perhaps most importantly, it is seen as being limited to looking at specific and narrow aspects of economic, environmental, social or technological development. One of the key elements of futures studies, in contrast, is held to be their effort to provide more holistic appraisals, bringing together knowledge about developments of very different kinds and considering their interaction. Thus scenario analysis, the depiction of alternative futures in terms of a large number of characteristics, is one of the main tools of the trade.

A wave of enthusiasm for futurology in the 1960s and early 1970s, during which time many research groups and associations were established, receded somewhat during the subsequent decades. The futures field became one in which opposing viewpoints argued with increasing sophistication, but little sign of resolution, about topics such as global environmental degradation and the liberatory or oppressive implications of new technologies. The importance of taking long-term views, and of relating together dimensions of change (see also SOCIAL CHANGE) that tend to be compartmentalized away from each other in the traditional academic and policy-making specialisms, has not diminished, however. As the millennium approaches, new interest in futures research – sometimes dubbed 'Twenty First Century studies', is apparent.

Reading

Coates, J.F. and Jarrat, J. eds 1992: *The Future: Trends into the Twenty-First Century*. Special issue of *Annals of the American Academy of Political and Social Science* 552, July.
Fowles, J. ed. 1978: *Handbook of Futures Research*.

IAN D. MILES

G

game theory A game is being played by a group of individuals whenever the fate of an individual in the group depends not only on his own actions, but also on the actions of the rest of the individuals in the group. Chess is the archetypical example. Whether White wins, loses or draws depends not only on the moves made by White, but also on the moves made by Black. Bridge and Poker are further examples which have the added interest that lack of relevant information complicates the player's decision problems.

The word 'game' is natural for the examples given above. But, for really interesting games, it would not be usual to use the word 'game' in ordinary English. Consider, for example, war, international treaty negotiations, competition for survival among animals or for status among humans, elections, wage bargaining or the operation of market economies. All these activities fall within our definition of a 'game'. The usage is not meant to imply that wars are fun or that economics is entertaining. It simply reflects the discovery made by John Von Neumann and Oskar Morgenstern in their monumental book *The Theory of Games and Economic Behavior* (1944) that both parlour games and real-life games raise similar problems and that an analysis which works for the former may therefore well be relevant to the latter.

This is not to argue that parlour games and real-life games are similar in every respect. The analogy noted by Von Neumann and Morgenstern between real-life games and parlour games lies solely in their strategic aspects. A person cast in the role of a player in a real-life game would be wise to consider reducing the problem with which he or she is faced to its essentials by discarding all detail that is not immediately relevant. Such detail is at best a distraction, and at worst may so obscure matters that no progress can be made at all. Once all irrelevant detail has been stripped away, the player will be left with an abstract decision problem. Von Neumann and Morgenstern's observation is that the basic structure of such decision problems is the same regardless of whether they are derived from parlour games or from real-life games.

The appearance of Von Neumann and Morgenstern's book raised great hopes that were only to be realized considerably later. The book introduced two approaches to the subject: a *non-cooperative approach* and a *cooperative approach*. The most successful and satisfying approach is the former since it seeks to deduce its conclusions from the theory of rational decision-making by individuals acting in isolation. However, Von Neumann and Morgenstern's non-cooperative analysis extended only to two-person, zero–sum games in which, whatever one player wins, the other loses. Their *minimax* theory for such games is justly celebrated. However, few real-life games are zero–sum. Their cooperative approach was concerned with the formation of *coalitions*. They formulated plausible 'axioms' about the coalitional structures that could survive the rational scrutiny of self-interested players and explored their consequences.

Although the cooperative approach is less satisfactory, it held the floor until comparatively recently since progress with non-cooperative theory proved to be difficult. However, over the last 15 years, great advances have been made in non-cooperative theory. These build on the idea of a *Nash equilibrium* introduced by Nash (1951). The strategies used by players constitute a Nash equilibrium when each player's strategy is an optimal response to the strategies of the other players.

These advances have revolutionized economic theory (see ECONOMICS). Great strides have been made in the theory of imperfect competition (Tirole, 1988), bargaining theory (Binmore and Dasgupta, 1987) and in the economics of information (Rasmusen, 1989). Progress has also been made in evolutionary biology (Maynard Smith, 1984). Elsewhere in the social sciences, the influence of new ideas in game theory has been more tangential. However, the study of how cooperation may arise among self-interested individuals has been a theme that has been of continuing interest (Axelrod, 1984). It is now hard to contemplate this issue at all without recourse to the theory of repeated games.

See also DECISION THEORY; RATIONAL CHOICE THEORY.

Reading
Aumann, R.J. ed. 1992: *The Handbook of Game Theory*.
Binmore, K. 1990: *Essays on the Foundations of Game Theory*.

KEN BINMORE

gender   As the social aspect of the relations between the sexes, gender is a concept which is distinguished from the biological one of sex. The question of whether and to what extent biological aspects of the sexes are pertinent to the understanding of gender is popularly contentious, but within the social sciences the question is widely regarded as settled – social organization is considered to be the overwhelmingly important factor.

Gender is constructed and expressed in many areas of social life. It includes, but is not confined to, culture, ideology and discursive practices. The gender division of labour in the home and in waged labour, the organization of the state, sexuality, the structuring of violence, and many other aspects of social organization contribute to the construction of gender relations. Social theories vary in their accounts as to the relative importance accorded to various social institutions in the construction of gender relations.

Gender relations take different forms in different societies, historical periods, ethnic groups, social classes and generations. Nevertheless, they have in common a differentiation between men and women, despite the immense social variability of the nature of the difference. A very common feature is that gender difference is combined with gender inequality, with men having power over women – some suggest universally so, others nearly universally so.

A related term is that of PATRIARCHY, which conceptualized gender inequality as socially structured.

Theories of gender
Three main perspectives on gender are often identified within social thought, though there are many more, especially if subcategories and partial syntheses between perspectives of FEMINISM are included. The traditional three are radical femi-

nism, socialist feminism and liberalism. Additional categories include conservatism (for instance, sociobiology), black womanist thought, postmodernism, dual systems theory, ecofeminism and materialist feminism. Some split the socialist feminist category, separating more orthodox Marxist currents from those which take more from radical feminism, as in a division between Marxism and socialist feminism. Some perspectives within social thought, of course, have an absence in the area of gender.

The following provides a summary of some of the main theoretical divergences. However, it should be noted that by its nature this overview is schematic and many individual texts defy such simple categorization.

Radical feminism   Radical feminist analysis suggests that gender differentiation is primarily a matter of gender inequality, with the male being the dominant gender. The chief beneficiary of the oppression of women is seen to be men. The subordination of women is seen as autonomous from other forms of social inequality.

While all aspects of women's lives are seen as affected by male dominance, radical feminists have more often analysed the issues of male violence towards women, men's abuse of women's sexuality, and issues around reproduction.

This perspective is often criticized for not taking other forms of social inequality sufficiently into account, but this flaw is a contingent rather than necessary feature of this type of analysis and some radical feminists have been sensitive to this issue. Another common criticism is that it has a tendency to biological reductionism. Again, while this is a feature of some thinkers, it is not a universal feature of this school of thought.

Socialist feminism   Socialist feminist analysis also focuses on gender inequality as an important feature of gender differentiation. However, gender inequality is seen not to be an autonomous system of social relations but intimately bound up with class relations. This means that capital as well as men – and sometimes to the exclusion of men – is seen as the beneficiary of the subordination of women.

Socialist feminists have often concentrated on different aspects of women's subordination than radical feminists. In particular they have developed analyses of labour, both waged labour and DOMES-

TIC LABOUR, though issues of culture and sexuality have also been addressed (the latter often in combination with psychoanalysis).

The debate between socialist feminism and radical feminism has often focused on the relative importance of men as active agents in women's oppression, the radical feminists considering that the socialist feminists underestimate this. There is also disagreement over the relative significance of different sites of gender inequality.

Liberalism   In comparison with the first two perspectives, liberal views on gender are often less structural. Analyses within this perspective tend to involve smaller scale phenomena and tend not to be integrated within a macro theory of gender relations. Topics covered here more often include issues such as education and representation in the formal political arenas, such as parliaments. Criticisms of this approach focus on the lack of systematic consideration of the interrelatedness of aspects of gender relations.

Structures

Patriarchy may be considered to be constituted by the following six structures:

Household   The family household is the institution which has most often been analysed for its role in producing both gender differentiation and gender inequality. However, the very considerable variation in household form between different cultures and times makes generalization hazardous. Functionalist analysis traditionally held that the family was a site of role differentiation – rather than inequality – between men and women. Much feminist analysis has argued that, on the contrary, women are subordinated to men in the family and that this is central for other aspects of their oppression (Barrett, 1980). The expropriation of women's household labour is a central feature of the theories of many socialist feminists and materialist feminists, such as Delphy (1984). This inequality in time expended on domestic labour has been confirmed by time budget analysis (Gershuny, 1983). However, the model of the family as composed of a husband/breadwinner and fulltime housewife plus children is an unusual phenomenon today. This is partly because it is ethnically specific; for instance, this form has rarely been found among people of African descent. Indeed, this ethnic variation is central to the analysis of some black feminists such

as hooks (1984), who argue that much feminist theory has illegitimately generalized from the experiences of white women to all women. The 'traditional' family household form is also uncommon among white families today partly because of the rise in the proportion of married women in paid employment in the postwar period and the increase in single parent households. Nevertheless, the entry of women into waged labour does not typically produce an egalitarian domestic division of labour. The increase in female headed households is partly a result of the rising DIVORCE rate, and partly a result of the rise in childbirth out of wedlock. However, this latter tendency has been accompanied by an increase in the proportion of unmarried and cohabiting couples (See MARRIAGE).

Employment   Women's employment differs from men's in two main respects. Firstly, women typically get paid less than men (about three-quarters of men's hourly rates in Britain). Secondly, women in many societies are less involved in paid work than men, and more involved in unpaid housework.

A major division in the explanations for these differences and inequalities is between, on the one hand, those who emphasize the importance of a woman's domestic commitments in reducing her ability to participate effectively in waged work, and, on the other, those who emphasize discriminatory structures within the labour market and the state.

Social theorists who are closer to Marxism have tended to stress the role of capital and the family in women's subordination in the labour market (Beechey, 1977). Mainstream economists have also tended to focus on the significance of women's domestic circumstances but, unlike the Marxists, they articulate this as a result of a free and rational choice by the women to engage in domestic work.

The emphasis on the discriminatory structures of the labour market and the state has typically come from dual systems theorists and liberal feminists. Dual systems writers combine a radical feminist analysis of men's active attempts to subordinate women with a socialist analysis of capital. Here the structuring of the labour market represented in occupational segregation by sex is seen as the outcome of a struggle between capital, organized male workers and women (Hartmann, 1979). Liberal feminists typically focus on the problems of a masculinist workplace culture and the difficulties of obtaining equal rights.

Sexuality The significance of sexuality for gender relations has been the subject of much debate. Some radical feminists see sexuality as the most important terrain of men's domination of women. Women are sometimes violently sexually abused by men, and at other times co-opted into patriarchal projects through particular constructions of heterosexuality. On the one hand, men rape and represent women pornographically as objects for men's desire, and on the other the ideology of romantic love seduces women into what is effectively compulsory heterosexuality. Sexuality is seen as a place where men force or manipulate women into close relations with men. Lesbianism is often seen as a desirable alternative.

Psychoanalysis has provided the concepts some Marxist feminists wanted to assist an analysis of sexuality. They have tried to shed the sexist parts of Freud's analysis and utilize core concepts, such as that of the unconscious (Mitchell, 1975). Sexuality is seen as closely bound up with gender identity and to be crucially shaped by early childhood experiences. Others have used a critique of Freud as a basis of radically different accounts of women's particular sexuality (Irigaray, 1985).

The concepts Foucault (1976) introduces are another route by which social theorists have tried to provide an account of sexuality. Sexuality is again seen as socially constructed, this time as a discourse.

Violence The awareness of the extent and significance of male violence to women is one of the products of the recent feminist wave. Radical feminists have analysed this violence as a form of social control over women. They have typically pointed up the significance and increasing incidence of such acts. Socialist feminists have had much less to say about such violence. Liberal analysis has pointed to the failings of the state in 'protecting' women and addressed questions as to how to reform this.

Culture Culture has traditionally been seen as of key significance in the construction of gender differences. Socialization theory has been very popular in its accounts of how boys and girls are treated differently from an early age and consequently grow up with different social-psychological characteristics. Education has been seen as an important part of this process, drawing boys and girls into different activities and achievements.

More recent analysis of gender and culture has drawn heavily on literary theory, with the deconstructionism of Derrida (1967) (see DECONSTRUCTION), and also on the DISCOURSE analysis of Michel Foucault. The emphasis has shifted from the individual's learning experience to the creation of the texts or representations or discourses which construct our notions of gender (Weedon, 1987). This work often speaks of difference, both between women and men, but also between women. Indeed some of the emphasis on differences between women has problematized the very concept of 'woman' as a unitary category.

State The state has usually been analysed as contributing to gender differentiation and gender inequality. For instance, radical feminists have analysed the lack of intervention of the state when men commit criminal acts of violence against women (Hanmer and Saunders, 1984), while socialist feminists have examined the way the welfare state reproduces the traditional form of family household (McIntosh, 1978).

Women have often tried to change their position in the world and we have had a number of waves of feminist activity. The two about which we know the most are 1850–1918 and the current one starting in the late 1960s in the USA and a little later in Britain (see WOMEN'S MOVEMENT). There is no monolithic movement, but rather a multiplicity of different feminist strategies and a corresponding complexity in the anti-feminist gendered responses. For instance, sometimes feminists have argued that the best way forward for women is to argue for the same rights and privileges and to be treated in the same way as men, while others have argued that women should demand special attention to the specifics of their situation, should recognize rather than deny difference.

Reading

Cockburn, C. 1983: *Brothers*.
Eisenstein, H. 1984: *Contemporary Feminist Thought*.
hooks, b. 1984: *Feminist Theory: From Margin to Center*.
Jaggar, A. and Rothenberg, P.S. eds 1978 (*1984*): *Feminist Frameworks*, 2nd edn.
Kelly, L. 1988: *Surviving Sexual Violence*.
Oakley, A. 1985: *Subject Woman*.
Spender, D. 1983: *Women of Ideas*.
Stanworth, M. ed. 1986: *Reproductive Technologies*.
Walby, S. 1990: *Theorizing Patriarchy*.
Weedon, C. 1987: *Feminist Practice and Poststructuralist Theory*.

SYLVIA WALBY

genocide   The concept was coined by Raphael Lemkin (1944) to refer to a principal objective of German population policy in World War II: to annihilate completely the Jews – the principal target entrapped throughout the German domain – and Gypsies, and to decimate and reduce selectively some Slavic nations. Although genocide has occurred throughout history, it has come to contemporary attention because of (a) its calculated and repeated use in the twentieth century and its justification by totalitarian ideologies; (b) the rationalization of its usage; and (c) the growth and specification of human rights norms.

The crime of genocide was a specification of crimes against humanity – an international crime under the Hague convention of 1907 – which was one of the charges against Nazi leaders at the International Military Tribunal at Nuremburg in 1946. Genocide and conspiracy to commit genocide are now a crime in international law in times of peace or war, in domestic or interstate practice, under the UN Convention on the Prevention and Punishment of the Crime of Genocide (UNGC), which came into force in 1951. Yet no genocides have been prosecuted under the UNGC despite the citation of over 18 cases by scholars, lawyers and human rights organizations (see Fein, 1990; Harff and Gurr, 1990). The failure of the United Nations and individual states to prosecute genocide has been related to: (a) structural faults in the UN; (b) the juridical paradox of the convention; and (c) the many political uses states have found for genocide in the twentieth century. As one observer has written in relation to (a) and (c): 'the sovereign territorial state claims, as an integral part of its sovereignty, the right to commit genocide, or engage in genocidal massacres, against peoples under its rule, and . . . the United Nations, for all practical purposes, defends this right' (Kuper, 1981, p.161). The UN has never established an international criminal court, and imposing sanctions depends on consensus among the great powers. Thus – and this is an example of (b) – although there is the theoretical possibility of such a court, the UNGC relies principally on state signatories to prosecute genocide despite the fact the state is most frequently the perpetrator of genocide.

The study of specific genocides – principally the 'Final Solution of the Jewish Question' of 1939–45 (see ANTI-SEMITISM) and the Armenian genocide of 1915 – together with the comparative study of genocides, which began in the 1970s, grew exponentially in the 1980s. Disagreement exists among scholars about the definition and best methods of explanation and analysis. Definitional disagreements focus on the usefulness and justification of the UNGC definition of genocide, especially the notion of intent and the inclusiveness of victim groups stipulated. According to the UNGC, genocide is 'any of the following acts [starting with killing group members] committed with intent to destroy, in whole or in part, a national, ethnical, racial or religious group as such'.

Many scholars today use the term genocide to refer to the deliberate annihilation of any group, including political (and non-violent) groups and social classes. A new definition is intended to parallel the terms of the UNGC definition: 'Genocide is sustained purposeful action by a perpetrator to destroy a collectivity directly or indirectly, through interdiction of the biological and social reproduction of group members, sustained regardless of the surrender or lack of threat offered by the victims' (Fein, 1990).

Explanations of genocide invoke several kinds of analysis: historical, structural and social-psychological. Genocide is viewed by Chalk and Jonassohn (1990) as first arising from the practice of empires seeking (a) to eliminate a real or potential threat; (b) to spread terror among real or potential enemies; and (c) to acquire economic wealth. Synthesizing their formulation and the typologies of others, we may distinguish four types: retributive; despotic; developmental; ideological.

Both structural and social-psychological theorists generally agree that a necessary but not sufficient precondition for victimization is the pre-existing 'definition of the victim as outside the universe of obligation' (Fein, 1979, ch. 1): an alien or stranger, an enemy or outsider, a pariah group or national community identified as foreign with no protective foreign nation-state to support them, and indigenous peoples who have never been conceived of as part of the polity. Structuralists focus on the interaction of preceding conditions which make genocide a likely outcome. These include crises of state decline and of legitimacy, the coming to power of revolutionary and totalitarian regimes, the implications of exclusive nationalist, fascist and communist ideologies, the competition for power between groups in new states, and the opening of new lands for development or plunder. Lastly, there are often common facilitating or enabling conditions: wars which render the victims less visible and make it unlikely, if not impossible, that other states will try to protect them; and the support of major world and regional powers for the perpetrators. Fein conceives the calculation of genocide as a rational choice (after taking all preconditions into account), viewing the precipitating factor as the change in the anticipated costs and benefits of genocide: this stems from 'a crisis or opportunity perceived to be caused by or impeded by the victim' (Fein, 1990).

Social-psychological theories focus on the inner states and motives of the perpetrators which interact with external events to lead them to blame victim groups for their problems, to follow authoritarian leaders, and to kill without shame and guilt (for a multilevel analysis, see Staub, 1989).

Genocide has been most prevalent in the postwar world in new states, especially states with communist or authoritarian governments. Before 1950, most twentieth-century perpetrators were totalitarian states, including major European powers: principally Nazi Germany and the USSR. One may relate recent patterns of genocide both to the range of options for multi-ethnic states to restructure their societies – expulsion and elimination are a radical way to avoid the resolution of conflict – and the increased use of repression and terror as means of social control among states in Asia, Africa and Central and Latin America.

Two recurrent interests unite many social scientists concerned with genocide: the acknowledgement of past genocides, and the prevention of future ones. In recent years, social scientists have begun to consider how to measure and monitor indicators of gross violations of human rights (including political killings and patterns of discrimination which may preface genocide), to propose 'early warning systems' and to assess the states and 'minorities at risk' (Gurr and Scarritt, 1989). See also EUGENICS.

Reading

Chalk, F. and Jonassohn, K. 1990: *The History and Sociology of Genocide*.

Charny, I. W. ed. 1988: *Genocide: A Critical Bibliographic Review*.

Fein, H. 1979: *Accounting for Genocide*.

——1990: Genocide: a sociological perspective. *Current Sociology* 38. 1.

Gurr, T. and Scarritt, J. 1989: Minorities at risk: a global survey. *Human Rights Quarterly* 11. 3, 375–405.

Harff, B. and Gurr, T. 1990: Victims of the state:

genocides, politicides and group repression since 1945. *International Review of Victimology* 1, 1–19.

Kuper, Leo 1981: *Genocide: Its Political Use in the Twentieth Century*.

Lemkin, R. 1944: *Axis Rule in Occupied Europe*.

Staub, E. 1989: *The Roots of Evil*.

HELEN FEIN

geography, human   *See* HUMAN GEOGRAPHY

gestalt psychology   The gestalt movement in psychology originated in Germany in the early part of the century. Gestalt psychologists argued that the psychological whole is greater than the sum of its parts: psychologists should analyse experience in terms of whole patterns of stimuli, or gestalts, rather than seek to break them down into component parts. Although many of their ideas were disputed by behaviourists, they have now been integrated into modern cognitive science.

The three major figures in the gestalt movement were Max Wertheimer (1880–1943), Kurt Koffka (1884–1941) and Wolfgang Köhler (1887–1967). Köhler explained the basic theoretical term of 'gestalt': 'beside the connotation of shape or form as an attribute of things, it has the meaning of a concrete entity *per se*, which has, or may have, a shape as one of its characteristics' (Köhler, 1947, p. 104). Gestalt theory suggested that the perceptual system registers the whole shapes of objects rather than their elements. Gestaltists often illustrated this principle with the example of music. It is possible to recognize a melody, even if played in an unfamiliar key. The separate notes cannot be recognized, for they have not been heard before. Therefore, it is the overall pattern, or gestalt, which is recognized.

The gestaltists set themselves the task of formulating the 'laws of perception', by which stimulus arrays are spontaneously grouped into meaningful patterns. These laws included principles such as 'closure and good gestalt', by which missing parts of a stimulus array are automatically 'filled in' by the perceiver. The gestaltists argued that such laws of perception are not learnt, and in this respect their ideas conflicted with the tenets of BEHAVIOURISM.

Gestalt theories of learning also differed from those of behaviourists. Gestaltists emphasized the role of insight, suggesting that problems are solved when grasped in their totality. Köhler illustrated these notions in his classic studies of apes. Bananas were placed just out of reach, but the apes would suddenly grasp the problem, or see the total gestalt; then they would use sticks to reach the distant objects (Köhler, 1925).

Although the basic notions of gestalt psychology were formulated in Germany, the three major gestaltists were to end their careers in the United States. Wertheimer and Koffka, as Jews, fled from Nazi Germany. Köhler was one of the very few non-Jewish German psychologists to oppose Nazism publicly. In 1935 he resigned his post at the Psychological Institute of Berlin University and left for America.

Gestaltist ideas have had a direct effect on the development of SOCIAL PSYCHOLOGY. Ideas about the structure of attitudes and the influence of attitudes on perception became influential in the psychological study of PREJUDICE and group dynamics. In recent years gestalt notions have been taken up by cognitive scientists. There is an affinity between the ideas of gestaltists and those of David Marr (1945–1980), who analysed how perceivers sort stimulus arrays into 'primary sketches' (Marr, 1982). There is a linguistic connection between gestalt psychology and a form of therapy, known as 'gestalt therapy'. However, the loosely defined concepts of gestalt therapy, with their anti-scientific themes, bear little relation to the ideas of gestalt psychology (Henle, 1986).

See also PSYCHOLOGY.

Reading
Ellis, W.D. ed. 1938: *A Sourcebook of Gestalt Psychology.*
Koffka, K. 1935: *Principles of Gestalt Psychology.*
Köhler, W. 1967: *The Task of Gestalt Psychology.*

MICHAEL BILLIG

globalization   This is the process whereby the population of the world is increasingly bonded into a single society. The term only came into wide use in the 1980s. The changes it refers to are highly charged politically and the concept is controversial because it suggests that the creation of world society is no longer the project of a hegemonic nation-state but the undirected outcome of social interaction on a global scale. In this way it brings the themes of POSTINDUSTRIAL SOCIETY and DEVELOPMENT AND UNDERDEVELOPMENT into the same discussion frame. The term has established itself in fields as diverse as economics, geography, marketing and sociology, which suggests that its use is more than a matter of passing fashion.

Critics of the concept point to the fact that the ideas of human beings belonging to one species, inhabiting a single world, or sharing universal principles are not new. Thousands of years of contact have been recorded between the great empires of history and an economic system involving most of the world's population can be traced back several hundred years. While accepting those facts proponents of the concept assert that a qualitative change has taken place in the last 30 years of world history. Universalism in social thought, INTERNATIONALISM in political thought, world commerce, imperialism, world wars are to be seen as preliminaries to a process which is more comprehensive and penetrating.

Use of the term 'global' is an indicator of the change which has taken place. In the 1960s this came to be used to mean 'belonging to the world' or 'worldwide'. Fowler's 1965 *Dictionary of Modern English Usage* considered it an unnecessary neologism, suggesting 'mondial' as an alternative. But Webster's, the Oxford English and Larousse French dictionaries all accepted it by the early 1970s. The Oxford dictionary cited its most famous use by Marshall McLuhan (1962) in his catchphrase 'the global village'. McLuhan's ingenuity was to capture a property of modern culture, namely the possibility of global communication, and to suggest that the instantaneous reception of far-off sights and voices changed the content of culture. His thought presaged a new focus on worldwide communication as a factor transforming local life of equal significance to the impact of capitalist markets. The Marxist theory of the development of capitalism as developed by Immanuel Wallerstein (1974) in his WORLD-SYSTEM theory had as its key image a centre or core extending its power over and linking peripheral regions. The image of influence in the idea of global culture resembles much more the picture of fall-out from an explosion. It gives extra impetus to those who see culture as an independent factor in the creation of one world (Robertson, 1990).

Culture and market combined in the 1970s in the activities of multinational corporations seeking to maximize the worldwide sales of products through global advertising. Perhaps most famously Coca-Cola offered the image of an assembly of people of all nations and colours singing of 'perfect harmony'. 'Globalization' became known as a marketing strategy soon after, although it remains contested just how far a global strategy allows for cultural difference. At the level of the corporation, the multinational, with its centre (usually in the United States) and its affiliates worldwide, gives way to the transnational, in which expatriates from many countries pursue the activities of the single corporation worldwide.

For economists, globalization has been associated with the dismantling of national barriers to the operation of capital markets which began in the early 1980s. This has resulted in simultaneous dealing in the main markets of New York, London, Tokyo and Frankfurt such that the movements of the markets are clearly outside the scope for control by any one national agency. The future of the capitalist system is no longer to be seen as linked to the fate of a particular modernizing nation, the United States. This suggests a qualitative change from a process seen variously as MODERNIZATION or imperialism towards an encompassing transformation in which new agents for global social change are potentially active in any part of the world. The Far East countries, Islam or Europe may take the centre of the stage at any one time, producing repercussions for lives in areas of the world far remote from them.

Ultimately it is the transformative effects of globalization on the lives of individuals and their relations with each other which are the test of the utility of the concept. They in turn are related directly to the arguments about postmodernity and the possibility of making sense of the idea of postmodern culture. One of the frequently noted aspects of postmodernism has been the juxtaposition of fragments from various ethnic and historical sources within one and the same cultural frame, whether in architecture, music, dress, or food, but it is still disputed whether this kind of cultural collage is to be seen as reaction against the rationality of modernity or as a stage towards a new global synthesis. (See also MODERNISM AND POST-MODERNISM.)

Globalization is attacked by those who see it as a new form of homogenization of culture, an extension of the MASS CULTURE which ironed out the variety of nineteenth-century local European cultures. It is however clearly linked to the advance of multiculturalism, the demand for cultural pluralism in unitary states, and movements for national self-determination. The process which has resulted in nation-states working towards supranational agencies, such as the United Nations, and intergovernmental accords, such as the General Agreement on Tariffs and Trade or the agreements of the 1992

Earth Summit, has facilitated worldwide travel, assisted migration flows, and highlighted issues of minority rights. The sense of a common fate for humanity is enhanced by recognition of global environmental issues, and political activism increasingly crosses national boundaries with the worldwide mobilization of social movements. Supranationalism therefore operates at the level of individual commitment to globalist values at one extreme and in the formation of an international class of capitalists, managers, bureaucrats, media and sports stars at the other. All these factors lead to the recognition that we have to move beyond the interplay of the economic, the cultural and even the political and clearly visualize globalization as a process of social transformation in the broadest sense. The most substantial treatment of the theme to date is by Anthony Giddens (1990).

Reading
Albrow, M. and King, E. eds 1990: *Globalization, Knowledge and Society.*
Featherstone, M. ed. 1990: *Global Culture: Nationalism, Globalization and Modernity.*
Giddens, A. 1990: *The Consequences of Modernity.*
King, A. 1990: *Global Cities: Post-imperialism and the Internationalization of London.*
Sklair, L. 1991: *Sociology of the Global System.*
MARTIN ALBROW

government   *See* STATE

green movement   Formed at the end of the 1970s, the West German Alternative Political Alliance or 'Green Party' was widely hailed as a major new departure in European politics. The movement brought together remnants of the student radicalizations of the 1960s, some elements of the extraparliamentary Marxist left, local 'citizens' initiatives' and 'new social movements' such as gay rights activists, ecologists, feminists, peace and anti-nuclear campaigners, together with more conservative and libertarian elements.

By the late 1980s there were green political parties in virtually all European countries, including the UK, where the tiny Ecology Party changed its name to the Green Party in 1985. So far the most impressive electoral achievement of the UK greens has been their showing in the 1989 elections for the European parliament when their candidates received a total of 3.25 million votes.

Although the most visible manifestations of the

rise of the green movement are the green parties and radical environmentalist pressure groups, it is important to keep in mind some distinction between the movement and its political expressions. Many greens remain suspicious of and even hostile to party politics, even where the party proclaims to be a radically new kind of party. Also the compromises of party structure and programme imposed by the vicissitudes of electoral politics have taken some green parties some distance from the radical green vision of many of their more 'fundamentalist' members and supporters. The unifying theme of the movement is deep disquiet about the environmental consequences of providing patterns of economic growth on a global scale. Unlike reform environmentalists, greens do not put their faith in technological advances and improved environmental management. For them, the environmental crisis demands nothing less than a profound transformation of social, economic and political life: the creation of a sustainable society. So much is common ground among greens, but it is questionable whether any determinate political programme follows from these concerns, and it is true that parties claiming the 'green' label are to be found espousing policies traditionally associated with both left and right of the political spectrum.

The German Green Party has been one of the most successful and has also been very influential as a model for green parties elsewhere. Its political programme has linked ecologically necessary economic transformation with questions of social justice, women's rights, peace, regional and local autonomy, civil liberties and radical democracy. Attempting to combine extraparliamentary action with electoral politics, the greens established themselves as a political party at federal level in West Germany in 1980. Their early electoral performances were uneven, reflecting local differences in popular awareness, and the pre-existing balance of forces, as well as divisions between left and right factions within the greens themselves. After the departure of the main right-wing groupings, the greens consolidated and extended their electoral support, breaking through the 5 per cent barrier to enter the federal parliament at the 1983 elections. Their electoral base has been broad, although it is nevertheless drawn disproportionately from the younger, more highly educated, middle-class and professional sections of the population. On social and economic issues, Green Party supporters are generally to the left of the Social Democratic Party

(SPD) and if they are not first-time voters they are likely to have a history of SPD support. Reflecting the radical–democratic values of green movement members, the Green Party set out to be a party of a 'new kind', with a constitution designed to maintain decentralized grass-roots control over policymaking, leadership, parliamentary representatives and the allocation of resources, and to ensure full participation by women members.

The policies of the greens are a compromise between the different political traditions which are brought together in the movement. In defence, opposition to nuclear weapons is combined with a vision of a non-aligned Europe, and the break-up of the major military blocs. Green economic policy favours decentralization, workers' self-management and a reorientation of production for the meeting of need in accordance with the self-regulating mechanisms of nature. The purely quantitative commitment to growth upheld by both state 'socialist' and capitalist regimes is rejected in favour of a selective approach geared to need, sustainability and quality of life. These democratic and egalitarian values are also evident in green support for feminist aims, the extension of civil liberties and Third World liberation movements.

Werner Hülsberg has distinguished four main tendencies within the West German greens. The 'ecosocialists' favour the consolidation of the greens as a political force to the left of the SPD, urge support for workers' defensive struggles and argue for an ecologically oriented socialism, built on a new material–technical basis. The 'fundamentalists' argue the necessity for a 'cultural' or 'spiritual' revolution, in which the false consumer needs engendered by capitalism are renounced in favour of a qualitatively different way of life. Small, self-managing and convivial communities would be responsible for meeting their own basic needs, and life would be sustained with a much lower level of material consumption. The most influential thinker in this tendency has been Rudolf Bahro. The 'ecolibertarians' are a diverse grouping who favour proposals for a 'basic income' unrelated to work, and for a 'dual' economy which would allow individuals more freedom for self-development, study and autonomous work.

Through the 1980s the West German greens served as a model for the emergent green movements across Western Europe, and there are close parallels as well as direct links between these movements and the environmental protest movements of Eastern Europe. Though they are so far predominantly a European phenomenon, there are comparable green movements in the USA, Australia and New Zealand, Japan, and in numerous Third World countries.

See also ENVIRONMENTALISM.

Reading
Bahro, R. 1984: *From Red to Green.*
Capra, F., and Spretnak, C. 1984: *Green Politics.*
Hülsberg, W. 1988: *The German Greens.*
Parkin, S. 1989: *Green Parties: An International Guide.*
Porritt, J. 1984: *Seeing Green.*
Ryle, M. 1988: *Ecology and Socialism.*

TED BENTON

group A social group can be defined as an aggregate of human beings in which (1) specific relations exist between the individuals comprising it, and (2) each individual is conscious of the group itself and its symbols. In short, a group has at least a rudimentary structure and organization (including rules and rituals), and a psychological basis in the consciousness of its members. A family, a village, a sporting association, a trade union or a political party is a group in this sense. However, there are also larger groupings of individuals – in a tribe, a nation or an empire – and sociologists have generally distinguished such entities, which are conceived as 'inclusive societies', from the smaller groups which exist within them. Some writers have also identified a third category of 'quasi-groups', characterized by more tenuous relationships among the members, less awareness of the group and perhaps a more fleeting existence, indicating as examples of this phenomenon crowds or mobs, age and gender aggregates, and social classes. But the boundary between groups and quasi-groups is not fixed or clearly marked, and Max Weber's observation on classes, that while they are not in themselves communities, they are frequently a basis for communal action, can be applied more widely. Thus crowds may develop into protest movements, age differences sometimes crystallize in age-sets or youth movements, gender has given rise to women's movements, and distinctions of social status, which produce quasi-groups such as the 'professions' or the 'intellectuals', may then become the source of more organized groups in the form of professional associations or specialized elites.

Social groups in the strict sense are extremely varied in character. Tönnies (1887), in a work which has had a considerable influence on later social thought, made a broad distinction between two types of group, *Gemeinschaft* (community) and *Gesellschaft* (society or association), in terms of the nature of the relations among the members. In a community individuals are involved as whole persons and are bound together by an accord of feeling or sentiment, and Tönnies gives as examples the family or kin group, the neighbourhood (rural village), and the group of friends. The members of an association, on the other hand, enter into the relationship in a more calculated and deliberate way, look to the satisfaction of specific and partial aims and are united by a rational agreement of interest, and the main examples given are those groups concerned with economic interests. Tönnies, it may be noted in passing, also applied this typology to inclusive societies, primarily in a contrast between feudalism and modern capitalism. So far as groups within society are concerned his distinction has some similarities with that made by Cooley (1909) between 'primary groups' and others (frequently called 'secondary groups' by later sociologists), the primary groups being those 'characterized by intimate face-to-face association and cooperation' which results in 'a certain fusion of individualities in a common whole'.

Many later studies of groups (Homans, 1948, and the sociometric researches of Moreno, 1934) concentrated on these 'primary' or 'small' groups, and although it was generally recognized that they are only one element in the social structure some writers tended to adopt Cooley's own view that such groups are primary above all in being fundamental in forming the social nature and ideals of the individual. Against this it can be convincingly maintained that small groups are shaped by the inclusive society to a much greater extent than they shape it, as is most evident in the impact of modern industrial society on such groups as the family and the rural village. Redfield (1955) in his study of the 'little community' recognized the importance of this issue, and explored very thoroughly, with reference mainly to tribal societies, the (diverse) relations which exist between small groups and the larger society in which they function.

A much more elaborate typology of groups was outlined by Gurvitch (1958, vol.1, sect.2, ch.1) who proposed 15 criteria of classification: content, size, duration, rhythm, proximity of members, basis of formation (voluntary and so on), access (open, semi-closed, closed), degree of organization, function, orientation, relation with the inclusive society, relation with other groups, type of social control, type of authority, degree of unity. This takes account of all the major differences between groups and of the diversity of their relations with each other and with the inclusive society. Thus it encompasses, for example, such issues as Georg Simmel raised, in a well-known essay (1902) which examined the relationship between the number of members in a group and its structure, and in another study (1903) which showed how the concentration of population in cities changed the nature of social relations.

More generally, Gurvitch's typology provides a more adequate starting point for a systematic investigation of the ways in which social groups establish a network of relationships in CIVIL SOCIETY which interact with, and modify, those tendencies towards the creation of a MASS SOCIETY where relatively isolated individuals confront an increasingly powerful state. On the other hand, it also makes possible an analysis of the conditions in which specific social groups such as elites or organized dominant classes (see ELITE THEORY) may themselves acquire an inordinate power. From various standpoints, therefore, the study of groups can illuminate some fundamental questions in social thought concerning the relation between individual and society, the sources of social solidarity and stability, and the prerequisites of a democratic order.

See also SOCIAL PSYCHOLOGY.

Reading
Homans, G.C. 1948: *The Human Group*.
Redfield, R. 1955: *The Little Community*.
Tönnies, F. 1887 (*1955*): *Community and Association*.

TOM BOTTOMORE

growth, economic See ECONOMIC GROWTH

guerrilla The origin of the word, in its meaning of 'small war', goes back to Napoleon's intervention in Spain (1808–12). But its tactics are as old as history. Guerrilla warfare is used by irregulars (often now themselves called guerrillas) and is based on surprise and harassment to weaken a regular army. Guerrilla warfare was often used as a form of resistance to foreign occupation (Roman, Ottoman, Napoleonic); later it was widely practised against European colonial expansion in Asia and Africa.

Guerrilla warfare once again occupied an important role during and after World War II (Greece, Yugoslavia, China). With Mao Zedong, guerrilla tactics become revolutionary warfare, a military tool aimed at seizing political power (See MAOISM). Mao's innovation was not military but political. He used the vanguard party originally created by Lenin to organize the urban proletariat to mobilize the peasantry. This mode, based on widespread propaganda, organization and the use of selective terrorism, is aimed at building a popular support and, above all, a political underground infrastructure. It was successfully used by the Viet Minh while fighting against French colonialism, and Vietnamese troops were able to win the battle of Dien Bien Phu. Later, the same model was also adopted by non-Marxist movements of national liberation. Middle cadres are an essential help to win the support of segments of the population through agitation and propaganda, the aim being to create a new order which challenges the legitimacy of the state. From beginning to end, military problems are closely related and subordinated to political aims.

Although many insurgencies were defeated (in Greece, the Philippines, Malaya, Kenya), many did succeed after long wars of attrition – sometimes with the sympathy of the public opinion of the colonial country – in gaining independence through a political victory. Democracies agreed to negotiate, since nothing vital to them was at stake. Dictatorships on the other hand would not negotiate and only a military victory (most of the time against a weak state) would end the conflict. This was the case in Cuba (1959) and, 20 years later, in Nicaragua. The Vietnam war (1965–73) confirmed the capacity of the weak to resist the strong. But in the 1960s, all Latin American guerrillas lacking popular support were defeated (Guevara in Bolivia, 1967).

Today there is an increasing variety of guerrillas:

- Marxist guerrillas aiming at seizing power for social change (as in Peru, El Salvador, the Philippines);
- against foreign occupation, as in Afghanistan where Soviet troops, after eight years of intervention (1979–88), withdrew;
- guerrillas fighting for the autonomy or the independence of an ethnic or religious minority (Eritrea, Sri Lanka, the Kurds in the Middle East);

– anti-Marxist guerrillas, first helped by South Africa (UNITA in Angola and RENAMO in Mozambique), then by the USA (Contras in Nicaragua).

Guerrilla warfare is not going to vanish, because the conditions that trigger it are still present. But with urban unrest, the increasingly crowded megalopolis is becoming more and more the epicentre of riots and insurgencies.

See also WAR.

Reading
Beaufre, André 1972: *La Guerre revolutionnaire: les forces nouvelles de la guerre.*
Chaliand, Gérard 1979 (*1984*): *Stratégies de la guerilla.*
Ellis, John 1975: *A Short History of Guerrilla Warfare.*
Laqueur, Walter 1977: *Guerrillas: A Historical and Critical Study.*
Sarkissian, Sam S. ed. 1975: *Revolutionary Guerrilla Warfare.*

GÉRARD CHALIAND

H

---

health In 1948 the World Health Organization promulgated a definition of health as 'a state of complete physical, mental and social well-being, not merely the absence of disease or infirmity'. This widely used definition, though commonly criticized as over-inclusive and difficult of achievement, draws attention to the major change which has taken place in the latter half of the twentieth century: the replacement of a strictly biomedical model of health by a more holistic and social concept.

This is not new, echoing as it does the classical Platonic model of health as harmony or Galen's concept of disease as disturbance of equilibrium. Some reasons for its reappearance in developed countries during this century, however, are held to be the rise in importance of chronic disease in 'ageing' populations, the eradication of many 'scourge' diseases and the general improvement in living conditions which gives emphasis to the STANDARD OF LIVING rather than simple survival. The human ecology movement is also relevant, encouraging a focus on health as a state of balance between human beings and their environment. A further strand in the development of holistic concepts has been the growing knowledge about mind–body links: at first, the place of psychosocial factors in the cause of disease was emphasized; more recently, concepts of stress, social integration, coping ability, a 'sense of coherence' (Antonovsky, 1987) or 'generalized susceptibility' (Marmot, Shipley and Rose, 1984) have been seen not only as causes of ill-health but as integral parts of the concept of social health. Thus health is now generally conceived of as multidimensional, encompassing but not confined to the absence of disease.

Disease

Concepts of disease itself have changed, with a challenge to the key suppositions – the definition of disease as deviation from normality, the doctrine of specific etiology, the universality of disease taxo-nomy, the scientific neutrality of medical science – which had shaped modern medicine during the nineteenth century (Dubos, 1961). The conviction that the universe of disease is finite, and that for every disease there is a unique cause and a cure to be found, has been shaken by the advent of new diseases (such as Aids) and the recognition of the multiple and interactive causes of many forms of ill-health. Further, it is suggested that the definition and categorization of disease is a social as well as a scientific process, and normality can be only a relative concept. The influence of Michel Foucault, arguing against naive acceptance of the theoretical models of the 'sciences of man', has been strong in creating the view that medical knowledge (no less than medical practice) is socially constructed, and connected with broader developments in social thought: it cannot simply be taken for granted.

Illness

Similarly, the experience of illness involves cultural meanings and social relationships. A major question of a considerable body of research in social anthropology and medical sociology during the last 30 or 40 years has concerned the perception and the meaning of health and illness among those who experience them. Bodily states and changes are interpreted differently in different cultures and at different periods: as Mary Douglas (1970) noted, the social body constrains the way the physical body is perceived. Many studies, following pioneering work by Claudine Herzlich (1973), have mapped the concept of health held by lay people. Several have found a threefold division: health as positive fitness or well-being, or as a 'reserve' or 'equilibrium' ('health as having'); health as the ability to function or perform social roles ('health as doing'); and health simply as the absence of symptoms of ill-health ('health as being'). The most positive concept of health is generally found to be associated with better education or more favourable social circumstances. A feature of all these studies is the strong moral meaning demonstrated to attach to the concept of health.

Health promotion and health behaviour

Growing public expectations have been associated with a marked trend in Western societies towards an emphasis on positive aspects of health and health promotion. From about mid-century, research strongly implicated personal behaviours – smoking, diet, lack of exercise – as agents in the cause of chronic disease. Meeting with the deepseated view of health as a moral issue, new concepts of disease as 'self-inflicted' and health as 'self-responsibility' have been fostered. 'Fringe' and alternative medicine and self-help movements flourish in this environment, as does the commercialization of health promotion. Critiques of the 'medicalization' of society (Illich, 1975) have fed into this trend, as, from different perspectives, have critiques of medicine's efficacy (Cochrane, 1972; McKeown, 1976). During the 1970s and 1980s there was, however, some reaction against the model of health promotion which emphasizes only lifestyle change and voluntary behaviour. The self-responsibility movement, it is argued, can empower individuals, but it can also reinforce guilt and foster victim blaming (Crawford, 1977).

Thus research began to reemphasize the social and environmental constraints within which health behaviour is determined. The concept of 'social inequality' in health reemerged strongly in Britain and in other countries of Europe (DHSS, 1980). In a sense, this represents a return to the 'public health' movement of the early years of the century, with its emphasis on specific causes of ill-health in the physical and social environment, but now informed by the more complex theories of holistic models.

See also PSYCHIATRY AND MENTAL ILLNESS.

Reading

Armstrong, D. 1983: *The Political Anatomy of the Body.*
Bury, M.R. (1986): Social constructionism and the development of medical sociology. *Sociology of Health and Illness* 8, 137–69.
Foucault, M. 1963 (*1976*): *The Birth of the Clinic.*
Fox, J. ed. 1989: *Health Inequalities in European Countries.*
Sontag, S. 1979: *Illness as Metaphor.*

MILDRED BLAXTER

hegemony The twentieth-century use of this term combines and extends earlier usages. It traditionally indicated the dominance of one country or ruler over others. Secondly, it also signified the principle around which a group of elements was organized. It is now not only applied to international relations, where it still means dominance, but – mainly under the influence of the Italian Marxist thinker Antonio Gramsci, who developed the concept significantly (1929–35) – has also come to indicate the organizing principle of a society in which one class rules over others not just through force but by maintaining the allegiance of the mass of the population. This allegiance is obtained both through reforms and compromises in which the interests of different groups are taken into account, and also through influencing the way people think. Whereas at first Gramsci (1921–6) used the term in the same way as other Marxists such as Lenin, Bukharin and Stalin with regard to the leadership of one class over others in a system of alliances, in extending the term he went beyond the usual Marxist concept of state POWER as the instrument of a class which employed a monopoly of force, to argue that the state in the modern period could only be understood as force plus consent.

This enriching of the meaning of hegemony is related to the increasing complexity of modern society in which the terrain of politics has changed fundamentally. In the age of mass organizations such as political parties and pressure groups, when the expansion of the suffrage requires any state, however restricted democratic liberties are, to attempt to maintain the consent of the governed – and with the development of the educational and cultural level of the population, its ideas, practices and institutions – the area of state action expands and the public and private spheres of society are increasingly intertwined. In this context the very meaning of political leadership or dominance has changed as rulers must claim to be ruling in the interests of the ruled in order to stay in power. Increasingly the demands and needs of society have come to be considered the responsibility of governments, when once they might have been relegated to the private sphere defined as outside politics. Ideas, culture and how people view themselves and their relationships with others and with institutions are of central importance for how a society is ruled and is organized, and underpin the nature of power – who has it and in what forms. Thus, as the very nature of politics has changed, the meaning of hegemony, as leadership, dominance or influence, has in turn evolved. It now also implies intellectual and moral leadership and relates to the function of systems of ideas or ideology in the maintenance or the challenge to the structure of a particular society. It is consequently instrumental not only in the continuance of the status quo but in the manner in which a society is transformed.

Reading
Anderson P. 1976–7: The antinomies of Antonio Gramsci. *New Left Review* 100.
Bocock, R. 1986: *Hegemony*.
Buci-Glucksmann, C. 1982: Hegemony and consent. In *Approaches to Gramsci*, ed. A.S. Sassoon.
Femia, J. 1981: *Gramsci's Political Thought: Hegemony, Consciousness and the Revolutionary Process.*
Mouffe, C. 1979: Hegemony and ideology in Gramsci. In *Gramsci and Marxist Theory*, ed. C. Mouffe.
Sassoon, A.S. 1980 (*1987*): *Gramsci's Politics*, 2nd edn.

ANNE SHOWSTACK SASSOON

hermeneutics This area of philosophical activity and enquiry is concerned with the theory and practice of understanding in general, and the interpretation of the meaning of texts and actions in particular.

Overview
In the two decades after the publication of Hans-Georg Gadamer's *Truth and Method* in 1960, hermeneutics came to represent a central topic in philosophy and cultural analysis, thereby vindicating the assertion contained in this seminal work concerning the 'universality of the hermeneutic problem'. Gadamer's position is pivotal in contemporary hermeneutics. Working from within the tradition of Heidegger's ontology, he could critically appropriate and develop earlier formulations of the 'hermeneutic problem' and provide the foundations for the subsequent application of hermeneutic insights to a wide field.

In the social sciences, the influence of hermeneutics has been pervasive. Debates concerning, for example, the scientific status of the social sciences, the relationship of subject and object, the meaning of 'objectivity', the formulation of appropriate methods, the meaningful constitution of the object have all been crucially shaped by hermeneutics and today proceed largely on its terrain.

The seminal influence of Gadamer's work can also be traced in a wide range of disciplines outside philosophy and the social sciences, ranging from medicine to business studies to architecture – in fact, anywhere where the dialogical constitution of meaning is reflected upon.

As a methodology
In so far as hermeneutics has been regarded as the methodology of the human sciences (*Geisteswissenschaften*), it referred to those disciplines ancillary to theology, jurisprudence and philology that attempted to provide rules and guidelines for the interpretation of texts. The term was coined as late as the seventeenth century but its field, the *ars interpretandi*, reaches back into the beginning of Western thought. It was, in particular, at times of social and cultural upheaval that hermeneutics was charged with the task of clarifying the self-understanding of an age in relation to traditioned frames of meaning. It is when taken-for-granted conceptions are shaken that the interpretation of meaning, as its method-guided appropriation, comes into play.

Hermeneutical theory as it developed before the nineteenth century, that is, as a set of practical rules, is in principle unable to provide a theoretical foundation for the interpretation of meaning. What is required for this purpose is nothing less than the contribution Kant made to the foundation and justification of the natural sciences. In this respect, Wilhelm Dilthey's 'Critique of historical reason' (see Dilthey, 1927) represents a widening of Kant's *Critique of Pure Reason* in accounting for the historical dimension in the development of human thought.

Dilthey's attempt to provide the foundation for the human sciences was continued in this century by Emilio Betti, who set himself the task of harvesting the wealth of hermeneutical thought that had by now accumulated, and putting it to good methodological use.

A major attraction of Emilio Betti's *objective-idealist* perspective on the study of meaning resides in the promise of being furnished with an account of the possibility of *verstehen*, here used in the sense of a method-based form of understanding leading to objective results.

Betti introduces his general theory of interpretation through a consideration of the relationship of subject and object in the intepretation of meaningful forms. The object of the human sciences is constituted by ethical and aesthetic values. They 'represent an ideal objectivity that unerringly follows its own lawfulness' (Betti, 1955, p. 9). The ideal objectivity of 'spiritual values' can, however, only be comprehended through the 'real objectivity' of 'meaningful forms'. These forms contain values which Betti regards as something absolute, that is, as containing within themselves the basis of their own validity. They are thereby removed from the perceiver's subjective arbitrariness and, as objectively existing, are accessible to intersubjective verification.

Hermeneutic philosophy

Betti's work represents a sophisticated exposition of hermeneutical theory as the methodology of the interpretation of objective mind. Hermeneutic philosophy, in contrast, shifts the focus of hermeneutics from the problem of *verstehen* to the existential constitution of possible understanding from the standpoint of active existence, especially in reference to our embeddedness in tradition and language.

Heidegger

In the later work of Edmund Husserl, the central figure in the development of PHENOM-ENOLOGY, the life-world – the world of everyday life that we uncritically accept as 'our world' – provided the ontological basis for any possible experiencing (Husserl, 1937).

Martin Heidegger's *hermeneutic* phenomenology develops this theme towards an analysis of *Dasein*, the human 'being-there' in the world, that is characterized by a search for meaning and a meaningful existence (Heidegger, 1927).

The meaning of *Dasein* can only be approached through an interpretive effort: 'hermeneutical' therefore becomes the central concept in existential analyses. Hermeneutical theory, on this basis, can be no more than a derivative of the more fundamental hermeneutic of *Dasein* where we are engaged in clarifying an already existing form of understanding of our world of everyday life.

But not only is methodically disciplined *verstehen* a derivative of existential understanding, it is also directed by the latter. The interpretation of something *as* something, that is, the 'as-structure of understanding', is based on the *fore-structure* of understanding. The circularity of argument apparent in the conception of interpretation as a movement within the fore-structure of understanding is that of the existential–ontological, or *hermeneutic*, *Circle*.

Hermeneutical theory stressed the movement from part to whole and reverse in the process of understanding. That methodologically guided interpretive procedure is now seen as a derivative of the existential structure of our Being-in-the world. In Heidegger's account, it is not a question of

getting out of this Circle (as in the pursuit of 'objective' findings) but of getting into it properly since it contains the possibility of original insight.

Gadamer

Hermeneutical theory conceives of understanding as an act residing in the interpreter's capacity to engage with meaningful forms. In Gadamer's view, however, understanding is not to be thought of as an act of one's subjectivity so much as the placing of oneself within a tradition in which past and present are constantly fused. The bringing together of past and present in the act of understanding Gadamer describes as the 'fusion of horizons'. In understanding, the interpreter's horizon is widened to encompass the initially unfamiliar object, and in this process forms a new, widened horizon. It is at this point, at the converging of initially differing positions, that true meaning can arise. Meaning is constituted in the dialogic formation of agreement. Only in this communicative experience do we come to understand and to know more fully what previously had remained an unclarified part of our pre-understanding, our initial horizon.

The stress on the historicity of understanding, on the situatedness of the interpreter within an active tradition, has already been referred to in terms of the 'fore-structure' of knowledge. Gadamer pursues this point further in the terms of a 'pre-understanding' and the inevitability of *Vor-urteile* (which can mean both prejudice and pre-judgement).

This aspect has been regarded as a 'rehabilitation of prejudice' by critical hermeneutics and as such a step back behind the questioning of unjustified assumptions that characterizes the Enlightenment tradition. At this point, though, this insight into the pre-judgemental structure of understanding can be developed further into an argument for the 'universality of the hermeneutic problem' on the basis of Gadamer's stress on the linguisticality of our Being.

Language is not merely an instrument of thought but it itself operates to disclose a world to us; we move within it and on the basis of it. Ultimately, it is language that forms the 'tradition', the 'pre-understanding', that generates our understanding of ourselves and our world.

Poststructuralism

Gadamer's emphasis on the productive rather than merely reproductive nature of interpretation parallels a shift in French philosophical and literary thinking towards a 'poststructuralist' position. One strand, often referred to as 'textualist', is of particular interest here, especially since its main representative, Jacques Derrida, has entered into a dialogue with Gadamer (see, for instance, Derrida, 1967). (See also DECONSTRUCTION.)

The figure of the 'fusion of horizons' that represents the dialogic constitution of meaning appears in poststructuralist thinking as 'intertextuality'. These terms, too, refer to an active relationship of reader and text, to an interaction and performance rather than passive consumption or detached analysis of a fixed meaning. This move, at the same time, forms the central point of departure from STRUCTURALISM and semiology (see SEMIOTICS) with its emphasis on the 'sign' as closure.

Where poststructuralism parts company with hermeneutics, however, is in its radical denial of any foundations of knowledge in the sense of operative assumptions regarding a self-evident basis of knowledge claims. For this tradition, it is impossible to use notions such as 'reaching a consensus' or 'arriving at a truth' without becoming entangled in a self-contradictory circular movement of thought.

Hermeneutics as Critique

The figure of the *hermeneutic circle* was used by Gadamer to reject the objectivism inherent in the historical–hermeneutical *Geisteswissenschaften*. When challenged by Betti to produce any criteria for judging the correctness or truth of proffered interpretations, Gadamer answered that he was only concerned with showing what it was that was always happening when we understand.

Gadamer's reference to the embeddedness of interpretation in a tradition was seen by Betti as a relapse into subjectivism. For *critical hermeneutics* this not only prevents hermeneutics from acquiring any methodological significance but also, and perhaps more importantly, it represents the forfeiting of the hard-won degree of autonomy from the forces of tradition which Enlightenment thought had secured.

In the work of social philosophers working within the wider orbit of the FRANKFURT SCHOOL, such as Karl-Otto Apel and Jürgen Habermas, an integration is attempted of hermeneutic philosophy with other traditions such as phenomenology, pragmatism, linguistic philosophy and Freudian analysis. Both aim towards an integration of Gadamer's analyses with sociopolitical concerns,

and with the formulation of a social science that can assist in freeing repressed social practice.

Adhering to the 'project of the Enlightenment', Habermas seeks to develop a critical social science that reconstructs suppressed possibilities for emancipation. As a critical–dialectical social science, Habermas's *depth hermeneutics* attempts to mediate the objectivity of historical forces with the subjectivity of actors. Since its aim is to free emancipatory potential through reconstructing processes of repression it is not suprising that Habermas should use psychoanalysis as a model.

Because repression takes place in and through language, the theoretical framework required for such a programme takes the form of a projected 'theory of communicative competence'. Ideologies provide an illusory account of societies that are characterized by the domination of one section over another. Consensus in such conditions is likely to be false or distorted, that is, the results of 'systematically distorted communication'. In conditions of inequality, consensus can only be a 'counterfactual' assumption, the anticipated aim of social interaction, rather than its unquestioned precondition.

Postmodernism

Habermas's *discursive ethics*, which centres on the idea of dialogue free from domination, has been rejected by philosophers who draw their inspiration from Heidegger and, further back, from Nietzsche.

The universalistic intention of Enlightenment thought and its emancipatory programme is now seen as, at best, illusory, but more likely as itself repressive. Such a project involves a philosophical justification, in Jean-François Lyotard's phrase a 'grand narrative' or 'meta-narrative' (1979), the function of which is to impose a unilinear, monological conception of the object and to legitimize its own rules of procedure.

One such grand narrative is represented by the 'hermeneutics of meaning', and it characterizes the postmodern condition that we have become 'incredulous' towards it. This attitude arises from the valued recognition of heterogeneity, plurality and local determination, and leads Lyotard to reject the unanimity of minds sought in the formation of consensus as not only unrealistic but even as dangerous, as 'terroristic'.

As far as the philosophical and practical–political concern with the formation of consensus is concerned, it is necessary to state that the dialogical constitution of meaning and the striving for communicatively achieved, rational agreement is unrelated to the monological imposition of one particular language-game. More to the point, critical hermeneutics is concerned with formulating the conditions of the possibility of plurality. It is only on the basis of consensual norms that diverging positions can freely be developed and be given a fair hearing. Critical hermeneutics seeks to expand that space through helping to initiate an emancipatory practice that removes obstacles in the way of genuine consensus formation.

Conclusion
Hermeneutic thought points to the situatedness of all activity within a particular interpretive framework. As such it draws our attention to the presuppositions, and limitations, of all forms of thought and social practice. The aim of its proponents has been to enhance communicative interaction and thereby to facilitate the development of humane and truly rational forms of social coexistence.

See also THEORY OF KNOWLEDGE.

Reading
Bauman, Z. 1978: *Hermeneutics and Social Science.*
Bleicher, J. 1980: *Contemporary Hermeneutics.*
——1982: *The Hermeneutic Imagination.*
Dallmayr, F. and McCarthy, T. eds 1977: *Understanding and Social Inquiry.*
Gadamer, H-G. 1960 (*1975*): *Truth and Method.*
Habermas, Jürgen 1967 (*1988*): *On the Logic of the Social Sciences.*
Hekman, S. 1986: *Hermeneutics and the Sociology of Knowledge.*
Hoy, D.C. 1982: *The Critical Circle: Literature, History and Philosophical Hermeneutics.*
Ricoeur, P., 1974: *The Conflict of Interpretations: Essays in Hermeneutics.*
Wachterhauser, B.R. 1986: *Hermeneutics and Modern Philosophy.*
Warnke, G. 1987: *Gadamer: Hermeneutics, Tradition and Reason.*

JOSEF BLEICHER

Hinduism and Hindu social theory   Hinduism is the name generally given to the beliefs and practices which have developed over many centuries in the Indian subcontinent. These are diverse but bear a family resemblance to each other. Three traditions: BUDDHISM, Jainism and Sikhism have emerged as distinct but cognate religions. The Western term 'Hinduism' derives from a Sanskrit word for the Indus river, and variants of the word 'Hindu' have been used for over 2,000 years by outsiders to describe the people of India. Hindus call their way of life 'sanatana' (eternal) 'dharma'.

Dharma, often translated as 'religion', is a fundamental concept which has no English equivalent and includes the notion of morality. It denotes the conduct appropriate to an individual's caste, gender and age. Human life is regarded as an opportunity for achieving moksha (liberation) from the soul's cycle of birth and rebirth. Hindus believe that suffering and good fortune can be explained by karma, the cosmic law of cause and effect, operating over many lifetimes.

Hindu social theory is the view of society which emerges from analysis of Hindu history and culture and as articulated by Hindu thinkers and by analysts of Hindu society. Hinduism has no single founder and no single book that is regarded as scripture. Its roots can probably be traced to the period of the Indus Valley civilization (2500–1500 BCE (before Christian Era)) and to the many local tribal religions of the subcontinent. The oldest texts, the Veda, which were probably written about 1,000 BCE in north India, record the sacrificial hymns of the Aryans (a term which has acquired connotations of racial purity or of pristine Hinduism but more accurately indicates speakers of an Indo-European language, who probably originated further west). The Aryans worshipped male gods such as Indra.

In the Upanishads, composed about 500 years later, there emerges the characteristically Hindu belief in the transmigration of the soul and the unity of atman (the individual soul) with brahman (the impersonal absolute which pervades all). Mystical experience assumed great importance and there subsequently arose systems of physical and mental control for advancing this (yoga), which are prefigured in the Bhagavad Gita.

The purpose of the Arthashastra, a fourth century BCE account of social relationships, is the preservation of a king's power. *Realpolitik* is combined with principle.

Underlying Hindu society are the twin concepts of varna (see CASTE) and ashrama (stage of life). Society is understood as a hierarchy of interdependent but unequal elements characterized by harmony rather than by competition. The life of a male from the 'twice-born' castes came to be thought of as a sequence of stages. The brahmachari (celibate student) would marry and become a grihastha (married householder). When his son's son was born (and his line assured) he could become a forest hermit (varnaprastha) before renouncing all ties with the world as a sannyasi (renunciant). This pattern persists in Hindu society as an underlying ideal of family life giving way to untrammelled preoccupation with religious pursuits. From the Rig Veda, the epics (Mahabharata and Ramayana) and the lawbooks (Dharmashastra) emerges an evolving view of society.

The prime concern of theologians and philosophers was not social theory but understanding the ultimate reality. Shankara (c. 800 CE) preached advaita (non-dualism). In other words all appearances of duality (for instance between God and matter) were illusory. For medieval mystics, such as Kabir and Ravidas, mystical experience left no place for caste division, but it would be anachronistic to describe them as social reformers or theorists in the modern sense.

Nineteenth-century India, ruled by the British and sensitive to Western thought and Christian teaching, threw up Hindu thinkers with programmes for transforming society. In Bengal the Brahma Samaj founded by Ram Mohan Roy (1772–1833) promoted social reform, especially the rights of women. In his thinking a form of theistic monism was defended by philosophical reasoning of a Western type. The Gujarati ascetic, Swami Dayananda Saraswati (1824–1883) exhorted Hindus to return to his conception of a pure Vedic society, purged of the superstitious overlay of subsequent centuries. He and the movement which he created (Arya Samaj) emphasized Hindu rather than Western philosophy, strove to eliminate untouchability, encouraged the education of women and enabled widows to remarry. Swami Vivekananda (1862–1902) preached mystical monism coupled with social reform without ruling out caste or the worship of images.

Bal Gangadhar Tilak (1856–1920) promoted social conscience and political nationalism. He argued for the antiquity of Aryan culture and that the Bhagavad Gita should be understood as an exhortation to selfless service. Mahatma Gandhi (1869–1948) strove to realize a society, free of foreign domination, and characterized by non-violence, in which all individuals were equally valued. He saw no justification in Hinduism for untouchability. His principle of sarvodaya (universal uplift), espoused by Vinoba Bhave (1895–1982) and other Gandhians, means practical action to improve the quality of life of the most needy. In the philosophy of the erstwhile political activist, Sri

Aurobindo Ghose (1872–1950), evolution replaces maya (illusion) as a fundamental principle of society and the universe.

For Jawaharlal Nehru (1889–1964), India's first prime minister, society must embody democracy, socialism and secularism – that is, loyalty to the basic unity of India – rather than communalism (the self-interest of communities as divided along religious lines). Sarvapelli Radhakrishnan (1888–1975), philosopher and president of India, saw an Indian Idealism as the potential saviour of civilization from exploitation by Western commercial technology. As defined by Radhakrishnan, secularism does not mean irreligion or atheism, but lays stress on spiritual values which may be attained in a variety of ways. Harmony rather than competition was the ideal incorporated in the caste system, as he expounded it (Radhakrishnan, 1927).

Twentieth-century Hindu social thought has been characterized by increasing tension between the principles of secularism and Hindutva (Hindu revivalism) in which Bharat (India) is emotively identified with Hinduism. This has developed in conjunction with a movement to unify Hindus of all sects, castes and regions. The aim of the Rashtriya Swayamsevak Sangh (National Volunteer Union), founded in 1925 by Dr Keshav Baliram Hedgevar (1889–1940) was to revive the self-confidence of Hindus and their sense of civil duty, largely through involving young people in disciplined social service. In 1964 the Vishwa Hindu Parishad (World Hindu Organization) was founded with the same ethos to unify Hindus. Many Hindus, angered by their perception that the Indian government was appeasing minorities, have asserted themselves more militantly, united by the struggle for a temple rather than a mosque to mark the birthplace of Rama in Ayodhya. This activism inspired by idealization of the Hindu past is represented politically by the Bharatiya Janata Party (BJP).

Analysts of Hindu society have understood it in terms of a variety of processes, for example the interactive relationship between the Great and Little Tradition (pan-India and local forms of Hinduism). Srinivas postulated Sanskritization (the process whereby lower castes change their behaviour to resemble that characteristic of the brahman castes). Other processes include secularization (whereby what is identifiably religious, such as a belief in the supernatural, plays a less significant role in people's lives), modernization, industrialization, urbanization (as unprecedented millions move from villages to the cities) and Westernization (denoting a shift towards, for instance, the consumption of meat and alcohol, behaviour at odds with Sanskritization).

Reading

Basham, A.L. 1954: *The Wonder that was India*.
Beteille, A. 1966: *Caste, Class and Power: Changing Patterns of Stratification in a Tanjore Village*.
Dumont, L. and Pocock, D. eds 1957–69: *Contributions to Indian Sociology*, vols 1–9.
Lannoy, R. 1971: *The Speaking Tree: A Study of Indian Culture and Society*.
Radhakrishnan, S. 1927: *The Hindu View of Life*.
Srinivas, M.N. 1967: *Social Change in Modern India*.

ELEANOR M. NESBITT

historicism   A stress on the historical variability of systems of ideas and practices, their subordination to broader processes of change, was one of the main characteristics of nineteenth-century thought, especially in the German-speaking world. The contextualizing approach to law and economics of the respective 'historical schools' and their critique of abstract systems with a pretention to universality was at the centre of important theoretical controversies (see METHODENSTREIT) which continued into the early twentieth century – when the terms *historismus* or *historizismus* came into general use. As the virulence of these disputes declined, and historicism was eclipsed by the rise of POSITIVISM and PHENOMENOLOGY, thinkers such as Ernst Troeltsch (1865–1923) and Friedrich Meinecke (1862–1954) offered retrospective critical evaluations of historicism (for Troeltsch, see 1922). Karl Mannheim's principle of 'relationism' attempted to do justice to historical and other differences in perspective without falling into a full-blown RELATIVISM.

There had always been a more speculative strand of historicist thinking which understood the stress on change and development not as a caution against generalization but as an invitation to construct grand schemes of historical development and progress (see EVOLUTIONARY PROCESSES IN SOCIETY). Karl Popper used 'historicism' in this sense in his critique of 'prophecy' in social theory, particularly MARXISM. This usage which, as Popper recognized, is directly opposed to the first one, became dominant in English-language discussions, leading many writers, including the translator of Meinecke's

book, to prefer the term 'historism'. Popper's critique of Marxist 'historicism', like Jean-François Lyotard's later critique of 'grand narratives' (1979) gave rise to considerable discussion within the Marxist tradition. Here, however, the term is also used to indicate a stress on the historical embeddedness, and hence changeability, of Marxist thought itself, in opposition to more scientistic versions of Marxism such as that defended for some time by Louis Althusser, who popularized this further usage in his critique of such Marxists as Lukács and Gramsci (Althusser, 1965).

Historicism or historism in the primary sense has been an important, if inexplicit, feature of philosophy and social theory in the later decades of the twentieth century. Peter Winch (1958) emphasized the need to understand 'alien' cultures in their own terms, making his identification with this central historicist principle explicit with a quotation from Nestroy in the frontispiece of his book. Quentin Skinner has emphasized the importance of understanding the texts of political theory in the context of their traditions (see Skinner, 1978, and also Tully, 1988), and this historical concern has affinities with 'contextualist' approaches in modern political theory which argue for a holistic approach to concrete forms of life and traditions, rather than the implementation of discrete moral and political principles. A more general valorization of diversity or 'difference' has been a pervasive theme of recent Western thought, as the legacy of imperialism gradually gives way to a less ethnocentric and more 'multicultural' awareness. Most recently, the label 'new historicism' has been applied to literary and cultural studies which, in opposition to the more abstract theorizing of the 1970s and early 1980s, engage closely with historical texts but with a focus on the ways in which they are produced and the complex mediations through which we have access to them. In these various and disparate ways, the legacy of historicism survives, and what was denoted by the term in the nineteenth and early twentieth centuries comes to seem, along with and opposed to more systematizing and universalistic approaches, a permanent pole of attraction in philosophy and social theory.

Reading

Mannheim, Karl 1952: Historicism. In *Essays on the Sociology of Knowledge*.
Meinecke, Friedrich 1946 (*1972*): *Historism: The Rise of a New Historical Outlook*.
Popper, Karl 1957: *The Poverty of Historicism*.

Schnädelbach, Herbert 1984: *Philosophy in Germany 1831–1933*, chapter 2.

Veeser, H.A. ed. 1989: *The New Historicism*.

WILLIAM OUTHWAITE

history   The invitation to write a short essay on history for a dictionary of twentieth-century social thought is an invitation to decide for that essay what the twentieth century is. For that purpose it will here be a short twentieth century – *the 75 years from 1914 to 1989*, from the onset of World War I to the multiple collapse of communism as effective actuality and as ideology in the world. In that 75-year 'century' the writing of history has undergone three sorts of major change, distinguishable but also mutually interrelated. The sources to which historians paid professional attention changed; the subject matter that the profession wrote about changed; and the framework within which they defined their discipline changed.

In the past 'century' historians have gained access to storehouses of information, hitherto beyond their reach for lack of technology or techniques to exploit them or lack of the perspective from which to make historical sense of them. For the first time historians systematically used sources such as aerial land surveys, registers of births, baptisms, marriages and deaths, physical measurements of men drafted into armies, catalogues of mail-order companies, records of school enrolments and university matriculations, automobile licences, guild memberships, telephone directories. This detritus of human life people had gathered and shaped into manageable form sometime, somewhere, for some purpose. Their purposes were other than those of the twentieth-century historians who ultimately reshaped the surviving data for their own uses. The common characteristic of these kinds of data was that they attained significance for historians only by aggregation. In the very nature of things the kinds of advancement of historical knowledge such sources lent themselves to were quantitative.

A second sort of data that engaged the attention of professional academically trained historians in the twentieth century was the mass of information that for 250 years or more local antiquarians had been unsystematically amassing in the publications of local learned societies. Professional historians had long been contemptuous of such antiquarian activities. Their contempt was well merited by the ineptness of some such efforts, and the triviality or mediocrity of much of the rest. In the twentieth century professional historians dug into kitchen middens of local history and amid much vacuous rubbish found precious artifacts of a past not hitherto explored. To the new quantitative data they added the letters (diaries, marriage settlements and wills, rentals and leases) of obscure men and women; and on both counts history was enriched by the increment.

Both kinds of new historical sources have provided data on the kinds of people to whom professional historians had hitherto paid only slight attention – agricultural workers, peasants, factory hands, foot soldiers, domestic servants, women, children, indeed the larger part of humankind since human life came to be. So in the twentieth century for the first time it became possible – and soon thereafter it became common practice – for professional historians to write coherently about phenomena that earlier historians had few means and less disposition to concern themselves with: diet, health, water power, energy sources and application, literacy, population, productivity, epidemics. (See also SOCIAL HISTORY.) The historians who undertook to open new fields of enquiry accompanied their pioneering effort with appropriately loud trumpet blasts and less felicitously with territorial claims that made those of the 13 original states of the USA seem modest by comparison.

The shift of interest to people whom historians of earlier generations had neglected or looked down on disrupted a complacency that the profession had cultivated. The reconception of the historical, protean sometimes to the point of appearing chaotic, had altered the visible practice of professional historians with a series of seismic shocks, the ultimate force of which was hard to gauge when the 'century' ended in 1989.

In the period of the founding of their profession from about 1815 to 1914, historians by training had given most of their attention to the past doings of leaders of white adult males, a minuscule minority of the persons who had hitherto lived on earth. The intensity of their dedication may have been overestimated, and their grounds for it misperceived by many of their successors in the twentieth century. Still the generality with which in the nineteenth century professional historians, all adult white males, pursued the study of the power struggles in war and peace of adult males, especially white ones, is conspicuous. The bringing to light of evidence about how the overwhelming majority of human beings not white, not male, not adult had lived and died in the human past resulted in a large and confused tumult over what to count as the significant past and how to count it. Clearly in the course of the four-and-a-half centuries between 1492 and 1942 adult white males had come to dominate, to have hegemony over the earth. To some historians in the twentieth century, even to some not easily chargeable with parochial or blinkered vision, it was evident that the rise of the West was *The Story* of the 450 years before that, in the same sense that World War II was *The Story* of the six years (1939–1945); it was the coherent story or text of which most other human doings within that interval could be seen as context or background. This way of looking at the past is of course older than the modern West. It had its origins in the literatures of two ancient cultures – the Graeco-Roman and Judaeo-Christian – which the rulers and writers of the West had found congenial well before the discovery of America. The story of the rise of the West thus comfortably fits the two narrative traditions with which the men of letters of the West were most familiar before 1492 and which almost all the founding fathers of the historical profession in the nineteenth century accepted as a given.

Not surprisingly many of the twentieth-century historians who took part in the discovery of history 'from the bottom up', considered this 'old' narrative history an evidence of the former subjection of other races, other classes, other age cohorts and the other sex to bondage by hegemonic white males. It was also an instrument of that bondage.

The devaluation of individual persons as the centres of historical stories and the devaluation of stories as the natural form of history therefore fit comfortably the kinds of evidence that the new types of sources yielded in the twentieth century. That evidence afforded answers to many historical questions that no historian had hitherto asked. It afforded no answers to the kinds of questions which had mainly preoccupied nineteenth-century historians and later successors who continued to share their concerns. In a culture which for 200 years had assigned an unprecedented honorific value to innovation, it was to be expected that twentieth-century innovators would cry down the value of kinds of story-telling history that their practices were no more apt to produce than a pile driver was apt to produce an etching. (This is said with no intent to compare invidiously the value of one to the other; they are not comparable.)

So the innovative sort of twentieth-century historical work marginalized writers of narrative history. It also marginalized human persons, or effectively disintegrated them, made into historical non-entities the actual players in those manifold stories of the past, that had been most of what most historians wrote about during the previous hundred years.

In the twenty-first century (beginning in 1989), historians may want to examine the confluence of the new sources of twentieth-century history writing, its new subjects, and the conceptions, indeed the *idées fixes*, that captured the minds of the most influential historians of the era. The longer they wait, the more the passage of time will diminish their capacity to empathize with the durable fascination – both attraction and repulsion – for twentieth-century historians of the particular cluster of ideas to which we will shortly return.

The confluence of sources, ideas and events occurred between 1914 and 1945. Its setting was two terrible wars, generated in Europe, which in 30 years left that violent civilization desolate amid the ashes of its own folly. The first years of the twentieth century thus witnessed a holocaust of the expectations, hopes, and aspirations of the nineteenth – expectations of the spread throughout the earth of the civilization of the states of Europe most advanced in science, technology and literacy, hopes for continuous PROGRESS on the way to feedom and democracy, aspiration for universal peace. In Europe since Waterloo there had been occasional short episodes of armed strife. But from the Urals to the Atlantic, north of the Danube, for the first time since the states of Europe had achieved the cohesion necessary for interstate conflict there had been no long major wars among the great powers. We need to remember that, lest with the advantage of hindsight we ascribe to historians teetering on the brink of mankind's most hideous century, idiocy – moral or political or both.

In the clash of arms of World War I, the greatest clash of human resources in Europe's history, this facile optimism of a century sank. It left as jetsam only the idiot smile of the naive transatlantic giant, the United States, which had bumbled on to the battlefield only long enough to determine the immediate military outcome, had muttered a ritual incantation, 'Make the world safe for democracy,' and then withdrawn into its wonted isolation, spiritual as well as geographical.

In the postwar years, in their dire and abandoned

plight, the best intellects of Europe turned back to those few prophets of woe who in the midst of the promise of the nineteenth century had seen omens of impending ill. Many turned especially to that succession of prophets who, although perceiving in their own time the threat of world catastrophe, saw dimly on the horizon the omens of a red dawn that appeared in the early 1920s – a new light in the East, the first socialist society.

One after another the socialist goals proclaimed by Karl Marx in 1848 were attained in the Soviet Union – the abolition of private property, the liquidation of an archaic class structure, the dictatorship of the proletariat, the destruction of that opiate of the people, organized religion, and – but 12 years into the Russian phase of the world revolution – the introduction of economic planning, and thus at last a society rationally organized to attain its stated goal. Never was the persuasiveness of doing more effective than it was in those early years of the communist experiment in Russia. It stood in stark contrast with the blind stumbling of the West in the ten years before World War II. On the one hand a firmly directed march through socialism to a communist society in the Soviet Union. On the other, the Great Depression, massive unemployment, the collapse of the prewar pseudo-democratic regimes of Italy and Germany into fascism and Nazism, the paralysis of capitalist economies, and the apparent death-throes of imperialism and the bourgeois world order.

Before World War I, the word Marxist had been applied to a polycentric cluster of political sects and factions with two shared traits. The first was an aversion to the political, economic and social structures amid which they lived, and the conviction that those structures were so exploitative and oppressive to most of humankind that they should be replaced by any feasible means. The second was the conviction that Karl Marx had effectively analysed how mankind had come to the pass it had in 1914; he had also discovered the route that it would and should follow in the future, the route called socialism to the goal called communism. By 1914, followers of Marx's teachings, from Russia to the Iberian peninsula, were in multifold disagreement about what the true Marxist philosophy was and about what course of action it required of them at the moment. All Marxists agreed, however, that the teaching of Marx required that his followers apply his doctrine, whatever it was, in the sphere of action; it provided a scientific law of life.

Especially via their impact on Marxism, the events of World War I produced a torsional effect on the perceptions of historians that, almost to the end of the short twentieth century, was to shape or twist the history written during its seven-and-a half decades. In the last years of World War I, the Muse of History played a sour joke on Marxism and on all but one of its main sects. At the very beginning of his *magnum opus, Capital* (1867), Karl Marx had set out the prime prior condition for a communist society, the kind of society he had envisaged in the *Communist Manifesto* of 1848. That condition was the abolition of private property. Capitalist society having passed from maturity into senile decay, the proletariat in a socialist revolution would overthrow an obsolete bourgeoisie and set society on the path toward its communist goal. This must be achieved through capitalist exploitation of the working class by the bourgeoisie before a society could be right for the socialist revolution. Late in 1917, however, under the leadership of Lenin, a small communist faction in Russia seized power. In the ensuing five years the Russian Communist Party succeeded for the first time in history in abolishing private ownership of the instruments of production. It also consolidated its own rule over almost the whole domain in Europe and Asia once under the Tsars of Russia, a domain hitherto viewed by Europeans, Marxists or not, as 'backward' and 'Asiatic'.

The time, the place and the substance of the triumph of communism in the Union of Socialist Soviet Republics, formerly the Russian Empire, imparted a unique and peculiar tilt to what went on in the world in the ensuing 75 years. It is therefore appropriate to begin the story of the twentieth century with the emergence of Soviet Marxist socialism and to end it between 1989 and 1992, when by official action the former Union of Soviet Socialist Republics became the Community of Independent States. The implications of that change for Marxism were not heartening and for communism were dire. So the shorter twentieth century was the Marxist Century. For 75 years the Soviet Union, of which Marx and Lenin were the official icons, presented to humankind the first 'acting out' of socialism on the world stage. Off and on in that century Britain, the United States, Nazi Germany, Japan, and Maoist China joined the Soviet Union centre-stage. The Union, the first great society explicitly founded on Marxist principles and precepts, was however from its inception constantly at one pole of humanity's current vision of the world as it was and ought to be.

To moderately observant people during the first three decades of the twentieth century, it seemed that on the most stringent human test for a scientific claim, the test of experience, Marxism had vindicated its assertion that it was the true science of human society or at least the place where that claim was being experimentally tested. Earlier Marxist predictions of the imminent collapse of capitalism were being confirmed by events all over the world. In Europe the Thirty Years' War among imperialist cultures, capitalist jackals and fascist hyenas looked as if it was winding down into assured mutual destruction.

For nearly the whole of the twentieth century the Communist Revolution and the success or survival of the Soviet Union were the decisive events in colouring the imagination of professional historians, not only in Russia but throughout the world. This was the case not only for explicitly Marxist historians but also for uncommitted historians who, self-consciously or not, regarded history as one of the policy sciences, aiming at human betterment. For them it was potentially a source of scientifically verified information that pointed towards a correct course of social, economic and political actions. They had to consider whether the Soviet Union was infallibly marking either the way other societies should follow or the way they should resist and reverse. Even in the few countries where up to 1945 the vocation of historians was not subject to irresistible guidance from above, many historians were attracted by the power exercised in the Soviet Union in the name of science. Others were hypnotized by the intellectual complexity and encompassing grandeur that Marxism achieved in its simultaneous missions of embracing the world and squaring the circle.

A good bit of serious historical evidence could be made to shape up in forms congruent with Marxism. So too, was a populous belt of the earth from the Elbe and the Adriatic on its western boundary all the way to the Pacific Ocean and the South China Sea on the eastern. Theoretical fascination joined with apparently imminent political triumph. That gave Marx's historical vision a particular piquancy for intellectuals of the few surviving free democracies. Many of the most articulate of those intellectuals inclined with varying degrees of acuteness toward Marxism. Those who did not so incline, rather than those who did, found that the unenviable burden of proof was tipping on to their shoulders. Some of them spent much energy, too much perhaps, in showing their reasons for not being Marxists. This entailed asserting that from where they were standing they did not see the inevitable Red Dawn – or any other shade of inevitable dawn for that matter – of a new day for humanity, not the message humanity finds most heartwarming. They spent considerable effort insisting on the inability of Marxists and quasi-Marxists to come to grips with the dilemmas, paradoxes and contradictions inherent in Marxism from the start. Such historians nibbled away at large Marxist assumptions that arbitrarily ruled out as inconsiderable or secondary (not basic, or unimportant in the long run) events and processes of which Marxism was unable to offer an adequate scientific explanation. In a world palpably intent on plunging towards wrack and ruin, rejection of the Marxist hope was not always popular with or plausible to intellectuals.

With the advantage of hindsight now, at the dawn of the twenty-first century, the preoccupations of historians in the previous century with a view of the nature and destiny of man so palpably flawed at its foundations as that of the Marxists may seem either mysterious or utterly ludicrous. When this happens – as it surely will – those present and future historians must try to see the world of the early twentieth century as those who lived in it saw it. Until 1989, no one – no layman, no expert – foresaw the end of the twentieth century as it actually happened: the implosion of the Soviet power structure and along with it of the ideology to which it was committed. At the time this article is being written no one has been able to make a plausible estimate of the devastation wrought by the inward collapse of communist institutional structures in much of the world and their probable imminent unhinging in China, the only major area where they have survived. There they are kept in being by the wiliness of a handful of men in their middle eighties; what will happen when the men die, as soon they must, is beyond knowing.

It is not the least irony of the twentieth century that the catastrophes at its end have been catastrophes of Marxism, the intellectual structure that attained dominance at its beginning, and of the institutional structures, those of Soviet communism, through whose agency that dominance was largely maintained. What this void in institutional structures will entail historians can begin to surmise at least to the extent of imagining a limited array of alternatives to them and of making exploratory moves toward understanding those alternatives.

As effectively to review and replace the dominant IDEOLOGY of the twentieth century presents historians with a more perplexing problem. Structures of ideas are far more durable than structures of institutions, their custodians more conservative, with more deeply entrenched vested interests in preserving them. Need for prompt disposal of institutions that send up suffocating fumes, and in the end produce nothing more than junk, sleaze, heartache and death is not all that hard to discern and the demolition tends to be evident to those trapped in the ruins. Being intangible, ideologies cling more persistently and are harder to clean away. For a historian – as for any intellectual who has invested his or her life in acquiring an expertise the contents of which the turn of events, that is, historical change, has made unsaleable – readiness to write down much less to write off the value of a life's work does not come easy. Already in the past 30 years, as the credit and credibility of the Soviet experiments slumped, historians who had most of their intellectual assets invested in communism have looked for ways to hedge their bets. Only rarely did a Marxist historian say 'I have spent all my life digging my way into a dead end.'

Reading
Barraclough, G. 1964: *An Introduction to Contemporary History.*
Braudel, Fernand 1980: *On History.*
Carr, E.H. 1961: *What is History?*
Collingwood, R.G. 1946: *The Idea of History.*
Hexter, J.H. 1961: *Reappraisals in History.*
—— 1971: *The History Primer.*
Le Roy Ladurie, E. 1973 (*1979*): *The Territory of the Historian.*

J. H. HEXTER

history, economic   *See* ECONOMIC HISTORY

history, social   *See* SOCIAL HISTORY

human geography   In their study of human occupancy of the earth's surface, the empirical efforts of human geographers throughout the twentieth century have been extremely heterogeneous, but they have almost always been associated with three underlying and frequently overlapping themes: the role of humans in transforming nature, in physically modifying the earth's surface; the organization of space by societal units and the impact of spatial organization on social and economic interaction; and the human activities or built-landscape features characterizing cities, regions or other delimited areas. A key common thread of these themes – the *situated* conduct of practice by human agents operating within a specific constellation of social relations – was long unrecognized and helped result in a disciplinary discourse which was largely oblivious to social theory; even though Vidal de la Blache and his fellow practitioners of *la géographie humaine* did regard the *genres de vie*, the ways of life, characteristic of regions together with the interactions of humans with their physical milieu as social phenomena above all else.

Adherents of environmental determinism, the most widely prevailing view during the early twentieth century, ignored the existence of social relations and insisted that livelihood practices, cultural characteristics, human physical attributes and mental abilities all varied geographically because of differences in the natural environment (and, in so doing, legitimated the persistence of European and American imperialism). 'Cultural geography', as developed by Carl Sauer and his followers from the mid-1920s onwards, avoided the social by adopting the superorganic view of CULTURE propounded by Alfred Kroeber and other anthropologists, by assigning culture an independent ontological and determinative status, by removing it from the realm of human agency and conflict and by allowing it magically to generate its own planted-on-the-ground forms. In the 1940s and 1950s those who pursued what Richard Hartshorne termed 'areal differentiation' abjured social theory through focusing on the areally *unique* interrelation of phenomena directly or indirectly bound to the earth, through stressing the variable and the different and through being inattentive to geographically extensive social structures and processes. Finally, the quantitative 'revolution' of the late 1950s and 1960s brought with it a new strict empiricism – now focusing on the statistically measurable rather than the field observable; a considerable concern for models derived from classical location theory and neoclassical economics; a search for geometric order; a preoccupation with spatial form rather than process; a positivistic disdain for theories that dealt with unquantifiable relations; and, as a result of all this, little attention to cultural and social theoretical issues.

In the context of the Vietnam war and the cascade of popular social movements in highly industrialized capitalist countries, there emerged an internal critique of mainstream human geography that at last came to grips with the social theoretical dimension of the discipline's subject matter through the introduction of a Marxist perspective. During the 1970s, behind the pioneering efforts of David Harvey, a growing minority of human geographers began theoretically and empirically to reinterrogate the world of spatial organization and regional differentiation in terms of political economy, uneven development and the 'logic of capital'. They began to explore the impact of contemporary capitalism on many of the urban and rural phenomena, many of the human–land relationships, that had traditionally been an object of the discipline's scrutiny. And they began – in an often combative manner – to examine the geographical dimension of social justice issues that had previously been beyond the realm of acceptable inquiry.

As Marx-inspired scholars became the target of criticism in the discipline and opened themselves to internal debate, and as Harvey (1982) himself expanded on the 'limits to capital', going beyond Marx in emphasizing the spatiality of capital and calling for a 'historico-geographical materialism', a number of human geographers became directly engaged in wider social theoretical developments. They embarked on the reformulation of social theory and a new discourse began to take form, especially on the pages of the journals *Antipode* and *Society and Space* and in a surge of important books, only a few of which appear in the suggested reading below. Sometimes calling on such dissimilar figures as Pierre Bourdieu, Michel Foucault and Anthony Giddens, those critical human geographers participating in this discourse have in various ways argued that history is no longer to be privileged in social analysis; that geography and history have equal ontological status; that the spatial, the temporal and the social are always inseparable; that all which is social is situated on the ground and context dependent; that the historical dynamics of social systems must be seen in concrete geographical context; that the spatial conditions, or structures, which enable and constrain human activity are themselves social products; that, in the unfolding of history, social and spatial structures

constantly play on one another. In so doing, and in one way or another acknowledging the transformational interplay of agency and structure, they have given a new set of meanings to Marx's famed dictum that people: 'make their own history, but they do not make it just as they please; they do not make it under circumstances chosen for themselves, but under circumstances directly encountered, given and transmitted from the past.'

With epistemological sensitivities awakened by the sceptical stance of postmodernist philosophers towards absolute standards of truth, many contributing to the new human geographic discourse in question have – following the stances of Keat and Urry (1975) and Sayer (1984) – become adherents of REALISM because of its assertion that science is possible and necessary; because of its contention that structures, with their impalpable relations and causal powers, exist to be identified; and because of the suggestions it provides for avoiding unwarranted causal conclusions in the empirical study of open and complex social systems.

The new discourse has yielded a number of theoretically informed and theory embellishing studies. Some of the most important explore the shifting articulations of the local and the global under late twentieth-century capitalism and investigate the ways in which gender relations, class relations, other power relations, the details of everyday life and elements of culture are restructured locally as different forms of capital are relentlessly restructured globally. Particularly significant advances have been made in the realm of industrial geography, where there has been a new focus on industrial restructuring and regional labour markets, on the concentrated production complexes resulting from flexible accumulation, and on the central role of geographically specific industrialization in growth under capitalism (Massey, 1984; Scott and Storper, 1986; Storper and Walker, 1989). Throughout all these developments critical human geography has not escaped the postmodernistic questioning of language and representation as a result of issues repeatedly raised by Gunnar Olsson since 1980 (Olsson, 1980).

Reading
Cosgrove, D. 1985: *Social Formation and Symbolic Landscape.*
Gregory, D. and Urry, J. eds 1985: *Social Relations and Spatial Structures.*
Gregory, D. and Walford, R. eds 1989: *Horizons in Human Geography.*

Harvey, D. 1985: *Consciousness and the Urban Experience.*

Harvey, D. 1989: *The Condition of Postmodernity: An Enquiry into the Origins of Cultural Change.*

Peet, R. and Thrift, N. eds 1989: *New Models in Geography: The Political-Economy Perspective*, 2 vols.

Pred, A. 1990: *Making Histories and Producing Human Geographies: The Local Transformation of Practice, Power Relations and Consciousness.*

Soja, E.W. 1989: *Postmodern Geographies: The Reassertion of Space in Critical Social Theory.*

Thrift, N. 1983: On the determination of social action in space and time. *Society and Space* 1, 23–57.

Watts, M.J. 1985: *Silent Violence: Food, Famine and Peasantry in Northern Nigeria.*

ALLAN PRED

human nature   There are many contending definitions of this notion. Each definition not only takes up a particular position but also claims for itself a uniquely privileged perspective that preempts all alternatives. This contentiousness is not an incidental matter because some notion of human nature is an indispensable component of social thought. The more significant twentieth-century contributions can be divided into two chief groups – the 'scientific' and the 'humanistic'.

Scientific interpretations
Sociobiology   E.O. Wilson defines human nature as 'a hodge podge of genetic adaptations to an environment largely vanished, the world of the Ice Age hunter gatherer' (1978, p. 196). In SOCIOBIO-LOGY the aim is to study human nature as an area of the natural sciences by creating an internally consistent network of causal explanation between biological and social sciences. The nodal point in this network is a notion of epigenetic rules. Every society is governed by these rules which cover everything from its economic policies to its moral tenets to its practices of childrearing (Wilson and Lumsden, 1981).

Ethology   Writers in this school, such as K. Lorenz (1966) and I. Eibl-Eibesfeldt (1971), focus on the fact that the human genotype shares 99 per cent of its history with that of the chimpanzee. The seeming narrowness of this difference means that the biological species *homo sapiens* emerged only recently in evolutionary time. Ethologists claim that the behaviour patterns of primates – their aggressivity, hierarchies and territoriality for example – have their counterparts in human society (see ETHOLOGY).

Behaviourism   While writers in this school do not question the tenets of neo-Darwinism, their focus is directly on human behaviour. This behaviour, like any other natural phenomenon, has antecedent causes which necessarily determine certain effects. In the terminology of B.F. Skinner (1971) human behaviour is subject to operant conditioning. One consequence of this, Skinner believes, is that many current social institutions and practices, such as punishment for crimes, are outmoded and should be replaced with an appropriate technology of behaviour (see BEHAVIOURISM).

What Skinner's position reveals, and what is present also in the other two schools, is the conviction that supposedly scientific statements have significant social as well as moral and political implications. All three assume human nature is a proper object of 'scientific' study and also assume that any social thought that does not comport with the findings of these studies is untenable. Despite the great prestige enjoyed by science, the appropriateness of this whole set of assumptions has been severely challenged. At the heart of these challenges is the contrary conviction that it is the humanness of human nature (not its 'nature') that should be the subject of enquiry.

Humanistic interpretations
Contextualism   According to this account human nature is specified or made concrete by the particular context within which it is necessarily found. Outside such a context only uninformative abstract generalizations (such as the number of chromosomes) are possible. No meaningful separation can be made between humans and their specific culture, since, as Clifford Geertz puts it, humans are 'cultural artifacts' (1972, p. 50).

Symbolism   Ernst Cassirer defines 'man' as an *animal symbolicum* (1944, p. 26). The way to understand that which is essentially human is to examine what is distinctive, and that lies in the fact that humans alone are linguistic beings. Human reality is not that of behaviour patterns but of symbolic action manifest in myths, art, religion and so on.

Large issues are involved in the differences between the various scientific and humanistic views of human nature. Of course neither position denies that the other has a role and one of the twentieth century's most far-reaching accounts can be seen as bridging the gap. The premise of Freud's (1915–17, 1923) psychoanalytic account of human nature is that its basic components can only be revealed by a scientific account of the way the Unconscious operates. But Freud's whole endeavour is to uncover pathologies in this operation and supply remedies to improve both individual and social life – religion, for example, he regarded as a 'neurotic relic' (1927, p. 72) (see PSYCHOANALYSIS).

All the views canvassed thus far accept that human nature is a meaningful concept. Perhaps the most characteristically twentieth-century view on this topic has been an attack on this meaningfulness. The most celebrated version is Sartre's (1946) EXISTENTIALISM. According to Sartre, human nature does not exist because there is nothing 'outside' it (such as God) to give it a 'nature' or essence. In humans, existence precedes essence; unlike natural objects which merely exist, humans decide to exist. Another criticism of the concept is that it only exists within certain historically specific discourses, so that M. Foucault (1966) is able to claim that it only emerged at the end of the eighteenth century and is not, accordingly, a universal transhistorical idea.

Within twentieth-century discourses human nature plays a prominent role in ideological argument. For example, integral to the differences between the socialist and liberal views of a 'good society' is whether cooperation or competition is central to human nature. Less overtly, the difference between the scientific and humanistic accounts is similarly disputatious. For example, the scientific claim that altruism is impossible, because selfishness is an ineluctable fact of human nature, is criticized for being rather an ideological defence of the status quo since it forecloses humanly possible futures. These examples illustrate why no uncontentious definition is possible.

Reading
Benthall, J. ed. 1973: *The Limits of Human Nature.*
Berry, C.J. 1986: *Human Nature.*
Forbes, I. and Smith, S. eds. 1983: *Politics and Human Nature.*
Hollis, M. 1977: *Models of Man.*
Jaggar, A. 1983: *Feminist Politics and Human Nature.*
Midgley, M. 1978: *Beast and Man.*
Platt, J.R. ed. 1965: *New Views of the Nature of Man.*
Rothblatt, B. ed. 1968: *Changing Perspectives on Man.*
Stevenson, L. 1974: *Seven Theories of Human Nature.*
Trigg, R. 1982: *The Shaping of Man.*

CHRISTOPHER J. BERRY

human rights *See* RIGHTS

I

ideal type The classification of phenomena into types is a common aspect of scientific work, as well as of ordinary life, and many scientific concepts involve an element of abstraction from concrete reality, or idealization in a non-moral sense: for example the concepts of frictionless motion or of a perfectly competitive market. Max Weber borrowed (from the political historian Georg Jellinek) the term *Idealtypus* (ideal type) to distinguish the analytical concepts of history and the other social sciences from merely classificatory concepts. The term 'exchange', for example, can be used either simply to refer to a set of similar phenomena, with what Wittgenstein later called 'family resemblances' between them, or as an analytical concept related to judgements about economic rationality, marginal utility and so forth. In the latter case, Weber claims, the concept is ideal typical in the sense that 'it removes itself from empirical reality which can only be *compared* or related to it' (Weber, 1904, p. 102, cf. pp. 93–4). Hence ideal types cannot be directly falsified if empirical reality seems not to fit them even approximately.

Weber's account of the ideal type is an aspect of his broader model of the relationship between the social sciences and VALUES, or more precisely value reference: '*There is no* absolutely "objective" scientific analysis of culture – or . . . of "social phenomena" *independent* of special and "one-sided" view-points according to which – expressly or tacitly, consciously or unconsciously – they are selected, analyzed and organized for expository purposes' (1904, p. 72).

Criticisms of Weber's account fall roughly into two categories, positivistic and hermeneutic. Positivists have tended to assimilate ideal types to the general class of theoretical concepts, emphasizing the possibility of measuring how far empirical phenomena diverge from the pure type and of mapping out a continuum between opposed types. Science, it is claimed, moves from the rather primitive classificatory and typological phase with which Weber was concerned to a more precise set of operationalized concepts linked together in laws. The hermeneutic critique inaugurated by Alfred Schutz (1932) stresses that the type-construction operated by the social scientist is parasitic on earlier processes of typification carried out in the life-world. Weber is too quick to replace actors' typifications of the meaning of social phenomena with his own ideal types, without concerning himself sufficiently with the fit between them – what Schutz calls 'adequacy'.

Both criticisms share a sense that ideal types, as Weber presents them, are too arbitrary; decisions to construct or to abandon them are left to the judgement, what Weber calls the 'tact', of the individual theorist. This suspicion of the conventionalism implicit in Max Weber's philosophy of science (see NEO-KANTIANISM) has led rationalists and realists to uphold a more ambitious conception of real DEFINITION – which Weber however would probably have accused of essentialism. The present mood in social science seems somewhat sceptical both of the positivist ideal of precision in measurement and of the radically distinctive contribution of 'phenomenological' and other forms of hermeneutic theory, and thus Weber's concept of the ideal type remains attractive.

Reading
Burger, Thomas 1976: *Max Weber's Theory of Concept Formation: History, Laws, and Ideal Types.*
Outhwaite, William 1983: *Concept Formation in Social Science.*
Papineau, David 1976: Ideal types and empirical theories. *British Journal for the Philosophy of Science* 27.2.
Schutz, Alfred 1932 (*1972*): *The Phenomenology of the Social World.*
Weber, Max 1904 (*1949*): 'Objectivity' in social science and social policy. In *The Methodology of the Social Sciences.*

WILLIAM OUTHWAITE

identity Derived from the Latin root *idem*, implying sameness and continuity, the term has a long philosophical history which examines permanence amid change and unity amid diversity, but in the modern period it is closely linked to the rise of INDIVIDUALISM, and its analysis is considered to start with the writings of John Locke and David Hume. It is not till the twentieth century, however, that the term comes into popular usage; reinforced especially since the 1950s in North America with the publication of books like *The Lonely Crowd* (Riesman et al., 1950) and *Identity and Anxiety* (Stein et al., 1960). These, along with much literature and drama, documented the increasing loss of meaning in MASS SOCIETY and the subsequent search for identity; and during this period the term became widely used in descriptions of the quest to establish 'who one really is'. Initially dealing with the crises faced by blacks, Jews and religious minorities, it was ultimately generalized to the whole of modern society. By the 1970s, Robert Coles could claim that the term was 'the purest of clichés' (Gleason, 1983, p. 913).

In the social sciences, discussions of identity take two major forms, psychodynamic and sociological. The psychodynamic tradition emerges with Sigmund Freud's theory of identification, through which the child comes to assimilate (or introject) external persons or objects (usually the superego of the parent). Psychodynamic theory stresses the inner core of a psychic structure as having a continuous (though often conflictual) identity. For Lichtenstein, it is 'the capacity to remain the same in the midst of constant change' (1977, p. 135). It was, however, the psychohistorian Erik Erikson who most developed the idea. He saw identity as 'a process "located" in the core of the individual and yet also in the core of his communal culture, a process which establishes, in fact, the identity of those two identities' (1968, p. 22). He developed the term 'identity crisis' during World War II with patients who had 'lost a sense of personal sameness and historical continuity' (p. 17), and he subsequently generalized it to a whole stage of life (as part of his epigenetic life-stage model – the eight stages of man). Here, youth is identified as a universal crisis period of potential identity confusion, which can ultimately be resolved through a commitment to a broader social ideology: there is 'a universal psychological need for a system of ideas that provides a convincing world image' (p. 31). Personal crisis and the historical moment are here strongly connected. Subsequently, the term 'identity crisis' moved into common parlance, as indeed did the later concept of mid-life crisis – coined in the 1970s through the work of Gail Sheehey (1976) and Daniel Levinson (1978).

The sociological tradition of identity theory is linked to SYMBOLIC INTERACTIONISM and emerges from the pragmatic theory of the self discussed by William James (1892, ch. 3) and George Herbert Mead (1934). For James, identity is revealed when we can say: '*This* is the real me!' (cited in Erikson, 1968, p. 19). The self is a distinctively human capacity which enables people to reflect reflexively on their nature and the social world through communication and language. Both James and Mead see the self as a process with two phases – the 'I' which is knower, inner, subjective, creative, determining and unknowable; and the 'Me' which is the more known, outer, determined and social phase. As Mead says: 'The "I" is the response of the organism to the attitude of others; the "me" is the organised set of attitudes of others which one himself assumes' (Mead, 1934, p. 175). It is the 'Me' which is most linked to identity – with the way in which we come to take ourselves as an object through the act of seeing ourselves and others. Identification, here, is a process of naming, of placing ourselves in socially constructed categories, and language becomes central in this process (Strauss, 1969). In the later works of Erving Goffman and Peter Berger, identity is clearly seen to be 'socially bestowed, socially sustained and socially transformed' (Berger, 1966, p. 116). People build their personal identities out of the culture they live in.

Both the sociological and psychodynamic approaches aim to link the inner world to the outer world, but their emphases differ. For both, however, the struggle to define the self is linked to the way in which a community constructs conceptions of people and life. In the modern world, both perspectives suggest that a shared community has largely dissolved – leaving modern people without a clear sense of identity (see also ANOMIE). This dilemma has spawned a huge literature, including many plays and novels where the 'quest for identity' or the 'breakdown of the self' are primary themes. These accounts have both an optimistic and pessimistic version, and can generate considerable ambivalence (Waterman, 1985). For the optimists, the modern world has brought with it increasing individuality and choice over a wider range of identities. Thus people are more likely to 'self-actualize' (Maslow, 1987); to discover an inner self which is not artificially imposed by tradition, culture or religion; to embark on quests for greater individuality, self-understanding, flexibility and difference. It is the 'democratization of personhood' (Clecak, 1983, p. 179). In contrast, pessimists portray a mass culture of estrangement: the psychodynamic tradition highlights the loss of boundaries between self and culture and the rise of the narcissistic personality; while the sociologists see a trend towards fragmentation, homelessness and meaninglessness, and bemoan the loss of authority in the public world through the growth of self-absorption and selfishness (Lasch, 1978; Berger et al., 1973; Bellah et al., 1985). Most popularly, all this is caught in the label given to the 1970s of the 'Me Decade' (Wolfe, 1976). Whatever analysis is made, most agree that there has been a profound shift in the modern self, making it more individualistic and impulsive than in former times.

Apart from the way ideas on identity have formed the basis of much therapeutic practice, they have also given rise to a distinctive form of politics. Identity politics became increasingly prominent from the late 1960s onwards, and is particularly associated with ethnic and religious minorities, as well as with feminist and lesbian and gay movements. It tacitly draws from Marx's model of class consciousness in which a subordinate group develops a self-conscious awareness of its position and becomes galvanized into political action (Marx's distinction between a class in itself and a class for itself). There is a clear move here from a class-based politics to a broader set of alliances. Experiences such as those of black, gay or women's oppression become highlighted as the focus for creating a separate group identity – as blacks, gays or feminists. Around this a strong culture of support develops and a political analysis takes shape. (See also COUNTERCULTURE.) There is hence a dialectic of culture, politics and identity which brings about social change (see Weeks, 1985). Towards the end of the twentieth century, some postmodernist commentators perceived 'identity' politics as the pattern for the future (see MODERNISM AND POSTMODERNISM). The traditional 'left–right' distinctions seemed to be breaking down as new alignments were being forged.

Reading
Baumeister, R.F. 1986: *Identity: Cultural Change and the Struggle for Self.*
Erikson, E.H. 1968: *Identity: Youth and Crisis.*
Lichtenstein, H. 1977: *The Dilemma of Human Identity.*
Mead, G.H. 1934 (*1962*): *Mind, Self and Society.*

Riesman, D., Glazer, N. and Denny, R. 1950 (*1966*): *The Lonely Crowd.*
Strauss, A. 1969: *Mirrors and Masks: The Search for Identity.*
Wiegert, A.J., Teitge, J.S. and Teitge, D. 1986: *Identity and Society.*

KEN PLUMMER

ideology   Literally referring to a science (or *logos*) of ideas, the term was used in that sense by the French philosopher Destutt de Tracy in his book *Eléments d'idéologie*, published in 1801. Ideas derive exclusively from sense perceptions, he believed, human intelligence is an aspect of animal life, and 'ideology' is, therefore, a part of zoology. Tracy and his colleagues felt that by this reductionist analysis, in the sense that mental activities were attributed to underlying physiological causes, they had arrived at scientific truth; and they demanded that educational reforms should be based on this new science (see ENLIGHTENMENT). When Napoleon was a general, he had proudly accepted membership in the Institut National made up of the learned societies, and – like the *idéologues* – he visited the philosophical salon of Mme Helvétius. But once in power, Napoleon wanted to uphold religion against its detractors. Hence he denounced Tracy and his circle as 'nebulous metaphysicians' and their science of ideas as a dangerous ideology: these enemies of the French people wanted to base legislation on the 'first causes' they claimed to have discovered, and hence do away with the laws of the human heart and the lessons of history. Ever since, the term 'ideology' has been inseparable from the pejorative implication that ideas are used to obscure the truth and to manipulate people through deception (see also PROPAGANDA). In this historical episode one finds assembled all the meanings associated with 'ideology': a science of ideas, the notion that ideas are derived from some underlying, extra-ideational basis (physiology, class, the struggle for power, and so on), the denunciation of ideas as visionary and subversive and hence the association of doctrines or myths with some group or movement bent on putting a dangerous political or cultural plan into effect.

The pejorative meaning of ideology became a standby of the political struggle during the nineteenth century, as the politics of notables gave way to the development of political parties with their appeals to the masses. Public affairs had been the concern of the privileged few, who took for granted that they knew what was best for their inferiors. In their own eyes, the privilege of their social position dispensed with the need to justify their actions. Conservatives of this persuasion typically accused their opponents of being ideological visionaries who subverted the social order by abstract schemes, out of touch with reality. Liberals and radicals, on the other hand, held that public affairs were a concern of the people and organized political clubs or parties to advance their ends. Typically, they accused the privileged few of exploiting the people under the pretence of benevolence. However, liberals and radicals also accused each other, because each group saw its opponents as hiding partisan goals under the guise of identifying them with the public good. The consequence was that the pejorative use of ideology became universal, leading Thomas Carlyle to quip that 'orthodoxy is my doxy, heterodoxy is thy doxy.' It was the ancient paradox of the liar: a man says that all men use ideas to deceive; he is a man; and so his own statement also deceives.

Here is one reason for the enormous appeal of MARXISM, which is diminishing only now. Marx and Engels denounced their opponents as 'ideologists', and in addition they elaborated a theory of 'historical truth' which, they claimed, proved their own views to be scientific. History is a history of class struggles, they asserted, arising from the organization of production and affecting all aspects of consciousness. Marx distinguishes successive social structures such as feudalism and capitalism in terms of the classes and the consciousness to which they give rise. And he identifies TRUTH with the historical role of the class which, because it was suppressed in the past, has the progressive future in its grasp. The reactionary rule of a class (aristocracy under feudalism, bourgeoisie under late capitalism) leads to ideological defences of the status quo; the progressive role of a class (bourgeoisie under feudalism, proletariat under capitalism) is the source of truth in the sense of access to the correct understanding of all present alienation and of human emancipation in the future. In the past, philosophers have only interpreted the world and produced ideological reflections of dehumanizing class relations, however abstractly. In the present and the future, the point is to destroy dehumanizing conditions once and for all. That can be done only by a unity of theory and practice such that in the final crisis of capitalism (and because of that crisis) those identified with the working class can

and will comprehend 'theoretically the historical movement as a whole'. In the socialist society of the future, the mystical veil of religion and all other ideological distortions of man's real condition will finally vanish, because 'the practical relations of everyday life offer to man none but perfectly intelligible and reasonable relations with regard to his fellow men and to nature.' These references (*Theses on Feuerbach*, 1845; *Communist Manifesto*, 1848; *Capital*, 1867) show that throughout his career Marx placed his own work at the centre of his world-historical distinction between ideology and truth. The idea of being on the 'right side' of world history, and hence 'scientific', distinguishes Marxism from all other social and political theories.

Since Marx, various other conceptions of ideology have been developed, though frequently in relation to his views. This persistent tendency in Western thought is due to the underlying assumption that ideas cannot and should not be taken at face value, but must be analysed in terms of the 'forces' that lie behind them. Among them are Marx's class struggle, Nietzsche's struggle for power, Freud's libidinal constitution of human nature, or a general preference for genetic explanations. Not what a person says, but why he or she says it has become a main focus of attention, so that an 'end of ideology' is not in sight.

Reading
Barrett, Michèle 1991: *The Politics of Truth*.
Larrain, Jorge 1979: *The Concept of Ideology*.
Thompson, John 1984: *Studies in the Theory of Ideology*.

REINHARD BENDIX

idiographic The distinction between idiographic and nomothetic method was first drawn by the philosopher Wilhelm Windelband (1848–1915). An idiographic approach is concerned with individual phenomena, as in biography and much of history, while its opposite, the nomothetic approach, aims to formulate general propositions or 'laws' (Greek: *nomos*). Windelband and Heinrich Rickert distinguished the idiographic method of history and other 'cultural sciences' from the nomothetic approach of economics and sociology, which they categorized as natural sciences. They recognized, however, that these categories have to be understood as ideal types (see IDEAL TYPE). Evolutionary biology, for example, is in large part idiographic, and an idiographic, historically specific approach to economics and law was upheld by the corresponding 'historical schools' in late nineteenth-century Germany (see HISTORICISM; METHODENSTREIT).

In much of the twentieth century, idiographic approaches were somewhat depreciated, under the influence of POSITIVISM and STRUCTURALISM, though they remained dominant in ethnographic field work (see ANTHROPOLOGY) and were formalized in social science methodology as the 'case study method'. 'Ethnographic' and historical case studies have recently played a growing part in sociology – notably in the SOCIOLOGY OF SCIENCE and the sociology of education. Biographical or 'life history' approaches are also attracting considerable attention.

Reading
Bertaux, Daniel ed. 1981: *Biography and Society.*
Hamel, Jacques ed. 1992: The case study method. *Current Sociology* 40.
Rickert, Heinrich 1902 (*1986*): *The Limits of Concept Formation in Natural Science* (abridged).

WILLIAM OUTHWAITE

illness *See* HEALTH; PSYCHIATRY AND MENTAL ILLNESS

immigrant workers *See* MIGRATION

imperialism The concept of 'imperialism' was introduced at the beginning of the twentieth century to deal theoretically and practically with an unexpected development of the capitalist world-economy. Nineteenth-century liberal and socialist thought had both assumed that the free-trade world order established under British hegemony in the first half of the century was there to stay and that, over time, this order would strengthen the tendency towards the supersession of interstate rivalries over territory. In the closing decades of the century there occurred instead a major resurgence of struggles over territory among the great powers of the state system, which threatened to destroy the very unity of the world market.

The concept of imperialism was first introduced by a liberal political economist (Hobson, 1902) but, with some notable exceptions (for instance, Schumpeter, 1919), liberal social thought generally ignored or dismissed its significance. Socialist thinkers working in the tradition established by Marx, in contrast, put the concept at the centre of their analyses and debates. The reason is quite

simple. The resurgence of interstate territorial rivalries continually undermined the solidarity of the world proletariat and pulled and pushed its various components into antagonistic national alignments under the hegemony of their respective ruling classes. Faced with the equally unpleasant alternatives of holding on to the principles of proletarian internationalism but losing the support of their constituencies, or going along with the nationalist predispositions of their constituencies and abandoning the principles of proletarian internationalism, Marx's followers were forced to question the assumed dominance of a unified world market over state action and engage in a major revision of received theories and doctrines.

Marxist theories of imperialism invariably focused on the relationship between the resurgence of interstate territorial rivalries and the development of capitalism on a world scale. Notwithstanding all their differences, Marxist theories of imperialism had one thesis/hypothesis in common: imperialism was the result of capitalist development and an expression of its maturity. Disagreements concerned the question of how and why capitalist development had generated imperialism, whether imperialism was the 'last' or the 'last-but-one' stage of capitalist development, and what political conclusions ought to be drawn from the hypothesized relationship between capitalism and imperialism. But whatever the disagreements, there was an underlying consensus that the resurgence of interstate territorial rivalries was a necessary consequence of the maturity of capitalism.

The two main variants of Marxist theories of imperialism were Rudolf Hilferding (1910) and Rosa Luxemburg (1913). Hilferding traced imperialism to a fundamental mutation in processes of accumulation due to three interrelated tendencies: the increasing concentration and centralization of capital; the spread of monopolistic practices; and the organic domination of finance capital over industrial capital. At a certain stage of their development – it was maintained – these tendencies heightened interstate territorial rivalries. Nevertheless, by centralizing the control of the industrial apparatus in the hands of a few financial institutions, they also created the organizational conditions for a 'socialist' takeover of national economies.

In contrast to this theory, Luxemburg saw the forcible incorporation of peoples and territories into processes of capital accumulation as a constant feature of the latter, due to the attempts of the agents of capital accumulation to overcome chronic overproduction tendencies. As capitalist development deepened and widened, the pressure to incorporate ever-new peoples and territories increased, but the availability of peoples and territories not yet incorporated decreased. Imperialism was thus conceived as 'the political expression of the accumulation of capital in its competitive struggle for what remains still open of the non-capitalist environment' (Luxemburg, 1913).

Early twentieth-century political debates among Marxists on what to expect and on what to do under the world-systemic circumstances created by the resurgence of interstate territorial rivalries came to be centred around Hilferding's theory, and paid little or no attention to Luxemburg's theory. The positions taken by Karl Kautsky (1913–14) and Lenin (1916) in these debates were both based on Hilferding's theory. For Kautsky, the joint tendencies towards the concentrations of capital, the spread of monopolistic practices and the organic domination of finance over industrial capital would, over time, lead to a supersession of interstate territorial rivalries and to the development of what he called 'ultra-imperialism'. Only at this ultra-imperialist stage of capitalism would conditions be optimal for the socialist transformation of the world.

For Lenin (1916), in contrast, *these same tendencies* did not unfold in a political vacuum. Rather, they developed 'under such stress' with such a tempo, with such contradictions, conflicts, and convulsions – not only economic, but also political, national, etc., etc. – that . . . before the respective national finance capitals will have formed a world union of "ultra-imperialism", imperialism will inevitably explode, capitalism will turn into its opposite' (Lenin's 1915 preface to Bukharin's *Imperialism and World Economy*). Only by actively intervening in these contradictions, conflicts and convulsions, while upholding the principles of proletarian internationalism, could Marxist parties hope to retain and expand their national constituencies and initiate the socialist transformation of the world.

The success of Leninist strategies of socialist revolution between 1917 and 1949 has been generally taken by Marxists to provide strong evidence in support of the validity of the theory of imperialism with which such strategies were associated. To some extent this is a legitimate point of view. In particular, there can be little doubt that throughout the first half of the twentieth century, Lenin's reconceptualization of Hilferding's theory of imperialism provided a far better guide to political action than any of the rival conceptualizations and theorizations. However, this does not mean that the Hilferding-Lenin theory of imperialism accounted accurately for all the relevant connections between capitalism and imperialism, or that the theory retained all its relevance and validity once it had been effectively applied in the anti-imperialist struggle.

On the contrary, the evolution of the capitalist world-economy since World War II has shown the historical limitations of the Lenin-Hilferding theory of imperialism and has made the entire body of early twentieth-century Marxist thought on the subject increasingly irrelevant to an understanding, let alone to a purposive transformation, of the present WORLD-SYSTEM. Ironically, this increasing irrelevance of Marxist theories of imperialism in the second half of the twentieth century has been at least in part the result of their success as a guide to political action in the first half of the century. As predicted by Lenin, inter-imperialist conflicts did create unique opportunities for socialist and national liberation movements to seize state power across the globe (see also COLONIAL LIBERATION MOVEMENT), and in the years immediately after World War II world capitalism did indeed seem to be about to 'turn into its opposite'. To be sure, socialist revolution failed to take root in the centres of world capitalist development as was generally expected by Lenin and most Marxists at the beginning of the twentieth century. But even in these centres the power and influence of working-class organizations at the end of World War II was at an all-time high.

Under these circumstances, capitalism survived by shedding its imperialist clothes. The tendency towards interstate territorial rivalries, which had prompted the introduction of the concept of imperialism, was reversed in an unprecedented wave of decolonization accompanied by the delegitimation of territorial expansionism and the reconstruction of the world market. Over time, it became quite clear that world capitalism could survive, and expand further, without being associated with the kind of territorial rivalries among core capitalist states that Marxists had assumed to be the necessary outcome of full capitalist development.

This capability of capitalism to survive imperialism is what all Marxist theories had failed to predict. Even Kautsky's prediction of an ultra-imperialist stage of world capitalism, which may seem to come close to what has happened after World War II, failed at least as much as rival Marxist predictions in foreseeing the course of twentieth-century capitalist history. For one thing, what came into being after World War II was not the kind of highly centralized, world-monopolistic structure envisaged by Kautsky's ultra-imperialism but a highly competitive world-economy. More important, whether ultra-imperialist or not, the capitalist world order established under United States hegemony was not the outcome of a self-acting development of capital accumulation. Rather, it was the result of 30 years of acute conflicts and convulsions in the world-system and of the active intervention in such conflicts and convulsions of socialist revolutionary vanguards, which Kautsky neither foresaw nor advocated.

The truth of the matter is that Marxist theories of imperialism in general, and the most influential among them (that is, Hilferding's) in particular, were all based on the historical experience of late nineteenth-century and early twentieth-century Germany, and assumed that that experience was prototypical of late capitalism. In reality, however, the relevance and validity of Hilferding's exemplary analysis of finance capital and imperialism were limited to Germany and other states of continental Europe in the period of transition from British to US hegemony. By no stretch of the imagination could it be said to have accounted for the relationship between capitalism and territorial expansionism as evinced in the experience of the declining hegemonic power (the United Kingdom) or of the rising hegemonic power (the USA).

From this point of view, J.A. Hobson's pioneering analysis of imperialism was far less limited than that of either Hilferding or Luxemburg. His conceptualization was better suited to capture system-level, long-term tendencies than those of his Marxist counterparts. He defined imperialism as one of several forms of expansionism and traced the particular form that expansionism took at the end of the nineteenth century to the policies and social structure of the declining hegemonic power.

Even though Hobson anticipated in many respects both Hilferding and Luxemburg, in tracing imperialism to capitalist development, he was careful in ruling out any necessary connection between capitalism and the generalized territorial expansionism of the late nineteenth century. In his analysis, the connection was purely contingent on the distribution of wealth and power among states and within the dominant world power. Hence the connection could be severed by greater political democracy and economic equality in the UK, and/or by a change in world leadership from the UK to a less oligarchic state.

Hobson's conceptual apparatus can be expanded without great distortions to accommodate both the acute interstate conflicts typical of the first half of the twentieth century, and the decolonization and recomposition of interstate conflicts typical of the second half of the century. In this expanded Hobsonian framework, imperialism, as originally conceived by liberal and Marxist thought, appears not as the highest/latest stage of capitalism but as a phase in a long cycle of world hegemony characterized by a strong evolutionary tendency towards the supersession of territorial expansionism in interstate relations (Arrighi, 1983). If this characterization is borne out by future trends of the capitalist world-economy, Schumpeter's thesis that in the very long run the correlation between territorial expansionism and capitalism is negative rather than positive may deserve greater credit than Marxists have been willing to admit.

Thus far, however, Marxists have shown little predisposition to engage in major revisions of received theories of imperialism. Their main reaction to the reversal of territorial expansionism after World War II has been to redefine imperialism to include the forms of world capitalist domination that were resurrected or created anew under United States hegemony. 'Imperialism' in Marxist writings has thus come to designate the development of underdevelopment and other international aspects of capitalism. The result has been a semantic confusion and an analytical impasse (Sutcliffe, 1972, pp. 313–14) which have never been resolved.

The traditional concerns of theories of imperialism have lately been taken over by WORLD-SYSTEM analysis and international political economy. Within these perspectives, the notion of imperialism has been superseded by the concepts of hegemony and world power. One can only hope that what remains relevant and valid of early social thought on imperialism is not lost in the process.

See also COLONIALISM; INTERNATIONAL DIVISION OF LABOUR.

Reading

Arrighi, G. 1983: *The Geometry of Imperialism.*

Hilferding, R. 1910 (*1981*): *Finance Capital.*

Hobson, J.A. 1902 (*1968*): *Imperialism: A Study.*

Kautsky, K. 1913–14: Der Imperialismus. *Neue Zeit* 32. 2, 908–22.

Lenin, V.I. 1916 (*1964*): *Imperialism: The Highest Stage of Capitalism.*

Luxemburg, Rosa 1913 (*1951*): *The Accumulation of Capital.*

Schumpeter, J. 1919 (*1951*): The sociology of imperialism. In *Imperialism and Social Classes*, ed. Paul Sweezy.

Sutcliffe, B. 1972: Conclusion. In *Studies in the Theory of Imperialism*, ed. R. Owen and B. Sutcliffe.

GIOVANNI ARRIGHI

individual, socialization of the *See* SOCIALIZATION

individualism This term embraces several ideas, doctrines and attitudes whose common factor is the according of centrality to the 'individual'. It originated in the early nineteenth century in post-revolutionary France, where it signified the dissolution of social bonds, the abandonment by individuals of their social obligations and commitments. In the German lands, its meaning was different: there it was associated with Romanticism and tended to signify the cult of individual uniqueness and originality and the flourishing of individuality. In England its meaning was different again: it contrasted with 'collectivism', and it typically served to refer to the virtues of self-reliance and initiative celebrated by Samuel Smiles, in the moral sphere, and was associated with LIBERALISM in the economic and political spheres. Another influential nineteenth-century usage was that of Jacob Burckhardt for whom the Italian Renaissance had engendered individualism, by which he meant (among other things) the recognition of the distinctness of unique individuals and the cultivation of PRIVACY (Burckhardt, 1860). All of these meanings have survived into our time.

Perhaps most influential on its twentieth-century uses has been Alexis de Tocqueville who wrote that it was 'a new expression to which a new idea has given birth . . . a deliberate and peaceful sentiment which disposes each citizen to isolate himself from his fellows and to draw apart with his family and friends', abandoning 'the wider society to itself', first sapping 'the virtues of public life', then attacking and destroying all others, eventually being 'absorbed into pure egoism' (Tocqueville, 1835–40, bk 2, pt 2, ch. 2). This usage has been influential among modern theorists of mass society and American social and cultural critics. It contrasts with another usage in which the term has been a catchword for free enterprise, limited government, personal freedom and the attitudes, forms of behaviour and aspirations held to sustain them. This usage was exemplified in Herbert Hoover's famous campaign speech of 1928 celebrating the 'American system of rugged individualism'.

Of a more abstract character are various further doctrines. One is *methodological individualism*. This is a doctrine about explanation which states that no explanation in social science or history can be adequate (or in another version 'rock-bottom') unless couched in terms wholly of features of individuals – their properties, goals, beliefs and actions. Social wholes, or aggregate patterns of behaviour, must always be explained, or ultimately explained, in terms of individuals. This doctrine has taken many forms and never ceased to be controversial, often passionately so. Karl Popper and Friedrich von Hayek have seen its defence as essential to the liberal defence of a free society. Others, from Emile Durkheim on, have seen its rejection as the first step to the sociological understanding of realities that are independent of and constraining on individuals. Yet others see the contests over it as combining useful caveats and insights with misleading exaggerations. Thus its defenders sensibly warn against the hypostatizing of social entities and collective forces and wisely insist that macro-explanation requires micro-foundations, yet they too often claim that social facts are really fictions and that social wholes are mere constructions of individuals. Conversely, its opponents rightly claim that impersonal structures and the behaviour of collectivities can have independent explanatory force, yet they all too easily detach these from a plausible theory of individual action.

A further doctrine concerns practical deliberation: it is sometimes called *atomism*. It holds that the ends of action are all individual and thus that social goods are no more than concentrations of individual goods, and hence that there are no irreducibly social goods, partly or wholly constituted by common actions and meanings. UTILITARIANISM and what is today called 'welfarism' exemplify this view, holding that the relative goodness of a state of affairs must be based exclusively on, and taken to be a function of, the various individual utilities it contains. Charles Taylor sees atomism as rooted in 'those philosophical traditions . . . which started with the postulation of an extensionless subject, epistemologically a *tabula rasa* and politically a presuppositionless bearer of rights' (Taylor, 1985, p. 210). Otto Gierke identified it with Natural Law thinkers from Hobbes to Kant, for whom all forms of social life were 'the creation of individuals' and merely 'the means to individual objects' (Gierke, 1868–1913, pp. 106, 111).

Apart from these, various other varieties may be mentioned. *Epistemological individualism* places the source of knowledge within the individual. It has been asserted in different ways by Descartes and various versions of EMPIRICISM. *Ethical individualism* sees morality as essentially individually oriented – either in the form of ethical egoism (according to which the sole moral object of an individual's action is his own benefit) or a further, more radical set of ideas, from which EXISTENTIALISM descends, according to which the individual is the very source of moral principles, the supreme arbiter of moral and other values.

Finally, there is a complex of ideas which may be labelled *political individualism* which proposes various connexions between 'the individual' and government: first, a view of government as based on the individually given consent of its citizens, its authority deriving from that consent; second, a view of political representation, not of orders or estates or classes or social functions, but of individual interests; and third, a view of the purposes of government as confined to enabling individuals' purposes to be satisfied and individuals' rights to be protected, allowing them maximum scope to pursue their interests. The first is rooted in social contract theories, but even where such theories are abandoned, it is the centre of justification for liberal democracy, though anarchists, since Henry David Thoreau, have drawn more subversive conclusions from it. The second was central to the framing of the United States constitution and the utilitarians' proposals for political reform and to modern constitutionalism in general. The third, which goes back to John Locke, is close to the heart of political liberalism.

Reading
Hayek, F.A. 1948 (*1980*): *Individualism and Economic Order*.

Lukes, S. 1973: *Individualism*.
O'Neill, J. ed. 1973: *Modes of Individualism and Collectivism*.
Taylor, C. 1985: Atomism. In *Philosophical Papers II*.
Tocqueville, A. de 1835–40 (*1966*): *Democracy in America*, trans. G. Lawrence, ed. J.P. Mayer and M. Lerner, esp. bk 2, pt 2, ch. 2.

STEVEN LUKES

industrial democracy The concept designates the idea and practice of cooperation between capital and labour to run in common workshops and enterprises. Industrial democracy aims to overcome the social division of labour, that is the hierarchical differences in the production process. In a broader sense it has to be associated with the general process of PARTICIPATION and democratization of society (Lauck, 1926). The term has also to be linked, and is sometimes identical, with 'economic democracy' (Naphtali, 1928; Carnoy and Shearer, 1980).

The idea of industrial democracy dates back to the early or utopian socialists at the beginning of the nineteenth century, the most famous protagonist being Robert Owen who founded in 1800 an industrial community in New Lanark, in Scotland (Owen 1812–16). It is the child of industrial societies which created the modern division between capital and labour, and the class of wage earners. From the very beginning two schools of social thought tried to overcome the conflicts and misery which accompanied the childhood of this society. The first is that of humanist, religious and philanthropic thinkers and practitioners who tried to integrate the proletariat into society to prevent revolutions and uprisings. The two churches – Protestant and Catholic – provoked many debates and activities. In Germany the Catholic priest Adolf Kolping created in the second half of the nineteenth century a broad social movement which resulted in Pope Leo XIII's social *Encyclica Rerum Novarum* of 1891. The second school is linked with the workers' movement in its different expressions as SOCIALISM, SYNDICALISM and TRADE UNIONS. Here industrial democracy might be understood as part of a process from alienation through participation to self-determination. The COOPERATIVE MOVEMENT is a specific form of industrial democracy so far as it covers producer cooperatives.

In 1916 England introduced joint management in the form of the Whitley councils. Certainly, as in other countries, the war situation facilitated a democratic opening into what had been until then mainly authoritarian, quasi-military decision structures in the economy. Joint management was also reintroduced into the American economy during World War II.

After World War II, labour legislation based on concepts of industrial democracy was introduced in many countries. The OECD and the International Labour Office also became active. The ILO itself may be regarded as the international part of industrial democracy. A number of reports and bibliographies have been published under its auspices and its International Institute of Labour Research carried out a number of studies itself (International Labour Office, 1981; Monat and Sarfati, 1986). Industrial democracy may be, and was, interpreted as a counter movement against 'scientific management' which alienated men and women even more from their product than capitalism had previously done.

The principal types of industrial democracy may be differentiated in various ways (ILO, 1981; King and van de Vall, 1978), but the following forms may be suggested as having developed historically and geographically.

Participative management has developed with the 'human relations' movement since the 1930s and new forms of work organization have been introduced since that time. It often takes the form of industrial democracy but remains one-sided and limits participation generally to the workplace level, with the final say reserved to management. Nevertheless, it can be regarded as a management response to growing demands by the workforce for more democracy at the workplace, and therefore promising for the future of democracy. 'Organizational development', 'socio-technical systems' (Emery and Thorsrud, 1969) and 'quality circles' are some of the methods used.

Collective bargaining is the most widespread form of industrial participation. It consists of regular negotiations over wages, working conditions, social benefits and so on, which may be held at the shopfloor, enterprise, industry or even national level. In the Anglo-Saxon countries this is in general the only form of industrial democracy accepted and practised. At the end of the last century Sidney and Beatrice Webb (1897) developed the general framework for this approach (see FABIANISM). Although there is a pluralist understanding of divergent economic interests at the base of the collective bargaining model, it tends never to question the economic system as such and is therefore not revolutionary. (Derber, 1970; Okamoto, 1981.)

Shop stewards as a form of industrial democracy have developed in England. This is a grass-roots democratic structure in which the elected representative of a shop negotiates directly with management on different issues of work-life. It may be regarded as complementary to the system of collective bargaining. (Coates and Topham, 1975.)

Worker ownership has always had a certain importance. Popular capitalism tried to integrate the workers through shareholding and profit-sharing schemes into the company and/or economy. Recently the so-called Employee Stock Holding Programme (ESOP) in the USA has been much discussed and scientifically studied. But often these participative schemes do not include voting rights, and they have not yet fundamentally changed labour relations. (*International Handbook of Participation in Organizations*, vol. 1, 1989, and Vol. 2, 1991.)

Guild socialism is linked with the name of G.D.H. Cole who formulated this concept from World War I on. In *Self-government in Industry* (1917) he developed the main principles, which may be summarized as follows: In the first place the guild constitutions have to achieve true individual self-government; secondly they have to combine efficiency with freedom. The means are decentralization to the utmost extent, that is, industrial democracy. He polemicized against the collectivists – that is, the communists – that their utopia is a world of public trusts, whereas the utopia of the guilds is a world of producer combines, which all work in the common interest. Consumer cooperatives were for him never democratic, since direct democracy is the only true DEMOCRACY. He developed a system which still guarantees unity through a federation of guilds with a central office.

Co-determination has been characterized as the typical German form of industrial democracy. It is a result of a historic compromise between capital and labour in 1920 after the Council Revolution of 1918–19 failed, and is based on the WORKERS' COUNCIL which is generally controlled by the trade unions. But there is a division of tasks between the works council – as it is named in Germany – and the unions. The unions are responsible for collective bargaining whereas the works councils are company oriented. Since 1951 different schemes of participation in the board of the companies or in the nomination of the works director – responsible for personnel and social affairs – have been introduced (Bruegmann, 1981). It is largely a legally codified system of industrial democracy, and there are various degrees depending on the industry and size of the enterprise. It has also been extended to the public sector. For many the relative success of the German economy after World War II, its *Wirtschaftswunder* (economic miracle), depends largely on its system of participation, also designated as *Sozialpartnerschaft* (social partnership). This concept was elaborated in 1928 by Fritz Naphtali and was seen as leading to a general system of economic democracy that would include a council system for all industries up to the national level, but although this feature was incorporated in the Weimar Constitution from 1919 and in the German Trade Union Federation's (DGB) Fundamental Programme of 1949 it has not yet been applied. Naphtali emigrated to Palestine and realized most of his ideas there in the *Histadrut* (trade union federation).

Workers' control was much discussed in the 1960s and 1970s in Britain and also on the Continent (Coates and Topham, 1975; Mandel, 1970). In this conception the collaboration with capital in all forms of participation schemes such as co-determination was radically rejected as collaboration with the capitalist economy.

Self-management has two different meanings in theoretical debate and in practice (see SELF-MANAGEMENT). One is linked with the theory and practice in Yugoslavia as it was formulated in opposition to Stalinism from 1950, mainly by Edvard Kardelj (1978), and is generally conceived as *workers'* self-management. Empirical research showed – at least until the 1970s – that the Yugoslav system gave workers most of the rights of management not only *de jure* but also *de facto* (Adizes, 1971; IDE, 1981; King and van de Vall, 1978). The other sense was developed especially in France as 'general self-management' (Bourdet, 1970). The introduction of industrial democracy in France is seen as secondary to a general transformation of society where all sectors are self-determined. Polish and other experiences seem to have shown that isolated experiments with full industrial democracy cannot survive. A general *political* framework has to exist on a national or even international level.

Without any doubt industrial democracy has been one of the main social ideas and practices in the twentieth century in almost all industrialized countries, and such schemes have also been introduced in many Third World countries. An ILO account lists a large number of them (Monat and Sarfati, 1986). With *perestroika* the socialist countries of Eastern Europe also began to democratize the economy after a long period of centralized management, and subsequent stagnation. The future of industrial democracy at the beginning of the twenty-first century seems to be open. There is a broad debate about the end of industrial society and the beginning of postmodernity. Participative management has become more and more widespread.

Slater and Bennis declared in 1964 (in the *Harvard Business Review*) that democracy is inevitable; and what socialists had asserted for more than a hundred years, namely, that political democracy must be complemented by economic democracy to realize full democracy, seemed to have received support from management as well. With the final dissolution of Stalinism the last defenders of Taylorism have been overthrown too. 'New production concepts' (Kern and Schumann, 1984) which are based on a historic compromise between management and labour seem to guarantee productivity and the reduction of costs. Social partnership under capitalist leadership on the one hand, and democratic socialism on the other both incorporate industrial democracy as the social basis of the economy.

Reading

Cole, George D.H. 1917 (*1972*): *Self-government in Industry*.

IDE (Industrial Democracy in Europe International Research Group) 1981: *Industrial Democracy in Europe*.

International Handbook of Participation in Organizations, 1989–92, 3 vols.

King, Charles D. and van de Vall, Mark 1978: *Models of Industrial Democracy: Consultation, Co-determination and Workers' Management*.

Monat, Jacques and Sarfati, Hedva 1986: *Workers' Participation: A Voice in Decisions, 1981–85*.

Széll, György 1988: *Participation, Worker's Control and Self-management*.

—— ed. 1992: *Concise Encyclopedia of Participation and Co-management*.

UNESCO 1984: Industrial democracy: participation, labour relations and motivation. *International Social Science Journal* 36, 196–402.

Webb, Sidney and Webb, Beatrice 1897: *Industrial Democracy*.

Woodworth, Warner, Meek, Charles and Whyte, William F. eds 1985: *Industrial Democracy: Strategies for Community Revitalization*.

GYÖRGY SZÉLL

industrial organization   The systematic analysis of the business enterprise, and groupings of such enterprises, are covered by this name. Such analysis comprises, broadly speaking: (1) data acquisition, organization and presentation; (2) economic theory, often expressed in a mathematical or rather tightly reasoned literary or geometrical form; and (3) statistical or econometric analysis (see ECONOMETRICS), involving tests of this economic theory on the data acquired. A common synonym for industrial organization is industrial economics, which makes it clear that the subject matter is the industry studied from the viewpoint of the economist.

The study of an industry involves the search for regularities in the behaviour of both the individual business enterprise in its many forms and the collection of such enterprises which constitutes the industry. That is, it is concerned with the firm at the individual level and varieties of competition at the group level. Such analysis is not confined to the industrialized or capitalist economies, but also embraces centrally or indicatively planned economies at various stages of economic development. The spectrum of industrial forms examined is wide, varying from the strongly decentralized, almost exclusively market oriented type to the highly centralized, largely bureaucratic type.

Given the sustained interest in the control and monitoring of industry at the level of economic policy in all types of economies, the data of industrial organization are generally rich and well supported by government agencies. A standard industrial classification (SIC) is widely accepted internationally and provides a comprehensive breakdown of industries, from broad groupings like transport and services down to fine groupings based on narrow product ranges. However, such data are not always in a perfect form for testing economic theories of the industry, and primary source data collection has always been an important activity of industrial economists, particularly by those who favour the case study approach (for instance, Fisher et al., 1983).

The theory of industrial organization focuses on the firm and on competition. Whereas in the most abstract forms of economic theory the type of firm may not be specified, in the theory of industrial organization it is crucial. Thus the small firm run by an entrepreneur (see ENTREPRENEURSHIP) is analysed in a different way (cf. Reid and Jacobsen, 1988) from the large corporate firm (cf. Jensen and Meckling, 1976). Competition assumes an immense variety of forms in practice, but in the theory of industrial organization it is often analysed along two dimensions, the degree of product differentiation (that is, the extent to which products produced are homogeneous, or distinguished by minor design variations, packaging or location) and the extent and nature of interactions between firms. Thus perfect competition is concerned with situations in which many firms, all producing a homogeneous good, are not in significant interaction. Heterogeneous oligopoly is concerned with situations in which few firms, producing differentiated products, are in significant interaction. Naturally, the methods used to analyse the former are simpler than those for the latter, and the progress of the theory of industrial organization in the twentieth century has been from the earlier rigorous analysis of perfect competition, as in Knight (1921), Hicks (1939) and Debreu (1959), to the later rigorous analysis of oligopoly, as in Fellner (1960), Telser (1972) and Shubik (1984). In looking at the more complex structures of oligopolies, where strategic considerations arise, theorists of industrial organization have worked extensively with the tools of mathematical GAME THEORY.

The testing of theories of industrial organization embraces many methods varying from a case study approach to an econometric, system of equations, approach. Throughout its development this century industrial organization has been distinguished from many areas of economic inquiry by its adherence to a non-degenerate scientific method, which has always insisted that theory should be confronted with evidence. A highly influential framework for the testing of theories has been structure, conduct and performance (S/C/P), as developed by Mason (1939) and codified by Scherer and others (Scherer and Ross, 1990). In its simplest form it holds that structure (such as numbers of firms, the degree of product differentiation) determines conduct (such as profit maximization, extent of collusion) which in turn determines performance (for example, provision of goods in qualities and quantities determined by consumers' preferences). This simple approach can be extended and modified to embrace more complex forms of causality, including feedback and bidirectional effects, and a great variety of types of structure, conduct and performance. Its flexibility accounts for its durability, and suitably modified it can be applied to modern theories of the industry and the firm of the late twentieth century, including those arising from mathematical game theory and from the approach particularly associated with Williamson (1985) which emphasizes the costs of transactions. However, the S/C/P framework, while widely used and respected, does not exert a dogmatic influence on empirical enquiry in industrial organization, which remains highly pluralistic in approach.

Reading
Davies, S. et al. 1988: *Economics of Industrial Organisation.*
Krause, C.G. 1990: *Theory of Industrial Economics.*
Reid, G.C. 1987: *Theories of Industrial Organization.*
Scherer, F.M. and Ross, D. 1990: *Industrial Market Structure and Economic Performance*, 3rd edn.
Schmalensee, R. and Willig, R. eds 1989: *Handbook of Industrial Organization.*

GAVIN C. REID

industrial relations   The term derives mainly from the work of a group of American researchers, Clark Kerr, John T. Dunlop, Frederick Harbison and Charles A. Myers; during the 1950s they conducted, with the financial support of the Ford Foundation, a large research programme on labour, 'The Inter-University Study of Labor Problems in Economic Development'.

The importance of this approach has to be understood through the research of the human relations school, carried out by Elton Mayo and his colleagues with large-scale experiments and observations on the Western Electric Company from 1927. Among their main results, these researchers pointed out the importance of the relationship between workers and their supervisors. Mayo and his colleagues also found that workers tended to restrict production even if their earnings were based on the level of production: the group, in an informal way, fixed output for each worker and constructed a system of social control. This system, protecting workers from outside and from inside, operated as an informal power against the formal power of managers (Mayo, 1933 and 1945). These findings differed greatly from F.W. Taylor's idea of 'scientific management', according to which workers' main motivation was income maximization. The studies of the human relations school, however, attracted many comments and criticisms.

Compared with the human relations school, industrial relations scholars are oriented towards the effect of the extra-organizational environment on the attitudes of workers and employers. For them, business conditions have a direct influence on matters such as turnover, absenteeism or workers' demands. The industrial relations approach considers workers not only as members of work groups, as does the human relations approach, but also as members of other social groups such as occupational groups, families, and economic or political groups. This system of relations has an effect on the attitude of workers towards their work, towards managers or towards the organization.

Industrial relations theorists criticize the human relations conception of the enterprise as a global social system. In their opinion this ignores conflict and glorifies a monolithic structure in which industry is supposed to provide individuals with an integrated social order (Kerr and Fischer, 1957).

J. Dunlop points out the interrelations between actors in the industrial system, showing that technological features of the workplace are often common to whole industries, to whole economic sectors, sometimes beyond national boundaries, and that those features are of prime importance. For this author, the distribution of power in society contributes to the structuring of industrial relations themselves. Dunlop conceives trade unions as a kind of equivalent of firms, with union leaders who have to adapt themselves to the labour market in order best to maximize economic returns to the workers (Dunlop, 1950 and 1958; Dunlop and Whyte, 1950).

Industrial relations studies show that workers' attitudes depend on factors far beyond the control of employers and that workers' protest has a positive impact on the process of industrialization (Kerr et al., 1960). They disagree with the conception of a labour movement as a response to capitalism and consider the labour movement as a whole, providing a much broader analysis than their predecessors. They analyse it as a response to INDUSTRIALIZATION, in its economic and social dimensions. In this way, the means of action and organization of labour movements are to be understood in terms of different aspects of industrialization such as the labour market, sources of investments, pace of development or types of rulers.

The studies of C. Kerr and his colleagues gave rise to the convergence theory, in which the world was perceived as entering 'the age of total industrialization'.

E. Mayo's works gave way to other theoretical developments and criticisms. On the one hand, the sociology of organizations is an attempt to explain the complex relationship between formal and informal organizational structure (for instance, Gouldner, 1954; Etzioni, 1961; Crozier, 1964). On the other hand, there is the French 'sociologie du travail' (sociology of work), in which work becomes a manifestation of social relations (Friedmann and Naville, 1961–2). In a broader analysis, social conflict becomes one of the main themes, with social actors fighting for the control of social development: the field open to social negotiation is unlimited (Touraine, 1965).

See also ORGANIZATIONAL BEHAVIOUR.

Reading
Dunlop, John T. 1958: *Industrial Relations Systems.*
Etzioni, Amitai 1961: *A Comparative Analysis of Complex Organizations: On Power, Involvement, and their Correlates.*
Gouldner, Alvin W. 1954: *Patterns of Industrial Bureaucracy.*
Kerr, Clark, Dunlop, John T., Harbison, Frederick and Myers, Charles A. 1960 (*1973*): *Industrialism and Industrial Man: The Problems of Labor and Management in Economic Growth.*
Mayo, Elton 1933 (*1946*): *The Human Problems of an Industrial Civilization,* 2nd edn.
—— 1945: *The Social Problems of an Industrial Civilization.*

SYLVAINE TRINH

industrial society The characteristics most often used to define industrial society are:

1 A change in the nature of the economy such that a very small primary sector can feed a population involved in the secondary and tertiary sectors;
2 The dominance of machine production within factories;
3 The urbanization of society (see URBANISM);
4 The growth of mass literacy;
5 The application of scientific knowledge to production;
6 An increase in the bureaucratic regulation of all aspects of social life.

On occasion, different characteristics are cited. This is understandable: social theory has tried to understand both capitalism and industrialism, and it is scarcely surprising that some of the characteristics of the former have been ascribed to the latter. One thing is absolutely clear, however: the emergence of industrial society marks a sea change in human affairs. The massive, Promethean increase in human powers that resulted meant that human beings were no longer at the mercy of nature – indeed, nature is now perhaps all too much at the mercy of human beings.

The first theorists of industrial society were aware that they were witnessing the birth of a new world. The roots of the concept lie in the Enlightenment thought of Turgot and Condorcet. But the most striking formulation of the idea came early in the nineteenth century from Henri de Saint-Simon and from Auguste Comte. Saint-Simon believed that industry would so change social life that traditional political struggle could be entirely displaced: instead of there being choices between different ends in life, what would matter much more would be the administration of the industrial machine. Saint-Simon's views had a considerable practical impact on French society, especially on its engineering profession. But Comte's thought proved to be even more important, not least in sociology, the very name of which he coined. Comte was as anti-political a thinker as Saint-Simon, but he added two important glosses to his teacher's work. First, he argued that the creation of affluence would lead to the end of wars between nations. Secondly, he believed that the industrial age would, once the false ideals of religion had been destroyed by science, have its own 'positive' beliefs – which he termed 'the religion of humanity'. (See also SECULARIZATION.)

The optimism of Comte in this last point was not maintained by most nineteenth- and twentieth-century social theorists. Novelists inveighed against the crass materialism and moral emptiness of modern life, and more academic writers echoed their characterization. Thus Karl Marx attacked the alienation brought on by industrial capitalism; somewhat similarly, Emile Durkheim argued that the 'anomic' lack of moral integration of modern life was responsible for an increase in suicide, scarcely the sign of some sort of universal progress. Interestingly, both Marx and Durkheim thought, albeit in very different ways, that modern industrial society could be combined with moral regulation: that is, they wrote, in the last analysis, in the spirit of Comte. This was not true of Max Weber, the greatest of all theorists of industrial society. This is not simply because he accurately predicted, against Marx, that the state socialist version of industrial society would be more bureaucratic than the capitalist model. Rather he insisted that there were opportunity costs to industrial society that could not be escaped. Knowledge can bring affluence, in his view, but the principles upon which science works are absolutely at odds with moral certainty: affluence is thus bought at the price of a measure of 'disenchantment', that is, by the loss of previous moral guidelines established by religious belief. It is important to note, however, that his tragic pessimism on this point was not endorsed by many other thinkers. Heidegger, for example, sought ways in which some 'real' morality could be created such that 'mere' technology would be kept in its place.

The concept of industrial society was given a fundamental restatement in the two decades after the ending of World War II. The concept underlay the optimism of Talcott Parsons, and it was quite as much behind the insistence of many thinkers – Clark Kerr being the most important – that development had become the key issue of the age. At its worst, this reworking of the concept led to the naive belief that the ideas and institutions of state socialism and liberal capitalism would simply converge. But it was possible to be much more sophisticated than this, and it was the great achievement of Raymond Aron to produce a judicious synthesis of the theory of industrial society. This synthesis was remarkable for paying proper attention to the political, that is, in refusing to grant that all change resulted from socioeconomic variables. This was particularly clearly seen in his various volumes on the autonomous logic of geopolitical conflict and in his masterpiece, *Democracy and Totalitarianism*, which described the alternate political systems by which industrial systems could be managed.

We can best understand the strengths and weaknesses of the concept of industrial society by considering four areas of debate which it has occasioned.

Origins

There has been much discussion, firstly, both of the origins of industrial society and of the extent to which we may now be passing into some new era. Capitalist society came, of course, before the emergence of industrial society, and we have some knowledge of the uniqueness of Europe – a historical pattern of nuclear families, the destruction of extensive kin networks, a multipolar state system, rainfall agriculture, the legacies of antiquity – that facilitated its rise. Industrialism first emerged on the basis of this pre-existent commercial background in a piecemeal manner. Exactly why this

process took place in England rather than, say, the Netherlands remains the subject of much dispute, with the most recent account by Wrigley stressing the importance of coal stocks and of a high level of demand consequent on the prior agrarian revolution. What is certain is that the industrialization or development of the Third World today cannot take place in the same gradual and piecemeal manner. The advantages and geopolitical need of industrialization have made it something that state elites wish to achieve as fast as possible; this tends to encourage authoritarianism of political regimes. All this is to say that many loose ends remain to be tied in understanding the crucial story of the rise of industrial society. In contrast, the concept of POSTINDUSTRIAL SOCIETY suggested by Daniel Bell (1974) and Touraine (1971) has little to recommend it, as Kumar has powerfully demonstrated (1978). While it is true that knowledge is ever more important in modern society, this amounts to intensifying rather than replacing the key principles on which modern society works. This is not, however, to say that no socially significant changes have taken place during the industrial era. The diminution in size of the manual working class is certainly a matter of importance, as is the increasing political salience of newly educated labour.

Capitalism and industrialism

A second general area of discussion concerns the respective virtues of the concept of CAPITALISM in contrast to that of industrialism. Marxists certainly have much in their favour when they insist on the greater cognitive power of the former concept. Industrial society theorists tend to see social stratification in functional, even meritocratic terms; Marxists are correct to point out that life chances are in fact determined by one's parents' position in the class system. This does not, however, mean that the Marxist paradigm is in every way superior to the concept of industrial society. Thus, while the working class certainly exists, it shows no sign of fulfilling the historic role ascribed to it by Marxism; more important still, Marxism's characterization of the nature of state socialist industrial society is nothing like as plausible as that offered by the theorists of industrial society. It is worth noticing in passing that the concept of capitalism is, however, in one unrecognized way distinctively superior to that of industrialism. The theorists of industrial society suggested that once affluence had been achieved all that then remained was to sit back and enjoy it; in this light there were even discussions of the benefits of a no-growth society. In fact, it is impossible to stand still within the world economy because it is organized on capitalist lines: to stand still means decline if others insist on making greater profits. International capitalist society remains restless and anarchic in a way foreign to the spirit of the theory of industrial society.

Industrialism and war

This general point can be highlighted by considering a third debate. The hope that the age of affluence would curtail war was proven illusory by two world wars. Much of that conflict can be understood in traditional terms, that is, as the result of rational action on the part of states within the 'asocial society' of state competition. This is extremely important. It means that we live within nation-states which have to swim quite as much within the larger society of interstate competition as that of international capitalist society. Geopolitics has affected the nature of social change quite as much as has capitalism; indeed it is the interaction between the two, still not properly understood, which has provided the dynamism for modern social change. Put negatively, we misunderstand our position if we say simply that we live inside industrial society. This is not, however, to say that both class and nation have not been affected by the industrial age. The fact that there have been no major wars between the major powers since 1945 is the result of the balance of terror that has resulted from the application of industrial principles to the waging of war.

Modernity and ideology

If industrial society did not bring peace in its train, the fourth area of discussion concerns the vexed question as to whether it might give birth to an age free of great ideologies. Was Max Weber right to suggest that the spread of science was incompatible with the retention of belief systems, whether ancient or modern, which sought to provide guidelines for social life? In the 1930s his claim looked decidedly unlikely given that the pace of political life was set by Bolshevism and fascism; the revival of Islam in the present-day world similarly represents an attempt to have the technology of modernity with an inclusive and total belief system. But these creeds appeal, as does the visceral force of nationalism, to societies in transition from the agrarian to the industrial era. The real question is

whether ideology can maintain its salience over time in regimes that were themselves founded on a claim to know the truth. The evolution of the Soviet Union under Gorbachev suggests that Weber's contention may have truth to it; but the whole matter is extremely complex, and it is best simply to say that history has not yet sat in judgement on the whole affair.

Conclusion

A summary of the strengths and weaknesses of the concept of industrial society can be offered in conclusion. There is no doubt, to begin by stressing the usefulness of the concept, that the emergence of industrialism marks a qualitative change in human affairs: it is nothing less than a moment of social evolution. Our lives are determined by this mode of production. However, the motor of change within the modern world order cannot be derived simply from some sort of 'logic' of industrialism. The dynamics of the modern world remain those created by the interaction of nation and capital. Industrialism has raised the stakes within that interaction, but it has not replaced it.

Reading
Aron, R. 1962 (*1966*): *Peace and War.*
——1965 (*1968*): *Democracy and Totalitarianism.*
Bell, D. 1974: *The Coming of Post-Industrial Society.*
Gellner, E. 1974: *Legitimation of Belief.*
Kerr, Clark, Dunlop, John T., Harbison, Frederick, H. and Myers, Charles, A. 1960 (*1973*): *Industrialism and Industrial Man.*
Kumar, K. 1978: *Prophecy and Progress.*
Polányi, K. 1944: *The Great Transformation.*
Saint-Simon, H. 1953: *Selected Writings*, ed. F. M. H. Markham.
Wrigley, A. M. 1988: *Continuity, Chance and Change: The Character of the Industrial Revolution in England.*

JOHN A. HALL

industrialization The process by which societies acquire the equipment, organization and skills necessary to engage in mass production using power technology is referred to as industrialization. Formerly the term 'industrial revolution' was often used. Social scientists now regard that term as misleading since it implies an abrupt discontinuity. The statistical record does not support such an assumption. Preindustrial economies, since most of their output originates in agriculture, are unlikely to experience a sudden surge in growth; the inertia of their dominant sector is too great. Discontinuities, if they occur, will be in sectors such as manufacturing which are initially much smaller. It is to these sectors that such terms as 'take-off' or 'spurts in growth' should be applied.

The modern tendency is to think of industrialization as a mode of economic growth rather than an event or short period of time. Its essential characteristic is the ever wider use of inanimate energy. It has its origins in an earlier phase of 'proto-industrialization', occurring within societies where agriculture and trade are still dominant. The success of industrialization is markedly influenced by the accumulations of capital that this earlier phase of growth facilitates, the types of labour force and skills that it brings into existence, the foreign exchange earnings that it creates and the cultural values and political structures that it engenders. Furthermore, social scientists now do not assume that industrialization has a definite end in time. Terms such as DE-INDUSTRIALIZATION or 'post-industrial society' refer to the rise of the service-based and information-based sectors of society; they do not imply that the process of industrialization has ended.

Historians conventionally date the first emergence of industrialization as around the middle of the eighteenth century; most of the important sites were in Great Britain. The process was rapidly diffused thereafter, first to regions in Western Europe, North America and Russia, later to other parts of the world. In the twentieth century it has become almost synonymous with economic development. Particularly in the new states that won national independence after World War II, the drive for higher living standards is essentially a drive for industrialization. Few of these states are willing to base their hopes for political autonomy and a higher standard of living on raw material production alone.

The technologies of industrial growth have changed over time and are still changing. Long before the eighteenth century, wind and water power had been used to supplement the energy of humans and other animals, but the widespread use of coal to smelt iron and generate steam-power vastly increased usable energy. Greater energy inputs were fundamental to later increases in output. Coal, steam-power and iron no longer play the critical role they once did in industrial growth but the essence of the process is unchanged: industrialization implies the tapping of inanimate energy sources on an ever-increasing scale. Human energy comes to be used primarily for control.

The increasing use of inanimate energy resources was of critical importance because of what it meant for man-hour productivity. Real incomes are closely linked to productivity, and industrialization, because of its use of inanimate energy, is one sure way to raise productivity. It is not the only way. Productivity can also be increased by better markets, better information, better organization and better division of labour. Industrialization, in fact, requires improvements in these social arrangements. Major policy errors can arise from concentrating on the technological shift alone and ignoring the institutional changes that must accompany it. It is not possible to alter drastically the mode of production without similarly transforming the social structure in which it takes place and, to a degree, the culture in which it is embedded.

From this arise many of the impediments to successful industrialization. Resistance to industrialization stems not from rejection of its prospect of higher material living standards but from opposition to its social, cultural and political costs. As industrialization has been diffused, so too has an appreciation of these costs. They include, first, an exploitative attitude towards the natural world and a propensity to undervalue the ecological and environmental damage that industrial growth can cause. Costs that do not appear on the account books of the corporations or government bureaus that direct the industrialization process tend to be ignored because they are not carried by those making the decisions. Second, industrialization in the past has been associated with an exploitative attitude toward labour. Labour under a regime of industrial capitalism comes to be treated as a commodity, and the attitudes that govern the exploitation of commodities are transferred to human beings. From this arises the aggravation of class conflict that often occurs during the initial phases of industrialization – phases when the social infrastructure of urban housing, education and public health is inadequate, when the rate of population growth is accelerating, and when labour is still learning how to influence wage rates and working conditions. Third, there typically occurs a breakdown in community and a rise in ALIENATION and ANOMIE. Industrialization breaks up traditional social formations, transforms traditional social roles and undermines traditional sources of authority. Sometimes referred to as the rise of individualism, this might better be called depersonalization, and in that sense it is as true of the state-directed industrializations of the twentieth century as of the more laissez-faire industrializations of the nineteenth. The technology of industrialization is the technology of standardization and uniformity and interchangeable parts; this often applies to consumers and workers as well as to processes and products.

In the hope of overcoming these obstacles, industrialization in the late twentieth century has often been undertaken not through decision making by private entrepreneurs but through direction by the state. The entrepreneurial groups are not private businessmen and corporations but politicians, civil servants and technocrats. The drive is to enter industrialization quickly, to make the 'giant leap' into modernization in one generation or less. Partly this is for reasons of national pride. Partly it is in the belief that obstacles can be overcome only by a 'big push'. And partly it is in the hope that the growth of output will outpace the predictable explosion of population as traditional restraints on family formation give way.

These are the problems that face many industrializing societies today. At the same time, many of the nations that made the transition to industrial growth earlier are finding their older industries hard-pressed to compete against later industrializing societies elsewhere. The tendency in these 'mature' economies is for an increasing proportion of the labour force to be employed in the tertiary or 'service' sector, where increases in productivity are hard to achieve, and a decreasing proportion to be employed in primary production or manufacturing, to which older technologies more readily apply. The output of such economies is becoming information intensive, rather than resource intensive or labour intensive. Some analysts call this the rise of postindustrial society. An alternative is to say that the technological base of industrialization is changing, as it always has been. In the late nineteenth century it moved away from the coal, iron and steam-power complex to the complex of hydrocarbon fuels, electricity, plastics and the light alloys. Now, in the late twentieth century, the technological base for further industrialization seems to lie in the information industries, based on electronics and the computer (see AUTOMATION; INFORMATION TECHNOLOGY AND THEORY).

Reading
Chenery, H. B., Robinson, S. and Syrquin, M. 1986: *Industrialization and Growth: A Comparative Study.*

Kemp, Tom 1978: *Historical Patterns of Industrialization.*
Kuznets, Simon 1966: *Modern Economic Growth: Rate, Structure, and Spread.*
Landes, David S. 1969: *The Unbound Prometheus: Technological Change and Industrial Development in Western Europe from 1750 to the Present.*
Mumford, Lewis 1934 (*1963*): *Technics and Civilization.*
Rostow, Walt W. 1978: *The World Economy: History and Prospect.*

HUGH G. J. AITKEN

inequality *See* EQUALITY AND INEQUALITY

information technology and theory Once the digitization of information was possible through the common language of the binary code, voice, data and video were able to become streams of digitized information which could be stored, manipulated and transmitted cheaply at great speed by digital computers. At the same time, the electronics, computing and telecommunications industries converged to become one all-embracing, global information technology (IT) industry, a trend noted over a decade ago (Nora and Minc, 1978; Barron and Curnow, 1979).

Many writers have seen IT as a pervasive 'core' technology at least as important as electricity or steam power and therefore probably the most important technological development this century. The key importance of IT stems from the fact that – unlike other technologies – decreases in the cost and size of electronic components have been accompanied by *increases* in their power, speed and sophistication. Thus powerful computers now sit neatly on individual desktops, whereas 25 years ago machines with the same processing power would have filled a huge room.

The term 'revolution' is frequently applied to IT and the 'IT revolution' is often compared in social significance to the Industrial Revolution two centuries ago. The economic, social and political implications of the ongoing IT revolution are the subject of continuing research and debate, but clearly some very important changes to society are under way, especially in the workplace, if not in homes and schools (Guile, 1985; Miles et al., 1988). Recent work, however, has cast doubt on the 'revolutionary' importance of IT and some see IT as part of the continuing evolution of control technologies which began in the last century (Beniger, 1986). The productivity pay-off from IT is also being seriously questioned (Forester, 1989).

Some writers have taken the opportunity to

proclaim new types of society arising from the IT revolution, with the 'information society' (Bell, 1979; Masuda, 1980) replacing the 'postindustrial society' as the front-runner. Both these notions have been subjected to critical scrutiny (see Lyon, 1988) and they raise important questions about 'paradigm' shifts, the process of social development, technological determinism and the importance of manufacturing industry as opposed to the services sector (Cohen and Zysman, 1987).

Commentators on the IT revolution (as with the issue of technology and society in general) tend to divide broadly into 'optimists' – Bell (1979), Toffler (1980), and Kranzberg – and 'pessimists' – Weizenbaum (1976), Roszak (1986) and Winner (1989) – although the latter three might more properly be called 'heretics' because they strongly oppose the orthodox view that computerization will have generally beneficial effects on society.

See also ARTIFICIAL INTELLIGENCE.

Reading

Forester, Tom ed. 1985: *The Information Technology Revolution*.
——1987: *High-Tech Society: The Story of the IT Revolution*.
Forester, Tom and Morrison, Perry 1990: *Computer Ethics: Cautionary Tales and Ethical Dilemmas in Computing*.

TOM FORESTER

intellectuals The term has been subject to a great deal of dispute ever since it made its appearance in France at the end of the nineteenth century during the debates between the defenders and the adversaries of Captain Dreyfus in the famous Dreyfus affair. To many, intellectuals are impractical dreamers unable to come to grips with mundane realities in society and state. To others they are the prime defenders of the moral and cognitive values and standards that sustain democratic or liberal political systems.

Certain scholarly analysts have tended to group under the term 'intellectual' all those persons involved in the sphere of culture, that is in the world of symbols. But others have objected that this is too wide a definition, which would include in its range winners of the Nobel Prize, on one hand, and schoolteachers and newspapermen, on the other, obscuring the necessary distinction between the creators of culture and those who distribute or apply it. It would, in addition, preclude the possibility of assessing and evaluating the status and influence of creators of ideas as distinct from related groups or strata. It makes it impossible to determine whether creators of ideas have a social weight different from that accorded other categories of symbol users.

Under these circumstances it appears more reasonable to define intellectuals more narrowly and to see in them those men and women in given societies who, while numerically small, are yet qualitatively important as creators of symbols, who possess attributes not to be found among the numerically much larger group of persons engaged in the arts, the sciences, the professions and religion. Academics or members of the professions are not necessarily intellectuals. Intellect, as distinct from the intelligence required in the arts and sciences, presumes a capacity for detachment from the immediate issues at hand, a movement beyond the pragmatic tasks of the moment, and a commitment to core values transcending professional or occupational involvement.

While most persons in the professions and elsewhere tend to be absorbed in the pursuit of concrete answers to specific problems, intellectuals are more likely to involve themselves with more general realms of meaning and values, with the sacred core of the culture. As such they seek to provide moral standards and to maintain meaningful common symbols. Modern intellectuals are descendants of the priestly upholders of sacred tradition even as they are also related to the biblical prophets whose message was far removed from the pieties of court and synagogue, castigating the men of power for the wickedness of their ways.

Those who see intellectuals in this way will also contend that they are persons who never seem satisfied with things as they are and with the sway of custom and habit, that they question the truth of the moment in terms of a higher truth: that they consider themselves special custodians of abstract ideas such as truth or justice and see themselves as guardians of moral standards when these are under attack in the marketplace and the house of power.

Intellectuals are not only gatekeepers of ideas and fountainheads of ideologies but, unlike medieval churchmen or modern political zealots, they tend at the same time to maintain a critical attitude. They are persons who think otherwise and they tend to be disturbers of complacency and adjustment.

It was only after the waning of the Middle Ages, after Reformation and Renaissance had fragmented the unified and monopolistic world-view of the church, that intellectuals could begin to raise an independent voice; only as multiple religious and secular powers began to emerge on the social scene and started competing for the allegiance of individuals could there arise a stratum of men and women of ideas no longer tied to the church or to secular patrons. With the emergence of a variety of centres of power and influence, with the thawing of a hitherto frozen culture, there arose conflicts of ideas carried by unfettered spokespersons for different trains of thought and winds of doctrine.

Some intellectuals were still partly dependent on patrons to sustain them before there emerged a literate public of wide scope in the eighteenth century, but at least they had the choice of patrons. From the eighteenth century on, however, a lay public began to provide a receptive audience for people of letters. From that point on the study of intellectuals needs to pay close attention to the complicated net of relations between them and the marketplace of ideas as well as with institutions such as the university or national academies. Attention must be paid to those social arrangements such as coffee houses, salons, periodicals, censorship, government bureaucracies, all of which impinge, be it positively or negatively, on the life of the mind in the world of modernity. Intellectuals in the modern world, be it in the East or in the West, have assumed crucial strategic positions. They are often wooed but also often persecuted by the men of power as well as by vested economic interests. At times their position seems fairly well established, at other times however they still seem an endangered species. Yet, in the last analysis, they are what Ezra Pound once called 'the antennae of the race'.

See also ENLIGHTENMENT.

Reading

Coser, Lewis A. 1965: *Men of Ideas: A Sociologist's View*.
Hofstadter, Richard 1963: *Anti-intellectualism in American Life*.
Mannheim, Karl 1929 (*1960*): *Ideology and Utopia: An Introduction to the Sociology of Knowledge*.
Shils, Edward 1972: *The Intellectuals and the Powers and Other Essays*.
Znaniecki, Florian 1940: *The Social Role of the Man of Knowledge*.

LEWIS A. COSER

intelligence test Like many concepts within psychology, intelligence may be easier to recognize than to define or measure. Thomas Aquinas offered 'the ability to combine and separate'; in the 1920s Charles Spearman proposed 'the ability to educe relations and correlates'. The problem is that intelligence is inferred from behaviour and behaviour is always relational. Intelligence is thus better seen as an emergent property of individuals in response to contingencies of their natural and social environments. That is, behaviour which is intelligent in one context may be quite inappropriate in another. In addition, a developmental perspective is essential. The intelligence of a child is not merely the intelligence of an adult writ small; development does not consist of simply 'filling up' the child to the adult level (the pint jug metaphor). For example a newborn baby evinces a rooting reflex by which it suckles; as the child grows, this reflex is replaced by chewing, qualitative transformation of one form of appropriate behaviour into another. However, a powerful tradition within psychology, dating back at least to Francis Galton in the 1860s, has seen intelligence (or for Galton 'mental capacity') as a fixed individual property, growing linearly with age to adulthood, and expressive of a largely inherited constitution.

Galton and his protégé Karl Pearson wrestled with methods for measuring this mental capacity. In 1904, the French government asked Alfred Binet to find ways to detect mentally deficient children. The result was a series of tests consisting of short problems designed to explore memory, verbal facility and so on. A child's score on these tests was used to define its mental age by finding the average age of children whose score on the tests it matched. The tests were brought to the USA by Henry Goddard in 1908 and revised by Lewis Terman at Stanford in 1912 to form the Stanford-Binet tests on which all subsequent versions have been based. Terman popularized the term IQ, or Intelligence Quotient, meaning the ratio of a child's mental age to its chronological age, times 100. The average IQ of the population – of children of a given age, or, in the adult version of the tests, of the entire adult population – is 100. IQ tests thus operationalize the definition of intelligence, reducing it to 'what IQ tests measure'. Originally intended in Binet's hands to predict school performance and identify for remedial education children who were performing below their 'mental age', in the 1920s and 1930s the tests, in the hands of the US psychologists and their UK counterparts, notably Cyril Burt, took on an increasingly reified character. Spearman used them to deduce that underlying all test performance there existed a unitary 'general intelligence factor' which he called 'g', thereby implying that it had some of the absolute character of a constant in the physical sciences. Others distinguished between 'fluid' and 'crystallized' intelligence, the former being seen as the ability for new conceptual learning and the latter as acquired knowledge and skills. At the same time efforts were made to develop tests which were 'culture fair' or independent of learned facts and skills. However, as such tests were themselves standardized against the Stanford-Binet, they must share many of its properties.

Mass application of the tests began on army recruits and would-be immigrants to the USA, and later on schoolchildren in the UK. They revealed large class and ethnic gradients in test scores; working-class children tended to score lower than middle-class, immigrants and blacks lower than the indigenous white population of the USA. Gender differences, apparent in early versions of the tests, were eliminated by revising the questions on which the scoring differences appeared, but the class and ethnic differences were widely regarded as indicating 'real' differences in intelligence. Claims such as that of Burt, ostensibly based on the measurement of IQ in identical twins reared apart (revealed in the 1970s to be entirely fraudulent), that variations in intelligence – or at least in IQ test score – were largely determined genetically, gave rationale to widespread eugenic concerns that immigration and class differentials in birthrate would lead to a decline in 'national intelligence' (see EUGENICS).

After 1945 group differences in IQ scores were generally attributed to environmental factors and, with the spread of comprehensive education catering for children of mixed abilities, reliance on IQ-related tests to discriminate between children and limit educational prospects diminished. The IQ issue became prominent again after 1969, when Arthur Jensen in the USA, followed by his popularizer Hans Eysenck in Britain, revived claims for the genetic determination of IQ differences not only between individuals, but also between groups, notably blacks and whites living in the USA. A vigorous debate followed in which the empirical and theoretical bases for these claims were intensely disputed. In the 1980s, evidence emerged that over the past 40 years there has been a substantial secular increase in average IQ scores in cohorts of children in Japan, New Zealand, the Netherlands and the UK. As this increase cannot be accounted for on any known genetic model, this debate may be regarded as at last concluded. Advances in the neurosciences mean that it is no longer seen as plausible to speak of intelligent behaviour, or even a person's score on an IQ test, as dependent on a single underlying, inherited property; the dialectic of biological, social and natural environments during development means that complex properties like intelligence cannot meaningfully be partitioned out into distinct 'genetic' and 'environmental' fractions.

See also COGNITIVE SCIENCE.

Reading
Blum, J. M. 1978: *Pseudoscience and Mental Ability*.
Evans, B. and Waites, B. 1981: *IQ and Mental Testing: An Unnatural Science and its Social History*.
Rose, Steven et al. 1984: *Not in our Genes*.

STEVEN P. R. ROSE

interaction   In everyday language, interaction means interrelated acts, actions, activities, and movements of two or more individuals, as well as animals and objects, such as machines. Generally, the term stands for reciprocal active influencing. In the social and human sciences the concept 'interaction' is used in a non-uniform way, although it has been one of the central themes. In sociological and psychological literature the term 'interaction' is used in the following contexts.

Social interaction   The interrelated behaviour of individuals who influence each other by means of communication is called social interaction. In the literature, interaction and communication are often used as synonyms. Watzlawick, Beavin and Jackson (1967) define interaction as a reciprocal sequence of communications (that is, messages) between two or more individuals. The term 'patterns of interaction' exists for the more complex units of human communication. Social interaction is sometimes referred to as interactional communication. According to Hare, interaction means 'all words, symbols, and gestures with which persons respond to each other' (1976, p. 60). In recent SOCIAL PSYCHOLOGY non-verbal communication (facial expressions, exchanged glances, body movement, spatial behaviour, extralinguistic behaviour and so on) is considered to be of great importance for understanding social interaction (Argyle, 1975; Weick, 1985).

The sociological and psychological interaction

theories will not be dealt with here in detail. It should be enough to mention social exchange theory and symbolic interactionism. Exchange theory (see Thibaut and Kelley, 1959) explains social interaction in terms of rewards and costs. The Thibaut-Kelley theory of interaction outcomes deals mainly with two-person relationships. The two-person interaction (dyadic interaction) forms the basic paradigm for most interaction theories. With regard to the empirical study of group interaction processes, the observational methods which have been developed so far actually start with the analysis of two-person interactions. The theory of symbolic interactionism (see Blumer, 1969) is an influential sociological interaction theory which is mainly associated with the philosopher and sociologist George Herbert Mead. Reference is made to it here because this theory and the related research strategy has experienced a certain renaissance in social psychology over the past years. The central assumptions imply that individuals behave on the basis of 'meaning' which comes from social interactions. Meaning is constantly modified by a continuing interpretation process of the individuals who participate in the interaction (Blumer, 1969). The self is seen as the result of interaction; the interactional behaviour of an individual can be understood only on the basis of reciprocal acts of interpretation between the interacting partners in a certain historical, cultural and situational context. In European social psychology greater attention is given to social interaction between members of different groups (intergroup behaviour; intergroup relations); see especially the social identity theory (Tajfel, 1978), where the role of group membership and social identity for intergroup behaviour and the self-concept is made the central theme.

Interaction analysis Based on the above given definition for interaction, interaction analysis means the systematic collecting, recording, analysing and interpreting of COMMUNICATION. Communication here does not refer only to verbal but also to non-verbal communication. A series of observational procedures (see Simon and Boyer, 1974) and recording devices (Krüger et al., 1988) has been developed to classify verbal and non-verbal communication. According to past orientation, these procedures are mainly concerned with the coding of verbal interacts in dyads or small groups (see Hare, 1976).

The Interaction Process Analysis (IPA), developed by Bales (1950), one of the founders of small group research, is still considered the prototype for an observational coding system. This system consists of 12 categories and is aimed at revealing patterns of interaction in leaderless problem-solving groups, and describing these processes over time (phases of group development). The categories follow the model of a problem-solving sequence. The central pair of categories illustrates the problems of collecting information in the initial phase (category 6: Gives Orientation; category 7: Asks for Orientation). Categories 5 (Gives Opinion) and 8 (Asks for Opinion) refer to the evaluation of information; categories 4 (Gives Suggestion) and 9 (Asks for Suggestion) refer to the problem of control. The next problem areas are: decision-making (category 3: Agrees; 10: Disagrees), regulation of tension (category 2: Shows Tension Release; 11: Shows Tension), and in the final phase coping with socio-emotional problems (category 1: Seems Friendly; 12: Seems Unfriendly). The further development of the IPA approach, which led to the more recent SYMLOG system (System for the Multiple Level Observation of Groups), linked the categories to a spatial model which was obtained through factor analysis and consideration of the content of messages (Bales and Cohen, 1979). The SYMLOG coding of interaction permits the description of the communication processes on three levels: the level of verbal and non-verbal observable behaviour, the level of communicated images, and finally the level of the value judgements which the actor communicates through his or her expressed images. The images can be then assigned to six levels (Self, Others, Group, Situation, Society, Fantasy). Shown behaviour and expressed content can be localized and interpreted in a three-dimensional space (dimensions: dominance versus submission; positive versus negative; task orientation versus expression of emotions). The data, which can also be processed with the help of computer programs, are graphically presented as field diagrams.

A theory-based interaction coding system (TEMPO), which seems to be easy to learn and applicable to a wide range of group task performance settings, has recently been introduced by Futoran, Kelly and McGrath (1989). The majority of the published observational methods is made up of systems of classroom observation (such as Flanders, 1969). In psychodiagnostics there is a wide range of concepts and procedures which go by the name of interaction diagnosis. In this frame of reference interaction behaviour is provoked by means of experimental techniques (tests, problem and conflict provoking tasks, role-play situations) and is analysed with the help of interaction coding systems (see McReynolds and DeVoge, 1978).

Statistical interaction   In research statistics the term interaction is connected with the statistical research method of 'factorial analysis of variance'. In this case it refers to a possible source of variance, the variation due to the joint action (that is, interaction) of two or more independent variables (see Kerlinger, 1973).

Interactionism   The term refers to a group of theories which deal with interactive effects, for example, the relation between body and mind, individual and society, and organism and environment. This is illustrated in the following examples. According to Drever, interactionism is 'a theory of the relation between mind and body, which assumes interaction or reciprocal causation between the two – that mind acts on body and body on mind – as the solution of the psycho-physical problem' (1964, p. 142). In the field of differential psychology and PERSONALITY psychology a collection of articles published by Endler and Magnusson (1976) led to the so-called person–situation debate during which interactionism was advocated as a more appropriate model for personality theory and personality research. This view assumes that actual behaviour is determined by a continuous and multidirectional interaction between person variables and situation variables (ibid., 1976). An optimistic provisional appraisal of this continuing debate is given by Kenrick & Funder (1988).

Reading
Bales, R.F. 1968: Interaction Process Analysis. In *International Encyclopedia of the Social Sciences*, vol. 7, ed. D.L. Sills, pp.465–71.
Danzinger, K. 1976: *Interpersonal Communication.*
Duncan, S. and Fiske, W. 1977: *Face-to-face Interaction.*
Goffman, E. 1959: *The Presentation of Self in Everyday Life.*
Homans, G.C. 1961 (1974): *Social Behavior: Its Elementary Forms*, rev. edn.
Jaffe, J. and Feldstein, S. 1970: *Rhythms of Dialogue.*
Jones, E.E. and Gerard, H.B. 1967: *Foundations of Social Psychology.*

Parsons, T. 1968: Social interaction. In *International Encyclopedia of the Social Sciences*, vol. 7, ed. D.L. Sills, pp. 429–41.

JOHANN F. SCHNEIDER

interest group   This is a private organization which seeks to aggregate the shared values and preferences of its members and, by articulating them, attempts to influence both public opinion and government policy.

The generic term interest group encompasses organizations that function primarily to represent the economic interests of their members (such as employer associations) and those that seek to promote a particular cause which reflects attitudes held in common by its members. Whereas economic interest groups are usually depicted as defending sectional, even selfish, interests, promotional groups are invariably portrayed as being engaged in the selfless advocacy of a cause which is pursued in the interests of all (for example, environmental groups). Though the terms differ, the categorization of interest groups into two such types is characteristic of the academic literature.

While distinguished from political parties by attempting to influence rather than constitute government, interest groups have acted as the progenitors of political parties (thus the British Labour Party's origins lay in the trade union movement). Moreover, the distinction between economic and cause groups is not always clear-cut, if only for the reason that the former do identify with causes that are wider than the particularistic interests of their members.

In the twentieth century, the preoccupation with interest groups as a field of study originated largely in the United States. It was rooted in a tradition of writing on the American political system which had interpreted its plethora of groups as a testament both to the energy of its people and the vitality of its democracy.

In the United States (Truman, 1951; Latham, 1952), and somewhat later in the UK (Mackenzie, 1955; Beer, 1956; Finer, 1958) and Western Europe (Lapalombara, 1964), the adoption of a group-centred approach followed in the wake of Bentley (1908). He had presented the study of groups and their interactions with government as a key to the understanding of the wider political process.

While freeing scholars from a single-minded concern with constitutions and political institutions, the fashion for group studies was criticized by some for neglecting or misunderstanding the motives of individuals (Olson, 1965) and for sub-ordinating the role of more traditional political institutions (Crick, 1959). Others (Bachrach and Baratz, 1962; Lukes, 1974) took issue with those like Dahl (1961) who interpreted the widespread existence of interest groups competing openly to influence policy as evidence of the diffusion of power (see also PLURALISM). They challenged this pluralist analysis, contending that power is concentrated in the hands of relatively few groups which are enmeshed with government because of their strategic economic role (Mills, 1956; Lindblom, 1977). The reinvigoration of the intellectual debate on the concept of POWER is a direct outcome of the study of interest groups.

The literature on interest groups, especially in relation to policy-making (Kimber and Richardson, 1974; Wilson, 1981; Marsh, 1983), has led to a more comprehensive knowledge of both the dynamics and substance of government actions. In addition, their study has underscored the necessity for institutions that mediate between the citizen and government, providing for individuals both the opportunity and motive for political representation and PARTICIPATION other than through the medium of political parties. For these reasons, and because of the question of whether they enhance or impair democratic government, interest groups have become an integral element in the analysis of political systems.

See also SOCIAL MOVEMENT.

Reading
Bentley, A.F. 1908 (*1967*): *The Process of Government*, ed. P. Odergard.
Berger, S. ed. 1981: *Organizing Interests in Western Europe: Pluralism, Corporatism and the Transformation of Politics.*
Dahl, R. 1961: *Who Governs?*
Jordan, A.G. and Richardson, J.J. 1987: *British Politics and the Policy Process.*
Olson, M. 1965: *The Logic of Collective Action.*

R.A. WILFORD

interests To say that an action, policy or state of affairs is in the interests of an individual or collectivity is to suggest that it would further their well-being in some significant respect. The attribution of interests may serve normative or explanatory purposes: in the one case it is used to recommend action or to justify action taken on behalf of others, for example, by governments, parents or social workers: in the other it is used to explain or to predict behaviour.

The normative usage raises questions of the physical, psychological and social conditions which make for the well-being of the relevant individual or collectivity. Since there are different views on what those conditions might be, the attribution of interests is frequently open to dispute. There is no reason to suppose the individuals or collectivities need be aware of the interests they are said to possess. The point rather is that their social situation is supposed to identify an interest *vis-à-vis* other relevant individuals or collectivities: the interests of a child as distinct from those of its parents, of the working class as distinct from those of the bourgeoisie, of different categories of tax-payers, of the community as a whole as distinct from merely sectional interests, and so on. The attribution of interests in this respect involves little more than a plausible argument relating their well-being to some policy or state of affairs. It need say nothing about what motivates the individual or collectivity in question.

The explanatory usage raises questions of a different order. Jürgen Habermas has suggested that human experience is organized in terms of *a priori* cognitive interests. However, the more usual understanding of interests is as contingent but relatively stable properties of individuals or collectivities (unlike transitory wishes or desires) which provide them with actual or potential reasons for action. Many authors would agree with Connolly's claim that every 'explanatory theory of politics includes . . . assumptions about persons and their real interests' (1983, p. 73). Interests have been regarded as an underlying source of social conflict and of differences in the political philosophies or world-views of different classes, and as accounting for important aspects of culture and of knowledge.

There have been many changes in the way interests are thought to relate to other sources of motivation but in the modern period the pursuit of interests is normally contrasted with behaviour that is not self-interested. Max Weber, for example, treats 'material' interests and values as independent sources of motivation, providing distinct and some-times conflicting reasons for action. American PLURALISM analyses political life as a matter of the interactions of organized groups who have banded together for the defence or promotion of their interests. This view suggests that organizations bring together and express independently existing interests, but it is now widely recognized that organizations themselves play an important part in determining what interests are effectively represented in political life.

Interests are sometimes regarded as possibly having effects even when they are not acknowledged by those who act on them. A common manoeuvre is to unmask what appears to be non-self-interested behaviour by claiming to reveal its true foundations in terms of interests. In *The 18th Brumaire of Louis Bonaparte* Marx insists that what distinguished the Legitimist and Orleanist factions of French royalism 'was not any so-called principles, it was their material conditions of existence, two different kinds of property . . .' (1852, p. 118). Here material conditions give rise to interests which then account for both action and ideas. The distinct interests of the two royalist factions account for their political differences and for the 'convictions, articles of faith' and the like which they use to justify their actions.

The interests at stake in this unmasking manoeuvre are sometimes described as objective, meaning that their existence and effectiveness does not necessarily depend on any subjective awareness on the part of those whose interests they are said to be. In the normative usage there is no great problem in treating interests as objective in this sense. However, if the attribution of interests is to serve an explanatory purpose those interests must provide some actor or actors with reasons for action. This condition gives rise to a number of difficulties. First, interests that are objective in this sense may well not be recognized by those who are said to act on them. In that case their explanatory significance is obscure, unless the interests in question are assumed to be unconscious.

Secondly, objective interests are attributed to individuals or collectivities by virtue of some significant feature of their social location such as class, ethnicity or gender. In the above example, Marx refers us to the forms of property that distinguish the interests of Legitimists and Orleanists. The concept of interests then appears to provide an explanatory link between the locations of individuals or collectivities within a structure of social relations on the one hand and their actions on the other: their locations provide them with interests which then provide them with reasons for action. Different features of social structure may well be used to specify different, and sometimes conflicting, sets of interests. The analysis of such conflicting interests and their effects has been an important theme in several traditions of political analysis, for example, in the 'affluent worker' arguments of the 1960s and in more recent treatments of contradictory CLASS locations.

Finally, the view that social location gives rise to objective interests poses a problem of explanation in the case of those who do not act on the interests attributed to them on these grounds. Marxism conventionally attributes an interest in socialism to the working class, but the majority of the working classes in the advanced capitalist societies neither acknowledge such an interest nor act on it. The problem is then to explain the failure of the supposed link between social location and action and an answer is frequently given in terms of the operation of power, false consciousness and ideology.

Reading

Barry, B. 1965: *Political Argument*.
Berger, S.D. ed. 1981: *Organizing Interests in Western Europe*.
Braybrooke, D. 1987: *Meeting Needs*.
Connolly, W.E. 1983: *The Terms of Political Discourse*.
Habermas, J. 1968 (*1971*): *Knowledge and Human Interests*.
Hirschman, A.O. 1977: *The Passions and the Interests*.
Mannheim, K. 1929 (*1960*): *Ideology and Utopia*.
Moe, T.M. 1980: *The Organization of Interests: Incentives and the Internal Dynamics of Political Interest Groups*.

BARRY HINDESS

international division of labour   *See* DIVISION OF LABOUR, INTERNATIONAL

international relations   All social phenomena not confined within a single state – the relations of states with one another, the operations of non-state actors such as international organizations, multinational corporations and religious movements, and the impact of abstractions such as the international economy – fall within the scope of international relations. Its study was stimulated, in this century, by such events as the two world wars, the Russian revolution and its global repercussions, the economic collapse of 1931, the invention of nuclear weapons in 1945 and their seemingly endless refinement thereafter, the decolonization of Asia, Africa and elsewhere, the subsequent confrontation of North and South, and the multiplication of novel forms of international organization, global and regional, including the European Community.

During and after World War I, international relations, as a subject, was often seen as the servant of INTERNATIONALISM, charged with helping states to civilize the conduct of their mutual relations and avoid future wars. In this perspective, which came to be known as 'rationalism' or 'utopianism', much emphasis was placed on the need to uphold and extend the rules and procedures of the League of Nations. With the coming of World War II, and, shortly afterwards, the Korean war in which 16 states, under the United Nations banner, associated themselves with the Republic of Korea (South Korea), 'rationalism' came under scathing attack from the 'realists', and in particular E. H. Carr and Hans Morgenthau.

Carr had long since insisted that the League's rules of political and economic conduct reflected, not an underlying harmony of interests among states, but simply those of the initially stronger and 'satisfied'. As the once weak grew in strength, they would naturally challenge these rules. For the 'satisfied', wisdom lay, not in treating every challenge as a crime, but in deciding which to resist and which to accommodate; 'a successful foreign policy must oscillate between the apparently opposite poles of force and appeasement' (1939, ch. 13). For Hans Morgenthau (1951), both 'political necessity' and 'moral duty' dictated that the sole guide to foreign policy should be the national interest. In the Korean war, bemused by the notion of North Korean aggression and the supposed obligation to resist it, the USA had, he argued, lost sight of that central truth.

Realists thus promoted an emphasis on states rather than international organizations or other non-state actors; on their interests rather than their doctrines or their leaders' beliefs; on the normality of force and thus the importance of strategic considerations; and on the distribution of power in the international system and the need to achieve or maintain a 'balance'. In the decades that followed, all these facets of Realism were to be vigorously challenged.

Initially, though, the debate over substance was overshadowed by one over method. Rather than replacing one set of dogmas and prescriptions by another, it was argued, scholars should investigate the reality of international relations by applying the techniques and philosophy of science, whereby theories would stand or fall according to the weight of the empirical evidence for or against them, and concepts would be so tightly defined that it was clear in advance of an investigation what findings would count in favour of a given theory or hypothesis and what against it, so that others could replicate the investigation. International relations was also widely seen as no more than a special case of human relations, to which the appropriately modified findings of other social sciences, notably economics, sociology and psychology, must apply. The scientific approach made much use of models, that is, attempts to portray the causal process implied by a theory in abstract and often mathematical form, and thus highlight the empirical assumptions on which it rests.

Lewis Fry Richardson's work on WAR was a forerunner of this mode of enquiry, and its posthumous publication in book form coincided with the appearance of several major new works in this vein (Kaplan, 1957; Rapoport, 1960; Boulding, 1962). In the ensuing methodological controversy, whose flavour is well captured in Knorr and Rosenau (1969), Hedley Bull's 'International theory: the case for a classical approach' (in that volume) was a conspicuous rallying point for the traditionalists. On the whole, the scientists won, at least to the extent of having their contributions to the subject accepted on their merits.

One notable field for this was that of international 'systems', in whose operation, and stability or instability, theorists detected the effects of holistic attributes derived from the behavioural tendencies of the units making them up (just as economists see the 'market' for a commodity as a holistic fact derived by aggregating the likely responses of the commodity's customers). Kaplan (1957) specified what he saw as the crucial differences between the nineteenth-century 'balance of power' system and the post-1945 'loose bi-polar' one, and explored four more systems which might conceivably arise. Deutsch and Singer (1964) contended that, in general, multipolar systems were likely to be more stable and more peaceful than bipolar ones; Waltz (1979, ch. 8) argued the reverse. Though difficult, it is possible, and instructive, to trace the different assumptions that lead to such diametrically opposed conclusions.

The substance of Realism came under attack from four main quarters. First, theories of international society, among them Bull (1977), contended that there is more to the relations of states than an unceasing struggle for power. Bull, following a classification Martin Wight had used in his lectures at the London School of Economics, delineated three traditions of thought about international relations, the Hobbesian, corresponding to Realism; the Kantian, a 'revolutionary' conception based on the centrality of the transnational bonds that make all people, as people, part of the community of humankind; and a Grotian (from the seventeenth-century jurist Grotius), asserting the existence of a society of states, bound by a set of norms manifest in international law and diplomacy. While acknowledging that elements of all three were discernible in the contemporary world, Bull regarded the Grotian conception as predominant. From a somewhat different perspective, Keohane and Nye (1977) reinforced this critique of Realism by showing that international 'regimes' – the rules accepted as applicable to a given set of international issues – did not simply reflect the preferences of the most powerful.

A second target was the assertion that states are, and for the foreseeable future will remain, the central actors of international relations. To attack it, Herz (1959), used a Realist, indeed Hobbesian, axiom, that political loyalties are given only in return for security. Since economic warfare, ideological penetration, aerial bombardment and finally the invention of nuclear weapons had rendered the state permeable and indefensible, Herz proclaimed its demise. As he was later to concede, this obituary was premature. States have indeed become vulnerable to violent separatist movements and transnational terrorism, but to a large extent they have survived, not because they are defensible, but partly because the organizational networks that sustain them remain 'going concerns', capable of clipping the wings of most alternative actors, and partly because of what the citizens of most states have in common – culture, religion, language, race or even a purely subjective sense of a common identity. It is the Hobbesian premise that is flawed.

Nevertheless, though the replacement of territorial states by a world government is not remotely in sight, they have come to share their powers to a significant extent with other bodies. Whereas once treaties could be concluded only between states, the United Nations Law of the Sea Convention, for instance, had to be open for signature not merely by the European Community's members, but also by the Community itself, because of the latter's centrally administered Common Fisheries Policy. Again, almost all parties to the European Convention on Human Rights, in what to an earlier generation would have seemed an unimaginable derogation of their sovereignty, have accepted the right of their citizens to appeal to an international body capable of overturning decisions of their highest national courts and even of overriding national legislation deemed incompatible with the convention.

'National interest' was the target of the third challenge to Realism. The cybernetic approach of Karl Deutsch (1963) attempted a more fundamental explanation of state policy. Like other actors, states, in responding to ever-changing circumstances, are seen as needing to combine receptivity to new concerns and new values with fidelity to old ones. Their performance, like that of motorists, depends heavily on the communications networks at the disposal of their decision-makers: on how far they can see ahead ('lead'), how quickly their decisions are implemented ('lag'), how much competes for their attention ('load'), what weight they can bring to bear in the desired direction ('gain' – a refined form of power) and how quickly and how accurately they can assess the results of their decisions (feedback). It is the state that cannot cope with its environment that is likely to fall back on power in its cruder form, 'the ability not to have to learn'. Conversely, states whose citizens are linked in a variety of close networks, official and unofficial, can create 'security communities' within which PEACE is assured.

States retain enormous military arsenals, but are less preponderant than they were, or than Realism would posit. Their functions and their power are being increasingly circumscribed by other layers of authority, intergovernmental, non-governmental and local, often in no orderly relationship. Bull warned that if the Grotian pattern of a society of states were thus to be superseded, which he thought to be unlikely, it could give rise to a possibly more violent condition of 'a new medievalism'.

The fourth attack on Realism came from Marxists, who have sought to portray human society, including global society, from the perspective of the poor and weak, in which classes, not states or nations, are the basic units. Events have not, however, corroborated some fundamental Marxist contentions, particularly about war; and explanations of imperialism and other aspects of foreign policy in terms of economic interests have not, on the whole, been convincing; but the Marxist prophecy of the ever-increasing concentration of economic power under capitalism has been borne out by the seeming lack of any natural limit to the size of firms, and it is hard to imagine that such power will not carry with it increasing political power, especially in the Third World.

Realism has thus been shown to oversimplify the complexity of international relations, but so, too, have most alternative approaches. The most fertile counterpart to it may prove to be cybernetics, which teaches us to assess the world's political and other systems in terms of their capacity to identify global problems and respond to them adequately. Any list of such problems, which would include famines, epidemics, environmental hazards, the exhaustion of resources and the continuing dangers of 'conventional' and even nuclear war, is inevitably incomplete, which underlines Deutsch's insistence that the first prerequisite of such systems is 'openness'.

Reading
Aron, R. 1962 (*1966*): *Peace and War*, trans. R. Howard and A.B. Fox.
Bull, H. 1977: *The Anarchical Society*.
Carr, E.H. 1939 (*1964*): *Twenty Years' Crisis*.
Claude, I.L. 1962: *Power in International Relations*.
Deutsch, K.W. 1963: *The Nerves of Government*.
Kaplan, M.A. 1957: *System and Process in International Politics*.
Keohane, R.O. and Nye, J.S. 1977: *Power and Interdependence*.
Knorr, K. and Rosenau, J.N. eds 1969: *Contending Approaches to International Politics*.
Linklater, A. 1982: *Men and Citizens in the Theory of International Relations*.
Wight, M. 1979: *Power Politics*.

RODERICK C. OGLEY

internationalism   The insistence that social and political problems must be considered from a standpoint transcending that of any one state is not new. Hinsley (1963) begins his history of internationalist theories with Dante's *De Monarchia*, thought to date from 1310. In the twentieth century, internationalism has taken three different, though not unrelated, paths: the promotion of action across state frontiers by those with similar interests and opinions (sometimes known as 'transnationalism'); opposition, in the Benthamite tradition, to narrowly nationalist state policies such as protectionism; and support for the creation, upholding and strengthening of international institutions.

Ethically, the main argument has been between those who hold that 'the state is fundamentally a nexus of special and general obligation' (Paskins,

1978, p. 163), and those who maintain that international society should be so structured as to express the rights and duties that 'each member of mankind might reasonably claim' from others (Linklater, 1982, p. 9), and see all 'particularistic moralities' as 'forms of human understanding which would be superseded in time as men grasped the nature of their capacity for self-determination' (ibid., p. 137).

The transnationalist path is exemplified by MARXISM, which, in its original form, held that the state was a mere instrument of the bourgeoisie and that 'the worker has no fatherland', but the very occurrence of World War I demonstrated the inadequacy of international proletarian solidarity. When the revolution in Russia of October 1917 failed to ignite an uprising of workers throughout the capitalist system, the internationalism of the Second International (founded 1889) and its successors became pragmatic rather than radical, and direct representation of workers (within national delegations) in the International Labour Organization gave socialists some scope for transnational collaboration. In contrast, the Third International, founded by Lenin, became a channel through which the USSR controlled communist parties of the rest of the world, until Soviet interventions in Hungary (in 1956) and more blatantly Czechoslovakia (in 1968) liberated most Western Marxists from this subservience. Non-Marxist manifestations of transnationalism in the late twentieth century have included charities and movements such as Oxfam, European Nuclear Disarmament (END), Amnesty International and Greenpeace.

The second, 'Benthamite' path has come under increasing challenge this century, and, in its economic aspect, not just from nationalists. Between the two world wars, repeated calls by League of Nations conferences for all-round reductions of tariffs exemplified the 'utopianism' denounced by E. H. Carr (1939) (see INTERNATIONAL RELATIONS). Followers of KEYNESIANISM also regarded free trade and multilateralism as misguided in the absence of a managed international economy with adequate mechanisms for sustaining effective demand, a view nominally embodied in the institutions created at Bretton Woods to manage the international economy after World War II, which J. M. Keynes helped to negotiate. Another aspect of this form of internationalism, the principle of freedom of movement across frontiers, has also had to fight a rearguard action against increasingly restrictive immigration controls and ever more formidable obstacles to the granting of asylum to refugees.

In the early part of the century, those who took the 'institutional' route to internationalism (see Angell, 1908; Woolf, 1916) usually made peace their goal, though, as indicated earlier, the newly created bodies commonly assumed other tasks. With the influx of new states, almost all of them underdeveloped, into the United Nations after 1950, internationalists also looked to such bodies to promote 'development' and correct the alleged biases of the existing economic system (see also DEVELOPMENT AND UNDERDEVELOPMENT). In the latter part of this century, 'institutional' internationalism has added to its concerns the worldwide upholding of human rights, the protection of the environment and the management of the resources of the sea, conceived of as the 'common heritage of mankind'.

Reading

Carr, E.H. 1939 (1964): Twenty Years' Crisis.
Dower, N. 1983: World Poverty.
Hinsley, F.H. 1963: Power and the Pursuit of Peace.
Linklater, A. 1982: Men and Citizens in the Theory of International Relations.
Paskins, B. 1978: Obligation and the understanding of international relations. In The Reason of States, ed. M. Donelan.

RODERICK C. OGLEY

invention The creation of new institutional structures, practices or objects, or any significant alteration in the above, is an ongoing feature of human history. For a variety of reasons, however, invention in the twentieth century has been largely reserved as a term describing scientific and technological developments (see TECHNOLOGICAL CHANGE). Additionally, theories with a determinist base (whether economic, biological, psychological or technological) assume that institutional or attitudinal changes are the functions of systemic requirements. But theory which attributes to invention itself an independent character makes more Promethean assumptions concerning the ability of people to alter radically their environment. On this view, the sonnet and the button were both inventions, one cultural and one technological, both of them representing 'different types of creativity' on the part of individuals in response to perceived needs (White, 1963, p. 114).

Theorists of invention, whether concentrating on technological or on social, economic, cultural and political acts of creation, focus on both the origins and the nature of inventive acts and patterns of diffusion. Many writers emphasize the fact that inventions are rarely the result of a single creative act but the result of a series of innovative responses, sometimes over many years, to the resolution of a problem. Invention often results from the application of differing perspectives to a problem. Bell's invention of the telephone was made possible by his very lack of expertise since the inventor saw possibilities for the instrument as a speaking device that experts in telegraphy did not (Hounshell, 1975). Architectural invention results from a playful inclusion of disparate cultural images and styles (Venturi et al., 1977). Some writers suggest that the development of certain kinds of inventions can be traced to the *Weltanschauung* of different historical periods. Robert Nisbet contends that the Middle Ages were rich in the creation of social inventions (the guild, marketplace, monastery, university) while in the twentieth century there is a dearth of social invention and a preoccupation with technological invention (1975). Other writers suggest that invention occurs more frequently in periods of political upheaval, particularly revolution. Georges Sorel, referring to the 'social poetry' of revolutionary activity, discusses the creation of myths of a future society as 'expressions of the will' (1906). Hannah Arendt argues that modern revolutions have regularly produced invented representative institutions which have thus far not succeeded in surviving (1965). The role of institutional sources of invention has also been explored, such as the impact of research laboratories on technological invention and ideological structures on political inventions. If major cultural, technological and political changes can be conceived as inventions, additional important questions arise as to the nature of the interaction among inventions and whether it is possible to categorize inventions in general. Some writers argue that recent inventions in electronic technology now permit the invention of new democratic practices (Barber, 1984). Others contend that technological invention crowds out other inventive forms through cultural reliance on a 'technological fix' to solve problems. Inventions themselves have been categorized by their impact on society and on one another, or in terms of their propensity to generate or forestall human liberation.

Reading
Abbott, Philip 1987: *Seeking New Inventions: The Idea of Community in America.*
Hughes, Thomas 1989: *American Genesis: A Century of Invention and Technological Enthusiasm.*
Illich, Ivan 1978: *Toward a History of Needs.*
Nisbet, Robert 1976: *Sociology as an Art Form.*
Pool, Ithiel de Sola ed. 1977: *The Social Impact of the Telephone.*

PHILIP ABBOTT

Islam A monotheistic world religion, Islam combines holy law, prophetic revelation and a sacred text to form a religious tradition that is detailed and all-embracing. Although there are a number of versions of Islam, there is an orthodox core which is still authoritative.

From the orthodox point of view, Islam is timeless. As a faith based on complete submission to the will of Allah, Islam has neither beginning nor end; Islam is self-sufficient in that it has not depended on any other religion, but it is also the last religion, which perfects all other versions of monotheism. From a sociological point of view, Islam is an Abrahamic religion which shares many beliefs and institutions with Christianity (see CHRISTIAN SOCIAL THEORY) and JUDAISM, such as a sacred book (the Qur'an), an ethical prophet (Muhammad), a normative tradition (the Sunnah), a doctrine of individual salvation and a view of Islam as a social community (the Ummah), which is essential if Muslims are to practise their religion fully. The principal differences, which are disputed by scholars, are that Islam has a stronger sense of the indivisible nature of law and religion, it has no sacramental priesthood and its orthodox core pays little attention to sacramental ritualism. Orthodox Islam has no tradition of baptism, eucharist or confession. Where such ritualism has developed in Islam, it has been associated with more popular or deviant traditions such as Sufism.

From a historical perspective, Islam arose in seventh-century Arabia in the cities of Medina and Mecca as a consequence of the preaching of Muhammad (570–632 AD). The Prophet received the Qur'an in the form of inspired verses or chapters (surat) which called all people to accept Allah as the one and only God, to renounce all aspects of their local religions, and to unite together in one community (the Household of Islam) in order to practise their religion faithfully. Out of these early practices, there developed a core of orthodox practice which is called the Five Pillars of Islam – the renunciation of polytheistic heresy by a proclamation that 'there is no god but God (Allah) and Muhammad is his Prophet' (shahadah), fasting during the month of Ramadan, the pilgrimage to Mecca (Hajj), alms giving (Zakah) and daily prayer (Salah).

Islam developed in a geopolitical niche between two declining empires – the Byzantine and the Sassanian. Having successfully overcome opposition to his preaching, the simplicity of Muhammad's message functioned as an important social bond which, during his lifetime, united the fissiparous nomadic tribes. Islam spread rapidly through the Middle East and North Africa. There has been much dispute over the causes of conversion to Islam. Critics emphasize the importance of holy war (Jihad) and the economic benefits of either conversion or protection. Islam has often been regarded as a warrior religion which spread by force, but it is important to acknowledge that Islamic expansion depended heavily on the expansion of trade and commercial links as the routes along which Islamic missionaries spread. Islam is essentially an urban religion of merchants, not a faith of desert nomads.

After the death of the Prophet, Islam split into a Sunni majority and a Shi'ite minority movement. Sunnism became the official ideology of the caliphate (the central institution of the Islamic polity). By contrast, Shi'ism, which became eventually the 'official' religion of Persia, was based on the idea of a charismatic succession of religious leaders (Imams) who drew their legitimacy from their descent from the Prophet. Its religious ethos gave greater emphasis to suffering and martyrdom; Sunnism remained a more sober, ascetic practice. These two branches of Islam eventually developed different legal and religious characteristics. Sunnism developed four major 'rites' (Hanafite, Malikite, Shafi'it and Hanbalite). Once the holy law (Shari'ah) had been fully developed by these four schools, it was said that no further or new interpretation of the sacred law was possible; the gate of judgement (ijtihad) was closed.

Intellectually Islam then went into a long period (from the tenth to the nineteenth century) of official ossification in which any change in the core doctrines was ruthlessly opposed. Although Islam continued to expand through the creation of new cultural and political centres in Spain, India, Persia and Turkey, social scientists have claimed that the failure of Islam to maintain a technical and military advantage over Europe has its origin in this rigid opposition to innovation. After a series of crucial turning points for Islam – the loss of Spain in 1492, the military defeats outside the gates of Vienna in 1529 and 1683, and the defeat of the Ottoman navy at the Battle of Lepanto in 1571 – the capitalist West acquired a strategic economic and military advantage within the world system. The heartlands of Islam became encircled as Western capitalism and COLONIALISM spread through Africa, India and Asia. By the nineteenth century, Islam was decisively on the defensive against Western imperialism as many Muslim societies came under direct or indirect European (and therefore Christian) control. Many Muslim leaders in the twentieth century, such as Colonel Mu'ammar al-Qaddafi of Libya, regard nineteenth-century territorial expansion as the final stages of the Crusades.

Between Napoleon's Egyptian expedition and World War I, Islam experienced three major social transformations. The first was the political decline of the Ottoman Empire in relation to Western expansion, resulting in its dismemberment after 1918; secondly, the economies of the various Muslim states were incorporated into global capitalism on a dependent basis; and thirdly there were important responses in the form of religious movements to these secular developments. The Wahhabi movement, which was founded by Muhammad ibn 'Abd al-Wahhab (1703–1787), sought to create a fundamentalist return to Islamic principles. Liberal responses on the part of the urban intelligentsia, particularly in Egypt, attempted to integrate a reform of Islam with Western principles of parliamentary democracy and secular education. The Islamic response to Western economic and cultural penetration was thus intensely ambiguous, swinging between outright acceptance of secular Westernization and violent anti-colonial nationalism.

In the twentieth century, these cultural and social dilemmas have continued, despite the successful process of decolonization which occurred after World War II. Immediately after the war, Islamic societies were significantly influenced by various forms of secular NATIONALISM, of which Nasser's Egyptian brand of nationalism and PAN-ARABISM is a significant example. In Algeria, the liberation movement had a strong attachment to both nationalism and Marxist SOCIALISM. In Indonesia, the anti-colonial struggle against Western, specifically Dutch, colonialism adopted a mixture

of Islamic universalism, paganism, nationalism and a personality cult around Sukarno. In Iran, the intellectual leader Ali Shari'ati (1933–1977) produced a revolutionary blend of Marxism and Shi'ism to inspire a mass movement for whom the word of Allah was the voice of the people.

These radical anti-colonial movements which combined secular nationalism with Islamic social principles have been slowly but globally challenged in the late twentieth century by a profound emphasis on FUNDAMENTALISM, which has rejected MODERNIZATION (both capitalist and socialist) and the traditional folk religiosity of the Sufi orders. In Egypt, Hassan al-Banna (1906–1949) founded the Ikhwan al-Muslimun (the Muslim Brotherhood) to fight imperialism, to foster Islamic unity and to defy Islamic governments which cooperated with Western control. The Ikhwan opposed secularist features of Nasserism, sought to compel Sadat to undertake a thorough Islamization of Egyptian social life and bitterly opposed any peace process with the Israelis. Because the Ikhwan has a mass following and extensive support in the army, it has remained a significant oppositional force.

In Pakistan, Maulana Abul A'la Mawdudi (1903–1979) created in 1941 the Jamaat-i-Islami, which had originally narrowly religious objectives. However, Mawdudi's writings assumed an increasingly political direction, because he condemned nationalism as a Western idea which divided the Muslim community. He called for the creation of an Islamic state which was to be based on exclusively religious principles. In the 1970s, the Jamaat played a major role in the struggle against the secularism of President Bhutto's Pakistan People's Party and maintained pressure on General Ziaul Haq to bring about the Nizam-e-Mustafa (the Islamic system).

In Iran, opposition to the Pahlavi dynasty and to the Western economic policies of Reza Shah drew considerable support from fundamentalist groups who came eventually under the leadership of Ayatollah Ruhollah Musavi Khomeini (1902–1989). Khomeini challenged the governments of all Muslim countries for failing to uphold the Shari'a, for accepting foreign influences and for neglecting the rights of their Muslim citizens. The fall of the Shah (1978–9) has resulted in a triumph of the jurists and the clergy (the mullahs) over the everyday regulation and imposition of religious practices and beliefs, especially in the symbolic return of the veil in women's attire. Khomeini continues to have many loyal Shi'ite followers in Iraq, Lebanon and the Gulf states.

Similar, if less spectacular, religious changes have taken place throughout the Islamic world. In Algeria, an uprising in 1988 in which Islamic fundamentalism played a part has forced the regime to adopt religiously inspired social reforms and to legalize the Islamic opposition party (the Front Islamique du Salut). In the Sudan, a military coup against Sadiq-al-Mahdi was undertaken by officers close to the Ikhwan in 1989. In Tunisia, Islamic opposition groups won 17 per cent of the popular vote in 1989. In the occupied areas of Palestine, Islamic forces have been influential in the intifadha struggle against Israeli forces.

The causes of Islamic fundamentalism are complex. It represents a response to the failures of capitalist experiments to raise the real standard of living of the masses, and also a response to political attempts to enforce secular communism. Islam's egalitarian message of revolutionary struggle has been successful in mobilizing the rural and urban masses against governments which have been sympathetic to Western influences and those which have sought Soviet support. Popular protest against urban elites have found a natural leadership in the mullahs, while the mosques were strategic meeting points for opposition which few governments dared to attack.

Two further changes in the twentieth century have been crucial. The development of a world communication system has enabled the world Muslim community to become a more united global political force. The Pilgrimage to Mecca has become a crucial feature of Islamic globalization. Secondly, the presence of Islam has become a political force inside Europe (partly as a consequence of extensive migration to Britain, France and Germany) and to a lesser extent in what was the Soviet socialist bloc. These conflicts came to a crisis in the Salman Rushdie affair, which involved a mass protest in 1989 against continued publication of *The Satanic Verses*. This struggle is one aspect of a broader campaign for Muslim schools, an Islamic curriculum, the right to wear Muslim clothing in public, and for recognition of Islamic personal law.

Islam, as a result of its association with the oil-rich states, has also played an important economic role in the development of Muslim societies, especially in the Third World. However, the Islamic prohibition on usury has often forced Islamic commercial leaders to depend on Western intermediaries. This relationship has had some disastrous consequences, as in the case of the collapse of BCCI in 1992.

Finally, the apparent triumph of fundamentalism has, however, been challenged by a number of prominent liberal intellectuals in Islam, and there is considerable opposition from radical Muslim women who reject the traditional seclusion of women, veiling and arranged marriages.

Reading

Arkoun, M. 1984: *Pour une critique de la raison islamique.*

Cragg, K. 1965: *Islamic Surveys: Counsels in Contemporary Islam.*

Esposito, J.L. ed. 1980: *Islam and Development: Religion and Sociopolitical Change.*

Hodgson, Marshall G.S. 1974: *The Venture of Islam.*

Hourani, A. 1962 (*1983*): *Arabic Thought in the Liberal Age 1798–1939.*

Roff, W.R. ed. 1987: *Islam and the Political Economy of Meaning: Comparative Studies of Muslim Discourse.*

Shariati, A. 1980: *On the Sociology of Islam*, trans. Hamid Algar.

Smith, W.C. 1957: *Islam in Modern History.*

Turner, B.S. 1974: *Weber and Islam: A Critical Study.*

Watt, W.M. 1988: *Islamic Fundamentalism and Modernity.*

BRYAN S. TURNER

IT *See* INFORMATION TECHNOLOGY AND THEORY

J

Judaism A belief system which, in the beginning of time, emerged with a single idea – monotheism – and in the course of time elaborated this idea by constructing ethical imperatives, first for the single God and then, through covenant and revelation, a corpus of timeless laws (Torah), which the people of Israel, elevated through the experiences of liberation and exodus, endorsed and then amplified into an eternal literature, the Bible. With the unique God and the unique Torah, there appeared, simultaneously and inseparably, the sense of peoplehood, of being the chosen, or better, the choosing people, and the identification of a plot of land as the only, the promised, the Holy Land. Time and space thus validated the ephemeral dreams of desert wanderers.

In a naive dialectic of human greed and social justice, political sophistication and crude force, ascetic learning and sensuous pleasure, the people were torn by and between external power and internal strife, guided, chided and occasionally comforted by that uniquely Judaic phenomenon – the prophet – fierce, fiery, uncompromising, but always proclaiming a rational ethic, teaching humanity (according to Max Weber) the first steps towards a disenchantment of the world. In a nation of dissenters, where even atheism is negotiated through the law, conflicts of principle, struggles between concepts, battles over issues, tended to take precedence over earthly realities and political discipline.

The price they paid was high. It gave Israel its first taste of exile, but left the creative impulse of the people unharmed. In Babylon the temple was replaced by the synagogue and daily prayers took the place of cultic sacrifice. For all the centrality of history in the Jewish world view, it has not protected the Judaic enterprise from falling a second time into the traps of defeat and dispersion through internal dissension and fraternal strife, which included the appearance of Jesus and the birth of Christianity. Nevertheless the conceptual unity of God–Torah–people–land was maintained and preserved and the carriers of Judaism – the Jews – became, in accordance with Torah prediction, 'a by-word among the nations'.

The second dispersion, more total and more widespread than the first, brought Judaism into contact, albeit limited and poorly tolerated contact, with a range of other belief systems and religions, resulting in many structural changes in Judaism which were frequently due to the catalytic impact of host cultures. Priests and prophets gave way to a rabbinic Judaism – with rabbis as teachers and guardians of Jewish law – in which the codifications of an 'oral' law, as opposed to the revealed 'written' law, offered an inexhaustible source of social and intellectual adaptation. It established a continuum of tradition and progress which has enabled the people to come to terms with almost all social, econonic or political variants. Although doggedly intolerant of heathenism and all forms of pagan worship, Judaism found it easier to accommodate itself to the two dominant religions of the Diaspora (countries of dispersion) – Christianity and Islam – than either of them did to the mother religion. Rabbinic Judaism found ways of incorporating theological and philosophical problems from the Christian West and scientific and mathematical thought from the Arab East without, in either case, sacrificing their expressly Jewish orientation. The frequent hostilities shown to Jews were utilized to create separate and closely knit communities led by this-worldly rabbis and supported by the spontaneous autonomy which an imposed segregation created. Just as the prophetic message was deliberately rational, so was rabbinic teaching on practical and metaphysical issues: freedom is a precondition of Judaism, but freedom can only exist under the law; equality is not merely social and economic but also spiritual – there can be no ecclesiasticism; salvation is itself a rational resolution of human conflict, hence the Messiah is not for individual salvation, his role is national in the first instance, but can be national only in a universal context. Judaism accepts, but does not invite proselytes. It has no doctrine of an only truth – other than the unity of God – and insists that righteousness is a human, not a Jewish, aspiration.

For almost 2,000 years the Jews lived as more or less tolerated minorities in Europe and Asia – from Scotland and Norway in the North, Morocco and Spain in the West, to Persia and Iraq in the East. They lived for the most part in a Jewish world whose external boundaries rarely extended beyond the regulations of and taxation by the host country. However problematic the material existence of the people may have been, Judaism enjoyed a long period of consolidation and creative innovation which enriched the prayer-book, enhanced internal discourse but shifted increasingly towards a rational intellectualism which gave rise to two dissenting movements within Judaism. The first originated in Palestine, where Jews, now representing a very small, barely tolerated minority, sought solace in a deeper, secretive and less formal approach to God. Jewish mysticism found expression in the *Kabbalah* (the literature of the mystic tradition) and initiated a new perspective in the Judaic tradition. A little later the same hard rationalism, now in marked contrast to the emotionally more satisfying mysticism, gave rise to a growing alienation of economically and socially deprived Jews in Eastern Europe. This led to the development of Hasidism, a movement of devoutly religious Jews, who put the service of God before the study of his law.

Although the creation of both these movements resulted in considerable conflict and communal tension they did not represent a true challenge to the principal norms and values of an established Judaism, nor did they alter the existing patterns of Jewish life. It was different with the next great impetus for change, which this time came from outside and which threatened to engulf the whole Judaic system. The French revolution aimed to restructure society at all levels in the spirit of new notions of social equality advocated by the Enlightenment. The Jew, too, was to be given the rights and privileges of citizenship in a Europe in which most of them were confined to ghettos and by petty restrictions which ensured their subservience. There was an expectation that in return for civil rights they would give up 'bad habits' of earlier times and adapt themselves to the demands of the new era. Neither the Jews nor the people of the host countries were any too eager to accept this change.

For the rabbis it was a threat to the survival of Jews as Jews. This led to diverging schools of thought, with those who clung to traditional Judaism forming an orthodox movement while those who saw a need to conform to the standards of the gentile environment developed a Reform movement which took its inspiration as much from Christian worship as from its Jewish roots.

For some Jews the new era called for a more radical response. They noted the growing secularization of society, the depressingly constant hostility of host nations, and the rising interest in one or another form of socialism throughout Europe. In one way or another they responded to one or two or all three of these factors by variously leaving Judaism altogether, forming a nationalist and/or socialist Judaism or seeking to preserve ancient loyalties in a modern garb through a Jewish humanism. The revolt against the emancipation of the Jews in Europe, which led to the extermination of six million Jews (see ANTI-SEMITISM), consolidated both the religious and the secular streams in Judaism. It led to the return of the Jews to their ancient homeland, a sharp polarization of religious and non-religious Jews, and, in the spirit of a reformed Europe, a Jewish pluralism which may be a first step towards a much desired messianic era, and which also reflects the tolerance which most host nations now show for the bearers of the Judaic tradition. While many of its adherents are assimilated into their host cultures, Judaism itself assimilated much of what is best in these host cultures into itself, thus giving it a vitality and resilience which has enabled it to survive in an essentially hostile world.

Reading

Selected from a huge literature:
Bulka, Reuven P. 1983: *Dimensions of Orthodox Judaism. Encyclopedia Judaica*, 1971, vol. 10.
Fackenheim, Emil 1987: *What is Judaism? An Interpretation for the Present Age.*
Glatzer, N. N. ed. 1968: *Martin Buber: Humanism.*
Levin, Nora, 1978: *Jewish Socialist Movements, 1871–1917.*
Meyer, Michael A. 1988: *Response to Modernity: A History of the Reform Movement in Judaism.*
Rabinowicz, H. 1970: *The World of Hasidism.*
Scholem, Gershom 1961 (*1973*): *Major Trends in Jewish Mysticism.*
Spero, Shubert 1983: *Morality, Halakha and the Jewish Tradition.*
Urbach, E.E. 1975: *The Sages, their Concepts and Beliefs*, 2 vols.

JULIUS CARLEBACH

justice Evaluations of the basic social and political institutions, particularly with respect to the consequent distributions of benefits and burdens, are standardly expressed in terms of justice or injustice. In its most general sense the concept of justice requires that each individual have what is due to him or her. Within this formula we may distinguish formal and material justice.

Formal justice requires distributions which are in accordance with existing or agreed criteria or rules. It is often identified with legal or individual justice. This involves standards of procedural justice ('due process' or 'natural justice') which are directed towards fairness and accuracy in the application of rules. It entails formal equality if it is assumed that every person in a society or group ought to be treated in accordance with the same rules.

Material (or substantive) justice concerns the identification of the appropriate distributive criteria (such as rights, desert, need or choice) that constitute competing conceptions of justice. Material justice may justify substantive inequalities of outcome or redistribution between different social groups. It is often identified with social justice.

Justice is often held to be the priority social value which overrides all other normative considerations, such as utility, at least with respect to the basic institutions of a society (Rawls, 1971, p. 3). This makes the choice of the specific criteria of a just distribution a matter of normative controversy (Miller, 1976, pp. 151ff.) If the normative priority of justice is not taken for granted then the selection of one of these competing conceptions of justice is largely a matter of conceptual convenience (Campbell, 1988, pp. 6ff.) However, criteria of substantive justice are normally confined to characteristics or properties of individuals (Honore, 1970, p. 63). More restrictively, it can be argued that criteria of justice, either always or mainly, refer in one way or another to the deserts or merits of those affected by the distribution in question (Sadurski, 1985, ch. 5).

Critics of the concept of social justice argue that the idea of distribution in accordance with a pattern (such that the extent and nature of a person's holdings depend on the extent and nature of his or her characteristics) is mistaken because the achievement of such patterns involves unwarranted curtailment of the liberties of individuals. An alternative, 'entitlement' model of justice (Nozick, 1974, part 2) takes holdings to be just if they are the result of legitimate behaviour. Justice is then the outcome of acquisitions and transactions which do not violate the pre-existing moral rights of the individuals, or which rectify the consequences of past illegitimate acquisitions or transfers (see RIGHTS).

The idea of socialist justice is controversial in that justice, particularly if it is associated with desert, may be regarded as a bourgeois value based on erroneous ideas of individual responsibility. However, a radically egalitarian conception of justice can be framed in terms of distribution in accordance with need, so that substantive justice favours outcomes in which individuals or groups are in a position of material equality (see Buchanan, 1982).

The most influential contemporary theory of justice seeks to combine a number of criteria of material justice under the idea of contract. John Rawls (1971) argues that the principles for determining the basic institutions of a society which would be chosen in a procedurally fair situation ('the original position'), and which are endorsed by our firmest reflective intuitions as to what is just, are

1　each person is to have an equal right to the most extensive total system of basic liberties compatible with a similar system of liberty for all (p. 250); and
2　social and economic inequalities are to be arranged so that they are both (a) to the greatest benefit of the least advantaged and (b) attached to offices and positions open to all under conditions of fair equality of opportunity (p. 83).

Recent 'communitarian' theories hold that criteria of justice depend on the 'sphere' in which distributions are being considered, so that, for instance, economic and political justice are distinct (Walzer, 1983, pp. 23–5), and that standards of justice are always relative to the understandings and expectations current in specific societies.

Reading
Ackerman, B. A. 1980: *Social Justice in the Liberal State*.
Barry, B. 1989: *Theories of Justice*.
Buchanan, A. E. 1982: *Marx and Justice*.
Campbell, T. D. 1988: *Justice*.
Honore, A. 1970: Social justice. In *Essays in Legal Philosophy*, ed. R. S. Summers, pp. 61–94.
Nozick, R. 1974: *Anarchy, State and Utopia*.
Rawls, J. 1971: *A Theory of Justice*.
Sadurski, W. 1985: *Giving Desert its Due: Social Justice and Legal Theory*.
Sandel, M. J. 1982: *Liberalism and the Limits of Justice*.
Walzer, M. 1983: *Spheres of Justice*.

TOM D. CAMPBELL

K

Kantianism, neo- *See* NEO-KANTIANISM

Keynesianism In its broadest sense Keynesianism is an approach to the political, social and economic affairs of advanced capitalism that validates the state taking a leading role in promoting material welfare and growth, and in regulating civil society. It also has a narrower meaning as a body of economic theory underlying macroeconomic policy. Both concepts of Keynesianism derive from the writings of John Maynard Keynes from the late 1920s and from the policies he attempted to implement from within British official circles then, and during World War II and postwar reconstruction.

The fundamental idea of Keynesian thought is that capitalist economies systematically fail to generate stable growth or fully utilize human and physical resources; markets, which are civil society's main economic mechanisms of self-regulation and adjustment, cannot eliminate economic crises, unemployment, or, in later versions, inflation. However, the meaning of Keynesianism, in either its broad or narrow sense, is open to interpretation and is the subject of continuing controversy, as is its validity.

Broad Keynesianism

The idea that the state has a special role in fostering material welfare and growth predates Keynes by many centuries, but Keynesianism provided an intellectual rationale for a type of state project not previously attempted under capitalism. Under it, full employment was given priority as a citizen's right which, since private enterprise itself could not be relied on, should be delivered by the state promoting investment directly or through managing markets to induce businesses to invest.

That project gained political and social momentum from apparently intractable mass unemployment in the 1920s, culminating in the crises of the 1930s, which put the legitimacy of the capitalist order in doubt and appeared to threaten that it could collapse into barbarism or give way to socialism. Keynesianism seemed to offer a 'third way' between laissez-faire capitalism and socialism which, by transforming capitalist society, would strengthen and preserve it.

The policy of 'public works' – direct state investment in infrastructure – which Keynes saw as one means to promote full employment had been on the agenda of political debate and partly implemented in Franklin D. Roosevelt's NEW DEAL in the United States before Keynes published his major theoretical work, *The General Theory of Employment, Interest and Money*. It illustrates the breadth of Keynesianism for, instead of public works being only a technical economic device, the programme's adoption required a fundamental reconstruction of political forces. In the United States that included the formation of the long-lasting Democratic Party coalition of the industrial working class, liberal middle classes, poor ethnic groups, and Southern interests, and its implementation involved an expansion of Washington-based executive agencies. In Britain the pressure for public works financed by credit was a struggle against the entrenched interests represented politically by the 'Treasury view'.

Public works programmes were generally opposed by banking interests in both America and Britain and the adoption of other elements of Keynesian economic policies, such as low interest rates to stimulate private investment, similarly required a political reorientation which demoted the power of financiers. The construction of a liberal corporatist state with institutionalized links between trade unions, employers' organizations and state agencies was one political shift that appeared consistent with Keynesianism; but public works and hostility to banking were also found in fascist states built on a rather different kind of CORPORATISM. In Britain moves toward corporatist cooperation (most famously the Mond–Turner talks) were in ferment in the years leading up to

Keynes's promulgation of his economic strategy in the 1930 hearings of the Macmillan Committee, but they made no significant progress until World War II. Then the growth of working-class social democratic and communist organizations created the basis for a postwar reconstruction of the state based on rights to full employment and social provision, control over financial institutions and markets, public ownership and investment in major industries. At the same time a dominant political ideology of Keynesianism, shared by the major parties, was constructed and held without effective challenge for three decades.

Although full employment, engineered through public spending and measures to manage private investment, was the goal around which that consensus and corporatist arrangements were constructed, its near achievement led to renewed attention being given to the control of inflation which, as M. Kalecki had warned in 1943, would be used as an argument against full employment policies. This prompted a new direction for Keynesianism. In the belief that full employment had been irrevocably achieved, its main tenet became the achievement of national growth with low inflation, and corporatist arrangements were increasingly used to manage the labour market in attempts to restrict wage inflation (through imposed or agreed 'incomes policies' and 'social contracts').

Although Keynesianism is most closely identified with the post-1945 domestic agendas of the United States and Western Europe, especially Britain's WELFARE STATE, it had a strong international dimension in Marshall Aid and the construction of the Bretton Woods system around the International Monetary Fund and World Bank. That system was originally based on the Keynesian notions of governmental management of international finance and exchange rates, and control over bankers' operations. Keynes's statesmanship in building the system was aimed at facilitating domestic management of interest rates and government finance to promote full employment investment policies, but politically it represented an international realignment with American economic management of the capitalist order.

Narrow Keynesianism
The broad political agenda of Keynesianism had its roots in the technical revolution Keynes and his followers believed he had achieved in economic theory. Although several key ideas were contained in his *Treatise on Money*, published in 1930, Keynes's definitive statement was *The General Theory of Employment, Interest and Money*, published in 1936. It claims to demonstrate that, contrary to the orthodox reasoning of 'classical theory', the capitalist system, left to itself, will not generally produce full employment. The key to this theoretical revolution was the development of two concepts, liquidity preference and effective demand.

Liquidity preference is a highly simplified model of the workings of financial markets which provided a basis for the conclusion that financial markets may systematically cause interest rates to be at a high level that depresses private industries' investment. Its formal presentation as the idea that the demand for the stock of money depends on the rate of interest is now an integral part of all modern economics, although the Keynesian conclusion derived from it is not.

Effective demand is the notion that aggregate demand, and hence saving, depends on disposable income; consequently, full employment may be unsustainable because its level of output is not matched by aggregate demand. It stands in contrast to the 'classical' or, more accurately, neoclassical view that the price mechanism automatically adjusts to ensure equality between demand and supply, for instead of demand responding only to prices it responds to income.

Placing these concepts in the framework of concepts of aggregate output and income which then became the Keynesian basis for modern National Income accounting, the Keynesian theorem stated that the aggregate investment plans of business will not, in general, be equal to aggregate saving chosen at full employment output. At its centre is the failure of the interest rate to adjust automatically to restore investment-saving to equality, a condition required for equilibrium. Consequently, with investment plans depressed, output and income have to be at a depressed level (with mass unemployment as a symptom) in order to depress saving to the same level.

Although that model of unemployment equilibrium has remained the core Keynesian model, it was extended in various ways. Applying the principle of effective demand and the notion that the interest rate does not determine firms' desired capital stock, Roy Harrod and Evsey Domar showed that in a growing economy full employment is not the general case. Their model became the basis of development planning for the Third World, holding a pre-eminent position until four decades after the *General Theory* appeared. However, in Western macroeconomics the most significant extension to the Keynesian model occurred in the 1960s when the notion of a relationship between unemployment and the rate of inflation (the Phillips Curve) was added. Within economic theory the Phillips Curve promised to remedy the silence of the core model on how the price level is determined, while in a broader Keynesian perspective it provided a basis for incomes policies.

Disputes over Keynesianism

The broad Keynesian agenda had been attacked from its earliest days as socialist, although its avowed role was the preservation of capitalism; but ultimately it was undermined by changed circumstances more than by that political attack on it. The Keynesian hegemony constructed after World Warr II lost its cohesion in the late 1970s as the international order anchored by the US dollar gave way to unregulated international finance, and the social consensus of domestic politics in advanced capitalist countries was fragmented by the phenomenon of high inflation coexisting with high unemployment. It was overturned as an official agenda when Margaret Thatcher gained power in Britain and Ronald Reagan in America, but important elements survived. In Britain, majority opinion continued its allegiance to the core of the Keynesian welfare state, America experienced a long boom generated by Keynesian-type deficit financing of state spending, and in continental Western Europe Keynesian types of state management promoted growth and modernization. Nevertheless, the fundamental Keynesian objective of permanently eliminating mass unemployment was lost in that period.

In economic theory, the interpretation of the Keynesian model that had dominated the first two-and-a-half postwar decades was fundamentally challenged by, on one hand, Keynesian theorists themselves and, on the other, MONETARISM and 'new classical' theory. The dominant existing interpretation of Keynes's theory, the 'neoclassical synthesis' inaugurated by J.R. Hicks in 1937 and developed by A.C. Pigou, F. Modigliani and D. Patinkin, had attempted to base his conclusions on the neoclassical theory of markets in which prices rather than quantities (such as income and output) were the adjustment mechanisms. In this interpretation, the economy's smooth working was the norm and unemployment appeared as a special case resulting from wage rigidity, in contrast to Keynes's own general theory of unemployment in which full employment was seen as the exception.

A 'neo-Keynesian' critical school emerged in the 1970s emphasizing the importance of quantities whenever any prices in the system are less than perfectly flexible and showing that unemployment is generally possible while full employment equilibrium is only one of many possibilities. That school retains but amends the choice theoretic foundations of the neoclassical synthesis. By contrast, POST-KEYNESIANISM attempts to return to the 'true Keynes', emphasizing complex phenomena that undermine those foundations. That school pays special attention to the role of unquantifiable business expectations; the lack of connection between the interest rate and the productivity of capital; the endogenous character of the money supply instead of its control by the central bank; the importance of credit and the whole structure of finance instead of money; and the influence of income distribution on macroeconomic developments.

The monetarist criticisms voiced by Milton Friedman and his school for many years took a new and powerful line at the end of the 1960s by interpreting Keynesian theory as depending on the Phillips Curve. Friedman gave the latter a neoclassical foundation by introducing expectations of inflation into a model of wage determination and obtained the anti-Keynesian result that in the long run unemployment, however high, is at its natural rate reflecting workers' choice instead of being involuntary and is not influenced by Keynesian demand-management policies. Because the dominant Keynesian model itself was based on neoclassical principles, its supporters were unable to argue effectively against this extension despite its anti-Keynesian conclusion. That criticism of the Keynesian model was carried further by 'new classical' writers, who demonstrated that in a model where expectations are 'rational expectations', unemployment is voluntary and at its 'natural rate' at all times, not only in long-run equilibrium. Although that refutation of Keynesian conclusions confounds common sense and experience, the dominant neoclassical synthesis version of Keynesian theory was unable to present a grand alternative in the way that Keynes had attempted. While unemployment at prewar levels returned, mainstream Keynesian theory accepted the concept of a natural rate of unemployment and was concerned only with the speed at which economies reached it.

Reading
Keynes, J.M. 1936: *The General Theory of Employment, Interest, and Money.*
Leijonhufvud, A. 1968: *On Keynesian Economics and the Economics of Keynes.*
Moggridge, D.E. 1976: *Keynes.*

LAURENCE HARRIS

Keynesianism, post-   *See* POST-KEYNESIANISM

kinship   A pre-eminent interest of anthropologists since the late nineteenth century, kinship remains both a keystone to the understanding of particular societies and a tool through which to explore theoretical issues such as human evolution, social organization and 'primitive' thought. It is also a topic of interest within other fields, including psychology, sociology and economic and social history.

The late nineteenth century
The importance of kinship in the late nineteenth century was related to its significance for the theory of social evolution. One early debate concerned the historical precedence of patrilineal (descent through men) versus matrilineal (descent through women) social organization. Some nineteenth-century writers argued for the primacy of patrilineal descent, as found for example in ancient Rome, in the foundation of society. Others argued that group marriage and matrilineal – and even matriarchal (with authority in the hands of women) – social organization preceded the development of patrilineal groups and rules of inheritance. Among the key thinkers who held this view were John F. McLennan and Lewis Henry Morgan. McLennan's (1865) version of the theory was based on his supposition that people knew their relationship to their mothers before they understood the role of fathers in conception. This, he argued, led to polyandry (the marriage of one woman to more than one man), then to bride capture, and then to exogamy (marriage outside the group). Morgan agreed with McLennan on the precedence of matrilineal descent but suggested errors in McLennan's line of reasoning. He argued instead that the best evidence for early forms of

social organization is to be found through the study of the classification of relatives (Morgan, 1871 and 1877). His supposition was that the relationship terminologies are conservative and reflect forms of social structure which have been rendered extinct. He propounded his argument with a vast array of ethnographic data collected worldwide, at his instigation, and from his own in-depth knowledge of the Iroquois, a matrilineal people of his native New York State.

McLennan's ideas on exogamy reemerged in the twentieth century as the foundation of alliance theory (see below). Morgan's ideas, and particularly his interest in relationship terminologies, remained important in kinship studies throughout the following century. Yet they took on a larger significance because he regarded the development of private property as the single most important cause of social evolution, particularly in the change from matrilineal to patrilineal descent. This interested Karl Marx and Friedrich Engels, who helped to popularize Morgan's ideas outside the realm of kinship studies (see especially Engels, 1884).

Descent theory
In the twentieth century, interests turned towards the understanding of particular kinship systems. Evolutionism declined among anthropologists as the new generation engaged directly in field research, a practice indulged in by few nineteenth-century thinkers. This fact, together with the impact of synchronic, ahistorical approaches, which were emerging in linguistics and sociology as well as in anthropology, led to the development of the idea of kinship as the foundation for the social organization and even the indigenous thought of the peoples anthropologists studied. In both the American and the British traditions, the key theoretical ideas which informed the next generation of kinship studies originated with the functionalist school.

The central idea of this school, especially its structural-functionalist branch, was one of society as being made of 'systems': economic, political, religious and kinship (for instance, Radcliffe-Brown, 1952, pp. 49–89, 178–87). Kinship systems came to be seen as pivotal to the workings of society in general, as social institutions within the kinship system affected the structure of those outside this domain. For example, bridewealth (payment, usually livestock, from a bridegroom to his bride's kin) has implications for the accumulation and distribution of wealth. It also has implications for political relations within and between kin groups which exchange wealth and people in marriage.

The dominant theme which resulted from studies in this tradition later became known as descent theory, in opposition to alliance theory which developed in the decades following World War II. Descent theorists were primarily interested in relations within kin groups. They stressed the idea of groups as corporate or property-owning units. Such 'property' could variously take the form of movable goods, land, sacred sites, ritual statuses, or simply a group name and its exclusive identity. Membership of the group could be derived from descent through the father, through the mother, through both, or through either (in the last case entailing an element of individual choice). Spouses might be incorporated into the group or remain members of their natal groups, according to custom. Groups might be localized or widely dispersed. These variations were of great importance for field researchers from the 1920s at least until the early 1960s. This was especially true for those in the British tradition who conducted their research among patrilineal peoples of the African continent (for instance, Fortes, 1949; Evans-Pritchard, 1951).

Alliance theory

While descent theory dominated anthropological thinking on kinship in Britain and the Commonwealth, alliance theory was developing in France, and to some extent in the Netherlands, where scholars had anticipated the trend through in-depth studies of the kinship systems of the East Indies. In France, Claude Lévi-Strauss was the key thinker, largely through his influential book *Les Structures élémentaires de la parenté* (1949). Lévi-Strauss and his structuralist disciples stressed the significance of marital alliance over the formation of descent groups. The word *alliance* itself is simply French for 'marriage'. In alliance theory it is taken to infer relations through marriage, between groups and categories, and the implications of these relations for the ordering of both social and cosmological structures. At the root of alliance is the incest taboo and the idea of exogamy.

Societies which were of special significance for alliance theorists were those in which alliance does in fact order such relations to a great extent. They include those of Aboriginal Australia, South America and parts of India, where individuals are required to marry kinsfolk of a specified category which includes relatives on both sides of the family (see, for instance, Dumont, 1975). This category is generally that of the cross-cousin (a mother's brother's or father's sister's child) and more distant terminological equivalents (such as second cousins). In some of these societies, notably those in Aboriginal Australia, marital alliance is often part of a larger indigenously defined system of world order in which relations between kin groups are thought to duplicate relations between animals, mythical beings and elements of the cosmos such as the sun and the moon (Maddock, 1973).

Other societies of interest to alliance theorists are found in parts of South and Southeast Asia, where individuals are required to marry kinsfolk on one particular side of the family. The typical form is one in which a man marries a member of the classificatory category that includes his mother's brother's daughter. Such a system is conducive to the generation and maintenance of social hierarchy, in that it defines absolute relations between kin groups as 'wife-takers' and 'wife-givers' in respect of one another. In Hindu societies 'wife-takers' are regarded as inferior. Elsewhere, 'wife-givers' are often regarded as superior. When bridewealth is paid, it will accumulate in the hands of those kin groups giving their sisters in marriage in exchange for such wealth (e.g. Leach, 1961, pp. 54–104, 114–23).

A third logical possibility would involve the marriage of a man to a member of the category of his father's sister's daughter. This possibility is largely unattested in the ethnographic literature, partly because it lacks both the logic of the symmetrical system of bilateral cross-cousin marriage which fosters egalitarianism, and that of the asymetrical system of mother's-brother's-daughter marriage which fosters hierarchical relations. For formal reasons, repeated father's-sister's-daughter marriage would result in asymmetrical relations within any given genealogical level, but symmetrical relations between any two groups over time (Needham, 1962, pp. 101–26). Yet it has been of interest to theorists (especially Lévi-Strauss) precisely because it is a logical and not a practical possibility.

A later interest of alliance theorists has been in those systems, including most in the world, which define the categories which one must *not* marry (for instance, that of close kin). These, more 'complex' systems are seen in opposition to the 'elementary' ones where there is less choice (Héritier, 1981, pp. 137–67). Finally, systems known as 'semi-complex' or 'Crow-Omaha' (after two North American tribes) involve such extensive prohibitions that they have been described as constituting an intermediate type (Héritier, 1981, pp. 73–136). Ironically, the existence of semi-complex systems in North America and Africa facilitated Lévi-Strauss's (1966) plea for recognizing all real kinship systems as only approximations of his ideal types. This precipitated a harsh confrontation between him and those British empiricists who in the 1950s and 1960s adopted an alliance theory approach.

Relationship terminologies
In the United States the dominant interest in the twentieth century has been neither descent nor alliance but the study of kinship or relationship terminologies. Nevertheless, there has been a lack of agreement as to the nature of relationship terminology structures. A.L. Kroeber (1909) argued that they represent not 'sociology' but 'psychology', by which he meant the formal properties of human thought. In this sense, to some extent he anticipated Lévi-Strauss. Yet his more direct intellectual descendants were the practitioners of componential and transformational analysis of the 1950s and 1960s. Componential analysts (such as Goodenough, 1956) drew on ideas in linguistics to develop methods with which to analyse the semantic components of relationship terms. The word *uncle* in English, for example, comprises the components 'male' (which distinguishes *uncle* from *aunt*), 'collateral' (which distinguishes *uncle* from *father*), and 'first ascending generation' (which distinguishes *uncle* from *cousin* or *nephew*). Transformational analysts (such as Scheffler and Lounsbury, 1971) adopted a quite different approach. It was characterized by the premise that some genealogical points of reference are more fundamental to the definition of a category than others. For example, in 'Crow-Omaha' systems of the 'Crow' type, one may call father's sister, father's sister's daughter, and father's sister's daughter's daughter (all members of the father's sister's matrilineal group) by a single kinship term. This term may be labelled simply 'father's sister' by the analyst, who then must explain with pseudo-mathematical logic the mechanism through which the term is 'extended'. For those who pursued these approaches, the place of social structure in determining the classification of relatives was a matter of

debate or, in some cases, was regarded simply as irrelevant.

Other American anthropologists stressed the variety of forms of classification above their formal properties. Chief among these was George Peter Murdock, who, like Morgan before him, saw in relationship terminologies a reflection of social evolution. Murdock (1949) identified six types of relationship terminology structure. He named these after tribal or geographical entities, in some cases not very accurately, but his intention in any case was that the names be regarded as exemplary rather than all-encompassing. For example, the 'Hawaiian' structure classifies all same-sex siblings and same-sex cousins by a single given term, unlike, say, the 'Eskimo' structure (that of the English language, as well as Inuit or Eskimo languages) which distinguishes *brother* and *sister* from *cousin*. The 'Hawaiian' type, structurally the simplest, is found not only in Hawaii but also, for example, in West Africa. To Murdock and his followers each type represented a terminology structure which could reflect a particular stage or stages of human evolution, but it did not necessarily imply a common linguistic or cultural origin of all peoples who possess it.

Recent developments
In the late twentieth century, the trend has been towards syntheses of the approaches of the past and towards the refinement of theoretical ideas with the paradigms of descent, alliance and terminology. Alliance theorists, in particular, have tried to tackle the problem of the relation between the highly theoretical models introduced by Lévi-Strauss and the ethnographic data (e.g. Needham, 1973 and 1986; Good, 1981).

Other developments have included interest in the social implications of *in vitro* fertilization by donor, surrogate motherhood, fostering and adoption (see FAMILY). All these practical concerns reflect a theoretical interest in explaining cross-cultural variation in the concept of 'kinship' and in understanding the grey area which separates nature and culture (see Héritier-Augé, 1985).

See also ANTHROPOLOGY.

Reading
Barnard, A. and Good, A. 1984: *Research Practices in the Study of Kinship.*
Bohannan, P. and Middleton, J. eds 1968: *Kinship and Social Organization.*

Dumont, L. 1971: *Introduction à deux theories d'anthropologie sociale*.

Fox, R. 1967: *Kinship and Marriage: An Anthropological Perspective*.

Goody, J. R. ed. 1971: *Kinship: Selected Readings*.

——ed. 1973: *The Character of Kinship*.

Graburn, N. ed. 1971: *Readings in Kinship and Social Structure*.

Needham, R. ed. 1971: *Rethinking Kinship and Marriage*.

Schneider, D. M. 1984: *A Critique of the Study of Kinship*.

ALAN BARNARD

knowledge, sociology of *See* SOCIOLOGY OF KNOWLEDGE

knowledge, theory of The philosophical theory of knowledge – or epistemology – is concerned with the nature, varieties, origins, objects and limits of knowledge. Plato distinguished knowledge (*epistēmē*) from mere belief (*doxa*). Traditionally knowledge has been defined as justified true belief. Among the questions that epistemology has been concerned with are: (1) is knowledge possible? (2) if so, are its objects real or ideal? (3) is its source experience or reason? (4) is knowledge unitary? From its birth, epistemology has been (5) *aporetic*: that is to say, its solutions have been forged in preoccupation with certain problems, or problem sets. So in this article I will look briefly at one such set, that clustering around the problem of induction, pronounced 'the scandal of philosophy' by C. D. Broad in 1926.

(a)   Sceptics have doubted whether the justification of knowledge claims is possible, while fallibilists such as C. S. Peirce and K. R. Popper have argued that the best that can be achieved are critically examined non-falsified conjectures. But the falsification of a conjecture seems to imply the recognition, and thus acceptance, of a mistake. Nevertheless apprehension of the relativity of knowledge has caused both twentieth-century conventionalists, and some sociologists of knowledge, to want to put that term in scare quotes.

(b)   The beginning of the century saw a realist reaction against the prevailing nineteenth-century subjective and objective idealisms, in which reality, and in particular the objects of perception and more generally knowledge, were viewed as consisting in, or at any rate dependent upon (finite or infinite) minds or (particular or transcendent) ideas. G.E. Moore proposed a commonsense perceptual REA-LISM, but neither this nor the more customary Cartesian–Lockean representative realism, in which some percepts were like their objects, provided a match for phenomenalism, in which objects were analysed as actual or possible sense-data and in which the logical empiricism dominant in the second quarter of the century was usually couched. (Logical empiricists, however, typically tended also to dismiss the whole realist/idealist issue as a characteristically undecidable, and therefore meaningless, 'metaphysical' question.) In the 1970s and 1980s the issue of realism – but now principally of scientific realism – has once more come to the fore, in the USA mainly in the epistemologically oriented forms put forward by H. Putnam and W. Boyd, and in the UK in the more ontological varieties proposed by Harré and Bhaskar. The latter holds that the objects of scientific knowledge are not events and their conjunctions, but causal structures, generative mechanisms and the like which exist and act, for the most part, quite independently of human activity, and in particular the activity such as experimentation which affords us empirical access to them. More generally it seems important to distinguish, at least in respect of science, two kinds of objects of knowledge: the (intransitive) objects of scientific investigation (such as the mechanism of electrical conductivity or the propagation of light) and the (transitive) cognitive objects – resources, not topics – used in the production or transformation of their knowledge (see MODEL).

(c)   At least since Leibniz and Hume, analytical knowledge has been clearly distinguished from empirical knowledge, though this distinction has come under attack in the third quarter of the century from W.V.O. Quine (and in a different direction from Friedrich Waismann). A principal dispute historically within epistemology has been that between rationalists such as Plato and Descartes who have regarded reason, and empiricists such as Aristotle and Locke who have seen experience, as a primary (or even sole) source of knowledge. Typically rationalists have conceived knowledge, on the paradigm of Euclidean geometry, as derived in a priori fashion from self-evident or rationally demonstrable axioms. Empiricists, by contrast, have assumed knowledge to be established by induction from (or tested by advertion to) incorrigible, or conventionally agreed, but uninferred observation statements. Kant attempted to reconcile the contending claims of reason and experience in his system of transcendental idealism by seeing reason as furnishing synthetic a priori principles imposing form on the matter received through the senses.

In the first half of the century EMPIRICISM, particularly in a logical form promulgated by the Vienna circle of M. Schlick, R. Carnap and O. Neurath, was well nigh hegemonic – though, outside the analytical mainstream, species of rationalism such as Husserl's PHENOMENOLOGY thrived, and even within it figures like R.G. Collingwood survived. It is worth going into the demise of logical empiricism in some detail. The Vienna circle employed the analytical/empirical dichotomy in the form of a criterion of meaningfulness (initially stated by Schlick as 'the meaning of a proposition is the method of its verification') and a criterion of demarcation (of scientific from non-scientific discourse). But difficulties soon appeared. First, the verifiability principle was neither analytic nor empirical and so should be meaningless. Secondly, on it, both historical propositions and scientific laws (which, being universal, could never be conclusively verified) turned out to be meaningless. To meet this difficulty Carnap weakened the criterion to allow a proposition as meaningful just in case some empirical evidence could count for or against it, that is if it was testable. Popper's response was to admit non-scientific propositions as meaningful, but to substitute falsifiability as a demarcation criterion. Finally, the principle seemed to entail solipsism or, if given a realist interpretation, loss of incorrigibility and, with this, of unique decisions.

More generally, the whole idea of theory-independent facts, constituting the incorrigible foundations of knowledge, was rendered suspect from a variety of quarters. Wittgenstein's critique of his own early philosophy, and in particular of the possibility of a private language, fatally undermined the sociological individualism implicit in the model. An increasing awareness of the mutability of scientific knowledge (and of the magnitude of actual scientific changes), for which the work of Karl Popper, T.S. Kuhn, I. Lakatos and P.K. Feyerabend were principally responsible, vitiated the point of fundamentalism. Further, it became apparent that key terms such as 'experience' were underanalysed and used equivocally, for instance by the failure to distinguish social practice, on the one hand, and experimentally controlled enquiry, on the other – both, moreover, deeply implicated in theory. Finally, the holistic character of both experimental outcomes and observational languages became clear. (Thus, in the former case, any result is, first, a test of a multiplicity of hypotheses (any one of which may be saved), second, consistent with a (generally infinite) plurality of further sets of hypotheses, and third, subject to subsequent revision or redescription in the history of science.)

The work of the later Wittgenstein and the ordinary language, then LINGUISTIC PHILOSOPHY centred on Oxford (and led by Gilbert Ryle and J.L. Austin), together with the conceptual analysis also practised at the same time, paved the way for the reemergence of neo-Kantian themes, most notably in the work of P. Strawson and S.N. Hampshire and in the philosophies of science propounded by W. Sellars, S.E. Toulmin, N.R. Hanson and Rom Harré. More recently a non-Kantian sublation of empiricism and rationalism has been essayed by Bhaskar in his system of transcendental or critical realism, on which scientific theory is viewed as generating, under the discipline of experimental control, knowledge of natural necessity a posteriori. On this system, Humean criteria of causality and law and Hempelian criteria of explanation are neither necessary nor sufficient. Ontology is re-vindicated and the mistake of the analysis of statements about being into statements about our knowledge of being – the epistemic fallacy – is seen to cover the generation of an implicit ontology, in the standard case that of empirical realism, incorporating the reduction of the real to the actual (actualism) and thence to the empirical. From this perspective, without a rethematization and critique of empiricist ontology, empiricism must mutate into some form of conventionalism, pragmatism such as represented by Rorty's influential *Philosophy and the Mirror of Nature* (1980) or even superidealism, entailing a subjective hyper-relativism in which criteria of objectivity and truth are altogether lost.

(d) Traditionally, the PHILOSOPHY OF SCIENCE has been treated as little more than a substitution instance of the more general theory of knowledge, and the PHILOSOPHY OF SOCIAL SCIENCE has been tacked on in turn as nothing more than an example of the general philosophy of (natural) science. These elisions have been increasingly questioned in the course of the twentieth century. Thus discriminations have been made between ordinary and scientific knowledge, with the latter requiring a socialization of its own, and between knowledge in the natural and human sciences (to which I turn in a moment). Moreover, following Ryle, a distinction is now customarily made between practical knowledge-how and propositional knowledge-that (and the more generic knowledge-of); following Polanyi, between tacit and explicit knowledge; following Wittgenstein, between practical and discursive consciousness (or between form of life and theory); and following Noam Chomsky, between competence and performance. These distinctions have all helped to break down the erstwhile unitary and undifferentiated concept of knowledge.

(e)   I now want to consider briefly the problem-field of induction. The problem of induction is the problem of what warrant we have for supposing the course of nature will not change. On the transcendental realist ontology, the stratification of nature provides each science with its own internal inductive warrant. If there is a real reason, located in the nature of the stuff, and independent of the disposition concerned, such as its molecular or atomic structure, then water *must* tend to boil when it is heated. It is inconsistent with this reason (explanation) that it should tend to freeze, blush shyly or turn into a frog. But it remains true that in an open world any particular prediction may be defeated. So transcendental realism allows us to sustain the transfactuality (universality) of laws in the light of the complexity and differentiation of the world, so as to enable us for example to infer tendencies in the extra-experimental context, thus resolving the problem of what could be termed 'transduction'. An ontology of closed systems and atomistic events is a condition of the intelligibility of the traditional problem of induction. Closely associated with this problem are the problems of distinguishing a necessary from an accidental sequence of events, of subjective conditionals and of N. Goodman's and C.G. Hempel's paradoxes. All these turn on the absence of a real (non-conventional) reason, located in the nature of things, for predicates to be associated in the way they are. In virtue of his genetic constitution, if Socrates is a human being he must die.

Turning, too, on the absence of a principle of structure is the traditional problem of universals. If there is something, such as the possession of a common atomic or electronic structure, which graphite, black carbon and diamonds possess in common, then chemists are justified in classifying them together. On the other hand, there is nothing of any scientific (structural) significance that, say, all greengroceries possess in common – in the latter classificatory context a resemblance, rather than a realist, theory works best. Science is only concerned with what kinds of things there are, in so far as it casts light on their reasons for acting (the generative mechanisms of nature); and it is only concerned with what things do, in so far as it casts light on what they are (the structured entities of the world). There is a dialectic of explanatory and taxonomic knowledge in science (Bhaskar, 1975, esp. ch. 3, sections 3–6). On the transcendental realist ontology, other traditional aporiai of epistemology – from the Platonic paradoxes of self-predication to the twentieth-century self-referential and set-theoretic paradoxes and the contemporary paradoxes of material implication – are dissolved. Thus it can be seen that Plato, for example, tries to account for some instance of blueness in terms of its participating in the Form 'blue' – instead say (as of course he could not say) of its reflecting light of wavelength 4400Å – invoking a new level or order of structure. It is easy to find other homologues of the problem of induction – for instance in Kripke's 1981 interpretation and generalization of Wittgenstein's private language argument; or analogues of it – as in the role played in sociological theory by the Hobbesian problem of order.

The field of the humanities and the social sciences has been dominated in the twentieth century by the dispute between the champions of an unqualified naturalistic POSITIVISM and an anti-naturalistic HERMENEUTICS. Arguably, it is resolved by the new critical naturalism, based on the transcendental realist philosophy of science. On this VERSTEHEN appears as the starting point for social enquiry, which seeks to uncover generative mechanisms at work in society, at least partially analogous to those in nature, which may render agents' own initial understandings subject to critique. On the new qualified naturalism a whole series of ontological, epistemological, relational and critical differences emerge between the sciences of nature and society (see NATURALISM). Social structure appears as an ever-present condition *and* the continually reproduced outcome of intentional human agency (this is a duality of structure in the terminology of Giddens's 'theory of structuration' and Bhaskar's 'transformational model of social activity'); and agency appears as a synchronically emergent power of matter (see MATERIALISM). Social science, for its part, appears as both easier to initiate and more difficult to develop than natural science.

Closely associated with the new critical realism is a reassessment of Marx as, at least in *Capital*, a scientific realist. But the nature of his *Ausgang* from philosophy into substantive sociohistorical science led to an underdevelopment of his critique of empiricism in comparison with his critique of idealism; of his scientific, as distinct from simple material object, realism; and of his conception of the intransitive dimension (thematized around 'objectivity') in comparison with the transitive dimension (thematized around 'labour'). This has resulted in a tendency for Marxist epistemology to fluctuate in the twentieth century between a sophisticated idealism (whether in the neo-Kantianism of Max Adler and the Austro-Marxists, the historicist Marxism of G. Lukács, K. Korsch and Antonio Gramsci, the anti-objectivism of the critical theory of the Frankfurt school, the humanist and existentialist Marxisms of the postwar period (most notably Jean-Paul Sartre's) or in the scientific rationalism of Louis Althusser and a crude materialism (whether in Engelsian–Leninist–Stalinist 'diamat' or G. Della Volpe's more sophisticated but scientistic positivism).

Outside the analytical mainstream, Husserl's phenomenology, especially after 1907, became increasingly rationalistic in tenor, practising an epoché or transcendental suspension of the reality or otherwise of the objects of acts of consciousness in order to investigate their pure forms. Heidegger responded to this by asking how the being of acts was related to the being of the *objects* of the acts, thus opening the way to his fundamental ontology of *Dasein* in *Being and Time* (1927) and then later to his influential meta-ontology and meta-history of the epochs of being, culminating in the contemporary age of technology and nihilism. Nietzsche and Heidegger are the main progenitors of the school called poststructuralist (after the STRUCTURALISM of Claude Lévi-Strauss and Althusser). The leading members of this are Jacques Derrida, Michel Foucault and the metapsychologist Jacques Lacan. Derrida's work follows up on Heidegger's critique of the metaphysics of presence – logocentrism – which he sees as informing traditional epistemology and turns on the deconstruction of the characteristic oppositions, such as universal/particular, of philosophy. Poststructuralism is normally associated with the motif of postmodernity, lately subjected to a devastating critique by Jürgen Habermas in *The Philosophical Discourse of Modernity* (1985). In the Anglo-Saxon world Richard Rorty has pursued his pragmatist approach, increasingly (although questionably) invoking J. Dewey as his mentor, contending that public pragmatism is compatible with private irony.

Meanwhile the SOCIOLOGY OF KNOWLEDGE, which has often appeared as a rival to epistemology, is a flourishing enterprise. It seems that philosophy, if it is to analyse the conditions of possibility of knowledge, must join hands with the empirically grounded study of its causes and effects, in an enquiry which must logically include both the questions of its own epistemological status and its own causal role as part of the totality it seeks to describe and explain.

Reading

Bhaskar, Roy 1991: *Philosophy and the Idea of Freedom.*
Dews, Peter 1987: *Logics of Disintegration.*
Giddens, Anthony 1979: *Central Problems of Social Theory.*
Harré, Rom 1970: *The Principles of Scientific Thinking.*
Kripke, Saul 1981: Wittgenstein on rules and private language. In *Perspectives on the Philosophy of Wittgenstein*, ed. I. Block.
Outhwaite, William 1987: *New Philosophies of Social Science.*
Polanyi, Michael 1967: *The Tacit Dimension.*
Rorty, Richard 1980: *Philosophy and the Mirror of Nature.*
Ryle, Gilbert 1949 (*1963*): *The Concept of Mind.*
Wittgenstein, Ludwig 1953 (*1967*): *Philosophical Investigations.*

ROY BHASKAR

L

labelling In a sociological or criminological context, the word should usually be read as a reference to a special set of ideas about the interplay between language and self in the formation of identity, and of deviant identity in particular. It should also be noted that most prominent 'labelling' theorists actually rather dislike the term and associate it with simplifications devised by its critics.

Labelling theory itself may be treated as a strand of symbolic interactionist and phenomenological sociology (see SYMBOLIC INTERACTIONISM; PHENO-MENOLOGY) that was fed into analyses of deviance and control in 1938 by Tannenbaum's *Crime and the Community*, in 1951 by Lemert's *Social Pathology* and, most importantly, in 1963 by Becker's *Outsiders*. It stems from the interactionist preoccupation with the self that came out of a philosophical response to Hegel formulated by C. S. Peirce, J. Dewey, W. James and G. H. Mead (see PRAGMATISM).

The self, interactionists maintain, is a reflective process in consciousness, a splitting of subjectivity into linked phases, a turning of the mind back on itself so that it becomes simultaneously observer and observed, 'I' and 'me'. It arises in conduct. People talk about themselves and the activities in which they are engaged. They can remember and review themselves as they were in the past; project themselves into new situations; ascertain something of the way in which others see them, rehearse their own response to those others, and foresee the answering response that may be made in return. They will be defined by others, and 'taking the role of the other' is a vicarious activity which affords a perspective on one's socially situated identities. People become social in that process, knitting themselves into the projected action of others, incorporating others' perspectives into their own. In what has been called the 'significant gesture', they can assume multiple interacting identities that are staggered over time; being themselves and others in interplay around an unfolding act. Selves thereby create and are created by other selves, they are constructed cooperatively with 'significant others' who help to define who and what one is at any time.

Selves are symbolic objects, and the chief medium of objectification is language. Language separates, classifies, generalizes, anonymizes, records and preserves. It permits users to become detached from their own subjectivity, making it thing-like. It allows one to react to oneself as one would to another. The character of a self is set by language: Peirce remarked, 'my language is the sum total of myself.' One may take as many stances towards oneself as there are names, and a renaming will prompt a transformation of the self. The drinker can become an alcoholic, the slimmer anorexic, the eater a glutton. Titles give form to the self, but the mere proffering of a title does not oblige one to accept it: one is repeatedly bombarded with offers of identity from parties, associations, occupations, critics and friends, and does not take them all. What counts is a sense of the limits, plausibility and possibilities of one's own and others' emerging characters; the effects which change could work on one's social world; one's attachment to the person or group who makes the offer; and one's capacity to resist or modify a self.

There is another way in which the organization of a self mirrors language. Interactionists have adopted conversation as a model for their own logic of explanation (see CONVERSATION ANALYSIS). Conversation proceeds by the making of indications which capture, create and order social life; it reacts to those indications; builds upon them; merges them; and manufactures its own distinct symbolic reality. The talk of different people can combine over time, becoming a form of communal property. It can refer and respond to itself, constituting itself reflexively. Interactionism in its turn depicts social life as actively mediated by conversational processes that are interactive, dialectical and emergent. It examines the interaction within the self, between the I and the me, and analyses it as dialogue. One may be heard to interrogate onself, praise oneself, commune with oneself conversationally. One talks to others.

Like all conversations, one rarely receives a full reply: knowledge of the self is incomplete, mediate and situated. It is endlessly being discovered. One tries to establish who one is and what one is doing by catching a glimpse of one's own gestures and the responses which others make to them. The self is an inference, a matter of guesswork based on quick surmise and rough working description. And, like any other inference, it need not be 'correct', 'truthful' or searching at all. One's own and others' understanding of oneself is often supplied by categories that possess more of caricature and stereotype than detail or nuance. The me is a reification confronting and working with others who have been similarly reified. A social relationship cannot be an encounter between people revealed in all the fullness of their 'true' selves. It is mediated by evolving, interacting interpretations that bear the mark of the participants' objectives, interests and knowledge. In the main, people lack the time and curiosity to enquire very deeply into their own and others' histories, motives and ambitions. There is a tendency to supply just enough detail to keep interaction going. Life is based on rough and ready labels.

Labelling theory is actually little more than an extension of this idea of the self into the arena of rule-breaking and social control (see also CRIME AND DEVIANCE). Becoming deviant is a transformational process which revolves around the acquisition of names, meanings, motives and perspectives. It is mediated by language and by the identities and interpretations which language confers. It is assisted and sometimes forced by the significant others who populate the environments through which the emerging deviant moves. Deviance, in short, is deeply implicated in negotiated definitions of people and behaviour. Reactions to deviance give it symbolic organization and public identity. In the central statement of the argument, Becker (1963) said:

Social groups create deviance by making the rules whose infraction constitutes deviance, and by applying those rules to particular people and labeling them as outsiders. From this point of view, deviance is *not* a quality of the act the person commits, but rather a consequence of the application by others of rules and sanctions to an 'offender'. The deviant is one to whom that label

has successfully been applied; deviant behavior is behavior that people so label.

What makes deviance special is that it is a morally devalued status accompanied by the actual or threatened imposition of sanctions. Major institutions are devoted to the detection, policing and punishment of deviance. Those who become deviant may well wish to escape penalty by becoming devious.

Most deviants do succeed in escaping attention. Yet even when they are unnoticed or tolerated, they will still form conjectures about the significance of their actions and selves, borrowing from wider, public typifications of conduct, and formulating meanings in exchanges with confederates, friends, relatives and victims. Deviance has been likened to scripted behaviour that is shaped in interaction.

When deviants do not escape, labelling may be foisted publicly to work major transformations of identity. Courts, police and prisons are invested with an awesome symbolism: they 'dramatize evil' in Tannenbaum's phrase. Becoming publicly deviant may be fateful indeed. At the very least, it will enforce the need to make an accommodation to the public response evoked by rule-breaking, although accommodation can take different forms and not every response amplifies conflict. Indeed, some labels actually have the ironic effect of preserving a deviant's self-esteem: the unwed mothers described by Rains (1971) were encouraged to think of themselves as virtuous women who had fallen, and it is useful to creditors to make their debtors believe of themselves that they are still honest. Some deviants become penitent or accept a sick role in which they become temporarily invalid.

Identities that are spurned can change selves too. A formal deviant label tends to be unwelcome; it reifies and 'overcategorizes' its subjects; the singular features of a person or phenomenon will become blurred or lost; and putative materials will be added. People may resist, preferring to describe themselves by other names; and the assumption of deviant identity will frequently be forced and theatrical in consequence, entailing what Harold Garfinkel called a 'status degradation ceremony', leading to a coerced rearrangement of the self. Very typically, the deviance becomes even more pronounced in such dramaturgical work, assuming symbolic centrality, becoming exaggerated in its denunciation, constituting a person's 'master status' and closing access to other selves and roles.

Many deviant characteristics may actually be explained by the form and content of the labelling process. Thus Schur (1971) argued that the identity of drug users is as much shaped by social control as by the 'intrinsic' qualities of illicit drugs themselves; Goffman (1961) described madness as a role that receives definition in the management strategies of asylums; and Scott (1969) wrote of blindness as a learned helplessness. It is not enough to describe the characteristics of the deviant and the deviant act alone; interactionists would maintain that there must also be recognition of the symbolic constituents and consequences of the experience of deviance.

Reading
Becker, H. 1963: *Outsiders.*
——ed. 1964: *The Other Side.*
Goffman, E. 1961: *Asylums.*
Lemert, E. 1951: *Social Pathology.*
Plummer, K. 1979: Misunderstanding labelling perspectives. In *Deviant Interpretations,* ed. D. Downes and P. Rock.
Rains, P. 1971: *Becoming an Unwed Mother.*
Schur, E. 1971: *Labelling Deviant Behaviour.*
Scott, R. 1969: *The Making of Blind Men.*
Tannenbaum, F. 1938: *Crime and the Community.*

PAUL ROCK

labour, division of *See* DIVISION OF LABOUR

labour, domestic *See* DOMESTIC LABOUR

labour, international division of *See* DIVISION OF LABOUR, INTERNATIONAL

labour market This is an abstract concept, used to describe the varied institutional arrangements governing the allocation and pricing of labour services in capitalist economies. Economists often use the analogy of a fruit market to elaborate the structure and workings of the market for labour. Like apples and pears, labour is said to be bought and sold under competition and its wages set by the interplay of supply and demand. Simple to understand, and remarkably enduring as a conceptual reference point, this approach nevertheless conceals several distinctive features of the labour transaction.

Most crucially, wages are exchanged for workers' mental and physical capacities, and not a definite quantity and quality of finished output. The productivity of labour is socially determined through a collective LABOUR PROCESS after human capacities have been procured. Put another way, the relationship between wages and work is determined not in the marketplace, but in the workplace, within a specific set of social relationships which transcend the forces of supply and demand. Most commonly, workplace organization is hierarchically structured, with employers exercising control and authority over their workers.

Comparisons with the fruit market also tend to obscure the fact that the institutions of the labour market are historically specific. In pre-capitalist societies, trade in the products of labour was well established, but the market for labour services did not emerge until the feudal order and its associated restrictions on labour mobility were progressively dismantled. Wage labour developed rapidly from the sixteenth century in the growing rural and urban industrial centres. Its growth was accelerated by the enclosure movement which denied the bulk of the population direct access to the land and means of subsistence, and hence rendered them dependent for their survival on paid employment within the emerging factory system.

This historical development of labour markets has been conditioned by the interplay of state, labour and employer institutions. With the Factory Acts in the mid-nineteenth century the state, for example, sought to regulate the terms on which employers engaged and utilized workers by restricting the use of child and female labour and the length of the working day. Other, more recent examples of state intervention in labour markets include the attempts to shape the wage setting process through incomes policies and the power relationships between workers and employers through the enactment of laws on employment and TRADE UNIONS.

A key institutional feature of the wage–labour relationship in the twentieth century has been the emergence of the internal labour market. A description of the often elaborate job, pay and promotion systems commonly found in large organizations, the internal market was developed first in US enterprises to forestall the growth of trade unionism. Employees were offered a career within their organizations, and steady improvements in pay and status, in return for a high level of commitment and loyalty. Core functions of the labour market were, in other words, progressively internalized, resulting in a redrawing of the boundaries between the market and hierarchical organization. The growing significance of the internal labour market for employment systems has been extensively documented in the research literature, and now forms the starting point for the analysis of UNEMPLOYMENT, labour market inequality and discrimination, and the management and development of personnel.

Reading
Dobb, M. 1946: *Studies in the Development of Capitalism.*
Doeringer, P. and Piore, M. 1971: *Internal Labor Markets and Manpower Analysis.*
Williamson, O. 1975: *Markets and Hierarchies: Analysis and Anti-Trust Implications.*

PETER NOLAN

labour movement   *See* TRADE UNIONS

labour process   As a general definition this is concerned with the ways in which human labour, working with tools or instruments of production, transforms raw materials into useful products, but while any type of working activity (contemporary or historical) is a labour process, the term derives its interest from its centrality to Marx's analysis of capitalism, and the ways in which this has been applied and developed in twentieth-century analyses of work, primarily, but not exclusively, within capitalist society.

Marx's analysis emphasized the subordination of labour to capital in production processes (see EXPLOITATION) which were subject to continual transformations in pursuit of productivity gains. In such transformations, mechanization fragments labouring activity into simple, uniform and repetitive tasks under a strict factory discipline, craft skills disappear, and new hierarchies of mental and manual labour are constructed on the basis of capital's control over labour. Marx provided extensive empirical illustrations of these theses, drawn in the main from mid-nineteenth century official documents.

These developments within the production process were not only noted by Marx. They informed the attempt by Frederick Taylor around the turn of the century to construct a theory of scientific management. Taylor's aim was to subject the physical actions of workers to the same principles of optimization as governed the inanimate factors of the production process. For workers' activity to

be rendered mechanical in this manner, management had to abrogate to itself the knowledge and the discretionary activity traditionally characterizing craft skills. Thus Taylor's emphasis in this extension of the division of labour was on the extension of managerial control, both at the level of individual motions and over the production process as a whole. When combined with the developing handling and transfer technologies of the period, Taylorism proved a potent ideology for management in the type of assembly-line mass market consumer durables industries pioneered by the Ford Motor Company.

After 1945 mechanization was increasingly extended from handling and transfer to the process of control itself, culminating to date in microprocessor technologies and their wide application, especially in small batch (non-standardized) production processes, and in industries specializing in information handling and retrieval. (This is sometimes held to characterize the transition from a Fordist to a neo-Fordist era; see FORDISM AND POST-FORDISM; LONG WAVES; REGULATION.) Within a Marxist framework, Braverman's analysis (1974) has proved particularly influential, emphasizing the twentieth-century relevance of Marx's theory in understanding the origins and development of hierarchy in the workplace, the evolution of the skills composition of the workforce and the fragmentation of work, and the ways in which science and technology are used in increasingly mechanized production processes. In his focus on capital's continual reorganizations of the labour process, and its attacks on areas of skill and worker discretion which hinder detailed capitalist control, Braverman also focused on the obverse: the increasing degradation of work as it is experienced in the labour process, and the associated alienation thereby engendered. Criticisms of Braverman tend to concentrate on his failure to allow adequately for the ways in which worker resistance at the point of production can shape developments in the labour process, and on his failure to explore the different mechanisms of capitalist control.

In contrast to the Marxist approach, in which class struggle determines the development of technology and indeed the very notion of technical efficiency, is an approach which sees the development of technology as the driving force, and the cost savings attributable to the economies of large-scale production as determining the development of factory production. (See also TECHNOLOGICAL

CHANGE.) Hierarchical control over labour is similarly attributed to cost savings and to the incentive difficulties of cooperative labour processes. The issues of the 'naturalness' of technology and technical efficiency, and their relation to the organization of the labour process, is part of the continuing divide between analyses based on a class approach and those based on a calculus of individual maximization.

Reading

Braverman, H. 1974: *Labor and Monopoly Capital: The Degradation of Work in the Twentieth Century.*

Edwards, R. 1979: *Contested Terrain: the Transformation of the Workplace in the Twentieth Century.*

Landes, D. 1986: What do bosses really do? *Journal of Economic History* 46.3, 585–623.

Marglin, S.A. 1974–5: What do bosses do? The origins and function of hierarchy in capitalist production. *Review of Radical Political Economics* 6.2, 60–112; 7.1, 20–37.

Nichols, T. ed. 1980: *Capital and Labour: Studies in the Capitalist Labour Process.*

Stone, K. 1974: The origins of job structures in the steel industry. *Review of Radical Political Economics* 6.2, 113–73.

Thompson, P. 1983: *The Nature of Work: An Introduction to Debates on the Labour Process.*

Williamson, O.E. 1980: The organization of work. *Journal of Economic Behaviour and Organization* 1.1, 5–38.

SIMON MOHUN

laissez-faire This phrase literally means 'to let do'. Most accounts attribute the politically charged slogan '*laissez-faire, laissez-passer*' which means 'let people do as they choose, let goods pass,' to Vincent de Gournay. The slogan became the rallying cry among advocates of free trade, such as Jacques Turgot and other physiocrats, and was quickly systematized in Adam Smith's *An Inquiry into the Nature and Causes of the Wealth of Nations*, as part of 'the obvious and simple system of natural liberty' (Smith 1776, book 4, ch. 9). Smith and other classical economists broadened the notion of *laissez-faire* from a free international trade policy to a comprehensive social philosophy. In Smith's words:

Every man, as long as he does not violate the laws of justice, is left perfectly free to pursue his own interests in his own way, and to bring both his industry and capital into competition with those of any other man, or order of men. The sovereign is completely discharged from a duty, in the attempting to perform which he must always be exposed to innumerable delusions, and for the proper performance of which no human wisdom or knowledge could ever be sufficient; the duty of superintending the industry of private people, and of directing it towards the employments must suitable to the interest of society. (Ibid.)

The duties of government were to be limited to national defence, administration of justice, and provision of certain public goods.

The classical liberal appeal for an unhampered MARKET system and limited government was never, however, realized in practice. The capitalist state failed to wither away. By the turn of the twentieth century, contemporary advocates of *laissez-faire*, such as Herbert Spencer (1879–92), were considered passé espousers of rugged INDIVIDUALISM and SOCIAL DARWINISM, and their claim that unrestricted, competitive markets would promote economic growth and stability was all but shattered by the Great Depression of the 1930s.

New interpretations of economic cycles and depressions have since appeared. Given the Progressive Era ideology of the day, the depression was considered the outcome of inherent market inertia. However, scholarship since has argued that the Great Depression may have had its origins in irresponsible monetary policy of the American Federal Reserve System (Friedman and Schwartz, 1963; Rothbard, 1972) (see MONETARISM). The claim that government intervention may largely explain such deep socioeconomic maladies as the Great Depression has helped rehabilitate the *laissez-faire* position among some intellectual circles, and the NEW RIGHT.

Contemporary restatements of *laissez-faire* social philosophy range from the neoconservatism of Milton Friedman (1962) and James Buchanan (1975), to Robert Nozick's (1974) and F.A. Hayek's (1973, 1976, 1979) libertarianism, to the 'anarcho-capitalism' of Murray Rothbard (1973). Although *laissez-faire* notions have coloured the rhetoric of New Right politicians in the West, as well as market reformers in the transforming East European socialist states, it has yet to be seen whether minimal government and unhampered markets is a real political alternative to twentieth-century statism. Recent Marxist criticisms of state intervention (such as Claus Offe, 1984) maintain that even though the interventionist welfare state disrupts the market order, dismantling it would create greater economic and social disorder, and therefore state intervention, as problematic as it is, is irreversible.

The debate over the practical limits to the actions of the state will surely continue through the next century.

See also COMPETITION; LIBERALISM.

Reading

Eatwell, John, Milgate, Murray and Newman, Peter, eds 1989: *The Invisible Hand*.
Fusfeld, Daniel R. 1990: *The Age of the Economist*, 6th edn.
Hofstadter, Richard 1945: *Social Darwinism in American Thought, 1860–1915*.
Lepage, Henri 1982: *Tomorrow, Capitalism: The Economics of Economic Freedom*, trans. Sheilagh Ogilvie.
Prychitko, David 1990: The welfare state: what is left? *Critical Review* 4.

DAVID L. PRYCHITKO

language The implications of the subject range so widely and are so varied that language can be said to be both central and marginal to twentieth-century social thought. Central in so far as conceptions of the nature of language and languages have provided leading ideas – or at least metaphors – for thinking about the nature of society. (The idea that 'society is like a language' has tempted many.) Marginal in so far as the sociology of language, as a subdiscipline of sociology, and SOCIOLINGUISTICS, as a subdiscipline of linguistics, have rarely been central preoccupations of professional sociologists or linguists.

Three examples may illustrate how conceptions of language can be central to social thought.

1 Of leading social thinkers this century, just one had an education in which linguistic studies figured largely, Antonio Gramsci (1891–1937). It has been argued persuasively by Ferruccio Lo Piparo (1979) that his enormously influential conceptions of HEGEMONY are largely informed by the understanding he acquired as a student of the history of the development of Italian as a national language. The linguistics which Gramsci studied was both historical and idealist in character. It stressed the active role of individuals – for example, creative writers – in shaping the development of a language, but equally recognized that the hegemony of 'standard' Italian as the language of a unified Italy was the outcome of collective action, conflict and the exercise of political power. Gramsci himself, in prison, wrote about the 'language question' (see Gramsci, *1985*, pp. 164–95).

2 More commonly cited is the influence of STRUCTURALISM in linguistics on the development of social thought and, indeed, its intersection with major currents of social theory. For it is not as if the founding work of structuralist linguistics, Ferdinand de Saussure's posthumous *Course in General Linguistics* first published in 1916 (see also Culler, 1976), is innocent of the vocabulary of social theory. It is full of it, and it has been a much debated question whether Saussure got his vocabulary (or his concepts) from Emile Durkheim's *The Rules of the Sociological Method* (1895). Whatever the genesis of Saussure's ideas, it is true that in the period after 1945 he and other structural linguists (notably Roman Jakobson (1895–1982)) provided anthropologists and sociologists with reasonably precise conceptions of structure and convention and also with clearer distinctions than had hitherto been available between structural (synchronic) states and historical (diachronic) processes and practices. In the 1960s and 1970s it did, indeed, become common to think that society is structured like a language and that all social action is like speech in being a rule-conforming or rule-violating practice enabled by the resources which social structure – as a sort of grammar – provides. For a critical discussion, see Giddens (1979). For a philosophically deep analysis of the key concept of convention, see Lewis (1969), and for subsequent discussion, Margaret Gilbert's lengthy *On Social Facts* (1989).

3 Often enough remarked upon, but rarely developed, there is an intersection between Noam Chomsky's influential emphasis on nature – as against convention – as shaping the languages we use, and anarchist social theory. As a linguist, Chomsky – who is also an anarchist – portrays human nature as a source of both linguistic order and linguistic disorder. It is because human beings share such a rich biological inheritance that their languages are as *similar* as they are – so nature is a source of order, as in optimistic ANARCHISM. But, equally, nature is a source of disorder, as in pessimistic anarchism. For with a system of universal grammar sufficiently elaborate, then it is both true that limited language input suffices for the development of complex and

similar individual linguistic competences, and also true that small changes in input can lead to, at least superficially, radical changes in the resultant language system. The insight here is basically the same as that recently generalized in chaos or catastrophe theories, that is, by theories of discontinuous change originating in meteorologists' problems with long-term weather forecasting (though the historical antecedent is the debate between catastrophists and uniformitarians in nineteenth-century geology). For the themes of order and disorder in language, see Chomsky (1986) and Bickerton (1981); the ideas are taken up and then applied in the theory of ideology in Pateman (1987).

Turning now to the sociology of language, it is not unfair to say that much of the work done is methodologically uninteresting, simply explaining the distribution of languages (such as the growth of English as a world language) as the overdetermined outcome of economic, political and cultural causes. Likewise, there is work on the creation or revival of languages as elements of a national identity – as with Irish Gaelic, Hebrew or New Guinea Tok Pisin. More sociologically interesting work has been done on how centralized language planning and standardization policies are often resisted, for example in educational settings. This leads to the realization that language has a 'symbolic' as well as 'real' value – it can be employed as an arbitrary mark of identity surplus to its use as a means of communication. Such an approach is developed by Pierre Bourdieu within the framework of his theory of cultural capital: see his *Language and Symbolic Power* (1991).

Some work in sociolinguistics actually has similar concerns, though approached from quite different methodological standpoints. Here the study of socially situated speech may reveal how its style or register varies systematically with social setting or the social status of speakers and hearers. Sometimes this looks like a 'passive' reflection of the operation of the 'independent' social variables; at other times, it looks like an active endeavour on the part of social agents to define and respond to social situations. See the first of William Labov's many influential (and broadly positivistic) sociolinguistic studies, *The Social Stratification of Language Use in New York City* (1966).

On the basis of such research, it becomes easier to understand some of the failures of language education policies. British speakers do not all speak with Received Pronunciation (RP) or write Standard English, not because they are stupid or their teachers ineffectual but because they are active in defining their own social and cultural identities, and do not wish to be what they are marked out to be. People are not cultural dopes. And they do not need to be: they succeed perfectly well – only too well – in communicating, with or without RP or Standard English. Many of the complex issues in this area of educational linguistics are explored in the writings of Peter Trudgill, beginning with *Accent, Dialect and the School* (1975).

Though much sociolinguistic work, including Labov's and Trudgill's, has been positivist in letter and spirit, and thus dubious to the theoretically sophisticated sociologist, there has been non-positivist work on linguistic interaction within the traditions of ETHNOMETHODOLOGY, largely inspired by the work of the late Harvey Sacks (see now Sacks, 1992). This aims to extract and formalize the full set of synchronic rules governing interactions in a domain, such as telephone calls (see also CONVERSATION ANALYSIS). Here there is thus a link into structuralist traditions of analysis, though ethnomethodologists have generally insisted on the ultimate ad hocness – the open-endedness or unfinalizability – of social interaction. This is also a dominant motif in the currently influential 'dialogism' of Mikhail Bakhtin (1895–1975) and the linguistics of his associate Valentin Vološinov, (1895–1936) (see for introductions, Holquist, 1990; Morson and Emerson, 1990; Vološinov, 1929). It is beyond the scope of this article to enter into dialogue with dialogism, but see Pateman (1989).

Reading

Bickerton, D. 1981: *Roots of Language.*
Chomsky, N. 1986: *Knowledge of Language: Its Nature, Origin and Use.*
Saussure, F. 1916 (*1983*): *Course in General Linguistics*, trans R. Harris.
Vološinov, V. 1929 (*1973*): *Marxism and the Philosophy of Language.*

TREVOR PATEMAN

law Contemporary usage requires that the term law be given a dual definition. In its broadest meaning, which derives historically from classical theological traditions but is currently also used in psychoanalysis, the term refers to any form of absolute injunction: the law is the law of the father, be it God the father or the dictate of the unconscious. In more pragmatic yet nonetheless related terms, the secular legal tradition generally defines law in a technical and largely tautological manner as those norms issued from or institutionally recognized by the existing legal hierarchy. In this latter professional definition rules of law or legal norms are the substantive constituents of a national legal system and their authority or legal validity is derived immediately from that membership of the system and only subsequently from the constitutional legitimacy of their actual statement or content. The two definitions given correspond in historical terms to the difference between a conception of *natural law*, the externally given law of God, nature, reason, Sovereign or some other absolute source, and the secular conception of *positive law*, of an artificial law created by human beings. This article will trace the complex relationship between these two historically competing conceptions of law as it affects contemporary debates as to the nature and function of legal order.

The twentieth-century history of the concept of law is the history of the apparent demise of theological or naturalistic conceptions of legal order in favour of a mundane science of positive law. The repression of the earlier doctrinal tradition, one which until the mid-nineteenth century simply defined common law as the unfolding of reason (*semblable reason semblable ley*: what seems to be reasonable seems to be law), is the key to any understanding of either the philosphical or the political characteristics of contemporary legal systems. Both on the continent, where national legal traditions are based on written law or Codes that have their ultimate model in Roman jurisprudence (Watson, 1981), and in the Anglo-American legal tradition based historically on unwritten or customary law laid down by the courts (Goodrich, 1990), the nineteenth century was in legal terms an era of secularization. Prompted most explicitly by the Napoleonic code or *Code Civil* of 1804, the legal systems of Europe transformed their shared historical background in the universal text of Roman law, the *Corpus Iuris Civilis*, and translated the Latin tradition into national codes of vernacular law. The Code was now to represent the spirit of the people in an authoritative and accessible written form which would bind its administrators and judges to the popular will. Despite differences of tradition and of the form of Anglo-American common law, most particularly its lack of explicit reference to Roman sources and its resistance to codification, the nineteenth century was also an age of reform and of written law in which statutory provisions came to dominate and legal records and legislation were translated from law Latin and law French into a species of the vernacular. In the latter part of the nineteenth century, the common law also developed a system of interpretation known as binding precedent (*stare decisis*) whereby prior decisions of the courts were to be binding on all future courts of coordinate or lower jurisdiction and thereby sought to transform the particularistic tradition of case law into a system of known and binding norms.

Accompanying the radical rewriting of the European legal orders of the nineteenth century was a corresponding movement to elaborate the details of a fully scientific discipline of legal governance, of the rule of law as opposed to the rule of persons. Within the continental tradition this science was based in and developed by the university law schools and its purpose was broadly that of maintaining the discrete hermeneutic tradition and professional authority of the legal institution into a secular and revolutionary age. The study of law was to be turned again to the study of the text and nothing but the text, the entire curriculum of legal studies being a complex induction into the authoritative designation and interpretation of the written law (Perelman, 1976). The authority of legal science lay in an intimate knowledge of textual detail combined with a much more classical knowledge of the procedural and interpretative maxims appropriate to legal construction and argument. In doctrinal terms the letter of the law dominated all legal causes and the textual science of that literal provision was the jurisprudential legacy of the nineteenth century, a legacy best expressed in twentieth-century LEGAL POSITIVISM and the Pure Theory of law.

Within the common law tradition a similar heritage dates from the second half of the nineteenth century and the emergence of common law in the universities, where prior to 1750 the scholarly study of law had been the study of Roman and canon law. The movement to found a science of the common law outside of the erratic educational practices of the profession itself had borrowed continental methods and had built on the tradition of institutional treatises (Cairns, 1984). The tradition that emerged was that of a textbook jurisprudence of what were termed 'black letter' laws. The principle underlying this new discipline of legal study was primarily that of empiricism. To convince the universities that law was a fitting subject of academic as opposed to vocational study and simultaneously to persuade the profession that, contrary to the traditional practice, academic legal study could contribute to the formation of competent lawyers, the existing substantive law had to be formalized in an uncontroversial manner (Twining, 1986). The result was an arcane but limited tradition of treatise writing in which existing divisions and categories of legal practice were systematized in an exhaustive but conventional manner without the development of any explicit theory of the logic of historical classifications such as contract, tort, public or private law, let alone of the rights, duties, interests or policies which had dominated pragmatically the development of the case law tradition (Samuel, 1990). Law was to be understood as the existent corpus of substantive rules of law and nothing else, a view well expounded in the practice of the treatise writers and subsequently presented as positivistic jurisprudence in the work of H. L. A. Hart (1961) and elaborated in somewhat revised form by Ronald Dworkin (1978).

The central theoretical consequence of the nineteenth-century tradition was the jurisprudential acceptance of an implicit metaphysical belief in the unity or homogeneity of the legal order as a system of rules, a belief which was more redolent of earlier traditions of natural law and of scriptural faith than it was of any more modern science (Kantorowicz, 1957). Primarily defined in terms of its source, either in the Code or in the diverse authoritative sites of enunciation of common law, the doctrinal exposition of the legal order was unified by no more cogent principle than reference to the library of legal texts, statutes and reports. In a not dissimilar manner, the sociology of law tended to accept the professional or scientific definition of law and to translate it into an equally unified conception of social practice: in empirical terms the law was simply what lawyers did, while in theoretical terms the juridical system was deemed to express certain structural features of the social order be they property relations, commodity production, bureaucratic rationality, ideological hegemony or simply social control (see Renner, 1904; Kamenka and Tay, 1980). An implicit faith in technical competence and professional knowledge left the doctrinal definition of law as a system of authorized rules unified by reference to exclusively legal

sources in its place. While social theory might endeavour to link legal norms to historical or political circumstances, to examine the social interests which underlay specific areas of regulation, to assess the impact of legal norms on social practice or to criticize the class or gender bias of legal rules, the self-evidence of a unitary legal system was seldom challenged (Hunt, 1978). More recent sociological theories of law self-consciously continue the attempt to depict a systematics of law predicated on the concept of a self-referential or autopoietic legal system. In short, the notion of an absolute source of law, inherited from the classical tradition and translated into jurisprudential theories of the sovereignty of the legislature or of the people, remained and to some degree remains in place: in the theory of law the king had yet to be beheaded (Foucault, 1975).

The break-up of the doctrinal paradigm of law in recent legal theory has been a product of the influence of theoretical trends external to legal studies, most notably in anthropology, linguistics, literary criticism, semiotics and philosophy. Within the Anglo-American tradition such theoretical influence has been almost exclusively a translation from continental sources. In philosophical terms a resurgence of interest in pragmatism has led, from the early and limited work of the American legal realists through the revival of legal rhetoric on the continent, to theses on the indeterminacy of linguistic and legal norms that are currently associated with poststructuralism and deconstruction (see MODERNISM AND POSTMODERNISM). The first major figure of influence within such a shift of paradigm was undoubtedly Foucault's major historical study *Discipline and Punish* (1975). The principal jurisprudential impact of that work lay in the move to conceptualize law as an integral part of a much larger set of institutional forms of normalization that spanned the asylum, the hospital, the school, the factory and the prison as variant forms of disciplinary discourse or, as he later termed it, governmentality (Rose, 1989). In more literary terms, the grammatological work of Jacques Derrida, of the French feminisms influenced by his work, and the elaboration of the concept of deconstruction in particular led to a more general scepticism with regard to the professional construction of a hermetic legal text separate from the play of intertextual features. For the critical legal studies movement, originating on the continent in the late 1960s (as *critique du droit*) and in America in the early 1970s (as the critical legal studies conference), the metaphysically determinate reference of legal terms and the more general doctrinal claims as to the objectivity of textual regulation and juristic knowledge were to be castigated as components of an antiquated and now defunct paradigm of legal truth.

In the place of the positivistic science of law or of legal systematics, contemporary legal scholarship concentrates on historical and particular reconstructions of substantive areas of legal regulation and of what is termed informal law, namely the exercise of normative control in areas traditionally conceived to be outside the domain of formal legal regulation. At the level of theory, jurisprudence has been opened to some considerable degree to the scholarship of other disciplines, in particular to anthropology, history, linguistics, accountancy, geography and semiotics as intrinsic to the study of substantive areas of legal regulation. So, too, other disciplines have come to study law, both as positive regulation and as the injunction issued from the place of the father. In substantive terms the break-up of the unitary paradigm of legal order accompanies significant changes in the domains and procedural forms of contemporary legal regulation. While it would be impossible to list the full parameters of the growth and corresponding fragmentation of the substantive areas and forms of legal intervention, certain general observations may be taken as indicative.

The principal trend in legal regulation in the industrialized jurisdictions has been that of the growth of public law. The last century has been the age of statute law and the principal substantive characteristic of such law has been bureaucratic and regulatory. The new areas of public law that have developed, largely haphazardly, in response to state intervention in both public and private realms of the social are immense. In a loosely conceptual order, the first area of such legal invention was the development of administrative law and the juristic category of judicial review, whereby the courts created a power to adjudicate on the formal reasonableness of administrative action. Prior to or contemporary with that development were a whole series of legislative innovations creating a variety of statutory regulations and bodies governing safety in the factory, working men's compensation, public health, environmental protection, schooling and policing. That trend towards social provision through public law later saw the emergence of

bodies of statutory governance of sexual relations, race relations, welfare provision, industrial relations, criminal injuries, damage to property, motor accident compensation, public services or utilities, air transport, the entertainments industry and further incursions on private law which regulated contractual relations, non-criminal or tortious injuries, private property and commercial standards. In one sense, the new regulatory form of law – only very inadequately evoked through the above list – was a direct politicization of traditional patterns of legal regulation. Not only were the courts to adjudicate on the arbitrariness or otherwise of virtually all forms of individual relation with the state but the bodies of law that governed such decisions were more often than not the product of delegated legislation by which is meant the internally devised rules of governmental departments or quasi-governmental agencies.

With the increasingly active role of the courts in a wide variety of contested areas of social relations it was increasingly difficult to maintain the traditional scientific view that the law was somehow free of political and other forms of discourse. In view also of the enormous range of substantive domains of legal intervention, ranging from the negotiation of marital breakdown to the arbitration of industrial disputes, the notion of the formal unity of law was equally abstracted from the experience of legal practice. That social theory should now account for legal regulation in terms of an amalgam of competing normative discourses and in terms of broadly political-administrative functions at one level simply reflects the growth of a public law substantively concerned with the demographic and actuarial control of populations. It also has the intriguing consequence that even within the traditional confines of jurisprudence, the classical forms of legal discourse are increasingly subordinated to psychological, medical, actuarial, political and economic forms of expertise, these being the discourses which directly govern the substantive subject-matters of legal intervention (Ewald, 1986).

It remains to conclude that the above reversal of the order of discourses has brought into play a variety of theories of the end of law. Certainly, if we mean by law the traditional procedures of classification of subject matter according to legal sources of validity then the Enlightenment form of legal regulation or rule of law is already dead. The sociological truth is that a variety of formal and informal species of normative control and of dispute resolution have a much higher profile and are of greater social significance than the onerous, expensive and infinitely time-consuming recourse to the courts. Economic blacking, for example, is of far greater practical significance in terms of multi-national corporate relations than the law of contract ever was or could be. Faith in the law, to revert to our starting point, is now to be understood as faith in industrial reason and in the dogmatics of economic regulation (Legendre, 1988). What remains of traditional legal classificatory procedures is a disparate series of pragmatically orientated forms of legal intervention in discourses and practices in which positive law is subordinate to broader economic, geopolitical and discursive forms of regulation and manipulation. Put differently, the law dwells elsewhere than in its traditional discursive habitus. If law is defined in terms of absolute injunction, in terms that is of the fealty of things to their place, then it is to be found in those corporate discourses of truth responsible for demographic management and actuarial control.

Reading

Cairns, John 1984: Blackstone, an English Institutist. *Oxford Journal of Legal Studies* 4, 318.

Dworkin, Ronald 1978: *Taking Rights Seriously*.

Ewald, François 1986: *L'Etat Providence*.

Foucault, Michel 1975 (*1977*): *Discipline and Punish*.

Goodrich, Peter 1990: *Languages of Law: From Logics of Memory to Nomadic Masks*.

Hart, Herbert 1961: *The Concept of Law*.

Hunt, Alan 1978: *The Sociological Movement in Law*.

Kamenka, Eugene and Tay, Alice Erh-Soon 1980: Socialism, anarchism and law. In *Law and Society: The Crisis in Legal Ideals*, ed. Kamenka et al.

Kantorowicz, Ernst 1957: *The King's Two Bodies*.

Legendre, Pierre 1988: *Le Désir politique de Dieu: étude sur les montages de l'état et du droit*.

Perelman, Chaim 1976: *Logique juridique, nouvelle rhétorique*.

Renner, Karl 1904 (*1949*): *The Institutions of Private Law and their Social Functions*, trans. Agnes Schwartzschild, ed. with introduction and notes by Otto Kahn-Freund.

Rose, Niklas 1989: *Governance of the Soul*.

Samuel, Geoffrey 1990: Science, law and history. *Northern Ireland Legal Quarterly* 41, 1–21.

Twining, William 1986: *Legal Theory and Common Law*.

Watson, Alan 1981: *The Civil Law Tradition*.

PETER GOODRICH

leadership This commonplace term can be defined quite simply as the quality permitting one person to command others. This implies that leadership is, above all, a mutual relationship between leader and led, individual and group. The term also suggests action: the leader and the group *do* something together. Finally, leadership is clearly a relation based on consent, not coercion – the robber holding a gun at one's back is not one's leader. It follows then that an investigation of leadership requires the insights of social and psychological theory, and is a prerequisite for a full appreciation of the ways in which power is held, legitimized and wielded.

However, despite (or perhaps because of) the apparent simplicity and fertility of the basic definitional framework, the study of leadership, though voluminous, has been marked by great controversy and little agreement – so much so that one well-known commentator concluded despairingly that 'the concept of leadership, like that of general intelligence, has largely lost its value for the social sciences' (Gibb, 1968, p. 91).

Nonetheless, the topic continues to fascinate social thinkers, and has stimulated two rival modes of approach. The classic studies of leadership focused primarily on the personalities of great men, portraying them as unique and heroic figures capable of transforming their disciples through sheer force of will. Examples of such overwhelming geniuses include Jean-Jacques Rousseau's Great Legislator, Friedrich Nietzsche's Superman, Thomas Carlyle's Hero, and Max Weber's famous 'ideal type' of the charismatic leader (see CHARISMA).

The idea of the active charismatic leader dominating a passive public remained central in the late nineteenth and early twentieth century in the writings of French crowd psychologist Gustave Le Bon, who provided pragmatic advice for many later power holders, and in the work of his fellow theorist, Gabriel Tarde, the founder of modern public opinion polling and political media consultation. A similar concept also animated Sigmund Freud's work on mass psychology. Essentially, these thinkers saw society as somnambulistically awaiting the voice of a hypnotic leader who could manipulate the deep human craving for authority and direction (see MASS SOCIETY). But unlike earlier writers in the heroic tradition, leaders were now portrayed not positively, but as irrational and emotionally charged theatrical figures of monomaniacal self-absorption.

During World War II, the debate between hero worshippers and diabolists, although never resolved, was set aside in favour of a more pragmatic focus on the needs and structure of the group and the surrounding situational context, and on the resulting dynamic between leaders and followers. This new emphasis reflected both a practical military concern with discovering and training effective combat leaders, and a revulsion against the charismatic personalized leadership styles of Hitler and Mussolini.

Leaders, according to this point of view, are hardly intrinsically heroic or extraordinary; instead, as Cecil Gibb wrote, 'leadership is not a quality which a man possesses; it is an interactional function of the personality and of the social situation (1951, p. 284). In fact, some studies indicated that leaders, far from being unusual, were often the group members closest to the statistical average whose very ordinariness allowed them to make innovations (see Hollander, 1958). But different situations made for less desirable types of leaders, including some displaying authoritarian personalities (as documented in Fiedler, 1964). Researchers therefore devoted themselves to discovering the interrelationship between leadership and context, with the pragmatic aim of developing the most efficient task organizers and of encouraging democratic leadership styles. But despite the empirical successes of the interactionist perspective, the emphasis on shifting circumstances and the denial of any universal characteristics to either groups or leaders soon made it difficult to tell if researchers were talking about 'leadership' or simply about 'management'.

Furthermore, qualifications quickly arose as to the actual purpose and character of the group and the functions of authority. For example, Robert Bales (1953) argued that while some groups give rise to instrumental leaders whose qualifications for command are ability and expertise, other groups have leaders who are primarily expressive, conveying to members a sense of emotional participation in the community. The leader's 'task' here is simply to maintain the group *as* group. It also became evident that even those who obviously are in command are not necessarily leaders; some are 'headmen' whose power derives solely from their position in a rigid hierarchy.

Followers too could be discriminated on various grounds: some were attached to the leader because of instrumental expectations of profit, others because of a belief in the leader's values, and others because of affection for the leader and the group. Much of the sociological and social psychological literature on leadership thus became an effort to categorize types of leaders and followers, and to outline the infinite and problematic vicissitudes of their interrelations in various situations.

Partially in response to the increasingly technical nature of situational and interactionist studies, there has been a return to the heroic tradition among a number of psychologically and biographically oriented writers who have accepted as given the leader's personal command over a passive following. But, in the disenchanting tradition of crowd psychology, the leader's appeal is portrayed in these studies not as a mark of charisma, but instead as an indication of psychological disorder. The precursor of this tradition is Harold Lasswell, who argued that leaders typically displace unmet psychic needs on to the political arena (1930). More sophisticated versions may be found in Erik Erikson's highly influential work on Gandhi (1969) and Luther (1958), although Erikson bows to the interactionist school in attempting to show why the public should find such neurotic displacements attractive; still, the masses remain essentially passive – reflecting, rather than acting.

Recent studies of leadership have continued to follow along these dichotomous paths, focusing either on the categorization of situations and pragmatic questions of a leader's influence and efficiency, or on the leader's psychology and motivations; efforts to reconcile these divergent theoretical tendencies regrettably remain few and far between, though there are welcome indications of a synthesis in, for example, the work of Kracke (1978), Willner (1984), Tucker (1981) and others, who combine psychological insight into the characters of leaders and followers, an awareness of the sociocultural context in which leadership arises, and a comparative framework that attempts to go beyond typologies.

See also AUTHORITY.

Reading

Burns, J. 1979: *Leadership.*
Carlyle, T. 1904 *(1966)*: *On Heroes, Hero-worship and the Heroic in History*, ed. C. Niemeyer.
Freud, S. 1921 *(1959)*: *Group Psychology and the Analysis of the Ego*, trans. J. Strachey.
Friedrich, C. 1958: *Authority.*
Gouldner, A. 1950: *Studies in Leadership: Leadership and Democratic Action.*
Hook, S. 1943: *The Hero in History: A Study in Limitation and Possibility.*
Le Bon, G. 1895 *(1952)*: *The Crowd: A Study of the Popular Mind.*

Nietzsche, F. 1901 (*1964*): *The Will to Power*, trans. A. Ludovici.

Paige, G. 1977: *The Scientific Study of Leadership*.

Rousseau, Jean-Jacques 1762 (*1967*): *The Social Contract*, ed. L. Crocker.

Tarde, G. 1903 (*1962*): *The Laws of Imitation*, trans. E. Parsons.

Weber, M. *1968*: *On Charisma and Institution Building*, a selection, ed. S.N. Eisenstadt.

CHARLES T. LINDHOLM

Left, New   *See* NEW LEFT

legal positivism   The term refers to any philosophy of LAW directed towards the value-free description of the Western legal institution in terms of a discrete system of social rules. In its broadest definition legal positivism is associated with a belief in the possibility of a science of law, classically a geometry of legal order, and a corresponding adherence to the methodological separation of questions of fact from questions of value, of law from morality.

The roots of this doctrinal philosophy of law lie in the medieval distinction between divine or natural law and secular or positive law, the latter being termed *ius positum*, law by position or, more pragmatically, law laid down by a human sovereign. In that generic description the order of positive law is identifiable as a distinct system of rules by reference to its supreme source: positive law was law which emanated from the monarch, Leviathan, the commonwealth or latterly the legislature.

In its initial definition legal positivism is associated in the English tradition with the writings of Thomas Hobbes and later with those of the nineteenth-century legal philosophers Jeremy Bentham and John Austin. Their positivism was that of defining law quite simply as the command of the sovereign and having once isolated that single source or oracle of national law they could argue that the task or province of jurisprudence was that of scientifically determining the pedigree and logical coherence of the established legal order. Positivistic legal philosophy was thus a systematizing discourse; one which took the content of law as 'given' or axiomatic and was merely concerned to arrange the sources and institutions of the legal system into a formally defined normative order or 'rule of law'.

In continental jurisprudence a similarly dogmatic tradition of positivistic legal philosophy dates back to the reception of Roman law – of the *Corpus Iuris Civilis* – in Europe in the late eleventh century. For the continental or 'civilian' tradition there was one law and one source of law for all of Europe, namely, the law codified in the early sixth century by the Emperor Justinian. Granted such a unitary and universal source of law the civilian tradition of dogmatic jurisprudence could easily adopt a positivistic legal philosophy in arguing the coincidence of law and reason in the texts – the written reason (*ratio scripta*) – of the code. Later continental codifications in the eighteenth and nineteenth centuries generally saw a resurgence of legal positivism, of the belief in the availability of all law in the code, in the logical and discrete world of the Text.

Modern legal positivism presents an often simplified and considerably more abstract version of the traditional lawyers' philosophy of the secular law. Its major philosophical proponent on the continent (though subsequently domiciled in the United States) was the Austrian neo-Kantian legal philosopher Hans Kelsen. In a series of highly influential works Kelsen attempted to construct a 'pure theory of law' or structural science of legal order. Replacing the unique sovereign source of law with the logical presupposition of 'the basic norm' or *Grundnorm* as the unitary foundation of any legal system, Kelsen posited the conditions of any positivistic legal science in terms of the exclusive study of the internal coherence of the normative order. Legal problems were to be studied as normative problems, as structural questions of order, and in that way legal science could be separated from those 'pre-scientific' disciplines such as sociology, psychology, history, economics or ethics which conflated the study of legal rules with the study of values, questions of what 'is' with questions of what 'ought to be'. A properly positivistic science of law would study the pedigree of 'formal authorization' of the legal norm, or in more pragmatic terms it would study the text of the law but simply in terms of its system membership.

In the common law world, modern legal positivism draws on the work of Kelsen but is principally associated with the work of the analytic legal philosopher and jurist Herbert Hart and his book *The Concept of Law*, first published in 1961. In a largely synthetic work Hart elaborated a positivistic legal philosophy in terms of the study of law as the study of a discrete system of primary and secondary rules. The separation of the legal order from other normative systems is, in Hart's version of legal positivism, attributable to a 'rule of recognition' whereby officials of the legal system identify and accept the discrete source and characteristics of legal rules. Legal positivism thus connotes the objective study of an isolated system of social rules. These rules are studied as official or professional knowledge and can be formally identified and analytically described without reference to any contextual, non-normative or other evaluative considerations. The existence of law, for the legal positivist, is one thing, its merit or demerit is a quite separate thing.

In critical terms legal positivism can be described as the indigenous, or commonsense, philosophy of the legal profession. It is in that sense a dogmatic philosophy, one which seeks to legitimate a professional knowledge on the basis of the profession's self-representation. It should be noted in this respect that legal positivism seeks to isolate law from its political and administrative contexts. It studies law as an activity apart from other social phenomena and as a discourse uniquely free of any such subjective or intertextual features as would threaten the overriding value of the 'rule of law'.

See also POSITIVISM.

Reading

Austin, John 1885 (*1955*): *The Province of Jurisprudence Determined and the Uses of the Study of Jurisprudence*.
Bentham, Jeremy *c*. 1780–2 (*1970*): *Of Laws in General*.
Goodrich, Peter 1986: *Reading the Law*.
Hart, Herbert 1961: *The Concept of Law*.
Hobbes, Thomas 1651 (*1973*): *Leviathan*.
Kairys, David ed. 1982: *The Politics of Law*.
Kelsen, Hans 1976: *Pure Theory of Law*.
Legendre, Pierre 1983: *L'Empire de la verité*.
Moles, Robert 1987: *Definition and Rule in Legal Theory*.

PETER GOODRICH

legitimacy The 'rightfulness' of a social or political order, its claim to support, as opposed to mere acquiescence, on the part of those subject to it, is of course a pervasive theme in political theory, often formalized in theories of 'political obligation'. Twentieth-century social thought, as well as continuing this normative and prescriptive tradition in relation to JUSTICE, freedom, equality, etc., has been greatly preoccupied with legitimacy as an empirical or behavioural concept, according to which a regime is 'legitimate' if it is *believed* to be legitimate by the population concerned. This line of thought, which recalls Machiavelli's *Prince* (1513), La Boétie's *Discourse on Voluntary Servitude* (1975) and, in the twentieth century, Georges

Sorel's *Reflections on Violence* (1906), has been dominated throughout the century by Max Weber's classic distinction (1921–2) between 'three pure types of legitimate authority'. Although domination or authority may be based, Weber says, on custom, interest, affectual or 'value-rational' motives, a secure order is usually characterized by a belief in its legitimacy. This may be based on tradition, on the CHARISMA of the ruler(s) or on a 'rational' acceptance of the legality of the order. As always with Weber's ideal types, these pure forms of legitimacy are found in combination, but one might take Saudi Arabia, Nazi Germany and Switzerland as illustrating the respective types. As in other areas of social life, charisma tends to become routinized or objectified, developing into traditional or constitutional rule or some combination of these.

The Weberian paradigm dominated Western political science in the middle decades of the century. It provided a useful framework for studies of POLITICAL CULTURE, though critics attacked the paradoxical and, as they saw it, cynical implication that secret police and propaganda could contribute to the 'legitimacy', in this 'value-free' sense, of a regime (Schaar, 1969; Pitkin, 1972, pp. 280–6). Jürgen Habermas, in his classic programmatic work (1973), suggested that advanced capitalist societies suffered from 'legitimation crises' resulting from the displacement of tendencies to economic crisis into the spheres of state policy and individual motivation. Habermas's analysis, unlike Weber's, is grounded in a normative conception in which the legitimacy of a regime depends on whether it is what those concerned *would have* agreed to as a result of a free, fully informed and exhaustive discussion (see Habermas, 1981). The distinction between legitimacy and a 'mass loyalty' often seen as manipulated has become popular in critical theory (see FRANKFURT SCHOOL) and more generally. At the more conservative end of the political spectrum, a model of legitimation by constitutional and other formal *procedures* (Luhmann, 1969) continues one of Max Weber's central motifs. This opposition between constitutional–processual and radical–democratic emphases has been mitigated in the 1990s as a result of two developments: the overthrow of state socialist regimes and their replacement, in some countries, by constitutional democracies; and a new interest among Western radicals and socialists, notably in Britain and Germany, in constitutional reform.

The twentieth century has seen the consolidation of what at the beginning of the century was still a rather revolutionary notion, that the legitimacy of a regime most fundamentally depends on the electorally expressed support of a majority of the whole adult population – though few parties quite attain this ideal. In a broader sense, the idea that all AUTHORITY exercised over sane adults should have to be justified in discussion and debate is becoming more prominent in the everyday practice of many countries – sometimes even in their armies. Political leaders and other authority figures find it harder than in the past to avoid giving press conferences and interviews to justify their policies, though public relations experts have become correspondingly skilled at turning such 'debates' into manipulated and propagandistic rituals.

Reading
Connolly, William ed. 1984: *Legitimacy and the State.*
Habermas, Jürgen 1973 (*1975*): *Legitimation Crisis.*
Merquior, J.G. 1980: *Rousseau and Weber: A Study in the Theory of Legitimacy.*
Schaar, John 1969: Legitimacy in the modern state. In *Power and Community*, ed. P. Green and S. Levinson. (Also in Connolly, 1984, above.)

WILLIAM OUTHWAITE

leisure   The word derives etymologically from the Latin verb *licere*, meaning 'to allow'. Built into the term, then, is a sense of the permissible. Even in Greek thought the notion of leisure was coupled with that of labour or work; for Aristotle, leisure was a serious business indeed: 'We conduct business in order to have leisure,' he wrote. Leisure in this sense is an ideal state to which the citizen can aspire, in which the living of a life of leisure is premised on minimizing necessities and ensuring that as much time as possible is free (Barrett, 1989, p. 14).

In modern English usage the term came to mean, by the fourteenth century, 'opportunity for free time' (Williams, 1976). WORK was becoming more narrowly defined as paid time, as measured and hired labour, and lesiure-time activities seen as those sorts of activities one could engage in away from the obligations of work. But in the key transitional period which laid the foundation of modern industrial society (in Britain at least) it was clear that the relation between work and leisure could be far from harmonious, and for many zealots of the new industrial order leisure was a potential problem. If the new industrial workers exhibited

initially the leisure and recreational mores of the preindustrial culture, the desired forms of the new labour discipline could well be threatened. This is why the suppression and marginalization of traditional recreational forms was one of the prerequisites of the new industrial order (Thompson, 1967). New forms of work and everyday living were seen as requiring new forms of leisure: for workers, rational recreation (respectable and often self-improving forms of non-work activity) was evolved by the reforming classes as one answer (Bailey, 1978); for the emergent Victorian bourgeoisie, there were expanding possibilities in the growing consumer market (Campbell, 1987). Without doubt, though, leisure activity in the early modern industrial period was a sphere of social, cultural and political struggle.

The truly 'leisured' were those who had no need to work: the privileged elite for whom a life of leisure was a serious life-project, and the ability to engage in an activity 'at your leisure' was a sign of status. This sense of leisure as a means of conspicuous consumption informed the first genuinely sociological treatise on leisure, in Thorstein Veblen's satirical *The Theory of the Leisure Class* (1899).

The 'problem' of leisure has been rediscovered regularly, usually during periods of potentially widespread unrest or UNEMPLOYMENT. A fascinatingly wide range of writers in North America in the 1920s was concerned with leisure. Hunnicutt (1988) describes one conservative figure as seeing leisure as the 'most serious educational and social problem' of the 1920s, and cites another commentator of the time: 'Alfred Lloyd, a sociologist at the University of Michigan, thought that leisure was essentially a way to democratic culture' (p. 104). These well-intentioned reformers grafted a humanist idealism on to the rational recreation model. Others, as Hunnicutt also observes (1988, p. 130), saw leisure as creativity: 'Society had to provide individuals with the opportunity to be creative and to find a practical way to direct sex drives into creative forms. Leisure offered that opportunity.'

In Britain, the labour movement at that time saw leisure more in tension with money than with sex drives (Cross, 1986). In the 1920s, Post Office unionists perceived a 'share-out of leisure and a betterment of life' as 'more vital than money'. Printers took the same view, and painters argued for a tripartite deal: extended pre-work education; a shorter working week; and holidays with pay (Jones, 1986). In the period after World War I organized labour won a great deal more free time and by 1920 seven million workers in Britain had achieved a reduction in the working week of six-and-a-half hours, while one-and-a-half million workers had been granted the right to holidays with pay. Legislation on holidays with pay was introduced in 1938.

The allegedly idle have always been a target for some social reformers. Rising unemployment in Britain in the 1980s provoked concern, and leisure schemes were evolved in the hope that these would compensate for the lack of work, and even promote forms of social and community responsibility. However:

> hopes of handing over the running of schemes to paid or volunteer unemployed leaders have rarely been realized. The unemployed, it seems, have more important things to do with their time – or lead such amorphous lives that they feel unable to commit themselves to anything. (Glyptis, 1989, p. 157)

In the educational sphere, working-class young have often been perceived as a potential problem (Clarke and Critcher, 1985, p. 129):

> in response, for concerned providers education for leisure aims to broaden the minds of young people by introducing them to the opportunities for constructive leisure, and by providing the social skills necessary to take advantage of the possibilities that exist.

The rhetoric of leisure has often been an individualist one, yet ironically the concern with leisure has frequently led liberal commentators to adopt the paternalistic tone of the critical moralist. David Riesman pointed to 'the best of our college students' as examples of an admirable use of leisure time – in their 'serious concern with current issues, with reading and companionship, and often a strong interest in music, drama, literature and nature' (Riesman, 1964, pp. 190–1).

An important sociological emphasis on the work–leisure relation has promoted a great deal of debate and research (Parker, 1976; Roberts, 1981), and few experts would disagree with the claim that 'the study of leisure time must . . . be approached within the context of the reduction of the working week, as well as the social norms associated with it, and the desired balance between work, family and leisure' (Pronovost, 1989, p. 57). Some of the most innovative social analysis of leisure has been from a feminist viewpoint, often challenging the very categories employed by male sociologists (McIntosh, 1981, pp. 93ff.; Wimbush and Talbot, 1988); and from critical perspectives (Horne et al., 1987; Rojek, 1989).

It has been convincingly argued that the formative social theorists of the modern age were concerned not just with capitalism and the labour process, but also, however implicitly, with the nature of leisure (Rojek, 1985). Debates about postmodernism and globalization focus on leisure: the contemporary consumer constructs the appropriate leisure lifestyle in her/his fragmentedly free fashion (Rojek, 1990) – at home, or anywhere on the world's tourist map (Urry, 1990). The leisure and culture industries are big business indeed, challenging social scientists to revise old models of the production/consumption dynamic, and the process of consumption in particular (Tomlinson, 1990 and 1991; Warde, 1990). (See also CONSUMER SOCIETY; MASS CULTURE). These issues also crystallize debates about freedom and constraint, agency and structure. Is leisure a sphere in which we are free to choose? If not, what is the nature of the constraints on our choices? The study of leisure can be a form of political as well as social analysis, casting light on processes and relations of power and privilege. The social order is not held together, threatened or negotiated exclusively at the workplace, but also in leisure (Elias and Dunning, 1986), where new identities can be sought and local cultural autonomy might be expressed (Finnegan, 1989; Bishop and Hoggett, 1986; Willis et al., 1990); where bargains might be struck between contested interests and contesting groups; where inequalities might be reproduced and forms of authority reaffirmed.

Reading
Barrett, Cyril 1989: The concept of leisure: idea and ideal. In *The Philosophy of Leisure*, ed. Cyril Barrett and Tom Winnifrith.
Clarke, John and Critcher, Chas 1985: *The Devil Makes Work: Leisure in Capitalist Britain*.
Finnegan, Ruth 1989: *The Hidden Musicians: Music-making in an English Town*.
Rojek, Chris ed. 1989: *Leisure for Leisure: Critical Essays*.
Wimbush, Erica and Talbot, Margaret eds 1988: *Relative Freedoms: Women and Leisure*.

ALAN TOMLINSON

Leninism   The term refers both to the ideas of V. I. Lenin, founder and theoretician of Russian Bolshevism; and to the numerous organizations and groups that have laid claim to and been inspired by them. This double reference has marked it with a particular ambiguity. As the thought of one man, Leninism was a developing corpus, adaptable to different circumstances and in the light of changing political needs and concerns. As an organized sector of international socialism on the other hand, it has often hardened into unbending sectarian doctrine and rigid practice. This has been so especially where it was joined to its parent 'ism' in the coupling 'Marxism-Leninism' – generally signifying a continuity traced back to Lenin by way of STALINISM. But it has also been true sometimes of groups that were politically opposed to Stalinism (see TROTSKYISM).

In its first sense, Leninism necessarily grew by a process of accretion, as Lenin grappled with the problems of the socialist movement in Russia. From an early stage his name became associated with a distinctive approach to questions of party organization and the party–class relationship. This was soon fused with a strategic vision of the projected Russian revolution, one characterized by a certain internal paradox. Later, in the shadow of world war, Lenin put forward a view of modern capitalism that would contribute in 1917 to altering that earlier paradoxical conception. He also outlined a theory of the capitalist state, of the necessary means of socialist revolution against it, and of the type of transitional institutions he envisaged on the road to a classless society.

Lenin's thinking about revolutionary organization took shape in the early years of the century, in connection with the campaign of the newspaper *Iskra* to establish a unified Russian party and with the split which then rent this infant party into Bolshevik and Menshevik factions. Lenin's view of the kind of party needed was of a centralized organization, with a group of full-time, professional revolutionaries at its core, whose theoretical formation and political training would enable the party to act as the vanguard of the working class. This view, elaborated in *What Is To Be Done?* (1902) and *One Step Forward, Two Steps Back* (1904), was explicated and defended in terms of four principal theses.

First, the party must be guided by the most 'advanced' theory. As Lenin wrote, 'Without revolutionary theory there can be no revolutionary movement.' Second, the spontaneous impulses and efforts of the masses of the working class would not by themselves produce a revolutionary class consciousness, but must inevitably remain confined within trade union limits. Third, socialist consciousness could only be brought to the workers' struggle from without. Lenin gave this thesis two different meanings: the source of socialist theory, he argued, was a section of the bourgeois intelligentsia; and the true ambit of that theory was much broader than the perspective of trade unionism, involving an overall grasp of the relationships of bourgeois society, particularly as focused through the state. On one meaning or the other, the party had to bring together under its programme and leadership all the disparate grievances, demands, campaigns and struggles of the exploited and oppressed, combining them into a unified revolutionary assault against the state. Fourth, in order to accomplish this task the party needed to be centralized and disciplined. Individual members were to be bound by the democratic decisions of the organization, and the local sections and other bodies coordinated by the central leadership in line with agreed policy. These norms later came to be known under the rubric 'democratic centralism'.

There is no doubt that some of Lenin's emphases here were due to the particular political – and polemical – context. He himself subsequently acknowledged that. The thesis concerning the trade union limits of proletarian spontaneity, and his arguments for a narrow, clandestine party, were both to be qualified in more revolutionary times. This ensemble of theses has, in any case, given rise to widely differing judgements regarding the import of the original Leninist project. Was it simply an attempt to give organizational focus and direction to the axiomatic Marxian goal of proletarian self-emancipation – creating an effective party *of* the working class, its own tool of analysis, criticism and struggle? Or was it, rather, a project of tutelage; the party (what so many would-be Leninist parties were to become) the final arbiter of Marxist 'truth'; this vanguard of the class in fact an elite bent on taking power for itself in the class's name? Again, was the project – in an intermediate interpretation – one of healthy, liberatory ambition, but the bearer also of more negative potentialities which eventually were to prevail? This has been part of a larger argument across the twentieth century: about how far Leninism was responsible for Stalin and Stalinism.

With the Leninist view of the party, one of the

two main pillars of early Bolshevism was in place. The other was fashioned during the upheaval of 1905: the conception of the Russian revolution Lenin advocated in *Two Tactics of Social Democracy in the Democratic Revolution*. In essence this revolution, according to him, was to be a bourgeois revolution carried through by the proletariat in alliance with the peasantry. Its bourgeois nature was an assumption he shared with the Mensheviks: the chief tasks were to clear the ground for a free development of capitalism and to create a democratic, republican state. However, against the Mensheviks, Lenin insisted that proletarian rather than bourgeois forces would have to lead it – the bourgeoisie being too weak and politically timid for any radical, thoroughgoing transformation. On the basis of the same premiss, Leon Trotsky for his part arrived at the thesis of PERMANENT REVOLUTION: the idea that the Russian workers would go further than the bourgeois aims of the revolution and begin the transition to socialism. Lenin resisted this idea. In Russian conditions it was impossible, he thought, to go beyond the first (bourgeois-democratic) to the second (proletarian-socialist) revolutionary stage. His view therefore, in sum, was of the proletariat taking political power with the peasantry, only to have to relinquish it in due course to the bourgeoisie.

In 1917 Lenin was to abandon this conception of two distinct stages and, in the face of opposition from many Bolsheviks, to urge that a proletarian revolution was on the agenda after all. His own thinking on the point had come together with that of Trotsky. One factor in changing his mind was probably the analysis of world capitalism that he had been prompted by the onset of war to undertake. In *Imperialism, the Highest Stage of Capitalism* (1916), he argued that the contemporary capitalist order was marked by the domination of large monopolies, the merging of bank and industrial capital, and fierce territorial competition among the largest capitalist powers for portions of the globe, driven by the need to secure a field for the export of capital. In this perspective of an international system shaken by competitive instability, war and crisis, the Russian revolution was now seen by Lenin as a breaking of the capitalist chain at its weakest link: the first of a series of proletarian revolutions in a global struggle for socialism. However, where the Leninism of Lenin himself could accommodate such a significant change of mind, derivative Marxism-Leninisms later did all

they could to obscure it. Concerned to make Lenin right about everything, the Stalinized Leninist tradition froze his viewpoints, including those he had left behind, into a rigid unity – rather as it erected statues of the man and even embalmed his corpse.

World war and revolution in Russia induced a more general reconsideration on Lenin's part. This involved a critique of the 'orthodox' Marxism of Karl Kautsky, one that symbolized the historical rift then opening up between Social Democracy and the world Communist movement, as Bolshevism and its international support were soon to become (see COMMUNISM; SOCIALISM). Lenin's critique centred on emphatic claims about the nature of the bourgeois state and of the transitional order – the 'dictatorship of the proletariat' – which must replace it. An effective socialist strategy, he argued in *State and Revolution* (1917), could not be based on simply taking over the institutions of the existing bourgeois state. These must rather be destroyed and something radically different be created in their place. For, the parliamentary-representative state and its executive machinery all but excluded the working class from influence and power, while socialism by its very nature required for its construction much more directly democratic institutions, of the workers' council type. Such was Lenin's conception of proletarian rule: of a state of a new kind, more democratic than any before it; an active, participatory democracy for the masses of working people.

If his views on party organization have often been seen as elitist, the argument of *State and Revolution* by contrast is sometimes regarded as being close to a form of anarchism – though Lenin would later vigorously oppose inside the Communist International the anarchist-style view of so-called 'left' communists, according to which the working class and its organizations should abstain altogether from participation in parliamentary politics even in non-revolutionary circumstances.

In any event, the participatory-democratic spirit of Lenin's pamphlet, penned on the eve of the Bolshevik revolution, was quickly subject to all of the pressures facing the new regime in power: of civil war, foreign intervention, economic and social dislocation, political opposition and discontent. In this situation Bolshevik rule under Lenin's guidance began to tighten into an autocratic monopoly of power. Other parties were banned, some but not all of them in open and violent revolt against the new political order. Factions inside Lenin's party itself were then prohibited, as they never had been hitherto. Whether these measures were just temporary and desperate expedients, or were instead perfectly in harmony with the 'substitutionist' logic of the Leninist project – this, again, forms part of the decades-long argument about the relationship between Leninism and Stalinism.

That Leninism in power laid some of the bases for the rise of Stalin cannot easily be denied. It did so institutionally, albeit under intense pressure, by eliminating the possible sites of a political pluralism. And it did so doctrinally as well – making a virtue out of necessity, as Rosa Luxemburg famously wrote – by fudging, in self-justificatory polemics, the distinction between proletarian and party rule. But equally, that Lenin himself would not have been able to go along with, much less preside over, what transpired with the triumph of Stalin, is also clear. Shortly before he died Lenin became alarmed at the forms of arbitrary power in process of development around him; sought to check them; and to have Stalin, in particular, removed from the strong position of influence he had achieved. The effort was too late and in vain.

Today the statues of Lenin are coming down in what were the lands of 'Marxism-Leninism'. It is part of the complex reality that evolved under the label deriving from his name – and an irony little noticed in recent comment – that Lenin himself could only have applauded their coming down: a renunciation of the rigidified, authoritarian cult that had been made out of his revolutionary project and his modest individual person. Whatever his judgement on connected events might have been, his applause for this at least seems a reasonable certainty.

Reading

Carr, E.H. 1950 (*1966*): *The Bolshevik Revolution 1917–1923*, vol. 1, pp. 15–111.
Colletti, L. 1972: *From Rousseau to Lenin*, pp. 219–27.
Harding, N. 1977, 1981 (*1982*): *Lenin's Political Thought*, 2 vols combined.
Lenin, V.I. (*1960–70*): *Collected Works*.
Lewin, M. 1973: *Lenin's Last Struggle*.
Liebman, M. 1975: *Leninism under Lenin*.
Luxemburg, R. *1970*: Organizational questions of Russian social democracy. In *Rosa Luxemburg Speaks*, ed. M.A. Waters, pp. 114–30.
——*1970*: The Russian revolution. In *Rosa Luxemburg Speaks*, ed. M.A. Waters, pp. 367–95.
Mandel, E. 1977: The Leninist theory of organization. In *Revolution and Class Struggle: A Reader in Marxist Politics*, ed. R. Blackburn, pp. 78–135.
Meyer, A.G. 1962: *Leninism*.
Miliband, R. 1983: *Class Power and State Power*, pp. 154–66.

NORMAN GERAS

liberalism This is a political doctrine which holds that the purpose of the state, as an association of independent individuals, is to facilitate the projects (or 'happiness') of its members. States ought not to impose projects of their own. Like its doctrinal partner CONSERVATISM, liberalism is one version of the Western political tradition, and both terms are employed, somewhat confusingly, in both a generic and a specific sense.

In a generic sense, 'liberalism' refers to the whole modern Western tradition of thought and behaviour, as contrasted with the traditional forms of order found in Asia and Africa. Critics of the modern Western world, such as Marxists, or various kinds of religious fundamentalists, attack liberalism as the doctrinal aspect of capitalism. Liberalism in this sense refers to the release of an individual's desires from many of the restraints of a traditional order. But within the actual politics of Europe and America, liberalism refers to a *specific* set of ideas which from time to time mark off its adherents from conservatives and socialists. Just what constitutes this specific form of liberalism changes from one generation to the next. In the nineteenth century, for example, liberalism incorporated such ideas as free trade, democracy and national self-determination. Towards the end of that century, however, a 'new liberalism' arose emphasizing that the state ought to be responsible for supplying the material needs of the poor so that they might more effectively exercise the liberty they ought to enjoy. This mediation towards socialism was clearly at odds with the minimal state which many earlier liberals had thought the only guarantee of freedom. Such classical liberalism of the mid-nineteenth century has been powerfully revived during the 1970s, and has generally found a home in parties calling themselves 'conservative'.

It will be clear that any attempt to define liberalism is like tracking a moving target. The meaning of 'liberalism' changes not only with its level of abstraction, and with the passing of time, but also from country to country. Anti-clericalism, for example, was an important component in nineteenth-century French liberalism, whereas anti-religious feeling has been at best intermittent in Britain and America. All such emphases change constantly.

The history of liberal ideas

The actual term 'liberalism' came into British politics from Spain and France in the 1830s, the decade in which most of the labels of modern politics gained their currency. It came to describe the old Whig party whose roots went back to the classical republicanism of the seventeenth century. The fluidity of these political ideas can be illustrated from Edmund Burke's appeal, in the 1790s, from the 'new Whigs' sympathetic to French doctrines of natural rights, to the 'old Whigs' who stood, as Burke saw it, by the tradition of the 1688 settlement. Burke's doctrinal founding of British conservative thought reveals much about where it is distinguished from liberalism. He agreed that society was a contract, but he rapidly dissolved the actual contracts of rational men in 'the great primaeval contract of eternal society' which left much less to their active discretion. Liberals, by contrast, are more willing to adapt the rules and arrangements of a civil association so as to accord with what is currently thought rational. As Burke's critic and contemporary, Tom Paine, put it, no generation has the right to bind its successors.

In its SOCIAL CONTRACT versions, liberalism explored a realm of private discretions (which included conscience, the family and opinion) which governments must not invade. Many of these themes became explicit in the Protestant Reformation of the sixteenth century, and a certain tension between liberalism and Catholicism has been a recognized feature of political life up until the later decades of the twentieth century. A classic expression of this attitude is John Milton railing in *Areopagitica* (1644) against the moral domination of their flocks by Catholic priests. But it was long generally agreed that the essential principles of liberalism were first stated in John Locke's *Second Treatise of Government* (1690).

Locke here argues that government is a kind of trust set up by individuals who have banded together to form a society the point of which is to secure order and protect property. 'Property' for this purpose includes 'life, liberty and possessions', and its management is a duty imposed upon us by God. Governments rule by law, and the broad outlines of their duty (and its limits) are given by what reason tells us about human nature and natural rights. Authority results from the consent of the ruled, and the people have the right, as a last resort, to overthrow a ruler who violates these conditions.

Locke's *Second Treatise* was a highly partisan work dressed up as if it were a philosophical argument, and historians of ideas now believe that to identify it with the much later doctrine of liberalism is to commit Whig history, in which historical personages are understood as animated by ideas of liberty which only emerged at a later time. An even more serious problem is that the central place accorded to natural law in Locke's argument severely limited the range of possible political disagreement. But it is of the essence of a liberal society that it is characterized by basic disagreement about all matters of substance. From this point of view, the thought of Thomas Hobbes, dismissed by many later critics as absolutist, indeed virtually totalitarian, begins to tell us more about liberalism.

The central point is that Hobbes's *Leviathan* (1651) takes with the utmost seriousness the fact of disagreement between the members of a modern state. Such disagreement threatens human associations with violence and breakdown, an outcome which can only be avoided by vesting authority in a sovereign whose decisions on matters of law and public business, including public doctrine, must be taken as final. Instead of basing the state on reason, as Locke did, Hobbes relied on authority. The subject of a modern state is bound by rules he may find neither rational nor desirable, and his freedom consists in those areas (assumed by Hobbes to be an immense continent) in which the law is silent. Later liberal thought has emphasized the fact that it is the logical character of rules – as being abstract and hypothetical – which facilitates liberty. Such 'adverbial' modifications of behaviour (to use an appropriate metaphor stemming from Michael Oakeshott) allow scope for ingenuity and imagination in the pursuit of desires. Laws qualify actions, but do not command them. The secret of the dynamism of modern liberal states lies in a continuing dialogue between a legislating government and a responding citizenry guided by a set of abstract rules. Hobbes himself compared laws to the hedges and fences which keep people from straying into private ground. As Oakeshott has remarked, 'without being himself a liberal, [Hobbes] had in him more of the philosophy of liberalism than most of its professed defenders.'

The liberal conception of political life

The essence of liberalism lies in its recognition of individual desiring as the basic fact of a modern civil association. There are no overriding values or norms to which man is comprehensively and permanently obliged. But this formula is frequently misunderstood. It must not be thought, for example, that a desire is the same as impulse, inclination or caprice. The 'desire' of liberal thought, like the 'happiness' of utilitarian theorists (see UTILITARIANISM), is highly rationalized. The identity of the person in liberal thought is to be discovered not in any natural feature (such as race or class) nor in any social relationship (such as status or station) but in a structure of coherent or rationalized desires. It is only such a person who can be made responsible for his or her actions. Such formulations suggest, of course, that each individual in a liberal state is a paragon of self-creation. All actual states, of course, are permeated by a living texture of patriotic feelings, and moral and religious attachments inherited from the past. The advance of liberalism, however, has diminished the authoritative status of religions, and opened up patriotic attachments to the competition of universalistic and cosmopolitan attachments. This dissolution of inherited attachments (which conservatives often argue will in the end prove fatal to modern Western societies) has largely been based on the growth of modern societies as economies, in which all members (rather than the traditional breadwinners of the past) participate in what Adam Smith called 'truck, barter and exchange'. Indeed, one of the most persuasive versions of liberalism – that advanced by F.A. Hayek (1960) – consists in an argument that the economy ought in substance to be beyond the range of political interference.

Critics of liberalism often charge it with being false to social and political reality. Such criticism is usually based on misunderstanding. The individualist emphasis of the social contract theory, for example, is often attacked as a form of atomism which does not recognize that man is a social animal. When the citizen of a liberal state is characterized as a 'bourgeois' (for example, in Marxist doctrines), he is often thought to be isolated and in conflict with his fellows. In fact, liberal theory has no difficulty recognizing social relations, and one of the most striking features of liberal societies is the flexible and fluent creativity of their social cooperation – of which the celebrated wealth of voluntary associations in Anglo-Saxon societies is a good example. Again, the similarity between liberal individualism and the theory of rational economic relations has led some critics to conclude that selfishness and greed lie at the heart of liberal societies. This muddle between selfishness (which is a moral fault) and self-interest (which is a formal criterion of rational behaviour) is both common and pernicious. It may best be refuted by pointing to the fact that at both the individual and governmental level, liberal societies have been the most spectacularly given to making gifts to the less fortunate of any groups in history.

The real deficiencies of liberal thought only appear when it issues in a kind of rationalism which assumes that all human beings have the same rationalizing character. Those late nineteenth-century writers whose liberalism was boosted by the heady wine of progress would have found that human nature in the twentieth century has badly let them down. Religious and ideological zeal have led to ferocious conflicts which many liberals have found, and often are still finding, difficult to understand.

Recent developments
Liberalism has been a major beneficiary of the revival of normative political thought since the 1960s. The two basic moral ideas in terms of which liberalism has been elucidated – those of rights, and of utility – have been ingeniously developed. The liberal emphasis on rational choice (see RATIONAL CHOICE THEORY) has revived the familiar social contract question: how can such creatures generate public goods? How can they be motivated to behave communally if it is not in their private interest to do so? A huge technical literature in this area has focused around the prisoner's dilemma and other forms of game theory. The idea of choosing basic social principles behind a 'veil of ignorance' in *A Theory of Justice* by John Rawls (1971) attempts to determine a framework of constitutional rules independently of the partiality we are assumed to exhibit in actual social and political life. In these terms, a liberal state appears as one which is indifferent or neutral as between the specific projects and opinions favoured by its members. This procedural ideal of liberalism has recently been expressed in terms of the priority of the right over the good.

The problems explored in this philosophical literature are academic in the sense that liberal–democratic societies do, as a matter of fact, work, and indeed work very well. But critics often argue that the freedom and neutrality liberals claim for their state is illusory. It is certainly true that religious believers who are entirely persuaded that they alone possess the truth of things may well find the pluralism of a liberal society intolerable, and in fact the consequence of centuries of such controversy on most Christian churches has been to induce a tolerant ecumenism which often abandons, at the level of literal revealed belief, the claim to truth. Academic discussion of liberalism is thus likely to conclude that nihilism lies at the end of the liberal road, while some sociologists have argued that the liberal emphasis on freedom is an acid dissolving the invisible bonds by which social order is sustained. Daniel Bell (1979), for example, has argued that modern capitalist societies require both an austere and thrifty Protestant ethic in the area of production, and a hedonist attitude to consumption; each propensity tends to destroy the other.

These explorations of danger might well, however, be taken as part of the resourcefulness of modern liberal societies, which certainly live dangerously, but have so far shown a considerable capacity for making adjustments which will save them from disaster. There is, of course, no guarantee at all that this will continue. But such danger, on the liberal view, is an unavoidable feature of the adventure of modernity.

Reading

Barry, Norman P. 1980 (*1986*): *On Classical Liberalism and Libertarianism.*

Bell, Daniel 1979: *The Cultural Contradictions of Capitalism.*

Gray, John 1989: *Liberalism.*

Haakonssen, Knud ed. 1988: *Traditions of Liberalism.*

Hayek, F.A. 1960: *The Constitution of Liberty.*

Hobbes, Thomas 1651 (*1973*): *Leviathan.*

Locke, John 1690 (*1960*): *Two Treatises of Government*, ed. Peter Laslett.

Mill, John Stuart 1859 (*1991*): *On Liberty and Other Essays*, ed. John Gray.

Milton, John 1644 (*1925*): Areopagitica. In *Milton's Prose: A Selection.*

Nozick, Robert 1974: *Anarchy, State and Utopia.*

Oakeshott, Michael 1975 (*1991*): *On Human Conduct.*

—— 1975: *Hobbes on Civil Association.*

Rawls, John 1971: *A Theory of Justice.*

Sandell, Michael 1982: *Liberalism and the Limits of Justice.*

KENNETH R. MINOGUE

liberation theology   The first theoretical construction of Christian faith elaborated in the Third World, liberation theology has the aim of presenting freedom from oppression as a matter of universal religious significance. Of Latin American origin and dating from the 1960s, liberation theology fuses concepts from the social sciences with biblical and theological ideas. In particular, in its use of Marxist and neo-Marxist social theory it may be superficially read both by undiscerning theologians and sympathetic sociologists as a form of radical social theory incorporating a secular ethic of justice. Indeed, a recent official response of the Catholic church to liberation theology questions the epistemological status of a theology which integrates elements of a Marxist theory (Congregation for the Doctrine of the Faith, 1984).

The hybrid form of liberation theology creates an initial impediment to definition. One might go further and say that the use of the noun in the singular, 'theology', to describe the corpus of liberation literature, as if it were in any way comparable to classical systematic theology, is misleading. There are a number of liberation theologies: black liberation theology (Cone, 1969); Jewish theology of liberation (Ellis, 1987); Asian liberation theology (Suh Kwang-sun, 1983); and Latin American liberation theology (Haight, 1985). In addition to these, there is so-called political theology, influenced by the Frankfurt school of critical sociology, which may be described as a liberation theology for Western capitalist society (Metz, 1969). In other words, it is accurate to speak of 'liberation theologies' rather than of 'liberation theology'.

Even if a univocal description is not yet available, these theologies may be linked together under one title because they share assumptions about the need for contemporary theology to be orientated by three values: first, the analysis of oppression and its corresponding form of liberation; second, the employment of social analysis and theory as a corrective to the 'privatized' mode of traditional theology; and, third, the use of the paradigm of liberation from the Book of Exodus.

Oppression and liberation

The distinctive mode of theologizing developed in liberation theology came from the combination of detailed empirical analysis of forms of oppression and the sociological and political analysis of these forms. In Latin America, the educational theories of Paulo Freire (1970) promoted descriptions of the poverty and powerlessness of the mass of the people. It was later realized that the socio-economic analysis of Marx was effective in identifying these forms of oppression as inevitable consequences of the alliance of wealth and power specific to capitalism. Those theologians who were reflecting along with the people on the experience of poverty began to speak of 'structures of oppression', and, interpreting the situation theologically, they adopted the term 'structures of sin'.

It is not clear whether liberation theologians have made textual connections between their own style of theologizing and Marx's usage in *Critique of Hegel's Philosophy of Right*, but the similarities are striking. Marx identifies the oppressing class by its 'embodiment of a limitation' ... 'which gives general offence' (in terms of liberation theology this might be the sinful structures which create widespread poverty), or by the deficiency of a particular sphere which becomes 'the notorious crime of a whole society' (which might describe the place of the Nazi holocaust in Jewish liberation theology) (see Marx, *1975*, p. 254).

The progression from a personal and psychological understanding of the foundations of theology to a sociological interpretation of reality is typical of liberation theology. For instance, the Catholic church's recommendation of a subjective lifestyle of poverty has been replaced in liberation theology by an objective 'option for the poor'. Since the church compromised itself with the oppressing wealth-owning class, it must now identify with the poor in the struggle for liberation. This recommendation to 'a fundamental option for the poor' reflects Marx's view that 'If one class is to be the class of liberation *par excellence*, then another class must be the class of oppression' (ibid.).

Marx's conclusion (with its own strange theological echoes) that social oppression of this kind means 'the total loss of humanity, which can therefore redeem itself only through the total redemption of humanity' (ibid., p. 256), presents in secular form the eschatological theme of the struggle to establish the universal Kingdom of God (with its social and political consequences) which is at the heart of liberation theology.

Radical social theory: deprivatizing the Christian message

The development and nature of liberation theology cannot be understood without seeing it, in part, as a reaction, first, against the individualism of classical Western theology; and, secondly, against the consensus theoretical approach of traditional Catholic social thinking. Two influences were brought to bear in correcting the first weakness: German political theology, which was defined by Metz as 'a critical corrective to the tendency of contemporary theology to concentrate on the private individual' (1968, p. 3); and, the other corrective, the recovery of the social meaning of the Gospel by Latin American Christians engaged in the struggle for justice. Liberation theology attempted to correct the second weakness by drawing on Marxist contributions to demonstrate that the analysis of social oppression entails a theory of conflict and action. It has tried to be selective in its use of Marxist insights, to avoid accepting, that is, the Marxist system; but many Christian commentators are doubtful if the analysis can be used without also accepting the materialist interpretation of history.

What distinguishes the approach of liberation theology from preceding forms, and more importantly what constitutes its distinctive epistemology, is summed up in its use of the term 'praxis'. Western theologians were trained in a tradition that gave primacy to theoretical knowledge. First came truth, and then its application. Liberation theologians question this order. They give primacy to action; praxis comes before theory; orthopraxis comes before orthodoxy. Without denying the usefulness of this approach to theology, it may be asked if this use of praxis is anything more than Aristotle's use of the term to describe those matters which have to do with life in the polis; whereas in Marx 'praxis' has specific reference to that action connected with the relationships of production. Once again, the intimate connections between the notion of praxis in Marxism and the materialist interpretation of reality must create difficulties for theological interpretation of history.

The Exodus paradigm

It would be misleading, however, to discuss liberation theology as if its coherence depended exclusively on exact correspondence with a definitive Marxism, especially at a time when Marxism finds itself more and more incapable of keeping intact the universalistic nature of its economic propositions. At this point Marxism may have something to learn from liberation theology.

In 1921, Ernst Bloch, in his original and independent interpretation of Marxism, argued against Engels and others that the language used by Thomas Münzer in the Peasant War of 1542 was not a disguised form of secular political aims, but an expression of deeply felt religious experiences which also fostered political commitment. In liberation theology the Book of Exodus occupies a central and paradigmatic place in promoting Christian endeavour to break the bonds of oppression. In the story of Exodus, faith and politics are set together; the action of the people and the action of God are one; political fact and theological event run together. Looked at from the point of view of the liberation process itself, the Book of Exodus identifies two moments: liberation from (the oppression of the Pharaoh); and liberation to (the Promised Land). It is this paradigm that directs much of liberation theologizing. Already in 1968, the Conference of Latin American Bishops in their famous Medellin document (which officially inaugurated liberation thematics) referred to the revolutionary force of reflecting on liberation in Exodus; and Gutierrez remarks that 'it remains vital and contemporary due to similar historical experiences which the people of God undergo' (1973, p. 159).

See also CHRISTIAN SOCIAL THEORY.

Reading
Boff, L. 1985: *Church, Charisma and Power*.
Boff, L. and Boff, C. 1987: *Introducing Liberation Theology*.
Bonino, J. 1983: Towards a Christian Political Ethics.
Concilium, 1987 part 1, pp. 83–106.
Guttierez, G. 1983: *A Theology of Liberation: History, Politics and Salvation*.
Institute of Jewish Affairs 1988: *Christian Jewish Relations* 21.1 (monograph issue).
Lane, D. 1984: *Foundations for a Social Theology*.
Segundo, J.-L. 1973: *The Community Called Church*.
Sobrino, J. 1978: *Spirituality of Liberation*.

FRANCIS P. McHUGH

libertarianism Asserting that individual liberty is the primary political value and that private PROPERTY is its most important institutional safeguard, the term came into use in the United States of America after the presidency of Franklin Delano Roosevelt (1933–1945) whose supporters appropriated the old name 'liberalism' for their branch of political and economic interventionism. Hence, those of their opponents who also rejected conservatism began to call themselves 'libertarians'.

Regarding themselves as the rightful heirs of the classical liberal tradition of John Locke and Adam Smith, most libertarians believe that liberty is of intrinsic value; according to them, it is an inalienable human right, a demand of reason, the natural condition of human beings. Some are inspired by the romantic individualism of the writer Ayn Rand (1957); others, taking their lead from Locke, base the right to liberty and property on the principle of self-ownership. Some libertarians, however, argue for liberty in the terms of the good consequences which seem to flow from it. (The two positions are not mutually exclusive.) They believe that liberty is the only means of coping with the diversity of individual values, views and lifestyles: people can agree to disagree. Moreover, these libertarians (many of whom are influenced by AUSTRIAN ECONOMICS or CHICAGO ECONOMICS) contend that the freedom to experiment, innovate and, inevitably, to make mistakes is a necessary prerequisite of progress.

Another division of libertarians is suggested by their views on government. Some, such as Murray Rothbard (1973) and David Friedman (1989), are anarchists, or anarcho-capitalists, holding government to be unnecessary (see ANARCHISM). They believe that individuals can, at least in principle, perform all the tasks by voluntary cooperation which are now undertaken by government, even the provision and protection of law and order and of money. Relying on modern price theory, libertarian economists have produced many ingenious free-market solutions of the problem of public goods. Other libertarians, like Robert Nozick (1974), are minarchists. According to them, a minimal state, limited to protecting individual rights, and supported by taxation, is necessary. All libertarians agree, however, in opposing the compulsory redistribution of income in the name of 'social justice'.

Libertarians think that the opposition to private property often derives from a misreading of history. They contend that the conditions of the working classes were not worsened by CAPITALISM in the early nineteenth century: on the contrary, capitalism enabled many more to live than would otherwise have survived. Libertarians also believe that the Great Depression between the two world wars is not evidence of any inherent instability of the market order; it was caused or at least much aggravated by government intervention. Libertarians take equally controversial positions on current affairs; monopoly (often maintained by government) is exaggerated by the foes of the market order; environmental problems can sometimes be solved through the price mechanism; not development aid, but free trade and the unhindered flow of capital, will enable poor nations to escape the poverty trap; and so on.

Conservatives and classical liberals agree with many of these positions (see CONSERVATISM and LIBERALISM). But classical liberals (like Friedrich

A. Hayek and Milton Friedman) can contemplate, in addition to the traditional functions of the minimal state, the enforcement of social security, for example a 'safety net' or a guaranteed minimum income for the poorest. Conservatives, on the other hand, take issue with the relentless pursuit of private satisfaction tolerated by libertarians: may consenting adults really do whatever they want with (or to) one another, including drug peddling and prostitution, provided only that they do not violate other people's rights in the process? To the classical liberals, libertarians respond by stressing the coercive nature of public (as distinct from private) charity, and some of its undesirable, but unintended, consequences. In the debate with conservatives, they emphasize the difference between acceptance and tolerance.

Reading

Barry, Norman 1980 (*1986*): *On Classical Liberalism and Libertarianism*.
Block, Walter 1976: *Defending the Undefendable*.
Friedman, David 1989: *The Machinery of Freedom*, 3rd edn.
Lepage, Henri 1982: *Tomorrow, Capitalism*.
Nozick, Robert 1974: *Anarchy, State and Utopia*.
Rand, Ayn 1957: *Atlas Shrugged*.
Rothbard, Murray 1973 (*1978*): *For a New Liberty: The Libertarian Manifesto*, rev. edn.

HANNES H. GISSURARSON

linguistic philosophy This is a somewhat misleading term, carrying the suggestion that it deals with the philosophy *of* language. In fact, the expression is mostly used, and is best reserved, for a certain philosophical movement, which crystallized in Cambridge under the leadership of Ludwig Wittgenstein (1889–1951) during the years immediately preceding World War II. This movement came to dominate the philosophical scene in England, and to a smaller extent in other English speaking countries, during the decades immediately following the war. Though originating in Cambridge, its headquarters after the war were located in Oxford, under the leadership of Gilbert Ryle (1900–1976) and J. L. Austin (1911–1960). It was also sometimes referred to as 'Oxford philosophy'.

The central idea of the movement was not that philosophy would illuminate language, but rather, that language would illuminate philosophy. Philosophical problems were held to be in an important sense spurious: they arose not because there really was a problem to solve or a question to answer, but because people seized by 'philosophical perplexity' (an expression much used) were possessed, without clearly or consciously realizing it, by mistaken ideas about the nature of language. These mistaken ideas manifested themselves to them in the form of a conceptual disquiet, which led those possessed by it to ask characteristically philosophical questions. This diagnosis was said to be applicable to *all* philosophy.

The attempt to answer philosophical questions, and, worse still, to try to substantiate these answers, was inherently misguided. The correct procedure, on this view, was to *describe* the linguistic custom which governs the use of the crucial expressions connected with the alleged 'problem'. This would lead the person seized by the perplexity to understand the real functioning of the relevant words, and thereby to come to be liberated from the temptation to ask, and to answer, the spurious question. It is this recipe for handling philosophical problems which led those who embraced this position to the practice of detailed – though somewhat impressionistic – observations of the use of words, accompanied by the conviction that this is the *only* proper method of philosophizing.

The movement secured a powerful hold over the younger generation of philosophers who entered the profession after the war, a hold not seriously challenged until around 1960. The movement did not at the time see itself as one position among others, but rather as a definitive revelation, abrogating past thought, and as the culmination of all previous philosophy. Its adherents had to 'cure' their rivals of their tacit self-deceptions, rather than argue with them as equals. It was all destined to lead, either to the final euthanasia of philosophy, or to the birth of a new subject altogether.

What were the mistaken assumptions concerning language which had the power to haunt humanity for so long and actually to engender a whole learned discipline and profession? The mistake(s) can be divided into one great generic error, on the one hand, and specific mistakes on the other. The generic mistake was that language does but one thing, and that this one role or function is *reference to the world*. Previous empiricist theories of language had often taken this for granted, and in particular, Wittgenstein's own youthful *Tractatus Logico-Philosophicus* (1921) had been based on this assumption. (It was the overcoming of this assumption which gave birth to the new revelation.) Such visions of language did not of course deny that language is also used for a variety of other social purposes, such as ritual, but they implicitly discounted such roles, treating them as minor irrelevances and excrescences, not modifying the real essence of language. This was *the* great error.

The specific mistakes were in a way but special concrete instances of the general mistake. For instance, there is the misinterpretation of evaluation as the attribution of a characteristic, or of 'dispositional' traits as directly obervable features. (To say that something is brittle is to say that it is liable to break, not that it has some perceptible characteristic right now.)

The hypothesis which underlay Wittgensteinian linguistic philosophy was that, whenever philosophical problems or theories are formulated, what is really happening is that the thinker has failed to realize this general truth about the diversity of function of language, and is trying to impose a homogeneous model on linguistic material which is inherently heterogeneous. Without such a mistaken assumption, the question would not arise. For instance, moral theorists try to assimilate moral discourse to descriptive or scientific discourse; proponents of theories of mind fail to see that discourse concerning intelligent performance refers to a wide variety of skills, and not to a distinct observable zone; and so forth. During the heyday of the movement, this hypothesis was seen as an established revelation; in practice, it was used as a *definition*.

It was an inherent and central part of Wittgenstein's 'mature' position that theorizing, explanation and justification had no place in philosophy, and were to be replaced by the *description* of linguistic custom. 'Forms of life', by which he appeared to mean the actual linguistic custom of concrete speech communities, were beyond either explanation or justification. Therefore this strategy was self-justifying. In this strange way, a philosophy which denied the traditional role of justification or of validation to philosophy, itself practised it in an oblique fashion. It did so in a curious new, indiscriminate and omnibus manner: *all* actually existing styles of thought were valid. Only the attempt to seek an external vantage point and justify, or damn, existing practice was invalid. This philosophy ignores the fact that the pursuit of the transcendence of the custom of any given community is itself an important and pervasive feature of human intellectual history: Platonism of all kinds, transcendent religion, the Reformation, the En-

lightenment, the Cartesian philosophical tradition seeking a foundation for knowledge, all exemplify it. Wittgenstein's indiscriminate relativism and linguistic immanentism would damn them all.

The first wave of deeply convinced and uncritical linguistic philosophers did not practise this implied relativism in any consistent or so to speak generalizing way: they concentrated on *their own* conceptual custom, 'ordinary language', endeavouring to show that philosophic theories were misreadings of *it*, and could be 'cured' by attention to its nuances. The most determined and celebrated attempt to practise this strategy was Gilbert Ryle's *The Concept of Mind* (1949), which claimed to solve, or 'dissolve', the mind–body problem (and the 'other minds' problem into the bargain). Probably the most influential practitioner of the method was J. L. Austin, who tried to show, in *Sense and Sensibilia*, that the problem of knowledge as previously presented by theoreticians of knowledge, was misguided (see also THEORY OF KNOWLEDGE). When our claim to knowledge was subjected to general doubt, there was, according to him, no case to answer.

This kind of classical Wittgensteinian philosophy, carried out within philosophy and in a markedly insular spirit – use of 'ordinary English' to show that earlier philosophies were nothing but clusters of muddles – eventually withered away after two or three decades of enthusiasm. The subsequent influence of Wittgenstein tended to be more among thinkers more clearly aware of his cultural relativism. These men were positively attracted by the general relativism. The outstanding formulation of this position is Peter Winch's *The Idea of a Social Science* (1958). Such thinkers no longer saw it as the diagnosis and terminal culmination of all philosophy, but as a philosophy among others, but better, and more generous in its endorsement of all cultures. In this kind of interpretation, what is valued in Wittgenstein is not so much his abrogation of previous philosophy (as an alleged misunderstanding of language), but his vindication of the equal value, dignity and autonomy of all cultural visions. In this form, Wittgenstein continues to exercise much influence in broader fields, such as literary studies or cultural anthropology.

Reading
Austin, J.L. 1962: *Sense and Sensibilia: How To Do Things with Words*.

Gellner, Ernest 1959: *Words and Things*
Magee, Bryan 1971: *Modern British Philosophy*.
Ryle, Gilbert 1949: *The Concept of Mind*.
Winch, Peter 1958 (*1976*): *The Idea of a Social Science*.
Wittgenstein, Ludwig 1953 (*1967*): *Philosophical Investigations*.

ERNEST GELLNER

linguistics   At the beginning of the twentieth century 'linguistics' could have been characterized as 'the study of the form and function of language', leaving the denotation of 'language' vague. This might include areas such as literary theory, philosophical, psychological or sociological aspects of LANGUAGE, and even animal communication. In its modern usage, however, 'linguistics' *tout court* has come to mean 'the study of the grammatical structures of human languages'. For some, this would exclude pragmatics (the interpretation of utterances in context) and even semantics. However, these are generally included in the purview of linguistics.

The subject has undergone immense changes during the century, resulting in a considerable degree of specialization, and a noticeable sharpening of the focus of research questions. At the same time the interface between linguistics and other areas of social relations and human cognition has become a serious object of inquiry, seeing the development of 'hyphenated' disciplines such as sociolinguistics, psycholinguistics, neurolinguistics, as well as mathematical linguistics and computational linguistics. Linguistics has also interacted fruitfully with formal logic, epistemology, cognitive psychology, artificial intelligence and 'cognitive science' in general.

The central concern of the nineteenth century was the historical development of languages, or diachronic linguistics. A shift of emphasis took place associated with Ferdinand de Saussure (1916). He distinguished diachronic linguistics from synchronic study, that is, the study of present-day language structures. Viewing language as an essentially social phenomenon, he famously distinguished *langue*, the abstract system underlying language, from *parole*, observed language use (cf. Noam Chomsky's psychological dichotomy between competence and performance). Central to Saussure's thinking was the structuralist notion that the essence of the organization of language is in sets of differences between abstract terms in a system.

Structuralism flourished in Europe and America, particularly in the fields of phonology (sound structure) and morphology (word structure), where the concepts of the phoneme and the morpheme (the minimal meaningful component of a word) were developed. The phoneme concept played a particularly important role. It is a speech sound conceived abstractly as a member of a set of contrastive sounds. Thus the 'th' sound of 'those' is a phoneme in English because it contrasts with other consonants, including the 'd' of 'doze'. However, in Castilian Spanish, the same sound turns out to be simply a variant of the phoneme /d/ when it appears between two vowels. That sound in Spanish, therefore, is not a phoneme in its own right.

In the prewar work of the Prague school, notably Roman Jakobson and Count Nikolai Trubetzkoy (1939), phonological theory became the study of the phonetic differences between phonemes, enshrined as distinctive features. For example, the set /p t k/ is distinguished from /b d g/ by the one feature of voicing. The sound pattern of a language was thus based not on an inventory of phonemes, but the more abstract universal set of distinctive features with language-particular rules for combining them into 'bundles' representing individual sounds. This view of phonology remains highly influential, having been incorporated into generative phonology (Chomsky and Halle, 1968).

In the USA structuralism was dominated by the views of Bloomfield (1933). He advocated a behaviouristic approach to linguistics, eschewing appeal to mentalist constructs. American structuralism developed the *immediate constituent*, or *phrase structure* approach to syntax, by which sentence structure is conceived of as a set of nested phrases each ultimately consisting of words and then morphemes. Thus, the words of the sentence *Black cats chase furry mice* might be grouped into the following phrases, or constituents: [black cats], [furry mice] and [chase furry mice] to give [[black cats] [chase [furry mice]]].

A feature of later American structuralism was concern with 'discovery procedures': the claim was that linguistic analysis had to proceed mechanically from the phonology to morphology then syntax, without any 'mixing' of levels, so that, say, information about syntactic structure could not influence decisions about morphological structure.

Structuralism was rapidly replaced as the dominant approach to linguistics by the theory of generative grammar initiated by Noam Chomsky.

Chomsky (1957, 1965) rejected concern with 'discovery procedures' as methodologically unscientific, and argued that the goal of linguistic theory should be the explicit characterization of the tacit grammatical knowledge of the (idealized) native speaker. This knowledge is technically called 'competence', distinguished from actual language behaviour – 'performance' – typified by errors and imperfections of various sorts. To characterize such knowledge it is necessary to construct a grammar, a set of rules which when applied algorithmically will deliver all and only the well-formed ('grammatical') expressions of the language. Such a grammar is said to 'generate' the (expressions of the) language.

Chomsky (1957) provided a mathematical formalization of the immediate constituent approach to syntax, by developing the concept of a phrase structure grammar (psg). A psg is a set of rules for constructing phrases, generally visualized as tree diagrams representing the hierarchical structures implied by nested phrases. He offered theorems demonstrating that a psg is inadequate to describe English. He argued that syntactic theory should be able to characterize formally relationships such as that between the statement *The man who is visiting us is American* and the corresponding question *Is the man who is visiting us American?* This requires a more powerful analytical tool, the syntactic transformation. In crude terms this is a grammatical rule which moves, deletes or adds parts of syntactic trees. In the present case a transformation would move the second token of the verb *is* to the front of the sentence. A grammar so endowed is called a transformational grammar. The example is noteworthy because it shows that transformations have to appeal to structure, in this case the fact that the sequence *the man who is visiting us* is a phrase (functioning as the subject of the sentence). The occurrence of *is* inside this phrase cannot be fronted, showing that the transformation operates over more than just a string of words. In a later refinement (Chomsky, 1965) a psg generates basic sentence structures (called 'deep structures', a term frequently misunderstood to refer to language and not sentences) which are then modified by transformations.

Chomsky's approach to language is thoroughly mentalistic, as is clear from his famous refutation of Skinnerian behaviourism (Chomsky, 1959). Chomsky regards linguistics as a particularly important window on the human mind, arguing that human languages are unique among animal communication systems in permitting an unbounded set of messages using finite means (i.e. a finite vocabulary and a finite set of grammatical rules). He distinguished three types of 'adequacies': a grammar is *observationally adequate* if it generates all the right data and no wrong data (where 'data' means simply a string of words, morphemes, or phonemes); it is *descriptively adequate* if it generates the appropriate structural descriptions, that is, structures which are not inconsistent with what is known of the organization of the language or of languages in general (such as the 'correct' tree structure for a sentence); it is *explanatorily adequate* if it embodies an explanation of how such structures could be acquired by the infant language learner. Explanatory adequacy is the most important of these goals, superseding the others as a matter of pragmatic methodological fact (hence, a grammar which appears explanatory but gets some of the facts wrong should not necessarily be rejected if there are good grounds for supposing that future technical improvements would allow those facts to be accounted for). This move puts language acquisition at the forefront.

A prime research question for linguistics is the *logical problem of language acquisition*: how it is that children learn grammars rapidly and effortlessly, despite the formal complexity of the task. A related question is why any child can learn any language with roughly the same ease, despite the superficially unlimited grammatical differences between languages. The standard approach to this puzzle in generative grammar is to argue for universals, highly abstract organizational properties shared by all human languages. Further, these universals are assumed to be unconsciously and innately known by all humans, being ultimately part of the genetic endowment. Linguistic theory therefore has to formulate these universals and account for their interaction with language-particular properties.

A problem arises with the earlier approach to generative grammar, under which the object to be acquired by the child is a (rather complex) set of rules, for it turns out that such rule systems have formal (i.e. mathematical) properties rendering them difficult to learn. Latterly (Chomsky, 1981, 1986), the emphasis on rules is dropped and replaced by a conception of language acquisition as the growth of a kind of 'mental organ', the language faculty, on the basis of triggering experience gained from the utterances to which the learner is exposed. The child innately knows a set of universal principles governing human language grammars, but these principles are subject to systematic variation, giving rise to the differences in grammatical structure found in the world's languages, such as the basic word order, or whether the language permits omission of the subject of the sentence. This variation is referred to as 'parametrization' and learning a grammar is a question of fixing values for these parameters.

The most significant inroads into the study of word meaning have been motivated by philosophical discussion of the nature of reference, analytic and synthetic TRUTH, and the nature of 'natural kinds', essential properties and questions of DEFINITION. In particular, Putnam (1962) argues that since tigers have no essential properties, a word such as 'tiger' can only refer to a stereotype of tigerhood; the word itself escapes definition.

Sentence semantics is generally studied within the framework created by formal logicians such as G. Frege, Bertrand Russell, A. Tarski, R. Carnap. Linguistics has been especially influenced by the model theoretic approach of Richard Montague (1974). The central aim of such models is to specify conditions under which sentences express true or false propositions. A representative puzzle concerns the notion of truth itself confronted, say, with non-referring definite descriptions (such as Russell's 'the present king of France'). Can assertions predicated of such a (non-)entity be true or false, or do we have to say they bear some intermediate truth value? Considerable effort has been devoted to the semantics of quantifiers, words such as *all*, *some*, *every*.

Truth-based approaches to meaning have difficulty coping with functional aspects of language, such as asking questions or giving commands. These functions, or speech-acts, are the province of the burgeoning field of pragmatics. In addition, pragmatics deals with the way we convey implicit content in an utterance. For instance, in answer to the question 'Would you like a cup of coffee?' the reply 'Coffee always keeps me awake' could implicitly be taken as a refusal of the offer (or an acceptance, depending on the context). Likewise, a claim such as 'Your office looks as though a bomb has hit it' would (usually) be literally false, yet it would generally be interpreted not as a lie but as a hyperbole. In fact, most discourse deviates in these ways from strict assertion of truths. Linguists and philosophers of language such as J.L. Austin, John Searle, and especially Paul Grice (1975) have investigated these questions in detail. Grice argues that speakers respect certain conversational maxims such as 'speak what you believe to be the truth' or 'be relevant', but that these maxims can be broken for special effect. Thus an apparently irrelevant statement about coffee flouts the maxim governing relevance but when this flouting is interpreted as deliberate by the hearer, it can be used to convey implicit meaning. More recently, D. Sperber and D. Wilson (1986) have argued that the maxim of relevance, together with other assumptions about the way information is processed, will account for all the cases subsumed under Grice's original set, and on the basis of this propose a general account of utterance interpretation and cognition, the Theory of Relevance.

Reading
Anderson, S.R. 1985: *Phonology in the Twentieth Century*.
Atkinson, R.M. 1992: *Children's Syntax*.
Chomsky, N. 1980: *Rules and Representations*.
Culler, J. 1986: *Saussure*.
Lyons, J. 1977: *Semantics*, 2 vols.
Newmeyer, F.J. ed. 1988: *Linguistics: The Cambridge Survey*, 4 vols.
Partee, B.H., ter Meulen, A. and Wall, R. 1990: *Mathematical Methods in Linguistics*.
Piatelli-Palmarini, M. ed. 1980: *Language and Learning: The Debate between Jean Piaget and Noam Chomsky*.
Robins, R.H. 1979: *A Short History of Linguistics*.

ANDREW SPENCER

linguistics, socio-   *See* SOCIOLINGUISTICS

literature   All printed books in the unrestricted sense constitute 'literature'. But in more restricted usage it refers to a circumscribed body of imaginative writings within a given language, a nation, a period of time or more broadly as in the concept of 'world literature', which is deemed to be particularly worthy of esteem, for its formal beauty, its affective power, or the 'truths' it expresses.

Three broad types of definition recur in writings on literature: in terms of some distinguishing qualities of the literary text which mark it off from other kinds of writing; in terms of an aesthetic response on the part of the reader; and in terms of social function.

The Russian formalists of the early decades of the twentieth century sought the literary in writing which is instantly recognizable for its departure from everyday language (see FORMALISM). Ordinary language invites the reader to look through the words to their meanings and referents, while literary language is self-reflexive, pointing towards its own formal properties *as* language, and in so doing 'making strange' the reader's everyday understanding of the world. On this view the proper study of literary theory is the structure of literary *form*, its organization and its devices (Matejka and Pomorska, 1971).

However, specification of literature in terms of qualities intrinsic to the literary text has been found wanting because of the failure to yield a satisfactory demarcation between literature and other kinds of writing. No defining quality has yet been advanced which does not have the effect of excluding what is normally included, and vice versa. Thus the formalist emphasis on linguistic play and reflexivity would include jokes and even crossword puzzles, but would exclude realist literature. Finally the formalist approach does not register the selective, evaluative dimension of the term, which cuts across typologies of literary form, to make judgements of good and bad, sifting out those texts which deserve a place in literary history from those which will be excluded in spite of belonging to a literary genre of writing. Even in those approaches which eschew critical evaluation in favour of scholarship, such as that which prevailed in the Oxford English school (Bergonzi, 1990), there is a built-in critical judgement in the determination of worthy objects of scholarship.

The attempt to find the distinctive mark of literature in the aesthetic response produced by the text on the reader, or in the adoption of an aesthetic stance by the reader towards the text, does not succeed much better. For the aesthetic stance may be taken towards almost any kind of writing, and the aesthetic response may not always be produced in every reader, and may be produced in some readers by texts which are not normally identified as literature. But the part played by the reader in determining textual meanings has been a recurrent theme in twentieth-century literary theory, which has also seen the authority of the author fundamentally challenged in a number of approaches to literary interpretation. Reception theorists drawing on HERMENEUTICS (Iser, 1978; Fish, 1980) have given primacy to the moment of reading, underlining the plurality of meaning in literature: an emphasis shared from a very different theoretical perspective with the work of Barthes (1970).

Literature as a social practice
The third type of definition in terms of social functions points to literature as an institutionalized and historically variable social practice. The institutions of literature include those of the literary marketplace – publishing, bookselling, reviewing, the journals, literary prizes, coteries and so on (Sutherland, 1978). It constitutes what has been termed an art world (Becker, 1982), one which has been obliged to take its bearings in relation to another powerful institutional practice, that of education. The academy has played a more vital part in relation to the art world of twentieth-century literature than any other, because of the central place which the teaching of national literatures came to occupy within the curriculum (Mathieson, 1975).

The selection of texts worthy of inclusion on the curriculum involves a multiple process of definition. First, the literary tradition itself is selected, defined and perpetuated. Nothing more powerfully fixes a text within the literary canon than its inclusion as an object of study on a national educational curriculum. In Britain, the A-level text, and the texts studied in departments of literature in institutions of higher education together constitute the core of the literary canon. Roland Barthes's aphorism that literature is what gets taught has resonance here.

Secondly, because the selective process is an evaluative one, it defines literary good taste which is always rooted in social class. Familiarity with literature is part of what the French sociologist Pierre Bourdieu terms cultural capital (1979). Bourdieu argues that the class-related values of literature are transmitted across generations through selective access to the dominant literary culture, as a range of literary references is acquired. Others such as Raymond Williams (1977) and György Lukács (1970) locate literature in terms of class, but acknowledge functions and values which transcend these origins. There are popular traditions, too, which have spoken to the interests of the working-class reader: English writers such as Shakespeare, Milton, Bunyan, Dickens and Hardy. Such literature has been a staple of adult working-class education. Finally, the selection of a national literature through the process of selecting the literary canon plays a significant part in defining the nation (Doyle, 1989).

Marxist theories of literature

This embeddedness of literature within the educational institution means that it is an agent of SOCIALIZATION, and within Marxist terminology, IDEOLOGY – the production and reproduction of social power relations. But Williams argues that the *reduction* of literature to its ideological functions poses as many problems as it solves: 'the assimilation of "literature" to "ideology" ... was in practice little more than banging one inadequate concept against another' (1977, p. 52).

In fact there has been a marked resistance to such reductionism in the history of Marxist criticism. The Romantic belief in literature and art as enclaves of opposition to industrial capitalism was drawn on by Marxist humanists such as Lukács, whose aesthetic of realism was rooted in pre-Marxist left Romanticism. He located in great literature a repository of authentic human values and aspirations created during the bourgeoisie's period as a progressive historical class up to 1848, but which it was the historical task of socialism and the working class to realize.

For Lukács great literature itself stood in no need of radical transformation. This conservatism was challenged by Bertolt Brecht (1938) and in a different register by the writers of the FRANKFURT SCHOOL for whom an art capable of saying 'no' to capitalism and resisting its powers of co-option had to be uncompromisingly radical to the point of near-total inaccessibility. Theodor Adorno sought an art which was 'non-affirmative' in the avant-garde, and this has proved more attractive to modern Marxist theorists of literature than Lukács's espousal of nineteenth-century realism (Adorno, 1967).

But it was structuralism which was to transform mid-twentieth-century Marxism. Structuralist criticism, drawing on modern linguistics and on the work of the Russian formalists, analysed the meaning of each part of the work in terms of its place in the whole. Structuralists such as Roland Barthes, Tzvetan Todorov (1973) and Gérard Genette (1972) aspired to produce a 'science of the text'. But the structuralist appeal to the authority of science has been disallowed by poststructuralist and deconstructionist theorists such as Jacques Derrida (1967) and Michel Foucault (1969), who have refused any distinction between scientific and ideological discourse (see STRUCTURALISM; DISCOURSE; DECONSTRUCTION).

Deconstructionism can be understood as an attempt to live with the heady vertigo which results from such a thoroughgoing relativism. Its strategy is to look to the margins: to what a text refuses, disguises or finds it impossible to say. There is no doubt that this approach has been a most productive one in terms of textual analysis. The skilled deconstructionist produces unexpected readings 'against the grain' of the text, and a greater degree of consciousness of form in a whole range of writing outside of that which is usually counted as literature. But the success of deconstructionism depends on never standing still long enough to be in turn deconstructed: move like a butterfly, sting like a bee. The sophisticated literary producer responds by producing a knowing text designed to be deconstructed. A sophisticated game ensues within the confines of the literary critical academy and while its ground rules are very different from those of more familiar regimes of criticism, of the American New Criticism (Lentricchia, 1978) and English followers of F. R. Leavis (Mulhern, 1979), dismissed by these newer theories as 'humanist', it is no more able to place itself outside, above and untouched by the surrounding social world than was Romantic humanism.

Committed literature

Some interesting challenges within literary theory and practice have been made by members of groups who have been excluded or marginalized, or whose own writing has been denied recognition as literature. Typically, the history of literature has been combed for 'lost' works by members of marginal groups, and in the process, the dominant literary tradition has come under interrogation. Claims have been advanced which link alternative narrative strategies, styles of writing, and so on, to the situation and identity of the group, and these styles then acquire a moral and a political value. In the past it was most often REALISM that was thus valorized, in a call for 'more realistic' or 'positive' cultural images. But realism has fallen out of fashion, and many radical theorists since the late 1960s have identified it *with* the dominant culture, and aligned the writings of marginal groups with styles of writing which challenge and disrupt realism. Today if an affinity is claimed between a certain marginalized category of writer – lesbian, for example (Zimmerman, 1985), or black (Gates, 1984) – and a distinctive style of writing, it is likely to be with an experimental style (see MODERNISM AND POSTMODERNISM).

Literature in the twentieth century has oscillated between a practice which sets itself apart, and one which is deeply concerned about its own relationship to society and politics. Jean-Paul Sartre was the twentieth century's most famous exponent of commitment in literature (Sartre, 1948). Or more precisely, in prose: he excluded poetry which he classified with music. All (prose) writing, he argued, was a form of 'secondary action', with real effects. The man of letters must take sides, consciously placing his writing in the service of a freedom which was posited for Sartre in the very act of writing and reading. Only in a classless society would the optimal conditions for writing and reading in full freedom exist. Short of that, degrees of radical writerly commitment vary in different historical epochs. The detachment of the *fin de siècle* writer was impossible for Sartre's generation because it was profoundly 'situated' by the experience of war. Because the conscious commitment of the writer must always be to freedom, the committed writer was placed on the side of the worker, the colonial subject, the racially oppressed group (see EXISTENTIALISM).

Writing from the margins
Under the impact of theories which have questioned the status of literature, interest has been directed towards a wider range of written forms, including working-class autobiography (Vincent, 1981). But outside the adult education context, the relationship of the working class to the literary text has been largely one of exclusion. René Balibar (1974) argues that in France, the level of educational attainment determines differential linguistic skills. Familiarity with literary French differentiates the higher levels to which few working-class children gain access. Thus literary French plays its part in reproducing the social and cultural relationships of class.

The relationship of (white middle-class) women to literature has also been analysed in terms of women's relationships to language and writing. American 'gynocriticism' – the study of women's texts in an attempt to identify a 'female' aesthetic – has stressed the difficulties which women faced when they attempted the pen in Victorian England

and America (Showalter, 1978; Gilbert and Gubar, 1979). It is an approach which characterizes the dominant culture as a male-produced one which denies women their subjectivity, so that in taking up the pen, women took on those alien cultural subjectivities.

'Gynocriticism' locates the separation of public and private spheres in the Victorian period as a major cause of the difficulty faced by women taking on the identity of the professional writer, over and above the marginalization of the feminine in language and culture. The new French feminism from the 1970s has little interest in the social circumstances under which women wrote, but shares gynocriticism's identification of the feminine in language and culture as marginal, although the understanding of language is more rigorous and theoretical (Marks and Courtivron, 1980; Moi, 1987). Julia Kristeva, Luce Irigaray (1974) and Hélène Cixous drew on Jacques Lacan's reworking of Freudian psychoanalysis (Lacan, ed. Mitchell and Rose, *1982*). Unlike the American critics, they refused validity to any search for women's *identity* in writing. For Cixous and Kristeva, 'woman' cannot be defined. Human subjectivity is produced in language and culture, and is always *in process*, never fixed (Cixous, 1975, 1976; Kristeva, 1986). The concern was less with women's writing than with what Cixous termed *écriture féminine*: a fluid, motile, playful form of writing. *Ecriture féminine*, like Kristeva's 'semiotic', is not exclusive to women writers, and, notoriously, these theorists have actually paid more attention to male-authored texts. Writing is identified as 'feminine' only in so far as both 'the semiotic' and the feminine are marginal to language and culture.

While American and French feminist criticism have very different theoretical roots, then, the former has proved open to the influence of the latter in a manner parallel to the way in which Derridean deconstructionism has crossed the Atlantic (de Man, 1979), and a synthesis has occurred (Jardine, 1985). Curiously, the marginality of 'woman' and the feminine in language and culture has been transformed into an advantage under the influence of the French feminism, for it is prestigious avant-garde, modernist and postmodernist forms which have been claimed as feminine forms.

What is absent from both terms of the synthesis is the identification and location of literature within a material and historically specific context. For the French feminists, writing which disrupts the structures of 'phallogocentric' language is in itself revolutionary, and an association is generated between such avant-garde writing and a variety of marginalized 'others' within society and culture – women, ethnic minorities, the Third World, the working class.

Yet the relationship of (white middle-class) women to literature and writing generally is very different from that of working-class men and women. Gender structures the relationship to writing and reading in a manner different from class. In the schoolroom, little girls have found themselves at home: 'The primary school celebrates the qualities that bind women; but this celebration does not put little girls at an *educational* disadvantage. In fact, as any confirmation of the known self will, it actually aids the learning process' (Steedman, 1982, p. 4). Verbal and literary skills have traditionally been expected and rewarded in girls and thereby reinforced. Sex *per se*, then, has not been a barrier to writing and reading in quite the same way as class, and women have been and remain key, if subordinate, actors in the process of the transmission of literary culture (Lovell, 1987). Ellen Moers (1978) drew attention to the ways in which, as mothers with the responsibility for the cultivation of the minds of young children, as teachers and as governesses, women might write with considerable authority. This authority from within the dominant culture may be linked to women's close association with the rise of the novel as a form (Spencer, 1986; Armstrong, 1987).

The relationship of black writers to the institutions of literary production and consumption adds further complexity, since black writing is gendered, and vice versa. The label 'black', like that of 'Third World', places together people whose only common cultural attributes may stem from the racialism or the imperialist domination they jointly and severally suffer. This label has nevertheless been consciously chosen in a historically important political act of oppositional solidarity in the United States and elsewhere (Gates, 1984; Spivak, 1988; Said, 1983).

Black and feminist criticism have interesting parallels and divergences. Even before the development of theories which made identity politics so problematic, there was less likelihood of black criticism slipping into ahistorical forms of essentialism. Critics such as Edwards (1984) who have discerned continuities between African and Afro-American and Caribbean literature are clear that these are cultural, and that common attributes of black literature, variously identified in figuration (Gates, 1984), in antiphony (Bowen, 1982) or in 'a topos of (un)naming' (Benston, 1984), are a function of cultural and social positioning. That positioning has produced, typically, a literature which is 'double-voiced', argues Gates, drawing upon, and speaking within, more than one cultural tradition. Black criticism has argued for the reinstatement of black vernacular and oral traditions as points of reference in criticism of black writings, in addition to the dominant European forms. But as with 'women's writing', the effect of poststructuralism and deconstructionism has been to push black criticism towards consciousness of difference and diversity rather than identity.

Reading
Bennett, Tony 1979: *Formalism and Marxism.*
Bloch, Ernst et al. 1977: *Aesthetics and Politics.*
Eagleton, Terry 1983: *Literary Theory: An Introduction.*
Gates, Henry Louis Jr, ed. 1984: *Black Literature and Literary Theory.*
Jameson, Frederic 1972: *The Prison-House of Language.*
Lodge, David ed. 1988: *Modern Criticism and Theory: A Reader.*
Seldon, Raman 1989: *Practising Theory and Reading Literature: An Introduction.*
Showalter, Elaine ed. 1986: *The New Feminist Criticism: Essays on Women, Literature and Theory.*
Williams, Raymond 1983: *Writing in Society.*

TERRY LOVELL

logic This is an old discipline. As it was conceived by its founder, Aristotle, in the fourth century BC, logic was not a 'theoretical' science, such as mathematics or physics, but a 'poietic' science, an *organon* or an instrument for science, which would set the criteria for proper scientific thinking. Aristotle also called 'logic' a more restricted inquiry into the nature of deductive arguments (where conclusions follow 'necessarily' from the premises), which came to be known as logic proper, by opposition to the idea of 'logic' in the broad sense of an enquiry into the nature and method of knowledge in general. Arguments which display this feature, for Aristotle, are syllogistic arguments, involving affirmative or negative propositions of subject and predicate form, quantified with such expressions as 'all' and 'some'. Syllogistics is the systematic study of these arguments and of the means of proving their valid forms, through various 'figures' and 'modes', or patterns of premisses and conclusions. Traditional logic, or the logic of terms, dominated the *curriculum* during the Middle Ages, and has been refined through the centuries, without any major changes. The place of logic in the THEORY OF KNOWLEDGE has been contested from the sixteenth century onwards, when the advent of modern science made dubious its use for the discovery and systematization of scientific truths. The renewal of the discipline came in the nineteenth century, when mathematicians such as George Boole (in his *Laws of Thought*, 1854) attempted to derive the laws of syllogistic logic from the laws of algebra (an attempt foreshadowed by Leibniz). But the advent of modern logic dates from G. Frege's *Begriffsschrift* (1879), where for the first time the traditional subject–predicate form of the proposition was replaced by the mathematical distinction of argument and function, yielding a new analysis of quantificational expressions which could account for a greater number of inferences than traditional logic, and in particular for the expression of mathematical concepts, such as the concept of number. Frege, and soon afterwards Bertrand Russell, attempted a derivation of mathematical concepts from logical axioms, according to the view known as 'logicism', which was codified in Russell and Whitehead's *Principia Mathematica* (1910–11). The logicist programme, however, proved difficult to carry out: Russell discovered a contradiction in Frege's system ('Russell's paradox'), and his own theory of 'logical types', framed to avoid the contradiction, was not sufficient to allow the derivation of mathematics from purely logical laws. One of the main features of Frege's and Russell's logic is that logic is 'universal' (van Heijenoort, 1967): it is a 'language' which expresses all that there is, and not a 'calculus', in which the relations between symbolism and the world, or relations within the symbolism, can be represented explicitly. On the contrary, logicians from the 1920s onward raised metasystematic questions, and the distinction between proof theory and semantics emerged. David Hilbert and his school attempted to prove the consistency of arithmetic by characterizing logic only in terms of axioms and rules of inferences of 'proof theory', without using semantic notions such as truth and validity (this view is known as 'formalism'). The main notion of modern logic is that of a formal system, composed of a vocabulary of primitive expressions, of a deductive apparatus of axioms and/or rules of inferences, and of a semantics, establishing the interpretations of the primitive expressions. The precise formalization of a semantics, as a theory of truth for formal languages, was given by Tarski (1930). In 1930, Gödel proved the completeness of the main part of modern logic, quantification theory, establishing the coincidence of the proof–theoretic and of the semantic concept of deduction. In 1931, he proved his celebrated incompleteness theorem for elementary number theory, according to which the consistency of arithmetic cannot be demonstrated. This ruined the hopes of Hilbert's programme, but opened the path for new developments in metamathematics and in the foundations of mathematics, either from the proof–theoretical or from the semantical (model–theoretical) point of view. Another major achievement of contemporary logic is the study of recursive functions and computability, which, with writers such as Emile Post, Alonzo Church and Allan Turing, was to give rise in the 1940s to the theory of algorithms and automata, and to the birth of computer science.

Although modern logic could not deliver its foundational promise for mathematics, philosophers were quick to appreciate its relevance for the theory of knowledge and the PHILOSOPHY OF SCIENCE, and attempted to treat logic as a new *organon*. Frege, Russell, and later the Viennese school of positivism showed how logic could help to reformulate the Kantian problem of *a priori* truth. Ludwig Wittgenstein's *Tractatus logico-philosophicus* (1921) assimilated logical truths to tautologies, which say nothing about the world, in opposition to statements describing facts. This led to the formulation of the logical empiricist criterion of meaning, according to which a statement is meaningful only if it is true from the meaning of its terms alone (analytic) or if it can be verified by its relation to experience, or if it can be deduced from empirical statements alone. This is known as the 'linguistic' theory of logical truths, for logical statements are, on this view, true by linguistic conventions alone. According to the positivist philosophy of science of writers such as Carnap, Schlick, or Reichenbach, logic serves not only to demarcate empirical from non-empirical science, but also to provide criteria for the analysis of scientific theories (see also POSITIVISM). On the classical neo-positivist view, a scientific theory has a dual structure: it is composed of a (partially interpreted) 'theoretical vocabulary', consisting in fundamental laws having an axiomatic or postulational status from which theorems or empirical predictions are derived, and of an 'observational vocabulary' consisting in verifiable terms. The two languages are related by 'correspondence rules' which allow us to interpret empirically the axioms or postulates. But the positivist ideal of the complete replacement of the theoretical language by this pure observational language of empirical predictions from the axioms could never be realized, for it was soon admitted that theoretical terms could not be eliminated through any logical procedure. Rudolf Carnap himself never renounced his project of giving a purely logical analysis of the language of science, and of formulating a sharp distinction between analytic and synthetic statements. In his *Logical Foundations of Probability* (1950), he sought to define induction on a purely logical basis. But these positivist hopes have proved impossible to realize. On the one hand, the analytic/synthetic distinction and the theory of meaning upon which it rests have been made dubious by W.V.O. Quine's criticism (1952), and the conventionalist doctrine of logical truth has been accordingly contested. On the other hand, the idea of giving an algorithm for scientific method, in the form of a 'logic of confirmation' or of induction, encounters difficulties so great (Goodman, 1955) that the realizability of the programme appears virtually impossible.

The failure of the positivists' hopes in the theory of knowledge does not imply, however, that logic ceases to play a role in the framing of hypotheses about the nature of cognitive rationality or of the rationality of action. This role is mainly normative, in the sense that logic sets certain standards of interpretation of human behaviour, without which this behaviour cannot be interpreted at all. The main question is whether these norms can be absolute, or whether they are mainly relative. From the beginning of the twentieth century, logicians have had an increased interest in the construction of non-classical logics such as modal, intuitionistic, quantum, relevance, three-valued logics, and so on, which all rest on various departures from classical logical principles, such as bivalence, excluded middle, or extensionality. According to the doctrine known as 'absolutism' (which was typically Frege's and Russell's), there is only one logic, applicable to all forms of discourse or areas of inquiry, and 'deviant' or 'non-classical' logics are

not really *logics*. According to the opposite doctrine known as RELATIVISM, there are as many legitimate logics as there are areas of discourse susceptible of being studied from the point of view of the inferences that they license.

This problem of the variety of the canons of inference describable as 'logics' is manifest in many domains, such as linguistic semantics, where the complexity of natural language seems to validate a variety of formal logical models applicable to its fragments (McCawley, 1981). It is also central in psychology, where the question has been asked whether human beings 'follow' the laws of logic, and in this sense are rational. According to the doctrine of 'mental logic', human logical competence owes its characteristics to an innate (or acquired – Piaget and Inhelder, 1955) medium encoded in the brain in the form of inference rules. But the fact that human beings make logical mistakes, and moreover systematic ones (Kahneman et al., 1982; Wason 1968), renders this doctrine dubious. Some writers prefer to renounce the mental logic hypothesis, and try to account for reasoning without rules framed according to standard logical calculi (Johnson-Laird, 1983). The standard objection to the normative character of logic is that most human reasoning does not conform to the ideal standards of rationality set by the norms of ordinary classical logic. Some writers (Stich, 1985; Nisbett and Ross, 1980) prefer to conclude that the evaluation of the rationality of human beings is an empirical matter. Others (Cohen, 1986) want to keep logic's normative status as an ideal theory of human competence, which can nevertheless be revised according to a 'reflective equilibrium method' comparable to John Rawls's (1971) similar conception of the revision of moral normative standards. Similar problems can be encountered in ARTIFICIAL INTELLIGENCE, since AI systems are built according to certain logical inference rules, which simulate natural intelligent performances only to a degree. Most AI researchers find here that classical deductive logic is of little use, and have widely used non-classical logics (in particular non-monotonic logic – Turner, 1984).

In the social sciences, the normative role of logic can be considered from two standpoints. The first is the framing of hypotheses about the rationality of action, according to the standards of game, decision and utility theories (von Neumann and Morgenstern, 1944; Jeffrey, 1965). In their normative part, the logic of decision and the logic of preference set out standards of ideal rationality, which have been used, in particular by economists, to define optimality models of rational behaviour. The descriptive adequacy of these models has been contested, and a theory of 'limited' or 'bounded' rationality (Simon, 1957) has been proposed to deal with the more 'real life' situations of individual and collective choice. The notorious paradoxes of decision theory (prisoner's dilemma, Newcomb's problem) serve here as instruments for the framing, testing and revisions of the general hypotheses of rationality embedded in the standard models. Here the role of a logic of individual or of collective action is not to impose strict standards or schemes of explanations, but to allow the study of the departures from these standards. In particular a study of the irrationality of individual and collective behaviour can come out from the analysis of different criteria of rationality (Elster, 1983).

The second standpoint is the anthropological study of the meanings of cultural beliefs. In anthropology, the rationalistic attitude of writers such as Lucien Lévy-Bruhl who attributed to primitive societies a 'pre-logical' mentality has been widely challenged by a cross-cultural relativism according to which rationality and logicity are only relative to schemes of understanding proper to given cultures. For philosophers like Quine (1960), such debates can only be evaluated in the context of a proper theory of translation and meaning. But the study of our criteria of translation shows that neither full-blown rationalism nor relativism can be consistently maintained: in devising a translation manual for an unknown language we need to rely on the general hypothesis ('principle of charity') that their speakers are on the whole rational, consistent, and do not hold contradictory beliefs. In this sense 'prelogicity is a trait infused by bad translators' (Quine). But relativism (and in particular linguistic relativism) also fails, for the very coherence of the claim that there can be people having radically different 'conceptual schemes' from our own presupposes that we can impose a common set of coordinates (a general presumption of rationality and coherence) in order to assess cultural divergence (Davidson, 1974). This does not mean that cultural divergences cannot be assessed on psychological and sociological grounds, but that they can be assessed only within certain limits. In this sense too, logic sets certain minimal constraints on a theory of human rationality.

See also RATIONALITY AND REASON

Reading
Cohen, L.J. 1986: *The Claims of Reason.*
Elster, J. 1983: *Sour Grapes: Studies in the Subversion of Rationality.*
McCawley, J.D. 1981: *Everything that Linguists Have Always Wanted to Know about Logic.*
Stich, S. 1985: Is man a rational animal? Notes on the epistemology of rationality, *Synthèse*, 64, 115–35.

PASCAL ENGEL

long waves   The popularity of long waves as a topic in economic theory exhibits a cyclical pattern. Since the beginning of the 1980s more empirical studies and theoretical analysis have been devoted to long waves than in the other years after World War II. This implies not only a return to the supply-side aspects of the economy, partly as a reaction to the long-standing emphasis on Keynesian demand-oriented views, but expresses also the remarkable turn-around in economic activity, entrepreneurial initiative and technical change.

The role the theory of long waves nowadays plays in economic discussions also goes along with what can be called the revival of Schumpeter. While most of the present century has seen Keynes on the pedestal of economic science, the last part has brought a reevaluation and deeper understanding of J. A. Schumpeter's writings and contributions to economic science. In particular, his emphasis on the role of the entrepreneur, combined with the process of innovation, has received much more attention and praise than in the past. In his view the idea of economic cycles with a period of 40 or 50 years is related to the emergence of a burst of major innovations which are at the start of a long-run upswing in economic life. Nowadays, one could think in this respect of information technology as a source for a long-standing upswing through the interlinked processes of diffusion, further innovation and imitation (see also INFORMATION TECHNOLOGY AND THEORY).

Schumpeter revived the discussion of long waves in the 1930s, but it did not start with him. Two Dutch economists, J. van Gelderen and S. de Wolff are both well known for their theoretical and statistical work on long waves. They really discovered the phenomenon, but in the literature it is mostly the Russian economist N. D. Kondratiev who is credited with the discovery. The main

A long-wave chronology

1st Kondratiev	2nd Kondratiev	3rd Kondratiev	4th Kondratiev
prosperity 1782–1792	prosperity 1845–1857	prosperity 1892–1903	prosperity 1948–1957
prosperity 1792–1802	prosperity 1857–1866	prosperity 1903–1913	prosperity 1957–1966
(war 1802–1815)		(war 1913–1920)	
recession 1815–1825	recession 1866–1873	recession 1920–1929	recession 1966–1973
depression 1825–1836	depression 1873–1883	depression 1929–1937	
recovery 1836–1845	recovery 1883–1892	recovery 1937–1948	

Source: J.J. van Duijn, Chapter 20, in S.K. Kuipers and G.J. Lanjouw, eds, *Prospects of Economic Growth* (Amsterdam, North-Holland, 1980), pp. 223–33.

question is, of course, whether one can depict one cause that produces long waves. In the beginning price fluctuations were related to changes in the total stock of gold. However, as new discoveries of gold-fields are a matter of chance, this can not be a very convincing approach. A more advanced approach can be seen in the theories that relate waves to movements in investment and, in particular, investment for replacement. S. de Wolff introduced, in this respect, the so-called echo principle.

Nowadays, the most important theory about long waves is cast in terms of innovations. Modern authors who are inclined to relate the long wave fluctuations in innovations over time are J. J. van Duijn and C. Freeman. Van Duijn presents in his book (1983) the scheme shown here for the long waves. According to this scheme, we have been since the beginning of the 1980s in a period of recovery. In this respect information technology has played and is still playing a major role. Freeman has stressed several times the interaction between the diffusion of new technologies and institutional changes in society. The idea, going back to Schumpeter, is that innovations come in bursts and spread over the economy, provoking imitation and preparing the ground for a booming economy.

In conclusion, of all possible explanations of long waves the cyclical pattern of innovations seems to be the most promising, but whether even this factor is at the basis of a systematic pattern over such a long period of time remains doubtful.

See also BUSINESS CYCLE.

Reading
Freeman, C. ed. 1984: *Long Waves in the World Economy.*
Van Duijn, J.J. 1983: *The Long Wave in Economic Life.*

ARNOLD HEERTJE

M

management science Management science
may be defined as the application of scientific
method and analytical reasoning to the decision-
making process of executives in the control of
business and industrial systems for which they are
responsible. These systems may involve specific
manufacturing, service or administrative operations, whole departments or plants, or even
complete enterprises.

An important characteristic of management
scientists is their endeavour to approach managerial
problems with the same kind of objectivity that is
expected from pure scientists in their studies of
physical phenomena. The application of the scientific method implies the need for data collection,
critical analysis of the assembled evidence, formulation of hypotheses used to construct models of
behaviour of the systems under scrutiny, specification of criteria for measurement of variables that
affect the performance of these systems, design of
experiments (where appropriate), prediction of
future outcomes, and testing the validity and
robustness of proposed hypotheses and models. In
the context of management science (MS) this
process also involves recommending courses of
action for executives to consider for implementation, and finally analysing the effect of managerial
decisions through measurement and feedback, for
the purpose of modifying and refining existing
models (or replacing them) and helping to improve
future decision-making and system performance.

It is difficult to pinpoint any date for the first
application of this methodology in the managerial
arena. Jethro's advice to Moses to delegate authority through a hierarchical structure for dealing with
cases that needed adjudication may be cited as one
of the early examples of applying logic to administrative problems (Exodus 18). Some point to an
investigation by Lanchester, published in 1916,
into the effect of military forces thrown into combat
as the first mathematical modelling exercise in the
study of warfare. Indeed, since problems of organization, strategy and logistics have always figured

prominently in the conduct of war, it may be argued
that MS, albeit not under that name, has been
around as long as humanity.

Most students of the subject, though, attribute
the rise of MS to the emergence of Operational
Research (OR) and the term OR/MS was then
coined to cover both. OR started in the UK in the
late 1930s and then expanded rapidly during World
War II both in the UK and the USA (where this
activity is called Operations Research) in order to
assist in the conduct of military operations (hence
the name). After the war, many scientists engaged
in military OR turned their attention to civilian
applications and many OR groups were formed in
industry and government departments on both
sides of the Atlantic in the 1950s and 1960s.

Industrial applications of OR/MS were first
concentrated on production and inventory control
in manufacturing industry, but in the last 25 years
these activities have spread to cover many other
functions of business, such as marketing, distribution, finance, manpower, project management, and
any other activity that involves allocation of scarce
resources. OR/MS has now penetrated almost
every sector of industry and business, including
service industries such as banking, fund management, insurance, health, education, transport, commerce and many others.

Essentially, there is no difference between the
definitions of OR and MS and the two terms have
developed side by side through the accident of
history. The first OR Society (ORS) was formed in
the UK in 1950, followed by the Operations
Research Society of America (ORSA) in 1952. OR
was then developed and taught at many universities, first at the graduate level, either as an adjunct
to industrial engineering and other academic programmes or as a discipline in its own right, leading
to a master's degree, and then it began to infiltrate
various undergraduate programmes. The highly
mathematical nature of academic OR and the
development of its analytical techniques have led to
the literature being dominated by theoretical expo-

sitions and many feared that applications in the real world and the potential contribution of OR to the solution of managerial problems would thereby be inhibited (a fear that is still widely held today). It is partly for this reason that The Institute of Management Sciences (TIMS) was established in 1953 in an attempt to emphasize the need for applications and implementation. Its proclaimed objectives are 'to identify, extend and unify scientific knowledge that contributes to the understanding and practice of management'.

In practice, though, there is not much to distinguish between ORSA and TIMS, which have a noticeable overlap of membership. The term OR/MS has become widely used to indicate the close affinity and relationship between the two societies and to indicate that OR and MS may be regarded as interchangeable labels, though many analysts still feel that the OR literature, particularly in the USA, has continued to be obsessed with theory and that a gulf has developed between OR theory and MS in practice.

The literature and many academic programmes often highlight certain analytical tools that are said to be the hallmarks of OR, such as probability theory and statistical methods, calculus of variations, linear and non-linear programming, dynamic programming, combinatorial analysis and scheduling, queuing theory, the theory of games, network analysis, and allied techniques. Such descriptors tend to characterize OR as a highly mathematical occupation (some academics in the USA even suggest that OR is merely a branch of applied mathematics). This picture is an unfortunate distortion of reality. In practice, formal techniques play a very small part in OR/MS investigations, which by their nature have to start with real problems that demand solutions and not with a toolkit in search of situations to which it can be applied. Even techniques such as linear and mathematical programming, which dominate the literature, cannot be said to be in common use in business and industry (with the notable exception of the oil and chemical industries), and as for queuing theory, its elaborate and convoluted models have been largely bypassed through the use of computer simulation.

The complex nature of industrial and business enterprises, which have to operate under severe competition and under many constraints, demands that managerial decisions have to rely increasingly on analysis of information and on the formulation of strategy based on scientific modelling. This is where MS, assisted by the phenomenal growth of computing power in recent years, has an important contribution to make.

See also DECISION THEORY; GAME THEORY.

Reading
Dennis, T.L. and Dennis, L.B. 1991: *Management Science*.
Eilon S. 1985: *Management Assertions and Aversions*.
——1992: *Management Practice and Mispractice*.
Hillier, F.S. and Lieberman, G.J. 1986: *Introduction to Operations Research*.

SAMUEL EILON

managerial revolution Referring in its most general sense to the process through which ownership and control in industry is supposed to have passed from entrepreneurs and family owners to professional, salaried managers, the term has also been used to refer to changes in the class basis of political rule. In this latter sense, it is the process through which a ruling capitalist class is replaced by a new ruling class of financial and technical managers.

The earliest formulation of the general thesis of the managerial revolution in industry can be found in the work of Berle and Means (1932). This book grew out of a concern in American liberal circles about the industrial power exercised by New York bankers. This concern has been expressed in the idea of a 'money trust' through which financiers such as J. P. Morgan were held to control industry on the basis of extensive shareholdings, loans and interlocking directorships. Adolf Berle, a corporate lawyer, and Gardiner Means, an economist, were more sanguine about this, seeing it as a mere phase in the move away from traditional owner control and towards a system of 'management control' in which business activities could more easily be harnessed to the public interest. In 1933, Roosevelt initiated his New Deal of economic and social policies aimed at overcoming the economic problems ushered in by the financial collapse of 1929. Berle was recruited to the 'brain trust' – a presidential think tank which came up with many policy ideas for Roosevelt. In this way, the thesis of the managerial revolution came to have a significant impact on official and business thinking in the United States.

Berle and Means held that the increasing scale of business enterprise meant that companies would have to draw on wider pools of capital in order to finance their activities. As a result, the ownership of company shares would become ever more widely dispersed. The owners of a company would own a diminishing percentage of the company's shares and would no longer be able to exercise the kind of control that was possible when they had personal ownership of the whole undertaking. They could initially exercise 'majority control', but when their shareholding fell below 50 per cent they could exercise only 'minority control'. Eventually, their holdings would become so small that they would be swamped by the mass of small shareholders. In this situation, the capital is subscribed by a large number of individuals, each with a very small percentage of the total, and no shareholder has sufficient shares to exercise control over the company. The top executives and directors – the 'management' – are no longer constrained by the interests of their shareholders and 'management control' has been achieved.

The work of James Burnham (1941) gave a more radical slant to this argument, seeing it as the basis for the rise to power of a new ruling class. Burnham argued that the growth of business enterprise was more than a mere matter of increasing scale. There was also an increasing technical complexity of the means of production, and Burnham argued that control over industry was passing away from the groups dependent on the framework of private property and profitability (shareholders and financiers) to those who have the necessary skills and knowledge to run the new means of production. Organizational skills and technical knowledge were the bases of managerial power. Burnham saw the knowledge base of managers as expressed in the new MANAGEMENT SCIENCE. The power of the managers in industry gives them a leading role in society as the agents of an evolving system of state ownership – their power in industry is matched by the growing power of 'managers' in the state. The vast and complex bureaucracies of the modern state, he argued, required skilled administrators who would increasingly supplant elected politicians. The managerial revolution, therefore, was the process through which managers in industry and the state consolidated their power and became a new ruling class. Burnham, writing in the 1940s, felt that this had been achieved in the Soviet Union, fascist Italy and Nazi Germany. Britain and the United States, he argued, would soon follow in the same direction.

In the postwar period, Burnham's thesis was especially influential among analysts of the emergent communist states, finding its expression in various views of 'totalitarianism' and in Djilas's (1957) notion of the new bureaucratic class of Eastern Europe. Among writers on Western capitalism, however, it was the formulation of Berle and Means that was most influential. This view was, however, allied with a claim that the managerial revolution was transforming industrial society and was creating a new society in which there would be no class divisions. The managers, as seen by writers as varied as Bell (1961) and Galbraith (1967), were merely the current occupants of positions in an open and meritocratic system. High rates of social mobility ensured that they did not form a closed social class, and their insulation from the demands of property and profit ensured that they acted in the general social interest. This view of POSTINDUSTRIAL SOCIETY became for much of the 1950s and 1960s the leading sociological perspective on modern society.

The thesis of the managerial revolution, as expressed in theories of postindustrial society, has been subject to considerable criticism during the last 20 years. The belief that shareholding was becoming irrelevant to control has been shown to be unfounded. The situation observed by Berle and Means in the early 1930s was, at best, a short-lived, transitional period. Since that time there has been a massive growth in share ownership by financial institutions – banks, insurance companies and pension funds. Shareholding has become more concentrated, not more dispersed. This has enhanced the power of the directors of the major financial institutions, who comprise an 'inner circle' of business leaders (Zeitlin, 1989; Useem, 1984). Research has also suggested that the evolutionism and inevitabilism of the managerialist position must be questioned and that more attention should be given to variations between countries in their experience of business development (Scott, 1985).

Reading
Berle, A.A. and Means, G.C. 1932: *The Modern Corporation and Private Property.*
Burnham, J. 1941: *The Managerial Revolution.*
Florence, P.S. 1951: *Ownership, Control and Success of Large Companies.*
Gordon, D. 1945: *Business Leadership in Large Corporations.*
Herman, E.O. 1981: *Corporate Control, Corporate Power.*
Mintz, B. and Schwartz, M. 1985: *The Power Structure of American Business.*

Scott, J.P. 1985: *Corporations, Classes, and Capitalism*, 2nd edn.

——1986: *Capitalist Property and Financial Power*.

Useem, M. 1984: *The Inner Circle*.

Zeitlin, M.R. 1989: *The Large Corporation and Contemporary Classes*.

JOHN SCOTT

Maoism This term refers to the revolutionary thought and practice of Mao Zedong (1893–1976), who spearheaded the victory in 1949 of a peasant-based communist revolution in China, resulting in the creation of the People's Republic, and then guided the development of the new state for most of its first 25 years of existence. Maoism therefore encompasses two aspects: firstly, Mao Zedong's unique strategy of protracted revolution in an economically backward country beset by foreign imperialism, relying on rural base areas and a peasant Red Army, and, secondly, his attempt to promote a 'Chinese road to socialism' once political power had been achieved after 1949. The former aspect provided inspiration for radical leaders of the THIRD WORLD in the 1950s and 1960s, struggling to achieve national independence from their present or former colonial masters and their internal allies (see COLONIAL LIBERATION MOVEMENT); while the latter aspect aroused the admiration of Western radicals, particularly in the 1960s.

Mao Zedong, who came from a well-to-do peasant family and who had received a secondary education, was one of the founding members of the Chinese Communist Party (CCP) in 1921. Between 1923 and 1927, in line with Moscow's advice that fledgling communist parties in the colonized world forge alliances with bourgeois nationalist parties, the CCP entered into a united front with the much larger Nationalist Party (Guomindang) of Sun Yatsen, whose aim was to defeat the militarists and reunify the country. It was during this period that Mao, in contrast to most of the CCP leadership, began to emphasize the importance of the peasantry in the revolution. In arguing that it was the 'semi-feudal' landlord system on which warlords and foreign imperialism depended, Mao attempted to shift the focus of the revolution from the cities to the countryside. He criticized the timidity of the party leadership for its negative attitude towards peasant 'excesses' and insisted that a mobilized peasantry (with or without party leadership) could sweep away all reactionary forces (Day, 1975, pp. 339–47).

When the United Front broke down in 1927 and the CCP leadership went underground in Shanghai, Mao retreated to the countryside and began the process of establishing a rural base and creating a Red Army, recruited from among poor peasants, agricultural labourers, vagrants, and even former bandits. Reflecting the voluntarist aspect of his thinking, Mao insisted that such a Red Army, its class origins notwithstanding, would become 'proletarianized' through the act of revolution itself. The party leadership, still assuming that the revolution would emerge from among the ranks of the urban working class, criticized Mao's 'peasant mentality' and his 'petit bourgeois military adventurism'. The failure of a series of armed attacks on the cities in 1927–30, however, only convinced Mao that the revolution would need to be a protracted one in which rural base areas would eventually surround the cities.

During the early 1930s, in the rural soviet he established in the southern province of Jiangxi, Mao formulated his theories of GUERRILLA warfare and underlined the need for close links between the army and people; stressed the leading role of poor peasant associations in the villages while at the same time emphasizing the necessity of winning over middle peasants (those who owned the land they cultivated) and of adopting a flexible attitude towards rich peasants; and exhorted cadres to remain in close touch with grass roots opinion, a leadership approach later defined in 1943 as the 'mass line'.

In criticizing the dogmatic approach of Moscow-trained rivals, and asserting his ideological as well as military and political leadership, Mao referred to the 'Sinification of Marxism', the need to adapt Marxism to Chinese conditions. The concept played a significant role in the rectification campaign Mao launched in 1942 to confirm his ideological leadership of the party (as well as reflecting Mao's determination to assert the CCP's independence from Moscow). The campaign also illustrated the Maoist emphasis on ideological remoulding, a process of small-group study and self-criticism to bring about changes in subjective attitudes and work style. Excessive formalism and bureaucratism were condemned and higher-level party cadres were urged to 'go down to the countryside (*xiafang*) to work and live among the peasants. At the same time, the campaign called for greater central discipline over party members. Local initiative was always to be balanced by control from the centre, what Mao called 'democratic centralism'. Writers, too, were now expected to be subject to closer party supervision, reflecting Mao's lifelong ambivalence towards intellectuals.

In order to meet the Japanese threat and to combat the economic blockade imposed on his Yanan base area by the Guomindang (the second united front had broken down by 1940) Mao emphasized self-reliance (which implied local economic initiative) and the need to mobilize the entire population in a genuine 'people's war'. Mao in his later years was to hark back wistfully to the 'Yanan spirit', which for him became associated with ideological commitment, egalitarian ideals and the close links forged between party and people.

The CCP constitution of 1945 officially proclaimed Mao's thought as the guide to party action. This was accompanied by the development of a Maoist cult, which sought to elevate his persona and ideas above those of his colleagues (Wylie, 1980). With communist forces from the rural hinterland poised to take over the Guomindang-held cities in the civil war of the late 1940s, CCP leaders also hailed the Maoist strategy of protracted rural revolution as a model for the colonized regions of Asia and Africa, thus implying that the Soviet Union should not be regarded as the only source of guidance for world communist movements.

Many of the features of Maoism as it had developed to 1949, such as the populist faith in the rural masses (see POPULISM), the voluntarist emphasis on the human will, an ingrained anti-bureaucratism and a suspicion of intellectuals, were to remain in evidence after 1949 when Mao sought to pioneer a 'Chinese road to socialism'. Internal and external circumstances, however, compelled the People's Republic to adopt initially the Soviet model of development. In the early 1950s, therefore, emphasis was placed on centralizing planning, heavy industry and technical expertise.

As in 1940, Mao was keen to distinguish China's revolution from that of the Soviet Union. He referred to the new regime in 1949 as a People's Democratic Dictatorship, an alliance of several revolutionary classes – workers, peasants, petit bourgeoisie and national bourgeoisie (that is, those not associated with foreign capital) – led by the CCP, which would practise 'dictatorship' over the reactionary classes of Guomindang remnants, landlords, counterrevolutionaries and rightists. Mao also envisaged a gradual transition to socialism. Land reform (1950–2), for example, while eliminat-

ing landlords as a socioeconomic class and redistributing land to poor peasants, allowed rich peasants to retain the land they cultivated. In the cities the private sector continued to exist until 1956.

By the mid-1950s, it was clear that Mao was dissatisfied with the Soviet model. Centralized planning had produced powerful economic ministries and increasingly differentiated state and party bureaucracies, symbolized by elaborate pay scales; emphasis on technical expertise diluted ideological fervour and threatened to create a technical and managerial elite divorced from the masses; and the priority given to heavy industrial development led to the draining of scarce agricultural resources in order to fund it. It was to be in the countryside, however, that Maoism in its post-1949 context had its first impact. Concerned with growing inequalities in the villages and the preponderant influence of rich peasants, Mao in 1955 encouraged the acceleration of the collectivization process. He dismissed the determinist (see DETERMINISM) argument of party planners that full-scale collectivization had to await prior mechanisation and industrial take-off (that is, the raising of the productive forces) and insisted that the transition to new socialist forms and an increase in production had to advance together.

The second initiative Mao took over the heads of his party colleagues revealed the anti-bureaucratic impulse of Maoism. In the Soviet Union, Khrushchev's denunciation of Stalin in 1956 had raised the issue of the relationship between party and people and it was with the concern that the CCP was becoming an entrenched bureaucratic elite that Mao in the same year called on intellectuals to voice their criticisms in what became known as the One Hundred Flowers Campaign (derived from the slogan 'let a hundred flowers blossom, let a hundred schools of thought contend'). The lack of enthusiasm shown by his party colleagues prompted Mao in early 1957 to renew his call for an 'open-door rectification' of the party in a speech given outside party channels. He warned that non-antagonistic contradictions in a socialist society such as those between leaders and led could become antagonistic if the party did not allow outside criticism of its mistakes. A key Maoist assumption underlying the campaign was the idea that class struggle would continue in a socialist society, although it was to be a class struggle between competing ideologies rather than socioeconomic classes. In Mao's view, the party's elitism and aloofness from the masses was an expression of the ideology of the old exploiting classes. Only by exposing itself to criticism from the people, who, Mao assumed, broadly supported socialism, could the party be rectified. As it turned out, Mao and his colleagues had to end the campaign when criticism from intellectuals overstepped the required bounds and began to question socialism itself.

The definitive break with the Soviet model occurred in 1958 when Mao launched the Great Leap Forward, an ambitious campaign to accelerate the transition from SOCIALISM to COMMUNISM and promote rapid economic progress. The ideological rationale behind the campaign was the Maoist concept of PERMANENT REVOLUTION, the idea that the attainment of communism could only come about through waves of unceasing struggle in which radical ideological advance accompanied (or even was the precondition for) an increase in economic production. In what has been described as a 'utopian' approach (Meisner, 1982), Mao also argued that China's very backwardness was a positive advantage since it provided more scope for mass enthusiasm and initiative, another indication of his voluntarist faith in the human will. Such enthusiasm, Mao believed, could best be harnessed by utilizing moral incentives (appealing to the virtues of selflessness, asceticism and concern for the collective welfare) rather than material incentives. The ideal party cadre was now to be both 'red and expert', combining the correct ideological outlook with technical or administrative expertise. At the same time the communes established during the Great Leap would help bridge the gulf between city and countryside by promoting rural industrialization and expanding rural educational and health facilities. The equally iniquitous gulf, in Mao's view, that separated mental from manual labour was to be eliminated by having cadres and intellectuals 'sent down to the countryside' on the one hand and, on the other, creating half-work half-study schools and colleges to enable the masses, in Mao's words, to become 'masters of technology' instead of remaining dependent on a technocratic elite.

The Great Leap had disastrous consequences. Natural disasters, an inefficient transportation system and the channelling of peasant labour into mass irrigation works and unrealistic industrialization projects led to a decline in agricultural production and, ultimately, wide-scale famine. There was also peasant hostility to the attempts by party cadres to usher in a communist society through the institution of a free supply system, the creation of communal mess halls and nurseries, and the confiscation of all private possessions. In the early 1960s Mao was compelled to withdraw from active leadership while his party colleagues proceeded to modify Great Leap policies. Centralized planning was re-established; the socioeconomic functions of the commune were reduced and private plots and rural free markets restored; resources were shifted back to the cities and rural schools and clinics closed down; expertise took priority over 'redness'.

Mao criticized such trends as 'revisionist' and warned that a restoration of reactionary classes was a possibility in socialist society. By 1965, having been thwarted in his attempts both to revive a collectivist spirit among the people and party and to root out revisionism in the cultural domain, Mao was claiming that persons within the party leadership were taking the 'capitalist road'. It was in this context that Mao launched the Cultural Revolution in 1966. Arguing that 'bourgeois ideology' had infected the superstructure (see BASE AND SUPERSTRUCTURE), Mao called on the masses to wage an onslaught on all forms of authority. Mao's major target was the party itself but he also attacked academic and cultural authorities who, in his view, had favoured a divisive education system that stressed academic over political criteria as well as encouraging reactionary bourgeois ideas (elitism, specialization, ideological neutrality and the downplaying of the importance of class struggle).

In an immediate sense the Cultural Revolution was the outcome of an intraparty leadership struggle between Mao and his opponents. The fanatical Maoist cult that was deliberately cultivated at this time (ascribing an almost supernatural power to Mao's thought) was also the grotesque culmination of a process begun in the 1940s that had sought to locate all-knowing wisdom within the person of Mao himself. In a wider sense the Cultural Revolution was to be a process of self-liberation, as the masses confronted and struggled with hierarchical structures in the attempt to revive a socialist ethos and rejuvenate party organization. (It was this aspect that attracted Western radical intellectuals and students.) Mao particularly appealed to the young since, in his view, they were more amenable to changing the status quo; the experience of struggle would also equip them to become worthy 'revolutionary successors'. High school and college students formed into Red Guards and were encouraged to attack all vestiges of the past, described as the 'four olds' (ideas, culture, customs and habits), as well as 'pernicious' bourgeois influences of the present. As such, not only party leaders but also writers, intellectuals and teachers were subject to criticism and humiliation. In the realm of culture, Confucian philosophy (see CONFUCIANISM) and Western art were equally condemned.

Mao's experiment to create a new socialist culture ended when increasing chaos and violence compelled him to call in the army (1967–8) to restore order and oversee the rebuilding of the party. Since Mao's death in 1976, and especially since 1980, his successors have implicitly rejected many features of Maoism: class struggle is now officially proclaimed to have ended and the possibility that an antagonistic contradiction might develop between party and people is denied; emphasis is now placed on developing the productive forces (the economy), in a way which makes use of material incentives and allows for disparities in wealth among individuals and between regions; education aims to create technical and managerial elites; and self-reliance has given way to greater economic ties with the capitalist world. This rejection has been paralleled by a growing disillusion with Maoism in the West.

It is important to note, however, that Maoism was, and still is, influential in other parts of the world. In the 1950s Ho Chi Minh in Vietnam, Frantz Fanon in Algeria and Amilcar Cabral in Guinea-Bissau, to name but a few, drew on Maoist ideas of people's war, reliance on the peasantry and a voluntarist approach to revolution, while the Shining Path (Sendero Luminoso) movement in present-day Peru explicitly refers to itself as Maoist in orientation.

Reading
Ch'en, J. 1970: Mao Papers.
Compton, B. 1952: Mao's China: Party Reform Documents, 1942–1944.
Mao Zedong, 1986: The Writings of Mao Zedong, vol. 1, ed. M. Kau and J. Leung.
Meisner, M. 1982: Marxism, Maoism and Utopianism.
——1986: Mao's China and After.
Schram, S. 1969: The Political Thought of Mao Tse-tung, revised edn.
——1989: The Thought of Mao Tse-tung.
——ed. 1974: Mao Tse-tung Unrehearsed.
Schwartz, B. 1979: Chinese Communism and the Rise of Mao, new edn.
Starr, J. 1979: Continuing the Revolution.
Wylie, R. 1980: The Emergence of Maoism.

PAUL BAILEY

marginalist economics This term is used to describe the kind of economic analysis which, after 1870, gradually superseded the doctrines of the English classical economists. Marginalist analysis, and, in particular, the concepts of marginal utility and marginal cost, were primarily devoted to questions of the efficient allocation of resources by individual consumers and firms.

Marginal utility (or marginal cost) is the addition to total utility (or total cost) of consuming (or producing) one more unit of a good. The need for a marginal concept may be found in the two fundamental principles – or 'laws' – of diminishing returns and diminishing utility. The principle of diminishing returns, or of diminishing marginal productivity, as it was later more precisely restated, was first explicitly formulated by the great French economist and administrator A.R.J. Turgot (1727–1781) and played an important role in the theoretical system of the English classical economists, who dominated the subject in the first two-thirds of the nineteenth century. In its original form the principle of diminishing returns was applied only to agricultural production, when successive units of labour were applied to a fixed area of land. The principle then stated that the additional product or return to each successive unit of labour would decline as additional units were applied. It was, therefore, necessary to distinguish between the *average* product of a unit of labour and the *marginal* product of an additional unit.

Apart, however, from agricultural production, there was little scope for marginal concepts in English classical theory. Utility and the principle of diminishing utility played a very minor part, while, as regards industrial production, it was generally assumed that costs were constant and that markets were competitive. There was, therefore, no role for the concepts of marginal cost or marginal revenue, since these were necessarily equal to average cost and average revenue. The need for marginal concepts arose when it was necessary to distinguish between average and marginal cost, or between average and marginal utility, or average and marginal sales revenue. A partial role for marginal concepts began to emerge in the middle decades of the nineteenth century when the production and pricing problems of monopolies and public utilities, such as railways, came to the front, with their sharply falling average costs, and therefore still more sharply falling marginal costs. It was with these problems that such major pioneers of marginal analysis as A.A. Cournot (1801–1877) and J. Dupuit (1804–1866) were concerned.

The marginal concept first took on a general, central and fundamental role with the development of the neoclassical, marginal utility theory of value in the early 1870s, following the seminal works of W.S. Jevons (1835–1882) in England, C. Menger (1840–1921) in Austria, and L. Walras (1834–1910) in Lausanne. These writers approached the problem of value and price from the side of utility and the demand for goods, rather than from the side of costs, or labour, as had their predecessors the English classical economists. There was now, therefore, a vital role for the principle of diminishing utility, and hence for marginal utility. According to the principle of diminishing utility, the utility forthcoming from each successive unit of a good consumed – (say, the marginal utility from consuming successive slices of bread) – falls with each additional slice consumed, though the total utility of *all* the slices consumed will continue to rise until the saturation point is reached when the consumption of a further slice yields no utility, and subsequent slices yield a *dis*utility. The rational consumer, concerned to obtain as much utility as possible from limited resources, will aim at equating the marginal utility of consuming an additional slice with the cost to him, or price, of that slice, or with the utility foregone by paying the price of this marginal slice.

The analysis of the decisions of the consumer, developed from the early 1870s onwards, was complemented, in the 1980s, by the marginal productivity analysis of the decisions of firms regarding how much of the different factors of production – (land, labour and capital) – to employ. The formula was propounded that the firm aiming at minimizing its costs and maximizing its profits would hire units of the various factors of production up to the point where the addition to its revenue, accruing from the additional product of one more unit of a factor, equalled the cost of employing that additional unit.

It may be noted that the adjective 'marginal' did not come into general use until the late 1880s and early 1890s, following its adoption by P. Wicksteed (1844–1927) and A. Marshall (1842–1924), and, in German (*Grenznutzen*), by F. von Wieser (1851–

1926). By the 1890s, however, with the marginal concept playing a central and essential role, an analysis of the logic of choice, and of the rational allocation of scarce resources by households and firms, was constructed, which, though it sometimes started from the highly simplified analysis of an isolated individual, such as Robinson Crusoe, possessed a very wide applicability. Though based on extreme abstractions and simplifications, and very tenuous in content, this marginal analysis could be applied to the valuation and allocation of scarce resources by individual consumers and producers, as well as by public utilities and government planners.

Subsequently, with the systematic development, by Keynes and others, of monetary and macroeconomics – that is, the analysis of the economy as a whole and of national income and employment – the marginal concept was applied to the analysis of aggregates, as with the marginal propensity to consume (measured by the percentage of an additional unit of national income spent on consumption) or as with the marginal propensity to import of a national economy. It would, therefore, now be misleading to apply the term 'marginalist' simply to the neoclassical, microeconomic analysis of individual households and firms. It would be even more misleading to imply that the use of the marginal concept necessarily, or usually, implies approval of any particular ethical or political assumptions.

See also NEOCLASSICAL ECONOMICS.

Reading
Howey, R.S. 1960: *The Rise of the Marginal Utility School 1870–1889*.
Hutchison, T.W. 1953: *A Review of Economic Doctrines 1870–1929*.
Marshall, A. 1890 (*1920*): *Principles of Economics*.
Schumpeter, J.A. 1954: *A History of Economic Analysis*.
Stigler, G.J. 1941: *Production and Distribution Theories: The Formative Period*.
Wicksteed, P.H. 1933: *The Common Sense of Political Economy* and *Selected Papers and Reviews on Economic Theory*, ed. Lionel Robbins.

T.W. HUTCHISON

market As the social institution in which people freely exchange commodities (goods, resources and services), generally through the medium of money, the market presupposes a social DIVISION OF LABOUR and (at least *de facto*) private ownership of the means of production. The nature of the market system has been the subject of a great deal of debate during the course of the twentieth century, concerning both the theoretical role of the market in coordinating economic activity and the practical possibility of improving upon the market system through either governmental monetary and fiscal policy, or outright comprehensive economic planning. We can identify three schools of thought in this regard.

The market as inherently crisis-ridden

The notion that the market system is fundamentally anarchic, and essentially crisis-ridden, finds its most complete expression in MARXISM. Marxists contend that the commodity form of market exchange, in which goods are produced by wage labour and sold by capitalists with the intention of securing monetary profit, alienates workers and promotes class conflict. Furthermore, because money acts as a cash nexus, which separates production of commodities from their ultimate uses, periodic crises are inevitable. Individual capitalists, not fully informed about consumer demands, may be forced to sell their goods at market prices that fall below their values. As Karl Marx (1885) maintained, and Rudolf Hilferding (1910) later explained, this may lead to widespread disproportions between supply and demand within various industries and a fall in the average rate of profit (see BUSINESS CYCLE). Bankruptcies will increase and the number of unemployed will grow. Over time, crises will become more severe, and coupled with increasing alienation and class conflict, conditions will eventually be ripe for a proletarian revolution.

According to some Marxist theorists, government intervention designed to manipulate and improve the market system will not be enough to ward off recessions and depressions. Only the outright abolition of private property, commodity production and money – in short, abandonment of the entire market system – will do. Rather than market competition, economic activities will be coordinated through a comprehensive economic plan (see NATIONAL ECONOMIC PLANNING).

The market as an end-state

The school of NEOCLASSICAL ECONOMICS, the leading school of twentieth century economic thought, hypothesizes that the market system works like a mechanism that tends towards a general economic equilibrium, in which all supplies and demands for scarce goods and services are perfectly coordinated. Rather than viewing the market as anarchic, full of

conflict and inherently prone to crises, neoclassical economists tend to explain markets in a static, Newtonian fashion, as if all market participants (producers, consumers, workers and so on) enjoyed full and complete information and were guided by prices that equate market supplies with demands. The formal general equilibrium model is no longer considered by leading neoclassical economists (such as Frank Hahn, 1973) to be an accurate description of real world markets, or even a practical possibility. Instead, the standard neoclassical explanation of markets is now understood as an imaginary construction of economic equilibrium as such, and not about the actual operation of real existing markets.

The Keynesian variant of neoclassical economics (Keynes, 1936; Samuelson, 1976) differs in the sense that it explains the market through the interaction of aggregate (macroeconomic) variables as opposed to decomposed (microeconomic) variables (see KEYNESIANISM). The Keynesian approach attempts to explain macroeconomic market failure, chiefly the phenomenon of economic depression, as a failure of Say's Law. Keynesian theory criticizes Jean Baptiste Say's (1803) argument that supply creates its own demand in an unhampered market system. Market participants' expectations about future economic events, as illustrated through saving and investment decisions, need not always mesh. Due to institutional inflexibility of money wages (particularly workers' unwillingness to accept reduced money wages), in addition to the potential for individuals to hoard money, Keynesians argue that aggregate demand may fall short of aggregate supply, and the market may get stuck in depression, an 'unemployment equilibrium', as it were (the ECONOMIC DEPRESSION of the 1930s is considered exemplary). Keynesians do not go as far as Marxists with regard to policy – they prescribe a mix of monetary and fiscal policies to fine tune the market economy, rather than comprehensive planning.

The market as a process

An alternative view of the market has gained force only since the mid-twentieth century. Primarily associated with Ludwig von Mises (1949) and F.A. Hayek (1948), the school of AUSTRIAN ECONOMICS argues that the market works as a rivalrous discovery process, a process that is set in motion by the myriad plans and activities of producers and consumers who cooperate and compete under the social division of labour. The market process is the result of all the activities of its participants, but it is neither willed nor designed by anyone in particular. Rather, the market order is an unintended consequence of individuals seeking their own interests. The notion that the market is an undesigned, dynamic process differs dramatically from the notion of its being an end-state equilibrium. From this perspective the market economy neither begins in an overall equilibrium nor can it ever achieve it. Instead, it spontaneously yields an ever-evolving order, a discernable pattern of events (see EVOLUTIONARY PROCESSES IN THE ECONOMY). Because the complexity of the market order is beyond what any mind can master, it is impossible for any person to know all the alternative uses of resources. Market participants therefore must rely on free market prices to expose relative values and promote a dovetailing of production and consumption plans. According to the market process explanation, an unhampered market system disseminates knowledge about relative scarcities of goods and services to market participants, who use monetary economic calculation and double entry bookkeeping to interpret the information embedded in competitive prices (see COMPETITION). Without a market system, society would not be able to calculate rationally the values of scarce goods.

Proponents of the view that the market is a spontaneous, orderly process admit that the market is essentially anarchic, in the non-pejorative sense that it is under nobody's deliberate control. They generally explain breakdowns in the market system, including recessions and depressions, as the unintended consequence of government intervention (such as wage and price controls, excessive growth in the money supply and Keynesian monetary and fiscal policies) which distorts relative prices, rather than an inherent feature of the market system as such. Of the three schools of thought, the market process approach tends to advocate the extreme LAISSEZ-FAIRE stance with regard to government's role in the market order.

Reading

Buchanan, James 1982: Order defined in the process of its emergence. *Literature of Liberty* 5, 5.
Cowen, Tyler 1982: Say's law and Keynesian economics. In *Supply-Side Economics: A Critical Appraisal*, ed. Richard H. Fink.
Hayek, F.A. 1978: Competition as a discovery procedure. In *New Studies in Philosophy, Politics, Economics and the History of Ideas*, ed. F.A. Hayek.
Kirzner, Israel M. 1973: *Competition and Entrepreneurship*.
Lachmann, Ludwig M. 1986: *The Market as an Economic Process*.
Lavoie, Don 1986: The market as a procedure for discovery and conveyance of inarticulate knowledge. *Comparative Economic Studies* 28, 1–19.
O'Driscoll, Gerald P. Jr and Rizzo, Mario J. 1985: *The Economics of Time and Ignorance*.
Offe, Claus 1985: *Disorganized Capitalism*, ed. John Keane.
Roberts, Paul Craig and Stephenson, Matthew A. 1971: *Marx's Theory of Exchange, Alienation, and Crisis*.
Weintraub, Sidney ed. 1977: *Modern Economic Thought*.

DAVID L. PRYCHITKO

market, labour *See* LABOUR MARKET

market socialism In its primary sense this is a theoretical concept (model) of an economic system in which the means of production (capital) are publicly or collectively owned, and the allocation of resources follows the rules of the market (product, labour and capital markets). At the same time the term has often been applied more loosely to cover the projects of reforming the economic system of the countries of 'real socialism' (communist countries) away from command planning (see NATIONAL ECONOMIC PLANNING) in the direction of market regulation (Yugoslavia after the early 1950s, Hungary after 1968, China, Poland, the USSR and Bulgaria in the 1980s). For ideological reasons the designation 'market socialism' was, however, largely avoided in some of the countries in question, with preference for the formula of 'socialist market' which was thought to be more acceptable for Marxists.

Marx's political economy had for a long time been interpreted to hold that socialism was incompatible with the market. Socialism makes the market redundant and overcomes its shortcomings as an allocation mechanism by bringing into the open the social nature of work, assigning it directly *ex ante* to a particular role in the economic process through the 'visible hand' of planning, which secures full utilization of resources, especially human resources, free of cyclical fluctuations.

After the Russian revolution of 1917, any application of the market mechanism was presented in the programmatic communist documents as only a temporary concession to underdevelopment (*Programme of the Communist International*, 1929, ch. 4). At the same time, however, the social democratic wing of Marxism began to recognize the relevance of the market in a socialist economy (Kautsky, 1922).

Theoretical debates on market socialism acquired a new dimension in the interwar period, particularly after republication by F. A. Hayek (1935) of an article by L. von Mises published originally in 1920, which categorically denied the possibility of rational economic calculation under socialism, because exchange relations between production goods and hence their prices could be established only on the basis of private ownership. Among the many attempts at refutation of this view (Taylor, 1929; Dickinson, 1933; Landauer, 1931; Heimann, 1932), probably the best known is that by Oskar Lange (1936–7). Similar ideas had been developed in the same period by Abba Lerner (1934, 1936, 1937), hence the often used designation of the 'Lange-Lerner solution'.

Lange not only denied the purely theoretical validity of Mises's stand (by pointing to Barone's (1908) demonstration of the possibility of dealing with the question through a system of simultaneous equations), but tried to present a positive solution. This was to consist of a 'trial and error' procedure in which a central planning board (CPB) performs the functions of the market where there is no market in the institutional sense of the word. In this capacity the CPB fixes prices, as well as wages and interest rates, so as to balance supply and demand (by appropriate changes in case of disequilibrium), and instructs managers to follow two rules: (1) to minimize average cost of production by using a combination of factors which would equalize marginal productivity of their money unit-worth; (2) to determine the scale of output at a point of equalization of marginal cost and the price set by the board.

Most of the subsequent accounts of the interwar debate acknowledged the validity of the theoretical argument presented by Lange, and accepted that Hayek retreated to the position of asserting the practical impossibility of reconciling socialism with rational economic calculation. This may be true when one follows – as Lange seems to have done – the type of model of static general equilibrium as developed by Walras (1954). The point made, however, increasingly forcefully by new students of the interwar debate (such as Lavoie, 1985) is that the Mises/Hayek challenge has come from the positions of the school of AUSTRIAN ECONOMICS, with the emphasis on the dynamic properties of the competition process, the central figure of which is the entrepreneur. This leaves unanswered the question of whether economic actors who are not principals operating at their own risk and responsibility but agents employed by a public body are actually capable of entrepreneurial behaviour.

Thus, Lange's 'competitive solution' had the merit of advancing the idea of an alternative to command planning as well as showing the indispensability of scarcity prices for rational allocation of resources under socialism. At the same time, however, it could not provide an adequate theoretical base for change when market-oriented reforms were put on the practical agenda in countries of 'real socialism'.

The first attempt to apply the ideas of market socialism in practice came in the early 1950s in Yugoslavia, after the Stalin–Tito break. The Yugoslav Communist Party searched both for greater economic efficiency and for ideological legitimacy vis-à-vis Stalinism. The latter was found in self-management, and as self-managed economic units must be autonomous, this engendered the process of replacement of the command system by market coordination, albeit not conducted in a consistent way.

In the countries of the Soviet bloc the main motive for the reform drive was dissatisfaction with the command economy's performance when this became openly discussed after Stalin's death. In Poland a relatively comprehensive blueprint of systemic changes was worked out in 1956–7; similar ideas in Hungary were quelled as a result of the suppression of the popular uprising of 1956.

Since then, a long string of attempts at economic reforms – of various degrees of consistency, but heading in the same direction of increasing the role of the market – occurred in Eastern Europe: Czechoslovakia in 1958 and in 1967–8; the New Economic System in the German Democratic Republic in 1963; the 1965 so-called 'Kosygin reform' in the USSR and its Bulgarian imitation; the Hungarian New Economic Mechanism (NEM) introduced in 1968; repeated attempts at reform in Poland. However, at the beginning of the 1980s, out of all these attempts only the Hungarian NEM remained basically operative; otherwise, what happened were, rather, secondary modifications within the framework of the command system. On the other hand, the tendency towards market-directed change persisted, clearly under the pressure of a progressive deterioration of economic performance, which reached crisis proportions in most communist countries in the 1980s. In 1978–9 China joined the reformist ranks, and from 1985 onwards the 'radical economic reform' became one of the fundamental elements of Gorbachev's *perestroika* in the USSR.

The reasons for the difficulties in carrying out market-oriented economic reforms are seen (Brus, 1979) in: (1) political resistance of the ruling elite; (2) vested interests of the administrative apparatus as well as of some sections of the workers, who may feel threatened in their job security; (3) substantive obstacles to grafting a market mechanism on to the existing structures of planning and management, property rights and the monopoly of power of the communist party. As a result, countries which made some headway in the reform process (Yugoslavia, Poland, Hungary) found themselves not only in economic trouble worse than those (Czechoslovakia, East Germany) which stuck to the old system (although non-systemic factors must be taken into account in any comparisons), but also actually failed to cross the threshold between administrative and market coordination of the economy. The examination of the Hungarian NEM in this respect led to the conclusion that, despite the abolition of obligatory output targets and physical allocation of producer goods, the overall effect of the reform by the mid-1980s was merely a change from direct to indirect 'bureaucratic coordination' (Kornai, 1986).

Experience seems to have shown that the earlier reform models, based on the idea of combining central planning with a 'regulated market' by limiting market regulation mainly to the product market (Brus, 1961), as well as on acceptance of the dominant position of state ownership of the means of production, have proved inadequate. In the course of the 1980s the projects for market-oriented change in communist countries underwent sharp radicalization: the need for a capital market, in the form both of commercial banking and of dealing in securities, was widely recognized (Tardos, 1986; Lipowski, 1988), and so was the need for a labour market, although sometimes not openly by name. Moreover, a successful market-oriented economic reform has become closely linked with fundamental transformation of the ownership structure (Abalkin, 1988). One of the factors which evidently contributed to the reconsideration of the ownership issue was the experience of much more favourable results of systemic reforms outside the state sector (cooperatives, private enterprise) in Hungary, and particularly the initial spectacular success of the 'family production responsibility' in Chinese agriculture. The acknowledgement of the necessity of a wide-ranging change in the ownership structure was reflected towards the end of the 1980s in a number of legal measures in various communist countries. In the USSR there was legislation about *arenda* (leasehold) of land, buildings and equipment with the intention of maintaining the position of the state as a freeholder, but of opening the way towards entrepreneurship to workers' collectives, partnerships or even individuals. In some other countries (Poland, Hungary) the principle of a mixed economy was adopted, with state enterprises, cooperatives and private enterprises (the latter without limits on size and employment) intended to compete on equal terms.

This conceptual, and to some extent also practical, development posed with renewed force the question of the link between economic and political transformations. On the one hand, marketization involving increased enterprise freedom, particularly when accompanied by ownership changes, raised the political aspirations of the people, who felt less subjugated by the all-pervasive state. On the other hand, in view of the resistance of the ruling elites and their supporting strata, political pluralism became an indispensable instrument for effecting the transition from the old to the new economic system, as well as of guarding the latter's continuing existence. A denial of this link based on examples of successful market economies with authoritarian political regimes (such as some of the 'newly industrialized countries' in Asia), was rejected by the reformers in communist countries as failing to recognize the true nature of the problems they were facing.

Consistent pursuit of market socialism – capital and labour markets, ownership restructuring, political pluralism – may be regarded as blurring the habitual distinctions between capitalism and socialism, and therefore denying to socialism the character of a bounded successor system to capitalism (Brus and Laski, 1989). This is not necessarily tantamount to the abandonment of basic socialist policy objectives – full employment, equality of opportunity, social care – as well as of government intervention as the method to achieve them. What it seems to imply, however, is the abandonment of the concept of socialism as a grand design requiring total replacement of the institutional framework of the past; in other words – abandonment of the philosophy of the revolutionary break in favour of continuity in change. From this point of view, market socialism as an aim of a consistent transformation of the countries of 'real socialism' may be said to share certain common features with market socialism as perceived by some Western social democratic parties (see also SOCIAL DEMOCRACY), including the British Labour Party (Fabian Society, 1986 and see FABIANISM); but any analogy must be very tentative, recognizing differences in starting position and profoundly different conditions of struggle for achieving the desired aim, as well as ideological implications.

Reading

Brus, W. 1961 (*1972*): *The Market in a Socialist Economy.*
——1979: East European economic reforms: what happened to them? *Soviet Studies* 31.2.
Brus, W. and Laski, K. 1989: *From Marx to the Market: Socialism in Search of an Economic System.*
Fabian Society 1986: *Market Socialism: Whose Choice? A Debate*, pamphlet 516.
Hayek, F.A. ed. 1935: *Collectivist Economic Planning.*
Kornai, J. 1986: The Hungarian reform process: vision, hopes and reality. *Journal of Economic Literature*, December.
Lange, O. and Taylor, F. 1936–7 (*1948*): *On the Economic Theory of Socialism*, ed. B. Lippincott.
Lavoie, D. 1985: *Rivalry and Central Planning: The Socialist Calculation Debate Reconsidered.*

W. BRUS

marriage This is regarded as the socially approved bond of a man and a woman for the puposes of sexual communion, procreation and economic cooperation yet, curiously, the direction of twentieth-century social thought has been to document and encourage the detachment of these functions from the marital setting, actions that call into question the future utility of the word.

Of course, traditional views have remained active. In the West, the religious affirmation of marriage as divinely ordained found its strongest champion in the Roman Catholic papacy. Pius XI's encyclical *Casti Connubii* (1933) reaffirmed the sacramental and irrevocable nature of marriage, stressed its sexual monopoly, celebrated the procreative function as a collaboration with God and defended the household economy.

However, philosophical currents of greater influence moved a different way. John Locke's basic redefinition of marriage as 'a voluntary compact' (1812, vol. 5, pp. 383–5), necessary only so long as small children needed protection, came in

the late seventeenth century. Two hundred years later, this shift from a spiritual to a contractual understanding of marriage had a powerful momentum. At the same time, Marxist theorists placed marriage within the context of class struggle, while early feminists emphasized the institution's exploitation of women (see FEMINISM).

Critical treatment of the specific functions of marriage developed particular force after 1900. Ellis argued against the sexual monopoly claimed by legal marriage (1912, pp. 53–66), a development later given statistical credence by the work of Kinsey (Kinsey, Pomeroy and Martin, 1948) and Masters and Johnson (1982, p. 229). Key argued that the economic factor in marriage had degraded women (1911, pp. 367–8). Even in marriage, she said, men and women ought to be economically independent, and all new mothers should draw support from the state, rather than from husbands. At the same time, the procreative monopoly of marriage faced mounting criticism for its cruel categorization of children. The reformed family law of the new Soviet Union set the model by eliminating the legal distinctions between legitimate and illegitimate births.

Ironically, as marriage faced this form of deconstruction, modern anthropologists affirmed the institution's universality. In his cross-cultural survey, Murdock defined marriage as existing 'only when the economic and the sexual are united into one relationship' (1949, pp. 7–8), and then claimed to find this institution 'in every known human society'. Also universal, he said, was 'a division of labor by sex' rooted in the natural and indisputable differences in reproductive functions. Malinowski acknowledged the forces cutting away at the marital union, but concluded that there is 'something bigger in human marriage' rooted in 'the deepest needs of human nature and society' (Briffault and Malinowski, 1956, pp. 27–8).

For their part, sociologists projected the development of new marriage patterns. Westermarck viewed marriage as a human instinct shaped by natural selection (1936, p. 20). No longer needed in the modern environment, marriage would survive only as a residual drive. Groves (1928) focused on the family's loss of functions, as discrete tasks such as economic cooperation and childrearing passed to professional entities. At mid-century, Talcott Parsons (1951) put a positive gloss on this change, emphasizing the new importance of marriage in adult personality adjustment. In the 1970s, resurgent feminist ideas led many sociologists to see a pure egalitarian marriage as the model for the future (Bernard, 1972).

Recent observers, though, suggest that marriage may be disappearing, rather than merely changing, in advanced societies. Looking particularly at Sweden, Poponoe (1988, pp. 188–94) charts a reduced propensity to marry, the postponement of marriage to a later age, a smaller portion of individual lives spent in wedlock, a shorter duration of marriage and a growing preference for alternative types of sexual union.

See also FAMILY; DIVORCE.

Reading
Key, E. 1911 (*1949*): *Love and Marriage*, trans. A.G. Chater.
Murdock, G.P. 1949: *Social Structure*.
Parsons, Talcott 1951: *The Social System*.
Poponoe, D. 1988: *Disturbing the Nest: Family Change and Decline in Modern Societies*.
Westermarck, E. 1936: *The Future of Marriage in Western Civilisation*.

ALLAN C. CARLSON

Marxism A body of social theory and political doctrine derived from the work of Karl Marx and his close collaborator Friedrich Engels. Only after Marx's death was Marxism developed as a comprehensive 'world view' and as the distinctive political doctrine of many socialist parties, initially by Engels who expounded the 'Marxist world view' as the outlook of the working class, likening its role to that of classical German philosophy in relation to the bourgeoisie (Engels, 1888), though at the same time he stressed its scientific character. Through his writings and correspondence, Engels had a strong influence on the first generation of Marxist thinkers, and by the end of the nineteenth century Marxism was firmly established, largely outside academic institutions, as a major social theory and political doctrine, assimilated in some cases into a general philosophical system.

In the social theory three main elements can be distinguished. First, an analysis of the principal types of human society and their historical succession, in which a pre-eminent place is given to the economic structure or 'mode of production' in determining the whole form of social life: 'the mode of production of material life determines the general character of the social, political and spiritual processes of life' (Marx, 1859, Preface). The mode of production itself is defined in terms of two factors: the forces of production (the available technology) and the relations of production (the way in which production is organized, and in particular the nature of those groups which either own the instruments of production or simply contribute their labour to the productive process). From this analysis two fundamental ideas of Marxist theory emerged: a periodization of history, conceived as a progressive movement through the ancient, asiatic, feudal and modern capitalist modes of production, and a conception of the role of social classes in constituting and transforming social structures.

The second element is an explanatory scheme covering the changes from one type of society to another, in which two processes are crucially important. From one aspect the changes are brought about by the progress of technology, and Marx himself emphasized this when he wrote (1847, ch. 2, sect. 1) that 'the hand mill gives you a society with feudal lords, the steam mill a society with industrial capitalists,' or again later, in the *Grundrisse* (1857–8, pp. 592–4), where he discussed most fully the consequences of the rapid advance of science and technology for the future of capitalism. From another aspect, however, social transformations are the outcome of conscious class struggles; but the two processes are intimately related, since the development of productive forces is bound up with the rise of a new class, and the existing dominant class becomes increasingly an obstacle to further development.

The third element is the analysis of modern capitalism, to which Marx and later Marxists devoted most of their attention. Capitalism is conceived as the final form of class society, in which the conflict between bourgeoisie and proletariat steadily intensifies along with the economic contradictions of capitalism, manifested in recurrent crises, and the process of SOCIALIZATION OF THE ECONOMY is accelerated by the development of cartels and trusts. This analysis, and the growth of mass socialist parties, necessarily led to a preoccupation with the forms that a transition to socialism might take, and to the elaboration of a Marxist political doctrine which would help to integrate and guide the working-class movement.

From an early stage, however, there were diverse interpretations of Marx's legacy and disagreements about its further development. In Germany, largely under the influence of Karl Kautsky, Marxism was conceived primarily as a scientific theory of social evolution (its affinities with Darwinism being strongly emphasized) and its more deterministic features seemed to be confirmed by the development of capitalism and the rapid growth of the socialist movement. In Russia, on the other hand, where capitalism had only begun to develop and there was no mass socialist movement, Marxism was a doctrine expounded by small groups of revolutionaries, and notably by Plekhanov, as a philosophical world view, from which Lenin developed the idea of a 'socialist consciousness' brought to the working class from outside; and this subsequently became a central element in the ideology of the Bolshevik party and the Soviet state.

This division between more deterministic and more voluntaristic interpretations runs through the later history of Marxism, in incessant revisions and reformulations of the social theory and of the political practice which was, at least in part, derived from it. By the first decade of the twentieth century, Marxism was also confronted by increasing critical discussion, both from outside, in the writings, for example, of Max Weber, Emile Durkheim and Benedetto Croce, and from within, notably in Bernstein's exposition (1899) of the results of his effort 'to become clear just where Marx is right and where he is wrong', which led him to criticize several aspects of Marxist orthodoxy, including the 'economic collapse' view of the end of capitalism and the idea of an increasing polarization of society between bourgeoisie and proletariat, and in later writings to argue that the socialist movement required an ethical doctrine as well as a social theory (see REVISIONISM).

Among those Marxists who responded to the criticisms of Marxism as a social science, and more generally to new conceptions in philosophy and economics, the Austro-Marxists acquired a distinctive influence through their elaboration of the principles of a Marxist sociology and their innovative research in new fields of enquiry, which included studies of nationalism, of law, and of the most recent development of capitalism in its imperialist stage (see AUSTRO-MARXISM). Lenin and the Bolsheviks, however, with the partial exception of Bukharin (1921), paid little attention to alternative social theories, and responded to Bernstein's criticisms by identifying revisionism with REFORMISM and the abandonment of revolutionary aims. Their versions of Marxism concentrated to a large extent on the creation of a disciplined revolutionary party which would be capable of leading the working class and its allies (especially, in the Russian case, the peasantry) to a successful conquest of power. In this way Marxism was converted into a doctrine emphasizing political will and party leadership as the crucial factors in social change.

The Russian revolution, which installed the Bolsheviks in power, created entirely new conditions for the development of Marxist thought. Leninism, and subsequently Stalinism, became established as a dogmatic official ideology which acquired great international influence with the foundation of communist parties on the Soviet model in other countries, while the German Social Democratic Party, deeply divided and weakened as a result of the war and the defeat of revolutionary uprisings in 1918–19, lost its former pre-eminence as a centre of Marxist theory and practice. In the interwar years and for some time after World War II Marxism became largely identified in the public mind with Soviet Marxism; although there was in fact a profound rift in Marxist thought, partly coinciding with the division in the international working-class movement, between the Soviet version and what was later called 'Western Marxism'. But the latter was itself quite diverse. In some of its forms, and especially in the work of the Austro-Marxists, it continued to develop as a field of scientific enquiry, analysing the further changes in capitalist society after World War I, the rise of fascism, and the development of a totalitarian state economy and political dictatorship in the Soviet Union.

Other Western Marxists, however, who became members of the newly formed communist parties, rejected the conception of Marxism as a scientific sociology and adopted a more Leninist view of it as a revolutionary consciousness embodied in a working-class party, although considerable differences existed or emerged among the principal exponents of this view, Korsch (1923), Lukács (1923), and Gramsci (1929–35). Korsch later (1938) rejected this whole outlook saying that 'the main tendency of historical materialism is no longer "philosophical", but is that of an empirical scientific method', and Gramsci's analyses of the state and civil society contained many elements which could be, and have been, incorporated into a sociological theory. Lukács also changed his ideas and in the preface to a new edition of his early work (1923 (*1971*)) he referred self-critically to its 'revolutionary, utopian messianism' and expressed doubts about the content and methodological validity of the kind of Marxism he had expounded. The earlier writings of Korsch and Lukács, however, also helped to promote another form of Marxist thought with the creation of the Frankfurt Institute of Social Research in 1923, which later (in the 1960s) bloomed luxuriantly in the critical theory of the FRANKFURT SCHOOL.

Difficulties of another sort for Marxist theory were raised by the practical problems of constructing a socialist society in post-revolutionary Russia, in a mainly agrarian country, ravaged by war, civil war and foreign intervention. Most of the early Marxists, like Marx himself, had in any case paid little attention to the question of how a socialist economy and new social and political institutions would actually be organized, confining themselves to such general descriptions as the 'associated mode of production' or a 'society of associated producers'; although Kautsky (1902) and the Austro-Marxists did discuss more fully some of the issues involved. In the Soviet Union the difficulties of socialist development were compounded by the urgent need to restore the shattered economy and to promote rapid industrialization, and this became the focal point of the intense debates of the 1920s about the policies of the 'transition period'; debates which were finally ended by Stalin's dictatorship and the ruthless imposition of forced industrialization and the collectivization of agriculture.

Western Marxists in the interwar period had to contend with an array of problems: the failure of revolutionary movements in advanced capitalist countries, the rise of fascism, the increasingly totalitarian character of the Soviet regime, and critical attacks on the whole idea of a planned socialist economy, initiated by von Mises (1920, 1922) and continued in a lengthy controversy between conservative economists such as Hayek (1935) and from the side of Marxism especially Lange (Lange and Taylor, 1938). Nevertheless the influence of Marxist thought, predominantly in a Leninist–Stalinist form, increased during the 1930s, largely because of the contrast between the quite rapid and sustained development of the Soviet economy and the conditions of economic crisis and depression in the capitalist world, as well as the recognition of the Soviet Union as a principal opponent of the fascist regimes. But among Marxists themselves the criticism of totalitarian socialism continued, and there were also increasing doubts, most strongly expressed by the Frankfurt

School thinkers, about the revolutionary political role of the working class in capitalist society.

These themes continued to dominate Marxist thought after World War II. The extension of the Soviet system into Eastern Europe, followed by a succession of uprisings against the new regimes from the 1950s to the 1980s, produced mounting criticism of what was called 'real socialism' and its orthodox defenders, and the influence of Soviet Marxism steadily waned. Concomitantly, the varied array of theories and doctrines known as Western Marxism acquired a much greater influence, including that which they exerted on dissident movements in Eastern Europe, but in very different conditions from those of the interwar years. After World War II capitalism entered a phase of exceptionally rapid and sustained economic growth, accompanied in Western Europe, under the influence of socialist movements which were now stronger than they had ever been, by an extension of public ownership, some degree of economic planning and the development of what came to be called the 'welfare state'. In Eastern Europe, the movements of revolt, especially in Hungary in 1956 and in Czechoslovakia in 1968, and the entirely different course embarked on by Yugoslavia from 1951 in the construction of a system of workers' self-management, seemed to point towards an eventual attainment in that part of Europe of a democratic socialist form of society. At all events they contributed to a notable revival of Marxist thought, which now became widely diffused, in Western countries, not only in history, sociology and political science where it had long had some kind of presence, but in economics and anthropology, philosophy and aesthetics. Marxism thus became a focal point of major controversies, which brought it into a new relationship with other currents of social thought.

But this renaissance also increased the diversity of Marxist conceptions, affected also by a wider diffusion of some of Marx's own lesser-known writings, such as the *Economic and Philosophical Manuscripts* (1844) and the *Grundrisse* (1857–8). The Frankfurt School, through the writings of Theodor Adorno, Max Horkheimer and Herbert Marcuse, gained widespread influence as a cultural critique of bourgeois society, conceived as being dominated by 'technological rationality' and by a corresponding positivist/scientistic orientation of the social sciences, rather than by a capitalist class. Against this the structuralist Marxism of Louis

Althusser, shaped partly by the wider structuralist movement (see STRUCTURALISM), asserted the importance of analysing the deep structures of human societies, and especially their modes of production, and portrayed Marxism as a 'new science' of the different levels of social practice, from which the human subject as an autonomous active being was eliminated. In another direction the *Praxis* group of Yugoslav philosophers and sociologists concentrated their attention on the problems of alienation in both capitalist and state socialist societies, and on the development and prospects of self-managed socialism, and their writings had a particular impact on intellectuals in Eastern Europe.

The Marxist thought of this period was divided not only between a vigorous Western Marxism and a moribund Soviet Marxism (with a brief incursion of Maoism as a political doctrine that captivated some student radicals), but between two alternative conceptions which can be broadly categorized as 'humanist' and 'scientific' (Bottomore, 1988, Introduction). Marxists in the first category laid stress on the humanist, democratic or emancipatory content of Marxist theory, and on the conscious, intentional actions of individuals and social groups, while those in the second category were primarily concerned with its scientific, explanatory character, and with the distinctive conceptual scheme and theory of knowledge that underlies it. Both orientations involved Marxist thinkers in much wider controversies over the whole field of the social sciences, history and philosophy, about 'structure' and 'human agency' in social life, about the relative importance of cultural (or ideological) and social factors in the development of society, and about fundamental methodological issues; and they themselves made substantial contributions to these debates.

Although Marxism has retained a more important place in social thought than it had earlier in this century, it became less influential in the 1980s than in the previous decade and had to face major problems. One of these is to provide some convincing analysis of the stability and growth of postwar capitalism, and in the light of that to reconsider the nature, or indeed the possibility, of a transition to socialism as hitherto conceived in the advanced industrial countries, taking account especially of the apparent decline of specifically working-class politics and the rise of various forms of non-class politics in the new kinds of SOCIAL MOVEMENT. A still greater problem is presented by the changes in the countries of 'real socialism', which culminated, at the end of the 1980s, in the overthrow of the communist regimes in most of Eastern Europe and the acceleration of fundamental changes in the Soviet Union towards a more market-oriented economy and a multiparty political system. Since most of the East European countries then embarked on a restoration of capitalism it is evident that the Marxist theory of history, which envisaged no such reverse transition from socialism to capitalism, stands in need of drastic revision, and it is a singularly inadequate response to these events to say that the countries concerned were not *really* socialist at all. What is required is a much more fundamental analysis of the development of capitalism and socialism in the twentieth century, and a reorientation of Marxist theory, if that is possible, from being primarily or even exclusively an analysis of the rise, development and anticipated surpassing of capitalism, to one which gives equal or greater prominence to studies of the emergence and development of socialism, and of the contradictions and crises which may arise within a socialist economy and society. Whether this reorientation of ideas will be accommodated within a scheme of thought that is still recognizably a form of 'classical Marxism', or whether it marks the beginning of a 'post-Marxist' era, remains to be seen. It is evident at least that over the past few decades Marxism had already developed in such a way that its character was less that of a single tightly knit theory, and more that of a broad, though still distinctive, paradigm within which diverse kinds of explanation and interpretation are possible; and that in this process its role as a political doctrine, separate from that of socialism in general, has been greatly attenuated, so that in the future 'Marxist' parties are likely to be something of a rarity.

Reading

Avineri, Shlomo 1968: *The Social and Political Thought of Karl Marx.*
Bottomore, Tom ed. 1983 (*1991*): *A Dictionary of Marxist Thought.*
Kolakowski, Leszek 1978: *Main Currents of Marxism.*
Lichtheim, George 1961: *Marxism: An Historical and Critical Study.*
McLellan, David ed. 1983: *Marx: The First Hundred years.*

TOM BOTTOMORE

Marxism, Austro- *See* AUSTRO-MARXISM

Marxism, Western *See* WESTERN MARXISM

mass culture Usually used pejoratively, to identify the culture of MASS SOCIETY or, more generally, of the mass of the population in modern societies, mass culture is so characterized not merely because it is the culture of the masses or because it is produced for the consumption of the masses, but because it is alleged to lack both the reflectiveness and sophistication of the 'high culture' of social, cultural or educational elites and the directness and simplicity of the folk cultures of traditional societies (see also CIVILIZATION).

Although originally an elitist reaction to the cultural consequences, real and imagined, of political democratization and the application of technology to the reproduction and diffusion of cultural products, the pessimism of the critics of mass culture has been mirrored in the work of left-wing critics of capitalist consumer societies, most famously in the Marxism of the FRANKFURT SCHOOL.

There are both elitist and broadly democratic versions of the critique of mass culture, although elements of the two are often conjoined. In the eyes of its elitist critics, what damns mass culture is that, in order to be easily accessible to the unlettered masses, it panders to their least noble but most nearly ubiquitous sentiments and emotions. Mass culture is, accordingly, superficial and sentimental: thus a contributor to the *New York Review* described popular music as expressing 'the deepest thoughts of the shallowest of men'. The democratic critique of mass culture contrasts it with autonomous popular culture and emphasizes the extent to which its production and distribution is in the hands of capitalist elites.

The position of the artist as creator of culture is a recurrent theme. Matthew Arnold's characterization of artists as 'aliens' is echoed in Karl Mannheim's conception of the culture-producing intelligentsia as a stratum relatively detached from the classes of modern society. (See also ART, SOCIOLOGY OF.) From this perspective, mass culture represents the threat that the remorseless commercialization of all aspects of modern life will integrate the intellectual too closely into the economic life of class society.

The poet and critic T. S. Eliot explicitly rejected Mannheim's diagnosis. Often represented as aristocratic or elitist, even Nietzschean, Eliot's critique of

mass culture is more accurately described as conservative. Eliot believed that the best guarantee against the levelling down and homogenization of culture was the maintenance of a stratified society in which the cultural creativity of each class might be protected and the common cultural heritage preserved.

Often bracketed with Eliot is the literary critic F. R. Leavis. However, if Leavis shared Eliot's alarm at what they believed to be the decline of artistic standards and of popular taste and, like Eliot, laid much of the blame on the development of the mechanical production of culture, whether in the form of cinema, gramophone records or paperback fiction, Leavis's critique of mass culture was nevertheless more democratic. Leavis bemoaned the loss of a 'common culture' whose destruction began with the arrival of the machine and was hastened by the development of the automobile which, because of the mobility it conferred, tended to uproot individuals from family and community. At the centre of Leavis's critique was a romantic myth of preindustrial society as a realm of real, organic communities innocent of the conflict between capital and labour. Modern mass production, by contrast, standardized the worker's emotional experience as surely as it did its physical products. The result was a spiritual impoverishment of the masses and an entertainment industry geared to passive diversion.

Despite the exalted role he proposed for literary critics, Leavis was not simply elitist. He believed, unlike Eliot, that the real threat to cultural vitality came from the alienation of creative thinkers from the common culture. Mass publishing, book clubs, newspapers and the MASS MEDIA in general undermined the organic relationship between creative elites and a broad readership. The threat of mass culture was not a threat from below, in the shape of the erosion of class distinctions, but from above, in the shape of profit-oriented capitalist mass media.

Similar themes are to be found in the work of the sociologist, C. Wright Mills. Mills argued that, in the American society of the 1950s, increasing specialization of function and the collapse of pluralism led to a mass society in which power was increasingly concentrated and culture was a matter of elite manipulation. Mass education, far from raising the general cultural level, produces only 'educated illiteracy' as education loses its critical function and becomes integrated with the demands of the economy, leaving only the bland, undemanding and conformist culture of white-collar suburbia.

American social criticism was conjoined with Frankfurt School Marxism in Herbert Marcuse's *One-Dimensional Man* (1964). Marcuse saw the mass media as the principal agent of an engineered social consensus that denied real human interests. Commentators even suggested that the availability of Marcuse's book in supermarket bookstalls was proof that culture had become a mere commodity.

Marcuse's was a less recondite version of the critique of mass culture advanced by the leading theorists of the Frankfurt School, T. W. Adorno and Max Horkheimer. They argued that 'high art', unlike mass culture, does not seek to reconcile the audience to the dominant economic and political order but has a transcendent, critical function. Because works of mass culture must appeal to a vast homogeneous public, they allow no room for imagination and do not engage the reader in a genuine dialectic but instead treat him or her as a passive object. The mass culture industry removes all genuine opposition to the reifying trends of capitalism and is, accordingly, the basis of modern totalitarianism.

The defenders of mass culture argue that, as a result of nearly universal literacy, diffusion of knowledge by mass media including television, and increased leisure time, 'high art' now enjoys a larger audience than ever before. Folk cultures may be 'contaminated', but cultural diversity has not disappeared, the impact of mass media is at least ambiguous, and cultural innovation continues. Perhaps, but when great works of art are acquired as investments by pension funds and it is its prospects of commercial success that determine whether a film is made or a book is published, the critique of mass culture and the 'culture industry' retains some force.

Reading
Giner, S. 1976: *Mass Society*.
Swingewood, A. 1977: *The Myth of Mass Culture*.

C. A. ROOTES

mass media   The term 'mass media' is commonly used to refer to a range of institutions concerned with the large-scale production and generalized diffusion of symbolic forms. These forms include books, newspapers, magazines, films, radio and television programmes, records, compact discs and so on.

The origins of the mass media can be traced back to the second half of the fifteenth century. Around 1440 Johann Gutenberg, a goldsmith working in Mainz, began experimenting with printing, and by 1450 he had developed his techniques far enough to exploit them commercially. Gutenberg developed a method for the replica casting of metal letters, so that large quantities of type could be produced for the composition of extended texts. He also adapted the traditional screw press for the purposes of manufacturing printed works. During the second half of the fifteenth century, these techniques spread rapidly and printing presses were set up in the major trading centres throughout Europe.

The early presses were generally commercial enterprises concerned with the reproduction of manuscripts of a religious or literary character, and with the production of texts for use in law, medicine and trade. In the early sixteenth century the presses began to print periodicals and news sheets of various kinds, and in the early seventeenth century regular newspapers began to appear. The book and newspaper industries expanded rapidly in the nineteenth century, when techniques associated with the Industrial Revolution were applied to the production of printed texts. Circulation increased significantly and, with the decline in illiteracy, books and newspapers became available to an increasing proportion of the population in industrialized (or industrializing) societies.

Radio and television broadcasting are phenomena of the twentieth century. The technical basis of broadcasting was developed by Marconi and others in the 1890s and early 1900s, and the first steps in large-scale radio broadcasting were taken in the 1920s. Television broadcasting was introduced on a large scale in the late 1940s and it quickly became one of the most popular media. In many Western industrial societies today, adults spend on average between 25 and 30 hours per week watching television, and television has become the most important source of information concerning national and international events.

Given their significance in the modern world, it could be argued that the mass media have not received the attention they deserve from social and political theorists. But a number of distinctive theoretical approaches to the mass media have been developed. Among the first social thinkers to study the mass media in a systematic way were the early 'critical theorists' associated with the Frankfurt Institute for Social Research. These theorists, including Max Horkheimer (1895–1971) and Theodor Adorno (1903–1969), were interested in the nature and impact of what they called 'the culture industry' (Horkheimer and Adorno, 1947). Writing in the 1930s and 1940s, they argued that the mass media have given rise to a new form of IDEOLOGY in modern societies. By producing large quantities of standardized and stereotyped cultural goods, the mass media were providing individuals with imaginary avenues of escape from the harsh realities of social life and were weakening their capacity to think in a critical and autonomous way. Horkheimer and Adorno suggested that these developments, among others, had rendered individuals more vulnerable to the rhetoric of Nazism and fascism.

A generally negative appraisal of the mass media and their impact can be found in the writings of other social and political theorists, particularly those influenced by Marxism. For many Marxist theorists, the mass media are viewed primarily as a medium of ideology; that is, they are regarded as a mechanism by virtue of which dominant groups or classes are able to diffuse ideas which promote their own interests, and which serve thereby to maintain the status quo. An example of this view is the approach developed by the French Marxist Louis Althusser, who treats the mass media as an integral part of what he calls 'ideological state apparatuses' (Althusser, 1971).

A different account of the nature and significance of the mass media was developed in the 1950s and 1960s by the Canadian authors Harold Innis (1894–1952) and Marshall McLuhan (1911–1981). Sometimes referred to as 'the media theorists', Innis and McLuhan argued that the very *form* of the medium of COMMUNICATION may affect the nature of social organization and human sensibility. Innis introduced the idea that every medium of communication has a certain 'bias' towards durability in time or mobility in space. He suggested that societies in which the dominant medium is biased towards temporal durability (for example, stone or clay) will tend to be small and decentralized, whereas societies with media which are biased towards spatial mobility (for example, papyrus or paper) will tend to be large and imperial, like the Roman Empire (Innis, 1950 and 1951). Innis's work was pathbreaking in the way that it linked the development of communication media to broader considerations of time, space and power.

McLuhan suggested that media technologies have had a fundamental impact on human senses and cognitive faculties. In contrast to traditional oral societies, the development of writing and printing created a culture which was dominated by the sense of vision and by an analytical, sequential approach to problem-solving. It enabled individuals to become more independent, rational and specialized. But the development of modern electronic media has, according to McLuhan, created a new cultural milieu in which the primacy of vision has been displaced by a unifying interplay of the senses, and in which individuals are bound together in global networks of instantaneous communication (see MODERNITY). In other words, electronic media have created a 'global village' (McLuhan, 1964) (see GLOBALIZATION).

The views put forward by Innis and McLuhan are rather idiosyncratic and are treated with caution by most media theorists and analysts. A large number of more detailed studies have been carried out to examine the role of the mass media in modern societies and their possible effects on social and political life. (For a review of this literature, see McQuail, 1987.) Nevertheless, the work of the media theorists, among others, has helped to highlight the fact that the development of the mass media has shaped, in a profound and irreversible way, the nature of social interaction and cultural experience in the modern world.

Reading
Curran, James and Seaton, Jean 1991: *Power Without Responsibility*, 4th edn.
Eisenstein, Elizabeth L. 1979: *The Printing Press as an Agent of Change.*
Golding, Peter 1974: *The Mass Media.*
Habermas, Jürgen 1962 (*1989*): *The Structural Transformation of the Public Sphere*, trans. T. Burger with F. Lawrence.
Meyrowitz, Joshua 1985: *No Sense of Place.*
Poster, Mark 1990: *The Mode of Information.*
Thompson, John B. 1990: *Ideology and Modern Culture.*

JOHN B. THOMPSON

mass society A term used to describe the condition of modern societies in which traditional forms of association such as community, class, ethnicity and religion have declined, and in which social organization is predominantly large-scale and bureaucratized so that social relationships are relatively impersonal. In more extreme formulations, 'mass society' is portrayed as one in which the population is an undifferentiated mass, uprooted from community, tradition and customary morality, incapable of discrimination in matters of cultural taste and politics alike, and consequently subject to waves of emotion and fashion and prey to the manipulations of unscrupulous charismatic politicians.

Mass society theory was influential particularly in the second quarter of the twentieth century as a diagnosis of the cultural and political ills that produced FASCISM and Bolshevism, and in the 1950s and 1960s as a critique of an American society that was seen as conformist and politically demobilized. In recent years it has become unfashionable, both because its elitist cultural pessimism seems unwarranted in light of the evidence of continuing and possibly increasing social and cultural pluralism, and because it has been associated with a conservative politics that did not comprehend the changed nature of POLITICAL PARTICIPATION since the mid-1960s.

The mass society perspective is, however, by no means a twentieth-century novelty. The threat posed by the uncultured, decadent or desperate urban masses to elites of talent or virtue has been a recurrent theme in political philosophy since classical antiquity but it was events of the late eighteenth and early nineteenth centuries which sharpened these concerns and laid the basis for the modern conception of mass society. So precipitately did the French revolution sweep away traditional aristocratic regimes across Europe that even thinkers who were not reactionary, like J. S. Mill, worried that democratization amounted to the political incorporation of people insufficiently educated to undertake responsibly the obligations of citizenship. Democracy might, accordingly, mean a levelling down in which the passions of the mass overwhelmed the reason of the educated elite and led to an intolerance of nonconformity.

The other major factor in this process was the transformation of predominantly agrarian societies by the interrelated processes of INDUSTRIALIZATION, bureaucratization and urbanization. Mass society theory draws heavily on the works of those nineteenth-century theorists (especially Alexis de Tocqueville, Ferdinand Tönnies, Emile Durkheim, Max Weber) who both identified these changes and who worried about their implications for social cohesion and political order. Just as the social relationships characteristic of preindustrial society were transformed by industrialization, so the political order was threatened by the collapse of the previous moral order and the loosening of the mechanical constraints which hitherto had helped to hold societies together.

But the classical sociologists did not, unlike the mass society theorists who later drew on their work, assume that the trends they identified were absolutes. The various versions of the 'community-society' polarity were intended as heuristic devices, and seen as dimensions of ongoing social processes rather than as end-states. Durkheim, in particular, saw that if social development entailed the destruction of traditional forms of community and morality, there were nevertheless possibilities of innovation. The mistake of mass society theorists was to be so blinded by nostalgia that they failed to see the development of new forms of community and morality even in societies dominated by modern forms of association.

It is as a contribution to political sociology that the mass society perspective attains its clearest theoretical specification. Kornhauser (1959) stresses the disruptive impact of rapid social, economic and political change but attaches centrality to the secondary associations de Tocqueville thought so important to the health and stability of liberal democracy. In the absence of such intermediate associations, the poorly integrated mass of the population was susceptible to mobilization by political elites while elites themselves were dangerously uninsulated from the pressures of mass opinion. The result was vulnerability to political volatility and extremism.

Kornhauser's book may be read as an attempt to generalize from the explanations of the rise of extremist movements and totalitarian societies in the 1920s and 1930s (especially those of Emil Lederer, Hannah Arendt and Franz Neumann). Most attention was, understandably, focused on Nazi Germany. The collapse of Germany into Nazism was attributed to the recency and speed of Germany's transformation into a democratic, mass society. So rapid was this change that the old associations of community, class and religion had collapsed leaving anomic and rootless masses as putty in the hands of manipulative politicians who disposed of distinctively modern means of organization and communication.

Plausible though it was, as an account of the rise of Nazism, mass society theory is flawed by the strong evidence that contradicts its central proposition. Germany was indeed a society which had suffered rapid and dislocating change, but that change was political rather than primarily social and Germany, before the accession of the Nazis to power, was not a society in which intermediary social organization was weak; on the contrary, it was stronger than in societies such as France in which the appeal of fascism was relatively limited.

Mass society theory reached its nadir when applied to the new social movements of the 1960s and 1970s, for in the case of such movements there was an abundance of evidence that it was not anomic, socially atomized individuals who were most prone to take radical political action but, on the contrary, people who were relatively well socially integrated and more than usually motivated by commitment to strong moral principles. Indeed it is this evidence that is most damaging to mass society theory. For all that rapid change is disturbing and frequently politically destabilizing, it is not usually the people who are most dislocated by rapid change who are most prone to taking radical political action, and for those who do, the character of their political involvements appears usually to be more a reflection of the values with which they were previously socialized than an unreasoning reaction to their changed circumstances.

See also COMMUNICATION.

Reading
Giner, S. 1976: *Mass Society*.
Halebsky, S. 1976: *Mass Society and Political Conflict*.
Kornhauser, W. 1959: *The Politics of Mass Society*.

C. A. ROOTES

materialism In its broadest sense, materialism contends that whatever exists just is, or at least depends upon, matter. (In its more general form it claims that all reality is essentially material; in its more specific form, that human reality is.) In the Marxist tradition, materialism has normally been of the weaker non-reductive kind. Materialism may be regarded as a 'holding operation', against forms of idealism, asserting the existence of abstract entities such as universals (unless identified as the properties of material things), supernatural beings or minds (unless identified with, or at least rooted in, bodily processes); and against explanations which invoke such entities. Materialists thus exclude the possibility of disembodied existence and are metaphysically oriented against dualism. In this article I will first consider materialism in the realm of the philosophy of mind, before turning to Marxist materialism.

Opposing classical Cartesianism, early and mid

twentieth-century BEHAVIOURISM argued that mind consists in outer acts or even movements. In the third quarter of the century it became clear that behaviourism traded, to say the least, on a confusion between meaning and empirical grounds. The dominant form of materialism, the central state materialism (CSM) advocated by D. Armstrong, U.T. Place and J.J.C. Smart, involved three steps: (1) the analysis of prima facie mental statements, such as 'I am thinking now,' as 'topic-neutral', that is, as saying nothing about the nature of the process involved; (2) the definition of a mental state, both in opposition to the classical view as an inner arena and to behaviourism as an outward act, as a (real) state of a person apt for the production of certain sorts of physical behaviour, so that the mind is seen as an inner arena identified by its causal relations to the outward act; and (3) the speculative identification of these inner processes with the physico–chemical workings of the brain, or more fully the central nervous system. CSM is most plausibly construed as a regulative principle or research programme, backed by neurophysiological evidence. But the notion of the reduction involved in step 3 is suspect; and it has been argued that CSM faces insuperable difficulties of analysis, and in sustaining causality and social interaction (Bhaskar, 1979 (*1989*), ch. 4, sections 4 and 5). Eliminative materialism (El M), perhaps most persuasively advocated by P. Churchland, following up on the writings of P. Feyerabend, W.V.O. Quine and R. Rorty, rejects the topic-neutral analysis (step 1), offering not a revisionary analysis of prima facie mentalistic terms, but denying that the statements in which they occur can be true. But it is not clear that El M can be consistently stated. Other realist philosophers, objecting to the deterministic and reductionistic implications of CSM and El M alike, have counterposed to it a view of minds as causally (and taxonomically) irreducible, but dependent, modes of matter. For instance, on the position of synchronic emergent powers materialism (SEPM) advanced by R. Bhaskar, mind is conceived not as a substance, whether material or immaterial, but as a complex of powers. This has analogies with H. Putnam's 'functionalism'.

'Double-aspect theories', revived by P. Strawson, are often regarded as species of materialism – because on them, mind and matter are two modes of a single substance. But they suffer from an ambivalent ontological commitment. If the mental attributes are real (irreducibly causally efficacious) then they amount to SEPM; if not to CSM. On the other hand, if this question is evaded, then there is no non-subjective criterion for the attribution of any mental states at all. Epiphenomenalism, still sometimes supported, has difficulties in doing justice to the phenomenon of our *agency*.

It is this that the early Marx stressed in elaborating his *practical materialism* (PM), asserting the constitutive role of human tranformative agency in the reproduction and the transformation of social forms. *Historical materialism* (HM), asserting the causal primacy of men's and women's MODE OF PRODUCTION and their natural (physical) being, or of the labour process more generally, in the development of human history consists in a substantive elaboration of PM. It is rooted in *ontological materialism* (OM), asserting the unilateral dependence of social upon biological (and more generally physical) being and the emergence of the former from and its subsequent causal efficacy on the latter (cf. SEPM). And it presupposes scientific realist or *epistemological materialism* (EM), asserting the independent existence and transfactual efficacy of at least some of the objects of scientific thought.

Only PM can be dealt with in any detail here. The First Thesis on Feuerbach (see Marx, *Early Writings*, 1975, pp. 421–2) implies a distinction between (α) objectivity or externality as such and (β) objectification as the production of a subject, or in the terminology of modern scientific realism between the intransitive objects of knowledge and the transitive activity of knowledge production. The Sixth Thesis (ibid, p. 423) entails a distinction between (β) intentional human activity and (γ) the reproduction or transformation of the antecedently existing, historically social forms, given as the conditions and media of that activity, but reproduced or transformed only in it. Failure adequately to distinguish (α) and (β) as two aspects of the unity of known objects has led to tendencies to both epistemological idealism (reduction of (α) to (β) from György Lukács and Antonio Gramsci to Leszek Kolakowski and Alfred Schmidt) and reversion to traditional contemplative materialism (reduction of (β) to (α) from Engels and Lenin to Della Volpe and the contemporary exponents of 'reflection theory'). And failure adequately to distinguish (β) and (γ) as two aspects of the unity of transformative activity (or as the duality of praxis and structure) has resulted in both sociological

individualism and voluntarism (reduction of (γ) to (β), as in, for instance, Jean-Paul Sartre) and determinism and reification (reduction of (β) to (γ) as in, for instance, Louis Althusser).

The hallmark of the dialectical materialist tradition (see also DIALECTICAL MATERIALISM) was a combination of a dialectics of nature and a reflectionist theory of knowledge. Both were rejected by Lukács in the seminal text of Western Marxism, *History and Class Consciousness* (1923), which also argued that they were mutually inconsistent. In general when Western Marxism has been sympathetic to dialectical motifs, it has been hostile to materialism. On the other hand, when Western Marxism has advertised its materialism, this has usually been of an exclusively epistemological kind, as in Althusser, G. Della Volpe and Lucio Colletti; and, where ontological topics have been broached, as in S. Timpanaro's re-emphasis of the role of nature in social life, discussion has often been vitiated by an unreflected empirical realism.

In any discussion of materialism there lurks the problem of a definition of matter. For Marx's PM, which is restricted to the social sphere (including of course natural science) and where 'materialism' is to be understood as 'social practice', no particular difficulty arises. But from Engels on, Marxist materialism has had more global pretensions, and the difficulty now appears that if a material thing is regarded as a perduring occupant of space capable of being perceptually identified and re-identified, then many objects of scientific knowledge, although dependent for their *identification* upon material things, are immaterial. Clearly if one distinguishes between scientific and philosophical ontologies, such considerations need not, as both Bertrand Russell and Lenin saw, refute philosophical materialism. But what then is its content? Some 'materialists' have subscribed to the idea of the exhaustive knowability of the world by science. This seems an extraordinarily anthropocentric – even idealist – conceit. On the other hand, the weaker supposition that whatever is knowable must be knowable by science, if not tautologous, merely displaces the truth of materialism on to the feasibility of NATURALISM in particular domains.

For such reasons one might be tempted to treat materialism more as a *prise de position* than as a set of quasi-descriptive theses, and more specifically as: (a) a series of *denials*, largely (remembering that Hegel could plausibly assert that the history of philosophy is the history of idealism) of claims of traditional philosophy, concerning the existence of God, souls, forms, ideas, sense-data, duties, the absolute and so on, or the impossibility (or inferior status) of science or earthly happiness; and (b) as an indispensable ground for such denials, a commitment to their scientific explanation as modes of false or inadequate consciousness or ideology. However such an orientation still presupposes some *positive* account of science (ideology, etc.). In fact it may be easier to justify materialism as an account of science and scientificity than it is to justify materialism *per se*; and perhaps only such a *specific* explication and defence of materialism is consistent with Marx's critique of hypostatized and abstract thought (for example, in the Second Thesis on Feuerbach (ibid p. 422)). It is significant here that a transcendental realist explication of materialism is congruent with an emergent powers naturalist orientation.

The importance of this last consideration is that, since Marx and Engels, Marxism has conducted a double polemic: against idealism and against vulgar, reductionist or 'undialectical' materialism (that is, contemplative (Marx) or mechanical (Engels) materialism). And the project of elaborating a satisfactory 'materialist' account or critique of some subject matter, characteristically celebrated by idealism, has often amounted in practice to the attempt to avoid *reductionism* without reverting to *dualism*. This has normally necessitated a war of position on two fronts – against various types of 'objectivism' and against various formally counterposed, but actually complementary or interdependent, types of 'subjectivism' (Bhaskar, 1989, pp. 131–2). It would then be the intention of Marxist materialism to transform the common problematic, thus throwing both the errors and the partial insights of the old symbiotes into critical relief.

Reading

Armstrong, D. 1968: *A Materialist Theory of Mind.*
Bhaskar, Roy 1979 (*1989*): *The Possibility of Naturalism,* 2nd edn.
Churchland, P. 1979: *Scientific Realism and the Plasticity of Mind.*
Labica, G. 1980: *Marxism and the Status of Philosophy.*
Putnam, H. 1976: The mental life of some machines. In *The Philosophy of Mind,* ed. J. Glover.
Rorty, R. 1980: *Philosophy and the Mirror of Nature,* part 1.
Soper, K. 1981: *On Human Needs.*
Timpanaro, S. 1976: *On Materialism.*

ROY BHASKAR

materialism, dialectical *See* DIALECTICAL MATERIALISM

measurement   Statements such as 'A is more X than B', 'A is n times more X than B' appear as grounded when adequate measurement procedures are defined thanks to which a set A, B, C . . . of objects can be compared with respect to X. Thus, a rod A can be said to be longer than B once a measure of length has been defined and applied to A and B. In the same way, a society A will be considered as more mobile socially once a measure of social mobility has been defined.

Measurement is a current operation in the social as well as in the natural sciences. Without measurement, it is impossible to answer such simple descriptive sociological questions as: Are rates of suicide greater now in country A than twenty years ago? Is social inequality decreasing or increasing in society A? Is social inequality greater in country A than in B? Has intergenerational social mobility been increasing or decreasing in country A in the last decade?

While these questions show that the social sciences cannot avoid measurement, they illustrate also the difficulties of measurement in these sciences. Ethnomethodologists and phenomenologists have rightly made the point that measuring, say, rates of suicide can be meaningless, since the social definition of suicide is variable with time and place and recording a death as a suicide is a social decision affected by many factors. These objections should be relativized, however: while it is true that such measures as suicide rates should not be taken at their face value, they can provide reliable 'weak' comparative statements (as in: 'rates of suicide appear to increase from time 1 to time 2'; 'they are greater in country A than in B').

A second methodological difficulty is even more crucial. Lengths can be measured in inches or centimetres: if a rod appears as longer than another in inches it will also be longer in centimetres. However, this property of alternative physical measures (according to which they are *monotonically* related to one another) is generally lost in the case of the measures used in the social sciences. Thus, social mobility can be measured by the so-called Glass index, by the Yasuda index or by many other indices (Boudon, 1973). In the same fashion, income equality/inequality, educational equality/

inequality, and so on, can be measured in several ways. Now, it is theoretically possible that, say, a society A appears as more mobile or more equal than B with regard to some variable when one measure is used, while the reverse will be true with another measure.

This means that concepts such as 'social mobility' or 'inequality' are actually much more ambiguous than 'length' or 'temperature': the various available indices correspond actually to various interpretations of these notions. In practice, however, these various measures often appear as convergent.

See also SOCIAL STATISTICS.

Reading
Douglas, Jack C. 1967 (*1970*): *The Social Meanings of Suicide*.
Pawson, Ray 1989: *A Measure for Measures*.

RAYMOND BOUDON

media *See* MASS MEDIA

medicine All societies have ways of interpreting and understanding the phenomenon of illness. Factors as diverse as the stars, sins, the weather and a person's constitution have been used in the past as the basis for explanatory frameworks; but the dominant explanation during the twentieth century in the West – and increasingly throughout the world – is based on a theory of disease which first emerged in the late eighteenth century in Parisian hospitals (Ackerknecht, 1967).

Whereas the previous medical view had held that an important characteristic of illness was its movement, the new medicine of hospitals made the radical claim that it could be localized to specific malformations of anatomic structures – so-called pathological lesions – inside the body. This analysis at once justified the hospitalization of the patient (to place the body in a neutral setting) where medical practitioners could practise their new-found skills of the clinical examination (to localize the lesion), and the post-mortem (which allowed the truth about the lesion to be revealed to the medical eye) (Foucault, 1963).

This new model of illness was remarkably successful: rival systems of medicine were soon swept away as hospitals were built throughout Europe and North America and the medical profession organized systems of state licensing to mar-

ginalize and eliminate the 'non-qualified' from treatment of the sick (Starr, 1982). Thus by the early twentieth century a strong pathology-based biomedicine, as it is often called, was firmly established and in a position to benefit from the enormous increase in resources devoted to health care during the rest of the century, particularly through the commitment of governments to health-care welfare programmes for their populations (see HEALTH).

Despite the continuance and dominance of a biomedical approach to illness throughout the twentieth century – with its narrow gaze directed on the pathological lesion deep inside the body – a parallel interest in the social and psychological world of the patient has emerged (Armstrong, 1983). During the mid-nineteenth century, the public health movement had successfully improved the living conditions of the population by measures directed to environmental hygiene, such as sanitation, food inspection and clean drinking water. Indeed, it has been argued that the improvements in the health status of the population since the mid-nineteenth century are the result of these social policies rather than the actions of individual clinicians (McKeown, 1979). After its 'golden age', public health became routinized and neglected; but it was revived in the early years of the twentieth century with the discovery of the social as a new space in which illness could manifest itself. Recognition of a link between 'social factors' and diseases such as tuberculosis and venereal disease formed the basis for this new social medicine. In its most recent form, often referred to as the 'new public health', emphasis is given to the regulation of lifestyles through health promotion activities, and to a belief that individuals should begin to take responsibility for maintaining their own health (Martin and McQueen, 1989).

In parallel with the emergence of concerns for the overall health of the population, clinical medicine began to recognize the importance of the individual patient's psychosocial world. This shift can be seen particularly in psychiatry, which moved away from its nineteenth-century exclusive preoccupation with insanity towards the everyday problems of coping, as found in the clinical problems of anxiety and depression (see PSYCHIATRY AND MENTAL ILLNESS; CLINICAL DEPRESSION).

The extension of medicine into areas of social life, both through social medicine and the concerns of an increasingly psychosocially orientated clinical medicine, has evoked a number of responses. One has been to welcome the shift in emphasis as a humanizing and liberating change. Instead of objectifying patients as nothing more than physical bodies, recognition of the psychosocial aspects of illness means that patients have their autonomy and dignity respected; late twentieth-century identification of the patient as a consumer is but one component of this more patient-oriented vision.

Other commentators have been more critical. If a medicine of bodies could be reproached for objectifying those same bodies, then a medicine which monitors the psychosocial functioning of the patient has analogous effects on the patient's wholeness. In short, medicine stands accused of medicalizing social life, reducing feelings, cognitions and behaviour to yet more 'factors' which need proper management (Arney and Bergen, 1984). On the one hand, this is said to remove responsibility from autonomous patients by persuading them to seek and become dependent on medical advice for all aspects of living (Illich, 1978); and on the other hand, the move to emphasize self-responsibility for health means an additional burden of stigmatization when people 'fail' in their task (Crawford, 1977).

A third response to the extension of medicine's purview into the psychosocial world of the patient has been to treat it as neither liberating nor repressive, but as reflecting another facet of the multilayered relationship between medicine and society. From the significance of medical diseases, such as cancer and tuberculosis, as metaphors in lay thought (Sontag, 1979), to the impact of organic models of equilibrium on social theory, medical ideas have fed into the social. The influences in the other direction are more subtle, yet more profound. These range from the recognition that much of what passes for esoteric and technical knowledge is in fact predicated on lay knowledge (Hughes, 1977), to the claim that all medical knowledge embodies social representations. Thus the category of disease, which medicine reads as a biological phenomenon, is itself a social artefact: the difference between normal and abnormal in medicine (physiology and pathology) must be rooted in normative assessments of how the body should be functioning. In this sense, all diseases, despite their biological manifestation, encode social evaluations of what is to count as normal in any particular society. A further extension of this approach is the argument that not only is the boundary between normal and abnormal socially derived, but the very content of pathology reflects a historically located way of reading the nature of the body (Armstrong, 1983) and the mind (Rose, 1990).

During the late twentieth century, medicine has held together an ascendency over an increasingly complex health division of labour: in many ways the move into psychosocial areas can be seen as part of a strategy for maintaining hegemony over the province of illness. Nevertheless, there are already signs of independence from other health-care professionals, such as nurses, and an increasing use of alternative and complementary practitioners by the public; at the same time biomedicine is having to cope with challenges to its effectiveness and efficiency (Cochrane, 1972), and major constraints on its future funding. Taken together these suggest a growing challenge to the dominant framework of medicine in which illness is conceptualized.

Reading
Armstrong, D. 1983: *Political Anatomy of the Body: Medical Knowledge in Britain in the Twentieth Century*.
Arney, W.R. and Bergen, B.J. 1984: *Medicine and the Management of Living: Taming the Last Great Beast*.
Foucault, M. 1963: *The Birth of the Clinic: An Archeology of Medical Perception*.
Illich, I. 1978: *Medical Nemesis: The Expropriation of Health*.
Starr, P. 1982: *The Social Transformation of American Medicine*.

DAVID ARMSTRONG

mental illness *See* PSYCHIATRY AND MENTAL ILLNESS

messianism A redeemer is awaited who will transform the present order, replacing it with a reign of universal harmony and bliss. This 'messianic' idea is crucial for the cultural complex emerging from Mediterranean history. While messianism originated in Mesopotamia, it took different forms in the Judaic, Christian and Islamic contexts and has taken on new meaning in modern times.

The prophetic books of the Old Testament contain the basic features of the messianic expectation: the centrality of prophecy itself; an active rather than contemplative attitude; the perception of present conditions as unbearable ('captivity' or 'exile'); a linear vision of history, where present suffering looks to the past for harmony and to the future for redemption; the visible and collective nature of that transformation; the extension of its scope towards universal limits, involving all peoples, friend or foe, and all nature, savage or domestic, earthly or cosmic; the affinity between messianism and later apocalyptic literature, symbolizing the traumatic passages from this to the other world order; redemption as an extraordinary feat which transcends human capacities in every way; the personal nature of reality's ultimate meaning, framed between divine sovereignty and human unrest; the personalization of the word and the act of redemption, made real by the coming of the 'Messiah'.

Jewish tradition projects His coming to the end of time, when all nations shall recognize the God of Israel. Christians believe that the Messiah has already been amidst us, and continues to dwell among us through sacramental and charismatic means (see also CHARISMA). Humankind is therefore internally divided between recognition and ignorance, or denial, of His presence, living through a time of transition between His first and second coming, when all division will be overcome.

Islam underlines the prophetic element in this tradition, subsuming Jewish and Christian memory as part of a revelation that reaches its ultimate point with and after Muhammad. Universal judgement, at the end of history, is reaffirmed and dramatized in the present struggles (*Jihad*, holy war) between the faithful and those who will not bow to the only true God. The messianic element common to Islamic culture is particularly developed by the Shiite branch.

Modern rationalism challenged transcendence. The religious symbolism was therefore translated into immanent and supposedly conceptual terms. Yet the messianic expectation was not forgotten. Rather, it was reinterpreted and integrated into the ideologies characteristic of modernity, shaping the historical horizon of 'nations', 'races' and 'social classes'.

The planetary expansion of modern culture has generalized that horizon, which became refracted in a great variety of local traditions. Travellers, missionaries, merchants and anthropologists gave notice of 'messianic movements' in other peoples, such as the 'cargo cult' of Melanesia or the 'land without evil' of the Guaraní in South America. The messianic notion has thus been expanded to include beliefs of a transhistorical and transcultural dimension. This more generalized use of the term,

however, has occurred in a discursive context, carried by travellers, laden with Western memories and expectations.

Although fundamental, messianism has never entirely dominated the culture of which it is a part. Law and tradition, on the one hand, contemplation and magic, on the other, have always formed fundamental counterpoints to the messianic expectation. Priests, legislators, merchants and philosophers have traditionally been mistrustful of prophecy. Even today most social scientists study messianism with a polemical bias, recalling the catastrophic results that may issue from radical promises of immediate redemption. This kind of criticism is as old as messianism itself.

Reading

Cohn, Norman 1970: *The Pursuit of the Millennium*, revised and expanded edn.

Sachedina, A.A. 1980: *Islamic Messianism: The Idea of the Mahdi in Twelver Shi'ism*.

Scholem, Gershom G. 1961 (*1973*): *Major Trends in Jewish Mysticism*, revised edn.

Wallis, Wilson D. 1943: *Messiahs: Their Role in Civilization*.

Worsley, Peter 1957 (*1970*): *The Trumpet Shall Sound: A Study of 'Cargo' Cults in Melanesia*.

RUBEM CÉSAR FERNANDES

Methodenstreit Formally, the 'dispute over method' dates from Carl Menger's critique of German historical economics as expounded in his *Untersuchungen über die Methode der Sozialwissenschaften* (1883) and Schmoller's review of this book (1883), together with Dilthey's *Einleitung in die Geisteswissenschaften* that appeared the same year (see Dilthey, 1923). Menger had drawn attention in his book to the absence of a systematic methodological appraisal of POLITICAL ECONOMY, especially in Germany. A major section of his work was given over to specific criticisms of German historical economics, and it is this aspect of the book that has come to characterize the nature of the dispute. Menger's critique and Schmoller's quick response initiated a dispute on the nature and relation of theoretical and practical knowledge in the social sciences that has survived to this day.

Menger argued in the preface to his critique that contemporary political economy was characterized by a plurality of methods that derived from a failure to distinguish consistently between the precepts of theoretical ECONOMICS and the methods to be followed in the practical investigation of economic forms. As a consequence, there was a lack of clarity and agreement concerning the nature and purpose of political economy that was becoming increasingly problematic. His treatise sought to correct this through a systematic critique of the conception that the principles of economics could be developed on the basis of a practical study of national economies – or, as Wilhelm Roscher had argued in 1843, that the laws of economics could be revealed through a study of the formation of economic systems. Menger drew attention to the fact that there was a lack of symmetry between the historical method as practised in law, and the method as practised in economics. Exponents of the former were capable of identifying clear principles that persistently eluded exponents of the latter such as Schmoller, Roscher and Karl Knies. In many respects, of course, the lines of his argument recapitulate aspects of methodological debate since the beginning of the century, but Menger does not situate his argument by reference to French and English debates on 'inductive' versus 'deductive' political economy, debates associated with the names of David Ricardo, Thomas Malthus and Richard Jones.

Schmoller in his review rejected the idea that theoretical *Nationalökonomie* could in fact aspire to the revelation of general economic principles: 'Economic phenomena are the outcome of individual economic desires and must therefore be considered from this point of view,' he stated. This focus on self-interest was necessarily a concrete one, identifiable only within the fabric of social activity. Only on this practical, concrete and historicizing basis could one advance to firm principles which would then permit a degree of deductive reasoning on forms. Schmoller further argued that Menger's proposed reform owed much to John Stuart Mill's 'natural scientific logic', hinting at a dimension to the controversy that was to develop in the next decade.

A difficulty in assessing the issues raised by the exchanges between Menger and Schmoller is that the former in no respect resembles our modern preconceptions of an abstract economist, while the latter's 'historical economics' is highly diffuse. Furthermore, as later writers pointed out, whereas Roscher as the founder of the German historical school of economics clearly stated his belief in the existence of laws of economic development, Schmoller at times denied any such economic regularity. Menger was able to mount a precise

epistemological critique of the manner in which 'history' and 'economy' combined in the work of Schmoller, but no such concise defence of 'historical method' was ever formulated by Schmoller. While this can be attributed to a lack of clarity in Schmoller himself over the nature of historical and economic method, a logical defence of historical method is a formidable task.

Max Weber avowed himself a member of the 'younger historical school' of German economics in the early 1890s, but the methodological principle of *Verstehen* that he went on to develop in his writings is more indebted to the principles espoused by Menger than to any historical understanding of social action. The present lack of any detailed account of German economics in the later nineteenth century makes it difficult to appreciate the finer aspects of the controversy, but it is possible to judge its effects as transmitted through the work of Weber, as well as in the existence of a translation of Menger's original critique.

Reading
Hasbach, W. 1895: Zur Geschichte des Methodenstreites in der politischen Ökonomie. In *Jahrbuch für Gesetzgebung, Verwaltung und Volkswirtschaft* NF Jg. 19, 465–90, 751–808.
Hutchison, T.W. 1981: Carl Menger on philosophy and method. In *The Politics and Philosophy of Economics*.
Menger, Carl 1883 (*1985*): *Investigations in the Method of the Social Sciences with Special Reference to Economics*.
Schmoller, G. 1883: Zur Methodologie der Staats- und Sozial-Wissenschaften. In *Jahrbuch für Gesetzgebung, Verwaltung und Volkswirtschaft* NF Jg. 7, 975–94.

KEITH TRIBE

methodology This notion, which describes the critical activity directed by scientists toward the procedures, theories, concepts and/or findings produced by scientific research, should not be confused with 'technology', that is, the activity of dealing with the techniques, devices and recipes used by scientific research.

Methodology is important for a simple reason: in the social and human sciences as well as in the natural sciences, it represents an essential (though of course not exclusive) path through which scientific progress is brought about. A better understanding of the world can be gained, in Karl Popper fashion, by generating theories and trying to make them as compatible as possible with observational data. But it can also be gained by a reflexive critical view addressed by the scientist toward his or her own activity. Thus, the special theory of relativity was probably born in part from the failure of the Michelson–Morley experiment, but also from Albert Einstein's critical analysis of the notion of simultaneity. Whereas previously most people treated this notion as unproblematic, Einstein noted that it is clear and unambiguous only as long as events do not occur on mobiles moving away from – or towards – one another at a speed significant with regard to the speed of light. This critical analysis of a familiar notion produced, as is well known, a revolution in our representation of the physical world.

Among classical sociologists, Max Weber as well as Emile Durkheim paid great attention to methodology and devoted important writings to this field. P. Lazarsfeld among modern sociologists insisted with particular force on the importance of methodology for the development of the social sciences. In several publications and notably in the volume he co-edited with M. Rosenberg, *The Language of Social Research*, he tried to illustrate and institutionalize methodology. Unfortunately, the very notion of methodology is often misunderstood: this is readily confirmed by the fact that in many places methodology courses are actually technology courses.

A few examples will show that methodology can effectively have an important impact in the social sciences. Thus, the study of socioeconomic development took a new course when the meaning of aggregate measures of the so-called *national product* was criticized and clarified and when it was realized that the GNP of a country would increase tremendously, given the way this quantity is defined, if each citizen would clean his neighbour's car rather than his own. In the same way, it has been shown that income inequality can be measured in several ways and that there is no guarantee that all the measures will lead to the same conclusion. While stick A will always be longer than stick B, independently of the way the two sticks are measured, incomes can appear as more *unequally* distributed in society A than in society B when a given index is used, while they appear as more *equally* distributed in A with regard to another acceptable index. As long as this point is not realized, many ill-grounded conclusions can be drawn from inequality measures (see MEASUREMENT).

One of the methodological points developed by Lazarsfeld has become particularly famous: that a correlation between x and y can be spurious, that is, correspond to no causal influence between x and y.

Several important studies can be mentioned, in fact, whose impact derives from the fact that they demonstrated the spuriousness of correlations which had been interpreted in a causal fashion. Thus, the post-Weberian controversy on *The Protestant Ethic* has shown that, while Weber saw a direct influence of the puritan *ethos* on the development of the capitalist spirit, this correlation should rather be interpreted as the product of a number of indirect effects. Writers such as H. Lüthy and H. R. Trevor Roper showed, for instance, that the countries which had been receptive to the new faith were also more open to business. Weber himself had already recognized that the French Huguenots were active in business because other professional opportunities, notably cultural or political, were closed to them, officially or in practice.

As in the case of the notion of simultaneity in physics, methodology can often take the form of a critical analysis of notions currently used in the social sciences. Thus Durkheim was not satisfied by the notion of 'primitive mentality' used by Lévy-Bruhl to explain the beliefs in magic, probably because he detected in it an *ad hoc* and circular character. At any rate, he developed a theory of magic of his own (close to Weber's) where he tried to show that magic could be explained by *good reasons*, without supposing that the 'primitive' followed logical rules and mental procedures different from ours. This criticism can be generalized: many contemporary authors are critical towards irrational, 'over-socialized' views of men, of social actors and of social behaviour and have proposed, following in this respect the Weberian tradition, to interpret behaviour and beliefs as inspired by reasons, at least so long as no proof to the contrary can be given. Actually, the importance of Weber's sociology of religion is above all methodological: its main innovation lies in the fact that it shows by many examples that even beliefs that are apparently the most strange can be explained as inspired by reasons. Thus, the Roman civil servants had good reasons for being attracted by the cult of Mithra: it included hierarchical values close to the values of the Roman administration itself.

Methodology can take the form of a systematic criticism of the notions, concepts, inferences from statistical or qualitative data, or models of behaviour proposed by the social sciences. It can also discuss the very nature of explanation in the social sciences. Thus, to some writers, the social sciences should consider themselves as interpretive rather than explanatory (see VERSTEHEN). To others, building or generating models is a major activity of the social as well as of the natural sciences and defines the very notion of explanation.

See also PHILOSOPHY OF SCIENCE; PHILOSOPHY OF SOCIAL SCIENCE.

Reading
Boudon, Raymond 1979: Generating models as a research strategy. In *Qualitative and Quantitative Social Research*, ed. R. Merton et al.
Durkheim, Emile 1895 (*1982*): *Les Règles de la méthode sociologique*.
Lazarsfeld, Paul and Rosenberg, Morris 1955: *The Language of Social Research*.
Pawson, Ray 1979: *A Measure for Measures*.
Pellicani, Luciano 1988: Weber and the myth of Calvinism. *Telos* no. 75 (Spring), 57–85.
Weber, Max 1922 (*1968*): *Gesammelte Aufsätze zur Wissenschaftslehre*.

RAYMOND BOUDON

middle class   There has been a longstanding series of controversies about the place of the middle class in the overall class system of advanced industrial societies. The controversies include whether there is one middle class or a number; whether such a CLASS (or classes) is in any sense in the 'middle' of society; whether the position of the class(es) is being changed through a process of 'proletarianization'; and whether such a class(es) will develop forms of politics and consciousness aligned to either the WORKING CLASS or the capitalist class or will be relatively independent of both.

The term 'middle class' appears to have been used first by the Reverend Thomas Gisborne in 1785, to refer to the propertied and entrepreneurial class located between landowners, on the one hand, and agricultural and urban labourers, on the other. This usage remained common during the nineteenth century, but in this century the term 'middle class' has come to refer to 'white-collar occupations'. These range from professionals, such as doctors, accountants, lawyers, academics and so on, to people in relatively routine and less skilled clerical jobs. Sometimes middle class is taken to refer to all those with 'non-manual' occupations; at other times owners of factories and the self-employed are excluded.

Whichever definition is used there is no doubt that such groups have increased in absolute numbers and as a proportion of the employed population in all the major Western countries. In Britain, for example, the proportion of non-manual employees has risen from 19 per cent in 1911 to 47 per cent in 1981. This increase has been particularly marked among female employees. By 1981 approximately three-fifths of female workers, but only about two-fifths of male workers, had non-manual jobs. However, there are marked differences in the gender composition of different non-manual jobs. Most professional workers are male; most lower level white-collar workers are female.

There are many theories which attempt to place such a class or classes within the overall class system of advanced capitalist societies. These can be divided between Marxist and Weberian theories. In the former it is argued that it is the relations of *production* which generate different social classes, while in the latter it is maintained that classes are produced through the different ways in which rewards from different occupations are acquired and distributed through the *market*.

Marx's own views were contradictory. On the one hand, he argued that there would be growing polarization between the 'two great hostile camps' of the bourgeois and the working classes with the result that the middle classes would be squeezed out and forced to join one or other of the hostile camps (see also BOURGEOISIE). On the other hand, he maintained that the middle class will in fact grow in size as a smaller proportion of the workforce would need to play a direct role in the production of material commodities – in particular there will be increased importance of 'commercial wage-workers'.

Many Marxists have argued however that such office workers are a fundamentally unstable grouping. Indeed some writers have asserted that there is no middle *class* as such, merely a number of intermediate strata. As a result of the insecurity of employment and the 'deskilling' of their labour, with office enlargement and mechanization, such strata will experience the 'proletarianization' of their class position (Braverman, 1974). And it is argued that over time the middle strata will come to adopt proletarian forms of class consciousness and politics, including union organization and voting for left-wing parties.

Other Marxist writers have argued by contrast that there is no general process of proletarianization. Poulantzas (1974), for example, maintains that there is a substantial 'new petty bourgeoisie' determined not only by economic but also by political and ideological structures, and which has a class position different from both capital and labour. Johnson (1972) has argued that certain professions will not be proletarianized where their power rests on forms of knowledge which cannot be easily expressed and codified in technical terms. In the USA Ehrenreich and Ehrenreich (1979) maintain that there is a distinctive 'professional-managerial class' based on the possession of a college degree, who function to reproduce capitalist culture and relations. This new class has given rise to new forms of politics which disrupt previously structured politics between capital and labour. Finally, Wright (1985) maintains that not all positions in the division of labour are in fact to be seen as *class* positions as such – they are rather to be viewed as 'contradictory class-positions'.

Weberian writers have developed a number of diverse arguments partly in opposition to Marxist claims. Lockwood (1958), for example, maintained that clerical workers were not being proletarianized because they occupied a work situation which still gave them a superior status compared with manual workers. Giddens (1973) maintained that dichotomous theories of social class must fail because they are unable to recognize how the market capacity of educational and technical qualifications generates middle-class occupations which possess considerable economic advantages over manual occupations. Other writers have claimed that there is no such single entity as *the* middle class. Rather there is a fragmentary class system made up of various social groups which possess different images and conceptions of what that system is like. Indeed it is further claimed that investigating people's work experiences over their lifetime shows that there is enormous diversity. Many male clerical workers, for example, are not to be viewed as 'proletarianized' because they experience career mobility and become managers. It is female white-collar workers who are much more likely to be in proletarianized jobs, although there is some evidence that young women are increasingly obtaining the educational credentials which are necessary for promotion. Finally, it does seem that many white-collar workers are willing to join trade unions which often take up 'proletarian' positions on issues. Indeed it is white-collar workers in the public sector who have been the most militant in the 1980s in many European countries.

In recent years, researchers have been emphasizing a number of points. First, the distinction between Marxist and Weberian theories became much less clear-cut in the 1980s. This is because, on the one hand, Marxist writers now analyse in much more detail labour market differences, particularly those resulting from the differential possession of educational credentials. And, on the other hand, Weberians have come to appreciate that lying behind occupational differences in the labour market are a wide array of structural transformations of production. In particular, the internationalization of production means that there are large differences in the relative size and importance of the middle classes between different societies, particularly depending on where the headquarters of the major companies are located.

Second, an example of this coming together of Marxist and Weberian approaches can be seen in the recent literature on the 'service class'. This notion was developed by the Austro-Marxist Karl Renner who argued that as capitalism expands its scale of operations, capitalists increasingly employ people to carry out those functions that they can no longer perform personally. This class serves capital, either directly within capitalist organizations or indirectly within professions and the state. Goldthorpe (1980) has developed this notion, both in showing its relatively heterogeneous origins, and in emphasizing the importance of career and trust to the service class. More recently, research in Britain has suggested that new kinds of service-class positions are being developed which do not involve lifetime service with a single organization. The development of a so-called 'yuppie' culture has been attributed to the increased numbers of people possessing high-level professional and managerial skills which permit them to move *between* organizations.

Finally, it has been strongly argued that there is no simple 'proletariat' whose interests can be unproblematically established and to which some sectors of the middle class may be moving. Whether 'proletarian' politics emerges depends on a calculation by workers as to whether they would benefit from such politics. Furthermore, it is suggested that contemporary society is much affected by the growth of a powerful service class which is changing the contours of social and political life and in particular affecting the 'proletariat' and its ability to develop its own distinctive forms of politics. People in modern societies are not all 'middle class' but as the middle class changes so it is having profound effects on everyone else.

Reading
Abercrombie, N. and Urry, J. 1983: *Capital, Labour and the Middle Classes.*
Bourdieu, P. 1979 (*1984*): *Distinction.*
Hyman, R. and Price, R. eds 1983: *The New Working Class? White collar Workers and their Organizations: A Reader.*

JOHN URRY

migration Movements of peoples from one place to another are extremely old phenomena. Invasions, conquests, exoduses, seasonal moves and definitive settlements on other territories and in different societies punctuate human history. Today, there are few societies that have not been shaped by the integration of groups and cultures which have been aggregating for ages. The European societies – sixteenth-century Spain, and then the industrial societies, with the notable exception of France – saw early important migrations towards the 'virgin lands' of America, Australia and of the colonial empires. Those migratory movements to new lands were explained by the same reasons that apply today: the overpopulation and destitution which prevailed in certain regions of Europe, such as Ireland, Scotland or the south of Italy, and the disorganization of the traditional economies due to a widening capitalist market, mainly in Britain. Occasionally, emigrations result from political or religious causes: the minorities, oppressed on political, ethnic or religious grounds, fly from the threatening regimes. To Jews, Protestant minorities, Armenians, political refugees and others, the new countries are symbols of freedom as well as of affluence.

The sociology of migrations is essentially devoted to immigration, to the process of integration and assimilation of a foreign community in a host society. Not unexpectedly, the United States is the country in which this sociology first developed, since immigration coincided with the very birth of American society. In Europe, since the middle of this century the migratory trend has been reversed, with the original countries of emigration in industrial Europe first drawing in workers, then their families, from southern Europe, and then from Africa, from the West Indies, south-east Asia and Indonesia, and from the old colonies. When the migratory flows began to stabilize and the population to settle, the European economies entered into troubled times, during the 1970s, and economic, demographic, cultural and political studies of immigration expanded.

In the 1920s, the sociologists of the Chicago school (see CHICAGO SOCIOLOGY) dealt with immigration in terms of urban integration, of change from the traditional to the modern way of life. How do the migrant communities coming from the rural South, the black community among others, or from various parts of the world, integrate into the town in a spatial way and into modernity from a cultural viewpoint? Robert Park and Ernest Burgess studied the trajectories of the various groups in the urban space by isolating cycles and regular processes which range from segregation to integration, through a transitional process of relationships of progressive reciprocity with the host society. These studies prove that the melting-pot pattern, the mixing in American culture, allows of very numerous exceptions: some immigrants happen to fail in their settlement plans and go back to their mother country; others cannot manage to put an end to segregation and to the obstacle of PREJUDICE; others even remain in a closed community space; and finally some merge into the modern town. With the passing of years, the signs of urban segregation in the American cities have hardly changed, and segregation of the various groups, mainly the black and white groups, is still the standard rule.

Immigration can be viewed as a process of cultural transformation, as an ordeal suffered by the actor who sees the norms, values and identifications of his or her group of origin moving away, without adopting for all that the patterns of their host society and without feeling accepted. The famous study of Thomas and Znaniecki, *The Polish Peasant* (1918), of the life stories of Polish immigrants who came to Chicago at the beginning of the century describes the mechanisms of 'acculturation' and of cultural transformation undergone by the migrant who has to change from rural to urban society, from a community structured by its religious values to the diversity of the town, from recognition to anonymity. The violent breaking of traditional ties, isolation and the normative uncertainties, may turn immigration into an experience of social disorganization leading to the deviant and marginal behaviours often associated with immigration.

But the migrant is not always alone, since he or she may also belong to a community which still has coherence in its new place, is able to welcome new arrivals, to offer them resources and a sense of security and continuity in identity, and to make the cultural change ordeal easier for them. In fact, the total assimilation of a group to the host culture as early as the second or third generation is something rare, and many societies appear as medleys of communities whose relationships of reciprocity transform little by little the culture of the host society. Immigration must be viewed as a process of progressive assimilation during which the identities of the actors who are present are changing and mixing without ever totally merging and there is no lack of historical studies revealing the dynamic and enriching nature of all this cultural 'work'.

However, the assimilation process does not always proceed in a more or less harmonious way. Immigrant groups, even those that are today the best assimilated and integrated, have almost all encountered the hostility of racist or xenophobic movements, with varying degrees of violence depending on economic and political circumstances. In times of economic difficulties, immigrants may be seen as dangerous economic competitors who take jobs away from workers in the host country, and insecure or downwardly mobile groups use them as scapegoats for their own difficulties, blaming them for threatening the unity of the country, or of the 'race'. The policies of the state vary noticeably with these circumstances, ranging from attempts to attract labour or increase population, to severe restriction of immigration under pressure from xenophobic groups. In the United States since the end of the last century, and in Europe in recent years, immigrant communities have tried to increase their capacity for political negotiation and social participation. Generally, three strategies appear among the immigrant movements. The immigrants can join existing social movements and so take part in the political life of the country, a strategy often chosen by immigrant workers who participate in trade unionism. Or they may identify with democratic movements which champion civil rights and fight against racism. On the other hand, they may fight for the recognition and respect of their cultural identities, and, instead of stressing their similarity with the host society, emphasize their differences and ETHNICITY, an 'ethnicity' thanks to which they can be acknowledged and become political actors. Eventually, the groups which are economically integrated and yet keep community links within an ethnic business enterprise or a culture may form lobbies, notably in the United States.

An old land of emigration, Western Europe, is now a land of immigration owing to the imbalance between rich countries and poor countries; thus the European countries become more and more multi-ethnic. At a time when economies and culture transcend their national limits, the migratory movements share in a notable transformation of the European pattern in which the nation-state defined a culture, a territory and a political framework. Consequently, the 'immigrant problem' is often a problem of the host societies.

Reading

Brubaker, W.R. ed. 1989: *Immigration and the Politics of Citizenship in Europe and North America.*

Castles, Stephen and Kosack, Godula 1973: *Immigrant Workers and Class Structure in Western Europe.*

Duchac, R. 1974: *La sociologie des migrations aux Etats-Unis.*

Eisenstadt, S.N. 1955: *The Absorption of Immigrants.*

Miles, R. 1982: *Racism and Migrant Labour.*

Myrdal, G. 1944 (*1962*): *An American Dilemma.*

Noiriel, G. 1988: *Le creuset français.*

Park, R.E. and Burgess, R.W. 1929: *Introduction to the Science of Sociology.*

Rose, A.M. 1970: Distance of migration and socio-economic status of migrant. In *Readings in the Sociology of Migration*, ed. C.J. Jansen.

Thomas, W.I. and Znaniecki, F. 1918 (*1958*): *The Polish Peasant in Europe and America.*

FRANÇOIS DUBET

military Definitions of the military are wide-ranging. Biderman (1971) stipulates that the military is a specialized institution for guarding and securing the ultimate and sacred value of society. Hackett (1983) focuses on the function of the profession of arms – the ordered application of force in the resolution of a social problem. In contrast, the earlier definition of Lasswell identifies the military with the management of violence (1941).

Conventionally, the analysis of the military is linked to three main themes; first, the status of the military as an organization; secondly, its role as a profession; and finally, its relationship to the parent society. This division is based on previously postulated concepts and each area of interest reflects facets of mainstream sociological theory (van Doorn, 1975).

The evaluation of the military as an organization recognizes that armed forces are a highly bureaucratized complex structure. The basic conceptual framework is linked to the model of the Weberian ideal-type BUREAUCRACY. Accordingly, a persistent area of interest is the structure of the military. Three basic models are identified: the mass army, the citizen army and the all-volunteer force. Yet despite differences in institutional format, considerable stress is consistently placed on the common structural features of all military organizations. These identify stability, continuity and homogeneity of values as being of critical importance. They also emphasize the degree of centralization of authority to be found in the military. The model is simple. The hierarchy rests on a broad base of basically unskilled enlisted men under the command of an officer, assisted by a few trusted non-commissioned officers to supervise the execution of orders. At each successive echelon or grade, there is an officer of higher rank. This rank structure creates the traditional hierarchical pyramid which is a defining characteristic of all bureaucratized organizations. One of the secondary issues which its existence engenders, however, is the complex question of the relationship between these office-holders and the staff of specialists needed to assist in the control of subordinate units.

These specialists are, essentially, professionals. Their activities reflect the role of the military as a fully developed profession which exhibits three identifying characteristics of the ideal-type professional model: expertise, corporateness and responsibility (Huntington, 1957). Janowitz, in treating the military as a social system, stresses, however, that these professional characteristics have changed over time. More importantly, he emphasizes that the concept of professionalism encompasses norms and skills which include, but exceed, the basic role of the military; that is, the management of violence. While he acknowledges the characteristics which make the military a profession: expertise, lengthy education, group identity, ethics and standards of performance, he identifies the profession not as a static model but as a dynamic institution which changes over time in response to changing conditions. This recognizes the extent to which the form of existing military organizations and professionalized officer-corps has been shaped by the impact of broad social transformations since the turn of the century. More specifically, this implies that armed forces are experiencing a long-term transformation toward convergence with civilian structures and norms (Janowitz, 1960).

The significance of these changes is recognized in a number of studies. Moskos stresses that the military is now moving from an organizational format that is predominantly *institutional* to one that is becoming increasingly *occupational* (1988).

The former is legitimated in terms of values and norms, that is, a purpose transcending individual self-interest in favour of a presumed higher good. Members are seen as following a calling identified with words such as duty, honour, country (Harries-Jenkins, 1977). The occupational model, in contrast, is identified with the economics and principles of the marketplace. The law of supply and demand rather than normative values is paramount. The priority of self-interest replaces the concept of altruistic service.

Notwithstanding the significance of such changes, the importance of the military in the parent society remains unaltered. Endowed with a near monopoly of arms, possessing a sophisticated communications network and constructed as a highly purposive organization, the military continues to be a dominant feature in contemporary society. Given the mood, motivation and disposition, the military may interfere in the domain of the civil power. More usually, it continues to be a major user of scarce resources thereby inviting critical discussion of the role of the military in contemporary society.

See also GUERRILLA.

Reading
Abrahamsson, B. 1972: *Military Professionalization and Political Power*.
Edmonds, M. 1988: *Armed Services and Society*.
Finer, S.E. 1962: *The Man on Horseback: The Role of the Military in Politics*.
Harries-Jenkins, G. and Moskos, C.C. 1981: Armed forces and society. *Current Sociology* 29, 1–170.
Janowitz, M. 1975: *Military Conflict: Essays in the Institutional Analysis of War and Peace*.
——1977: *Military Institutions and Coercion in the Developing Nations*.
——ed. 1981: *Civil–Military Relations: Regional Perspectives*.
Little, R.W. ed. 1971: *Handbook of Military Institutions*.
Moskos, C.C. 1976: The military. *Annual Review of Sociology* 2, 55–77.

GWYN HARRIES-JENKINS

mobility, social   *See* SOCIAL MOBILITY

mode of production   According to most twentieth-century understandings of MARXISM, history can be periodized into different modes of production, each with its own internal dialectic of class struggle. This 'materialist conception' of history was outlined in the *German Ideology* (Marx and Engels, 1845–6) and developed in subsequent works by both Marx and Engels, although they did not always use the concept of a mode of production in this way. In the twentieth century, it became the central concept of what has become known as 'dialectical materialism', adherence to some version of which continues to distinguish Marxist from other forms of social thought (see MATERIALISM).

According to this view of history, the fundamental difference between types of society occurs in the way production takes place. Any society's 'mode of production' consists of two elements: its forces and its relations of production. The forces of production refer to society's productive capabilities, not just in a technological but also in a social sense, and include not only material means of production but also human abilities both physical and conceptual. The relations of production refer to the social relations under which production is organized: how resources and labour are allocated, how the labour process is organized and how products are distributed. It is the specific combination of both forces and relations of production which defines the pattern of class relations in any society and thus its internal dynamic.

Within Marxism, classes are defined by their relation to the process of production, in particular to the production of a surplus. A surplus is produced in any mode of production in which not all available labour time is needed to provide for the direct consumption needs of the population, and some members of society work more hours than those needed to produce their own means of subsistence. If the producers of the surplus and those who control its use are distinct, such societies will have at least two classes. The ruling class of any mode of production is the one that has the control of the surplus, consuming some of it but also using it in other ways to enhance its own power and to further the process of surplus extraction or EXPLOITATION.

It is the specific way in which the surplus is extracted by the ruling class that defines a particular mode of production. For example, under capitalism the bourgeoisie's ownership of the means of production enables it to employ workers for less than the value of their product and thus extract a surplus in the form of profit. This method of surplus extraction is thus purely economic, grounded in the apparently fair rules of exchange. In other modes of production, such as feudalism, the method of surplus extraction, initially direct labour on the lord's land, later the payment of rent, is due to customary right backed up where necessary by the use of force.

All class, or surplus producing, modes of production hold within them the seeds of their own destruction. Particular relations of production will be appropriate to a particular stage of development of the forces of production. A mode of production will be relatively stable when its forces and relations of production are appropriate to each other, allowing for their mutual reproduction. However, through the existence of a surplus and thus the potential for change, the forces of production will develop in all modes of production, however slowly. Ultimately a point will be reached at which existing relations of production become a fetter on the further expansion of the forces of production and the mode of production will be overthrown to give way to a new one under which the forces of production can continue to develop.

The process by which this takes place is class struggle. Classes, defined in the Marxist sense to exist only when there is a surplus to be fought over, are inherently antagonistic and engage in struggle over the extent and control of the surplus. This provides the internal dynamic of modes of production, an internal dynamic which eventually leads to revolution as a previously subordinate class overthrows existing relations of production to set itself up as the new ruling class based on a new mode of production more appropriate to the further development of the forces of production. Thus, for example, the growing but subordinate capitalist class overthrew feudal relations of production when their restrictions on the labour market held back the development of more efficient capitalist methods of surplus extraction.

The above rather deterministic account of the materialistic conception of history is one that became general currency only in the twentieth century. The Second International, the international organization of social–democratic parties which collapsed into nationalistic splinters in 1914, promulgated an official Marxism which, influenced by Engels's interpretations, tended towards economism. According to this official view, the mode of production formed an economic 'base' which determined all other 'superstructural' aspects of society (see also BASE AND SUPERSTRUCTURE). This view was also adopted by the Third International or Comintern, founded to unite the nascent communist parties after the Russian revolution, and restated by Stalin (1938) to be the correct understanding of Marx, thus becoming the foundation of 'Diamat' (for dialectical materialism). Although there is evidence in Marx's writings to support this particular reading of the historical process, his own usage of the term 'mode of production' was more varied and his account of history less rigid.

There are a number of problems with the official version. First it can be criticized for technological determinism. Although mediated through a consideration of the relations of production and the agency of class, the development of the forces of production alone form the ultimate driving force of history and it appears that revolution is not only possible but inevitable at the appropriate stage of their development. Early twentieth-century history, with the success of revolution in backward Russia yet the failure of revolution in advanced Germany, would appear to throw doubt on this; although events in the Soviet Union nearer the end of the century could be interpreted to give support to the view that revolution in a backward country was ultimately doomed to failure.

But more fundamentally, the unpredictability of the revolutionary process has led to a questioning of the whole role of the economic, that is, the relations and forces of production, in the above account. For it has not appeared possible to map the process of class struggle on to changes in the mode of production in such a clear-cut manner as the base/superstructure analogy would imply. In particular it would seem that the role of consciousness has at times been crucial and that the apparently 'superstructural' factors of ideology and politics can affect the economic to the extent of bringing about or preventing a transformation of the mode of production.

A highly influential attempt to grapple with this problem was made in the 1960s by the French structuralist Marxists, Althusser and Balibar (1970), who tried to find a way to retain the centrality of the concept of a mode of production, while dispensing with the crude base/superstructure model. In their view a 'social formation' is reproduced at a number of different levels: ideological and political as well as economic. They replaced the notion of determination with one of structural causality between levels in which the non-economic levels are also necessary to the reproduction of the whole 'social formation' including its mode of production. However, within such an interdependent structured totality, the economic sets limits within which the other levels can be only 'relatively autonomous' because they have to function in ways which reproduce the mode of production. Revolution occurs when this process becomes 'overdetermined'; contradictions between the levels, rather than within the economic alone, providing the motor of change.

But this formulation has been criticized for missing the dialectical element in Marx's materialist conception of history by making too much of a conceptual separation between the mode of production (the economic level) and the (non-economic) conditions of its reproduction (Clarke, 1980). Making the levels relatively 'autonomous' could not resolve the problem of economic determinism, because all other levels remained constrained to a privileged economic one, and neither did it grasp the Marxist idea of the dialectic as consisting of interconnected elements, because the levels were disconnected.

In Althusser and Balibar's notion of the economic level, the mode of production was defined to consist of two sets of relations, those of 'the real appropriation of nature' (relations of production) and those of 'expropriation of the product' (property relations and those of distribution). Thus in this formulation, production is hypostasized to consist only of relations with nature, while the scope for social relations is found in the mode of expropriation of the product alone, the relations of property and distribution. But this, according to their critics, is to miss Marx's fundamental insight that not only are relations of distribution socially specific, but that the labour process itself forms the core of the social relations of the capitalist mode of production, and indeed, in a different form, of any other mode of production.

Reading
Althusser, L. and Balibar, E. 1970: *Reading 'Capital'*.
Banaji, J. 1977: Modes of production in a materialist conception of history. *Capital and Class* 2.
Bettelheim, C. 1978: *Class struggles in the USSR*.
Brenner, R. 1977: The origins of capitalist development: a critique of neo-Smithian Marxism. *New Left Review*, no. 104.
Clarke, Simon 1980: Althusserian Marxism. In *One-Dimensional Marxism: Althusser and the Politics of Culture*.
Cohen G.A. 1978: *Karl Marx's Theory of History: A Defence*.
Colletti, L. 1972: *From Rousseau to Lenin*.

SUSAN F. HIMMELWEIT

model An interpretation of a formal system and/or a representation, normally by analogy (but sometimes by metaphor or even metonymy), of one thing by something else (for instance for heuristic, explanatory or test purposes). The century opened with a blistering attack by Pierre Duhem in his *La Théorie physique: son objet, sa structure* (see Duhem, 1906) on the mechanical models (and 'broad but shallow', pictorializing minds) of English physicists such as James Clark Maxwell, Lord Kelvin and Oliver Lodge, in support of his own Cartesian conception of science. Theory should bind together experimental laws, but any model associated with the (partially) interpreted axiom system is logically and epistemologically quite redundant. Agreeing with Duhem's position that a theory consisted in a deductively organized structure of empirical laws, Norman Campbell nevertheless argued, in his *Physics, the Elements* (1920), that to be intellectually satisfying or capable of growth, a theory must also involve a (non-deductive) relation of analogy with some known field of phenomena. Thus, on Campbell's view, it is not merely the consideration that Boyle's law, Charles's law and Graham's law were all deductive consequences of the kinetic theory of gases, but the corpuscularian model associated with this theory – in virtue of which gas molecules are imagined to be, in certain respects (the positive analogy), like billiard balls bouncing off each other and exchanging their momentum by impact – which secures our intellectual assent to it. In the theory, the respect in which gas molecules are unlike billiard balls, that is colour, size (the negative analogy), are just ignored; while the respects in which we do not know whether or not gas molecules are like billiard balls (the neutral analogy) are used as a source of 'surplus (or unbound) meaning' to suggest ways in which the theory can be refined.

In the positivism that characterized PHILOSOPHY OF SCIENCE until the late 1960s, Duhem's approach was triumphant. Moreover there were substantial difficulties with Campbell's own position. Thus Braithwaite argued that the intellectually satisfying nature of models could not justify the choice of any particular one. Moreover the implicit notion of explanation – as a reduction of the strange or unknown to the familiar – is suspect. For scientific revolutions may involve transformations in our conception of what is plausible. At the core of these problems lies Campbell's continuing empirical REALISM and deductivism, and in particular his unwillingness to admit models, as Max Black, Mary Hesse, Rom Harré and Roy Bhaskar have urged, as possible or hypothetical descriptions of an unknown but knowable reality, and in consequence to see science as essentially developing. Thus Bhaskar's transcendental realism sees deducibility as neither necessary nor sufficient for explanation and allows that in the scientific process even the positive analogy may be overturned.

Any model of a subject possesses a source (which may itself be a model). Models may be conventionally divided into those in which the subject is the same as the source, the homoeomorphs, and those in which it is different, the paramorphs. A doll is a model of a baby, modelled *on* a baby. Homoeomorphs may be classified into scale models, class representatives, idealizations and abstractions. But it is clearly paramorphic model-building, that is the construction of a model utilizing antecedently available cognitive resources (Bachelard's 'scientific loans') for an unknown subject (whose reality can be eventually empirically ascertained), which is most important in creative, knowledge-extending science. Such models may be based on one, more than one or just aspects of a source, that is singly connected, multiply connected and semi-connected paramorphs respectively, as exemplified by the kinetic, Darwinian and Freudian theories. Thus Darwin worked the theory of domestic selection and Malthus's theory of population together with the facts of natural variation into a novel theory of a new kind of process: natural selection. Harré has argued that multiply connected paramorphs must lead to the postulation of new kinds of entities or processes. But imaginative model-building, so essential in science, is always subject to rigorous empirical test.

Reading
Bhaskar, R. 1975 (*1978*): *A Realist Theory of Science*, 2nd edn, esp. ch. 3, section 2.
Campbell, N.R. 1953: *What is Science?*
Duhem, P. 1906 (*1962*): *The Aim and Structure of Physical Theory*.
Harré, R. 1970: *The Principles of Scientific Thinking*, esp. ch. 2.
Hesse, M.B. 1966: *Models and Analogies in Science*.
Losee, J. 1980: *A Historical Introduction to the Philosophy of Science*, esp. ch. 9.

ROY BHASKAR

modernism and postmodernism Modernism, as a general term in cultural history, denotes a richly varied set of aesthetic breaks with the

European realist tradition from the mid-nineteenth century onwards. Realism is premised on an identity between the work of art and the external nature or society with which it deals, an identity which is secretly guaranteed by the metaphor of the mirror which lies at the very core of realist AESTHETICS. The realist artwork offers modestly to 'reflect' the reality which is set before it, neither adding anything to nor subtracting anything from it. The metaphor of 'mirroring' seeks to guarantee the objectivity and impersonality of the work, avoiding the potential distortions of personal caprice or class bias on the author's part.

Modernist artists, from a whole variety of positions, rejected these basic realist tenets. Reflectionist aesthetics, they argued, were unacceptably passive, reducing the work of art to an empty echo or 'ghost' of more fundamental social processes, bleeding it dry of any distinctive substance of its own. That substance, in their view, resided not in the work's content, which necessarily came to it from elsewhere (history, nature, psychology), but in its *form*, in its stylistic or technical reworkings of its raw materials. Form is thus the central term of modernist aesthetics – with Russian FORMALISM, appropriately, being one of its major schools – and it is the practical and theoretical emphasis on form which guarantees the 'autonomy' of the artwork, that irreducibly aesthetic dimension which prevents it from being mere historical document (realist novel) or emotional expression (romantic lyric poem).

But as soon as we start trying to date the origins of the modernist 'turn to form', we see that this is no simple internal debate in aesthetic theory but itself a complex 'reflection' of profound social anxieties (see also SOCIOLOGY OF ART). If Charles Baudelaire and Gustave Flaubert are taken as the pioneers, then the origins of modernism can be assigned (as they often have been by Marxist critics) to the politically bloody year of 1848; the brutal suppression of the revolutions of that year is seen as throwing the would-be universalism of classical or realist writing into terminal crisis. Alternatively one can hunt for origins in movements rather than individuals, and see modernism as only truly getting under way with the accelerating series of avant-garde experimentalisms from the 1880s onwards: naturalism, symbolism, cubism, expressionism, futurism, surrealism, constructivism, and others. The social factors which form the matrix of this great carnival of aesthetic experiments would then include the rise of mass culture, working-class militancy and revolution, feminist political agitation, the new technologies of the second industrial revolution, imperialist war between 1914 and 1918, and – bringing all these to an intense experiential focus – the dynamism and alienations of life in the great European capitals: Paris, London, Berlin, Vienna, Petersburg.

'History is a nightmare from which I am trying to awake,' says Stephen Dedalus in James Joyce's *Ulysses* (dating from 1922). For most modernisms, contemporary history is in one way or another nightmarish or (in another key category of modernist aesthetics) 'inauthentic', and the work of art seeks to 'awake from' it into a more authentic or even utopian mode of being. Yet these general emphases can be fleshed out in detail in violently contradictory ways. History may be seen as bogged down by the dead hand of tradition, by a social and aesthetic conservatism which weighs like a nightmare on the brains of the living. The modernist work must then, by a huge effort of technological imagination, lift itself out of this ruck of dead, inauthentic past styles, and purge them away by the pitiless rigour of its 'functionalism'. Such is the aesthetic logic of the modernist architecture of Le Corbusier and the International Style or of Walter Gropius and his Bauhaus. Alternatively, the modernist artist can look for forces of dynamism already at work within society and align himself or herself with them in an attempt to blast away the stifling cobwebs of the cultural and political past. Such is the project of Italian and Russian futurism, which celebrates the vast energies of contemporary science and production: ocean liners, aeroplanes, motor cars; factories and skyscapers; machine guns and tanks. Such prodigious 'forces of production', wielded by the new, dynamic breed of modern men and women that urban life was generating, would blast apart the claustrophobic social 'relations of production' which fettered them in bourgeois society. Such an aesthetics, clearly, at once implies a revolutionary politics, but futurism (in the person of Filippo Marinetti) could serve the cause of Fascist counter-revolution as enthusiastically as it did (through Vladimir Mayakovsky and others) the Bolshevik socialist project.

If, with futurism and International Style architecture, you can judge the present to be 'inauthentic' in the name of the future, so too can you in the name of the deep past. Contemporary history, for this other wing of modernism, is nightmarish in its philistine rationalism and crass mass culture; and against such a degraded present the work of art must, in both theme and form, reactivate the forces of *memory*. This project takes many varying specific forms. The work may appeal to a personal past, a Proustian *temps perdu* or lost wholeness, by which to condemn a deracinated adult present; or it may, as with the representations of medieval Gothic cathedrals in some of the great texts of the period, hark back to a lost *cultural* past, an epoch of unified sensibility and 'organic community' or *Gemeinschaft*, before the 'fall' into bourgeois individualism. Alternatively, little pockets of 'memory', of authentic being, may still residually exist in the capitalist present: in geographically remote corners of the earth, in neglected dimensions of our physical experience, or in a Jungian, myth-informed collective unconsciousness which the modernist work, by virtue of its dislocations of form, may tap into.

Dislocated, perceptible form, then, may enact both the dynamism of the future and the unsettling return of the archaic past, but perceptible form also characterizes another strand of modernism which repudiates any such ideological investment of technical innovation. For this vein of modernism, from Gustave Flaubert and Henry James onward, history is chaotic flux which must be redeemed by the formal symmetries of the work of art. By virtue of its intense craftsmanship, its obsessive quest for the *mot juste* or self-conscious intricacy of plot, the work transcends history, constructing a realm of aesthetic autonomy which bears no relation whatsoever to past, present or future. Such transcendentalist aesthetics – sometimes termed 'aestheticism' or 'high modernism' – have come to be contrasted with the 'historical avant-garde' (futurism, surrealism, Dadaism), which aims to break open this sealed realm of aesthetic value and return the aesthetic to everyday life (see Bürger, 1984).

If modernism is a multiple rather than unitary phenomenon, then *post*modernism, from the late 1950s or early 1960s on, will be no less polysemantic: its force in any particular context will depend on precisely *which* version of modernism it is presumed to negate. The concept of postmodernism emerged early in architecture, but has since been generalized to virtually all fields of culture. Postmodern architecture is an attack, above all, on the International Style. While it does not repudiate the emphasis on technological innovation in Le Corbusier or Walter Gropius, it does problematize some

of the key values associated with technological advance in modernist architecture: universalism, elitism, formalism. The austere, rectilinear white facades and flat roofs characteristic of the International Style claim to be universal architectural forms, adhering to the canons of a pure, scientific reason independent of the idiosyncracies of any particular time or place. Postmodernism finds such claims arrogant and even authoritarian, and invests heavily instead in localism, particularism, regionalism, reinventing the traditionalist and vernacular styles and building materials which modernist aesthetics had consigned to the dustbin of history. The white surfaces and flat roofs of universal Reason may gratify the avant-garde architect, but they are, objects postmodernism, not much fun for anybody else, including those who have to live in them. Some of the best-known postmodernist manifestos, including Robert Venturi's *Learning from Las Vegas* in the 1970s and Tom Wolfe's *From Bauhaus to Our House* of 1982, thus launch a populist assault on the elitism of International Style architecture; and this attack involves not only the defence of traditionalist building styles that people happen to like but also praise for the wit and vitality of mass-cultural commercial styles. The postmodern work, Venturi insists, must 'learn from' such forms, incorporating them pleasurably into its very substance rather than austerely negating them. This dissolving of the rigid modernist distinction between 'high culture' and MASS CULTURE, first manifest in architecture, has its equivalent in many other cultural fields, and is indeed often cited as *the* central characteristic of postmodern culture.

The elitism of modernist art lies in the difficulty of its forms, that 'organized violence upon ordinary language' or conventions which for Roman Jakobson defined modernism as such. Any attack on its elitism is, accordingly, necessarily a critique of its obsession with form. In this sense, postmodern art can be seen as the 'return of content', a content which was either radically subordinated by the modernist preoccupation with form or, on occasion, abolished by it altogether. Such a model, extrapolated from developments in architecture, is finely developed by Linda Hutcheon in *A Poetics of Postmodernism* (1988). She defines the postmodern novel, exemplified by such authors as Gabriel García Márquez, Günter Grass, John Fowles, E.L. Doctorow and others, as 'historiographic metafiction'. Such novels return to questions of plot, history and reference which had once seemed to be exploded by modernist fiction's concern for textual autonomy and self-consciousness, but without simply abandoning such 'metafictional' concerns. This suggestive model can be readily extended into other areas, including the return of representation and the body in painting, and so on.

The attack on modernist universalism, elitism and formalism constitutes what we might call the attractively 'ecological' moment of postmodernism, its decentralist openness to repressed styles or experiences and to cultural Otherness (women, gays, blacks, the Third World). However, to build a thatched cottage or narrate a Victorian love story in 1990 is not the same as to construct these artefacts in the seventeenth or nineteenth century. It is, in effect, to construct an image or simulacrum of such entities; and this is the point where reservations about postmodern culture tend to come to the fore. The modernist obsession with time gives way, in the postmodern, to a concern with space and geography, with synchronic rather than diachronic differences. There is much that is liberating about this, as Western modernity abandons its imperialist arrogance towards those 'primitive' cultures which surround it; but there may also be a 'freezing' of history, a loss of imagination and thus of the practical possibility of radical social change. The styles of the past may be welcomely reinvented, but only, perhaps, as one-dimensional images in the 'heritage industry' of an eternal present. In a world dominated by mass media and technologies of cultural reproduction, the modernist dream of a utopian, 'authentic' experience beyond mass culture vanishes. Saturated as we are from birth by the images, stereotypes and narrative paradigms of a ubiquitous mass culture, we have long since lived on the pulses that 'death of the subject' which poststructuralism has recently articulated at the level of theory. Again, there are progressive dimensions to this development; along with the dream of authenticity, modernism's contempt for ordinary people has also vanished. But if we can no longer appeal to Nature or the unconscious, to authentic Lawrentian sexuality or Third World precapitalist enclaves against the image-ridden First World in which we live, what now *is* the basis of political critique – above all in the wake of the collapse of a Communist project which seems to have shared in the very universalism and elitism of modernist culture itself?

Such ambivalences about the value of postmodern culture also infiltrate any attempt to sketch the social matrix from which it emerges. By general consent, postmodernism comes into being as capitalism shifts from its Fordist to its post-Fordist moment (see FORDISM AND POST-FORDISM), from the standardized products of monolithic production lines in giant factories to the decentralized use of information technology sophisticated enough to allow 'flexible specialization'. This shift from the One to the Many within capitalism itself then poses new questions about the trends toward pluralism and difference we have noted in postmodern culture. Are these genuine steps towards a democratization of the unacceptable absolutism of some forms of modernism, or are they rather, perhaps, merely the latest ruses of a global economic system which, having seen off its Communist antagonist, now has us more firmly in its grip than ever before?

Reading
Berman, Marshall 1983: *All that is Solid Melts into Air: The Experience of Modernity.*

Bradbury, Malcolm and McFarlane, James eds 1976: *Modernism 1890–1930.*

Bürger, Peter 1984: *Theory of the Avant-Garde.*

Connor, Steven 1989: *Postmodernist Culture: An Introduction to Theories of the Contemporary.*

Harvey, David 1989: *The Condition of Postmodernity.*

Hutcheon, Linda 1988: *A Poetics of Postmodernism.*

Jameson, Fredric 1991: *Postmodernism, or, The Cultural Logic of Late Capitalism.*

Lyotard, Jean-François 1979 (*1984*): *The Postmodern Condition.*

Williams, Raymond 1989: *The Politics of Modernism.*

TONY PINKNEY

modernity This is a 'contrast concept'. It takes its meaning as much from what it denies as what it affirms. Hence the term can appear at different times with widely differing meanings, depending on what is being denied and, by contrast, what is affirmed. For Augustine in the fifth century AD, the late Latin word *modernus* expressed the rejection of paganism and the inauguration of the new Christian age. Renaissance thinkers, recovering classical humanism, fused this with Christianity to make the distinction between 'ancient' and 'modern' states and societies. The eighteenth-century Enlightenment not only interposed 'medieval' between 'ancient' and 'modern' but made the crucial identification of the modern with the here and now. This added a new fluidity to the concept. From now on, modern society was *our* society, the kind of societies we lived in, whether in the eighteenth or the twentieth century. Western society, as showing the sharpest contrast with earlier or other – the two came to seem synonymous – societies, became the emblem of modernity. This evolution determined the contours of modernity. To modernize was to Westernize.

Modern society therefore carried the hallmarks of Western society since the eighteenth century. It was industrial and scientific. Its political form was the nation-state, legitimated by some species of popular sovereignty. It gave an unprecedented role to the economy and economic growth. Its working philosophies were rationalism (see RATIONALITY AND REASON) and UTILITARIANISM. In all these ways it rejected not just its own past but all other cultures that did not measure up to its self-understanding. It is wrong to say that modernity denies history, as the contrast with the past – a constantly changing entity – remains a necessary point of reference. But it is true that modernity feels that the past has no lessons for it; its pull is constantly towards the future. Unlike other societies, modern society welcomes and promotes novelty. It can be said to have invented the 'tradition of the new'.

Modernity – modern INDUSTRIAL SOCIETY – received a comprehensive analysis in the writings of the principal social theorists of the nineteenth century, Hegel, Marx, Tocqueville, Weber, Simmel and Durkheim. Their analyses remain relevant in many respects for present-day societies – Marx included, despite the failure of state socialism in several parts of the world. But the growth of certain features in our time – the globalization of the economy, the decline of the nation-state, the great migrations of population – have led some thinkers to postulate the end of modernity as it has generally been understood. Geoffrey Barraclough has proposed 'contemporary history' as something different from 'modern history'; others have gone further and announced 'the postmodern age'.

None of these claims carry conviction. Nearly all the developments picked out can be shown to have their roots firmly in classic modernity. This is particularly true of the renewed emphasis on transience, fragmentation and the loss of a sense of meaning to the historical process. Thinkers such as Baudelaire, Nietzsche and Burckhardt had already remarked on these tendencies of their time. Nietzsche's 'last man' was already experiencing the difficulties and dilemmas of 'postmodern' man.

Modernity was never of a piece, as Max Weber and Georg Simmel in particular were at pains to emphasize. Its dynamism constantly threw its parts into conflict with each other – the polity against the economy, culture against instrumental rationality. Much of what appears as 'postmodernity' first found its expression in the cultural revolt against modernity which marked the movement of 'modernism' at the turn of the century (see MODERNISM AND POSTMODERNISM). Modernism certainly echoed modernity in its stress on functionalism and technological sophistication; but equally, in such currents as surrealism and Dadaism, it subverted certain tenets of modernity by espousing the claims of the 'pleasure principle' against those of the 'reality principle'.

It is undeniable that today's modern society is in many ways not the modern society of Marx or Weber's time. But modernity is not Western society in any of its particular phases. It is the principle of Western society as such. The commitment to continuous growth and innovation requires that existing forms be regarded as provisional. It is therefore entirely to be expected that new features emerge. The important question is how far the essential dynamism of industrialism has been checked or redirected. The worldwide spread of the industrial way of life is a testimony to its continuing force. At the same time industrialism is threatening the life-support systems of the planet. It is here that industrialism might run up against its limits; and the rethinking and redirection that this would involve might well unpick some of the fundamental strands of modernity. Whether this would take us 'beyond modernity' is something we cannot yet tell.

Reading

Berman, Marshall 1983: *All that is Solid Melts into Air: The Experience of Modernity*.
Bradbury, Malcolm and McFarlane, James eds 1976: *Modernism*.
Frisby, David 1988: *Fragments of Modernity*.
Giddens, Anthony 1990: *The Consequences of Modernity*.
Habermas, Jürgen 1990: *The Philosophical Discourse of Modernity*.
Kumar, Krishan 1988: *The Rise of Modern Society*.

KRISHAN KUMAR

modernization   This is a process of economic, political, social and cultural change occurring in undeveloped countries as they move towards more advanced and complex patterns of social and political organization. It has been closely studied and defined in American postwar sociological theories which start with an implicit or explicit reference to a dichotomy between two ideal types:

the traditional society (which in some versions can also be called 'rural', 'backward' or 'underdeveloped') and the modern society (or 'urban', 'developed', 'industrial'). These types of social structure are somehow historically connected by means of a continuous evolutionary process which follows certain general laws. The idea is that all societies follow a similar historical course of increasing differentiation and complexity from one polar type to the other.

As some societies have already industrialized, they become the basis on which the modern society paradigm and the ideal typical process of transition can be constructed. Some theories emphasize the endogenous nature of the process of change (Rostow, 1960; Hoselitz, 1965; Parsons, 1951) while others emphasize the importance of exogenous factors such as the diffusion of values, technology, skills and forms of organization from advanced nations of the West to poor nations of the Third World (Lerner, 1958). But in any case traditional societies are supposed to follow the same pattern of change undergone earlier by the developed nations. Modernization theories, therefore, seek to identify in the organization and/or history of industrial countries the social variables and institutional factors whose change was crucial for their process of development in order to facilitate this process in the newly developing countries.

A convenient classification of modernization theories is that which distinguishes sociological, economic and psychological versions. The sociological versions highlight the role of a wide variety of social and institutional variables in the process of change. Thus Germani (1965) describes the process in terms of changes from prescriptive actions to elective actions, from the institutionalization of the traditional to the institutionalization of change; and from a conjunction of relatively undifferentiated institutions to their increasing differentiation and specialization. Most of these versions have been influenced by Max Weber through Talcott Parsons's interpretation of his ideas, and use the PATTERN VARIABLES to describe the ideal typical social structure of 'traditional' and 'modern' societies: affectivity versus affective neutrality, ascription versus achievement, diffusion versus specificity, particularism versus universalism and orientation towards collective interests versus orientation towards private interests.

The psychological versions emphasize internal factors and psychological motives as the motor

forces of the transition. Thus McClelland (1961) proposes the 'need for achievement', a desire to do well, as a crucial motivation which, by spreading among the entrepreneurs of a country, leads to economic development. This motivation is not innate or hereditary and can be developed in a country in transition to modernity by means of education.

The economic version is well represented by Rostow (1960) and his theory of stages of economic growth. He suggests that all societies pass through five stages: traditional society, preconditions for take-off, take-off, road to maturity and the age of high mass consumption. Rostow believes that the process of development going on at present in Asia, Latin America, Africa and the Middle East is analogous to the stages of preconditions and take-off in Western societies in the late eighteenth and nineteenth centuries.

The theories of modernization have been criticized in a number of ways. Most important are the accusations of abstractness and lack of historical perspective. First, it is a mistake to treat underdevelopment as a universal original situation, as lack of development in general, as a stage which all developed countries went through. Second, modernization analyses tend to assume a prescriptive character and instead of studying historically the structural context of the specific features of underdeveloped societies they only seek to establish whether these features follow or depart from the ideal Western model which is supposed to be the norm. Third, implicit in all the theories of modernization is the idea that present-day developing countries should go through the same stages and processes as developed countries went through previously. Even when they recognize the existence of some historical differences (Germani, 1965, and Rostow, 1960, acknowledge them) they refuse to accept that they could essentially alter the pattern of change. History can be repeated, developing countries can industrialize in the same way as the older industrial countries and in some respects they have even more advantages in doing so. There is hardly any discussion of the international order as a system dominated and manipulated by certain industrial countries in their own interest. Modernization theories assume that the process of modernization and industrialization is inevitable and that newly developing countries have the same if not better opportunities to industrialize. As Hoogvelt has put it, they have turned the abstracted, generalized history of European development into *logic* (Hoogvelt, 1982, p. 116).

See also DEVELOPMENT AND UNDERDEVELOPMENT.

Reading
Eisenstadt, S.N. 1961: *Essays on Sociological Aspects of Political and Economic Development.*
Frank, A.G. 1972: Sociology of development and under-development of sociology. In *Dependence and Underdevelopment*, ed. J.D. Cockcroft, A.G. Frank and D.L. Johnson.
Larrain, J. 1989: *Theories of Development.*
Smelser. N.J. 1964: Toward a theory of modernization. In *Social Change*, ed. A. Etzioni and E. Etzioni.

JORGE LARRAIN

monarchy While monarchy is the institution of rule over a state by the head of a hereditary family, monarchism is the doctrine that this is best. Monarchy or kingship is one of the most ancient types of government and, until this century, the most common. The most ancient claim for AUTHORITY is either that a king is a descendant of a god or that the office is sacred. This makes obedience a natural duty. But the power of kings was not perceived as absolute or sovereign. Until the seventeenth century, there was no clear idea of absolute sovereignty: for if monarchy was a divine institution, kings themselves were bound to obey God's laws. Medieval monarchs in Europe were seen as the steward or guardian of the realm on God's behalf. Christianity had, indeed, introduced a potentially civilized complication to simple claims to absolute authority: Christ had preached that some things were Caesar's and some God's. The theology was dualistic: the church claimed a large degree of autonomy but even laymen (if they were powerful) could question if secular power was rightly used.

Under monarchy there were always some justifications for rebellion and some ambiguities about succession. Both in the Christian and the Muslim world an incompetent elder son could be passed over for another member of the immediate family. In the Caliphate, succession was often determined by assassination or limited warfare between royal brothers or cousins.

In the seventeeth century the idea became common, as formulated most powerfully by Thomas Hobbes, that for the sake of peace and avoidance of civil war an abstract entity called the STATE should exercise all power and be the exclusive object of loyalty. No longer 'open in the name of the king!' but 'in the name of the state'. The doctrine of the 'divine right of kings' was a belated and largely unsuccessful attempt to claim this sovereignty for the person of the monarch. Louis XIV might claim that 'L'état c'est moi,' but it was a conscious paradox. For by then monarchy was everywhere coming to be seen as an office, to be exercised on advice and prudently, not the disposable property of a person or dynasty.

Loyalty to persons was the great virtue preached by royal apologists, but this proved easier in modern times if their powers were limited. Walter Bagehot (1867) famously distinguished between the 'dignified powers' of Queen Victoria and her 'efficient powers', which he believed to be few. The dignified, symbolic or ritual powers were a focus of loyalty and continuity to the nation, otherwise difficult to locate in a competitive party system, especially in a multinational state. In the United States the constitution itself is the symbol of unity, not the elected president.

A few constitutional monarchies survive, none exercising real political power but some (like the British) serving to legitimize a hierarchical social order; others, as in Holland, Denmark and Norway, contrive to appear more democratic in style, and are more bourgeois than aristocratic. Modern social theorists show surprisingly little interest in why such seeming anachronisms endure.

Reading
Cannadine, D. 1983: Context, performance and meaning of ritual: the British monarchy and the invention of tradition, *c.*1820–1977. In *The Invention of Tradition*, ed. E. Hobsbawm and T. Ranger.
Martin, K. 1937: *The Magic of Monarchy.*
—— 1962: *The Crown and the Establishment.*
Nairn, T. 1988: *The Enchanted Glass: Britain and its Monarchy.*
Shils, E. and Young, M. 1953: The meaning of the coronation. *Sociological Review* NS 1, 63–81.

BERNARD CRICK

monetarism This is the modern name, dating from 1968, for several old economic doctrines linked to the 'quantity theory of money', and the political and social project associated with them.

The fundamental, basic proposition of monetarism is that the rate of growth of the money supply in an economy determines the rate of inflation of prices; that is the quantity theory proposition whose origins are traceable at least to David Hume's essays of 1750–2. Subsequently the idea and its foundations were refined and developed, especially in the first 40 years of the nineteenth century (David Ricardo through the currency school), the first 30 years of the twentieth century (especially K. Wicksell, A.C. Pigou and I. Fisher), and the quarter century from 1956 (initiated by Milton Friedman) (see also CHICAGO ECONOMICS).

That quantity theory proposition is associated with the idea that the quantity of output or volume of activity does not vary in response to increases in the money supply, for otherwise the effect of the latter would partly increase the amount of goods produced instead of wholly making itself felt on their prices; the quantity of goods can be treated as if it were always equal to the amount produced with full employment of labour. That idea (Say's Law) was rarely held in absolute form and, in rescuing the quantity theory from Keynes's demolition of Say's Law, Friedman's 1956 restatement explicitly dropped it, arguing that the money supply affects either output or the price level. However, subsequent work by Friedman and his successors uses the direct money–price relation as frequently as the more general idea that money affects either prices or output.

Those ideas underpin the monetarist concentration on controlling inflation through controlling the money supply which is generally counterposed to the Keynesian focus on controlling unemployment through fiscal (budgetary) policy (see KEYNESIANISM). That characteristic policy causes monetarism to be widely identified with deflationary policies that induce recession, but monetarist economists apply their beliefs in both directions; for example, seminal monetarist studies of the 1930s concluded that the depression could have been avoided by policies to reverse a fall in the money supply.

Nevertheless, in politics the monetarist label is associated with rightwing governments whose policies have a deflationary bias, frequently sharply deflationary. Their ideology of controlling inflation is linked to a belief in reducing state spending and borrowing which claims two intellectual bases: first, the idea that controlling state borrowing produces control of the money supply; and, second, the idea that reducing expenditure and borrowing by the state liberates the dynamism of private capital in expanded spheres.

Since controlling the money supply has proved to be a chimera in advanced capitalist societies, the monetarist project has increasingly been defined in residual terms as a hostility to state expenditure, especially 'welfare state' spending, promotion of unregulated private capital, and hostility to organized labour. In those forms monetarism has defined the strategic views of many governments and political elites for long periods since 1975. Nevertheless, the rationale articulated for it, especially by the International Monetary Fund over a long period, continues to turn on control of the money supply despite the impracticality of such controls in a complex, growing economy.

Reading

Friedman, M. 1968: Quantity theory. In *International Encyclopaedia of the Social Sciences*, vol. 10, pp. 432–47.

Friedman, M. and Schwartz, A.J. 1963: *A Monetary History of the United States, 1867–1960*.

Mayer, T. ed. 1978: *The Structure of Monetarism*.

LAURENCE HARRIS

money   This everyday phenomenon is the supreme social fact of modern society, yet the social theory of money has been largely neglected by social scientists. This neglect has arisen because money has been reduced to a rational instrument, seen alternatively as a means of *exchange* (see NEOCLASSICAL ECONOMICS), or as a means of *communication* (see AUSTRIAN ECONOMICS). The historical development, forms of existence and modes of operation of money have been reduced to its economic and social *functions*, its primary function being conventionally identified as its role as means of exchange. While various theories of money differ in their specification of these functions, and in the hierarchical relationship proposed between them, they have in common the dissolution of the specificity of money as a social phenomenon, reducing it to a means of representation of non-monetary phenomena. However, in stressing the symmetry of *exchange* relations as the basis of the instrumental rationality of money, such theories neglect the essential asymmetry of relations of *domination* through which money asserts itself not as a mere *symbol*, but as an *autonomous social power*.

The dominant conception of money dates back at least to Aristotle, who explained the emergence of money in terms of the inconvenience of barter, defining the primary function of money as its role as *means of exchange*, but recognizing also its derivative functions as the *measure of value* and, at least implicitly, also as a *store of value*. The subsequent development of monetary theory has added remarkably little to Aristotle's analysis, the main debate being between those who have insisted that money must itself have a value, and those who have argued that primitive forms of commodity money could be replaced by purely symbolic forms of money, whose value was determined by convention and, for some, endorsed by the state. This debate has overlapped with that between those who follow Aristotle in seeing the function of means of exchange as primary, and those heretics who have attributed primacy to other functions of money. The political significance of the debate centres on the 'quantity theory of money': if the primary function of money is as means of exchange, an increase in the supply of money will lead to rising prices. If its primary function is as store of value, an increase in the money supply will lead to falling interest rates.

Adam Smith (1776), following David Hume (1752), laid the foundations of modern economics by reasserting the Aristotelian orthodoxy against the 'mercantilist' heresy, which saw the primary function of money in its role as store of value. Knapp's 'state theory of money' (1905) stressed the primacy of the function of money as means of payment, validated by its status as legal tender. Keynes (1930) followed Knapp, stressing the primacy of 'money-of-account' over money as means of exchange. However neither the mercantilists nor Knapp developed a systematic theory of money to challenge the classical orthodoxy, while Keynes did not develop the implications of his undoubted insights, restricting himself to the analysis of the motives for holding money as the basis of his theory of interest and employment (1936). Thus Keynes's theory was soon reabsorbed into the classical orthodoxy, in the form of the 'neoclassical synthesis', the primacy of the function of money as store of value, expressed in Keynes's theory of 'liquidity preference', being reduced to an irrational deviation from the normal functioning of the monetary system, based on the primacy of money as means of exchange.

The economists have not been so naive as to believe that their theory is adequate to the everyday reality of a society in which money is transparently not merely a rational instrument, but is also both the substance and symbol of wealth, status and power. Nevertheless the irrationality associated with a developed monetary system is treated as a pathological phenomenon, separable in principle from the normality embodied in the ideal system of the economists' theories, to be explained by sociologists and social psychologists, or even by theologians and moral philosophers. Such irrationality is explained not in terms of the objective irrationality of capitalist society, but in terms of the subjective irrationality of social actors, which is called on to explain all the evils of modern society: the 'trade cycle', mass unemployment, persistent poverty, growing inequality, the 'abuse' of power, industrial conflict, urban decay all result from the failure of human beings to live up to the ideals of rationality embodied in the theories of the economists.

Sociology, for all its concern with the non-rational dimensions of social action, has not offered an effective challenge to the economists' orthodoxy. Weber (1921–2) concurred without question with the economists' conception of money as the instrument and means of expression of economic rationality. Parsons (1967) went further, seeing the economists' conception of money as a model for the analysis of other social subsystems, considered as systems of symbolic exchange, an approach which has been further developed in the postmodernist conception of society as a communication network (Habermas, 1981; Luhmann, 1983, 1984; c.f. Ganssmann, 1988; see MODERNISM AND POSTMODERNISM) in which money is analogous to the linguistic sign (a conception which brings the theory of money full circle, since Saussure's theory of the sign (1916) was inspired by the economists' conception of money).

Sociologists have not ignored the irrational aspects of money, nor have they been content with the economists' psychologistic conception of such irrationality. Nevertheless sociologists have followed the economists in viewing such irrationality as a pathological phenomenon, as a social institution whose primary function to serve as a rational instrument acquires secondary meanings which may subvert its original purpose. Simmel's *Philosophy of Money* (1907), the only serious sociological contribution to the theory of money, is a brilliant exploration of the pervasive influence of money on social life, but the irrationality of a society dominated by money is attributed to a universal metaphysic, the psychological process through which means and ends come to be inverted. Thus the essential feature of money in a capitalist society, that it can serve as a means only because it is the supreme end, is attributed to a mysterious psychological process that has to be invoked because of the original, and erroneous, designation of money as the instrument of reason.

The only social theorist systematically to challenge the orthodox conception of money has been Karl Marx. Until recently interpretations of Marx's theory of money have remained within the functionalist framework, generally insisting that the primary function of money lies in its role as the independent form of value, and so as *capital*. This conception of money accords with the Marxist conception of capitalism as a society based not on exchange and communication, but on EXPLOITATION and domination, whose development is determined not by human needs and aspirations, but by the accumulation of capital. This theory leads Marxists to argue that the 'substantive irrationality' of capitalist society is inseparable from, and more fundamental than, its 'formal rationality'. However, it does not define a distinctively Marxist theory of money, validating the orthodox view of Marx as a minor heretic, whose monetary theories were derivative and flawed.

Within the functionalist interpretation of Marx, money remains an instrument, an instrument not of reason but of capital. The irrationality of money is not inherent in money, but lies outside itself, in the social relations which it serves to symbolize. The implication, seized on by the reform movement in the Soviet bloc, is that money is socially neutral, and can as well serve as an instrument of socialist planning as it can serve as an instrument of capitalist exploitation.

The publication of Marx's early works and of the *Grundrisse* has opened the way to an alternative, and more radical, interpretation of Marx's theory which gives a central role to his critique of money. This approach represents a convergence of the analysis of the 'value-form', pioneered in Germany, and of money as a mode of domination, pioneered by the Italian *autonomia* movement, in the early 1970s (Backhaus, 1969; Negri, 1972). This interpretation reverses the conventional relationship between form and function, seeing the *functions* of money as deriving from the properties of money as a particular *social form*. This approach rejects the analytical separation of the 'real' from the monetary system, which marks both orthodox economics and orthodox Marxism, and which appears in inverted form in post-modernist theories. Money does not symbolize a real relationship which lies behind it. Still less does money constitute the 'economy' as a purely symbolic realm. It is only with the develop-ment of capitalism that money dissolves all 'prehistoric ties', so that relationships between individuals can only be constituted as *social* relationships, and so acquire a determinate social character, through the form of money. In a developed capitalist society money is not, therefore, merely a symbol, it is the primary mediating term between individual and society. This apparently trite observation has quite fundamental consequences, for it implies that the theory of money, far from being a technical economic theory, must be at the very heart of the theory of capitalist society (Merrington and Marazzi, 1977; Negri, 1979, Lesson 2; Clarke, 1982, Chapters 3 & 4; Clarke 1988, chs 4 and 5; Ganssmann, 1988; cf. Aglietta and Orlean, 1982, who develop a comparable, but non-Marxist, anthropological theory of money).

Reading

Aglietta, M. and Orlean, A. 1982: *La Violence de la monnaie*.

Backhaus, H.-G. 1969 (*1980*): On the dialectics of the value-form. *Thesis XI* 1, 94–120.

Clarke, S. 1982 (*1991*): *Marx, Marginalism and Modern Sociology*.

Ganssmann, H. 1988: Money: a symbolically generalized medium of communication? *Economy and Society* 17.3, 285–316.

Knapp, G.F. 1905 (*1924*): *The State Theory of Money*, abridged edn.

Luhmann, N. 1983: Das sind Preise: ein soziologisch-systemtheoretischer Klärungsversuch. *Soziale Welt*, 34.2, 153–70.

——1984: Die Wirtschaft der Gesellschaft als autopoietisches System. *Zeitschrift für Soziologie*, 13.4, 308–27.

Merrington, J. and Marazzi, C. 1977: *Notes on money, crisis and the state. CSE Conference Papers*.

Negri, A. 1984: *Marx Beyond Marx*.

Simmel, G. 1907 (*1990*): *The Philosophy of Money*.

SIMON CLARKE

monopoly capitalism   The term was used by Lenin to define a new stage in the development of CAPITALISM at the end of the nineteenth century, in which economic life was dominated by large corporations, bank capital had merged with industrial capital to form financial oligarchies, and the major capitalist nations were engaged in imperialist expansion. Lenin was indebted to Hilferding's *Finance Capital* (1910) for his basic conceptions, but he expounded them in the context of an entirely different political doctrine which envisaged socialist revolutions as an outcome of war between the imperialist powers. Subsequently, Lenin and later Marxist-Leninists elaborated a conception of 'state monopoly capitalism' (see Hardach and Karras, 1978, pp. 47–50, 63–8) to take account of the increasing involvement of the state in the capitalist economy. These ideas too, had affinities with Hilferding's later conception of 'organized capitalism' (see Bottomore, 1981, pp. 14–15), but they differed profoundly in being embedded in an increasingly dogmatic and intellectually barren Bolshevik ideology.

Monopoly capitalism was given a different meaning, however, in the book by Baran and Sweezy (1966), where it was argued that new 'contradictions of capitalism' had taken the place of those analysed by Marx. The high rates of economic growth, and an apparently greater stability of postwar capitalism, reflected a significant change in the character of the capitalist economy, from competition to monopoly. This results in a steady and continuing increase in the profits of monopolistic firms, approximating society's 'economic surplus' according to Baran and Sweezy, who then went on to argue that this rising economic surplus necessarily leads to stagnation unless it is counteracted in some way (see Hardach and Karras, 1978, pp. 61–3). But this conception, like those elaborated by Marxist-Leninist thinkers, in fact paid little attention to various important counteracting influences, such as the development of welfare capitalism and a number of more 'socialistic' changes in the economy. In the future social theorists are likely to be concerned less with what are called – often misleadingly – 'monopolies', and more with studying the structure and influence of large corporations in the context of welfare capitalism and extensive state regulation in its diverse forms.

Reading
Baran, Paul and Sweezy, Paul 1966: *Monopoly Capitalism*.
Hardach, Gerd and Karras, Dieter 1978: *A Short History of Socialist Economic Thought*.
Lenin, V.I. 1916 (*1964*): *Imperialism: The Highest Stage of Capitalism*.

TOM BOTTOMORE

morality In its prescriptive sense, it is that consideration or set of considerations providing the strongest reasons for living in some specified way; in its descriptive sense, such a consideration or set of such considerations adhered to or avowed by some person or group. (See also VALUES.)

Thus, if we assume that the Ten Command-

ments are a correct representation of the demands of morality, morality (prescriptive) requires us to live without killing one another, to keep the Sabbath holy, and so on; while, even if we assume that the Decalogue is mistaken, we can describe it as constituting the morality (descriptive) of any person who avows or lives by it.

Work on descriptive morality this century has centred on the content and explanation of moral beliefs. Anthropologists have continued to document the moral systems of other cultures and subcultures, one of them (Turnbull, 1973) describing the apparent absence of morality among the Ik. Historians of ideas have attempted to explain how particular moral ideologies, such as that of Nazi Germany, developed, while sociologists have tried to account for and analyse morality in general.

Durkheim (1925) argues that there are three elements in morality: an imperatival aspect; attachment to social groups; and the autonomy of moral agents (cf. Max Weber's 'ethics of responsibility'). Like Durkheim, Westermarck (1906) sought a non-individualistic explanation of the origin of moral beliefs, being influenced also by William Sumner, Ferdinand Tönnies and Vilfredo Pareto in stressing the importance of the sentiments. The moral ideas have their roots in custom, and develop in the light of reason. Modern writers have concentrated on the morality of modernity; see for instance the view of P. Berger, B. Berger and H. Kellner (1973) that modern morality is to be understood in terms of the pluralization of 'life-worlds'.

Explanations have also been offered of why humans tend to develop moral beliefs. Freud (1923) claimed that morality consists in the internalization of parental commands in the form of demands made by the superego. He allowed development from mere obedience to these commands into the reflective morality of the ego ideal. Lévi-Strauss (1949) stressed the importance of reciprocity and exchange in the development of institutions such as marriage, which are partly constituted by moral expectations and beliefs. Advocates of game theory have put notions of cooperation at the centre: many moral institutions, such as promising, can be seen as social solutions to coordination and cooperation problems such as the Prisoner's Dilemma (see Elster, 1989).

Philosophical work on prescriptive morality can be roughly categorized as either second order (metaethical) or first order. (See ETHICS.) Metaethics has concerned itself with three main questions: the truth value of moral judgements, the nature of moral reality, and moral epistemology.

A.J. Ayer (1936) introduced the logical positivism of the VIENNA CIRCLE into mainstream Anglo-American philosophy. According to his emotivist position, moral judgements have no truth value, being mere expressions of attitude (the 'Boo/Hurrah theory'). Through the writings of R.M. Hare (1981), prescriptivism – the view that moral judgements are essentially imperatival – became influential. J.L. Mackie (1977) argued that all moral judgements are false, because there is no objective moral reality to which they refer.

Mackie's view demonstrates the interconnection of the three metaethical themes mentioned. Discussion of the nature of moral reality revolved around the so-called 'fact/value distinction'. G.E. Moore (1903) argued that evaluative facts are unlike those facts which constitute the subject matter of the natural sciences. Rather, goodness is a non-natural property of things. A more common view was that there are no evaluative facts: the world is evaluatively neutral and to be described in scientific terms. This view, of course, provided the impetus for accounts of moral judgements as not primarily assertive such as emotivism. In North America, there has been a recent revival of realist naturalism, according to which moral facts are natural facts of the same broad kind as say chemical or biological facts (see Brink, 1989).

Discussion in moral epistemology has revolved around the question of how we might be said to know moral facts, and the nature of moral knowledge. Intuitionism was dominant after Moore. We are held to possess a 'moral sense' which enables us to intuit the rightness or goodness of concrete particulars or the correctness of certain fundamental moral principles (see Ross, 1939). This is a form of moral foundationalism. According to coherentism, moral knowledge consists in the most consistent and coherent set of moral beliefs (see Brink, 1989).

In first order ethics, questions have been asked about the nature of morality with a more obvious relation to how we should live. A central issue has been that of RELATIVISM: is there a universally true morality, or are moralities relative, perhaps through being grounded in specific social practices or 'forms of life' (see MacIntyre, 1981)? Also, how important are specifically other-regarding moral considerations as opposed to, say, considerations of self-interest or aesthetics (Williams, 1985)?

Modern first order moral philosophy has been dominated by the development of moral theories, according to which morality consists in one or a small number of pertinent considerations. According to utilitarianism, as espoused for example by Moore and Hare, the only consideration which is directly relevant to the question of how to live is the overall maximization of welfare.

Non-utilitarian theories have tended to be rooted in the work of Kant. Such theories have been described as deontological (Greek *dei* = 'one must'). One example is that of Ross, who thought that we ought, for instance, to keep promises for reasons independent of welfare.

Since the publication of Elizabeth Anscombe's article 'Modern moral philosophy' (1958), a new strand has emerged in moral theory, putting greater emphasis on the nature of moral character and the virtues (see French et al., 1988).

Because of the dominance of metaethics, the philosophers of the first half of this century paid little academic attention to practical first order moral problems. Since the Vietnam war this has changed, and discussions of issues such as abortion, war, and the environment are now widespread (see Singer, 1986).

See also JUSTICE; NORM; RIGHTS.

Reading
Anscombe, G.E.M. 1958: Modern moral philosophy. *Philosophy* 33, 1–19.
Hare, R.M. 1981: *Moral Thinking.*
MacIntyre, A. 1981: *After Virtue.*
Mackie, J.L. 1977: *Ethics.*
Moore, G.E. 1903: *Principia Ethica.*
Ross, W.D. 1939: *Foundations of Ethics.*
Singer, P. ed. 1986: *Applied Ethics.*
Westermarck, E. 1906: *The Origin and Development of the Moral Ideas.*
Williams, B. 1985: *Ethics and the Limits of Philosophy.*
ROGER CRISP

movement, social *See* SOCIAL MOVEMENT

music While the relationship between music and society has been studied by musicologists, ethnomusicologists and sociologists, development in all three disciplines has, to a greater or lesser extent, been fragmentary and characterized by fundamental theoretical problems.

Musicology and musical analysis, focusing on the study of Western art music, have been orientated to the explication of the formal properties inherent in the musical work. This concern with structures has led to a conception of the musical work as being divorced from its social or cultural context. Consequently, the social researcher must either establish some explanatory or analytical link between musical structures and society, or redefine and marginalize musicology's concept of autonomous music.

The historical study of music has been influenced by musicology's formalism. Music is grasped through a stylistic development, such that the work of any given period is understood in terms of a style that is formally related to, and logically develops, the style of the preceding period. Reference to social history concerns only the ambient conditions within which musical creation took place, with little or no consideration of any explanatory links between society and the musical product. Only recently has there been a significant shift of emphasis, away from formalism and towards the consideration of music within a 'web of culture' (Tomlinson, 1984). The social history of music is increasingly seen in terms of the goal of recovering the meaning of a given piece of music, by consideration of the culturally specific values that informed its production, consumption and dissemination. While formal analysis is not abandoned, emphasis shifts to the recognition of the values and meanings attributed to music in a specific CULTURE.

Ethnomusicology is divided between more or less explicit biases to musicology, and as such to the analysis of the inherent structure of non-Western musics, and to anthropology, and thus to the consideration of music within its cultural context. The latter approach has led to the challenging of the universality of Western conceptions of music. From an initial concern with the comparison of different cultures' musics, increasingly sophisticated explanations have been suggested in terms of the uses to which music is put by groups, and the functions that music serves for the society as a whole. More recently, and in line with the developments in social history, music has been interpreted as an integral part of a symbolically expressed culture. Increased scope has therefore been made for the interpretation, as opposed to causal or functional explanation, of the music.

The sociology of music has tended to be concerned with a positivistic documentation of the social conditions of musical activity. Here the formalist definition of music is ignored rather than challenged. At its weakest, the concern is exclusively with the extramusical social phenomena that occur in the presence of music, or that determine its production, consumption and distribution. The music itself is neither explained nor interpreted.

An engagement with formalism occurs most profoundly, although not uniquely, in the work of Max Weber and Theodor Adorno. Weber used music to illustrate and explore the limitations of RATIONALIZATION. The musical system of a given culture is examined in terms of the degree to which it manifests a rationalization of the natural musical phenomena. Adorno similarly broke down the formalist approach by suggesting that music is at once autonomous and yet a social fact. The seemingly autonomous development of music, charted by orthodox music history, is sociologically decoded by recognizing the social basis of the materials and forms of thought that music uses, albeit that music manifests a development of that material autonomously from the all-embracing economic purposes of capitalist society.

PHENOMENOLOGY, SEMIOTICS, and STRUCTURALISM have had an increasing influence on the sociology of music, allowing more sophisticated analyses of musical meaning, in terms of its social construction within specific situations, and its determination through culturally specific codes.

Most recently a more concerted attack has been launched on the presuppositions of traditional musicology. Directly or indirectly, ethnomusicology and sociology have led to a new questioning within musicology of the assumption of the aesthetic autonomy of the musical work. Increasingly music is seen to be produced and defined within a social context, suggesting that notions of 'autonomy' are ideological constructs.

Reading
Adorno, T.W. 1976: *Introduction to the Sociology of Music*, trans. E. B. Ashton.
Frith, S. 1978: *The Sociology of Rock*.
Leppert, R. and McClary, S. eds 1987: *Music and Society: The Politics of Composition, Performance and Reception*.
Nattiez, J.J. 1990: *Music and Discourse: Toward a Semiology of Music*, trans. C. Sabbate.
Nettl, B. 1983: *The Study of Ethnomusicology*.
Supičić, I. 1987: *Music in Society: A Guide to the Sociology of Music*.
Weber, M. *1958: The Rational and Social Foundations*

of *Music*, trans. D. Martindale, J. Riedel and
G. Neuwirth.

ANDREW EDGAR

myth   A sacred narrative involving supernatural
beings and embodying the *conscience collective*,
myth has woven into it popular beliefs about
mankind, the social world and the nature and
meaning of the universe. Twentieth-century theories of myth can be divided into psychological,
functionalist, structuralist and political.

Nineteenth-century anthropologists interested
in EVOLUTION and diffusion of cultures sought to
discover the origins of myths, interpreting them as
unscientific thought and incomplete records of historical events. Psychoanalytic approaches developed by Sigmund Freud (see PSYCHOANALYSIS)
instead tended to seek in myth themes of universal
psychic conflict (repression, incest taboo, sibling
envy, Oedipus complex), or archetypal images arising from the 'collective unconscious' (Jung, 1964).

The functionalist anthropological tradition, best
represented by Malinowski, criticized these theories
for abstracting myths from their social context.
From empirical studies of the Trobriand islanders,
Malinowski argued that 'myth fulfils in primitive
culture an indispensable function': it is a product of
a living faith which serves to codify and reinforce
group norms, safeguard rules and morality, and
promote social cohesion (1948, p. 79) (See FUNCTIO-
NALISM).

Contemporary approaches, including those of
Leach (see Leach and Aycock, 1983) and Barthes
(1973), have been heavily influenced by STRUCTURA-
LISM, and in particular, Lévi-Strauss (1964–72).
Using theories developed within psychoanalysis and
linguistics, Lévi-Strauss has interpreted myths not
as charters for action providing explanations or legitimation for existing social arrangements, but as
systems of signs; a language whose meaning is coded
and lies below the narrative surface. Myths are
cognitive devices used to reflect upon and resolve
the contradictions and principles underlying all
human societies, each myth being a variation on
universal themes, endlessly recombining the symbolic elements constituted by sets of binary oppositions (mother/father, nature/culture, female/male,
raw/cooked), which reputedly reflect the fundamental conceptual categories of the human mind. Lévi-
Strauss's structuralist techniques have provided
useful insights into motifs underlying myths, but

critics claim the approach is reductionist, a kind of
'verbal juggling with a generalised formula' which
'cannot show us the truth' (Leach, 1970, p. 82).

In political science the meaning of the term has
sometimes been extended to include political philosophy, IDEOLOGY and religion. The most famous
writer in this tradition was Sorel for whom myths
(including the General Strike and Proletarian
Revolution) were images capable of evoking
instinctively all those sentiments which enable a
people, party or class to bring its energies into play
for political action. For Sorel (1906) all great social
movements develop by the pursuit of a myth, which
supplies the necessary idealism to bind and unite
people behind a cause. The idea of myth as an
essential element woven into the fabric of a general
ideology was echoed in Mussolini's conception of
fascism as a living faith. Political myth is a
mobilizing device, a celebration of the irrational
impulses whose appeal to mythmakers lies more in
its lucid and compelling vision of redemption and
salvation than arguments based on abstract principles (Tudor, 1972, p. 130).

Central to most theories is the idea that myths are
unconnected to, and outside of, ordinary space and
time. 'Once upon a time', the 'Golden Age', the
'Dawn of Time' or the 'end of history', all imply past
or future events that are not diachronically linked to
the present. In this respect myths have been interpreted as 'liminal phenomena' told at times or places
that lie 'betwixt and between' normal states of being
(Turner, 1968, p. 578). Thus, according to Eliade
(1968, p. 34), those who participate in myth are
transported temporarily from the everyday world on
to a plane where time is deemed to be 'sacred',
'concentrated' and of 'heightened intensity'.

Reading
Barthes, Roland 1973: *Mythologies*.
Eliade, Mircea 1968: *Myths, Dreams and Mysteries*.
Leach, Edmund, 1970: *Lévi-Strauss*.
Leach, Edmund and Aycock, Alan 1983: *Structural
    Interpretations of Biblical Myth*.
Lévi-Strauss, Claude 1964–72 (*1970–8*): *Mythologiques*, 3
    vols.
Malinowski, Bronislaw 1948: *Magic, Science and Religion
    and other Essays*.
Sorel, Georges 1906 (*1972*): *Reflections on Violence*.
Tudor, Henry 1972: *Political Myth*.
Turner, Victor 1968: Myth and symbol. In *International
    Encyclopaedia of the Social Sciences*, ed. D. Sills, vols
    9–10.

CRIS SHORE

N

nation   There is not and probably cannot be a universally agreed, so to speak neutral, definition of this term. The inherently contested nature of the definition is a consequence of the complex and tangled nature of the raw material to which the term is applied. Humanity is subdivided into many diverse cultures (groups distinguished by language, custom, faith and so forth), and into diverse political units (groups committed to mutual aid, sharing an authority structure, and so forth). *Neither* cultural *nor* political boundaries are generally neat; cultural traits such as language, religous adherence or folk custom frequently cut across each other. Political jurisdictions may be multilayered, so that obedience to a local authority in some contexts may coexist with submission to a more general higher authority for other purposes. Political and cultural boundaries seldom converge with each other.

It is impossible to apply the term 'nation' to all units which are either culturally or politically distinguishable, and there is little temptation to do so. If one were to do so, there would be too many nations, and too many individuals would have multiple national identities. The question is – which of the either culturally or politically distinguishable groupings are in fact plausibly called 'nations'?

The sheer existence of a political unit does not in most cases give rise to the presumption that its boundaries define a nation. Characteristically, many historic political units are either smaller or larger than what are normally called nations: empires are multinational; city-states or tribal segments are smaller than a nation. Nevertheless, political units which are clearly willed and endorsed by their members can sometimes be called nations even when multicultural: it is natural to speak of the Swiss nation, notwithstanding cultural-linguistic differences within it, or the presence inside the polity of politically significant subgroups, 'cantons'.

Likewise, it would not correspond to actual usage to allow *any* given cultural differentiation to define a nation. Arabic dialects differ to the point of mutual unintelligibility, but this on its own neither undermines the idea of an Arab nation, nor automatically turns the speakers of a distinguishable dialect into a nation. What then is the answer?

In premodern times, the question was not merely devoid of a general answer but, more significantly, it was seldom asked. Human beings were members of kin-groups or of local organizations, subjects of dynasties, adherents of faiths often linked to political legitimation, members of ritually or legally defined social strata, and so forth. Cultural identification and political loyalty was complex and variable. The question of *the* nation was seldom asked, and only becomes pervasive and insistent in the context of a special kind of sociopolitical organization which has become pervasive since the turn of the eighteenth into the nineteenth century.

Characteristic of this kind of society is the replacement of an agrarian economic base by an industrial one. People working the land become a minority, sometimes a very small one, and moreover one no longer markedly distinguished from the rest of the population. Most work is semantic, involving manipulation of meanings and people, rather than of physical objects. Occupational mobility is the norm. Both the nature of work (involving constant anonymous communication with many people, mostly strangers) and the nature of all social contact presuppose near-universal literacy and a good measure of formal education. Such education ceases to be a privilege, and becomes instead the precondition of social effectiveness and acceptability and employability. In *these* circumstances, a shared and standardized education-based culture does become the main criterion of social identity; one of the main roles of the state is the maintenance and protection of such a culture. Human beings identify with their literate culture, and states protect such cultures. The state in turn is legitimated by providing protection for a national culture, and the symbols it primarily employs are national rather than dynastic or religious.

In this kind of world, a 'nation' is a large, anonymous population which both shares a common CULTURE and either has, or aspires to have, its own political roof (see also STATE). 'National' identity becomes a general preoccupation *and* a criterion of political legitimacy. Both the external criterion of shared culture and the subjective criterion of political will are present in this definition, though their relative weight may vary. The Swiss, as indicated, are defined by a shared will rather than culture: the same criterion also makes Gaelic-speaking Scottish Highlanders into Scots, notwithstanding a linguistic distinctiveness.

The *applications* of this definition remain contentious. The disagreements are not a fault of the definition, but are inherent in the situation. The point is that on the way to the establishment of nation-states, each providing a single political roof for a single shared culture, conflicts occur, often of great severity, concerning just *which* of the pre-existing cultures are to be granted a state, or which of the pre-existing political units are to be granted a culture as its ward and its *raison d'être*. While from a theoretical point of view it is essential to distinguish between modern 'nations' on the one hand, and 'mere' tribes, castes, dialects, religious minorities on the other, this does not tell us *which* of these multiple premodern differentiations are to be allowed to turn themselves into a modern nation. Only historical destiny, not some independent criterion, can decide this issue.

The term 'nation' does occur in premodern contexts, describing, for instance, regionally based corporations of students in medieval universities, or the totality of the gentry in a given political unit (Poland). But in the interests of logical tidiness, it is best to restrict the term to the modern phenomenon of a large anonymous population, *both* sharing a literate culture *and* endowed with a will to possess a single political authority (though sometimes one or the other of these two elements may predominate). This definition cannot provide us with the ability to tell in advance of the event just which premodern groupings will or will not succeed in becoming nations. Nationalists imbued with a strong sense of the justice of their cause tend to feel that their culture *really*, 'objectively' defines a nation (see NATIONALISM): but this feeling engenders the historical reality of the nation, rather than being, as the nationalist supposes, its reflection.

Reading
Armstrong, John 1982: *Nations before Nationalism*.
Bauer, Otto 1907 (*1924*): *Die Nationalitätenfrage und die Sozialdemokratie*, 2nd enlarged edn with new preface.
Gellner, E. 1983: *Nations and Nationalism*.
Smith, A. D. 1991: *National Identity*.

ERNEST GELLNER

national economic planning The classical economists in the past and the neoclassical economists in modern times have been concerned mainly with the behaviour and interactions of two groups of economic actors, enterprises and households. The actors would be typically assumed to be maximizing private benefits, profits and utilities respectively. They interact by trading private goods and services on terms determined in (economy-wide or international) competitive markets.

Central to the traditional case for national economic planning is the recognition that apart from private goods, private interests and individual preferences, there are also, and in any modern society even more so, non-private goods, common interests and social preferences. Markets for such goods do not exist or can be grossly inefficient. The decisions about the economic resources needed to satisfy these common interests must therefore be made in a different way. National planners are, or are supposed to be, the representatives of such interests, acting on behalf of a whole society. These representatives form the third group of economic actors. They are or should be the elected representatives of the society, acting in their resource allocation roles through various agencies of the national government. These bureaucratic agencies and the process of bargaining which national planners initiate and over which they preside are the counterparts, respectively, of market institutions and market competition. The regulations and direct resource allocation decisions of the agencies are what may be called the visible hand of bureaucracy, or the bureaucratic coordination mechanism, the counterpart of Adam Smith's invisible hand of the price mechanism, or the market coordination mechanism (Kornai, 1980).

In the course of the twentieth century, excepting the 1980s and probably the 1990s, the worldwide tendency has been for governments to devote an increasing proportion of national resources to the provision of public goods, such as national defence, public transport, law and order, and to the provision of merit goods, such as health, education and housing. National plans, though of a limited kind, are needed for the purpose of arriving at the decisions about the size and composition of current and investment spending in these areas in the course of time.

However, a truly spectacular advance of national economic planning was in socialist countries with centrally managed economies and, to a much lesser extent, in newly industrialized countries with market-based economies. The origins of this advance can be traced in large part to the spread of socialist doctrine for much of the twentieth century, promoting non-private ownership as socially superior and advocating the new role for state authorities as an all-purpose entrepreneur either alongside, in place of or in the absence of private entrepreneurs (Gomulka, 1986, ch. 1). National planning in these countries became macroeconomic as well, concerned not just with individual sectors or regions, but with the development of the entire economy, taking into account the mutual intersectoral and intertemporal relationships. Socialist national planners tended to see markets as failing to mobilize adequate financial savings and human resources for development, and as promoting myopic and erratic behaviour of investors, one leading to potentially serious underinvestment, especially in activities where social benefits exceed private benefits. A major boon for the spread of national planning in market economies was also the Great Depression of the 1930s and the direct and successful involvement of governments in the supply side of economies during World War II.

In the countries in which state ownership prevails, the scope, the ends and the instruments of national planning depend largely on the decision-making autonomy of state-owned enterprises and on the extent to which community preferences, effectively planners' preferences, dominate over the preferences of individual consumers in determining the economy-wide demands. Under the traditional Soviet-type system (the USSR between 1928 and 1990), much production and investment activity was planned and managed from the centre, while consumers' sovereignty and enterprise autonomy were highly restricted. By contrast to market economies where supplies and demands are closely interrelated, in any centrally managed economy (CME) the direction of causality tends to run from resources to supplies, and then to demands. In particular, consumer supplies would reflect planners' preferences and may deviate considerably from the levels which would have existed if freely determined by the market. Administered prices and subsidies would have been used to bring the levels of consumer demands closer to those of such supplies (Kushnirsky, 1982).

National plans in a CME vary in terms of the periods of time they cover and in terms of the degree of aggregation. Annual plans are the most operational and the most disaggregated. These plans would themselves be subdivided into quarterly and monthly plans. Medium-term plans, usually to run for five years, would be more aggregated and often only indicative rather than obligatory. Purely indicative and highly aggregative would be long-term national plans. To ease the task of plan formulation and subsequent implementation, state enterprises producing similar goods would typically be grouped together to form a production association, several associations would form a branch, headed by a ministry, and the activities of the industries would be coordinated by the central planning authority. These enterprises negotiate with their higher authorities production plans which specify the minimum output targets and maximum input quotas, including new capital investment. These enterprise-specific plans are drawn in terms of a limited number of products, the total number of which is some 5,000 to 50,000 at the association level and some 200 to 2,000 at the central level. Most of these 'products' are large groups of similar goods, usually expressed in both physical terms (tons, square metres and so on) and value terms. The immediate aim for central planners is to select from a set of feasible alternatives the volumes of enterprise-specific demands and supplies of such products in a manner which would ensure balance at the economy-wide level for each of the products. The additional and more demanding aim is to do the national balancing in a way that final or net outputs of the economy would maximize some sort of index of national welfare or, at any rate, that these outputs would meet planners' objectives in a manner considered satisfactory (Manove, 1971; Heal, 1973; Ellman, 1979).

Crucial to the efficient operation of such a planned economy is the behaviour of enterprises. Since both output targets and input quotas are typically large aggregates, an enterprise-specific plan imposed from above can be viewed as representing a set of (resource, demand and financial) constraints defining the set of choices still open to the enterprise. The choice of its own plan by the enterprise (agent) depends in turn on the incentive system imposed by the centre (principal), particularly on the credibility of its disciplining threats (Schaffer, 1989). The terms of both the imposed plan and the incentive system are enterprise-specific and therefore open to bargaining between the enterprise and the centre. The bargaining asset for the enterprise is the limited access to the information on its true production possibilities by the centre. In the bargaining process enterprises are therefore in a position to seek both greater input quotas than necessary and lower output targets than possible. They are also typically better off by not revealing present production possibilities, since this information may be used by the centre to increase their future output targets. This practice of planning whereby achieved levels of performance are used as a starting point to determine new targets is known as the application of the 'ratchet principle' (Berliner, 1976; Cave and Hare, 1981).

When many dissimilar goods are included in composite output targets, these targets have to be expressed in value terms. The producer has in this case an interest, given the cost-plus principle of price formation, to use expensive inputs in order to minimize effort needed to implement a given plan. This leads to a bias in CMEs to produce material-intensive products (see Gomulka and Rostowski, 1988, for an estimate of the bias). Most product prices in CMEs were state imposed and rigid, responding little to market disequilibria. Such *ad hoc* prices are likely to differ substantially from the marginal social cost of production. To reduce their allocative role, and as a response to the effort-minimizing behaviour of enterprises, central planners would typically set high output targets and low input quotas, so that the set of choices from which an enterprise selects its own plan is small. This practice of 'taut planning' attempts to bring to the fore the allocative role of quantities, which for planners are meaningful, and diminish the role of prices. However, inflexible prices lead to widespread and persistent microeconomic disequilibria, and this in turn causes the phenomenon of 'forced substitution' (of shortage goods by surplus goods). Given the poor quality of prices, profits could not be relied upon as a measure of performance. This feature of CMEs led to the practice of tolerating loss-making. This tolerance helped to develop, and was itself enhanced by, 'paternalistic attitudes' of the centre to enterprises (Kornai, 1980).

Despite the widespread presence of microeconomic disequilibria and inefficiency, socialist central planners were on the whole capable of maintaining macroeconomic control. They kept wages low and this ensured that profit margins were usually exceptionally high by Western standards. These profits were used to finance large investment activity and to fund current expenditure of the state budget, a large proportion of which was consumer subsidies. Except in Yugoslavia, central planners were also able to control well the growth of wages and other incomes and thereby limit price inflation to rates typically below 10 per cent per annum (Wiles, 1980). However, in some countries and in certain periods, this control was seriously eroded or nearly lost (Poland in 1950–1, 1980–1, 1988–9, the USSR in 1989–91), leading to bursts of what Kolodko and McMahon (1987) call 'shortageflation'. Politically motivated attempts to keep state controlled prices below market-clearing levels led in turn to the growth of black markets and the phenomenon of 'forced savings'.

The early reformers of CMEs, in the quest for combining economic efficiency and socialist principles, did not advocate the reduction of state ownership or central planning, but merely the abolition of enterprise-specific plans. Enterprises would as a consequence be financially and managerially independent. To elicit better performance it was vital that they also operate in a competitive market environment. However, according to the reformers, key prices, performance criteria and incentives would be set by the centre to induce enterprises to produce, although no longer individually but jointly, what the centre wanted them to produce. In this 'planned socialist economy with a regulated market' (Brus, 1961) the competitive market mechanism was intended to be used as an instrument to implement central plans (Malinvaud, 1967, proposed a possible implementation of this idea in a fully developed mathematical model; for a survey of possible implementations see Heal, 1973). This idea of indirect or parametric central planning was at the heart of the Hungarian reform between 1958 and 1990, the Polish reform from 1982 to 1989, and the Chinese reform initiated in 1982. Under those reforms shortages were reduced and price flexibility increased. However, competitive markets were not established, paternalistic and interventionist attitudes of the state owner to enterprises persisted, and as a result the old deficiencies, particularly high inefficiency and low innovation, continued unabated. This failure of reforms within the system subsequently led, in

Eastern Europe and the former USSR, to a frontal attack on the twin pillars of the system itself: central planning and state ownership. In Eastern Europe and the former USSR central planning was abandoned in the period 1989–92. The original arguments of von Mises (1935) against the feasibility of rational economic calculation in the 'Socialist Commonwealth' appear to have been vindicated (see Lavoie, 1985, for a recent review of the arguments).

There has been a parallel shift in developed market economies of Western Europe and Japan, as well as in most newly industrialized developing countries worldwide, away from active and extensive 'indicative' central planning (Brada and Estrin, 1990). In many of the countries privatization policies have also reduced the size of the public sector. However, the more traditional economic role of central authorities in the provision of public and merit goods, as well as macroeconomic stabilization management, regulations and enforcement, remains largely intact in both West and East.

See also SOCIALIST ECONOMICS; SOCIALIZATION OF THE ECONOMY.

Reading

Cave, J. and Hare, P. 1981: *Alternative Approaches to Economic Planning*.
Ellman, M. 1979: *Socialist Planning*.
Gomulka, S. 1986: *Growth, Innovation and Reform in Eastern Europe*.
Heal, G. M. 1973: *The Theory of Economic Planning*.
Johansen, L. 1978: *Lectures on Macroeconomic Planning*, vols 1 and 2.
Kushnirsky, F. I. 1982: *Soviet Economic Planning, 1965–80*.

STANISLAW GOMULKA

national popular regime   A system of government that derives its legitimacy from affirmations of mass popular support and from the defence of national interests, while not following too strictly the rules of liberal democracy, can be called a national popular regime. Countries in the process of development, in most of Asia, Africa and Latin America, as well as in Eastern Europe before World War II, are especially likely to experience this kind of rule. Its origins can be basically twofold. In some cases, conservative or foreign-dominated political systems are toppled by a violent takeover by alienated sectors of the elite – often the military – which use the state apparatus to reorient economic and social policy and acquire mass support. In other cases, mass movements are organized from below, and only after a long period of oppositional politics, either reformist or revolutionary, do they accede to power.

In the first case, that is, when the national popular regime has been installed from above, the result is often of a highly authoritarian kind, with the addition of officially controlled mass demonstrations. Many countries in the Middle East have followed this pattern since World War II, and so to a lesser extent has Turkey since the days of Mustafa Kemal Atatürk in the 1920s. The mass component of the regime generally takes the form of an official single party. In Turkey, however, the regime eventually generated a system of competitive parties, in a slow process of liberalization punctuated by renewed military interventions.

The degree of popular support obtained by national popular regimes is difficult to ascertain, as it is not genuinely tested in free elections. That support, however, is often present, particularly during the early periods of consolidation, as a result of nationalist, revolutionary or radically reformist policies and of the monopoly or near monopoly of the mass media. Public opinion is usually polarized by those policies, and a large sector of the erstwhile dominant classes is thrown into opposition or exile, while a new ruling class is formed on the basis of the bureaucracy, the military and the new capitalists.

In the second case considered, that is, when a national popular regime has its origins in insurrections from below, mass politics take a somewhat different character, because of the more genuine and spontaneous nature of the party representing the revolution. However, structural constraints determine a convergence in the nature of these regimes with those originating from above. In Mexico, whose 1910 revolution can be considered to have generated, after a few years of civil war, the first national popular regime in the twentieth century, the formation of a dominant party took almost a couple of decades, and was compatible with the existence of minor opposition parties. The regime has evolved in a clearly capitalist direction, and the ruling party has become increasingly conservative, while opposition from both the right and the left has been growing and becoming capable of challenging the regime. As a result trends are discernible towards the consolidation of a more competitive and free political system, unless a military coup stops this process.

In Algeria the regime established in 1962 was based on a successful national insurrection which had to wage a protracted struggle against French colonialism. The ensuing legitimacy of the freedom fighters gave them an extended credit from the masses and the new elites, and enabled them to establish important reforms and elements of a socialist economy. In Iran the fundamentalist Islamic revolution of 1979 enthroned a religious and highly bellicose version of a national popular regime, apparently quite capable of receiving continued, though regimented, popular support.

National popular regimes, particularly those originating from below, can evolve in a socialist direction, or at the very least adopt a socialist phraseology, in an attempt at maintaining support among the masses or the radicalized middle sectors and the intelligentsia. Some revolutionary socialist regimes, such as those in Cuba and from 1979 to 1990 in Nicaragua, have come to power with a complex pattern of social support, and share some of the traits of national popular regimes, including the cult of personality and a preference for one-party systems.

Some instances of national popular regimes are a mixture between the two polar types considered before, those originating from above and those originating from below. In Argentina the military coup of 1943, with Juan D. Perón as a leading figure, established a regime with national popular traits. Forced by the opposition to grant free elections, the political party formed by Perón revalidated its credentials of representing the masses. The ensuing constitutional presidencies of Perón (1946–55) saw a progressive deterioration of the recently reestablished liberal democratic system, ending in a military coup in 1955. Peronism in opposition retained its character of a mass party, and has since become a permanent feature of the Argentinian political system. In other Latin American countries as well governments originating from above or from a combination of civilian and military force (like that of Vargas in 1930) evolved towards becoming the basis of popular parties capable of maintaining their strength in a reconstituted democratic regime.

In Eastern Europe between the two world wars several governments partook of the traits here assigned to national popular regimes, and of those of fascism. Often national popular regimes or their associated populist parties have been branded as fascist. It is a fact that in some of them fascist elements have a presence, but the traits of the two systems are quite different. It is, however, probably no coincidence that the fascist components of national popular regimes are greater in relatively more developed countries, such as Argentina, Brazil and in Eastern Europe. The presence of authoritarian and mass mobilization traits is not enough to classify a regime as fascist, as these traits are also present in communist countries. They do establish a contrast with liberal democracy, but the Latin American experience shows that the heirs of those regimes can become permanent participants in a competitive political process, in which they occupy a position nearer to the left than to the right.

See also POPULISM; NATIONALISM.

Reading
Almond, Gabriel and Coleman, James S. eds 1960: *The Politics of Developing Areas*.
Apter, D.E. 1965: *The Politics of Modernization*.
Dahl, Robert ed. 1973: *Regimes and Oppositions*.
Linz, Juan and Stepan, Alfred eds 1978: *The Breakdown of Democratic Regimes*.
O'Donnell, Guillermo, Schmitter, Philippe and Whitehead, Lawrence eds 1986: *Transitions from Authoritarian Rule: Prospects for Democracy*.

TORCUATO S. DI TELLA

National Socialism The earlier confidence in general explanations of National Socialism – as a political movement, ideology, and regime – has been undermined by the progress of detailed research and the emergence of 'postmodernist' paradigms. The theories of Hitlerism, TOTALITARIANISM, FASCISM, or the German *Sonderweg* (see Grebing, 1986; Blackbourn and Eley, 1984) now appear usable only for the light they shed on particular features, or as incentives to further reflection and analysis. It seems problematic today whether the National Socialism of the 1920s, such as developed in industrial-capitalist Germany under Adolf Hitler's leadership, established a dictatorship (1933–45) which brought suffering to a great part of humanity through World War II and the policy of mass extermination, can simply be subsumed under the general category of fascism, even though it was historically associated with it (see Larsen et al., 1980).

One of the roots of National Socialism in European history is to be found in the intellectual and political efforts, even before the turn of the century in France and in Central Europe, to unite a bellicose nationalism with mass politics in the early phase of democratization, and with socialist conceptions. Although this 'new nationalism', not yet fully realized by such diverse parties as Adolf Stoecker's 'Christian-Social Workers' Party' in Berlin or Georg von Schönerer's Pan-Germans in Vienna, is often assimilated in traditional political thought to the extreme right, it did in fact, like fascism generally, evade this left–right schema (see O'Sullivan, 1983, chs 2 and 3). This Janus-faced attitude also explains why controversy among social scientists and historians has persisted over whether National Socialism should be regarded as revolutionary or reactionary, backward-looking or modernizing (see Prinz and Zitelmann, 1991), as an attempt to achieve social stability by reactionary means or as an (unintended) economic and societal modernization achieved by a 'conservative' political revolution (see Schoenbaum, 1966).

In contrast with Mediterranean and West European fascism, National Socialism started from a national culture which was characterized by conceptions of a mythical common descent, of 'blood and soil', of 'race' and the '*Volk*'. Another essential element was 'modern' ANTI-SEMITISM based on Christian traditions. These elements were combined in a distinctive way in Germany from the time of national unification 'from above' in 1871. The belief in the German 'Volk', expressed through national monuments, public festivals, popular novels and writings, and Wagner's operas, became established as a kind of 'secular religion' in many sections of German society (see Mosse, 1964). This 'German ideology' was communicated in symbols and liturgical forms as 'theatrical politics'. This was another, still more important source of National Socialism, and at the same time a precondition for its diffusion when German society was convulsed by the economic and social crises of the interwar years.

Forerunners of National Socialism, both in name and organization, emerged before 1918 in the nationalist struggles in German Bohemia of the multi-national Habsburg empire (1903 saw the foundation of the German Workers' Party), and after World War I they had a resurgence in Austria, Czechoslovakia and Germany. The National Socialist movement was at first only a splinter party of the 'völkisch' workers in postwar Munich, but soon found in Hitler an outstanding propagandist and eventually a mythically transfigured leader. As the National Socialist German Workers' Party (NSDAP) it adopted in 1920 a programme in which

radical nationalistic and imperialistic claims, and demands for the revision of the international and domestic postwar order were combined with wide-ranging anti-Semitic issues and middle-class and social demands (such as the nationalization of trusts, profit-sharing in large enterprises, communalization of wholesale distributors, and the division of large landed property) subsumed under the comprehensive notion of a classless 'people's community'. The heterogeneity of this programme was indeed constantly emphasized by contemporaries and by historians, and little significance was attributed to it in the political practice of National Socialism. Nevertheless, it enabled the NSDAP to present itself as being uncommitted to specific social groups, and during the world economic crisis to respond to contradictory elements of dissatisfaction and protest, uniting them in a mass movement.

Hitler's world-view (expounded in 1925 in *Mein Kampf*), which was formed in the Vienna of the late Habsburg monarchy and refined in the counter-revolutionary climate of postwar Munich, serves the historian to some extent as the main formulation of National Socialist ideology. Its basic principles are the social Darwinist struggle for existence (see SOCIAL DARWINISM); belief in the superiority of the 'Aryan race'; and an elitist view of individuals. The central aims set out are the conquest of 'living space in the East' and a radical 'removal of the Jews' from society, which in practice became merged in the struggle against 'Jewish Bolshevism'. Unlike the National Socialist agrarian romantics Richard Darré (1895–1953) and Heinrich Himmler (1900–1945), Hitler, who accepted the existence of private property though wanting it to be subordinated to a 'people's community', conceived the future transformed Germany as a highly industrialized and technologically advanced society (see Zitelmann, 1987; Kershaw, 1991, ch. 1 and conclusion).

The principles of a charismatic leadership, violent 'anti-Marxist' and anti-democratic agitation, and paramilitary politics (the 'private army' of the SA and later the SS 'private police') were perfected by the NSDAP after the failed Munich Beer Hall putsch of 1923, although the party leadership restrained many 'revolutionary' combative tendencies among its militant members and avoided any appearance of trying to seize power unconstitutionally. The party membership and electoral supporters in the early 1930s gave the impression of a modern, if asymmetrical, people's party much more than that of a middle-class or petty bourgeois party which many Marxist and liberal theorists of fascism emphasized. Equally dubious are the assumptions about the financing of the NSDAP's rise, mainly by 'big capital', but the seizure and consolidation of power in 1933 is hardly conceivable without the support of national and conservative elites of the late Weimar Republic (the Prussian landed aristocracy, military leaders and high officials).

The establishment of National Socialist rule raises fundamental questions about its structure and functioning. In particular, German historians debated in the 1980s whether the 'Third Reich' depended in fact on the will of Hitler as the all-powerful leader, or was a polyarchy of rival subordinate leaders and bureaucracies which, in the final analysis, can be reduced to the structural dichotomy of 'state' and 'party' factors in the power structure of the Nazi dictatorship ('dual state') (see Fraenkel, 1941 and Neumann, 1942). In the same context, diverse answers have been given to the question whether in the Nazi regime a direct realization of the National Socialist, or Hitler's, programme can be discerned, or whether the brutal reality of the 'Third Reich', lacking a proper foundation on a distinctive ideology, was the consequence of an unplanned process of self-radicalization, resulting from latent tendencies in the German or in any modern society. Above all, in explaining the origins of the 'final solution' of the Jewish question, this debate gave rise to diametrically opposed and politically diverse evaluations, to which corresponded different judgements on the everyday reality of the National Socialist system: as a terroristic totalitarian dictatorship to which the whole population was subjected (Arendt, 1951), or as a regime of consensus, partial 'popular resistance' and a significant degree of latitude in private life, which was outside the public rituals of assent and the horrible events of the persecution of political opponents and Jews, and – for a long time – the effects of the war.

These suggested limits to the 'totalitarian' penetration of German society by National Socialism created the impression after the defeat of 1945 that there had been scarcely any convinced National Socialists, but only fellow-travellers, opportunists and deluded individuals. Postwar 'denazification' implemented by the occupying Allies was limited in West Germany and superficial in East Germany, but there was little revival of National Socialist ideas in the proper sense. Neo-Nazi organizations and parties have had little influence, except briefly in the late 1960s with the emergence of the German National Democratic Party (which was not neo-Nazi in the full sense) and more recently since 1990, although the 'Republicans' are right-wing nationalists rather than neo-Nazis (see Benz, 1989).

Reading

Baldwin, Peter 1990: Social interpretations of Nazism. *Journal of Contemporary History* 25, 5–37.
Bracher, Karl Dietrich 1970: *The German Dictatorship*.
Broszat, Martin 1981: *The Hitler State*.
Jäckel, Eberhard 1972: *Hitler's Weltanschauung*.
Kershaw, Ian 1989: *The Nazi Dictatorship*, 2nd edn.
Mayer, Arno J. 1988: *Why Did the Heavens Not Darken?*
Mosse, George L. 1975: *The Nationalization of the Masses*.
Noakes, Jeremy and Pridham, Geoffrey eds 1983–8: *Nazism 1919–1945: A Documentary Reader*, 3 vols (vol. 4 forthcoming).
Peukert, Detlev 1987: *Inside Nazi Germany*.

GERHARD BOTZ

nationalism The doctrine requires that the political and the ethnic group must be congruent. More specifically and concretely, nationalism holds that the national state, identified with a national culture and committed to its protection, is the natural political unit; and that it is scandalous if large numbers of members of the national community are obliged to live outside the borders of the national state. Nationalism is also not too well disposed to the presence within the borders of the nation-state of large numbers of non-nationals. But the political situation which quite specially scandalizes nationalists is one in which the ruling stratum of a political unit belongs to an ethnic group other than that of the majority of the population (see also NATION).

The principle of nationalism, as outlined, is very widely held and even more commonly taken for granted in the modern world. To a very large proportion of our contemporaries, it simply seems obvious and self-evident that people should prefer to live in political units with fellow members of the same 'nationality' or culture and, above all, that they should find rule by foreigners offensive. The national and political unit is the one which represents and expresses the will of the majority of *one* nation, protects its interests and ensures the perpetuation of its culture.

Under the impact of nationalism, both the ethnographic and the political map of Europe, and in a different manner that of the rest of the world, has come to be redrawn. The principles which had governed the drawing of the map of Europe in 1815, after the Napoleonic wars, were dynastic or religious: little if any attention was given to bringing the nationality of subjects and of rulers into harmony with each other. In many parts of Europe, this would in any case have been quite impossible: the ethnic map of much of Europe was extremely complex, and implementing the nationalist principles to respect it would have required that the political map should resemble a jigsaw puzzle. Moreover, it was often quite impossible to project the ethnic boundaries on a territorial map at all: ethnic, cultural and religious groups were frequently separated not by territory, but by their place in a social structure. They often inhabited the same territory, but their role in society was distinct.

It is important to note that styles of drawing political boundaries which respected dynastic, religious or community links but which ignored the principle of nationality were at that time and at previous times taken for granted. They were seldom challenged or found offensive. The question arises as to why a principle, once largely ignored or weak, should in the course of the nineteenth and twentieth centuries have become so very strong and effective. A number of answers have been proposed for this crucial and important question:

1 There is an atavistic instinctual drive within human beings, which makes them wish to be close to others of the same 'blood' or culture (or both) and to hold territory together, and which also leads them to detest those they consider alien, resent their proximity (especially in large numbers), and resent even more strongly the rule of foreigners. The reawakening of these drives may be attributed to various causes, such as the decline of religious faith, the disruptions of modern life, or a general tendency to a return to a 'naturalistic' vision of human beings.

2 The impact of nationalism is due to the formulation and dissemination of nationalist ideology, worked out by various thinkers at the turn of the eighteenth into the nineteenth century, then elaborated further and subsequently disseminated. The main proponent of this theory is Elie Kedourie.

3 A theory held by many Marxists to the effect that the real underlying conflict in history is between classes, so that inter-ethnic conflict is an irrelevancy; but nevertheless, it acquires importance because dominant classes foster nationalist sentiment, in order to distract the attention of those whom they dominate from their real interests. Nationalism is a plot to prevent the oppressed from fighting their real enemies. (But see also Bauer, 1907).

4 Nationalism arises in the course of economic 'development', that is, during the diffusion of industrialism, interpreting this term broadly as an economy based on a rapidly growing and very powerful technology. The diffusion of such an economy leads 'backward' areas and their populations to be incorporated in the industrial economy on terms disadvantageous to them, both economically and socially. To protect themselves, they must organize with a view to creating their own political units, ones which will guide their economic development, especially during its earlier and fragile stages.

5 Nationalism is a by-product of conditions prevailing in the modern world, when most people no longer live in closed village communities, when work is semantic, not physical, and requires the capacity to communicate in a shared, fairly context-free idiom and in writing, when the occupational structure changes rapidly and cannot easily tolerate an ethnic division of labour, and when contact with and dependency on large bureaucracies, both political and economic, pervades all aspects of life. In these conditions, universal literacy and the use of standardized codes become the norm. A person's mastery of such a code becomes his or her most important asset and means of access to employment, social and political participation, acceptability and dignity. Only the state can protect and maintain the required cultural homogeneity, and the principle of *one state, one culture* tends to operate. It then becomes of great concern to any individual that the state in whose territory he or she resides should use the same culture as the one to which the individual in question is committed. Individuals will struggle so that this congruence be achieved, either by assimilating into the dominant culture, or by trying to turn *their* culture into the dominant one. They will endeavour to create new states around this favoured culture, and/or modify existing political frontiers.

The present author is inclined to believe that the

truth of the matter is to be found in a combination of positions (4) and (5). The objection to the 'atavistic' theory is that the dark instinctual drives of human beings, powerful though they are, have not in the past prevented an intensity of hate and murderousness between members of the same 'blood' or cultural groups. There is no good reason to believe that the call of *Blut und Boden* ('blood and soil') should have become more powerful in our age. The 'ideological' explanation fails to explain why just these ideas, in an age of over-production of ideas, should have had more appeal than their rivals, often propagated by more zealous and more talented thinkers and writers. Some Marxist theories of nationalism as a cunning ploy of ruling classes seem to have little factual support.

However, the issue is in no way closed, and the empirical or historical evidence is more than ambiguous. The theories favoured by the present author apply better to Europe than they do to much of the Third World, where nationalism has certainly led to a powerful anti-colonial movement (see COLONIAL LIBERATION MOVEMENT; NATIONAL POPULAR REGIME), but where subsequently colonial frontiers have been, to a remarkable extent, perpetuated and maintained. Plural, multi-ethnic polities have also survived, as have a proliferation of states sharing the same culture (Arab and Hispano-American states). The linking of the political saliency of nationhood to the industrial era has also been challenged, for instance, by one of the most active and serious scholars of nationalism, Anthony Smith.

Reading

Anderson, Benedict 1983: *Imagined Communities: Reflections on the Origin and Spread of Nationalism.*
Armstrong, John 1982: *Nations before Nationalism.*
Breuilly, J. 1982: *Nationalism and the State.*
Deutsch, K. 1966: *Nationalism and Social Communication,* 2nd edn.
Hobsbawm, Eric 1990: *Nations and Nationalism since 1780.*
Kedourie, Elie 1960: *Nationalism.*
Kohn, Hans 1962: *The Age of Nationalism.*
Renan, Ernest 1945: Qu'est-ce qu'une nation. In *Ernest Renan et l'Allemagne,* ed. Emile Bure.
Seton-Watson, Hugh 1977: *Nations and States.*
Smith, Anthony 1971: *Theories of Nationalism.*
—— 1979: *Nationalist Movements in the Twentieth Century.*
—— 1991: *National Identity.*

ERNEST GELLNER

nationalization   *See* SOCIALIZATION

natural selection   According to NEO-DARWINISM, natural selection is the primary mechanism in terms of which the adaptation of organisms to their environment is to be explained. It depends on three subsidiary mechanisms: variation, inheritance and COMPETITION. Individual organisms vary in many of their traits, some variants being better adapted to the environment than others. Given competition for scarce resources, better adapted individuals will prevail over those less well adapted and, if the superior variant is heritable, it will come to be more common in successor generations, and the species to be better adapted to its environment.

Some notable developments in recent social thought show signs of the influence of the idea of natural selection. Cultural ecology explores, anthropologically, the adaptation to the environment of ideology and other aspects of culture (Sahlins and Service, 1960) and exploits, analogically, the idea of selection, as does the theory of Talcott Parsons (1966), associated with his functionalism, of adaptive upgrading via differentiation (see EVOLUTIONARY PROCESSES IN SOCIETY).

The idea of adaptation via variation and selection provided a model for BEHAVIOURISM, as B.F. Skinner acknowledges (1971, ch. 1), and is invoked by F.A. Hayek (1973) to account for the development of the market (see EVOLUTIONARY PROCESSES IN THE ECONOMY) and to justify the OPEN SOCIETY. This idea, which also provided inspiration for the evolutionary epistemology of Karl Popper (1972), had earlier grounded the PRAGMATISM of John Dewey (1938) and, in the biological domain, provided theoretical foundations for SOCIOBIOLOGY and ETHOLOGY.

Ideas about adaptation through selection were invoked by advocates of SOCIAL DARWINISM to defend the inequalities generated by unconstrained economic competition, and by advocates of eugenics to justify programmes of restrictive reproduction.

Perhaps the most important long-term influence of the idea of natural selection is its contribution to the process of SECULARIZATION. For selection provides, for the explanation of the adaptation of organisms to their environment and to each other, an alternative to the creationism associated with religious fundamentalism.

One common misunderstanding of natural selection should be noted. Selection-driven processes of evolution are oriented to no final goal and need not generate any fixed sequence of stages in which

PROGRESS is manifested. The theory of natural selection thus stands opposed to the HISTORICISM with which it is often identified.

Reading
Darwin, Charles 1859: *The Origin of Species.*
Gould, S.J. 1980: *Ever Since Darwin.*
Maynard Smith, J. 1958 (*1975*): *The Theory of Evolution,* 3rd edn.

FRED D'AGOSTINO

naturalism In this century naturalism has usually connoted three related ideas:

1 the dependence of social, and more generally human, life upon nature, i.e. materialism;
2 the susceptibility of these to explanation in essentially the same way, i.e. scientifically;
3 the cognate character of statements of fact and value, and in particular the absence of an unbridgeable logical gulf between them of the kind maintained by David Hume, Max Weber and G.E. Moore, i.e. ethical naturalism.

This entry is mainly concerned with the second sense. It has been the dominant issue in the philosophy, and a controversial issue in the practice, of the human sciences. Naturalism, in this sense, must be distinguished from two extreme species of it: scientism, which claims a complete unity, and reductionism, which asserts an actual identity of subject matter, between the natural and social sciences.

Three broad positions can be delineated: (a) a more or less unqualified naturalism, usually associated with POSITIVISM, dominant in the philosophy and practice of the social sciences (at least in the Anglophone world) until *c.*1970; (b) anti-naturalism, based on a distinctive conception of the uniqueness of social reality, that is as preinterpreted, conceptualized or linguistic in character – HERMENEUTICS, the 'official opposition' to positivism, strong in the Germanic world and in the practice of the humanities; and (c) more recently, a qualified critical naturalism, grounded in an essentially realist conception of science and a transformational conception of social activity, which has begun to come to the fore in the last quarter of the century (see REALISM).

Positivism finds expression in the Durkheimian sociological tradition and in behaviourism, functionalism and structuralism. Its immediate philosophical antecedents lie in the work of David Hume, J.S. Mill, Ernst Mach and the Vienna circle, providing the spine of the orthodox conception of science. The immediate philosophical ancestry of hermeneutics comes from Wilhelm Dilthey, Georg Simmel, Heinrich Rickert and Max Weber. They fused Kantian and Hegelian distinctions so as to produce a contrast between the phenomenal world of nature and an intelligible world of freedom, grounding distinctions between causal explanation (*Erklären*) and interpretive understanding (*Verstehen*), the nomothetic and the IDIOGRAPHIC, the repeatable and the unique, the realms of physics and of history. It finds expression in the Weberian sociological tradition and in phenomenological, ethnomethodological and interpretive studies in general. A discrimination must be made within this second camp between those who seek to synthesize or combine positivist and hermeneutical principles such as Weber or Jürgen Habermas, and those dualists who deny positivism any applicability in the human sphere such as H.G. Gadamer or P. Winch. The third, critical naturalist tradition is immediately based on the realist philosophy of science developed by Rom Harré, E.H. Madden, Roy Bhaskar and others and the conception of social activity independently proposed by Pierre Bourdieu, Anthony Giddens and Bhaskar. It has been taken up and developed by a number of writers including Russell Keat, Ted Benton, William Outhwaite and Peter Manicas. Most of these authors locate an early sociological expression for it in aspects of the work of Marx and more recently in social theory (both Marxist and non-Marxist) aiming to draw on both structuralist and Verstehende traditions in a geohistorically and ecologically informed way. It is not easy to characterize the work of poststructuralist, and more generally postmodernist, thinkers. For the most part they adopt a Nietzschean epistemological perspectivism on a Humean or positivist ontological base.

While positivists have based their naturalism on relatively a priori epistemological theory, hermeneuticists have grounded their anti-naturalism in ontological considerations, particularly the meaningful or rule-governed character of social reality. Moreover while positivists insist that hypotheses about such features must be subject to the normal procedures of any empirical science, hermeneuticists can correctly point to the complete absence of laws and explanations conforming to the positivist canon. In response to this positivists plead that the social world is much more complex than the natural

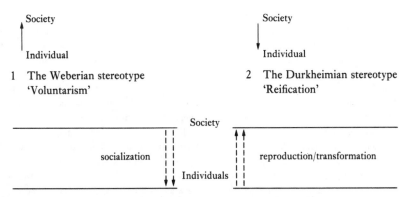

1 The Weberian stereotype 'Voluntarism'

2 The Durkheimian stereotype 'Reification'

3 The transformational model of social activity

world or that the laws that govern it can only be identified at some more basic, for instance neurophysiological, level. Both positivists and hermeneuticists have accepted a fundamentally positivist account of natural science. If this, as the realists argue, is false, then positivists have to make out a special case as to why positivism should be uniquely (and most implausibly) applicable to the human realm; and hermeneuticists, for their part, have to reassess their contrasts. Thus both of Winch's two main arguments are parasitic on a positivist ontology. Constant conjunctions of events are neither necessary nor sufficient either for natural or for social scientific understanding: both alike are concerned with the discovery of intelligible connections in their subject matter. Nor do the conceptual and the empirical jointly exhaust the real. Realism can allow that conceptuality is distinctive, without supposing that it is exhaustive, of social life. Further, realists have argued that transposed positivist themes enter directly into hermeneuticists' substantive metatheories.

The case for critical naturalism turns on the extent to which an independent analysis of the objects of social and psychological knowledge is consistent with a realist theory of science. Thus whereas on the Weberian tradition social objects are seen as the results of, or constituted by, intentional or meaningful behaviour, tending to voluntarism (see figure 1), and on the Durkheimian tradition social objects are seen as possessing a life of their own, external to and coercing the individual, tending to reification (see figure 2), on the critical naturalist conception society is seen as both pre-existing and a (transcendentally and causally) necessary condition for intentional agency (Durkheim's insight) but equally as existing and consisting only in virtue of it (see figure 3).

On this conception, then, society is both the condition and outcome of human agency (the duality of structure) and human agency both produces and reproduces (or transforms) society (the duality of structure). On this model, in contrast to the hermeneutical perspective, actors' accounts are both corrigible and limited by the existence of unacknowledged conditions, unintended consequences, tacit skills and unconscious motivation; but, in opposition to the positivists' view, actors' accounts form the indispensable starting point of social enquiry. The transformational model entails that social life possesses a recursive and non-teleological character, inasmuch as agents reproduce and transform the very structures which they utilize (and are constrained by) in their substantive activities. It also indicates a relational conception of the subject matter of social science, in contrast to the methodological individualist and collectivist conceptions characteristic of the utilitarian (and Weberian) and Durkheimian traditions of social theory.

Certain emergent features of social systems which, on the invocation of a causal criterion for describing reality, can be regarded as *ontological* limits on naturalism, are immediately derivable from this model. These may be summarized as the concept dependence, activity dependence and greater space–time specificity of social structures. The causal interdependency between social science and its subject matter specifies a *relational* limit; while the condition that social systems are intrinsically open – the most important *epistemological* limit – accounts for the absence of crucial or decisive test situations in principle, necessitating reliance on exclusively explanatory (not predictive) criteria for the rational assessment of theory. However subject to (and, arguably, just in virtue of) these qualifications, both the characteristic modalities of theoretical and applied explanation which realists specify (see PHILOSOPHY OF SOCIAL SCIENCE) appear possible in the social, just as in the natural, sphere. On critical naturalism, then, the social sciences can be 'sciences' in exactly the same sense as natural ones, but in ways which are as different (and specific) as their objects.

A fourth *critical* difference, necessitated by the consideration that the subject matter of social science includes not just social objects but beliefs about those objects, makes possible an explanatory critique of consciousness (and being), entailing judgements of value and action, without parallel in the domain of natural sciences, vindicating a modified form of substantive ethical naturalism, that is (3) above. However, it seems vital to see such critique, and social science generally, as conditioned by human beings' dependency on the natural order, that is materialism or naturalism in sense (1) above.

Reading

Benton, Ted 1981 (*1985*): Realism and social science. In *A Radical Philosophy Reader*, ed. R. Edgley and P. Osborne.

Bhaskar, Roy 1989: *The Possibility of Naturalism*, 2nd edn.

Giddens, Anthony 1976: *New Rules of Sociological Method*.

Harré, Rom and Secord, Paul 1972: *The Explanation of Social Behaviour*.

Keat, Russell 1971: Positivism, naturalism and antinaturalism in the social sciences. *Journal for the Theory of Social Behaviour* 1.3.

Outhwaite, William 1983: *Concept Formation in Social Science*.

ROY BHASKAR

needs   A term for essential human requirements, necessities for subsistence, needs have only really become the subject of theory in the twentieth century. Previously philosophers had argued either that need was an essentially contested concept, or that there was no essential distinction between needs and wants. Thinkers as early as Plato and Aristotle had postulated human needs as the basis for the city (*polis*), a social aggregate whose economic foundation was market exchange. But so undefined was the Greek concept of need that it was frequently translated as 'demand'. Stoic and Epicurean writers of the Hellenistic period used needs as a criterion to distinguish between virtuous and corrupt lives, promoting the ideal of 'the man of few needs'. Thinkers like Epictetus and Seneca argued that needs have an elasticity that permits them to proliferate if the moral will does not intervene to check them. This was a line of thinking taken up by Enlightenment thinkers such as Jean Jacques Rousseau, who in both his First and Second Discourses follows Seneca in arguing that analysis of the decline of civilization turns on the distinction between 'natural' and 'artificial' needs. French environmental psychologists and early socialists of the late eighteenth and early nineteenth centuries, such as Helvétius, d'Holbach and La Mettrie, drew an obvious conclusion from this distinction: that the good society depends on appropriate need formation in the individual (compare AFFLUENT SOCIETY).

The break between early moralistic and unsystematic treatments of needs and the use of the concept in a quasi-technical way comes with Hegel in the *Philosophy of Right*. Influenced no doubt by the Scottish political economists, Hegel defined civil society as 'a system of needs', referring to the economic function of society as the provider of necessaries for subsistence through the mechanism of market exchange. While this option harks back to Aristotle, who had in the *Politics* already made the distinction between use value and exchange value on which it turns, Hegel produced a wider conception of society as a tissue of institutions and structures created in the process of need satisfaction. Marx, who owed so much to Hegel, expanded this notion in the concept of a mode of production, society's base, on which institutional superstructures were erected as needs dictate. Marx, too, neglects to define needs or to address them specifically, however. In the *1844 Manuscripts*, for instance, he makes a Rousseauian distinction between human and inhuman needs, whereas in *Capital* he refers to needs as indistinguishable from demands, adding that it matters not whether they are real needs or spring from fancy in terms of their system effect (Springborg, 1981, ch. 6).

In the twentieth century a focus on human needs has been prompted by two considerations: problems in Marxist theory, and issues in public policy. Classical Marxists were faced with explaining the unexpected longevity of capitalism, predicted to collapse due to overproduction and underconsumption. A number of Marxist revisionists, marrying Freudian notions of instinctual desires to observations about the role of the media by theorists of mass society, came up with an explanation in terms of 'false needs'. Beginning with Erich Fromm, who first propounded the idea in the 1930s, and including Wilhelm Reich, Herbert Marcuse and members of the Frankfurt school, these thinkers argued that capitalism has a unique capacity to introject into the psyche of its subjects the needs it requires them to have for the system to survive.

A second stimulus to the theoretical discussion of needs has been the development of policy studies. Education theorists, town planners, social workers and civil servants address themselves to 'need-based' policies. Thresholds for needs and criteria to discriminate between conflicting needs command attention in their theories. The distinction between true and false needs, as formulated by neo-Marxists, is now generally seen to be essentially moralistic and unscientific, lending support as it does to the 'dictatorship over needs' (Fehér et al., 1983) established by the command economies of socialist countries. With the imaginative work of Michael Ignatieff (1984), theorists are once more focusing on the problem of needs for the have-nots: those for whom the institutions of private property leave no public space, squeezed by the debt burden created by the collusion of capitalist economies of the First World and dictatorships in the Third World. The WELFARE STATE whose legitimacy rests on its claim to guarantee subsistence and security cannot fail to address the problems raised by the poor and the homeless, whose needs are desperate.

Reading
Heller, Agnes 1976: *The Theory of Need in Marx.*
Ignatieff, M. 1984: *Needs of Strangers.*
Leiss, William 1976: *The Limits to Satisfaction: An Essay on the Problem of Needs and Commodities.*
Soper, Kate 1981: *On Human Needs: Open and Closed Theories in a Marxist Perspective.*
Springborg, Patricia 1981: *The Problem of Human Needs and the Critique of Civilization.*

PATRICIA SPRINGBORG

neoclassical economics   The development of neoclassical economics dates from the break with classical economics which took place in the last third of the nineteenth century. All schools of

ECONOMICS seek to explain in their different ways the disjunction between use value and exchange value. The classical school had the labour theory of value as its central mode of explaining the worth of different commodities – the rates at which they exchange. There were many anomalies with this theory, especially concerning the difficulty of valuing rare things – 'masterpieces' – and commodities in the production of which durable capital played a major role. The labour theory relied on the role of labour time expended in the production of a commodity to explain its rate of exchange against another good. The use value – the usefulness or utility of the good – played no active role in this explanation.

Almost simultaneously, though in different ways, three authors argued for replacing the classical theory with a theory based on subjective considerations as well as objective or resource cost considerations. Use value or utility become one side of the equation explaining exchange value. Leon Walras (1834–1910), William Stanley Jevons (1835–1882) and Carl Menger (1840–1921) within three years of each other proposed an anti-classical approach. Their work came to be known as the 'marginal revolution', because they used the notion of marginal utility as the explanation for exchange values (see MARGINALIST ECONOMICS). The marginal revolution is often thought of as synonymous with neoclassical economics, but this is a misconception. The marginalist pioneers, especially Jevons and Menger, were explicitly anti-classical.

It was Alfred Marshall (1842–1924) who consciously sought to emphasize continuity rather than rupture with earlier English economists, and who created *neoclassical* economics as the legitimate successor of classical economics. He incorporated marginalism into the main body of economics but also integrated it with classical theories of rent and of international trade.

Neoclassical economics thus emerges as a conscious result of Marshall's efforts to propagate a rounded synthetic blend of classical economics (though without the labour theory of value) and marginalism. But modern economics, especially in the 1960s and since, has one major difference from Marshallian economics. Marshall thought of markets in separate, partial equilibrium fashion; Walras had earlier put forward a simultaneous general equilibrium way of theorizing about economics. Modern economics has gone much more along the Walrasian lines.

Basic propositions

(1) Methodological individualism. The individual consumer is the starting point and end point of neoclassical economics. He (let us face it, it is he) maximizes his utility, and his attainment of an optimum provides the criterion for evaluating economic alternatives. The individual producer or the firm, if specified separately, only derives its rationale as being ultimately consumer or owned by consumers.

(2) Economic rationality. The consumer seeks to optimize. Optimization involves maximizing an objective function (utility) subject to constraints. Income, or resources in general, acts as constraint. The consumer faces a multiplicity of ends but scarce means, which leads him to optimize.

(3) Choice and substitution. Faced with optimization as a task, the individual is helped by the fact that he has a choice. Apart from the resource constraint, there are no other constraints that he should ideally face. Thus the range of goods and available opportunities in general is such that he can choose one rather than another good. Goods are substitutes of each other: either in satisfying a single want, or because wants are competing and if not one, another can be satisfied. In general there is no hierarchy of wants or needs. On the production side as well, the technology is such that alternative ways of producing a good or, if not, substitute inputs or substitute final goods, are always available. If for some reason such substitutes are not available and the scarce good is unique then a sufficient rise in its price will encourage a search for substitutes and such searches will be successful.

(4) Equilibrium. Optimization by a consumer is successful and defines an equilibrium for him; equilibrium is a situation such that in the absence of new information the individual has no reason to change his behaviour. The same applies to producers.

(5) Competition. In arriving at his decision, the individual consumer takes the prices of the goods as given; the consumer is too small a part of the total economy to exert any power by virtue of his actions, for instance to influence the price. Producers are in a similar situation only in perfectly competitive industrial structures. These are desirable but not universal. In non-competitive situations, individual producers (and very rarely consumers) exert market power and affect the price at which they sell or buy. The competitive case is the norm.

(6) Market clearing. In the absence of outside arbitrary constraints, a world of individual consumers and producers will so act that the market for the commodity in question (in partial equilibrium) and all commodities (in general equilibrium) will clear, that is demands will equal supplies. There will therefore be no excess demand or excess supply of an involuntary nature.

(7) Welfare maximum. In competitive general equilibrium situations consumer welfare will be at a maximum. This can be either on utilitarian grounds which allow the adding up of the utilities of the several consumers, or on the Pareto criterion, which states that a situation is optimal in the sense that no one can be made better off without at least one person being made worse off. In either calculus, a competitive equilibrium is a situation of maximum welfare.

Around these basic propositions, neoclassical economics has extended and enriched its ability to model an increasing number of human activities within its framework. Thus, crime, marriage, childbearing and the choice of family size have all been studied, as well as the more narrowly defined economic activities such as occupational choice, investment, consumption, production and so on. Given the methodological individualist starting point, neoclassical economics has an uneasy time of theorizing about aggregate, macroeconomic relationships. Aggregation over individuals or firms or commodities leads to internal problems of coherence. A search for microfoundations of macroeconomics is thus endemic and an unsolvable part of neoclassical economics.

Its detractors criticize neoclassical economics for being static, too equilibrium oriented, making unrealistic assumptions, ignoring institutional, cultural, social data, for neglecting power or (class) conflict. Its continued dominance in economics is, however, sustained not only by its institutional hegemony in universities but also by the commitment of its practitioners to a rigorous adherence to the small number of basic propositions, and to active and ferocious internal critical mechanisms which try to assure that at least by its own internal standards only high quality and rigorous work passes muster.

Reading
Blaug, M. 1962 (*1985*): *Economic Theory in Retrospect*, 4th edn.
Boland, L.A. 1985: *The Foundations of Economic Method.*
Hahn, F.H. 1984: *Equilibrium and Macroeconomics.*

Hey, J. and Winch, D. eds 1990: *A Century of Economics*.
Stigler, G. 1965: *Essays in the History of Economics*.

MEGHNAD DESAI

neo-colonialism *See* COLONIALISM

neo-Darwinism The synthetic theory of evolution (Huxley, 1974), combining Charles Darwin's ideas about NATURAL SELECTION with Gregor Mendel's about genetics, is the basis of neo-Darwinism, which provides, largely through the statistical techniques of population genetics, an account of the adaptation of organisms to environments.

Neo-Darwinism is an advance on Darwin's own theory of evolution which depended on concepts of variation and inheritance which were poorly understood in his time. Mendel's results provided a basis for distinguishing between an organism's constitution (genotype) and its physiological and behavioural traits (phenotype), and for our understanding of genetic recombination during reproduction, now recognized as the primary source of heritable variation, on which selective processes depend.

Neo-Darwinism should be distinguished from neo-Lamarckian theories of EVOLUTION, briefly (and tragically) dominant in Russia (Medvedev, 1969), according to which maladaptation of organism to environment elicits a response by the organism which results in its acquisition of a trait which better fits it to its environment and which is inherited by its offspring. According to this account, environment 'instructs' organism. This idea is repudiated in neo-Darwinism, according to which processes of recombination and mutation 'randomly' throw up variants of all kinds, better *and worse* adapted, from which the environment 'selects' those which better fit organism to environment (Maynard Smith, 1958, ch. 2).

Three common misunderstandings of evolution are clarified by neo-Darwinism.

First, natural selection does not *optimize* organism–environment fit, but merely tends to improve it. Herbert Spencer's 'survival of the fitt*est*' is thus misleading; 'survival of the fitt*er*' would be more accurate. Evolution fails to optimize, in part, because it can only select from actually occurring variants, which are unlikely to include the optimally adaptive one (Simon, 1983, ch. 2).

Second, neo-Darwinism does not imply that *all* traits have been selected for their adaptive superiority. Distinct traits may be genetically 'linked',

enabling neutral or maladaptive traits to 'hitch-hike' with traits of positive adaptive value (Gould, 1983, ch. 3).

Third, evolution is not necessarily a 'struggle for survival' involving direct competition between organisms; species can establish or occupy hitherto unoccupied environmental niches and thus avoid conflict with other species (Hutchinson, 1965).

Important questions about neo-Darwinism include its scientific status (Ruse, 1973, sect. 3.2) and its adequacy, particularly in relation to SOCIOBIOLOGY, to account for genetically grounded dispositions to altruistic behaviour (Maynard Smith, 1975, ch. 12).

Reading
Dawkins, R. 1986 (*1988*): *The Blind Watchmaker*.
Simpson, G.G. 1949: *The Meaning of Evolution*.

FRED D'AGOSTINO

neo-Kantianism The term may be applied to any philosophy or social theory that interprets itself as developing and revising analytical methods from Kant, or responding to the problems, for example of epistemology and ethics, posed by Immanuel Kant (1724–1804). The term is used with greatest precision to refer to a movement within German philosophy, prior to World War I. This movement consisted of two major schools, based at Marburg and at Heidelberg, the latter being significant in its influence on Max Weber. Other sociologists, such as Georg Simmel and Emile Durkheim, while not presenting themselves explicitly as neo-Kantians, may be seen to develop sociology by attempting to find preconditions in society for Kant's *a priori* rules.

The return to Kant in the 1860s was a response to the apparent failure of both idealist and materialist post-Kantian philosophies. It was an attempt to rebuild philosophy, not through slavish imitation of Kant, but by seeking to reinterpret him in the light of the foregoing generations of Kantian critics. Neo-Kantian schools are characterized as much by what they reject in Kant as by what they adopt.

Hermann Cohen (1842–1918) and Paul Natorp (1854–1924) were the major figures in the Marburg school. Their work is centrally concerned with epistemology, and specifically with the construction of the object domain of the individual natural sciences. However, this entails a movement away from Kant's transcendental analysis, towards the formation of a general logic. Transcendental inquiry involves explicating the necessary preconditions of the possibility of experience. For Kant, *a priori* rules determined the synthesis of sensations into objects of experience. Hence, only when a subjective sensation is legitimately subsumed under *a priori* particulars and categories (according to what Kant terms schemata) does it become objective, and only thus does the subject have knowledge of objective reality. The transcendental analysis therefore presupposes that the *a priori* rules are necessarily applied in experience. However, the formal or general logics that Cohen and Natorp sought to develop are explicated independently of experience. They are rather methodologies for the conceptualization of the objects of particular sciences, and so not applicable to experience in general. Further, these logics are not presented as necessary, *a priori* rules, but rather as desirable. This leads to the 'never-ending task' of perfecting the constitution of the scientific object domain, until conceptual thought comes to correspond to the thing-in-itself.

The leading representatives of the Heidelberg (or Baden) school were Wilhelm Windelband (1848–1915) and Heinrich Rickert (1863–1936). By giving primacy to Kant's *Critique of Practical Reason* they offered an analysis of the constitution of knowledge grounded in values. Windelband argued that all judgements, in logic, ethics and aesthetics, are guided by the subject's presupposition of the universal values of truth, goodness and beauty. The values themselves cannot be proven, in so far as they are, as Kant argued, beyond the jurisdiction of theoretical reason. The empirical subject is not then seen to create values, because values are posited by a transcendental consciousness behind any empirical consciousness. A Kantian division of the practical and theoretical reason is maintained, but transformed in so far as values are made the transcendental precondition of theoretical reason.

The Heidelberg school concentrated on the methodology of the cultural sciences. Rickert, in an attempt to overcome the fact–value dualism inherent in Windelband's philosophy, postulates a 'third realm', of culture, containing both fact and value. Through practical judgement subjects create cultural goods. That is to say that sensible objects, and hence objects accessible to theoretical reason, are placed in relation to values, and are thereby given a value dimension. Again, the subject does not create values, for culture, as a system of prevailing values,

is the transcendental precondition of the possibility of apprehending cultural goods. Rickert seeks to clarify his position by distinguishing between the value judgements of a historical actor and the activity of the historian. The actor is guided by what he/she believes 'ought to be'. The historian, however, responds to values only in so far as they are actually accepted by the actors. This serves in fact to undermine the transcendental nature of Rickert's argument. The comparison with the constitution of nature fails, because the historical subject, as well as the theorist, actively creates values. The constitution of culture thereby occurs empirically, not transcendentally.

Weber develops Rickert's arguments, but within the context of an empirical sociology. Weber does not merely accept that the social actor actively creates values, but argues further that in the rationalized and disenchanted modern world, actors create a proliferation of competing values. In so far as rationalization may be seen as the predominance of theoretical reason, there no longer exist commonly accepted means of assessing competing values. Weber's methodology of the IDEAL TYPE may then be seen as a development of Rickert's analysis of the historian's activity. An ideal type is a heuristic, and so without transcendental import. Yet it 'constitutes' the meaning of a cultural phenomenon for the theorist. Value is given to the cultural phenomenon only through recognition of the values that are actually accepted by the actors.

Neo-Kantian elements may also be seen in the work of Simmel. He responds to the problem of the transcendental constitution of society with a theory of forms of sociation. Simmel recognizes that the unity of society is constituted by the social actors, and not merely by the theorist. His concept of forms therefore refers both to the multitude of general types that actors use to constitute a structured totality out of the diversity of social life, and to the sociologist's understanding of them, as processes that give rise to the actors' 'consciousness of sociation'. However, the relationship between transcendental and empirical processes again becomes ambiguous.

Finally, Durkheim's sociology, and especially the sociology of religion, is an example of an attempt to ground Kant's *a priori* categories of understanding in some social substrate. Durkheim, following Kant, accepts the actuality of categories and values, but looks for the conditions of their possibility in society, as a reality *sui generis*. Society thereby becomes a moral force, having a transcendental objectivity. With this approach Durkheim can trace variations in the categories of understanding, by reference to concrete variations between societies.

Reading

Arato, A. 1974: The neo-idealist defence of subjectivity. *Telos* 21, 108–61.

Coplestone, F. 1963: *A History of Philosophy*, 9 vols. Vol. 1: *Fichte to Nietzsche*, pp. 361–73.

Durkheim, E. 1912 (*1968*): *The Elementary Forms of the Religious Life*, trans. Joseph Ward Swain.

Habermas, J. 1968 (*1971*): *Knowledge and Human Interests*, trans. Jeremy J. Shapiro.

Rickert, H. *1962*: *Science and History; A Critique of Positivist Epistemology*, trans. George Reisman.

Rose, G. 1981: *Hegel Contra Sociology*.

Simmel, G. *1959*: *Georg Simmel 1858–1918; A Collection of Essays with Translations and a Bibliography*, ed. K. H. Wolff.

Weber, M. 1947: *Methodology of the Social Sciences*, ed. and trans. E. A. Shils and H. A. Finch.

ANDREW EDGAR

new classical economics   Following the marginalist revolution in the 1870s, the structure of economic orthodoxy constituted a set of individuals with given preferences, given initial endowments, and access to a given technology, each of whom optimized their objectives (utility or profit) in competitive markets on the basis of parametric prices. Prices themselves were then determined by the interaction of all individuals together, by, that is, supply and demand. If markets are competitive then, if supply and demand are not in balance, fluctuations in prices will lead optimizing individuals to alter their actions and hence supplies and demands. Only when supply and demand are in balance will prices cease to fluctuate; in such a situation prices are 'equilibrium' prices, and are said to 'clear the market'. The economic theory based on optimizing individuals and competitive market-clearing prices was called 'classical economics' by J. M. Keynes, to denote the theory from which he was trying to escape in the 1930s. It is also known as pre-Keynesian theory, and Walrasian theory.

One implication of this body of theory is that output, employment and real wages are determined in the labour market. A profit-maximizing entrepreneur will hire labour up to the point at which the revenue obtained from selling the output produced by the last person hired just equals the wage paid to that person (marginal product equals the real wage); a utility maximizing individual will supply labour until that individual's psychological rate of exchange between leisure and labour hours exactly matches what is gained in terms of goods by an extra hour's work (marginal rate of substitution of leisure for consumption equals the real wage). In a competitive labour market, fluctuations in the real wage will clear the market and the equilibrium labour demanded and supplied then suffices to determine aggregate output produced. Finally, given prevailing monetary institutions and arrangements, with output determined in the labour market, the supply of money serves to determine the price level, and the rate of interest equates the supply and demand for loanable funds. This is the classical dichotomy: real variables are determined in the labour market, and monetary variables by the quantity theory of money. And perhaps its most striking implication is that all unemployment is necessarily voluntary.

Keynes rejected this analysis in the 1930s and substituted for it a macroeconomics with interdependent markets in which quantities adjusted faster than prices, and with government intervention to prevent an equilibrium with involuntary unemployment (see also KEYNESIANISM). While the theoretical details remain the subject of continued controversy, the postwar era was one of apparent Keynesian success in macroeconomic management. However, the end of the postwar boom was coterminous with the end of this success, and Keynesian innovations began to be questioned. Particularly important was the divorce between conventional Keynesian macroeconomics and any foundation or grounding in the behaviour of individuals at the microeconomic level. This latter was increasingly emphasized in the late 1960s and through the 1970s.

Two routes were taken to the microeconomic foundations of macroeconomics. Both retained the starting point of optimizing individuals, but one saw these individuals as operating in imperfectly competitive markets in which market-clearing prices were not necessarily established, whereas the other made a virtue out of the standard Walrasian assumptions of perfect competition and no trading out of equilibrium, and hence instantaneous adjustment to full equilibrium. This latter approach is called 'new classical macroeconomics', Walrasian

macroeconomics, or sometimes, slightly misleadingly, 'rational expectations macroeconomics' (see
also RATIONAL EXPECTATIONS HYPOTHESIS), and it is
particularly associated with the work of Robert E.
Lucas and Thomas J. Sargent in the USA.

The approach has many obvious similarities with
pre-Keynesian theory, but it is much more rigorous
and often mathematically demanding in its detailed
analysis. Three propositions stand out. First is the
Lucas critique of econometric modelling (see ECO-
NOMETRICS). If individuals optimize, then they
must be allowed to take account of changes in
government policy; and so in the new equilibrium
consequent upon a policy change, behaviour will
not be what it was prior to policy change. Consequently one cannot expect the parameters of
macroeconometric models to remain invariant
when policy changes, and so existing models cannot
be used to evaluate the effects of such changes. The
influence of this critique extends to all schools of
contemporary micro-based macroeconomics.

Second is the policy invariance result. Because
individuals optimize and full equilibrium is presumed, predictable alterations in the money supply
can have no effect on real output or employment:
the behaviour of these latter is not affected by any
predictable countercyclical policy by the monetary
authorities. Only unanticipated movements in the
money stock can affect output; these create random
fluctuations in output around the full employment
level. The classical dichotomy is thus reproduced.

Third is how UNEMPLOYMENT is understood.
Optimizing individuals make judgements as to
whether perceived price changes are temporary or
permanent. If the former, arbitraging opportunities
exist and will be exploited. Hence individuals
intertemporally speculate and take more leisure
when the price of leisure time is lower. So-called
involuntary unemployment is just a utility-maxi-
mizing intertemporal substitution of leisure for
labour.

New classical theory was very influential in the
1970s and 1980s, its laissez-faire implications and
supply-side emphases harmonizing with the political ideologies prevailing in the advanced capitalist
countries. But the new classical results are crucially
dependent on the Walrasian market-clearing
assumption and the starting point of optimizing
individuals. Other mainstream economists reject
the former, and Marxist and other radical economists the latter as well.

Reading

Begg, D.K.H. 1982: *The Rational Expectations Revolution
in Macroeconomics.*
Blanchard, O.J. and Fischer, F. 1989: *Lectures on Macro-
economics.*
Hahn, F.H. 1984: *Equilibrium and Macroeconomics*, chs
15, 16.
Lucas, R.E. 1981: *Studies in Business Cycle Theory.*
Sargent, T.J. 1987: *Macroeconomic Theory*, 2nd edn.
Sheffrin, S.M. 1983: *Rational Expectations.*

SIMON MOHUN

New Deal   A group of economic policy measures
taken in the United States between 1933 and 1940,
under the leadership of President Franklin Roosevelt, intended to produce recovery from the Great
Depression and to correct defects in the system
believed to have been revealed by the depression.
There was no single theory underlying the steps
taken. All kinds of things were tried. Many
measures were discarded because the conditions to
which they were addressed passed, because they
failed or because they were found to be unconstitu-
tional. Among the more durable policy changes
were:

1   Substantial liberation of monetary policy from
    the constraints of the gold standard and greater
    acceptance of the responsibility of monetary
    policy for stabilization of the economy.
2   Increased reliance on government budget
    policy for achieving and maintaining high
    employment. This came at first pragmatically
    in the form of public works and other work
    relief programmes and was later rationalized in
    terms of theory by Keynesian economics (see
    KEYNESIANISM).
3   The beginning of the federal WELFARE STATE in
    America. The main ingredients of this were:
    (a) the social security system, providing retire-
    ment benefits for workers;
    (b) the unemployment insurance system;
    (c) the provision of financial aid to poor families
    with dependent children.
4   Government intervention to control prices and
    production in agriculture.
5   Government promotion of trade union organ-
    ization.
6   New or enlarged government control of prices,
    entry or other aspects of transportation, power,
    communications and financial industries.
7   Movement towards a more liberal international
    trade policy.

The fiscal and monetary measures helped to bring about the recovery of the American economy, although the fiscal measures were weak and vacillating. Some of the other measures probably retarded the recovery, by raising costs and increasing uncertainty in the business community. The recovery was still incomplete and unemployment was still high at the time World War II became a dominant factor in the economy.

All of the New Deal measures were hotly contested at the time, mainly on the ground that they were improper interferences with economic freedom. On the other hand there were complaints that the New Deal was propping up a basically flawed system that needed more radical restructuring. But the measures were overwhelmingly popular, as evidenced by Roosevelt's electoral successes.

Fifty years later American policy has gone far beyond the New Deal in almost every respect – more regulation, more transfer payments, for social security, unemployment insurance welfare and medical care, and more active fiscal and monetary policy. Even those who are most concerned by the increased power of government in the economy would regard a return to the New Deal as a return to small and limited government. From the perspective of the 1990s the complaint about the New Deal, if there is complaint, is not about the steps taken in the 1930s but about the path on which the federal government then entered.

Reading
Lehergott, S. 1984: *The Americans: An Economic Record*, pp. 453–65.
Stein, H. 1969: *The Fiscal Revolution in America*.
—— 1988: *Presidential Economics: The Making of Economic Policy from Roosevelt to Reagan and Beyond*, pp. 27–64.

HERBERT STEIN

New Left   A descriptive term loosely applied to a variety of political doctrines and social movements which emerged in the late 1950s, after the 1956 uprising in Hungary, and then developed strongly during the 1960s, particularly in opposition to the American intervention in Vietnam and the military occupation of Czechoslovakia by Warsaw Pact countries. The New Left brought together in an uneasy alliance diverse social movements – radical students, sections of the peace movement, and the early feminist and ecology movements – along with intellectuals of extremely varied origins and orientations, including dissident communists, anarchists, left-wing socialists and cultural critics.

A great wealth of ideas flourished in these movements, among them two which had more or less universal appeal: 'participatory democracy', and radical criticism of what was called 'the system'. These were closely related, since participatory democracy meant the full and continuous involvement of all individuals in decision-making which directly affected their lives, while the system being contested was elitist and excluded those who were subordinated to it from any effective part in controlling it or determining its policies. The universality of these ideas was strikingly illustrated by their diffusion in the countries of 'real socialism' as well as in capitalist countries, reflecting the fact that in both types of society elitist forms of domination prevailed, whether it was that of the large corporations and the 'military-industrial complex' or that of party officials and bureaucrats, and excluded any genuine participation by ordinary citizens. Only in Yugoslavia (and for a short period in China, where the agricultural communes and the 'cultural revolution' were seen by some as embodying policies of popular involvement in decision-making) were the elements of participatory democracy to be found in the system of self-management, and the Yugoslav experience, as it was interpreted and discussed especially by the *Praxis* group of philosophers and sociologists (Marković and Cohen, 1975), became an important influence on some sections of the New Left.

At the same time there was a general renaissance of Marxist thought in philosophy and the social sciences, influenced by the earlier writings of György Lukács and Antonio Gramsci, now rediscovered and widely read, by the new 'structuralist' Marxism of Louis Althusser, and by the ideas of the FRANKFURT SCHOOL of critical theory. The last of these probably had the greatest influence, through the writings of Herbert Marcuse in the USA, of Theodor Adorno, Max Horkheimer, and (in the second generation) Jürgen Habermas in Germany. Their work raised many of the most acute problems facing the radical movements in the 1960s: the political role of the working class in relation to new social movements which were not class-based; the power of mass culture and ideology in sustaining structures of domination, and their connection with the scientific and technological orientation of modern societies; and the need for a critical analysis of the basis of authoritarian-bureaucratic socialism. But critical theory itself became more diverse, and, among the older generation of thinkers increasingly non-political and pessimistic, engaged in a despairing cultural criticism, with ever fainter hopes of the emergence of a 'counterculture'. In any case, Marxism in its revived and variously reconstructed forms was only one of the intellectual influences (mainly among students) on the New Left, along with anarchism, utopian socialism and the new ideas of ecology and feminism.

The New Left reached the peak of its development in the USA in the late 1960s, in the civil rights movement and the opposition to the Vietnam war, in Europe in 1968 in widespread student protests, especially the 'May movement' in France, and in the 'Prague spring' in Czechoslovakia. Since then its influence has gradually diminished, the onset of its decline signalled by the failure of the student movements in France, West Germany and elsewhere to bring about any substantial social changes, and by the suppression of the Czechoslovak reform movement in August 1968, though its ideas contributed to the eventual success of the opposition movements in Eastern Europe in 1989. Its later disintegration in the Western capitalist countries, during the 1980s, had as its counterpart a strong revival of conservative doctrines in the NEW RIGHT. Nevertheless, although the New Left as a broad movement has ceased to exist, some of its component elements have continued to develop in other forms, and in particular the peace movement, feminism and the ecology movement; and the central idea of 'participatory democracy' is far from having exhausted its influence, especially in the green parties which have grown rapidly in Western Europe during the past decade and emerged more recently in Eastern Europe.

Reading

Caute, David 1988: *Sixty-Eight: The Year of the Barricades.*
Habermas, Jürgen 1968–9 (*1970*): *Toward a Rational Society.*
Jacobs, Paul and Landau, Saul eds 1966: *The New Radicals: A Report with Documents.*
Marcuse, Herbert 1964: *One-Dimensional Man.*
Marković, Mihailo and Cohen, Robert S. 1975: *Yugoslavia: The Rise and Fall of Socialist Humanism.*
Touraine, Alain 1968 (*1971*): *The May Movement.*

TOM BOTTOMORE

New Right This originally left-wing expression was generally adopted in the 1980s to denote a widespread reaction among Western intellectuals against SOCIALISM, an ideology to which many of them previously subscribed, and which, in dilute form, has underlain the postwar democratic consensus. The title is misleading, however, not least in its implied symmetry with the NEW LEFT. First, the 'New Right' is more diverse even than socialism as a whole. Secondly, though ideologically inclined (a feature to which it owes its intellectual success), it is not a self-conscious 'movement', and is united by few articles of belief beyond a shared antipathy to socialism. Thirdly, few New Rightists would accept the title or regard it as useful (contrast 'New Left', which is self-ascriptive). Finally, most New Right thought is neither new nor particularly 'right wing'.

Socialism's historic rivals are CONSERVATISM and LIBERALISM, and New Right thought is usually one or the other, or a mixture. There are four main schools.

Neoliberalism (or 'liberal-conservatism')
Of all New Right doctrines, neoliberalism has been by far the most influential on governments (even some socialist and communist governments). Leading figures include F. A. Hayek, Karl Popper and Milton Friedman (who also has libertarian leanings: see below). All prize the 'spontaneous order' supposedly exemplified in free markets, common law and (the more conservative would add) tradition, and deplore any politics (notably socialism) which pretends to definitive knowledge of human needs. Such absolute knowledge is available to no central observer, and hence to no government. Nevertheless it exists, but only as diffused throughout the myriad unpredictable transactions between individuals living in a free or OPEN SOCIETY. As many decisions as possible, therefore, should be transferred to the market, which, in maximizing choice, is the only genuine democracy. When insufficiently restrained by law or constitutional provisions, formal democracy becomes a *political market*, in which votes are traded against welfare benefits, subsidies, trade union privileges and so on, and the cost, in the shape of excessive taxation or inflation or both, falls jointly on the most productive and the weakest, least politically organized members of society (See also NEOCLASSICAL ECONOMICS.)

Neoconservatism

This title denotes two somewhat divergent approaches:

1 the conservatism represented in the UK by the *Salisbury Review* (edited by Roger Scruton), which nevertheless gives space to nearly all shades of New Right opinion, and in the USA by the *National Review* (edited by William F. Buckley). Burkean and anti-individualist, it stresses, not rights or abstract, unqualified liberty, but duty, authority, morality, religion, tradition, culture, society and national identity. Such things resist translation into 'market' desirabilities, and are thus proper objects of political concern, being as much under threat from unfettered capitalism and the liberal doctrines which promote it as from socialism. Especially in the USA, some thinkers of this stamp (such as Russell Kirk) idealize the small, agrarian COMMUNITY under patrimonial or aristocratic rule.

2 the ethos of the New York Jewish journal *Commentary*, which is anti-communist, fiercely patriotic, 'hawkish' in foreign affairs (especially where Israel is concerned), and generally liberal or social-democratic on domestic issues. Often descended from desperately poor immigrants, members of this circle understandably have an urban perspective, little nostalgia for tradition and a high regard for capitalism, on account of the wealth and social mobility it creates.

In the intervals of their economic experiments (which have been broadly neoliberal), recent US and UK administrations have so far borrowed from neoconservatism much of its rhetoric, but little of its policy.

Libertarianism (or 'anarcho-capitalism')

This ingenious doctrine is largely confined to the USA. Except in economics its influence on government has been minimal. This is not surprising, since libertarians regard most state action bar the enforcement of property rights as either unnecessary or illegitimate.

The following prescriptions are typical: abolition of all statutory restraints concerning planning, pollution, industrial safety, drugs and sex (relevant action to come from interested parties); privatization of all public property and infrastructure (such as roads); ditto welfare, law and order and defence (to be supplied through private insurance and protection agencies). Libertarianism is INDIVIDUALISM in its extremest form, and evenhandedly stresses both freedom and personal answerability for one's actions. Its patron saints are John Locke and Ludwig von Mises, and its fundamental tenet is the slogan of the US novelist-philosopher Ayn Rand, 'Hands off!' (The maxim also applies in libertarian foreign policy, which is isolationist.) Other representative figures are Murray Rothbard and Robert Nozick.

French and Eastern European anti-communism

There are several links between these two outlooks: (1) Continental existentialism; (2) experience of Marxism (either as former believers, or as subjects thereof); (3) the influence of Alexander Solzhenitsyn (especially *The Gulag Archipelago*). The French *nouveaux philosophes* (such as B.-H. Lévy and A. Glucksmann) are mostly ex-1968 student radicals, who, rejecting Marx, Sartre and the French revolutionary tradition, have somewhat naively embraced a mixture of the neoliberalism and neoconservatism described above. The Eastern European New Right may be divided into the older, ex-communist, emigrés (such as the Polish philosopher Leszek Kolakowski and the writer Czeslaw Milosz), who are now mostly neoliberals or social democrats, and the younger ex-dissidents. The latter are largely neoconservatives of popular rather than aristocratic sympathies who, after the collapse of the Soviet empire, nearly all succeeded to positions of considerable power in their various countries. (The most notable, perhaps, is the dramatist Václav Havel, who became president of Czecho-Slovakia). Preoccupied with cultural and religious questions, they strongly distrust all instrumental, goal-directed politics, though it is doubtful whether their newly democratic circumstances will permit them any longer to do so. For them goal-directed politics includes not only communism, but also Western consumer society, and even the Slavophile mysticism which Solzhenitsyn (an otherwise admired figure) advances against both.

These various doctrines are the positive creed only of a minority, and are still quite frequently reviled (especially by *littérateurs* unfamiliar with the detailed arguments used to support them). Nevertheless, the New Right has for the moment completely wrested the initiative from socialism, and has finally deflated the century-old, and previously impregnable, assumptions of intellectual superiority which have constituted no small part of socialism's appeal. But for all that, the really crucial factor in socialism's eclipse has been its historical record. That test the New Right has yet to pass, or even fully to face, despite the fact that many of its policy prescriptions have already had dramatic (and controversial) short-term consequences.

Reading

Friedman, Milton and Friedman, R. 1962: *Capitalism and Freedom*.
Havel, Václav et al. 1987: *Václav Havel or Living in Truth*, ed. J. Vladislaw.
Hayek, F. A. 1944 (*1962*): *The Road to Serfdom*.
—— 1960: *The Constitution of Liberty*.
Kirk, Russell ed. 1982: *The Portable Conservative Reader*.
Nozick, Robert, 1974: *Anarchy, State and Utopia*.
Oakeshott, Michael 1962 (*1974*): *Rationalism in Politics and Other Essays*.
Popper, Karl R. 1945 (*1966*): *The Open Society and its Enemies*.
Scruton, Roger 1980 (*1984*): *The Meaning of Conservatism*.
—— ed. 1988: *Conservative Thoughts: Essays from the Salisbury Review*.

ROBERT GRANT

nomenklatura This system of names played a very important role in the control methods of the monolithic, Stalinist type of socialism (see also TOTALITARIANISM); its revision and radical change became the main problems in the efforts to achieve democratic reforms.

In line with the decisions of leading organs, nomenklatura included a list of jobs or posts of different elected organs where personal changes (appointments, disciplinary procedures and so on) were decided by the party at different levels (from local to the highest central institutions). The most important jobs covered by nomenklatura were those in the chain through which the leaders to be elected by party organs at lower levels were determined by the next higher level. This gave party democracy a purely formal character, which, during political crises which preceded the more recent sweeping away of party regimes, provoked some of the party membership to revolt (Hungary in 1956 and 1988; Poland in 1956 and 1980; Czechoslovakia in 1968).

Appointment to various state and economic functions was also decided by party organs. It happened frequently that rational requirements, abilities and skills were pushed into the background in favour of political reliability. In state and economic life this contraselection by the apparatus reduced the effectiveness of the economy. Thus it was natural that one aim of the economic reforms was to liberate the economic leadership from the pressure of nomenklatura.

The appointed and elected leaders of mass organizations also belonged to nomenklatura, including those of the trade unions, youth organizations, the association of writers and the official peace movement. This meant that the leaders of these bodies did not depend on their own movements or organizations but on various party institutions. The renaissance of CIVIL SOCIETY which is taking place in the East European countries has released the leaders of these organizations from the old framework of nomenklatura and in this way the opportunity arises for leaders to be elected democratically and for the organizations to achieve their own independence.

Nomenklatura also played a highly significant role in culture and the mass media because of the information blockade typical of the Stalinist system (see also ELITE THEORY). This was more important than the different offices of censorship. All the leaders of institutions which formed public opinion depended for their existence on different party organs, which largely prevented the aspiration of intellectuals for *glasnost*.

Bold theoretical conclusions have been developed concerning nomenklatura as an important component of monolithic STALINISM. Especially important among them is the work entitled *Nomenklatura*, by Vozlensky, who regards those belonging to nomenklatura as the ruling class of these societies. This is actually the concretization of Milovan Djilas's theory about the 'new class' which developed in these societies.

These theories, however, ignore the main characteristics of the power-holders, so that the use of the term 'class' to denote these strata can be questioned. It is precisely their inclusion in nomenklatura which indicates that their existence depends on the relevant organ of the party, and if they lose its confidence they drop out of the power situation. One of these counter-arguments is that in contrast to ruling classes in other socioeconomic formations, position cannot be passed on to the next generation, although the offspring of those belonging to nomenklatura start in life with better chances. Yet very often in practice they tended to avoid jobs belonging to nomenklatura. Instead they chose occupations which provided greater independence and more income.

Reading
Deutscher, Isaac 1954: *The Prophet Armed: Trotsky, 1879–1921.*
Djilas, Milovan 1957: *The New Class: An Analysis of the Communist System.*
Lozovsky, S. 1925: *Lenin i professional 'noe dvizhenie.*
Vozlensky, Michail 1985: *Nomenklatura.*

ANDRÁS HEGEDÜS

norm   At its most general the idea of a norm is the idea of a pattern. There are two main ways in which this idea has been developed in social theory, where social norms have been the focus of concern. First, there is the idea of a norm as an *actual* pattern of behaviour, as what is 'normal' in the sense of being regularly or standardly done by members of a population. (The labels 'social habits' and 'usage' are used of some such patterns.) Second, there is the idea of a norm as a *prescribed* pattern: as what is considered in a given population to be the thing to do. (The labels 'convention', 'social rule' and LAW are used of certain patterns in this category.)

Social norms are often associated with expectations. Two different kinds of expectation need to be distinguished: *predictive* expectations about what will in fact be done by members of a population, and *normative* or *deontic* expectations. Normative expectations involve a belief that the 'expected' behaviour *ought* to occur, in some more than merely predictive sense. Actual patterns are likely to be associated with predictive expectations, prescribed patterns with normative expectations.

The term 'norm' itself is relatively recent in standard social theory usage. The more established terms 'custom', 'tradition', 'convention', 'law' and so on tend to be used for specific types of norms. They have all been variously defined by different authors in sociology, philosophy and elsewhere. We can in any case make many distinctions among norms. For example, there are those prescribed patterns which are seen as special to and typifying the group, as 'what we do' or 'our way' (customs?), and those which are seen as typifying the group by virtue of a long past history of conformity (traditions?).

W. G. Sumner distinguished and discussed a wide variety of types of norm in *Folkways: A Study of the Sociological Importance of Usages, Manners, Customs, Mores, and Morals* (1906). He stressed the variety of contents norms may have, and the difference in importance that may be attached to different norms: thus *laws* alone are given the 'specific sanction of the group as it is organized politically' (p. 56).

Norms may relate to any area of human life, from everyday greetings and dress to sexual conduct and political processes. In *The Rules of the Sociological Method* (1895) Durkheim noted a continuum between the 'fixed' norms of written law and uncodified and even ephemeral norms such as those of etiquette. In *Suicide* (1897) he emphasized the importance of norms as a framework for human life. Many have stressed the need for some prescribed patterns as a way of producing and maintaining social order in a context where instinctive drives are insufficiently determinate (as in coordination problems, see below) or where people's desires are in conflict (as in the 'prisoner's dilemma' type of situation). In *Suicide* Durkheim used the term ANOMIE to describe a state of society in which there were relatively few clear-cut norms. Such a state, he conjectured, can cause an increase in a society's suicide rate. Norms, then, are important for human psychological well-being. A way to reduce the suicide rate, he suggested, is to strengthen the individual's ties to particular smaller groups such as the conjugal family and occupational groups. Norms can of course characterize both large-scale societies and small groups such as a marital couple or medieval guild.

In the *Rules* Durkheim proposed that while social norms are associated with 'external' sanctions ranging from informal criticism and ostracism by others to legal penalties for deviance, a major factor in producing conformity to norms is the SOCIALIZATION process whereby individuals come to internalize norms: following the norm becomes 'second nature' and the external constraints of society are relatively rarely called into play any more.

Max Weber, though differing from Durkheim on many aspects of social theory, also emphasized the importance of norms in his discussion of fundamental sociological concepts (1921–2, pp. 29–36). Weber distinguished 'custom' and 'usage' from convention, where conformity is regarded as binding on the individual, as it is with law. With convention, any member of the relevant population may apply sanctions for deviance. With law a limited 'staff' of people are the expected purveyors of sanctions, physical or psychological. More recently Parsons argued for the crucial role of norms and values in society; in particular they enable people to predict what others will do, which is of enormous practical importance.

There will be many social norms in any social group. Durkheim, Parsons and others emphasized the importance for societal functioning of a harmony or integration among these norms.

Many questions can be raised about norms in general and particular types of norm. Norms can and do change over time or cease to exist. Any theory of social change will need to explain how this comes about. Sometimes (as with some norms governing gender roles) important needs of one group in society may be slighted or ignored by the existing norms. Consciousness of this may lead to pressure for change, which may or may not succeed. The factors involved in such processes of change will be complex. Other important topics include deviance from established norms (how much occurs, who deviates and why?), conflict among norms and the genesis of norms.

There remains the question of how best to understand the notion of a prescribed pattern. In recent philosophy, jurisprudence and economics careful attention has been paid to the related questions of how to analyse the everyday notion of a social convention and a social rule.

The game-theoretic approach is exemplified by the influential work of Lewis (1969) who follows a suggestion of Schelling (1960). Lewis focuses on a special type of situation involving more than one person and argues that where a situation of this type recurs in a population an actual pattern of behaviour may be expected to result. He refers to patterns that arise in this way as 'conventions'. The type of situation in question is called by Lewis a 'coordination problem'. Such problems are common in human social life. A small-scale example is of two people whose telephone call has been cut off. Who should call back? In such situations people may reach a successful outcome by chance at first, then be inclined to repeat what worked last time, or to expect that others will do so. Thus there may arise a 'self-perpetuating system' of expectations of conformity, preferences for conformity, and conformity by all to a certain regularity (such as the original caller calling back) (Lewis, p. 42). Lewis suggests that a general belief that this regularity *ought* to be followed is likely to arise in this case (p. 97). However, he sees emergence of an actual pattern of behaviour as the primary phenomenon; a general prescription of conformity is merely a probable consequence. Lewis does not make any kind of prescription part of his definition of convention.

Critics have argued that Lewis has not captured the vernacular concept of a social convention, as he had hoped. Among other things it does not appear that conventions only arise in the context of prior coordination problems; the question of aetiology is not preempted by definition. Further, a convention appears to involve a prescription at its core.

What is it for a group to have a rule or prescription about action? According to Hart (1961) the members must take a certain 'critical reflective attitude' to some actual pattern of behaviour. They must regard it as a standard to be conformed to by all members. Hart stresses that most members must believe that they are *entitled to criticize* one another for deviance from the standard, and that they are *entitled to demand compliance* if deviance is threatened.

The question then arises of what is the basis for any such belief. It would not obviously be justified by the simple fact that each member personally believed that members should conform to the standard, for instance. Certainly an entitlement to take another to task for deviance from a standard does not flow directly from that person's own acceptance of the standard or from one's own acceptance of it.

Gilbert's account of *jointly accepted principles* (1989a, esp, pp. 373ff.) shows how a special type of acceptance of a standard may directly generate an entitlement to criticize others for deviance. Joint acceptance of a standard or principle involves an agreement-like process by virtue of which those involved understand themselves to be mutually obligated to uphold the standard, and hence to conform to it. One who deviates from the standard violates his obligations to another. This gives the other grounds for complaint or criticism. It seems that explicit agreement is not essential to this process. What is needed is that the parties indicate to each other that they are willing to be committed in the relevant way, a way strongly analogous to the commitments involved in an explicit agreement. One way of doing this is to acquiesce in criticisms and demands of the type described by Hart. (Compare Williams, 1968, p. 207.) A plausible way of analysing the idea that a group has a rule, then, is in terms of joint acceptance of the rule.

Gilbert (1990, see also 1989b) has argued that something agreement-like is required for the emergence of a stable regularity in behaviour among the purely rational agents of classical game theory where there is a recurring coordination problem.

Agents who are moved to action on the basis of reasons for acting, as opposed to instinct or habit, cannot appeal to the existence of a successful precedent, or to the salience of a given solution, since these do not of themselves provide reasons for choosing the precedented or the salient option. To the extent that humans function as rational agents, then, jointly accepted principles are likely to be a major force in the organization of their life in society.

See also VALUES.

Reading
Gibbs, J. P. 1965: Norms: the problem of definition and classification. *American Journal of Sociology* 70, 586–94.
Parsons, T. 1937: *The Structure of Social Action.*
Raz, J. 1975: *Practical Reason and Norms.*
Ullman-Margalit, E. 1977: *The Emergence of Norms.*

MARGARET GILBERT

O

old age As anthropological research has shown, each society divides the lifespan into a definite number of stages embedded in the culture. It assigns a meaning to these stages and defines, for individuals, the conditions of transition from one stage to another during the life course, that is, the socially organized lifespan. Old age designates the last stage and thus has to be understood as a continually renegotiated social construction. It cannot be reduced to a biological reality of decrepitude and invalidity resulting from senescence. During each epoch of its history, a society reinterprets the chronological and biological differences among individuals so as to organize the life course and assign specific social statuses and roles to each age group (Balandier, 1974). Historians have shown how the roles and statuses of the aged have fluctuated (Laslett, 1976; Minois, 1987). The aged in preindustrial societies were not systematically assigned a prestigious status, nor was value always attached to their wisdom and experience. Although industrialization tended to reduce old people's social status, this does not hold equally true for all social classes. For instance, becoming old in our society, a process characterized by entry into the economically inactive population as well as the loss of both a parental role and social bonds, takes place at different chronological ages depending on the social class. Lessened social integration, reduced roles and even 'social death' occur earlier in the working than the upper classes, since persons from the latter may profit from their social resources (contacts, education and so on) in order to prolong the roles and functions they assumed at maturity (Guillemard, 1982).

Along with the growth of industrial society, pension systems have been set up and expanded with, as a consequence, the age of retirement becoming a significant threshold for entry into old age. Retirement thus shapes this last stage of life, which has gradually been divided into old age and extreme old age – categories that reflect both the considerably longer lifespan (in France, life expectancy at the age of 60 is about 20 years) and the fact that old age is considered to be a social problem and not just a private, family affair. The WELFARE STATE and society's increasing interventions on behalf of the aged have led to distinguishing an old age dependent on social and medical institutions from one that is autonomous and supported by social service policies aimed at integration (Guillemard, 1983). Social policies have an active part in redefining the life course and old age. Measures providing for early withdrawal from the labour force, which have been adopted in most industrial countries during the last decade, are reshaping old age and lowering its threshold by constructing a category of 'occupational old age' that starts before the retirement age (and often as early as 55) (Kohli et al., 1991). As a consequence, old age is ever more 'socially defined' as a time of social uselessness, when the aged may become dependent wards and social outcasts (Guillemard, 1986a, 1986b).

Reading
Balandier, George 1974: *Anthropo-logiques*.
Guillemard, Anne-Marie 1982: Old age, retirement and the social class structure: toward an analysis of the structural dynamics of the later stage of life. In *Ageing and the Life Course*, ed. T. Hareven.
—— 1986a: *Le déclin du social: formation et crise des politiques de la vieillesse.*
—— 1986b: State, society and old-age policy in France from 1945 to the current crisis. *Social Science and Medicine*, 23, 1319–26.
—— ed. 1983: *Old Age and the Welfare State.*
Kohli, Rein et al. 1991: *Time for Retirement: Comparative Studies of Early Exit from the Labor Force.*
Laslett, Peter 1976: Societal development and ageing. In *Handbook of Ageing and the Social Sciences*, ed. R. Binstock and E. Shanas.
Minois, Georges 1987 (*1989*): *History of Old Age: From Antiquity to the Renaissance.*

ANNE-MARIE GUILLEMARD

oligarchy As originally defined by Plato and Aristotle, this term for rule by the few, based generally on the possession of wealth, was contrasted with monarchy (rule by a single person) and democracy (rule by the people). In modern social thought the term has been largely displaced by that of elite (see ELITE THEORY), although references to oligarchical tendencies are still made in analysing the structure of power in organizations of various types.

The best known use of the term in twentieth-century social thought is by Roberto Michels (1911) who argued, from his study of the German Social Democratic Party, that a sharp distinction between the leading officials and the rank and file, resulting in rule by the few, necessarily developed in all large-scale organizations (even socialist ones). This view, formulated as the 'iron law of oligarchy', is clearly related to Gaetano Mosca's proposition that the 'organized minority' will always dominate the unorganized majority, and Michels went on to examine the 'technical and administrative causes' which produced such domination. Michels's conception was largely derived from the elite theorists, and it was later developed in a particularly anti-democratic form when he became a supporter of Mussolini and the fascist movement, invoking Max Weber's notion of the 'charismatic leader' to explain his new allegiance (Mommsen, 1981).

The iron law of oligarchy has been contested in various ways, by the numerous critics of elite theories, among them notably Marxist thinkers whose class theory envisages an eventual 'classless society', and by others who conceive the possibility of an extension of democracy, or even a wide-ranging 'participatory democracy', which would hold in check the elitist and oligarchical tendencies of large-scale organizations. Among the latter, some commentators on Michels's law have questioned the view that organization is necessarily accompanied by oligarchy, especially in the case of socialist parties (Beetham, 1981), and have drawn attention to the existence of counteracting forces, so that it is possible in some cases to speak of an 'iron law of democracy', and more generally of an ebb and flow of oligarchical and democratic tendencies in political and other organizations (Brym, 1980, ch. 3). It is in relation to such opposing tendencies, and especially to the consequences of the growth of bureaucratic administration, that recent discussions of oligarchy, or more frequently of elites, have taken place.

Reading
Beetham, David 1981: Michels and his critics. *European Journal of Sociology* 22.1, 81–99.

Brym, Robert J. 1980: *Intellectuals and Politics.*

Michels, Roberto 1911 (*1962*): *Political Parties: A Sociological Study of the Oligarchical Tendencies of Modern Democracy.*

Mommsen, Wolfgang J. 1981: Max Weber and Roberto Michels: an asymmetrical partnership. *European Journal of Sociology* 22.1, 100–16.

TOM BOTTOMORE

ontology   Two senses of the term can be distinguished: either (1) the branch of philosophy concerned with the nature of existence or being as such, apart from any particular existent objects (philosophical ontology); or (2) the entities posited or presupposed by some particular substantive scientific theory (scientific ontology). Sense (2) is relatively unproblematic and may be generalized to extrascientific contexts. Traditional philosophical ontology reflected on the nature and relations between different kinds of existents – the sense in which, for example, numbers, minds and qualities could be said to exist. Immanuel Kant and David Hume criticized such enquiries as necessarily undecidable, or even meaningless, attempts to transgress the bounds of possible experience, and proposed a rejection of ontology not just in the styles practised by Leibniz or John Locke, but generally.

In the mainstream of analytical philosophy the prohibition on ontology has been generally upheld in the twentieth century. But working from within this tradition, Roy Bhaskar has recently argued that philosophical ontology need not be dogmatic and transcendent, but may be conditional and immanent, taking as its subject matter not a world apart from that investigated by science (a Platonic or Lockean-Leibnizian noumenal realm), but just that world from the standpoint of what can be established about it by conditional a priori or transcendental argument. Bhaskar has further argued that any THEORY OF KNOWLEDGE presupposes an ontology of what the world must be like for knowledge, under the descriptions given it by the theory, to be possible. Thus the Humean theory of causal laws presupposes, in J.S. Mill's words, that 'what happens once will, under a sufficient degree of similarity of circumstance, happen again', that is, that there *are* constant conjunctions, or parallel cases, in nature.

From this perspective, the post-Humean dogma that statements about being can always be analysed as statements about our knowledge of being is a mistake – which Bhaskar calls the 'epistemic fal-

lacy'. It is, however, a mistake with consequences. In the first case, it merely glosses the generation of an *implicit* ontology – in the dominant (in the twentieth century) Humean case, of atomistic events and closed systems – and *a fortiori* of an implicit realism (in this case, of an empirical realism). Secondly, it conceals a deepseated anthropocentric bias in non- (explicitly) realist philosophies of science, underlying which is what we may call the *anthropomorphic fallacy* – the analysis of being in terms of human being. Thirdly, it coexists with an esoteric naturalization of knowledge – for example in the Humean case through the reification of facts and the fetishism of their conjunctions; that is to say, with in effect the compulsive determination of knowledge of being by being – in the reciprocal *ontic fallacy*. Finally, transposed to the social domain and in a hermeneutical or otherwise linguistified key, the collapse of what critical realists call the 'intransitive (or ontological) dimension' takes the form of the analysis of being in terms of our discourse about being – the *linguistic fallacy*. Indeed the linguistic fallacy is the form in which in ordinary language or LINGUISTIC PHILOSOPHY, on the one hand, and poststructuralist and more generally postmodernist thought (for instance, in 'discourse analysis'), on the other, the epistemic fallacy is most characteristically committed.

Substantively, on the transcendental realist ontology the world appears as structured, differentiated and changing. Applied to the social domain this ontology requires, as critical naturalism, further elaboration, e.g. to incorporate what has been called the duality of structure and praxis and a relational conception of the subject matter of social science. On the critical realist research programme, transcendental ontology is only in its infancy, and much remains to be done – on other categories such as negation or reflexivity, on the ontological presuppositions of further sciences and on those of social practices besides science.

Outside the analytical tradition, *the* philosopher of being has been Martin Heidegger. In his early *Being and Time* (1927) Heidegger argued that fundamental ontology or the 'science' of being, as enquiry into being, was itself dependent upon human being or *Dasein*. Traditional philosophies have forgotten the salient features of human being as being-in-the-world: from our manipulation of tools to authenticity in respect of our finitude. In his later work Heidegger moved from a concern with ontology to what might be called meta-ontology – for instance, why is there being rather than nothing? – and to a meta-history of the epochs of being, starting with the mere traces of being in the pre-Socratics and culminating in the contemporary age of nihilism and technology. His critique here overlaps with that of the Lukácsian and critical theoretic traditions in Western Marxism. There are interesting historical connections here. Heidegger knew Lukács's work and Jürgen Habermas began his philosophical career strongly influenced by Heidegger, for all his subsequent disdain for ontology.

Reading
Bhaskar, R. 1975 (*1978*): *A Realist Theory of Science*, 2nd edn.
—— 1989: *Reclaiming Reality*.
Habermas, J. 1974: *Theory and Practice*.
Heidegger, M. 1927 (*1962, 1970*): *Being and Time*.
—— 1947 (*1971*): Letter on humanism. In *Poetry, Language and Thought*.
Lukács, G. 1923 (*1971*): *History and Class Consciousness*.
ROY BHASKAR

open society The phrase has now entered the vocabulary of politics, being quite commonly employed by leader writers and politicians, though hardly by the man in the street. It is usually used to denote a society where no ideology or religion is given a monopoly, where there is a critical interest in new ideas whatever their source, where political processes are open to public examination and criticism, where there is freedom to travel and where restrictions on trade with other countries are minimal, and where the aim of education is to impart knowledge rather than to indoctrinate. For a long time the Soviet Union epitomized the antithesis of an open society, but under the policy of *glasnost* the countries that have replaced it seem to be moving away from that negative extreme.

The term 'open society' (together with its antonym, 'closed society') first gained currency from a famous book by Karl Popper (1945). As he acknowledged, this pair of terms had been introduced previously by Henri Bergson (1932). These two thinkers' conceptions of a closed society had much in common. Both saw it as a small, tightly knit, face-to-face community. According to Bergson, it is a centralized, static and unprogressive society, its religion authoritarian, its morality absolutist, its customs rigid. Popper stressed its anti-scientific, magical, tribalist outlook. A point made by Bergson but not by Popper was that war with neighbouring societies will usually be seen by the leadership of a closed society as a desirable way of fostering tribal loyalty and corporate unity.

However, their conceptions of an open society diverged considerably. For Bergson, the emergence of an open society will come about only when the multiplicity of closed societies eventually gives way to one all-embracing world society in which progress and diversity are encouraged, and religious dogma and authoritarian morality give way to mystical intuition and spontaneity.

For Popper, by contrast, the essential characteristic of an open society is not mystical intuition but the unfettered use of critical reason. And such a society may be quite small; he instanced Athenian society under Pericles (when its slaves are not regarded as integral to it). And the attainment of an open society is not a consummation lying in some distant future. Indeed, Popper claimed, successful moves in the past towards greater openness, especially in the West, have generated among some influential thinkers, most notably Plato in ancient Greece, a longing to return to a closed society. For life in an open society can be arduous and people are not necessarily happier there than they would be in a closed society. They may suffer from what Popper called 'the strain of civilization'. Some people would gladly give up the burden of individual responsibility in return for the imagined warmth and security of a closed society.

Popper agreed with Bergson, however, concerning the temporal priority of a closed to an open society; according to Popper, the former came naturally, as it were, whereas the latter always had to be struggled for. He gave two reasons for this.

(1) To be open, a society has also to be, to a considerable degree, what he called an 'abstract' society; here face-to-face transactions with known persons give way to impersonal dealings with anonymous, role-playing individuals. And the transition to such a society will be a late development.

(2) It is natural for people to regard the taboos and rigid customs of a closed society as natural and unalterable, as if they were laws of nature. Thus the move to an open society also requires the revolutionary recognition of the man-made, conventional character of social institutions, another late development.

In his book Popper (1945) attacked various doctrines that are hostile to the idea of an open society. One was the dream of utopian engineering, epitomized by Plato's idea that the philosopher-king should begin by *cleaning his canvas*. This is an impossible dream, if only because the canvas cleaner and the cleaning instruments are part of the picture to be wiped out. The closer a revolutionary political leadership approximates this impossible ideal, the more havoc and destruction it will cause. (See also TOTALITARIANISM.) The alternative is *piecemeal engineering*: this allows for large-scale reforms, but requires them to proceed in a step-by-step manner, making it possible to monitor the process and keep a check on the sociological hypotheses being relied on. Error may have got into these, with the result that the intended aim is not achieved, or is accompanied by consequences that are both unintended and unwanted. Critical surveillance becomes impossible when too many reforms are going on in the same area. (See also SOCIAL DEMOCRACY.)

A related idea of Popper's (1945) was *negative utilitarianism*; this says that governments should aim, not directly at increasing overall happiness, but at reducing known suffering.

Another doctrine Popper saw as hostile to the open society was HISTORICISM and the related doctrine of *moral futurism* (What *will* be, is right). Popper recommended an individualistic methodology (see INDIVIDUALISM).

Some critics have questioned whether early human societies were closed. Charles Darwin (1871) emphasized how important inventiveness and imitativeness had been in helping primitive humans to gain an ascendancy over the other primates. This argues for a certain openness to novelty alien to the cast of mind characteristic of a closed society.

See also FREEDOM.

Reading
Levinson, Ronald B. 1953: *In Defense of Plato*.
Magee, Bryan 1973: *Popper*, chs 6 and 7.
O'Hear, Anthony 1980: *Karl Popper*, ch. 8.
Popper, Karl 1976: *Unended Quest*, ch. 24.
Schilpp, Paul Arthur ed. 1974: *The Philosophy of Karl Popper*, 2 vols, pp. 820–924.

J.W.N. WATKINS

operations research   *See* MANAGEMENT SCIENCE

opinion   Among many different definitions two elements are commonly found: that opinions deal with controversial matters, and that they are capable of rational justification.

The first critical point is that one cannot have an opinion about a matter of demonstrable truth or falsehood. One cannot have an 'opinion' that the three angles of a triangle are equal to two right angles, nor can one legitimately hold an opinion that Australia does not exist. This is not quite as simple or straightforward as it might seem. We are confronted regularly with the tentative nature of knowledge, for the universe is not the certain place many assume it to be. Even within a specific time – space setting, where a body of settled 'facts' are not seriously challenged and therefore are not matters of opinion, circumstances change so that what was settled may become disputed. Many once supposedly incontrovertible facts – the indivisibility of the atom, for example – have been proved to be errors. There may well develop a controversy about whether a question formerly not debated is now controversial. Many who hold views on controversial matters firmly deny there is anything in the least questionable or disputable about their convictions. It is a matter of opinion whether a subject is a matter of opinion. In an increasingly sophisticated society, as the certainties of an older, more homogeneous order come to be challenged, the range of things on which we can hold opinions widens. All new areas of thought, all reexaminations of orthodoxy, raise questions of opinion.

The second element proposes that opinions are those views which are capable of being accepted by the rational mind as true. This is not to suggest that each opinion, as propounded by each individual, has a logically reasoned foundation. Opinions may be acquired in many ways, among which logical deductions from objective premises or empirical observations are only sometimes a factor. Many hold their opinions out of habit, or accept them from the authority of others. The essential requirement is that in their internal content they be consistent with some defensible interpretation of public data, and that they could be reached by the normal processes of reason.

However formulated or arrived at, opinions have their roots in the related concept of attitudes. An opinion may in fact be described as an expressed attitude, perhaps modified by the need for expression. Attitude itself is another complex idea in which certain common threads run through scores of detailed definitions. The first point is that attitudes are internal mental states, reflected in an inclination to respond to external stimuli in a favourable or unfavourable manner. Attitudes embody a basic evaluation of the world – a combination of beliefs about 'reality', together with moral judgements of approval or disapproval, likes and dislikes.

There is no exact correlation between an individual's set of attitudes and the expressed opinion on a specific situation. This is because the voiced opinion may be derived from two, possibly conflicting, attitudes – one to the stimulus itself, and the other to the circumstances in which it must be expressed.

See also PROPAGANDA; IDEOLOGY.

Reading
Childs, H.L. 1965: *Public Opinion: Nature, Formation, and Role.*
Lippmann, Walter 1922: *Public Opinion.*
Petty, R.E. and Cacioppo, J.T. 1981: *Attitudes and Persuasion.*
Qualter, T.H. 1985: *Opinion Control in the Democracies.*

TERENCE H. QUALTER

organization   The starting point for this increasingly frequently used notion in the social sciences is the analogy between animate organisms and society. In biology the organism is an entity producing beings similar to itself, while in society organization appears as a unit of persons and groups separated by the division of labour but also cooperating with each other. Entity and reproduction are significant features of organization in society, as of the organism in nature.

The organizations emerging in society can be classified in many different ways, and the classification to be adopted can be decided on the basis of the requirements of a specific research approach. Ferdinand Tönnies made a classic differentiation between two basic types of social organization which is still in use: *Gemeinschaft*, which is characterized by being born into something and living one's life in it, for instance village communities and ethnic subcultures; and *Gesellschaft*, a type of organization which comes into being by the conscious will of the participants, where membership is normally decided by the free decision of the people concerned. (See also SOCIAL STRUCTURE.) An essential feature of modern societies is the diversity of these organizations, which spread more and more widely through social life. They can also be classified from several viewpoints, and this is a major theme of organization theory. The most important differentiations are the following.

Military organizations, a very old form of organization in history, in which a strict relationship of leadership and subordination asserts itself, although in recent times professional competence is gaining ground, and parallel with this the functional elements are being reinforced alongside the linear chain of command.

Work organizations, a main type of which is the hierarchically structured enterprise (see MANAGEMENT SCIENCE). This form is predominant in economic life and as a result of various reformist efforts it is assuming a more and more humane character, gradually losing its original rigidity.

Political parties and political organizations. In Western societies parliamentarianism has promoted to the rank of the most important organization of civil societies the political parties which, on the basis of general elections, have a smaller or greater share of power. Some of them do not get the chance to acquire real power but as institutions for holding the executive accountable they may have an important role in society. The latter role was especially important in the process of reforming socialist countries, where the introduction of parliamentarianism encountered very severe obstacles in the constellation of power.

Professional interest-protection organizations, the most typical form of which is that of the TRADE UNIONS organized by occupation. They play an important role not only in the protection of workers' interests but also as mediators between the power-holders and the masses. In the USSR, Stalinism emphasized only the latter role of the trade unions, but in the course of recent reforms the role of interest protection is increasing, and against organization on the basis of economic sectors the principle of professional organization is becoming more prominent.

Local interest-protection organizations, which are often connected with the conservation of historic monuments on the basis of local patriotism. More recently, however, in these organizations the significance of environmental protection and the elimination of problems caused by the ecological crisis is growing (see also CIVIL SOCIETY).

Religious organizations, which are organized partly within the official churches and partly outside them. Especially important among the latter are the basic communities, an indicator of a possible future renaissance of religion.

Of course, this list could be continued and within each category new subcategories could be distinguished. Instead it is more useful here to underline the significance of two aspects of organizations through which they can be classified and analysed. First, the degree of bureaucratization of organization (see also BUREAUCRACY). Three main groups can be differentiated here: (a) bureaucratic organization which is clearly governed by bureaucratic subordination; (b) dichotomous organization where bureaucratic leading organs are operated by lay persons; (c) organization fully managed by lay persons (self-management). Secondly, the relationship between the organization and state power. Three main types can again be differentiated: (a) organization subordinated to state power and identified with it; (b) organization in opposition to state power; (c) organization neutral with respect to state power.

See also FORDISM AND POST-FORDISM; INDUSTRIAL ORGANIZATION; ORGANIZATIONAL BEHAVIOUR; ORGANIZATIONAL THEORY; SYSTEM THEORY.

Reading
Simpson, R.L. 1959: Vertical and horizontal communication in formal organisations. *Administrative Science Quarterly*, no. 4.
Tönnies, Ferdinand 1887 (*1955*): *Community and Association*.
Whyte, W.H. 1960: *The Organisation Man*.

ANDRÁS HEGEDÜS

organization, industrial *See* INDUSTRIAL ORGANIZATION

organizational behaviour This interdisciplinary study focuses on the human and social aspects of management in formal organizations as a 'technical' problem. It draws primarily on sociology and psychology, but also on economics, MANAGEMENT SCIENCE and production engineering to study the structure and functioning of organizations and the behaviour of groups and individuals within them. The application of this subject to practical problems of managing change in organizations is referred to as organizational development. In the twentieth century the impact of social science on management thinking has built up to become the major force.

From the point of view of organizational behaviour the task of management may be considered as the organization of individuals' behaviour in relation to the physical means and resources to achieve desired goals. A basic problem then becomes: how much organization and control of behaviour is necessary for efficient functioning, and what form should it take? It is in the implied answer to this question that two sides of a continuing debate can be distinguished – characterized by Pugh (1990) as the 'organizers' and the 'behaviouralists'.

The organizers stem from the work of Henri Fayol, Frederick W. Taylor and Max Weber. They maintain that more precisely determined structures, plans and programmes, with improved specification, monitoring and control of the behaviour required to achieve them, are necessary for effectiveness. They point to the advantages for efficient goal achievement of specialization of function and task, clear job definitions, standardized procedures and clear lines of authority, that is, the form of organization for which Weber (1922) used the term BUREAUCRACY.

Fayol's (1916) definition of what management is, and Taylor's (1947) approach to the extreme subdivision and control of the tasks of shopfloor workers (called 'scientific management') had and continue to have a considerable impact on both management thinking and practice. While Fayol and Taylor were enthusiastic advocates of full management control, Weber expressed considerable concern about the social implications of the spread of bureaucracy in terms of the bureaucrats' ability to usurp democratic functions. But since this concern was based on his belief in the overwhelming technical efficiency of the bureaucratic approach, its impact on the field of organizational behaviour was to underline the arguments of the organizers.

These ideas have been developed, for example, by spelling out the minimum required characteristics of an effective bureaucratic structure (Jaques, 1976).

The behaviouralists stem from the work of Elton Mayo, Kurt Lewin and Abraham Maslow. Mayo (1933) studied shopfloor work groups in the 'Hawthorne experiments' and developed the 'human relations' approach which emphasizes the human and social needs of workers (see also INDUSTRIAL RELATIONS). Lewin studied the strengths of democratic as opposed to autocratic leadership (Lewin et al., 1939). Maslow (1968) identified 'self-actualization' – the need to grow and develop as an individual – as an important motivator. All three argue that the continuing attempt to increase control over the behaviour of members of the organization is self-defeating. Management control leads to rigidity where flexibility is required, and apathy in members' performance when commitment and high motivation are required. Increasing control generates efforts devoted to countercontrol through informal relationships to defeat the aims of the organization. It does not generally lead to increased efficiency, and when it does it is only in the short term and at the cost of internal conflict. Subordinates must be given considerable autonomy in decisions and opportunities for self-development if the organization is to function efficiently.

Studies of decision-making have also suggested that it is not possible to take a completely rational approach to management (Simon, 1947). A partially rational piecemeal approach normally occurs (Lindblom, 1959). Even non-rational approaches to decision-making are encouraged as a spur to innovativeness (March, 1976).

Further developments stem from those who take a 'contingency approach' arguing that a balance must be kept between the concerns of the organizers and the behaviouralists. This balance will be contingent on the particular contextual situation of the organization which will cause differences in its structure (Burns and Stalker, 1961; Pugh and Hickson, 1976) as will the technology used in producing the output as demonstrated in the sociotechnical system approach (Emery and Trist, 1960). Similarly, different tasks of a work group, and the needs of its members, will require differences in leadership (Fiedler, 1967).

The Marxist approach (Braverman, 1974) has been to argue that the extreme organizers will always be preferred by managements since their aim is not efficiency in performance, but efficiency in the control of the working class in the interests of capital.

An important recent development, with the expansion of international trade and the rise of multinational corporations, has been the systematic identification of cross-cultural differences in organizational behaviour in regard to work values, leadership style and control structures (Hofstede, 1980).

Reading

Morgan, G. 1986: *Images of Organization.*
Pugh, D.S. and Hickson, D.J. 1989: *Writers on Organizations*, 4th edn.

DEREK PUGH

organizational theory An interdisciplinary body of knowledge with close ties to sociology, psychology, political science and economics, it originated mainly in the United States, France and Germany in the period following World War I, partly in response to the need for practical and professional, as well as scholarly, knowledge for managers and administrators in both public and private sectors. The American contribution focused on problems of industrial organization and the growth of the administrative state after 1933, the French on industrial organization as a key problem area of the social division of labour, following on the work of Emile Durkheim, and the German on the phenomenon of bureaucracy as the organizational embodiment of what Max Weber called 'legal-rational' authority in both the state and the large enterprise.

These three strands of research, scholarship and professional advice to managers and administrators began to come together in a relatively coherent form only after World War II, and achieved full recognition as a discrete field of research, teaching and training by the mid-1950s. Since 1970, organizational theory has split into a number of different areas of study, including ORGANIZATIONAL BEHAVIOUR and interpretive and radical organization studies. While organizational behaviour is more empirical and less formal and prescriptive than organizational theory, interpretive and radical organization studies focus respectively on reality construction from the actor's standpoint and organization as a locus of political struggle, labour exploitation and class domination and control.

Organizational theory traditionally has concerned itself with the relationship or 'fit' between the individual personality, the structure of authority and the organization of work and role of technology, as well as with issues bearing on the small group, goals, motivation, leadership, communication, decision-making, alternate organizational and suborganizational systems, and the 'environment' of organizations. Cutting across these concerns was the question whether personality, role or decision-making constituted the best conceptual basis for carrying out research and theory in the field. More recently, key journals in organizational theory and behaviour have begun to treat both areas as forms of *social* theory and research, thereby collapsing to a far greater extent than was true in the 1950s the boundaries between organizational theory and the study of problems bearing on social, economic and political structures and processes.

This tendency has intensified since the late 1970s as a consequence of the rise of neo-conservatism, the withdrawal of government and the public sector from traditional and established functions, services and regulatory activity, and the consequent rise of privatization strategies of various kinds, particularly in the United States, Great Britain and Australia. For whatever reason, these trends appear to constitute a return to the focus pioneered in both France and Germany from the very beginning, for in both cases the study of formal or complex organizations was intimately related to larger order concerns of social organization, state and economy like alienation, anomie, rationality, class and class conflict and power, authority and control. Meantime, management theory, once a central part of organization theory, continues to constitute a discrete body of knowledge, even as it too has been required to respond to social, political and economic concerns related to globalization, social responsibility and ethics.

See also MANAGEMENT SCIENCE.

Reading
Burrell, Gibson and Morgan, Gareth 1979: *Sociological Paradigms and Organizational Analysis.*
Etzioni, Amitai 1969: *A Sociological Reader on Complex Organizations.*
Krupp, Sherman 1961: *Pattern in Organization Analysis.*
March, James and Simon, Herbert 1958: *Organizations.*
Perrow, Charles 1967: A framework for the comparative analysis of organizations. *American Sociological Review* 32.
Thompson, James 1967: *Organizations in Action.*
Thompson, Victor 1961: *Modern Organization.*

H.T. WILSON

oriental despotism Referring to a form of political organization in which a centralized bureaucracy controls water supplies and irrigation works, the concept was made famous by Karl Wittfogel who wrote a book with this title (1957), but it nevertheless has a complicated history and wider reference.

The term despotism is very old, but it is generally considered that Montesquieu (1749) was the first to use it systematically in drawing a distinction between monarchy and despotism. While the former system of government comprised a number of ranked levels, the latter, thought to be characteristic of Asia, featured a chasm between the ruling despot and the people who were all alike in being 'nothing'.

Many other writers were interested in Asiatic societies in the eighteenth century. Adam Smith (1776), for example, argued that despotism, linked to agriculture rather than commerce, was a type of society at a low level of evolutionary development, and largely in a stationary state. In the nineteenth century the focus of attention switched from government and ruler to the supposedly self-sufficient and largely isolated village communities that constituted the individual units of oriental society.

With Karl Marx oriental society became the Asiatic system. The development of this concept within the tradition of Marxism is difficult to trace both because Marx's ideas on the evolution of social formations changed over time, and because his own writings on this topic became available only gradually and in piecemeal fashion. In an early argument Marx and Engels (1845–6) advanced the view that there are various stages in the social division of labour which correspond to specific forms of property. The first stage is the primitive commune in which all property is held communally. Out of this comes the development of ideas of private property and the contrast between town and country (and between free man and slave), which is linked to the separation of industrial and commercial labour from agricultural labour, and hence to the rise of the ancient city-state. The third stage of property is feudal ownership. Because this does not involve concentration of population in cities, however, it is debatable whether feudalism succeeds the ancient city-state or is an alternative route out of the primitive commune. The next stage is capitalism emerging out of the economic contradictions of feudalism.

After ten years of further intensive research Marx modified this version of historical periodization. In that section of the *Grundrisse* (1857–8, first published only in 1953, and published in English as *Pre-capitalist Economic Formations*, 1964), Marx set out a more elaborate treatment of this issue. In this, the Asiatic system, not mentioned in the previous scheme, has become one of three alternative routes out of the primitive commune, along with the ancient and the Germanic systems. Here Marx also drew attention to a distinction between those social formations 'which resist and those which favour historical evolution' (Hobsbawm, 1964, p. 33), oriental society being a clear example of the former.

By this time then it is evident that Marx did not entertain a simple unilinear theory of evolution.

In the primitive commune 'the earth provides the means and the materials of labour' and men 'regard themselves as its *communal proprietors* (Marx, *Pre-capitalist Economic Formations*, p. 69). In such a social form the bounty of nature constitutes a precondition of existence, but is not itself the product of labour; rather it appears as a natural and divine precondition conceived as a sort of unity over and above the group. The Asiatic system, seen as the most elementary form of the state, is but a short step away from the primitive commune because the divine unity takes the substantial form of a ruling despot seen as a representative or reincarnation of the divine. The higher unity thus stands in as the 'father' of the smaller communities and appears as the sole proprietor to whom surplus labour is given as tribute. Objectively, in so far as property is still held communally, the Asiatic form is a state without classes (or at least without the corrosive effect of classes, see Bloch, 1985, p. 112) and hence stagnant. Asiatic states may break down and re-form at the higher level but the social organization of the village communities remains immune from the turbulence of changes in ruling dynasties.

With the adoption in the Soviet Union of a simplistic unilinear historical materialism in which the various forms of society were seen to succeed one another through the dynamic of class struggle, the notion of a stagnant oriental despotism (Asiatic society) posed a major theoretical and political problem. Much of the early work of Soviet thinkers was devoted to reinterpreting this social form as really a version of feudalism, and the fact that Engels did not mention Asiatic society in the *Origin of the Family, Private Property and the State* (1884) made their task somewhat easier.

Karl Wittfogel's *Oriental Despotism*, as a theory of 'hydraulic society', argues that the special ecological conditions of Asia make large-scale irrigation by canals and waterworks the necessary basis of agriculture, which also requires the interference of a centralized bureaucracy to coordinate water control. This consolidates into despotic political systems in which the ruling elite appropriates a surplus from primary producers and possesses a monopoly of military power. In such systems the local village communities remain atomized and culturally distant from their overlords. *Oriental Despotism* is also noteworthy for its extended polemic against Stalinist Russia. According to Wittfogel both Lenin and Stalin ignored and suppressed the concept of the Asiatic system, even though Marx had stressed it, because they were aware that Russia was itself at such a stage of evolution and because they wanted to play down the possibility that a communist state might assume the character of despotism. As far as Wittfogel was concerned Stalin was just another in the long line of oriental despots.

Though very influential, Wittfogel's work has been widely criticized. One obvious problem is that there are many south-east Asian states based on irrigated rice production but lacking effective and centralized bureaucracies. Another criticism is that the linking of a specific form of society with a particular geographical area (and a type of ecological setting) seems to limit the universal applicability of Marx's theory of the evolution of socioeconomic formations.

With the recent publication of *Grundrisse* and other of Marx's later works, debate in the West now focuses on the issues of the conditions for the emergence of states, the nature of classes in pre-capitalist societies and the symbolism of state power. More recently the idea that oriental society constitutes a specific and coherent object of study has come under intense scrutiny (Said, 1978).

See also STATE; MODE OF PRODUCTION.

Reading
Bailey, A.M. and Llobera, J.R. 1974–5: The Asiatic mode of production. *Critique of Anthropology* 2, 95–103; 4–5, 165–76.
—— 1979: Karl Wittfogel and the Asiatic mode of production: a reappraisal. *Sociological Review* 27, 541–59.
Geertz, G. 1980: *Negara: The Theatre State in Nineteenth-Century Bali.*
Hindess, B. and Hirst, P. 1975: *Pre-capitalist Modes of Production.*
Krader, L. 1975: *The Asiatic Mode of Production.*
Mitchell, W. 1973: The hydraulic hypothesis: a reappraisal. *Current Anthropology* 14, 532–4.
Service, E. 1975: *The Origins of the State and Civilization.*
Steward, J. 1977: *Evolution and Ecology.*
Winzeler, R. 1976: Ecology, culture, social organization and state formation in Southeast Asia. *Current Anthropology* 17, 623–40.

LEO HOWE

orientalism A term that was given currency recently by the work of Anouar Abdel-Malek (1963) and Edward Said (1978), 'orientalism' refers to the peculiar perspective on the East of scholars of the Orient representing the old colonial powers. The view of the classical 'orientalists' was one from the 'centre' to the 'periphery'; a view that saw the East as 'other', the foil and the prey of the triumphant and civilizing West. Said (1978, p. 222) has shown very well how the Orient was seen by the orientalists – using this term technically to refer to scholars of the Orient – as a field for the expert whose role in society was to interpret it for compatriots. A long line of thinking from the travellers' tales of European gentlemen to the scholarly treatises of Jesuit missionaries and works representative of the Western Enlightenment contributed to this very positional image of the Orient. But not surprisingly orientalism's heyday coincides with the power of COLONIALISM at its height.

In fact, one can show that the notion of the East as the foil of the West, and 'other', dates back to classical antiquity, in Aristotle's remarks about 'servile Asiatics' (in the *Politics*) and speculations by Greek philosophers and orators on the Persian Great King and why he ruled his people like slaves. While it was clear that to the Greeks, ancient Persia, Egypt, Mesopotamia and Syria represented venerable and respected cultures with which they saw themselves competing, it was not uncommon for the Greeks to rewrite history in such a way that in the struggles between the 'giants' and the 'barbarians' they were always the victors. For instance, Plato, in the *Timaeus* and *Critias*, which recount the story of the legendary Atlantis, now thought to be Crete, whose civilization was destroyed by the eruption of Thera, referred to allegorically by Plato, clearly reverses the results of the battle between the armies of Egyptian Ramses III and the Greeks in favour of the latter. Plato, who is reputed to have journeyed to Egypt and perhaps to have spent as long as three years there, at the same time makes several favourable references to Egypt, as having invented 'number and calculation, geometry and astronomy, not to speak of draughts and dice, and above all writing' (*Phaedrus*, 27c–d; *Philebus*, 18b–d), and of already showing 10,000 years of continuity in religion, art and law by the time that he wrote (*Laws*, 656–7). Egypt, in fact, he claims, better preserved Greek historical records than the Greeks, due to the devastations following the eruption of Thera (*Timaeus*, 22–3). Herodotus, our principal ancient authority on Egypt and Mesopotamia, maintained that Greece acquired her gods and cultic practices from Egypt as the repository of ancient wisdom (Herodotus, *Histories*, 2.44–5, 1972 edn, 146). While Herodotus's view was long discredited by Plutarch's smear that he was 'the father of lies', or 'a barbarian lover', who credited non-Greeks with more than any Greek should, Plutarch himself, in his *Isis and Osiris* (*Moralia*, bk 5) and other works, showed himself well acquainted with, and in a certain admiration of, the highly developed cultures of Egypt and Persia.

In that period of classical revival, the European Renaissance of the fourteenth and fifteenth centuries, we do not find, as we might expect, a carry-over of xenophobic Greek attitudes. This is partly because the Italian Renaissance was more Roman than Greek in inspiration, not surprisingly given that this was also a nationalist movement. So far was the East from being stigmatized as 'despotic' in the European Renaissance, a period which saw fascination with power in all its modes, that in fact we have several indications that the Orient was a source of inspiration and political models. Indeed, the East's role to 'regenerate the West' was a recurrent concept that gained in strength with time, a dream of the novelist Gustave Flaubert in his later years, for instance. Niccolò Machiavelli was, it seems, representative of Renaissance Florentine humanists in his admiration of the ancient Eastern empires and the efforts of Alexander the Great to conquer and then reconstitute them. Quattrocento Florentine humanism owed a good deal to Byzantine scholars responsible for the reintroduction of Greek language and classical texts, some of them, in particular Gemistus Pletho, schooled in the Arabic commentaries, just as medieval humanism had owed its rich source of Greek classical texts to the Arabs.

The second phase in the rise of 'orientalism' as a specific phenomenon dates precisely from the emergence of the Western nation-states from the sixteenth century on, and the tradition of classical republican theory in terms of which they legitimated themselves. It is a peculiar achievement of this tradition of Western political theory that it succeeded in characterizing the great landed monarchies of Western Europe as essentially 'democratic', and the polities of the East, which had most probably pioneered republican social forms – the bicameral assembly, voting by ballot and by lot, the roster of magistracies tenurable for a year, the liturgy and a judicial system based on common law justiciable in the courts – as essentially 'despotic'. From Thomas Hobbes, James Harrington and John Locke, to Jean Bodin, Jean-Jacques Rousseau and Montesquieu, different though the specific content of the work of these political theorists was, the net result was to cast in stone the boundaries between East and West, as between despotic and representative regimes respectively (see also ORIENTAL DESPOTISM). The struggle for the mantle of the *polis* became the arena in which Western state formation was carried out. Among the permitting conditions was the fortuitous circumstance that the church, itself an institution whose wellsprings were in the East, and responsible for the educational function in the West, had nurtured indigenous elites on an exotic literature, from Greece and Rome and the ancient Near East. Classical literature constituted the fund of examples from which models were drawn, and on this basis, early modern dynamic factions in Western European states persuaded their monarchs, some under pressure, to convert aristocratic clan councils into representative assemblies on the Greek and Roman models. That they succeeded in doing so was due in no small measure to the threats held out to them of the Muslims, particularly the dreaded Turks, who at the battle of Poitiers were turned back from the very heartland of Europe and whose traditions and institutions were deemed to be the very antithesis of everything Western Europe stood for.

The case against the Orient is clearly to be seen in the writings of James Harrington and Edward Gibbon, who compared the 'slothful effeminacy of the Syrians and Egyptians' with the 'fierce independence of the Germans and Caledonians', appealing to Tacitus's celebrated encomium to Teutonic probity. Montesquieu, for his part, uses the Turk as a scare figure to warn the court of Louis XIV against the hazards of despotism. On the rising tide of philologically based ethnocentrism that produced the 'Aryan model' as the defining instrument to divide the Greeks and the barbarians, this ancient Battle of the Giants achieved new heights. Climatological theories, theories about the movement of peoples and the origins of civilization on the Iranian steppe, combined to favour Indo-European as opposed to Semitic cultures (Bernal, 1987). Here we have the context for 'orientalism' as a professional academic disposition toward the East theorized as 'the Asiatic mode of production' by nineteenth- and early twentieth-century thinkers as influential as James Mill in *The History of British India*, J. S. Mill, in *Dissertations and Discussions*, Karl Marx and Antonio Gramsci. The belief that oriental cities differed from either ancient or medieval Western cities, in being founded on the 'armed camp', and that oriental society, exemplified by India, lacked 'history' in its changelessness (Karl Marx, in the *Grundrisse* and *Capital*), combined ideas of backwardness and stationariness that favoured Western society in Social Darwinist terms, then current, legitimating colonial projects of the nineteenth-century Western powers.

It is without doubt the case that orientalist stereotypes have infected much of the 'development' literature analysing Third World polities in relation to the First World, evident in the very concept of 'underdevelopment', a readiness to ascribe national character traits in the diagnosis of systemic weaknesses, and the wholesale transportation of Western institutions as political and economic panaceas (see also DEVELOPMENT AND UNDERDEVELOPMENT). Orientalism is a form of racism that has in the nineteenth and twentieth centuries, as in the heyday of Roman imperialism, had strong institutional backing in colonial and neo-colonial administrative structures. Thus departments like the Colonial Office which once bore the White Man's Burden have been replaced by the international aid agencies, strongly committed to a 'civilizing mission' which includes 'development', that is to say Western education, economic and political 'growth', the transportation of Western culture and values and the integration of non-Western economies into the world market.

Reading

Abdel-Malek, Anouar 1963: *Civilization and Social Theory*.

Bernal, Martin 1987: *Black Athena: the Afro-Asiatic Roots of Classical Civilization*.

Said, Edward 1978: *Orientalism*.

Springborg, Patricia 1986: Politics, primordialism and orientalism: Marx, Aristotle and the myth of *Gemeinschaft. American Political Science Review* 80, 185–211.

——1992: *Western Republicanism and the Oriental Prince*.

Turner, Bryan 1978: *Marx and the End of Orientalism*.

—— Orientalism and the problem of civil society. In *Orientalism, Islam and Islamists*, ed. Asaf Hussain et al.

Wittfogel, Karl A. 1957: *Oriental Despotism*.

PATRICIA SPRINGBORG

P

pacifism The protracted slaughter of World War I gave fresh impetus to the old doctrine that resort to war, even in response to attack, is always wrong. Its twentieth-century adherents have, however, faced peculiarly acute dilemmas. In the face of threats, actual or potential, from brutally dictatorial regimes, capable, in some cases, of genocide, the question arises: how can a state that deprives itself of the military weapon survive, or fulfil its obligation to its own people or others? And if it does not survive, how can its people preserve their values? In the twentieth century war has become a moral obscenity, but so, often, have the alternatives to it.

Apart from those that follow the biblical injunction to 'take no thought for the morrow', pacifists answer this in two ways. In the first place, they argue that no one is likely to attack a patently undefended state. Secondly, they claim that if such an attack were to occur, the population could preserve the values of their society, and eventually induce the invader to withdraw, by organized non-violent resistance.

Cases can be found which support their first contention. Costa Rica has long survived without an army, and Austria, though certainly not pacifist, has owed its survival and security since the State Treaty of 1955 more to its recognized status as an unthreatening and constructive neutral than to its capacity to defend itself against the military alliances of either NATO in the West or the Warsaw Pact in the East; but given the fate of Denmark in 1940, Czechoslovakia in 1968 and Grenada in 1983, it cannot convincingly be maintained that to pose no military threat is enough to assure immunity.

The feasibility of pacifism thus very much depends on the efficacy of non-violence. Gandhi's 'civil disobedience' campaigns against British rule in India in the interwar years, and the challenges mounted by the National Association for the Advancement of Colored Peoples, under the leadership of Martin Luther King, to the segregation and disfranchisement of blacks in the American South, seemed to show that non-violence can sometimes succeed in changing the minds of powerful and often brutal opponents, though other factors were undoubtedly at work, and in each case the activists were able to appeal to a democratic public opinion with ultimate control over their oppressors. Gandhi was not himself a pacifist, but his campaigns, which made much use of fasts, consistently renounced violence and disavowed any to which his professed supporters resorted. His teaching drew much on Hindu religious writings. 'The way of the spirit . . . is one of detachment, of self-abnegation, of being unattached to all desires' (see Gandhi, 1951, p. 26).

Gene Sharp (1971) reported having identified 125 different forms of non-violence, falling into three main categories: protest, non-cooperation and intervention, and discerned three mechanisms of change: conversion, accommodation and coercion. Given that the resisters are capable of explaining the reasons for their resistance, which he sees as a *sine qua non*, their non-violence, and the respect won through their willingness to suffer if necessary for their beliefs, will, he claims, make opponents readier to reconsider their policies. Alternatively, such resistance may induce accommodation in an opponent who, while not (yet) convinced of the rightness of their case, is prepared to comply with the activists' demands because 'he does not think the matter worth the trouble caused by the struggle' (p. 156). COERCION can be applied when the resistance is sufficiently widespread, and protracted, as to 'succeed in withholding, directly or indirectly, the necessary sources of the ruler's political power'. Thomas Schelling (1971, p. 179), who in his previous writings had cold-bloodedly analysed the logic of violent coercion, conceded that 'the potential of non-violence is enormous [with] implications for peace, war, stability, terror, confidence and domestic politics that are not yet easy to assess.'

Nuclear pacifism, which holds that the use of nuclear weapons is always wrong, even in retaliation, and therefore calls for their renunciation, unilaterally if necessary, offers a less drastic prospect. Such weapons have not been used since the closing stages of the war against Japan in 1945, and it cannot be said that those states that are not able to rely on their own nuclear threats, or those of their allies, are impotent. Vietnam, for instance, had no such threat at its disposal but that did not prevent it from defeating the world's most advanced nuclear power. Opposition to their use now often invokes the theory of the 'just war', whereby, for military force to be legitimate, not only must the end be good (and attainable), but the violence must be restricted to those actually resisting such force, that is, to combatants.

Reading
Bondurant, J.V. ed. 1971: *Conflict: Violence and Non-Violence.*
Ceadel, M. 1987: *Thinking about Peace and War.*
Hinton, J. 1989: *Protests and Visions.*
Roberts, A. ed. 1967: *The Strategy of Civilian Defence.*
Sharp, G. 1973: *The Politics of Non-Violent Action.*

RODERICK C. OGLEY

pan-Africanism   This may be defined as a sense of solidarity among Africans and people of African ancestry. That awareness of shared identity has sometimes been intellectualized into a theory or translated into political action. At its most ambitious, pan-Africanism seeks to create one government for the whole of Africa, combined with strong economic and political ties with people of African descent elsewhere in the world.

Pan-Africanism may take the form of *emotions*, *ideas* or *action*. When African-Americans burst into the Security Council at the United Nations in 1961, interrupting proceedings in protest against the murder of the former premier Patrice Lumumba in the Congo (now Zaire), that angry protest constituted pan-African emotions translated into political action. When the civil rights activist Reverend Jesse Jackson recommended in 1989 that the term 'black American' should be replaced by 'African-American', that was a pan-African idea which was soon widely adopted as policy by many public institutions in the United States. In Africa itself pan-African manifestations have ranged from Nigerian students protesting the murder of black consciousness leader Steve Biko of South Africa to such regional economic experiments as the defunct East African Community (EAC) and the more recent Economic Community of West African States (ECOWAS). Pan-Africanism can be primarily *sub-Saharan* (focusing mainly on black Africans south of the Sahara as when in the 1980s President Mobutu Sese Seko of Zaire recommended an organization of only black African states), or *trans-Saharan* (seeking to unite black Africa with Arab Africa), or *trans-Atlantic* (solidarity between Africans and blacks of the Western hemisphere), or *global* (a sense of a shared identity among people of African descent everywhere). Descendants of Africans who are located outside Africa constitute what is often called 'the African diaspora' or 'the black diaspora'.

History of pan-Africanism
At the turn of the century black people were suffering political oppression, economic exploitation and social degradation under COLONIALISM and systematic racial discrimination. Apart from black-ruled Ethiopia, Haiti and Liberia, the lives of people of African origin were under the control of Europeans. The 'pan-European' domination fostered the belief that the liberation of blacks hinged on their political unity. Moreover, 'pan' movements were a fashion from the middle of the nineteenth century to the outbreak of World War II; prominent among these were pan-Slavism, pan-Germanism, pan-Arabism, pan-Turanism, pan-Islamism and pan-Asianism (see also NATIONALISM).

In 1900 the first Pan-African Conference took place in London. It was organized by the African Association founded by Henry Sylvester Williams. The preparatory session in 1899 was attended by, among others, Booker T. Washington. The actual conference had about 60 participants from the USA, the West Indies, Britain and Africa, including W.E.B. Du Bois and Bishop Alexander Walters. The resolutions dealt with slavery, forced labour, segregation and other violations of human rights. In an appeal 'to the nations of the world' the conference declared:

> The problem of the twentieth century is the problem of the colour line, the question as to how far the differences of race . . . are going to be made . . . the basis of denying to over half the world the right of sharing to their utmost ability the opportunities and privileges of modern mankind. (Geiss, 1974, p. 190)

After World War I, the Pan-African Congress movement began. This was a series of meetings held in 1919 (Paris), 1921 (London, Brussels and Paris), 1923 (London and Lisbon), 1927 (New York), 1945 (Manchester) and 1974 (Dar es Salaam). The prime mover and main organizer of the conferences in the inter-war years was W.E.B. Du Bois. The most important of these was the fifth Pan-African Congress in Manchester in 1945; many of those who took part (for example, Obafemi Awolowo, Hastings Banda, Jomo Kenyatta and Kwame Nkrumah) became major political figures in post-independence Africa. The Manchester resolutions set the agenda for mainstream pan-African thinking thereafter. The major positions of past Pan-African Congresses had been to promote the well-being and unity of people of African origin, to demand their self-determination, to insist on the abolition of racial discrimination and to condemn capitalism. The Manchester Congress also declared: 'the struggle for political power by colonial and subject peoples is the first step towards, and the necessary prerequisite to, complete social, economic, and political emancipation' (Legum, 1976, p. 137). This shift to anti-colonialism was particularly relevant for Africa and the Caribbean which were still under imperial rule.

Ghana's attainment of independence in 1957 reinforced this dramatic shift to an anti-colonial struggle and a continental focus in pan-African thinking. As a result, the All-African Peoples' Organization launched by Ghana's Kwame Nkrumah, which met first in Accra in 1958 and later had meetings in Tunis and Cairo, confined full participation to residents of Africa. The All-African Peoples' Conferences were not restricted to governments but included liberation movements and trade unionists. Their resolutions provided a further advance in pan-African thinking: there should be the 'African personality' in international affairs and 'neo-colonialism' must be fought.

The biggest ambition of continental pan-Africanism was to create an all-African suprastate. The creation of the Organization of African Unity (OAU) in 1963 was a modest compromise because, in part, its charter includes the following stipulations: non-interference in the internal affairs of member states as well as respect for the sovereignty and territorial integrity of each state. This intergovernmental organization has made no significant moves towards creating a United States of Africa. Indeed, within the OAU, there is the added tension between pan-Africanism and pan-Arabism.

A distinction can be made between *pan-African-*

ism of liberation and *pan-Africanism of integration.* Pan-Africanism of liberation is a solidarity in pursuit of liberty and self-determination. Pan-Africanism of integration is a solidarity in pursuit of regional, economic and political integration. Pan-Africanism of liberation is a success story: a united African voice of anti-colonialism and anti-apartheid has helped to mobilize the rest of the world. Pan-Africanism of integration is still, as we have noted, a failure.

Trans-Atlantic pan-Africanism declined in the second half of the twentieth century. Nevertheless, W.E.B. Du Bois from the USA and George Padmore from the Caribbean became Ghanaian citizens after independence. Malcolm X and other black muslims were often both pan-Islamist and pan-African. The civil rights movement in the USA had links with the politics of decolonization in Africa. The Rastafari movement in Jamaica identified with Ethiopia as the Promised Land and Haile Selassie as Divine King. Cultural pan-Africanism in the diaspora ranged from adopting African religious rituals to the popularity of African hairstyles, from adopting African personal names to the proclamation of an African substitute for Christmas (the African-American festival of *Kwaanza*, based on a Swahili word for *beginning*). Artistic trans-Atlantic pan-Africanism has included the periodical festivals of arts and cultures which have been held in both Africa and the diaspora. The most famous of these artistic events was FESTAC held in Lagos, Nigeria, in 1976. Singers, dancers, poets, dramatists, drummers and others converged on Lagos.

After a break of nearly 30 years, a 'call to the sixth Pan-African Congress' was issued by radical diaspora intellectuals who had become disenchanted with continental pan-Africanism. More than 500 delegates and observers met in Dar es Salaam in 1974. It was the first congress to be held in Africa, and although it consisted largely of governmental officials, it also included liberation movements and leading African and diaspora intellectuals. It was thus the most comprehensive of all the Pan-African Congresses. The congress was a major attempt to bring pan-African thinking up to date. While the fifth Pan-African Congress in 1945 had resulted in *narrowing* the pan-African focus to the African continent (instead of the black world as a whole), the sixth congress in 1974 *broadened* the relevant constituency to encompass oppressed people everywhere. In Dar es Salaam, pan-Africanism was trying to become a cornerstone of 'pan-humanism'. One central debate was whether *class* was more salient than *race* in the global struggle against oppression and exploitation.

Pan-African movements

Pan-Africanism has seldom been a *mass* movement; it is mainly a movement of elites. The main diaspora exception to this was Marcus Garvey's movement. Garvey himself was Jamaican; his followers were mainly African-Americans in their hundreds of thousands. The movement's goals were pan-African, but no mass membership existed outside the USA.

Pan-Africanism in the *continental* sense has also failed to become a mass movement. The inspiration of pan-Africanism, in this sense, is not *nationhood* but *continental* solidarity; however, for this very reason, the impact of continental pan-Africanism has been thwarted by the cultural, economic and political diversity among various African states which manifested themselves after independence. For most Nigerians, Ethiopians and Zambians, to name but a few, pan-Africanism was bound to be of lower priority than 'nation-building' within each country. That, however, leads to another problem: pan-Africanism and this kind of nation-building are at odds with each other. As Nyerere put it:

the truth is that as each of us develops his own state we raise more and more barriers between ourselves. We entrench differences which we have inherited from the colonial period, and develop new ones. Most of all, we develop a national pride which could easily be inimical to the development of a pride in Africa. (Nyerere, 1968, p. 211)

Pan-Africanism has never been a unified movement, for in addition to the splits already mentioned, there have always been liberal and radical versions, representing different organizations. There is also the diaspora/indigenous split. There have always been the black/Arab divide and the francophone/anglophone split. Except for the sixth Pan-African Congress in Dar es Salaam in 1974, all the other tendencies (including those leading up to the formation of the OAU) have manifested these stresses. Nevertheless large numbers of people identify with the ideals of pan-Africanism without joining any pan-African organization.

Pan-Africanism as an ideology

Pan-Africanism is less than a full ideology because it is neither a systematic explanation of political phenomena nor a specific programme for political change. There is no theorist who has provided a set of interrelated principles and definitions that conceptually organize, in a systematic fashion, the condition of Africans and those of the diaspora. Not even W.E.B. Du Bois and Kwame Nkrumah, for all their writings on pan-Africanism, provide such an ideology. There is also disagreement over what pan-Africanism is. Some have claimed that its constituent concepts are the following: Africa as the true homeland of all persons of African origin wherever they now are; solidarity among people of African origin; belief in a distinct 'African personality'; rehabilitation of Africa's past and respect for African culture; Africa for the Africans in terms of sovereignty; and the hope for a united Africa. However, based on the resolutions of the Pan-African Congresses, it could be justifiably claimed that there are only four essential components of pan-Africanism:

1 a concern with the common problems of all African peoples wherever they may be;
2 self-determination for all African peoples;
3 pride in and of things African; and
4 insisting that the economic system governing African peoples be socialistic.

There is significantly more consensus behind 1, 2 and 3 than behind 4. Although pan-Africanism is not as yet a complete ideology, it does constitute a set of interrelated ideas and values comprehensive enough to add up to a world-view in search of a thinker.

Reading

Ajala, A. 1973: *Pan-Africanism: Evolution, Progress and Prospects.*
Du Bois, W.E.B. 1965: *The World and Africa: An Inquiry into the Part which Africa has Played in World History.*
Geiss, I. 1974: *The Pan-African Movement: A History of Pan-Africanism in America, Europe and Africa,* trans. A. Keep.
Legum, C. 1976: *Pan-Africanism: A Short Political Guide.*
Mazrui, A.A. 1977: *Africa's International Relations: The Diplomacy of Dependency and Change.*
Nkrumah, K. 1963: *Africa Must Unite.*
Nyerere, J. 1968: *Freedom and Socialism.*
Padmore, G. 1972: *Pan-Africanism or Communism.*
Resolutions and Selected Speeches from the Sixth Pan-African Congress 1976. Dar es Salaam: Tanzania Publishing House.

Thompson, V.B. 1969: *Africa and Unity: The Evolution of Pan-Africanism.*

ALI A. MAZRUI AND A.M. SHARAKIYA

pan-Arabism As an ideology pan-Arabism is a development of Arab NATIONALISM, which first appeared as a literary and political phenomenon in the Arab provinces of the Ottoman Empire towards the end of the nineteenth century. Arab nationalism itself came into being partly as a consequence of the literary and linguistic revival movement known as the *nahda*, which began in Greater Syria. A wave of rediscovery, editing and publishing of classical Arabic texts, and lexicographical activity, encouraged Arab intellectuals to reflect on their past greatness and their present weakness under Ottoman domination.

By the beginning of the twentieth century the legitimacy of Ottoman rule over the Arab provinces was beginning to be challenged by Muslims and Christians alike. A number of Muslim writers and thinkers, increasingly conscious of the relative backwardness of the Islamic world, and more specifically the Ottoman Empire, *vis-à-vis* Europe, seized on the notion that the decline and decay of ISLAM was due to the Turks' usurpation of the caliphate. If Islam was to be revitalized, some thought, the caliphate should be restored to the Arabs, and, later, by extension, that the Arab lands should be liberated from the 'shackles of Turkish rule'. For their part a number of Christian intellectuals, in company with some more secular-minded Muslims, believed that the ideals of liberty and equality, on which they considered the prosperity and progress of contemporary Europe to be based, were largely incompatible with the style and substance of Ottoman rule.

In theory, and to a considerable extent in practice, the Ottoman Empire was a theocratic Islamic state, in which the majority group, the Sunni Muslims, enjoyed a privileged status which the empire's religious ideology made it difficult to challenge. If language, ethnicity and co-residence, rather than religion, were to become the criteria of association, Arabs could associate with each other politically on equal terms across the boundaries of religion and sect, and a secular society would come into being in which no group had a built-in superiority over any other. Since it envisaged a society in which they would not be inferior in status to anyone else, this notion was particularly attractive to Arab Christians, especially the Greek Orthodox of Greater Syria, who regarded themselves as in some sense more authentically Arab than their Maronite and Catholic co-religionists, since the closeness of the latter's association with France as their patron and protector was regarded as compromising both their independence and their 'Arabness'.

As World War I drew nearer, it became clear that some Arabs were prepared to seek the aid of Western powers, notably Great Britain, to achieve their aim of independence from the Ottomans; paradoxically, in Egypt, which had been under British occupation since 1882, many nationalists had wanted to enlist the Ottomans' help to obtain independence from Britain. Here it is worth mentioning that at this stage the notion of an 'Arab nation' was generally confined to Greater Syria; thus an Egyptian who wanted to take part in the first Arab National Congress in Paris 1913 was refused permission to contribute to the discussions.

The Ottoman Empire collapsed at the end of World War I, but although many Arabs had fought with Britain in the Arab Revolt against the Ottomans assuming that they would gain some sort of political independence as a result, this goal was not to be achieved for several decades. In addition, rather than creating a single political entity in the former Arab provinces of the Ottoman Empire as some Arabs had hoped, the peace settlement brought into being the states which are now Iraq, Syria, Lebanon, Israel/Palestine and Transjordan (now Jordan). These territories were designated mandates and assigned to the tutelage of Britain and France, under the overall supervision of the League of Nations. Thus, with the exception of Saudi Arabia and northern Yemen, the whole Arab world was now under European control: Egypt, although not a mandated territory, was ruled by Britain in a somewhat similar manner, while Libya had been an Italian colony since 1910, Morocco and Tunisia French protectorates since 1881 and 1912, and Algeria had been annexed to France since 1848.

It was not until the interwar period, largely under the influence of the writings of the educationalist and publicist Sati' al-Husri (1882–1968), that the idea of an 'Arab nation', perhaps the most important tenet of pan-Arab ideology, began to take shape. It is important to stress this, since certain features of Arab nationalist thought have been implanted in the minds of subsequent generations as if they were self-evident, quasi-eternal truths, in such a way as to obscure the recentness of their origin. Hence pan-Arabism, postulating the *a priori* existence of a single Arab *nation*, was formulated at precisely the moment when the modern Arab *state* system came into being.

The basic tenets of pan-Arabism are that the Arab world, from the Atlantic to the (Arab) Gulf, forms one NATION; that this nation has been artificially divided, first by the Ottomans and more recently by imperialism and Zionism, and that its regeneration can only be achieved by Arab unity. In al-Husri's formulation, 'the Arabs' are defined in the following somewhat totalitarian terms:

> Everyone who speaks Arabic is an Arab. Everyone who is affiliated with these people is an Arab. If he does not know this or if he does not cherish his Arabism, then we must study the reasons for his position. It may be a result of ignorance – then we must tell him the truth. It may be because he is unaware or deceived – then we must awaken him and reassure him. It may be a result of selfishness – then we must work to limit his selfishness.

Of course, the notion that the Arabs are a single nation is an assertion rather than the expression of a historical reality. Apart from the fact that 'the nation' as an idea does not antedate the latter part of the eighteenth century, even in the heyday of the medieval Arab empire, there is only a very limited sense in which this particular region was ever a single *political* entity. The most cursory glance at a historical atlas or chronological handbook shows the rise and fall of numerous territorially based dynasties in areas such as 'the Maghrib', 'Tunis', 'Egypt', 'Syria' and so forth. Of course, as all contemporary analysts of nationalism have indicated, committed nationalist historiography, in this case Arab nationalist historiography, must be considered as a contribution to the making of a myth rather than part of an objective historical discourse.

Perhaps the two most visible manifestations of pan-Arabism have been 'Nasserism' and Ba'thism. Jamal Abd al-Nasir (Nasser), the leader of the Free Officers, who seized power in Egypt in 1952 and subsequently became the country's president until his premature death in 1970, had a deep distrust of political parties and did not himself build up any formal pan-Arab organizations, but the founders of the Ba'th party in Syria in the 1940s saw their organization as genuinely pan-Arab, and in the 1950s and 1960s party branches were established in each Arab country, or 'region of the Arab nation', in party parlance. Nasser's appeal was probably less purely ideological, in the sense that the support he attracted stemmed from his achievement as the first Arab leader to present a significant challenge to the West; he was above all a populist-nationalist, merging himself with 'the nation', both Egyptian and Arab. The most concrete political expression of pan-Arabism was the United Arab Republic of Egypt and Syria, which lasted from 1958 to 1961; initially rushed into as a desperate expedient by the Syrian Ba'th who feared the effect of communist popularity in Syria on its own fortunes, it rapidly turned into a device for Egypt to exploit its smaller partner economically, and as a result became profoundly unpopular in Syria.

In spite of the Ba'thist slogan of 'One Arab nation with an eternal mission' the reality has been very different. The Ba'th Party split in 1966, and its two separate wings have been in power in Damascus since that time and in Baghdad since 1968. The 1970s and 1980s were characterized by a bitter battle for ideological legitimacy between the two rival factions; in an important sense, the legitimacy of the one was defined in terms of the illegitimacy of the other. In fact, the only logical destiny for the two states (in terms of the ideology each professed) would have been the merger of the one with the other. In both cases, political power was seized by small well-organized political factions, whose members shared elements of a common ideology but whose principal concern was to seize power. When they had done so, both in Damascus and Baghdad, they proceeded to set up mass political parties to give themselves legitimacy. The ideology of pan-Arabism is sufficiently vague to have enabled both these regimes to justify a wide variety of political activity in its terms – so that Syria's incursion into Lebanon in 1976 and Iraq's invasion of Iran in 1980 could both be characterized as 'preserving the integrity of the Arab nation'.

On a popular level, the idea of Arab unity has had considerable attraction in the Arab world, since most of the population speaks Arabic, is Muslim, and does share a wide range of common cultural assumptions and social attitudes. In practical terms, however, the weakness, lack of legitimacy and the profoundly undemocratic or anti-democratic nature of almost all Arab regimes, coupled with the fact that the existing individual national states are at very different stages of socioeconomic and political development, has meant that however immediately desirable the idea may be, the practical realization of pan-Arabism is as far away today as it was when al-Husri first formulated it in the 1920s. In addition, it is probably true to say that the pursuit, or the excuse, of pan-Arabism, has had a generally negative effect on the process of state and nation building in the Arab world, since it has tended to focus attention on a distant external enemy rather than on the glaring problems of poverty, inequality and the absence of the rule of law within the existing states.

In addition, one of the most visible features of political developments in the region over the past few decades – underlined by the Gulf crisis of 1990–1 – is the gradual adoption of more autonomous and inward-looking policies on the part of all the Arab regimes, notwithstanding loud public claims to the contrary. Events in one Arab state no longer necessarily assume the character of matters of fundamental concern to the other Arab states, unless their own vital interests are thought to be at stake, with the result that 'national' rather than 'Arab' priorities have largely taken over the political arena, indicating that the 'artificial' nation-states of the Arab world are gradually turning into discrete entities – like the states of South America – and growing apart rather than closer together. It is only in this light that any sense can be made of the feebleness of the 'Arab' response to the Israeli invasion of Lebanon in 1982, the ambiguous attitudes of the Arab states towards Palestine and the Palestinians, and the generally rational and 'political' responses of the various Arab states to Saddam Husain's invasion of Kuwait.

Although some Arab political writers defend the concept of pan-Arabism, it must be regarded largely as a spent force; the Arab League, founded in 1944, is more a forum for the discussion of matters of common concern than a mechanism for Arab integration. The heyday of pan-Arabism came to an end in June 1967, when the balloon of nationalist rhetoric was massively punctured by Israel's devastating defeat of Egypt, Jordan and Syria. Palestine is perhaps the quintessential symbol of the failure of pan-Arabism, in the sense of providing a constant reminder of the continuing inability of the Arab states to present a common or united front which might bring the issue towards resolution. The reason for this failure is not hard to find; however 'artificial' the boundaries which were drawn up before and after World War I, these have now been in place for some 70 years, and bodies of vested interests have grown up around them which make the maintenance of the existence of a separate Lebanon, or a separate Jordan – not to mention a separate Kuwait – take precedence over the pursuit of the idea of a wider suprastate. Whether this phenomenon is to be deplored or applauded is less important than that it should be acknowledged as taking place – or, more accurately, as having taken place.

Reading

Ajami, Fuad 1981: *The Arab Predicament: Arab Political Thought and Practice since 1967*.
Antonius, G. 1938 (*1969*): *The Arab Awakening*.
Haim, S. 1962 (*1976*): *Arab Nationalism: An Anthology*.
Hourani, A.H. 1962 (*1983*): *Arabic Thought in the Liberal Age, 1798–1939*.
—— 1991: *A History of the Arab Peoples*.
Tibi, B. 1981: *Arab Nationalism; A Critical Enquiry*.
Zubaida, S. 1988: *Islam, the People and the State*.

PETER SLUGLETT

paradigm   Most generally defined as a pattern, template or exemplar, this concept is important for twentieth-century social thought in two contexts: (1) in the deployment of what came to be called 'paradigm case arguments'; (2) for its centrality in T.S. Kuhn's enormously influential *The Structure of Scientific Revolutions* (1962).

Paradigm case arguments were used by the Oxford school of LINGUISTIC PHILOSOPHY in mid-century and they, or close relatives of them, are arguably to be found in the work of the late Wittgenstein also. The argument infers from the fact that a word is taught by reference to clear (paradigm) cases that examples of the thing or state (such as material objects, free will) denoted by the word must exist. It seems open to the obvious objection that our language game may be grounded in mystification or illusion, as with the use of the word 'witch' in the seventeenth century.

Kuhn's use of the term 'paradigm' in *The Structure of Scientific Revolutions* has been subjected to an exhaustive analysis by Margaret Masterman who differentiates 21 senses of the term in the first edition of the book. In his postscript to his second edition (*1970*), Kuhn himself distinguishes two main meanings: (a) 'the entire constellation of beliefs, values, techniques and so on shared by the members of a given community', that is, a disciplinary matrix; and (b) 'one sort of element in that constellation, the concrete puzzle-solutions which, employed as models or examples, can replace explicit rules as a basis for the solution of the remaining puzzles of normal science', that is, an exemplar. Examples of the latter are Isaac Newton's *Principia Mathematica* (1687) and John Dalton's *New System of Chemical Philosophy* (1808). These provide the paradigms for the work of normal science – resources to be exploited, not hypotheses to be tested – in the elaboration and development of the disciplinary tradition. Eventually, when sufficient anomalies appear, a crisis will occur and a period of revolutionary science begin until a new paradigm is formed, around which the (now changed) scientific community can once more cohere. Kuhn's account generated a vast secondary literature in which it was argued *inter alia* that normal science was not nearly as monolithic as Kuhn had described it, that his claims about the 'incommensurability' of paradigms were overstated, that revolutions were (or at least could be) quite rational affairs, not quasi-religious conversions, and that his work suffered from a systematic realist/superidealist equivocation.

I only have space here to deal with the last two questions. Kuhn uses in several places, in a self-consciously paradoxical way, the metaphor of scientists after a revolutionary upheaval working in 'different worlds'. Now it seems clear that after a revolutionary upheaval it makes sense to talk of scientists working in a different cognitive or social world – in the terminology of modern critical realism, in the transitive dimension – but they are still describing and seeking to explain for the most part the same object or natural world – that is, in the intransitive dimension. It is Kuhn's failure to make this distinction which is the source of his paradox. Secondly, Kuhn formulates in a number of places criteria for judging a new paradigm 'later', including number of problems solved, accuracy of predictions, etc., but draws back from calling it 'better'. This seems doubly wrong. In the first place it ignores the possibility of historical regression. Secondly it overlooks the consideration that epistemic relativism might be coupled, especially if conjoined with ontological realism, with judgemental rationalism (as argued by critical realists). Kuhn's criteria for historical lateness are in fact instead (partial) criteria for rational choice.

Reading
Austin, John 1961: *Philosophical Papers.*
Bhaskar, Roy 1989: *Reclaiming Reality*, esp. ch. 3.
Gellner, E. 1968: *Words and Things.*
Kuhn, T.S. 1962 (*1970*): *The Structure of Scientific Revolutions*, 2nd edn.
Lakatos, I. 1970: Falsification and the methodology of scientific research programmes. In *Criticism and the Growth of Knowledge*, ed. I. Lakatos and A. Musgrave.
Masterman, M. 1970: The nature of a paradigm. In *Criticism and the Growth of Knowledge*, ed. I. Lakatos and A. Musgrave.

ROY BHASKAR

participant observation In this method, the researcher is involved in the system of relations, the community or the organization which he or she studies. The sociologist endeavours to take part in the experiences of the actors, joins them in their daily life, and occasionally becomes one of them. Most anthropological studies rely on this method, since it is important that the researcher should be accepted and recognized by those who are studied and who belong to a different culture. Sometimes it is a member of the studied group itself who becomes a sociologist. In the large sphere of influence of the school of CHICAGO SOCIOLOGY, some important sociological monographs have given a preferred place to participant observation. For instance, F. W. Whyte was able to describe and analyse the life of gangs of teenagers by participating in the inhabitants' life in a poor Italian suburb of an American city. Moreover, he tried to derive some general principles from this method: such as favouring a few regular informants, not aiming for complete assimilation, avoiding any direct intervention in the group's affairs. The method has been used in various fields. The early studies in the sociology of work at the Western Electric plant used this method. In the 1960s new theoretical movements, keen to understand the social interaction and the LABELLING process, brought new life to the method of participant observation. H. S. Becker studied some types of marginal behaviour by sharing the experience of a few groups, and notably Erving Goffman renewed the analysis and description of social interaction and the social 'show' by becoming a full member in the daily life of exchanges.

The methodological status of participant observation is far from obvious. On one hand, participant observation is essential to the sociologist in so far as the researcher has to be in contact with the subjects of study and to understand their orientations and sensibilities. Any such enquiry involves the researcher in a relation with the people or society under scrutiny and this is also a social relationship.

On the other hand, participant observation does not provide the means to control the techniques the researcher uses, or the changes in the subject studied introduced by the researcher's own presence. The researcher often has a higher social status than that of the actors studied, and the search for a close relationship does not necessarily avert ethnocentric prejudices. Or the sociologist may identify with the actors and be turned into their advocate and ideologist, more or less manipulated by the group. Participant observation may appear as a necessary phase of the study, but without being a reliable method for the whole, since it is not independent of the spontaneous sociology of the subjects, and the distortions this introduces, which it is unable to evaluate or control.

However, in spite of these methodological weak points, many of the most convincing works in sociology use this research method as a basis. In these cases, the sociologist or anthropologist has undertaken an analysis and criticism of his or her own values and cultural background, and has employed the method with talent and above all with a desire to regard himself or herself, too, as the object of the research.

See also ETHNOMETHODOLOGY.

Reading
Becker, H.S. 1963: *Outsiders: Studies in the Sociology of Deviance.*
Goffman, E. 1961: *Asylums: Essays on the Social Situation of Mental Patients and Other Inmates.*
——1967: *Interaction Ritual: Essays in Face-to-Face Behavior.*
Lewis, O. 1961: *The Children of Sanchez: Autobiography of a Mexican Family.*
Roethlisberger, F.J. and Dickson, W.J. 1939 (*1961*): *Management and the Workers: An Account of a Research Program Conducted by the Western Electric Company, Hawthorne Works, Chicago.*
Whyte, W.F. 1943 (*1965*): *Street Corner Society: The Social Structure of an Italian Slum.*
——1951: Observational field-work methods. In *Research Methods in Social Relations: With Special Reference to Prejudice,* ed. M. Jahoda, pp. 496–501.

FRANÇOIS DUBET

participation An ambiguous concept in the social sciences, participation can have a strong and a weak meaning. In the first, it means that given the size and the complexity of contemporary mass societies, the centralization of political power, the growth of bureaucracy, and the concentration of economic power, the traditional guarantees of democracy need to be strengthened, protected and extended in order to counterbalance the tendency for an ever-increasing number of decisions affecting people's lives to be made by small groups; these groups are often remote and not easily identifiable or called to account, since they act in the name of the state, of a local authority, or of some large business corporation. (See also POLITICAL PARTICIPATION.)

In this sense, and in so far as politics is concerned, the principle of participation is as old as democracy itself, but it is made vastly more difficult by the scale and comprehensiveness of modern government and by the need for clear-cut and rapid decisions – failure to produce which is no less a matter for protest by those who demand greater participation. In the postwar period the tendency has been to extend participation to fields other than politics, for instance to higher education, where it was the major demand of all student protests in the late 1960s and again in the late 1980s; and, of much greater importance and scope, to industry, business and, since the late 1970s, to local government. It is at this stage that the 'weak meaning' of participation began to develop. The practice by which employees take a greater part in management decisions was introduced in the 1950s by the federal government in West Germany; it has spread in various forms to other countries in Western Europe (Italy's similar decision dates from the early 1970s, France's from the late 1980s) and has been adopted as an objective, still not entirely fulfilled, by the European Community to express what it calls 'the democratic imperative', defined as the principle that 'those who will be substantially affected by decisions made by social and political institutions must be involved in the making of these decisions.' In the UK the very influential Bullock report on INDUSTRIAL DEMOCRACY, proposing a variant of the German system of *Mitbestimmung*, was rejected by the employers. Since then the trade unions have resolutely failed to agree on a common policy. Other forms of participation, notably the growth of interest in cooperatives and profit-sharing and share-ownership schemes, have superseded the EC initiative. Within the EC, the concept of 'social partners' has attempted to provide a platform for participation from the top down.

More recently, a broader workers' participation in technological change appeared as a realistic solution to the numerous conflicts that the widespread adoption of 'information technologies' was creating. In order to prevent or reduce the importance of conflict, 'participative methods' of technological change have been developed, varying according to the different socioeconomic conditions and to the strengths of unions in Europe, the USA and Japan: thus 'participative design', 'participation in technological choices' have become buzzphrases widely used but extremely vague in content and meaning. The solutions proposed to avoid the expected consequences of technological change can be divided into two categories: procedural and substantive. The first are more a normative set of regulations based on legislation, standards and rules, mostly advocated by unions and concerned with the methods of introducing new technologies. Substantive issues relate more to operational conditions once technological change has been implemented. The fundamental aim of participative methods is to establish a strong consensus around technological change, by promising a more democratic decision-making process and providing information to the unions at an early stage of the process, long before the final decision is to be taken and while it is still possible to influence the choice; by creating joint union and management bodies to discuss, negotiate and supervise the changes, with the possibility of consulting independent experts; and by stimulating users' involvement in the design of future organization and, in part, in the use of the technology.

Substantive issues are oriented to the protection of existing status, salary and qualifications, and ensuring that the same level of employment will be maintained; inhouse displacement is allowed only if associated with substantial retraining programmes.

In spite of significant results, in particular a reduction in the number and intensity of actual, visible social conflicts, it appears that 'participative methods' reveal some new problems, more difficult to solve.

Reading
Pateman, Carol 1970: *Participation and Democratic Theory*.
Poole, Michael 1978: *Workers' Participation in Industry*.
MARCO DIANI

participation, political *See* POLITICAL PARTICIPATION

party, political *See* POLITICAL PARTY

patriarchy Women are systematically disadvantaged in twentieth-century society in most arenas of social life. Patriarchy is a social system in which men dominate, oppress and exploit women. It is a concept which emphasizes the interrelatedness between the various ways in which men have POWER over women. The social relations through which men dominate women have been considered to include reproduction, violence, sexuality, work, culture and the state (Walby, 1990). Others consider that GENDER inequality is best theorized in ways other than through the concept of patriarchy.

The traditional approach to patriarchy saw it as based on men's position as head of a household and family. More recent usage has tended, though not exclusively, to broaden the meaning so that this household form is merely one aspect or one form of patriarchy. All theories of patriarchy consider that there is a fundamental division of interests between most men and most women as a result of the social structuring of gender relations. A few of these make reference to the biological aspects of reproduction, for instance, Firestone (1970), but this is uncommon, especially in more recent writings. A more frequent feature of such analyses is the control of women through sexuality, with reference to the institution of heterosexuality (Rich, 1980) and such phenomena as pornography (Dworkin, 1981). Male violence as the basis of male control over women is the focus of some analyses of patriarchy (Brownmiller, 1976; Daly, 1978). Other analyses have a more materialist emphasis, with an examination of how men benefit from women's labour, both as unpaid housework and as poorly paid work in the labour market. These latter accounts often integrate an analysis of patriarchy with other structures of social inequality such as capitalism (Hartmann, 1979).

The concept of patriarchy is controversial. Some critics, for instance, have suggested that it leads to an underemphasis on other forms of social inequality such as class and 'race'. This is countered by writers such as Hartmann, who combines an analysis of patriarchy with that of capitalism in a dual-systems theory.

Essentialism, false universalism and ahistoricism are further criticisms which suggest that the term does not enable the variety of forms of gender relations between cultures, ethnic groups and different historical periods to be adequately appreciated. In response, accounts have been developed which do analyse the variety of the forms of patriarchy and how these change over time.

The usefulness of the concept is that it provides a focus to theorize gender relations which takes into account the interconnectedness of the different aspects of women's oppression by men.

Reading
Daly, Mary 1978: *Gyn/Ecology: The Metaethics of Radical Feminism.*
Mies, Maria 1986: *Patriarchy and Accumulation on a World Scale: Women in the International Division of Labour.*
Rich, Adrienne 1980: Compulsory heterosexuality and lesbian existence. *Signs* 5.4, 631–60.
Walby, Sylvia 1990: *Theorizing Patriarchy.*

SYLVIA WALBY

pattern variables These are types of orientation to action, roles or social relations which present some dichotomous choices in giving meaning to a situation (Parsons and Shils, 1962, pp. 76–7). They were originally proposed by Parsons (1951, pp. 58–67), who systematized, elaborated and extended the Weberian ideal-typical approach to society by arguing that social actions and roles can be classified in terms of five dimensions which present polar alternatives. They can be used to compare cultures or subsystems and groups within a society; but one of their most important and frequent applications has been the description of the ideal-typical social structure of 'traditional' and 'modern' societies (see MODERNIZATION). Particularism versus universalism is one of them. Particularistic actions are carried out for specific actors in terms of their particular situation which cannot be transferred (friendship, family relations). Universalistic actions can be defined for a more general category of persons according to objective criteria (salesman–client relation). A second pattern variable is diffusion versus specificity. Some relations are functionally diffuse in that they cover a series of unspecified dimensions (friendship, family roles). Others are functionally specific in that their content is clearly definable and delimited (bureaucratic roles).

A third pattern variable opposes ascription to achievement. Some roles are accessible and provide status according to and depending on performance. Others accrue to actors and provide status according to their physical and non-achievable social

attributes (class, sex, age, family, and so on). Fourth, affectivity versus affective neutrality. Some roles provide immediate gratification in the very performance of their expected activities whereas others postpone gratification and become purely instrumental for an ulterior goal. Finally, there is orientation towards collective interests versus orientation towards private interests. Some roles are exclusively oriented towards the collective interest (public servant); some others entail the pursuit of private interest (entrepreneurs). Parsons (1951, pp. 176–7) claims that in traditional societies roles tend to be ascriptive, diffuse, particularistic and affective. In industrial societies, on the contrary, roles which are performance oriented, universalistic, affectively neutral and specific tend to predominate. The transition from traditional society to industrial society implies, in general, a progressive expansion of the sphere of application of the latter type of roles and a contraction of the sphere of application of the former. Parsons leaves out the last pattern variable, probably because of some difficulties in making a clear-cut argument in either direction. Hoselitz (1965, p. 40) has made the point that in underdeveloped societies self-orientation predominates among the ruling elites, whereas in advanced societies collectivity orientation predominates. But it can equally be argued that actors in underdeveloped societies tend to be more oriented towards collective interests than actors in individualistic industrial societies, who tend to seek their private interest.

Reading
Hoogvelt, A.M.M. 1976: *The Sociology of Developing Societies.*
Parsons, T. 1967: Pattern variables revisited: a response to Robert Dubin. In *Sociological Theory and Modern Society.*

JORGE LARRAIN

peace A strict conception of peace, as the antithesis of WAR, the 'beating of swords into ploughshares', is more fruitful, intellectually, than one which extends its meaning to make it synonymous with utopia.

Much twentieth-century thinking about peace has taken the form of recipes for the creation or transformation of international institutions in response to the two world wars. Inis Claude (1956) listed six approaches to peace through international organization: peaceful settlement of disputes, collective security, disarmament, the 'grand debate', trusteeship and functionalism. Later, in the third edition of his book, he added a seventh, preventive diplomacy. Peaceful settlement involves persuading states to postpone violent responses to situations of high tension, so that passions may cool, facts may be impartially investigated and alternative solutions considered. Collective security, more ambitiously, stresses the 'indivisibility of peace', promising to deter acts of aggression, from any quarter, by committing all states to resist them. Disarmament assumes that arms races threaten peace by fostering belligerence and (in a nuclear age) making unintended war more likely. Claude is sceptical about these three approaches, which all go back to the founding of the League of Nations and earlier. He sees more potential in the others. The value of the 'grand debate', epitomized by the proceedings of the United Nations General Assembly, lies in providing states with feedback about how their policies appear to others, thus inducing adjustment and compromise. Trusteeship, as Claude defines it, includes all attempts, from the League onwards, at the international supervision of colonial rule. His assessment of the remarkably successful United Nations pressures for decolonization as 'possibly the last chance for European civilization to make up for its shady past in dealing with non-European peoples' now seems excessively sanguine. Certainly, decolonization has not brought peace in its wake. Functionalism, expounded by David Mitrany (1946), holds that if experts of a variety of nationalities, free from foreign office interference, are allowed to collaborate in solving international economic, social and other problems, they will, in time, lay the foundations of a more lasting peace by generating new international loyalties in the relevant populations to replace the divisive pull of the old national ones. Finally, preventive diplomacy represents the innovative UN responses to crises through the dispatch of forces, missions and presences, and the active intervention of the Secretary-General, following the dramatic precedent set in the Suez crisis of 1956.

Unlike world federalists such as Emery Reves (1945), Claude clearly believes that peace is possible without attempting to create a world state. Strong support for this view came from a study by Karl Deutsch and his colleagues (1957) examining the growth and disintegration of communities in the 'North Atlantic area' since the Middle Ages. They sought to identify 'security-communities' characterized by the ability to ensure, for a 'long' time, dependable expectations that social problems will be resolved without resort to large-scale physical force, and they show that amalgamation (including federation) is neither necessary nor sufficient for the establishment of such communities. Thus Canada and the United States form a 'pluralistic security-community', and the Scandinavian countries (and perhaps now most of Western Europe, including non-members of the European Community) another. The crucial elements are communication networks, multiple points of contact and 'institutions and practices' that are both reliable and flexible.

Other peace theorists have addressed themselves to the processes by which peace can be brought to highly charged international (and intercommunal) situations. John Burton's device of 'controlled communication', well articulated by Mitchell (1981), approaches human conflict 'as an essentially subjective phenomenon' and therefore as dynamic and malleable. Representatives of the parties to a specific conflict are brought together privately and informally encouraged each to express its own case and listen to the other side doing the same, and eventually to formulate suggestions, not for 'compromise' but for 'resolution'. This emphasis on 'integrative' bargaining fosters a creative approach to conflict resolution, but it would be an unnecessarily stringent view of the latter that would deny any role to 'distributive' bargaining in the peacemaking process.

See also INTERNATIONAL RELATIONS; PACIFISM.

Reading
Claude, I.L. 1956 (*1964*): *Swords into Plowshares*, 3rd edn.
Curle, A. 1971: *Making Peace*.
Deutsch, K.W., Burrell, S.A., Kann, R.A., Lee, M., Lichterman, M., Lindgren, R.E., Loewenheim, F. L. and Van Wagenen, R.W. 1957: *Political Community and the North Atlantic Area*.
Hinsley, F.H. 1963: *Power and the Pursuit of Peace*.
Mitchell, C.R. 1981: *Peacemaking and the Consultant's Role*.
Mitrany, D. 1946: *A Working Peace System*.

RODERICK C. OGLEY

peace movement Something that can be identified as a peace movement has been in existence in Europe for at least two centuries, if not longer. Yet, unlike other movements, the Labour movement for example, or liberalism, the peace movement has no collective memory (see also COLLECTIVE ACTION). It has always been based on the energies of volunteers and, with the honourable exception of the Quakers, has had no permanent institutions. Each new outburst of peace protest has had to discover for itself its ideas, methods and slogans. There is very little in the way of a continuous peace tradition.

The emergence of a peace movement coincided with the rise of capitalism and the construction of a European states system. Just as economics and politics became separate spheres of activity, so during this period the concept of peace became clearly distinguishable from the concept of war. War became a discrete social activity in two respects. First, it became an external activity directed against other states. This was a period when private armies were eliminated, violence was increasingly removed from domestic, that is internal, social relations, and armed forces were professionalized and monopolized by states. Secondly, war became a temporary activity, an exception, an abnormal state of affairs. With the increase in all kinds of relations and treaties, accepted regulations, congresses and so on among European states – what became known as the 'public law of Europe' – wars became less frequent, alternating with long periods of PEACE. It was out of this experience of peace, both domestically and over long periods, that a body of activity, arguments and campaigns which could be called the peace movement came together to work for what Kant called 'perpetual peace'.

Yet while it is possible to identify a common interest in preventing war in general, or particular wars, the term 'peace movement' covers a wide spectrum of opinions, tendencies, theories, even subjects. Broadly speaking, one can distinguish two strands of peace movement thinking. One strand has been concerned with government policy, with putting forward and campaigning for a variety of proposals, schemes or rules to be carried out or followed by governments in order to develop peaceful mechanisms for regulating relations between states. This approach dates back to the international peace projects of the late eighteenth and early nineteenth centuries put forward by thinkers like Immanuel Kant, Abbé St Pierre, Emeric Crucé or Jeremy Bentham, to name but a few, which envisaged the extension of civil society and the rule of law to the international arena. The establishment of the League of Nations after World

War I and the United Nations after World War II owes much to these proposals.

During the twentieth century, this strand of peace thinking has increasingly focused on disarmament. The (almost) infinite expansion of destructive capabilities, as a result of the application of science and technology to military purposes, has focused the attention of those who oppose war on arms races and the threatening nature of destructive potential. The growth of peace research after World War II has been largely devoted to the study of armaments and methods of limiting them.

The second strand of peace movement thinking has been much more concerned with what one might describe as peace culture, the notion that, however ingenious or ambitious, international peace projects cannot be implemented unless human beings, as individuals and social animals, become more peace-minded. From this perspective, the construction of peace, either within nations or at an international level, is not so much the consequence of the establishment of some kind of governmental or intergovernmental authority responsible for ensuring peace and security; rather it has more to do with individual values and social relationships.

This strand of peace thinking includes the tradition of absolute PACIFISM, that is, the individual commitment to non-violence, to be found among the early Christians, the Quakers whose movement was founded during the English Civil War, conscientious objectors, organizations like War Resisters International, and has been expressed by writers such as Leo Tolstoy and Mahatma Gandhi. It also includes a wide range of theories or beliefs that focus on the social causes of war and militarism.

In the early nineteenth century, the peace movement was often synonymous with the free trade movement. There was a widely held proposition that the elimination of the vestiges of feudalism, the warrior classes, would also eliminate war. Travel, trade and democracy would remove the causes of international misunderstanding. However, the rise of nationalism and militarism in the late nineteenth century called into question these assumptions. Socialist anti-militarists, writers like Rosa Luxemburg or Karl Liebknecht, attributed wars and arms races to capitalist rivalries and to the drive for markets and sources of raw materials. The victory of the working classes was expected to secure peace. 'Do you know what the proletariat is?' asked the French socialist, Jean Jaurès in 1912, 'Masses of men who collectively love peace and abhor war.'

The emergence of the women's peace movement in the twentieth century introduced another element to this strand of peace movement thinking: the notion that the causes of war are rooted in the gender division of modern society and, in particular, can be linked to domestic violence, that is, within the family.

The so-called new peace movement which emerged in Western Europe, and to a lesser extent North America, Japan and Australasia, during the 1980s was probably unprecedented in scale and in the transnational nature of the movement. (Although it is worth noting that the peace movement has always been international; regular European congresses were held in the middle of the nineteenth century.) Some five million people protested against the introduction of a new generation of nuclear weapons in Europe in the autumn of 1981 and again in 1983. A peace movement developed in Eastern Europe as well and was to play an important part in the peaceful revolutions of 1989 which toppled communist regimes and marked the end of the Cold War.

However, the peace movement in the West was very different from the peace movement in the East. The former was primarily a disarmament movement, an anti-nuclear movement. It belonged to the first strand of peace movement thinking and was primarily concerned with policies at an international level. It can perhaps be said that, during the postwar period, the separation between war and peace became even more stark. Overtly, Western society appeared less militarized, there was less emphasis on patriotism, discipline or military education. Missile bases were hidden away in the countryside. War became remote and abstract – partly because war in Europe was unthinkable, and partly because war in the Third World, which was concrete and ever present, became a kind of spectacle, to be observed on television, difficult to distinguish from fictional presentation. Western peace activists were protesting about an external reality, not obviously of immediate relevance to everyday life. This is not to say that there was no interest in the development of a peace culture, but it was under the rubric of anti-nuclearism. Particu-

larly important was the role played by women who established a long-term camp outside the missile base at Greenham Common in pioneering new forms of protest.

In contrast, the movements that emerged in Eastern Europe, like Swords into Ploughshares in East Germany, Freedom and Peace in Poland, the Dialogue group in Hungary and the Independent Peace Association in Czechoslovakia, were much more concerned with immediate domestic issues – militarism in their society (military-patriotic education, conscription, war toys), non-violence, and the link between peace and democracy. For them, concern about nuclear war seemed like an abstract luxury; they were less afraid of dying than of living under totalitarianism, which they considered to be inseparable from war and militarism. They criticized the Western peace movements for an excessive concern with symptoms, such as armaments, rather than causes. In this sense, the East European movements could be said to have rediscovered some of the nineteenth-century traditions of the peace movement.

In the late 1980s, the dialogue between parts of the peace movements in East and West led to some common approaches. On the one hand parts of the Western peace movement put increasing emphasis on 'détente from below', on dialogue between citizen's movements in East and West and the need to support democracy movements as one way of ending the Cold War and initiating a disarmament process. On the other hand, Eastern peace movements and parts of the Eastern democracy movements, particularly Charter 77 in Czechoslovakia, became interested in alternative approaches to European security, the concept of 'common security' and the proposals for strengthening the Conference on Security and Cooperation in Europe, better known as the Helsinki process. This was because European peace projects of this kind potentially offered a framework in which efforts to change society and struggle for democracy could be protected from a military crackdown.

In the aftermath of the Cold War, peace energies have been exhausted. Yet despite the end of East–West confrontation and the beginnings of a disarmament process, perpetual peace has not broken out even in Europe. The rise of nationalism, populism and fundamentalism, the 1991 war in the Gulf, and the conflicts in Yugoslovia seem to herald a turbulent era. Can we expect a fusion of peace ideas as a result of the opening up of Eastern Europe which could provide a conceptual basis for future protest? Or will the ideas of the 1980s be forgotten once again?

Reading
Brock, P. 1968: *Pacifism in the United States.*
Carter, April 1992: *Peace Movements: International Protest and World Politics since 1945.*
Gallie, W.B. 1978: *Philosophers of War and Peace.*
Hinton, J. 1989: *Protests and Visions: Peace Politics in Twentieth Century Britain.*

MARY KALDOR

peasantry The attitude towards peasants in the preindustrial world combined hostility and silence. The term 'peasant' denoted 'a countryman' (from Latin *pais*, countryside), but it carried a powerful negative connotation; acting as a synonym of boorishness it was often used as a word of abuse. In sixteenth-century English the verb 'to peasant' meant to subjugate, while in other European languages the tacit message of the term was similar (Russian *smerd* from the verb 'to stink', Polish *cham* assuming for all peasants the inferior racial origins ascribed in the Bible to the 'sons of Ham', etc.). The *Declinatio Rustico* of medieval Europe defined 'six declensions of the word peasant' as 'villain, rustic, beggar, robber, brigand and looter'. But, as a rule, chronicles simply did not speak of them. Later, in the modern world of industrialization and science, peasants came to be treated as an anachronism in all the basic senses of that term and thereby an irrelevance. With the major exception of Eastern Europe peasants were largely absent from scholarly discourse.

All this changed dramatically with decolonization in the 1950s and awareness of the 'developing societies' in which peasants formed a major part of the population. (See also DEVELOPMENT AND UNDERDEVELOPMENT.) Problems of development planning, perceptions of growing social crises, and famine, brought the issue of peasantry into focus. From the 1960s a rapid development of peasant studies took place all around the globe, posing the issue of the characteristics and the analytical delimitation of this social group. This analytical effort has had broader significance where such topics as 'informal' economies, ecological history, oral culture and civil society are concerned.

As a first approximation we can describe peasants as small agricultural producers who, with the help of simple equipment and the labour of their families, produce mostly for their own consumption, direct or indirect, and for the fulfilment of obligations to holders of political and economic power. A more developed general type would include four interdependent facets:

The peasant family farm as the basic multidimensional unit of social organization The family mostly provides the labour on the farm. The farm mostly provides for the consumption needs of the family and the payments of its dues. Such units are not autarkic; peasants are universally involved in daily exchange of goods and in labour markets. Their economic action is, however, closely interwoven with extramarket social relations. Family division of labour and the consumption needs of the family give rise to particular strategies of survival and use of resources. The family farm operates as the major unit of peasant property, production, consumption, welfare, social reproduction, identity, prestige, sociability and welfare. In it, the individual tends to submit to a formalized family role-behaviour and patriarchal authority.

Land husbandry as the main means of livelihood Peasant farming includes a specific, traditionally defined combination of tasks on a relatively low level of specialization. What would elsewhere be considered different occupations are combined in peasant productive activities. Related to this is informal and family-based vocational training. The impact of nature is particularly important for the livelihood of small production units with limited resources, defining its rhythms: seasonal cycles deeply influence the life of the family, family events are reflected in the dynamics of the farm. Of the forces/factors of production, land and family labour are central – a 'licence' to enter the occupation and a major way in which the local status of the families is defined.

Specific cultural patterns linked to the way of life of a small rural community/neighbourhood The characteristic context is a small and localized community within which most of the peasant needs of social living and social reproduction can be met. Particularities of residence, social network and consciousness are linked and interdependent. Peasantries' cultural features, in the sense of socially determined norms and cognitions, show some characteristic tendencies, such as the pre-eminence of traditional and conformist attitudes (such as the justification of action in terms of past experience and the views of the community), particular norms of inheritance, of solidarity, of exclusion, etc. (See also TRADITION AND TRADITIONALISM.) Peasant culture both reflects and reinforces the characteristics and life experience of a small village community, with its lack of anonymity and its face-to-face relations being related to strong normative controls and the common experience of growing up in a similar physical and social environment affecting the attitudes to 'outsiders'.

The 'underdog' position – the domination of peasantry by outsiders   Peasants as a rule have been kept at arm's length from the social sources of power. Their political subjugation has been interlinked with cultural subordination and economic exploitation through tax, rent, corvée, interest and terms of trade unfavourable to the peasants. Subordination has also entailed repeated attempts by the peasants at self-defence through the extensive use of the 'weapons of the weak', such as economic sabotage, avoidance, boycott, etc., and, in some conditions, of massive revolts which turned peasants into a major revolutionary force of our century.

The four 'facets' suggested must be treated as a Gestalt, the elements of which reinforce each other. When any of the major characteristics is removed from the set, the nature of each of its further components changes. Different schools of thought concerning peasantry have often expressed their diversity of vision through the accentuation of one of the suggested characteristics – treating it as the cutting edge of definition. In this author's view it is the family farm which is the most significant characteristic of peasantry as a social and economic entity.

The next step in unfolding the concept would be to consider its analytical 'margins', that is, to look at social groups which share with the 'hard-core' peasants most but not all of their main characteristics. Analytical marginality does not imply here numerical insignificance or particular 'instability'. Also, such groups share rural environments with the 'hard-core' peasants and may be supplementing them or be supplemented by them within a historical process. Many of them are colloquially referred to as peasants.

The most significant of these groups (ordered by the type of characteristic they do not share with 'fully fledged' peasants) are:

1 Agricultural wage labourers (and also the worker-peasants who adopt a 'man in town, rest of the family on the land' division of labour).
2 Family farmers who use capital-intensive equipment, transforming thereby the nature of the agriculture they engage in. We shall return to this category presently.
3 The village-less peasants – like, for example, some of the squatters at the Latin American agricultural frontiers, and 'gauchos'.
4 The 'uncaptured' peasants, peasant communities penetrated and controlled only to a limited degree by the 'national' networks of state, market and acculturation (in the past, often an armed and independent 'peasantry of the frontiers').

Like every social entity, peasantry exists only as a process. The typology suggested can be used as a yardstick in historical analysis, for instance to 'measure' the extent of peasantization or depeasantization. One should beware, however, of forcing multidirectional changes into schemes which presuppose a necessary one-track development. Considerable differences among peasants, ecological as well as historical, are reflected in diverse regional peasantries.

In so far as social dynamics are concerned one must keep in mind cyclical rhythms which do not lead to changes of social structure but rather reinforce its stability. As to the structural changes, these can be ordered into five analytical categories which, in social actuality, may be parallel or interrelated. These have been:

1 Socioeconomic differentiation, such as polarization of rural wealth followed by mutation of some peasants into capitalist farmers or wage workers.
2 Pauperization, when the increase of rural population in relation to land, without alternative sources of income, leads to an aggregate economic decline for the mass of peasants.
3 'Farmerization', when the family farm proceeds as the major unit of agricultural production while its character changes. Such 'peasant-into-farmer' development is linked to massive investment which ties the family farmer into a capitalist economy via credit, supplies and sales, often organized by agrobusiness. It also relates to specialization and 'narrowing' of the occupational profile of farmers, making them more akin to the urban populations.

4 Collectivization/statization, when the state takes over responsibility for agriculture, structuring it into large production units under governmental control. (One should not overstate here the exceptionality of this form of rural organization. The difference between collectivization in one country and the monopoly of state-controlled boards of trade over the smallholders' produce elsewhere is often only one of degree.)

5 Peasantization by an egalitarian land reform, and at times a repeasantization as peasants' children return to the farm because of state inducement, political pressure or, alternatively, because of new opportunities to do so profitably. The current privatization and redivision of 'collectivized' land in the former USSR etc. would also belong here.

Peasants form part of broader societies and of their histories. The rapid extension of those ties during the last decades has made this issue central to any effort at understanding peasantry. It has often been referred to as one of 'insertion' or of 'subsumption' of peasants. However, peasant particularity does not reside simply in what they 'are' as against the transforming pressures of 'change' or 'society', 'capitalism' or 'development plans'. It is also expressed in the ways peasants respond to those forces. These characteristic responses are reflected in the particularity of methods of analysis expressed in contemporary peasant studies. Also, the particular peasant experience and peasant agenda clearly linked into such diverse political and social movements as Russia's *narodnichestvo* (a movement 'to the people'), the guerrilla strategies of MAOISM, cooperative movements and contemporary nongovernmental organizations.

Finally, the many definitions of peasantry which view it as representing an aspect of the past in the present are valid but should be treated gingerly. Even in our 'dynamic' times we live in a present which is rooted in the past, and that is where our future is shaped. It is therefore worth remembering that – as in the past, so in the present – peasants and peasants' offspring are the majority of humankind and will remain so well into the twenty-first century.

Reading

Chayanov A.V. 1987: *The Theory of Peasant Economy.*
—— 1991: *The Theory of Peasant Cooperatives.*
Galeski, B. 1972: *Basic Concepts of Rural Sociology.*
Harriss, J. ed. 1982: *Rural Development.*
Kautsky, K. 1899 (*1987*): *The Agrarian Question.*
Ladurie, E. Le Roy 1980: Peasants. In *The Cambridge Modern History*, vol. 13.
Scott, J. 1986: *The Weapons of the Weak.*
Sen, A. 1981: *Poverty and Famines.*
Shanin, T. 1990: *Defining Peasants.*
—— ed. 1987: *Peasants and Peasant Societies*, 2nd edn.
Sorokin, P.A., Zimerman, E.F. and Golpin, C.J. eds 1965: *Systematic Source Book in Rural Sociology.*
Wolf, E.R. 1966: *Peasants.*

TEODOR SHANIN

penal institution   *See* PUNISHMENT

performing arts   *See* CINEMA; DANCE; MUSIC; THEATRE

permanent revolution   The phrase has come to stand for a running together, into one continuous process, of two types of revolutionary transformation. Of obscure origin, it was introduced into Marxist thought by Karl Marx himself. But the full-blown theory of permanent revolution is associated with the name of Leon Trotsky who, from 1905 until his death in 1940, developed, defended and systematized the idea of such a double revolutionary transformation, for countries at an early stage of capitalist development.

The term itself is not altogether apt to the meaning it has acquired, seeming to suggest, rather, an outlook of never-ending upheaval or radical change. Except when caricatured by opponents, however, it has not been put forward in this sense. Marx's discussion of Germany's political prospects in the mid-nineteenth century indicates the principal themes. A merely democratic or 'bourgeois-democratic' REVOLUTION – one, that is, directed against political autocracy and pre-capitalist economic relations – was, he thought, problematic in that country. For, the chief beneficiary of such a partial revolution, the bourgeoisie, lacked the political will to carry it through, being afraid of the class beneath it, the proletariat. The latter, as the only truly radical class, could and must take the initiative: fighting, though, not just for the democratic revolution that was necessary for a still-backward Germany to free itself from the legacy of the Middle Ages; but for a more complete emancipation, involving the abolition of private property and of classes. It was the telescoping of these two revolutionary stages – bourgeois-democratic and social-ist – into one more or less unbroken process, that constituted the 'permanence' of the revolution. Marx anticipated, also, that the political efforts of the German workers would be assisted by a victory of the proletariat in France.

Despite the presence of these themes in Marx's work, it was a different view, also to be found there, that came to define Marxist 'orthodoxy' and, therewith, the shared expectation of Russian Marx-ists in the early years of the twentieth century. This was that, before existing economic relations could be replaced by more advanced ones, the appro-priate material forces and conditions must already have matured. Socialism must be based on a high level of capitalist progress. The two main currents within the Russian socialist movement accordingly, although they disagreed about the proletariat's role in a future Russian revolution – the Bolsheviks seeing it as a leading, the Mensheviks as a merely supporting, role – were united in thinking that that revolution could only be bourgeois-democratic in content: its aims, in a backward, largely peasant country, had to be political democracy and a period of capitalist economic and social development, as a separate stage prior to any socialist revolution.

Into this relative harmony one voice projected a solo, discordant note. What had been for Marx only an occasional line of thought was now given an independent foundation by the young Trotsky, the resulting theory of permanent revolution serving him as a guideline for the rest of his life. First formulated after the defeated Russian revolution of 1905, its point of departure was what Trotsky was later to call the 'law of combined and uneven development'. The unequal degree and pace of capitalist development in different countries, taken together with capitalism's tendency to cross natio-nal boundaries, carrying with it its products, its methods, its technology and communications, had the effect in less economically developed regions, he argued, of producing a distinctive historical 'com-bination': of archaic, pre-capitalist social and politi-cal structures on the one hand, with a relatively advanced, albeit small, sector of capitalist industry, on the other. So it was in Russia, where capitalism had been fostered by the state itself and hastened by the foreign investment it encouraged. The most modern methods of production had been projected suddenly into an economically backward milieu, rather than developing organically with the more gradual evolution of an indigenous entrepreneurial

class. The Russian bourgeoisie and Russian libera-lism, consequently, were weak, and fearful of popular revolution; whilst the working class was highly concentrated, politically militant and self-confident. Though small, this class would have, Trotsky held, to lead the peasants behind it against Tsarism, the peasantry being too heterogeneous and geographically dispersed to take the lead itself.

It was from this hypothesis of proletarian politi-cal leadership in Russia that Trotsky derived the then heterodox projection that the first anti-capitalist revolution might well occur outside the advanced capitalist world. For, should the repre-sentatives of the working class come to power through revolution, they would not be able to limit themselves to pursuing the objectives of a bour-geois-democratic programme. The dynamics of the class struggle would oppose major bourgeois forces even to this 'minimum' programme, compelling the working class to move against the very bases of capitalist wealth and power, if the revolution was not to fail in its most elementary objectives. There could be no strict division, therefore, between bourgeois-democratic and socialist stages. The content of the two revolutions would be merged.

If Russia, however, could begin the transition to socialism, it could not on its own complete it. Here Trotsky sustained the orthodox Marxist thesis that socialism requires both an international framework and a high level of development of the productive forces. Unless the revolution in Russia was soon followed – as he confidently expected it would be – by revolutions in other key European countries, conjointly producing an international project of socialist transition, the new workers' state in Russia would be doomed in short order. This was the second limb of the theory of permanent revolution: insistence on the urgency of socialist victories elsewhere. Less prominent, before 1917, than the argument about the running together of revolution-ary stages, it was to become in the 1920s and 1930s a main theme in opposition to Stalin's advocacy of 'socialism in one country'.

Despite some parallels between his own views on Russia and those of other thinkers (Rosa Luxem-burg, for example), on the crucial matter of the anti-capitalist dynamic of the coming Russian revolution, Trotsky stood alone amongst Marxists for over a decade. Rejecting his theory right up to 1917, Lenin, and the Bolshevik Party behind him, then adopted a perspective in all essentials identical with Trotsky's, as the programme of their October revolution. This has frequently been denied by apologists of Stalinism, and in the tradition of orthodox COMMUNISM more generally; but the denial is not intellectually credible.

The perspective of permanent revolution was in one respect remarkably prescient, anticipating the broad lines of what was actually to happen in Russia, in face of a strong and dismissive orthodoxy that the anticipation was absurd. In that perspective, at the same time – as in classical Marxism generically – the facility and speed with which socialist revolution might extend from one national arena to another was clearly overestimated. Trotsky, on the other hand, underestimated the capacity of a post-revolutionary regime in Russia to survive in isolation; foreseeing initially its imminent fall, where later he would come to speak rather, in connection with Stalin's rule, of the regime's prolonged degeneration. But if the absence of socialist revolutions in the advanced capitalist world leaves, in one way, a general question mark over the theory of permanent revolution (as, indeed, over a central classical Marxian expectation), events now unfolding in the Soviet Union and Eastern Europe may, in another way, belatedly confirm it, should they lead to a full restoration of capitalism there.

See also TROTSKYISM.

Reading
Deutscher, I. 1954: *The Prophet Armed. Trotsky: 1879–1921*.
Geras, N. 1976: *The Legacy of Rosa Luxemburg*.
Knei-Paz, B. 1978: *The Social and Political Thought of Leon Trotsky*.
Löwy, M. 1981: *The Politics of Combined and Uneven Development*.
Marx, K. 1843 (*1975–*): Contribution to the Critique of Hegel's Philosophy of Law: Introduction. In K. Marx and F. Engels, *Collected Works*, vol. 3, pp. 175–87.
Marx, K. and Engels, F. 1850 (*1975–*): Address of the Central Authority to the League, March 1850. In *Collected Works*, vol. 10, pp. 277–87.
Trotsky, L. 1930, 1906 (*1962*): *The Permanent Revolution* and *Results and Prospects*.
—— 1922 (*1972*): *1905*.
—— 1932 (*1977*): *The History of the Russian Revolution*.

NORMAN GERAS

personality 'There is very little difference between one man and another,' said William James early in this century, 'but what little there is, is very important.' That very important matter is personality. It is composed of biological and psychological attributes and processes, each of them when taken in isolation shared either with all or with some other human beings, but unique to the individual in their configuration. Theorists of personality are therefore confronted with a wide choice of approaches: they can concentrate on the structure of the configuration or select out of the vast possible number of attributes and processes those which they regard as significant for the understanding of individual differences. That they have fully availed themselves of that freedom of choice was documented by Gordon Allport (1937), who identified almost 50 different conceptions of personality then in use.

There is, however, one approach which has dominated thinking about personality throughout the century: Sigmund Freud's (1923, for example). Not that it has been universally accepted; on the contrary, an argument could be made that its lasting influence is due as much to its detractors (such as Eysenck, 1947, 1982) as to its proponents. It has penetrated the humanities and, often in vulgarized form, the entire culture. In any case, there is hardly a systematic approach to thinking about personality that does not refer, positively or negatively, to Freud's global conception. The essence of his approach lies in his threefold structural view of personality, which is a comprehensive classification of continuously interacting psychological processes: ego processes, that is transactions with the real world, including perception, learning, memory, thinking and acting as well as unconscious defense mechanisms; id processes, including biological needs, pleasure seeking and repressed experiences, all unconscious; and superego processes, that is the application of internalized moral standards to oneself. This view of personality structure is reminiscent of Aristotle's classification of the basic goals in human actions as profit, pleasure and morality. In their dynamic interaction the three types of processes can pull in different directions and thus account for the experience of inner conflict as well as for personality disorders.

Freud's basic ideas about the structure of personality were elaborated and modified partly by himself, but largely by his followers, including his daughter Anna who identified additional defence mechanisms, by Heinz Hartmann who postulated the autonomy of ego processes, and by Erik Erikson who put ego development into its social context and described its stages throughout the life cycle.

Alfred Adler and Carl Jung, early followers but later critics of Freud, developed their own views on personality. Adler, father of the term 'inferiority-complex', understood personality as the early acquired habitual manner of trying to overcome the infant's inevitable sense of inferiority, an experience that tends to recur with new social encounters and external demands. In contrast to Freud's pessimism he regarded the drive for superiority, the will to power, as the root of all improvements in human affairs.

Jung deviated somewhat less than Adler from the Freudian basic concept, though his imaginative new vocabulary for psychological processes, tinged with mystical ideas, disguises the similarities. He added to Freud's model the notion of a collective unconscious transmitted from our ancestors, shared by all and containing the archetypes of thought and emotion. He also introduced the terms 'extraversion' and 'introversion' into personality psychology which later on began to play a major role in a very different approach.

Many other modifications of the psychodynamic model have been and still are being proposed. Notwithstanding differences and often antagonism between them, their proposers share some common features and assumptions: they deal with the whole person, not with isolated aspects; they assume more depth to personality than meets the naked eye; they develop their ideas over prolonged contact with individuals; most of them emphasize the social component in the constitution of personality; they are practising therapists and function largely outside academic institutions.

Intellectual opposition to the psychodynamic model arose inside and outside psychology and inside and outside academia, based on two major arguments: objections to determinism by early childhood and unconscious processes on the one hand; and objections to the 'unscientific' methods of psychoanalysis on the other.

The first of these gave rise to humanistic psychology, for a time regarded as the third force in psychology between PSYCHOANALYSIS and BEHAVIOURISM. Under the influence of Jean-Paul Sartre's existentialism and Martin Heidegger's phenomenology the idea of the unconscious was rejected in favour of regarding free will, agency, being-in-the-world and becoming as central aspects of personality. Ludwig Binswanger in Switzerland, Carl Rogers and Abraham Maslow in the United States, and Ronald Laing in Great Britain were the leading exponents of this conception; whether it will survive their deaths is an open question.

To object to psychodynamic conceptions because they are 'unscientific' presupposes adherence to a particular view of science that excludes systematic thought unless it leads to hypotheses which can be experimentally tested. While there is, of course, no doubt that experimentation presents a stringent test of ideas (in practice some of Freud's ideas have been tested in hundreds of experiments), basic approaches are notoriously difficult, if not impossible, to test experimentally.

Henry Murray (1959) and Gordon Allport (1961) made significant contributions both to basic assumptions about personality structure and to methods. Both men concentrated on normal people in their natural habitat, with their natural concerns; both regarded motivation as the centre around which personality is organized. Murray, acknowledging influences from Freud and Jung, rejected Freud's two basic motives – life and death drives – as too limited. He proposed some 20 needs with origins in the brain which interact with 'presses', that is, properties of the social environment which enhance or hinder the satisfaction of needs. Allport was much more critical of the Freudian model. He regarded personality as motivated by relatively enduring traits and rational intentions whose combined organization he termed the 'proprium', by which he meant a psychophysical system that tends toward functional autonomy of motives (independent from childhood motivation).

Both personality theorists constructed ingenious methods for collecting empirical evidence. Murray's contribution in that area was above all the Thematic Apperception Test (TAT), Allport's the advocacy and practice of idiographic methods, though he was also inventive in designing nomothetic methods.

The influence of these two personality theorists on their students was profound, but their ideas on the structure of personality were not further developed. Instead a large number of personality inventories and scales were constructed and standardized. There now exist instruments for many personality attributes, such as extraversion/introversion, anxiety, depressiveness, machiavellism, anomie, moral judgement, values, prejudice, and more. They are widely used for comparisons between groups, less often for comparisons over time periods, though they could help to clarify ideas about the enduring or flexible nature of such dispositions.

Those who postulate a large hereditary component in personality are, of course, satisfied with a once-and-for-all measure; their emphasis on the biological determination of personality type has taken differing routes. William Sheldon (1942) saw personality as determined by body structure; Hans Eysenck (1982) by the nervous system.

Following a tradition going back to Hippocrates, Sheldon regarded temperament as the essence of personality, postulated its dependence on a person's somatotype and found indeed very high correlations between these two variables. For Eysenck the essence of personality is determined by as yet not well understood brain processes whose result can, however, be measured along four continuous dimensions which are independent from each other. They are: extraversion/introversion, neuroticism, psychoticism, and intelligence. Eysenck's scales for three of these dimensions are now widely used in research even by those who do not share his overall approach.

The leading textbook on personality theories (Hall et al., 1985) presents many other contributors, including several learning theorists, foremost among them B. F. Skinner. It is, however, debatable whether he and other behaviourists have made a contribution to thinking about personality, however important they may be in other contexts; they certainly do not claim so. To assume an internal organization that accounts for the interpretation of the external world, as personality theorists must, seems to contradict Skinner's entire way of thinking.

At the end of the twentieth century there exists, then, no generally accepted approach to understanding personality. The major split is between psychodynamic models with their assumption of unconscious mental events and the other models, though there is controversy also within each side. Efforts to bridge the major gap were made periodically throughout the century; they failed. The most recent effort in that direction (Westen, 1985) is a demonstration of the compatibility of rigorous empirical research results with psychodynamic ideas by one who is qualified in both camps. Whether it will fare better than its forerunners remains to be seen.

Reading

Hall, C., Lindzey, G., Loehlin, J.C. and Manosevitz, M. 1985: *Introduction to Theories of Personality*.

Westen, D. 1985: *Self and Society*.

MARIE JAHODA

phenomenology In philosophy this is (a) the pure description of the 'phenomena' of human experience as they present themselves in direct awareness, disregarding the history, particularity, causation and social context of such experiences; and (b) the twentieth-century European philosophical movement, associated in particular with Edmund Husserl (1859–1938), advocating this method of investigation in various forms. Secondly, in sociology – and inspired in particular by the writings in social phenomenology of Alfred Schutz (1899–1959) – it is the study of the ways in which people directly experience EVERYDAY LIFE and imbue their activities with meaning. Thirdly, in the psychology of perception, it is a school influenced by the philosopher Maurice Merleau-Ponty (1908–1961), asserting that the body and behaviour are immediate, prelinguistic bearers of meaning in experience (Shapiro, 1985) (see PSYCHOLOGY). This entry focuses on phenomenology in philosophy and sociology.

Phenomenology is an abstract, rigorous and specialized branch of philosophy, with various schools and national traditions. However, it is not incorrect to say that in opposition to scientific REALISM, all phenomenologists have given priority to describing lived experience (*Erlebnis*) in the everyday human life-world (*Lebenswelt*). Those in the movement influenced by EXISTENTIALISM (such as Jean-Paul Sartre or Maurice Merleau-Ponty) stressed more the experience of situated, concrete human subjects living together, while those in the tradition of Cartesian rationalism (such as Husserl) started from the experience of the individual Ego and tried to discover the ultimate foundations of knowledge.

Phenomenological inquiries in general are not intended to produce factual statements, but rather non-empirical or 'transcendental' philosophical reflections on knowing and perceiving and on human activities such as science and culture. Husserl aimed to establish nothing less than pure TRUTH, independent of time, place, culture or individual psychology. He was not interested in the perception of particular, concrete objects but in 'the perceived as such', which he called the *noema*. In order to arrive at such abstract essences of objects, Husserl advocated a procedure he called the 'transcendental reduction' or *epoché*, whereby matters of ONTO-

LOGY were held in abeyance. By a shift of attitude, belief in the actual world of human existence in any society, community or historical period was suspended, or 'bracketed'. By placing individual concrete social or natural objects in brackets in this way, it was possible, he believed, to vary many examples of things to discover the essential features that any given thing must possess in order to be recognized as an example of that thing. In phenomenology this method is known as the *eidetic* approach (Husserl, *Ideas*, 1931).

The doctrine of *intentionality* is important in Husserl and in phenomenology in general and derives from Husserl's teacher Franz Brentano. The most fundamental characteristic of consciousness is held to be that it is always consciousness *of* something. Regardless of the existential status of the object concerned, consciousness is 'directed'. Individuals single out entities in their experience for attention and thus constitute them as objects. But one cannot infer from the fact that a conscious act is directed towards something that that thing exists. For Husserl, every act is 'directed' because even if it has no obvious object, it will be directed towards a noema. During the artificial procedure of the epoché, 'intentional' acts such as hoping, expecting or fearing become important for establishing the essence of perception as such (Husserl, *Cartesian Meditations*, 1931).

Through following this reasoning and using the method of the epoché, Husserl hoped to show that it was possible to reach a realm of purified consciousness, or 'transcendental subjectivity', held to be a self-contained realm of experience outside time and space. The method would produce non-empirical, apodictic truths, *a priori*, which would be universally valid and free from presuppositions. These would provide a solid bulwark against sceptical doubt, historicism, relativism and political irrationalism. In this respect phenomenology was also a humanistic WELTAN-SCHAUUNG, the nature of which Husserl made explicit in his last work *The Crisis of European Sciences and Transcendental Phenomenology* (1937).

The social phenomenology of Alfred Schutz leaves aside the project for a presuppositionless philosophy and sidesteps the resultant Husserlian problem of how the 'transcendental Ego' (which he was forced to posit to avoid subjective idealism) is constituted in the individual 'empirical Ego'. Schutz assumes at the outset that people encounter each other in an already constituted, meaningful,

intersubjective life-world, which is the 'paramount reality' for human beings, and advocates the study of the ways in which people experience this everyday life-world. The characteristic commonsense posture people take in this sphere Schutz calls the 'natural attitude'. The existence of others is taken for granted in everyday life since we assume a 'reciprocity of perspectives'. The concept of 'simultaneity' describes the idea that our experience of the Other occurs in the same present as the Other experiences us. People orientate themselves using 'typifications', such as business competitor, American, jovial type, through which meaningful interaction is effected (Schutz, 1932).

Schutz shared Husserl's humanistic belief, which he had set out in the *Crisis*, in the primacy of the *Lebenswelt* as the ultimate reference point and basis in meaning for all experience as well as for the scientific theories that humans construct. Highly influential on ETHNOMETHODOLOGY and on sociological methodology was Schutz's insistence, in pursuance of that principle, that to avoid REIFICATION, the 'second-order' constructs created in social science should be based on the 'first-order' ones already in use in the everyday life-world. Social science as a 'context of meaning' was possible and humanly legitimate only if it effected a two-way translation between itself and the 'stock-of-knowledge-at-hand' available and in use in the meaning contexts of the *Lebenswelt*. (A version of this idea appears as the 'double hermeneutic' in the influential writings on sociological theory by Anthony Giddens (1976) – see HERMENEUTICS.) Schutz said one should observe typical meaningful acts and events and coordinate them with constructed models of typical actors or 'homunculi'. In social science it was thus possible to construct, as all sciences do, analytical conceptual systems (in this case of social action) of maximum anonymity, but based in real experience and, by the two-way dialogue, retaining links with the uniqueness of ordinary individuals.

Controversy continues within and surrounding phenomenology. Two recurring focuses of debate are the following.

1 Problems arising from the transcendental status of phenomenological reflections. In the sociological versions there is an ambiguous relationship between the transcendental categories and the real world depicted by empirical social science. This relation is always the Achilles heel of any transcendentally informed inquiry, phenomeno-

logy included (Kilminster, 1989) (see NEO-KAN-TIANISM). Strictly speaking, Schutz was outlining only the preconditions for humanistic social science inquiry, not attempting an empirical description of any society, or providing concepts for direct use in social research. As Thomas Luckmann (1983, pp. viii–ix) put it, social phenomenology is 'proto-sociology' which 'uncovers the universal and invariant structures of human existence at all times and places'. But such a claim to universality, based as it was solely on philosophical reasoning, was always challengeable. From where does the abstract catalogue of basic structures of the life-world derive? What empirical evidence, if any, could change them? Are values and prejudices about human nature being smuggled in?

Moreover, the clarificatory, *a priori* nature of the enterprise that the phenomenologists had garnered for themselves meant that – as they acknowledged – they were not competent to make any systematic, concrete statements about the urgent questions of social power and domination in specific societies. Such a social scientific task was outside their sphere. Their main claim to fame thus became the humanistic critique of objectivism and POSITIVISM where they existed in mainstream social science. Once this corrective had been taken on board by sociologists, phenomenology gradually lost its appeal.

2 The 'egological' focus of phenomenology has had important repercussions for both the social and philosophical variants. This individualistic cast is obvious in Husserl, but also clear in Schutz's view of society as consisting of concentric circles around himself:

> In reference to Us whose center I am, others stand out as 'You', and in reference to You, who refer back to me, third parties stand out as 'They'. My social world with the *alter egos* in it is arranged, around me as the center, into associates (*Umwelt*), contemporaries (*Mitwelt*), predecessors (*Vorwelt*), and successors (*Folgewelt*), whereby I and my different attitudes to others institute these manifold relationships. All this is done in various degrees of *intimacy* and *anonymity*. (Schutz, 1940, p. 181)

Such a nominalistic starting point for social science has been the subject of considerable criticisms in sociology from Karl Marx and Emile Durkheim onwards, but recently notably in the theoretical and empirical work of Norbert Elias, where it has been

seen as an unacceptable form of *monadology* (Elias, 1978 and 1991).

The same egoism has meant that philosophical versions, particularly that of Husserl, have always been haunted by the ghost of *solipsism*. His solution – the universal self-experience of the 'transcendental Ego' – was assailed by existential phenomenologists (Sartre, 1936–7; Merleau-Ponty, 1945). They tried to circumvent this danger by shifting the emphasis towards ontology. They created concepts such as the 'being-in-the-world' of humankind, to try to describe the pre-theoretical togetherness of people in societies. The anti-subjectivist and anti-humanist movement of STRUCTURALISM in European social thought in the 1950s and 1960s was also partly a reaction to the more individualistic forms of phenomenology.

The individual subject, or empirical Ego, in phenomenology always had an analytic status, though implicitly it was assumed to be a grown-up individual. Reference to the development of this individual was made formally, for example in Husserl's distinction between the 'active' and the 'passive' genesis of the Ego (*Cartesian Meditations*, 1931, sect. 38). In his early work Schutz explicitly described the individual actor assumed in his analyses as the 'wide-awake adult'. This static assumption is corrected in his posthumous *The Structures of the Lifeworld* (Schutz and Luckmann, 1974) which contributed to developing what has become known as 'genetic phenomenology'. In this work the fact that adults used to be children, who learned from a pre-existing culture via socialization, was acknowledged. This viewpoint can be found in a sophisticated form in Berger and Luckmann's influential work of metatheory *The Social Construction of Reality* (1961). However, consonant with the transcendental character of phenomenological analysis in general, genesis is inevitably handled here, too, only in a formal, abstract way, as part of a universal framework of subjective orientation for the social sciences, with the world of real, empirical genesis placed in brackets.

Sociologists have drawn attention to the fact that phenomenology is a pre-eminent product of the ego-centredness of traditional European philosophy from Descartes to Kant and Husserl. This tendency has been cogently explained by the development of complex, internally pacified Western nation-states. It can be seen as one expression of the self-experience of the highly self-controlled modern individual characteristic of such societies (Elias, 1939). The dominant emerging direction of contemporary inquiries in the sociology of individuality is away from transcendental towards empirical investigations simultaneously on the two fronts of what Norbert Elias called *psychogenesis* and *sociogenesis* (Burkitt, 1991).

Reading

Elliston, Frederick and McCormick, Peter eds 1977: *Husserl: Expositions and Appraisals.*
Hammond, Michael, Howarth, Jane and Keat, Russell 1991: *Understanding Phenomenology.*
Landgrebe, Ludwig 1966: *Major Problems in Contemporary European Philosophy, from Dilthey to Heidegger.*
Luckmann, Thomas ed. 1978: *Phenomenology and Sociology.*
Natanson, Maurice ed. 1970: *Phenomenology and Social Reality: Essays in Memory of Alfred Schutz.*
Pivčević, Edo 1970: *Husserl and Phenomenology.*
Spiegelberg, Herbert 1982: *The Phenomenological Movement*, 2 vols, 3rd rev. and enlarged edn.
Thomason, Burke C. 1982: *Making Sense of Reification: Alfred Schutz and Constructivist Theory.*

RICHARD KILMINSTER

philosophy In the nineteenth century it was impossible for *fin de siècle* philosophical thought to avoid the consequences of the development of modern science. The responses of Nietzsche, neo-Kantians, evolutionary naturalists, Marxists, pragmatists and idealists, each different, met with unequal success. Least successful were idealists, whose efforts to comprehend the world as constituted by a system of ideas were no longer persuasive.

In Germany, Hegelianism had already been routed. Not so in the USA and Britain. In the USA, Josiah Royce, and in Britain, T.H. Green, F.H. Bradley and Bernard Bosanquet were providing powerful metaphysical backgrounds to liberal Christianity. Although varieties of 'personalist' idealism, promoted by the American G.H. Howison and by Cambridge philosophers J.E. McTaggart and James Ward, rejected 'absolutism' as 'oriental', all these idealist philosophers shared in rejecting empiricist commitments to nominalism, atomism and 'external relations' – the idea that 'things' retain their identities irrespective of the relations in which they stand.

From at least Parmenides, philosophers have struggled with the double-barrelled problem of the relation between the one and the many and of thought and reality. Bradley (1846–1924) charac-

teristically attempted a solution which began with 'immediate experience' and argued that all judgements, including those of science, are 'riddled with contradictions'. For Bradley, thought can be true only when the intellect is *fully* satisfied – and it cannot be fully satisfied as long as thought contains contradictions. As John Passmore (1957) writes: 'Nowhere short of the Absolute . . . can this self-consistency be found.' For idealists, the world in its infinite complexity was, ultimately, a unity.

Idealism all but disappeared with World War I. Indeed, all the more successful twentieth-century developments, including Marxism, had opposed it. In America, PRAGMATISM, and a string of 'realisms' – the 'new' realisms of, for example, E.B. Holt and R.B. Perry (Holt, 1912) and the 'critical' realisms of A.O. Lovejoy and R.W. Sellers (Drake, 1920) – were direct responses to idealism. The same was true in Britain with the dominating figures of Bertrand Russell and G.E. Moore. In Germany and Austria, Husserl's PHENOMENOLOGY, Heidegger's philosophy of existence and Vienna POSITIVISM, also enormously successful movements, were efforts to overcome the late nineteenth-century impasse between idealists and realists.

In response to materialist attacks on 'scientific socialism', Engels had belatedly tried to provide a philosophy of science for Marxism. Following him, Lenin's *Materialism and Empirio-Criticism* (1908) became the source of what became, with Stalin, DIALECTICAL MATERIALISM, the 'official' philosophy of Marxism. So-called 'Western Marxism', of which more subsequently, would be a recent response to this.

Pragmatism was not one thing. The writings of Charles S. Peirce, William James, George Herbert Mead and John Dewey are perhaps as different as they are similar. All are properly pragmatists in accepting Kant's critique of metaphysics, but in rejecting his transcendental move.

Peirce (1839–1914) came closest to traditional 'realism'. Not only was there an independently existing external world which was lawful, but it was intelligible. Peirce (1877) responded to Cartesian anxiety by arguing that the problem was to find the preferred mode of fixing belief in the community. This was, of course, the 'scientific method', preferred because, as public and fallible, it alone was self-correcting.

Peirce's famous 'pragmatic maxim' (1878) that our conception of the practical effects of an idea gives the whole meaning to it, was misappropriated by later verificationist theories of meaning. His work on semiotic and logic remain topical especially since they provide a radical alternative to the dominant views of Frege/Russell.

The pragmatism of James (1842–1910) was meant to reap benefits from both the 'tender' and 'tough-minded', to include not merely 'facts' and 'principles', but science *and* religion. To do this, James demystified both. Science and religion spring from 'the sentiment of rationality' (1878) and both aim at 'ideal and inward relations' which can 'in no intelligible sense whatever be reproductions of the order of outer experience'. James's definition of truth (1908) outraged the epistemologists since it seemed to allow that a *sufficient* condition for truth was that a belief be useful. Similarly, his 'radical empiricism' has found favour with more recent, widely opposing, views. While a wonderful prose writer, James had little interest either in narrowly conceived 'philosophical' problems or in meeting the standards of recent technical philosophy. His main point was to insist that the world is plural, relational and 'in the making'. Accordingly, beliefs have value as truth claims only in so far as they respond to specific needs, wants, aims and interests.

Dewey's 'instrumentalism' was a naturalism which involved de-essentializing Aristotle and ignoring traditional epistemology in favour of a frank avowal of the method of science. But if Dewey (1859–1952) was comfortably abstract about what this meant, he was not 'scientistic'. On the contrary, he sought to 'humanize' science and to bring its methods into everyday affairs, including a democratic politics. Since democracy was 'the idea of community itself' and community requires that 'face to face relationships have consequences which generate a community of interests, a sharing of values' (1927), the problem of democracy was precisely the problem of establishing the conditions in which consequences can be identified and values conjointly established.

Overcoming a host of dualisms, mind and body, experience and nature, and importantly, fact and value, was crucial to Dewey's project. On his view, these dualisms, and with them the 'chief divisions' of modern philosophy, 'have grown up around the epistemological problem of the general relation of subject and object' (1917). Inquiry was the central idea of his theory of knowledge, and his approach, in many ways comparable to Marx's, was to begin

with concrete practice, to raise questions as to 'the genuineness, under present conditions of science and social life, of the problems [of philosophy]' and then to articulate the 'problems of men' in terms which are amenable to inquiry. Dewey is currently undergoing a renaissance, both as a premature postmodern thinker in the mode of Richard Rorty *and* as a thinker whose philosophy remains viable for modernist reconstruction.

While Dewey evaded many of philosophy's traditional problems, G. E. Moore (1873–1958) insisted that these resulted from unclarity. His essay, 'The refutation of idealism' (1903a) exhibits this and sets the tone for the (later) conception of philosophy as linguistic analysis. For Moore, the concept of an existing thing required that it be externally related to some other thing. Idealism, committed to internal relations, could not coherently be stated. Moore (1903b) used the same tactic against 'naturalistic ethics', arguing that views which try to define good in terms of some 'natural property', such as utility, commit a 'fallacy'. Even if we grant, he insisted, that something is useful, we can still ask, 'but is it good?'

Russell (1872–1970), a giant of modern logic, was not content to seek solutions to problems in logical theory and mathematics. Rather, by employing techniques generated in his effort to construct mathematics from logic ('logicism'), he could argue that 'every philosophical problem, when it is subjected to the necessary analysis and purification, is found to be not really philosophical at all, or else, to be, in the sense in which we are using the word, logical' (1914a).

He owed his early Platonist metaphysics to Moore. But given Moore's dubious notion that we perceive 'sense data' which were, presumably, the *surfaces* of things, Russell was forced to conclude that ordinary objects were *inferences* from sense data. With the principle that 'whenever possible, logical constructions are to be substituted for inferred entities' (1914b), he was able to argue that ordinary objects, like numbers, could become 'logical constructions'. But while defending 'logical atomism', he acknowledged that 'general facts' could not be analysed as 'molecular facts' (Russell, 1918). For example, all swans are white did not 'reduce to' this swan is white *and* that swan is white, etc. By 1948, his optimism had waned. With all the ingenuity in the world, empiricism could not be sustained. Not only did science require 'the inductive principle' which he could find no way to ground, but it needed 'the postulate of quasi-permanence' – 'things'.

As science industrialized, a host of nineteenth-century physicists became philosophers of science (see PHILOSOPHY OF SCIENCE). They shared in rejecting metaphysics and, as part of this, they insisted that science did not aim at explaining why things happen as they do. Explanation, if possible at all, meant deduction, subsumption under law. There were, however, some important differences between them.

G. R. Kirchhoff (1874), Ernst Mach (1886) and Karl Pearson (1892) offered a phenomenalist and descriptivist version of science. Henri Poincaré (1902) and Pierre Duhem (1906) urged a more 'conventionalist' position, holding that laws and theories were definitions in disguise. Finally Heinrich Hertz (1894), student of the more realistically inclined Herman Helmholtz, provided a neo-Kantian response in which theories were 'representations' of the world in the form of mathematical models (*Bilder*).

These philosophers established the *Weltanschauung* for 'logical positivism', perhaps the century's most influential movement. Russell and Whitehead's *Principia Mathematica* (1910–11), and Ludwig Wittgenstein's *Tractatus Logico-Philosophicus* (1922) were, however, the immediate resources. Wittgenstein (1889–1951) seems to have followed Hertz in arguing that language needed a comprehensive 'model'. He turned, accordingly, to the work of G. Frege and Russell. But Wittgenstein's effort seems to have been designed *not* to show that non-scientific discourse was cognitively meaningless. On his view, it is precisely what we must be silent about which constitutes all that really matters in life! Either way, philosophy had backed itself into a corner. Relieved of the responsibility to say what ought to be, philosophers turned to 'meta-ethics'. John Rawls's *A Theory of Justice* (1971) would be the first significant mainstream philosophical tract in normative ethics and political philosophy in perhaps two generations.

The story of recent positivism is a hoary one indeed, not merely in regard to the disappointments of the programme, but, today, even in getting clear as to what it was. For example, W.V.O. Quine, himself deeply implicated in the movement and one of its sharpest critics, held that Rudolf Carnap's 1928 *The Logical Structure of the World* was a rigorous, but failed, effort to carry out Russell's 1914 programme to account for the external world as a 'logical construct of sense data'. Carnap later argued that it had a more general aim, namely to show the possibility of translating scientific statements into an ontologically neutral 'constructional system' in which phenomenalist language was not privileged. On this view, Carnap was already committed to the idea of pragmatically justified linguistic frameworks and of truth defined relative to these. This was to become a theme of later analytic philosophy, for example, as in the work of Donald Davidson.

Phenomenalist 'reduction' was a main theme of A. J. Ayer's influential *Language, Truth and Logic* (1936) whose formulation of the famous 'verifiability principle' introduced it to countless readers. In its terms, the meaning of a proposition is given by its method of verification.

The principle instantly ran into problems. Thus, if it was not a tautology or a verifiable empirical generalization, what was its status? By 1936, at least, verifiability had become 'confirmability' and there were no longer any hopes for phenomenalist reduction (Carnap, 1936). Assuming a naive realism, the problem became the status of theoretical terms. They were endowed with partial meaning by means of 'reduction sentences', for example, 'If challenged, then if someone is anxious, he fidgets.' The relation to 'operational definition' and to 'behaviourism' is clear. But without much notice by social scientists whose affection for these ideas was not easily disturbed, it quickly became clear to Carnap that 'reduction sentences' would not suffice. By 1956, he had shifted to 'correspondence rules', considerably loosening the hold on the 'empirical' (Carnap, 1956).

There was also the continuing problem of a 'logic of confirmation', the skeleton in the closet of logical empiricism. Carnap and C. G. Hempel recognized that what was needed was an inductive logic which, like *Principia*, would allow us to discriminate between 'valid' and 'invalid' predictions. Others were less sanguine, including Karl Popper (1934). He bit the Humean bullet and insisted on 'falsifiability', based on the deductive rule of *modus tollens*. 'Bold conjectures' are the stuff of science, conjectures which are then tested by trying to falsify them. Non-falsifiability, accordingly, would define non-science. But, as already noted by Duhem, it was hardly clear, given the holistic character of theories, whether falsification was ever possible.

By the 1950s, criticism from within had eaten away at all the central pillars of positivism. Goodman (1947) showed that no extensional analysis could deal satisfactorily with the intimately related problems of induction, confirmation and the analysis of scientific law; Quine (1951) showed both that verifiability and the analytic/synthetic distinction could not be sustained; Hempel (1958) acknowledged that if theoretical terms were understood as positivists had understood them, they could not play the role they were presumed to play. Hanson (1958) argued that the distinction between terms in the observation language and the theoretical language could not be made. One could go on, but it was perhaps T. S. Kuhn's *Structure of Scientific Revolutions* (1962) which brought the issues to a head. The main upshot was that if Kuhn was even approximately correct, actual science in no sense conformed to the 'reconstruction' being promoted by empiricist philosophy of science.

Putting aside earlier marginalized writers, for example Cassirer (1923), Whitehead (1925) and Bachelard (1934), two alternatives to the 'standard view' emerged, the 'methodological anarchism' of Paul Feyerabend (1971) and the 'realism' of Rom Harré (1970) and others. For Feyerabend, Kuhn was insufficiently radical; for Harré, once the 'myth of deductivism' was expunged, one could make sense of scientific practice in ways unnoticed by previous philosophies.

Logical empiricism was one strain in the predominating 'analytic' posture of Anglo-American philosophy. The other, with Moore in the background and the later Wittgenstein in the foreground, was 'ordinary language analysis' (see LINGUISTIC PHILOSOPHY). Getting a handle on the Wittgenstein of the *Philosophical Investigations* (1953) is not easy. But the slogan 'the meaning is the use' quickly came to typify analyses which, even to old-guard Wittgensteinians, seemed to be exercises which lacked philosophical consequence, even consequences of the 'therapeutic', anti-metaphysical sort which had presumably motivated Wittgenstein's later work.

Two of the best known 'ordinary language' analysts were Oxford philosophers, Gilbert Ryle (1900–1976) and J. L. Austin (1911–1960). Ryle (1949) analysed 'mental concepts' and concluded that 'mind' was not a 'ghost in the machine'. Ryle, who initiated 'philosophy of mind', was, however, close to Carnap (and B. F. Skinner!), in holding that mental concepts were best analysed dispositionally, as hypotheticals which make reference to behaviour. Austin joined in the attack on phenomena-

lism (1962) and identified (1962) a critical difference between 'performatives', for example, 'I now pronounce you man and wife,' and 'constatives', such as 'Today is Monday.' Only the latter had truth-conditions. Austin's 'speech-act' analysis pushed analytic philosophy towards a rethinking of the relevance of the social.

But we need here to go back to an entirely different response to the maturing of science. Edmund Husserl (1859–1938), like Frege, Russell, Peirce and Dewey, thought of logic as a theory of science, but for him it had to be considered 'transcendentally'. Logic should provide an *a priori* elucidation of the conditions of possibility of science (Husserl, 1900). To this end, he developed a 'presuppositionless' PHENOMENOLOGY. The idea was to begin with 'the total, unanalysed cognitive situation' as experienced, and then through rigorous description 'to account for the sameness of meanings and their reference to an objectivity, whether real or fictive in character'. In this way, questions of the existence of ordinary objects, as of space and time are 'bracketed', so that the method is ostensibly neutral between realism and idealism. Objectivity, then, 'is not constituted in the "primary" contents (i.e., sensed contents), but rather in the characters of meaningful apprehension and in the laws which belong to the essence of these characters.' But Husserl went on to argue that objects 'can only be "in" the system of knowledge'. This, of course, is idealism.

The philosophies of 'existence' of Martin Heidegger (1889–1976) and Jean-Paul Sartre (1905–1980) (see EXISTENTIALISM) owe much to phenomenology, but not only to phenomenology. Kierkegaard (1813–1855) and Nietzsche (1844–1900), each responding to Hegel, saw reason as threatening to swallow up humanity. Heidegger's central theme became 'man's estrangement from Being' (1927). He sought, then, to describe, without preconceptions, what human existence is. Attempting to undercut Cartesian subjectivity, *Dasein* is the 'field' of human existence, the name for persons in relation to others and their environment. For Heidegger truth does not concern propositions, but, following Greek etymology, a-*lēthia*, or unhiddenness, regards 'understanding', a primordial condition of existence. This is a theme of 'hermeneutical' approaches, for example, that of Hans-Georg Gadamer (1960) (see HERMENEUTICS).

While Hitler was attracting Heidegger, he was also driving countless notable philosophers to

England and America, among them members of the FRANKFURT SCHOOL. Herbert Marcuse, Theodor Adorno and Max Horkheimer attempted a revision of the Hegel/Marx Enlightenment project of finding reason in history. If the working class did not provide a privileged perspective, then reason was 'without its condition of possibility'. Jürgen Habermas remains a powerful voice in this effort.

Indeed, the 'decisive philosophical event' in postwar France was the rediscovery of Hegel's DIALECTIC. This owed much to Alexander Kojève and Jean Hyppolite. Between them they taught a host of French intellectuals, including Raymond Aron, Maurice Merleau-Ponty, Jacques Lacan, Michel Foucault, Gilles Deleuze, Louis Althusser and Jacques Derrida. As Simone de Beauvoir reported, speaking for both Sartre and herself, 'we had discovered the reality and weight of history.'

In Sartre's first novel, 'nausea is existence revealing itself' (1938). *Being and Nothingness* (1943) developed a radical existentialism which focused on freedom, but which foundered on 'the reef of solipsism'. By 1947, Sartre had confronted Marxism and Stalinism (Sartre, 1947). The result, the *Critique of Dialectical Reason*, completed in 1960, was an assimilation which drew criticism from both 'structuralists', including Claude Lévi-Strauss (1962), and close colleagues, Albert Camus (1951) and Maurice Merleau-Ponty (1955), who gave us the term WESTERN MARXISM.

Like Herbert Marcuse, François Lefèbvre, and G. Della Volpe, Sartre emphasized the recently 'discovered' writings of the young Marx. For the 'structuralists' this reintroduced metaphysics, the *bête noire* of twentieth-century philosophy. Lévi-Strauss thus defended 'Kantianism without a subject', and Louis Althusser (1965), although committed to a strong form of realism, defended history without agents. On his view, Marx had made an 'epistemological break', rejecting his former 'humanism' and 'historicism'. But Althusser shared with Sartre in rejecting 'diamat' and in seeking to redefine a philosophy for MARXISM.

The response to structuralism, 'poststructuralism', is characterized by ontological anti-realism and Nietzschean anxiety over the will to power. Although Foucault (1966) rejected Sartre's idea that 'totalization' could answer Nietzschean criticism of objective knowledge, he would seem to admit a kind of immanent critique, exposing through 'genealogies' alternative understandings of present practices. While it is unlikely that Derrida

(1967) would approve, epigones of 'deconstructionism' have tended to reduce philosophy to rhetorical genres, obliterating, en route, the very idea of truth. But 'postmodernism' (see MODERNISM AND POST-MODERNISM) is perhaps too diffuse a phenomenon to characterize briefly.

Philosophy, then, is in a far different condition than it was as the century began. It is not so much that the idealism/realism debate has disappeared; rather, its terms have changed. As important, perhaps, the incapacity of anti-metaphysical empiricisms to make sense of science, still less of our world, has forced recent philosophy to reject both easy solutions and its 'foundationalist' aspirations. The upshot remains unclear.

Reading
Ayer, A.J. ed. 1959: *Logical Positivism*.
Barrett, William 1958 (*1962*): *Irrational Man: A Study in Existential Philosophy*.
Callinicos, Alex 1990: *Against Postmodernism*.
Caton, Charles E. ed. 1963: *Philosophy and Ordinary Language*.
Farber, Marvin 1943 (*1967*): *Foundation of Phenomenology*.
Flower, Elizabeth and Murphey, Murray G. 1987: *A History of Philosophy in America*, vol. 2.
Passmore, John 1957: *A Hundred Years of Philosophy*.
Poster, Mark 1975: *Existential Marxism in Postwar France: From Sartre to Althusser*.
Suppe, Frederick ed. 1974: *The Structure of Scientific Theories*.
Tiles, J.E. 1988: *Dewey*.
Tiles, Mary 1991: *Mathematics and the Image of Reason*.
Toulmin, S. and Janik, A. 1973: *Wittgenstein's Vienna*.
Urmson, J.O. 1956: *Philosophical Analysis: Its Development Between the Two World Wars*.

PETER T. MANICAS

philosophy of history   *See* HISTORICISM; HISTORY; TELEOLOGY

philosophy of science   This branch of enquiry encompasses questions about science in general (such as, are at least some theoretical entities real?), about particular groups of sciences (such as, can social objects be studied in the same way as natural ones? – the problem of NATURALISM), and about individual sciences (such as, what are the implications of relativity theory for our concepts of space and time?). It arose as a discipline separate from the more general theory of knowledge in the mid-nineteenth century – at about the time that distinct sciences bearing names such as 'physics', 'chemistry' and 'biology' were becoming 'professionalized'. The leading figures of its first generation were Auguste Comte, the inventor of the label 'positivism' (as well as 'sociology'), the ultra-empiricist J.S. Mill (who thought that even mathematical propositions were empirical) and the Kantian historian of science, William Whewell. Much of the subsequent history of the philosophy of science can be seen as a continuation of the controversy between Mill and Comte, on the one hand, and Whewell, on the other, with the former hegemonic until *c*.1970. The dominant view of science has been squarely based on Humean empiricism, epitomized in the claim of E. Mach (1894, p. 192) that natural laws were nothing but 'the mimetic reproduction of facts in thought, the object of which is to replace and save the trouble of new experience'. Thus the late nineteenth century saw such spectacular triumphs for the empiricist camp as Benjamin Brodie's construction of a chemistry without atoms, which were widely held to be, in Alexander Bain's words, merely 'representative fictions'.

The logical POSITIVISM of the Vienna circle of the 1920s and 1930s married the epistemological empiricism and reductionism of Mach, Pearson and Duhem with the logical innovations of Frege, Russell and Wittgenstein to form the backbone of the dominant view of science in mid-century. Its principle members were M. Schlick, R. Carnap, O. Neurath, F. Waismann and H. Reichenbach. C.G. Hempel, E. Nagel and A.J. Ayer were intellectually close to it. Ludwig Wittgenstein and Karl Popper were on its periphery. Formalism and linguisticism were characteristic of the circle. It shared the latter bias with the conventionalism that had grown up in France under the influence of H. Poincaré and E. Le Roy in the first decade of the century and which was to be radically historicized by G. Bachelard and G. Canguilhem from the 1930s on. Against the grain, Whewell's legacy was taken up by N.R. Campbell in the twenties, arguing for the necessity of models in science. Altogether outside the mainstream were the biologically inspired cosmologies produced by H.L. Bergson, S. Alexander and A.N. Whitehead at about the same time; and the dialectical materialism that was being systematically codified and disseminated in the USSR under Stalin.

The positivist vision of science pivoted on a *monistic* theory of scientific development and a *deductivist* theory of scientific structure. The former came under attack from three main sources. First, from Popper and (ex-)Popperians such as I. Lakatos and P. Feyerabend. They argued that it was falsifiability, not verifiability, that was the hallmark of science and that it was precisely in revolutionary breakthroughs such as those associated with Galileo or Einstein that its epistemological significance lay. Second, from Kuhn and other historians (such as A. Koyré) and sociologists (such as L. Fleck) of science. They drew scrupulous attention to the real social processes involved in the reproduction and transformation of scientific knowledge – in what has come to be called the transitive or epistemological or historical-sociological dimension of the philosophy of science. Finally, from Wittgensteinians, such as N.R. Hanson, S.E. Toulmin and W. Sellars, who latched on to the non-atomistic, theory-dependent and mutable character of 'facts' in science.

One problem which arose in the early days of the debate about scientific change concerned the possibility, and indeed according to people like Kuhn and Feyerabend the actuality, of meaning variance as well as inconsistency in scientific change. Kuhn and Feyerabend suggested it might come to pass that no meaning was shared in common between a theory and its successor. This seemed to render problematic the idea of a rational choice between such 'incommensurable' theories, and even encouraged (superidealist) scepticism about the existence of a theory-independent world. However, if the relation between the theories is one of conflict rather than merely difference, this presupposes that they are alternative accounts of the *same* world; and if one theory can explain more significant phenomena in terms of its descriptions than the other can in terms of *its*, then there is a rational criterion for theory choice, and *a fortiori* a possible sense to the idea of scientific development over time.

The deductivist theory of scientific structure initially came under fire from Michael Scriven, Mary Hesse and Rom Harré for the lack of *sufficiency* of Humean criteria for causality and law, Hempelian criteria for explanation and Nagelian criteria for the reduction of one science to another more basic one. Their critique was then generalized by Roy Bhaskar to incorporate the lack of *necessity* for them also. Bhaskar argued that positivism could sustain neither the necessity nor the universality – and in particular the transfactuality (in open and closed systems alike) – of laws; and for an ontology – in what he characterized as the intransitive dimension of the philosophy of science – that did not identify the domains of the real, the actual and the empirical. It is of some significance that the attack against deductivism was both initiated and carried through by philosophers with a strong interest in the human sciences where what one writer has called the 'law-explanation orthodoxy' (Outhwaite, 1987b) was never even remotely plausible (Donagan, 1966).

The linchpin of deductivism was the Popper-Hempel theory of explanation, according to which explanation proceeded by deductive subsumption under universal laws (interpreted as empirical regularities). It was pointed out, however, that deductive subsumption typically does not explain but merely generalizes the problem (for instance, from 'why does this x ϕ?' to 'why do all x's ϕ?'). What is required for a genuine explanation is, as Whewell and Campbell had insisted, the introduction of new concepts not already contained in the explanandum, models, picturing plausible generative mechanisms, and the like. But the new – critical or transcendental – realists broke with Campbell's Kantianism by allowing that, under some conditions, these concepts or models could denote new and deeper levels of reality; and science was seen as proceeding by a continuing and reiterated process of movement from manifest phenomena, through creative modelling and experimentation, to the identification of their generative causes, which now became the new phenomena to be explained. . . . Moreover it was argued that the laws which science identified under experimentally closed conditions continued to hold (but transfactually, not as empirical regularities) extra-experimentally, thus providing a rationale for practical and applied explanatory, diagnostic, exploratory etc. work.

In the 1980s further arguments for scientific realism were adduced by I. Hacking, A. Chalmers and others. But there was also a partial resurgence of positivism in B. van Fraassen's 'constructive empiricism', which would once more restrict the ascription of reality to observables and in N. Cartwright's actualism, on which the laws of physics, in so far as they are not empirically true, literally lie. At the same time critical realists started to explore the question – in what was called the 'metacritical dimension' – of the conditions of the possibility of both positivism and REALISM alike (for example, the empirical identification permitted by twentieth-century technology of the novel enti-

ties and strata denoted by terms like 'atoms', 'electrons', 'radio stars', 'genes'). In this way they linked up with the 'strong programme in the sociology of knowledge' associated with Barry Barnes, David Bloor and the Edinburgh school. From here the century seems set to end, in the philosophy of science, on a pluralist and ecumenical note, with (arguably) the great questions of realism and naturalism resolved and perhaps more attention being given to the metacritical, metatheoretical and conceptual problems posed by particular sciences.

Reading
Bhaskar, R. 1975 (*1978*): *A Realist Theory of Science*, 2nd edn.
Chalmers, A. 1982: *What is this Thing called 'Science'?*, 2nd edn.
Feyerabend, P. 1975: *Against Method*.
Hacking, I. 1983: *Representing and Intervening*.
Harré, Rom and Madden, E. 1975: *Causal Powers*.
Kuhn, T.S. 1962 (*1970*): *The Structure of Scientific Revolutions*, 2nd edn.
Nagel, E. 1961: *The Structure of Science*.
Popper, K.R. 1959: *Conjectures and Refutations*.

ROY BHASKAR

philosophy of social science The social sciences have always existed in closer relation to their metatheories or philosophies than the natural sciences – that is to say, to invoke G. Bachelard's useful distinction, the diurnal philosophy of the scientists here has been more steeped in the nocturnal philosophy produced by their philosophers. Moreover each social science and each school within it has had ontological, epistemological, methodological and conceptual problems peculiar to it. But a grand contrast can be drawn between a naturalist positivism, strong in economics, psychology and sociology in the moulds of Emile Durkheim and Talcott Parsons and prominent in the Anglophone countries, and an anti-naturalist hermeneutics, strong in the more humanistically oriented social sciences and sociology in the vein of Max Weber and prominent in the Germanic world. This contrast cuts across the Marxist/non-Marxist divide. Thus traditional dialectical materialism of the sort of Friedrich Engels, G. Della Volpe and Louis Althusser may be ranged on one side, György Lukács, Jean-Paul Sartre and the FRANKFURT SCHOOL on the other. Only relatively recently has a third alternative, a critical or qualified naturalism, based on a non-positivist realist account of science come to the fore. This article will be mainly concerned with some of the issues that have arisen in the philosophy of the social sciences in the twentieth century.

Explanation and prediction

The canonical positivist model of EXPLANATION holds that to explain an event etc. is to deduce it from a set of universal laws plus initial conditions. Unfortunately examples of explanations conforming to this model are completely absent in the social sciences. This provides the strongest negative argument for hermeneutics. The deductivist model posits a symmetry between explanation and PRE-DICTION but social science, operating as it must in open systems, has a notoriously bad predictive record. And strangely enough it was one of the leading exponents of the deductive-nomological model of explanation, Karl Popper, who was most virulent in his attack on what he called historicism, that is, the making of unconditional historical prophecies. Clearly the falsity of this does not imply that the social sciences cannot make conditional predictions, subject to a *ceteris paribus* clause. But the absence of closed systems means that decisive test situations are in principle impossible, so the social sciences must rely on exclusively explanatory criteria for confirmation and falsification. As for explanation, the new critical realists posit a distinction between theoretical and applied explanations. The former proceeds by *d*escription of significant features, *r*etroduction to possible causes, *e*limination of alternatives and *i*dentification of the generative mechanism or causal structure at work (which now becomes the new explanandum to be explained) (DREI); the latter by *r*esolution of a complex event (etc.) into its components, theoretical *r*edescription of these components, *r*etroduction to possible antecedents and *e*limination of alternative causes (RRRE).

Understanding

The strongest positive argument for hermeneutics is that since social phenomena are uniquely meaningful or rule governed, social science must be precisely concerned with the elucidation of the meaning of its subject matter – either by immersion in it as in the Wittgenstein-inspired account of P. Winch or by the dialogical fusion of horizons or meaning frames as in the Heideggerian account of H.-G. Gadamer. To this it can be objected that the conceptuality of social life can be recognized without assuming:

1   that such conceptualizations exhaust the subject matter of social science (consider the social states of famine, war or imprisonment or the psychological ones of anger, courage or isolation);

2   that such conceptualizations are incorrigible (rather we know since Marx and Freud that they may mask, repress, mystify, rationalize, obscure or otherwise occlude the nature of the activities in which they are implicated); or

3   that recognition of the conceptuality of social being rules out its scientific comprehension (at least once the restrictive empiricist ontology of *esse est percipi* is abandoned).

The hermeneutical paradigm is, however, consistent with a realist metatheory of science. Moreover critical realists typically insist that *Verstehen* must be the starting point for social enquiry.

Reasons and causes

The hermeneutical position is often buttressed by the argument that the human sciences are concerned with the reasons for agents' behaviour and that such reasons cannot be analysed as causes. For, first, reasons are not logically independent of the behaviour they explain. Moreover, second, they operate at a different language level (F. Waismann) or belong to a different language-game (Wittgenstein) from causes. But natural events can likewise be redescribed in terms of their causes (for instance, toast as burnt). Furthermore unless reasons were causally efficacious in producing one rather than another sequence of bodily movements, sounds or marks, it is difficult to see how there can be grounds for preferring one reason explanation to another, and indeed eventually the whole practice of giving reason-explanations must come to appear as without rationale (see also MATERIALISM).

Structure and agency

Both positivism and hermeneutics have been coupled with each of individualism and collectivism or holism; and positivists at least have accentuated either human agency or social structure. But the new realists suggest a relational paradigm for, in particular, sociology; and a resolution of the antinomy of structure and agency in the 'theory of structuration' (Anthony Giddens) or the 'transformational model of social activity' (Roy Bhaskar). According to this, social structure is both the ever-present condition and the continually reproduced outcome of intentional human agency. Thus people do not marry to reproduce the nuclear family or work to sustain the capitalist economy. Yet it is the unintended consequence (and inexorable result) of, as it is also a necessary condition for, their activity. Related to this is the controversy about ideal types. For critical realists the ground for abstraction lies in the real stratification (and ontological depth) of nature and society. They are not subjective classifications of an undifferentiated empirical reality, but attempts to grasp (for example in real definitions of forms of social life already understood in a pre-scientific way) precisely the generative mechanisms and causal structures which account in all their complex and multiple determinations for the concrete phenomena of human history. Closely connected with this is a reassessment of Marx as, at least in *Capital*, a scientific realist – contrary to pre-existing Marxist and non-Marxist interpretations. In its wake, too, is a reassessment of other founding figures in the social sciences (such as Durkheim and Weber) as combining aspects of a realist and some or other non-realist method and ontology.

Facts and values
Positivism upholds an unbridgeable gulf between fact and value statements. But the value impregnation of social-scientific factual discourse seems a patent fact. It is clearly bound up with the value-impregnated character of the social reality the social sciences are seeking to describe and explain. (Marx and Engels were just wrong not to see this.) Less obviously, it has been suggested by Bhaskar that social science has value implications. In so far as we can explain this necessity for systematically false consciousness (distorted communication and so on) about social phenomena then we can move *ceteris paribus* to negative valuations on the objects which make that consciousness necessary and to positive valuations on action rationally designed to transform them. Marx's 'critique of political economy' is an obvious paradigm here. This conception of social science as explanatory, and thence emancipatory, critique links up with Jürgen Habermas's early work on the 'emancipatory cognitive interest'; and with his more recent project for a *necessarily* (cf. Outhwaite, 1987) realist reconstructive science of communicative competence.

Naturalism
The new realists posit a series of ontological, epistemological, relational and critical differences between the social and natural sciences (see NATURALISM). The normal backcloth for this contrast has been (standard conceptions of) physics and chemistry. But more recently a number of writers have urged different disciplines for comparison – for instance, biology (Ted Benton), drama (Rom Harré and P.F. Secord, following up on the work of Erving Goffman and Harold Garfinkel). As the century draws to a close there seems plenty to keep social scientists talking.

Reading
Benton, Ted 1977: *Philosophical Foundations of the Three Sociologies*.
Bhaskar, Roy 1979 (*1989*): *The Possibility of Naturalism*, 2nd edn.
Giddens, Anthony 1984: *The Constitution of Society*.
Habermas, Jürgen 1968 (*1971*): *Knowledge and Human Interests*.
Harré, Rom 1979: *Social Being*.
Keat, Russell and Urry, John 1975 (*1981*): *Social Theory as Science*.
Manicas, Peter 1987: *A History and Philosophy of the Social Sciences*.
Outhwaite, William 1987: *New Philosophies of Social Science*.
Sayer, Derek 1979: *Marx's Method*.

ROY BHASKAR

planning, economic *See* ECONOMIC PLANNING

planning, social *See* SOCIAL PLANNING

pluralism The same word denotes three quite different bodies of ideas in the social sciences. One of them may be dealt with quite briefly: pluralism in this first sense refers to an institutional pattern in a non-Western preindustrial society under colonial or post-colonial rule. Plural society is a concept proposed by J. S. Furnivall (1948) and further developed by L. Kuper and M. G. Smith (1969). In such a society self-regulating and enclosed social groups live side by side, but each has a distinct communal existence. Such groups are externally linked by the state and the market. Such a pattern of pluralism does not imply equality of influence or importance between the groups; rather relations of hierarchy or domination are typical. Such communalistic relations are an obstacle to the development of the modern nation-state or the modern integrated economy.

American pluralism

The second sense of pluralism is by far the more influential and is much better known, so much so that references to 'the pluralist approach' or 'pluralism' almost invariably mean the American pluralist theory of political democracy. This theory claims to develop the insights of a number of premodern sources in political thought. Often cited is *The Federalist Papers* of 1787–8, but the most important precursor is Alexis de Tocqueville who argued in *Democracy in America* (1835–40) that a democratic polity is sustained by a society in which the conditions of plural political influence are secured and perpetuated. That is, democracy, in the sense of widespread and relatively evenly shared opportunities to influence public opinion and governmental decision-making, depends less on formal constitutional mechanisms like representative elections than on the existence of a plurality of secondary associations in CIVIL SOCIETY separate from and uncontrolled by the state. Such social dispersal of opinion and influence, such competing organized bodies of citizens, prevent majoritarian democracy from becoming tyrannical or the state from exclusively controlling the lives and loyalties of its citizens. Tocqueville's ideas are in direct opposition to those of Jean-Jacques Rousseau, who argued that all organizations that intervened between the state and the individual citizen perverted majoritarian democracy and ensured the rule of self-interested factions. That the French revolution and the Terror had intervened is clearly of some consequence. Tocqueville saw that if political society is composed of competing *minorities*, none able to prevail on each and every issue, it will be relatively secure against tyranny.

These insights have been developed more formally by American political scientists particularly since the 1940s. Notable pluralist theorists were Talcott Parsons (1969) and David Truman (1951). The most rigorous formulation is that of R. A. Dahl in *A Preface to Democratic Theory* (1956). In Dahl's hands pluralism becomes a theory of stable and relatively open political competition and of the institutional and normative conditions that sustain it. Power and influence will only be dispersed under definite social and political conditions: political participation must be at least potentially inclusive of all adult citizens who enjoy the same formal rights; the formation of competing interest groups and parties independent of state control must not be systematically monopolized by one minority group. In addition, the majority of competing groups seeking to control or to influence decision-making must subscribe to the norms of a democratic political culture, that is they must accept the circulation of office, the right of other groups to exist and limits on the methods of political competition (see INTEREST GROUP). Modern Western industrial societies and some Third World countries like India tend to meet these conditions to a sufficient degree that they can be classified as instances of satisfactorily functioning 'polyarchy'. No state is ever likely to meet in full all the ideal-typical conditions of a fully functioning democracy. Democracy exists under modern conditions in the form of 'polyarchy', that is the plural and successive influence of interest groups. Modern democracies are formed of competing constellations of such groups, not the formal rule of the representatives of a majority of individual citizens' opinions. Pluralism is the rule of minorities. At a minimum each of these minorities has some influence on some of the issues which concern it. So long as this is true, and groups deem the contest for influence sufficiently open that it is worth competing, and no group seeks or attains a monopoly of influence, then the system is pluralist. Pluralism neither requires an absolute equality of influence for all groups, nor does it assume politics is without conflict; it tries to argue that inequality and conflict have to be confined below definite thresholds if the system is to be polyarchical. It is, therefore, perfectly possible for a pluralist system to fail either on the dimension of inclusiveness, whence it becomes an oligarchical system, or on the dimension of competition, whence it becomes an 'inclusive hegemony', that is, power is monopolized by a specific minority group.

Dahl is the most explicit pluralist, in the sense of constructing a theoretical model of the conditions a polity must meet to guarantee a minimum of democratic competition for influence and office. It is the function of his model to show the degree to which concrete societies approximate to its conditions for polyarchy. Pluralism, and Dahl's work in particular, has been subject to much hostile criticism from radicals such as C. Wright Mills (1956) and Marxists such as R. Miliband (1969). They argue that pluralism is a systematic apologia for Western capitalist societies, that the pluralists wrongly claim that power and influence are widely distributed, and are at fault in claiming that there is no systematic inequality in access to political competition. Mills and Miliband argue that power is in fact monopolized and that a minority is able to control all major decisions affecting its interests. Bachrach and Baratz (1962) argue that the dominant group is sufficiently powerful that it can define the political agenda, such that issues of importance to other groups simply never become formal matters of political decision.

In fact, *pace* the critics, all pluralists need to argue is that a polyarchy exists if less successful groups still deem it worthwhile to compete and that over time the system shows a tendency to become more inclusive and more openly competitive. Dahl argues that on both counts Western societies show themselves minimally pluralist. He cites the rise to influence of labour parties and movements in Europe – having previously been excluded, they have both competed for and attained office and influence – and in the United States he cites the inclusion of blacks within the political system and the destruction of the Jim Crow system in the South. By and large radical and Marxist critics have lacked the methodological sophistication necessary to construct a serious empirical test of the pluralist model, while Dahl in particular had produced powerful criticisms of both Mills's power elite model (Dahl, 1958) and Marxist approaches to democracy (1948). The conventional wisdom of the 1960s radicals was that pluralism was obsolete ideology; on the contrary, pluralism has survived into the 1980s and worn better than the ideas of the critics.

The radical and Marxist criticism of pluralism is understandable in the context of the Cold War. Pluralism was often used uncritically as an apologia for and an endorsement of Western democracies. The ideological exploitation of a theory can clearly compromise its explanatory value. Rigorously specified, pluralist theory enables us to see how far many Western democracies are from a fully functioning polyarchy. It has to be said that, with the exception of the later work of Dahl (1982; 1985), it has seldom been used in this manner. When used in comparisons with the Soviet Union and its satellites, pluralism was able to show that Western democracies exhibited incomparably greater political influence and open political competition. Yet this encouraged and created an open target for hostile critics all too aware of the limits of democratic functioning in the West.

It must be added that pluralism is rigorous only as a specific theory of political competition and not as a general approach to political science. It does have major explanatory limitations, the chief of which is that it tends to treat the state and governmental agencies as if they are no more than a medium through which successfully influential groups are able to give effect to their aims. The state is thus an intermediary network through which competing groups strive to influence policy and decision-making, the state reflecting in its actions the objectives of the dominant organized interest on any particular issue. This could rather flippantly be called the telephone exchange theory of the state. It is extremely difficult to accommodate within pluralist theory the propositions that the state is an extremely exclusive institution and that groups and agencies within it have distinct interests and objectives of their own. However, the theory of a ruling elite or the Marxist theory of a ruling class are by no means effective substitutes, since they are generalizing theories which in turn systematically underplay the role of political competition and plural political influence. They in turn make the state both too impermeable and homogeneous, and too subservient to the dominant minority social group: the military-industrial complex or the capitalist class. While pluralism correctly challenges the zero–sum conception of power as a fixed quantity, it tends to ignore the institutional rigidities of government that prevent influence from being infinitely extendable.

An important area of pluralist empirical research has been the analysis of community power. Pluralists and neo–elitists have argued pro and contra the proposition that power in American regions and cities is widely diffused, the classic pluralist statement being Dahl (1961) and the classic statement of the monopolization of power being Floyd Hunter (1953). For overviews of this debate see Nelson W. Polsby (1963) and Arnold M. Rose (1967).

English political pluralism

The third sense of pluralism is that of English political pluralism. This current in political theory was very influential in Britain and internationally in the first quarter of this century, and then suffered a rapid and radical eclipse. Pluralism in this sense is less a doctrine of political competition, like the American, than a critique of state structure and the basis of the authority of the state. The English pluralists challenged the theory of unlimited state sovereignty and the conception of a unitary centralized state embodying such sovereign power in a hierarchy of exclusively controlled authority. The English pluralists gave a central role to voluntarily formed associations of citizens in civil society, but their main thrust in this respect was normative: to argue, that is, that the sovereign state restricted and inhibited the growth and freedom of such associations, that the state was an obstacle to the existence of plural self-governing associations and therefore should itself be 'pluralized' to correspond more closely with the needs of free associations in a free society. American pluralism, on the contrary, argues that the diffusion of power is a fact and it pays little attention to state structure.

The main English pluralist thinkers were the legal historian F. W. Maitland, his collaborator the Anglican clergyman John Neville Figgis and the socialist intellectuals G. D. H. Cole and Harold J. Laski. Maitland and Figgis were directly influenced by the German legal theorist Otto von Gierke and his theory of associations (1900). They challenged the 'fiction' theory of corporate personality and the concessionist conception of the legal right of associations. Such conceptions stemmed from the view that the sole legitimate organizations in society are the state, representing the will of the people, and individuals as bearers of rights. The grant of corporate personality is dependent on the state and the body so formed is limited in its power by its articles of association. Figgis in his major work *Churches in the Modern State* (1913) argued powerfully that such a view must inhibit both the free development of individuals and the internal democracy of associations. He argued that individuals can only pursue and enjoy certain of their most important freedoms in association with others, and that the concessionist view inhibited the autonomy of self-governing associations like churches and trade unions.

The notion of state sovereignty was challenged by all the pluralists. By 'sovereignty' they meant that a particular political body, typically a legislature, claimed for itself a plenitude of power and a right to exercise control over and to make rules for every person, agency and circumstance within a definite territory. Sovereignty is a defective concept because no such body can actually possess such a plenitude of power and because in claiming to do so it tended to strike at the plural sources of power, influence and administration in a society. Laski (1921) summed this opposition up well when he argued that in modern societies all power and organization are necessarily and *de facto* federative.

The state should thus concede autonomy and self-government to those agencies and associations most appropriate to performing a particular task – he claimed that as 'the railways are as real as Lancashire' they should be left to conduct those affairs peculiar to them no less than the county was left to manage its local affairs. Cole and Laski argued strongly for the participation of workers in the government of their industries and for those industries to build up federatively the patterns of codetermination and collaboration one with another they found necessary and appropriate. Cole explicitly linked the pluralization of state authority with the Guild Socialist government of industry in *Guild Socialism Re-stated* (1920).

The pluralists believed in dispersing state power into distinct and functionally autonomous domains of authority. Because of this they were strongly opposed to the representative democratic legitimation of the centralized state, the claim that only such a body could represent the will of the people, other bodies being partial and self-interested. Cole, in particular, strongly challenged this view, arguing that the representation of the actual wills of a diverse mass of citizens was impossible. The pluralists denied that society could give rise to a general will, claiming in contrast that the interests of citizens were both specific and diverse. Although all the pluralists believed that centralized state power should be dispersed and that associations should enjoy the greatest measure of freedom consistent with the liberty of others, they did not agree about the nature of the remaining public power in such a system. Cole, in particular, strongly favoured replacing the system of representative democracy with a system of functional democracy based on the industrial guilds. Laski favoured a combination of a representative territorial system with functional self-government.

Pluralism waned after the mid-1920s. The 1929 crash finished it off completely, as radicals advocated more rather than less central state action to revitalize the economy – Cole and Laski among them. It is now returning to intellectual prominence as excessive centralization loses support and the devolution of power seems more attractive in Western countries. For an excellent account of English pluralism see Nicholls (1975).

Reading

Dahl, R.A. 1956 (*1966*): *A Preface to Democratic Theory.*
Hirst, P.Q. ed. 1989: *The Pluralist Theory of the State:*

Selected Writings of G.D.H. Cole, J.N. Figgis and H.J. Laski.

Hunter, F. 1953: *Community Power Structure.*

Kuper, L. and Smith, M.G. eds 1969: *Pluralism in Africa.*

Nicholls, D. 1975: *The Pluralist State.*

Polsby, N.W. 1980: *Community Power and Political Theory*, 2nd edn.

Rose, A.M. 1967: *The Power Structure.*

PAUL QUENTIN HIRST

police   Whether referring to the function of maintaining social control in society (policing) or to the agency set up to carry out this function (the police), we are dealing with a complex, contentious and highly charged issue. While we are all policed in some way (society requires some minimum of organization and conformity to persist), the question of who is policed, by whom, in what way(s) and with what justification(s) gets to the heart of debates about social and political processes (see SOCIETY; POWER; STATE). Policing can be: formal or informal; public or private; open or secret; locally or centrally controlled; reactive or proactive; peaceful or violent; community based or paramilitary; by consent or in the teeth of opposition and resistance. Traditionally policing has been legitimated (see LEGITIMACY) by the need to control crime and apprehend the lawbreaker. However, much police work is not related to crime and the police also have a central role in maintaining public order and controlling political dissent.

There are variations both historically and across cultures in terms of police structures, powers and performance. In preindustrial societies crime control tends to be carried out by the whole community without an organized police force. With increasing differentiation (see INDUSTRIALIZATION) specific officials are appointed to maintain order leading to the proliferation of specialist forces. As with any group wielding considerable power, there is the ever-present danger of corruption, violence and racism and this forms a major focus for debates about policing. Policing tends to generate reactionary, defensive, inward-looking cultures, resistant to criticism and reform. Typically police are armed, uniformed and male.

Not surprisingly, theories about the police are closely related to wider political ideologies (see IDEOLOGY). Three approaches can be distinguished: (a) a conservative view focuses on the police as crime fighters, emphasizing and (implicitly) supporting the integrative role they play in promoting social harmony; (b) a radical view (such as Marxism) regards the police as a repressive state agency, necessarily operating in the interests of the ruling class in controlling working-class resistance against exploitation, that is, the police are seen as the enemy, to be abolished; (c) a policy-oriented approach (emerging more recently) accepts the need for policing and examines various styles and methods of policing in a more empirical way, utilizing criteria like efficiency, effectiveness and public acceptability (Morgan and Smith, 1989).

Two current developments suggest possible sources of change. First, prevailing masculinist values in policing emphasizing toughness, aggression, machismo, drinking, not losing face, and so on, are now being challenged by feminists, who point out that the concerns of women both in the police and in being policed are shamefully neglected. However, with more women joining the police it remains an open question whether 'the image of the traditional cop is about to change fundamentally' (Chessyne, 1989, p. 20), or whether women will simply become integrated into the macho 'cop culture' that has become ingrained throughout the world. Second, recent radical changes to social and political organization in Eastern Europe may well open the way for a more democratic and accountable style of policing in countries hitherto dominated by repression. This may challenge conventional assumptions about the relative openness of policing in the West and add an interesting new twist to debates about powers, accountability and acceptability.

See also CRIME AND DEVIANCE.

Reading
Benyon, J. and Bourne, C. eds 1986: *The Police: Powers, Procedures and Proprieties.*

Dunhill, C. ed. 1989: *The Boys in Blue: Women's Challenge to the Police.*

Hanmer, J., Radford, J. and Stanko, E.A. eds 1989: *Women, Policing and Male Violence: International Perspectives.*

Morgan, R. and Smith, D.J. eds 1989: *Coming to Terms with Policing.*

Reiner, R. 1985: *The Politics of the Police.*

Roach, J. and Thomaneck, J. eds 1985: *Police and Public Order in Europe.*

CHARLES R. M. WILSON

policy, social   *See* SOCIAL POLICY

political culture   The concept dates from the 1950s when it became an analytical tool of political science. Gabriel Almond, one of the pioneers of the new approach, defined political culture as 'a particular pattern of orientations to political action', a 'set of meanings and purposes' within which every political system is embedded (1956, p. 396). Political culture therefore refers to the beliefs, values and expressive symbols (the 'flag', the monarchy, and so on) that comprise the emotional and attitudinal context of political activity. The analysis of political systems in terms of their cultural attributes has distant antecedents. As far back as the eighteenth century, Montesquieu thought it appropriate to relate the constitutional principles of a nation to its 'morals or customs'. The revival and systematic development of this approach during the past 30 or 40 years must be understood against the background of the 'behaviourial revolution', which rejected the formal legal-institutional study of politics and instead stressed empirically observable behaviour (see BEHAVIOURISM). For this reason, most analysts are careful to draw a conceptual distinction between political *culture* and political *behaviour*, since the former is meant to explain – at least partially – the latter. In particular, political scientists have been concerned to explore the links between stable democracy and certain types of political culture. The concept is seen as a powerful explanatory variable in accounting for the failure of Western-style democracy to take root in the less developed countries of the Third World, where cultural fragmentation and traditional habits of passivity supposedly undermine constitutional patterns (Almond, 1956, pp. 400–3). It has also been argued that a cultural approach can help to explain the diversity of communist systems, as revolutionaries must inevitably adapt their Marxist model to suit the specific politico-ethical heritage of the country in question (Tucker, 1973).

Whether political culture actually succeeds in explaining anything is open to doubt. In the first place, it is difficult to determine the precise components of a nation's political culture. Early studies were impressionistic and seemed to infer subjective orientations from the practical behaviour that the orientations were meant to have caused. Thus, in Almond's first treatment of the subject, the 'log-rolling' antics of American politicians were taken to demonstrate that America possessed 'a rational-calculating, bargaining, and experimental political culture', while – at the same time – these antics were explained by the 'culture' (1956, p. 398). The circularity of this reasoning did not escape critical notice, and by the 1960s attempts

were made to discover mass attitudes through rigorous survey methods (Almond and Verba, 1963). But it is by no means obvious that popular VALUES and beliefs can be elicited by techniques of data gathering and analysis. As critics have shown, it is notoriously difficult to frame unambiguous questions to put to respondents, and such questions may in any case be too clear-cut to capture the ambivalent and shifting attitudes of ordinary people (Femia, 1979). At any rate, 'hard' data do not obviate the need for intuition and interpretation on the part of the analyst. For example, how widespread must an attitude be before it can be included in a country's political culture? If, say, 51 per cent of the adult population are classed as 'deferential', does this mean that the political culture is a deferential one? Small wonder that the literature abounds in vague and even banal observations (such as 'The British political culture is a mixture of tradition and modernity').

Even if we could determine a particular political culture with mathematical precision, it would not follow that the cultural orientations so determined would have any causal efficacy. Some critics argue that what passes for political culture is largely the creation of the political system it is supposed to explain. If, to take one example, Italians are alienated from their political institutions, this disaffection must to some degree result from the inadequate performance of those institutions. The way a system performs, moreover, will be influenced by its own characteristic features. In Italy political immobilism can be seen as an effect of proportional representation, which – given the nature of the country's social cleavages – ensures unstable coalition government (Sartori, 1969).

Orthodox Marxists have also questioned the validity of cultural explanations. In their perspective ideas and beliefs are merely derivative from the social and economic structure. Political behaviour is therefore ultimately explicable in terms of class conflict or other material pressures. Under the influence of Antonio Gramsci, however, some present-day Marxists have conceded the explanatory potency of cultural phenomena. It is no longer considered 'bourgeois' to account for the persistence of liberal democracy by reference to widely shared perceptions and norms. Yet no Marxist would assume that this CONSENSUS emerged fully formed from the national soil; he or she would attempt to trace the dominant cultural outlook back to its socioeconomic roots.

This brings us to the central defect of political culture analysis as normally practised. Its practitioners appear to forget that culture is the product of many and various influences, and that its use as an explanatory variable should never be other than as an intervening factor. The actual relationship between the normative order and political or social or economic structures is likely to be one of mutual reinforcement over time, and this interaction makes it hard to decide which, if any, factor is most important. Political culture must form *part* of an explanation of the performance of political systems, but eventually we must examine how cultural orientations came to be formed. Still, man is a symbolic animal living a mental life. His actions will reflect the way he interprets his environment, and this interpretation will be shaped by his 'cognitive map' (Almond, 1956, p. 402), his beliefs and attitudes. With this truism in mind, we may conclude that the concept of political culture can, at least potentially, increase our understanding of political life.

Reading
Kavanagh, D. 1972: *Political Culture.*
Nordlinger, E. 1967: *The Working-Class Tories: Authority, Deference, and Stable Democracy.*
Pye, L. and Verba, S. eds 1965: *Political Culture and Political Development.*
Rosenbaum, W.A. 1975: *Political Culture.*
White, S. 1979: *Political Culture and Soviet Politics.*

JOSEPH V. FEMIA

political economy This designation has acquired a variety of meanings, not all of which are consistent with one another. Historically, the term 'economics' referred to the management of the household budget. When the household was that of the monarch, such economic concerns were obviously political. Hence 'political economy' originated as the study of the problems concerning the monarch's revenues (from taxes and loans) and expenditures (on the court, civilian administration and army and navy) in an era when nation-states were beginning to consolidate and when debasement of the currency was common. In particular, the sixteenth-century European inflation associated with the influx of silver from the New World prompted issues concerning the determinants of balance between revenues and expenditures, and their association with the nation's trade, production and, more generally, wealth. The seventeenth-century mercantilists located the origins of wealth

in the acquisition of precious metals through trade surpluses, reflecting the predominant merchant capitalism of the time. This doctrine was superceded in the following century by that of the physiocrats who located the source of all wealth in agriculture (reflecting the slow growth of agricultural capitalism). Later still, the origins of wealth were sought (by Adam Smith in the 1770s) in the extension of the division of labour, reflecting the increase in economic activity leading up to the industrial revolution. In the early nineteenth century, during the industrial revolution (David Ricardo), and rather later (Karl Marx), there is the recognition that the origins of wealth lie more generally in production. In particular, the focus is on how an economic surplus (surplus, that is, to the reproduction of a subsistence stationary state) is produced, and how it is distributed; what the relation of such production and distribution is to economic growth and class conflict (between landlords and capitalists for Ricardo, and between capitalists and workers for Marx); and what the implications are for prices, profits, wages and employment.

Marx further distinguished 'classical' political economy, which 'investigated the real internal framework of bourgeois relations of production' and which he regarded as thereby scientific, from the activities of 'vulgar' economists who 'flounder around within the apparent framework of those relations . . . systematizing in a pedantic way, and proclaiming for everlasting truths, the banal and complacent notions held by the bourgeois agents of production about their own world, which is to them the best possible one' (*Capital*, vol. 1, 1867 (*1976*), p. 174, n34). For Marx, the break occurred in 1830: the conquest of political power in France and England by the bourgeoisie and its class conflict with a rapidly increasing proletariat marked the end of any possibility of further development of scientific political economy; thereafter all that was possible was either apologetics for the status quo (vulgar political economy) or scientific critique (his own work).

More conventional successors to Ricardo increasingly regarded Ricardo's foundation of his theory on a labour theory of value as unsatisfactory, and by the 1870s his theory of rent had been successfully generalized to other so-called factors of production such that, in competitive equilibrium, each factor receives the monetary equivalent of its marginal contribution to output. Several consequences immediately followed. First, issues of growth and aggregate economic activity were displaced by concerns of resource allocation. Second, class conflict was displaced by the focus on maximizing individuals (utility maximizing consumers and profit maximizing producers) with given initial endowments and given technologies of production (both matters of history) and given preferences (a matter of psychology). Third, the very notion of an economic surplus disappeared. And fourth, the term 'political economy' was displaced by the term 'economics'. (See VALUE.) While Marxists found these developments 'vulgar', and continued to use the term 'classical political economy' to describe the work of Ricardo and his predecessors, other economists increasingly followed J. M. Keynes's usage of the term 'classical economics' to describe the economic orthodoxy in the century after Ricardo (treating Marx as a follower of Ricardo) and prior to Keynes's own *General Theory* of 1936. The term political economy only survived in the non-Marxist orthodoxy in two senses. First, it occurs as an occasional term in the theory of public finance, an obvious reference to its historical origins. Second, it has been appropriated by a growing body of work, largely originating in the USA in the 1970s, which investigates the interaction between democratic political processes and the economic relations of commodity exchange in free markets; the former are regarded as hindering the latter and require restructuring and subordinating to the latter. Again the reference back to the historical origins of the term is clear.

While a Marxist tradition in the twentieth century was maintained by economists such as Paul Baran and Paul Sweezy in the USA and by Maurice Dobb and Ronald Meek in the UK, it was the conjunction of the civil rights movement in the USA with massive US military involvement in Vietnam which led to a revival of the concerns of classical political economy. Hymer and Roosevelt (in Lindbeck, 1977) describe the consequences of the use of 'reason, technical knowledge, legal maneuvering, and electoral reform politics' by student activists in the 1960s and early 1970s:

They discovered personally the violence backed up by law and government that was used against blacks; in underdeveloped countries they saw ruling elites cooperating with international business to obstruct the most obviously needed reforms; they saw that their university adminis-

trators would resist mild demands with incredible tenacity; they saw how social welfare programs and prisons terrorized and degraded the very people they were supposed to uplift; and, in politics young people found that even if they could rouse a large groundswell against the War and force a President to give up, it did not stop the War. From this experience, they began to wonder if there is not something fundamentally at fault in the system itself. (p. 121)

This questioning led to the construction of an alternative world-view to that of the prevailing economic orthodoxy, which rejected the latter's focus on efficient patterns of resource allocation produced by the optimizing activities of rational (and often omniscient) individuals in favour of many of the concerns of the classical political economy tradition which had culminated in the work of Marx. In particular, economists of the New Left (as they came to be called) did not deny the focus on competition and voluntary exchange in markets so central to economic orthodoxy; but they argued that such a focus was too one-dimensional to represent the reality of capitalism in anything other than a misleading manner. What was required in addition was, first, a recognition of the relationships of power, coercion and hierarchy characteristic of both the workplace and the marketplace in capitalist society; and second, a recognition that capitalist societies are not in static or even dynamic equilibrium, but are constantly changing, such changes being produced by their systemic existence.

The focus on power is particularly important. Explanation of the inequalities of capitalist society in terms of the optimizing behaviour of individuals is, for radical political economists, particularly otiose, since it constructs at best misleading, and more typically quite mythical, representations of capitalist reality. Political economy instead focuses on aggregates of individuals, on how power relations distribute resources between such aggregates and on how these distributions of resources maintain relations of domination and subordination. This type of analysis of distributive relations has been widely used in analyses of poverty in class stratified societies, in analyses of gender and patriarchal relations between men and women, in analyses of racial conflict within the richer capitalist countries, and in a wide variety of analyses of the situation facing underdeveloped countries both in terms of their domestic environment and in terms

POLITICAL PARTICIPATION 479

of their insertion into a world market dominated by the richer capitalist countries.

But it is not only with respect to power relations between aggregates in distribution that radical political economy distinguishes itself from economic orthodoxy. Marx himself thought that the relations of domination and subordination in the process of production itself were particularly important to the analysis of capitalism. But there was little development after Marx's own writings in this area, and in the twentieth century these Marxist concerns were rather neglected. However, they were revived, and indeed reached a much broader constituency with the publication in 1974 of Braverman's work on the capitalist LABOUR PROCESS which attempted to apply Marx's analysis to the modern workplace and its twentieth-century evolution. A large number of empirical studies have drawn their inspiration from Braverman's work and sought to understand the evolution of a wide variety of workplace situations. In this, there is some connection with the concerns of REGULATION theory. A related if distinct focus has been an analysis of the twentieth-century corporation; one strand of analysis draws on the American institutionalist school from Thorstein Veblen to J. K. Galbraith; another relates the evolution of the multinational corporation to Marxist theories of imperialism.

This itinerary of rediscovery of theoretical concerns of the past no longer a part of economic orthodoxy has simultaneously discovered how the work of many influential economists can be read and interpreted in a light different from how those works have been appropriated by economic orthodoxy. One prominent example is that of the work of Keynes: while the orthodox interpretation sees Keynesian economics in terms of equilibrium states, Joan Robinson and her associates have always insisted that this is to distort the disequilibrium processes with which Keynes was concerned. Thus Nell for example argues that the economic orthodoxy 'misrepresents the nature of circulation and distribution' (1980, p. xi); a more accurate understanding of these requires a return to Keynes's theory of effective demand and its extension to link pricing and investment decisions (see POST-KEYNESIANISM). Other examples include Piero Sraffa's interpretation of Ricardo's economics, and the rediscovery of Marxian economics as something other than a minor variant in the Ricardian tradition.

The concerns of radical political economy are thus heterogeneous; united by hostility to the prevailing economic orthodoxy, they remain eclectic, partly complementary to, and partly competitive with, each other. In the USA, the Union for Radical Political Economics (URPE), publishing the *Review of Radical Political Economics*, is the major umbrella organization of dissenting economists; in the UK there is the analogous Conference of Socialist Economists (CSE) with its journal *Capital & Class*, but the concerns of political economy pervade a number of other journals, including the *Cambridge Journal of Economics*, *Critical Social Policy*, and *Race and Class*, testifying to its influence in challenging economic orthodoxies.

Reading
Bowles, S. and Edwards, R. 1985: *Understanding Capitalism: Competition, Command and Change in the US Economy*.
Edwards, R.C., Reich, M. and Weisskopf, T.E. 1978: *The Capitalist System*, 2nd edn.
Green, F. and Sutcliffe, B. 1987: *The Profit System*.
Lindbeck, A. 1977: *The Political Economy of the New Left: An Outsider's View*, 2nd edn.
Nell, E.J. ed. 1980: *Growth, Profits and Property: Essays in the Revival of Political Economy*.

SIMON MOHUN

political participation This means the number and intensity of individuals and groups involved in decision-making. From the time of the ancient Greeks it was thought ideally to consist of free citizens debating publicly and voting on decisions of government. The simplest theory has always been that good government depends on high levels of participation. But that is difficult to achieve outside small units, so participation is found both in indirect modes – the distinction between representative rather than direct DEMOCRACY – and in minimal modes, such as simply voting in occasional elections. Most decisions of governments are taken independently of the wishes of their citizens. To try to bridge this huge gap between the power of the state and the authenticity of the individual, Jean-Jacques Rousseau famously propounded his doctrine of the General Will: that a person can only be truly a citizen (with all the rights and duties entailed) when he or she wills the general, not the particular good. Although this doctrine is democratic in the sense that any human being, however ignorant, can express the general will, yet it makes virtue not numbers the test.

Liberal theorists in the nineteenth century made education the test of fitness for participation; in the twentieth century democratic power has simply demanded compulsory primary and secondary education. While increasing popular participation was seen as the strength of representative government, some worried that such mass participation was increasingly vulnerable to manipulation by elites (see ELITE THEORY). Old autocracy had followed the adage or theory of government, 'let sleeping dogs lie,' only needing passive obedience; but modern political leaders, of both left and right, demanded positive enthusiasm, 'mobilizing the masses' to create unprecedented power for social transformation. So theories of participation have taken both totalitarian and democratic forms.

Roberto Michels (1911) posited an 'iron law of oligarchy': above every democratic base there stood a bureaucratic hierarchy. Others argued that this is not necessarily undemocratic so long as these elites are competitive, circulate or are penetrable. Syndicalists, Guild Socialists, anarchists and pluralists all, however, denied the premise that societies are simple hierarchies of leaders and masses, seeing them rather as a plurality of groups constituting participative and overlapping communities.

Some thinkers (especially those in the American federalist tradition) argue that participation must be limited by institutional checks and balances, that legal rules and a constitutional framework alone create a just CIVIL SOCIETY. Others (especially those in the French revolutionary tradition) argue that civil society is nothing other than an unhampered evolution of popular participation.

The necessity for a skilled and literate working class in modern industrial societies forces governing classes to tolerate, even encourage, high levels of participation, whether controlled by a single party mass movement, or open, voluntary and habitual. Some still argue, however, that high levels of political apathy denote social stability; but this is doubtful, and statistics meant to prove this usually measure participation only in formal political parties, rather than in the whole range of social groups in which rates of participation are higher.

See also PARTICIPATION; SELF-MANAGEMENT.

Reading
Keane, J. 1988: *Democracy and Civil Society.*
Kornhauser, W. 1960: *The Politics of Mass Society.*
Michels, R. 1911 (*1962*): *Political Parties.*
Pateman, C. 1970: *Participation and Democratic Theory.*

Schumpeter, J.A. 1942 (*1987*): *Capitalism, Socialism and Democracy.*

BERNARD CRICK

political party   To fulfil their aims of achieving power or of preventing others from coming to power, political parties typically build large apparatuses with ramifications throughout the country; they adopt programmes which they propose to or press on the population; and they recruit future generations of politicians.

Political parties are essentially nineteenth-century innovations. They did exist spasmodically previously, but in certain types of polities, such as Republican Rome, Italian Renaissance cities, or Stuart and Hanoverian England. Their spread in nineteenth-century Western Europe and North America coincided with the emergence of political systems based on popular sovereignty where a link was needed between the rulers and the ruled. Where politics takes place exclusively within a closed elite which is not responsible to the rest of the population, parties do not exist; where, on the contrary, some form of representation exists, even if it is limited or very constrained, parties emerge. They develop fully, however, when three conditions are fulfilled – and these tend to be present almost everywhere in the contemporary world. The first condition is the existence of social cleavages (ethnic, religious or class-based, for instance) – otherwise parties tend to be personal coteries; second, the government has to be based on popular support, even if this is more in words than in deeds; and, third, there has to be a belief that victory will be achieved only if the mass of the population or at least a substantial proportion of it has to be organized – small conspiracies are then not felt to be adequate.

These three conditions were not fulfilled in most parts of Western Europe in the early part of the nineteenth century. Parties tended therefore to be dominated by small cliques or by members of the old social elite; they were 'cadre' parties. Under the pressure of the extension of the suffrage, party organizations began to expand; they acquired members and appointed substantial numbers of officials, increasingly drawn from the ranks of the ordinary middle class and even from the working class; they became 'mass' parties, of which the best examples were the labour or social democratic parties set up at the end of the nineteenth century.

These were ostensibly democratic in that their policies were officially decided by congresses representing the membership; in practice, leaders wielded substantial power and were often accused of exercising bureaucratic control. In order to fight effectively their new opponents, parties of the right and centre gradually adopted many of the organizational characteristics of their competitors. The age of the mass party seemed to have arrived with the twentieth century.

At the same time, however, another type of political party, with a rather different purpose, began to take root, first in Eastern and Central Europe, and after 1945 in many newly independent states of the Third World. This type of party was set up to buttress governments wanting to impose their authoritarian or even totalitarian rule, whether of the right (fascism and Nazism being the clearest cases) or of the Left (communism, but also various forms of Third World 'populism'). In those regimes, the single party was the instrument of the dictatorship, as it provided a means of spreading the message of the rulers across the country. The purpose was essentially to mobilize the population and control it, although these efforts needed typically to be combined with the popularity of a 'charismatic' leader (see CHARISMA). However, even in these cases, the success of the single party was often shortlived and rarely truly durable: the fall of communist regimes in Eastern Europe and the Soviet Union after several decades of apparently unshakeable power showed the intrinsic weakness of the single-party system.

Competitive party systems appear more stable overall, at least in Western Europe and North America. They have spread to other parts of the world, with varying degrees of success, Latin America in particular having known periodically periods of competitive politics followed by periods of military rule. Indeed, even in Western Europe, competitive party systems have been subjected to major criticisms and to reappraisals. The stability of the mass party is in question, with the decline of party 'identification' and the growth of the 'independence' of the electorate. Party programmes have lost much of their clarity as they take increasingly into account demands made by groups putting forward new 'postmodern' issues, in particular with respect to the environment.

These developments have led to the role of parties being put in question. Their programmatic function appears to be shrinking; they are sometimes by-passed by direct appeals to the people by way of referendums; the personalization of leaders, pushed by the mass media and by television in particular, means that intermediate party elites and party structures in general are becoming redundant. While this is taking place in the West, the collapse of many single-party systems and in particular of most communist single-party systems constitutes a major blow to the prestige of parties as mobilizing organizations.

Yet there are no real substitutes for parties in the contemporary world, whether in industrial or in developing countries. Some relationship between people and government has to exist, even if the links are becoming less tight; there has also to be a place where programmes and policies are formally adopted and publicized and where the demands of groups can be presented and discussed; and there has to be a channel through which future politicians can be recruited. For all these reasons, parties will continue to play a major part in the political life of our societies, even if the enthusiasm which characterized their earliest development gives way to lukewarm support and even continuous criticism.

Reading
Castles, F.C. ed. 1982: *The Impact of Parties*.
Duverger, M. 1955: *Political Parties*.
Janda, K. 1980: *Political Parties: A Cross-National Survey*.
Michels, R. 1911 (*1949*): *Political Parties*.
Randall, V. ed. 1988: *Political Parties in the Third World*.
Sartori, G. 1976: *Parties and Party Systems*.
Wolinetz, S. ed. 1988: *Parties and Party Systems in Liberal Democracies*.

J. BLONDEL

political ritual   As formal or standardized activity typically performed at certain specific times and places, ritual differs from mere habit and custom in being symbolic and often dramatic, expressing and communicating ideas but also often powerful feelings. It does this through symbolic scenes, acts and words that bring diverse ideas together. Often a single symbol can stand for many ideas, and the interpretation of ritual symbolism is often ambiguous. Political rituals typically occur before the public; what they express and communicate typically concerns, or helps to shape, central interests of those who participate in them and those who observe them. In this way, they can help to determine what is politically significant in a community, representing its past and future, and the social relations within it. (See also POLITICAL CULTURE.)

The effects of political ritual are hard to estimate but are probably both cognitive and emotional, conveying both a certain stereotypical picture of the social and political world and of the identities of those who inhabit it, and strong sentiments associated with these, often inducing or reinforcing strong loyalties and sometimes hostilities. (See also IDENTITY.) The result may be either socially cohesive or divisive. Political rituals may be integrative, a means of legitimation, inculcating and consolidating a civil religion, as, say, coronations are supposed to do, or Memorial Day commemorating the American war dead (see Warner, 1959), or they may be conflictual, as when, say, the Protestant Apprentice Boys march in Catholic areas in Northern Ireland or Chinese students erect a Statue of Liberty in Tienanmen Square, or they may serve to mark out, and thus reinforce, social divisions within a plural society, as in ethnic parades or May Day parades in capitalist societies.

To say that political rituals are expressive is not to deny that they may be instrumentally or strategically used, whether to consolidate or resist power, or to express limited opposition to an existing social order. Moreover their interpretation is often a matter for contest, even struggle. Nor should one suppose that political ritual is 'merely ritual', an illusion essentially irrelevant to the 'real' business of politics. Both dictators and revolutionaries have clearly believed its effects to be very powerful: even the rationalist leaders of the French revolution thought it important to establish elaborate rituals of Reason, and thereby obliterate the symbolism of the Catholic past (see L. Hunt's chapter in Alexander, 1988).

Political rituals may be distinct solemn or festive occasions, like coronations or parades. They may be apparently non-ritual activities, such as elections, which are then interpreted as political rituals. Or one may see *aspects* of political ritual in ordinary political activities, as when, say, a ritual aspect is seen in the budgetary process.

Reading
Edelman, M. 1971: *Politics as Symbolic Action.*
Kertzer, K.I. 1988: *Ritual, Politics and Power.*
Moore, S.F. and Myerhoff, B.G. eds 1977: *Secular Ritual.*

STEVEN LUKES

political science This discipline is concerned with the study of political phenomena. Such phenomena are often regarded as characterizing exclusively the national government together with local and regional authorities, and this is indeed where politics is the most visible, but in reality the activity of politics is general. It occurs in all organizations, be they businesses, trade unions, churches or social organizations. Politics can thus variously be described as being concerned with power, as dealing with conflict resolution, or as providing decision-making mechanisms. In truth, politics embraces all these things, as it is the mechanism by which collective action can be undertaken in any community as soon as there is no unanimity and as long as the community remains in existence. While the general character of political activity is now widely recognized, this activity is still mainly analysed in relation to public bodies, in part for historical reasons, in part because politics within these bodies affects directly all those who live in a given area, and in part because public bodies, and the state in particular, are formally entitled to control the structure of the other organizations existing within their geographical boundaries.

The word 'science' applied to the study of politics is regarded by some as controversial, at any rate if it is given a truly rigorous meaning. This controversial character stems from profound differences among scholars both about the nature of political phenomena and about the capacity of observers to analyse these phenomena 'objectively'. These differences are also reflected in the sharp distinction often made by the political scientists themselves between political science as such and a branch of POLITICAL THEORY which is close to political philosophy and is normative: while political science is the study of political phenomena, normative political theory is concerned with the characteristics of political values.

Despite a very old ancestry, political science as it is now known developed only recently; partly as a consequence, the profession of political scientist is still rather small, especially outside the United States. Admittedly, the study of politics can be traced back to the Greeks, Plato and Aristotle being the originators of the discipline; the contrast between these two authors' approaches does indeed illustrate the point that the divide between an emphasis on the observation of phenomena and an emphasis on the analysis of values has existed from the start. Yet the development of political science throughout the Middle Ages, the Renaissance, and the modern period was at best very patchy. There have been a number of brilliant writers, primarily Machiavelli, Bodin, Hobbes, Locke, Montesquieu, Rousseau and Tocqueville, whose interest in political life as it occurs was large, in part because they wanted to improve on a *status quo* which they felt to be highly unsatisfactory; but, while these authors exercised great influence, they did not develop an academic branch of learning which could be regarded as a science, even in embryo.

Political science did not therefore emerge as a discipline before the second half of the nineteenth century; yet even then and for several decades subsequently the growth of the discipline remained slow. Constitutional law, political philosophy, and political history were variously involved in this growth, with philosophy and history playing a larger part in Britain, while philosophy, and even more law, played a major part on the continent of Europe. Indeed, by the end of the twentieth century, political science had still not acquired fully independent status in many parts of the world; in reality, only in the United States as well as perhaps in Scandinavia and in some countries of the British Commonwealth can political science be regarded as having become truly established.

This lack of disciplinary autonomy affected the growth of political science; it also had an effect on the nature and vitality of political theory, especially on the non-normative aspects of this theory. As in all disciplines, political science needs to develop a theory if it is to understand the phenomena which it observes. Admittedly, it has already been pointed out that some believe a truly scientific theory of politics to be impossible given the nature of human behaviour, both individually and in groups. The grounds for such a standpoint range from the view that human actions are basically unpredictable to the notion that political situations are too complex for any scientific analysis to be able to discover, let alone measure, all the variables involved in the process; it is also claimed that observers' biases are inevitable and that what passes for 'observations' is often only a reflection of these biases.

While these views are undeniably partly correct, there is also a need to understand politics better, and especially to discover broad regularities, even if these do not turn out to constitute truly scientific 'laws'. To take only a few examples: there has been much interest in examining the relationship between electoral systems and party systems, or the socioeconomic conditions under which liberal democracy is likely to emerge and be stable, or which system, parliamentary or presidential, is likely to result in more effective government. Regularities which may be discovered in this way need to be based on and guided by a theory which can account for these broad trends.

A movement in this direction did indeed begin to take place in the 1950s. In a first phase, the goal was overambitious: it was felt possible to discover truly general explanatory models. These models were primarily drawn from philosophy of history or from sociology (see POLITICAL SOCIOLOGY), as was the case with the two most successful among them, MARXISM and FUNCTIONALISM. There was subsequently a shift of emphasis towards approaches more akin to those prevailing in economics, such as rational choice (see RATIONAL CHOICE THEORY). By and large, efforts made at such a level of generality have provided frameworks of analysis rather than true explanations of the characteristics of political life; they none the less have constituted a spur by helping to structure research.

Meanwhile, the debate about the feasibility of a science of politics continued despite and in a sense because of these general models – for, deep down, the origin of this debate can be found in the part played by historical 'accidents' and by the idiosyncratic context in which political phenomena often take place. Two camps or at least two tendencies unavoidably divide political scientists; those who feel that 'accidents' and idiosyncrasies play a truly major part in political life have tended to shy away from broad generalizations and maintained that the study of politics should provide lessons rather than aim at giving scientific explanations.

One of the reasons why such a debate is likely to continue and not even abate is that political life, and in particular political life at the level of the national decision-makers, is shaped markedly by the POLITICAL CULTURE of countries and in many cases even of regions; political and social traditions are the mechanisms through which historical specificities come to play a part. Yet another reason which also militates in favour of stressing the role of 'accidents' is the prominent part which some great political leaders seem to play in shaping the destiny of their country. Of course, not all is accident in the context of LEADERSHIP. One can discover regularities, for instance, in the background or in the career development of those who are at the top, be they government ministers, party leaders or senior civil servants. But the way in which these men and women are likely to behave will depend on more than these characteristics, and on more than the political environment: personality also plays a part and personality is first and foremost an individual feature. Some tend to play down the role of leaders – there is indeed a great debate on the matter – but most political scientists naturally find it hard, and at the limit impossible, to deny that leaders 'make a difference'. For, if they do so, they have at the same time to deny any influence to one of the most visible elements in political life and thus to reduce markedly the role of political factors. Full-scale generalizations can thus lead to pitfalls: they are likely to leave unexplained a large part of the concrete reality. They have therefore to be combined with the recognition of the importance of the particular context and of particular actors. This is perhaps the most difficult and the most challenging problem facing political scientists: more than other social scientists, they need to combine the general and the particular.

Such a state of affairs naturally affects the methodology of political science: political scientists must use a wide range of tools and techniques if they are to come to grips with reality. There is no single and common methodology. Those who are concerned with the study of leadership must collect evidence in the manner of historians, that is to say mainly from documents, although interviews also play a large and increasing part. Case studies of important events, for instance of major decisions in home or international affairs, need also to be based on documents and interviews, even if efforts are often made to undertake analyses within a structured framework. On the other hand, where regularly repeated happenings are examined, as in the case of the analysis of the careers of politicians, or where the behaviour of large numbers of individuals is examined, as in election studies, quantitative techniques are not only more appropriate but have to be used if general trends are to be discovered and associations between variables identified. As a matter of fact, studies of decision-making processes have been increasingly based also on formal mathematical models, especially those which developed (relatively) recently, such as GAME THEORY. Finally, straightforward arguments borrowed from law and philosophy prevail in those aspects of political science primarily concerned with constitutional and administrative arrangements as well as in normative and much of analytical political theory.

Political science has thus great diversity; it is not a truly united branch of learning. As we have seen, it never was. This does not necessarily constitute a handicap. Nor does this characteristic single out political science: other branches of learning do not appear to be appreciably more united. As a result of these divisions, one currently finds not only the old distinction between the study of values and empirical investigations, but five aspects of empirical studies which have become increasingly separate fields of inquiry: the study of government *stricto sensu*, of public administration, of international relations, and, more recently, of political behaviour and of public policy analysis.

The study of *government* is the oldest branch of the empirical study of politics. In its modern form, it has been often closely associated with (in some countries it proceeded from) constitutional law, in particular on the continent of Europe. It is concerned with the examination of the institutions and procedures characterizing political systems across the world: the institutions and procedures which are being studied may either be constitutionally set up (as legislatures or executives) or emerge *de facto* (political parties, for instance). The study of government is also concerned, indeed increasingly so, with the examination of behavioural patterns and especially with the way in which and the extent to which institutions and procedures affect behaviour. From a geographical standpoint, many studies of government are concentrating on one institution or on one country: the remarks made earlier about the idiosyncratic character of each political system apply here and are often strongly put forward by specialists of particular areas. Yet there are also (and increasingly) cross-national studies, either involving the governments of one region (such as Europe), covering governments in different regions (industrialized and developing), or attempting to be truly general. This branch of the discipline, known as *comparative government*, is thus a central element of the study of politics.

Public administration analyses the structure and characteristics of public bodies and the conditions of employment of those who run these bodies. From being essentially descriptive (in Britain and America) or concerned with legal arrangements (on the European continent), it has become primarily devoted to the analysis of the types of relationships which emerge within and between public agencies as well as between these agencies and the public. Public administration thus endeavours to discover the broad conditions under which public decisions are taken; it attempts to determine which of these conditions are the most efficient and the most effective in achieving particular goals. With the expansion of the public sector, the increasing variety of public agencies, as well as the tendency towards a reduction in the distinction between public and private organizations, the specificity of public administration has diminished, it has come closer to (and may even be regarded by some as part of) the study of organizations, which is a lively branch of SOCIOLOGY.

INTERNATIONAL RELATIONS studies have also changed markedly in their character, moving from being a not altogether distinct branch of history to becoming a section of political science. This is in part out of the recognition that they are markedly concerned with politics among nations and in part because the distinction between internal state matters and interstate relations has become less sharp; as a result of the increased number and variety of types of associations among states, and the growth of international non-governmental organizations, international and national affairs have tended to be linked. Meanwhile, at a more theoretical level, international relations scholars have looked for general models to structure their analyses. This, too, has brought the field closer to what can be regarded as mainstream political science. Although these general models have not succeeded so far in providing more than broad guidance, they have tended to suggest frameworks of analysis, as in other aspects of political science. Consequently, as in other branches of political science, too, the debate between the role of structural factors and the role of the specific context of given events has remained lively.

The last two important subfields of empirical political analysis have developed more recently, at least as fully fledged branches of the discipline. The study of *political behaviour* is in many ways the by-product of the eruption of mass politics in modern societies, in particular in the West. There has naturally been increasing interest in understanding the bases on which the people make their political choices, above all in the context of elections. This type of inquiry has to use different approaches and different methods from those conventionally adopted in the study of government or of public administration. Sociology and psychology have

markedly helped the development of analyses of political behaviour in providing conceptualization and techniques, while economics has more recently also played a significant part in the assessment of electoral choices. Meanwhile, political behaviour studies have expanded to the analysis of elites, in particular with respect to party members, to legislators, and to public servants. The goal is to discover the motivations of those who belong to these groups and to see how these motivations are translated into behaviour.

The study of *public policy analysis* is the newest subfield of political science. It proceeds from public administration but it differs from it in a way which is not altogether dissimilar from the way in which political behaviour studies have proceeded and also differed from the study of government. Public policy analysis is concerned with the manner in which the behaviour of political actors can affect decisions, while public administration is primarily concerned with structures and the effect of these structures. This branch of study emerged because scholars wished to understand better how decisions were concretely taken and especially how far they were (and indeed could be) taken 'rationally'. Thus the origin of public policy analysis can be found in the description of specific cases; it has moved rapidly towards a more systematic second stage, however, in which it has been markedly helped by the development of a number of mathematical tools, especially drawn from economics. These tools have made it possible to follow the ramifications of decisions and to classify types of outcomes. Given the complexity of public decisions at the national and even at the subnational level, the study of public policy-making is regarded by many as of major importance for decision-makers as it helps them to analyse better the problems with which they are confronted.

While political science was thus enjoying a major expansion in the course of the last decades of the twentieth century, its influence naturally increased appreciably. It still experiences major difficulties in predicting outcomes, whether the outcome of elections or of major decisional problems, but other social sciences also experience difficulties in making accurate predictions. Meanwhile, the need to engage in a systematic study of political trends and thus to make sense of political events is increasingly recognized both by the public at large and by the decision-makers themselves, be they politicians or career public servants. Perhaps naturally, the latter have often been reluctant to give major importance to the analysis of the structures in which they operate, as well as to the study of their own behaviour within these organizations; yet these sentiments are gradually overcome as patterns of political life are being identified more precisely at many levels. In this way, political science fulfils an essential function, which is that of helping citizens to acquire a better understanding of political phenomena and thus to have greater influence in their community and in the society at large.

Reading

Almond, G.A. and Powell, G.B. 1976: *Comparative Politics.*
Barry, B. 1965: *Political Argument.*
Blondel, J. 1981: *The Discipline of Politics.*
Dahl, R.A. 1963: *Modern Political Analysis.*
Downs, A. 1957: *An Economic Theory of Democracy.*
Easton, D. 1953: *The Political System.*
Harrop, M. and Miller, W.L. 1987: *Elections and Voters.*
Inglehart, R. 1977: *The Silent Revolution.*
Morgenthau, H.J. 1968: *Politics among Nations.*
Simon, H. 1947 (*1957*): *Administrative Behavior.*

J. BLONDEL

political sociology This discipline has been primarily concerned with the study of parties, electoral systems and voting behaviour, social movements, political leadership and elites, bureaucracy, nationalism and the formation of nation-states, types of political system, and political change. Many studies of parties have concentrated on their class basis, and in particular on the opposition between bourgeois and working-class parties, but in another direction the division within all types of party between the leaders and the mass of party members has been emphasized and was formulated in a classic study (Michels, 1911) as the 'iron law of oligarchy'. Political leadership was also a salient issue in the work of Mosca (1896), Pareto (1915-19), and Max Weber (1918, 1920), writing from the perspective of ELITE THEORY. Connected with such questions is the growth of BUREAUCRACY in modern societies which Weber saw, in the context of conditions in Imperial Germany, as producing a bureaucratic domination of politics as well as a general rationalization of social life. The role of bureaucracy in socialist societies has also been a major concern, though very differently evaluated by Weber and by Schumpeter (1942).

Social class differences have been given prominence in analyses of voting behaviour, while electoral systems themselves have come to be more closely studied in recent work, especially with regard to proportional representation, which is often seen as expressing more adequately the diversity of political opinion in modern democracies.

In recent decades there has been a growing interest in social movements (Scott, 1990), inspired partly by the rise of radical movements in the 1960s, though nationalist and neo-fascist movements have now also become more prominent again. Such movements are seen as alternative major forms of political action alongside previously dominant class movements. The various movements may, however, overlap to some extent, and they may also – and frequently do – give rise to new parties.

NATIONALISM and the creation of nation-states have been intensively studied by social scientists of different persuasions, who have emphasized their connection with the rise of the bourgeoisie (Bauer, 1907) and the subsequent emergence of imperialism, with the struggles for democracy (Kohn, 1967), or with industrialization and modernization (Gellner, 1983). The issues thus raised retain all their importance in the late twentieth century when movements for national independence within existing states have again become widespread.

Political sociologists have also given much attention to the differences between political systems, and in the second half of the twentieth century this interest has been largely concentrated on the contrast between democratic and totalitarian regimes (Aron, 1965), and on the new political systems that emerged in post-colonial developing countries. The latter studies have been closely related to theories of political change and conflict, which also encompass such large issues as the origins and development of modern capitalism (which may be conceived in Marxist, Weberian or Schumpeterian terms) or, still more widely, of the modern world system. Political conflict involves the clash of opinions, doctrines and ideologies, and much research has been concerned with the ways in which political opinions are formed, and the role of intellectuals and the mass media in this process.

In the postwar period the scope of political sociology has been greatly extended, so that it now covers virtually the same territory as POLITICAL SCIENCE. The remaining differences seem to derive mainly from traditional preoccupations, on one side with the formal 'machinery of government', on the other side with the social context of all political thought and action, but these differences, too, have been much attenuated, particularly in so far as political science itself has become more sociological.

Reading

Avineri, Shlomo 1968: *The Social and Political Thought of Karl Marx.*
Barry, Brian 1970: *Sociologists, Economists and Democracy.*
Bottomore, Tom 1979: *Political Sociology.*
Brym, Robert J. 1980: *Intellectuals and Politics.*
Mommsen, Wolfgang J. 1974: *The Age of Bureaucracy: Perspectives on the Political Sociology of Max Weber.*
Runciman, W.G. 1969: *Social Science and Political Theory.*
Scott, Alan 1990: *Ideology and the New Social Movements.*

TOM BOTTOMORE

political theory   This may briefly be defined as systematic reflection on the nature and purposes of government, characteristically involving both an understanding of existing political institutions and a view about how (if at all) they should be changed. It is an intellectual activity with a long pedigree, dating back at least as far as ancient Greece, and embodied in a series of classic works from Plato's *Republic* to John Stuart Mill's *Considerations on Representative Government.* It has not on the whole flourished in the twentieth century, and we may begin by asking why this is so. Two tendencies have conspired to discredit political theory, one being social determinism and the other positivism. Both tendencies, however, have weakened as the century has progressed, and the last twenty or so years have witnessed a revitalization of the subject, in the USA especially but also to a lesser extent in the European democracies.

Social determinism, whose roots lay deep in nineteenth-century thought, undermined political theory in an obvious way. If the shape of social and political institutions was governed by factors outside of human control, intellectual speculation about the best form of society or government was plainly a pointless activity. Various forms of social determinism were adumbrated, each pointing to a different factor as the basis of the laws which governed the evolution of human society: technological change, the ownership of the means of production, forces within the human psyche, genetic evolution, and others. In each case the implication was that society's course of development was preordained, so that rational thought could only

record (and in some cases predict) this course, while being powerless to intervene to change its direction.

Such theories, however, are rarely now advanced in the strong forms that once prevailed. This can be seen in the case of the most influential of all the determinist philosophies, MARXISM. The twentieth century has seen a steady retreat by Marxists away from the thesis that a society's economic structure exercised a controlling influence on all its other components, especially its political system and its ideology. The most influential thinker here has been the Italian Marxist Antonio Gramsci, who recognized that the culture and politics of any given society developed in ways that were not directly governed by economic factors. Similar ideas were expounded by the members of the FRANKFURT SCHOOL in Germany and by the French structuralists headed by Althusser (see STRUCTURALISM). If political and other institutions enjoyed such a measure of relative autonomy, then questions could again be asked about which institutions were 'progressive', measured in terms of human needs and interests, at any historical moment. (It made sense, for instance, to mount a defence of liberal democracy against fascism). Thus Marxists found themselves grappling with traditional questions of political theory, although it must be added that Marxism itself lacks the resources to offer any very illuminating answers to such questions.

Other versions of determinism – such as Freudian theory, which at one point threatened to reduce all political behaviour to the play of non-rational instincts – have waned in similar fashion. Yet the attempt to discover general laws of social development, and in particular to explain political phenomena in terms of more rudimentary factors, has left its mark on political thought, most notably in a strong tendency to connect political questions in the narrow sense to wider social issues. The line of demarcation between social and political theory has been eroded: questions about the form and function of the state are normally now treated together with questions about the economy, class and ethnic divisions, and so forth. The assumption is that it no longer makes sense to speculate about the ideal form of government in isolation from the social, psychological and cultural environment in which that government has to function.

The second force threatening to derail political theory by destroying its intellectual credentials was POSITIVISM. By positivism, I mean the view that the only genuine forms of knowledge are empirical knowledge and formal knowledge; the knowledge embodied in the empirical sciences, derived ultimately by induction from observational data, and the knowledge embodied in logic and mathematics, derived by deductive reasoning. This had the immediate implication that all prescriptive and value judgments, including the judgements about different forms of society and government offered by political theory, were subjective in character; in the most extreme version, they were seen simply as expressions of personal feeling on the part of the person making them. Positivism had a powerful influence on philosophy and social science in the middle years of the century, and it led to two parallel developments: philosophers turned their attention away from problems in ethics and political theory to concentrate on logic, epistemology, philosophy of science and (later) philosophy of language, while social scientists attempted to develop a purely empirical science of social behaviour, freed of all evaluative elements. This latter development was especially marked in political science, where the postwar years witnessed the so-called 'behavioural revolution', the application of quantitative methods to political phenomena such as voting behaviour with the aim of creating a science of politics on positivist lines. The combined effect of these two developments was to cast in doubt the continued viability of political theory as an intellectual enterprise, a concern epitomized in the title of an essay by Isaiah Berlin, 'Does political theory still exist?' (1964).

For reasons that were partly intellectual and partly political, the hold of positivism steadily weakened during the 1960s, paving the way for a major revival of political theory at the end of that decade. In the Anglo-Saxon world, the most important single event was the publication of John Rawls's *A Theory of Justice* (1971), hailed by some commentators as the most significant work of political thought since John Stuart Mill. At about the same time, Jürgen Habermas (1968) mounted a frontal attack on the positivist model of knowledge and paved the way (in Germany especially) for the renaissance of critical theory.

Like social determinism, however, positivism left a legacy to political theory, here in the form of persistent uncertainty about criteria of validity: how, ultimately, could the claims of a political theory be tested? Subsequent theorists can broadly be divided into foundationalists, who maintain that it is possible to find objective and universal grounds for accepting or rejecting a theory, and conventionalists, who argue that a theory can only be tested against the beliefs and attitudes prevalent in a particular culture and can claim no deeper grounding than that. Among foundationalists, there is again a broad division between neo-Aristotelians, who attempt to move from general observations about human nature to claims about the human good, and from there to specifications of the institutional structure best suited to promote that good, and neo-Kantians, who begin with minimal claims about rationality, and go on to argue that only certain institutions and practices could command the support of every rational person in a situation of free choice.

Both Habermas and Rawls are neo-Kantians. They try to derive valid political principles by appeal to an artificially constructed setting in which reason alone would operate. Habermas claims that legitimate norms are those that would emerge consensually from an 'ideal speech situation' from which coercion and domination are absent and in which participants have to persuade one another by the force of argument alone. Rawls resorts to an 'original position' in which people are imagined to be ignorant of their personal characteristics, tastes, positions in society, and so forth; valid principles of justice are those which would be chosen by rational individuals placed in such a position. The question both must face is whether any determinate results can be derived from such thought experiments. It is significant here that both Habermas and Rawls have recently retreated from their original bold claims. Both now concede that their ideal choosers must be conceived as bearers of certain culturally specific traits if substantive political conclusions are to emerge from the 'ideal speech situation' or the 'original position'.

This amounts to a narrowing of the gap between the foundationalists and the conventionalists. The conventionalists argue that political theory can only proceed by drawing out and making explicit the beliefs and ideals of a particular culture; there is no external vantage point from which these beliefs and ideals can be assessed. Recent theorists in this category include Alasdair MacIntyre (1981, 1988) and Michael Walzer (1983). MacIntyre has tried to diagnose the condition of modern liberal societies – where dispute about principles of distributive justice, for instance, is apparently interminable – by contrasting them with older societies with well-established practices and traditions where justice and other values had stable criteria of application. Walzer argues that modern societies do embody a relatively coherent conception of justice, but one that is radically pluralistic. They comprise a number of separate 'spheres' within which different kinds of goods are distributed according to different criteria (welfare on the basis of need, office on the basis of equality of opportunity, and so forth). Both the meaning of the goods and their distributive criteria are socially constituted, and criticism of a society's distributive practices must take place from within this set of understandings.

For those who aspire to the grand tradition of political theory, these attempts to erect a structure of political argument on what is recognized as a basis of convention may be dismissed as nothing better than parochialism – succumbing to the illusions of the epoch, as Marx would have said. Nevertheless, given that the twentieth century has produced no work of political thought that unequivocally stands in that tradition, and given the way in which would-be foundationalists have been forced to back down from their bolder claims, we may have to conclude that some form of conventionalism is the only viable option for political theory in the late twentieth century.

Turning our attention from questions of method to questions of substance, the main feature of twentieth-century political thought has been the predominance of LIBERALISM in its various guises. Of the major nineteenth-century ideologies, neither conservatism nor socialism nor anarchism has generated any major new theoretical statement in our period, and the one unquestionably novel ideology – fascism – was inherently hostile to theoretical reflection. (I shall later refer briefly to feminism.) Thus the main lines of debate have been internal to liberalism, broadly conceived: we may roughly distinguish right, centre and left strands.

Central to right-wing or conservative liberalism have been sceptical arguments which recommend limiting the power of governments on the grounds of their incompetence. In the 1930s and 1940s this frequently took the form of scepticism about democratic institutions: evidence from mass psychology was cited to show that ordinary people were incapable of arriving at rational political decisions, hence the scope of democratic decision-making must be severely limited (see MASS

SOCIETY). The most influential text in this category was Joseph Schumpeter (1942), which argued that the people's role should be confined to choosing between competing elites, the successful team then being responsible for all policy decisions in the ensuing period.

An alternative approach argued that governments of whatever stripe necessarily lacked the cognitive capacity to reshape society in radically new ways. This took the form of an attack on rationalism, understood as the view that social processes could be understood scientifically and transformed through an act of political will. Prominent here in the postwar period have been Karl Popper (1945, 1957), who attacked the idea of historical laws and 'utopian social engineering'; F. A. Hayek (1944, 1960), who argued against central planning and in favour of the free market on the grounds that the knowledge needed to make economic decisions was always dispersed and local; and Michael Oakeshott (1962), who argued that political knowledge was a type of practical knowledge embodied in tradition and incapable of being cast in scientific form.

Finally here mention should be made of attempts to model politics in economic terms as the unintended outcome of actors pursuing their own private interests, financial or otherwise. This is the domain of PUBLIC CHOICE theory whose major exponent has been the American political economist James Buchanan. The upshot of the public choice approach is that government cannot be seen as the disinterested representative of the collective will; hence it is pointless to set it tasks such as promoting social justice. All the strands of conservative liberalism converge on the following three propositions: that the economic role of government should be strictly confined, with most tasks being left to the market economy; that democratic procedures cannot be expected to produce a genuine popular will; and that in this light the powers of government should be limited by a formal constitution which disables it from taking on tasks it is inherently unsuited to perform.

Centrist liberalism sees its task as identifying the set of social and political institutions that best promotes personal FREEDOM; it envisages a more positive role for government than liberalism of the right, especially in the form of market regulation and welfare provision. Again different routes may lead to a broadly similar conclusion. One begins with a definition of freedom that expands on the classical definition: freedom is not merely the absence of external constraints on action, but the positive capacity to achieve valued ends. There is a lineage here which runs from the idea of positive freedom used by early twentieth-century liberals such as L. T. Hobhouse (1911) through to recent arguments about the conditions for personal autonomy, such as those of Joseph Raz (1986) and Stanley Benn (1988). What all these theorists claim is that, although it is essential for each individual to have a wide sphere of discretion in personal and economic life, the state is responsible for guaranteeing the preconditions for effective choice. This means among other things providing education, cultural opportunities and economic security.

A second line of argument revives the idea of a social contract. It asks what individuals would want their government to do in advance of knowing how precisely they would be affected by its workings. The contract approach has been used to defend both right and left liberalism, but its major exponent has been John Rawls (1971), whose conclusions are centrist. Rawls argues that, alongside the familiar liberal principles of equal liberty and equality of opportunity for all, people placed in a suitably defined contractual setting (the 'original position') would choose the difference principle, which permits social and economic inequalities only to the extent that they act to the benefit of the least advantaged members of society. This then licences progressive taxation, welfare provision, economic management and similar measures: the state's job is to see that its least fortunate members have the best life it is possible to provide for them. In practice, centre liberalism converges with SOCIAL DEMOCRACY as it has come to be understood in the postwar period.

Left liberalism is a more recent and less developed tradition. Its central claim is that freedom must be distributed equally to everyone, and the emphasis this places on the egalitarian component of liberalism drives it in practice to quite radical conclusions. For instance, left liberals are likely to argue that capitalist ownership of the means of production constitutes an effective barrier to the freedom of all those who are not owners, and this calls for a remedy that is stronger than the standard liberal prescription of economic protection for employees; for instance it may lead to advocacy of a form of MARKET SOCIALISM in which all enterprises are owned and managed by those who work in them. More radically still, the liberal assumption that each person is entitled to enjoy the fruits of his or her talents may be challenged. The argument here is that our genetic and other natural endowments are features for which we can claim no credit, and for which, therefore, we deserve to receive no rewards. Egalitarian liberals are thus led to look for institutions which may serve to nullify the effects of natural advantages, while still allowing individuals to bear the consequences of their choices. Broadly this points to some scheme for distributing society's resources equally, with compensation for those who fare badly in the genetic lottery.

A different (though not incompatible) development of the left liberal position lays stress on political freedom, and the requirement that this should be made available equally to everyone. This points towards a form of participatory democracy where existing institutions are restructured in such a way that every member of society has the opportunity to contribute to the making of public decisions, for instance though a system of primary assemblies in each locality. Underlying this is the claim earlier made by Jean-Jacques Rousseau and John Stuart Mill that political participation is an essential prerequisite of individual self-determination. Recent theorists are notable mainly for their ingenuity in suggesting ways in which this claim can be made relevant to the circumstances of an advanced industrial society.

The hegemony of liberalism in its various guises should not surprise us, given that twentieth-century political thought has taken shape in societies that are mobile and pluralistic, and in which personal freedom has acquired supreme status as a value. It is also in this context that we should view the rise of feminist thought in the period since 1970. Although FEMINISM is conventionally divided into liberal, radical and socialist versions, its central insight is that the exclusion of women from the freedoms, rights and opportunities enjoyed by men is the last great anomaly of liberal society; the competing versions are best seen as offering different accounts of the conditions under which women's claim for equal treatment between the sexes can be made good. Feminism has so far generated a number of pioneering works (see Millett, 1970; Mitchell, 1974; Pateman, 1988), some of a markedly speculative nature. We are now entering a period of consolidation, but it is too soon to say whether it is likely to yield major works of political theory that will win a place in the classic tradition.

Reading

Barry, B. 1965: *Political Argument.*
Barry, N. 1981: *An Introduction to Modern Political Theory.*
Dunn, J. 1979: *Western Political Theory in the Face of the Future.*
Gamble, A. 1981: *An Introduction to Modern Social and Political Thought.*
Goodwin, B. 1987: *Using Political Ideas.*
Kymlicka, W. 1990: *Contemporary Political Philosophy.*
Miller, D. and Siedentop, L. eds 1983: *The Nature of Political Theory.*
Parekh, B. 1982: *Contemporary Political Thinkers.*
Plant, R. 1991: *Modern Political Thought.*
Runciman, W.G. 1969: *Social Science and Political Theory.*
Skinner, Q. ed. 1985: *The Return of Grand Theory in the Human Sciences.*

DAVID MILLER

politics and terrorism Two major sorts of terroristic behaviour should be distinguished. First, terrorism may be a method of action that an actor uses to achieve precise goals. In this case, violence is pragmatic, more or less under the control of the actor who may, if circumstances change, turn away from this method and resort to other strategies, not necessarily violent. Terrorism as a method of action is a specifically political phenomenon situated within a boundary that may circumscribe one country or delimit an international, geopolitical space. It may be the work of groups or movements but also of governments.

Secondly, terrorism may be a logic of action – no longer a political actor's ultimate or conjunctural means of action but a political and ideological combination of thought and action, a phenomenon wherein the 'clerisy' has a concrete role of organizing terrorist actions. In this case, violence reverses ends and means, and the actor seems to be caught up in a chain reaction that is endless unless stopped by repression, imprisonment or death. This actor is born within a politically bounded space, but he leaves it following a process of 'inversion' (Wieviorka, 1988, pp. 95–118) involving both his ideology and his relationship to the experiences of those of whom he claims to be a part. Terrorist ideologies do not directly prolong an earlier ideology; they change it, turn it around and alter it

considerably, as can be seen in the numerous groups throughout the world since the 1960s that claim to be Marxist-Leninist but have broken with Lenin's thought or even with the theses of classical communism. The community to which such terrorists refer is an artifical paradise, the reference itself a dream, as can be observed in certain cases of nationalistic terrorism that have lost all roots – and any significant audience – in the reference community. This holds true also of a far leftist terrorism that has usually left the working class (if this class, for whose sake actions are carried out, really does exist) indifferent, if not averse, to it.

According to a current thesis inspired by functionalism, terrorism arises where there is a crisis, particularly a political one. Several authors have proposed explaining the emergence of a terroristic process by the crisis of a state that is torn apart (citing Lebanon), corrupt (citing Italy) or excessively repressive (citing West Germany). Others have drawn up arguments based on the observation that the political system is blocked (as happened in Italy during the 1970s owing to the 'historic compromise' between the Christian Democrat and Communist parties). These explanations are to be taken more seriously than those that, without evidence, consider terrorism to result from manipulations conducted by distant powers. They have the advantage of explaining the conditions propitious for the emergence of terroristic logics of action, but they leave aside a major aspect, namely the work of managing meaning that political or intellectual actors perform with reference to a social or community reality that is, in fact, elusive.

Terrorism affects the political system, and its effects are all the more spectacular whenever it attacks a democracy. Whether domestic or international, terrorism shifts the balance within each of the three branches (executive, legislative and judicial) of government and also causes tension between them. In particular, it makes it harder for each to maintain its autonomy. Unless there is an overall crisis of the state, terrorism's principal consequence is to reinforce the executive's power at the expense, mainly, of the judiciary, which may be forced into a very subordinate position. For this reason, terrorism is a challenge to democracies (Dror, 1983).

How can a government respond? This question has hardly been explored by the social or political sciences. Law enforcement is the essential means for dealing with domestic threats from the far left or right or from separatist groups. It relies on several tested methods, some of which are universal (police infiltration and files of suspects) whereas others may not be accepted in certain political cultures. For instance, what is thought, in West Germany, to be a civic action (the population's participation in tracking down and turning in suspects) is felt, in France, to be 'informing' or 'squealing'. Economic, social and political measures may also be useful for depriving terrorists of any popular base or for handling the conditions that generate VIOLENCE.

In response to international terrorism, governments have, for a long time, tended spontaneously to take an apparently firm stand in the eyes of international public opinion but to be lax behind the scenes. In recent years considerable effort has gone into developing international cooperation; and certain countries (in particular, the United States and Great Britain) have brought pressure to bear on governments accused of encouraging, even practising, terrorism.

Terrorism breaks out sporadically, and the event itself may precipitate an overall crisis in a country. If so, a variety of actors – political authorities, justice officials and the police but also political parties, public opinion and the media – are concerned. Their complex interactions are determined, above all, by the government's ability to control the situation. The less the government manages to do so the more the media blow up the event, the more autonomous the police becomes, the more panicky and rigid public opinion grows, and the less and less compatible are the demands formulated by political forces (Wieviorka and Wolton, 1987).

All these problems define a considerable field of research in the social sciences. However, few scholars have delved into this subject, and most research has been journalistic, mainly based on police information or the accounts of former terrorists and political leaders.

Reading
Crenshaw, M. ed. 1983: *Terrorism, Legitimacy and Power.*
Della Porta, D. and Pasquino, G. 1983: *Terrorismo e violenza politica.*
Fetscher, I. and Rohrmoser, G. 1981: *Ideologien und Strategien: Analysen zum Terrorismus*, vol. 1.
Hacker, F. 1976: *Crusaders, Criminals, Crazies: Terror and Terrorism in Our Time.*
Laqueur, W. 1977: *Terrorism.*
O'Sullivan, N. ed. 1986: *Terrorism, Ideology and Revolution.*
Wieviorka, M. 1988: *Sociétés et terrorisme.*
Wieviorka, M. and Wolton, D. 1987: *Terrorisme à la une.*

MICHEL WIEVIORKA

population Transformation of the question of human numbers from an exogenous to an endogenous element in systems of social thought characterizes most new insights related to population in this century. Both social influences on population and demographic influences on society (see also DEMOGRAPHY) fall into three general subcategories, focused on births, deaths and MIGRATION.

Social influences on population

Social forces shaping death rates constitute the oldest dimension of social thought on population determinants, dating back to John Graunt's work (1662) over three centuries ago. In the twentieth century this theoretical heritage was extended and applied to a widening array of specific mortality differentials and trends. The theory of the epidemiologic transition (Omran, 1971) illustrates such integration of mortality into a social theoretical perspective. The search also continues for clearer understanding of the social roots of mortality differentials between sexes, races, occupational groups, religious denominations, urban and rural residents, geographic regions within nations, and different nations of the world.

The twentieth century fundamentally changed the place of human migration in social thought, not so much from new theoretical insights or debates, but from changes in that demographic phenomenon itself. The beginning of the twentieth century roughly separates the eras of free and controlled migration. Closed borders controlled by proliferating nation-states reduce the volume of migration and change its character to a trickle of two extremes: refugees and skilled manpower. This shift reinforces the distinctive twentieth-century direction of social thought concerning population, emphasizing societal control over migratory flows of people.

A socially grounded understanding of reproduction is undoubtedly the greatest change and contribution to population theories of the twentieth century. For Thomas Malthus (1798), as for Johann Süssmilch (1761–2) before him and for Karl Marx (1867) after him, human fertility was a fact of nature. The consequences of a continual flood of babies might be lauded or lamented, but the stream itself flowed from an unquestioned well-spring somewhere beyond the realm of social interactions. Kingsley Davis and Judith Blake (1956) provided the most succinct twentieth-century revision of this shortcoming in social thought. Now high birth rates as well as low birth rates must be explained as social outcomes, as products of different constellations of social forces.

Demographic influences on society
Consequences of low death rates (particularly infant death rates) figure prominently in twentieth-century social thought. Philippe Ariès (1960) thus assigned a crucial role to mortality decline in changing the institution of the family. Mortality decline together with unchanged fertility yields rapid population growth and younger age structure. Both of these outcomes take a prominent place in theories of modernization, social change and the stability of societies.

Migration and migrants figure in twentieth-century social thought in two quite different interpretations. Robert Park (1928) viewed the marginal social position of migrants as a source of potential innovations, change and progress in societies. Other scholars carry on this basically positive view of migrants as catalysts of societal transformation. On the other hand, Oscar Handlin (1951) and others present a picture of migrants and migration as a source of social disorganization, deviance, anomie, crime and mental illness. Both traditions stress the marginal role of migrants, but draw different conclusions about the impact of this marginality on society as a whole and on the migrants themselves.

For much of the world, population growth due to continued high birth rates and declining mortality rates poses a serious social problem. Social theories generally stress the positive results expected from lower birth rates: lower consumption by young dependants, fewer dependants per productive adult, less restriction on the activities of women and slower population growth. Beyond this dominant perspective, however, another theoretical debate of long standing concerns the societal consequences of demographic ageing due to low birth rates. Some scholars fear a possible lack of flexibility (whether in terms of ideas, the mobility of labour or other terms) in ageing societies (see also AGE), and view low birth rates and population ageing as social problems in need of remedies.

Population as threat or asset?
In all its manifestations, population continues to figure in social thought in two contrasting interpretations. One view holds, with Jean Bodin, that 'there is no wealth nor strength but in men', and advocates population growth as a means to various ends falling under the general heading of progress. The other view holds, with Malthus, that population growth forms an obstacle to progress, bringing difficulties that 'must necessarily be severely felt by a large portion of mankind'. Both approaches treat population (its size, dispersion or concentration, age structure and so on) not as an end in itself but as a parameter to be manipulated with a view towards other goals. To some extent, these two views of population also reflect the classic distinction of the French philosopher Auguste Comte between social statics and social dynamics.

The view that progress is best served by restricting population gained popularity around the world during the twentieth century. This restrictive element in social thought chiefly refers to the dynamic aspects of population, maintaining that high rates of population growth create many problems.

The other view stresses the advantages of a large population, such as greater division of labour, larger economic markets, or even more potential military manpower. This static view of population is usually not concerned with the processes leading to large aggregations of people, but population growth has also been advanced by some twentieth-century theorists as a motor of social change (Boserup, 1965; Clark, 1968).

The balance between these two orientations to population depends on one's position in society and on the structure of that society. Absolute rulers and ruling elites, insulated from their subject populations, most often stress positive aspects of large population size and ignore the social costs of rapid population growth. To the extent that such insulated elites are replaced by more open, pluralistic or democratic social structures, social thought shifts towards greater attention to the costs of population growth and less support for maximizing numbers of people. Such a shifting balance provides a key to understanding much of the changing rhetoric concerning population in the twentieth century.

Reading
Ariès, Philippe 1960 (*1962*): *Centuries of Childhood: A Social History of Family Life.*

Boserup, Ester 1965: *The Conditions of Agricultural Growth.*

Davis, Kingsley and Blake, Judith 1956: Social structure and fertility: an analytic framework. *Economic Development and Cultural Change* 4, 211–35.

Handlin, Oscar 1951: *The Uprooted.*

Malthus, Thomas 1798 (*1970*): *An Essay on the Principle of Population.*

Omran, A. 1971: The epidemiologic transition: a theory of the epidemiology of population change. *Milbank Memorial Fund Quarterly* 49, 509–38.

Park, Robert 1928: Human migration and the marginal man. *American Journal of Sociology* 33, 881–93.

Süssmilch, Johann 1761–2: Die göttliche Ordnung in den Veränderungen des menschlichen Geschlechts aus der Geburt, dem Tode, und der Fortpflanzung desselben Erwiesen, 2nd edn.

ELWOOD CARLSON

populism Political movements with high capacity to obtain popular support, but without the traits typical of European socialism, have been called populist, especially in Latin America during the twentieth century. What they have in common is:

1 the presence of a socially mobilized mass with little or no autonomous class organization;

2 a leadership predominantly drawn from upper- or middle-class sectors; and

3 a charismatic type of connection between leaders and followers.

Demographic alterations due to rapid urban expansion, running ahead of industrial growth, and the effects of the 'revolution of rising expectations', impinging on the mentality of elites, make this type of political expression highly likely in countries at the stage of development usually found in Latin America. In Asia and Africa populism as a form of free competitive political organization is less widespread than in Latin America, though some traits are to be found in a NATIONAL POPULAR REGIME.

The Mexican revolution, beginning in 1910, was an early example of a rebellion with an extended mass following and multiple class support, accompanied by an eclectic ideology including elements of liberalism, nationalism and socialism. The Peruvian Aprista Party, founded by Víctor Raúl Haya de la Torre in exile in 1924, was partly inspired by the Mexican experience and is usually reckoned as one of the main examples of populism. In opposition to Lenin, Haya argued that in typically Third World countries imperialism is the first and not the last stage of capitalism, and hence a peculiar strategy has to be used in order to harness its economic potentialities, while preventing its attempts at political domination. An explicit alliance was proposed between the middle classes, the peasantry and the manual workers, in contradistinction, again, to the Marxist formula for developed countries, which emphasized the role of the urban proletariat. The Peruvian branch of what was expected to be a Latin American International was founded in 1930, and soon acquired an important following among trade unionists and Indian communities, though its backbone was formed by the impoverished provincial middle classes. After attempts at violent overthrow of the authoritarian – often militaristic – native regimes, 'Aprismo' became more moderate after World War II, and in 1985 obtained the presidency. Other parties with traits similar to Aprismo are Acción Democrática of Venezuela, Liberación Nacional of Costa Rica, the Revolucionario Dominicano of the Dominican Republic, and, somewhat more distantly, the Movimiento Nacionalista Revolucionario of Bolivia.

In Brazil, in 1930, a civil-military movement took Getúlio Vargas to power, where he remained for 15 years. He had been a pragmatic governor of one of the states of the previous highly federal regime, and remained a pragmatist. He obtained the support of an important group of young officers known as the *tenentes*, intent on reform, with a motley of ideological convictions ranging from liberalism to nationalism and local versions of fascism, which was perceived as a developmental regime suited for countries in the process of change from a predominantly rural to an urban and industrial society. Vargas ruled the country with an iron hand, enacting in 1937 a constitution inspired by Mussolini's CORPORATISM. During the later years of World War II Brazil experienced an important advance in its industrialization, and Vargas took the opportunity to appeal to the mass of new entrants into the urban labour force, initiating the populist phase of his rule. This led to a military-conservative reaction against him, in 1945, but after five years he returned to power in free elections. Under Vargas trade unions obtained favourable legislation and state support, at the cost, though, of administrative control, and of being subjected to a corrupt leadership. In more recent years, after the long military interlude (1964–85), the heirs of Vargas's followers are still strong, divided into two parties, a moderate one (Partido do Movimento Democrático Brasileiro), and a more radically populist one (Partido Democrático Trabalhista), led by Leonel Brizola.

In Argentina populism is expressed in Peronism, a political movement launched by the then Colonel Juan D. Perón, while Secretary of Labour in the 1943–6 nationalist military regime. He was successful in forging an alliance between the military, some sectors of the industrialists, and the popular classes, among them large numbers of new migrants from the rural interior who had arrived in the large cities, though also obtaining the allegiance of some old trade union leaders. Peronism combined ideological elements from the Catholic intelligentsia and the nationalist right, including some with clearly fascist sympathies, together with more pragmatic or traditional socialist ones, and some middle of the road politicians from the Radical Party. The movement passed through a period of radicalization and violence during the 1970s, generating from its bosom a guerrilla formation, the Montoneros, who were finally expelled from the organization by 1974. In 1989, after several years of internal change and democratization, Peronism recovered from the impact caused by the death of its leader, and gained the presidency, with a programme of moderate reform and respect for civil liberties.

In Chile the working class movement has proved to be rather immune to populism. From its early days it was organized in Marxist parties, based on grass roots activity with little or no bureaucracy. The left in Chile is thus clearly associationist rather than mobilizational, but in other Latin American countries socialism, especially of the Leninist persuasion, can also take populist forms, as under Fidel Castro in Cuba.

In some countries of the area populism has been losing some of its grip on the working class, allowing a Marxist left to grow on its flank. On the other hand, with the acculturation into urban and industrial ways of life, social–democratic patterns of organization and ideology tend to develop within populist parties.

Reading
Di Tella, Torcuato S. 1989: *Latin American Politics: A Theoretical Approach.*
Germani, Gino 1978: *Authoritarianism, Fascism, and National Populism.*
Ionescu, Ghita and Gellner, Ernest eds 1969: *Populism: Its Meaning and National Characteristics.*
Laclau, Ernesto 1977: *Politics and Ideology in Marxist Theory; Capitalism, Fascism and Populism.*
Murmis, Miguel and Portantiero, Juan Carlos 1971: *Estudios sobre los orígenes del peronismo.*

Weffort, Francisco 1978: *O populismo na política brasileira.*

TORCUATO S. DI TELLA

positivism Much like the concept of ideology, which first came into wide currency around the same period, the notion of positivism boasts a contentious and ironic trajectory. Originating as a positive self-designation in the writings of Auguste Comte, offered as a 'philosophy to end all philosophies' by the VIENNA CIRCLE, and equated with science *tout court* by the advocates of FUNCTIONALISM and BEHAVIOURISM in postwar America, it has become a term of polemical indictment, if not abuse, in contemporary social science – few sociologists today would claim or welcome the label. And, like ideology, it has assumed a multiplicity of meanings so that there are nearly as many definitions of positivism as there are critics of it; Halfpenny (1982), for instance, distinguishes no fewer than 12 subspecies. The dispersion and inversion of the semantic charge of the word is indicative of the changes that have transformed the PHILOSOPHY OF SCIENCE since the 1960s and challenged the long hegemony of positivism in social enquiry by raising anew the question of the 'dualism of the natural and cultural sciences' (Habermas, 1967).

In its broadest philosophical sense, positivism refers to the theory of knowledge proposed by Francis Bacon, John Locke and Isaac Newton which asserts the primacy of observation and the pursuit of causal explanation by way of inductive generalization (Kolakowski, 1966). In the social sciences, it has become associated with three related principles: the ontological tenet of *phenomenalism* according to which knowledge can be founded on experience alone (verging on the fetishization of 'facts' as immediately available to sense-perception); the methodological tenet of the *unity of the scientific method* which proclaims that the procedures of natural science are directly applicable to the social world with the goal of establishing invariant laws or lawlike generalizations about social phenomena; and the axiological tenet of *neutrality* which refuses to grant normative statements the status of knowledge and maintains a rigid separation between facts and values.

Three broad successive traditions of positivism may be schematically distinguished, the French, the German and the American. The French lineage originates with Auguste Comte and his mentor

Saint-Simon (who was in turn indebted to Condorcet) and is best exemplified by the sociology of Emile Durkheim. Comte's ambition was to found a naturalistic science of society capable of explaining the past of humankind and to predict its future by applying to it the same methods of enquiry as had proved so successful in the study of nature, namely observation, experimentation and comparison. In his *Course of Positive Philosophy* (Comte, 1830–42), he argued that the human spirit had evolved through three necessary stages. In the 'theological or fictitious' stage, phenomena are explained by the intervention of supernatural entities, and in the 'metaphysical or abstract' stage by reference to abstractions. In the 'scientific or positive' stage, the search for the ultimate causes of facts is abandoned in favour of establishing their 'laws', that is, the 'invariable relations of succession and resemblance' which connect them. Comte coined the term 'sociology' to designate the science which would synthesize all positive knowledge, unlock the mysteries of the statics and dynamics of society, and guide the formation of the positive polity.

Durkheim abandoned the substance of Comte's philosophy but retained its method, insisting on the logical continuity between the social and natural sciences and on the application of the principle of natural causality to society. 'Our main goal', he wrote in *The Rules of Sociological Method* (Durkheim, 1895), his revolutionary manifesto for scientific sociological explanation, 'is to extend scientific rationalism to human conduct. . . . What has been called our positivism is but a consequence of this rationalism.' To establish the definitive independence of sociology from all philosophy and thus its autonomy as a distinctive scientific field, Durkheim put forth a conception of society as an objective reality *sui generis* whose constituents, structure and functioning obey regularities that impose themselves on individuals as 'ineluctable necessities' independent of their volition and consciousness. He also proposed a set of methodological principles encapsulated by the famous injunction to 'treat social facts as things': reject common preconceptions in favour of objective definitions, explain a social fact only by another social fact, distinguish efficient cause from function and normal from pathological social states, etc. These principles were forcefully illustrated in *Suicide*, arguably the exemplar of French positivism, in which Durkheim (1897) shunned the analysis of the meaning of suicide in favour of uncovering its social types and causes via a statistical analysis of its group correlates and variations.

The German-Austrian tradition of positivism finds its roots in the METHODENSTREIT ('conflict over method') which had embroiled neoclassical and historical economists and neo-Kantian philosophers from the 1880s over the question of whether social life is amenable to causal explanation or solely to interpretive understanding as in the philosophy of VERSTEHEN. The group of analytical philosophers, mathematicians and scientists (among them Moritz Schlick, Ernst Mach, Rudolf Carnap, Carl Hempel and Otto Neurath) that came to be known as the Vienna circle in the years 1923–36 sided with explanation and the unity of science. Their aim was to effect a synthesis of Humean empiricism, Comtean positivism, and logical analysis that would forever rid philosophy of the vacuous speculations of metaphysics by firmly grounding all knowledge in experience (Ayer, 1959). According to this *logical positivism*, scientific knowledge rests on a bedrock of facts formulated by way of 'protocol sentences' (Mach) that provide an unadulterated because immediate recording of sensory experience, or elaborated via 'correspondence rules' (Carnap), forming a bridge between theoretical language and the language of observation. Aside from the analytic propositions of logic, the only meaningful statements are those that can be subjected to the 'verification principle', that is, tested by observation. In frontal opposition to the idea of *Geisteswissenschaften* premised on a schism between the sciences of nature and culture, the Vienna circle asserted that scientific explanation in sociology or history follows the same 'covering-law' or 'deductive-nomological' model as the natural sciences (Hempel, 1965) in which an explanandum is deduced from a combination of initial conditions and universal law and explanation synonymous with prediction.

In the United States, a kindred understanding of social science evolved into what Bryant (1985) calls *instrumental positivism*, an incrementalist, naturalistic tradition of social research committed to attaining standards of rigour comparable to those of physics or biology. Based on a nominalist and voluntaristic conception of society as a mere aggregate of individuals, this tradition reigned unchallenged from the 1930s to the 1960s by encompassing a variety of theoretical orientations and it continues to permeate American sociology. It is distinctive for its preoccupation with issues of method and measurement, including the refinement of statistical techniques, its emphasis on operationalization and verification (Zetterberg, 1954), and the priority it accords to quasi-experimental designs, quantitative surveys and team research. It is 'instrumental' in that the instruments of enquiry largely determine the questions asked, the definition of concepts (through the construction of empirical indicators) and thus the knowledge produced, with testability, replicability and technical feasibility superseding theory as guides of scientific practice and evaluation.

Instrumental positivism was first articulated by George Lundberg, who adapted from physics P.W. Bridgman's doctrine of 'operationalism' (which holds that the meaning of a variable is defined by the operations necessary to measure them), and by William F. Ogburn (1930), who equated scientific sociology with the quantitative verification and accumulation of 'little bits and pieces of new knowledge' – he proudly predicted that all sociologists would one day be statisticians. But it fell to Viennese scholar-in-exile Paul Lazarsfeld to institutionalize positivism in the American university. Lazarsfeld not only introduced into sociology a number of methodological innovations (multivariate analysis, snowball sampling and latent structure analysis, among others) and techniques borrowed from market research such as panel studies; he invented the organizational vehicle that would carry forth the professionalization, bureaucratization and commercialization of positivist social research in America and its satellite countries: the 'bureau of applied research' (Pollak, 1979).

The rise and dominance of positivism have met with criticism and opposition of two kinds, antipositivist and post-positivist. *Anti-positivist* dissenters have long argued that the natural and the human sciences are ontologically and logically discrepant and that the very idea of an explanatory science of society is untenable (Winch, 1958). Proponents of HERMENEUTICS and 'interpretive' sociology – recently joined by advocates of postmodernism and DECONSTRUCTION, as well as certain strands of FEMINISM – maintain that causal accounts of social behaviour cannot be constructed because human practices, institutions and beliefs are inherently meaningful, nay constituted by the understandings that participants have of them

(Taylor, 1977). The task of 'human studies' therefore cannot be to specify invariant laws of human behaviour but to make that behaviour intelligible by interpreting it in relation to subjective intentions. For Gadamer (1960), furthermore, all such interpretations involve a projection of cultural prejudices grounded in a network or 'horizon' of expectations and assumptions constitutive of a cultural tradition. It follows that the goal of interpretive sociology cannot be to duplicate or confirm previous research but to revise prejudice by illuminating new dimensions of a phenomenon.

The feminist critiques of positivism which proliferated in the 1980s join in this attack but for a different reason. Arguing that science is a gendered institution which reflects the truncated and oppressive point of view of males, they have evolved from a reformist outlook seeking to achieve gender parity in the scientific field to a revolutionary stance aimed at overhauling the very foundations of science so as to uproot its constitutive 'androcentrism' (Harding 1984). These critiques span a gamut from feminist empiricism (for which sexism can be corrected by more rigorous enforcement of the standard methodological dictates of scientific enquiry) to standpoint epistemology (which holds that women's subjugation puts them in a privileged position to produce true knowledge) to postmodern feminism, which questions the very notions of universality and reason that undergird science. For Sandra Harding, the accepted tenets of impartiality, value-neutrality, and objectivity are tools of social control that serve men in their project to make science a male preserve. Genuine objectivity, she argues, arises not from embracing the 'patriarchal' idea of the unity of the scientific method but out of a commitment to the 'participatory values' of antiracism, anticlassism, and antisexism. Therefore not science but moral and political discussion provides a paradigm for rational enquiry.

Rather than dismissing it outright, exponents of *post-positivism* have sought to reform the received understanding of science. The attacks of W.V.O. Quine, Karl Popper, Thomas Kuhn, Paul Feyerabend, and Imre Lakatos have converged to undermine the very foundations of the positivist philosophy of natural science (Chalmers, 1982) by demonstrating that scientific theories are neither built inductively nor tested individually on the sole basis of phenomenal evidence, for there is no such thing as theory-neutral observation. Nor is their adjudication effected strictly on rational grounds in so far as rival theories are always 'underdetermined' by data and generally partake of 'paradigms' or broad scientific frameworks whose criteria of evaluation are incommensurable (Giddens, 1978). The REALISM of Bhaskar (1975) also repudiates phenomenalism and verificationism by differentiating three levels of reality (the real, the actual, and the empirical) and by asserting the existence of hidden structures and mechanisms which may operate independently of our knowledge of them but whose causal powers and liabilities are nonetheless empirically investigable. The 'applied rationalism' of Pierre Bourdieu – resulting from the importation into sociology of the historicist epistemology of A. Koyré, G. Bachelard, and G. Canguilhem – similarly overturns the epistemological scaffoldings of positivism by positing that scientific facts are 'conquered, constructed, and constated' (Bourdieu et al., 1973) through rupture with lay and scholarly common sense, systematic application of relational concepts, and methodical confrontation of the model built with the evidence generated by different methodologies. The critical theory of the FRANKFURT SCHOOL combines elements of both the anti-positivist and post-positivist critiques in rejecting SCIENTISM (the idea that only science produces knowledge), the conflation of explanation with prediction by means of universal laws, and the dichotomizing of facts and values, while at the same time combatting the idealism of hermeneutics and refusing to forsake claims to scientific TRUTH. Thus Habermas (1968) argues that, lest it becomes complicit with the technical rationality that undergirds positivism and turns into another ideological instrument of domination, social science cannot keep to an analysis of external causal relations. Because the social universe is a 'pre-interpreted' world, it must *also* explicate internal relations of meaning and purpose and therefore reconstruct the concept of objectivity bequeathed by the natural sciences in a way that recovers the critical dimension of science as a tool for emancipation.

Eclipse is not death: positivism may have been discredited as a philosophy of science, but it still actively informs and arguably even dominates the design and implementation of empirical social research. And it promises to survive, if not thrive, both as a foil and as a surreptitious working epistemology so long as Max Weber's project of bringing interpretation and explanation 'under one roof' is not fully realized in the day-to-day practice of social scientists.

Reading
Adorno, Theodor, Albert, Hans, Dahrendorf, Ralf, Habermas, Jürgen, Pilot, Harald and Popper, Karl R. 1969 (*1976*): *The Positivist Dispute in German Sociology.*
Alexander, Jeffrey C. 1982: *Theoretical Logic in Sociology*, vol. 1: *Positivism, Presuppositions, and Current Controversies.*
Apel, Karl-Otto 1979 (*1984*): *Understanding and Explanation: A Transcendental-Pragmatic Perspective.*
Fuller, Steve 1988: *Social Epistemology.*
Giddens, Anthony ed. 1974: *Positivism and Sociology.*
Harding, Sandra and Hintikka, Merrill eds 1983: *Discovering Reality: Feminist Perspectives on Epistemology, Methodology, and Philosophy of Science.*
Keat, Russell and Urry, John 1978: *Social Theory as Science.*
Outhwaite, William 1987: *New Philosophies of Social Science: Realism, Hermeneutics, and Critical Theory.*
Philips, D.C. 1987: *Philosophy, Science, and Social Inquiry.*
Simon, Walter M. 1963: *European Positivism in the Nineteenth Century.*

LOÏC J.D. WACQUANT

positivism, legal   *See* LEGAL POSITIVISM

postindustrial society   The term postindustrial society seems to have originated with Arthur Penty, a British Guild Socialist and follower of William Morris, at the turn of the century. Penty looked forward to a 'postindustrial state' based on the small craft workshop and decentralized units of government. The concept was not taken up significantly until the late 1960s, when it was given an entirely new twist. In its present meaning the term was coined, almost simultaneously, in the writings of Daniel Bell and Alain Touraine, to describe the new social structures and social movements marking the evolution of industrial societies in the latter part of the twentieth century. In more recent years, many of the more common uses of the term postindustrial have also included, or have been defined alongside, a concept of contemporary society as a postmodern society, for instance by Jean-François Lyotard (see MODERNITY; MODERNISM AND POSTMODERNISM). Economically, the postindustrial society is marked by the change from a goods-producing to a service economy; occupationally, by the pre-eminence of the professional and the technical class; and in decision-making by the widespread diffusion of 'intellectual technology'.

Bell, particularly in *The Coming of Post-Industrial Society* (1974), defined the 'axial principles' of postindustrial society as the centrality of theoretical knowledge as the source of innovation and of policy formation for the society. He argued that this type of society differs as much from classical INDUSTRIAL SOCIETY as the latter did from preindustrial, agrarian society. It is mainly concerned with the production of services rather than goods, the majority of its workforce is in white collar rather than manual occupations, and many of these workers are professional, managerial or technical employees. The old WORKING CLASS is disappearing, and with it many of the characteristics and conflicts of industrial society. New alignments, based on status and consumption, are supplanting those based on work and production. Postindustrial society, both Bell and Touraine argue, is also a highly educated society, and the key idea of a knowledge society is central to all various theoretical versions. If industrial society ran on material and practical knowledge, postindustrial society depends much more on immaterial and theoretical knowledge, as it is developed in universities, research centres and new types of workplaces. It not only looks to theoretical knowledge for many of its characteristic industries, such as the computer, chemical and aerospace industries, but also puts an increasing part of its national resources into developing such knowledge, by support for higher education, research and development activities. This shift in emphasis is reflected in the growth in importance of a 'knowledge class', composed of scientists and professionals, and of 'knowledge institutions'.

It is evident that the discussion of postindustrial society has represented in the last 20 years a major and radical renewal in the social thought about large-scale change in modern societies; Kumar (1976, p. 441) and others have claimed that 'at the very least, post-industrial theorizing marks a welcome renewal of one of the central tenets of the formative period of sociology, that the study of being and becoming are indissolubly linked.' The coming of the postindustrial society has in effect brought about a very particular 'terminology war', which reflects some confusions or, at least, the different insights to be gained from approaching the subject of postindustrial society from the vantage point of the new classes and new conflicts which appear or develop alongside it. Three main

definitions can be distinguished. *White collar workers* are those whose work is now performed under conditions and circumstances which are close to factory conditions and follow highly structured work patterns. *Office workers* are those who, as automation and artificial intelligence increase in commercial and administrative settings, need a greater amount of knowledge to operate and interact with such equipment; in that sense the term does not encompass, by far, only the people working under office conditions. *Information/knowledge workers*, as a term, supersedes the rigidity of census and statistical classifications, but in practical use is charged with an optimistic overtone that often prevents a better understanding of the changes in the nature of work and the structure of organizations.

Touraine (1971) and Bell are in complete agreement over the central importance of the universities, of research and the role of the 'knowledge class' for the overall productive and managerial apparatus of the new society. But they differ about its foreseeable results. Whereas Bell sees the promise of greater social integration and political and institutional harmony, Touraine – more alarmed by its manipulative potential and clearly sensitized by the ideas of May 1968 and the generalization of social movements in Europe – foresees a deepening conflict between those (teachers and students) who uphold the humanistic values of liberal education, and a different breed of their peers who man the technocratic apparatuses, dedicated to the goal of economic growth. In this sense, the concept of postindustrial society has been widely used by other social thinkers who emphasize different features, for instance, the search for a world beyond materialism by young people, or the displacement, as a result of TECHNOLOGICAL CHANGE, of the working class from the role assigned to it by Marxists as the historic agent of change in modern society.

Although industrial and postindustrial society are not simply linked by the fundamental changes in the nature of WORK, technology and social classes, five problematic areas can be indicated which constitute the central challenge for all the social actors involved; scientists and producers, ergonomic experts and users are all faced with the 'architecture of complexity' of fundamental changes and unprecedented novelties that go beyond the conventional theoretical tools and methods of industrial society. These have been at the core of all theoretical debates about post-industrial, and more recently, postmodern society.

(1) Symbols without decision

Information technology and ARTIFICIAL INTELLI-GENCE make it increasingly possible to formalize knowledge, and favour the integration of a pro-gramme which can command a machine or a series of machines. As a result, the more activities are planned in advance and contained in information processes, the less need there is for a decision system at every single level of work, whether in its formalization or in its execution. (See also INFOR-MATION TECHNOLOGY AND THEORY.) Moreover, the use of information machines entails an increase in new symbols, which are not only difficult to learn but also call for a special effort to be correctly attributed to what they conventionally designate. The problem lies in the fact that for the moment we possess only new symbols but not a new language; this could come about only if, in the designing of information machines, we take into consideration new behavioural patterns and new collective cul-tures. Postindustrial work then, despite its techno-logical possibilities, becomes a binary type activity, with stimuli reactions and information rules to apply, which are already contained in the informa-tion program. At all levels of power, responsibility, and integration of the work system, managers, technicians and employees find themselves occu-pied with the control of work in which decision-making is less and less in evidence.

(2) Abstraction and solitude

Information technology makes most operations and gestures in work abstract and 'immaterial'. Thus, symbols, figures and languages of a 'varied nature' become the essential mediating factor between workers, work, previous knowledge and the com-munity of work. Thus, besides distinctions in category, and differences in salary, company status, or career, the centre of gravity is shifting towards a series of functions which call for intense mental activity, the actual cognitive mediation of work and of its social and organizational context. Moreover, the stereotyped image of an intelligent, creative and rewarding activity on the one hand, and of a repetitive and intellectually boring job on the other, is now giving way to a vision which is the hybrid product of the information revolution: despite job status and cultural differences, there now exists a series of tasks which are marked by the same standards, which use the same symbolic mediation, and which create the same sense of loss of identity in dealing with the intelligent processes of the machine.

(3) The involuntary and paradoxical recomposition of work

It is not only that the machine and work procedures require a certain amount of mental commitment, which may vary with the complexity of the machines and the operator's knowledge and experi-ence, but in postindustrial society a new component is added: the 'organizational load', that is, the component dealing with the effects of the variables that define the organization of social relations and work in the workplace. At the centre of an ever-increasing number of activities in postindustrial society we find the processing, checking and sometimes the analysis of the symbolic data and mediating information produced by information-based systems. The borderline between jobs and their respective cultures becomes blurred, giving place to a much larger group of activities in which work is performed in similar conditions, with processes of the same kind, content and intelligib-ility, and above all in similar organizational con-texts. This 'recomposition of work' carries with it, however, at least one major consequence: the conditions of work and of the weight of the organization – once its 'mechanical' and material side disappears – vanishes from view, while the abstraction inherent in the new conditions of work changes the individual's psychological sense of the work itself. With new information technologies, work may indeed recompose, but the meaning of each activity becomes murkier and more inacces-sible both for individuals and for the organization.

(4) Cognitive pressure and accelerating tempos

Contrary to widespread belief, this process of symbolic abstraction and mediation of work is not an 'unexpected consequence' but an intrinsic ele-ment in information technology. The alteration of the experience, contents and finality of a job takes place independently of the way in which the postindustrial type of work is conceived, planned and introduced. The most dramatic example, perhaps, is the rapidity of access to information and the speed of its processing, which make possible a considerable increase in the number of operations and lead to an intensification of work tempos.

(5) *Modifications in the social life of workplaces*
Postindustrial society has introduced profound changes in the social life of the workplace as it affects the identity of individuals and groups. One of the fundamental bases of the ideology of work, therefore, might become nothing but an empty myth: the community, the work group, which was central and absolutely necessary for the efficient running of industrial society, is being detached from the technological base on which every workplace rests. The form of collective organization inherited from industrial society, which was based on the need to gather management, machines and workers in the same space, has now been basically compromised by the possibility of automation. What will happen in the workplace, then, if for example the employees no longer need or have no chance to intermingle at the workplace, or if they no longer have any control of the deeper significance of both individual and collective work? In such a context the new problems have shifted from the positive or negative myths of automation and focused on how to plan and manage an organization and work which have become abstract for all three of the most important levels: the individual-cognitive, social and managerial.

If one of the main characteristics of the new technologies which characterize postindustrial society is their pervasiveness and their adaptability, then 'office' work becomes the dominant structural form of work. Rapid technological change from human- or machine-mediated work to computer-mediated work leads to changes in how workers adapt to their particular work environment. Concomitant with these technological shifts are societal and cultural transformations, reflecting changes from a society based on manufacturing and producing material goods to a society based on a service economy.

Under these new conditions, the study of postindustrial society becomes a more complex and multidisciplinary operation than in the recent past, resulting from interdisciplinary research, with contributions stemming from many different disciplines, including engineering, computer science, industrial psychology and sociology, ergonomics, technology assessment, management science, economics, system science, social and economic history, political science, and probably others. The task is to manage the architecture of complexity which is the most important and vulnerable element of a society dominated by computer-mediated work.

Reading
Bell, Daniel 1974: *The Coming of Post-Industrial Society: A Venture in Social Forecasting.*
Diani, Marco 1992: *The Immaterial Society: Design, Culture and Technology in the Postmodern World.*
Kumar, Krishan 1976: Industrialism and post-industrialism: reflections on a putative transition. *Sociological Review* 24. 3, August, 439–78.
—— 1978: *Prophecy and Progress: The Sociology of Industrial and Post-industrial Society.*
Lyotard, Jean-François 1979: *The Postmodern Condition: A Report on Knowledge.*
Rose, Margaret A. 1991: *The Post-modern and the Post-industrial: A Critical Analysis.*
Touraine, Alain 1968 (*1971*): *The Post-industrial Society.*

MARCO DIANI

post-Keynesianism A term which encompasses a variety of attempts to construct an alternative to orthodox microeconomics and macroeconomics, post-Keynesianism is not a unified school of thought, but an amalgam of elements drawn from different traditions in economic theory, with its proponents often differing over which elements to emphasize.

Common to all proponents are a rejection of equilibrium analysis in favour of considerations of unbalanced growth, and hence an interventionist rather than a laissez-faire policy stance; and a rejection of microeconomic explanations of price determination in terms of supply and demand. Consequently, the orthodox theory of the (functional) distribution of income (determined by supply and demand schedules created by decisions of optimizing individuals and therefore generally involving marginal productivity considerations) is rejected in favour of a macroeconomic theory of income distribution related to the growth of aggregate demand and national product: aphoristically, workers spend what they get and capitalists get what they (the capitalists) spend. Similarly, any understanding of the labour market in terms of supply and demand analysis is rejected, so that the level of unemployment is explained not in terms of labour pricing itself out of the market, but is rather related to the macroeconomic volume of output, and its incidence is explained in terms of a labour force which is segmented by an industrial structure of an oligopolistic and therefore protected core, and a competitive and therefore exposed periphery. Within such a structure, prices are determined by oligopolistic mark-ups over costs, the size of the mark-up being related to the necessity of obtaining sufficient profits to finance future investment in a world of inherent uncertainty. Finally, the orthodoxy is criticized for its barter approach to the economic system; post-Keynesians consider it essential to integrate money into the theory of the workings of the economy from the outset. At the macro level, the money supply is seen as endogenous, passively adjusting to whatever level is necessary to sustain current levels of output. Inflation is not then interpreted as the result of an excessive expansion of the money supply, but is rather seen as the outcome of struggle between contending classes over the division of national product into wages and profits.

Much of post-Keynesianism traces its ancestry back to J. M. Keynes, but emphasizing Keynes's approach to uncertainty and instability as the starting point of his analysis. Subsequent Keynesian economics (see KEYNESIANISM) has tended to disregard this starting point, thereby, according to post-Keynesians, misinterpreting the import of Keynes's analysis. This emphasis on an uncertain future is then allied to an analysis of investment and profitability taken largely from the work of M. Kalecki: current investment determines the rate of growth which in turn determines the level of profits, while future investment is determined by the profits firms anticipate through an appropriate pricing mark-up over their costs. Superimposed upon this is a sociological account of class conflict taken from the Marxist tradition, but reduced to a conflict over wages and profits as a struggle over the distribution of what is surplus to the requirements of exactly reproducing the economy in a stationary state.

Post-Keynesianism is thus not a single rigorous approach but a collection of themes which proponents see as emphasizing the sterility and irrelevance of orthodox economics and the contrasting realism and relevance of post-Keynesian alternatives. But the very eclecticism of these is also a major weakness, for it is doubtful whether Marxian and Keynesian concerns can be allied quite so easily except by divorcing them from the theoretical structures within which they are embedded and from which they derive meaning.

Reading

Eichner, A.S. ed. 1979: *A Guide to Post-Keynesian Economics.*
Harcourt, G.C. 1982: Post-Keynesianism: quite wrong and/or nothing new? *Thames Papers in Political Economy*, Summer.
Kalecki, M. 1971: *Selected Essays on the Dynamics of the Capitalist Economy.*
Minsky, H. 1975: *John Maynard Keynes.*

SIMON MOHUN

postmodernism *See* MODERNISM AND POST-MODERNISM; MODERNITY

poverty The use of the concept has grown rather than lessened with the passage of the years. It is one of the organizing concepts for statements about 'the social condition' – whether applied to rich or poor societies, and in the late twentieth century the consistency of meaning across all societies has become a critical scientific issue. Books about poverty in the Third World during this time have been more critical, and theoretically more radical, than those about poverty in the First World. Divergencies of meaning have produced, or reflected, divergencies in the methodologies of measurement, modes of explanation and strategies of amelioration.

The concept has attracted intellectual and political interest for many centuries (see Himmelfarb, 1984; Woolf, 1987), as governments and ruling groups grudgingly came to feel obliged to define the needs of the poor in relation to the income of the poor. Thus in Britain and much of Europe those in charge of small areas like parishes developed forms of indoor and outdoor relief for the poor long before the Industrial Revolution, but economies newly based on manufacturing industry and an incentive wage system posed new problems of regulating the amounts to be received by the poor outside as well as inside Poor Law institutions. The costs of maintaining institutions and their inmates had given concern to ruling groups and in the formulation of a new scheme to manage the poor from 1834 in Britain, for example, the principle of 'less eligibility' played a crucial part in the thinking both of politicians and of those undertaking scientific enquiries. (*Report ... of the Poor Laws*, 1834, p. 228)

There was pressure to define the *minimum* needs

of institutional inmates and of the able-bodied poor outside institutions, and the early work of nutritionists in Germany, the United States and Britain was addressed to such questions. (For Germany, see for instance Leibfried, 1982; Leibfried and Tennstedt, 1985; for the USA, Aronson, 1984.)

During the twentieth century three alternative conceptions of poverty have evolved as a basis for international and comparative work. They depend principally on the ideas of *subsistence*, *basic needs* and *relative deprivation*. In Britain the 'subsistence' standard came to fruition in two stages, first in conjunction with surveys carried out by entrepreneurs like Rowntree (1901 and 1918) and then in the war years 1939–45 by means of a report on social security drawn up by Beveridge (1942). As a result of work prompted by the nutritionists, families were now defined to be in poverty when their incomes were not 'sufficient to obtain the minimum necessaries for the maintenance of merely physical efficiency' (Rowntree, 1901, p. 86). A family was treated as being in poverty if its income minus rent fell short of the poverty line. Although allowance was made in the income for clothing, fuel and some other items, this allowance was very small and food accounted for much the greatest share of subsistence.

The formulation by Rowntree, A. L. Bowley and others during the 1890s and the early decades of the twentieth century had a powerful influence on both scientific practice and international and national policies, examples being the statistical measures adopted to describe social conditions, within individual countries, and later by international agencies such as the World Bank. Beveridge's particular interpretation of 'subsistence' was carried over after 1945 as a means of justifying the low rates of national assistance and national insurance that were then adopted. The idea of subsistence was also freely exported to member states of the former British Empire (Pillay, 1973; Maasdorp and Humphreys, 1975). In the United States 'subsistence' remains the linchpin of the government's measures of poverty (US Department of Health, Education and Welfare, 1976). The use of 'subsistence' to define poverty has been heavily criticized (Rein, 1970; Townsend, 1979), principally on the grounds that human needs are interpreted as being predominantly physical needs – that is, for food, shelter and clothing – rather than as social needs.

A second formulation – of 'basic needs' – was taken up in the 1970s, although strictly the idea had a longer history (Drewnowski and Scott, 1966). Basic needs were said to include two elements:

Firstly, they include certain minimum requirements of a family for private consumption: adequate food, shelter and clothing, as well as certain household furniture and equipment. Second, they include essential services provided by and for the community at large, such as safe drinking water, sanitation, public transport and health, education and cultural facilities. (International Labour Office, 1976, pp. 24–5; and see also ibid., 1977).

This concept has played a prominent part in a succession of national plans (Ghai et al., 1977; Ghai and Lisk, 1979) and in international reports (UNESCO, 1978; Brandt, 1980). The term is quite clearly an enlargement of the subsistence concept. Emphasis is placed on minimum facilities required by local communities as a whole and not only individual and family needs for physical survival and efficiency. However, proponents of the concept have had great difficulty in producing acceptable criteria for the choice and definition of items included. One of the attractions of the 'subsistence' concept for some thinkers has been its limited scope and therefore limited implications for sociostructural reform, and its easier reconciliation with the strong emphasis given to individualism within liberal pluralism. One of the intellectual attractions of the 'basic needs' concept, on the other hand, has been its emphasis on establishing at least some of the preconditions for community survival and prosperity in all countries.

For such reasons some social scientists have been turning to a third, more comprehensive and rigorous *social* formulation of the meaning of poverty – that of RELATIVE DEPRIVATION (Townsend, 1979, 1985 and 1992; Chow, 1982; Bokor, 1984; Mack and Lansley, 1984; Ferge and Miller, 1987; Desai and Shah, 1988; Luttgens and Perelman, 1988; Lister, 1991). Societies are passing through such rapid change that any standard devised at some historical date in the past is difficult to justify in new conditions. People are subject to new laws and obligations and consume different goods and services. Therefore incomes cannot be adjusted by an index of prices. Poverty may best be understood as applying not just to those who are victims of a maldistribution of resources but, more exactly, to those whose resources do not allow them to fulfil the elaborate social demands and customs which are placed upon citizens of that society in the first place. This is a criterion which lends itself to scientific observation, measurement and analysis.

The driving motivation for putting forward poverty as 'relative deprivation' could be said to be scientific and international. There are respects in which the 'subsistence' concept minimizes the range and depth of human need just as the 'basic needs' concept is restricted primarily to the physical facilities of the communities of the Third World. People are relatively deprived if they cannot obtain, at all or sufficiently, the conditions of life – that is, the diets, amenities, standards and services – which allow them to play the roles, participate in the relationships and follow the customary behaviour which is expected of them by virtue of their membership of society. People may be deprived in any or all of the major spheres of life – at work, where the means largely determining position in other spheres are earned; at home, in neighbourhood and family; in travel; in a range of social and individual activities outside work and home or neighbourhood in performing a variety of roles in fulfilment of social obligations.

As with any formulation, there are problems in defining poverty operationally. Under the 'relative deprivation' approach a threshold of income is conceived, according to size and type of family, below which withdrawal or exclusion from active membership of society becomes disproportionately accentuated. Whether that threshold exists depends on the scientific evidence which can be marshalled on its behalf (for an introduction to the controversy see Townsend, 1979, ch. 6; Desai and Shah, 1988; Desai, 1986; Sen, 1983 and 1985; and Townsend, 1985). Detailed and comprehensive scientific observation is necessary to demonstrate both the extent and severity of non-participation among those with low incomes and meagre other resources, because people lead different roles during their lives and may have complex patterns of association.

We are at a relatively early stage of the recognition of the *social* needs of individuals and the full social effects of low income remain to be systematically described and scientifically investigated, but this is not an unfamiliar stage in the evolution of scientific definition and theory.

See also NEEDS; WELFARE STATE; SOCIAL STATISTICS.

Reading
Atkinson, A. 1989: *Poverty and Social Security*.
George, V. 1988: *Wealth, Poverty and Starvation*.
Sen, A. 1981: *Poverty and Famines: An Essay in Entitlement and Deprivation*.
Townsend, Peter 1979: *Poverty in the United Kingdom*.
—— 1992: *The International Analysis of Poverty*.

PETER TOWNSEND

power At its most general, power is the capacity to produce, or contribute to, outcomes – to make a difference to the world. In social life, we may say, power is the capacity to do this through social relationships: it is the capacity to produce, or contribute to, outcomes by significantly affecting another or others. These broad general definitions offer a general framework for characterizing some of the major differences in how power has been viewed in twentieth-century debates. Focusing on social power, we may ask various questions.

First, who or what possesses it? Most have seen power as a capacity of agents, individual or collective, though some have seen it as an impersonal property: the capacity of social systems to achieve collectively binding goals (Talcott Parsons) or to reduce complexity (Niklas Luhmann) or of social mechanisms to 'discipline' individuals, shaping their discourse, their desires, indeed their very 'subjectivity' (Michel Foucault). But there is no need to speak of such impersonal structures as 'having power': all such 'structuralist' views are reformulable as stating various conditions which facilitate or reduce the power of agents, as individuals or collectively, to act (see ACTION AND AGENCY).

Second, which outcomes count as the effects of power? Many agree with Bertrand Russell and Max Weber who insisted that the outcomes be intended. For Russell, power is 'the production of intended effects' (1938, p. 25); for Weber, it is 'the probability that an actor in a social relationship will be in a position to carry out his will, regardless of the basis on which this probability rests' (1921–2). But is intention *sufficient*? What if, like the Stoics, I want only what I can get, or like a conformist only what others want, or like a sycophant only what (I think) others want me to want? Am I powerful, as opposed to you, if the effects I can intentionally produce are produced because you have threatened or induced me, or because I anticipate that you will do so, or if I can only produce them at enormous cost (say by sacrificing my life, or what gives it value) or if I can produce nothing but trivial effects? And are the intentions actual or hypothetical? Is power not also the capacity to achieve what I might, but do not actually, want? And is intention *necessary*? Must all power's effects be intended? Can power not be exercised in routine or unconsidered ways, as when by making investment decisions I deprive unknown people of work, or provide them with it? Perhaps, rather, the outcomes of power are to be identified as affecting the *interests* of the powerful and those their power affects. That the former are advanced only at the expense of the latter is an unduly restrictive assumption found in much of the existing literature on power, even though this is clearly only one possibility.

Third, what distinguishes power relationships? In what ways can the powerful significantly affect others to produce, or contribute to, outcomes? Some, again like Weber, have focused on relations of domination – on *power over* another or others, the securing of compliance by means that may range from VIOLENCE and force through manipulation to AUTHORITY and rational persuasion (though whether this last is a form of power is controversial and depends on whether you think that, in persuading me, my mind is changed by you or the reasons you offer me). Others, like Hannah Arendt, see power relations as essentially cooperative, defining power as 'the human ability to act in concert', contrasting with violence and force and 'the command–obedience relationship': power, in this view, 'belongs to a group and remains in existence only so long as the group holds together' (1970, pp. 44, 40). Others attempt to combine both aspects in a more comprehensive view, stressing both the need of the powerful to enlist cooperation and form coalitions and their need to avert or overcome opposition.

Fourth, how is the capacity in question to be conceived? Does 'power' identify what an agent can do under various conditions, or only under the conditions that actually obtain? On the first view, you are powerful if you can produce the appropriate outcomes in a wide range of possible circumstances; on the second, only if present circumstances enable you to do so (for example, a particular configuration of voting preferences enables you to decide the outcome). The first view identifies an ability which can be deployed across a range of contexts, the second what can be done in a specific time and place. A further view (common among sociologists

of stratification) would include as part of power access to, or the capacity to command, desired outcomes (such as resources or privileges) whatever the agent does. On this view, power can be seen as the ability to secure advantage without effort. But others think this is best thought of as luck rather than power.

Fifth, how is power to be identified, even measured? Robert Dahl and his followers have looked at who prevails in decision-making where there are conflicting interests; Peter Bachrach and Morton Baratz have recommended a further focus on agenda setting (1970); and Steven Lukes has further suggested that power can involve the shaping of beliefs and desires, which, in turn, may not be deliberate (1974). Some have focused on the possession of resources as a 'power index', others on the ability to make a difference, as a 'pivot', in voting decisions, others on the measurement of the opportunity costs of attempting to secure compliance as against the costs of that attempt failing. Plainly, how we answer this last question depends on how we answer all the others.

Reading
Arendt, H. 1970: *On Violence*.
Dahl, R.A. 1961: *Who governs? Democracy and Power in an American City*.
Lukes, S. 1974: *Power, A Radical View*.
Morriss, P. 1987: *Power: A Philosophical Analysis*.
Weber, M. 1921–2 (*1978*): *Economy and Society*, trans. and ed. G. Roth and C. Wittich, esp. ch. 10.

STEVEN LUKES

pragmatism This is the name usually given to the classical philosophical movement in the USA. It emerged in the last decades of the nineteenth century and achieved a certain hegemony in the country's intellectual life during, and immediately after, the so-called Progressive Era (1896–1914). From the 1930s, and even more after 1945, it was largely displaced by other currents of thought in philosophy, the social sciences and public political discourse. American pragmatism also attracted considerable attention in Europe, especially around 1910, though exposition and critical discussion of pragmatism displayed widespread misunderstandings and the tendency to depreciate it by reducing it to an expression of alleged American national characteristics.

The everyday sense of the term 'pragmatic'

certainly contributed to these misunderstandings, connoting as it does a kind of 'muddling through' which is oriented to immediate requirements, disregards theoretical or moral principles and treats the given features of the situation simply as part of a calculation. The term pragmatism has the same Greek roots as PRAXIS, practical etc. The founder of pragmatism, Charles Sanders Peirce (1839–1914), coined the term as a result of his reflections on Kant's use of the terms 'pragmatic' and 'practical'. Peirce's lectures and writings around 1878 are now regarded as the original documents of pragmatism. These first became known only to narrow circles of intellectuals in Cambridge, Massachusetts, and did not achieve wider notice until some 20 years later, when William James (1842–1910) delivered his lectures on 'Pragmatism'. Peirce came to distance himself from James's pragmatism and to call his own philosophy 'pragmaticism'.

Along with Peirce and James, the inner core of pragmatism is usually taken to include John Dewey (1859–1952) and George Herbert Mead (1863–1931). The differences between all these thinkers were so evident, not least to the 'pragmatists' themselves, that their subsumption into a single school or movement has constantly been questioned. The most widely accepted view, however, has been that despite the differences there is enough of a core of shared views to justify speaking of 'pragmatism' as a distinct philosophical orientation.

What are the basic themes of pragmatism? Peirce's approach starts from his critique of Descartes' methodological principle of radical doubt and the resultant programme of making the thinking ego's certainty of itself into the firm foundation of a new philosophy. The pragmatist questions the meaningfulness of Cartesian doubt, not in order to defend unquestionable authorities against the emancipatory claim of the thinking ego, but arguing for a more substantial doubt, that is, the grounding of cognition in real problem situations. In pragmatism, the guiding idea of the doubting ego is replaced by the idea of a cooperative search for TRUTH in order to overcome real problems of action (see ACTION/AGENCY). Real doubt occurs in action, conceived as a cyclical succession of phases. Thus every perception of the world and every action in it are anchored in an unreflective belief in self-evident conditions and successful habits. But these habitual ways of acting constantly come up against the resistance of the world, which is seen to be the source of the destruction of unreflective expectations.

The resultant phase of real doubt leads to a reconstruction of the interrupted context. Perception must grasp new or different aspects of reality; action must attach itself to other elements of the world or reorganize its own structure. This reconstruction is a creative accomplishment by the actor. If he or she succeeds, via a change in perception, in acting differently and thus getting going again, then something new has come into the world: a new way of acting which can be institutionalized and itself become an unreflectively followed routine. Thus pragmatists see all human action in the opposition between unreflective habits of action and creative accomplishments. This means also that creativity is seen here as characterizing achievements in situations which demand a solution, rather than the unconstrained creation of something new without a constitutive background in unreflective habits.

From this basic model of pragmatism, in which action and cognition are combined in a particular way, we can derive the other central claims of pragmatism. In the metaphysics of pragmatism, reality is not deterministic: rather, it enables and demands creative action. In the epistemology of pragmatism, knowledge is not the reproduction of reality but an instrument for dealing with it successfully. The semantics of pragmatism locates the meaning of concepts in the practical consequences for action resulting from their use or their difference from other concepts. Thus in pragmatism's theory of truth, the truth of sentences can only be determined by way of a process of agreement on the success of action based on them, and not on, say, their correspondence with an uninterpreted reality. The misunderstanding of pragmatism as principally a movement aiming at the destruction of the ideal of true knowledge resulted primarily from the isolation of individual sentences, such as William James's statements about truth, from the whole complex of pragmatist thought.

The leading representatives of pragmatism contributed to different fields of inquiry. Peirce was primarily interested in developing a general theory of scientific knowledge and a broadly conceived theory of signs or SEMIOTICS. His multifaceted work, which is hard to summarize, includes important thoughts on the intersubjective use of signs and on the creative production of hypotheses ('abduction'). This theory of signs, particularly in its emphasis on the 'discourse' of scientists in an experimental community, has been of decisive importance for the 'discourse ethics' developed by Karl-Otto Apel and Jürgen Habermas (see DIS-COURSE; ETHICS) and for Habermas' 'theory of communicative action'.

William James worked mainly in psychology, in which he saw the prospect of a way out of the dilemma between a religiously based belief in the free will of the moral agent and the scientific image of the world as a universe governed by causal processes. The solution, for James, lay in the functionality for the survival of the human organism in its environment which he saw in the human capacity to pay deliberate attention to perceptual impressions and to choose between alternative courses of action. A 'functionalist' psychology (see FUNCTIONALISM) could proceed by understanding all mental achievements in terms of their function for the organism's active mastery of its environment.

John Dewey, whose thought at first developed independently of the first pragmatists, abandoned his earlier neo-Hegelian approach and increasingly tried to link up with the epistemological and psychological aspects of pragmatism as developed by Peirce and James. His aim was to construct a philosophy which extended the core ideas of pragmatism into all the traditional domains of philosophy (metaphysics, logic, ethics, aesthetics), and in particular the field of social and political philosophy. He gave more explicit emphasis than the others to a radical version of democracy as the normative core of pragmatism.

George Herbert Mead, a friend of Dewey, did most to develop James's strategy of the translation of pragmatist themes into the programme of a biologically based empirical social science. His decisive contribution to social theory consists in his theory of the specific features of human communication and hence the attempt to thematize the constitution of personality structures in the dynamics of interpersonal relationships. Mead attacked the assumption of a pre-social substantial self and replaced it by a theory of the genesis of the self in which even the interaction of a person with himself or herself is conceptualized as the result of social structures. Mead also pursued this line of thought in the direction of problems of cognitive development, such as the constitution of permanent objects in experience and the constitution of structures of time (see TIME AND SPACE).

Certain of Mead's concepts and models formed the basis of the school of SYMBOLIC INTERACTION-ISM in sociology. The influence of the other pragmatists on sociology, outside the Chicago school and symbolic interactionism, has so far, despite spectacular exceptions such as C. Wright Mills and Jürgen Habermas, been rather slight. The unmistakable renaissance of pragmatism in philosophy has so far no similarly striking parallels in sociology.

Reading
Joas, Hans 1985: George Herbert Mead: A Contemporary Re-examination of his Thought.
—— 1993: Pragmatism and Social Theory.
Mead, G.H. 1934: Mind, Self and Society.
Smith, John E. 1978: Purpose and Thought: The Meaning of Pragmatism.
Thayer, Horace S. 1981: Meaning and Action: A Critical History of Pragmatism, 2nd edn.

HANS JOAS

praxis Definition (1), in Aristotle, is acts performed as an end in themselves, for their own sake; distinguished from *poiesis*, meaning productive activity in pursuit of ends; and from *theoria* or contemplation. These are the three basic activities or walks of life of human beings (Lobkowicz, 1967). Meaning (2), in Marx and in the writings of a number of philosophers within WESTERN MARXISM is: (a) a type of creative practical activity peculiar to human beings whereby they construct their world, an idea basic to Marx's model of HUMAN NATURE; (b) an epistemological category describing the practical, object-constituting activity of human subjects as they confront Nature, that Marx called 'practical, human sense activity' (Marx, 1845, p. 83); and (c) as 'revolutionary' praxis (Marx, ibid.), the putative point of fundamental social transition whereby in practice the proletariat's objective social circumstances and their complete understanding of them are said to coincide.

Although the three separate Marxist senses have come to be established in modern social thought, the concept generally remains imprecise, obscure and elastic in its application. This is partly because it has been associated with the slogans of the NEW LEFT in recent times and partly because its origins lie in the obscurities of the philosophy of action elaborated by Young Hegelian writers of the 1840s such as Arnold Ruge, August von Cieszkowski, Moses Hess and Marx himself (Stepelevich, 1983). Furthermore, Marx's early writings on this subject were largely unpublished drafts and a number of important passages on the topic are open to interpretation.

Sometimes the phrase 'the unity of theory and practice' is said to be the meaning of the concept of praxis, and it does seem to capture loosely the speculative meaning 2(c). In fact, the phrase is employed in orthodox MARXISM and refers to ongoing sequences of organized, theory-informed political activity, including the application of the principles of Marxism-Leninism in the former Soviet Union. The idea of praxis, on the other hand, particularly in sense 2(a), was prominent in the socialist countries of Eastern Europe, as part of the ideological armoury of dissidents' criticisms of the regimes (Marković, 1974).

The usage (2a) relates to the image of human beings or model of human nature found in Marx: 'free, conscious activity is man's species character' and 'In creating an objective world by his practical activity... man proves himself a conscious species being' (Marx, 1844, p. 71). Praxis, in this sense, is bound up with ALIENATION, as a general historical process in which human beings, in their creation of human history and society, have become successively estranged from Nature and from the objective products of their labouring praxis.

The category of praxis (2b) as object-constituting human action in Marx's early writings (notably 1844, 1845 and 1845-6) can be read with hindsight as making a contribution to epistemology (see THEORY OF KNOWLEDGE); in particular to the supersession of idealism and materialism and to a sociological approach (Kilminster, 1982). Marx saw that traditional materialism was implicitly individualistic and implied a passive view of human beings, whereas the idealism of Hegel stressed the active, historical, cultural dimension of human knowing but restricted this activity to the realm of consciousness. Marx's social version of materialism achieved a new synthesis. Humans are part of nature and the objectivity of their social world is a result of their practical, collective sense-activity in appropriating non-human nature through productive labour over many generations. By working on nature to satisfy our needs we come to know it, but only in a 'humanized' form. Nature thus has a socially imprinted character and an autonomous role in human affairs at the same time (Kolakowski, 1971).

The social scientific theory of knowledge Marx developed out of these abstract reflections was the BASE AND SUPERSTRUCTURE model of social consciousness. Despite his early ambitions, this model is flawed by a dualistic ONTOLOGY and suffers also from an overemphasis on economic relations, and Marx also projected into COMMUNISM not only the overcoming of the major epistemological antinomies but also solutions in practice to all other theoretical problems (Marx, 1844, pp. 95, 102, 114). Nevertheless, this was a pioneering effort. By shifting the problem of knowledge on to the ground of structured, practical social activity, and away from the individualism of the traditional subject-object epistemology, Marx contributed to the growing realization of the social nature of the knowledge process (see SOCIOLOGY OF KNOWLEDGE).

Revolutionary praxis (2c) constitutes the most speculative dimension, involving not only knowledge, but also ETHICS. Marx's theory survived in its uncorrected and more mythological form in the extravagant millenarian flourishes of later Marxists such as György Lukács, Karl Korsch and Antonio Gramsci in the 1920s (Kilminster, 1979). For them, in various versions, proletarian class consciousness potentially overturns the objectivity of society itself. They also (wrongly) identified all social science with POSITIVISM, seen as articulating the dominant social experience in an alienated, capitalist society. Hence, social laws could be falsified by mass action or cumulative cultural and political changes.

There is some evidence that the Left Hegelian idea of 'realizing philosophy in practice' was an important motif in the formation of Marx's ideas. Hegelian radicals compared social reality as it *is* with what it ideally *ought* to be, but Marx thought this was ineffectual verbal radicalism which changed nothing, and enjoined instead 'practical-critical activity', that is, the project of bringing reality up to what it ought to be *in practice*:

> Communism is for us not a state of affairs which is to be established, an ideal to which reality will have to adjust itself. We call communism the real movement which abolishes the present state of things (Marx and Engels, 1845-6, p. 48).

Communism would effectively be a society which no longer required ethics because there would no longer be, in the reality of people's lives, any significant discrepancy between how they lived and how they thought they could ideally live. In Marx's materialistic version of Hegel's philosophy of history, there was no need to develop a separate ethical justification for socialism or communism. The scientific economic theory describing the historical stages of human development and the moral desirability of the end state of communism were essentially the same thing. It was only bourgeois rights and morality that were ideological (Lukes, 1985).

Later, Marx's theory lent itself to buttressing the power of bureaucratic elites in the former Soviet Union and in Eastern Europe, who stifled dissent by claiming that not only were their policies based on a correct Marxist scientific analysis of society and history, but were by definition also *morally* right. In opposition to these claims Marx's model of man-as-praxis was emphasized as embodying the 'authentic' Marxist vision of human life.

The demise of the idea of the historical inevitability of socialism, together with the experience of TOTALITARIANISM in the twentieth century, has had important consequences. The grounding of moral questions could no longer be put off by subsuming their future solution in a necessary historical movement or, prior to that, in the scientific, political and moral infallibility of the Party. These realizations formed the starting point for the neo-Marxist project of critical theory (Habermas, 1974), and after the collapse of communism in Eastern Europe in 1989 and the break-up of the Soviet Union, the issue of the good society is very much back on the agenda.

Reading
Habermas, Jürgen 1971 (*1976*): *Theory and Practice*.
Kilminster, Richard 1979: *Praxis and Method: A Sociological Dialogue with Lukács, Gramsci and the Early Frankfurt School*.
—— 1982: Theory and practice in Marx and Marxism. In *Marx and Marxisms*, ed. G.H.R. Parkinson.
Kolakowski, Leszek 1971: Karl Marx and the classical definition of truth. In *Marxism and Beyond*.
Lobkowicz, Nicholas 1967: *Theory and Practice: History of a Concept from Aristotle to Marx*.
Lukes, Steven 1985: *Marxism and Morality*.
Marković, Mihailo 1974: *From Affluence to Praxis: Philosophy and Social Criticism*.
Rotenstreich, Nathan 1965: *Basic Problems of Marx's Philosophy*.
Stepelevich, Lawrence S. ed. 1983: *The Young Hegelians: An Anthology*.

RICHARD KILMINSTER

prediction As the determination of the future states of a physical or social system, prediction is an important epistemological issue because the ability to produce accurate and reliable predictions is often considered as the ultimate criterion by which science should be distinguished from other types of intellectual activity.

That predictions can be made and are often successfully made in the social sciences is beyond doubt: thus, short-term or middle-term predictions of employment, birth or death rates or educational opportunities are often reliable (see also SOCIAL STATISTICS). On the whole, the social sciences have successfully developed an actuarial dimension. The crucial distinction between prediction and prophecy is not always clearly made by the social sciences, however. At the beginning of this century, W. Sombart predicted that a powerful socialist movement would develop in the United States. In the middle 1980s, many sociologists and political scientists predicted a long life to the communist regimes in the East European countries. As is well shown by Anthony Giddens (1990), the predictions of Karl Marx and Max Weber on modern societies must be seriously relativized.

In the recent past, social scientists have become increasingly aware of the difficulties confronting prediction in the social sciences. This can be seen from the fact that 'futurologists' no longer pretend that they can predict social change accurately, and develop instead alternative plausible 'scripts' of the future stages of social systems. This more modest attitude towards the possibility of prediction is due notably to the decline of positivism in the social sciences and to the progression of the idea that social facts are the products of individual actions, behaviours and/or beliefs. While some interaction systems are as predictable as physical systems, others are not. Thus 'cooperative games' are accurately predictable, while interaction structures of the 'repeated prisoner's dilemma' or of the 'chicken' type are highly unpredictable (Boudon, 1986; Boudon and Bourricaud, 1989). On the other hand, social change research has led to the view that contingent factors cannot be ignored. Moreover, many prophecies appear as self-destroying by essence: if the prediction is made that some social catastrophe is coming, something will probably be done to prevent it, so that it will possibly not occur. On the whole, the old tendency to define science by its predictive capacity is now perceived as naive: the objective of science is primarily to gain knowledge and understanding of the world and only secondarily to predict its future states. It is important to know, say, that a given interaction structure is unpredictable or that the course of a given process can be affected by contingencies, even though this knowledge makes prediction impossible.

See also CAUSALITY; MEASUREMENT.

Reading
Boudon, Raymond 1986: *Theories of Social Change*.
Ferkiss, Victor 1977: *Futurology*.
Giddens, Anthony 1990: *The Consequences of Modernity*.

RAYMOND BOUDON

prehistory *See* ARCHAEOLOGY AND PREHISTORY

prejudice Defined here as a rigid negative pre-judgement of an individual or a group, the concept is derived from the Latin *prejudicium*, referring to a preceding judgement or decision, a precedent, or damage. The basic connotations include bias, partiality, predisposition, preconception. In modern usage the term carries many variant meanings. Common to most of these, however, are the notions of an unfavourable previous judgement made in advance of full consideration, and rigidly held even in the face of evidence which contradicts it.

Because of its broad scope and complex connotations in ordinary language, the term always should be interpreted in the specific context in which it is used (see Williams, 1964, pp. 28–9). In modern social science the typical usage refers to categorical prejudgements that have cognitive components (beliefs, stereotypes), affective components (disliking, aversion), and evaluative or conative aspects (such as dispositions toward public policies) (see Blalock, 1967, p. 7; Klineberg, 1968, p. 439).

Definitions of prejudice are necessarily range-definitions which focus on certain characteristics, selected from a wider range of other characteristics. For example, some authorities specify that preju-dices are not only unfavourable and categorical but also inflexible, rigid and based on inadequate knowledge or false judgement. Thus Allport (1976, pp. 515–16) holds that prejudices are overgenera-lized and erroneous attitudes – misconceptions that are not reversible by new knowledge. On the other hand, Klineberg (1968, p. 440) argues that reversi-bility by new knowledge is not an appropriate criterion of prejudice. Accordingly, it seems best to regard reversibility as a correlate for empirical study rather than as part of a formal definition of the concept.

Numerous research findings show that the atti-tudes usually labelled as prejudices in ordinary speech may be specific to one group or generalized to many; they may be primarily cognitive, or affective, or evaluative; they may concern only personal social interactions or be directed towards broad public policies; and they may be important or peripheral to the individual actor. Confronted with these variations, social science research generally has focused on unfavourable orientations directed towards racial and ethnic groups or categories, leaving other correlated characteristics to be inves-tigated for particular purposes (Williams, 1964, pp. 22–77; Klineberg, 1968, p. 439). The accumulated research evidence has established a large number of empirical generalizations concerning prejudice in this sense. Among the more important findings are these:

1 Such negative prejudices, although widespread, are not universal.
2 Prejudice is not a monopoly of any one society or culture.
3 Prejudice is not inborn but must be learned.
4 Prejudices towards different groups tend to go together: persons who manifest prejudice to one ethnic group typically show similar attitudes to other 'outgroups'.
5 Individuals vary greatly in the intensity and kind of their prejudices.
6 Prejudices both encourage and are generated by actual discriminatory behaviours and public policies.
7 Prejudices and behaviour need not be con-gruent: specific situations can greatly affect actual conduct, even in spite of generalized attitudes (see also Pettigrew, 1976, p. 525).

Ethnocentrism
A concept closely related to prejudice is ethnocen-trism. In its less intense forms ethnocentrism may mean no more than a positive attitude towards one's own group and its ways. Generally, however, the term also connotes some feelings of group superior-ity in comparison with outgroups. In either case, ethnocentrism varies greatly in both intensity and in specificity (Levine and Campbell, 1972). Never-theless there is a marked empirical tendency for ethnocentrism to become generalized – at the extreme, one's own group is superior to all others in all important ways (see Williams, 1964, pp. 22–8). In general, historical and comparative studies

indicate that the more prevalent and intense in a society are the beliefs in the superiority of the ingroup, the greater will be the likelihood of blaming outsiders for any undesired conditions or events. As ethnocentrism becomes more unconditional, emotionally intense and rigid, the greater is the likelihood of conflict with outgroups; such conflicts, in turn, reinforce and accentuate ethnocentrism. In this way, diffuse ethnocentrism often turns into strong prejudice.

The objects of ethnocentrism and prejudice

Ethnic and racial categories are social constructions (see also ETHNICITY; RACISM). They develop reciprocally with social differentiation and interaction among people who presumably were initially rendered distinctive by kinship, geographic community and modes of subsistence. Interactions among persons linked by networks of kinship and marriage and living in close proximity inevitably produce distinctive cultural characteristics. When such ingroups come into contact with others who differ from them in salient ways, the basis is laid for ethnic relations. As long-distance trade, military conquests and migrations and other population movements develop, the range of potentially salient sociocultural differences widens, and when the populations that come into contact differ both in culture and in obvious physical characteristics, there is the possibility that ethnic relationships will be defined as 'racial'. Thus modern race relations, so-called, are an outgrowth of the world-wide expansion of trade and political interactions after the fifteenth and sixteenth century 'voyages of discovery' (Williams, 1977).

Sources of prejudice

When distinctive ethnic and racial groups have come into contact, economic COMPETITION enhances prejudice. Similarly, group boundaries and negative attitudes are accentuated by struggles for political power or social prestige and deference. Threats to vested interests in such scarce values, then, are potent stimuli for group conflict. Much research has revealed psychological processes (frustration, displacement, rationalization, among them) and personality structures (such as authoritarianism) that are important in the development and maintenance of prejudice in individuals (LeVine and Campbell, 1972; Simpson and Yinger, 1953). But aside from psychological sources, what social conditions affect the extent and intensity of categorical prejudices?

Negative prejudice and discrimination are mutually reinforcing. Whatever the causes, increases in hostility, negative stereotyping and attitudes of social distance typically lead to increased discrimination, including exclusion and enforced segregation. In the reciprocal sequence, increased discrimination leads to more pervasive and more intense prejudice. The experience in the United States has been that reduced discrimination against black persons (primarily through legal and political action) was often followed by reduced prejudice. In short, discrimination generates and reinforces prejudice; prejudice creates a base for and rationalization of discrimination (see also IDEOLOGY).

Once formed, a particular ethnic prejudice as a complex cluster of beliefs, values and sentiments may become widespread and normative in a population through ordinary processes of SOCIALIZATION and conformity. Through indoctrination and example children learn prejudices as part of the total cultural repertoire absorbed in family and other ingroups. When such prejudices become normative, the interlocking expectations and demands of authorities and peers create pressures and inducements to conformity. In these ways, a cultural 'tradition' of prejudice can acquire great strength and persistence.

Reading
Blalock, H.M. Jr 1982: Race and Ethnic Relations.
Ehrlich, H.J. 1973: The Social Psychology of Prejudice.
Francis, E.K. 1976: Interethnic Relations: An Essay in Sociological Theory.
Rex, J. 1983: Race Relations in Sociological Theory.
van den Berghe, P.L. 1981: The Ethnic Phenomenon.
Williams, R.M. 1977: Mutual Accommodation: Ethnic Conflict and Cooperation.

ROBIN M. WILLIAMS, JR.

pressure group See INTEREST GROUP

privacy One way of understanding this concept is as an alchemical laboratory housing those minute creative processes punctuating EVERYDAY LIFE which contribute to the 'recreation' of the self and to the maintenance of a sense of IDENTITY without which personal resilience and resistance would be impossible. This phenomenon emerges clearly from a survey carried out on young people. In analysing so called 'inner emigration', the survey highlighted how individuals search out 'niches' in time allowing daily periods of withdrawal from the outside world (Duvignaud, 1975, p. 233). One could extend this analysis by showing how, even if its manifestations are not predictable in detail, such private niches are a constant of all social structures. Underlying the tradition of *smucke dei heim* ('decorate your home') in Nordic countries, workers' gardens or the predilection for kitsch, all of which have been extensively studied, not to mention the taste for converted barns and rural cottages, the same quest can be sensed, namely for the womb-like refuge of the 'nocturnal realm' (G. Durand), in other words of a privacy which persists despite, or in defiance of, any kind of progressive mythology. (See also MODERNISM AND POSTMODERNISM.)

This regenerating retreat from the world, it must be remembered, is linked to what might be called the 'return to the forests' (Ernst Jünger) which has a distinguished pedigree stretching from 'Robin Hood' to the many clandestine resistance groups of modern history right up to present-day urban guerrillas. Such extreme forms of social behaviour throw into relief the truth about many more ordinary ones. They exhibit a mechanism whereby individuals who have withdrawn into a private shell of inertia are able to rally and achieve a collective identity so as to confront the multifarious encroachments of external reality. It is within the weft of everyday life, immune from the sphere of politics with all its slogans and power games, that social sovereignty is located. It might even be argued that it derives all its strength from the fact that it remains hidden, that it is an occult force which has nothing to do with the appearance of power.

One example of privacy could be seen in the 'culture of the poor' so perceptively described by Richard Hoggart (1957). The vast corpus of witticisms, maxims, sayings and slang, satirical theatre or popular literature, has quite rightly been presented by many observers as a social space preserving an effective tradition of resistance (see also MASS CULTURE). It should be added that such resistance works precisely because its gestures of defiance cannot be carried out in any meaningful sense except on a symbolic level, where they act as factors of socialization. They are the passwords through which mutual recognition takes place. Recognition of oneself via recognition by the group. It is, in fact, an ancient anthropological reality;

ethnologists have documented what the 'shalako' of the Zuni Indians, the 'condomblé (Bahia), the 'Kula' (Melanesia) to mention only a few examples, represent in their respective social structurations.

There is, in Gaston Bachelard's use of the word, a 'poetics' of privacy which, although never officially recognized, sanctioned or canonized, remains a valuable generator of socialization. Such a 'poetics' is made up of all those humdrum social activities, trips to see someone, pub conversations, do-it-yourself, cooking, walks, shopping expeditions to buy clothes and so forth, through which individuals recognize themselves as belonging to a particular social group. This recognition or sense of identity, far from being homogeneous and stable, is in constant flux, but nevertheless constitutes, across the plurality of its expression, a dense weft, as varied in texture and colouring as all the threads which make up, in their multiple weavings, the resistant cloth of familiar everyday reality. In *The Soul and the Forms* (1910) Lukács, in the attempt to take stock of this volatile and yet intense community, talks about an 'internal sociality' which manifests itself in the lyricism of human relations.

The lyricism found in pop-songs, escapist fiction and magazine stories written for teenage girls is very illuminating in this respect. It is not the content of such lyricism that counts, but its signifier. What is being said is not so important, as long as it is something which can give structure to the community, a form of structuration to which the 'discreet', womb-like niche of the local neighbourhood or the village is particularly conducive.

It can thus be seen that recourse to privacy is extremely common, and represents the renewal of bonds with the community which can be traced throughout human history and without which none of the specific crystallizations of social life (such as civilizations, customs, institutions, governments) could take place. But while those crystallizations have given rise to a historiography capable of articulating them, the privacy which underpins them has no other guarantee of survival than its own persistence. It is the strength of the abyss, the kingdom of the shadows, the *via negativa*, the dark night of the soul, the black hole of astrophysics. Whatever the name given to it by different centuries and mythologies, this constantly repressed substratum of social life continues to confront demanding and clear-minded thinkers with new metamorphoses which are just as powerful as ever before. Today we seem to be witnessing another forceful resurrection of the 'private', a fact which cannot leave the sociologist indifferent.

See also CIVIL SOCIETY; PUBLIC SPHERE.

Reading
Durand, G. 1969: *Les Structures anthropologiques de l'imaginaire*.
Duvignaud, J. 1975: *La Planète des jeunes*.
Hoggart, R. 1957: *The Uses of Literacy*.
Lukács, G. 1910 (*1974*): *The Soul and the Forms*.
Maffesoli, M. 1976: *Logique de la domination*.

MICHEL MAFFESOLI

problem, social *See* SOCIAL PROBLEM

problematic The concept refers to the configuration of theoretical concepts presupposed in a text or discourse. The problematic defines the 'field' of questions which can be posed and the forms answers must take. It also *excludes* the posing of certain questions, renders some problems unthinkable and some objects 'invisible'. The concept emerged in the late 1940s in the work of the French historian and philosopher of science, Gaston Bachelard. In Bachelard's work, the concept was used to oppose the view of scientific concepts and their real-world referents. Scientific concepts were held to acquire their specific meaning from their place within a structured theoretical whole, advances in science taking the form of fundamental reorganizations of theoretical problematics.

The concept obtained a wide currency in the social and political debates of the 1960s and 1970s by way of its utilization by the French Marxist philosopher Louis Althusser, who made use of the affinities between the concept of problematic and the currently fashionable structuralist approaches in linguistics and psychoanalysis (see STRUCTURALISM). In Althusser's work the primary use of the concept is to achieve a periodization of Marx's writings in terms of underlying transformations in their problematics. Central to this periodization is a contrast between the 'humanist' problematics of Marx's early writings and the 'scientific' problematic of historical materialism which was constituted from 1845 onwards. Verbal correspondences between early and late texts can be reconciled with this thesis of an 'epistemological break' on condition that a 'symptomatic reading' is employed: the empirical 'surface' of a text does not immediately display its problematic. Theoretical work (on the model of a psychoanalytic investigation) has to be done to expose the often contradictory underlying theoretical determinants of the texts. Althusser and his associates also employed the concept of problematic as a way of representing the logical structure of Marx's own critique of classical political economy in *Capital*.

Reading
Althusser, L. 1965 (*1969*): *For Marx*, esp. the glossary entry.

TED BENTON

professions There is no single, generally accepted definition of a profession. Indeed, a considerable literature exists – often referred to as the 'trait' or 'attributional' perspective – which consists of a largely fruitless attempt to identify the elements common to all such occupations (Greenwood, 1957; Millerson, 1964). Despite the difficulties involved in reaching agreement about what a profession is, it is generally recognized that the twentieth century has been marked by a great increase in the number of occupations claiming professional status, seeking legal monopolies of title and practice and attempting to create systems of colleague control over entry and training. It is also agreed that this process of professionalization has, since the early nineteenth century, been gaining in impetus in association with the increasing complexity of the DIVISION OF LABOUR. The literature is, however, acutely divided over the issue of professional power. There are those, such as Daniel Bell (1974), who have identified professionals with the newly powerful knowledge-holders of postindustrial society, while others (Haug, 1973) have pointed to the declining status and power of professionals in an increasingly bureaucratic and sceptical age.

Two questions have characteristically governed social thought about the modern professions. First, to what extent have professional occupations been a unique product of the division of labour? Weber (1921–2), for example, saw professionalization as a process crucial to the emergence of modern society, with the rise of occupations characterized by 'rational' criteria of recruitment and performance. This question has also informed the 'trait' approach to the analysis of the professions. The second seminal question posed the problem: do the professions perform a special role or function in modern society? The general implications of this question were explored by Emile Durkheim (1950) who argued that in industrializing societies, increasingly fragmented by a 'forced' division of labour, the 'occupational corporation' or profession was the only social institution capable of generating a new moral order, mediating between the bureaucratic regulation of the modern state and the anomic individual. Once again, however, this question has often been reduced to a search for some essential quality shared by all professionals, such as their collective altruism or service orientation (Parsons, 1951). This perspective suggests that the relatively high levels of status and power enjoyed by professionals are explained by their authority or competence and that this knowledgeability renders the client vulnerable and exploitable. Likewise, the collective altruism of a profession is observable in the fact that the client is protected, the community is serviced and practitioner privileges are ultimately justified by colleague-imposed ethical codes of conduct.

This 'altruistic' or 'functional' view of the professions (see FUNCTIONALISM) is rooted in Durkheim's work on the division of labour (1893) and Carr-Saunders and Wilson's *The Professions*, published in 1933, the same year as Durkheim's *The Division of Labour in Society* appeared in English. Durkheim sought to encourage the development of professional associations in all areas of fragmented, specialized work, so replacing kinship as the main source of social solidarity. Carr-Saunders and Wilson regarded the English professions as equally pivotal to the well-being of democratic society, identifying in their ethical codes and forms of collegial – as against bureaucratic – authority the best defence against those 'crude forces which threaten steady and peaceful evolution of society', namely the state and the 'exploiters' of public opinion.

These 'functionalist' themes were further developed in the period after World War II by American sociologists who stressed the positive functions carried out by associations of professional colleagues in ensuring that those systems of knowledge which exerted a 'powerful control over nature and society' (Barber, 1963, p. 672) were mobilized in the community and individual interest. It was also argued that because only professionals fully understood the implications of their own practice it was also natural that they should be given a dominant role in controlling their application, and rewarded highly in material and status terms for so doing.

Since the mid-1960s, however, there has been a loss of faith in professional altruism, an increasing focus on monopolistic professional power as an exploitative force, and scepticism about the beneficial effects of professionalism as a strategy for collective, occupational advancement or mobility. This 'radical' perspective has concentrated on the dysfunctional effects of professionalism, both as a mechanism of market domination and as the product of a collusive state/profession relationship generating structures of social control (Gilb, 1966; Navarro, 1976). An influential source of this alternative tradition is the classical liberalism of Adam Smith, with its hostility towards all clubs, corporations, cliques, cabals and cartels threatening the free operation of the market; a tradition expressed in the writings of economists such as Milton Friedman (1962) as well as the policies of the 1980s associated with Thatcherism in the UK and Reaganism in the USA.

Scepticism has also characterized more recent sociological thought, particularly with the emergence of what has been called 'dominance' or 'monopoly' theory. This literature identifies professionalism as both a collectivist strategy for monopolistic control over occupational jurisdictions (Larson, 1977) and a system of exclusionary practices, significant in the formation of the division of labour rather than a product of it – part of the wider process of class formation (Parkin, 1979).

While 'monopoly' theorists generally agree with 'functionalists' that a successful strategy of professionalism is associated with an occupational claim to special skills and knowledge, requiring extensive training, they have tended to disagree about the direction of the causal link. That is, while 'functionalists' argue that esoteric knowledge and scarce skills are the primary conditions for securing professional privilege, 'monopoly' theorists reverse the claim, arguing that occupational power to control the market – often backed by the state – has led to public acceptance of the knowledge base and the legitimation of jurisdictional skills (Abbott, 1988). The implications of such a perspective has led to a focus on the self-interest inherent in the strategy of professionalization as well as the potential for an exploitative relationship between professional and client.

Given such fundamental disagreements, the absence of a shared definition of a profession is unsurprising. The most successful attempt to overcome the seeming contradictions exists in the work of Eliot Freidson, who in his analysis of the American medical profession argues that it is possible for a profession to be autonomous even while submitting to the 'protective custody' of the state (1970, p. 24), as modern states whatever their ideological leanings uniformly leave in the hands of professionals control over the technical aspect of their work (see also TECHNOCRACY). Consequently, state intervention in medicine does not undermine the autonomy of professional judgement.

However, while most analysts accept that medicine and law are 'classical', autonomous professions in Freidson's sense, there is little unanimity beyond that point. Difficulties are experienced in equating 'true' autonomous professionalism with the *commercial* ethos of the pharmacist, the *bureaucratic* work locations of accountants, the subjection of the architect to the *patronage* of the client, or the *public/official* role of the civil servant. Consequently, a range of concepts have developed to cope with the problem of the 'semi-', the 'marginal-', the 'bureaucratic-', the 'sub-' and the 'pseudo-professions'. Such terms have been applied to most of the hybrid occupations staking a claim to professional status in the course of the twentieth century. The 'monopoly' theorists have responded by claiming that the identification of an occupation as professional has less to do with the reality of a division of labour in which a colleague association effectively controls its own work practices than with the collective strategy of professionalism as a means of occupational advancement (Johnson, 1984).

Reading

Abbott, Andrew 1988: *The System of Profession: An Essay on the Division of Expert Labor.*

Bell, Daniel 1974: *The Coming of Post-industrial Society: A Venture of Social Forecasting.*

Carr-Saunders, A.M. and Wilson, P.A. 1933 (*1964*): *The Professions.*

Durkheim, Emile 1950 (*1957*): *Professional Ethics and Civic Morals.*

Freidson, Eliot 1970: *Profession of Medicine: A Study in the Sociology of Applied Knowledge.*

Greenwood, E. 1957: Attributes of a profession. *Social Work* 3, 44–55.

Haug, M.R. 1973: Deprofessionalization: an alternative hypothesis for the future. *Sociological Review Monograph* 20, 195–211.

Johnson, Terence 1972: *Professions and Power.*

Larson, Magali Sarfatti 1977: *The Rise of Professionalism: A Sociological Analysis.*

Parsons, Talcott 1949 (*1951*): The professions and social structure. In *The Social System*, chapter 10.

TERRY JOHNSON

progress Strides forward have occurred throughout the human experience. Even in the Middle Ages, long thought to have been almost stagnant, major advances in technology were made. There were, for example, the great achievements in architecture and engineering required to build the Gothic cathedrals. Francis Bacon cited three before his time: the inventions of the compass, of gunpowder, and of the printing press. But they occurred as it were unconsciously. None was thought of as 'progress' – simply as ingenious contrivances of persons, mostly anonymous, to meet immediate needs. Philosophy, reasoning about the laws of nature, had no part, and their creators were artisans or mechanics.

Lacking was the *idea* of progress; namely, the idea that purposive, concentrated effort, often of an organized group, guided by increasing knowledge of nature, could achieve defined goals of improving 'man's estate' in objectively measurable ways – and that such effort is of great moral, and indeed spiritual value. This idea, along with the institutions of representative government based on universal suffrage, has been the most enduringly influential force in the modern world.

Progress, as idea and ideal, emerged suddenly in the seventeenth century, in England, and its classic formulator was Sir Francis Bacon, who in the *New Atlantis* (published 1627) called for a great enterprise, with workshops, laboratories and so on, which would give mankind greatly expanded and corrected knowledge of nature, ending the stagnation of many centuries. Then wretched humanity, like a long-denied heir, would come into its own: 'power and empire of mankind in general over the universe.' The key to everything is concentrated on a coherently planned and directed operation. A significant corollary is that these undertakers would, unlike their humble predecessors in earlier times, become in effect cultural heroes.

Bacon emphatically did not regard this great undertaking as part of any pattern of history, moving upwards, either in the past or for the future. He postulated cycles, ups and downs, for nations as well as individuals; but, unlike the medieval notion of fortune, his theory assumed that the cycles could be controlled by conscious effort. There could be no guarantee that the reversal he envisaged would last forever; only constant alertness can prevent slipping back. Again, his investigation of nature is not what we would call pure science. Indeed, natural philosophers of the Middle Ages, with an aristocratic attitude towards their study and bound by the paralysing authority of Aristotle, had been too 'pure', existing isolated from the practical concerns of society. The test of scientific endeavour is pragmatic: 'what in operation is most useful, that knowledge is most true.' This vision of the possibilities of human advancement, mediated through Thomas Hobbes, became the inspiration of the Royal Society (founded in 1660). It was dominant in the Enlightenment, which indeed it did much to create. The idea of progress represents one of the greatest changes in human consciousness of all time; yet it would have been inconceivable in any place at any time before seventeenth-century Britain. And its dominance in 'developed' nations is the most important difference between them and others.

The immense benefits which this idea has indirectly caused are so evident that the problems which it has also brought tend to be obscured; yet they are among the most important of the late twentieth century. 'Progress' has become the ideal that drives out all others, such as spirituality and personal cultivation. The fact that it must be determined by objective, inescapably quasi-quantitative standards is especially significant. It has produced a cult of change (see also SOCIAL CHANGE; TECHNOLOGICAL CHANGE), a major source of alienation between Western nations and others for whom preservation of a heritage, of a divinely revealed way of life, is the primary purpose. The invocation of the magic word is self-justifying: thus political parties have preempted the word 'progressive', its presence in their names automatically guaranteeing their worthiness and rightness. Its dominance has brought about a neglect, even rejection of the past. Such an attitude has extended even to fields where change and objective standards of 'advancement' are not primary criteria – such as progress in poetry, progress in religion.

This Enlightenment idea of progress should be clearly distinguished from another concept of progress, with which it is usually confused – the notion of inevitable progress through history, or even in the cosmos, to a terminal utopia. The schoolmaster Deasey, in James Joyce's novel *Ulysses*, proclaims that 'all human history moves towards one great goal, the manifestation of God.' This idea, also, is 'modern'; it would have been inconceivable at any time before recent times. Its root is not in the Baconian idea of progress as possibility only, but in apocalyptic patterns of history. The Book of Revelation, supposed to predict the future on divine authority, has been the single most influential book of the Bible throughout most of Christianity. It was long thought to predict a steady increase of evil, and general decline until divine intervention with judgement, after which history would cease and the earth would be transformed. This linear model of world history replaced the classical one of an unending succession of cycles and pointless changes. The apocalyptic linear pattern was replaced, after the Reformation, by another linear model, this time in the opposite direction: that God is judging and guiding historical events in a progressive elimination of evils, until the end, a millennial age of peace, prosperity and justice. The Reformation and the American civil war were interpreted by many Protestants as two great examples of God's action in history.

Schemes of historical interpretation which are non-religious, or even opposed to religion – as Comteanism, Hegelianism and Marxism – owe two essential elements to this change of historical interpretation. First, history is seen as linear, moving upwards. Second, apocalyptic theories see the great events as foreordained, making it the duty of the individual to play his appointed part in the great drama. Conflicts of various kinds, like the great battles of Revelation, are the engines of this universal progress. (See also HISTORICISM.)

Finally, the idea of progress proper should not be confused, either, with progress through EVOLUTION. Thus Erasmus Darwin, in *Zoonomia* in 1794–6, outlined a determined evolutionary movement upwards along the Great Chain of Being. Although his grandson Charles effectively undermined this vision of optimism, by the theory of natural selection, the idea of progressive evolution has endured, culminating in the philosophy of Teilhard de Chardin, who sees the universe moving to an Omega Point, the merging of individual and Christ consciousness. Yet, different as these conceptions of 'progress' are, they have in common the atmosphere of optimism that emerged in the seventeenth century, with the faith in the supreme value of change.

The two ideas of progress defined above have dominated the history of the twentieth century. The limited, Baconian one has in effect been employed innumerable times, producing immense advances in areas from medicine to warfare. It may be a major reason for the great technological success of Western European and North American nations as contrasted with others which have only recently encountered this idea.

The faith in historical teleological progress has, in contrast, had a determining and generally negative influence on the history of the century. It is at the heart of the great ideologies – Manifest Destiny, national communisms, Nazism – all of which are founded on some notion of predetermined movement towards a UTOPIA, however much the conceptions of that utopia may vary. These meta-narratives, dominating and determining all aspects of society and culture, are in essence variants of the original apocalyptic pattern, as, for example, the Nazi Reich, 'to last a thousand years', is a version of the millennial age. These ideologies envisage a fixed pattern of actions, destined inevitably to succeed, but susceptible of being hindered and delayed by 'evil' persons or groups, as the Jews in Germany, the 'bourgeois' and religions in communist countries, etc. Such individuals and groups must be eliminated, for they are preventing the achievement of the glorious culmination of history, with its infinite advantages for all. The profound disillusionment of postmodernism with the 'grand narrative' is in considerable part a rejection of tyrannical schemes of 'progress' (see MODERNISM AND POSTMODERNISM).

The influence of historical teleological progress in a democratic country is demonstrated by the fact that it has been incorporated into US constitutional law. In a recent decision, the US Supreme Court spoke of 'evolving standards of decency that mark the progress of a maturing society' (*Hudson v. McMillan* in 1992). Thus it seems to be assumed that moral progress accompanies the ageing of a society, each stage representing a refinement of sensibility over the previous ones – an assumption which is open to question, as the history of Germany in this century would indicate.

The collapse of the ideology of inevitable progress has left an enormous vacuum which it will be perhaps the principal task of the next century to fill.

Reading
Bury, J.B. 1923: *The Idea of Progress*.
Giuberg, Achsch 1986: *The Map of Time: Seventeenth Century English Literature and Ideas of Patterns in History*.
Jones, Richard Foster 1961 (*1982*): *Ancients and Moderns: A Study in the Rise of the Scientific Movement in Seventeenth Century England*.
Kumar, Krishan 1987: *Utopia and Anti-Utopia in Modern Times*.
Nisbet, Roger 1980: *History of the Idea of Progress*.
Rossi, Paolo 1968: *Francis Bacon: From Magic to Science*, trans. Sacha Rabinovich.
Tuveson, Ernest Lee 1949 (*1964*): *Millennium and Utopia: A Study in the Background of the Idea of Progress*.
—— 1968: *Redeemer Nation: The Idea of America's Millenial Role*.
Webster, Charles 1975: *The Great Instauration*.

ERNEST TUVESON

propaganda   This may be defined as the deliberate attempt by the few to influence the attitudes and behaviour of the many by the manipulation of symbolic communication. In English, to a greater degree than in other European languages, the word 'propaganda' has a pejorative connotation that makes its objective analysis extremely difficult.

Its origins, in the seventeenth-century organization of the Roman Catholic church responsible for missionary activities in the New World and for defending the faith in the old, were largely neutral. But in Protestant England the promotion of Catholicism had a sinister taint. Thus when progaganda began to attract attention during World War I, both as a large-scale, institutionalized activity and as an object of academic study, it was easy to focus on its shady associations. Although Britain did for a while have a Department for Propaganda in Enemy Countries, it soon became policy to grant the enemy exclusive use of the term. Against their 'propaganda' we would spread 'information and truth'. Today propaganda is still largely thought of as a device for undermining the credibility of opponents. Their arguments, discredited by the propaganda label, don't merit reasoned rebuttal. They can simply be dismissed as, by definition, dishonest and invalid. When we are ourselves charged with being propagandists, most of us go on the defensive, trying to refute the allegation.

A further difficulty arises from a continuing idealistic image of liberal democratic politics which combines a freedom to persuade with a fear of being persuaded. Despite evidence from the conduct of all election campaigns, in all the liberal democracies, for at least the past hundred years, innocents still dream of a perfect political world in which choices are made by the rational evaluation of objective, unpressured information.

Most popular definitions focus on the attempt to distinguish the 'truth' which we uphold from the 'falsehoods' or propaganda of the other side. It is invariably a futile exercise, for truth and falsehood are not the objective dichotomies many believe them to be. For the most part, assertions of fact offered in all good faith are assertions of opinions or beliefs about facts, which others, with equally good faith, might dispute. Further, 'the facts' are rarely the same as 'the truth'. Much depends on the knowledge of speaker and audience. An incorrect statement made by someone sincerely believing it to be true is not a lie. An objectively true statement, made with the intention to deceive, by someone who believed it to be false, may well be. There is a further difficulty in that one may adhere strictly to the facts and still be a liar. In proffering only some of the facts, in ignoring uncomfortable counter-facts, in exaggerating or downplaying the signifi-cance of facts, or in asserting as unique attributes of one side facts that are common to both, one may totally distort or deceive while not saying anything that is actually untrue. Two elements seem to be necessary for a lie: the statement must be believed to be false in the light of currently available knowledge, and it must be made with the intention to deceive. These conditions make it extremely difficult to determine whether or not a speaker is a liar. The same kind of objections can be made to attempts to describe propaganda in terms of irratio-nal, or controversial, or dysfunctional statements.

A serious consequence of the attempt to identify propaganda by some element of its content – a lie, a deceitful device, or an exaggeration – is the assumption that propaganda may be rendered ineffective by exposing its tricks. But propaganda involves much more than the message content. It is a persuasive communication set in a particular context. Propaganda effect stems from the interac-tion of a communication and an audience, through a specific medium, in a particular cultural and ideological environment, at a particular time and place.

There are, it seems, five key elements common to all propaganda, whatever its ideological bent or the cause advocated, whatever the tactics or levels of honesty, duplicity or irrationality engaged, and whatever the nobility or baseness of its goals. It is, first, something consciously or deliberately done to achieve certain objectives. All propagandists are trying to influence an audience. None has a monopoly on any particular technique or virtue. Any act of promotion can be propaganda, and will be propaganda to the extent that it is part of a deliberate campaign to influence behaviour. Second, propaganda attempts to affect behaviour through the modification of attitudes rather than through direct force, intimidation or bribery. It

seeks the apparent willing compliance of its audience. And it assumes that while each individual may have a unique set of attitudes, those of a common national, cultural, social or economic background will share sufficient common attitudes to respond meaningfully to group-oriented stimuli. Third, it is behaviour that is the major concern. Attitudes and opinions are important only because they are assumed to be the root of action. It is what people do, not what they think, that finally matters. Fourth, propaganda is of political and sociological interest because it is essentially an elitist phenome-non. It is the attempt by the few who have access to the media as disseminators to influence the many who have access only as an audience. Finally, the propagandist's link to the audience is through symbols: objects which can be perceived by the senses and which convey meanings beyond their own physical existence; meanings that are attri-buted to them by their users. Symbols include all forms of language, all graphic representations, music, displays and exhibitions, art, and generally anything that can be perceived. The conscious employment of symbols to lead to some intended effect can be called the manipulation of symbols. All these elements together are contained in the definition at the head of this article.

See also OPINION.

Reading
Altheide, D.L. and Johnson, J.M. 1980: *Bureaucratic Propaganda.*
Chandler, R.W. 1981: *War of Ideas: The US Propaganda Campaign in Vietnam.*
Choukas, M. 1965: *Propaganda Comes of Age.*
Ellul, Jacques 1965: *Propaganda: The Formation of Men's Attitudes.*
Jowett, G.S. and O'Donnell, V. 1986: *Propaganda and Persuasion.*
Qualter, T.H. 1962: *Propaganda and Psychological War-fare.*
—— 1985: *Opinion Control in the Democracies.*
TERENCE H. QUALTER

property As a social institution, regulated by law and/or custom, property has assumed very diverse forms in different types of society. According to Hobhouse (1913, p. 6) property 'is to be conceived in terms of the control of man over things', a control which is recognized by society, more or less permanent, and exclusive; and it may be private (individual or collective) or common (public). In all societies there is some *personal* private property, and as Lowie (1950, ch. 6) observed in a study using comparative material from tribal and from later state-organized societies, personal property among the former may include such things as names, dances, songs, myths, ceremonial regalia, gifts, weapons and household implements. On the other hand, the principal economic resources (and especially land) are communally owned in many tribal societies, but with the development of agriculture, and still more in modern times with the growth of industry and the emergence of capitalism, private ownership comes to predominate.

The distinction between personal property (which in the advanced industrial societies of the late twentieth century may be considerable for a large part of the population) and private ownership of means of production by a small minority of people has been central in the doctrines of socialist parties and in political controversy since the nineteenth century, and it has profoundly influenced social thought and policy. Earlier property systems, Hobhouse (1913) argued, were largely concerned with property for use, and even where private ownership was highly developed there remained a significant degree of community control and responsibility; whereas property for power and the unlimited acquisition of individual wealth reached a peak in nineteenth-century capitalist Europe and North America. During the twentieth century, however, fresh restraints and limitations have been imposed on private property, in various ways.

One way is through the development of democratic citizenship and the expansion of social rights which provide the whole population with a basic minimum of control over resources for personal consumption. Another is the redistribution of resources through progressive taxation and the transfer of some major means of production from private to public ownership (see SOCIALIZATION OF THE ECONOMY). Accompanying these changes there has been a generally increasing involvement of the state (at local and regional as well as national levels) in the regulation of the economy to achieve various policy objectives, among them that of limiting economic inequality. Modern industrial economies and the political movements to which they gave rise transformed the context in which the idea of property was debated, and as one historian (Schlatter, 1951, p. 273) suggested:

Property rights can no longer be defined as a relation between the individual and the material objects which he has created; they must be

defined as social rights which determine the relations of the various groups of owners and non-owners to the system of production, and prescribe what each group's share of the social product shall be.

Nevertheless, in spite of redistributive measures and the growth of welfare services, great inequality in the distribution of property in industrial societies has persisted, and in some respects has increased. There has been a massive concentration of productive capital in large corporations, and much of this capital is owned or controlled by a small number of wealthy individuals and families; landownership remains very unequal in some countries (and notably so in Britain); and the ownership of property still determines large differences in standards of living (see EQUALITY AND INEQUALITY). Thus in twentieth-century social thought the controversies about property have involved above all a confrontation between CAPITALISM and SOCIALISM as alternative forms of economic and social organization, and the confrontation became more intense when socialist societies were established, first in Russia, then after 1945 in other East European countries, in China and elsewhere. But these societies developed subsequently in ways – involving political dictatorship and repression, authoritarian (and often inefficient) planning, and the formation of new privileged and dominant groups – which aroused widespread popular opposition, leading ultimately, in Eastern Europe, to their collapse; and as a consequence more individualistic conceptions of property rights, emphasizing market freedom and private initiative, have been vigorously reasserted since the 1980s.

In the closing decade of the twentieth century, therefore, the terms in which property rights are analysed and debated have altered significantly. According to some thinkers, public ownership has been shown to be a failure, not only economically but also socially, in so far as it engenders new (and sometimes more onerous) structures of power; but others argue that in democratic political systems some degree of public ownership, and public investment in basic infrastructural services, have had manifestly beneficial results, and that a technologically advanced society in fact depends heavily on a high level of provision of such services, particularly in the field of education. The issues posed in much recent discussion of property thus concern the nature of a desirable and effective balance between public and private ownership in some form of 'mixed economy'; the tolerable degree of inequalities of wealth and power in a democratic society; and particularly over the past decade, the need for greater public regulation of the use of productive property in order to safeguard the natural environment.

Reading
Hegedüs, András 1976: *Socialism and Bureaucracy*, ch. 6.
Hobhouse, L.T. 1913: The historical evolution of property, in fact and in idea. In *Property: Its Duties and Rights*, ed. Charles Gore (Bishop of Oxford).
Ryan, A. 1984: *The Political Theory of Property*.
Schlatter, Richard 1951: *Private Property: The History of an Idea*.
Scott, John 1982: *The Upper Classes: Property and Privilege in Britain*.

TOM BOTTOMORE

Protestant ethic thesis   Max Weber's thesis on the relationship between Puritanism and the 'spirit of capitalism', first published in 1904, engendered a discussion among scholars that continues today. Yet a great deal of the controversy has concerned the correct understanding of the thesis and, in particular, whether Weber intended to claim that CAPITALISM was the effect of Puritanism (or more specifically Calvinism). This debate should be understood in terms of abiding twentieth-century concern with questions of historical method and the genesis of MODERNITY.

The thesis is derived from three writings: Weber's essays in *The Protestant Ethic and the Spirit of Capitalism* (1904–5); his essay on Protestant sects in America (1906); and his replies in 1910 to Karl Fischer and Felix Rachfahl (in Winckelmann, 1968). His book develops three observations. First, that in the sixteenth and seventeenth centuries most economically developed countries were Protestant, and within them the most economically advanced bourgeoisies were associated with the Reformation. Secondly, the new spirit of capitalism differed from money-making or greed in general (which are ubiquitous) in that the capitalist spirit was defined by an ethically regulated conduct of life and the pursuit of accumulation as an end in itself. (See also ETHICS.) Thirdly, there was an affinity between the theology of Puritanism, especially its concept of a 'calling', and the secular spirit of capitalism (as advanced by writers such as the American moralist Benjamin Franklin).

The essence of Weber's argument is that a theological movement grounded in the Reformation had the unintended consequence of contributing to the worldly and materialistic ethos of capitalism. The link between the two is reconstructed through the Calvinist doctrine of predestination. If God had determined the pattern of Creation for eternity, then the saved (the elect) and the damned were also predetermined. This must have created for Calvinists an unprecedented inner loneliness, since salvation could not be achieved, for example, through the sacraments or 'good works'. Weber claims that 'The question – am I one of the elect? – must sooner or later have arisen for every believer and have forced all other interests into the background' (Weber, 1904–5 (*1974*), p. 110). Calvinists sought proof of election through success in worldly activity, for to be profitable in life was to have been chosen as one of 'God's stewards'. Yet Calvinists proscribed the relaxed enjoyment of life, and this prevented profits from being spent on conspicuous consumption. Thus commerce came to be regulated by motivational dispositions that had never before existed. Be prudent, diligent, never idle (for time is money), cultivate credit-worthiness, be punctual in repayment of loans and frugal in consumption. The reward of endeavour became 'the irrational sense of having done [one's] job well' (p. 71).

The thesis offers an explanation of why capitalism developed specifically in north-western Europe, even though preconditions (such as wage labour, markets, technology, or separation between home and production) had existed elsewhere. Yet it also makes a statement about modernity, rationality and history. Capitalism is 'rational' as a system of accounting and planning, but its central value – accumulation as an end in itself – is as non-rational as any other goal. Thus, 'If this essay makes any contribution at all, may it be to bring out the complexity of the only superficially simple concept of the rational' (Weber, 1904–5 (*1974*), p. 194). Further, Weber argued that the transposition of the idea of a 'calling' from a religious to a secular realm was *wholly unanticipated* by Puritan theology. History follows a logic of unintended consequences, governed by accidental affinities and could not therefore follow the kind of laws of development proposed by historical materialism.

Issues such as the genesis of capitalism and the nature of historical explanation also preoccupied Weber's contemporaries Werner Sombart, Karl Fischer, Felix Rachfahl and Ernst Troeltsch, and the publication of the *Protestant Ethic* prompted a debate that continued throughout the twentieth century. Weber was often (mis)understood as having argued that capitalism (as opposed to the capitalist ethos) was the effect of Puritanism. Thus R. H. Tawney, in *Religion and the Rise of Capitalism*, which in some ways echoed Rachfahl's critique of 1909, argued that capitalism in fifteenth-century Venice and Florence predated Puritanism, that political theorists such as Machiavelli gave an impetus to the capitalist spirit, and that Calvinism itself was anti-capitalist. Protestantism, Tawney concluded, was the ideological ground on which capitalism asserted itself. In *The Quintessence of Capitalism* (1913), Sombart argued that Catholicism had not prevented profitable activity, and that the impetus for capitalism had derived from marginalized groups such as Jews, and from merchant adventurers. Such arguments about chronology and causal influence were not confined to the early twentieth-century debate, but arise today, as Pellicani's work indicates (1988).

Weber's response to critics such as Rachfahl, Sombart or Fischer, in which he was supported by Troeltsch, was to restate that he had claimed no more than an 'elective affinity' between Puritanism and the spirit of capitalism. Certainly there were merchant adventurers unaffected by Puritan theology. Yet it was the spirit of accumulation as part of an ascetic lifestyle that differentiated capitalist activity in the sixteenth and seventeenth centuries from money-making in general. It was this spirit that embodied the congruence between Reformation theology and the economic motivations of capitalism (Weber, 1910). Moreover, Weber had already anticipated accusations of 'idealism' when he observed, 'of course it is not my aim to substitute for a one-sided materialistic an equally one-sided spiritualistic causal interpretation of culture and history. Each is equally possible . . .' (Weber, 1904–5 (*1974*), p. 183).

Yet this disclaimer hints at the kind of ambiguities in the thesis that have fuelled seven decades of debate. Did Weber really only mean to suggest an elective affinity between Puritanism and the capitalist ethos? If so, then the claim is suggestive (prompting C. P. Hill and Robert Merton to examine links between Puritanism and natural science for example) but not strong. Further, what does it mean for historical writing if each account is equally possible? Karl Löwith, a Marxist sympathetic to Weber's project, interpreted him to mean

that 'both are equally impossible' (Löwith, 1932, p. 103); hence historical accounts must be 'many-sided' (p. 104). Yet the Protestant ethic thesis also implies a renunciation of history as a structured narrative, such as historical materialism expounds, in favour of multiple connections amid the chaos of unintended consequences. Puritan values found affinity with a materialistic system that in its developed form would have horrified Reformation theologians. One can detect here an idea of history and modernity as tragic phenomena, in the sense also suggested by Weber's colleague Georg Simmel. Modern culture is 'tragic' when the forces that destroy it are necessary consequences of properties essential to the phenomenon itself. Yet this is not explicitly stated in Weber's work. It merely indicates the kind of broader inference that the thesis admits, which has occupied scholars throughout the twentieth century.

Reading
Eldridge, J.E.T. ed. 1972: *Max Weber*.
Fischoff, E. 1944: The Protestant ethic and the spirit of capitalism: the history of a controversy. *Social Research* 11, 61–77.
Green, R.W. ed. 1959: *Protestantism and Capitalism: The Weber Thesis and its Critics*.
Hennis, W. 1988: *Max Weber: Essays in Reconstruction*, trans. K. Tribe.
Marshall, G. 1982: *In Search of the Spirit of Capitalism: An Essay on Max Weber's Protestant Ethic Thesis*.
Mommsen, W. 1977: Max Weber as critic of Marxism. *Canadian Journal of Sociology* 2, 373–98.
Poggi, G. 1983: *Calvinism and the Capitalist Spirit*.
Ray, L.J. 1987: The Protestant ethic debate. In *Classic Disputes in Sociology*, ed. R.J. Anderson, J.A. Hughes and W.W. Sharrock.
Schluchter, W. 1981: *The Rise of Western Rationalism: Max Weber's Developmental History*.
Sprinzak, E. 1972: Weber's thesis as an historical explanation. *History and Theory* 11, 294–320.

L.J. RAY

psychiatry and mental illness Psychiatry – a way of both defining and treating mental illness – has seen important changes since World War II in both its practice and its intellectual roots. This has included a greatly diminished role for psychoanalytic thought (see PSYCHOANALYSIS), particularly marked in the USA where it had been a dominant influence. With this there has been an increased concern with the biological origins of the wide range of disorders that make up psychiatric practice. During the last 20 years the complex task of their classification has returned, together with a biological perspective, to the centre of psychiatric attention as seen in the highly influential third, 1980, edition of the American Psychiatric Association's Diagnostic and Statistical Manual of Mental Disorders (DSM-III). The coming together of nosology (classification of diseases) and biology has undoubtedly been partly prompted by the success of pharmacological treatments and the hope that they would prove to be specific for certain diagnoses. DSM-III largely reflects clinical experience rather than research findings, and it is possible to find described in it well-recognized conditions such as severe mental illnesses (psychoses) like schizophrenia and manic depressive psychosis, the less severe neuroses and emotional disorders, psychosomatic disorders, organic states of dementia, mental retardation and behavioural anomalies such as the addictions. But, at every point there are complexities. Neurotic states, for instance, can in practice be severely handicapping over a long period while schizophrenia may represent a passing episode of 'madness' with a complete remission. There is also a worrying essentialist thrust to the thinking of DSM-III. For example, its definition of schizophrenia requires continuous signs of disturbance for at least six months, but this rules out the possibility of establishing possible environmental factors leading to a brief episode. It furthermore assumes something has actually been established about the nature of the disease entity involved. This is certainly not so, although a fair amount is known about the somewhat disparate group of conditions currently classified as schizophrenic.

But leaving aside such technical issues of definition, psychotic disorders for the most part involve peculiarly unpleasant forms of suffering and, in so far as they can be seen as an exaggeration of ordinary emotional affective responses to experience, represent an important route to the understanding of society at large – something, of course, recognized by Emile Durkheim in his classic study, Suicide, published at the end of the nineteenth century. However, this remains disputed ground, not least because evidence for psychosocial influences inevitably tends to move psychiatry somewhat away from its traditional medical role. It is of significance that psychiatrists first qualify in medicine and spend a good deal of their subsequent training involved in the care and treatment of severe conditions within a mental hospital setting. Although the aetiology of core conditions such as schizophrenia and manic depression remains elu-

sive, their peculiar severity encourages a biological perspective. That similar symptoms can be produced by drugs, tumours, epilepsy and metabolic and hormonal changes only whets medical appetites for more of the often exciting developments in neuroscience and physical treatment. The term 'medical model' in this context is more often used by social scientists than medical practitioners since the clustering together of symptoms and signs into syndromes which can then be correlated with hypothesized biological disorder is so intrinsic to clinical practice as to be rarely explicated.

However, those seen by psychiatrists have been changing and many more are now seen in outpatient clinics – most of whom would never have contacted a psychiatrist even 40 years ago. This, and the recognition that there are even more potential patients in general practice and general hospital medicine, has made clear that mental hospital patients form only a small minority of those who might be classed as suffering from a clinically relevant psychiatric disorder – particularly of depression or anxiety. This diagnostic variety and the fact that individual psychiatrists may have experience of only a selected sample of potential patients has enabled quite disparate ideas about aetiology to flourish – although most can be formulated in biological or psychodynamic terms. A social perspective on these matters has never been central in psychiatry, but developments since World War II have made it more difficult to ignore. Early efforts largely consisted of the speculations of psychodynamically orientated workers, which, although sometimes influential, largely lacked an empirical base. The notion of the 'schizophrenogenic mother', for example (considered by some in the 1940s and 1950s to be central in the aetiology of schizophrenia), failed to survive systematic testing. Fortunately there have been somewhat sounder developments.

One had its origins in the obvious shortcomings of the large mental hospital. The growing population in mental hospitals following the decline in death rates from intercurrent infections in mid-century had brought about overcrowding, particularly involving long-stay schizophrenic patients, and the terrible revelations of the European concentration camps perhaps had some impact on opinion. By the 1950s a few medical superintendents in the UK had initiated a policy of early discharge and begun to develop ideas of how the hospital could be a genuinely therapeutic community. With the introduction of the major tranquillizing drugs in the mid-1950s these changes spread to other mental hospitals. (The movement got under way much later in the USA.) In this climate the anti-psychiatry movement led by figures such as R. D. Laing had an important impact on general and academic opinion. However, its excessive claims and almost total lack of concern for evidence has meant that it has had a limited impact on psychiatry itself. Nonetheless, with hindsight, it is possible to see that one message was important – that those with even the most severe mental illness are still human beings and responding to this humanity can importantly influence the course of their disorder. Indeed it is a remarkable experience to see a previously severely handicapped patient acting with confidence and some insight, despite continuing 'voices' and delusions, within a setting devoted to encouraging independence, pride and vocational activities. Nonetheless the concern during this period of many in the social sciences with doubting the relevance of diagnostic labels and arguing for their likely baleful effect ran totally contrary to the increasing concern in psychiatry to improve and systematize its diagnostic usage. Sadly one effect has been a growing distance between mainstream social science and psychiatry.

Another postwar development was an interest in recording the rates of psychiatric disorder in general population samples. Early surveys indicated surprisingly high rates, particularly among working-class populations. Despite a good deal of scepticism within psychiatry, interest persisted. New clinical-type interviews (instead of questionnaires) were introduced which could be used in the general population together with more sophisticated measures to investigate the role of social factors. For the latter there has been concern to deal with the meaning of experience, something ignored by traditional epidemiology, and with this has come a greater sensitivity to the measurement of stress.

Studies within mental hospitals concentrated on the question of the impact of the organization on the course of the illness, and those studies outside (particularly on the role of the family) considered factors influencing both onset and course. Two things have emerged. First, that what are almost certainly essentially biological conditions such as schizophrenia are importantly influenced in their course by the external environment and particularly by the quality of core interpersonal ties. (The matter of original onset remains more obscure.)

The importance of considering social factors in terms of course has been confirmed by cross-cultural studies where the long-term outcome of schizophrenia appears to be more favourable in developing countries. Given the somewhat mixed effectiveness of physical treatments (including long-term iatrogenic effects), the significance of these findings has been increasingly recognized and also the need to harness such knowledge to everyday clinical practice. A second conclusion to emerge is that affective disorders (which make up the great majority of psychiatric conditions) are common in the general population, and social factors, including adverse experiences in childhood and adolescence, probably play an important role in onset and course. There is also often a link with low social class: for example, in inner-city areas of London, approaching one-fifth of working-class women with children at home appear to suffer from a clinically relevant psychiatric disorder within the space of one year and the majority of these have a significant depressive component (see CLINICAL DEPRESSION).

While some dispute particular aspects of such claims, there is already fairly broad agreement within psychiatry about the importance of the social world and about the need for a genuinely biopsychosocial perspective. Someone depressed for social reasons can still respond to pharmacological therapy and there is no reason in such circumstances why chances of onset (and a deteriorating course) should not also be influenced by underlying biological factors. The impetus for a biopsychosocial perspective has been underlined by the views of John Bowlby about the importance of the attachment system in the genesis of affective disorders and how the system, although greatly influenced by early experience, has essentially an evolutionary and biological basis. It becomes clear that both biological and social systems serve to create meaning and they often do so in tandem. Added to this coming together of disparate perspectives, there is a dawning realization that it is possible to acquire what is apparently the same disorder in quite different ways.

Such developments, of course, have implications for clinical practice. If the current claims for the role of psychosocial influences turn out to be broadly correct, the population-based methods of intervention will be quite beyond psychiatry on its own to provide. It has also become clear that the much debated policy of 'community care' has been largely a matter of talk. Except for a handful of impressive local initiatives, procedures to cope with the running down of mental hospitals have been *ad hoc* and unplanned – the result of pressure for liberal reform, changing treatment regimes and ill-coordinated higher level policy decisions. This has had serious consequences for those with long-term handicaps. We still lack services based on reasonably well-founded principles focusing on the vulnerabilities of particular classes of patient, and services that are capable of remaining in touch with individuals, if necessary, for long periods of time. We are even further away from any effective means of helping the large numbers suffering in the general population, especially those with chronic conditions, few of whom see psychiatrists and probably only half of whom are recognized as psychiatrically disturbed by a medical practitioner.

Psychiatry undoubtedly requires social science; fortunately such collaboration is bound to be useful to social science itself. It is difficult to pursue aetiological research in this area without quickly facing fundamental theoretical issues – say about the nature of social support or the relevance of traditional concepts such as integration or alienation. It is doubtful whether the current extreme emphasis on the biological basis of psychiatry will continue, particularly since so much has stemmed from a particular political climate in the USA. Biological processes of possible relevance are turning out to be of extraordinary complexity and major returns are more likely in the longer than the shorter term. The results of current social research, although modest in terms of what needs to be known, are sufficiently secure to form a foundation for expansion, and there is also some sign that the narrow focus and parochialism of the relevant social science disciplines might be lessening. There is an increased awareness that each needs to do more than develop enticing and stimulating ideas for consumption by its own students. Ideas need to be tested in the setting of actual psychiatric practice. So far, when this has been done, it has proved difficult to sustain the one-sided ideas that have been so popular in individual disciplines (such as the emphasis in sociology on the key role of labelling in producing disorder). However, it must be recognized that there is considerable inertia, if not opposition, to the kind of integrative trends that have been outlined, and it might well be that too much weight has been given to the likely impact on psychiatric thought and practice of reasonably well-established empirical generalizations. The attraction of a drug prescription for a busy clinician will remain considerable. But, at the same time, psychiatry has throughout its history been the most open of medical specialities to social ideas, and as yet there is no reason for outright pessimism about the development of an effective social perspective within psychiatry.

Reading
Bebbington, P. and McGuffin, P. 1988: *Schizophrenia: The Major Issues.*
Gelder, M., Gath, D. and Mayou, R. 1986: *Oxford Textbook of Psychiatry.*
Newton, J. 1988: *Preventing Mental Illness.*

GEORGE W. BROWN

psychoanalysis As one of the most significant intellectual movements of the twentieth century, it is arguable that psychoanalysis is second only to Marxism in the range of its impact on the thought and language of the Western world. The elaboration and formulation of the ideas of this movement was largely the work of one man, Sigmund Freud (1856–1939). Although Freudianism, unlike Marxism, never became the official faith of any state, it is conceivable that its influence may outlast that of Marxism.

The intellectual ancestors of Freud, who foreshadowed his general ideas, were Arthur Schopenhauer (1788–1860) and Friedrich Nietzsche (1844–1900). Whether Freud actually studied them and was directly influenced by their writing, or whether, as he himself suggested, he deliberately kept clear of them (which would not preclude indirect influence through the intellectual 'climate') is not well established. Schopenhauer taught that the underlying reality of the world, the thing-in-itself about whose nature his predecessor Kant taught us to be agnostic, was a dark blind Will, inaccessible to reason, and never given any real satisfaction. The Will sometimes turned in upon itself, but there was no salvation to be had in either indulging or opposing it. The only escape lay in passive, aesthetic contemplation, accompanied by compassion. Schopenhauer's pessimism blended elements drawn from biology, from Indian philosophy, Kantian theory of knowledge and Western aestheticism.

Nietzsche accepted Schopenhauer's overall picture but inverted the valuation: if the Will was everything, why not endorse it rather than damn it? Nietzsche related the theme of the Will turning in on itself to a more historical account of the emergence of moralities of meekness, which he saw both in early Christianity and what he held to be its modern secular continuation, humanitarian-socialist ideals. The entire Schopenhauer-Nietzsche tradition offered, above all, a sensitivity to the conflict-ridden, instinct-dominated, irrational nature of human beings, and the superficiality and inadequacy of facile, optimistic visions of them, promising contentment on the basis of reason, brotherhood or prosperity.

The Freudian or psychoanalytical picture of human beings undermined any more facile optimism and perpetuated this sombre recognition of harsh realities; but it also endowed them with a new twist, which won them an incomparably wider audience. Schopenhauer and Nietzsche were merely writers and philosophers: but Sigmund Freud was a doctor and teacher of medicine, and moreover one espousing a rather materialistic or positivistic or scientific vision of the world. Moreover, he did not present his ideas in the abstract, but in the context of a definite therapeutic technique, aimed at curing specific neurotic disorders. Freud did not merely say that human beings were prey to violent, powerful and unconscious drives, operating in hidden and devious ways: he traced the alleged mechanisms of those operations, and the technique of exploration was at the same time also presented as the technique of the cure.

Freud discovered a new technique claiming to penetrate the defences of the realm of the UNCONSCIOUS, within which our psychic destiny is forged, and offering access to its secrets, thereby securing therapeutic results: the patient 'free associates', ideally without any constraints whatever, in the presence of the analyst-therapist, who after a time tentatively proposes interpretations to the patient. When these interpretations, or some of them, are eventually agreed and accepted, a cure ensues. The process is intensive and long: an hour five times every week, stretching over five years, is considered fairly normal. It should be added that during the early years of the movement, analyses-initiations were often much shorter; that no terminal date can be given in advance of the event; and both in theory and in practice, it is often found that psychoanalysis has no termination.

Freud did not merely invent a new investigative and therapeutic technique (which is what *psychoanalysis* mainly means); he also created what was in fact a major new organization around it. This is in fact the guild, or guilds, of qualified, recognized psychoanalysts, practitioners. The most interesting and significant feature of this guild is the manner of initiation it imposes. Although conventional pedagogic methods are present in the training of an analyst – seminars, lectures, reading – unquestionably the central and crucial place is taken by the 'training analysis', the analysis undergone by the trainee with a senior analyst. The assumption and doctrine is that what makes an analyst is not abstract, cold information acquired, but the transformation of his own psyche, attained by his own successful analysis. Having penetrated his own Unconscious, and no longer prey to the illusions it had imposed, the properly trained analyst is now capable of avoiding self-induced error and helping his own patients, in turn, eventually to attain similar illumination. Unquestionably presupposed in psychoanalysis, though never formally stated and defended, is that there is a very distinctive theory of knowledge: the attainment of truth is basically unproblematic (at any rate in psychic spheres) *provided* there is no interference by the wiles of the Unconscious. The removal of these obstacles leads to the recognition of truth, and truth liberates the psyche from unnecessary suffering. Hence the secret is to obviate these inwardly imposed errors, and the rest is then plain sailing.

This eccentric theory of knowledge can also be presented as a new version of the Socratic approach, but one adapted no longer to a rationalist, but to an irrational and variously more plausible vision of man. The Socratic method of question and answer was based on the assumption that truth is not to be sought by an external inquiry, but to be elicited from within: the questions and answers, so to speak, brought out, by logical midwifery, the concepts which had been ever present. The Freudian variant of the midwifery elicits the truth not by precise questioning, but by unrestrained free association, a cognitive antinomianism, more suited to an Unconscious which is passionate and undisciplined. The marks of the truth eventually elicited are emotional recognition and therapeutic success, rather than logical cogency.

Whatever the therapeutic or investigative effectiveness of this method (a highly contentious matter), there can be no doubt of the truth of one particular psychoanalytic doctrine, namely that of 'transference'. The therapeutic technique described is claimed to engender a powerful emotional bond between the two partners involved in it.

This appears, in a very large proportion of cases, to be the case. The 'transference' so produced would then also appear to be the social bond of the organization produced by Freud. Transference, however, is claimed (plausibly) to be both positive and negative, either in succession or even simultaneously. Correspondingly, the psychoanalytical movement is marked not only by powerful cohesion, but also by equally characteristic fission, accompanied by mutual denunciations. The fact that the theory makes truth hinge, not on external and public criteria, but on the possession of a pure and enlightened psyche, so to speak, means that the mutual criticisms then tend to be framed more in terms of the inner defects and imperfections of the opponents, than in appeals to logic or evidence. The fissions which have occurred in the movement have been of two kinds: either leading to the permanent hiving-off of the dissident sect (secession of Carl Jung and Alfred Adler), or to milder sectarianism which is contained within a broader church (for instance, the existence of an orthodox Freudian, Kleinian and 'Middle' group within the British psychoanalytical guild, continuing to work within the same organization on the basis of an understanding that no one of the three segments will dominate). The various national guilds (at least one country, the USA, has more than one) are loosely linked in an international association. One of the practical issues which divides the movement concerns the question whether analysts must be medically qualified, or whether 'lay analysts' are permitted.

Apart from reasonably tight and well organized psychoanalytical guilds, striving (not always successfully) to retain a monopoly of the appellation 'psychoanalyst', there is also an enormous, volatile, fluid, ill-defined and as yet largely uncharted world of psychotherapists and 'counsellors', organized in various large or small groupings and sometimes freelance, and blending the doctrine in various ways and proportions with other systems of ideas (existentialism, phenomenology, conventional religion, and so on). The central ideas and techniques of most of these do, however, remain indebted to the Freudian inspiration, even if they modify it in various ways. There can be no doubt but that these movements have taken over a very major part of what might be called pastoral care, in a mobile and agnostic industrial society. The influence of the ideas is even more pervasive in literature, ordinary language, the humanities and social sciences. It is fair to say that Freudian terminology has become *the* language in which people discuss their psyches and personal relationships.

There is no simple way of assessing the claims of psychoanalytic doctrine and therapeutic practice. Its persuasiveness is not the same in all spheres, and it is perhaps best to discuss various aspects separately:

Idiom Psychoanalysis has not merely conquered our language, but, one might add, rightly so. The simultaneous recognition of the importance of instinctual drives, and of the complexity and deviousness of the semantic forms in which they appear in consciousness, does seem to do justice to the truth of the matter.

Specific theories The more specific doctrines found within psychoanalysis are difficult to assess, on account of the over-endowment of the system with evasive practices, when confronted by apparent falsification. The loose and even detachable operationalization of its concepts, the ready availability of *ad hoc* evasions, makes these theories survive apparent refutations with great ease.

Therapeutic success Researches actually carried out do not support the idea that the technique is therapeutically effective, or even that it is preferable to 'no treatment'. Though the initial impact of psychoanalysis was related to its clinical involvement and plausible therapeutic promise, claims in this sphere are now muted and carefully hedged.

Theory of knowledge, and method These are not merely at variance with standards customary in other spheres of scientific inquiry, but are exceedingly odd, and barely defensible when subjected to impartial investigation.

Ontology The underlying picture of human beings, stressing both the importance of instinctual drives and the extreme complexity, deviousness and disingenuousness of their conscious expression, would seem to be far more convincing than their rival available models, such as 'associationist' psychology. Whether this model is also a good basis for a more genuinely explanatory psychology is not clear.

Pastoral usefulness In a mobile, atomized, competitive society, in which personal relations are extremely important, not provided or ready-made, or prescribed by a stable social structure, and where they are the objects of great anxiety, the psychoanalytical technique of encouraging people to speak freely to a professional attentive listener, in the expectation that the interaction will bring illumination and an inwardly sanctioned direction of purpose, seems more attractive, or at any rate, to have wider appeal, than any available alternative.

Reading

Gellner, Ernest 1985: *The Psychoanalytic Movement*.
Jones, Ernest 1963: *The Life and Work of Sigmund Freud*, abridged edn, ed. Lionel Trilling and Steven Marcus.
MacIntyre, A.C. 1958: *The Unconscious*.
Magee, Bryan 1983: *The Philosophy of Schopenhauer*.
Malcolm, Janet 1982: *Psychoanalysis: The Impossible Profession*.
Rycroft, Charles 1966: *Psychoanalysis Observed*.
Sulloway, Frank J. 1980: *Freud, Biologist of the Mind*.

ERNEST GELLNER

psychological depression *See* DEPRESSION, CLINICAL

psychology The term is used to describe an academic discipline as well as a professional activity. Academic psychologists are engaged in the systematic study of behaviour and/or mental life. They have used a variety of different theories and methodologies to this end. Although the majority of academic psychologists have sought to make their discipline a scientific one, there have been fundamental disagreements about the nature of psychological enquiry. Professional psychologists have been involved in a number of different activities, such as the diagnosis and treatment of mental or behavioural problems and the selection of individuals for industrial and educational purposes. Professional psychologists typically have studied academic psychology; they normally possess further professional qualifications, enabling them to practise, for example, as clinical or educational psychologists. The majority of academic psychologists have not trained to practise professionally.

Psychology, both as an academic discipline and as a professional activity, has firmly established itself during the twentieth century. Nowadays, most universities in the Western world offer specialist degree courses, yet at the turn of the century there was little formal teaching of psychology. The number of people calling themselves 'psychologists' has greatly increased. For example, the American Psychological Society, founded in 1892, has grown from a small 'learned society' to an organization currently numbering over 55,000 members; in keeping with the dual nature of psychology, these members include both academics and professional practitioners. There are also people without the official qualifications granted by the professional organizations, but who claim to be psychologists and offer services to the public in return for payment.

In the first part of this century, academic psychologists were concerned to create an independent discipline, which would be separate from philosophy. Psychologists claimed that they were scientifically examining matters which previously had only been the object of philosophical speculation. Despite the agreement that empirical science should replace philosophizing, there was little agreement about what the new science should be like. At this time, academic psychology was characterized by deep divisions between competing schools, such as associationism, behaviourism, eugenics/psychometrics and psychoanalysis. Each of these schools claimed to have discovered the basic principles for building a scientific and unified science of psychology, but they disagreed profoundly about these principles. In short, they possessed different philosophies of psychology.

Associationism
Dominant in Germany at the turn of the century, associationism concentrated on analysing the contents of mental life. Using laboratory techniques, associationist psychologists were concerned to investigate the images and mental states experienced under differential experimental conditions. They were particularly concerned to discover the elements of experience, and especially to break down perceptual experience into its basic components. The theoretical assumptions of associationists were to be strongly questioned by gestalt psychologists. Although the gestaltists agreed with the importance of studying experience, especially by means of laboratory experiments, they stressed the need to consider the whole pattern of perception rather than decompose experiences into their individual elements (see GESTALT PSYCHOLOGY).

Behaviourism
In reaction to associationism, behaviourists denied the validity of studying experience. They suggested

that scientific psychologists should be concerned only with outwardly observable behaviour and they dismissed the study of inner experience as intrinsically unscientific. All mentalistic concepts were to be rigidly excluded from the vocabulary of the behavioural psychologist. In the United States this position was first advocated by John B. Watson (1878–1958) and later by B. F. Skinner (born 1904). A similar anti-mentalist programme was developed in the Soviet Union by Ivan Pavlov (1849–1936). Both programmes laid great stress on the experimental study of learning, with Watson, more than Pavlov, emphasizing the role of rewards and punishments. Both behaviourism and Pavlovianism claimed to have discovered through careful experimentation the fundamental principles for changing behaviour. It was suggested that these principles provided the basis not only for scientific psychology, but also for the solution of social problems: if the principles of learning were discovered, then there would be limitless possibilities for changing behaviour by altering the environment (see BEHAVIOURISM).

Eugenics/psychometrics
This school of thought owed much to the early work of Francis Galton (1822–1911) and has had a major impact on the development of British psychology. Unlike behaviourism this school of psychology assumed that the possibilities for changing behaviour were strictly limited by genetic inheritance. Not only were psychological characteristics assumed to be inherited, but they were also thought to be measurable. Much emphasis was placed on 'psychometrics', or the construction of tests to measure individual differences in personality, intelligence, vocational aptitudes and so on. On the basis of test results, psychologists such as Charles Spearman argued that IQ ('intelligence quotient') was largely inherited, and Raymond Cattell produced similar arguments for personality traits. In addition to the argument that some individuals were constitutionally more intelligent than others, there were also racial themes: it was alleged that some 'races' were more or less intelligent than others. This school of psychology has been less optimistic than behaviourism in its approach to social issues: because psychological characteristics were presumed to be genetically fixed for the most part, social problems would not be solved by changing the environment. Some psychologists advocated eugenics, suggesting policies which restricted the

breeding patterns of the 'less fit' and encouraged the 'most fit' to reproduce. These themes, together with those of racial and individual differences, were taken up in the 1930s by fascist politicians (see EUGENICS; INTELLIGENCE TEST).

Psychoanalysis
This school of psychology is associated with the work of Sigmund Freud (1856–1939), who, in Vienna at the turn of the century, formulated both a theory of mind and a therapeutic practice. Like associationism, psychoanalysis concerned itself with the mental life of individuals rather than with overt, measurable patterns of behaviour. However, psychoanalysts argued that the most important elements of mental life were the unconscious ones. According to psychoanalytic theory, the mind was fundamentally divided: the unconscious, instinctual part of the mind (the 'id') was in perpetual conflict with both the 'ego' (conscious, rational elements) and the 'superego' (the sense of conscience). Psychological disturbances such as neuroses and lapses of memory could be traced to the conflict between the unconscious instinctual forces, especially sexuality, and those of the ego and superego. Psychoanalytic therapy aimed to give the patient insight about their unconscious mental life. Freud also proposed a psychoanalytic social psychology which tried to explain the growth of civilization in terms of the child's repressed feelings towards parents. (See PSYCHOANALYSIS.)

The four schools of thought represented competing visions of what psychology should be like. Although they agreed that psychology should be a science, they proposed very different methods for conducting psychological enquiry. Moreover, each suggested that psychologists should study different phenomena: conscious experience, behaviour, genetic abilities, unconscious feelings. In addition, the schools proposed very different types of training for professional psychologists, and envisaged dissimilar roles for them within society.

Within the world of academic psychology, the period from 1930 to 1960 saw the steady triumph of the behaviourist school, especially in America. The major journals of psychology reflected a growing preoccupation with behavioural experimentation and with the processes of learning. The analysis of experience was increasingly considered to be old-fashioned, even pre-scientific, as psychologists sought to discover experimentally the behavioural responses to stimuli. Since the aim was to construct a general stimulus–response psychology, it mattered little whether the experimental subjects were humans. There was a growth of animal experimentation as psychologists accumulated vast amounts of laboratory data about the frequency with which hungry rats press levers in pursuit of food.

The triumph of behaviourism was by no means absolute or universal. The psychometric tradition remained strong, especially in Britain and in parts of America, where A. R. Jensen has continued to argue that Afro-Americans are genetically less intelligent than whites. Psychometric tests were much in demand from educationalists, industrialists and military authorities, who wanted convenient and scientifically warranted procedures for classifying large numbers of people. Moreover, this period saw the publication of some classic works of gestalt psychology, which directly analysed experience and criticized the philosophy of behaviourism.

During the behaviourist heyday, psychoanalysis was largely a peripheral interest within universities. However, psychoanalysts tended to earn their living as therapists rather than university teachers, and they established their own professional organizations. During the 1930s the American psychoanalytic movement was considerably augmented by the arrival of a number of eminent Jewish refugees, fleeing from Nazi persecution in Germany and Austria. Despite intellectual and other prejudices, these refugees succeeded in shifting the major focus of psychoanalysis from Europe to the United States.

The growth of behaviourist psychology coincided with another development within psychology, which ensured that in the long run no single system, neither behaviourism nor any other, would attain complete dominance. There was a growth and separation of specialisms. These included physiological psychology, drawing on new advances in neurology and biochemistry, and seeking to identify the physiological mechanisms underlying psychological processes; child development, pioneered by the Swiss psychologist Jean Piaget (1896–1980), who analysed the stages of children's mental development; and social psychology, which was intellectually closer to the social sciences than the biological ones. New journals were established for these subdisciplines, and technical vocabularies were developed. No longer was it possible for a single individual to be acquainted with, let alone understand, all the

developments in psychology. As psychology became more diffuse, the prospects for an integrated discipline, unified around a single theoretical perspective, became more remote.

Some of the developing specialisms were directly influenced by non-behaviourist ideas. There was a pronounced gestalt influence on social psychology as researchers sought to discover the structure and function of attitudes, values and roles (see SOCIAL PSYCHOLOGY). It was linguistics rather than traditional psychological theory that provided much of the impetus for the study of language which developed in the 1960s, and the emphasis was on studying mental processes rather than overt behaviour (Miller, 1981). Nevertheless, most of the new specialisms shared a commitment to experimental methodology, and behaviourist styles of inquiry were frequently retained. In this sense, there was more methodological unity in the discipline of academic psychology than there was theoretical unity.

Since the 1960s this methodological commitment to the laboratory experiment has weakened. There have been a number of direct attacks. 'Humanistic' psychologists have complained that the experimental approach has led to a trivialization of psychology and a dehumanization of its subject matter (Shotter, 1975). Some social and developmental psychologists have also reacted against the commitment to laboratory experimentation. They have claimed that behaviour should be studied in its social context (Harré and Secord, 1972), with particular attention paid to the study of natural conversation (Potter and Wetherell, 1987).

The major weakening of the behaviourist tradition has not come from critics on the margins of the discipline, but from a central change of interest. The past 15 years have seen the growth of cognitive psychology, devoted to the study of thought processes (Neisser, 1976). Many mentalist terms, which behaviourists had wished to eradicate from the psychological vocabulary, are now commonplace, and have even been incorporated into the writings of 'neo-behaviourists'. The growth of cognitive psychology has been stimulated by developments in information technology. Models of thinking have been constructed, viewing the human brain as an information-processing form of computer, albeit one which is far more complex than any created by human hand (Newell and Simon, 1972; Marr, 1982). A significant number of cognitive psychologists design computer-run models of thinking, rather than conduct traditional laboratory experiments (Winograd, 1972). It is a matter of current controversy whether such models reveal the mental processes which actually occur when people think, or whether the primary value of such models is to assist the construction of machines which can recognize patterns or 'read' documents (see ARTIFICIAL INTELLIGENCE).

The direct influence of psychological ideas on social theory has not been as great as might have been expected. Although some left-wing social theorists have adopted psychoanalytic notions (see FRANKFURT SCHOOL), other sociologists have chosen to create their own social psychology rather than borrow wholesale from the works of psychologists (see SYMBOLIC INTERACTIONISM). On the other hand, the influence of Piagetian ideas on educational theory and practice has been widespread. In addition, psychology has had a major influence on the wider society through the activities of professional practitioners and through the training of educationalists, personnel managers and advertisers. Over and above such direct influences, there has been the more diffuse impact of psychological notions on ordinary, non-specialist ways of thinking. This impact is illustrated by the way that technical phrases have passed into lay vocabulary: extravert, IQ, neurotic, 'Freudian slip' and so on. Such concepts may not be elements in the sort of unified scientific theory which the early psychologists had hoped for; yet they now belong to twentieth-century common sense, and this itself demonstrates the social significance of psychology.

Reading
Ash, M.G. and Woodward, W.R., eds 1987: *Psychology in Twentieth-Century Thought and Society*.
Freud, S. 1933 (*1964*): New introductory lectures on psycho-analysis. In *Standard Edition of the Complete Psychological Works of Sigmund Freud*, vol. 22, ed. J. Strachey.
Hearnshaw, L.S. 1987: *The Shaping of Modern Psychology*.
Köhler, W. 1947: *Gestalt Psychology*.
Norman, D.A. ed. 1981: *Perspectives on Cognitive Science*.
Pavlov, I.P. 1932 (*1958*): *Experimental Psychology and Other Essays*.
Piaget, J. and Inhelder, B. 1955 (*1958*): *The Growth of Logical Thinking*.
Skinner, B.F. 1953: *Science and Human Behaviour*.
Spearman, C.E. 1927: *The Abilities of Man*.

MICHAEL BILLIG

psychology, gestalt *See* GESTALT PSYCHOLOGY

psychology, social *See* SOCIAL PSYCHOLOGY

public choice People behave in much the same way whether they are acting in markets or political office or the civil service: they pursue their self-interests. This is the arresting premise of a theory that attempts to unify politics and economics by providing what is also sometimes known as an economic theory of politics. This application of the rational choice model has had a powerful impact on both the theory and practice of modern politics. Notably, it has fuelled arguments for the extension of constitutional restraint on government through its analysis of 'government failure'.

Public choice theory began with a revival of interest in voting systems (see Downs, 1957; Black, 1958). Two insights, in particular, became building blocks in the public choice school. First, the possibility of cycling in voting systems was (re)discovered and this helped undermine the traditional idea that government action reflected 'the will of the people' (see SOCIAL CHOICE and the discussion of the Arrow Impossibility Theorem). In part as a consequence, public choice theorists now adopt a version of the contractarian approach to government (Buchanan, 1974). Thus they argue that there are only individuals (as distinct from some 'group mind' or a 'general good' which government might reflect); and the authority of government comes when individuals establish it to resolve their differences as part of a constitutional settlement which enables them to live advantageously together.

Secondly, it was recognized that information is costly to acquire. This insight combines dramatically with the assumption that political actors pursue their own self-interests to produce the prospect of 'government failure' – that is, government which fails to behave as an institution of mutual advantage. For example, politicians attempt to maximize their chances of re-election by responding to electors who, given the costs of acquiring information, are more aware of issues directly relevant to their interests (like particular expenditure programmes and taxation levels) than those of more indirect and less immediate interest (like the state of public finances and future debt service). The result, in the absence of any constitutional constraint, is a bias towards high expenditure, low taxes and public deficits (see Buchanan and Wagner, 1977). Likewise, the politicians' poor knowledge of the actions of their bureaucrats leaves scope for the pursuit of bureaucratic self-interests; and these are likely to be best served, under the reward systems of most civil services, through the growth of their departments (see Tullock, 1965). Hence, inadequate information here fuels excessive bureaucratic growth and this, in turn, interacts with the phenomenon noted earlier to create a growing constituency of voters whose immediate interests also favour a large public sector.

Thus the scene is set for a modern Leviathan which has neither the capacity nor the inclination to satisfy the needs of its citizens; it is out of control and the need for reform is all the more pressing because the growth of government also encourages rent-seeking activity. (Rents in this sense are created, for instance, through government actions that create monopolies of one kind or another, as when certain activities are licensed by government, or when public pay exceeds the private counterpart. Such rents encourage individuals to invest resources wastefully in actions which are designed to increase their chances of acquiring the titles to them.) There is an obvious solution: the constitutional restraint on government action. Specifically, for instance, there should be requirements to balance the budget, a monetary constitution, and bureaucracies should be exposed to the forces of competition through opting-out, tendering, privatization and the like.

Some may want to jib at the precise informational assumptions, and at reliance on the model of 'utility' maximizing individuals (see also UTILITARIANISM). But few doubt that the recognition of 'government failure' has proved an important corrective to a common view (in economics, at least) which simply held that the government would act to compensate for 'market failure', once identified. Nevertheless, it should not be forgotten that markets do fail, and hence the real questions in public choice theory now relate to how different constitutional regimes affect the relative incidence and size of 'market' and 'government' failures.

Reading
Black, D. 1958: *The Theory of Committees and Elections.*
Buchanan, J. 1974: *The Limits of Liberty: Between the Anarchy and Leviathan.*
Buchanan, J. and Wagner, R. 1977: *Democracy in Deficit: The Political Legacy of Lord Keynes.*
Downs, A. 1957: *An Economic Analysis of Democracy.*
Tullock, G. 1965: *The Politics of Bureaucracy.*
                                    SHAUN P. HARGREAVES HEAP

public sphere   Although the distinction between public and private goes back to Greek and Roman times, the concepts of the public sphere and of publicity are intimately linked to eighteenth-century conceptions of CIVIL SOCIETY. Twentieth-century social thought has continued to be concerned with what is seen as excessive 'privatism' (see PRIVACY) and a corresponding decline of public life. Jürgen Habermas (1962) argued that publicity as a critical principle, the opening-up of public affairs to discussion by concerned citizens, had given way to a manipulated public opinion, while Richard Sennett (1978) diagnosed *The Fall of Public Man.*

FEMINISM has both documented the gender bias in the distinction between 'public man' and 'private woman' (Elshtain, 1981) and questioned the public/private distinction itself. The feminist slogan that 'the personal is political' has been complemented by research showing, for example, that the nineteenth-century 'private sphere' not only lacked privacy but was a major area of economic activity (Davidoff, 1979), and that women are not so much uninterested in 'public', political life as excluded from it and, where they are present, overlooked (Siltanen and Stanworth, 1984). As Marx implied in his critique of Hegel, the pathologies of the public and private spheres can reinforce rather than mitigate one another, as when a politicized private sphere which is made the object of 'moral panics' and legislation (Donzelot, 1977, 1984) coexists with a personalized and degraded political sphere, whose dissatisfactions are in turn relieved in the 'niches' of private life. These ways of thinking about the relation between public and private are also affected by an overdue recognition of the importance of the MASS MEDIA (Thompson, 1990, esp. pp. 238–48).

Reading
Elshtain, J. 1981: *Public Man, Private Woman.*
Habermas, Jürgen 1962 (*1989*): *The Structural Transformation of the Public Sphere.*
Keane, John 1984: *Public Life and Late Capitalism.*
Sennett, Richard 1978: *The Fall of Public Man.*
Siltanen, Janet and Stanworth, Michelle 1984: *Women and the Public Sphere.*
                                    WILLIAM OUTHWAITE

punishment   To punish is to impose a penalty in response to and in condemnation of a rule violation. The process of punishment is thus the deliberate imposition of some form of hard treatment and stigmatization on an agent deemed responsible for violating a norm. Penalties which lack any element of condemnation – such as library fines – are not, strictly speaking, punishments. Nor are measures such as 'preventive detention' which are imposed on the basis of predicted future conduct rather than past offences. The status of compulsory measures of care and treatment, where these are imposed in response to deviant conduct – for instance by a juvenile court – is ambiguous. Such measures may be experienced as punitive and stigmatizing because of their context or use, even though they aim to provide help or therapy for the recipient.

Punishment occurs in a variety of social contexts, and in one form or another is probably an intrinsic property of all settled forms of human association. Families, schools, workplaces, networks of friends or even nation-states all punish their deviant members from time to time, using sanctions which can range from a mild rebuke to a full-scale military assault. However, the central case of punishment in modern society is judicial punishment – the legal process whereby violators of the criminal law are sanctioned in accordance with specified legal rules and procedures, and undergo a punishment which is administered by state officials. It is thus judicial punishment which has formed the focus of attention for most modern thinking about punishment, although the behavioural effects of punishment in other contexts have been the subject of much psychological research.

The philosophy of punishment

Because judicial punishment entails the deliberate infliction of harms by state officials on individual citizens, it is a social practice which is susceptible to criticism and has need of legitimation. A large philosophical literature has developed around the issue, setting out justificatory arguments for the institution, identifying circumstances in which penal power may be exercised and describing the proper purposes which punishments should pursue. The major debate here tends to be between utilitarian and deontological approaches to the problem. The former argues that punishment is itself an evil and is justified only when, and in so far as, it can produce useful effects – such as social defence or the prevention of future crime (see also CRIME AND DEVIANCE). Deterrence, incapacitation, reformation and denunciation are thus acceptable objectives on this view and should be used to the extent that they can be shown to be effective. Against this, the rival position claims that punishment is justified as the proper response to certain evils because justice, or natural law, or the social contract demands that crimes be avenged and appropriate retribution be exacted. The purpose of punishment should therefore be to ensure proper retribution or 'just deserts', such retributive measures being morally imperative whether or not they can be shown to be instrumentally useful.

In practice, penal measures and institutions usually claim to pursue several of these aims simultaneously, though empirical research suggests that only the more negative aims (retribution, denunciation, incapacitation) can be pursued with any likelihood of success. Attempts to achieve reformative ends by means of penal sanctions have not succeeded in more than a small minority of cases. Similarly, although the existence of a penal system which enforces social norms does produce a basic deterrent effect (as compared with no enforcement), the deterrent effects of specific sanctions, or specific levels of sanctioning, appear to be severely limited. Rational, calculating offenders who believe it likely that they will be apprehended and punished and for whom that risk is unacceptable are the best targets for deterrence.

The practice of punishment

For much of the twentieth century, penal systems espoused to a greater or lesser degree a 'rehabilitative' ideology which insisted that offenders should be dealt with in a positive, reformative way, adapting measures of treatment and training to their individual needs and disregarding punitive concerns. Characteristically, there was the introduction of more refined modes of assessing and classifying offenders, an extended repertoire of specialized institutions, legislation to allow indeterminate sentencing and the employment of experts at key points in the system. This 'penal welfare' approach never fully displaced older concerns with punishment and just deserts, not even in the sphere of juvenile justice where treatment philosophies were best established. Since the 1960s there has been a marked turn away from the rehabilitative approach and a revival of an explicit concern with retributive and deterrent concerns on the part of policy-makers, politicians and criminologists (see also CRIMINOLOGY).

Contemporary systems of punishment utilize a diversified range of sanctions, providing a hierarchy of measures which allows a scale of severity together with a horizontal set of alternatives adapted to different types of offenders. These include fines, community service orders, various forms of supervision (which can be geared towards counselling and support or towards surveillance and control), psychiatric orders, custodial sentences of one kind or another and, in some jurisdictions, judicial execution. There is great diversity in the patterns of sanctioning and levels of punishment experienced by countries which are in other respects (including crime rates) very similar. Rates of imprisonment are, for example, subject to enormous variation, both between states and within the same jurisdiction over time. Similarly, the levels of punishment deemed appropriate for particular offences can vary markedly from one nation to another.

The sociology of punishment
Sociological and historical research has endeavoured to explain these variations in penal patterns, usually by exploring the social functions and determinants of punishment and the ways in which penal institutions are related to broader social configurations. Emile Durkheim argued that punishment represents a collective response to acts which violate the shared sentiments and values of society. It is a passionate reaction which expresses collective feelings and at the same time reaffirms the force of social mores. The rituals of punishing are thus one means whereby the moral order is upheld, social solidarity is reinforced and the boundary between acceptable and unacceptable conduct is redrawn (although, as G.H. Mead pointed out, this form of solidarity is based on hostility and can promote intolerance). On the Durkheimian view, punishment forms an important element within society's moral circuitry, and the form and intensity of penal sanctions will be determined by the character of society's moral life. Advanced societies, featuring an extended division of labour, diversified moral codes and a commitment to the values of liberal individualism, are thus more likely to develop more lenient systems of punishment, organized around the deprivation of individual liberty.

In contrast, Marxist interpretations portray punishment as an instrument of state control, functioning repressively and ideologically to preserve ruling class dominance, and being shaped primarily by the MODE OF PRODUCTION. The centrality of the fine in modern penality; the emphasis on labour in prisons; the principle of 'less eligibility' which insists that prison conditions must be set below those of the poorest classes in society; even the idea that offences should be 'exchanged' for an equivalent penalty, measured in abstract units of time – all of these characteristics are cited as evidence that punishment is shaped as much by the structures of market society as by the requirements of crime control.

The most recent interpretation of punishment – developed by Michel Foucault – emphasizes the 'disciplinary' and 'normalizing' aspects of modern penal methods, and highlights the ways in which an increasingly knowledgeable penal apparatus is able to exert deeper and more positive forms of control on those caught up in the system. Punishment here is viewed as a form of power and governance, operating by means of detailed principles of surveillance, inspection and individuation, its concern being less to 'punish' offenders than to mould their behaviour and to manage the risks that they collectively represent. The 'panoptic' regime of the modern prison – which subjects individual inmates to continual surveillance in order to identify and correct any deviance from institutional norms – is taken to represent a model of the kinds of 'power-knowledge' relations that are prevalent in contemporary society.

It is widely recognized that, as a control technique, punishment has serious limitations. Psychologists point out that positive reinforcements are often more effective means of shaping conduct, that the effects of punishment are often shortlived, and that the recipients of punishment tend to build up a resistance to it. Similarly, criminologists argue that the capacity of the penal system to transform individuals or to reduce crime rates is severely restricted. Critics of punishment argue that criminal justice should rely less on a punitive response and more on alternative methods of handling social conflicts and troublesome individuals, such as mediation, reparation and crime prevention. That such criticism has had so little impact on modern penal systems is one reason why so much attention is currently being given to the social dynamics which underlie the institution of punishment.

Reading

Christie, N. 1982: *Limits to Pain*.

Cohen, S. 1985: *Visions of Social Control*.

Durkheim, E. 1893 (*1984*): *The Division of Labour in Society*.

Foucault, M. 1975 (*1977*): *Discipline and Punish*.

Garland, D. 1990: *Punishment and Modern Society*.

Mead, G.H. 1918: The psychology of punitive justice. *American Journal of Sociology* 23, 577–602.

Rusche, G. and Kirchheimer, O. 1968: *Punishment and Social Structure*.

Sharpe, J.A. 1990: *Judicial Punishment in England*.

Walker, N. 1980: *Punishment, Danger and Stigma*.

DAVID GARLAND

Q

quality of life   *See* STANDARD OF LIVING

R

race   This concept as it has been popularly used in politics has had profound effects on recent world history. The National Socialists in Germany believed in the existence of a superior Aryan race as well as in the existence of inferior races. They also regarded the Jews as a race and proceeded to try to exterminate them. In South Africa in recent times the political domination of whites has been justified in terms of a doctrine of racial superiority of whites over blacks. In many other countries there have been similar if less dramatic developments in which the struggle between ethnic groups has seen the emergence of theories that these groups are races. The implication of the use of the term race in all of these cases is that the factual inequalities existing between groups are inevitable because they are naturally given. Such views, however, are at odds with scientific knowledge.

In 1950 UNESCO called together a meeting of experts to review what was known scientifically about races and to indicate how the term 'race' should be used scientifically (see Montague, 1972). This experts' committee reached the following conclusions:

1   All human beings belong to the same species, *homo sapiens*; they are also probably derived from the same stock. The differences which exist between groups of humans are due to 'isolation, the drift and random fixation of material particles which control heredity (the genes), changes in the structure of these particles, hybridization and natural selection'.

2   *Homo sapiens* is made up of a number of populations each of which differs from the others in the frequency of the occurrence of one or more genes.

3   The larger distinguishable populations have been referred to as races and there is some agreement among anthropologists that humanity can be divided into three major groups: (a) the Mongoloid; (b) the Negroid; and (c) the Caucasoid. Mongoloids have lank hair and relatively sparse bodily hair. Their skin has a yellowish tinge and in most cases there is a fold of skin (the epicanthic fold) overhanging the eye opening. Negroids have dark brown skin. Their hair is of the tightly curled 'peppercorn' sort. They have little bodily hair. Their heads tend to be long, the nose is frequently flattish with wide nostrils, the lips are usually thick and everted and there is a slight forward projection of the upper jaw. Caucasoids have a variety of hair forms. Hair on the face and over the body is well developed. Skin colour varies from white to brown. The nose is narrow and lips are thin.

4   Many subgroups may be distinguished within these major groups, but there is far less agreement among anthropologists about their distinguishing characteristics.

5   In making these classifications the only characteristics which anthropologists use as a basis for classification are physical and physiological. According to present knowledge there is no proof that the groups of humanity differ in their innate mental characteristics, whether in respect of intelligence or temperament.

6   Social and cultural differences between groups are not genetically determined and social and cultural development have been independent of changes in inborn constitution. .

7   The different racial groups are capable of interbreeding and producing fertile offspring. There is no evidence, moreover, that interbreeding produces results which are bad from a biological point of view.

The final and most important conclusion however is stated as follows:

All normal human beings are capable of learning to share in a common life, to understand the nature of mutual service and reciprocity and to respect social obligations and contracts. Such biological differences as exist between members of different ethnic groups have no relevance to problems of social and political organization, moral life and communication between human beings. (in Montagu, 1972)

Quite clearly then there is no justification in biological science for the popular usage of the term race. We should not speak of Germans, French and British, or Protestants, Muslims and Jews as races. These are in fact national, religious, or ethnic groups (see ETHNICITY) bound together by political organization and shared culture.

Nonetheless, even if it has no justification, the existence of the popular usage of the term race does raise problems for the sociologist. There is a difference between situations in which ethnic and national groups simply interact with one another and those situations in which this interaction is seen as a racial one. In these latter situations an element of RACISM is present.

Several sociologists have sought to explain the popular usage of the term race and the existence of racism by defining 'race relations' or race relations situations. The first of these is van den Berghe (1978) who sees race relations as one of the bases on which social systems make 'invidious distinctions' between individuals. Such invidious distinctions lead to the emergence of status systems. Race relations exist where the invidious distinctions are based on differences of phenotype (physical appearance).

Rex (1983, 1986), on the other hand, suggests that a race relations situation may occur not merely between groups distinguished by phenotype but between any groups in certain conflict situations if the differences are explained in terms of racist theories. Thus he argues that a race relations situation has three aspects:

1 the situation is one of severe competition, exploitation, oppression or discrimination, going beyond that to be found in free market situations (free markets being seen here as producing class rather than race relations situations);
2 the relations which exist are between bounded groups and it is impossible or at least very difficult for an individual to move from one group membership to another;
3 the whole system is justified by dominant groups in terms of some sort of deterministic theory, usually of a biological kind.

It is to be noticed here that neither in the definition of the kinds of groups involved nor in the theories referred to in the third part does Rex confine

himself to phenotypical or even biological factors. What he seeks to do is to emphasize that 'deterministic' theories and especially racist theories of the biological sort arise when the basic group relationship is severely conflictual. This draws attention to an important aspect of the popular usage of the term 'race', namely that it arises in conflict situations and is used to justify the dominance of a particular group.

This definition of a race relations situation, however, involves a deliberate overemphasis in order to bring together all the many kinds of situation which are popularly thought to be based on race. It includes the situation of the Jews in prewar Germany and that which prevails between Catholics and Protestants in Northern Ireland, not because it accepts that the groups involved here are races in a scientific sense, but because they are sometimes popularly described as races (in the latter case, in Northern Ireland itself), and the situations have much in common with conflictual situations between groups distinguished by phenotype.

This point having been made, however, and with the recognition that race relations situations are always involved with severe 'competition, conflict, exploitation, oppression or discrimination', it might nonetheless clarify matters if it were recognized that two types of groups, one distinguished by phenotypical, the other by cultural characteristics, may be involved. The essential point made by Rex was that 'race relations situations' always referred to situations of conflict rather than of harmonious cooperation. The general view amongst sociologists, however, would be that it is worthwhile distinguishing those situations in which phenotype was involved as the true race relations situations and recognizing a separate category of situations of ethnic conflict.

But with this said, it has still to be noticed that both race relations situations and ethnic relations situations may be justified by dominant groups in terms of deterministic theories, including racial ones. What the popular usage of the term race does is precisely to extend the usage of the term to cover situations based on cultural difference. From a sociological point of view it is important to recognize that there is a group of conflictual situations which are marked by racism. These are race relations situations even though the groups involved are not in a scientific sense races.

As a later meeting of experts called by UNESCO

recognized, one of the main types of situation giving rise to racist definitions is that which derives from colonialism (both UNESCO statements, of 1953 and 1967, in Montagu, 1972). Such definitions are particularly evident in what Furnivall (1939) and Smith (1963) have called plural societies. Such societies, according to Furnivall, involve culturally distinct groups which come together only in the marketplace, so that, whereas relations between individuals within any group are harmonious and cooperative, relations between groups are brutal and oppressive. According to Smith, on the other hand, each of the groups has a nearly complete institutional system in itself, but the political institution binds them together under the domination of one group. These are the sorts of situations which Rex refers to as being marked by severe competition, conflict, exploitation, oppression and discrimination and they nearly always give rise to racist definitions producing race relations situations.

If colonialism is peculiarly productive of racism, however, it is not the only circumstance under which it might occur. Another common situation occurs when societies with ongoing systems of class and class conflict attract immigrants who enter the society on less favourable terms than the lowest native-born class. These immigrants may then form what is sometimes called an underclass and be subject to more severe exploitation and oppression than that experienced in the labour market by native-born workers (see MIGRATION). Very often in these circumstances the immigrants may be defined as racially different by dominant groups. Such distinctions may rest on a recognition of physical differences but also occur when distinctions are cultural, resting on the false assumption that mental and cultural characteristics are biologically inherited. Finally there are other situations in which a racial or ethnic group is not an underclass but performs an unpopular pariah role in the society, as classically, in the case of the Jews in medieval Europe and amongst secondary Indian or Lebanese traders in colonial societies. In times of political, economic and social stress such a group might become a scapegoat for the society's ills. If it does, even if the group is an ethnic group rather than a racially distinct population, it may be subject to racist definition and the scapegoating situation becomes one of race relations as defined above. This is what happened in the case of European Jews in Nazi Germany.

In summary, what may be said in definition of the term race is that correctly used in a scientific sense it is a taxonomic term of limited usefulness. It has no relevance to the explanation of political differences among human beings. The popular use of racist terminology, however, does mean that there are many situations in which physically and culturally distinguishable groups are defined as races, and where such definitions exist we have what may be called race relations situations, even though the groups involved are not races in a scientific sense.

Reading

Furnivall, John Sydenham 1939: *Netherlands India: a Study of Plural Economy.*
Montagu, Ashley 1972: *Statement on Race.*
Rex, John 1983: *Race Relations in Sociological Theory.*
——1986: *Race and Ethnicity.*
Smith, Michael Garfield 1963: *The Plural Society in the British West Indies.*
van den Berghe, Pierre Louis 1978: *Race and Racism: A Comparative Perspective.*

JOHN REX

racism Any set of beliefs which classifies humanity into distinct collectivities, defined in terms of natural and/or cultural attributes, and ranks these attributes in a hierarchy of superiority and inferiority can be described as racist. Under social and political conditions favourable to them, these beliefs are associated with sets of discriminatory practices and institutions which favour one such collectivity over another, in line with the supposed difference and superiority.

'Racism' is a European notion, which came into use in the 1930s to designate the beliefs and practices of the Nazi regime in Germany, based on the alleged superiority of the 'Aryan' race, the importance of racial 'purity' and the consequent policy of 'purification' which culminated in the horrors of the Holocaust (see ANTI-SEMITISM; NATIONAL SOCIALISM). In that instance, racism was directed primarily (but not exclusively) against Jews. The ideas behind this hostility formed a system of classification of 'races' on the basis of supposedly distinct biological constitutions, which in turn had attached to them distinct moral and cultural qualities. Subsequently, 'racism' has been generalized to designate other ideas of systematic group differences of superiority/inferiority, most commonly those which relate to black/white relations in South Africa, the United States and Western Europe.

'Racism', of course, is linked to the notion of RACE as a principle of classification of humanity. This notion has been highly variable in content, following the political and cultural contexts of its use. In the earlier periods of European history, prior to the eighteenth century, 'race' referred generally to national 'stock', say French as distinct from English, each having particular attributes, customs and traditions. One can only speak of 'racism' in this context in general and vague terms of 'national pride'. Overriding this differentiation between European nations was distinction, on the basis of religion, between Christian and heathen. The main non-Christian adversary was the world of Islam. As such, negative stereotypes of others were formulated on the basis of religious difference, and the assumptions of moral and cultural superiority and inferiority which followed from these differences.

The main modern notion of race, however, developed in the eighteenth and nineteenth centuries, based on the idea of biologically distinct types of humanity. European geographical explorations, and later colonial expansion, heightened curiosity and interest in different peoples. The later period of this expansion coincided with the intensification of scientific activity and the increasing prestige of science. Systems of classification and, later, theories of evolution marked the biological sciences. The classification of human races was seen as an extension of this scientific endeavour. On the basis of the criteria of classification, rankings were developed of orders of superiority/inferiority, in which the Europeans, naturally, regarded themselves as superior. However, classifications did not stop there, but were extended into the different European nations. For instance, the negative stereotype of the Irish in England in the nineteenth century was incorporated into this racist classification of difference and attribution of inferiority.

It was this biological idea of race hierarchy which animated the racist thrust of Nazism and fascism in Europe in the 1920s and 1930s. The atrocities committed by these regimes in line with their racist ideologies alerted the liberal world to the dangers of these beliefs, and, as we have seen, led to the formulation of the very concept of 'racism'. After the Nazi defeat, liberal world opinion was concerned to ensure that these concepts would never again be employed for political purposes. To that

end, during the 1950s and 1960s UNESCO convened four meetings of leading scientists (in biology and the social sciences) to pronounce on the scientific status of the concept of 'race'. Their conclusions were that there was no scientific basis for racial theories. This view was facilitated by developments in biological science, especially genetics, in terms of which classifications on the bases of 'phenotypical' characteristics like skin colour are arbitrary (Montagu, 1972).

Reactions to the Nazi horrors made 'racism' into a label of moral and political disapprobation. The near consensus of scientific opinion on the invalidity of the concept of 'race' undermined the credibility as well as the respectability of racist beliefs. To some writers on the subject, this signified the end of biological racism, and therefore of racism as such, though not of 'ethnocentrism' (Banton, 1970, pp. 31–2). Others have disagreed with this conclusion (Miles, 1989, pp. 42–8). First, the demise of biological classifications at the intellectual and official levels did not lead to their extinction at the levels of popular culture and 'commonsense' knowledge. Second, biological racism is not the only possible form: there are many beliefs and ideologies in the modern world which classify people and evaluate them on the basis of cultural and 'ethnic' differences. These beliefs, it is argued, function in similar fashions to biological beliefs: whether hostility to Jews or blacks is based on the belief in their biological inferiority or culturo-ethnic inferiority makes little difference. Indeed, the terms 'race' and 'race relations' continue to enjoy wide currency. On the other side, it is argued that this wider usage of 'racism' does not distinguish it from 'ethnocentrism' or even nationalism. The argument then revolves on choice of definitions, and the necessity or otherwise of distinguishing between closely related and, in any case, fluid concepts.

An important sociopolitical context for the operation of racist ideas at present is constituted by Western European societies containing Afro-Caribbean, Asian, North African and Southern European communities originating in waves of migrant labour in recent history. Political conflicts and communal tensions surrounding this phenomenon have featured a wide range of racist ideas. Given the politically and morally negative connotations of racism, only a few, generally disreputable ultra-right groups would acknowledge being 'racist'. Most forms of hostility or discrimination against these 'ethnic groups' are disguised or covert, especially when practised by governments and official bodies. A good example is British immigration controls, widely thought to be racist in their effects, but which nevertheless do not use explicit racial or ethnic categories in their legal or administrative specifications. Nevertheless, a new form of explicit ideas on 'race relations', which are thought by some to be racist, are increasingly voiced from respectable quarters on the 'New Right'. These ideas assert the common propensity of people to prefer intercourse with 'their own kind', this being defined in cultural and national terms. It follows that it is desirable to segregate culturally and ethnically different populations in the interests of peace and harmony. Proponents of these views would deny that they are racists: they classify differences of humanity, but without asserting superiority or inferiority of different categories, merely the desirability of their segregation. Yet these were the explicit justifications of apartheid in South Africa, now universally condemned.

Explanations of racism

Why are hostile sentiments and actions directed against certain groups under particular conditions on the grounds of their supposed natural or cultural inferiority or offensiveness? Various explanations have been advanced.

Psychological explanations These are framed in terms of patterns of emotional reactions by particular personality types, dubbed in one set of studies in the 1950s as the 'authoritarian personality' (Adorno et al., 1950), in effect a type of psychopathology generated by certain patterns of childhood experiences. Whatever the merits of this explanation, it cannot account for situations, like that of Nazi Germany, in which a whole political culture, which must include many different personality types, is geared to waging violent racist campaigns.

Social tensions explanations The idea here is that racism derives from particular social conflicts and stresses which generate the need for 'scapegoats'. Social frustrations lead to generalized aggression which cannot be directed against the sources of frustration because they are too powerful or not clearly identifiable. The aggression is then directed against vulnerable minority groups who are blamed for economic and social ills.

Structural explanations If certain minority groups are regularly under attack in a whole range of different situations, then, it is argued, there must be systematic social processes which activate and institutionalize these sentiments and actions. Inferiorization of blacks and Asian communities in the United States and Western Europe, it is pointed out, is the product of a long history of European domination, first in colonial situations where native populations were exploited, then in the metropolitan countries themselves into which they were imported as convenient labour, sometimes as slaves, and more recently as migrant cheap labour. The weak economic and political position of these minorities renders them vulnerable to racial categorization and 'scapegoating'. This would then serve to legitimize their exploitation and disadvantage in the dominant society. Critics of this line of thought have pointed out that the groups in question do not constitute uniform economic or social categories, but occupy varying positions, ranging from poorly paid workers to prosperous businessmen who are sometimes the employers and landlords of the poorer individuals. A more complex analysis of racism, combining 'class' with the communal factors, is advocated by some writers (for a discussion of these issues, see Miles, 1982 and 1989).

An examination of the wide and variable range of historical and modern situations of racism would indicate that it is not a uniform phenomenon amenable to a common explanation. There are many different phenomena of racism, characterized by the socioeconomic and cultural factors of which they form a part. Explanations of racism must arise from the analysis of each situation.

Reading
Adam, Heribert 1971: *Modernizing Racial Domination.*
Banton, M. 1987: *Racial Theories.*
Benedict, R. 1983: *Race and Racism.*
Castles, S., Booth, H. and Wallace, T. 1984: *Here for Good: Western Europe's New Ethnic Minorities.*
Fanon, F. 1961 (*1983*): *The Wretched of the Earth.*
Husband, C. ed. 1982: *'Race' in Britain: Continuity and Change.*
Miles, R. 1982: *Racism and Migrant Labour: A Critical Text.*
—— 1989: *Racism.*
Mosse, G.L. 1978: *Toward the Final Solution: A History of European Racism.*

Rex, J. 1983: *Race Relations in Sociological Theory*.
Zubaida, S. 1970: *Race and Racialism*.

SAMI ZUBAIDA

radicalism   The word is of Latin derivation and means literally 'of or pertaining to a root or to roots' (*OED*). Not suprisingly, it has been extended to mean relating to that which is central, essential, fundamental, primary, or the source and origin of any phenomenon. It has, consistently with this broad connotation, acquired technical meanings in mathematics, geometry, philology, music, botany and chemistry.

The word or its derivatives came to be applied in politics to what were perceived as far-reaching and thoroughgoing reforms, those seeking them, and their advocacy as a more or less systematic belief system. This use originated in English politics in the late eighteenth and early nineteenth centuries in the course of the ferment arising out of the French revolution and later became prominent in France as well. Radicalism initially referred only to the left in politics, that is, to proposals, programmes and ideologies advocating change in existing institutions and practices (the left–right distinction itself had its origin in the politics of the French revolution).

'Radical' may be used to characterize either the *content* of desired changes, suggesting that they are far-reaching, the *methods* recommended for achieving them, methods seen as going beyond the conventional norms regulating political conflict, or both in combination, envisaging a 'totalistic' transformation of the political or social order to be attained by armed struggle or violent REVOLUTION. 'Radical' in this sense is distinguished from 'moderate', 'conventional', and even from 'legal', terms that may also be applied both to the ends and to the means espoused by a political movement. Radicalism, therefore, lacks any specific substantive content. It describes an abstract property of a belief or programme, that of opposing and wishing to replace features of an existing order that are seen as central and even definitive.

'Radicalism' resembles such political labels as 'left', 'right', 'conservative' and 'progressive' in identifying a political viewpoint solely by its attitude towards change or its relation to other political positions. Radicalism suggests a more extreme, absolute, uncompromising commitment; in addition, one that is comprehensive, embracing a large number of concrete issues in the sweep of its condemnation or endorsement. So understood, 'radicalism' stands in contrast to such labels as 'liberalism', 'socialism', 'communism' or 'anarchism', which possess a definite content pointing to substantive conceptions of a desirable political or social order, however distorted and ambiguous those conceptions may have become in the course of nearly two centuries of political contestation over their meaning. Because radical as a label is vacuous in conveying no concrete image of the institutional order it seeks, while simultaneously suggesting extreme rejection of whatever exists, it has rarely been adopted as a self-sufficient name by power-seeking parties and movements. In this it differs from such similarly non-specific all-purpose labels as 'progressive', 'populist' or 'democratic', the first indicating no more than a general predisposition towards change, the other two merely that they reflect the will of the people or the majority. These terms are frequently favoured by vote-seeking parties in democratic politics precisely because of their vacuity and ability to mean all things to all persons, whereas nuances of both extremism and elitism inescapably cling to radicalism except perhaps in times of acute social crisis.

Nevertheless, the Radical and later Radical Socialist Party was the leading political party of the French Third Republic and survived into the Fourth Republic. Similar parties of the same name and outlook existed in several smaller European countries in the first half of the present century. The French Radicals laid claim to the Jacobin heritage of REPUBLICANISM. They were strongly anti-clerical, opposed to traditional conservative elites, and also to large-scale capitalism and socialist collectivism. Although basically a conservative party by the 1920s, the French Radicals did participate in the Popular Front government of the left in 1936–7.

Despite its original restriction to the left, some political tendencies that are in no sense of the left have also been described as radical in recognition of the truth of the dictum that '*les extrèmes se touchent*' – extremes touch each other. Reactionary or rightwing movements have on occasion resembled the revolutionary left in their zealous rejection of the status quo, their readiness to countenance new and even extralegal methods of political advancement, and their disposition to see their political aims as expressions of all-encompassing ideologies or *Weltanschauungen* purporting to explain human nature, society and history. The fascist movements of the interwar years were called radical, unsurprisingly, since they largely patterned themselves on the mass movements of the radical left and were often led by renegade leftists. The term 'radical right' came into use in the 1950s when it was applied by a number of well-known American political sociologists and intellectuals to McCarthyism – the indiscriminate exploitation by the conservative former isolationist wing of the Republican Party of anti-communist sentiment as a weapon against the Democrats in office and the left in general.

When it was coined by Seymour Martin Lipset, the phrase 'radical right' possessed the resonance of an oxymoron. It reflected, however, the widespread sense before and immediately after World War II that movements such as fascism and communism and even paler reflections of them like the McCarthyite tendency in the United States had common traits that transcended the 'normal' left–right interest cleavages of democratic politics. Radicalism, therefore, came to stand for a particular style of politics characterized by extreme and conspiratorial images of the enemy and a willingness to resort to undemocratic methods of political conflict and ones of questionable legality.

After the 1950s the older, primarily leftwing, overtones of 'radicalism' were largely restored. Indeed, it was the aim of the NEW LEFT movements in the major Western democracies to reinstate the left–right division as the major axis of political conflict and to cleanse the label 'radical' of the totalitarian implications it had acquired in the fascist and early Cold War era. In the late 1980s, however, the collapse of communism once again made the term ambiguous, for some of the opponents of communist rule in the Soviet Union and Central Europe were often described – and described themselves – as 'radicals' or 'leftists', although they wished to establish democratic governments and capitalist market economies on the Western model in their own countries.

Despite its abstract and formal nature, radicalism has always tended to acquire a particular ideological colouration from the major historical events of a period. Its meaning in use, therefore, is likely always to be highly relative and context-bound.

Reading
Bell, Daniel ed. 1963: *The Radical Right*.
Lasky, M.J. 1976: *Utopia and Revolution*.
Lipset, S.M. 1960 (*1981*): *Political Man*, expanded edn.
Mannheim, Karl 1929 (*1960*): *Ideology and Utopia*.

DENNIS H. WRONG

rational choice theory   The distinctive feature of this approach is the view that social life is to be explained by means of models of rational individual action. Rationality can mean many different things in modern social thought (see RATIONALITY AND REASON). In this case it is understood in utilitarian terms as a matter of maximizing the satisfaction of the individual's preferences (see UTILITARIANISM). Models of maximizing behaviour are widely used in contemporary economics, and rational choice theory can be understood as proposing to extend that 'economic approach' to other areas of social life. It claims to be rigorous and able to generate powerful explanations on the basis of a few, relatively simple assumptions. Outside of economics proper, influential examples can be found in the literature on public choice, and increasingly in contemporary political science and sociology and even within academic Marxism.

The assumption of individual rationality does not imply the rationality of collective behaviour. First, Arrow (1951) has shown that individual preferences cannot normally be aggregated into a well-defined collective preference structure. In that case there may be no outcome that can be said to maximize collective preferences. Secondly, collective behaviour involves the strategic interaction of rational individuals (see GAME THEORY). Each will act on the basis of calculations of the effects of the possible actions of others. In a 'prisoner's dilemma' situation, characterized by the absence of effective communication (imagine two prisoners interrogated separately for a crime they have jointly committed), the rational actor fears the worst of others and acts to minimize the damage. Each therefore avoids the worst possible outcome, but collectively they fail to obtain the best.

The 'free rider' problem is another example. Unless there is some device (like compulsory taxation) to make individuals contribute to provision of a collective good, rational individuals will leave the contributions to others. The free rider obtains the benefits of a collective good without incurring the costs of its provision. If there are too many 'free riders' then the collective good will not be provided at all. Olson (1965) has developed this argument to suggest that just because all members of a group share a common interest it does not follow that they will organize to pursue that interest. Collective action by large groups depends on the existence of selective incentives for activists, and sometimes on an element of compulsion. Groups with few members (such as an oligopoly) are normally better placed to organize and to agree on an optimal course of action.

Rational choice theory does not require its models of rational action to be entirely realistic. The point rather is that they are intended to provide successful predictions in many cases and, in the event of predictive failure, to provide means of identifying the place of non-rational elements in human action. Electoral behaviour is a frequently cited example. In most cases one person's vote will have little effect on the outcome, and the difference the outcome makes to that person will also be small. The assumption of rational, self-interested behaviour therefore 'yields a notoriously poor explanation of voting behaviour, since it suggests that almost no one would voluntarily vote in, say, American national elections. It helps us to understand why half of eligible Americans do not vote, but it does little to help us understand the other half' (Hardin, 1982, p. 11).

Evidence of significant irrationality in human behaviour therefore does little damage to the claims of rational choice theory. More serious critical issues relate first to the character and location of rationality, and secondly to its role in explanation. Critics have argued that rational choice theory has too simple a view of the actor: for example, that it takes inadequate account of altruism and other commitments, that human rationality is a matter of long-term projects of self-construction, not just of short-term maximization, and that human cognitive capacities are too limited for their decisions to be fully rational in all cases.

These critical positions suggest a more general issue for the methodological individualism of rational choice theory. There are two quite distinct senses in which rationality might be attributed to human individuals. It might refer to what used to be called a faculty of reason, a generalized capacity to develop a connected chain of reasoning or argumentation. It might also refer to the consistency of chains of reasoning themselves and to the concepts and other intellectual tools (horoscopes, dice, cost–benefit analysis) employed in their construction – and, by extension, to particular courses of action and items of behaviour. The assumption that human individuals are normally endowed with

a faculty of reason and that they are therefore capable of developing chains of reasoning tells us nothing about the character of the conceptual tools they might employ in the process. Since the greater part of the conceptual tools available to an actor will be culturally acquired, there is an important sense in which the rationality or otherwise of individual action will depend on cultural and social conditions external to the actor concerned.

Finally, there is the question of the explanatory role of the assumption of rationality. That assumption leads us to expect a certain consistency in the behaviour of individuals but it tells us nothing about their motivations. Explanations of significant features of social life as resulting from the rational actions of individuals therefore depend on auxiliary assumptions regarding the content of their motivations – another respect in which the overt individualism of rational choice theory often involves a covert reference to supra-individual cultural and social conditions. There are two further issues here. First, the validity of these motivational assumptions may well be open to question. The above explanation of why so many Americans do not vote in national elections simply assigns them an assumed motivation, from which the decision not to vote then follows. It is not compatible with the results of one recent study of their reasons for not voting (Fox-Piven and Cloward, 1988). Secondly, it is debatable whether the strict assumption of rationality adds much to the explanatory power of the auxiliary assumptions themselves (Simon, 1986).

See also SOCIAL CHOICE.

Reading
Barry, B. and Hardin, R. eds 1982: *Rational Man and Irrational Society.*
Elster, J. ed. 1986: *Rational Choice.*
Hardin, R. 1982: *Collective Action.*
Hindess, B. 1988: *Choice, Rationality, and Social Theory.*
Hollis, M. 1987: *The Ruse of Reason.*
Journal of Business, 59 (1986), 4. Part 2: The behavioural foundations of economic theory.
Olson, M. 1965: *The Logic of Collective Action.*
Sen, A. 1987: *On Ethics and Economics.*

BARRY HINDESS

rational expectations hypothesis According to this hypothesis, an individual's expectations regarding future events should not suffer from systematic errors. The reason is simple: you ought to be able to learn about the systematic components of your errors, and there is every incentive to do so since you will profit by removing them. Thus it is the instrumentally rational agent's 'eye for the main chance' (see RATIONAL CHOICE THEORY) which is responsible for the generation of rational expectations; and not unsurprisingly it has been hailed as the natural hypothesis to use in NEOCLASSICAL ECONOMICS. Indeed, together with the so-called natural rate of unemployment hypothesis, it has constituted one of the main planks in the extremely influential NEW CLASSICAL ECONOMICS. In addition, it has greatly simplified the estimation of relationships in econometrics.

Muth's (1961) original statement of the rational expectations hypothesis was phrased slightly differently. Expectations were to be the 'predictions of the relevant economic theory', or more generally the 'subjective probability distribution of outcomes' should tend to the 'objective probability distribution of outcomes'. This way of putting the hypothesis reveals, perhaps, more of the difficulties which have come to be associated with it. Individuals may wish to avoid making systematic errors but closing the gap between the 'subjective' and the 'objective' is not some simple exercise in the social world. It is not just a question of allowing time to elapse as it might be for someone forming expectations about the landscape as the fog disappears. There are no 'objective' outcomes in this sense because outcomes in the social world depend on the 'subjective' expectations which we entertain about them. This interdependence generates two principal problems for the hypothesis and they combine to suggest that this account of expectation formation will remain incomplete unless it is supplemented by some additional sense of individual agency.

The first concerns the characterization of the process of learning as an individual moves from non-rational to rational expectations. Formally, since the pay-off to a particular person of holding one set of expectations rather than another depends on actual outcomes and these outcomes depend on the expectations of others, a person is actually in a game with others (see GAME THEORY). A Nash equilibrium in this game constitutes a rational expectation and it is the out-of-equilibrium behaviour of agents in this game which corresponds to a learning process. However, it is now generally accepted that an analysis of such out-of-equilibrium behaviour must have recourse to a notion of rational agency which differs from the simple

instrumental sense which is normally assumed in neoclassical economics.

Secondly, there are a variety of social settings where this dependence of outcomes on expectations yields multiple rational expectations equilibria. That is to say, there are many expectations which if widely held would reproduce themselves but for white noise random errors (the errors have an expected value of zero and are not serially correlated). Again, this raises a problem for the normal instrumental sense of rationality: which expectation is to be held when many potentially satisfy this condition of being a rational expectation? This dilemma is characteristic of situations where there is genuine uncertainty (see DECISION THEORY).

Thus the rational expectations hypothesis has contributed enormously to our understanding of how individuals form expectations about the future. In particular, whereas it once promised to fill the informational gap in the instrumental account of rationality, it has actually served to underline the need for additional rationality assumptions if we are to understand action in conditions of uncertainty.

Reading

Attfield, C.L.F., Demery, D. and Duck, N.W. 1985: *Rational Expectations in Macroeconomics.*

Begg, D. 1982: *The Rational Expectations Revolution in Macroeconomics.*

Bray, M. 1985: Rational expectations, information and asset pricing. *Oxford Economic Papers* 37, 161–95.

Frydman, R. and Phelps, E.S. 1983: *Individual Forecasting and Aggregate Outcomes.*

Hahn, F. 1980; *Money and Inflation.*

Haltiwanger, J. and Waldman, M. 1985: Rational expectations and the limits of rationality. *American Economic Review* 75, 326–40.

Hargreaves Heap, S.P. 1989: *Rationality in Economics.*

Muth, J.F. 1961: Rational expectations and the theory of price movements. *Econometrica* 29, 315–35.

SHAUN P. HARGREAVES HEAP

rationality and reason   Enlightenment thinkers declared the human mind and human society to be as rational as the other operations of nature and as amenable to scientific reason. The history of the social sciences could be written as an unfinished debate about the truth of this conjecture. Definitions of 'rationality' and 'reason' would be part of the debate, and so cannot usefully be given at the start of this entry.

The conjecture is 'rationalist' in three very

different senses. Firstly it involves a broad contention that nature is a rational (in the sense of ordered) system of causes and effects, governed by laws which a scientific method (Reason) can discover. In whatever exact way this causality is construed, it excludes meaning and purpose from the workings of nature and absolves science from thinking in these older terms about God's designs. It also excludes chance; but there is scope for a reluctant compromise by means of theory of probability, which allows for a limited element of unpredictability. 'Positivism', as the term is used in the social sciences, applies this broad philosophy of nature and science to the social world.

To philosophers, however, 'positivism' suggests 'logical positivism', a sharp form of empiricism and hence opposed to rationalism. In this second sense rationalists think of causal laws in terms of hidden forces and necessities, in the spirit of the Cartesian and Newtonian systems of the seventeenth century. Reason is the power of the mind to penetrate the veil of perception and its model is mathematics. Empiricists retort that observation, experiment and statistical generalizations provide the only warrants of science and hence that causal 'laws' are projections of experience upheld by experience. This dispute continues in the social sciences, with, broadly, systemic, structural and strongly functional approaches on the rationalist side and behavioural and statistical approaches on the empiricist. Be it noted, however, that it is possible to disagree with both parties. For instance Quine (see as an example 1951) has argued both that experience cannot be described without invoking a prior theory and that how the theoretical web is spun is a matter of convention. Kuhn's (1962) claim that scientific thought is governed by 'paradigms' suggests a similar theme for a sociology of knowledge.

Thirdly there is a rationalism which rests on the assumption that human behaviour is rational. The leading example is that of microeconomics, where agents are rational, in that they always calculate the most effective way to satisfy their preferences. They are the utility maximizers found in decision theory, rational choice theory and game theory, agents whose rationality is of an instrumental, means-to-given-ends kind. To act rationally is to maximize an objective function subject to constraints. The assumption of rationality is often taken to imply that agents are self-interested. Strictly, however, it implies only that they pursue their own goals in a systematic maximizing (or

satisficing) way, thus leaving it open whether they are self-interested (see RATIONAL CHOICE THEORY).

The power and elegance of economic theories based on rationality assumptions have attracted other social sciences. There are 'economic' theories of, for instance, democracy, international relations, race relations, gift giving, friendship and marriage, all treated as exchange between rational bargainers. Such theories are individualist and, at their most ambitious, try to account also for the emergence of the institutions within which exchanges occur. The grandest example is the theory of the social contract, rejuvenated lately by Rawls (1971), which analyses the very being of society as norms which it is rational for individuals to create or accept to their mutual advantage.

Alternatively, however, human behaviour may be deemed rational in the different sense of conforming to rules and institutional procedures. This is how Max Weber viewed the rational-legal systems of the modern world and, especially, the activities of bureaucrats. It also invites the relativistic suggestion that every culture or institution is rational in its own terms and is therefore to be understood by identifying its rules from within. Disputes about whether to take rational action as instrumental or rule governed, and whether to allow scope for both readings, are notably alive in anthropology but also to be found elsewhere, even in economics.

The 'economic' reading is usually held to be consistent with positivism and hence to allow for purposive behaviour in humans without threat to the unity of scientific method. The other reading opens up a dispute between positivism and hermeneutics (or 'interpretation' as the key to the understanding of action), which challenges the scope of causal explanation in the social world. A break may be perceived between 'nature' and 'culture' and, with it, between the natural and the social sciences. If so, 'reason' is to be connected to 'interpretation' for social understanding. For a starting point see Weber (1921–2) on adequacy at the level of meaning and causal adequacy.

Questions of scientific method are distinct from historically specific questions about the forms and limits of human rationality, as raised in the twentieth century by, for instance, Freudian psychoanalysis, B. F. Skinner's behaviourism, Chomskyan linguistics or computational models of the mind. The widest is perhaps Weber's problem of modernity and whether the spread of rational-legal order, necessary for capitalism, can sustain itself in a wholly secular world. It may be that whether the human mind and human society are as rational as the other operations of nature depends on whether human beings make them so – a disturbing thought which brings abstract discussion of the definitions of 'rationality' and 'reason' abruptly down to earth.

Reading

Chomsky, N. 1966: *Cartesian Linguistics: A Chapter in the History of Rationalist Thought.*
Hollis, M. and Lukes, S. eds 1982: *Rationality and Relativism.*
Kuhn, T.S. 1962 (*1970*): *The Structure of Scientific Revolutions.*
Quine, W.V.O. 1951 (*1963*): Two dogmas of empiricism. In *From a Logical Point of View.*
Rawls, J. 1971: *A Theory of Justice.*
Weber, M. 1921–2 (*1979*): *Economy and Society.*
Wilson, B.R. ed. 1970: *Rationality.*

MARTIN HOLLIS

rationalization   This is a richly ambiguous concept, covering a 'whole world of different things' (Weber, 1904–5). Its ambiguity parallels and reflects that of the related concepts of reason, rationality and rationalism (see RATIONALITY AND REASON). Because of this ambiguity, it is impossible to give a general definition of rationalization. Two meaning clusters, however, can be identified, reflecting what can be called the *special* and the *general* conceptions of rationalization. (A third conception of rationalization, unrelated to the first two, will not be addressed here: rationalization as a false or self-serving explanation or justification of the beliefs or practices of an individual or group.)

The special conception of rationalization, restricted to the economic domain, developed in Germany in the late 1920s. 'Rationalization' became a widely current catchword during these years of spectacular economic recovery and reorganization, used to denote – and to promote – the development of new instances of inter-firm coordination, integration, standardization and planning, on the one hand, and the systematic institutionalized exploitation of scientific research, knowledge, techniques, methods and attitudes in production, management, distribution and finance, on the other. It quickly became clear, however, that what was rational from one point of view might be irrational from another. Technical rationalization might be economically irrational; the administrative rationality of coordinated planning might be irrational from the point of view of market efficiency; organizational rationalization to curb excess capacity might be socially irrational. Perhaps because of this inescapable ambiguity, the vogue of 'rationalization' as a programmatic rallying point quickly passed. The term was adopted in other countries, but it never had the same currency it had in Germany. In English, the term has generally had a narrower meaning, referring mainly to organizational changes aimed at reducing inefficiency, waste or overcapacity.

The general conception of rationalization has a much wider frame of reference. The forces of rationalization – science and technology, markets and bureaucracies, discipline and self-discipline – are understood as permeating all spheres of life: culture, sexuality, and the personality itself as much as production, warfare, law and administration. This sweeping civilizational conception of rationalization owes most to Max Weber, whose entire *oeuvre* can be read as an attempt to characterize and explain in world-historical perspective the 'specific and peculiar rationalism' of modern Western civilization (1904–5). As Weber demonstrated in detail, exceedingly various modes of rationalization have existed in every sphere of life and in every great civilization. In any particular domain, moreover, there are competing modes of rationalization, oriented to different ends and values. For example, Weber stressed the rationalism of both Confucianism and Puritanism, but noted that the former enjoined 'rational adjustment to the world', the latter 'rational mastery of the world' (Weber, 1951, p. 248).

Weber's concern, then, was not to set rationalization in the West against its absence elsewhere; it was to specify and explain the distinctiveness of the Western pattern of rationalization. This distinctive pattern involves six fundamental and widely ramifying social and cultural processes:

1   the disenchantment and intellectualization of the world, and the resultant tendency to view the world as a causal mechanism subject, in principle, to rational control;
2   the emergence of an ethos of impersonal worldly accomplishment, historically grounded in the Puritan ethic of vocation;
3   the growing importance of specialized technical knowledge in economy, administration, and education;
4   the objectification and depersonalization of law,

economy and polity, and the consequent increase in the regularity and calculability of action in these domains;

5 the progressive development of the technically rational means of control over man and nature; and

6 the tendential displacement of traditional and value-rational (*wertrational*) by purely instrumental (*zweckrational*) action orientations.

Despite their different historical roots, these processes are linked by the fact that they all further *formal* rather than *substantive* rationality. They enhance, that is, the calculability of action while remaining indifferent to its informing ends or values. What is 'specific and peculiar' about the Western pattern of rationalization, then, is the fact that the 'end' in terms of which the social order is rationalized – maximum calculability – is not really an end at all but a *generalized means* that indiscriminately facilitates the purposeful pursuit of all substantive ends.

In his investigations of rationalism and rationalization, Weber recast in sociological terms a problem belonging originally to the philosophy of history. In so doing he broke decisively with the faith of the Enlightenment – and with that of Hegel – in the realization of reason in history. The dream of reason, Weber suggested, might turn out to be a nightmare: rationalization might engender a world without meaning, without *caritas*, without freedom, dominated by powerful bureaucracies and by the 'iron cage' of the capitalist economy. It is this mood of cultural pessimism – representing, to be sure, only one aspect of Weber's deeply ambivalent response to modern Western rationalism – that informed the subsequent development of the general conception of rationalization in the work of Max Horkheimer and Theodor Adorno. More recently, Jürgen Habermas has undertaken a systematic reconstruction of the notions of rationality and rationalization, aiming to link the normative philosophical concern with reason and the empirical historical-sociological concern with rationalization. Basing this reconstruction on the distinction between cognitive-instrumental rationality and communicative rationality, Habermas arrives at a more differentiated and less pessimistic appraisal of the course of Western rationalization than that of the FRANKFURT SCHOOL theorists, while retaining and amplifying their critique of instrumental reason.

See also SCIENTIFIC-TECHNOLOGICAL REVOLUTION; MODERNIZATION.

Reading
Brady, R. 1933: *The Rationalization Movement in German Industry.*
Brubaker, R. 1984: *The Limits of Rationality: An Essay on the Social and Moral Thought of Max Weber.*
Habermas, J. 1981 (*1984, 1989*): *The Theory of Communicative Action*, 2 vols.
Horkheimer, M. 1947: *The Eclipse of Reason.*
Levine, D.N. 1985: Rationality and freedom, inveterate multivocals. In *The Flight from Ambiguity: Essays in Social and Cultural Theory.*
Weber, M. 1921–2 (*1978*): *Economy and Society*, ed. G. Roth and C. Wittich.
——1920 (*1946*): *From Max Weber: Essays in Sociology.*

WILLIAM ROGERS BRUBAKER

realism Generally, 'realism' in philosophy asserts the existence of some disputed kind of entity (such as universals, material objects, causal laws; propositions, numbers, probabilities; social structure, moral facts). But the three most historically important types of realism have been:

1 *predicative realism*, asserting the existence of universals independently (Plato) or as the properties (Aristotle) of particular material things;

2 *perceptual realism*, asserting the existence of material objects in space and time independently of their perception; and

3 *scientific realism*, asserting the existence and operation of the objects of scientific enquiry absolutely (for the most part in natural science) or relatively (for the most part in social science) independently of the enquiry, or more generally of human activity.

Modern (late twentieth-century) scientific realism entails, but is irreducible to, realist positions in (1) and (2). This article will be mainly concerned with (3) and with the PHILOSOPHY OF SCIENCE generally. (But see also PHILOSOPHY OF SOCIAL SCIENCE; NATURALISM.) But for the first half of this century it was (2) that was at the forefront of philosophical debate.

Thus the turn of the century saw the beginnings of a reaction against the prevailing idealisms – in Britain, especially in the work of G.E. Moore and (for some of the time) Bertrand Russell, and in the USA, William James. Moore, in defending a commonsense realism, prefigured the devastating attack against phenomenalism provided in mid-century by the later Wittgenstein and the Oxford school of LINGUISTIC PHILOSOPHY, led principally by J. Austin, G. Ryle and F. Waismann. But the theoretically dominant form of perceptual realism in the first half of the century was 'representative realism', which posited a causal chain between object and percept, mediated by sensation or sensa, in virtue of which some percepts were like their objects. This suffered from the defect that it was unverifiable. For, on representative realism, there was no way object and percept could be directly compared. For this reason, the dominant epistemology, POSITIVISM, was normally formulated in phenomenalist terms (that is, material objects were analysed as actual or possible sense-data) – though occasionally given physicalist (for instance by O. Neurath) or operationalist (for instance, by P.W. Bridgman) declensions. Phenomenalism was, however, at least as untenable as representative realism. For there was no way to define sense-data save in material object terms. ('I seem to be seeing' – or 'I am sensing' – 'a pink elephant now'.) A way out of this impasse seemed to many late-century realists to be provided by the ecological perception theory of J.J. Gibson and his school. According to this theory human beings were organisms which actively sought out invariants – as affordances (such as, this cheese as edible) – in their environment. Many have hailed this as a Darwinian revolution in (2).

Modern scientific realism takes off from criticism of the logical positivism of the 1920s and 1930s which formed the basis for the received view of science until the late 1960s. One of the first decisive attacks on this was mounted by W.V.O. Quine who argued against the canonical analytical/empirical and theory/fact distinctions for a holistic view of knowledge as in effect 'a field of force whose boundary conditions are experience'. Drawing upon this, Mary Hesse and others argued that scientific language should be seen as a dynamic system constantly growing by the metaphorical extension of natural language. Observational predicates were not isomorphs of (physical, sensual or instrumental) objects, but 'knots' attaching the network to the object world in a theory dependent and mutable way.

This was powerfully reinforced by a growing awareness, induced by the work of Karl Popper, T.S. Kuhn, I. Lakatos, P.K. Feyerabend and, in France, G. Bachelard and A. Koyré, of the reality of scientific change. Theories were social constructions, offering competing descriptions and explana-

tions of a theory-independent world. Rom Harré, invoking the tradition of W. Whewell and N.R. Campbell, drew attention to the role of models in theory growth. Theoretical entities and processes, initially imaginatively posited as plausible explanations of observed phenomena, could come to be established as real, through the construction of either sense-extending equipment or of instruments detecting the effects of the theoretical phenomena (in the latter case invoking a causal criterion for attributing reality). All this strongly suggested a vertical '*theoretical*' realism. This was further supported by the linguistic arguments of Saul Kripke and H. Putnam that the use of natural kind terms, such as 'gold' and 'water', presupposed that those substances have real essences, although not necessarily known to us.

Shortly afterwards Roy Bhaskar produced, in his system of transcendental or critical realism, an argument for a horizontal 'transfactual' or nomic realism, alongside the theoretical realism already established. He argued that it is a condition of the possibility of experimental and applied activity that the objects of scientific enquiry (causal laws, generative mechanisms, structured things) not only exist but act independently of that activity – transfactually, in open and experimentally or otherwise closed systems alike. Both theoretical and transfactual realism involve what a recent writer has called, following Mandelbaum, 'transdiction', that is, inference to the (in practice and in principle) unobservable (Manicas, 1987, p. 10). Many have hailed this as a Copernican revolution in (3).

Arguments for (3) may be divided into three broad types: (a) transcendental arguments from the possibility of specified social practices (such as Bhaskar's); (b) inductive arguments from the successes of the sciences; and (c) *reductiones ad absurdum* of irrealist (non-realist) positions. An example of (b) is Putnam and Boyd's argument that the cumulative character of scientific growth strongly indicates that theories are (fallible) attempts to describe real states and structures as they succeed one another in providing better (fuller) accounts of a theory-independent reality. (Putnam (1978, p. 25) now rejects this on the grounds of the possibility of a 'disastrous meta-induction' from the failure of reference in some actual cases, e.g. phlogiston. Hesse has also criticized it on the grounds that the history of science reveals no convergence.) Another example is Harré's and Aronson's argument from the determinate outcome of searches for hypothesized beings for a pragmatic policy realism. Examples of (c) are the paradoxes, antinomies and aporiai into which irrealist philosophies fall, such as the problem of induction (see THEORY OF KNOWLEDGE). One kind of problem may be specifically mentioned. If realism is transcendentally-axiologically necessary, this means that irrealist accounts will presuppose in practice some ontology, and thence some or other type of realism (for instance, an empirical or a subjective or objective conceptual realism). Moreover if a particular form of realism, such as transcendental realism, is necessary, this implies that actually generated and historically efficacious philosophies will always take the form of internally inconsistent compromise formations. Here philosophy in pursuing its critique must join hands with empirically grounded sociology of knowledge.

Until very recently most debates about realism have turned on the epistemological question of the truth of our knowledge, rather than the ontological question of the reality of structures and things (as defined at the onset of this article). But critical realists have argued that ontological realism is consistent with epistemological relativism (and that the latter does not entail judgemental relativism). We know the same world but under irreducibly historical (and better or worse) descriptions.

A final word on social objects. Bhaskar (1989, p. 47) has contended that although the processes of the development of knowledge and their objects are causally interdependent, the latter must still be regarded as existentially intransitive, so that realism, in this modified sense, appears as an a priori condition of any investigation, irrespective of domain. (Thus it applies, for example, even to 'Cartesian doubt', ibid., pp. 91–2.)

Reading

Bhaskar, R. 1986: *Scientific Realism and Human Emancipation.*

Gibson, J.J. 1966: *The Senses considered as Perceptual Systems.*

Harré, Rom 1986: *Varieties of Realism.*

Hesse, Mary 1974: *The Structure of Scientific Inference.*

Isaac, J. 1990: Realism and reality: some realistic considerations. *Journal for the Theory of Social Behaviour* 20.1.

Outhwaite, W. 1990: Realism, naturalism and social behaviour. *Journal for the Theory of Social Behaviour* 20.4.

Putnam, H. 1983: *Philosophical Papers*, vol. 3.

Quine, W.V.O. 1952 (*1963*): *From a Logical Point of View.*

ROY BHASKAR

reason *See* RATIONALITY AND REASON

reformism Initially a debate inside Western SOCIALISM at the end of the nineteenth century and beginning of the twentieth century about the most appropriate and desirable political methods for bringing about the transformation of CAPITALISM and the transition to socialism, reformism embraced the idea of a peaceful route.

Because Karl Marx (1818–1883) had left no clear or authoritative theory explaining the social processes by which socialism replaces capitalism, divisive political controversy was inevitable. However, there were broadly two opposed views. Orthodox Marxists like Rosa Luxemburg (1871–1919) and Karl Kautsky (1854–1938) argued that capitalism could only be finally destroyed by violent revolutionary methods. Revolution was necessary for the establishment of the dictatorship of the proletariat, the destruction of the capitalist state and the end of bourgeois law. Luxemburg supported the strategy of the mass strike to develop a revolutionary consciousness. Those who adopted reformism like Eduard Bernstein (1850–1932) claimed that the transition to socialism could be achieved by peaceful means, for example by the electoral victory of the organized working class within liberal democracy.

After Marx's death, MARXISM became the official ideology of the German Social Democratic Party (SPD) which represented the German working class. Under the influence of Bernstein, the reformist wing of the SPD gradually accepted the position that a crisis of the capitalist economy was no longer imminent or inevitable, and that there could be an evolutionary reform of capitalism resulting in socialism. Bernstein published a number of important articles in the *Die Neue Zeit*, *Sozialdemokrat* and *Justice* in the 1890s on the general problems of socialism. He noted that as capitalism became a more complex and differentiated social system, social class divisions became equally complex. As a result, the likelihood of a violent class struggle between capitalists and workers became more remote. The middle classes were thriving, the workers' standard of living had improved and the dominant class had reluctantly accepted the role of a socialist opposition in the parliamentary system. Bernstein argued that Marxism was a set of useful but tentative guides to action and, rather than playing a scientific role, socialism had to provide moral leadership to counteract the negative effects of factory conditions on the lives of the working class. In short, Bernstein's programme for the social reform of the capitalist system was also associated with REVISIONISM, because he rejected economic determinism.

The question of reformism which dominated socialist debates in the period 1890–1918 is by no means resolved. Similar issues reemerged after World War II in social democracy and eurocommunism. The political and economic integration of Europe has produced a major rise in real incomes, thereby making the possibility of armed insurrection against the capitalist state even more remote. In a liberal democracy, communism could only win votes by adopting a more reformist, legalistic strategy and, as a consequence, moving towards a more central position. Many social scientists came to believe that the EMBOURGEOISEMENT of the workers would turn them further away from socialism. The WELFARE STATE was an alternative to revolution, because it transformed the exploitative relationship between capital and labour; the worker was no longer faced with a choice between starvation or employment.

The gradual de-Stalinization of Eastern Europe, the crises of Hungary and Czechoslovakia, the split between Chinese and Russian versions of socialism, and the continuous problems of centralized economic planning in the 1960s contributed to the emergence of the NEW LEFT, which rejected the tradition of revolutionary political violence, whereby the working class would carry the sole burden of destroying capitalism by a direct assault. The progressive reform of capitalism would in fact require the participation of all oppressed social groups, namely blacks, women and students, and not just the militant workers.

The apparent collapse of the command economies of the Soviet bloc, the erosion of the communist party legitimacy and the restoration of multiparty democracy in 1989–90 has once more transformed the character of political debate. The idea that capitalism could be destroyed by revolutionary violence is no longer an issue. Instead social reformers inside Eastern Europe returned to the task of restoring the vitality of civil society, while in Western capitalism attempts to reform society are often couched in terms of a revitalization of the liberal principles of CITIZENSHIP as the essential foundation of welfare rights; such reforms are no longer perceived as necessary steps towards social-ism. However, critics of capitalism still argue that fundamental reforms of society (in terms of health, education and welfare) cannot be realized without a radical attack on the underlying inequality in property and power which characterizes a free market system. Radical critics claim that the expansion of citizenship and welfare is merely a cooptation of radical dissent, and therefore the welfare state is not in fact a major reform of laissez-faire economics. Although these criticisms are obviously contested, it is important to compare different patterns of social reform, because there are major differences within capitalism between for example Sweden, Great Britain, Japan and the United States in terms of the relationship between inequality, economic growth and welfare expenditure.

Reading
Anderson, P. 1976: *Considerations on Western Marxism*.
Mann, M. 1988: Ruling class strategies and citizenship. *Sociology* 21, 339–54.
Maravall, J.M. 1979: The limits of reformism: parliamentary socialism and the Marxist theory of the state. *British Journal of Sociology* 30, 267–90.
Marshall, T.H. 1981: *The Right to Welfare and Other Essays*.
Schram, S.G. and Turbett, J.P. 1983: Civil disorder and the welfare explosion: a two-step process. *American Sociological Review* 48, 408–14.
Tudor, H. and Tudor, J.M. eds 1988: *Marxism and Social Democracy: the Revisionist Debate 1896–1898*.
Turner, B.S. 1986: *Citizenship and Capitalism: The Debate over Reformism*.

BRYAN S. TURNER

regionalism   This is a term used to indicate a sociopolitical movement which is inspired by the culture of a particular region and aims to defend local identity from being submerged by national homogeneity, as well as to make the region more independent of central government.

Regionalism is a particularly strong and recurrent phenomenon in those countries in which the formation of the nation-state (Tilly, 1975) has not obliterated diverse regional cultural identities but, rather, fostered centralized government strategies for repressing or subordinating these identities to uniform and unified national standards. Regionalist movements are magnified by relative geographical isolation, as is the case with large islands like Corsica and Sardinia or mountain districts like Savoy and the Aosta Valley, or by specific religious – Ulster, Kossovo, Azerbaijan – sociocultural or socioethnic – Catalonia, the Basque country, Quebec – or ethnic national – the Kurdish or Armenian movements in various Middle Eastern countries – factors. In many cases where there is a cumulation of conditions of regional diversity, it is difficult to distinguish between regional identity and a separatist national movement, especially in nations which have historically encompassed regions with different religious, linguistic and cultural traditions; examples are the Basque country and, above all, most of the local states which formerly constituted the federal republics of Yugoslavia and the Soviet Union. Recent events in the latter show how difficult it is to draw a dividing line between regionalism and separatism, apart from concrete historical developments. which have witnessed, at least in the Baltic republics, a rapid transition from regionalism to national separatist movements.

When the conflict between regionalism and national governments does not take on separatist overtones, regionalist political organizations claim as their objective the devolution of wide governmental powers to an intermediary level between the national and the provincial and municipal levels (see Rousseau and Zariski, 1987).

Regional movements are often magnified also by marked imbalances resulting from economic development (see Holland, 1967). This applies both to regions that are less developed, like southern Italy, and to those that are affected by strong economic growth and end up by seeing national centralism as a limit to their own prospects for development, as in the case of Slovenia. Highly imbalanced periods or trends of regional development may give rise to instances of regionalism even in contexts where cultural heterogeneity is limited, like France, or where federative regional autonomy is strong, like the United States (see also FEDERALISM).

Although this phenomenon more often brings to mind industrialized countries, it is also found in many underdeveloped countries, above all in Asia and Africa. Here the formation of nation-states under the dominant influence of colonialism has led to the aggregation of highly diverse local entities into fragile centralized states, continually beset by economic difficulties; take, for example, India, Indonesia or the Philippines where the regional map coincides with deep ethnic, religious, linguistic and cultural divisions.

Reading
Holland, Stuart 1976: *Capital versus the Regions.*
Rousseau, Mark O. and Zariski, Raphael 1987: *Regionalism and Regional Devolution in Comparative Perspective.*
Tilly, Charles ed. 1975: *The Formation of National States in Western Europe.*

ENZO MINGIONE

regulation The 'regulation approach' to the analysis of contemporary capitalism derives from a disparate group of French Marxists writing in the late 1970s and early 1980s. Economies are analysed as more or less cohesive structural combinations of a two-sector productive system (means of production and means of consumption), a wage relation, a monetary relation and banking structure, and a state relation, all embedded within an international division of labour of production and finance.

Primarily, regulation theory identifies 'regimes of accumulation' as extensive or intensive, and 'forms of regulation' as competitive or monopolistic. These distinctions have narrower and wider interpretations. Thus on a narrow interpretation, an extensive regime of accumulation is one in which accumulation does not alter the technology of production (at least in the consumer goods sector) and in which productivity growth is low, whereas an intensive regime continually alters both technical and social organizations of work in pursuit of rapid productivity growth. And again on a narrow interpretation, forms of regulation refer to predominant practices of price formation, freely fluctuating prices characterizing the competitive form of regulation, and administered pricing practices the monopolistic. Wider interpretations of these terms are also used to describe the social structure as a whole.

On this basis, capitalist history is periodized, with particular emphasis being placed on the changing organization of work and on the way in which the wage system facilitates the realization of the products of labouring activity. Thus from the mid-nineteenth century to 1914 is an extensive regime of accumulation with competitive regulation. The interwar period is a transitional phase in which an organization of work known as 'scientific management' or Taylorism is generalized in the USA and appears partially in Europe. In addition, the incorporation of Taylorist principles into automatic systems of production, known as Fordism, appears embryonically. But the rapid rates of growth of productivity thereby engendered were not extended to the purchasing power of the wage, whose growth was comparatively slight. Hence the economic crises characterizing world capitalism after 1929 are seen not in terms of the conventional business cycle but rather as a structural breakdown: the developing intensive regime of accumulation could not properly establish itself on the basis of competitive regulation, but required a policy of active regulation of the wage relation itself. This was achieved by the post-1945 reconstruction and the following long boom: Fordist methods of mass production were able to establish themselves as the preponderant organization of work, because of the mass consumption allowed the working class by the variety of institutional forms collectively constituting monopoly regulation. Particularly important here are collective wage agreements, backed up by the social security and unemployment insurance provisions of the WELFARE STATE and the huge increases in the economic interventions of the state (seen not so much in terms of Keynesian public expenditure policies, but rather with respect to the management of money, and to the reproduction of the labour force). Accordingly, intensive accumulation (the generalization of Fordism in production) and monopoly regulation (the management of mass consumption via the establishment of the welfare state and the partial incorporation of trade unions into economic management) characterize the 'golden age' of capitalism in the 1950s and 1960s. Finally, the problems of the 1970s are seen as the breakdown of this golden age; Fordism is in the process of giving way to the flexible specialization of post-Fordism. This requires an organization of consumption which is in the process of being worked out in the 1980s and 1990s, through the alteration of the state's economic role, privatization, mass unemployment and the restructuring of the labour force, and the alteration of the legislative framework defining both trade union activity and the boundaries and scope of the welfare state.

There is also an international dimension. The pre-1914 era is characterized by British hegemony, and the interwar transitional era by international rivalry and US isolationism; the golden age to 1970 is dominated by the USA, and in the post-1970 transitional era neither the USA nor the EC nor Japan is able unambiguously to regulate the world economy through its international economic domination.

Regulation theory is all-embracing. It is stronger on description than on analysis, because it is difficult to conceive a single analytical account of the very wide variety of different national experiences and their institutional forms. It is therefore best understood as an indicative or suggestive research agenda rather than as a polished theory. It is for detailed research to confirm or invalidate both premises and conclusions of regulation theory, and this remains in its infancy.

Reading
Aglietta, M. 1976 (*1979*): *A Theory of Capitalist Regulation: The US Experience.*
——1982: World capitalism in the eighties. *New Left Review* 136, 5–42.
Boyer, R. 1979: Wage formation in historical perspective: the French experience. *Cambridge Journal of Economics* 3:2, 99–118.
De Vroey, M. 1984: A regulation approach interpretation of contemporary crisis. *Capital & Class* 23, 45–66.
Lipietz, A. 1986: Behind the crisis: the exhaustion of a regime of accumulation: A 'regulation school' perspective on some French empirical works. *Review of Radical Political Economics* 18.1–2, 13–32.

SIMON MOHUN

reification   This term refers to the process by which the products of the subjective action of human beings come to appear as objective, and so autonomous from humanity. However, two broad uses of the term may be identified. In the Marxist tradition the term is used critically, to describe a process that is specific to capitalism, and that serves to maintain the inequalities of a capitalist society by concealing actual processes of exploitation. In the non-Marxist tradition, and especially in phenomenological approaches (see PHENOMENOLOGY), reification is presented as an inevitable feature of all societies, as part of the social construction of reality.

Within Marxism, the term 'reification' occurs as the standard English translation of the German *Verdinglichung*, which was introduced by György Lukács (1923, pp. 83–222) and does not occur in Marx's writings. Lukács's theory of reification is a generalization of Marx's theory of COMMODITY FETISHISM. For Marx, the process of exchanging the products of human labour on a commodity market leads to the social relationship between people appearing as a relationship between things (Marx, 1867, pp. 163–5). Lukács attempts to extend Marx's economic analysis to the total life of society. He does this through reference to Weber's analysis of the growth of rationality. Instrumental rationality is integral to the development of the capitalist economy, and further reflects the process of commodity exchange, in so far as it facilitates the equating of different objects. For Lukács, this equation works only by emphasizing the quantitative characteristics of the object at the expense of the qualitative. Lukács suggests that these qualitative aspects are the uniquely human properties of the object, and hence are systematically concealed by reification.

While reification has been referred to widely in Marxist writing, the theory has been developed most precisely by Theodor Adorno. Reification becomes a theory of the social determination of language and thinking. This emphasizes the relationship between concepts and the objects to which they refer. In so far as concepts are products of social processes, they cannot be presupposed to correspond wholly to their objects. Under reification, concepts serve either to impute properties to the object that are absent (as for example with the concept of 'freedom'), or to conceal or distort existing properties, so that they appear objective rather than subjective (Adorno, 1966, pp. 183–92).

While the Marxist tradition sees reification as a historically specific phenomenon that is at once undesirable but potentially open to change, the non-Marxist tradition uses the term to refer to a more general process by which human beings come to forget the human authorship of the social world. As such, reification is not uniquely situated in relation to Marx's theory of commodity fetishism. Rather, it is argued that all social reality is constructed by social actors, and that reification is merely 'an extreme step in the process of objectification' (Berger and Luckmann, 1967, p. 89). Further, it may be argued that only in so far as human beings forget that social reality is constructed does that reality attain any permanence. Reification thereby becomes a necessary feature of society, rather than something undesirable.

Reading

Adorno, T.W. 1966 (*1973*): *Negative Dialectics*, trans. E.B. Ashton.

Berger, Peter L. and Luckmann, Thomas 1961: *The Social Construction of Reality: A Treatise in the Sociology of Knowledge.*

Lukács, G. 1923 (*1971*): *History and Class Consciousness: Studies in Marxist Dialectics*, trans. Rodney Livingstone.

Rose, G. 1978: *The Melancholy Science: An Introduction to the Thought of Theodor W. Adorno.*

Thomason, Burke C. 1982: *Making Sense of Reification: Alfred Schutz and Constructionist Theory.*

ANDREW EDGAR

relative deprivation This attracted prominence as a subjective and later as an objective concept – with alternative but quite distinct meanings. People can *feel* deprived relative to others and also relative to their observed conditions or situation. Alternatively, people can *be* deprived relative to others: their conditions are demonstrably worse than those of others. First, people's feelings, or their behaviour arising from their feelings, may provoke surprise and even seem irrational. 'Relative deprivation' was originally coined to help explain why some objectively well-off soldiers in the American army were discontented (Stouffer et al., 1949, p. 125). The term was taken up by social psychologists, sociologists and political scientists (Merton, 1949, is one example) to call attention to both differences of feeling between groups and differences between feeling and reality. Feelings of deprivation relative to some condition or situation perceived as attainable or achievable irrespective of people's actual condition or situation were clearly relevant to a large part of social life. The distinction helped to explain variations of opinion but also spontaneous protests and the organization of collective action. Runciman (1966, p. 10, and 1989, esp. pp. 36 and 97) applied the term rigorously to the problems of class structure, minority status and variation between cultures.

Second, the need to use the term in an objective and not only an individually or collectively subjective sense has subsequently emerged. Work on social rank, class, social mobility, income distribution, poverty and patterns of ill-health in the population has directed attention to the importance of measuring, for example, social distance, the material and social conditions of different groups, classes or ranks in the population and the disjunction between met and unmet needs. In the process the meaning of 'deprivation' itself has come under more searching scrutiny. It has been distinguished from ideas like POVERTY by applying it directly to material and social inadequacies rather than indirectly to the low incomes which may, or may not, underlie those inadequacies. Some have distinguished between objective forms of *material* and *social* deprivation as well as between subjective forms of *individual* and *collective* deprivation (for example, Townsend, 1979, pp. 46–53, and 1987).

The objective social context or framework and reference points for the ascertainment and understanding of individual and group grievances of the kind encouraged by studies of feelings of deprivation demands elucidation. Thus, a group of skilled manual workers may feel deprived in relation to a group of office staff. Before jumping too readily to the conclusion that subjective and objective states are out of line, information has to be collected in detail about pay but also many other highly relevant features of working and social life. And this can involve a much broader investigation of working conditions, security of employment, promotion prospects, fringe benefits and social location than may be suggested in the original discoveries about feelings of deprivation. Analysis of the history of the concept shows that the importance of subjective or collective deprivation as an explanatory variable cannot be assessed independently of actual deprivation.

Reading
Runciman, W.G. 1989: *A Treatise on Social Theory*, vol. 2: *Substantive Social Theory*.
Townsend, P. 1979: *Poverty in the United Kingdom*.

PETER TOWNSEND

relativism If true belief is defined as belief which matches an independent reality, relativism denies that beliefs can be, or can be known to be, true in this sense. 'What is truth on one side of the Pyrenees is error on the other,' Pascal remarked drily in his *Pensées* (*V* 294), commenting on the diversity of moral beliefs. The apothegm also serves to capture a broader relativism, which asserts the relativity of all cognition. Meanwhile it is worth starting with the case for moral relativism. Ethical variety within societies and between them is a plain fact which, while not proving that there is no absolute or objective truth in ethics, tends to suggest it. The rise of science has brought a sharp fact/value distinction, which seems to cut the ground from under moral beliefs. The social sciences offer ways of explaining their variety as a function of correspondingly various social systems. Philosophy has cast doubts on the very idea of moral knowledge, especially those put scornfully by Nietzsche or analytically by emotivism. In short, traditional claims to truth in ethics have been a natural casualty of 'modernity', with Reason now undermining what it used to support.

Yet even in ethics relativism is not always meant to subvert all objectivity. As with utilitarians, it may demand only that local preferences be respected, when deciding what it is right to do. So one must distinguish a limited relativism, which in effect injects an element of perspective into what is meant to remain an objective point of view, from a more radical scepticism, which contextualizes every point of view in order to deny that there is anything objective or universal under the sun. The former is symptomatic of social thought in the spirit of the Enlightenment, which treats human beliefs and relations as objects for scientific study. The latter, attractive to critics of Enlightenment rationalism (see RATIONALITY AND REASON), is not merely destructive, if it leads on to hermeneutics or into various forms of 'postmodernism'. The crux is whether a limited relativism can find a defensible stopping place.

The case for the relativity of all cognition is best taken in three stages. The first is *conceptual relativism*, which sets off from the enormous diversity of classificatory and explanatory schemes. The facts of experience never fully detemine what it is rational to believe about the order in (or underlying) experience. To classify or explain is to apply the concepts in local use. Thus the Karam concept of 'yakt' groups bats with most birds but excludes cassowaries (Bulmer, 1967); physics employs concepts like 'ether' or 'phlogiston' at one time and drops them at another. Each scheme of classification imposes a grid, backed by theoretical concepts which rely finally on categorial concepts, like time, deity, causation and agency. That is not a subversive thought, if science can be marked off and shown to be progressive. The subversive thought is that categorial concepts are essentially contestible within their own conceptual scheme, and that conceptual schemes are incommensurable, for instance because they rely on 'absolute presuppositions' (Collingwood, 1940) or 'paradigms' (Kuhn, 1962) which have the status of myths.

That there are any given facts of experience is denied, secondly, by *perceptual relativism*. Quine (1960) maintains that 'there is no such thing as unvarnished news.' Even to describe, one must interpret with the aid of theories and in language permeated by theory. So, it seems, 'the "real world" is to a large extent built on the language habits of the group' (Sapir, 1929), implying perhaps that those with deeply different theories or languages inhabit 'different worlds' (Kuhn, 1962; cf. Winch, 1958).

Thirdly, a sweeping *epistemic relativism* contextualizes even the criteria of truth and logic. If there can be fundamentally alternative logics, then the basic tenets of Aristotelian logic lose their title to be 'the laws of thought'. If truth is finally 'a mobile army of metaphors, metonyms and anthropomorphisms' and 'truths are illusions about which one has forgotten that this is what they are' (Nietzsche, 1873), then there can be no ultimate cognitive fixtures. The case is encouraged both by philosophical disputes about truth, which thereby unsettle the possibility of a neutral criterion, and by anthropological evidence that, one might say in echo of Pascal, what is a good reason (for any belief or action) on one side of the Pyrenees is a bad reason elsewhere. If so, all cognition is in the end held up by its own bootstraps.

In contextualizing or internalizing thought, what is one making it relative to? Answers divide broadly into materialist and idealist. The former relates cognition to something external to cognition – behavioural or neural conditioning, perhaps, or social structure or relations, construed independently of whatever beliefs they determine. The latter relates cognition to itself after the manner of a network, in effect internalizing social relations, or even nature, to the network too. Perhaps different languages are ultimately different networks. Perhaps 'what has to be accepted, the given, is, so to say, *forms of life*' (Wittgenstein, 1953). Materialist answers involve a stopping place, so that a scientific observer can establish a relativist perspective, presumably one which exempts properly scientific thought from contextualization. Idealist answers tend to refuse exemptions and so lead readily to, for example, the replacement of all traditional objectivity by a postmodern 'conversation of mankind' (Rorty, 1980).

On the one hand, if there is anything universal under the sun, it is not obvious. On the other, variety is in itself never a proof that all viewpoints are equally valid, and, if they were, a global relativism would be no more valid than its denial. Disputes remain fraught, since a distinction between the cognitive and the social, with the aim of explaining one in terms of the other, is easy neither to draw nor to defend.

Reading

Bernstein, R. 1983: *Beyond Objectivism and Relativism.*
Bulmer, R. 1967: Why is the cassowary not a bird? *Man*, NS, 2.
Collingwood, R.G. 1940: *An Essay on Metaphysics.*
Hollis, M. and Lukes, S. eds 1982: *Rationality and Relativism.*
Kuhn, T.S. 1962 (*1970*): *Structure of Scientific Revolutions.*
Nietzsche, F. 1873 (*1954*): On truth and lie in an extra-moral sense. In *The Portable Nietzsche*, ed. W. Kaufman.
Quine, W.v.O. 1960: *Word and Object.*
Rorty, R. 1980: *Philosophy and the Mirror of Nature.*
Sapir, E. 1929: The status of linguistics as a science. *Language* 5.
Winch, P. 1958 (*1976*): *The Idea of a Social Science.*
Wittgenstein, L. 1953: *Philosophical Investigations.*

MARTIN HOLLIS

religion In referring to experiences, feelings and ideas which suggest that there may be an immeasurably more profound, powerful and significant dimension of life than the everyday or mundane, religion concerns itself most distinctively with matters of ultimate significance such as the meaning of life, suffering and death, and the means of maintaining hope for a better future. This 'added' or other dimension takes widely different forms in different cultures and is, of course, subject to individuals' differing sensibilities and interpretations. There is no less variation in the social forms in which the religious dimension takes shape. The sedimentation of these added meanings in cultural, experiential and social forms over long periods of time has helped to establish religion as a powerful and enduring institution in virtually all known societies, although there is no necessity for individuals to be responsive to it. In other words, religion is a potential quality of human experience to which no limits can be set by definition. Rather, it makes good sense to think about it in terms of varying degrees of such things as distinctiveness, significance, formality, plausibility, scope, salience, applicability, coherence, consistency, methodicalness, emotionality and integration with other social phenomena.

Judaism, Christianity and Islam tend to dichotomize the religious and the secular, treating them as categorically separate domains. But Hinduism, Buddhism, Shinto and numerous tribal or folk cultures regard religion as an immanent quality of all existence. Nevertheless, all religions symbolize and 'manage' the points of disjunction or continuity between secular and religious registers of meaning by means of myth, symbol, ritual, sacred text and concepts of sacred space, time, community and being.

If it is objected that this inclusive and relativistic way of conceptualizing religion runs the risk of confusing religious with other kinds of intense or profound experiences, the response would be that the attribution of religious significance is itself a cultural variable and would, therefore, vary with the extent to which religious meanings had been identified, symbolized and codified in any particular culture. Thus, the religious meanings of, for instance, childbirth or warfare are not fixed but, depending on the context, they can be made more or less salient, systematic or distinctive. This means that there is no justification for confining the term 'religion' to particular beliefs or experiences, although, true to the canon of methodological agnosticism, the possibility that non-human powers or agents may directly affect the meanings attributed to human events has to remain open.

One of the twentieth century's major contributions towards the understanding of religion is the recognition that no single definition of the phenomenon can be adequate for all purposes. By contrast to the confident characterizations of religion produced by many Western thinkers of the late nineteenth century, there has been a tendency in the current century to prefer definitions which are more nuanced and more sensitive to the growing body of knowledge about cultures other than those dominated by Christianity, Judaism or Islam and about the varieties of religious expression on different levels of culture. Thus, whereas the founding generations of anthropologists and sociologists seemed content to reduce religion to a matter of 'a general theory of the world' (Karl Marx), 'belief in spiritual beings' (E. Tylor), or propitiation or conciliation of powers superior to humans (J. Frazer), it is now common for social scientists to adopt a more relativistic and less intellectualistic approach.

The force of evolutionary, rationalist and organicist thinking has slowly declined in this century, but there is no unanimity among twentieth-century thinkers. Current thought falls roughly into two categories. On the one hand, there are thinkers who insist on the need to conceive of religion in *substantive* terms of belief in certain kinds of spirits, divinities or other transcendental forces. Robertson's definition is representative of this approach:

> Religious culture is that set of beliefs and symbols (and values deriving directly therefrom) pertaining to a distinction between an empirical and a super-empirical, transcendent reality; the affairs of the transcendent being subordinated to the non-empirical. (1970, p. 47)

On the other hand, there is a long tradition of thinking about religion in terms of its alleged *functions* or purposes. An influential example of this approach is the claim that 'religion is a system of beliefs and practices by means of which a group of people struggles with the ultimate problems of human life' (Yinger, 1957, p. 9).

While the substantive approach offers the advantage of appearing to stick closely to what many people report about religion, it also runs into the criticisms that it arbitrarily emphasizes belief or knowledge, that it creates an artificial boundary between religion and magic, and that it is insensitive to cross-cultural differences between religions. By contrast, the functionalist approach benefits from its cross-cultural applicability and from its abstraction from the level of empirical detail, but it also incurs costs which, according to its critics, cancel out its benefits. In particular, it tends to attract criticism for imputing teleology to social and cultural arrangements, for reducing the meaningfulness of religion to its consequences, for confusing religion with ideology, and for implying that everything which exists must, for that very reason alone, fulfil a function. The relative strengths and weaknesses of these basic approaches are discussed in Spiro (1966), Berger (1974) and Bellah (1970).

The twentieth century has witnessed the fruition of academic disciplines which have constituted religion in rather distinctive ways. Older disciplines such as the history of religions, theology, and comparative religion tend to accord priority to philological, historical, philosophical and doctrinal aspects. But the growing influence of phenomenological thinking in the 1930s inspired more intuitive studies of religious experience, ritual sacredness and the holy (see Otto, 1950; van der Leeuw, 1938; Wach, 1958; Eliade, 1958; Sharpe, 1975). Meanwhile, psychological and psychoanalytical approaches found favour, especially among practitioners involved in training religious professionals for liturgical, counselling and social service functions (see Rieff, 1966). The influence of sociological thought increased dramatically in the 1960s when liberal American denominations were about to lose some of their popularity (Berger, 1961) and when, unexpectedly, conservative churches and allegedly deviant new religious movements began to grow in size and public impact (Kelley, 1972; Wilson, 1976). But it was the vogue for structuralism in the human sciences which probably gave most prominence to the study of religion in the forms of myth, ritual, symbolism and processes of sacralization. Finally, religious studies, as a deliberately interdisciplinary approach, began to flourish in the 1970s and fostered, in particular, a more critical attitude towards methodological issues as well as a more policy oriented stance both in the increasingly multicultural and ethnically diverse context of advanced industrial societies and in former colonies rediscovering their religious heritage.

As for the contributions that religions have made to the major currents of twentieth-century thought, it must be recognized that they are probably not among the most formative influences. Whether it be on the level of the ideologies which have shaped nation-states and international conflicts (such as clerical fascism, Christian Democracy, Hindu or Japanese nationalism, and Islamic anti-imperialism) or whether it be on the level of the changing fashions in philosophy (such as Catholic phenomenology, Christian existentialism, or theologies of struggle), the contributions of religious ideas and sentiments have in some cases been important but rarely decisive. And, in the Western world at least, religious themes have inspired relatively few artistic achievements of outstanding merit in the twentieth century.

These developments conform with the dominant interpretations of modernity, namely, that religion has ceased to serve as the 'sacred canopy' for modern existence (Berger, 1967), as the principal instrument of cultural and societal integration (Wilson, 1982), or as the social system's form of reflecting on its own integrity (Luhmann, 1977). On the other hand, religion that is not church oriented may still be implicit in basic socialization processes (Luckmann, 1967) and may still function as a metalanguage which transcends the domain of objective facts (Bellah, 1989) or which permits 'serious' things to be said 'for real' (Fenn, 1981).

Indeed, as the century draws to a close, there are indications that religious thought and sentiment may be reasserting themselves in response to the possibility of genuinely global communication *and* destruction (Robertson, 1985) and that religious themes are resurfacing in social movements concerned with such globe-wide issues as peace, human rights, genocide and protection of the natural environment (Beckford, 1989, pp. 143–65). Religion is also proving to be a remarkably durable and effective medium for the cultivation and expression of ethnic and national identities in

countries as different as Poland, Nicaragua, Iran and Sri Lanka. The results may, depending on historical circumstances, be integrative or distintegrative.

See also CHRISTIAN SOCIAL THEORY; LIBERATION THEOLOGY; THEOLOGY.

Reading
Berger, P.L. 1967: *The Sacred Canopy: Elements of a Sociological Theory of Religion.*
Bowker, J. 1973: *The Sense of God.*
Durkheim, Emile 1912 (*1968*): *The Elementary Forms of the Religious Life.*
Glock, C.Y. and Hammond, P.E. eds 1973: *Beyond the Classics? Essays in the Scientific Study of Religion.*
Smart, N. 1973: *The Science of Religion and the Sociology of Knowledge.*
Waardenburg, J. ed. 1973–4: *Classical Approaches to the Study of Religion: Aims, Methods and Theories of Research*, 2 vols.
Wilson, B.R. 1982: *Religion in Sociological Perspective.*

JAMES A. BECKFORD

republicanism   The Roman expression *res-publica* implies that things that are public must be of public concern: active citizens should manage the state, not kings, aristocratic oligarchies or even single parties. Citizens treat each other as equals. The public culture of politics is quite different from the private decision-making in autocracies. But the citizen body, until this century, always excluded women and slaves, and usually excluded debtors, servants, the poor and the illiterate. Republicanism is not necessarily democratic, but it is more participative in spirit than individualistic liberalism.

Machiavelli provided the classic theory of republicanism in his *Discourses* (ed. Crick, *1970*). A state is stronger if it can trust a citizen class with arms. Freedom means tolerating social conflict, but conflict if well managed, if handled by political compromise, can be a source of strength; it gives liveliness to political life. This realistic restatement of an idealized Renaissance picture of the Roman republic was immensely influential, especially in the Dutch republic, Sweden, England and Scotland of the civil wars, the British American colonies and above all in the French revolution. Antonio Gramsci produced a Communist variant, partly to refute Lenin's obsession with the state and *the* party, arguing that the participative cooperation of the skilled industrial worker was now the key to the rise and fall of societies rather than Machiavelli's armed citizen.

Republicanism was strong in the early United States, where the ideology of Jeffersonian democracy was based on a cult of active CITIZENSHIP, making simplicity of manners, plain speaking and candour virtues to be universalized by personal example. The name of the modern Republican Party in the USA is misleading, as is that of the 'IRA' (Irish Republican Army), except in the narrow sense that they oppose the British crown. In a MONARCHY the term has this narrower connotation. But republicanism is not necessarily anti-monarchical; it is essentially anti-aristocratic. 'Red republicanism', in the Jacobin tradition, is fiercely egalitarian and populist in spirit, in deliberate contrast to bourgeois republicanism which cares less for 'sovereignty of the people' and more for 'the rule of law' and 'the constitution'. But neither developed, like socialism, a distributive economic theory; both accepted liberal economics because historically it had replaced aristocratic mercantilist policies.

Republicanism is compatible with both democratic socialism and radical liberalism, but is best understood by contrast to that kind of liberalism which sees the state as ensuring the rights of individuals to lead a private life protected by legal safeguards both from itself and from each other. The republican spirit says that these laws must be made and changed by active citizens working in concert; the price of freedom is not simply eternal vigilance but perpetual civic activity. Between the state and the individual there is the creative tumult of CIVIL SOCIETY.

Reading

Bock, G., Skinner, Q. and Viroli, M. eds 1990: *Machiavelli and Republicanism*.
Crick, B.R. 1992: *In Defence of Politics*, 3rd edn.
Keane, J. ed. 1988: *Democracy and Civil Society*.
McWilliams, W.C. 1973: *The Idea of Fraternity in America*.
Pocock, J.G.A. 1975: *The Machiavellian Moment: Florentine Political Thought and the Atlantic Republican Tradition*.
Williams, G.A. 1989: *Artisans and Sans-Culottes: Popular Movements in France and Britain during the French Revolution*, 2nd edn.

BERNARD CRICK

revisionism A term which was introduced into Marxist thought at the end of the nineteenth century to refer to critical reassessments and reformulations of Marx's ideas, and in particular those concerning the development of capitalism and the nature of a transition to socialism. It gained wide currency in the revisionist debate initiated by Eduard Bernstein's articles (written from 1896–8), later expanded into a book (1899), on the problems of socialism, in which he attempted 'to become clear just where Marx is right and where he is wrong'. The main targets of Bernstein's criticism were the 'economic collapse' theory of the end of capitalism, and the idea of an increasing polarization of society between bourgeoisie and proletariat, accompanied by more intense class conflict. Against these doctrines, which had become part of Marxist orthodoxy, he argued that alongside the concentration of capital in large corporations there was a growth of new small and medium-sized businesses, more widespread property ownership, a rise in the general level of living, an increase in the numbers of the middle class, the emergence of a more complex and differentiated system of stratification in capitalist society and a diminution in the scale and intensity of economic crises.

In the course of this debate, revisionism became identified with REFORMISM and the abandonment of revolutionary aims, or even of any strong commitment to the achievement of socialism. But the opponents of revisionism were themselves divided, with Kautsky and the Austro-Marxists attempting to incorporate various new phenomena into the orthodox Marxist view of the development of capitalism, while Rosa Luxemburg and Lenin expounded a revolutionary political doctrine in terms of which some other critics of revisionism were themselves treated as revisionists.

The denunciation of revisionism as counter-revolutionary reached a peak with the outbreak of World War I in 1914 and the collapse of the Second International, and this usage as a term of abuse was perpetuated by the consolidation of Bolshevism as a new orthodoxy in the Soviet Union and then, after 1945, in Eastern Europe. By the end of the 1980s, however, Bolshevik orthodoxy had itself collapsed, totally in its Stalinist form and to a large extent in its Leninist form; and in historical perspective revisionism can now be seen as a succession of modifications of Marx's theory of society, and of its implications for political practice, resulting from major social changes in both capitalist and socialist societies, from particular historical circumstances and from changes in knowledge and ideas. What was once called revisionism is now better described as the development of numerous and diverse schools of Marxist thought (and of socialist thought more generally) in response to changing conditions; that is, as a normal feature in the unending effort to comprehend through the concepts of social theory an ever-changing historical reality.

Reading
Bernstein, Eduard 1899 (*1961*): *Evolutionary Socialism.*
Gay, Peter 1952: *The Dilemma of Democratic Socialism.*
Kolakowski, Leszek 1978: *Main Currents of Marxism*, vol. 2, ch. 4.
Labedz, L. ed. 1962: *Revisionism.*

TOM BOTTOMORE

revivalism   The idea that religious traditions tend towards entropy unless periodically revitalized either by a return to primitive truths or by the injection of new truths is central to many meanings of revivalism, especially in cultures affected by Christianity. Revivals, as collective searches for a radically better world, stem, therefore, from religious reasons for shared dissatisfaction with the present state of affairs. They may take such varied forms as millenarian, messianic, prophetic, nationalistic, nativistic, evangelical or charismatic movements, but in each case the emphasis is on the processes whereby vitality and creativity are infused into a putatively declining or threatened tradition. Religious revivals have also been said to herald periods of wide-ranging social reforms and, in the case of the American Great Awakenings, long-term cycles of spiritual renewal and social reconstruction (McLoughlin, 1978).

In elaborations of these ideas, Barkun (1974) has interpreted millennial movements as responses to disasters, while Lanternari (1963) and Worsley (1957) have argued that millennial revivals in preindustrial societies are creative responses to socioeconomic exploitation and oppression. Other theories have stressed relative deprivation, the search for short cuts to magical and healing power, the psychology of the 'true believer', cognitive dissonance and collective paranoia. There seems to be agreement among these competing interpretations, however, that successful revival requires the weakening of old meanings and commitments before the transition to new values and identities can take place (Burridge, 1969). Except in small-scale tribal societies, religious revival rarely transforms an entire society but is more likely to be confined to particular movements, orders, sects or churches. Examples include the Methodist revivals in eighteenth-century Britain and the series of revivals which transformed various Protestant churches in New York State in the first half of the nineteenth century (Cross, 1950).

In advanced industrial societies where Christianity has been the dominant form of religion, twentieth-century revivalism has been limited to occasional movements of heightened emotion, intensified feelings of guilt and spontaneous expressions of personal faith in the power of Jesus Christ to redeem sin and to heal minds and bodies. Circuit riders, hellfire preachers, camp meetings and tent revivals were all precursors of modern Protestant revivalism, and present-day innovations include charismatic renewal, televangelism and the Moral Majority. The Roman Catholic church has had revivals led by Benedictines and Cistercians, and Dolan (1978) has documented the specifically Catholic form of revivalism in nineteenth-century America.

Studies of current campaigns to reassert the power of Islam in some countries also show that activists tend to have *regained*, rather than acquired for the first time, their strong religious convictions. Moreover, the transformative effects of modern revivalism tend to be shortlived. Nevertheless, and contrary to most expectations about modernization, collective revivals of Islamic fervour have powerfully shaped political and social developments in, for instance, Iran, the Sudan, Pakistan and Malaysia in the recent past (Esposito, 1980). Hindu revivalism is also becoming an important factor in Indian politics, and Buddhist revivals have marked the history of several nations of South Asia.

See also FUNDAMENTALISM.

Reading
Barkun, M. 1974: *Disaster and the Millennium.*
Burridge, K. 1969: *New Heaven, New Earth.*
McLoughlin, W. 1959: *Modern Revivalism.*
——— 1978: *Revivals, Awakenings and Reform.*

JAMES A. BECKFORD

revolution   In political thought, this refers to an illegal, usually violent, seizure of power that produces a fundamental change in the institutions of government. However, the concept of revolution has been used in many ways, with some variation in meaning. 'Revolution' is sometimes used to describe *any* fundamental change, whether or not it was violent or sudden. In this sense we speak of the 'Industrial Revolution' or the 'scientific revolution'. Fundamental changes in government that occur through elections rather than through violent seizures of power are also sometimes described as revolutions, for example the 'Nazi revolution' in Germany which followed Hitler's electoral victory in 1933.

In most revolutions, the seizure of power depends on uprisings by urban crowds or rural peasants. These uprisings are usually what we mean when we refer to 'revolutions'. However, in some cases popular groups do little, while an individual or small elite group seizes power and implements sweeping political changes (as in the Turkish revolution under Atatürk in 1921, or the Egyptian revolution under Nasser in 1952). Such events are often described as 'elite revolutions' or 'revolutions from above' (Trimberger, 1978).

Revolutions vary in their scope. Those that change only government institutions are sometimes labelled 'political revolutions'. Those that also change the distribution of wealth and status in a society – for example, by destroying the advantages of a nobility – are often called 'social revolutions' or 'great revolutions'. When groups seeking fundamental change attempt to seize power, but that attempt fails, we speak of 'unsuccessful' or 'failed revolutions', such as the revolution of 1848 in Germany. (An attack on a government that seeks only to change the ruling personnel or policies but makes no attempt at fundamental change in institutions is usually called a 'rebellion', rather than a 'revolution'.)

Properly speaking, revolution is a process rather than an event. There is an initial period in which criticism of the state mounts and opponents of the government strive to gain support. Then ensues a period of contention between the government and its opponents; this may entail a long guerrilla war, or a sudden explosion of popular tumults. If the government falls, there follows a period in which revolutionary leaders contend with each other, and with adherents of the old regime; this period commonly includes both civil and international wars, and often a period of domestic 'terror' against opponents of the revolution. A successful revolution then leads to the consolidation of power and the construction of new political institutions. Because this process may take decades, the dating of revolutions is frequently imprecise. However, for convenience revolutions are typically dated by the year in which the old regime falls – thus the French revolution of 1789, the Chinese communist revolution of 1949 – even though revolutionary struggles and state reconstruction may continue for decades afterwards.

The concept of revolution as fundamental change is strictly a modern development. From ancient Greece to the Renaissance, 'revolution' meant a cyclical motion, such as the revolution or turning of the planets. In politics, the term 'revolution' therefore also implied a cyclical pattern, a movement from aristocracy to democracy to tyranny and back, in an endless circle. Only in the eighteenth century, particularly after the French revolution of 1789, did the term 'revolution' come to refer to a permanent and fundamental, rather than cyclical, change.

Moral evaluations

The concept of revolution is often used with moral, as well as descriptive, overtones. Many thinkers, particularly those inspired by Karl Marx, use the term 'revolution' to imply change that is valuable and progressive. In politics, this usually means reducing inequality and providing greater justice; in other fields, it simply implies progress in knowledge or productive output – as with the 'agricultural revolution', or the 'computer revolution'. These thinkers view revolutions as necessary to achieve social progress; indeed, they often argue that revolution is the only way to overthrow established ideas or institutions.

Others, however, use the term revolution to imply a time of chaos, of unfettered struggle for power with destructive consequences. They see revolution as a violent and dangerous departure from the normal course of political life. These thinkers consider revolutions as something to be avoided; they advocate that desired social change should be brought about through gradual reform.

This argument is long-standing and far from settled. Different writers continue to view revolutions with optimism or pessimism, depending on their individual judgement as to whether the benefits of revolutionary change are worth the costs. Additional debates over the nature of revolutions have centred on two issues – why do revolutions occur, and what have they accomplished?

Causes of revolution

Thinking about the causes of revolution has grown more sophisticated throughout the twentieth century. Early thinkers focused chiefly on crowds, seeing revolution as the product of uncontrolled and spontaneous popular enthusiasm. Such crowd action might be triggered by a burst of economic hardship, or a particularly flagrant act of government corruption or oppression.

In the 1950s and 1960s, there was great concern that revolutions would flare in countries undergoing a shift from more traditional to more modern patterns of economic and political life. Populations caught 'in between' old and newly emerging lifestyles were considered unusually vulnerable to popular frustration and enthusiasm for rapid change. There was also concern over ideologies – such as communism – that might lead crowds to adopt extreme and violent behaviour. The roots of revolution were seen in both modernization and ideological subversion.

By the 1970s, however, particularly as a result of the work of Charles Tilly (1978), scholars had become aware that revolutionary crowd behaviour was not simply spontaneous and emotional. Instead, revolutionary activity was seen to require leadership, organization and mobilization in pursuit of political objectives. This 'resource mobilization' view led scholars to seek the causes of revolutions in shifts of resources among politically active groups.

In addition, Theda Skocpol (1979) and Jack Goldstone (1990) drew the attention of scholars to the resources of the state. They pointed out that the state's own resources might be strained by the costs of war or economic development, weakening the state and creating opportunities for state opponents. Moreover, they noted that conflicts within the political and economic elite were often crucial in diminishing the effectiveness of the state in defending itself, and providing leadership to opposition groups.

The currently prevailing view of the causes of revolution is the 'structural' theory. This combines attention to resource mobilization and state resources. In this view, revolutions will occur only when a *combination* of factors creates a 'structural situation' favourable to revolution. This situation includes a weakened government; internally divided and alienated elites; and an opposition with leadership, resources (including popular support) and organization. Revolutionary ideologies – which might include communism, liberalism or Islamic fundamentalism – are considered to be capable of gaining wide appeal only when a structural situation arises which favours revolution.

Outcomes of revolution

Thinking about the outcomes of revolution is less advanced than thinking about its causes. Only two conclusions seem well established. First, revolutions generally produce a growth of state power, as post-revolutionary regimes tend to attack the problem of state weakness by building states with larger armies and bureaucracies than the pre-revolutionary regime. Second, revolutions generally increase the likelihood of international wars, since the change of regime usually results in a change of international alliances. This often leads to tests of the strength of the new regime or the new alliances via international aggression, whether initiated by the new regime or its opponents.

On a host of other important issues, such as whether revolutions can create stable democracies, reduce inequality or enhance economic development, the evidence is highly ambiguous. Systematic study of these matters has only just begun.

Goals regarding outcomes are what differentiate 'rebellions' from 'revolutions'. In rebellions, the goals of state opponents usually extend no further than rectification of a particular grievance, or forcing a change of state personnel or policy. In revolutions, however, state opponents are motivated by an ideology which depicts existing institutions as fundamentally flawed or evil, and in need of total replacement or reconstruction. Though the causes of rebellion and revolution may be similar – state weakness, elite divisions and popular mobilization – the impact of revolutionary ideology in promoting radical goals and outcomes makes revolutions distinctive.

Future prospects of revolution

In the early and mid-twentieth century, when revolutions were viewed as the product of popular emotional response to the stresses of modernization, it was expected that revolutions would become less common as the world grew more rational and developed. However, the realization that revolutions are grounded in rational pursuit of political objectives and arise when shifts in power occur between states, elites and popular groups has altered this expectation. Changes in technology, international politics and the world economy bring new resources into the hands of various groups, while strengthening some states and weakening others. Such shifts have been particularly marked in those countries heavily involved in the strategic competition between the USA and the USSR.

Thus revolutions (and attempted revolutions) have been frequent in the late twentieth century – in Iran, Nicaragua, Afghanistan, Poland, the Philippines – and will likely remain a recurrent feature of world politics.

See also COLLECTIVE ACTION, MARXISM, PERMANENT REVOLUTION.

Reading

Dix, R. 1983: Varieties of revolution. *Comparative Politics* 15, 281–93.

Eckstein, S. 1982: The impact of revolution on social welfare in Latin America. *Theory and Society* 11, 33–94.

Goldstone, J.A., Gurr, T.R. and Moshiri, F. eds 1990: *Revolutions of the Late 20th Century.*

Paige, J. 1975: *Agrarian Revolution.*

Walton, J. 1984: *Reluctant Rebels.*

JACK A. GOLDSTONE

revolution, managerial   *See* MANAGERIAL REVOLUTION

revolution, permanent   *See* PERMANENT REVOLUTION

revolution, scientific-technological   *See* SCIENTIFIC-TECHNOLOGICAL REVOLUTION

Right, New   *See* NEW RIGHT

rights   For anyone to have a right, a corresponding duty must fall on some other or others, specific or general. The right might be to do something, or to keep possession of something, or to receive something (including an abstraction like respect). The respective duty would be to tolerate the activity, refrain from interfering with the possession of the good, or to proffer the benefit or response. Legal rights, that is, those rights recognized by LAW, serve as a model for extralegal, or 'moral' rights. Those who invoke the latter in support of their claims imply that such claims would be upheld by an imaginary moral tribunal, and typically seek to change the law so as to give effect to them.

The question arises, on what grounds rights can be posited. The traditional answer is that human beings have 'natural rights'. John Locke main-

tained that, even in a 'state of nature', individuals are moral beings, and in abandoning that state of nature, they conceded only limited powers of constraint to the government they thereby established. When it exceeds these, it violates the 'natural rights' of its subjects. The Bill of Rights attached to the Constitution of the United States neatly exemplifies this mode of thinking. By the middle of the twentieth century, though, claims as to the existence of such rights had come under attack from a variety of quarters. Some, reflecting a logical positivist perspective which denies that moral judgements can be true or false, see such claims more as 'decisions' or 'the taking of a stand' (MacDonald, 1947–8, p. 49); others, while accepting the validity of moral judgements, have regarded collective entities – the nation, the class – as the sole repositories of worth; and, in a more practical vein, Mabbott (1958), while viewing collective entities with extreme scepticism and proposing to 'banish [the term] "society" in the interests of clear thinking' (p. 83), dismissed natural rights as 'indeterminate and capricious' (p. 58) and as a political weapon invariably used by opponents of reform (p. 62).

In the later part of the century, 'rights' have reasserted themselves in political thinking, though, following World War II and the subsequent exposure of the Nazi holocaust, much of the emphasis worldwide has been on what have been called 'human rights'. In delineating such rights, the debate has been not so much about what rights individuals once had, or would have, in a 'state of nature', as on what rights all should have in the world as it is today. Moreover, whereas natural rights tend to be thought of as 'active', that is, options which their holders might choose to exercise, or not, in any given case, 'human rights' extend the concept to cover 'passive' rights as well, that is, entitlements which impose duties on others regardless of the rights bearer's choice. Thus a child may be said to have a 'right to education' without implying that it should have the option of refusing to be educated.

Rights may be specific or universal. Whereas a universal right is one which everyone should recognize, a specific right is due only from a specific other, or set of others, and arises either from explicit undertakings the latter have made, or out of the relationship between them. Thus Melden (1959) contends that a father has the right to expect respect from his son, and, by analogy, some go on to claim that a group has a specific right to the loyalty of its members and a state to that of its citizens.

It is not, however, characteristic of 'natural rights' theorists to champion the rights of collectivities against individuals. On the contrary, 'rights' are seen as being based on freedom (Hart), and freedom is defined negatively as the absence of constraint (Cranston 1953; Berlin 1958). Jean-Jacques Rousseau's claim that we can be 'forced to be free' is held to be a misuse of language. In Hart's words

> if there are any moral rights at all, it follows that there must be at least one natural right, the equal right of all men to be free ... [whereby] any adult human being capable of choice (1) has the right of forbearance on the part of all others from the use of coercion or restraint against him save to hinder coercion or restraint and (2) is at liberty to do (i.e. is under no obligation to abstain from) any action which is not one coercing or restraining or designed to injure other persons. (Hart, 1955, p. 174)

This is not, in Hart's view, an absolute right, but good reasons would have to be given for overriding it.

Milne, by contrast, following Green (1941) and Bosanquet (1951), sees freedom as positive. He agrees with Hart that 'the right to freedom from arbitrary constraint is a necessary condition for having any other rights at all,' but maintains that this is possible only in a free society, one whose members 'are in substantial agreement about the fundamental character of their way of life' (Milne, 1968, p. 177). He envisages that the established morality of such a society might authorize constraints on grounds other than those mentioned by Hart (road safety might be one example). What distinguishes a free society is that each member shares in the responsibility of maintaining it and determining its direction, and must therefore be autonomous under the law. Rights, he argues, are essentially social in character. By presupposing the autonomy of each member, the free society depends on each acting in the spirit rather than merely the letter of its established MORALITY. It must therefore accord each person the chance to convey his or her own insight into public affairs, and thus preserve everybody's freedom of expression. Moreover, in what he calls a 'critical humanist' perspective, members of a society may appraise the prevailing understanding in their society, and seek to improve it. The rights of association, of political participation and of non-violent political action will tend to facilitate this process.

According to Mabbott (1948, p. 57), 'natural rights must be self-evident and must be absolute if they are to be rights at all.' Milne, by linking 'natural rights' with the conception of a free society, showed that they do not need to be self-evident; and both he and Hart concede that they may sometimes have to be overridden.

This last admission does however take 'natural rights' theorists down a slippery slope. If rights could be overridden simply on utilitarian grounds, that is, whenever overriding them would promote the 'greatest happiness (or greatest good) of the greatest number', they would be nugatory. As Waldron, following Dworkin, puts it,

> an individual has a right when there is a reason for assigning some resource, liberty, or opportunity to him even despite the fact that normally decisive considerations of the general interest (or other collective goals) would argue against that assignment. (Waldron, 1984, p. 17)

Utilitarians, by contrast, 'are necessarily and profoundly committed to ... trading off the interests in life and liberty of a small number of people against a greater sum of the lesser interests of others' (ibid., pp. 18–19).

To preserve this distinction, advocates of natural rights would contend, first, that even though a right were not absolute, a powerful case would have to be made before it could be overridden, which could mean requiring that those seeking to override it could not simply use their discretion but would have to convince an independent court or tribunal of the necessity for doing so; and secondly that, in overriding a right, the infringement should be kept to a minimum, the right should be restored as soon as the necessity for overriding it had passed and compensation should be paid for the transgression.

It is also argued that some rights are absolute. Gewirth (1984) proposes that a mother's right not to be tortured to death by her own son would be one. Thus even if terrorists credibly threatened to destroy a large city with nuclear weapons unless this happened, it would be wrong for the son to do it. The son would be responsible for the torture he inflicts but not for the lethal actions of the terrorists in response to his refusal to inflict it.

Gewirth's thinking, however, seems primarily concerned with the son's duty rather than the mother's rights. The latter would hardly be less totally violated if she were tortured to death by someone else. To echo Hart, if there are any 'natural rights' at all, the right not to be tortured, or delivered to a prospect of torture, is surely absolute.

Theories of rights (and especially of 'natural' or active rights) often present the individual as everything and society as nothing. As Milne shows, this is an exaggeration, which the broader concept of human rights, incorporating such 'passive' entitlements as those to food, shelter, medical attention and education, to some extent redresses, at least in principle. To claim that there are limits beyond which the individual's freedom and welfare may not be subordinated to what a government sees as the common good is hardly now disputable, though the contrary consideration posed by Mabbott's argument suggests that there should also be limits to the extent to which governments ought to be impeded from the promotion of genuinely common purposes by individuals invoking their rights. Nevertheless, it is difficult to disagree with the contention that, in this century, and particularly since the zenith of laissez-faire in the Great Depression of 1929 onwards, the grimmest outrages against humanity have, on balance, come more from an excess in the power of governments than from a deficiency in it. If that is conceded, the revived emphasis on rights represents a salutary trend.

See also JUSTICE.

Reading
Dworkin, R. 1978 (*1990*): *Taking Rights Seriously*, rev. edn.
Gostin, L. ed. 1988: *Civil Liberties in Conflict*.
Hart, H.L.A. 1955: Are there any natural rights? *Philosophical Review* 64, 175–91.
MacDonald, M. 1947–8: Natural rights. *Proceedings of the Aristotelian Society*, 35–55.
Melden, A.I. 1977: *Rights and Persons*.
Milne, A.J.M. 1968: *Freedom and Rights*.
Waldron, J. ed. 1984: *Theories of Rights*.

RODERICK C. OGLEY

ritual, political *See* POLITICAL RITUAL

role Denoting sequences of behaviour emitted by individuals occupying, or seeking to occupy, a particular position in a social situation, the concept of role has, of course, been borrowed from litera-

ture, and in more recent centuries, from drama. As such, individuals are viewed as playing characters and orchestrating their gestures in accordance with a script on stage in front of an audience of others who judge and evaluate their performance. As is examined below, each element of this portrayal of dramatic roles – individual actors assuming a character, orchestrating their gestures in a performance, following a script, acting on a stage, and playing for an audience – has been a point of debate among social scientists. Stated more positively, each of these elements has been the subject of considerable conceptual elaboration and empirical research, thereby refining the concept well beyond its more literary and dramatic connotations.

What is the nature of individuals who play roles? Several intellectual traditions – utilitarianism, BEHAVIOURISM, pragmatism, interactionism and PHENOMENOLOGY – have all influenced the conceptualization of those behavioural capacities of individuals that are crucial to playing roles. The composite portrayal that emerges produces an image of individuals as (1) possessing calculative, deliberative, and manipulative capacities; (2) seeking rewards and avoiding costs; (3) attempting to adjust and adapt to situations; (4) using implicit stocks of information about people and situations to do so; and (5) maintaining a conception of themselves as certain kinds of individuals. This imagery appears in all role theory and research, although some elements are more emphasized than others by varying researchers (J. H. Turner, 1991).

What is the nature of the characters that individuals assume? This question gets at the issue of what force or forces constrain individuals to act in certain ways. For some (Parsons, 1951; Linton, 1936, p. 28), the individual is seen as behaving in ways appropriate to incumbency in a status position in a system of interconnected positions comprising a social structure – worker, father, teacher, student, and so on. For others, individuals are viewed as behaving in ways, even when incumbent in a clear status position, to gain rewards, avoid costs and sustain self; and hence individuals are conceptualized as actively creating a character rather than just assuming one that is assigned by virtue of occupying a position (R. H. Turner, 1974 and 1962; Strauss, 1978). Because role is typically considered the point of interface between the individual person and the larger social structure, the stance taken on this issue implies very different views on humans and society (Handel, 1979). If role is behaviour associated with, and dictated by, incumbency in the positions of social structure, then humans are less spontaneous and creative, while the power of social structure is pre-eminent. In contrast, if role is behaviour emitted in negotiation with self, others' idiosyncratic needs or utilities, and positional prescriptions, then individuals are more ontologically significant than social structure.

What are the dynamics of gesturing? It was American pragmatist philosophers who made the initial breakthroughs on this topic. In particular, George Herbert Mead (1934) recognized that gestures mark people's dispositions, feelings and likely courses of action. For Mead, then, a role is a sequence of gestures denoting and highlighting an individual's dispositions and actions. Mead introduced the concept of role-taking to emphasize that as humans read each other's gestures, they take on each other's orienting perspective and, as a result, are better able to predict each other's actions. The phenomenologist Alfred Schutz (1932) made similar observations about humans' mutual reading of significant signs or gestures to achieve a sense of intersubjectivity. But, as all these early twentieth-century figures recognized, an individual reacts and interprets another's gestures through the prism of its own self, needs and stocks of accumulated knowledge. As a consequence, role-taking is always somewhat reflexive.

Not only do individuals role-take, but in Ralph H. Turner's (1962) terms, they role-make. That is, they orchestrate gestures in order to assert a role in a situation that meets their needs and affirms their self-conception. This process occurs even in highly structured situations where individuals in status positions will attempt to make for themselves a particular kind of role – good student, sensitive mother, hard worker and so on. Such capacity for role-making assumes that individuals – both those role-making and role-taking – have inventories of role conceptions in their stocks of knowledge. That is, individuals possess conceptions of syndromes of gestures marking certain kinds of roles; and individuals in INTERACTION reciprocally seek to find the underlying role denoted by another's gestures. There is some disagreement, however, over whether the roles in these inventories involve understandings of fine-tuned sequences of gestures or more loosely structured gestalts of gestures denoting more general and vague meanings that must be finalized during the course of role-making (see J. H. Turner, 1988; R. H. Turner, 1962).

What is the nature of the script guiding role behaviour? Some scholars (Parsons, 1951; Linton, 1936) argue that there are norms (expectations of appropriate behaviour) attached to each status position in a social structure; and so, roles are simply the behaviour of people in particular positions following a normative script. Others (R. H. Turner, 1962; Turner and Colomy, 1987; Handel, 1979) would not dispute that there are norms guiding behaviour, but would contend that norms are only broad parameters within which individuals make roles confirming self and meeting their needs. And, if there is a script to the interaction, it is more likely to be the inventories of roles that individuals carry and use in role-making and role-taking. Still others (Blumer, 1969) would go even further and view norms as one of many objects in a situation that individuals may, or may not, take account of when mapping out a line of conduct.

One of Erving Goffman's (1974) last important theoretical ideas was the notion of frames, which are cognitive enclosures (much like the physical material around a picture) that individuals use to delimit the range and type of responses in their roles. Interaction involves, Goffman argued, the keying and rekeying (that is, framing and then reframing) of an interaction, shifting the roles to be played as the frame is changed. For example, when a conversation shifts from polite talk to more personal intimacy, there has been a shift of frames which, in turn, rewrites the script for each actor in their role-playing. Others have extended Goffman's ideas in ways that posit certain basic types of frames and keying processes (J. H. Turner, 1988).

What is the nature of the stage? Beginning with Emile Durkheim's (1912) early twentieth-century discussion of religious ritual, several thinkers have extended the analysis of how co-presence, per se, influences the course of normal interaction. Erving Goffman (1967, 1959) was the first to recognize that the distribution of actors in space, their positioning, their movements on social stages, and their use of physical props determine what roles people play and how they want to present themselves to others. More recently, Randall Collins (1988, pp. 223–6, and 1975) has borrowed from both Durkheim (1912) and Goffman (1959) to emphasize that ritual behaviour in normal interaction settings is influenced primarily by the density of individuals co-present on stage and by patterns of inequality in their respective resources (for example, the greater the density and inequality among individuals, the more everyday rituals are formal, explicit, stereotyped and short term).

What is the nature of the audience? Obviously, the individuals co-present in a situation are an audience; and depending on staging requirements, they influence role behaviour – role-taking, role-making, framing, ritual and awareness of norms. However, in a vein converging with Durkheim's (1893) analysis of the collective conscience, George Herbert Mead (1934) argued that individuals not only role-take with others who are present in a situation but also with others who are not present and, moreover, with communities of attitudes or generalized others. These specific others who are not physically co-present and these generalized others who personify the perspectives appropriate to a situation constitute an important part of the audience for individuals' self-evaluations and role-playing on stage. These ideas fostered a large research tradition on reference groups, which are those varying types of groupings that individuals employ as a frame of reference for self-evaluation and for mapping out courses of action (Hyman and Singer, 1968).

Thus social scientific work on roles has followed the analogy to drama and the theatre – perhaps more than is often recognized. In addition to this work on normal role processes, a large theoretical research tradition examines problematic and deviant role processes. Early work (Goode, 1960; Merton, 1957) focused on problematic situations, particularly those involving role strain (difficulties in meeting the expectations in the script for a role) and role conflict (incompatible demands among the various roles that individuals play). Another large research tradition has focused on deviant roles (crime, mental illness and sexual behaviours, for example) that violate general institutional norms about appropriate behaviour. Some research in this area emphasizes structural and cultural forces that push individuals into deviant roles (Merton, 1938; Quinney, 1979), whereas other work examines how micro interactions can label and channel people into deviant roles (Lemert, 1951; Goffman, 1961; Scheff, 1966).

In sum, then, the concept of role is one of the most central constructs in modern social science. It is viewed as the point where more inclusive social structures impinge on individuals, and reciprocally, as a central force in constructing behaviours that produce, reproduce, or change social structures. Work on role processes cuts across all the social sciences, although it is most prominent in sociological and social psychological work. While the lay connotations of a concept still influence how roles are conceptualized and researched in social science, the concept has been extended considerably beyond its original literary and dramatic usages.

See also SYMBOLIC INTERACTIONISM.

Reading
Bandon, M. 1965: *Roles: An Introduction to the Study of Social Behavior*.
Biddle, B.S. 1979: *Role Theory: Expectations, Identities and Behavior*.
Heiss, J. 1981: Social roles. In *Social Psychology: Sociological Perspectives*, ed. M. Rosenberg and R. H. Turner.
Stryker, S. 1980: *Symbolic Interactionism*.
Turner, J.H. 1988: *A Theory of Social Interaction*.
——1991: *The Structure of Sociological Theory*, 5th edn, chs 18–23.
Turner, R.H. 1968: Role: sociological aspects. In *International Encyclopedia of the Social Sciences*, vol. 13, ed. David L. Sills.
—— 1979: Strategy for developing an integrated role theory. *Humboldt Journal of Social Relations* 7, 114–22.

JONATHAN H. TURNER

S

science, philosophy of *See* PHILOSOPHY OF
SCIENCE

science policy   At the level of policy-making,
science policy is usually defined as those policies
which are designed to influence the allocation of
resources to scientific and technical activities, the
effectiveness of this allocation and the social consequences. At the level of academic research, it may
be defined as the study of these activities, drawing
on the history, economics, sociology and philosophy of science as well as on contemporary observation and analysis of the policy-making process.
There is no consistency of usage with respect to
technology. Some authors (and some governments)
confine the expression 'science policy' exclusively
to science in the narrow sense of the word. Others
use it to embrace both science and technology
policy. It is in this sense that the expression is used
here. Abortive attempts have been made at various
times to introduce other expressions, such as the
'science of science' (Goldsmith and Mackay, 1964)
or 'scientific policy', but they have generally fallen
into disuse. Most of those involved, whether in
theoretical analysis or practical policy-making, are
uncomfortable with expressions which might convey too strong an impression of certainty and
coherence in a very uncertain and controversial
area.

The emergence of science policy as a distinguishable and significant area of policy-making and of
academic interest was closely related to the professionalization and scale of various scientific and
technical activities, particularly research and development (R & D). Already in the seventeenth and
eighteenth centuries there were of course organizations such as the Royal Society, academies of
science, and other flourishing scientific societies
and journals (Price, 1963). Some of these were
recognizable as of national importance and there
were embryonic forms of patronage and government assistance even earlier than the seventeenth

century. The promotion of invention through
patent legislation and attempts to limit the transfer
of technical know-how also go back for many
centuries. But it was in the latter part of the
nineteenth century that the professionalization of
R & D activities and their rapid growth led to
pressure for a more consistent and methodical
policy formation process in the leading industrial
countries, notably Germany and Britain. Poole and
Andrews (1972) have documented this growth of
government involvement in the period from 1875 to
1939 particularly well with selected original source
material. Of special interest is the eighth report of
the Royal Commission on Scientific Instruction
and Advancement of Science, which in 1875
recommended the establishment of a Ministry of
Science and made various other proposals which
had to wait between 30 and 90 years before their
implementation.

However, government involvement with science
continued to increase before, during and after
World War I, spurred on both by trade competition
and by military rivalry. The establishment of
inhouse R & D laboratories, in the first place in the
German chemical industry in the 1870s but later in
many other industrial firms, intensified technological competition and accelerated the growth of
professionalism in a wide range of scientific and
technical activities. At the same time university
science departments and technical schools became
the object of greatly increased industrial and
government interest because of their dual role as
performers of research and the source of educated
professional scientific and technical personnel.

It was this new and rapidly growing complex of
government industrial and university scientific
activities which was the subject of the pioneering
book by J. D. Bernal on the *Social Function of
Science* (1939). Without doubt this was the most
influential book on science policy in the first half of
the twentieth century. The book is divided into two
parts which matched the scientific concerns of the
author and his commitment as a Marxist to political

action: 'What science does' and 'What science could do'. In the first part Bernal made an attempt to measure the scale of all R & D activities in Britain at that time. It was not until the 1950s that governments made the first official measurements of R & D, which have since become a regular feature of social statistics and an important tool of analysis in much science policy research. In the second part he proposed both a massive increase in the scale of R & D and related scientific activities and a redirection of resources away from military towards welfare and humanistic goals. His proposals for increasing the scale of R & D by at least an order of magnitude, although at the time they seemed farfetched and impractical, have in fact been implemented in most industrial countries since World War II. His fundamental proposals for the reorientation and reorganization of scientific activities still await implementation and remain the subject of deep controversy, ranging from the goals of industrial R & D in large corporations through to the social responsibility of scientists, the planning of science and the dangers of technocracy.

Bernal's ideas were heavily criticized (see, for example, Baker, 1942) because of his advocacy of planning and his rather uncritical admiration of Soviet science policy. However, his insistence on the necessity of a major government role in science policy and his somewhat utopian vision of the enormous potential contribution of science to overcoming poverty and underdevelopment have remained an abiding influence in science policy research. The awesome achievements of scientific research during World War II marked the universal recognition that science was now one of the most powerful influences in society generally and led to the acceptance of a greatly enhanced role for science policy, which would have been difficult to achieve in the prevailing prewar climate of ideas in most countries.

Advisory councils and committees proliferated in the 1950s and 1960s and it was not long before ministries 'of Science', of 'Education and Science' or of 'Science and Technology' became quite a normal feature of government. International organizations such as the United Nations Education, Scientific and Cultural Organization (UNESCO) and even more the Organization for Economic Cooperation and Development (OECD) played a very important role in the standardization of statistics (OECD, 1963a), and in stimulating policy research and the interchange of experience at

ministerial meetings (see, for instance, OECD, 1963b). They also organized a periodic review of the science policy of various member countries conducted by outside 'experts' (policy-makers and academic researchers), thus conferring on science policy some of the attention normally devoted to the economic, social and foreign policies of governments.

The growth of science policy research followed and interacted with this rapid growth of R & D and of science policy institutions. It was, and is, pursued both by scholars from a variety of disciplines (for instance, Merton, 1973; Nelson, 1987; Price, 1963) and increasingly by multidisciplinary research groups in universities or elsewhere (see, for instance, Spiegel-Rösing and Price, 1977). Whereas much of the early impetus came from physicists such as J. D. Bernal or biologists such as Julian Huxley, social scientists have become increasingly involved, often in multidisciplinary research groups such as the Science Policy Research Unit established at the University of Sussex in 1965, or at similar institutions in Manchester, Lund, Heidelberg, Karlsruhe, MIT, Limburg, Tokyo and other centres.

Among the many streams of research which have flourished in the 1970s and 1980s have been the growing attempts to use so-called 'output indicators' of science and technology, including bibliometric indicators of publication and citation, patent statistics and patent citation, measures of innovation and diffusion. Obviously such indicators are open to much misinterpretation and abuse, as well as providing helpful clues for policy-making. A great deal of research is therefore devoted to the critical assessment and development of these indicators (see, for example, *Research Policy*, 1987). As science policy research has matured it has also begun to have a greater reciprocal influence on other disciplines, as for example, in the reformulation of economic theory through the economics of technical change (Dosi et al., 1988).

See also SCIENTIFIC-TECHNOLOGICAL REVOLUTION; SOCIAL PLANNING.

Reading
Annerstedt, J. and Jamieson, A. 1988: *From Research Policy to Social Intelligence: Essays for Stevan Dedijer*.
Bernal, J.D. 1939: *The Social Function of Science*.
Dickson, D. 1984: *The New Politics of Science*.
Freeman, C. 1987: *Technology Policy and Economic Performance; Lessons from Japan*.
Krauch, H. 1970: *Prioritäten für die Forschungspolitik*.

Lakoff, S.A. 1966: *Knowledge and Power: Essays on Science and Government.*

Mowery, D.C. and Rosenberg, N. 1989: *Technology and the Pursuit of Economic Growth.*

Nelson, R.R. 1987: *Understanding Technical Change as an Evolutionary Process.*

Poole, J.B. and Andrews, K. 1972: *The Government of Science in Britain.*

Ravetz, J. 1971: *Scientific Knowledge and its Social Problems.*

Spiegel-Rösing, I. and Price, D. de Solla 1977: *Science, Technology and Society: A Cross-Disciplinary Perspective.*

CHRISTOPHER FREEMAN

science, sociology of *See* SOCIOLOGY OF SCIENCE

scientific management *See* FORDISM AND POST-FORDISM; INDUSTRIAL RELATIONS

scientific-technological revolution One of the most significant transformations in the modern era has been the revolution in science and technology in the twentieth century. It represents a fundamental transformation in science, in the linkage between science and technology and in the relationship between science and society. Differences from earlier times include the social mechanisms for supporting research, the environments in which researchers work, the ways in which they are recruited, the organization of scientific/technological research, the manner in which problems are formulated, chosen or assigned, and the reward structures that largely direct the quest for knowledge. In essence, the relationship between science and society has been altered substantially in this century, and one aspect of this has been increased efforts to link science more closely to technology in an attempt to achieve economic or other national goals.

As with most transformations affecting the intellectual sphere, it will take some time before its full import is recognized and interpreted. But even before the revolution has run its course it is clear that not only has science and technology been affected but so also has the whole process by which social thought takes form, and – indeed – perhaps the very substance of future social thought.

The earlier scientific revolution, at the beginning of the modern era, provides a useful basis for comparison. The revolution of the sixteenth and seventeenth centuries was a cognitive revolution.

Ways of thinking about nature, the kinds of questions asked and the methods of seeking (valid) answers were transformed. Before the scientists of this era, the scholastics reigned supreme – with their worship of ancient classical thought and their disdain for empirical work. With this scientific revolution came the formulation of theories (ideally expressed mathematically) testable against empirical observations (where possible obtained from experiments). Galileo's work in the seventeenth century was a pathbreaking contribution that stimulated, embodied and defined this scientific revolution. Political changes accompanied this cognitive revolution and ultimately science gained some independence from state (at the time, church) oversight.

Later, newer sciences emerged or matured but though these might have varied in perspective or approach from sciences established earlier, each was shaped to the theory–observation template, each was a product of the earlier revolution. Examples include epidemiology, medical science, and ecology. Similarly for the application of scientific methods to the study of society, including the use of purposively designed experiments of a social or economic nature. In this case, simplifying assumptions about the nature of social actors are made and the presupposition has been that social research guided by a suitably adapted theory–observation template could lead to a better understanding of social action – on the average – and society.

In contrast, the recent scientific and technological revolution has been entirely different in character. Beneath the bedazzling distraction of discoveries and inventions seemingly without end, there has been a revolution in organization. What has changed most radically in this century has been the social organization of science, and it is this that has constituted a fundamental transformation. Many of the trends leading up to the current revolution – such as greater specialization, closer coupling between science and technology and between science and the state – have been visible for some time. In this century, however, interconnected changes of a cumulative nature have produced a threshold effect – a revolution in science and technology.

In its general form this new revolution has been a consequence of the drive for rationality that has been a motive force in the rise of the West, especially since the Protestant Reformation (see also PROTESTANT ETHIC THESIS). Methods of accounting that made capitalist enterprise possible have been extended and applied, initially to technology and subsequently to science. Concepts once thought to belong exclusively to the world of business – contracts, time budgeting and time management, output, production runs, ownership, productivity, and so on – have come to figure prominently in the administration (now management) of science and technology. Moreover, in many societies, relevance – especially relevance to the economic prosperity of those contributing to the support of research through their taxes, whose degree of contentment may determine the fate of governments in democratic societies – has become a criterion of some importance in the evaluation of science.

The relentless pursuit of economic rationality has been nowhere as evident as in the bureaucratization of research. For individual scientists this has meant a transformation from independent explorers to employees positioned on hierarchical career ladders in large organizations, from wide-ranging generalists to ever narrower specialists, and from personal participants in self-regulating communities to anonymous members of large professional associations. (See also BUREAUCRACY.)

Historically, a number of factors have helped to fuel this revolution. For example, the recognition – particularly from early in the twentieth century – that technology and science could be harnessed to the production of weapons provided a stimulus to the revolution, and to a considerable extent steered its subsequent course. When scientists or engineers studying the nature of matter or materials could furnish expertise useful for designing war-winning weapons, little effort was required to convince governments to provide ample support. In addition, the belief that science and technology could enhance considerably the well-being of nations, as defined in material terms and measured with economic indicators, has served as a further stimulus to the transformation of science and technology. (See also ECONOMIC GROWTH.)

The result has been a science and technology that has received more financial support than ever before, in which research has been carried out in industrial or government laboratories to a much greater extent than previously, often with its direction determined beforehand by organizational mandate, or in fulfilment of contractual obligations. Research, inside universities as well as outside, has become team research to a large degree, and the scientific-technological enterprise justified in terms of production . . . of patents, of publications, of personnel. The focus of research has shifted from the scientific problem to the published paper or patent. Whereas in times past a scientist or technologist – an independent thinker – could have wrestled with a single problem for some years, the accountability demands on organizations (and on their employees), and the career aspirations of the men and women of science and technology, have combined to ensure widespread acceptance of numbers of publications or patents (and/or page counts or successful grant applications or contracts or citations or students) per year as valid indicators of adequate production rates.

Any consideration of the scientific-technological revolution of the twentieth century must recognize one of its main features – its apparent success. Whether problems have been assigned by capitalist corporations or by the state, or chosen for their relevance to the concerns of the day, disciplinary or societal, on the whole science and technology have been remarkably adept at offering widely accepted solutions.

A critical question, however, is whether this present social organization permits the kinds of transformations in scientific and social thought associated with pioneering scientists such as Copernicus, Kepler, Galileo, Newton, Faraday, Snow, Darwin, Mendel, Pasteur and Einstein, or with Adam Smith, Marx, Durkheim, Weber and other seminal social scientists.

As it becomes clear that the social organization of science and technology usually does not encourage – indeed that it often discourages – truly innovative work, a sobering thesis emerges. Put simply: as the human population – growing in numbers and in material consumption – pushes ever harder against the limits of the carrying capacity of the planetary ecosystem, serious problems appear and pressure increases on science and technology to produce solutions. As a result of the scientific-technological revolution of the twentieth century, mechanisms translate this pressure into demands for greater economic rationality – more accountability, more efficiency, more productivity – in the use of resources allocated by society for research. Higher levels of scientific/technological productivity may result, as measured by contemporary performance indicators, but so also do inevitably lower rates of significant scientific discovery and technological innovation. In the end, following the transformation in its social organization, science and technology cannot craft enough work of the quality needed to sustain industrial society. In essence, modern society contains within its core values the seeds of its own demise.

Viewed historically, the same rationality that made possible the industrial revolution in the West has spread from its initial – largely commercial – focuses to all other areas of society. No area has escaped its influence. Yet, pushed to its extreme, economic rationality leads to the consumption – without replacement – of the very resource that made possible modern society: the contributions of the scientists, the engineers, the independent thinkers impelled by unconstrained curiosity, by an interest in ideas for their own sake, by a passion to understand – or by similar 'irrational' motivations. Persons with these motivations have not disappeared, but the twentieth century revolution in social organization – affecting corporate and government laboratories, research institutes and universities – defines most people with these kinds of motivations as unproductive, unworthy of serious consideration or financial support, and – at best – marginalizes them.

Ultimately, the question is whether the social organization of science and technology – and of the creation of knowledge more generally – will allow any effective contribution to the fundamental revolution in social thought and societal values that would be required for the long-term survival of the human species, with a reasonable quality of life, within its natural environment. As science and technology are ever more securely harnessed to the production machinery of present-day capitalism, as the critical capacities of individual scientists, engineers and – more generally – intellectuals are increasingly anaesthetized (often by their own personal ambitions for success, or needs for survival, within the present system), as societies around the planet strive ever harder to emulate the mass consumption models of the materialist West, possibly remaining windows of opportunity close.

See also RATIONALIZATION; SOCIOLOGY OF SCIENCE; TECHNOCRACY; TECHNOLOGICAL CHANGE.

Reading
Bernard, C. 1865 (*1961*): *An Introduction to the Study of Experimental Medicine.*
Harré, R. 1981: *Great Scientific Experiments: Twenty Experiments that Changed our View of the World.*
International Sociological Association 1977: *Scientific-Technological Revolution: Social Aspects.*
Kanigel, R. 1986: *Apprentice to Genius: The Making of a Scientific Dynasty.*
Kuhn, T.S. 1962: *The Structure of Scientific Revolutions.*
Latour, B. and Woolgar, S. 1979: *Laboratory Life: The Construction of Scientific Facts.*
Lemaine, G., Darmon, G. and Nemer, S. 1982: *Noopolis: Les laboratoires de recherche fondamentale: De l'atelier à l'usine.*
Martin, B.M., Baker, C.M.A., Manwell, C. and Pugh, C. 1986: *Intellectual Suppression: Australian Case Histories, Analysis and Responses.*
Merton, R.K. 1973: *The Sociology of Science: Theoretical and Empirical Investigations.*
Pirsig, R. 1974: *Zen and the Art of Motorcycle Maintenance: An Inquiry into Values.*
Szent-Gyorgyi, A. 1971: Looking back. *Perspectives in Biology and Medicine* 15, 1–5.

ALDEN S. KLOVDAHL

scientism Since the rise of modern science in the sixteenth and seventeenth centuries, its advocates have claimed an especially authoritative status for its judgements and a universally beneficial outcome from its potential technical applications. An early expression of this enthusiastic optimism on behalf of science was Francis Bacon's utopian text *The New Atlantis*. The subsequent integration of science with the development of industrial and military technology led to successive waves of disillusioned hostility to science, in which its vision of nature was decried as impoverished and its practical project denounced as an exploitative, destructive, and self-defeating quest for mastery.

The term 'scientism' figures in the verbal armoury of the modern inheritors of this critique of science, but it is not exclusive to them. In its most widespread usage, the term reproaches any extension of science or scientific method beyond its legitimate scope. But just what constitutes this 'legitimate scope' is, of course, deeply controversial. For some, Western science as a whole is profoundly suspect, embodying a form of rationality and an orientation to nature which is intrinsically destructive and oppressive with respect to both its natural and human victims. On this view, prevailing patterns of social and cultural oppression are rooted in a projected domination of nature which is implicit in the very rationality of science. Another approach (characteristic of the neo-Marxist writers of the FRANKFURT SCHOOL of Critical Theory) recognizes a realm of legitimate application for the empirical-analytical methods of science, but denounces as 'scientistic' attempts to subordinate such disciplines as psychology, sociology and cultural analysis to this methodological regime. The wider political pertinence of this critique of 'scientism' derives from the view, also widely shared among the Critical Theorists, that the forms of reason associated with science, and the cognitive authority conferred on it, have become the primary sources of legitimacy in modern industrial societies. The appeal to expertise and the scientistic representation of inherently controversial moral and political issues as matters for technical calculation are associated with an ever-narrowing public sphere and the withering of democratic participation. At the same time the technical capacities of modern industrial societies to 'deliver the goods' *and* to manipulate the desires of mass consumers are tending to render all opposition seemingly irrational and nugatory.

Opposition to science as an intrinsically totalitarian form of social domination is also a widespread theme in poststructuralist thought, and especially in the work of Foucault, who links the formation of the human sciences with distinctively modern forms of social power in institutions such as the prison, the asylum and the hospital. It is arguable that the critiques of 'scientism' mounted both by Foucault and by the Critical Theorists fail to distinguish between science, on the one hand, and the utopian or dystopian projects of its propagandists, on the other. If science is employed in a predominantly oppressive and destructive way, this may be because it is employed in a *society* which is oppressive and destructive.

See also SCIENTIFIC-TECHNOLOGICAL REVOLUTION.

TED BENTON

sect At the root of most uses of the term 'sect' in the twentieth century is the notion of a voluntary collectivity which has separated itself from the mainstream of religious or political ideas and which jealously preserves its social, cultural and ideological exclusiveness. The implicit contrast is usually with the more inclusive and universalistic stance of the church type, with the 'denomination' representing a midpoint between the sect and the church. Church, sect and denomination, with refinements such as established sect and cult, have formed the conceptual framework for numerous studies of the organizational and ideological dynamics of religious groups.

Max Weber (1864–1920) emphasized the fact that membership of a sect was not only voluntary but also conditional on the display of specific qualifications. The role of charismatic leaders in some religious sects also formed a bridge to his theorizing about the functioning of all social organizations. And, in combination with its strict procedures for preserving purity, Weber (1920) credited the sect type of Protestant organization with the capacity to instil the kind of this-wordly asceticism which had a strong affinity with the spirit of capitalism in general and with the ethos of American small businesses in particular. Weber's colleague, Ernst Troeltsch, preferred to emphasize the capacity of the sect type of religious collectivity to foster particular kinds of 'social doctrines' (1912) which were distinct from those of the church type and of mysticism. This focus on the interplay between the sociological, the doctrinal and the ethical aspects of religious collectivities subsequently inspired many studies of the relationships between the exclusivism of religious sects and the social background, cultural tastes and political dispositions of their members (see, for instance, Niebuhr, 1929; Wilson, 1961; Beckford, 1975). There have also been attempts to explain the continuing popularity of such sects as Jehovah's Witnesses and Seventh Day Adventists, not only in Western Europe and North America but also in Latin America, Japan and Sub-Saharan Africa in terms of their offer of ethical and doctrinal certainty at a time of widespread religious indifference (Wilson, 1976) or in terms of their strongly communal forms of organization and activity (Lalive d'Epinay, 1969).

By extension, O'Toole (1977) has tried to explain the inner dynamics and the external relations of some extremist political organizations in terms of their sectarian characteristics; and Jones (1984) has observed sectarian tendencies in some psychotherapeutic groups. Thus, although the implicit contrast with the church type and with mysticism has lost much of its relevance in secularizing societies, the concept of sect can still serve as a useful point of reference in studies of exclusive religious, political and ideological organizations. The concept's usefulness has been further enhanced by Wilson's (1970) specification of as many as seven subtypes of sect and by attempts to understand the processes whereby only some types of sect appear to lose their exclusivism and become sufficiently pluralistic and tolerant to warrant the label of denomination (Yinger, 1970). There has been a tendency since the

1970s, however, to apply the terms 'cult' or 'new religious movement' to groups which depart from the religious mainstream without necessarily displaying high degrees of social, doctrinal or ethical exclusivism (see, for instance, Wallis, 1975 and 1976; Westley, 1983). Nevertheless, in advanced industrial societies where organized religion has lost much of its former power, the activities of dynamic, and in some cases intolerant, sectarian groups have elicited hostile responses and strenuous efforts to control them. In particular, sociological attention has focused on the ways in which the mass media portray sectlike movements and on the dilemmas facing agencies of putatively secular states which intervene in religious controversies (Wallis, 1976; Beckford, 1985). This new focus for studies of the sect type weakens the concept's links with theology and ethics.

The concept of sect has also been applied to forms of religion other than Christianity, but the results are mixed. On the one hand, the concepts can serve as useful shorthand summaries of complicated configurations of doctrines, ethics and forms of organization. But, on the other, they illicitly smuggle Christian assumptions into the analysis of cultures that actually rest on very different foundations. So, while there are undoubtedly sectarian characteristics (such as separatism and exclusivism) in some reform movements in Hinduism (Bhatt, 1968) and Buddhism (Ling, 1980), it would be misleading to expect them to conform in other respects with the ideal-type of a Christian sect.

See also RELIGION; REVIVALISM.

Reading
Beckford, J.A. 1975: *The Trumpet of Prophecy: A Sociological Study of Jehovah's Witnesses.*
—— 1985: *Cult Controversies: The Societal Response to the New Religious Movements.*
Wallis, R. 1976: *The Road to Total Freedom: A Sociological Analysis of Scientology.*
—— ed. 1975: *Sectarianism.*
Wilson, B.R. 1970: *Religious Sects.*
—— 1976: *Contemporary Transformations of Religion.*
—— ed. 1967: *Patterns of Sectarianism.*

JAMES A. BECKFORD

secularism   The doctrine can be defined as the attempt to establish a body of principles concerning human behaviour based on rational knowledge and experience rather than THEOLOGY or the supernatural. It essentially seeks to improve the human condition by material means alone, and achieved its greatest success in Britain in the nineteenth century following the passing of the 1832 Reform Bill. It was a protest movement, espousing a positivistic theory of knowledge linked to a utilitarian philosophy, and reacting against the hegemony of wealth and established religion which prevailed in the middle years of the century. Its major proponent was G. J. Holyoake (1817–1906) who, although brought up in a religious, artisan family, became an Owenite 'social missionary' and avowed agnostic, with close associations with the Co-operative Movement (Waterhouse, 1920).

Secularism as a doctrine was not atheistic, although some of its later success was due to its associations with the anti-religious movements of the late nineteenth century through the work of Charles Bradlaugh. In some ways it is better seen as part of the disestablishment thesis springing from the reformation. There are close similarities with the French concept of laicization arising from the outcomes of the Enlightenment and the French revolution (Bosworth, 1962). Church and state became clearly separate entities, with the state holding a position of religious neutrality, rather than pursuing an anti-religious philosophy.

In France, the constitutional separation of church and STATE was only completed early in this century. Religious instruction in state schools had been abolished in 1882 and replaced by general ethical instruction. Similar occurrences took place elsewhere, notably in some 'third world' countries (Smith, 1971), Turkey (Beckes, 1964), Japan (Bellah, 1970), and of course the USA (Parsons, 1958). Secularism seen as laicization is therefore conceived of as a doctrine of complete freedom and non-interference from religions.

Elsewhere, however, secularism was more closely associated with conscious attempts to replace religion with a reliance on human reason and experience. This can be found, for example, in the work of Saint-Simon and Auguste Comte in the late nineteenth century, who developed a new religion of humanity and saw society reorganized on rational, positivist principles. Max Weber saw technological development as transforming not only the physical world of space and matter but human beings themselves. This disenchantment of the world means that individuals come to master their environment without recourse to the supernatural. Such a process of rationalization is anti-religious, an inexorable part of the development of a society rooted in the Judaeo-Christian tradition.

Present-day society still has its unbelievers who fail to experience the sacred or to feel subject to its authority. To what extent they stem directly from the secularist movement of the previous century is a more difficult question. Secular movements such as communism, or humanism, have been cited as examples of modern manifestations of secularism (Glock, 1971; Campbell, 1971). However, the functional similarity between such examples and the religion of which they are a secularized form make it more difficult to decide whether irreligion and unbelief are truly the heirs to Holyoake's legacy.

See also RATIONALIZATION; SECULARIZATION.

Reading

Campbell, C. 1971: *Towards a Sociology of Irreligion.*
Caporale, R. and Grumelli, A. eds 1971: *The Culture of Unbelief.*
Holyoake, G.J. 1896: *The Origin and Nature of Secularism.*

PETER E. GLASNER

secularization As the concept is conventionally defined, it describes ways in which religious thinking, practice and institutions lose their social significance (Wilson, 1966). Such a definition assumes that there existed a point in history when these aspects played a significant role in social life. It also implies that this is no longer the case. Many writers, particularly sociologists of religion, have commented on the difficulties of using such a concept, since it is necessarily closely related to definitions of religion and religious change over which there is much disagreement. In fact, secularization has come to be seen as a multidimensional concept encompassing the variety of forms of religious involvement in society within a unified, classificatory framework (Dobbelaere, 1981).

Most definitions of religion fall into one of three categories, institutional, normative, or cognitive, which provide a basis for discussing the variety of meanings subsumed under the secularization process. Thus an example of religion defined in primarily institutional ways is that located in the Judaeo-Christian tradition and called a church. Many of the mystic religions of the East, on the other hand, are based upon normative rules of behaviour. Cognitive definitions of religion allow such concepts as the sacred to provide the basis for religious organizations. The processes of secularization which relate to these three different views of religion will also vary, providing one basis for an

early plea to dispense with the concept altogether because of the confusion it engenders (Martin, 1969). Another concerns the doubtful methodological underpinnings of the concept: idealization of the past; assumptions about religious homogeneity within society; and a preoccupation with the historical categories of religious experience (Glasner, 1977).

Several forms of secularization stem from a definition of religion in primarily institutional terms, including the conventional one of decline mentioned above. The major variables used to discuss the process normally include formal religious practices, denominationalism, ecumenicalism and the liturgical movement. Religious practice is seen to encompass such aspects of conventional Christianity as baptism, confirmation, marriage, Sunday School attendance, Easter Communicants, and church membership and attendance. These are used as indices to chart the overall decline in religious practice since the Industrial Revolution. Denominationalism, while possibly a sign of religious revival at its inception, provides, at least in Britain, an example of a process of secularization starting with the Reformation. Since weak rather than strong organizations seek amalgamation, the ecumenical movement is a further example of the secularization process, compounded by the call for a return to traditional, professional standards of worship exemplified in the liturgical movement.

Another form of secularization, based on institutionally defined religion, relates to the dichotomy of church and SECT first discussed by Max Weber (1904–5) and Ernst Troeltsch (1931). The church is defined in the limiting case as an integral part of the existing social order. This is typically rejected by sectarian organization which strongly objects to the necessary routinization which church organization implies. Later writers have extended this typology to suggest that sects are the least secularized, and churches and denominations the most secularized forms of religious organization (Herberg, 1955).

A more evolutionary view of the secularization process sees it as a form of differentiation as society develops and becomes more complex. It argues that religious organization becomes less hierarchical as society becomes modernized, symbolism becomes more varied, individualism more significant, and hence institutional religion finally atrophies (Bellah, 1964). Underlying this discussion of societal evolution was the view that the social and religious communities, once identical, become differentiated so that the secular aspects of life emerge with a new order of religious legitimation.

A related view of the secularization process, developed from a definition of religion rooted in the normative sphere, concentrates on the increased generality of the religious dimension in society rather than its institutional differentiation. Thus religious norms and values are said to exercise low-level specific prescriptions regarding social behaviour in traditional societies, when almost everything from details of the cosmetics used or the clothes worn by ordinary people was judged in religious terms. In modern, secularized, societies a generalized, overarching integrative system which recognizes differentiation and diversity is more appropriate. Thus an all-embracing, unified church is replaced by a civil religion (Bellah, 1967) or, in America, a tri-faith system of Protestant–Catholic–Jew (Herberg, 1955).

Other forms of overarching normative systems have been used to illustrate a process of secularization based on the transformation of religious values, grounded in divine power, to specifically worldly ones. The emancipation of capitalism from ethical control is just one example, where the driving force of the Puritan ethic gave rise to a sober and regulated life devoted to the accumulation and investment of wealth (see PROTESTANT ETHIC THESIS). The Protestant emphasis on individual liberty and independence of thought transforms religious authority over such aspects of life as morality, education, work, into a secular state (Troeltsch, 1912).

Secularization which stems from cognitively based definitions of religion is a process of change using perhaps the most overworked distinction in this area of social thought: society is seen to move from being primarily sacred in character, with associated elements of ritualism, tradition, communality and harmony, to being primarily concerned with the secular or profane, where individuality, rationality and specificity reign. This distinction is linked to a continuum from *Gemeinschaft* to *Gesellschaft* (Tönnies, 1887), mechanical to organic solidary ties (Durkheim, 1912), and folk to urban society (Redfield, 1947). However, no single society exhibits either polar type to the exclusion of all else, so that different balances and mixes give rise to the empirical diversity found in world history.

It is therefore clear that secularization is by no means a unitary concept in twentieth-century social thought. Its various manifestations arise both from its relationship to different definitions of religion, and to the methodological limitations posed by attempting to operationalize it. The careful use of the term in a generic fashion based on a broad system of classification could, however, provide the basis for its continued inclusion by social scientists in their conceptual armoury.

See also EVOLUTIONARY PROCESSES IN SOCIETY; RATIONALIZATION; SECULARISM.

Reading
Bellah, R.N. 1970: *Beyond Belief: Essays on Religion in a Post-Traditional World.*
Dobbelaere, K. 1981: Secularization: a multi-dimensional concept. *Current Sociology* 29.2.
Fenn, R.K. 1978: *Toward a Theory of Secularization.*
Glasner, P.E. 1977: *The Sociology of Secularization: A Critique of a Concept.*
Luckmann, T. 1967: *The Invisible Religion: The Problem of Religion in Modern Society.*
Martin, D.A. 1978: *A General Theory of Secularization.*
Wilson, B.R. 1976: *Contemporary Transformations of Religion.*

PETER E. GLASNER

self-management The equivalent of the French *autogestion* and the German *Selbstverwaltung*, this is a form of self-determination of human beings as autonomous and conscious beings depending on concrete social conditions; such conditions include a given structure of production, the social and technological division of labour, political institutions, the level of culture, and the prevailing traditions and habits of human behaviour. Self-management should be considered, from the philosophical point of view, as a process aiming at overcoming the alienation of human powers within social relations.

Self-management is a key notion for the theory and praxis of 'economic democracy' or INDUSTRIAL DEMOCRACY. Applied more widely to global society, it is at the basis of 'participatory democracy' (see PARTICIPATION) or 'self-governing socialism'. In the first case we are usually speaking of workers' self-management; in the second, of social self-management. But in both spheres, productive and political, there is an increasing demand of the people for more control and power within social organizations, mostly in the form of the WORKERS' COUNCIL or the citizen's council.

Workers' self-management
This means the full participation of the producers (workers and employees) in managing all essential

functions of the process of production within the enterprise (planning, execution, control and disposal of the products). The basic ideas of workers' self-management were elaborated by the utopian socialists (Robert Owen, François-Charles Fourier, Pierre-Joseph Proudhon), by Karl Marx, by anarchists, guild socialists, the 'council communists' and others, and focused on the following themes:

1 the idea of the withering away of the state and its replacement by a 'free association of the producers'; hence decentralization of productive and political organizations;
2 the idea of the 'expropriation of the expropriators', the owners of the means of production (private owners as well as state capitalism), and direct control of workers' councils over the produced surplus value or surplus labour;
3 the idea of abolishing the technological division of labour or 'fragmented labour' and the crippling of the workers' personality. In opposition to Taylorism and Fordism, democratic and socialist theories emphasize personality growth, the development of individual potential and efficiency, and mental health in the context of a work community.

Participation and industrial democracy
In the recent sociological and political literature the term 'industrial democracy' has come to be used as the standard term for all forms of company management where the employers give greater importance to 'human relations', 'social climate' or 'human management', though often without affecting the system of relations based on rank and power distribution. It is concerned essentially with more democratic behaviour within the given formal organizational structure. But more precisely used, the term encompasses many different forms of participation of workers and employees in decision-making within the firm.

In 1967 an International Labour Office commission in Geneva noted that it was extremely difficult to arrive at a universally acceptable definition of participation. Concretely this notion makes it possible to estimate

the influence of workers on the preparation, making and follow-up of decisions taken at the undertaking level in various matters (such as . . . wages and conditions of work, discipline and employment, vocational training . . . technological change and organization of production, as well as their social consequences, investment and planning etc.), by methods as different as joint consultation and communications, collective bargaining, representation of workers on managerial bodies and workers' self-management . . . (ILO, 1981, p. 6)

Many typologies have been elaborated concerning different systems of participation, taking particularly into account:

1 decisional machinery (the preparation, taking and implementation of decisions);
2 organizational arrangements (at the level of the individual job, workshop, firm, industrial sector, the economy);
3 production relations (general questions, social questions, organizational and technical matters, economic matters and so on);
4 legal status (collective contracts, laws, constitution). For instance, German codetermination (*Mitbestimmung*) has been legally established in the constitution, but generally there are special laws or collective arrangements.

It is important to understand that all these typologies are founded on a historical process going from partial to full participation; that is, to full control of the productive process by workers' councils. But the process itself is controversial from the point of view of radical or reformist thinkers. The radicals claim that any form of 'participation' is a form of compromise with the class enemy and propose to replace it by the term 'workers' control' as conforming more closely with the sense of class struggle. But in practice they do not propose to abolish already achieved levels of participation. It seems that the new trade unionism (Coates and Topham, 1975) is more adequate to the general movement of the actual working class when it speaks of reformist means with a radical goal, attaining self-management by different forms of participation, or 'revolutionary reformism' (Gorz, 1980).

Some confusion in the usage of the term 'industrial democracy' is possible if it is interpreted in the sense of codetermination, of equal rights of different organized parties or productive factors – employers, workers and the state – and not as equal rights of every individual involved in the productive process. It is only then – when the right of decision is extended to all those engaged in production as one of their basic human rights, and not simply as a result of the class struggle between labour and capital – that it is permissible to speak of self-management. Therefore G.D.H. Cole (1917) was right when he insisted that industrial democracy is a form of direct democracy, with active participation by all members of a social community in decision-making, while indirect democracy is another form of slavery.

Nationalization and socialization

Decentralization is a means of attaining direct democracy and replacing the controlling hierarchy by a coordinating hierarchy. Private property is a cause of hierarchical organization, but nationalization of the means of production is not always associated with the abolition of a hierarchical order. On the contrary, it can strengthen it, as is the case with state ownership in state socialism, which is highly centralized and hierarchical. Nationalization of the means of production by the state, regardless of whether the state is bourgeois or proletarian, means only the transformation of the state into a 'general capitalist' one, and, as Engels noted in a letter to August Bebel in 1891, even worse, the concentration of 'political repression and economic exploitation of workers in the same hand'. Consequently the theorists of workers' self-management emphasize socialization of the means of production and not nationalization. Private or state ownership should be replaced by social ownership, which signifies that the means of production belong to the society as a whole, to everybody and nobody. The work community and workers' council are obliged to manage the production as 'good managers', enjoying the right of use and of appropriation of benefits, but not the right of abuse (ius abutendi). Social property represents a special type of property with distinct legal, social and economic characteristics designed to make exploitation impossible, but in the light of experience in the former Yugoslavia, it has been widely discussed as being ambiguous and insufficiently precise in legal terms.

Participatory democracy

Industrial democracy, like any other kind of democracy, is a constitutional form guaranteeing human rights, in this instance the rights of the producer. The constitution, in giving a right to the individual, protects him or her from abuse from others, but does not, of course, guarantee anyone the capacity to exercise that right. It establishes formal standards and ideals of behaviour, but it is left to the freedom of individuals themselves to turn these into reality. They must be in some way educated for democracy, and that is the task of participatory democracy. It is a broader concept, rooted in a wide range of intellectual currents and traditions (including small group democratization, concepts of group therapy and of individual participation and self-education, religious movements such as the Quakers, movements inspired by Gandhi, and diverse socialist, libertarian and anarchist movements), to be implemented through group or community participation of autonomous individuals in a spontaneous manner. The motivation for collective projects must come from inside, and be a free identification and personal involvement. Hence this form of participation necessarily transcends any kind of particular organization, since organization and institutions tend to foster functional, depersonalized relationships. Participatory democracy could be considered as a method and as a deeper basis of democratic behaviour. It is an ideal and a doctrine intended to equip individuals for a democratic way of life without external constraints or repression.

Reading

Horvat, B., Marković, M. and Supek, R. 1975: *Self-Governing Socialism.*

Szell, György 1988: *Participation, Workers' Control and Self-Management.*

UNESCO 1986: *Participate in Development.*

RUDI SUPEK

semiotics The term was coined by John Locke to capture a long tradition of Western thought about signification, going back to Greek philosophy. In modern thought, semiotics refers specifically to twentieth-century theories of signs and sign systems, and their role in COMMUNICATION. Although some include in semiotics the study of natural signs – zoösemiotics for animal communication, and even phytosemiotics for networks of plants and connecting animals (see Sebeok, 1976; Krampen, 1981; discussion in Deely, 1990, chs 5, 6) – semiotics usually focuses on the study of *human* communication systems. Semiotics in this respect gives priority to language, or the linguistic code, which is used as a paradigm for other non-linguistic signs of widely differing cultural micro- and macro-phenomena of a specific or a general nature. It thus crosses the boundaries between the arts and the social sciences, creating an overarching framework for the study of sign systems, which include, apart from the linguistic, also, for example, the 'language' of gestures, of dance, fashion, music, pictures, traffic signs, architecture, cock-fights, kinship systems and so on (see, for example, the different semiotic analyses of Roland Barthes, Umberto Eco, Claude Lévi-Strauss, Clifford Geertz and others). Eco (1976) differentiates between specific and general semiotics. Specific semiotics aims at producing 'the grammar of a specific sign system', 'a given field of communicative phenomena, ruled by a system of signification'. General semiotics, in contrast, would attempt to find common systematic laws for all specific semiotics: 'A general semiotics is simply a philosophy of language which stresses the comparative and systematic approach to languages by exploiting the results of more local enquiries' (Eco, 1976, introduction).

Currently there are three main trends in semiotics, with considerable overlap, especially between the first two. *Semiotics*, in the tradition of the American philosopher C.S. Peirce, is part of logic and philosophy (see PRAGMATISM). Peirce and Morris (Morris, 1971) postulate a semiotic triangle of sign, object, and interpretant. Signs are differentiated as symbol (=a token for a type, such as a verbal utterance), index (for example: smoke as index of fire) or icon (a map or diagram, which has structural similarity to the object it represents). As a total system, semiotics was to connect 'natural' and 'artificial' signs.

Semiology usually refers to a European tradition based on the work of the Swiss linguist Saussure (see LINGUISTICS; STRUCTURALISM). Saussure postulated, though he did not himself develop, a new science of semiology that would study sign systems in society. (See the 1974 edition of Saussure, based on lectures from 1906 to 1911.) To Saussure, semiology was thus part of social psychology.

The terms semiotics and semiology are often used interchangeably; both words are based on the Greek word for 'sign', *semeîon*, though they differ in the prior role which Saussure, more than Peirce, gives to the linguistic paradigm in formulating the shared laws. Saussure's linguistic sign divides into two parts: the 'signifiant' (usually translated as signifier/sound-image/expression) and the signifié (translated as signified/concept/content). Signs are arbitrary, that is, the connection between signifier and signified is unmotivated and based on convention, not on any natural link between form and meaning (see FORMALISM).

Critique of the assumed independence of the linguistic sign from its context comes especially from *social semiotics*, an Anglo-Australian development based on Hallidayan linguistics (see for example Halliday, 1978; Hodge and Kress, 1988). Social semiotics explores more strongly the role of context, the interconnection between the social system and the way it is realized in language (=text) or other semiotic signs.

A social reality (or a culture) is itself an edifice of meanings – a semiotic construct. In this perspective, language is one of the semiotic systems that constitute a culture; one that is distinctive in that it also serves as an encoding system for many (though not all) of the others . . . 'language as a social semiotic' . . . means interpreting language within a sociocultural context, in which the culture itself is interpreted in semiotic terms – as an information system. (Halliday, 1978, p. 2)

Social semiotics traces the correspondence between social system and discourse/text where the latter is seen as the systematic realization of a 'meaning potential' (see DISCOURSE). Social semiotics in recent years has been influenced by the work of V. Vološinov and his critique of 'abstract objectivism' (i.e. structuralism) which dates back to 1929, but was only made available in English translation in 1973, insisting instead on the ideological nature of the sign (Hodge and Kress, 1988).

Reading
Deely, J. 1990: *Basics of Semiotics.*
Eco, U. 1976 (*1984*): *A Theory of Semiotics.*
Halliday, M.A.K. 1978: *Language as Social Semiotic.*
Peirce, C.S. 1931–58: *Collected Papers.*
de Saussure, F. 1906–11 (*1974*): *Course in General Linguistics*, ed. J. Culler.
Vološinov, V.N. 1929 (*1973*): *Marxism and the Philosophy of Language.*

ULRIKE MEINHOF

sex The term refers to sexuality, eroto-sexual reactions, motives and behaviours and their cultural representations (see also GENDER). In the nineteenth century it was conceived as an instinctual drive rooted in reproductive biology and only externally regulated by social and cultural norms. Contemporary sexology is a multidisciplinary field, a kind of equilateral triangle, uniting medicobiological, sociocultural and psychological perspectives. Different disciplines emphasize specific aspects of sex: physiological, evolutionary, anthropological, ethological, socionormative, cognitive, motivational, semiotic and so on. These approaches are complementary in spite of the old opposition between biological reductionism and sociological constructivism.

Human sexuality is not a simple biological given which can be explained in terms of reproductive biology. Even among higher animals sex is a multifunctional behaviour, presupposing some sort of socialization, social learning, etiquette. Even some elementary sexual reactions like erection or penile display may serve non-sexual purposes, signifying power relationships, aggression, friendliness and so on. Human sexuality is a kind of sociocultural, historical construct. Its forms and meaningful content are comprehensible only in the context of a socionormative culture as a whole, including gender stratification, stereotypes of masculinity and femininity, the language of emotions, representations of the body and rules of verbal decency. The distinction between eroto-sexual and non-sexual motives and actions both on the individual and social level is conventional, depending on the general values of a society. The rigid opposition of sexual and non-sexual attractions or of love and friendship is to a considerable degree the function of a traditional anti-sexual attitude, an attempt to isolate the tabooed 'base' erotic feelings and experiences from the other aspects of life. Not only can sexuality appear in non-sexual disguise, but 'it is just as plausible to examine sexual behavior for its capacity to express and serve nonsexual motives as the reverse' (Gagnon and Simon, 1973, p. 17).

Every society makes some kind of difference between the 'right' and 'wrong' kind of sex. These normative prescriptions are often formulated in medicobiological language so that morally or socially disapproved behaviour or orientation is labelled 'abnormal' and 'pathological'. But some behavioural patterns that are obviously dysfunctional or incorrect in one context, for example the context of reproduction or the maintenance of family relationships, can be quite functional and useful in another context (say, giving emotional satisfaction, a sense of well-being). Behind any normative definitions of 'right' and 'wrong' sexuality relations of power are always hidden, such as the social control of men over women, parents over children, the state over individuals. The struggle over these rules and definitions is the core of the whole history of sexuality.

At present this struggle is particularly sharp.

The 'sexual revolution' of the second half of the twentieth century is a result of several macrosocial trends, including the breakdown of a traditional system of gender stratification based on male dominance; changes in masculinity/femininity stereotypes and corresponding sex role prescriptions and expectations; increased instability and psychologization of marital relationships; new liberal attitudes towards the body and emotions; a general increase in social tolerance for individual differences and non-conformity; the weakening of parental, school and peer-group control over adolescent sexuality; earlier sexual maturation of adolescents; the progress in contraceptive techniques, especially the invention of the birth control pill, liberating women from the fear of unwanted pregnancy; the progress of sex research and education.

All these trends have a profound influence on sexual attitudes and behaviour. In all industrial countries young people are now beginning their sexual life earlier than did older generations. Attitudes towards premarital sexuality have become more permissive, and in most cases such relationships are considered socially and morally acceptable. Sexual satisfaction has become one of the most important factors in marital success and stability. Sexual techniques are becoming more sophisticated and diversified; people demonstrate higher demands, expectations and worries about the quality of their sex life.

The changes in women's sexuality are especially important. The age differences in the beginning of sexual life for boys and girls have been considerably reduced or have even completely disappeared. Women strongly object to the 'double standard' in sexual morality. As a result of more liberal social attitudes there is a continuous decline in the rate of female sexual frigidity and anorgasmia. Sexuality is becoming an important aspect of the new female social and personal identity.

The new tolerance is gradually changing the social status of sexual minorities. Homosexuality, instead of being treated as a moral vice or, later, an incurable illness, is now considered rather as a specific lifestyle and, whatever the causes of this sexual orientation may be, not to be used as a reason for social or moral discrimination or legal prosecution. In most European countries the laws against homosexuals have been abrogated, and gay and lesbian organizations, fighting for their human rights, have emerged.

Taken as a whole this process means individualization and personalization of sexuality, and a move from external social control to internal moral self-control. But these changes are not unilateral and are very contradictory. Sexual scripts have important gender, cohort, ethnic, cultural and other variations. The weakening of the social regulation of sexuality combined with inadequate information and knowledge has several undesirable social and psychological consequences: the rise in some countries of the rate of adolescent pregnancies and abortions, sexual abuse, epidemics of sexually transmitted diseases. Commercialized erotica help to manipulate human sexuality, and extensive contacts without love or emotional involvement are transforming sexual freedom into sexual alienation. The dangers of unrestricted sex are strongly emphasized by the AIDS epidemic, which has revitalized many old sexual anxieties and fears, provoking a situation of moral panic. Conservative people consider sexual liberation as a state of total moral disorganization leading to the self-destruction of culture and society. The alternative to these fears is the development of moral self-regulation and the promotion of an adequate sex education.

Reading

Foucault, M. 1976 (*1981*): *The History of Sexuality*. Vol. 1: *An Introduction*.
Freud, S. 1905 (*1949*): *Three Essays on the Theory of Sexuality*.
Geer, J.H. and O'Donohue, W.T. eds 1987: *Theories of Human Sexuality*.
Kon, I. 1985: *Einführung in die Sexologie*.
Money, J. and Musaph, H. eds 1977: *Handbook of Sexology*.
Reiss, I.L. 1986: *Journey into Sexuality: An Exploratory Voyage*.
Weeks, J. 1985: *Sexuality and its Discontents*.

I.S. KON

slums The movement of people into the towns in the early decades of the Industrial Revolution led to the creation of large areas of housing of poor construction, lacking in essential services and grossly overcrowded. These slums contrasted with neighbourhoods in preindustrial cities and rural villages in that rich and poor were markedly segregated. As a result the pejorative connotations of the term were transposed to the inhabitants of these slums. They were portrayed, by the more affluent, as people who had rejected the dominant norms and values of their society, rather than striven to uphold them.

Thus the distinction emerged between the 'deserving' and the 'undeserving poor' – the latter being termed also the 'disreputable poor' (Matza, 1966), the 'dangerous classes' (Chevalier, 1973) and in Marxist literature the 'lumpenproletariat'. Stereotypical characteristics of the slum dwellers included the breakdown of family structure and the lack of community organization. The consequent apathy led to high levels of unstructured violence and crime. Explanations of this behaviour ranged from attributions of individual moral weakness – to be rectified by education and/or punishment – to imperfections in the state of society, to be remedied by social reform (Waxman, 1977). The inevitability of the intergenerational transmission of these behavioural characteristics was popularized in Lewis's (1967) concept of the 'subculture of poverty'; he argued that in most conditions of POVERTY children were socialized at an early age into the values of their parents; the concept of 'cycles of deprivation' suggested that the multitude of interlinked problems faced by the very poor made their escape from poverty almost impossible. Both of these approaches have been widely criticized (see Leacock, 1970; Coffield et al., 1980).

As the nineteenth-century slum neighbourhoods have been cleared and redeveloped, they have been replaced by other forms of low cost housing, high rise apartments and so on, which have in turn become labelled with the same stigmatizing characteristics.

This image of the slum generated by nineteenth-century Western industrial development has not proved entirely appropriate to the growth of the Third World in the second half of the twentieth century. Here annual growth rates of 10 per cent a year have been common due both to massive in-migration from the rural areas and to a high birth rate consequent on the youth of the migrants. Some of these migrants find homes in decaying property in inner city areas, others in purpose-built tenements. But the supply of such housing is far exceeded by demand; the vast majority of recent migrants have been obliged to build their own houses in the city peripheries. These areas, designated shanty towns, squatter settlements and by a multitude of local terms, now house a half of the total population of many cities.

The shanty town population tends to be characterized by the more affluent of their society by the same pejorative attributes cited above. Studies of these areas have however revealed very different attributes and have led to the distinction between 'slums of hope' and 'slums of despair' (Stokes, 1962). Typical of the former are rural in-migrants aspiring to a better life, adhering as far as possible to the dominant social values, often engaged in vigorous community activity; contrasted are the latter, the home of those who see themselves as downwardly mobile, having failed to cope with the problems of urban life, and who evince those characteristics of apathy associated with this form of extreme poverty. The equation of shanty towns with slums of hope, and inner city areas with slums of despair is not necessarily valid; for as Turner (1967) has shown for some Latin American cities the typical in-migrant stays first in rented accommodation in the inner city to establish a 'bridgehead' and then 'consolidates' his position by building his own dwelling in a developing shanty town.

The sharp contrast between the degradation of the classic slum and the achievement orientation found in the shanty town is undoubtedly overdrawn. Just as there have been many inhabitants of the former who have not possessed the attributes stereotypically associated with extreme poverty, so too are there many shanty town dwellers who do. Wide variations in success in finding urban employment contribute to differential living standards and social attitudes. Within the shanty town social differentiation is resulting from the commercialization of the housing market as successful early residents become petty landlords, their tenants then being unable to accumulate savings sufficient to build their own homes.

The shanty towns have not become the 'flash points' of civil unrest, as was so widely predicted in the late 1960s. But tensions arising from poverty, itself manifest in poor housing, certainly exist, though they are frequently diffused through political clientage, community organization and ties of ethnicity, rendering inappropriate the labelling of the majority of the urban poor as 'disreputable' or 'dangerous classes'.

See also URBANISM.

Reading
Chevalier, L. 1973: *Labouring Classes and Dangerous Classes.*
Lloyd, P. 1979: *Slums of Hope?*
Rutter, M. and Madge, N. 1976: *Cycles of Disadvantage.*
Waxman, C.I. 1977: *The Stigma of Poverty.*

PETER LLOYD

social change   The twentieth century has seen massive social change, and it is not surprising to discover that the concept has dominated much modern social investigation. There has been a certain ambivalence in the way in which change has been seen. At the back of the minds of most theorists, on the one hand, has been the nineteenth-century Promethean expansion of collective power occasioned by the industrial revolution; this has led to an implicit assumption that change is 'good' and even natural, such that social orders which do not allow it are seen as somehow 'flawed'. But there have been a fair number of theorists, on the other hand, who have doubted the virtue of change, largely on the grounds that settled stability is a value as much chosen and as worth defending. This viewpoint has particularly appealed to those members of the modern intelligentsia who have felt displaced by the arrival of an age of mass literacy: the loss of prestige that has accrued has encouraged romantic and naive longings for various types of communitarian stability.

Most work in the area of social change has sought to explain the causes, nature and direction of social change. Some indication of the most important debates can be given by looking first at key twentieth-century theorists, then at recent theoretical advances and finally (and crucially) at social change outside the advanced industrial world.

Many concepts of social change have been put forward during the twentieth century: attention has variously been directed to acculturation, diffusion, technological innovation, DEMOGRAPHY and MIGRATION as key causes of social change. Some of these make undoubted sense, it being impossible, for example, to understand the creation of Israel without an appreciation of migration or to predict its future without paying attention to differential fertility rates. Nonetheless, the concept of social change is best approached by examining, in rough chronological order, a handful of important general theories.

The study of social change has been, and probably continues to be, dominated by evolutionary assumptions. This is scarcely surprising given that much modern thought is the child of the Enlightenment. In the optimistic liberalism of thinkers such as L. T. Hobhouse and J. A. Hobson, the course of social evolution would guarantee peace, prosperity and the spread of rationality. These hopes were badly dented by the geopolitical conflicts of the period from 1914 to 1945. In contrast, Marxist ideas (which share much of liberal hopes with the key exception of presuming that peace and prosperity only ensue in tandem with the socialist mode of production) gained in credence for the first half of the twentieth century, especially when periods of economic crisis seemed to suggest that the Soviet Union might be able to bring a prosperity that eluded capitalism. Marxism has an advantage over most evolutionary theories in any case since it can specify a mechanism, that of class conflict, by means of which social change takes place. The interwar years also witnessed the emergence of another great revolutionary force, that of fascism. In principle, this theory, especially in the work of Oswald Spengler, opposed social change – or, more precisely, it regarded all change as merely cyclical, without developmental import. In practice, however, fascism was a reactionary modernism seeking to combine preindustrial ideological certainty with modern technology. This was a powerful and unstable mixture.

Intellectual life depends on geopolitical events. After 1945 the study of social change has been dominated by American and by Marxist categories. American thought, as exemplified by Talcott Parsons, allowed for incremental reform but had little to say about (although much disapproval of) fundamental social change. This led to the emergence of various conflict sociologies, often influenced by Marx but more generally indebted to the work of Max Weber. However, the stability of the postwar era meant that no great advances were made in the study of social change.

Conceptual advances are now being made. The first advance concerns the impact of political forces. Social change does not, as both liberal evolutionists and Marxists presume, always emanate from socioeconomic conditions: rather, political events can force society to change. Thus geopolitical defeat in the war led to the democratization of both Germany and Japan. More generally, we are beginning to understand that the character of social movements often results from the regime with which they are in contact: there are few revolutions inside capitalism, but those there are, whether in agrarian or industrial circumstances, seem caused by political exclusion. The second advance concerns capitalism. Most social thought was produced in opposition to political economy, and sought to go

beyond it. But the speed of change within capitalism and the extension of its social reach are ever more striking. The relations between capitalist society and nation-states – the latter, crucially, having to find a way to live within the larger society of the former – constitute the agenda for study of social change at the present time.

Social change outside the European heartland and its cultural offshoots, that is, the search of Third World countries, especially since 1945, for development and security, is of unquestioned world historical importance. The establishment of such countries was the result of nationalism, probably the most striking single force for change in the twentieth century – albeit the remarkable maintenance of the borders established in 1945 is the result both of superpower stalemate and of generalized agreement on the norm of non-intervention. Much discussion has taken place as to whether the advanced economies control the Third World through informal economic means. That 'dependency theory' cannot be true in any complete sense is clear given the remarkable rise of East Asian industrialism. But there is very much truth to this general view precisely because so few countries have escaped DEPENDENCY; the exceptions, whose extraordinary social portfolios are now being investigated, prove the rule. Nonetheless, the economic weakness of most Third World states does not mean that they will not effect large-scale social change. Such countries will soon possess nuclear weapons: this is bound to influence economic arrangements.

Reading
Collins, R. 1975: *Conflict Sociology.*
Gellner, E. 1983: *Nations and Nationalism.*
Hoffer, E. 1963: *The Ordeal of Change.*
Mann, M. 1986: *The Sources of Social Power.* Vol. 1, *From the Beginning to 1760 AD.*
Smith, A.D. 1973: *The Concept of Social Change.*

JOHN A. HALL

social choice   How do and how should governments and other public agencies decide their actions? There are various accounts of how governments make decisions (see, for instance, DEMOCRACY; ELITE THEORY) but it is a basic liberal democratic presumption that governments should act in the interest of their citizens. The public interest, so to speak, cannot be defined independently of the interests of the individuals from whom the government gains its authority. This democratic formula works smoothly enough when public action is in the interests of all. But inevitably there are situations where the choice of action involves a conflict between the interest of one individual or group and another. It is these difficult cases that have set the agenda for discussions in social choice. Unsurprisingly, with the rise of democracy and the growth of the public sector in various forms, these discussions have rarely been far from the centre of debate in both politics and economics.

There have been two important modern approaches to the origin of the principles which should be used in the difficult cases. One involves an appeal to the ballot box. It constitutes a natural extension of the ideas of individual choice found in economics (see NEOCLASSICAL ECONOMICS and RATIONAL CHOICE THEORY) to politics. And it has also been very influential in some discussions of how governments actually make decisions (see, for instance, Downs, 1957; Riker, 1982; and PUBLIC CHOICE). Individuals are assumed to have preferences over the possible outcomes (sometimes termed ethical preferences as they refer to the outcomes for society and can involve an ethical judgement as to whose interests should be favoured). A constitution then aggregates them, via some mechanism of voting, to produce a social ordering of the possible outcomes. Thus, just as consumers acting on their preferences over commodities in markets produce a social valuation of different commodities in the form of a set of relative prices, so the individuals vote according to (ethical) preferences and the ballot box produces a social ordering of outcomes and with it a judgement over whose interests to favour.

This is attractive because it offers a procedural solution which avoids any commitment to the moral form of the good life. However, Arrow (1951) demonstrated an impossibility result which casts doubt on the coherence of this approach. When individual preferences satisfy the standard axioms of choice theory then no system of aggregating these preferences can guarantee to produce a social ordering which satisfies a set of apparently minimal conditions. Specifically, it cannot avoid inconsistencies of the form 'x is preferred to y and y is preferred to z but z is preferred to x', while at the same time satisfying simple conditions like nondictatorship and Pareto optimality (the Pareto principle in this context entails that if all individuals prefer 'a' to 'b' then 'a' should be preferred to 'b' in the social ordering). The simplest intuition

behind this impossibility result is that Arrow is generalizing the famous Condorcet voting paradox. (To appreciate this paradox, suppose there are three individuals with the following preference ordering over three outcomes $\{x,y,z\}$: $[x,y,z]$; $[y,z,x]$; $[z,x,y]$. Then the use of a simple majority voting system to decide between pairwise comparisons of $\{x,y,z\}$ will yield that 'x is preferred to y (since the first and third individual outvote the second), y is preferred to z but the majority also prefers z to x'.)

This has been an immensely influential result for democratic theory, but it has also been the object of sharp criticisms directed at its foundations in the utilitarian tradition of economics (Sen, 1982). Although the Arrow approach explicitly rejects the interpersonal comparisons of utility which might require a social choice utilitarian to countenance torture if it yields more utility for the torturer than disutility for the victim, it is still based on an ordinal utility representation of individuals and is capable of generating a similar sort of problem because, notoriously, the majority could always vote to produce tyranny over minority groups. What seems to be lacking is an acknowledgement that individuals are more than bundles of preferences: minimally, that they have rights which need to be respected.

These rights are central to the alternative contractarian approach to social choice. The hallmark of contractarianism is an argument which justifies an outcome by showing how individuals, endowed with rights like basic liberties, would have agreed to such an arrangement had they started from some hypothetical original contracting position. It is an attractive argument because it seems there could be little cause for complaint over government actions when it can be shown that individuals, had they been given the chance to negotiate, would have agreed to them. Nevertheless, its appeal can be deceptive. It does not dissolve many of the fundamental controversies in this area because there are various ways of specifying the original contracting position and the subsequent hypothetical agreements are extremely sensitive to these specifications. (See also SOCIAL CONTRACT.)

For instance, those who follow Rawls (1971) might suppose that social choice in the difficult cases where interests conflict involves a matter of justice, and since justice should be impartial, the original position for the derivation of these principles of justice should be characterized by a 'veil of ignorance'. Individuals should decide on what social outcome they prefer without knowing, among other things, which individual position they will occupy. Formally, individuals must decide under these conditions of uncertainty and Rawls argues that the appropriate decision rule is maximin, once a condition of equal basic liberties has been satisfied. This means social outcomes are judged according to the welfare of the worst-off person, with a consequent presumption in favour of equality. Indeed, individuals under this rule will only choose a social outcome where there is inequality when the worst-off member under that arrangement is made better off than would be the case under an outcome with greater equality. Thus, a Rawlsian approach to justice when applied to social choice often seems to sanction interventionist state activities designed to promote equality.

This is a controversial implication. Firstly, it is not obvious that maximin commends itself as the appropriate decision rule for conditions of uncertainty. There is a stronger claim in the economics literature or rational choice theory for an expected utility maximization rule, and its use could restore a species of utilitarianism (Harsanyi, 1955). Secondly, it presumes that governments should decide whose interest to favour when conflicts arise. In other words, it presumes that justice demands some type of state intervention, whereas it has been famously argued by Robert Nozick (1974) that a system of justice based on rights requires nothing of the sort.

Nozick's original position is defined by a Lockean state of nature (roughly a state where individuals can enforce their rights to their property, including their labour, so long as this does not infringe another's rights); and he argues that individuals will contract with each other to form a state which upholds property rights, but no more. Specifically, any attempt by the government to follow a redistributive programme will contravene the fundamental right of individuals to dispose of their time and property as they see fit. It will upset or undo the actions which individuals have freely undertaken and thus constitutes an infringement of the rights of that individual.

Thus, the contractarian approach has not settled the disputes in social choice since its arguments can license both an interventionist and a minimal state. Nevertheless, what has been revealed by the recent contractarian turn of argument is the sensitivity of social choice to both the presumed model of

individual decision-making and to what is regarded as the relevant relationship between individuals in some original position.

Reading
Arrow, K. 1951 (*1963*): *Social Choice and Individual Values*.
Buchanan, J.M. 1986: *Liberty, Market and the State*.
Downs, A. 1957: *An Economic Theory of Democracy*.
Hamlin, A. 1986: *Ethics, Economics and the State*.
Harsanyi, J.C. 1955: Cardinal welfare, individualistic ethics and interpersonal comparisons of welfare. *Journal of Political Economy* 63, 309–21.
Nozick, R. 1974: *Anarchy, State and Utopia*.
Rawls, J. 1971: *A Theory of Justice*.
Riker, W.H. 1982: *Liberalism against Populism*.
Sen, A. 1982: *Choice, Welfare and Measurement*.
Sugden, R. 1981: *The Political Economy of Public Choice*.

SHAUN P. HARGREAVES HEAP

social contract   Any agreement between independent individuals concerning the basic institutional arrangements which are to determine their social or political relationships constitutes a social contract. The agreement may be between all relevant persons, or between one person (the potential sovereign) and all other persons, or it may involve agreements between pre-existing groups. The concept is used to explain, justify or deduce the positive rights and obligations which naturally autonomous persons have in relation to each other within a society and/or a state.

The idea of social contract exemplifies many of the presuppositions of traditional liberal political theory. Thus, a recent commentator suggests that social contract theory is *voluntaristic* (in that political authority 'depends on acts of human will'), *consensual* ('the theory postulates a consensus of wills among all those subject to a given legitimate authority'), *individualistic* ('grounding legitimate political authority on its acceptance by individuals') and *rationalistic* (in that the individual wills which reach consensus are rational rather than wilful) (Lessnoff, 1986, pp. 6f.).

In the early twentieth century it was assumed that social contract theory had rightly been discarded because of its erroneous historical and sociological assumptions and on account of its philosophical failure to provide an account of the basis of the foundational obligation to abide by the original social contract. Recently, however, the social contract approach has been revived in various forms.

In a tradition stemming from the seventeenth-century political philosopher Thomas Hobbes (1651) the social contract approach is once again being utilized as a way of reconciling egoistic individualism (according to which the rational person seeks, or ought to seek, only his or her own welfare) with the acceptance of defined and limited societal obligations (as being in the long-term interests of those involved). This transfers to the general social and political sphere economic models relating to the free market, where contractual relationships between individuals are central. In what is called collective choice theory, Buchanan and Tullock (1962) explore the decision procedures which are relevant to the determination of when it is rational for egoistic individuals to accept the restrictions involved in collective action.

In a less egoistic vein, derived from the Enlightenment theories of Locke (1690), Rousseau (1762) and Kant (*1977*), the methodology of social contract theory has also been used to underpin a modern liberal theory of JUSTICE which combines a commitment to strong individual rights with extensive redistributive mechanisms (Rawls, 1971).

Modern social contract theorists accept that there was no actual historical contract pre-dating the origins of social or political life, and rely instead on the idea of a hypothetical contract which is explicated in terms of what rational (and perhaps well-informed and impartial) persons would have agreed to in specified circumstances. Rawls, for instance, postulates an imaginary 'original position' in which generally knowledgeable, free and equal individuals agree on the basic institutions of society without knowing their own personal characteristics or what place they will occupy in such a society (the 'veil of ignorance') (Rawls, 1971, pp. 118–94). This formulation abandons the idea that individuals have societal and political obligations only if they have actually made certain undertakings and substitutes for it the more nebulous idea that what *would* be agreed in certain circumstances determines or explains what is obligatory independently of whether or not all or any actual individuals have made such agreements. In this way morality is analysed as a combination of long-term self-interest and impartiality or fairness. The practical implications of this approach may be difficult to distinguish from those of classical utilitarianism (to which contract theory is normally contrasted as giving more protection to individuals and minorities). Further, the hypothetical contract approach cannot easily explain why people conform to the require-

ments of such morality when it is not in their (even long-term) interests to do so (Gauthier, 1977), although it may explain why they sometimes have good reason to do so.

A more historically oriented form of hypothetical contract is set out by Robert Nozick (1974) who follows Locke in accepting that individuals have some presocial natural rights, such as the right to life, and constructs a conjectural history depicting what such individuals could have agreed to without violating each other's rights. He concludes that they would consent to a libertarian or minimal state, but nothing beyond that. No contractarian (or other) justification or explanation is given for the presupposed natural rights.

Nozick's theory is characteristic of contemporary social contract theory in being justificatory or normative rather than descriptive or explanatory, although it is usually assumed that there is sometimes empirical overlap between the asocial situations in which the contract is said to take place and the realities of actual social and political life. Hypothetical contract theories do not avoid the epistemological problems which arise concerning our alleged knowledge of the content of the contracts in question and the prescriptive outcomes of applying the social contract methodology tend to reflect the values of their users.

Reading
Barker, E. 1947: *Social Contract*.
Lessnoff, M. 1986: *Social Contract*.
Macpherson, C.B. 1962: *The Political Theory of Possessive Individualism*.
Rawls, J. 1971: *A Theory of Justice*.
Scanlon, T.M. 1982: Contractualism and utilitarianism. In *Utilitarianism and Beyond*, ed. A. Sen and B. Williams.

TOM D. CAMPBELL

social control The concept describes the capacity of society to regulate itself and the means by which it induces conformity to its own standards. It rests on the belief that order is not maintained only, or even mainly, by legal systems or formal sanctions but is the product of wider social institutions, relationships and processes.

Social control has, historically, been a central concern of sociology, arguably barely separable from the term sociology itself. The main issue for social control theorists was how to achieve a social order consistent with moral principles without imposing an excessive degree of coercive control. According to this view, all social problems were at base problems of social control. This view was developed in the 1950s by sociologists such as Paul Landis whose concept of social control derived from a highly conservative vision of society. Traditionally, order in society was the product of a deep-seated consensus maintained without any conscious effort on the part of any particular group in society. As the bonds of traditional society such as church and family weakened and the disintegrating forces of modern industrial, urban life proliferated, consensus became increasingly fragile. Maintaining continued stability through social control became, in Landis's view, 'the major problem of our time'. Seen in this way social control is barely distinguishable from SOCIALIZATION.

If socialization is the informal process by which individuals come to learn and adhere to social norms (see NORM), social control comes into play when these means fail to ensure conformity. To illustrate: socialization might entail internalization of norms through peer group opinion, social pressure or familial expectations. Social control, too, may operate informally through family, church or school or formally through the state, the legal system, the police or other instruments of force. Mechanisms of social control, according to Talcott Parsons, operate as 'secondary defences' to combat deviance which, if left unchecked, might disrupt the social equilibrium (see also CRIME AND DEVIANCE).

A more negative usage of the term was adopted in the 1960s by radical sociologists seeking to explain how authority is maintained in a conflict-ridden society. New sociologists of deviance inverted Parsons's premise that social control was a response to deviance, arguing instead that 'the reverse idea, i.e., that social control leads to deviance, is equally tenable and the potentially richer premise' (E. Lemert quoted in Donajgrodzki, 1977, p. 13). Social control was not merely a reactive or reparative force which came into play when other mechanisms failed but instead actively created deviance. Howard Becker, for example, using Emile Durkheim's concept of social solidarity, argued in *Outsiders* that institutions of social control create 'outsiders', be they criminals, the mentally ill, religious or racial minorities who serve both as social scapegoats and also as the outer boundaries of 'respectable society'. This radical view was readily embraced by movements such as anti-psychiatry, anti-medicalization and de-schooling.

Social historians, too, have been eager to embrace the concept as a means of understanding the mechanisms by which the working classes were conditioned into accepting and adopting the norms and conduct necessary to sustain the rapid industrialization of society. F.M.L. Thompson, for example, characterizes historians' understanding of the term as the means by which 'a group or class imposes its notions of what are suitable habits and attitudes for another class upon that class' (Thompson, 1981, pp. 190–1). According to Marxist historians, the aim of the middle and upper classes was to produce obedient, submissive members of the working class properly equipped for their inferior role in society, conditioned to respect law and order, and the authority, property and persons of their superiors.

At its extreme, social control theory posits all state activities, however benign or progressive they appear, as camouflaged mechanisms of control and repression. Welfare, education and health policies are revealed to be 'really' mechanisms of social control, indistinguishable in their aims from police, courts and prisons. Defined in this way, social control has limits as an explanatory tool. 'Casual usage of social control metaphors', argues the social historian Gareth Stedman Jones, 'leads to non-explanation and incoherence' (1983, p. 42). It promotes a tendency to see subjects of control as passive recipients, overlooking their ability (however constrained) to reject, adapt, distort or counter the forces of conformity. It assumes a monolithic notion of power, unanimity of purpose among the 'controllers', or simply buries questions of their identity or aims within 'bourgeois hegemony'. Finally, such usage leaves unchallenged the efficacy of the mechanisms of social control, overlooking the possibility that many may have quite other than their intended effects.

Growing disillusionment with social control as little more than 'a Mickey Mouse concept' (Cohen 1985, p. 2), has led to rejection of its broader usage. Sociologists like Stanley Cohen have chosen to restrict their understanding of social control to 'the organized ways in which society responds to behaviour and people it regards as deviant, problematic, worrying, threatening, troublesome or undesirable' (Cohen, 1985, p. 1). In this narrower, more specific sense, social control remains a central tool of the sociology of deviance.

Reading
Becker, H. 1963: *Outsiders.*
Cohen, S. 1985: *Visions of Social Control.*
Cohen, S. and Scull, A. eds. 1983 (*1985*): *Social Control and the State.*
Donajgrodzki, A.P. ed. 1977: *Social Control in Nineteenth-Century Britain.*
Landis, P.A. 1956: *Social Control: Social Organisation and Disorganisation in Process.*
Ross, E.A. 1929: *Social Control: A Survey of the Foundations of Order.*

LUCIA ZEDNER

social Darwinism   Theories that social organization is or is like a living organism, that societies undergo developmental change, and that such sequences of EVOLUTION are or can be progressive, emerged in the mid-nineteenth century. The unintended or even biologically determined consequences of individual actions, their aggregation into mechanisms such as competitive behaviour and the market, and intentions on the part of the theorist to draw normative and policy oriented conclusions have distinguished twentieth-century continuations of this trend.

Evolutionary theories of transformation in terms of biological make-up and observable behaviour, and of human transformation in similar senses, long preceded Charles Darwin (1859). However, social Darwinism and its descendant theories are in contradiction in a number of respects with Darwin's original views. Darwin rejected any notion of progress in the transformation of individuals and the origin of species, and he was highly suspicious of attempts to draw conclusions from his work applicable to human society. NATURAL SELECTION referred to non-patterned variation, interaction with the environment and mere reproductive success, not to normative concepts such as 'survival of the fittest'. This phrase was popularized by Herbert Spencer, the chief theorist of social Darwinism, and mocked by Karl Marx.

Marx's theory was evolutionary and progressive, sketchily rooted in a natural history of human biological requirements, but crucially dependent on premises of linguistic skills and ratiocination. However, Frederick Engels subsequently likened Marx's theory to Darwin's in method and importance, and strove to link natural selection with the development of human productive skills. This licensed a plethora of loosely formulated attempts within MARXISM to reconcile class struggle as a route to historical progress with biological mechan-isms of survival and extinction. However, the gap between a Darwinian theoretical premise of self-regarding individual behaviour and a Marxist view that individuals must act purposively in a collective entity such as a social class has proved difficult to bridge.

As a theoretical premise, the self-regarding individual organism battling competitively for existence and for betterment represents a notion akin to that underlying the anti-Marxist philosophies of Friedrich Hayek and Karl Popper. However, as theorists who extol the virtues of the market in goods and ideas, their arguments function at a level far above the simple biological mechanisms that a Darwinian theory of society would require. In the late twentieth century SOCIOBIOLOGY has emerged as a successor to social Darwinism. The consequences for the human collectivity of unintended behaviour, such as genetically determined AGGRESSION, are conceptualized theoretically, though sociobiologists by no means agree on the extent to which authoritative action can or should interfere with these supposed processes in society.

Reading
Hayek, F.A. 1983: *Knowledge, Evolution and Society.*
Holbrook, D. 1987: *Evolution and the Humanities.*
Jones, G. 1980: *Social Darwinism and English Thought.*
Peel, J.D.Y. 1971: *Herbert Spencer.*
Ruse, M. 1985: *Sociobiology*, 2nd edn.

TERRELL CARVER

social democracy   The political doctrines and action covered by this term can be clarified by considering what social democracy is and what it is not. Germany, France, Britain, Austria, New Zealand, Australia, Belgium, the Netherlands, Spain, Sweden and the other Scandinavian countries all have strong social democratic traditions and parties (which may call themselves socialist, social democratic, or labour parties; see SOCIALISM), and some of these parties have formed governments at various times, especially since World War II. Several generations of welfare programmes and legislated social reforms have left permanent imprints, affecting not only their state formation but prevailing attitudes about social responsibility. Russia also had an important social democratic movement at the beginning of this century, later suppressed by the Bolsheviks; and social democracy has been influential to a lesser extent in countries as diverse as Argentina, Canada, Northern Ireland (the Social Democratic and Labour

Party), India and Japan (where it remains strong despite the virtual monopoly of power by the governing Liberal Democratic Party, and receives considerable support from women, as well as farmers and the middle class).

Originally socialist, trade unionist and anti-capitalist, social democracy shares a common origin with other nineteenth-century working-class movements fighting against different versions of state repression – Bismarckian, militarist, Bona-partist, anti-Dreyfusard (see below), clerical (Cath-olic and Protestant), or other (see WESTERN MARX-ISM). The more successful they have been at the polls and the better organized as political parties, and as some of the social changes for which they campaigned were achieved in the WELFARE STATE, the more social democrats have tended to move from left to centre-left. Such flexibility is in part a result of the hybrid of social democracy as a political doctrine. Lacking a single founding father (a John Locke, Adam Smith or Karl Marx), its pedigree includes Marxism, utopian socialism, and that form of revisionism inspired by Engels's insight (in the 1890s) that evolutionary political action relying on the franchise and parliament was more likely to favour working-class struggles than revolutionary means.

Early social democrats shared a common com-mitment to the proletariat as the class of the future, and they differed from Jacobins and revolutionaries more in terms of method than principle. They believed that the proletariat as a class would take both economic and political power by such means as universal suffrage, parliamentary democracy and control over the executive branch of government. Once the proletariat was in power, nationalization and planning would eliminate the business cycle, abolish war and end colonialism. With some doctrinal variations, social democrats shared an egalitarian, secular, scientific vision, a socially responsible version of the Enlightenment tradition.

Social democrats still favour a strong democratic state in sharp contrast to liberal political minima-lism. They still reject the market as sole arbiter of justice, and continue to elevate the public over the private sphere. But they have distanced themselves from revolutionary socialism, and virtually all social democratic parties broke decisively with communism after 1919. Since World War II many of them have come to accept, or even favour, markets over planning, private over public enter-prise, and a growth-first redistribution-later policy.

Today, as the main alternative to social welfar-ism, social democracy shares with the latter a belief in pluralism whose model might be called the politics of a 'moving equilibrium', together with a politics of accountability, checks and balances, elections and laws, and an interactive relationship between the private and the public; but it empha-sizes continuous rebalancing between the economic and political within the framework of a double market. In social democratic theory, the economic marketplace is less a matter of private ownership than a mechanism providing *information* on the basis of which consumers and producers make choices about material needs and wants. In turn the political realm functions to provide *information* on the basis of which leaders can be selected according to policy priorities, with choices made according to programmes and preferences. Since individual citizens are simultaneously consumers and voters, the point of such a model is that inequities arising in the first sphere may be compensated for in the second, the private sector serving to prevent concentrations of power in the public, and the public sector to prevent concentrations of wealth in the private.

What separates social democrats from propo-nents of the social welfare state (see SOCIAL WELFARE) is a higher priority placed on equality and the institutional arrangements facilitating that goal. For them a deficiency of the social welfare state is that it results in ad hoc arrangements, temporary in nature, consisting of improvised strategies and legislative practices so grudging in character that they are likely to fail. In short, social democrats see social welfare reforms as grafts on the liberal state designed to ameliorate the worst effects of inequali-ties rather than eliminating their causes. In contrast the social democratic agenda is, to one degree or another, designed to alter or reduce substantially concentrations of private wealth, industry and capital. Indeed, according to social democrats, these are so powerful and the role of business so privileged that when compensatory and reform programmes are established in a social welfare state they prevent the double marketplace from working very well.

Social democrats, then, take a strong position on egalitarianism and the need to eliminate the causes of social inequities. They also believe that 'equilib-rium' will not be achieved without state interven-tion on behalf of those penalized or especially disadvantaged, including minorities (ethnic, religious, racial, linguistic) and classes. In recent years, however, experience has shown that intervention may bureaucratize the state, making it less politically responsive. Thus social democrats have become interested in experiments with multiple and pluralistic forms of representation, workplace democracy and self-management, hoping through such mechanisms to supersede competitive group conflict and transform it into cooperation. Modern pluralist theory and especially theories of participatory democracy and polyarchy have developed the political side of social democracy in the last 30 years (see, for example, Dahl, 1956, 1961; Polsby, 1963; Bachrach, 1967; Pateman, 1970; Lukes, 1974; Gould, 1988). At the same time social democrats have recognized that equity claims need to be balanced with developmental needs, and Dutch, Austrian, German, New Zealand and Scandinavian social democrats have shown considerable inventiveness in their policies of low-cost housing, workers' councils and novel educational programmes.

Social democrats have been close to the green parties on environmental issues (especially in Germany) while dividing on matters of nuclear energy and weapons (see GREEN MOVEMENT). Today, as membership and voting clienteles have become more middle class, some parties have also come to moderate their programmes of public ownership, and to emphasize the reform rather than circumscription of state welfare responsibilities (Hindess, 1971). Like the social welfare state, social democracy has been much influenced by KEYNESIANISM, though favouring those with a higher propensity to consume than to save. In general, social democrats favour the *collectivization of risk* while advocates of the social welfare state favour the *individualization of risk*. For some social democrats the state acts as an economic and political stabilizer, stimulating growth and preventing recession, as a form of crisis management (Offe, 1984, p. 148).

How these principles work can best be illustrated perhaps by some cases. While there is neither a definitive social democratic theory nor an exemplary social democratic state, Germany, Austria, Sweden, Holland and certain other countries such as Australia can serve as models. The German case illustrates particularly well the transformation of social democracy from a left to a centre-left doctrine. In the early 1860s liberal-inspired workers, educational associations and craft guilds began enlisting support for constitutional reform,

national unification, universal male suffrage, trade-oriented education, savings institutions, cooperative programmes and producers' cooperatives. The initial liberalism soon gave way to socialism, and two major workers' associations emerged in the 1860s; the General Association of German Workingmen, inspired and led by Ferdinand Lassalle, and the Social Democratic Workers' Party led by August Bebel and Wilhelm Liebknecht, who had close ties with Marx and Engels (Guttsman, 1981, ch. 1).

A period of radicalization occurred in the aftermath of the Franco-Prussian War. The two existing parties were united in 1875 as the Social Democratic Party of Germany (SPD), which within two years had 12 members in the Reichstag and received more than half a million votes. Like other socialist and social democratic parties, in France and elsewhere, it affirmed the priority of working-class solidarity over national affiliations, and in 1878 workers' organizations were prohibited by the Anti-Socialist Law. When the law expired in 1890 the SPD developed rapidly (Kocka, 1986, pp. 278–351), gaining nearly one and a half million votes in the elections of that year and sending 35 deputies to the Reichstag (Braunthal, 1961, pp. 200–1). Its programme included Lassallean corporatism (as embodied in the Gotha Programme of 1875) emphasizing state socialism, legal political means, universal suffrage, civil liberties and democracy, but as a direct consequence of Bismarck's repressive legislation against working-class organizations it now also included a call to radical proletarian action, a Marxist and revolutionary programme announced in its 1891 Erfurt programme. However, its Marxist doctrine had diverse strands, extending from the revolutionary Marxism of Rosa Luxemburg and Karl Liebknecht, through the 'centrism' of Karl Kautsky, to Eduard Bernstein's REVISIONISM.

All the social democratic parties in the Socialist International firmly opposed war, but despite such opposition, regularly reaffirmed at its congresses, the French socialists in the Chamber of Deputies and the German SPD in the Reichstag voted for war credits in 1914, setting the stage for a decisive split between socialists and social democrats, and revolutionary socialism and Bolshevism (Braunthal, 1961, ch. 21). Revolutionary Marxism remained a powerful force in the SPD until 1920 when the left wing of the party broke away to form the Communist Party (KPD). Relations between the mainly revisionist SPD and the KPD became increasingly bitter with the rise of National Socialism and the transformation of the KPD into a Stalinist party (see COMMUNISM). During the Nazi period members of both parties were persecuted and many of their followers killed or imprisoned. Reconstituted after World War II, a rejuvenated SPD officially abandoned even a diluted version of Marxism at its Bad Godesberg congress in 1959, accepting a liberalized market system. The SPD now stands in the main for free economic competition, but in a 'social market' economy, and largely rejects state ownership of the means of production (Lipset, 1990).

One of the problems in discussing social democracy is that most social democratic parties use socialist labels. In France, for example, socialists have made determined efforts to avoid social democracy, preferring the revolutionary pedigree and rhetoric of an original Jacobin inheritance. Its left 'tendency' derived from the revolutionary Marxism of Jules Guesde which was opposed to the more reformist or 'possibilist' programme of Paul Brousse. Where German social democrats favoured electoral means to socialism, some French socialists favoured the general strike, which they regarded as a weapon of peaceful reform in contrast to revolutionary action. Proudhonist, Marxist, Blanquist, Guesdeist, Sorelian in origin, the Dreyfus affair of 1894 helped to bring various socialist groups together under Jean Jaurès, so that by 1903 the socialists received 600,000 votes, elected over 50 deputies to parliament, and made it possible for Alexandre Millerand to become the first socialist minister. Guesdeists paid particular attention to municipal reform and obtained seats on numerous municipal councils. Then came the inevitable split between social democrats and communists at the Congress of Tours in 1919. Léon Blum, Jean Longuet and Paul Faure reestablished the socialist party around Longuet's paper Le Populaire, while the communists organized around Jean Jaurès' organ, L'Humanité. Social democracy, associated with the shortlived premiership of Léon Blum and the Popular Front government of 1936, declined thereafter until the 1970s when it began to revive, largely at the expense of the Communist Party. But it remained out of power until the presidency of François Mitterrand in 1981.

Sweden has of course long been regarded as an exemplary social democratic state, representing the 'third' or middle way. Founded in 1899 under the leadership of Hjalmar Branting (a fairly orthodox Marxist who became the first socialist prime minister) the Social Democratic Party quickly established itself as a major political force. Like German social democracy its original position was on the far left, and it was chiefly responsible for establishing Sweden's permanent neutralism. Despite being favourably influenced by the Russian revolution, successive social democratic governments (suffering only brief interruptions since the 1930s) have nevertheless preferred pragmatism to ideology, and growth over equality (a very strong position on this matter was taken at the famous Zimmerwald conference of 1915). One consequence is that while Sweden has long had the best social welfare programmes of any modern state, it has the lowest corporate taxes of all countries in the OECD (Organization for Economic Cooperation and Development), but also very high rates of income tax, social security and value-added tax (Lipset, 1990). It continues to favour schemes for worker participation in industrial decision-making, though these have proved less successful than originally anticipated (Tingsten, 1973; Meidner, 1978; Olsen, 1992).

The Austrian Social Democratic party was perhaps more doctrinal. Formed in 1888, it had received within ten years one-third of the votes cast and had 87 members in parliament; and AUSTRO-MARXISM represented a significant alternative to LENINISM. During World War I the party was split between Victor Adler, the party leader who favoured supporting the Austrian proletariat rather than an international proletariat, and his son Friedrich who took a militant anti-war position. After the war social democrats took office in several major cities, and Vienna in particular became a showcase of highly successful programmes in education, public health, provision of recreational facilities and new designs for workers' housing. In the 1920s it was the largest opposition party, and after World War II became the most powerful national party.

The Dutch Social Democratic Union was formed in 1878 under the leadership of Romela Nieuwenhuis who by 1888 was elected to the States General. The party registered steady success, with membership expanding from 13,000 voters and three parliamentary representatives in 1897 to 144,000 votes and 19 parliamentary representatives a year later, but the party refused to enter a coalition government on the grounds that this would mean compromising with capitalism. Since World War II, Dutch social democracy has been responsible for such elaborate welfare programmes and so greatly concerned with the less advantaged that today one might call Holland (rather than Sweden) the prototypical social democratic state.

The British Labour Party is a different and rather more puzzling case. Its origins differ substantially from those of European social democratic parties. Some trace its roots to authentic seventeenth-century evangelical radicalism (Levellers, Diggers), some to the later Owenite, Chartist and Chapel movements. Its most clearly working-class organization was the Independent Labour Party under the leadership of Keir Hardie, which drew much of its original support from the coalminers. In a real sense, however, modern British social democracy is best embodied in the Fabian Society. Founded in 1883, and officially unaffiliated to any party, the Fabians played a unique political role. The working papers they issued in considerable numbers were based on extensive empirical research, investigations into factory conditions, local government, public finance, housing, the condition of the poor, education, colonialism and other similar matters (see FABIANISM). They significantly influenced Labour Party policies, and their programme on Labour and the New Social Order, published just after World War I, provided a basic framework not fundamentally altered until relatively recently. Much of it was enacted into law, including a national welfare minimum, nationalization of mines, railways, utilities and insurance, redeployment of surpluses for the common good and a steeply graduated income tax.

Less significant strands included William Morris's semi-anarchist Socialist League, and H.M. Hyndman's Social Democratic Federation, a Marxist body founded in 1885 whose aim was collective ownership of the means of production, a democratic state, and social and economic equality between the sexes; among its members being Karl Marx's daughter Eleanor (Beer, 1948).

From its first paliamentary 'Lib-Lab' coalition of 1906 the Labour Party was, compared with European social democrats, eminently practical and pragmatic rather than doctrinal and ideological. It had rather a dismal record before World War II, first coming to power under Ramsay MacDonald in the 'Khaki election' of 1924. But after the war social democracy became so successfully entrenched that succeeding Conservative governments were unable to alter it until the Thatcher government's programme of privatization and devolution in the 1980s. From 1975 on, political polarization between left and right in the Labour Party intensified, leading in 1981 to a breakaway Social Democratic Party formed in alliance with the Liberal Party. After some initial successes, however, this party declined without establishing a clear power base, more of a 'media' party than anything else (Pridham, 1988, pp. 229–56).

Some former communist parties in Eastern Europe have followed the lead of the Italian and Spanish communists who, after first becoming eurocommunists, have now embraced social democracy. Social democracy has been extremely important both in Australia and in Western Canada, in sharp contrast to the United States where it declined steadily after 1912 (Weinstein, 1967). In Russia, after being the major radical influence before the split between Bolsheviks and Mensheviks, social democracy was eliminated after 1922. How it will fare in the present chaos of Eastern Europe and the former Soviet Union is difficult to predict.

While there is no *definitive* social democratic experience, with its move towards the centre of the political spectrum, social democracy, the product of a long political evolution in European radicalism, has now universalized itself as the main alternative to the social welfare state.

Reading
Braunthal, Julius 1961, 1963 (*1966, 1967*): *History of the International 1864–1914*, 2 vols.
Gould, Carol 1988: *Rethinking Democracy: Freedom and Social Cooperation in Politics, Economy, and Society.*
Guttsman, W.L. 1981: *The German Social Democratic Party, 1875–1933.*
Harrington, M. 1989: *The Next Left: The History of the Future.*
Judt, T. 1986: *Marxism and the French Left.*
Lindblom, C.E. 1977: *Politics and Markets.*
Meidner, Rudolf 1978: *Employee Investment Funds: An Approach to Collective Capital Formation.*
Miliband, R. 1989: *Divided Societies: Class Struggle in Contemporary Capitalism.*
Offe, Claus 1976: *Industry and Inequality.*
Olsen, Greg 1992: *The Struggle for Economic Democracy in Sweden.*
Panitch, L. 1976: *Social Democracy and Industrial Militancy.*
Pelinka, A. 1983: *Social Democratic Parties in Europe.*
Ross, G., Hoffman, S. and Malzacher, S. 1987: *The Mitterand Experiment.*
Schumpeter, J. 1942 (*1987*): *Capitalism, Socialism and Democracy.*

Tingsten, H. 1973: *The Swedish Social Democrats.*
Weinstein, James 1967: *The Decline of Socialism in America, 1912–1925.*

DAVID E. APTER

social differentiation   The concept refers to the recognition, and the constitution as social facts, of differences between particular groups or categories of individuals. Not all individual characteristics are distinguished in this way, but many are, in diverse ways in different societies and with varying degrees of rigour, sometimes codified in law. Among the most significant types of differentiation are those between the sexes (expressed in social terms as gender differences), between age groups (especially important in early tribal societies), between ethnic and linguistic groups, between occupational categories, and between status groups and classes. On a world scale, thoughout history, the distinctions between tribal groups, separate political communities, empires and modern nation-states, as well as between adherents of the major world religions or of the innumerable lesser creeds that have grown out of them, have been a powerful force in binding together human groups and at the same time separating them from, and frequently bringing them into conflict with, others.

Although social differentiation within particular societies or types of society has long been a subject of comment by philosophers, religious teachers (for example, in accounts of the origins of the Hindu caste system, or of feudal ranks) and political thinkers, it was studied systematically only from the end of the eighteenth century, and more particularly in the nineteenth century, when it was increasingly associated with economic development and the specialization of occupations. Thus Adam Smith discussed not only the economic consequences of the expanding division of labour, but also its effects in determining the characteristics and lifestyles of individuals; and Herbert Spencer subsequently conceived the division of labour as the primary element in social differentiation and traced its development in the specialization of functions in all areas of social life. Similarly, Karl Marx based his theory of classes on an analysis of the division of labour in different modes of production, while distinguishing between a social division of labour involving the ownership or non-ownership of means of production, and a technical division of labour within the productive process (see MARXISM). From another aspect Emile Durkheim (1893) emphasized the importance of the division of labour as the source of the individualism characterizing modern societies.

Undoubtedly, the type of economic system and the division of labour are major factors in creating social differentiation within societies, and in many cases between them (as, for example, in the present relationship between the advanced industrial countries and the Third World), but it is generally recognized that they are far from being the only factors. The writer who brought out most clearly the complexity of social differentiation in modern societies was Georg Simmel. In his volume of essays *Über soziale Differenzierung* (1890), and in other works, he considered the great variety of influences that had contributed to the growth of individualism and the diversification of social groups in the Western European countries during the nineteenth century: the rapid development of a money economy, the growth of cities, the mobility of individuals and the emergence of new social and cultural interests. In particular, city life afforded the stimulus of diverse and competing intellectual and cultural outlooks, from which new kinds of differentiation could again arise, while the increase in the number of associations and 'social circles' of all kinds allowed individuals to develop specific aspects of their character and purposes.

In the twentieth century these processes have continued, while being affected in some degree by opposing tendencies that arise from the development of MASS SOCIETY. At the same time two other kinds of social differentiation – those of gender and of race, ethnic origin or nationality – have acquired much greater prominence in social thought. In all human societies men and women have been treated differently (usually unequally), and many nineteenth-century social scientists (among them Marx and Spencer) suggested that the economic division of labour began with the division of tasks between the sexes, which was the source of many later social and cultural differences, including male dominance of political life. In the new industrial societies of the nineteenth century, women were still denied many basic social and political rights, and although these rights have been slowly acquired in most modern societies, various forms of invidious differentiation persist (see GENDER).

Differentiation by race or ethnic origin is also an important feature of modern societies, and similar distinctions occur in many post-colonial, multitribal societies of the Third World. In the industrial countries, partly as a legacy of colonialism, but more particularly, in the postwar period, as a consequence of large-scale immigration, such differentiation is frequently associated with substantial economic and social inequality and with manifestations of RACISM. Differentiation in terms of gender or race is connected with biological differences (as is that by age group), but the social distinctions that are made arise independently, and where biological factors are emphasized this is always intended to establish or reinforce some kind of inequality. Nationality, in the sense of a distinctive language and culture, is an important differentiating factor in those nation-states which incorporate national minorities, and in this case, too, often involves inequality of treatment, but it is also a source of separatist movements.

The cases just considered reveal as one major feature of social differentiation that it is almost invariably associated with SOCIAL STRATIFICATION. Inequalities of power, wealth and social prestige, in their diverse forms, are fundamental aspects of the process of differentiation (see ELITE THEORY) and need to be considered in relation to the 'individualism' of modern societies. In this respect, the analysis of social differentiation contributes greatly to understanding the relation between the individual and society. Individuals, with their array of personal qualities, are not located in neutral and unstructured positions in society, but are born into particular, distinctive groups and categories which do much to determine their character and outlook, opportunities and achievements. The extent to which each individual is able to fashion a personal and fulfilling style of life depends very largely – as Simmel, Durkheim and Marx argued in their different ways – upon the system of social differentiation and its changes, especially in the economic sphere.

Reading
Durkheim, Emile 1893 (*1984*): *The Division of Labour in Society.*
North, C.C. 1926: *Social Differentiation.*
Simmel, Georg 1890: *Über soziale Differenzierung: Soziologische und psychologische Untersuchungen.*
Tönnies, Ferdinand 1887 (*1955*): *Community and Association.*

TOM BOTTOMORE

social exchange theory   Dealing with reciprocal interactions that involve groups and persons exchanging items of social and symbolic value from which they benefit, the theory originally developed from early French sociological concerns with sources of social solidarity; it has also been elaborated in Anglo-American social science as ground for power differentiation in social relationships.

Origins in French sociology
In a review of French sociology in the 1800s, Durkheim (1900) attributed the resurgence of the discipline in the nineteenth century to the crisis that followed France's defeat in the Franco-Prussian War of 1870. It led sociologists to search for solutions in the societal order, 'the facade ... of the imperial [state] system [having] just collapsed' (p. 12). In the first decades of the twentieth century, Durkheim and his disciples expanded their scope of research to non-industrial societies, which were being opened up to scholarship by European imperialism, in the methodological faith that the principles gained from discovering how such simple societies cohered would shed light on the more complex value problems in the West (Durkheim, 1912; Durkheim and Mauss, 1903). The social exchange perspective emerged as a grounded theory of social solidarity from these inquiries. (See also DURKHEIM SCHOOL.)

Using ethnographic data from various non-Western societies, including especially Malinowski's (1922) documentation of *Kula* exchange in the Trobriand Islands, Mauss (1925) combed for evidence of gift and exchange traditions that would enable him 'to draw conclusions of a moral nature about some of the problems confronting us in our present economic crisis' (p. 2). Continuing in the same line of research, Lévi-Strauss (1949) discovered a connection between exchange practices and social solidarity in his comparative studies of kinship and marriage rules: direct (or *restricted*) exchange, in which two groups give and take from each other ($A \longleftrightarrow B$), generates mechanical solidarity; whereas indirect (or *generalized*) exchange, involving a network of several exchange partners who do not give to those from whom they receive (for instance, $A \rightarrow B \rightarrow C \rightarrow D \rightarrow A$), promotes organic solidarity (see Ekeh, 1974, pp. 37–77). In these studies, the unique individual is insignificant; it is groups, not individuals, that form exchange partnerships.

American reactions: individualism and social exchange

Rejecting the subordination of the individual to societal needs in Lévi-Strauss's theory (Homans and Schneider, 1955), Homans (1961) launched an individualistic social exchange theory in which interactions are limited to direct reciprocities. This version of social exchange theory underscores the significance of the unique individual by employing such key concepts in economics and psychology as rewards, costs, punishment, profits and investments, as well as the paired constructs stimulus and response and demand and supply. Homans's theory has provided the growth point for social exchange theory in the USA. While Blau (1964) developed its economic aspects, upgrading it to statements of emergent macrostructural relationships (although he later doubted the validity of such generalizations, see Blau, 1987), its psychological viewpoints have been elaborated by behaviourists who have linked them with Skinnerian psychology (Burgess and Bushell, 1969; Chadwick-Jones, 1976).

Social exchange theory in the USA has had its main application in the interpretation of POWER. While this can be traced to Homans's preoccupation with status differences in social interactions, Blau's extrapolation of power from small groups, and extensions of Emerson's (1962) seminal essay on power–dependency relations to the exchange situation, have been dominant in recent American discussions on this subject (see Cook, 1987). Their central contention is that power and dependency result from exchange relationships, with the greater giver being compensated with power and the lesser contributor embargoed with dependency. This view of power has been attacked by political sociologists (such as Birnbaum, 1976) and political philosophers (such as Lively, 1976) who argue that power has a wider basis in societal values and cannot be derived from the immediacy of the social exchange situation.

Other uses

Social exchange theory's versatility has enabled it to be used with similar theoretical perspectives in interpreting various other features of social relationships. The following two uses are particularly noteworthy.

Social exchange and rational choice Rational choice denotes actions motivated by personal gains in the course of economic activities that constrain actors to make choices from scarce means. From its beginnings, the Anglo-American brand of social exchange theory has used rational choice arguments, borrowed from economics and game theory, to conceptualize social exchange behaviours in Western and non-Western societies (Heath, 1976; Sahlins, 1965; see also RATIONAL CHOICE THEORY). While reflecting the dominance of economic reasoning in the USA and Britain, such reduction of social life to economic motivation contrasts sharply with the extra-economic conception of social exchange in French sociology.

Social exchange and justice Social exchange partners make judgements on their contributions to, and benefits from, groups in which they participate. They also compare their costs and benefits with those of other persons with whom they interact (see Thibaut and Kelley, 1959). These attributes make JUSTICE a central unit-idea of social exchange theory. Considerations of justice in social exchange may be along its two main variants identified by Barry (1989): *justice as impartiality*, emphasizing the distribution of benefits on common grounds and thus discounting privileged status as a bargaining edge, and *justice as mutual advantage*, stressing shared benefits among exchange partners. However, following Homans's (1961, pp. 71–5) initial formulations, social exchange theorists have conservatively embraced status as the principal criterion of justice. Social exchange theory may also help to account for the justice of citizenship defined as the exchange of rights for duties in the individual's relationship with the state (Marshall, 1950).

Conclusions

As Gouldner's (1960) essay on reciprocity intimates, the social exchange perspective derives its significance from a basic human impulse to give and take in social interactions, with contrary behaviours tending to destabilize social relationships. This assumption is widely shared by the social and behavioural sciences, making social exchange theory appealing to many disciplines (Gergen et al., 1980). Its French and Anglo-American variants also help to illuminate the value premises that separate collectivistic social thought, dominant in France, from individualistic perspectives which are pre-eminent in Anglo-American social science.

Reading

Chadwick-Jones, J.K. 1976: *Social Exchange Theory: Its Structure and Influence in Social Psychology.*

Cook, K.S. ed. 1987: *Social Exchange Theory*.

Ekeh, P.P. 1974: *Social Exchange Theory: The Two Traditions*.

Emerson, R.M. 1962: Power–dependency relations. *American Sociological Review* 27, 31–41.

Gergen, J.G., Greenberg, M.S. and Willis, R.H. eds 1980: *Social Exchange: Advances in Theory and Research*.

Gouldner, A.W. 1960: The norm of reciprocity: a preliminary statement. *American Sociological Review* 25, 161–79.

Heath, A. 1976: *Rational Choice and Social Exchange. A Critique of Exchange Theory*.

PETER P. EKEH

social history This branch of history has emerged greatly strengthened as the professional study of history has become more specialized in the twentieth century. It has been given many different definitions ranging from 'history with the politics left out' to 'economic history with the politics put in'.

At the beginning of the century the content of social history was often contrasted, sometimes favourably, sometimes unfavourably, with the content of constitutional, political and military history. Unlike them, it dealt, it was claimed, not with people of power or with acts of state or battles, but with 'ordinary people' and with their everyday ways of life. For critics, the past was being trivialized: for spokesmen of such an approach to history, particularly British historians following in the wake of J.R. Green, it was right to substitute knives and forks for drums, trumpets and swords. The past lived most vividly when historians focused on the history of 'the people'. When G.M. Trevelyan published his bestseller *Social History* in the midst of war in 1942 he was more interested in describing scenes, in narrating, in recapturing moods and in inspiring readers, than in theorizing about or explaining why society changed. The approach has remained popular, particularly in English-speaking countries, where for 20 years history workshops have explored what E.P. Thompson and other twentieth-century historians called 'history from below'.

Social history is directly related to experience and the perception of it and to communication. Yet there were obvious varieties of approach as the search for evidence broadened to include landscapes, buildings, machines, artefacts and ephemera as well as documents and literature, and as theory was injected into explanation. Some social historians concentrated on limited, often local, themes. Others were prepared to draw comparisons across space and time. There was a contrast, therefore, between 'micro' and 'macro' history.

Already at the beginning of the twentieth century different strands had been evident in the practice of the subject in different countries, and ambitious attempts had been made to theorize and to explain. Karl Marx approached 'the science of society' through history. This encouraged a view of social history that conceived of it not in terms of particular branches of history, what came to be thought of with increasing specialization as subhistories, but as synthesizing history. This was macro history with its theme the whole history of societies at different stages of development. There was a similar concern with major historical development in the writings of Max Weber. Marxist interpretations have remained influential in the late twentieth century in relation not only to working-class struggles as Marx identified them, but to more general analyses of social structure and social change.

In both Marxist and non-Marxist approaches to social history the subject was often bracketed with economic history, and the study of ways of life with the study of standards of life. How it was bracketed, however, was a matter of argument which centred not only on content but on methodology and on ideology. A distinction between substructure and superstructure was basic to Marxist history as was the sense of struggle through phases. Yet there were varieties of Marxism, and the influence of the Italian Marxist Antonio Gramsci was considerable as interest grew in the relationship between social history and cultural history, including the history of popular culture. Non-Marxist methodology became more quantitative during the same period, with developments in DEMOGRAPHY influencing a wide range of studies from family history to city history.

Whatever the ideology, economics as a subject, Marxist or non-Marxist, influenced economic history more than sociology as a subject influenced social history. Indeed, part of the argument about the academic role of history, particularly in Germany, concerned the relationship between history and sociology, the former often being considered as 'idiographic', dealing with the particular and the unique, and the latter as 'nomothetic', dealing with the general and the repetitive. The distinction was unhelpful since in practice social historians often generalized, for example when they wrote about 'feudalism', 'capitalism' or 'industrialism', while sociologists often particularized. Another theme in the argument concerned the use of 'types' and 'models'.

Drawing dividing lines between social history and SOCIOLOGY proved less attractive for most practising social historians than seeking a working partnership. It is difficult to distinguish between historical sociology and social history. Yet the partnership was never simply two-way. Other social sciences were also drawn on in what came to be thought of as a social science approach to history. Anthropology and psychology, particularly the former, greatly influenced the operations of a large number of social historians from the 1960s onwards.

In France geography had often done so in the past; the ANNALES SCHOOL of social historians, formed in 1929 and named after its influential periodical, developed a consciously new history. This turned to the social sciences both for concepts and techniques, widened the repertoire of social historians by spotlighting problems rather than events and states of mind as expressed in human behaviour. The history of events was separated from the long-term movement of history, and efforts were made, notably by Fernand Braudel, to reach new syntheses aspiring to present 'total history'. Nonetheless, for Marc Bloch, who explored many periods of history and ransacked many kinds of evidence, history was a small conjectural science.

Outside France there were eager explorers of the 'whole past', notably Gilberto Freyre in Brazil who integrated art and literature into his social history of plantation and city but insisted that 'in dealing with the human past room must be left for doubt and even for mystery.'

Reading
Abrams, Philip 1982: *Historical Sociology*.
Bloch, Marc 1954: *The Historian's Craft*.
Braudel, Fernand 1980: *On History*.
Briggs, Asa 1966: History and society. In *A Guide to the Social Sciences*, ed. Norman Mackenzie.
Burke, Peter 1980: *Sociology and History*.

ASA BRIGGS

social mobility The movements of people exchanging membership of one social category for another – most typically movements between social classes – have been explored by sociologists under the rubric of social mobility. Although there had been earlier interest in such movements as a facet of class analysis, in particular in response to Vilfredo Pareto's proposal of a circulation of elites (Bottomore, 1964), it was the publication of Sorokin's *Social Mobility* in 1927 that provided the first systematic conceptual treatment. Its broad view of a complex of movements across many different social dimensions was then narrowly refocused on mobility through education and occupation in the key work carried out at the London School of Economics (LSE) and published in 1954 as *Social Mobility in Britain* (Glass, 1954). This established a paradigm for subsequent mobility analysis, stimulated comparable studies of other nations, and produced the empirical evidence for later accounts of class boundaries, the rigidity of the social hierarchy and mobility between classes in Britain (see also CLASS; SOCIAL STRATIFICATION; STRUCTURATION). It also promoted the use of the term social mobility in popular parlance and political rhetoric. Major social surveys in Britain in the 1970s rekindled interest in the field, introducing new research techniques, generating fresh data and stimulating renewed debate about the causes, rates, consequences and forms of mobility (see Goldthorpe, 1980; Payne, 1987, 1989).

Glass and his colleagues had two main interests. First, what were the social characteristics of the senior civil servants who could be seen as a powerful elite in British society? Second, how far would educational reform (the 1944 Education Act) and the rising importance of educational qualifications for job entry produce an equalization of opportunity, so enabling able working-class children to obtain 'better' middle-class employment in which their talents were fully utilized? By comparing the positions of fathers and their now adult sons the LSE study showed little movement from the lower parts of the social hierarchy to the top, although there was considerable short-range mobility. The findings implied that the upper middle class was socially closed to those below, and that educational reform would take some time to alter the structured social inequalities existing in postwar Britain.

Over the next quarter of a century, this basic approach was developed in three main ways. A.H. Halsey, Jean Floud, John Westergaard and others demonstrated that welfare reforms benefited middle-class as well as working-class children, and that the move to credentialism did not in itself equalize opportunity. Writers such as Tom Bottomore,

Ralph Miliband, Frank Parkin, Anthony Giddens and Westergaard used the Glass empirical evidence to elaborate models of a class structure with substantial blockages to upward mobility. Abroad, new studies fuelled debate about the openness of American and other societies, and the mobility patterns associated with social democracy and liberal capitalism. In Britain, virtually no new empirical data were collected; the results of the Oxford and Aberdeen studies did not become recognized until the end of the 1970s (Payne, 1989).

These and other recent studies suggest higher rates of mobility, including moves from the bottom to very near the top of the occupational hierarchy, and throw doubt on the reliability of the original Glass data. A simple count of mobile people, for example, shows 28 per cent upwardly mobile in the Glass study, 40 per cent in the Oxford study, and 42 per cent in the 1984 Essex study. The upper middle, or 'service', class has 19 per cent, 28 per cent and 33 per cent recruited from the sons of manual workers in the same three studies (Payne, 1989, pp. 476–7).

However, it would be misleading to conclude, from these two examples among the many available measures of inter- and intragenerational mobility, that a new consensus perceives British society as being more open. Goldthorpe in particular has argued that the important measure of mobility is not the *number* of mobile people ('absolute mobility') but the *'relative' chances* of mobility for people with different origins. One reason for this is that he wishes to examine mobility as a product of class relations and welfare reforms, whereas the increasing absolute rates of mobility owe more to the structural expansion of new white collar jobs characteristic of postindustrial societies.

His position has been challenged by the New Right. Saunders (1990) claims that Goldthorpe underplays the high absolute rates of mobility out of a politically biased wish to support a negative view of capitalism. He also argues that standards of living have risen; as a result, an intergenerational comparison showing immobility in the working class can mean material enhancement even for those who fail to be upwardly mobile. While there are considerable flaws in Saunders's argument, it can be shown that even relative mobility rates are changing in the direction of greater equality of opportunity: whereas the sons of men in the service class had more than 3.5 times better chance of getting a service class job in 1972 than did the sons

of manual workers, a dozen years later this had dropped to a 3 times better chance.

A more substantial challenge to Goldthorpe's view has come from those who wish to broaden the definition of mobility, in the tradition of Sorokin. Research teams at Cambridge, Essex, Surrey and Plymouth have drawn on the ideas of the LABOUR MARKET, the household group, material inheritance, occupational change and gender studies to question whether a conception of mobility as a movement in terms of an undifferentiated idea of social class is adequate. The absence of any close connection between mobility experience and political or class behaviour and attitudes is taken as supporting evidence for this view. The appearance of new work will go some way to rectify the other major limitation to understanding social mobility, namely the virtual absence of women from the reports of the major studies (Payne and Abbott, 1991).

Reading
Heath, A. 1981: *Social Mobility.*
Marshall, G., Newby, H., Rose, D. and Vogler, C. 1988: *Social Class in Modern Britain.*
Payne, G. 1987: *Employment and Opportunity.*
—— 1991: Competing views of contemporary social mobility and social divisions. In *Class and Consumption,* ed. R. Burrows and C. Marsh.
Payne, G. and Abbott, P. 1991: *The Social Mobility of Women.*
Westergaard, J. and Resler, H. 1975: *Class in a Capitalist Society.*

GEOFF PAYNE

social movement   Most social theorists agree that this mode of collective action involves a specific type of socially conflictual relationship. The classical type is the workers' movement that marked nineteenth- and early twentieth-century industrial society. More recently, in the 1960s, most Western countries experienced important social movements, such as the STUDENT MOVEMENT, civil rights movements and peace movements, while in Third World countries, national liberation movements emerged. During the 1970s and early 1980s a multitude of social movements proliferated throughout North America and Europe – women's, ecological, anti-nuclear and peace movements, and movements for regional autonomy. Elsewhere, fundamentalist movements arose emphasizing cultural specificity. China, in 1989, experienced a democratization movement which was suppressed; and in Eastern Europe popular movements overthrew the communist regimes.

Many social movements challenge institutional structures, ways of life and thinking, norms and moral codes. In fact, social movements are closely linked to social change, and several features of contemporary societies are likely consequences of the actions of social movements.

From a theoretical point of view, too, social movements stand in the centre of social scientific discussion. Herbert Blumer (1939) claimed early on that collective behaviour and social movements are core concepts of sociological theory, as does Alain Touraine today. That the current use of the term is quite loose, even in the professional literature, might be largely due to the excessive variety of empirical phenomena to which the notion potentially applies. Are all the diverse movements just mentioned to be covered by the same concept? To employ the notion on a descriptive level is very convenient, but a more restrictive conceptual use is to be recommended. Like most notions in the social sciences, social movement does not describe part of reality, but is an element of a specific mode of constructing social reality.

The theoretical paradigms of social movements may be considered under different headings. Besides the *neo-Marxist* paradigm, theoretical approaches dominant until the early 1970s are the *interactionist* conception of collective behaviour and social movements of the Chicago school, and the *structural-functional* model. This latter paradigm with its many variants was the most widely shared perspective on social movements at that time. In the 1970s *resource mobilization* theories propose a neo-utilitarian, rationalist approach to the study of social movements. They are, however, severely criticized by more hermeneutically oriented approaches which attempt to conceptualize what is new in *new social movements*. And the *sociology of action* approach adds a comprehensive theoretical perspective to the study of social movements.

Neo-Marxism

The important influence of Marxist and neo-Marxist approaches to the study of social movements is well known, and will be discussed here only briefly (see MARXISM; NEW LEFT). Marxist theory asserts that, in industrial society, social movements and revolution spring from the central structural contradiction between capital and labour. The main actors in social movements – antagonistic social classes – are defined by this fundamental systemic contradiction. However, they are also considered as historical actors, and as such they must become conscious of their historical role and destiny. For this reason, social researchers are not only required to study the objective conditions, but also to account for more subjective processes through which social movements arise.

Interactionism

Der Streit (conflict) was understood by Simmel (1908) as a process of interaction. In the 1920s, theorists of SYMBOLIC INTERACTIONISM of the Chicago school adopted a similar approach to the study of collective behaviour and social movements. Starting out from the assumption that individual persons and groups of people act on the basis of shared understandings and common expectations, they maintained that social movements arise in non-structured situations. These are situations where shared cultural guidelines are lacking or have broken down and must be newly (re)defined. Social movements are the expression of such collective reconstructions of social situations, they are 'collective enterprises to establish a new order of life' (Blumer, 1939).

The symbolic interactionist approach to the study of social movements suffers from the fact that its theoretical paradigm remains insufficiently developed. Overall, the approach is still receiving increasing attention, for it stresses such social-psychological features of collective action as emotion, feelings of solidarity, expressive behaviour and communication, on the one hand; while on the other hand, it places the emergence of social movements within an ongoing process of social relationships and interactions.

Structural functionalism

Three variants may be distinguished within the structural-functional model of social movements. Although very different in its basic approach from the logic of social movements based on interaction, it is however not as far away as it may seem from Marxism in its analytical mode, albeit proposing a quite dissimilar vision of social life.

Mass society theories postulate the atomized individual (Kornhauser, 1959). Uprooted through rapid social change, urbanization and loss of traditional bonds, isolated from group relations and normative reference groups, the individual in mass society is both free and prone to participate in new kinds of social groups, such as social movements, which therefore find in mass societies an easy breeding ground.

Structural stress theories see the main cause for the emergence of social movements in the distorted equilibrium of social systems (Smelser, 1962). Non-correspondence between professed values and actual practices of society, blocked institutional functioning, dysfunctional elements challenging the survival of the system, are all features that can put the social system out of balance, provoke structural strains that, in turn, trigger off social movements.

Theories of relative deprivation are a sort of social-psychological variant of stress theories. The stress is not objectively given by structural discrepancies, but is a subjectively felt condition: people feel deprived relative to their expectations. Expected and actual need satisfaction do not correspond. Improvement of economic and political conditions, entailing growing expectations in some groups, are particularly favourable to the emergence of social movements, when reality seems not to keep pace with expectations. Dissatisfaction and frustration will follow, leading to the formation of social movements.

Despite the fact that the structural-functional model claims to provide a causal theory of the emergence of social movements, it does not give any precise explanation of how the passage from isolation, stress and frustration to the action of the movement occurs. This passage cannot be assumed to be automatic.

Resource mobilization

Neo-utilitarian approaches to the study of social movements appeared in the 1970s, and have expanded rapidly since then. Their basic assumption is that social movements develop in the wake of conscious organizational activity – if they succeed in mobilizing material and symbolic resources available to them, such as money, people's time and legitimacy. Social movements are thus accounted for in terms of opportunities, strategies, modes of communication, sophisticated organizational forms, and competition with groups and authorities having opposing interests. Such reasoning adds some evidence to the comprehension of how social movements arise, but hardly suffices to elucidate the meaning collective social mobilizations may bear.

The different variants (Olson, 1965; Oberschall, 1973; Tilly, 1978) within the resource mobilization perspective share a common logic: they think that social movements employ strategic-instrumental reasoning, cost–benefit calculations, and pursue their goals and interests rationally. They share still another important point: for them social movements are not abnormal occurrences but part of normal social life, which is seen as full of potential conflicts. For this reason, they reject the idea that stress or discontent can account for the emergence of social movements; on the contrary, it is social movements that focus stress and discontent. Whether a movement is able to do this will depend, however, on its organizational capacities.

New social movements

Several social theorists currently use the term 'new social movements' to refer to the great variety of protest movements during the 1970s and early 1980s in the West. Broadly speaking, these movements form a loose network of contestation and alternative life styles, but they have also entered official politics (see GREEN MOVEMENT).

What makes the newness of the new social movements? Most theorists conceive them in terms of conflictual collective behaviour that opens up new social and cultural spaces. They are seen as politicizing institutions of civil society, thereby redefining the boundaries of institutional politics (Claus Offe); as offering through their own existence a different way of naming the world and challenging the dominant cultural codes on symbolic grounds (Alberto Melucci); as creating new identities comprising non-negotiable demands (Jean L. Cohen); as expressing evolutionary collective learning processes (Klaus Eder); as being new social articulations that crystallize new shared experiences and common problems, in the wake of a general disintegration of experience based on economic class (Ulrich Beck). The overall significance that the above formulations confer on the new social movements, is that they have gained enhanced awareness of their capacity to produce new meanings and new forms of social life and action. A systematic outline of this increased reflexivity of social movements can be found in the paradigm of communicational rationality. The process of communicational rationalization of the life-world is posited here as a conspicuous feature of modernity, running parallel to systemic rationalization processes (Habermas, 1981). Within this theoretical framework, social movements are placed in a double perspective. As the expression of communicational rationalization, the new social movements call in question the validity of existing patterns of the life-world, such as norms and legitimacies, and subsequently enlarge public space. Simultaneously, as defensive movements, they offer resistance to the pathological encroachment on the life-world, which is being colonized by systemic economic and political rationalization mechanisms that abrogate communicational processes.

Sociology of action

An elaborate and complex theoretical perspective on social movements is put forward by the sociology of action which aims at integrating various approaches into a general representation of social life defined as conflictual self-production (Touraine, 1973). In this view, the very centre of social life is the permanent struggle over the use of new technologies and the social control of society's own transforming capacities. For this reason, social movements, considered as essential agents of conflict, are of major concern to social scientists.

Hence, social movements are conceptualized as social actors involved in a conflict for the social control of the main cultural patterns, which are knowledge, investment and ethics. Three components, I (identity), O (opponent), T (totality), provide the paradigm describing analytically the conflict field, which is therefore understood in relational terms. That is to say that the adversaries opposing each other (I–O), nevertheless share a common cultural field consisting of what is at stake in their conflict (T). In other words, social conflict must not be separated from cultural orientations in the analysis of social movements.

Moreover, it is necessary to differentiate between various kinds of social conflicts, and to place them on different levels of analysis. Movements that advocate economic demands act on an organizational level; political pressure groups and movements defending minorities act on a political level; the highest level is that of the system of historical action, on which social movements act by both contesting and creating cultural patterns. Historical action, or *historicity*, then, is the capacity of societies to develop and alter their own orientations, to generate their normativity and objectives by means of a central social conflict, of which social movements are the main expression (Touraine, 1981). A specific method of *sociological intervention* has been developed to assess these different meanings that are always combined in a concrete empirical movement, and to appreciate to what extent a given movement can be considered as a social movement defined in the above terms.

Reading
Hobsbawm, Eric J. 1959: *Primitive Rebels.*
Nelkin, Dorothy and Pollak, Michael 1981: *The Atom Besieged.*
Oberschall, Anthony 1973: *Social Conflict and Social Movements.*
Scott, Alan 1990: *Ideology and the New Social Movements.*
Social movements. *Social Research* 52 (1985), 660–890.
Tilly, Charles 1978: *From Mobilization to Revolution.*
Touraine, Alain 1984: *Le retour de l'acteur.*
Turner, Ralph, H. and Killian, Lewis M. 1957: *Collective Behavior.*
Zald, Mayer N. and McCarthy, John D. eds 1979: *The Dynamics of Social Movements.*

KARIN D. RENON

social planning   There exist many interpretations of planning in general, and social planning in particular. In the simplest approach social planning is planning applied to social institutions and resources. It may refer to global or to partial objectives. It may cover planning for an entire social system or may relate only to the planning of specifics of a project in a social service agency. Planning itself has to be described in more detail to avoid the circularity in this definition. According to H. J. Gans:

> In its generic sense, planning is a method of decision making that proposes or identifies goals or ends, determines the means or programs which achieve or are thought to achieve these ends, and does so by the application of analytical techniques to discover the fit between ends and means and the consequences of implementing alternative ends and means. (Gans, 1968b, p. 129)

Rationality is one of the characteristics of planning (see also RATIONAL CHOICE THEORY). In the technocratic approach to planning, rationality and calculation are of prime importance. Sensible policy-making and planning mean 'designing a system whereby society can *rationally weigh the costs and benefits of alternative[s] . . .*' (Owen and Schultze, 1976, p. 10). In a sociological perspective the rationality of planning depends, however, on the nature of the target and of the society in which the plan operates. Decision-making in societal matters is a political process in which the values and interests of the participants play a predominant, if not always open role. Also, the realization of the plan is a social process which is seldom, if ever, fully guided by the *intentions* of the planners. Various social actors operating on other levels of intentionality participate in these processes. The outcome will therefore depend on the strength of non-planned actions and so-called unintended consequences will inevitably occur. These may be seen, from the planner's perspective, as spontaneous. The divergence between the plan and the outcome depends on a number of factors. Some of the most important are the complexity of the target system; the internal contradictions and conflicts between components of the target system; the impact of outside (such as natural) forces; or the stochastic nature of intrasystemic links in a society (Sztompka, 1981).

Levels and actors of planning

Theoretically all social actors may take more or less rational decisions about their own future action and behaviour. Thus plans may be made by households, firms and other organizations, local communities and self-governing units, up to the body of central decision-makers. We are concerned here with planning which goes beyond the boundaries of one self-contained unit such as a household or a firm, and especially with planning on the global, societal level.

In market societies planning has emerged as an answer to various market failures. It remained for a long time partial or oriented to specific programmes, as illustrated by city planning, which appeared in some countries at the end of the nineteenth century. Macro-level – four-year or five-year – plans appeared after the world crisis of 1929 in some, mainly non-democratic, capitalist societies, such as Nazi Germany in 1933 (Madge, 1968). More comprehensive planning has developed since World War II. One trend first described by Chandler (1977) is the increasing coordination between large corporations of big business, so that their 'production and distribution nowadays increasingly are determined not by market forces, but by planning and administrative coordination' (Himmelstrand, 1981, p. 201). The other trend has been the emergence of state planning operating on the macro level (Kahn, 1969).

In (former) state socialist societies the trend has been reversed. Global, macro-level plans elaborated by the central organs predominated from the start (see also NATIONAL ECONOMIC PLANNING). Partial plans initiated from below have been non-existent. In conformity with ideological tenets, the market was abruptly replaced by central planning (the first five-year plan started in the Soviet Union in 1928). Planning proposed to eliminate the spontaneous operation of the market, and to replace by 'central rationality' all other initiatives and rationalities in all the fields of social life. The exclusive role of central planning has been questioned several times by economic reformers from the early 1920s on, without lasting success. The ultimate collapse of state socialism in 1989–90 can be attributed to a large extent to central planning, forcing an exclusively political rationality on all social subsystems, harming thereby economic rationality and efficiency, the tenets of political democracy, and so forth.

Types of planning

There are stricter and milder, more 'imperative' or more 'liberal' forms of planning (Rostow, 1962, p. 22). In the practice of state socialism, *planning by direct commands* was predominant for a long while. In this case the inputs, outputs and all the conditions of activity of all the units were centrally set. In the last 20 years *indirect planning* has appeared. This still means centrally defined targets, but the direct commands have been replaced by fiscal and other regulators. This method was followed by countries which had accepted, like Hungary from 1968 on, the 'market regulated by the plan' (Brus, 1961). In reality, under the given political conditions, the market remained a 'simulated' market, and could not produce the expected result. The change of the political system carries the promise of liberating the social subsystems, including the market. As a reaction to the former practices, all the forms of planning have become delegitimated in those societies. In capitalist (market) societies the state may accept some form of *indicative planning*, stressing goals without insisting on specified means (for instance, France), or may adopt only 'broad objectives and loosely-defined policies, which are expected to move them in the general direction sought' (Kahn, 1969, p. 44).

Techniques of planning

The stages of planning may be defined as policy development, policy implementation and policy evaluation (Rein, 1968). In all the stages adequate knowledge about the conditions and relationships affected by the plans and a continuous flow of information about their implementation is of the utmost importance. Since the early 1970s the improvement of management and the evaluation of projects have attracted a great deal of attention and funding (Meyers, 1981). One of the techniques is the planning-programming-budgeting system (ppbs), which serves goal setting and evaluation simultaneously (Kahn, 1969, p. 43). *Evaluation studies* have become a practically autonomous branch of social research. Since the end of the 1970s *cost–benefit analysis*, a method based on the logic of WELFARE ECONOMICS, is increasingly used in decisions about social projects and in the assessment of their outcomes. All these instruments seem to be useful in the case of partial projects which are well circumscribed, but are less well adapted to comprehensive, macro-level programmes. It has to be remembered, too, that these methods cannot solve the political problem of value-conflicts and divergent interests. The decisions about the factors to be included in, and to be excluded from, the various analyses remain influenced by social and political considerations.

Social planning
Where social planning has broad ambitions, it may be termed societal planning: 'Societal planning is concerned with evaluating social goals and developing in broad outline the kinds of programmes to achieve the goals chosen' (Gans, 1968b, p. 129). Partial planning, city or community planning, or the planning of welfare projects, have long been the main forms of social planning in market societies. This type of planning has been frequently discussed, including the problems of coordination, the competition for funds, and the machinery of planning (Gans, 1968a; Rein, 1968; Kahn, 1969).

The emergence of the WELFARE STATE, and even more the idea of a *welfare society*, have put on the agenda more comprehensive issues. In this case social planning may or should become the process of developing, implementing and evaluating social policies, its essence being the determination of social priorities. In other words, social planning has to be concerned 'with the distribution of welfare and the shaping of structural relationships' (Walker, 1984, p. 3). This issue is socially highly controversial, so that, at least for parts of the intelligentsia and the opposition, social planning has become a field of ideological struggle by means

of which 'they tried to find the means of overcoming economic development fostering inequalities' (Jobert, 1981, p. 238).

In former state socialist societies economic planning used to be predominant. The ideological assumption was that economic development would automatically entail social progress and the achievement of socialist objectives such as the growth of people's well-being, improvement of the style and quality of life, reduction of social differentiation between classes and groups, further improvement of social relations, and, finally, the creation of necessary conditions for many-sided personal development offered to every citizen (Zaslavskaya, 1981, p. 192).

Despite broad and often radical social goals, in both types of society social planning has often remained narrowly bureaucratic, centralized, unresponsive to need and subordinate to economic policy and planning (Walker, 1984). The gap between goals and reality used to be particularly wide in most state socialist societies. This failure had several reasons. The technical reason was that in the case of direct planning the targets had to be numerically and exactly defined. Social planning therefore was restricted to goals which could be defined in this way, such as the number of hospital beds or places in kindergartens, neglecting the quality of the services offered. The ideological reason was the emphasis on economic development, which has been supposed to entail in an automatic way social development. The main political or structural reason was, though, the political system itself. Successful planning for change and planning for needs has to be based on democratic participation in, and on control of planning, that is, on social and economic rights. The necessary – even if not the sufficient – prerequisite of these rights is the existence of civil and political rights. Since these have been underdeveloped or absent in totalitarian systems, planning has represented a 'dictatorship over needs'. The absence of political democracy has been delegitimating planning and its outcomes even if the standard of living or its components have been objectively improving.

More generally, since the crisis of Eastern Europen socialism and the spread of neoliberalism, planning in general, and social planning in particular, have lost much of their former legitimacy and appeal (Johnson, 1987). The negation of planning may, however, intensify the shortcomings of 'automatic' social mechanisms such as the market. Technological changes, for instance, seem to entail unemployment on a large scale with grave consequences for income distribution. In general, unequal and hierarchical social structures, if left to themselves, automatically and spontaneously reproduce themselves, usually with increased inequalities and strengthened hierarchies, and worsen the plight of the weakest groups in society. This is true even on an international level. Recent world tendencies seem to accentuate the inequalities of development between the three worlds.

The spontaneous consequences had to be attended to in order to avoid mounting social tensions on the national, but also on the international, level. Under the current political conditions this is not very likely to occur. Social plans are even more controversial than economic planning, partly because interventions in social affairs are especially suspect of 'dirigisme', and partly because the stakes are high: the outcomes may directly affect many social groups and individuals. The effectiveness of social plans will depend on whether societies can find ways to democratize and decentralize the processes of planning and implementation, whether they can involve citizens in those processes – whether, in short, they can build up a planning system from below.

Reading
Balogh, T. 1965: *Planning for Progress: A Strategy for Labour.*
Booth, T.A. ed. 1979: *Planning for Welfare.*
Gans, H.J. 1968a: *People and Plans.*
Hall, P. 1981: *Great Planning Disasters.*
Himmelstrand, U. ed. 1981: *Spontaneity and Planning in Social Development.*
Kahn, A.J. 1969: *Theory and Practice of Social Planning.*
Marris, P. 1982: *Community Planning and Conceptions of Change.*
Mayer, R.H. 1972: *Social Planning and Social Change.*
Paris, C. ed. 1982: *Critical Readings in Planning Theory.*
Walker, A. 1984: *Social Planning.*

ZSUZSA FERGE

social policy There is no universally accepted definition of social policy. The descriptions based on the historically changing practice and scope of social policies may complete and complement each other. Ideologically based explanations may offer conflicting accounts. The approaches themselves may be grouped in different ways.

Pragmatic approaches
Social policy may be conceived of as a field of action consisting of institutions and activities positively affecting the welfare of individuals. The scope of action is usually limited to publicly provided welfare services, that is, to the intervention of the state in the domain of distribution or redistribution. According to T.H. Marshall, for instance, social policy is 'the policy of governments with regard to action having a direct impact on the welfare of citizens by providing them with services or income' (Marshall, 1967, p. 6). It usually includes 'state provision of social security, housing, health, personal social services and education' (Walker, 1984, p. 15). To these branches, considered as the core of social policy, some authors add employment services and some the treatment of crime. Equating social policy with the formal administrative division of state services is the dominant tradition of British social administration and is often qualified as the 'textbook definition' of social policy.

The descriptive approach may be useful in analysing the operation of an administrative logic and may promote the in-depth analysis of various institutions. It may however be criticized on several grounds, as Titmuss (1958) and Townsend (1975) have pointed out. Thus it is shaped by tradition and is therefore insensitive to new developments (such as, for example, the increasing importance of free legal services). It does not spell out its own underlying rationale. It does not explain, for instance, why it leaves out indirect state intervention in the distribution of resources by means of fiscal policy, or why it focuses on individual welfare, leaving out all central or local state activities affecting the quality of life of communities, such as all communal services from road construction to water supply, or, more recently, environmental policy. It does not clarify why it ignores all non-state efforts to affect the welfare of citizens or their communities, from occupational welfare to the activities of voluntary agencies.

The functionalist approach
The proponents of this view focus on the problems which at any given time have disturbed the smooth reproduction of social systems, especially since the advent of capitalism. According to George and Wilding (1976, p. 7), 'Changes in the industrial system upset the equilibrium prevailing among the various parts of the social and economic system

with the result that social policy measures become necessary to restore stability and balance.' The flaw in this approach is the underlying assumption that the normal state of affairs is social equilibrium, and that instability and imbalances are signs of social disorganization and deviance (ibid.). It is helpful, though, in viewing social policy as a systemic element operating in the context of social and economic reproduction, and in bringing home the point that all societies have had 'social problems', and hence that they have all had some sort of social policy. Also, the emphasis on change promotes the analysis of social policy in historical perspective, identifying the variations in the nature of social problems and in the answers given to them. Thereby the different stages of the evolution of social policy may be identified.

Historical periods
The social policy of precapitalist societies has not been systematically studied, but there are many useful analyses of the different institutions of social help such as the Catholic church (see Troeltsch, 1912) or feudal institutions (see Bloch, 1940), or of the treatment of poverty in general (Mollat, 1978). A theoretical framework for a possible typology is offered by the 'patterns of integration' of Karl Polányi (1944), which helps us to understand the access to need satisfaction in early societies in terms of reciprocity, or redistribution, or production for one's own use.

There is more accord on the stages of development following the advent of the market society. It is generally agreed that the state started to intervene after the disintegration of feudal and local networks, and that its intervention served simultaneously policing and helping purposes, 'deterrence and therapy' (Pinker, 1971). In this first period state action was centred only on the poor, and remained piecemeal, marginal and very often inhuman. This politics of POVERTY remained dominant by and large until the mid-nineteenth century.

Rapid industrialization entailed the emergence of the working class and its political and social movements pressing for state action against new miseries and new uncertainties. Also, the acceptable functioning of the new system made necessary at least some public health, public education, public housing and so forth. The most important welfare institution created in this period is – in all

probability – social insurance or social security. Social policy provisions spread considerably, covering in most European countries between a third and a half of the population.

World War II created a divided Europe. The WELFARE STATE was developed in Western market economies, thanks to the effect of a number of factors. The war forged new solidarities. The challenge of the socialist bloc in the East triggered competition in the field of welfare. Socialist or labour parties increased their influence on politics, sometimes as a parliamentary majority. And most importantly, the economies underwent a period of unprecedented economic growth during the 'glorious thirty years' between the end of the war and the first oil shock. The welfare state has transformed many of the former selective or corporative welfare provisions into universal services. Systems of public health and public education largely replaced market or means-tested solutions. Societies have accepted on a large scale the 'right to existence', that is, the enforceable right to a social minimum. In the mid-1970s the industrialized Western countries spent 15 to 30 per cent of their gross domestic product on state social welfare (OECD, 1988). Since the oil crisis there has been a differentiation among Western countries. In some of them the legitimation crisis of welfare has become acute, and neo-liberalism has become the dominant ideology. In others the new ideologies have not as yet entailed any significant change. In a few of them, the idea of a 'welfare society' has been developed, characterized by a blend of decentralization, participation, 'welfare pluralism' (Johnson, 1987) and state commitment in welfare provisions (Wiman, 1987).

In the East European socialist countries social policy has been largely built into the operation of the economy by means of formal full employment, subsidized prices and so forth. Social provisions have considerably expanded there, too, albeit in most countries with the gap that has always existed between ideological promises and reality. With the collapse of socialism, it has become apparent that totalitarian practices have profoundly delegitimated the system and practically all its achievements. New solutions have to be found. One important element of the expected changes is the emancipation of economic policy and social policy from the domination of politics, and the creation of an autonomous sphere of social policy alongside an autonomous market.

Ideological and theoretical constructs

There are deep divisions in the perception of the role of social policy which are shaped by conflicting values and ideologies. George and Wilding (1976) distinguish the 'anti-collectivists' who reject all interference with the market in the name of freedom and efficiency; the 'reluctant collectivists' who realize the impossibility of a self-regulating market and accept some state intervention in reducing major injustices and inefficiencies; the (Fabian) socialists who are committed to the three central socialist values – equality, freedom and solidarity – and assign a positive role to the state in optimizing their interplay in a democratic and gradual way; and some Marxists who share the socialist values but reject the possibility of peaceful societal reform.

From another perspective there is the distinction made by Wilensky and Lebeaux between 'two conceptions of social welfare ... the residual and the institutional. The first holds that social welfare institutions should come into play only when the normal structures of supply break down. The second, in contrast, sees the welfare services as normal, 'first line' functions of modern industrial society' (1965, p. 138).

One of the important debates is concerned with the relationship between social policy and the economy. Social policy may be differentiated from the economy, or it can be more or less integrated with it (Mishra, 1981). In another view the economic interest may dominate the social interest; or they may acquire by and large an equal footing, if there is enough social support to limit the scope of market or profit interests. The domination of social interest over the economy has remained up to now only a theoretical possibility, assuming the replacement of formal economic rationality by a humane or substantive economy, concerned essentially with the satisfaction of needs (Polányi, 1944; Fournier and Questiaux, 1979).

Structural approaches

The pragmatic and functionalist approaches have largely left out of consideration the social processes which trigger the changes of social policy. Social tensions and conflict have always played an important role in the processes of defining the needs to be covered by non-market procedures, and especially in emphasizing the importance of the reduction of social inequalities. Owing to these struggles charity has been transformed into rights. The existence of civil and political rights helped to spell out 'social rights', the rights to decent incomes, housing, health and culture (Marshall, 1965). Social rights relate to the needs of the consumers, and may be satisfied by intervening in the sphere of distribution. 'Economic rights' spell out the needs of the producers not only for socially acceptable work, but also to participate in economic life on the level of the firm (termed industrial democracy) or on the macro level (economic democracy). By this extension of the field of non-market elements in social and economic reproduction social policy is transmuted into societal or structural policy (Ferge, 1979). All these struggles may be seen as aiming at the *decommodification* of needs (Esping-Anderson, 1985).

Social policy described in structural terms means that: 'Social policies are those that determine the distribution of resources, status and power between different groups' (Walker, 1984, p. 39). The dual and contradictory nature of social policy also becomes evident if structural forces are taken into account: 'social policy is not only one of the means of the existing social order. It is also the locus where tensions and injustices related to this order are most evidently revealed' (Jobert, 1981).

See also SOCIAL PLANNING.

Reading

Beveridge, W.H. 1942: *Social Insurance and Allied Services*. Cmnd 6404.

Evers, A. and Wintersberger, H. 1988: *Shifts in the Welfare Mix*.

George, V. and Wilding, P. 1984: *The Impact of Social Policy*.

Greffe, X. 1975: *La politique du social*.

Klein, R. and O'Higgins, M. 1985: *The Future of Welfare*.

Miller, S.M. and Riessman, F. 1968: *Social Class and Social Policy*.

Piven, F.F. and Cloward, R.A. 1971: *Regulating the Poor*.

Rein, M. 1979: *Social Policy*.

Rimlinger, G.V. 1971: *Welfare Policy and Industrialization in Europe, America and Russia*.

Titmuss, R.M. 1968: *Commitment to Welfare*.

ZSUZSA FERGE

social problem   This can be defined as a harmful condition identified by a significant number of people and recognized politically as needing improvement. Harm comes in many forms: people's economic interests, their political interests, their moral values, the environment and countless other phenomena can be damaged. In every case, to be expressed as a social problem, the harm must be a factual situation whose international, historical, social psychological and other dimensions can be observed systematically and objectively. The facts are important because they provide a realistic basis for action. Moreover, ignorance can be costly, since what people do not know can still harm them (Merton, 1961). Nonetheless, merely showing the harmfulness of a phenomenon is not, in itself, sufficient to identify a social problem. Conditions involving little harm, such as deaths from drug use (about 4,000 yearly in the USA), are often defined as social problems, while conditions involving great harm, such as deaths from auto accidents (about 50,000 yearly), are not so defined.

In addition to harm, a significant number of people must identify a social problem and debate it politically (Spector and Kitsuse, 1987). While controversy about how many is 'significant' has occurred, this issue can be resolved by noting the feedback between the number of people who claim a condition is harmful and their location in society. Sometimes a situation is identified as harmful, whether by citizen groups, victims, or influential individuals, and others respond by taking up the issue politically. Alternatively, sometimes research reveals a condition that prompts public outcry and the cause is taken up by politically significant advocates. For purposes of identifying a social problem, it does not matter why an issue is considered harmful or who originates concern about it: people can be motivated by moral values, economic interests or other factors.

Yet people's motives are important, since no scientific criteria exist for deciding that one harmful condition is a social problem but another is not. Public life, at least in democratic societies, is a competitive process in which individuals and groups vie for the attention of policy makers and ordinary citizens. The task involves transforming the harmful dilemmas experienced by individuals as private troubles into public issues, into social problems that can be improved (Mills, 1959). This political process means that social problems change over time, often without reference to changes in the extent of harm. Sometimes a known condition accepted at one point becomes unacceptable subsequently and, hence, a social problem. For example, the inequality that is intrinsic to traditional marriages became a social problem recently. Sometimes a known condition defined as harmful at one time becomes acceptable later; marijuana use, for example. Finally, a previously unknown harmful condition can become salient due to new scientific data and thereby become a social problem, such as global warming. The examples suggest the dynamism underlying identification of social problems.

This continuing activity reflects a belief in the possibility of improvement. In Western culture, people tend to be optimistic, to have a sense that their lives and the society in general can get better and to believe that progress has occurred (Nisbet, 1969). Social science can be enormously helpful in this context, since it can provide reasonably objective analyses of the dimensions of a harmful condition, assess the potential consequences for individuals and societies of various strategies for solving the problem, and suggest the possible side effects of actually reducing the harm. Wisdom, however, does not necessarily follow from knowledge and no guarantee exists that social scientific analyses will lead to improvement in a social problem (Rule, 1978). This is partly because many harmful conditions are unintended results of historical progress and provide benefits for certain segments of the population. Hence, people disagree over what 'improvement' means and, depending on their economic interests or moral values, one person's solution is often another's problem (Merton, 1961).

A social problem can be studied from at least three angles. The first is the SOCIOLOGY OF KNOWLEDGE: the process by which reality is socially constructed (Berger and Luckmann, 1966). In this case, the task is to understand how and why one harmful condition rather than another is identified as a social problem. Spector and Kitsuse (1987) have proposed a model for the study of this process that focuses on the claims people make about the harmfulness of some condition and the political debate that follows. The second perspective is that of SOCIAL PSYCHOLOGY: the way people interact with one another, influence groups to which they belong and are influenced by groups. Thus it is possible to specify how individuals' parents and friends, and others who are significant to them, influence them to become poor, use drugs, obtain an abortion or engage in any action identified as a social problem. The third approach is in terms of SOCIAL STRUCTURE: the way social organization influences rates of behaviour. For example, the high rate of poverty in the USA reflects the impact of the structure of the electoral process, macroeconomic policies and other factors that have little to do with why particular individuals become poor (Beeghley, 1989). More generally, it is possible to show how the social structure influences the rate of drug use, abortion or any issue defined as a social problem. A structural approach to a social problem is useful as a means of discovering its hidden dimensions, especially the distribution of conflicting interests and benefits in a society (Merton, 1949). When the insights from all three angles of vision are taken together, then a relatively complete picture of a social problem emerges.

Reading
Beeghley, L. 1989: *The Structure of Social Stratification in the United States.*
Merton, R.K. 1949 (*1968*): Manifest and latent functions. In *Social Theory and Social Structure*, ed. R.K. Merton.
Mills, C.W. 1959: *The Sociological Imagination.*
Spector, M. and Kitsuse, J.I. 1987: *Constructing Social Problems.*

LEONARD BEEGHLEY

social psychology In broadest terms the central task of social psychology is the systematic study of the relation between individual and collective phenomena. This daunting task overlaps with that of other social sciences, particularly SOCIOLOGY. Mainstream social psychology, however, clearly bears the stamp of its origin in psychology. Like its parent discipline it views science as a hypothetico-deductive enterprise; it interprets its central task psychologically as the study of individuals under the influence of the actual, implied or imagined presence of others. Its phenomenal rise in productivity began in the 1930s when the geographical centre of all psychology had shifted from Europe to the United States. There the concentration on individuals was further strengthened by the ideological individualism of American culture.

From its very beginning mainstream social psychology adopted a cognitive orientation. The central concept of the discipline is 'attitude', recognized already in 1935 as indispensable for social psychological thought (Allport, 1935). Attitude is defined as a combination of beliefs, feelings and intentions to act *vis-à-vis* aspects of the external world or the self. While all social sciences use this concept, it is social psychology that clarified it, made it measurable and studied it in its own right, not just as an adjunct to other concerns.

Because attitudes to minority groups, particu-

larly colour prejudice and anti-Semitism, were so disturbing a feature of the social scene not only in the USA but also in the totalitarian regimes in Europe, their study became, and continues to be, one focus of social psychological research. The structure of attitudes, their origin, influence on behaviour, proclivity and reluctance to change have been fully documented. The best known substantive contribution to the study of prejudicial attitudes is *The Authoritarian Personality* (Adorno et al., 1950). This influential but also much criticized work conceived authoritarian attitudes as manifestations of personality, not just as surface opinions, not innate but bred in authoritarian families which, in turn, reflect aspects of the social scene.

Current thinking in this field has broadened the approach in two directions: there is a growing realization that aspects of the social structure within which such attitudes are held must form part of their explanation (Hewstone and Brown, 1986). Secondly, identification with the in-group and consequent in-group favouritism has been put on a broader basis. Henri Tajfel (1981) has postulated that this is a universal cognitive predisposition, whatever the defining attributes of the in- or out-group. (See also GROUP.)

A second strand of concerns developed under the powerful influence of Kurt Lewin: the study of small groups. Group dynamics investigated the influence of leadership styles on the productivity and cohesion of groups, identified communication patterns, compared individual judgements with group decisions, documented the regular emergence of informal roles in continuing groups and other structural aspects. The repeated experimental demonstration that group pressure can induce individuals to deny the evidence of their senses (Asch, 1952) made conformity a much studied subject. For a time, interest in the experimental study of group functioning receded, although the application of what had been learned flourished in group training and group therapy. Now interest has revived in the study of leadership and in two previously neglected issues: the polarization of opinions in a group (in contrast to the earlier emphasis on group consensus); and the power of a determined minority to influence the majority.

Because of mainstream social psychology's commitment to hypothetico-deductive procedures, work on these major and many minor strands is as a rule guided by middle-range theories, designed specifically for social psychological topics, although the major theories of general PSYCHOLOGY – behaviourism, learning theories, gestalt psychology and psychoanalysis – have also provided hypotheses. The dominant social psychological theories have two common features: their subject matter is the striving for equilibrium when confronted with discordant information; and second, their common origin lies in the seminal work of Fritz Heider (1958), who analysed commonsense psychology and found there a tendency to avoid contradictions and asymmetrical relations. Several models of the striving for consistency, balance, conformity and symmetrical exchanges exist which differ from each other more in terminology than substance. Dissonance and attribution theory have created the most voluminous body of experimental work.

Dissonance theory (Festinger, 1957) proposes that when confronted with two mutually contradictory items of information people feel uncomfortable and hence strive to eliminate the discomfort by either disregarding one item or minimizing its significance. Numerous ingeniously designed experiments have shown that this is indeed the case for a majority of experimental subjects.

Attribution theory (Kelley, 1967) concerns the manner in which people analyse social events and attribute reasons or causes for them. This is currently the dominant theoretical approach; it is continuously developing and is used in the investigation of a large variety of topics. It owes its position in the field to the relatively high level of abstraction at which it is formulated. More specific theories, like that of the 'just society' which explains the tendency to blame the victim, or the theory of 'learned helplessness', can easily be subsumed under the attribution of causes or reasons for any given state of affairs.

The progressive refinement of attribution theory was in part stimulated by dissident voices within the discipline which arose not only in the United States but also in Europe. After the middle of the century these voices acquired momentum and initiated a critical self-examination on both continents. Mainstream social psychology, it was pointed out in this wide-ranging debate, had emphasized predominantly individual cognitive processes and had neglected the social context; it had relied too exclusively on experiments in laboratory settings, thus restricting the social side of the discipline, and had assumed cultural and temporal universality for its findings. The events at most

universities during the late 1960s added strength to the demand for reorientation.

By and large this self-criticism was salutory. Mainstream social psychology has become much more relevant to the understanding of everyday life and broadened its repertoire of methods. Substantive matters are now less often based on hypothetical social situations, more often studied where they are actually experienced. Attribution theory now guides research in a wide array of circumstances with people from many walks of life. The distinction between the biological concept 'sex' and the social psychological one of 'gender' is producing a necessary corrective to research results. Some areas of investigation that had always been studied in their natural setting, such as the social psychology of illness and health, or employment and unemployment, have received new impetus.

Parallel to this flourishing mainstream, radical new thinking about some fundamental issues in social psychology is now taking place. While most of these contemporary approaches have still to prove their mettle by contributing substantive knowledge about the two-way interaction between individuals and the social world, the ideas they propose find adherents, particularly in Europe but also in the USA, and give rise to much discussion and controversy. As a rule they take off from a critique of mainstream social psychology and proceed to programmatic formulations.

Kenneth Gergen (1973) argues that the mainstream is insensitive to the passage of time; theories are formulated as if they pointed to timeless regularities, but the empirical observations which support them are inevitably tied to the time of investigation and cannot claim transhistorical validity. According to Gergen, social psychology is therefore a historical and not a scientific discipline. This is in sharp contrast to the parental discipline which aims at discovering universals in the functioning of human and animal organisms.

Just like unconcern with time, others maintain, so unconcern with culture is in need of correction; American social psychology, in particular, is often accused of a parochialism that mistakes itself for a culture-free enterprise. Once again it is a question of whether social psychologists could aim at discovering universals or have to make do with specifics.

From different quarters comes the demand for changing the manner of theorizing in the discipline. Originating in the Frankfurt school, the construction of critical theory (termed 'generative' in the USA), that is a theory not about what is but about what could be, is being advocated; in the Frankfurt version for all social sciences, in the American formulation by and for social psychologists.

The widely recognized relative neglect of the social context in mainstream social psychology is now being challenged in a variety of ways. Some social psychologists are finally bridging the gap between the psychological and the sociological branches of the discipline. The study of social representations, that is the shared ideas, values and rules in a group or culture which are so powerful that they are taken for granted by individuals, has become the centre of a new approach. Perhaps the most widely shared social representations are encapsulated in a common language; modern studies have demonstrated that grammatical and semantic language habits can explain some psychological phenomena.

Another approach to the study of social influences on attitudes and behaviour distinguishes levels of explanation, each of them legitimate in its own right, but yielding full understanding only when all levels are considered. Psychological phenomena can be explained on at least four levels: by personal attributes, by the actual situation in which the psychological phenomenon is studied, by reference to people's social position and by the ideologies or belief systems to which they adhere. How complementarity rather than conflict between explanations on these levels can be achieved in empirical work is still an open question.

Even though these and other recent developments are not necessarily compatible with each other, they have common features and common functions. All of them transcend a narrow definition of social psychology; all of them require that their proponents be versed in one or more neighbouring disciplines, above all sociology and cognitive psychology, but also ANTHROPOLOGY, politics, philosophy or linguistics; all of them contribute to the intellectual vitality of the field in all its branches. Whether the debate among them will lead to a more unified social psychology or to greater separateness only time will tell.

Reading
Brown, R. 1986: *Social Psychology*, 2nd edn.
Israel, J. and Tajfel, H. 1972: *The Context of Social Psychology*.

MARIE JAHODA

social science, philosophy of *See* PHILOSOPHY OF SOCIAL SCIENCE

social statistics These compilations of quantified information about people, populations, property and so forth go back a long way. Counting and recording features of the social world began in ancient times and there are notable examples throughout history. In the Middle Ages there was the Domesday Book, a catalogue of the ownership of land in England, made for tax purposes by order of William the Conqueror in 1086. In the sixteenth century, vital statistics, describing baptisms and burials, began to be recorded in the registers of parish churches in Britain and France. In the early seventeenth century, the spread of merchant capitalism fostered systematic empirical enquiry and stimulated the gathering of demographic and economic facts in order to inform government policy, for example, by determining the human and material resources available for the military, and by estimating the cost of poor relief. In the early nineteenth century in Britain and France and the late nineteenth century in Germany and America, the advent of industrial capitalism brought renewed interest in systematically collecting economic and vital statistics to guide government policy. Centralized state agencies were established to coordinate the collection of what are now known as official statistics. For example, the General Register Office for the civil registration of vital statistics was established in London in 1836 (Nissel, 1987). (It is now known as the Office of Population Censuses and Surveys, OPCS.) Other Western countries instituted similar agencies during the nineteenth century, and national decennial censuses were initiated over the same period.

In addition to state records, social statistics may be collected by means of a SOCIAL SURVEY. Surveys have often been the tools of social reformers. For example, the nineteenth-century bourgeoisie in several countries, concerned about the fate of the newly urbanized industrial working class and about their own position in society, formed statistical societies. The purposes of these were to organize large-scale surveys and publish learned journals in support of the reforms they believed would stabilize society. A second phase of privately sponsored social surveys began in England during the economic depression at the end of the nineteenth century, with the aim of documenting the levels of poverty among urban dwellers. Charles Booth's survey of the London poor, conducted at the turn of the century, is the best known of these (Booth, 1892–7). It was followed by many more, which gradually became more technically sophisticated in both the use of sampling and inferential STATISTICS to generalize the results to the wider populations from which the samples were drawn, and the use of multivariate techniques to establish the magnitudes of relationships between the factors investigated, such as the influence of age and sex on voting. In Britain, the state too began to undertake wide-ranging social surveys, with what is now the Social Survey Division of OPCS emerging out of the Wartime Social Survey set up during World War II.

Criticisms of social statistics are of two sorts. First, there are technical criticisms of the quality of the data recorded and of the way in which it is presented. For example, should measures of people's incomes be based on their tax returns if there is a substantial black economy of undeclared earnings, and should average income be presented using the mean or the median?

Second, there are criticisms that spurious scientific or objective status is accorded to social statistics simply because they are numbers (Irvine, Miles and Evans, 1979). Such criticisms contend that just because social statistics are quantitative, it must not be forgotten that they are social products, influenced by the production methods and interests of their producers like any other social creation. Numerical information is no more neutral and free from political opinion than more qualitative accounts of the social world.

The lesson to be learned from these criticisms is that it is easy to lie with social statistics (Huff, 1954) and they must therefore be assessed carefully by asking how the features of the social world that they record were defined and measured.

Reading
Abrams, P. 1968: *The Origins of British Sociology*.
Bulmer, M. ed. 1985: *Essays on the History of British Sociological Research*.
Lazarsfeld, P.F. 1961: Notes on the history of quantification in sociology: trends, sources and problems. *Isis* 52, 277–333.
Oberschall, A. ed. 1972: *The Establishment of Empirical Sociology: Studies in Continuity, Discontinuity and Institutionalisation*.
Shaw, M. and Miles, I. 1979: The social roots of statistical knowledge. In *Demystifying Social Statistics*, ed. J. Irvine, I. Miles and J. Evans.
Slattery, M. 1986: *Official Statistics*.

PETER HALFPENNY

social stratification   In all complex societies, the total stock of valued resources is distributed unequally, with the most privileged individuals or families enjoying a disproportionate amount of property, power or prestige. Although it might be possible to construct an exhaustive rank-ordering of individuals based on their control over these resources, the approach taken by most scholars is to identify a set of 'social classes' or 'strata' that reflect the major cleavages in the population. The task of stratification research is to specify the shape and contours of these social groupings, to describe the processes by which individuals are allocated into different social outcomes (see SOCIAL MOBILITY) and to uncover the institutional mechanisms by which social inequalities are generated and maintained.

Forms of stratification

It has been conventional among contemporary theorists to distinguish between modern 'class systems' and the 'estates' or 'castes' originally found in advanced agrarian societies (see Mayer and Buckley, 1970; Svalastoga, 1965). The table defines these forms of stratification in terms of their underlying assets (column 1), their most important social groupings (column 2) and the structure of their mobility opportunities (column 3). It should be kept in mind, of course, that the foregoing systems are best seen as 'ideal types' rather than descriptions of existing societies (Weber, 1921–2). Indeed, the stratification systems of human societies are complex and multidimensional, if only because the institutional forms of their past tend to 'live on' in conjunction with new and emerging forms (see Wright, 1985, for a related typology; also, see Lenski, 1966; Runciman, 1974).

The first line in the table lists some of the basic principles underlying ethnic castes (see CASTE). As indicated in column 1, the castes of India can be ranked on a continuum of ethnic purity, with the highest positions in the system reserved for those castes which prohibit activities or behaviours that are seen as 'polluting' (such as eating meat, scavenging). In its ideal-typical form, a caste system does *not* allow for individual mobility of any kind (see line 1, column 3); the newborn child is

Principal assets, major strata and mobility process for three forms of social stratification

Stratification system	Principal assets (1)	Major strata (2)	Mobility process (3)
1 Caste system	Ethnic purity	Castes	Hereditary
2 Feudal system	Land and labour power	Kings, lords and serfs	Hereditary
3 Class system	Means of production	Capitalists and workers	Competitive

permanently assigned to the caste affiliation of its parents. Although a caste system of this form is often seen as the 'limiting case' of stratification, it should be noted that feudal systems (see FEUDA-LISM) are also based on a rigid system of quasi-hereditary groups (see line 2, column 3). The distinctive feature of feudalism is the institution of personal bondage (Bloch, 1940); that is, serfs were obliged to live on a manor and pay rents of various kinds (for instance, 'corvée labour'), since the feudal lord held the legal rights to their labour power. If a serf took flight to the city, this was nothing less than a form of theft; the serf was stealing that portion of his labour power which was owned by his lord (Wright, 1985, p. 78). It might be said, then, that 'labour power' was one of the principal assets in a feudal system (see line 2, column 1).

The most striking development of the modern era has been the rise of egalitarian ideologies (see line 3). This can be seen, for example, in the revolutions of the eighteenth and nineteenth centuries, where the ideals of the Enlightenment were directed against the privileges of rank and the political power of the aristocracy. In the end, these struggles eliminated the last residues of feudal privilege, but they also made it possible for new forms of inequality and stratification to emerge. It is usually argued that a 'class system' developed in the early industrial period, with the major strata in this system being defined in largely economic terms. There is, of course, considerable controversy over the contours and boundaries of these economic classes (see below). As indicated in line 3, a simple Marxian model might focus on the cleavage between capitalists and workers, whereas other models represent the class structure as a continuous gradation of 'monetary wealth and income' (Mayer and Buckley, 1970, p. 15). The important point, however, is that these positions in a class system are allocated in a *formally* competi-

tive fashion (see line 3, column 3). Although the results from contemporary surveys indicate that occupations are frequently 'passed on' from parents to children (Goldthorpe, 1980), this reflects the operation of indirect mechanisms of inheritance (socialization, on-the-job training and so on) rather than legal sanctions that directly prohibit mobility.

Sources of stratification
The foregoing sketch makes it clear that a range of stratification systems has emerged over the course of human history. The question that naturally arises, then, is whether some form of stratification is an inevitable feature of human societies. In addressing this question, it is useful to begin with the functional analysis of Davis and Moore (1945), since here we find an explicit effort to understand 'the universal necessity which calls forth stratification in any social system' (p. 242; also see Davis, 1953; Moore, 1963). The starting point for their approach is the premise that all societies must devise some means of motivating their most competent workers to fill the important and difficult occupations. This 'motivational problem' might be addressed in a variety of ways, but the simplest solution is to fashion a hierarchy of rewards (such as prestige, property, power) that privileges the incumbents of functionally important positions. As noted by Davis and Moore (1945, p. 243), this amounts to setting up a system of institutionalized inequality (a 'stratification system'), with the occupational structure serving as a conduit through which unequal rewards and perquisites are disbursed. It follows that the stratification system might be seen as an 'unconsciously evolved device by which societies insure that the important positions are conscientiously filled by the most qualified persons' (ibid.).

This approach has been criticized for neglecting the 'power element' in stratification systems (Wrong, 1959, p. 774; also see Huaco, 1966, for a comprehensive review). It has long been argued that Davis and Moore failed 'to observe that . . . incumbents [of functionally important positions] have the power not only to insist on payment of expected rewards but to demand even larger ones' (Wrong, 1959, p. 774; also see Dahrendorf, 1957). In this regard, the stratification system might be seen as self-reproducing: the workers in important positions can use their power to influence the distribution of resources and to preserve or extend their own privileges. It would be difficult, for instance, to account fully for the advantages of feudal lords without referring to their ability to *enforce* their claims though moral, legal or economic sanctions. According to this line of reasoning, the distribution of rewards not only reflects the 'latent needs' of the larger society, but also the balance of power among competing groups and their members (Collins, 1975).

The structure of modern stratification

The recent history of stratification theorizing is in large part a history of debates about the contours of inequality in advanced industrial societies. Although these debates have been waged on a wide variety of fronts, it will suffice for our purposes to distinguish between 'Marxist' and 'Weberian' models of inequality. It is probably fair to say that most contemporary theorists can trace their intellectual roots to some combination of these two traditions.

Marxists and neo-Marxists   The debates within the Marxist and neo-Marxist camps have been especially contentious, not only because they are frequently embedded in wider political disputes, but also because the discussion of class within *Capital* (Marx, 1894) turns out to be fragmentary and unsystematic. At the end of the third volume of *Capital*, we find the now-famous fragment on 'the classes' (Marx, 1894, pp. 885–6), but this breaks off at just that point where Marx appeared ready to advance a formal definition of the term. It is clear, nonetheless, that his abstract model of capitalism was resolutely dichotomous, with the conflict between capitalists and workers constituting the driving force behind further social development. This simple two-class model was designed to capture the 'developmental tendencies' of capitalism; however, whenever Marx carried out concrete analyses of existing capitalist systems, he recognized that the class structure was complicated by

the persistence of transitional classes (such as landowners), quasi-class groupings (peasants), and class fragments (the 'lumpenproletariat'). It was only with the progressive maturation of capitalism that Marx expected these complications to disappear as the 'centrifugal forces of class struggle and crisis flung all *dritte Personen* to one camp or the other' (Parkin, 1979, p. 16).

The recent history of modern capitalism suggests that the class structure will not evolve in such a precise and tidy fashion. Of course, the old middle class of artisans and shopkeepers has declined in relative size, but at the same time a 'new middle class' of managers, professionals and non-manual workers has expanded to occupy the newly vacated space. The last 50 years of neo-Marxist theorizing might be seen as the 'intellectual fall-out' from this development, with some commentators seeking to minimize its implications, and others putting forward a revised mapping of the class structure that accommodates the new middle class in explicit terms. Within the former camp, the principal tendency is to claim that the lower sectors of the new middle class are in the process of being proletarianized, since 'capital subjects [non-manual labour] . . . to the forms of rationalization characteristic of the capitalist mode of production' (Braverman 1974, p. 408). This line of reasoning suggests that the working class may gradually expand in numerical size and thereby regain its earlier power. At the other end of the continuum, Poulantzas (1974) has argued that most members of the new intermediate stratum fall *outside* the working class proper, since they are engaged in 'unproductive labour' of various kinds (see Wright, 1985, for a comprehensive review of these positions).

Weberians and neo-Weberians   The rise of the 'new middle class' turns out to be less problematic for scholars working within a Weberian framework. In fact, the class model advanced by Weber suggests a *multiplicity* of class cleavages, because it equates the economic class of workers with their 'market situation' (Weber, 1921–2, pp. 926–40). This model implies that wealthy property-owners are in a privileged class situation; indeed, members of this class can outbid workers for valued goods in the commodity market, and they can also convert their wealth to capital and thereby monopolize entrepreneurial opportunities. However, Weber emphasized that skilled workers are also privileged under modern capitalism, since the services that they provide are in high demand on the labour market. The end result, then, is that a new middle class of skilled workers intervenes between the 'positively privileged' capitalist class and the 'negatively privi-leged' mass of unskilled labourers (ibid., pp. 927–8). At the same time, the stratification system is further complicated by the existence of *status groupings*, which Weber saw as forms of social affiliation that often competed with class-based forms of organization. Although an economic class is merely an aggregate of individuals in a similar market situation, Weber defined a status grouping as a community of individuals who share a 'style of life' and interact as status equals (the nobility, an ethnic caste, and so on). Under some circum-stances, the boundaries of a status grouping might be determined by purely economic criteria, yet Weber notes that 'status honor need not necessarily be linked with a class situation' (ibid., p. 932). The *nouveaux riches*, for example, are never immediately accepted into 'high society', even when their wealth clearly places them in the uppermost economic class (pp. 936–7). The implication, then, is that the class and status systems are potentially indepen-dent forms of stratification.

This approach was elaborated and extended by sociologists seeking to understand the 'American form' of stratification. During the postwar decades, the Marxist model of class was typically dismissed by American sociologists as overly simplistic and one-dimensional, whereas the Weberian model was seen as properly distinguishing between the numerous variables which Marx had conflated in his definition of class (see, for instance, Barber, 1968). In the most extreme versions of this approach, the dimensions identified by Weber were disaggregated into a multiplicity of stratification variables (such as income, education, ethnicity), and it was then shown that the correlations between these variables were weak enough to generate various forms of 'status inconsistency' (that is, a poorly-educated millionaire, a black doctor, and so on). The overall picture that emerged suggested a 'pluralistic model' of stratification; that is, the class system was represented as intrinsically multidi-mensional, with a host of cross-cutting affiliations producing a complex patchwork of internal class cleavages. It should be noted that the competing forces of ETHNICITY and GENDER appear to be especially important in undermining class-based forms of solidarity (see Hechter, 1975; Firestone, 1970). Indeed, given the rise of feminist and nationalist movements throughout the modern world, it could well be argued that ethnic and gender-based groups have become *more* effective than economic classes in mobilizing their members to pursue collective goals.

Reading
Bendix, Reinhard and Lipset, Seymour M. eds 1966: *Class, Status, and Power*.
Bottomore, T.B. 1965 (*1991*): *Classes in Modern Society*.
Dahrendorf, Ralf 1957 (*1959*): *Class and Class Conflict in Industrial Society*.
Giddens, Anthony 1973: *The Class Structure of the Advanced Societies*.
Goldthorpe, John H. 1980 (*1987*): *Social Mobility and Class Structure in Modern Britain*, revised edn.
Lenski, Gerhard E. 1966: *Power and Privilege*.
Ossowski, Stanislaw 1957 (*1963*): *Class Structure in the Social Consciousness*.
Parkin, Frank 1979: *Marxism and Class Theory: A Bourgeois Critique*.
Weber, Max 1921–2 (*1978*): *Economy and Society*, vol. 2 (2-vol. edn).
—— 1946: Class, status, and party. In *From Max Weber: Essays in Sociology*, ed. H.H. Gerth and C.W. Mills.
Wright, Erik O. 1985: *Classes*.

DAVID B. GRUSKY

social structure   Although this is one of the most important concepts in the social sciences, since most social scientists do not define terms precisely it is often difficult to distinguish it in its use from such alternative terms as social organization and social system. The first explicit use of the term social structure was probably made by Herbert Spencer (1858). However, the concept of social structure dates to a much earlier period and is central to Ibn Khaldun in his book *Muqadimmah* written in the late fourteenth century.

Structure may be defined as an organized body of mutually connected parts. In social structure the parts are relationships among persons and the organized body of the parts may be considered to be coincident with the society as a whole. Also implicit in the concept of social structure is that there is some degree of permanence over time. Here, emphasis will be placed on theorists whose profes-sional careers began or ended in the twentieth century. However, twentieth-century thought is indebted to the thinking of persons who lived in previous centuries. Their contributions cannot be ignored. In what follows I shall focus on two basic questions about the nature of social structure that have been of paramount importance to social theorists. Concerning each of these questions scholarly agreement has not yet been reached.

The first question concerns the extent to which social structure is based primarily on consent or on coercion. In 1858 Herbert Spencer paired the term structure with the term function. In doing so, he invoked a metaphor of society as similar to the human organism. This analogy implies that all parts of society are integrated and that each serves to uphold the existing whole. Since there is no room for conflict in such an analogy, it also follows that the basis of societal existence is CONSENSUS and not COERCION. Karl Marx's theory (1845–6; 1848), advanced in the mid-nineteenth century, is in direct opposition to this view of society. For Marx each existing form of society (such as feudalism or capitalism) was based on the coercion exercised by the dominant class on subordinate classes. Nevertheless, in Marx's theory, conflict would disappear after the proletarian revolution and the establishment of socialism. Among twentieth-century theorists, the importance of consensus was emphasized heavily by Emile Durkheim (1893), A. R. Radcliffe-Brown (1952), and Talcott Parsons (1951). On the other hand, a conflict view of society is presented in the work of Ralf Dahrendorf (1957). Unlike Marx, Dahrendorf has emphasized that conflict will be present in both socialist and capitalist societies. Most sociological theorists have believed that social structure is partly based on consensus and partly on coercion. Twentieth-century theorists of this ilk have included Max Weber (1922), Vilfredo Pareto (1916–19), and Robert Merton (1949). Merton's term dysfunction explicitly denotes that certain elements of the social structure may work against the maintenance of the other elements.

All social theorists have recognized that change in social structure occurs over time. However, the nature of such change has been debated. Some theorists have viewed change in social structure as cyclical. Others have argued that social change occurs in a linear direction and have espoused theories of evolution.

Ibn Khaldun (1377) was the first of the cyclical theorists. Based on his empirical observations of Arab societies in medieval North Africa, he postulated the existence of two types of society, a nomadic herding society in which social solidarity was strong, and an urban society with a relatively low level of social solidarity; he pictured a cycle in which the herding society conquered the urban and established a new state. However, decreasing social solidarity in the urban society gradually led to its disintegration and finally to its conquest by another herding society. In the twentieth century the two most prominent cyclical theorists have been Oswald Spengler (1918–22) and P. A. Sorokin (1937–41). Spengler, in a work published shortly after the end of World War I, rejected the idea of progress and saw civilization as a continuing cycle of growth, decay, and death; in particular, contemporary Western civilization was seen as moribund. Sorokin, in a work published shortly before World War II, saw society as passing through a cycle with three stages, ideational (religious), idealistic, and sensate. According to his principle of immanent change, each type laid the seeds of its own destruction and the transition from one stage to another was accompanied by war and social crisis.

The idea that change in social structure moves in a single direction was first advanced by Henri de Saint-Simon early in the nineteenth century, and it was elaborated by his protégé Comte (1830–42), who postulated three stages in the development of social structure: the theological, the metaphysical, and the positive. Marx also believed that change in social structure evolved in a single direction, the driving force being change in the mode of economic production. Spencer was also very much interested in stages of human evolution, particularly with respect to the family, the state, and religion (Spencer, 1876–96).

In 1911 Franz Boas criticized attempts to make excessively precise descriptions of the evolution of social structure (Boas, 1911). Perhaps because of his influence, during the remainder of the first half of the century, scholarly interest in how social structure might evolve over time waned. Interest was revived after World War II, particularly following the publication of a book by Walter Goldschmidt (1959) detailing five stages of society as dependent on levels of technology, and in one of his last works, Parsons (1966) examined the evolution of social structure in terms of the process of differentiation of both structure and function in a manner reminiscent of Spencer.

See also STRUCTURALISM.

Reading
Leach, E.R. 1968: Social structure: the history of the concept. In International Encyclopedia of the Social Sciences, ed. D.L. Sills, vol. 14.
Moore, W.E. 1963: Social Change.

Moseley, K.P. and Wallerstein, I. 1978: Precapitalist social structures. *Annual Review of Sociology* 4, 259–90.

Smelser, N.J. 1988: Social structure. In *Handbook of Sociology*, ed. N.J. Smelser.

Udy, S.H. 1968: Social structure: social structural analysis. In *International Encyclopedia of the Social Sciences*, ed. D.L. Sills, vol. 14.

DAVID M. HEER

social survey In the earlier part of the twentieth century this referred to large-scale collection of social data by any or several means, usually about a single community treated as a unit. It was especially associated with studies of the poor and a desire to improve social conditions. Nowadays it has come to mean the collection of standardized data on a relatively large number of cases by asking questions, either in a face-to-face interview or by a self-completion schedule. It is no longer usually about a community, and the method is no longer associated with any particular topic. While the change in usage did not take place at one point in time, World War II may be treated practically as the dividing line.

The earlier social survey was an integral part of Anglo-American movements for social reform. In the USA it was part of the Progressive movement and the social gospel, while in Britain it fed discussion of 'the condition of England question'. The major British contributions were made by the great poverty studies: Charles Booth's massive *Life and Labour of the People of London* (1892–7) and B. S. Rowntree's York studies (1901, 1941). A. L. Bowley, a social statistician, also did important work in applying the theory of sampling to surveys, and showing that information about a smaller number of people, if they were systematically chosen by an appropriate method, could give a good estimate of the figures for a whole population (Bowley and Bennett-Hurst, 1915). In the USA, a 'social survey movement' developed in which the model was for communities to study themselves in order to devise a plan for collective civic improvement (see Elmer, 1917). By the 1930s, this movement was no longer important, although rural sociologists in the land-grant universities and the US Department of Agriculture still continued to carry out similar studies in rural areas.

This had by then, however, become one of the developing strands which were eventually to be combined to produce the modern survey. These strands included political polls, market research, and the Census and other data collection by government (Converse, 1987). The institution of the survey research agency, available to carry out surveys for anyone with the money to pay, began to emerge. Whatever it was called, the survey was thus becoming professionalized. During World War II, both British and American governments found it expedient to collect survey data on their civilian populations, on such topics as the response to rationing. In America there was also large-scale study of the armed forces, and some of the results of this were later published in the famous *American Soldier* volumes (Stouffer et al., 1949–50).

As a result of all this activity, significant technical advances were made, many of them associated with Paul Lazarsfeld's programme of development and codification of method. The postwar expansion of the social sciences meant that the survey could and did become institutionalized within the universities, where it is used in most social-science disciplines, as well as in government and commerce.

The stereotype of the modern social survey is based on a large representative sample of individuals and collects its data by a questionnaire with a few 'open-ended' questions (where the respondents answer in their own words) and more closed ones (with a fixed set of alternatives to choose from); the questionnaire is completed by an interviewer, who will have received some training in interview technique; the answers will be quantified, with those to open-ended questions being 'coded' (classified into categories) to make this possible, and analysed on a computer. In practice there are many variations from this stereotype. A whole population may be studied, and samples are frequently not designed to be representative of areas; the units may be organizations or families rather than individuals. The 'questionnaire' may have so many open-ended questions that it converges with intensive unstructured interviewing. The questionnaire may be completed entirely by the respondent, with or without assistance, and telephone interviewing is becoming increasingly common.

There is, of course, no right answer to the question of where 'survey' ends and other types of research begin. C. Marsh (1982, p. 6) redefined 'survey' to mean any social investigation where systematic measurements are made on a set of cases, and the co-variation across cases is analysed for patterns. The function of this redefinition is to direct attention to the structure of the data and how they can be analysed, and away from the means by which they were collected, which are seen as less important. This stimulates useful thought, but is unconventional.

The method has been much criticized. A fundamental criticism is that most surveys provide reports of behaviour rather than direct observation of it. However, this fact is not likely to create serious problems for every topic. It must also be borne in mind that a report may be better than no information, and that direct observation – especially of a large sample – is often impracticable. Surveys have also been criticized as 'positivistic', often as part of a general attack, of a kind which became fashionable in the late 1960s, on all quantification. Marsh (1982, ch. 3) has responded to these criticisms. Here it is merely noted that surveys differ so considerably from each other that it is not helpful to treat them as all the same. Moreover enormous technical advances have been made, on aspects ranging from statistical techniques to the qualitative nuances of question wording. Critics of the method in general have seldom taken the range into account, or shown familiarity with recent standards of good practice.

See also SOCIAL STATISTICS.

Reading
Converse, J.M. 1987: *Survey Research in the United States: Roots and Emergence, 1890–1960.*
Marsh, C. 1982: *The Survey Method: The Contribution of Surveys to Sociological Explanation.*
Moser, C.A. and Kalton, G. 1971: *Survey Methods in Social Investigation.*
Rossi, P., Wright, J. and Anderson, A. eds 1983: *Handbook of Survey Research.*

JENNIFER PLATT

social theory, Christian *See* CHRISTIAN SOCIAL THEORY

social theory, Hindu *See* HINDUISM AND HINDU SOCIAL THEORY

social welfare This term is the definition of the well-being of society as a whole. As such, it is a concept which assumes (however weakly) the possibility of measuring personal welfare, of comparing individual welfares, and of establishing the relationship between those (comparable) individual welfares and the sum of welfare of society as a whole. In its most ambitious form, it has assumed the guise of a *social welfare function*, an idea most closely associated with two economists, Bergson

(1938), and Samuelson (1947). Their model, effectively an exercise in transposing so-called 'individual preference scales' on to a 'social preference scale' (presumed to be the sum of individual preferences) sought to define the total well-being of society as a function of its resource allocation. This model was criticized by Arrow, who argued that any function or rule which sought to map individual preference orderings on to a social preference scale, and which obeyed minimal conditions of Universal Applicability (that all the logically possible variations of individual preferences be accommodated), Independence of Irrelevant Alternatives (that no unnecessarily detailed information violating personal privacy be required), and a Weak Pareto Principle (that at least someone be better off and no one worse off) must admit a dictator, that is, an individual whose strict preferences were imposed on society.

Various efforts to transcend Arrow's so-called 'impossibility theorem' have led to the modern discipline of *social choice theory*, or the pursuit of a normative rationale for social decisions in societies where individuals have different preferences about the use of available resources. To that end, this discipline is concerned with the aggregation of individual interests, preferences or welfares into notional aggregates of social interest, preference or welfare. And this has developed at least theoretical methods of measurement and comparability whose subtlety and ingenuity can only be admired; they cannot even be summarized here (for a short account, see Sen, 1987; see also SOCIAL CHOICE). Yet, for all its undoubted sophistication, social choice theory remains bound by the logical possibility of different aggregation exercises depending on exactly what is aggregated (interest, preferences, welfares, or even moral judgement about those three); and on what is deemed to be a proper conclusion from the exercise itself, whether simple measurement or active alteration (for example, towards equality of welfare), as a result of that exercise (see Sen, 1977 and 1986).

Similarly, social choice models, as axiomatic models of resource allocation and preference, tend to assume (for the most part) the possibility of full but not intrusive information on behalf of the decision-maker, and the legitimacy of dictatorial methods of decision-making in pursuit of maximized social welfare as a result of those calculations. In this respect, perhaps the most intriguing developments in the discipline have resulted from the systematic study of voting procedures, not merely as models for the theoretical calculation of aggregated social preferences, but as pointers to the possibility of their practical calculation at some point in the future; alternatively, there may be something to be said for Barry's (1991) plea to remove the notion of social (and individual) welfare from the assumption of collective provision altogether.

See also WELFARE ECONOMICS; WELFARE STATE.

Reading
Arrow, K.J. 1951: *Social Choice and Individual Values.*
Barry, N. 1991: *Welfare.*
Bergson, A. 1938: A reformation of certain aspects of welfare economics. *Quarterly Journal of Economics* 52, 310–34.
Samuelson, P.A. 1947: *Foundations of Economic Analysis.*
Sen, A.K. 1977: Social choice theory: a re-examination. *Econometrica* 45, 58–89.
—— 1986: Social choice theory. In *Handbook of Mathematical Economics*, vol. 3, ed. K.J. Arrow and M. Intriligator.
—— 1987: Social Choice. In *The New Palgrave: A Dictionary of Economics*, vol. 4, ed. John Eatwell, Murray Milgate and Peter Newman.

S.J.D. GREEN

socialism   Socialist ideas, in various forms, were expressed in earlier centuries but socialism as a distinctive doctrine and movement emerged only in the 1830s, when the term itself first came into general use. It then spread rapidly in Europe, particularly after the revolutions of 1848, and by the end of the century large socialist parties had developed in several countries, notably in Germany and Austria, while socialist thought had been widely diffused throughout the world.

In continental Europe MARXISM was the main intellectual foundation of socialism, combining a theory of society which explained the development of modern CAPITALISM, the division of society into two main classes, and the emergence and growth of the socialist movement itself, with a sociopolitical doctrine concerning the organization, aims and tactics of socialist parties. Elsewhere, however, and especially in Britain and North America, Marxism had less influence and alternative conceptions of socialism were formulated, for example by the Fabian Society (1889, see Shaw, ed., 1931). Nevertheless, there were common elements in all the versions of socialist thought: opposition to capitalist individualism, embodied in the very term 'socialism' which emphasized community and the well-being of society as a whole; a commitment to equality and to the idea of a future 'classless society'; and an assertion of the character of the socialist movement as a continuation of the democratic movement of the eighteenth and nineteenth centuries. All the European parties, indeed, were particularly active in the campaigns for universal suffrage, which they were largely instrumental in achieving, and some of them adopted the name 'social democratic' to express their aim of proceeding beyond political democracy to establish economic or industrial democracy.

By the beginning of the twentieth century, however, with the continuing development of capitalism, a greater diversity of socialist ideas had manifested itself, and differences had emerged between the socialist movements in various countries. In the European Marxist parties a fierce controversy erupted about REVISIONISM, following the publication of Bernstein's (1899) study in which he argued that the later development of capitalism made necessary a reassessment of Marx's theory, with regard to economic crises, the polarization of classes and the intensity of class conflict, taking into account particularly the growth of the middle classes and the general rise in standards of living. The division of opinion on these issues led in due course to a differentiation of two main tendencies, labelled 'reformist' and 'revolutionary' (though there were also some 'centrists', represented notably by Kautsky and the Austro-Marxists), which became more clearly marked after the emergence of Bolshevism as a separate tendency at the second congress of the Russian Social Democratic Labour Party in 1903. In Britain, a mainly reformist and gradualist socialist doctrine, strongly influenced by Fabian ideas, prevailed when the Labour Party (calling itself at first the Labour Representation Committee) was founded in 1900, while in the USA the socialist movement never established itself as a major political force (Sombart, 1906), reaching its peak in the vote for the Socialist Party of America in the presidential election of 1912 and declining steadily thereafter (Weinstein, 1967; Laslett and Lipset, 1974).

World War I had a profound effect on the whole socialist movement. Internationalism had been a central feature of socialist doctrine particularly since the founding of the First International (International Working Men's Association) in 1864, and by the end of the century, in face of the growing threat of war between the major imperialist powers, the socialist parties had also become anti-militarist. When war broke out, however, most of the European parties were overwhelmed by the tide of nationalist fervour and supported their own governments, though small minority groups maintained an anti-war stance. Lenin and the Bolsheviks, on the other hand, were vigorous opponents of the war from the outset, and after the Russian Revolution in 1917 they became the major force in an alternative revolutionary socialist movement. The division between this movement and the old social democratic parties of the Second International was then consolidated in an organizational form by the foundation of the Third (Communist) International in 1919, and the creation of separate communist parties in many countries.

From that point the development of socialist ideas and movements was dominated by the division and antagonism between Bolshevism and SOCIAL DEMOCRACY, which passed through various phases and generated many new problems. The attempt to establish a socialist society in Russia took place in circumstances never imagined by Marx, by most later Marxists (including Lenin and other leading Bolsheviks, who themselves had doubts about whether it could be successful without a revolution in one or more of the developed capitalist countries), or by socialists generally: in a mainly agrarian country with a very small industrial working class and a vast peasantry; devastated by war, a protracted civil war, and foreign intervention; lacking an efficient bureaucracy or experience of democratic institutions; and surrounded by hostile states. The overwhelming need was for economic reconstruction and rapid industrialization, which came to be identified with socialism. These conditions, together with some of the traditions of the Bolshevik party, provided fertile ground for the emergence of dictatorship and a totalitarian system, which Stalin finally implemented in an extreme form.

The later development of a socialist economy in the Soviet Union, with highly centralized planning and comprehensive public ownership, also raised questions which socialists had largely neglected about whether such an economy could actually function effectively in practice; and these issues were central in the debate about SOCIALIST CALCULATION of the 1920s and 1930s. During the 1930s, however, this controversy came to be overshadowed by the largely successful industrialization of the Soviet Union, reflected in very high rates of economic growth, at a time when the capitalist world was suffering a severe depression; and by the rise of fascism, which constituted a new danger both for the Soviet Union and for the democratic capitalist countries. World War II itself created a more sympathetic attitude to the Soviet Union as an ally and a major contributor, at the cost of immense sacrifices, to the defeat of Nazi Germany; and communist parties in the West benefited from these changed perceptions.

At the end of the war the Soviet Union emerged as the second industrial and military superpower, able to impose a totalitarian system on the countries of Eastern Europe, and to increase substantially its influence in world politics. Partly as a consequence of this Soviet influence, socialism also became an important force in some newly independent and developing countries: in India and several African countries in a mainly social democratic form, in China in a communist form but with its own distinctive variations, including the introduction over the past decade of a more liberal economic system which has avoided some of the problems of the Soviet economy, while still resisting a democratization of the political system.

In Western Europe the influence of socialist parties, and in some countries communist parties, also increased greatly, and in Britain the Labour government elected in 1945 with a large majority began the construction of a WELFARE STATE, at the same time extending public ownership and continuing some elements of wartime planning. In varying degrees such changes took place thoughout Western Europe, bringing into existence a new type of welfare capitalism which was successful for more than two decades in achieving exceptionally high rates of economic growth, full employment and steadily rising standards of living.

These postwar changes did not, however, overcome the division in the socialist movement between Bolsheviks and democratic socialists. On the contrary, although the Bolshevik regimes slowly became less harsh and terroristic after the death of Stalin in 1953, the monopoly of power by communist parties and the basic features of TOTALITARIANISM continued, provoking a series of popular uprisings in the 1950s and 1960s, and large-scale opposition movements in the 1980s. Social democratic socialists continued to voice their criticism of these regimes, reaffirming their view that socialism is inseparable from democracy, and that it can only be attained through a democratic and gradual process of change, in which the creation of a welfare state represents a new stage in the extension of a wide range of social rights to all citizens. Such criticism of the East European regimes, and of their monolithic ideology, took a distinctive form in the broad current of thought that came to be known as WESTERN MARXISM, much of which was assimilated to some extent by the internal opposition movements.

The collapse of the Bolshevik regimes since 1990 has removed from the political and intellectual map a form of socialist thought and practice which for more than 70 years profoundly divided the socialist movement, and in the view of most socialists distorted beyond recognition many of the fundamental ideas of socialism. But this collapse itself has posed many new questions for socialist thought. Since the Bolshevik regimes were identified with extensive state ownership (as a specific form of social ownership) and central planning, which most of the successor regimes have been abandoning in favour of some form of capitalist economy (while sacrificing at the same time some of the important social rights which were a more positive achievement of their predecessors), discussion about the basic principles of a viable socialist economy (Nove, 1983; Breitenbach et al., 1990) has become more intense. Earlier criticisms, formulated in the 'socialist calculation' debate, have been renewed (Lavoie, 1985), while the ideas of MARKET SOCIALISM – involving some combination of planning and markets, and a mixed economy of private and public enterprise – which aroused much interest and support in the 1970s and 1980s, both in Western and Eastern Europe, have been subjected to a more critical scrutiny (Brus and Laski, 1989).

Present-day socialist thought is thus beset by a great deal of uncertainty. For some thinkers, earlier socialist ideas of an egalitarian, collectively planned and self-directing society are impossibly utopian – a beautiful dream, but still only a dream – ignoring the limitations of human nature and such realities as bureaucracy, power-seeking and corruption. The real possibilities of socialism are then reduced to the implementation of a more advanced kind of welfare state within a basically capitalist economy. These thinkers also observe that postwar economic growth in the capitalist countries has created more prosperous, mass consumption societies, and a very different class structure in which earlier class opposition and conflict has substantially diminished (see CLASS), in a process to which Bernstein

(1899) perhaps only prematurely drew attention. Against these views others have argued that fundamental problems and deficiencies of capitalism – the cyclical character of economic development, with phases of expansion succeeded by depression and large-scale unemployment, massive inequalities of wealth and income, and a general instability and uncertainty – persist, and will continue to generate conceptions of an alternative economic and social order in which they might be overcome. It remains to be seen whether the present disagreements within socialist thought and socialist movements will eventually be resolved in some new and coherent formulation of socialism for the twenty-first century.

See also LENINISM.

Reading
Brus, W. and Laski, K. 1989: *From Marx to the Market: Socialism in Search of an Economic System.*
Cole, G.D.H. 1953–60: *A History of Socialist Thought*, 5 vols.
Kolakowski, L. and Hampshire, S. eds 1974: *The Socialist Idea: A Reappraisal.*
Schumpeter, J.A. 1942 (*1987*): *Capitalism, Socialism and Democracy*, 6th edn.

TOM BOTTOMORE

socialism, market *See* MARKET SOCIALISM

socialist calculation A term used with reference to controversies of the 1920s and 1930s about whether, in an economy characterized by extensive public ownership and central planning such as was being constructed in the USSR, rational economic calculation would be possible. The debate was initiated by Ludwig von Mises (1920) who argued that in a developed, complex economy such calculation requires a free market which establishes the exchange value of all goods. The planning authority in a socialist state, he claimed, can determine what consumption goods are most urgently needed, but it cannot establish a precise valuation of the means of production, so that investment decisions would depend at best upon 'vague estimates'; and he concluded tersely that 'where there is no free market, there is no pricing mechanism; without a pricing mechanism, there is no economic calculation.' The argument was then pursued by F. A. Hayek (1935) in a volume of essays which included von Mises's article, and by others.

The major response to this critique came from Oskar Lange, with contributions from Abba

Lerner and Fred M. Taylor (Lange and Taylor, 1938). At this time Lange argued for a form of MARKET SOCIALISM in which there would be a genuine market for consumer goods and labour services, but no market for capital goods and productive resources other than labour, whose prices would simply be indices of alternatives available, fixed for accounting purposes. The debate then petered out at the end of the 1930s, with both sides being able to claim a degree of success. Hayek conceded that rational economic calculation in a planned socialist economy was not in principle impossible, through the use of 'accounting prices', but maintained that it was a practical impossibility because of the great mass of (constantly changing) data involved; to which Lange replied by expounding a 'trial and error' method of establishing such prices. Hayek (1940) later argued, however, that what he called the 'competitive solution' for the organization of a socialist economy abandoned 'much of the original claim for the superiority of planning' in so far as the planned society would now rely to a great extent on competition for the direction of its industries.

This debate, or at least one side of it, revived strongly in the 1980s, especially in Britain and the USA, as an important element in the social and political doctrines of the NEW RIGHT extolling the virtues of private enterprise and free markets. The original debate itself was reinterpreted (Lavoie, 1985) in terms of the notion of 'economic rivalry', which gives prominence to alertness to new opportunities, futurity and knowledge dispersal, and conceives the function of rivalry as being to disperse decentralized information and then marshal it, through market prices, to achieve overall coordination of the economy.

The collapse of the East European communist regimes at the end of 1989, and the economic problems of the former USSR (which were also strongly affected, however, by various non-economic factors), and in another direction the economic difficulties of Britain and the USA in particular, have given a new importance to the issues raised by this debate, especially with regard to the role of NATIONAL ECONOMIC PLANNING, the MARKET and COMPETITION in promoting economic development and diffusing its benefits and costs.

Reading
Bottomore, Tom 1990: *The Socialist Economy: Theory and Practice.*

Brus, Wlodzimierz and Laski, Kazimierz 1989: *From Marx to the Market: Socialism in Search of an Economic System.*
Hayek, F.A. ed. 1935: *Collectivist Economic Planning: Critical Studies on the Possibilities of Socialism.*
—— 1940 (*1948*): The competitive solution. In *Individualism and Economic Order.*
Lange, Oskar and Taylor, Fred M. 1938 (*1964*): *On the Economic Theory of Socialism.*
Lavoie, Don 1985: *Rivalry and Central Planning: The Socialist Calculation Debate Reconsidered.*
von Mises, Ludwig 1920 (*1935*): Economic calculation in the socialist commonwealth. In *Collectivist Economic Planning*, ed. F.A. Hayek.

TOM BOTTOMORE

socialist economics   In the nineteenth century there were two broad schools of thought regarding how a socialist economy would function. First there were 'utopian socialists' such as Robert Owen and William Morris, who tried to construct detailed elements of what a new society could look like by appeal to reason and to socialist principle. Second, there were 'communists' such as Karl Marx and Friedrich Engels, who by and large eschewed such constructions in favour of an examination of contemporary capitalism. Both schools understood a socialist economy as one characterized by social rather than private ownership and control of the means of production. Since such an economy only existed in theory rather than in practice in the nineteenth century, socialist economics was basically speculative, and Marx called those who tried to construct blueprints for socialism 'utopian idealists', arguing that socialism could only evolve out of specific historical circumstances which could not be predicted in advance. His own remarks about socialism were generally confined, first, to polemics aimed at what he saw as the false ideas of other political programmes; and second, to remarks made in the course of his analysis of capitalism which emphasized the historical transience of capitalism together with the potentialities exhibited for the further development of the productive forces if privatized relations of production were socialized.

With the Bolshevik revolution of 1917 in Russia, such approaches were no longer sufficient. But while the organization of a socialist economy became a matter of practical importance, approaches to theorizing the basis of such organization differed according both to the extent of sympathy with the socialist project and to the degree of identification of the socialist project with the organization of the post-1917 Soviet economy.

This was particularly marked in an important debate begun in 1920 by Ludwig von Mises. He argued that if the means of production were no longer in private ownership, but owned and controlled collectively in some sense, then there could be no markets on which to trade means of production, for without an assignment of property rights to individuals, buying and selling becomes impossible. Hence there could be no prices for means of production. This in turn implies that costs of production cannot be calculated, and von Mises concluded that rational economic calculation in these circumstances was impossible. The socialist project was in principle doomed because of the inevitable lack of economic criteria for rational use of the means of production, and von Mises interpreted the chaos of civil war in Russia in the immediate post-revolutionary years as some evidence for his argument.

That von Mises was wrong was implicit in earlier writings of Vilfredo Pareto and Enrico Barone, but it was not until the mid-1930s that the theory underpinning these writings was used explicitly to counter his argument. This was achieved by Oskar Lange (1936–7). He assumed that people could exercise free choice in consumption and occupation, so that consumer goods markets and labour markets would operate freely. As regards means of production, he developed an iterative algorithm of price determination in the following manner. Managers of production units would be instructed to choose that combination of inputs which minimized the average cost of any given output, and produce that quantity of output at which marginal cost (the addition to costs of producing one more unit) equalled price (the addition to revenue of producing one more unit). Cost minimization is the criterion for technical efficiency in production. Marginal cost pricing is profit maximizing, and as long as prices accurately measure opportunity costs (the costs of the best alternative use of the resources in question), marginal cost pricing is socially efficient in the sense that no other use of resources could yield a more desirable outcome. The prices underlying these computations would be determined by the market in the case of labour inputs and consumer goods outputs, and by a central planning board (CPB) in the case of means of production whether as input or output. That is, the CPB would announce a set of prices, the various calculations would be performed, and input and output quantities determined and communicated to the CPB. The CPB would then raise (lower) the prices of goods in excess demand (supply), announce a new set of prices, and the procedure would continue until prices were found at which demand equalled supply for each good. Von Mises's argument was thus wrong, confusing price determination by markets with the (shadow) price determination implicit in the trade-offs which are embedded in any set of consumer preferences and production technologies. Because the CPB mimics the (perfectly competitive) market mechanism, Lange's approach became known as the 'competitive solution'. But Lange claimed advantages for his approach over the freely competitive economy. First, the rate of investment and hence growth would be determined socially, rather than in the anarchic pursuit of private profit, thereby eliminating a major cause of business cycles. Secondly, income distribution would not be tied to the inequality inherent in the ownership of or exclusion from the means of production, as in capitalism, but would be based on economic justice determined by labour performed together with a social dividend. Thirdly, prices would genuinely reflect opportunity costs, thereby enabling a solution of environmental problems which market prices reflecting only private costs cannot manage. And fourthly, the wastes of imperfect competition and monopoly inherent in capitalism would be avoided.

Lange's model of MARKET SOCIALISM was soon criticized from both 'right' and 'left', although in some respects the criticisms had a common theme. For while the market socialist model was based on the standard microeconomic theory of optimum resource allocation, much of the criticism centred on whether any sensible account of dynamics could be incorporated within this static framework.

From the left, Dobb (1939) doubted whether the decentralized allocation of investment resources was compatible with the achievement of any desired growth rate. For suppose the supply of investment funds is determined by the profitability of consumer goods production. Then as investment goods industries expand, the supply of consumer goods falls, which drives their price up (since demand has not fallen), which makes them more profitable, which increases the rate of investment; the ensuing cumulative process would make it impossible to equalize the demand and supply of investment funds at the rate of interest previously assumed. The only way out would be to tax the excess profits of consumer goods industries; but this would require a very fine differentiation of taxes between different production units which would be very complicated indeed to administer with the degree of precision required. Dobb concluded that rather than attempt indirect influence over production managers via the rate of interest and taxes (and subsidies, for the cumulative process can also work in reverse), it would be preferable for the CPB to allocate investment funds directly. This, however, runs quite counter to the decentralization of Lange's model. Such a dynamic was part of a more general argument by Dobb (reflecting on the Soviet experience) that a static optimum allocation of resources will in general conflict with typical post-revolutionary efforts to transform the socioeconomic structure and to achieve increases in growth. Further, the rationale for using a decentralized mechanism, as in Lange's model, is to reduce the burdens on the CPB, which would otherwise be faced with an enormous number of complicated alternatives; but Dobb argued that this misrepresents the situation. The CPB would not typically be faced with an impossibly large number of small problems, but would rather have to choose between a small number of technological alternatives involving input requirements not subject to marginal variation. Particularly in societies requiring major structural transformation in which economic growth is prioritized, Dobb concluded that a centralized planning mechanism was likely to be superior to any decentralized variant.

The most important criticisms from the right were made by F. A. Hayek (1940, 1945). These revolved around the issues of institutional structure, informational burden, dynamics and incentive compatibility. First, Hayek questioned whether production units could maintain any sort of independence from the centre if there were strong central preferences (for example, for growth maximization) that they act in a particular way. And he identified a further institutional problem in the lack of specificity as to who was to bear responsibility for the consequences of decisions which turn out unexpectedly. Secondly, if the CPB were to behave like a perfect market, it would have to solve millions of equations in millions of unknowns, a computational burden so heavy and requiring so much accurate information that rational economic planning – while possible in principle – would be impossible in practice. With the rapid recent development of computers, the force of this argument concerning computational burden is obviously less

today than it was in the mid-twentieth century, and the focus of the criticism has shifted more towards the difficulty of obtaining the requisite information on which to base the calculations. Hence thirdly, Hayek pointed to the absence of incentives for reducing costs of production at plant level, and for introducing technological innovations. And as regards the centre he questioned whether any CPB could react to changing conditions with the speed and accuracy required for the mechanism to work. These arguments about the economic inefficiency of socialism were embedded in more general themes concerning the incompatibility of any sort of planning with individual freedom. But there was one economic argument which assumed increasing importance with the passage of time: in Lange's model there is nothing to motivate production managers to obey the rules of the iterative (shadow price) game which it proposed.

While the 'socialist controversy' was debated in the West, the USSR after 1929 was developing a highly centralized hierarchical command system of planning (see NATIONAL ECONOMIC PLANNING). This was interpreted by supporters and some opponents alike as an attempt (in admittedly adverse conditions) to put into practice classical Marxist principles. Thus the division of labour was regulated *ex ante*; input coefficients were determined directly; supply and demand were equated in physical units; savings and investment decisions were centralized; and distribution was determined according to centrally determined wage rates together with a social dividend in kind (cheap housing, education, medical care and so on). Yet this was crudely to caricature classical Marxism. The system set in place by Stalin and his bureaucracy managed an industrialization process which ruthlessly transformed peasant labour into factory workers on the basis of a massive replication of US and German capital equipment imported in the early 1930s. Traditional factory divisions of labour were enforced, inequalities of access to individual and collective consumption goods established, traditional bourgeois freedoms (of association, speech, publication, organization) abolished, and a vast repressive state apparatus established with an ideology of emancipation and a practice of the cultivation of oppression. With traditional socialist aspirations thereby rendered a cruel joke, opposition to the status quo generally took inspiration either from the USA or from pre-revolutionary Tsarism, and was thereby easy to represent as counter-revolutionary. But the economic system established was extremely inefficient. Productivity was low relative to other economies at similar levels of development; queuing was a pervasive form of rationing consumer goods in perennial short supply, in limited assortment and of poor quality; the quality of housing, education and health care was poor by international standards; innovation rates were low with long gestation periods for investment projects such that equipment was often obsolete by the time it was installed; and there were common and ridiculous biases in both quality and quantity of output according to the particular measurement units used in the plan.

From 1962, reform proposals were allowed to be discussed openly in the USSR. These generally involved either more sophisticated methods of data collection and processing or the decentralization of significant areas of decision-making to the production unit. But few reforms were actually put into practice, for too many interest groups within the bureaucracy had a vested interest in the status quo. In particular, any partial decentralization tended to pit production units against the central planners, thereby encouraging recentralization measures as the planners sought to regain the control which the reforms had forced them to cede. By the early 1980s, Soviet economic performance had worsened markedly, to such an extent that there was widespread recognition that the existing system could not continue, coupled with little consensus as to what to do. The intelligentsia was advocating virtually complete decentralization to a market economy, whether in the Lange framework or along the lines of Scandinavian social democracy; Stalinist bureaucrats were reluctant to contemplate the dismantling of their *raison d'être*; workers were opposed to the widening of wage differentials implicit in a greater reliance on market forces; but all were agreed on the necessity for improving living standards. Considerations deriving from classical Marxism all but disappeared in what seemed a triumphant vindication of all that the critics of socialism had said all along.

The only dissent came from those who had always opposed Stalinism from the left, primarily from the Trotskyist tradition. Socialist revolution in such a backward economy as 1917 Russia could only be considered a viable project according to classical canons of historical materialism if the revolution were internationalized. With the failure of this latter by 1923, there was no way in which an isolated economy in a hostile environment could achieve levels of productivity surpassing those realized in an international capitalist world order. That bureaucratic dictatorship emerged out of the isolation of the USSR was tragic (and fatal for millions) but it did not vitiate the socialist project. What was required for the implementation of the latter was the sort of revolutionary democratization envisaged by Marx in his reflections on the Paris Commune of 1871 and endorsed by Lenin in 1917 in his *State and Revolution*, together with its international extension. But this was anathema to Soviet bureaucracy and Western capitalism alike.

Whether anathema or not, an influential polemic by Alec Nove (1983) also asserted that this combination of central planning and far-reaching democracy could not work. The reasons adduced by Nove were the standard problems of information and incentives. In addition he emphasized that economic linkages in a centrally planned system were necessarily vertical and hierarchical; only the horizontal linkages established by market relations (in however regulated a manner) were compatible with democracy. While this was denied by Mandel (1986, 1988), for example, other socialists addressed the challenge presented by Nove's reflections on the Soviet experience in a different manner. Building on elements of Lange's model, Devine (1988) sought to preserve the socialist vision through procedures of administered coordination between different democratized levels of the planning hierarchy, decisions being implemented by the use of the market mechanism. And Elson (1988) began to theorize how the market itself could be socialized by freeing labour power from commodity status. Both of these attempts were motivated by the realization that Lange's market socialism provided few of the benefits of planning that socialists had traditionally advocated. While the challenge remains to embed these benefits within a framework of genuine socialist democracy, the collapse of Stalinism in the late 1980s and early 1990s has provided the impetus for more creative thought than has existed in this area for the preceding half-century.

See also SOCIALIST CALCULATION.

Reading
Bergson, A. 1966: Socialist economics. In *Essays in Normative Economics*, ch. 9.
—— 1967: Market socialism revisited. *Journal of Political Economy* 75, 655–73.
Devine, P. 1988: *Democracy and Economic Planning*.

Elson, D. 1988: Socialization of the market. *New Left Review* 172, 3–44.

Gregory, P.R. and Stuart, R.C. 1986: *Soviet Economic Structure and Performance*, 3rd edn.

Hayek, F.A. 1940: Socialist calculation: the competitive solution. *Economica*, NS, 7, 125–49.

—— 1945: The use of knowledge in society. *American Economic Review* 35, 519–30.

Lange, O. 1936–7 (*1964*): On the economic theory of socialism. In *On the Economic Theory of Socialism*, ed. B.E. Lippincott.

Mandel, E. 1986: In defence of socialist planning. *New Left Review* 159, 5–38.

—— 1988: The myth of market socialism. *New Left Review* 169, 108–21.

Nove, A. 1983: *The Economics of Feasible Socialism*.

—— 1987: Markets and socialism. *New Left Review* 161, 98–104.

Nove, A. and Nuti, D.M. eds 1972: *Socialist Economics*.

Trotsky, L. 1937 (*1972*): *The Revolution Betrayed*.

von Mises, L. 1920 (*1972*): Economic calculation in the socialist commonwealth. In *Socialist Economics*, ed. A. Nove and D.M. Nuti.

SIMON MOHUN

socialization The processes by which human beings are induced to adopt the standards of behaviour, norms, rules and values of their social world are termed socialization. They begin in infancy and continue through life. Socialization is a learning process that relies in part on explicit teaching and in part on latent learning – that is, on the inadvertent absorption of taken-for-granted ways in relating to others. While everybody is exposed to socializing influences, individuals vary considerably in their deliberate or unwitting openness to them, from chameleon-like change in response to every new situation to complete inflexibility.

Early in the century the systematic study of these processes concentrated on infancy and childhood. Psychologists, social anthropologists and sociologists were forced by the nature of the process to borrow each others' concepts and approaches, but maintained their specific points of view. Psychologists emphasized the interaction processes, particularly in mother–child relations; social anthropologists concentrated on the transmission of culture in small, relatively homogeneous societies; and sociologists studied institutions and subcultures in complex societies as agents of socialization. The differing intellectual traditions of these disciplines are one reason why there exists no unitary theory of socialization, though many studies under each disciplinary label were, until about the middle of the century, much influenced by psychoanalytic

theory. More recently socialization studies have expanded to processes in adulthood and are guided by less global theories and use a large variety of approaches. Another reason for the absence of a unifying theory is the very broadness of the term which encompasses such diverse processes as child-rearing, schooling (see also EDUCATION AND SOCIAL THEORY), the acquisition of an occupational or workplace ethos, propaganda and brainwashing.

The early dominance of psychoanalytic thought led to some agreement on the great power of primary socialization in the family. In small, isolated cultures and in large complex societies, patterns of childrearing were investigated and used as explanation for similarities in social behaviour among people exposed to the same practices. There exists at Yale University a culture file which contains among other matters descriptions of the childrearing practices in about 300 cultures. Studies based on this material (such as Whiting and Child, 1953) have established systematic relations between these practices and the projective systems (religion, cosmology) of these cultures; they have also pointed to similarities in psychological functioning (for instance, willingness to take responsibility). In complex societies considerable variety exists in primary socialization in various subcultures, particularly social classes; this has been linked to systematic variations between them of, for instance, class-specific toleration for frustration, or differences in time perspectives.

These studies demonstrate that early socialization is inextricably interwoven with personality formation, though they are conceptually distinct processes: the former is concerned with the acquisition of shared patterns, the latter with individual differences. The conflation of the two processes led at one time to now rejected explanations of national differences entirely in terms of primary socialization.

In mid-century Talcott Parsons's influential but controversial approach to socialization kept this distinction in mind by defining socialization as the process by which people learn to fill the roles prescribed by the social system. Implicit in his thought is a normative component: achieved socialization into a given social system is always positively evaluated (Parsons et al., 1955). In this respect Robert K. Merton (1949) went beyond Parsons in his analysis of ANOMIE: socialization to the dominant success goals of a society is dysfunctional for that part of the population to which institutional means for the pursuit of the goals are denied.

The difficulty of distinguishing between personality formation and socialization leaves the question of the extent to which the results of early socialization can be undone or reversed, unanswered. Where early influences have resulted in individually or socially destructive behaviour, the helping professions have applied their range of methods with widely varying results in efforts to reverse early acquired habits; it is never an easy undertaking (see CRIME AND DEVIANCE). There is no doubt, however, that later influences can add to a person's repertoire of social behaviour.

After the family the major socializing agencies in Western societies are: the school and peer groups, entry into economic life, exposure to mass media, foundation of a family and marriage, participation in organized community life, and finally retirement conditions. A vast number of studies have dealt with the influence of each of these agencies. Other studies have started from the end product of socialization, for instance, high achievement motivation (McClelland, 1961) or gender identity, and have searched for agencies that could produce such results. Yet other studies have looked at the recipients of socialization pressures as active agents who make deliberate choices. Willis (1977), for example, has demonstrated that active, clever and rational resistance to the goals of school socialization led a group of underprivileged schoolboys to contribute actively to their socialization into unskilled and unsatisfying jobs.

This study and its interpretation by Anthony Giddens (1984) exemplifies current trends in socialization studies: they deal predominantly with adults and are often set in work situations. The once widely accepted notion of an all-powerful process resulting in 'organization man' is now replaced by studies of interaction processes and conflict between individual needs and external pressures with the aim of identifying possible changes in the socializing agency rather than in individuals (see Bailyn, 1989).

The study of socialization and socializing agencies bears on such major controversial issues in the social sciences as the nature of human nature, the nature/nurture debate and the place of values in social research. No amount of empirical evidence can finally solve these perennial questions; but evidence can and does illuminate the variety of processes that induce people to share rules and norms with some, but not with others. Socialization is a key concept in understanding the vast diversity of the social world.

Reading
Giddens, A. 1984: *The Constitution of Society.*
Graumann, C.F. ed. 1972: *Handbuch der Psychologie*, vol. 7, pp. 661–1106.

MARIE JAHODA

socialization of the economy   This conception of the development of capitalism was first outlined by Karl Marx in the manuscripts of the *Grundrisse* (1857–8) and of the third volume of *Capital* (1861–79, published 1894). In the *Grundrisse* Marx related socialization to the rapid progress of science and technology and the advent of automated production, arguing that the creation of real wealth had come to depend, not on labour time, but on the application of science to production, and that in this transformation it is the human being's

> understanding of nature and his mastery over it by virtue of his existence as a social entity – in a word the development of the social individual – which now appears as the great foundation of production and wealth.

In this process, 'general social knowledge has become a direct force of production' and 'the conditions of the social life process have been brought under the control of the general intellect' (1857–8, pp. 704–6). In *Capital* (vol. 3, chs 23 and 27) Marx emphasized another aspect in his observation that 'money capital assumes a social character with the growth of credit' while 'the mere manager performs all the real functions of the investing capitalist as such', and he concluded that this 'is the abolition of the capitalist mode of production within capitalist production itself' (see also MODE OF PRODUCTION).

Marx's conception was later elaborated by Rudolf Hilferding (1910, p. 366), who argued that

> finance capital puts control over social production increasingly into the hands of a small number of large capitalist associations, separates the management of production from ownership, and socializes production to the extent that this is possible under capitalism.

Subsequently (1927) he analysed the 'organized capitalism' of the period after World War I as a 'planned and consciously directed economy' which 'supports to a much greater extent the possibility of the conscious action of society' through the state. It was not only Marxist thinkers, however, who adopted this conception. J. A. Schumpeter (1942, p. 219), influenced no doubt by Hilferding as well as by Marx, observed that a large part of his argument about the development of capitalism 'may be summed up in the Marxian proposition that the economic process tends to socialize *itself*.'

After World War II the idea of a gradual socialization of the economy received a new impetus from the accelerating growth of large corporations, the enhanced role of financial institutions, a more thoroughgoing internationalization of the capitalist economy and a new wave of scientific and technological innovation, all of which were accompanied by more extensive state involvement in the economy, including various forms of economic planning, and a much higher level of social expenditure in the new 'welfare states'. To a degree quite unknown in earlier periods, living standards and general well-being came to depend on public expenditure and to be matters of public debate and policy making. These developments could be regarded, as they were by Schumpeter, as tending towards a socialist economy, and they were also compatible with broader views of what Touraine (1973) called the 'self-production of society' – that is to say, the conscious recognition that societies are 'the product of their labour and social relations'.

But the socialization of the economy itself may have very different outcomes depending on the context of social relations and political action in which it takes place. Hilferding argued that organized capitalism prepares the way for a socialist economy in which the major economic decisions would be made by the democratic state, while Schumpeter, analysing the 'obsolescence of the entrepreneur' as the functions of innovation and entrepreneurship are increasingly taken over by a rationalized, bureaucratic form of management, envisaged the probable emergence of a socialist system in which control over the means of production and the production process would be in the hands of a central authority. During the twentieth century, however, the growth of large corporations, state intervention and attempts to create centrally planned socialist economies have produced very diverse types of economic system. Among these are what has been described as 'corporatism' (Panitch, 1980), characterized by a mixture of public and private production, regulated by negotiation and agreement between the state, the large capitalist corporations and the trade unions; a totalitarian state economy such as came into existence in the USSR and the countries of Eastern Europe; a new kind of capitalism in which the role of the state in economic management is limited so far as possible to maintaining the conditions favourable to private enterprise while ensuring a basic level of social welfare; and, on a small scale, attempts (as in Yugoslavia) to combine central planning with the self-management of enterprises.

Taking different forms, and conceived in diverse ways in social thought, the idea of a progressive socialization of the economy has also been rejected, or excluded from consideration, by those who emphasize individual action and the unplanned evolution of society through accumulated experience (Hayek, 1973–9). What is evident, at all events, is that any process of socialization thus far has not created on a large scale a public awareness of the economy as a *social* enterprise, or forms of action corresponding with such an awareness, although this may perhaps be changing as a result of increasing concern about the human environment.

Reading
Habermas, Jürgen 1973 (*1976*): *Legitimation Crisis.*
Hilferding, Rudolf 1927 (*1978*): Die Aufgaben der Sozialdemokratie in der Republik. Trans. in *Austro-Marxism*, ed. Tom Bottomore and Patrick Goode.
Panitch, L. 1980: Recent theorizations of corporatism. *British Journal of Sociology* 31.

TOM BOTTOMORE

society Probably the most frequent use of the word today is in reference to the totality of human beings on earth together with their cultures, institutions, skills, ideas and values. But a considerable diversity of usages has reached the twentieth century. For example: animal society, primitive society, civil society, national society, political society, Society for the Prevention of Cruelty to Animals, high society, and so on. There is also the common use the intent of which is to stress the opposition between individual and society, which often comes down to conflict between the genetic and the social or cultural. The common denominator of most uses of the word society is the fact of sociation, animal or human. There is a society of amoebae but not a society of rocks.

In the social thought of the twentieth century two uses of the word are distinctive. In one, society has a negative, even pejorative cast; in the other, laudatory. In the first, society is contrasted deprecatingly with COMMUNITY. In the second, society is counterposed to the political state's sovereign power.

Ferdinand Tönnies's book of 1887, *Gemeinschaft und Gesellschaft*, translated commonly as *Community and Association*, was based on the first use. Community is made to represent relationships which are close and cohesive, rooted in family, place and tradition. Society on the other hand connotes relationships which are heavily economic and contractual in character, loose, impersonal, generally urban, and both mobile and individualistic. The distinction between community and society as made by Tönnies and others is more than classificatory; it is also the basis of a historical and developmental typology. Tönnies, Sir Henry Maine, Fustel de Coulanges, Graham Wallas, John Dewey and Walter Lippman all presented Western society in terms of the crisis involved in the spreading replacement of old and traditional community ties by the new, more impersonal and segmented ties of industry, city, mass democracy and secular individualism. In his *The Great Society* (a book dedicated by its author Graham Wallas to the young American Walter Lippman) Wallas made the contrast between community and the 'great society' an invidious one, implying that the latter contained within it the seeds of social breakdown or erosion because of its lack of social ties deeply and closely felt.

In America, John Dewey, in *The Public and its Problems* (1927), proceeding from Wallas, wrote: 'Our concern at this time is to state how it is that the machine age in developing the Great Society has invaded and partially disintegrated the small communities of former times without generating a Great Community.' That theme has been a powerful one in literary and philosophical works of the twentieth century, beginning in particular strength immediately after World War I. Utopian thought in the twentieth century has overwhelmingly taken the route of celebration of the cohesions and interpersonal mutualities of family society in contrast to the larger, impersonal and heterogeneous relationships of the city, factory and other characteristic ties of the modern Great Society. The quest for community that we find in so much political and social thought of the century is one in which 'society' is made the adversary.

Side by side with the pejorative meaning of 'society' is to be found another in twentieth-century thought that focuses on the differentiation between the STATE and society and on the vital necessity of keeping the latter as free as possible of encroachments by the state, in the interest of the freedom alike of individual and social group. In the writings of pluralists from Johannes Althusius down to Maitland and J.N. Figgis, the problem of freedom has been cast first of all in terms of the relationship between state and society – the latter word made to embody particularly the smaller associations and groups in the social order – and only secondarily in terms of individual versus state. 'More and more', wrote Figgis in 1911, 'it is clear that the mere individual's freedom against an omnipotent State may be no better than slavery; more and more it is evident that the real question of freedom in our day is the problem of the smaller unions to live within the state.'

When totalitarianism burst upon the twentieth-century scene defying older phrasings of despotism, monarchy or dictatorship, such writers as Ortega y Gasset, Hermann Rauschning, Emil Lederer and, somewhat later, definitively, Hannah Arendt saw the essence of the total state as the political state's absorption to its own sovereign power of all the authorities composing society such as family, church, local community, trade union, etc. It is worth emphasizing that Edmund Burke in some measure, Alexis de Tocqueville more sweepingly, foresaw the despotic potentialities of popular democracy very much in these terms; that is, the state's progressive swallowing up of society in its traditional forms. Perhaps the most famous chapter in Tocqueville's *Democracy in America* is 'What sort of despotism democratic nations have to fear'. His answer is: the slow, relentless bureaucratization of human existence through the state's supersession and then assimilation of all social authorities.

At the present time as communist totalitarianism shows strong evidences of inexorable retreat in the former Soviet Union and such Eastern European countries as Poland, Hungary, East Germany and Czechoslovakia, the idea of society, or civil society, has come to the fore. These are nations in which, under the auspices of socialism or communism, society – including economy, education, church, family and other component units of society – was calculatedly weakened, even at times destroyed. The question of the hour is: can the Eastern European countries and those of the former Soviet Union so strip themselves of pervasive and bureaucratized political power that a return to civil society and its inherent mechanisms and authorities is made possible? If state and party are to be divested of the powers and functions they have held in despotic fashion for several decades, to what entities are they to be transferred? For the rest of the century this will be the central drama: the ways by which the transfer from state to society is effected without a paralysing breakdown in which no kind of order whatever reigns.

See also CIVIL SOCIETY.

Reading
Hayek, F.A. 1960: *The Constitution of Liberty.*
Jouvenel, Bertrand de 1948: *On Power.*
Maine, Henry 1861: *Ancient Society.*
Mertz, J.T. 1914: *History of European Thought in the Nineteenth Century*, 4 vols. Vol. 4: *On Society.*
Nisbet, Robert 1953: *The Quest for Community.*
Polányi, Karl 1944: *The Great Transformation.*
Tönnies, F. 1887 (*1955*): *Community and Association.*
Tocqueville, Alexis de 1854 (*1955*): *The Old Regime and the French Revolution.*

ROBERT NISBET

society, affluent *See* AFFLUENT SOCIETY

society, civil *See* CIVIL SOCIETY

society, consumer *See* CONSUMER SOCIETY

society, corporate *See* CORPORATISM

society, evolutionary processes in *See* EVOLUTIONARY PROCESSES IN SOCIETY

society, industrial *See* INDUSTRIAL SOCIETY

society, mass *See* MASS SOCIETY

society, open *See* OPEN SOCIETY

society, postindustrial *See* POSTINDUSTRIAL SOCIETY

sociobiology A major change of emphasis in behavioural biology took place in the mid-1970s. Most obviously, the shift was marked by the

publication of E. O. Wilson's *Sociobiology: The New Synthesis* (1975), which brought together the insights derived from ecology and population biology with those obtained from ETHOLOGY and comparative psychology. In the previous decade the fruits of numerous field studies of animals had begun to suggest coherent explanations for the ways in which social behaviour might be related to ecological conditions. With the increasingly powerful use of Charles Darwin's evolutionary theory, a mass of seemingly unrelated and even contradictory evidence made sense and the subject looked exceptionally promising.

The term 'sociobiology' has been in use since the late 1940s; indeed the present-day Animal Behavior Society in the United States grew out of a section of the Ecological Society of America and the American Society of Zoologists called 'Animal Behavior and Sociobiology'. However, the most important influence on the birth of modern sociobiology in 1975 was probably the publication a decade earlier of an elegant theory by W. D. Hamilton (1964). This explained the evolution of self-sacrificial behaviour and, more generally, the delivery of benefits to kin other than offspring at personal cost to the donor. Hamilton formalized the conditions under which a gene that was needed to generate such a behaviour pattern could spread from being uncommon to being widespread. When the conditions are satisfied, any character that improves the chances of kin surviving can increase in frequency because the relatives are likely to carry the genes necessary for the expression of the character.

Hamilton's ideas were important because they repaired what looked like a defect in Darwin's evolutionary theory. Darwin proposed a process which involved some individuals surviving or breeding more readily than others. If the ones that survived or bred most easily carried a particular version of the character, the character would be more strongly represented in future generations. Hamilton's theory of kin selection explained how the outcome of the competitive evolutionary process is often social cooperation. In truth, it was an extension of the intuitively obvious point that animals often put themselves at risk and do things that are bad for their health in the production and care of offspring.

Another evolutionary explanation for cooperation, developed by modern sociobiologists, is that all the participants benefit directly. Cooperating individuals are not necessarily related, but each one is more likely to survive and reproduce itself if it works with others. In many species, individuals clean each other. Mutual assistance may be offered in hunting so that all get more to eat; for instance, cooperating members of a wolf pack will split into those that drive reindeer and those that lie in ambush. Emperor penguins huddle to conserve warmth. Cattle press tightly together to reduce the surface exposed to biting insects. Robert Trivers (1971) suggested that in highly complex animals, aid may be reciprocated on a subsequent occasion. Indeed, if one male baboon helps another to fend off competition for a female on one day, the favour will be returned on a later occasion. Both the males benefit by working together.

The emphasis on the necessary genetic conditions for the expression of social behaviour, which was explicit in Hamilton's work, gave rise to the most famous parable in modern biology, namely that of the selfish gene. In the work of Richard Dawkins (1976) evolution was thought about in terms of genes with intentions to do the best for themselves. Undoubtedly, this way of approaching evolution helped a great many people to understand the complex dynamics of evolution.

The genetic emphasis also lay behind many of the other classic proposals which were made by those who came to be known as sociobiologists. Robert Trivers (1972) proposed that, in sexually reproducing species, the genetic composition of an offspring is not identical to that of either of its parents which are also genetically different from each other. On this basis, offspring would not be expected to harmonize their behaviour with those of their care-giving parents since the offspring stand to gain from continued care whereas the parent may be in a position to maximize its reproductive success by saving its efforts for other offspring. For this reason a parent might start to withdraw its care of an offspring at a time when the offspring could still benefit from such care. Modern empirical evidence from mammals suggests that behavioural conflicts around weaning are less pronounced than had been expected from the theory of conflicting interests. This may be because it is crucial to their own development that offspring monitor carefully the state of their care-givers.

Trivers (1974) developed similar arguments to those used in his theory of parent–offspring conflict to explain sex differences in parental behaviour. Each parent might be expected to employ different methods of maximizing its reproductive success so that while one was still delivering intense care to its offspring, the other pursued opportunities for mating again. Once more the explicit idea was introduced of a trade-off between conflicting requirements to care for existing offspring and producing more, the optimum being different for the two sexes. Even on this argument, however, a balance may be struck between enlightened and naked selfishness. In many species of birds, in which both sexes normally care for the young and one parent dies or disappears, the remaining parent increases the time and energy it devotes to caring for the young. This suggests that each bird strikes an optimal balance which maximizes its own reproductive success. The cooperation observed when both parents are present is best explained in sociobiological terms as enlightened self-interest.

Optimality arguments played a central role in many other developments in sociobiology. One was the introduction of game theory to explain, for instance, the mixture of seemingly incompatible mixtures of aggressive, hawk-like behaviour and docile, dove-like behaviour. The simple models showed that stable combinations of evolutionarily stable strategies (ESS) could be formed. If one type of behaviour became more frequent than the optimum by chance, the other type would be at an advantage and, in the course of further evolution, would return to its former proportion at the optimum. John Maynard Smith was the most prominent figure in these theoretical developments. These models made very substantial simplifying assumptions, such as asexual reproduction and discrete either/or behavioural repertoires, but helped to clarify thought about the ways in which behaviour might have evolved.

Search for optimal solutions to foraging activity has been a major concern of behavioural ECOLOGY, a subject which has come to be closely associated with sociobiology. What, for instance, should an animal do after having eaten steadily in one place when the food in that patch starts to run out? At what point does the likely benefit of searching for a much better stocked patch outweigh the steadily diminishing benefit of staying where it is? The well-focused nature of the problem has brought with it an abundance of mathematical modelling. The models had the great virtue of providing precise expectations about what animals should do. These could then be tested against what the animals do in practice. Doing a good job in engineering terms depends on the availability to the animal of appropriate information about its environment, on its computational ability and on the time available for performing the necessary computations. Also, of course, the models assume that the biological function of the behaviour is known.

It is perfectly possible for models which are very different in character to generate the same result. So, even though scientists may think they have specified the right design requirements, the animal's behaviour may well be adapted to a rather different job. The least plausible model in biological terms may give the best fit in mathematical terms. In the long run, there will really be no substitute for good biological intuition and the theorists have to work hand-in-hand with people who are good observers of animals.

Sexual behaviour, as always, continues to be a subject of absorbing interest. What do animals look for when choosing mates? What does mate choice do to the dynamics of evolution? Why have sexes at all? These are evolutionary questions that continue to excite and tease people and are likely to go on doing so well into the next century. Direct evidence from history is usually lacking for behaviour, so biologists typically begin with attempts to distinguish between hypotheses about current use. Whether or not an answer will be a substitute for history is a moot point, since a behavioural system adapted to some other use might be coopted for its present function. Nevertheless, deductions about current use provide one indirect way for drawing conclusions about the shaping role of Darwinian evolutionary processes on behaviour in the past. Another indirect approach has been to use comparative knowledge of the many different species and their habitats to analyse the ways in which different characters evolved, the order in which they emerged and the functional significance of the evolutionary change.

In the book which gave modern sociobiology both its name and its character, E. O. Wilson attempted to incorporate a broad sweep of research on behavioural biology under a single banner. Imaginations were captured by the revitalizing of Darwin's great evolutionary theory and by the ways in which studies of behaviour had been attractively married to population biology. Even so the new subject was born in controversy, partly because the study of the development and integration of behaviour, which had been central concerns of ethology and comparative psychology, were deemed to be irrelevant or uninteresting to the new approach.

Opinion was particularly polarized by the attempt to inject a particular brand of biology into the social sciences and moral philosophy. The lacerations resulting from the ensuing academic and political conflict took a long time to heal and, for many years, 'Sociobiology!' was either a battle cry or a term of abuse. The claims were gradually moderated and the disputes have died down. As this has happened the agenda for sociobiology has merged with behavioural ecology and is now little different from the subjects it was supposed to have displaced.

Reading
Dawkins, R. 1976: *The Selfish Gene.*
Hamilton, W.D. 1964: The genetical evolution of social behaviour. I, II. *Journal of Theoretical Biology,* 7, 1–52.
Trivers, R.L. 1971: The evolution of reciprocal altruism. *Quarterly Review of Biology,* 46, 35–57.
—— 1972: Parental investment and sexual selection. In *Sexual Selection and the Descent of Man, 1871–1971,* ed. B.G. Campbell.
—— 1974: Parent–offspring conflict. *American Zoologist,* 14, 249–64.
—— 1985: *Social Evolution.*
Wilson, E.O. 1975: *Sociobiology: The News Synthesis.*

PATRICK BATESON

sociolinguistics   As its name implies, this covers areas of study which connect language with society. As an interface between two such enormous fields of enquiry, with theoretical and methodological concerns arising from a whole range of disciplines, including linguistics, sociology and anthropology, sociolinguistics cannot yet be defined in any strictly theoretical fashion. Nor is there much agreement as to the various demarcation lines between different exponents of sociolinguistic theories and methodologies. This uncertainty about its precise nature, and disagreement about its theoretical status has not, however, diminished its popularity as an academic subject. Publications which refer directly or in their subtitle to 'sociolinguistics' have been plentiful in the last two decades, with the content differing substantially according to the author's view of the nature of the discipline. The following references are only small selections from the range of introductory textbooks and monographs (cf. Hymes, 1974; Trudgill, 1974; Dittmar, 1976; Hudson, 1980; Downes, 1984; Fasold, 1984 and 1990), of collections of essays (cf. Giglioli, 1972; Pride and Holmes, 1972; Gumperz and Hymes, 1972), of sociolinguistic studies of particular speech communities (cf. Labov, 1970; Trudgill, 1978) and/or of the variations within a particular 'standard' language (for the sociolinguistics of German, see for example Barbour and Stevenson, 1990; Clyne, 1984).

Some writers draw a dividing line between 'two large subdivisions in the field' of sociolinguistics, and assign one to LINGUISTICS and the other to sociology. In this context, the first of the subdivisions 'starts with language, and social forces are seen as influencing language, and as contributing to an understanding of language,' whereas the latter 'takes society as the basic starting point and language as a social problem and resource (Fasold, 1984, introduction). Such a division echoes what other writers would see as a split between sociolinguistics proper with largely linguistic aims and a 'sociology of language' (Fishman, 1968) with largely sociological ones. The former would centrally comprise work by and in the style of one of the key figures in the development of sociolinguistics, William Labov, who has shown how variation in the linguistic system in a particular speech community is functionally related to the SOCIAL STRATIFICATION of that same group. The isolation of 'sociolinguistic variables', as for example, the class stratification of final and pre-consonantal (r) in the speech of native New York adults (cf. Labov, 1966 and 1970), which is perceived as prestigious in that community, allows predictions, formulated as variable rules, about the likely occurrence of this form according to the attention that speakers pay to their speech. There is thus both social and stylistic differentiation: the more attention a speaker gives to speech (as for example in the reading of word lists rather than in spontaneous speech) the more likely is the occurrence of the prestige variable. Labov infers from this an interdependence of 'functional varieties' of speech and 'cultural levels' such as norm perception (Labov, 1970, p. 190). He also takes the existence of style shifts between more or less prestigious forms, and the accompanying 'hyper-corrections' of lower-class speakers trying to adjust to the more prestigious form, as evidence of conscious change in progress (Aitchison, 1981, ch. 4). This example makes clear why even at the most microlinguistic level of sociolinguistics the demarcation to the macrolinguistic concerns of a 'sociology of language' has to be blurred, since the latter crucially involves speaker attitudes to language varieties, and how this influences language choice, language loss or maintenance, and language planning, though here the emphasis lies more at societal level. Apart from class and region,

other key sociolinguistic variables include most notably gender, race and age, with researchers often pointing up controversies in the interpretation of the correlation between linguistic and sociological category (for excellent discussions of this in respect of gender, see Cameron, 1985; Coates, 1986).

Obvious sociolinguistic concerns at macro level include *inter alia*: (1) the categorization of societies or nations as bilingual or multilingual according to the number of different languages spoken within their boundaries, irrespective of the offical recognition of these languages as national languages; (2) the political and social role of minority languages; (3) the study of 'diglossia', which refers to the strict functional differentiation of language varieties within a speech community according to a high (H) or a low (L) variety which usually corresponds to public (H) and private (L) domains – famous examples include diglossia between classical and vernacular Arabic, standard German and Swiss German, but also the switch between Spanish (H) and Guarani (L) in Paraguay (see Ferguson, 1959; Fishman 1967; for summary Fasold, 1984, ch. 2); (4) the definition and study of 'pidgins' and 'creoles' (Fasold, 1990, ch. 7; Barbour and Stevenson 1990, ch. 7).

The analysis and description of the sociolinguistic situation in a particular speech community, society or nation naturally depends on the way certain crucial categories are defined. There is, for example, disagreement as to whether the standard variety of a language counts as a dialect on a par with the other equally systematic and rule-governed regional and social varieties, and whether a simple division into standard and dialect is enough to cover the many different levels of regional and social variation in different countries (see Trudgill, 1974; Barbour and Stevenson, 1990, ch. 5). The definition of a 'language' as that overarching entity which contains dialects that are mutually comprehensible is equally problematical if one considers the mutual comprehensibility existing between speakers of 'different languages' such as Norwegian and Danish, or local dialect speakers at the Dutch/German border (Trudgill, 1974), as against the lack of such comprehensibility between speakers of several German dialects. Controversies also surround Labov's generalizations on the basis of the empirically unreliable abstraction of a 'speech community' (Romaine, 1982).

Apart from these concerns with defining its own objects of study, sociolinguistics is centrally concerned with methodology. In contrast to work in linguistics, which accepts and often relies on speaker or researcher intuition about questions of grammaticality of a particular form or sentence, sociolinguistics is firmly based on observation of actual, preferably spontaneous, speech behaviour. A great deal of sociolinguistic methodology is thus concerned with overcoming the difficulties of obtaining such data. This is not only true for the work relating to sociolinguistic variables such as Labov's famous elicitation of (r)s in New York department stores by making shop assistants include 'fourth floor' in their answers. It is also applicable to the substantial work in linguistic attitudes, where it is no longer deemed sufficient to ask people about whether they do or don't like a particular dialect, accent or speech variant, but to find out about such preferences by various indirect methods, such as different variations of 'matched guises'. Note, for example, the ingenious methods which Giles and Bourhis employed for tracing attitudes to Birmingham-accented, and in another study to Welsh-accented, English in contrast to received pronunciation (RP), by measuring how listeners responded to comments and requests made in different accents (Giles and Bourhis, 1976; Bourhis and Giles, 1976; excellent summary in Fasold, 1984, ch. 6).

In the light of the broad areas of interest in the interrelation of language and society and the range of methods employed, some writers prefer to see sociolinguistics as defined post hoc, by the topics and areas of enquiry which linguists, anthropologists, sociologists, social psychologists conduct at the various intersections between language and society (Fasold, 1990, introduction). This deprives sociolinguistics for the moment of a rigorous theory of its own, but has the advantage of not constraining the range of productive lines of enquiry to a particular set of methods. It does not preclude Hymes's conception of sociolinguistics, namely as 'an attempt to rethink perceived categories and assumptions as to the bases of linguistic work, and as to the place of language in human life' (Hymes, 1974, p. vii), but instead could be seen as a stepping stone towards such a theory. An alternative approach towards a unified theory of the place of language in social life and social process which would no longer be part of a 'hyphenated' sub-branch of linguistics, with its emphasis on rule-governed behaviour, or a subset of sociology, can be found in Halliday's work on systemic grammar

(Halliday, 1978, 1985, 1987), embedded in a general social semiotic.

See also DISCOURSE.

Reading
Barbour, S. and Stevenson, P. 1990: *Variation in German.*
Fasold, R. 1984: *The Sociolinguistics of Society.*
—— 1990: *The Sociolinguistics of Language.*
Giglioli, P.P. ed. 1972: *Language and Social Context.*
Pride, J.B. and Holmes, J. eds 1972: *Sociolinguistics.*
Trudgill, P. 1974: *Sociolinguistics.*

ULRIKE MEINHOF

sociology   A latecomer among the academic social sciences, sociology nevertheless had its origins in the eighteenth century, in the philosophies of history, the early social surveys, and the general ideas of the Enlightenment. In its early stages, and notably in the writings of Auguste Comte who gave the new science its name, sociology had a generally evolutionist and positivist orientation, and these characteristics persisted through much of the nineteenth century in the works of Herbert Spencer, and in quite a different fashion in those of Karl Marx, connecting the discipline in various ways with Darwinian theory (see SOCIAL DARWINISM), with theories of progress, and with projects of social reform or revolution. Towards the end of the century, however, sociology assumed a different form, and slowly established itself as an academic discipline, through the writings of two major thinkers, Max Weber and Emile Durkheim, who can be regarded, together with Marx whose work gave rise to a distinctive Marxist sociology (see MARXISM), as the founders of the modern subject. Although they differed widely in their ideas and approaches, these thinkers had in common a new and more precise conception of 'society' as an object of study to be clearly distinguished from the state and the political realm, from a vague universal history of humanity, and from the particular histories of 'peoples', 'states' or 'civilizations'; and they set out to define and demonstrate the principles and methods of this new 'science of society'. They also concentrated their attention primarily on the specific problems of the structure and development of modern Western capitalism, responding to the profound changes in social life which it brought about, the growth of the working-class movement, and the spread of socialist ideas. Marx's analysis of the capitalist economy and class structure had a profound influence on both Durkheim and Weber, especially the latter whose concepts and interpretations were elaborated to a large extent in critical opposition to Marxism (Löwith, 1932). More generally, a considerable part of European sociological thought in the early decades of the twentieth century came to be centred on a confrontation between Marxist and other theories.

At the same time, however, sociology also had very marked national and regional characteristics. In the first place it was largely confined to Western Europe and North America, that is, to those regions where industrial capitalism had developed most rapidly, but within these regions it also assumed a different character in particular countries. In the USA some early sociologists, especially W.G. Sumner, were strongly influenced by Spencer's ideas of individualism, *laissez-faire*, and the survival of the fittest (Hofstadter, 1955), but an opposing view and a reorientation of social thought emerged at the turn of the century (White, 1957): sociologists such as Lester F. Ward, E.A. Ross, Albion Small and Thorstein Veblen, influenced to some extent by Marxist ideas, reasserted the association of the discipline with social reform movements and advocated increased state intervention, an outlook which was particularly evident in the work of the sociology department at the University of Chicago, created by Small, which dominated American sociology for two decades up to the mid-1930s (see CHICAGO SOCIOLOGY). In Britain, Spencer's evolutionary theory was refashioned by L.T. Hobhouse into a more collectivist and reform-oriented scheme of thought, associated with a theory of progress (Collini, 1979), which continued to dominate the subject until after World War II, largely through the work of Morris Ginsberg. Sociology, however, had a very minor place in British universities, while the influence of Marxism as an economic or sociological theory was also minimal, and it was only in the second half of the century that the discipline became firmly established, in forms that were largely influenced by American and European ideas.

The situation in some continental European countries was very different. In Germany and Austria, Marxist social theory, developing at first mainly outside the universities, retained a major place from the beginning of the century until the early 1930s and had a strong influence on the work of other sociologists. The principal themes of Weber's sociology – the origins of modern capitalism, the problems of historical interpretation, economy and society, class and status, political power – all arose directly out of his encounter with Marxist thought. But in the course of his reflection on Marxism, and influenced by wider debates about the nature of social analysis and explanation, Weber also raised more general questions concerning historical explanation, the problems of objectivity in relation to value orientations, and the role of causal explanation, as against interpretive understanding, in sociology and other social sciences (Outhwaite, 1975). Not only Weber's methodological writings, but his critique of Marxism and above all his conceptualization of the development of modern society as a process of rationalization of the world (Brubaker, 1984) have had a pervasive influence on later sociology. Raymond Aron and C. Wright Mills both adopted, though in the context of different political orientations, Weber's distinction between class structure and the system of political power, and Aron, in particular, elaborated a scheme of thought in which the role of elites (see ELITE THEORY) was analysed in relation to social stratification, and undertook comparisons between the plurality of elites in Western societies and the unified elite in the Soviet Union (Aron, 1950). More generally, he developed a historical sociology which owed much to Weber, in his conception of the emergence of modern industrial society as a unique, initially Western, phenomenon which marked a radical break in the evolution of human societies (Aron, 1967). More recently, Weber's central theme of rationalization has been critically reexamined by Habermas (1981) in a comprehensive study of different theoretical approaches to the subject, which he concluded by distinguishing two main types of rationalized society in the present-day world, organized capitalism and bureaucratic socialism.

In France, Durkheim's sociology was also developed partly in opposition to Marxist theory, in his account of the division of labour and class relations (1893), his lectures on socialism (1928), and his rejection of historical materialism in his study of the social causes and functions of religion (1912), but it was greatly influenced too by positivist and neo-Kantian conceptions of science and by his critical view of Comte's evolutionist philosophy. But Durkheim, like Weber, also raised larger questions about the scope of sociological theory (Lukes, 1973; Nisbet, 1974), expounded most systematically in his book on sociological method (1895) where he set out a scheme of causal and functional analysis, and notably separated sociological explanation very sharply from psychological explanation. His sociological conceptions were widely diffused in France in the interwar years through the journal which he founded, *L'Année Sociologique*, around which a DURKHEIM SCHOOL was formed, and they also became influential elsewhere, notably in British social anthropology and in a different form in American sociology, as a major factor in the development of the functionalist school, which took as a principal aim of sociology the analysis of the ways in which differentiated institutions and groups contribute to the integration and persistence of a whole society (see FUNCTIONALISM).

Elsewhere in Europe the most influential contributions were made by Vilfredo Pareto (1916–19) and Gaetano Mosca (1896), particularly in their elite theories, developed in opposition to Marxist class theory, which gave rise to enduring controversies about elites and democracy, and the relation between elites and classes (Bottomore, 1964). Pareto's work also had a more general influence through the distinction he made between 'logical' and 'non-logical' action (dealing with some of the same issues that Weber raised in his analysis of the types of social action), and his argument that by far the greater part of human action is non-logical, the outcome of impulses and sentiments which he called 'residues', often camouflaged in doctrines and theoretical systems, termed 'derivations' (see IDEOLOGY; SOCIOLOGY OF KNOWLEDGE). There had also been an early interest in sociology in Russia, and after the revolution Bukharin (1921) expounded a Marxist 'system of sociology', but Stalin's rise to power put an end to such developments and sociology was replaced by an official doctrine of historical materialism, presented for the most part in the form of a crude evolutionary theory that was insulated from any kind of critical reflection or empirical testing.

By the 1930s sociology had become established in diverse forms in many of the leading industrial countries. In the USA, where the subject was most widely taught in universities, it had a predominantly empirical and reform-oriented character, exemplified in the work of the Chicago school, but was increasingly influenced by European theories, which provided the starting point for a major theoretical work by Talcott Parsons (1937), although the theory of social action which he expounded there had its greatest influence after the war. In Germany and Austria sociology was strongly influenced by Weber, but also by the work of Georg Simmel (1908) whose conception of the discipline as a new approach which involved analysing the 'forms' of sociation or interaction as distinct from the historical content was elaborated by Leopold von Wiese (1933) into a general 'systematic sociology', and by a Marxist sociology that was most rigorously formulated in AUSTRO-MARXISM. But this varied and vigorous development was brought to an end after 1933 by the National Socialist regime. In France, the discipline was dominated by Durkheimian conceptions, though these were challenged by Marxist critics, and some of Durkheim's followers – Halbwachs (1938) in his studies of social classes, and Simiand (1932) in his economic sociology – came closer to Marxist sociology in emphasizing the primary importance of economic phenomena.

Only after World War II, however, and particularly in the 1960s, did a rapid expansion of sociology take place and the subject become established as a major academic social science, for the first time on a truly international scale. Initially the influence of American sociology, because of the scale of the discipline in the USA, the level of development of empirical research, and the availability of research funds, was paramount in the revival of sociology in Western Europe and its extension to other parts of the world, and this was manifest in two different directions: in a rapid growth of more sophisticated, and also comparative and cross-national, empirical research, and in the impact of Parsons's theory of action on sociological thought, which was all the greater because Parsons drew extensively on earlier conceptions, in the work of Pareto, Durkheim and Weber, in constructing his own theory. This theory, in its original version, raised, among other questions, and attempted to resolve, the longstanding issue of the relation between individual action, or human agency, and the encompassing social structure, as it had been posed by Simmel and Weber; but in Parsons's later work the emphasis came to be placed on the analysis of social structure, or the 'social system' (1951) and of processes of social evolution (1966), and his mature theory was regarded by some critics as belonging clearly to the category of a (deterministic) sociology of social systems as opposed to a sociology of social action which would emphasize the construction of the social world by its members as active, purposeful and creative beings (Dawe, 1978).

For two decades, however, Parsons's systems theory (also referred to as structural-functionalism), modified in various ways by R.K. Merton (1949), provided to some extent, and more particularly in American sociology, a dominant paradigm for sociological theory. But it was always contested from other perspectives, not only by those who attributed greater importance to human agency, but by more historically minded sociologists, Marxist or Weberian, by many who continued to work in a positivist-empiricist framework, and by radical thinkers who criticized what they saw as the political conservatism implicit in it.

The decline of the functionalist paradigm began in the 1960s when a great transformation of sociology took place. International conflicts, and especially the Vietnam war, the emergence of new social movements, the growth of dissent and opposition in Western countries and in Eastern Europe, the widening gap between rich and poor nations, provoked a radical reorientation of social thought. Social change and conflict, instead of social integration and the regulation of social life by shared norms or a presumed 'common value system', now became central issues for analysis. As Weber had written in his essay on objectivity (1904): 'a time comes when the atmosphere changes . . . The light of the great cultural problems has moved on. Then science too prepares to change its standpoint and its conceptual apparatus.' In this new intellectual climate sociology flourished, while the influence of Western Marxist thought (see WESTERN MARXISM) rapidly increased, even spreading significantly into Eastern Europe as Stalinist orthodoxy disintegrated.

This reorientation and expansion of the discipline was accompanied by increasing specialization and a proliferation of new or redefined areas of research – for example, into the social context of economic growth, new forms of imperialism, the role of force in social life, gender, ethnic groups, and social movements – many of which brought sociology into a closer relationship with other social sciences, especially economics, anthropology and political science. At the same time, however, the multiplicity of paradigms also tended to increase, and the division of the discipline into competing schools of thought, which has always existed, became more pronounced. Marxist thought, which might have been supposed capable, during the period of its greatest influence, of fostering some

degree of theoretical unification, itself became more differentiated as a result of manifold reinterpretations and reconstructions of Marx's ideas, the extreme positions being represented by Louis Althusser's structuralist Marxism (see STRUCTURALISM) and the critical theory of the FRANKFURT SCHOOL.

There are, to be sure, controversies of long standing in all the social sciences about fundamental theoretical approaches, but in sociology, which claimed, and with greater or lesser conviction still claims, to formulate the principles of a general social science, they have always been exceptionally acute and sharply expressed. Three main issues are involved. The first concerns the relative importance in social life of social structure – established patterns of behaviour, formal institutions – and the conscious, intentional actions of individuals or groups of individuals: whether, and to what extent, society should be conceived as a resultant of these actions, or whether, on the contrary, individual and group intentions and possibilities of action should be seen as the product of society. The problem has been posed and debated from the origins of the discipline up to the present time: by Marx (1852) in his observation that 'human beings make their own history, but they do not make it just as they please'; by Simmel (1908) in his formulation of 'two logically contradictory characterizations' of the human being as 'a product and content of society' and as 'an autonomous being'; by Berger and Luckmann (1966) in their statement of three fundamental aspects of social life, 'Society is a human product. Society is an objective reality. Man is a social product'; and by many recent sociologists who are committed to social determinism in structuralist or other versions or on the contrary to conceptions of individual action (in particular rational action; see RATIONAL CHOICE THEORY) and the interpretation of interaction among individuals in everyday life (Wolff, 1978; see also PHENOMENOLOGY), or who attempt to transcend this opposition through such conceptions as 'destructuration' and 'restructuration' (Gurvitch, 1958; see STRUCTURATION), or the 'self-production of society' (Touraine, 1973).

A second major issue is that concerning the relation between social structure and historical change. The kind of structuralism introduced into social anthropology by Lévi-Strauss (1958) and afterwards diffused in sociology, partly in a Marxist version, was generally unhistorical and frequently rejected altogether the possibility or relevance of historical explanation, thus coming into conflict with sociological theories of social change and development, whether these were Weberian, Marxist or evolutionist. In the case of Marxist theory the problem might perhaps be resolved by invoking the idea of 'structural contradictions' (Godelier, 1972), but the general tendency of structuralist thought was to question the value of historical explanations and to see them as more or less arbitrary ideological constructions. Goldmann (1970), however, outlined a 'genetic structuralism' and argued that from this standpoint the structures which constitute human behaviour are not 'universally given facts', but 'phenomena resulting from a past genesis' whose transformation foreshadows 'a future evolution' (see also Piaget, 1968).

The third major issue, overlapping with the other two, concerns the general nature of sociological explanation and in particular the notion of CAUSALITY in social life. Here there is a broad division between the adherents of causal explanation, in positivist or realist forms (see POSITIVISM; REALISM), those committed to explanation in terms of end-states (functionalism), and those who, distinguishing sharply between the natural sciences and the social sciences, reject the idea of any causal explanation of social processes in favour of interpretations of the meaning of human action (see HERMENEUTICS). All the major sociologists have grappled with this question: Marx, in whose work some have discerned a 'latent positivism' (Wellmer, 1969), others a realist or dialectical (see DIALECTIC) or phenomenological method; Weber, whose complex view of the nature of sociology juxtaposed causal explanation and the understanding of meaning, both being necessary for a full comprehension of social life; and Durkheim, who advocated both causal and functional explanation, though the latter predominated in his actual studies.

Despite these fundamental problems and disagreements, sociology has had a profound influence on modern social thought; indeed, partly because of this preoccupation with the nature and first principles of a social science, it has become a focal point for debates which, if they have not resolved the problems, have undoubtedly illuminated in many ways the specific difficulties of generalization and explanation in the realm of social events and processes (Outhwaite, 1987). But sociological thought has also been influential in other respects

by conveying into more specialized disciplines a sense of the broader social context. Many of the most interesting sociological studies have been made in conjunction with other disciplines: for example, in economic sociology where an earlier tradition of political economy has been revived and such investigations as those of Weber (1921) and Schumpeter (1942) have been reassessed as a starting point for new studies; in political sociology where the accounts of formal political institutions have been greatly extended by studies of parties, elections, pressure groups and social movements, as well as by analyses of such concepts as democracy, bureaucracy and citizenship; in the considerable expansion of research in social history, in some cases conceived as a history of social structures (Burke, 1980); and in numerous studies of Third World development in which sociologists, anthropologists, economists and political scientists have participated and sometimes cooperated. In another domain sociology has also had some impact on postwar economic and SOCIAL POLICY, through research on the development of the welfare state in the industrial countries (Marshall, 1970) and subsequently in newly independent industrializing countries, and on the nature of social problems and the effectiveness of measures to deal with them (Wootton, 1959; Merton and Nisbet, 1961).

The achievements of sociology in these different spheres are real and substantial, in extending the range of a systematically ordered knowledge of social life, and in providing to some extent an empirical and rational basis for policy-making. Nevertheless, there is a pervasive dissatisfaction with the continuing divisions and fragmentation within a discipline which seems to range at will over a vast field, from the philosophy of science to the most detailed microscopic investigation of some bizarre form of human activity which may or may not shed light on the general human condition. It remains an open question whether a more unified and intellectually coherent discipline will eventually emerge, fulfilling some part of the original hope and promise of a single paradigmatic science of society, or whether increasing specialization will be accompanied by a further proliferation of models and intensified disputes between the proponents of alternative theories. For the foreseeable future the latter seems more likely, but the consequences are not all to be deplored; controversy will at least help to ensure that sociology remains a lively and critical discipline, not a celebration of the status quo, and new ideas may emerge that will have a fresh impact on social thought and on the forms of social life.

Reading
Abercrombie, N., Hill, S. and Turner, B.S. eds 1984: *The Penguin Dictionary of Sociology.*
Aron, Raymond 1965, 1968: *Main Currents in Sociological Thought*, 2 vols.
Bottomore, Tom and Nisbet, Robert eds 1978: *A History of Sociological Analysis.*
Giddens, Anthony 1971: *Capitalism and Modern Social Theory.*
Nisbet, Robert 1966 (*1967*): *The Sociological Tradition.*

TOM BOTTOMORE

sociology, Chicago *See* CHICAGO SOCIOLOGY

sociology, comparative *See* COMPARATIVE SOCIOLOGY

sociology of knowledge The nature of knowledge has been a central problem of philosophy at least since Graeco-Roman times. Plato, for example, in *Theætetus* adopts a scientific approach to knowledge and cognition, and his dualistic ontology rests on epistemological foundations. The philosophers of the French and Scottish Enlightenments recognized that all social differences had social origins and were thus the result of factors subject to human control. They were aware that a wide range of social, economic and political factors shape the genesis, structure and content of human consciousness, thereby anticipating one of the major propositions of the sociology of knowledge proper.

In general, however, philosophers have attempted rather to demonstrate that a sociology of knowledge is neither possible nor desirable. Kant thus argued that while there cannot be perception without conception, the constitutive components of cognition remain *a priori*. Similarly, empiricists of various persuasions have maintained that (scientific) knowledge is warranted by direct experience unaffected by social conditions. At most, these philosophies concede that extratheoretical factors influence the genesis of ideas but not the structure and the content of thought. Otherwise quite different philosophies of thought have shared an often explicit rejection of sociological RELATIVISM and attempted to overcome doubts by placing know-

ledge on a firm foundation, even outside the realm of sociohistorical experience.

The sociology of knowledge, by contrast, investigates the interconnections between categories of thought, knowledge claims and social reality – the *Seinsverbundenheit* (existential connectedness) of thought (Karl Mannheim). Marx was a significant precursor of the field, with his theory that at least under certain historical conditions economic realities ultimately determine the ideological 'superstructure' by way of various socioeconomic processes. This conception remains a central issue in the sociology of knowledge, and it has directly inspired some exemplary analyses of problems of cultural production, for example in the works of György Lukács.

Emile Durkheim, too, is an important pioneer of the sociology of knowledge, even though he failed to develop a general model of the classificatory process. He argued, especially in *The Elementary Forms of the Religious Life* (1912) and in *Primitive Classification* (1903, with Marcel Mauss), that the basic categories which order perception and experience (space, time, causality, direction) derive from the social structure, at least in simpler societies. Durkheim, Mauss and also Lucien Lévy-Bruhl, examined the forms of logical classification of 'primitive' societies and concluded that the basic categories of cognition have social origins. But they were not prepared to extend this kind of analysis to more complex societies. Their basic assumptions have been heavily criticized, but much sociological work continues to take as its starting point the Durkheimian proposition that the classification of things reproduces the classification of people.

The sociology of knowledge owes its decisive development to the work of Max Scheler and Karl Mannheim in the 1920s. It may be seen as the symptomatic intellectual expression of an age of crisis, and the recognition of its own rootedness in social structure and determination by social factors is perhaps its most characteristic trait. The mood of the German historical and social sciences during the period in which the sociology of knowledge developed in Germany may be described as one of 'tragic consciousness'. Georg Simmel's view of the 'tragedy of culture' as well as Max Weber's assertion that an inescapable process of rationalization leads to the disenchantment of the world and to new forms of bondage are symptomatic expressions of a period in which historians, philosophers and especially social scientists argued intensely about the issues raised by historicism, relativism, philosophical scepticism and the pervasive distrust in *Geist*.

It is in this period that the sociology of knowledge emerges as analysis of the regularities of those social processes and structures that pertain to intellectual life and to modes of knowing (Scheler), and as a theory of the existential connectedness of thought (Mannheim). Both orientations distance themselves from the Marxist critique of ideology which sees ideologies as mystifying representations of social reality and as disguises of the interests of powerful groups in society. The sociology of knowledge, by contrast, is concerned with intellectual and spiritual structures as inevitably differently formed in different social and historical settings (Mannheim).

It was Max Scheler who first introduced the term *Wissenssoziologie* (sociology of knowledge) in the early 1920s, and in *Problems of a Sociology of Knowledge* (1926) provided a first systematic introduction. He extended the Marxist notion of substructure (see BASE AND SUPERSTRUCTURE) by identifying different 'real factors' (*Realfaktoren*) which, he believed, condition thought in different historical periods and in various social and cultural systems in specific ways. These 'real factors' have sometimes been regarded as institutionalized instinctual forces, and as representing an ahistorical concept of substructure. Scheler's insistence on the existence of a realm of eternal values and ideas limits the usefulness of his notion of 'real factors' for the explanation of social and cultural change.

It was Karl Mannheim who provided the most elaborate and ambitious programmatic foundation for a sociological analysis of cognition. Like Scheler, he extended the concept of substructure, suggesting that biological factors, psychological elements and spiritual phenomena might take the place of primary economic relations in the substructure, but (just like the dominant theory of science) he did not think that scientific and technical knowledge could be subjected to sociological analysis. He conducted research into the social conditions associated with different forms of knowledge, and some of his studies are still considered first-rate examples of the kind of analysis of which the sociology of knowledge is capable. In addition to *Ideology and Utopia* (1929) these include his studies of competition as a cultural form, of conservative thought, of the problem of generations, and of economic ambition.

Mannheim believed that the sociology of knowledge was destined to play a major role in intellectual and political life, particularly in an age of crisis, dissolution and conflict, by examining sociologically the conditions which give rise to competing ideas, political philosophies, ideologies and diverse cultural products. He persistently pursued the idea that sociology of knowledge is somehow central to any strategy for creating a rapprochement between politics and reason, and this pursuit connects his various essays in the sociology of knowledge. Throughout, he believed that such a sociology has an important transformative effect on its practitioners: sociology of knowledge calls intellectuals to their vocation of striving for synthesis. It changes their relationship to the parties contending in society, giving them distance and overview. But Mannheim's conception of the specific ways in which such a sociology might affect the state of political knowledge fluctuated and changed. There are three main versions:

1 Sociology of knowledge as a pedagogical but also political mode of encountering and acting on the other forces making up the political world;

2 Sociology of knowledge as an instrument of enlightenment, related to the dual process of RATIONALIZATION and individuation identified by Max Weber, and comparable to psychoanalysis, acting to set men and women free for rational and responsible choices by liberating them from subservience to hidden forces they cannot control;

3 Sociology of knowledge as a weapon against prevalent myths and as a method for eliminating bias from social science, so that it can master the fundamental public problems of the time and guide appropriate political conduct.

The sociology of knowledge has recently experienced a reorientation in the direction of an analysis of everyday life and of natural scientific and technical knowledge (both neglected by the classical sociology of knowledge). Peter Berger and Thomas Luckmann's *The Social Construction of Reality* (1966), written in the tradition of Alfred Schutz's PHENOMENOLOGY and Arnold Gehlen's philosophical anthropology, represents a clear departure from the preoccupation of the classical sociology of knowledge with issues of epistemology and methodology. Everything that is regarded as knowledge in society is now accepted as a legitimate subject matter for sociological investigations.

Inspired by developments in the history of science, the sociology of knowledge has also turned in the direction of empirical analyses of the social construction of scientific facts, frequently by way of ethnographic studies of laboratory life. Such research on the 'manufacture' of natural-scientific knowledge has led to a reassessment of traditional assumptions about the unique rationality of scientific knowledge. Seen through the lens of the 'strong programme' of the sociology of knowledge, scientific knowledge and everyday knowledge are in fact extraordinarily similar in certain respects (see SOCIOLOGY OF SCIENCE).

Knowledge has no doubt always played a significant role in human life. Human action has to a greater or lesser extent always been steered by knowledge. Power, for example, has never exclusively been based on brute physical force, but frequently also on a knowledge advantage. At present, however, knowledge is assuming a greater significance than ever before. Advanced industrial societies may even be regarded as 'knowledge societies'. A thoroughgoing scientization of all spheres of human life and action, the transformation of both traditional structures of domination and of the economy, as well as the growing impact and influence of experts are all indications of the rapidly increasing role of knowledge in the organization of modern societies.

Reading

Berger, Peter and Luckmann, Thomas 1966: *The Social Construction of Reality*.
Latour, Bruno and Woolgar, Steve 1979: *Laboratory Life*.
Mannheim, Karl 1929 (*1936*): *Ideology and Utopia*.
Meja, Volker and Stehr, Nico eds. 1990: *Knowledge and Politics: The Sociology of Knowledge Dispute*.
Stehr, Nico and Meja, Volker eds. 1984: *Society and Knowledge: Contemporary Perspectives in the Sociology of Knowledge*.
Woolgar, Steve ed. 1988: *Knowledge and Reflexivity: New Frontiers in the Sociology of Knowledge*.

VOLKER MEJA AND NICO STEHR

sociology of science This branch of study explores the social character of science, with special reference to the social production of scientific knowledge (see SOCIOLOGY OF KNOWLEDGE). In present day society, the term 'science' has great potency. Not only is 'science' more or less equivalent to 'valid knowledge', but it also merges with 'technology', that is, the useful application

of knowledge (see SCIENTIFIC-TECHNOLOGICAL REVOLUTION). Consequently, those people known as 'scientists' are widely regarded as the purveyors of a superior kind of knowledge which represents the real world with a degree of precision and reliability that makes possible extensive control over its natural processes. In such a context, to be deemed 'unscientific' is, in the realm of ideas, to be dismissed as intellectually inept and also as irrelevant to the paramount world of practical affairs. Sociology itself emerged and developed as one small part of the scientific movement in modern society. Despite many reservations and differences of opinion among its practitioners, sociology has largely adopted the conception of knowledge that has come to be associated with the 'advanced' physical and biological sciences. As a result, the sociology of science necessarily has a self-referential element; that is, the practice of sociology falls within its scope and its general conclusions concerning the social process of knowledge production must be taken to apply also to sociology. The sociology of science is a critical area of analysis, therefore, not only because it deals with the dominant form of knowledge in our society, but also because its findings may have important implications for its own discipline and for other realms of social investigation.

During the last two decades, sociologists have looked in ever greater depth at the social production, and application, of scientific knowledge. They concentrated initially on the most advanced physical sciences such as physics and radio astronomy. Subsequently, much attention has been given to the biological sciences. These unequivocally scientific disciplines were chosen for study partly because they appeared to be the least amenable to a fully fledged sociological analysis. It has, of course, long been accepted that many aspects of science are obviously social in character: for instance, its form of organization, its patterns of communication, its internal hierarchy and its allocation of symbolic awards, with its emphasis on scientists' collective commitment to particular intellectual frameworks. But sociologists' own acceptance of the belief that science is a privileged form of knowledge led them to exempt the intellectual products of science from their investigations. When sociologists eventually took up the challenge of attempting to give a sociological account of the content of scientific knowledge, it seemed advisable to take what appeared to be the hardest cases first. For if the most advanced sciences were to prove susceptible, all other disciplines would follow automatically.

The sociological analysis of scientific knowledge received much of its initial impetus from outside the discipline. Thomas Kuhn's (1962) historical thesis concerning the occurrence of revolutionary upheavals in science (see Merton, 1973) was particularly important in freeing sociologists from the traditional assumption that scientific knowledge is largely independent of social influences. Kuhn's analysis enabled sociologists to envisage the possibility of furnishing a social interpretation of cognitive change in science. Furthermore, from the late 1960s onwards, there was an influx of scientifically trained investigators into the discipline who were able to cope with the intellectually demanding technical culture of science. These intellectual migrants contributed significantly to the series of detailed studies of specific areas of natural science which were completed during the 1970s, using interviews and documentary sources. These case studies were followed by a wave of anthropological investigations of the minutiae of scientists' laboratory practices, based on extended periods of participant observation.

As a result of this body of research, the traditional sociological model of scientific knowledge and of the METHODOLOGY of science was radically revised. Scientific knowledge was seen to derive, not from the impartial application of clear technical criteria of adequacy, but from such factors as practitioners' rhetorical skills and from their socially negotiated allegiances. Careful observation of scientists at work seemed to show that scientific knowledge is not an objective, detached representation of an independent natural world, but an active, engaged creation of that world in the course of social interaction. The conclusions of science are socially contingent formulations that have been deemed to be adequate by specific groups in particular cultural and social situations.

By the 1980s, it had become clear that the previous failure to understand the social processes of science was bound up with scientists' flexible use of language. In publicly accessible settings, scientists tend to use forms of discourse that depict their actions and beliefs as a neutral medium through which the realities of the world make themselves evident. In more private contexts, however, which have only recently become visible, they often employ repertoires which allow them to furnish much more socially and personally contingent accounts of the activities of science. In the last few years, some authors have tried to explore the implications of such findings for the textual practice of sociology. They have argued that the univocal texts of the social sciences, modelled on the conventional forms of the scientific literature, are unsuitable for expressing the interpretative diversity of the social world. They have maintained that the unitary language of sociological analysis hides away the social contingency and contextual dependence of its own representations of the world; and that this kind of textual subterfuge is inappropriate in a discipline committed to a fully sociological perspective. They have begun to devise new, multivocal formats which are intended to give greater voice to the interpretative multiplicity of the social world and to place sociologists in active dialogue with the subjects of their studies. This new form of analysis is an attempt to find an alternative language with which to escape from the restrictions of the dominant world-view of science in our approaches to the social realm.

Reading
Ashmore, M. 1989: *The Reflexive Thesis: Wrighting the Sociology of Scientific Knowledge.*
Knorr-Cetina, K.D. 1981: *The Manufacture of Knowledge: An Essay on the Constructivist and Contextual Nature of Science.*
Latour, B. 1987: *Science in Action.*
Mulkay, M. 1985: *The Word and the World: Explorations in the Form of Sociological Analysis.*
Woolgar, S. ed. 1988: *Knowledge and Reflexivity: New Frontiers in the Sociology of Knowledge.*

MICHAEL MULKAY

sociology, political *See* POLITICAL SOCIOLOGY

soviet *See* WORKERS' COUNCIL

Stalinism Iosif Vissarionovich Stalin (real name Dzhugashvili) (1879–1953) was a ruthless politician, who presided over the transformation of peasant Russia into an industrial superpower, the horrors of famine and purges in the 1930s and Russian resistance to the Nazi invasion of 1941–5. He is often portrayed as a man of mediocre intellect, but his pervasive ideology, which became known as 'Stalinism', played a major part in shaping the Soviet regime and the world communist movement in his lifetime and for some decades beyond.

As early as 1924, the year of Lenin's death,

Stalin's political doctrine began to display distinctive characteristics. He insisted that LENINISM was not merely a version of Marxism applicable to a peasant country, but was of worldwide validity in 'the era of imperialism and the proletarian dictatorship' and he emphasized the authoritarian characteristics of a Leninist political party. In the same year he declared, against Trotsky's bitter opposition, that it was possible to complete the building of SOCIALISM in the Soviet Union without a socialist revolution elsewhere (see TROTSKYISM).

As the Soviet Union embarked on forced industrialization and the collectivization of agriculture at the end of the 1920s, Stalin modified Leninist doctrine in major respects. In 1928 he argued that the class struggle would not die away but would become intensified during the transition to socialism, and two years later he declared that owing to the capitalist encirclement of the USSR the state would not wither away but become stronger during this transition.

In the early 1930s the Soviet definition of 'socialism' was also changed. The Bolsheviks, following Marx, had assumed that socialism would be a moneyless economy, without commodities or trade; but from the mid-1930s Soviet Marxists held that the personal plot of the collective farmer, the free market for some peasant products, and an inegalitarian wage system within industry were all part of the socialist economy, which must remain a money economy.

Stalin accordingly announced in December 1936 that socialism had been established 'in principle' in the Soviet Union. At this time he also developed his doctrine that there were no antagonistic contradictions within socialist society, so that all hostile actions and beliefs (which in practice meant all criticism of Stalin) were due to the influence of the hostile capitalist world. This provided an ideological justification for the repressions of 1936–8. In the last years before his death he conceded, however, that even within socialist society certain contradictions might develop, and stressed the value of a 'clash of opinions'; but this change in doctrine did not lead to any softening of his harsh despotic rule.

In 1956 Khrushchev launched his attack on the 'cult of the individual', and rejected Stalin's doctrine of the intensification of the class struggle during the transition to socialism. But the Soviet definition of socialism remained sacrosanct, as did the principle that the system must be controlled by a single united party.

After the appointment of Gorbachev as party General Secretary in 1985, the existence of a distinctive ideology of 'Stalinism' was officially admitted in the Soviet Union for the first time, and Stalinism was subjected to far-reaching criticism as a distortion or betrayal of socialism. Features of Stalinism strongly condemned as erroneous or outdated included its emphasis on the power of the state and on state property as the highest form of social property; the replacement of democracy by bureaucracy; and the establishment of what Gorbachev termed an 'administrative-command system of state-party management of the country'. Following the collapse of Soviet communism in August 1991, Eltsin's close associates argued that Stalinism was essentially a continuation of Leninism and even of Marxism, and rejected the whole course of Soviet development since October 1917.

Reading

Carr, E.H. 1958: Stalin. In *Socialism in One Country, 1924–1926*, vol. 1.
Davies, R.W. 1989: *Soviet History in the Gorbachev Revolution*, chs 3–8.
Lewin, M. 1985: *The Making of the Soviet System: Essays in the Social History of Interwar Russia*, especially chs 11 and 12.
Rigby, T.H. ed. 1966: *Stalin*.
Stalin, Joseph V. 1952–5: *Works*, vols 1–13.
—— 1972: *The Essential Stalin: Major Theoretical Writings*, ed. B. Franklin.
Tucker, R.C. 1973: *Stalin as Revolutionary, 1879–1929: A Study in Personality and History*.
—— 1991: *Stalin in Power: The Revolution from Above, 1928–1941*.

R.W. DAVIES

standard of living   The justification for activities aimed at economic development is generally supposed to be the improvement of the welfare of the population. Economic development in turn is assessed by means such as Gross National Product (GNP), and a comparison of GNP or per capita GNP levels has become established as a primary basis for estimating countries' comparative performance and progress over time. However, GNP is a measure of activity in the formal (waged) economy, and was not originally constructed as a welfare measure. It fails to deal with social EQUALITY AND INEQUALITY, with informal economic production, with environmental sustainability, and with a number of other equally important aspects of welfare.

The concepts of 'level of living' and 'standard of

living' refer to the circumstances of populations and subgroups of populations, and are reflected in statistics that seek to index them directly rather than to infer these from economic activity. Such SOCIAL STATISTICS are typically obtained by direct enquiry through household surveys and censuses. Conventionally they are concerned with such issues as household income, housing conditions (for instance, whether there is access to a toilet, and if so whether it is an indoor or outdoor one), material possessions (such as ownership of household appliances), and consumption practices (including foodstuffs being consumed). It is common practice for many such statistics to be produced routinely and frequently in most industrialized countries, though this is often not the case in poorer regions of the world. (In less industrialized countries, too, the specific questions posed may be rather different – for instance, access to clean running water may be a problem for much of the population, and the precise composition of the shopping basket may be less important than how far away one is from a basic nutritional standard.)

'Standard of living' is commonly used to refer to actual living conditions, although in the mid-1950s a United Nations expert committee recommended that 'level of living' be used for this purpose. Standard of living would then refer to people's aspirations or expectations for their living conditions. Technical literature sometimes abides by this distinction, but it is most often elided; however, statistical studies do sometimes contrast actual levels of income with those required to meet particular requirements for food, shelter, and so on, and consumption levels are frequently contrasted with a given standard (typically a minimum level, though sometimes the average level or the situation in a reference social group or country).

The focus of such data may be regarded as still being too economistic, and there have been many attempts to develop sets of indicators that encompass wider aspects of living circumstances – such as access to education and health services, life expectancy, mobility and even cultural facilities. However it is most common for 'standard of living' to be restricted to material well-being, and for this to be indexed in terms of possession of commodities and access to basic amenities.

Various other terms have been introduced in efforts to move beyond this, especially, in the last decades of the century, so as to include environmental dimensions of living circumstances such as exposure to various forms of pollution and environmental degradation – chemicals, radiation, waste products, noise, and so on. The term 'quality of life' is easily the most widely used term. It is often counterposed to 'standard of living' explicitly to underline the point that there is more to life than the accumulation of commodities. In this role its positive meaning, as opposed to the criticism of the limits of the economistic perspective, remains very open-ended. In some countries the term has been associated with particular political movements (for instance, campaigning against the excesses of CONSUMER SOCIETY), in others it signifies the emphasis of religious groups on spiritual issues, and so on. Despite this scope for misunderstanding, there has been substantial work on developing wider sets of social and environmental indicators which can capture a broader view of people's ways of life. The issues preoccupying conventional studies of standard of living are still represented in such compilations, since the fundamental importance of material welfare in our lives has not diminished. Some of the newer concerns – such as environmental damage – may well have an impact on material welfare in the long term, too; and some of these may lead us to rethink a simplistic reading of quantitative data which suggests that more of a commodity (for instance, multiple motor cars) is necessarily better.

Reading
Ekins, P. and Max-Neef, M. eds 1992: *Real-Life Economics.*
Miles, I. 1985: *Social Indicators for Human Development.*
Moll, Peter 1991: *From Scarcity to Sustainability: Futures Studies and the Environment.*

IAN D. MILES

state   There is a great deal of agreement among social scientists as to how the state should be defined. A composite definition would include three elements. First, a state is a set of institutions; these are manned by the state's own personnel. The state's most important institution is that of the means of violence and COERCION. Second, these institutions are at the centre of a geographically bounded territory, usually referred to as a SOCIETY. Crucially, the state looks inward to its national society and outwards to larger societies in which it must make its way; its behaviour in one area can often only be explained by its activities in the other. Third, the state monopolizes rule-making within its territory. This tends towards the creation of a common political CULTURE shared by all citizens.

It must be stressed that statehood is often an aspiration rather than an actual achievement. On the one hand, most historic states have had great difficulty in controlling their civil societies, and in particular in establishing their own monopoly of the means of violence; and what was true of feudal states is as true of present-day Lebanon. On the other hand, the search by a state for its prime goal, that of security, is normally made necessarily incomplete because of the presence of larger societies which it cannot control. One such society is that of the system of states, present for a thousand years in European history and now characteristic of what is genuinely a world polity. A second such society is that of CAPITALISM, which clearly has laws of motion all of its own. Much interesting and important work is now being done in modern social science on the interrelations of capital and the state, both domestically and internationally.

Contesting the state

The nature of the state has been the subject of intellectual debate and of power politics in the twentieth century. Two principal opposing camps can be identified, namely those of Anglo-Saxon liberalism and of a looser school best dubbed that of Germanic realism.

While there are many versions of liberalism, most show suspicion towards the activities of the state. All that is virtuous is seen as residing in society, with state forces being seen as obstacles needing to be diminished. The most active role for the state envisaged by some liberals is that of a nightwatchman, protecting a framework within which market forces can then operate according to their own logic. This is the philosophy of LAISSEZ-FAIRE; its explanations are society-based rather than state-centred because no fundamental reality is accorded to the polity. Liberalism's view of international relations is as strikingly dismissive of state power. The 'Manchester school' of laissez-faire liberalism hoped that nothing less than peace would be assured by the growing interdependence of the world economy; as importantly, trade rather than territorial conquest was now held to be the route to progress and prosperity. Other liberals, following the lead of Immanuel Kant, have suggested that the era of peace will depend not just on trade but on other states recognizing the principles of nationalism and of democracy.

Germany was created as the result of the actions of its state, and it is scarcely surprising that a greater appreciation was shown of the reality of state POWER. Internally, this tradition sees the state as an actor in its own right, able to represent the general interest. Externally, the state is seen as the guarantor of survival. This recognition of the logic of the 'asocial' world of state competition came especially easily to Germans. Social thought in general was massively influenced by the long peace between 1815 and 1914 in which the brute social transformation of industrialization did seem all-important. But Germans achieved statehood in part because of war, and it is scarcely surprising to find that thinkers such as Max Weber, Ludwig Gumplowicz, Gustav Ratzenhofer, Otto Hintze and Franz Oppenheimer all lent great weight to the impact of geopolitical transformation on social life.

Germany started two world wars and the Anglo-Saxon powers emerged victorious. This meant in consequence that for a long period a concern with the state was ruled out of court. Since the 1970s, however, this has thankfully changed. One source of such change has been modern WESTERN MARXISM. To fight an enemy influences one's own mind, and Marxism in the last analysis resembles liberalism – with which it shares, albeit with a different time-scale in mind, hopes both of universal peace and of the 'withering away' of the state – in proffering society-based rather than state-centred explanations. Nonetheless, the attempt to specify the way in which a 'relatively' autonomous state could serve the interests of capital by providing it with a necessary infrastructure led to questions being asked that rapidly escaped the Marxists' own paradigm. More generally, historical perspective is now such that no one can deny that the history of economic development beloved by liberals was rudely interrupted by geopolitical conflict between 1914 and 1945, or that this period profoundly changed social life. The different organization of social class in East and West Germany, to give but a single example, was the result of geopolitical settlement rather than of any logic internal to class in its own right.

All in all, there is no doubt but that 'the state is back'. Social science has, however, a regrettable habit of delighting in new approaches rather than of ensuring that they really do help us understand the world. Happily, renewed interest in the state has led to advances in our knowledge; the specification of some of these comprises the remainder of this entry.

The paradox of state power

We have come to understand, in part because of the work of Michael Mann (1988), that there are two faces or dimensions to state power. Traditional theory concerned itself, indeed was fixated by, the extent of the state's arbitrary powers, that is, the polar opposition between despotic and constitutional regimes. However, studies of agrarian states show that claims to universal power were more pretension than reality since the state had relatively few servants to penetrate and organize social life. Hence, a second dimension of state power deserves the appellation infrastructural.

A paradox results from this. State strength is often the result of the extent to which it can cooperate with groupings in civil society, and such cooperation is often ensured by some limitation on a state's despotic powers. Thus in the eighteenth century, the absolutist French state may have been autonomous in the sense of being 'free from' parliamentary constraint, but it was nonetheless weaker – as the test of warfare showed – than its constitutional rival, Great Britain. In that state, agreement between the upper classes and state actors allowed for higher levels of taxation and greater general efficiency: the British state was 'free to' do much more. This paradox applies equally well to the modern world: the war mobilization of Great Britain in World War II exceeded that of Germany, while recent scholars of the Japanese state have stressed that its great strength results from a 'politics of reciprocal consent'.

States and markets

A much clearer picture, drawn in comparative perspective, is now available of the role of the state in the emergence of the capitalist economic dynamism of north-west Europe that allowed Europe to dominate the world. Two theoretical points are of especial importance.

First, it is necessary to distinguish between different types of state in the preindustrial world. Very roughly speaking, Oriental civilizations had states which were at once too powerful and too weak – that is, despotically powerful but infrastructurally weak – to allow for the emergence of any capitalist dynamic. Such states sought to control all social forces that had the capacity to mobilize people, on the grounds that any independent force could rapidly undermine their own rule; this led to the blocking of capitalistic forces time and again. On the other hand, such states tended

not to cooperate with their upper classes, and were thereby prevented from gaining significant tax revenues; this meant that they had insufficient funds to provide a framework of rational expectations in matters of money and justice from which emergent capitalism would have benefited. In contrast, Occidental civilization saw the emergence of states which were powerful and weak in the 'right' places for the emergence of capitalism. Limits to arbitrariness meant that the state could not finally control capitalist actors, while the greater state revenue that resulted from cooperation with upper classes working through parliaments allowed for the provision of regularized justice and, with time, of decent money.

This European pattern is partly explicable, secondly, as the result of forces external to any single state. European states were long-lasting, and in consequence engaged in endless competition with each other. In these circumstances, it became rational not to kill the goose that laid the golden egg – that is, rulers eventually realized that predatory behaviour towards their capitalists would lead to their flight and consequently to an increase in the tax revenue of their geopolitical rivals. A large measure of decent behaviour towards nascent capitalism is explicable by means of the simple statement that capitalism had states: had Europe reverted to imperial rule after the fall of Rome, there would have been nothing to prevent rulers again preferring control over the social mobilization that resulted from allowing civil society a certain autonomy.

These patterns of state power are equally useful in understanding the ways in which states prosper economically in the industrial era. It seems increasingly the case that the ability of a nation-state to swim within capitalist society is related to its ability to cooperate with national capitalists and to provide a massive social infrastructure of educational training and of class compromise that allows for flexibility in the face of changing patterns of international trade. Thus the state in many East Asian countries is relatively (and increasingly) despotically weak but infrastructurally very powerful: that the opposite tends to be true of Latin America helps explain its poorish record of economic development. Furthermore, it is now quite evident that socialist planning works only at the stage of initial industrialization; the further economic success of socialist societies seems to depend on them changing their patterns of state control.

One final point is worth making about international markets. Such markets are geopolitically created. This was particularly true after World War II when an 'American system' was created whose institutions stabilized the advanced world, at the probable cost of the development of the Third World. One important theory about these matters, on which history has not yet sat in final judgement, suggests that capitalist society needs one leading state to order capitalism as a whole – that is, to provide a key currency and to insist on free trade. Certainly, the United States performed this role, although it is doubtful that Britain ever did. But as important a question for the late twentieth century as the liberalization of state socialist societies (see SOCIALISM) is the extent to which American decline may lead to renewed conflict between the leading capitalist powers.

States and politics

As noted, political developments internal to national societies often result from geopolitical forces. What was true of changes in class behaviour is as true of social revolution. Revolutions tend to occur in regimes which have been debilitated by excessive participation or actual defeat in war. State breakdowns give revolutionary elites their chance.

In addition, social scientists increasingly realize that the form of 'social movements' often results from the characteristics of the state with which they interact. Two examples deserve to be noted. First, working classes tend to be militant when a state excludes them from participation in civil society, that is, workers take on the state when they are prevented from organizing industrially and arguing with their immediate capitalist opponents. Thus a liberal state with full citizenship sees no working-class revolutionary movement, whereas authoritarian and autocratic regimes see the emergence of Marxist-inspired workers: this principle helps explain the difference in working class behaviour in the United States and Tsarist Russia at the end of the nineteenth century. The same principle – that political exclusion breeds militancy – seems, secondly, to explain the incidence of revolution in the Third World since 1945. Central American societies share a mode of production, but only a few witness revolutions. The possibility of participation in Costa Rica diffuses social conflict; its absence in Nicaragua under Somoza led to the creation of a revolutionary elite with popular support.

Reading
Aron, R. 1962 (1966): *Peace and War.*
Gilpin, R. 1981: *War and Change in World Politics.*
Hall, J. and Ikenberry, J. 1989: *The State.*
Katzenstein, P. 1985: *Small States in World Markets.*
Maier, C. 1988: *In Search of Stability.*
Mann, Michael 1988: *States, War and Capitalism.*
Poggi, G. 1978: *The Development of the Modern State.*
Skocpol, T. 1979: *States and Social Revolutions.*
Tilly, C. ed. 1975: *The Formation of National States in Western Europe.*
Waltz, K. 1959: *Man, the State and War.*

JOHN A. HALL

state, welfare   *See* WELFARE STATE

statistics   Statistics is the science of handling quantitative information. It is concerned with how data should be collected and with how they should be analysed and with what conclusions can legitimately be drawn from the analysis. It is especially relevant where the basic patterns in the data are obscured by extraneous variation arising from uncontrolled factors, poor measuring instruments or the effects of sampling. Statistical methods thus find a role in almost all branches of human enquiry though their importance varies considerably according to the degree of quantification which is possible.

The word 'statistics' itself has several other specific meanings. It is often used, for example, as a somewhat pretentious synonym for 'figures'. In the singular it refers to any number, such as an average, calculated from the members of a sample. It is also associated with a large number of qualifying adjectives indicating fields of application of which agricultural, biological, actuarial, business and medical are typical examples. Mathematical statistics is that branch of mathematics which formalizes statistical ideas and procedures and it is particularly concerned with determining 'best' procedures.

Statistics in the modern sense did not arise readymade but is woven from a number of different strands which began to coalesce about the end of the nineteenth and beginning of the twentieth century. One strand traces its origins to early attempts in biblical times to 'number the people' for military or other purposes. As functions of government became more centralized and complicated the need for good quantitative information about the 'condition of the people' became more pressing. In the nineteenth century this led to the formation of statistical societies, notably in 1834 of the Statistical Society of London, later to become the Royal Statistical Society. Its founders included people eminent in public life like the Marquis of Lansdowne and the Bishop of London and thinkers like Charles Babbage and T. R. Malthus. They were united in their concern to provide reliable factual information about all aspects of society. This movement grew to include public and private studies of such matters as the condition of the poor as outlined in Bartholomew (1988) (see also SOCIAL STATISTICS).

Most of these early studies would now be classified as descriptive statistics, their principal aim having been to condense and present the salient features of a large mass of figures in a form, often tables or charts, where their import could be readily grasped. This has remained the backbone of official statistics but the methodological aspects languished until the advent of powerful computers. These enabled very large quantities of data to be handled and made it possible for the first time to explore the interrelationship of many different variables. This is now sometimes regarded as a distinct activity called data analysis.

The second main strand of modern statistics has its origin in problems of dicing and gaming which gave birth to probability theory in the seventeenth century (see also GAME THEORY). Its relevance to the interpretation of data is that it gives formal expression to the inevitable uncertainty which attends any attempt at generalization. A simple and familiar example of what this means is provided by opinion polling. Suppose we are told that a poll of about 1,500 people shows that 48 per cent, say, of those questioned would vote for the return of the present government if an election were called. We are implicitly invited to believe that much the same percentage of the whole population of voters would behave like this sample. The purpose of inferential statistics is to provide a framework within which such generalizations can be made and justified. It is the formal equivalence of the throwing of dice and the drawing of members of a sample which enables the mathematical description of the one process to be applied to the other. (See also SOCIAL SURVEY.)

The recognition that probability theory was the key to inference effected the link between the descriptive tradition and inference, transforming the former into a tool of scientific inference. Sir Ronald Fisher (1890–1962), perhaps the greatest statistician of all time, exemplifies this synthesis. He was able to build on the work of those like Sir Francis Galton (1822–1911) and Karl Pearson (1857–1936) who sought to quantify the biological processes of natural selection and heredity which had been thrown into prominence by Charles Darwin's evolutionary theory. This work had an important influence on the eugenics movement between the wars.

The greater part of the twentieth century in statistics has been taken up with working out the implications of these seminal ideas in an ever expanding range of applications. A shift of emphasis associated especially with Abram Wald (1902–1950) and Jerzy Neyman (1894–1981) saw inference as a matter of decision-making in the face of uncertainty and sought to incorporate the consequences of the action to be taken into the evaluation of strategies of inference. (See also DECISION THEORY.) L.J. Savage (1917–1971) in his *Foundations of Statistics* again shifted the ground from objective probabilities expressed as frequencies to personal probabilities seen as guides to consistent behaviour in the face of uncertainty. His work found its inspiration in a theorem of the eighteenth-century Presbyterian minister Thomas Bayes (1702–1761) whose name is now given to this school of inference.

If the introduction of probability ideas into statistics marked the first revolution in the subject, the second is unquestionably the result of the power of the computer. This has not simply allowed much larger data sets to be handled more speedily but has had a far-reaching effect on what analysis is done and on who does it. It has enabled researchers to investigate the interdependency of many variables and hence to construct more realistic models of real phenomena, especially in the social sciences. Now that libraries of computer software are widely available, researchers can carry out their own analyses without recourse to expert advice. This has proved a mixed blessing since it not only leads to inappropriate analyses being done but encourages the proliferation of poorly designed studies and consequent waste of scarce resources.

Many biological and social systems evolve in time with a marked degree of internal randomness. Such things as mutation and competition in populations of organisms or the free choice of individuals in such matters as purchasing or voting make the evolution of such systems a highly uncertain affair. The theory of stochastic processes has been developed to deal with systems of this kind and the provision of statistical methods for such systems is one of the most difficult and challenging areas of current research.

In spite of the ubiquity of uncertainty and variability and the extent to which statistical ideas have permeated scientific work of all kinds, the influence of statistical thinking in Western culture, more generally, is still limited. Schools teach elementary statistics but often in a narrow technical manner which fails to inculcate the modes of thinking needed for life in a highly uncertain world. The desire for certainty and the deeply ingrained belief in a deterministic mode of operation of the world are difficult to eradicate. Nevertheless, some change is discernable. It is rare nowadays for anyone to say, as the television journalist Malcolm Muggeridge once did, that it is absurd to suppose that the replies of a few hundred people can tell us what millions think. Experience, if not theory, has taught us that there is a measurable link between what we find in a sample, properly drawn, and the population from which it comes. Scientists frequently despair that, though the fruits of scientific research are everywhere enjoyed, the manner of thinking which gives rise to them is still foreign to the vast majority – as the prevalence of superstition and interest in the occult demonstrates. Statisticians are in no better case and society is the poorer for failing to grasp and propagate the insights which it yields.

Reading

Clogg, C.C. 1992: The impact of sociological methodology on statistical methodology. *Statistical Science* 7.
Federer, W.T. 1991: *Statistics and Society*. 2nd edn.
Kotz, S., Johnson, N.L. and Read, C.B. eds 1988: *Encyclopaedia of Statistical Sciences*, 9 vols.
Pearson, E.S. ed. 1978: *The History of Statistics in the Seventeenth and Eighteenth Centuries*.
Sprent, P. 1988: *Taking Risks: The Science of Uncertainty*.
—— 1988: *Understanding Data*.
Stigler, S.M. 1986: *The History of Statistics: The Measurement of Uncertainty before 1900*.

D.J. BARTHOLOMEW

statistics, social *See* SOCIAL STATISTICS

stereotype *See* LABELLING

strategic studies Concerned with the role of military power in international politics, strategic studies can focus on microquestions related to the development of armed forces, their choice and procurement of equipment, and also on macroquestions such as the efficiency of military as compared with economic and diplomatic means in achieving the objectives of states. The major focus is on the distribution and employment of military means to achieve the ends of policy. This includes deterring war, strengthening alliances and engaging in arms control negotiations as much as the conduct of war. It involves looking not only at what military activities might naturally support particular objectives but also at how the ends might need to be altered to come in line with available military means, and also at unintended consequences.

Strategic studies has an interdisciplinary character and in the postwar period has benefited from contributions from economics and engineering as well as the more expected contributions from history and politics. It also has an unavoidably applied character in that much, although by no means all, work in this field has been deliberately undertaken to influence or support national policy.

The intellectual starting point for most thinking on strategy is the classic work *On War* by Carl von Clausewitz, who stressed the importance of viewing war as a continuation of politics. Since then many others have followed his attempt to develop a systematic theory to underpin the development of strategy in practice. A leading twentieth-century theorist was Basil Liddell Hart. Until the nuclear age there was little scholarly work in this area. The challenge posed to traditional concepts of military power by the arrival of means of mass destruction at a time of severe East–West antagonism proved to be a spur to the intellectual development of strategic theory. Much of this was undertaken in the USA, including work in 'think tanks' such as the RAND Corporation; there was work at the International Institute of Strategic Studies in Britain, and also important studies by individual scholars, among them Raymond Aron (1962).

Given the need to avoid a catastrophic total war, the critical concept became 'deterrence'. Theories of deterrence addressed such questions as whether it was possible to deter through the mere threat that a conflict could get out of hand through 'escalation' or whether any deterrent threats must be backed by credible military options and, if this was the case, whether punitive nuclear strikes could ever be credible when the enemy could retaliate in kind. The analysis of these issues initially made substantial use of such methodologies as GAME THEORY. More recent years have seen a greater stress on political analysis as it has become apparent that there are no technical fixes to the basic dilemmas of nuclear deterrence, and as the upheavals in the former Warsaw Pact countries of Eastern Europe have recast the basic questions of European security.

The concepts initially developed for the consideration of nuclear strategy have also been applied to conventional strategy. This has not been wholly successful as the conflicts in question have tended to be much more complex than supposed in the nuclear sphere. There has also been a separate and vigorous tradition of theorizing on GUERRILLA warfare, including study of such figures as T. E. Lawrence and Mao Zedong.

See also WAR.

Reading

Aron, Raymond 1962 (*1966*): *Peace and War*.
Baylis, John et al. 1987: *Contemporary Strategy*, 2 vols.
Clausewitz, Carl von 1832 (*1976*): *On War*, trans. Michael Howard and Peter Paret.
Freedman, Lawrence 1989: *The Evolution of Nuclear Strategy*, 2nd edn.
Liddell Hart, B.H. 1967: *Strategy: The Indirect Approach*.
Paret, Peter ed. 1986: *Makers of Modern Strategy: From Machiavelli to the Nuclear Age*.

LAWRENCE FREEDMAN

stratification, social *See* SOCIAL STRATIFICATION

structuralism This method of enquiry or paradigm became prominent and influential during the 1960s and 1970s, although it had several antecedents in earlier periods. In sociological analysis the concept of structure, in various formulations, has long had a central place (Bottomore and Nisbet, 1978, ch. 14), and a number of commentators (Piaget, 1968; Kolakowski, 1971; Schaff, 1974) have noted that the concept was a major element in the general philosophical and scientific outlook of the 1930s, reflected in the influence it acquired in such fields as mathematics, biology, linguistics and gestalt psychology. The more recent structuralist movement, however, made larger claims, emphasizing the paramount importance of identifying and analysing the 'deep structures' that underlie and generate observable phenomena, in which respect it has affinities with the modern realist philosophy of science (Bhaskar, 1975); and extending the structuralist approach more widely into the social and human sciences. Originating in linguistics, where

its beginnings are to be found in the theses outlined by the Prague Linguistic Circle in 1929 (Robey, 1973, Introduction), it then made its way into literary criticism, aesthetic theory and some of the social sciences – particularly anthropology, through the work of Claude Lévi-Strauss, sociology, mainly in the form of Louis Althusser's structuralist Marxism, and history, where the idea of 'structural history' in the work of the ANNALES SCHOOL was related, in some respects, to more general structuralist conceptions (*Review*, 1.3–4, 1978).

As a broad theoretical approach in the social sciences, structuralism can be distinguished by its opposition to humanism, historicism and empiricism. It is anti-humanist in the sense that the conscious, purposive actions of individuals and social groups are largely excluded from analysis and its own explanatory propositions are conceived in terms of 'structural causality'. This view was clearly expressed by Maurice Godelier (1966) when he distinguished two kinds of conditions for the emergence, functioning and evolution of any social system – intentional activity and unintentional properties inherent in social relations – and assigned a decisive importance to the latter, arguing that the ultimate reason or basis for social transformations is to be found in the compatibility or incompatibility between structures and the development of contradictions within structures. The humanist/structuralist opposition is also evident in the contrasting discussion of 'dialectical' and 'analytical' reason by Claude Lévi-Strauss (1962, ch. 9), and by Jean-Paul Sartre (1960), whose methodological investigations were designed to clarify the relation between structural conditions and the intentional actions – the 'projects' – of individuals, and to introduce into a sclerotic Marxism something of the individualistic and humanist outlook of existentialism.

Anti-historicism is manifested in the work of Lévi-Strauss by a general preference for synchronic rather than diachronic investigations, with the aim of discovering the universal structural characteristics of human society and, more remotely, relating these characteristics to universal structures of the human mind; and here structuralism shows its very close affinity with modern linguistic theory (Lyons, 1970, p. 99). Some Marxist structuralists, notably Hindess and Hirst (1975, Conclusion), expressed an anti-historicist view with particular force, denying that Marxism is, or could be, a science of history, since all attempts to formulate historical explanations emerge as teleological doctrines, not scientific theories. Structuralism was also anti-empiricist, in the same sense as the realist philosophy of science, by virtue of its insistence on the causal efficacy of a deep structure underlying the immediately given, surface appearance of events. This aspect was set out clearly by Godelier (1973, p. 35) in his criticism of 'classical empirical functionalism', which, he argued, 'by confusing social structure with external social relations ... is condemned to remain a prisoner of appearances within the social system studied, and there is no possibility of uncovering any below-surface logic'.

One of the salient features of the structuralist movement was its close connection with Marxism. Lévi-Strauss considered Marx the point of departure for his own thought, and structuralism became the main vehicle for conveying a significant Marxist orientation into anthropology (Godelier, 1973; Bloch, 1975; Seddon, 1978). In sociology, as well as in anthropology, Althusser's structuralist Marxism, very close to the general orientation of structuralist thought but focusing attention on those elements that were central in Marx's theory – the modes and relations of production, the relations between different levels of social life (economic, political and ideological) and structural contradictions – had a wide influence, notably on studies of different forms of society, social classes and the state.

The structuralist approach was criticized at an early stage by adherents of other methodological standpoints in the social sciences (for instance, Leach, 1967), and in its Marxist form by thinkers belonging to other schools of Marxist thought. By the late 1970s its influence was waning and in the following decade it was overshadowed by the rise of poststructuralism, or postmodernism (see MODERNITY), in which the idea of a fixed and objective structure of meaning or of social relations is abandoned (Eagleton, 1983, ch. 4). In a less extreme way, other social theorists have reintroduced into methodological discussion those questions about the relation between structure and human agency, or structure and historical change, which have been recurring themes of social thought.

Reading

Bottomore, Tom and Nisbet, Robert eds. 1978: *A History of Sociological Analysis*.
Eagleton, Terry 1983: *Literary Theory*.
Leach, Edmund ed. 1967: *The Structural Study of Myth and Totemism*.
Lévi-Strauss, Claude 1958 (*1963*): *Structural Anthropology*.
Lyons, John 1970: *Chomsky*.
Piaget, Jean 1968 (*1970*): *Structuralism*.
Robey, David ed. 1973: *Structuralism: An Introduction*.
Schaff, Adam 1974: *Structuralisme et Marxisme*.

TOM BOTTOMORE

structuration   References to structuration appear in anglophone social science as early as 1927, and in a more comprehensive theoretical scheme in the work of Georges Gurvitch (1955; 1962, pt. 2, ch. 4), who also introduced the useful concepts of 'destructuration' and 'restructuration'; but the term now refers mainly to the ontological theory of social life expounded by Anthony Giddens (1976, 1979, 1984), which expands on the insight that all elements of social life are constituted in the skilful enactment of social practices.

The structurationist ONTOLOGY provides generic presuppositions regarding the subject matter of social science, but contrary to presuppositions identifiable in classical ontologies (Thomas Hobbes, Adam Smith, Jean-Jacques Rousseau), functionalist theories (Talcott Parsons), and teleological theories of evolution (Emile Durkheim, Karl Marx), it does not postulate trans-historical inevitabilities, needs, or mechanisms of change. Instead, it addresses the unique capacities which permit social agents to institute, maintain and alter social life in manifold forms. Social constraints and enablements, and the form and direction of social change, are constituted in social practices which may differ in execution and outcome from one historical domain to another. Structuration theory therefore provides social science with an ontology of potentials rather than an ontology of fixed social traits (see Cohen, 1989). Because these potentials may be realized in a variety of ways, no historically specific concepts or explanations can be deduced from the structurationist ontology. Giddens's studies of modernity (see, for instance, 1990) illustrate the propaedeutic utility of postulates in structuration theory (see also Boden, forthcoming).

Because structuration theory ascribes a central role in the constitution of social life to enacted social practices, it disputes the ontological validity of the deeply entrenched division between collectivist and individualist traditions in social thought. Unlike collectivist theories, it treats the patterns and properties of social groups as realities produced through routinized practices, rather than as realities *sui generis*. Unlike individualist accounts, it treats the exercise of agency as logically prior to a concern for the actor's subjective choices or interpretations of social practices. It follows that broadly similar instances of an institutionalized practice may be reproduced through the agency of many different actors extending beyond a given cohort or generation. It also follows that actors need not (although they may) recognize that their exercise of agency reproduces or alters an institutionalized practice.

Giddens's theory of the acting subject is designed to complement the centrality of PRAXIS in structuration theory. Although reflective (discursive) consciousness is not overlooked, many social practices are reproducible on the basis of agents' tacit (practical) consciousness of the skills involved. Giddens grounds a diffuse motivation to participate in social life, along with elements of human personality development, in an unconscious sense of ontological security sustained in the enactment of familiar routines. However, he has yet to address the constitution of human will as well as important issues regarding human needs and interests.

Although structuration theory conceives the skilful enactment of practices much in the manner of Erving Goffman and Harold Garfinkel (see Giddens 1977, ch. 4; 1987), an emphasis on the trans-situational aspects of these practices is introduced in Giddens's innovative account of the duality of structure. In this account, knowledge regarding the enactment of practices in company with appropriate others in suitable settings is treated as a necessary condition for the reproduction of these practices. In turn, the enactment of these practices reinforces participants' awareness of the constitution of their social circumstances. Knowledge regenerated in this way serves to structure the ongoing reproduction of routine ways of life. The structural properties of social practices may be analytically decomposed into rules and resources. Both of the latter, however, are inextricably interrelated in the concrete reality of institutionalized ways of life.

Inspired by developments in time-geography, structuration theory substantially alters current accounts of systemic patterns in social life by conceiving them as institutionalized interactions and relations articulated across time and space (see Giddens 1987, ch. 6). The strength and permeability of systemic boundaries depend on how articulations are produced in social praxis. Interactions between co-present agents are institutionalized in systems of all kinds, but far-flung systems (those having a high degree of time-space distanciation) also involve institutionalized relations between agents in remote settings. Articulations of all kinds communicate, transmit or transport outcomes of various practices.

The structuration (that is, reproduction or alteration) of systemic relations across time and space may occur exclusively through unintended consequences of praxis, or involve the intentional administration of rule across time and space. Unlike pluralist and elitist political theories, structuration theory postulates a dialectic of control in systems of all kinds. While dominant groups have access to superior resources to achieve outcomes through the doings of others, subordinate groups never completely lack resources to resist or redirect dominant control. Therefore systemic power relations are constituted in institutionalized or contested balances of autonomy and control (Giddens 1981, ch. 2; 1985, ch. 1).

Reading
Bryant, C.G.A. and Jary, D. 1990: *Anthony Giddens.*
Clark, J., Modgil, S. and Modgil, C. eds 1990: *Anthony Giddens: Consensus and Controversy.*
Cohen, Ira J. 1989: *Structuration Theory: Anthony Giddens and the Constitution of Social Life.*
Held, D. and Thompson, J. eds 1990: *Social Theory of Modern Societies: Anthony Giddens and his Critics.*
Kiessling, B. 1988: *Kritik der Giddensschen Sozialtheorie: Ein Beitrag zur Theoretisch-methodischen Grundlegung der Sozialwissenschaften.*

IRA J. COHEN

structure, social   *See* SOCIAL STRUCTURE

student movement While recent student-based movements emerged in close relation to internal university problems, they soon focused critically on more general features of society. During the 1960s, student movements became a massive social phenomenon. The Free Speech campaign in 1964 on the Berkeley campus in California, set off the movement and student unrest and activism spread across universities throughout the United States, Europe, the Far East and Latin America. Student movements developed new forms of protest: sit-ins, mass picketing, sit-down strikes, happenings and mass meetings were almost daily occurrences. Students became deeply involved in the black civil-rights movement, organized huge meetings opposing the war in Vietnam, and demonstrated in support of national liberation movements in the Third World. In France, the government of de Gaulle was replaced in the aftermath of the student movement of May 1968. Elsewhere, in London, Rome, West Berlin, Tokyo, student protest often played a key role in political and social life and embodied major forms of cultural renewal. Student movements, however, were suppressed or disintegrated after a decade of protest, and since that time they have not impinged on society in the same conspicuous way. Nevertheless, they laid the foundations on which future movements of the 1970s and 1980s were partially to build (see SOCIAL MOVEMENT).

Social theorists and student actors alike have offered differing interpretations of student protest, which has been conceived as expressing both crisis and conflict.

The crisis of the university

Functionalist analysis looked for an explanation of the emergent student movement primarily in terms of an institutional crisis of the university. The changing function of universities, from elite educational institutions to mass production and professionalism (Jencks and Riesman, 1968), entailed internal university problems, dysfunctions, and decline of the academic community, which were held to explain the student unrest. Students criticized the university establishment for its large-scale technocratic structures and impersonal bureaucracies – which were hardly bent on satisfying the concerns of education and research – for its intellectual mandarinate and its undemocratic attitudes (Lipset and Wolin, 1965). On the whole, the crisis of the university was seen as being provoked by a modernization process of higher education.

The social significance of student protest

In the 1960s much heated discussion, among both students and social theorists, related to the question of what kind of social actors students were. Had they to be considered in terms of social class? Were they revolutionary subjects? These controversies profoundly marked the so-called New Left in the student movement. By some, students were seen as an *ally of the workers' movement*. Large sections of the student movement gained their self-awareness

from neo-Marxist theoretical analysis which considered them as revolutionary actors engaged in an anti-capitalist, anti-state, and anti-imperialist struggle. The student movement did not supplant the workers' movement, but acted as its avant-garde, becoming the custodian of proletarian consciousness, and deriving its social significance from the fact that it was fighting in the name of the proletariat, aiming at a total break with bourgeois institutions and culture. Others saw students as a *potentially revolutionary fringe element*. The assumption of critical theory (see FRANKFURT SCHOOL) was that, due to science and technology, social misery had been largely reduced and the conditions that objectively motivate revolution had faded away. Highly integrated, manipulated and dominated by large-scale technocratic structures, advanced capitalist society allowed critical potentials to originate only at the fringes of the integrated system. This could be students, hippies, sexual minorities or other marginal social groups. Escaping to some extent total domination, their subjective refusal of existing need structures and dependencies rendered them potentially revolutionary categories (Marcuse, 1964).

Criticizing the above interpretations, the student movement was placed, instead, in the symbolic realm, in the sense that it was seen as creating new sensibilities and enlarging public space. Student protest was understood to be highly significant on symbolic grounds, provided it remained non-violent and student activists did not misunderstand themselves as being directly revolutionary actors (Habermas, 1969).

Finally, student protest was interpreted as a *social movement*. This theoretical approach maintained that modern societies were entering a postindustrial stage, where it was no longer the factory, but cultural areas such as education, health, mass media, information, which were becoming the central locus of social conflict. It is this perspective that conferred a potentially central social significance on student movements. Student protest was therefore examined to discover in it the possible presence of a new social movement, that is to say, to ask whether it involved conflict between social adversaries over the control of a cultural field. Close analysis of data on the May movement in France showed, however, that the student movement retained a multiple significance. It did not satisfy the conditions of a social movement in so far as it did not designate technocracy as its main opponent, did not develop a clear view of its own identity, and did not consider knowledge produced in universities as a principal stake of the conflict (Touraine, 1968).

The student movement as cultural criticism

Several theorists considered the student movement as countercultural protest opposing certain cultural and structural features of contemporary societies. In this way, a new political culture was seen to be initiated by the student movement of the 1960s. Direct democracy became a key word. Being personally concerned, engaging in grass-roots participation, were essential mechanisms on which the new political culture was based. By means of extra-institutional forms of action, like sit-ins, civil disobedience and solidarity, student movements attempted to democratize social and political life by capturing public attention. They were committed to new ways of making politics outside institutionalized channels.

The new political culture was closely related to cultural protest denouncing authoritarian attitudes and social structures. The student movement attempted to alter existing social relationships in everyday life. The many criticisms that were levelled at the oppressive nature of authoritarian family structures, sexual repression, the subordination of women, the values of work and industrial society, were often psychoanalytically founded. The anti-authoritarian protest wanted to break with the patriarchal model of culture that gave prominence to masculine societal values and hierarchical social structures.

Furthermore, the student movement claimed that universities should recognize their social responsibility and must not lose interest in the social applications of scientific knowledge; and they criticized the illegitimate appropriation of the universities by the state, the military establishment and large-scale organizations.

Reading

Bergmann, Uwe, Dutschke, Rudi, Lefebvre, Wolfgang and Rabehl, Bernd 1968: *Rebellion der Studenten oder die neue Opposition*.

Flacks, Richard 1967: The liberated generation: an exploration of the roots of student protest. *Journal of Social Issues* 23, 52–75.

Keniston, Kenneth 1965: *The Uncommitted Alienated Youth in American Society*.

Morin, Edgar, Lefort, Claude and Coudray, Jean-Marie 1968: *Mai 68: la brèche*.

Touraine, Alain 1972 (*1974*): *The Academic System in American Society*.

KARIN D. RENON

suburb   In this kind of settlement, lying on the outskirts of a city and made up mainly of housing and shops and separated from industrial zones, there is not the concentration and intermingling of various uses of the territory typical of cities in the industrial age. Furthermore, suburbs are generally inhabited by homogeneous social groups and are either mainly working-class or middle-class.

These kinds of settlements already existed in preindustrial times, as the French term *banlieue* suggests; it refers to the space beyond the medieval city walls but under the jurisdiction (*ban*) of the city. Subsequently, the wave of industrial urbanization and the development of transport and communication networks have stimulated a vast expansion of suburbs, a process of 'suburbanization' (Walker, 1981).

The first systematically built suburban settlements go back to the second half of the nineteenth century in England (suburbia, with the variation of the 'garden cities') and in the United States (Mumford, 1966). These were settlements for the middle classes and represented a compromise between the need to live near the industrial city, the place for work and the high-quality services, and an Arcadian culture aiming to reproduce certain aspects of rural life: single family dwellings surrounded by private gardens and public parks far from urban chaos. As Ruth Glass (1955) has noted, the development of these suburbs is linked to the influence on lifestyles and townplanning of English and American anti-urban culture.

In this century, urbanization (see URBANISM) has largely altered the original suburb. Settlements for workers and middle and low income groups have sprung up, particularly in continental Europe, where high-income groups with their strong urban traditions have mainly stayed in the old city centres. One exception to this model of suburbanization is the residential districts for young well-off families with children in the period of the maximum influence of the American lifestyle, between 1945 and 1970. These developments have radically changed the suburban way of life, especially in the working-class peripheries, which are densely populated 'dormitories' lacking services and green spaces.

In many industrialized countries, working-class

suburbs contain mainly public housing while in others, above all the United States, private building has predominated (see Ball et al., 1988). Despite this and other differences, and the fact that in England and the United States anti-urban culture has also influenced the type of housing in suburbs by discouraging large multi-dwelling condominiums (with some exceptions like the famous 'towers' of the Bronx in New York City), working-class suburban settlements constructed on the outskirts of large industrial metropolises during the postwar years are very similar in kind and have the same problems. The *banlieue* of Paris, the new settlements on the peripheries of Moscow, New York and south of London all display the consequences of high-density cheap building, the lack and inadequacy of services and, in general, of social and family life marked by all the forms of urban deprivation. These range from anonymity and the difficulty of socialization to high costs, congestion and pollution and they are not compensated for by the usual advantage of living very close to the centres of quality services and of economic, financial and political power. To this can be added the fact that the privations involved in commuting have increased as cities have grown in size, and because public transport systems have not been modernized and traffic has become seriously overcongested. Hence, the word suburb, originally positive in meaning, has now taken on a decidedly negative connotation.

The most recent trends towards decentralization of factories and offices, the marked decline in employment in manufacturing industry (Mingione, 1991), economic and technological restructuring (Castells, 1989), as well as the impact of all these trends on urban systems (Scott, 1988; Soja, 1989), are modifying in turn the significance of suburbanization, but in directions that are still too controversial to permit a clear interpretation.

Reading
Ball, M., Harloe, M. and Maartens, H. 1988: *Housing and Social Change in Europe and the USA.*
Castells, Manuel 1989: *The Informational City.*
Glass, Ruth 1955 (*1989*): Urban sociology in Great Britain. In *Clichés of Urban Doom.*
Mingione, Enzo 1991: *Fragmented Societies.*
Mumford, Lewis 1966: *The City in History.*
Scott, Allen J. 1988: *Metropolis: From the Division of Labor to Urban Form.*
Soja, Edward W. 1989: *Postmodern Geographies: The Reassertion of Space in Critical Social Theory.*
Walker, Richard 1981: A theory of suburbanization. In

Urbanization and Urban Planning in Capitalist Society, ed. M.J. Dear and A.G. Scott.

ENZO MINGIONE

suicide   Emile Durkheim's work (1897) remains the most complete, comprehensive and influential social theory of suicide. Durkheim argued that the consistency of suicide rates was a social fact, explained by the extent to which individuals were integrated and regulated by the constraining moral forces of collective life. Egoistic and altruistic suicide arose from the respective under-integration and over-integration of the individual by society, while anomic and fatalistic suicide were caused by under-regulation and over-regulation. Durkheim used correlations between suicide and various rates of external association to demonstrate the validity of his key concepts. For example, Catholic populations had lower suicide rates than Protestant ones because Catholic society bound the individual more tightly to the collectivity. According to Durkheim, increasing egoism and ANOMIE were causing the steadily rising suicide rates of Western societies. However, egoism is not a necessary consequence of industrial society. Iga (1986) has shown how most suicides in modern Japan result from individuals' shame at failing to meet the demands of the group.

Post-Durkheimian sociological works, while approving of Durkheim's pioneering efforts in defining the suicide rate as an object of enquiry and correlating it with a range of social variables, tended to be sceptical of his attempt to explain both in terms of 'real but invisible' moral forces inclining individuals towards suicide. For these empiricist-orientated sociologists, Durkheim's notion of a science of moral phenomena was an impossibility. Thus most later sociological work, while appearing to support Durkheim's 'findings', has confined itself to the relationship between suicide rates and *external* social factors. From this perspective some of the best-known studies have positively linked suicide to, for example, urbanization and isolation (Halbwachs, 1933; Sainsbury, 1955; Cavan, 1965), lack of status integration (Gibbs and Martin, 1964), lack of external restraint (Henry and Short, 1954; Maris, 1969) and imitation following media coverage (Phillips and Carstensen, 1988).

Phenomenological or subjectivist approaches have tended to explore how individuals come to construct 'suicidal' meanings for themselves or for others. The latter concern has been developed into a critique of official data that goes beyond a traditional concern with the 'accuracy' of the statistics. Douglas (1967) argued that the ideas that different cultures and subcultures have about suicide determine what officials finally classify as 'suicide'. Developing Douglas's ideas, Atkinson (1978) and Taylor (1982) have shown that a suicide verdict will only be brought in if officials can find evidence consistent with accepted cultural ideas about why people kill themselves and how they go about doing it. Thus both the regularity of suicide rates and their consistent correlation with factors such as isolation and loss may both be functions of the way in which the data are collected.

Subjectivists have argued that attempts to understand suicide must be based on the meanings that suicidal actors give to their own actions (Douglas, 1967; Baechler, 1979). Douglas, for example, in rejecting statistics in favour of ethnographic data, refers to the latter as 'concrete and observable'. However, in assuming some kind of direct access to the world through observation, he is coming very close to the positivist tradition he is criticizing.

Psychoanalytic theory on suicide, stimulated initially by Wilhelm Stekel and Alfred Adler, has focused on displaced aggression as an unconscious motive for suicide. Freud (1917), comparing mourning with melancholia, argued that, in the latter, the free libido becomes withdrawn into the ego which establishes an identification with the lost object. If animosity towards the part of the ego with which the lost object is identified is great enough, the ego acts to destroy that identification and thereby destroys itself. Freud's later hypothesis in *Beyond the Pleasure Principle* that suicide represents a precocious victory of the death instinct has been less influential, even amongst psychoanalysts. However, the idea was developed in a celebrated book by Menninger (1938), who interpreted a range of damaging and potentially damaging behaviour as partial, or chronic, suicides. For full suicide, the individual not only had to have the wish to die, but also the wish to kill and be killed.

Durkheimian and Freudian theories have a lot more in common than is often realized. Both use theoretical analysis to try to reveal the underlying causes of human action, both explain suicide in terms of the normal development of individuals and societies, and both explore the tensions arising from the precarious relationship in persons between the 'animal' and the 'social being'. In contrast, modern 'suicidology' (now a discipline in the United States, with its own association and journal) tends to be informed by an empiricist epistemology with 'theories' of particular trends in suicide 'emerging' from the data.

Psychological and biological theories of suicide tend to search for the 'factors' which characterize, or are more prominent in, the suicide-prone individual. Cognitive psychology has, for example, suggested the suicidal are characterized by more polarized, less imaginative and more constricted thought processes (Neuringer, 1976). A range of social psychological studies have identified suicidal individuals scoring higher on scales of, for example, 'hopelessness', 'hostility' and low self-esteem. However, lack of consistency and difficulties in making comparisons arise from the fact that such context-bound scales are not 'measures' in any objective sense.

Biological and genetic factors offer potentially more objective indicators. For example, a number of studies have found links between suicidal behaviour and low levels of the serotonin metabolite 5-hydroxy-indoleacetic acid (5-HIAA) in the cerebrospinal fluid (Brown et al., 1982). However, attempts to *explain* this relationship, rather than merely document it, are faced with the problem of relating increasingly sophisticated biological measures to crude psychometric scales. Korn et al. (1990) argue that without improved 'measurement' of psychological functions, 'the biological revolution in psychiatry may indeed appear chaotic.'

Defining suicide has not generally been seen as a problem. Suicide is intentional self-killing. However, research into the nature of suicidal acts, fatal and non-fatal, has challenged the conventional notion that all 'genuine' suicidal deaths are aimed at death and can thus be distinguished from a variety of 'false' suicidal acts, such as 'cries for help', where the intention is to live. Stengel was one of the first to show that most suicidal acts, including the majority of those which end in death, are manifestations of risk-taking behaviour, undertaken with ambivalent intent and characterized by uncertainty of outcome (Stengel and Cook, 1958). Some researchers have used the term 'parasuicide' to describe behaviour which, while falling short of a full suicide attempt, is more than a mere manipulative gesture. These observations have implications for defining and theorizing about suicide. Stengel (1973) has defined suicide as 'any deliberate act of self damage which the person committing the act cannot be sure to survive'. Perhaps the key question for current research is not, why do people kill themselves, but why do so many more (possibly as many as 100,000 a year in England and Wales) risk their lives in what Stengel has likened to a medieval ordeal?

The ethics of suicide tend no longer to focus on the attempter's moral culpability. Twentieth-century thought sympathizes with the suicide, but puzzles over the mystery of what drives individuals to seek to detach themselves from the good society. In the twenty-first century, with an ageing population and diminishing resources, the reemergence of suicide as social responsibility, even a duty, cannot be discounted.

See also CLINICAL DEPRESSION; PSYCHIATRY AND MENTAL ILLNESS.

Reading
Douglas, J. 1967: *The Social Meanings of Suicide.*
Durkheim, E. 1897 (*1963*): *Suicide: A Study in Sociology.*
Freud, S. 1917 (*1957*): *Mourning and Melancholia.*
Lester, D. ed. 1990: *Current Concepts of Suicide.*
Menninger, K. 1938: *Man Against Himself.*
Stengel, E. 1973: *Suicide and Attempted Suicide.*

STEVE TAYLOR

superstructure   *See* BASE AND SUPERSTRUCTURE

surrealism   A revolutionary socio-artistic movement, which aimed at effecting nothing less than a change in society through revelation of the marvellous behind the everyday, and the methodical exploitation of the resources of the unconscious. The poet Guillaume Apollinaire described his play *Les Mamelles de Tiresias* (of 1917) as a 'drame surréaliste', and the word was adopted by a number of younger poets associated with the magazine *Littérature*, notably André Breton, Philippe Soupault, Louis Aragon and Paul Eluard, from 1922 onwards. Breton became the undisputed leader and theoretician of the group, which in time acquired the apparatus of a political party, with membership, trials, expulsions and heresies, and even its own dictionary.

Deriving initially from the nihilistic, anti-art attitudes of the Dada movement, surrealism took over from it the demonstrations, manifestos, shock tactics and desire to '*épater les bourgeois*', and added a profound interest in the discoveries of Sigmund Freud. The surrealists took their preoccupation with chance – '*hasard objectif*' – from the elegant, philosophical anti-artworks of Marcel Duchamp, a member of the Dada group, and its aesthetic method from a much-quoted phrase from *Les Chants de Maldoror* (of 1869) by Isidore Ducasse, Comte de Lautréamont: 'as beautiful as the unexpected meeting, on a dissecting table, of a sewing machine and an umbrella'. This juxtaposition of contrasting or contradictory realities to reach a new, surreal state was associated by Breton with Hegel's DIALECTICS, and was facilitated in particular by the relatively new idea of *collage*, the sticking together of printed or photographic elements.

The do-it-yourself nature of this technique accorded with another maxim of Lautréamont: 'poetry must be made by all.' *Collage*, the serious use of children's paper games such as 'consequences' (known as *cadavres exquis* from the first two words obtained by this method), the use of dream and trance material and automatic writing, and later the discovery of 'found objects', made for a theoretically democratic movement. New media like photography (with Man Ray) and film (with Luis Bunuel) seemed particularly well adapted to the production of contrasting realities. Primitive and naive art, cheap thrillers and early Hollywood movies were discovered and acclaimed. It is ironic, in view of all this, that the surrealists are now largely perceived as an elite group of poets and painters.

During their years of peak activity in the 1930s, at the time of the Popular Front and anti-fascist activity generally, they persistently tried to ally themselves with the French Communist Party, with predictably tragi-comic results; such free spirits, however sincere, had no place in a rigid party hierarchy.

Though they regarded themselves as anything but an art movement, it is also ironic that surrealism is best known today as the breeding ground of a number of exceptional painters: Max Ernst, André Masson, René Magritte, Salvador Dali; their varying nationalities testify to the international spread of the movement.

Love – *l'amour fou* – and Woman provided the inspiration. Violently anti-clerical, it is as if the surrealists took metaphysics and replaced divine love with physical love. A considerable number of their 'muses' became artists in their own right: women such as Elsa Triolet, Lee Miller, Meret Oppenheim and others found themselves through the movement. Surrealism reached its apogee in the great exhibitions in London (in 1936) and Paris (in 1938), though it carried on until the death of Breton in 1966, and has had a continuing influence, notably on 1960s Pop Art.

See also SOCIOLOGY OF ART.

Reading
Aliquié, Ferdinand 1965: *The Philosophy of Surrealism.*
Cardinal, Roger and Short, Robert Stuart 1970: *Surrealism: Permanent Revelation.*
Jean, Marcel 1970: *The History of Surrealist Painting.*
Nadeau, Maurice 1968: *The History of Surrealism.*
ADRIAN HENRI

survey, social   *See* SOCIAL SURVEY

symbolic interactionism   A branch of American sociology, this is an offspring of CHICAGO SOCIOLOGY. For decades it was a 'loyal opposition' to the dominant theory of Talcott Parsons (see FUNCTIONALISM) and to the more quantitative empirical approaches. In the 1960s interest in symbolic interactionism became almost a fashion, and it was connected, in an unclarified way, with phenomenological and other approaches. Today, this theory continues, on the one hand, relatively unbroken, while on the other hand there are tendencies, first, to overcome the concentration on microsociological phenomena and, second, to gain a historical understanding of itself.

The term 'symbolic interaction' was coined by Herbert Blumer in 1937. It denotes that this branch of sociology and social psychology focuses on processes of interaction – immediate reciprocally oriented social action – and that it has an underlying concept of interaction which stresses its symbolically mediated character. One should not think here of social relations in which action is a mere actualization of pre-given rules, but of those in which common and reciprocal definitions of the relation are proposed and established. Social relations, then, do not appear as fixed once and for all, but as open and depending on constant common approval. This basic principle of symbolic interactionism explains its methodological affinity with so-called qualitative methods, particularly the participant observation approach and the use of biographical data. On the level of content, processes of family interaction, processes of emergence and definition of deviant and subcultural behaviour were opened up as fields of research.

However, it would be insufficient to describe this approach only by a vague characterization of its basic assumptions. Above all it should be noted that Blumer's programme is a more or less simplifying condensation of the complex theoretical work of G. H. Mead, read with a social psychological interest. Without using the term, Mead elaborates the concept of symbolically mediated interaction in the framework of an anthropological theory of communication, for instance, in a comparison of animal and human modes of communication and sociality, emphasizing the meaning of self-perception and anticipation of behaviour and showing how these transform mere vocal gestures into meaningful symbols. On this basis he introduces a changed view of personality structure and a new concept of mind. The ability of the individual to indicate something to itself and to interact with itself is central in both cases. Then follows an analysis of the onto- and phylogenetic origin and development of self, reflexive thinking and intentional action. Mead considers the integration of individual behaviour into group activity by means of mutual anticipation of behaviour instead of fixed biological patterns as the characteristic feature of human sociality.

Criticism of symbolic interactionism is mainly directed against Blumer's methodological programme, asserting (1) an alleged reduction of social phenomena to forms of immediate interpersonal relationships; (2) a neglect of power and domination; (3) a conceptualization of macrosocial processes in terms of mere horizons for life-worlds; (4) a complete disregard of the human domination over nature and the increasing independence of social processes from the intentions and orientations of individual and collective actors. Many of these objections to Blumer's programme and its adherents may be justified, at least in part, but they seem odd if the whole range of the theoretical and empirical contributions of this approach is taken into account, for example by including the work of Everett Hughes and his school on the sociology of work and the professions.

The importance and potentiality of symbolic interactionism can only be understood in the context of the old Chicago school which it succeeded but also limited. In a sense it marks a decline of the loose interdisciplinary network of theorists, social researchers and reformers at the University of Chicago, which had a certain unity although the inner coherence of the various elements has never been worked out and was not even recognized for a long time. This coherence has to be understood as resulting from, first, a conception of social order which is guided by democratic ideals; second, the primacy of sociality derived from a theory of action; and third, the concept of action developed by pragmatism. But one has to admit that the analyses of social problems in the United States at that time produced – for example in R. E. Park's work – a dualism of two types of social order: one dominated by competition, the other dominated by COMMUNI-CATION.

It is an important point for the reconstruction of the history of symbolic interactionism to see whether this dualism was dissolved or merely covered by restricting research to the second type, the communicatively created social order. The productiveness of this tradition – beyond micro-sociological phenomena – has been shown in the analysis of the division of labour in the case of professional organizations and in the analysis of collective behaviour and social movements. This might be reason enough to give this sociological approach, which has for decades suffered from a lack of theory, a coherent theoretical self-under-standing, which would contribute to current theoretical debates.

Reading

Becker, H. 1963: *Outsiders: Studies in the Sociology of Deviance.*
Blumer, H. 1937: Social psychology. In *Man and Society*, ed. E.P. Schmidt.
—— 1969: *Symbolic Interactionism: Perspective and Method.*
Glaser, B. and Strauss, A. 1967: *The Discovery of Grounded Theory: Strategies for Qualitative Research.*
Hughes, E. 1971: *The Sociological Eye: Selected Papers.*
Joas, H. 1985: *G.H. Mead: A Contemporary Re-examination of his Thought.*
Mead, G.H. 1934 (*1962*): *Mind, Self, and Society*, ed. C.W. Morris.
—— 1964: *Selected Writings*, ed. A.J. Reck.
Park, R.E. 1967: *On Social Control and Collective Behavior: Selected Papers.*
Thomas, W.I. and Znaniecki, F. 1918 (*1974*): *The Polish Peasant in Europe and America*, 2 vols.

HANS JOAS

syndicalism   It was characteristic of syndicalists to subordinate theory to action; they celebrated spontaneity and were often ostentatiously anti-intellectual. The doctrinal origins of syndicalism were eclectic, and its central dynamic was typically *negative*: a reaction against the perceived failings of the mainstream labour movement, a protest against new forms of alienation and deprivation afflicting the working class. Since the precipitating forces

differed across countries, so syndicalism itself was internationally variable.

'Syndicalism' is merely the English rendering of the French word for trade unionism. *Syndicalisme révolutionnaire* commonly denoted the aims and principles expounded by Fernand Pelloutier (1867–1901), secretary of the Fédération des Bourses du Travail; and the policies embraced by the Confédération Générale du Travail (CGT) after the two union organizations merged in 1902.

If one can distil a coherent body of thought from the programme of the CGT, it involves the insistence that unions must keep clear of entanglement with political parties, should encourage localized rank-and-file initiative and should challenge capitalism through escalating militancy (including sabotage). Spontaneity and violence (spearheaded by a militant minority), together with the 'myth' of a revolutionary general strike, were celebrated in the writings of Georges Sorel (1847–1922) – though his connection with syndicalist trade unionism was neither close nor lasting. His writings particularly influenced the Italian left, some of whom – notably Mussolini – later turned to fascism (see Roberts, 1979).

The heyday of syndicalism as an internationally influential body of ideas was in the years immediately before the outbreak of war in 1914. This coincided with social and economic transformations in many countries, involving the displacement of traditional peasant and artisan relations of production, the imposition of the new disciplines of large-scale factory labour and the rise of giant capitalist combines and cartels with intimate links with the state. At the same time, the very successes of established trade unions and social-democratic parties often seemed to spell bureaucratization and the loss of their radical dynamic (Beetham, 1987).

Syndicalism seemed to provide an alternative for the working class, its meaning varying according to local circumstances. Often it involved a strong *ouvriériste* orientation: a hostility to what was seen as the malign influence of bourgeois intellectuals within labour movements (an attitude vigorously expressed by Victor Griffuelhes (1874–1923), secretary of the CGT from 1902 to 1908. Linked to this was a rejection of parliamentarism – considered a source of careerism and compromise – and of political parties (or at least those primarily committed to parliamentary action). Instead, syndicalists emphasized trade union struggle, while denouncing the spread of peaceable collective bargaining (see TRADE UNIONS); for them, industrial militancy was essential to defend workers' economic interests, while encouraging their confidence in preparation for a concerted challenge to capitalism through the revolutionary general strike. SOCIALISM itself was conceived in terms of workers' control rather than administration by a centralized state. Finally, most syndicalists were strongly opposed to militarism and nationalism.

By 1914, revolutionary syndicalism had become the official position of significant sections of the trade union movement, mainly in countries with traditions of ANARCHISM (Joll, 1964; Woodcock, 1963), with a substantial artisan base and with little background in institutionalized collective bargaining. As well as the CGT in France, notable examples were the Confederación Nacional de Trabajo in Spain (Payne, 1970) and the Unione Sindicale Italiana. Where syndicalists were in a minority they often led the opposition to official union policies and practices. In Britain an Industrial Syndicalist Education League was formed in 1910 by activists such as Tom Mann (1856–1941); they rejected centralized collective bargaining and proclaimed the slogans of solidarity and direct action. In the United States the term syndicalism was rarely used, but the Industrial Workers of the World (IWW) showed many parallels with revolutionary syndicalism in Europe (Dubofsky, 1969).

In much of northern Europe, the dominant meaning of syndicalism was rejection of the need for a socialist party. Social democracy had become bureaucratic, corrupted by parliamentarism, ready to compromise with the bourgeois state; the working class must return to the industrial battlefield. An intermediate position was expressed by the faction of the IWW led by Daniel de Leon (1852–1914), and their British followers, notably James Connolly (1870–1916). While insisting that industrial struggle was of primary importance, they perceived some role for a revolutionary party, and also accepted the need for centralized organization (encapsulated in the ideal of the 'one big union').

An attempt in 1913 to form a Syndicalist International proved abortive (Westergard-Thorpe, 1978); with the outbreak of war, many erstwhile syndicalists abandoned their former anti-patriotism. Those who sustained an anti-war position were often in the lead of the wartime industrial struggles, in some cases helping develop theories of socialist industry based on the principle of the WORKERS' COUNCIL. But revolution in Russia pro-

voked a further crisis for the movement. As early as 1907, Lenin had attacked syndicalism for perpetuating the 'economist' policies which he had earlier denounced. The Bolshevik model of revolutionary organization and socialist production contradicted syndicalism on many key principles; and after 1917, many leading syndicalists showed their commitment to the Russian example by recanting their former 'infantile' policies. Some specific aims of prewar and wartime syndicalism – workplace organization, industrial unionism, direct action – were indeed carried over into the new communist parties. But the underlying theories of socialism from below and of workers' management (expressed in Russia itself by the Workers' Opposition) were systematically eradicated.

Those syndicalists who refused to join, or broke with, the Comintern position tended to reject the Moscow model of the workers' state as well as the Leninist conception of the party. Increasingly, anarcho-syndicalism came to dominate the surviving syndicalist movements, which associated in a Syndicalist International in 1922. But with the widespread working-class defeats of the 1920s, syndicalism became displaced as a serious rival (at least outside Spain, Portugal and Latin America) to socialist, communist and trade union orthodoxies. One may detect some continuities between early syndicalist ideas and more recent theories of workers' control. But even on the left, 'syndicalism' itself has become little more than a term of abuse. Will the collapse of orthodox communism bring renewed attention to the syndicalist tradition?

Reading
Cole, G.D.H. 1956 (1967): A History of Socialist Thought, vol. 3.
Geary, Dick 1981: European Labour Protest.
Holton, Bob 1976: British Syndicalism 1900–1914.
Ridley, F.F. 1970: Revolutionary Syndicalism in France.
Stearns, Peter 1971: Revolutionary Syndicalism and French Labour.

RICHARD HYMAN

system theory The term system includes machines, organisms and social and psychological systems, as opposed to individual actions and parts. Systems are complexes of elements and relations, separated by boundaries from their environment, which is always more complex than the system itself (see Hall and Fagen, 1968; Allport, 1968). For Niklas Luhmann, 'This difference in complexity' between the system and the environment in which it is located is 'the fundamental problem for system theory, the ultimate point of reference of any functional analysis' (Luhmann, 1970–90, vol. 2, p. 210; see also FUNCTIONALISM).

Social systems may be interactions, organizations or whole societies. Social systems, like psychological systems, may be characterized by their use of *meaning*. Their elements, however, are not persons, human beings or subjects, but intersubjective or communicative actions (see COMMUNICATION). Social systems coordinate actions. They are not, however, life-worlds or sociocultural forms of life, characterized by the fact that they coordinate actors' intentions in such a way that these appear, in the perspective of the actors themselves (the participant perspective), as a meaningful and interpretable context. Social systems are as such neither understandable nor misunderstandable, neither the expression of an antecedent consensus nor the implementation of a conscious consensus. Social systems coordinate the *consequences* of actions, which objectively make up a functional whole from the perspective of an observer or an observing system.

Economic acts, for example, which are meaningful and therefore interpretable from a participant perspective, are combined by markets into a system in which one economic act follows from another. What determines the link and the sequence of actions in space and time is, however, not the meaningful intention but merely whether the buyer has money or not and whether or not he or she spends it. The money mechanism is blind to intentions and to any beliefs, programmes, ideas and interests. All that counts are the consequences of decisions to buy. The system of science operates in a similar way: it is not the concrete research programmes and the multifarious implications of research, such as its social value, which are decisive, but whether what is produced is true or false. The system of science as such is blind to everything else, in particular to the complex meaningful relation between science and life-world. The most important effect of functional differentiation is that 'the soldiers march, the writers write and the ministers rule – whether or not they care to in a given situation' (Luhmann, 1970–90, vol. 2). Earlier sociology had given a one-sided account of this process as one of bureaucratization, based on the model of purposive-rational action. System theory tends to treat the same process just as one-sidedly as a gain in freedom resulting from the removal of the burden of individual responsibility (cf. Luhmann, 1976, pp. 287ff.).

Abstracting from the perspectives and orientations of the actors has important consequences for the methodological status of system theory. As a theory it is concerned with explanation, not with understanding. It cannot, however, make any claim, or at best a very limited one, to offering causal explanations. Sociological system theory, at least, has reconciled itself to its virtual inability to provide causal explanations, along with strongly empirical concepts, observability, etc. It explains the imprecision and circularity of its functional explanations, however, not by the ontological peculiarity of its symbolically structured object domain or, like *verstehende* sociology, by the impossibility of escaping the hermeneutic circle, but by the complexity and opacity of system structures which are in principle not amenable to causal analysis. Autopoietic (self-forming) systems alter themselves by discovering completely new structures in an unpredictable manner. System theory itself, however, now sticks increasingly to its own method and explains the limits of its causal explanatory power by its social function and the functional conditions of its own self-reproduction as scientific theory (Maturana, 1982; Schmidt, 1987; Luhmann, 1988).

The interpretation of meaning complexes, as practised by W. Dilthey or Max Weber, is not rejected by system theory, but rather presupposed. Niklas Luhmann, like Talcott Parsons, starts from the fact that, for example, in Protestant cultures economic action was structured by different world-views and meanings to orthodox Catholic or in Islamic fundamentalist regions of the world. Only where action forms an intelligible life-world can a modern economic system coordinate actions exclusively by means of the effects of flows of money on the consequences of action. To this extent societies are always 'systemically stabilized complexes of action of socially integrated groups' (Habermas, 1981, vol. 2).

In a modern, functionally differentiated society, however, it no longer matters *where someone comes from*. Community, religion and collective consciousness, historical origin, social status and place in a traditional hierarchy, family ties and kinship obligations are irrelevant, although their socially integrative force is still presupposed. The only thing that counts in a juridically institutionalized, free and equally accessible market system is whether someone can pay or not. Through their legal institutionalization, free markets have cut themselves off from kinship ties and orders of privilege, from family and stratification as well as from the political sphere. As Marx already recognized, the order of social strata and classes has lost its old autonomy and become itself almost totally dependent on the autopoietic self-organization of the economic system.

Relying primarily on Max Weber's theory of value spheres, Talcott Parsons (1966, 1971) developed a theory of MODERNITY in terms of functional differentiation. This process turns the individual components of action – latent constitutive values, integrative norms, purposive motives, adaptive resources – which are integrated in communicative action into the specialized *performances* of differentiated functional systems. Both at the level of the 'general action system' and at that of the 'social system' and the integrative subsystem of the action system, the systems which take over the *internal* tasks of information processing, innovation and the symbolic-communicative reproduction of values and norms separate out from those systems which secure the adaptation of action system and social system to *external* environments.

The process of evolutionary change (see EVOLUTIONARY PROCESSES IN SOCIETY) which has led to the development of the system of modern societies can then be explained by the shift from social stratification to functional differentiation. The rise of autonomous cultural institutions makes possible, by way of the generalization of values, the legitimation of concrete norms which are binding for the social community. A post-traditional educational system, a self-organizing economy, autonomous art and individualized religion (the Protestant ethic) are the most important historical examples. By means of generalized influence, social integration can be organized as the inclusive and open-ended formation of free associations into a system of social communities. Parsons's 'societal community', juridically institutionalized in CITIZENSHIP, is the site of associative freedom as understood by Tocqueville. One could also describe the self-organization of the social community as the higher-level, reflexive 'social union of social unions' described by John Rawls. In intersystem exchange, this supplies the political system with loyal support, through its influence over the citizens, while the political administrative system supplies the social community of citizens with the necessary power through the juridical sanctioning of freedom of association on an equal basis.

The decoupling of political power from the influence of communicative action in social associations then gives the political sphere the necessary freedom to impose functional differentiation and to implement, in a purposive-rational manner, the corresponding juridical and administrative structures; these are necessary, for example, to separate the modern organization of work from the *oikos*, the diffusely functioning peasant family household, but also for example to protect the socializing function of the family from the economic mobilization of the individual family members. An economic system, freed by massive political intervention from all value commitments, normative restraints and political tasks can concentrate on the maximization of performance and develop the productive forces without which the system of modern societies would lack all motive power.

This model of functional differentiation suffers from a fundamental difficulty. For Parsons, every form of system formation by means of functional differentiation appears as a broadly unproblematic decoupling of system and life-world – unproblematic only because he conceives the life-world only in terms of traditionalism, particularism, diffuseness and affectual collectivism. For him, functional differentiation is the emancipation from the limits of nature and from traditional forms of sociation. Thus, for example, he could describe the development of the Soviet Union, even at the end of the 1960s, as a progressive modernization on the road to the Western system of modern societies and lagging only in certain domains. This one-sidedly optimistic interpretation of Soviet development, not based on any ideological prejudice in favour of communism, was due to a categorial blindness. The concept of functional differentiation permits an adequate analysis of the modern transformation and dissolution of traditional forms of socialization, but the question whether there are modernization processes (such as the Stalinist terror) which destroy not only traditional forms of socialization but the very possibility of socialization itself cannot even be posed. If this is so, functionalist system theory cannot escape the charge that it embodies a concealed philosophy of history. It seems, at least, as if system theories are forced by their categories into a certain blindness to possible *pathologies of modernization.* Habermas's anxieties go in this direction, and Michel Foucault's polemical discourse analyses gain considerable force as a corrective to the one-sided optimism of system theory's view of modernity.

Reading

Habermas, Jürgen 1981 (*1984, 1989*): *The Theory of Communicative Action*, vol. 2.

Parsons, Talcott 1951: *The Social System.*

—— 1966: *Societies: Evolutionary and Comparative Perspectives.*

HAUKE BRUNKHORST

T

taste   The *ability* to judge and appreciate what is beautiful, excellent, good or proper, and the *propensity* to produce or to consume objects (such as works of art) that embody this capacity make up the two sides of the coin of taste. While the notion has a long and illustrious past in Western social thought, stretching from Kant back to Hume and Plato, it has been surprisingly neglected by the social sciences. Indeed, until recently, save for Max Weber's considerations on the stylization of life and Thorstein Veblen's theory of conspicuous consumption, it was the near-exclusive province of philosophers and specialists in art history or criticism (Osborne, 1970), not to mention biologists – in short, it was relegated either to the realm of high culture or to that of nature. Thus the entry on taste in the *International Encyclopedia of the Social Sciences* (Wenzel, 1968) treats taste, along with smell, solely as a physico-chemical phenomenon and contains not a single line on its social dimensions.

The attitude of modern economics is emblematic of the traditional social-scientific disregard for taste. By assigning preferences the status of an 'exogenous' variable, neoclassical theory obviates the need to study their social genesis, structure and change and reduces taste to the outcome of a wholly individual process of internal learning, as in Tibor Scitovsky's 'cultivation' hypothesis. In their famed piece 'De gustibus non est disputandum', Stigler and Becker (1977) go as far as to argue for the radical irrelevance of taste to the social analysis of all human conduct, contending that differences in behaviour are best explained strictly in terms of variations in prices and incomes. Even such 'taste-based' phenomena as addiction, habitual behaviour, advertising and fashion, they say, can best be studied in light of the 'hypothesis of stable and uniform preferences'.

It was therefore incumbent on philosophy and AESTHETICS to explore taste and its contours. Twentieth-century philosophical thinking on the topic is anchored in Kant's treatment and may be characterized as a search for a transhistoric essence of taste. In the first half of his *Critique of Judgement* (1790) devoted to aesthetic judgement, Kant raised the 'problem of taste' thus: how can we issue judgements which claim 'universal validity' when 'their determining ground' is that most private response to the objects of the world, namely, pleasure? Or, is it possible for taste, springing spontaneously from our subjective feelings, to exclude 'decision by means of proof' and yet to meet the 'necessary agreement of others'? Kant's answer was to separate 'pure taste' and 'coarse pleasure' so as to isolate the disinterested disposition to 'differentiate' and 'appreciate' beauty (Cohen and Guyer, 1982); the latter rejects the easy submission of the senses to the common and the vulgar (*das Vulgäre*) to celebrate the finality of form. To be sure, not all philosophers have adopted the Kantian notion of a pure faculty of appreciation and distinction. Wittgenstein (*Lectures and Conversations*, n.d., p. 8), for one, clearly pointed to an anthropological as opposed to a charismatic conception of taste when he insisted that 'to describe what you mean by a cultured taste, you have to describe a culture.'

It is only in the last two decades that research in the sociology of CULTURE has broken the monopoly of philosophical and literary aesthetics, replacing the latter's *essentialist* notion of taste with a *relational* conception firmly tying taste to the dynamics of CLASS inequality. Whereas the thrust of pure aesthetics has been to *ontologize* taste in a quest for a Platonic entity with a history of its own, sociology labours to *historicize* it. For Norbert Elias (1939), our standards of taste are the historic product of a centuries long 'civilizing process' involving the progressive multiplication of constraints and prohibitions on the physical functions of the body (eating and evacuation, sleeping, sex and violence). The transformation of European sensibility recorded by these standards appeared first in royal courts before trickling down from the aristocracy to the middle and working classes due to the establishment of strong unified states and to the ensuing physical pacification of society. Corbin (1982) has developed a kindred argument in the domain of smell by uncovering how modifications in olfactory standards – what is considered foul and fragrant, what odours are deemed tolerable, what groups are considered 'offensive' – in nineteenth-century France expressed the growing conflict between classes in the appropriation and domestication of space in the industrializing city.

In fact, the very categories we use to establish hierarchies of taste, such as 'highbrow' versus 'lowbrow', find their origins in the historical process of *sacralization of culture* whereby the artistic matters and manners of the privileged classes were instituted into a universal canon of aesthetic judgement. Levine recounts the long struggle it took in America 'to establish aesthetic standards, to separate true art from the purely vulgar' so that, by the turn of this century,

the taste that ... prevailed was that of one segment of the social and economic spectrum which convinced itself and the nation at large that its way of seeing, understanding, and appreciating music, theater and art was the only legitimate one. (Levine, 1988, p. 231)

To create cultural consumers as a collection of persons reacting *individually* with 'tasteful' restraint to the performance required an active work of fragmenting, taming and segregation of audiences, actors, styles and genres, which entailed systematic denigration of 'popular' entertainment. Taste in art had grown into a means of social separation linked to the rise of the new middle and upper classes.

But it is in *Distinction* that we find a radically sociological answer to the Kantian conundrum of taste. In it, Pierre Bourdieu (1979) effects a Copernican revolution in the science of taste by breaking with three central tenets of the dominant perspective. First, he abolishes the sacred frontier which makes legitimate culture a separate universe by repatriating aesthetic consumption into everyday consumptions: the same set of dispositions – what Bourdieu calls habitus – determine one's choice in matters of music and sport, painting and hairstyle, theatre and food. Second, against charismatic ideology, Bourdieu observes, not only that cultural needs and capacities are a product of class upbringing and education, but also that there exists a *homology* between the hierarchy of goods and the

hierarchy of consumers, such that aesthetic preferences mirror in their organization the structure of social space. Consequently, taste can only be grasped relationally, within a system of oppositions and complementarities between lifestyles and between corresponding social positions in the class structure.

In matters of taste, more than in anywhere else, any determination is negation: tastes are no doubt first and foremost distastes, disgust provoked by horror or visceral intolerance ('sick-making') of the taste of others. (Bourdieu 1979, p. 56)

Thus the 'taste of liberty' of the upper class, which gives primacy to manner over matter based on an elective distance to economic necessity, defines itself by the refusal to surrender to primary drives, which they take to be the taste of the working classes. The latter evidence a 'taste of necessity' which expresses a class ethos and does not, properly speaking, constitute an aesthetic in so far as it refuses to separate art and life and to subordinate function to form. In between them, the taste of the petite bourgeoisie is a manifestation of cultural goodwill determined by the gap between their high recognition of the legitimacy of bourgeois culture and their low capacity to appropriate it. Bourdieu's third innovation is to show that the manner in which the specific code necessary for deciphering cultural works is acquired – through imperceptible immersion in the familial environment or via explicit teaching at school – survives in the way it is put to use and deeply affects all cultural practices. More importantly, when it takes the form of cognitive categories that appear individual yet are unevenly allocated across groups, this code automatically provides profits of social distinction: it functions as *cultural capital* naturalizing class differences.

Far from being the ultimate repository of spontaneous individuality, then, taste turns out to be the form *par excellence* of social destiny (*amor fati*), 'a class culture turned into nature, that is, *embodied*' (Bourdieu 1979, p. 190) and destined to operate as a code of power. By revealing taste as simultaneously weapon and stake in the classification struggles whereby groups seek to maintain or improve their position in society by imposing their lifestyle as the sole legitimate *art de vivre*, Bourdieu brings *homo aestheticus* back into the world of the mundane, the common and the contested, that is, back into the heartland of social science.

See also ART, SOCIOLOGY OF.

Reading
Bourdieu, Pierre et al. 1970 (*1990*): *The Love of Art*.
—— 1987: The historical genesis of a pure aesthetics. *Journal of Aesthetics and Art Criticism*, special issue on analytic aesthetics, 201–10.
Gamboni, Dario 1983: Méprises et mépris: éléments pour une étude de l'iconoclasme contemporain. *Actes de la recherche en sciences sociales* 49, 2–28.
Gans, Herbert 1974: *Popular Culture and High Culture: An Analysis and Evaluation of Taste*.
Gombrich, E.H. 1963: *Meditations on a Hobby Horse and Other Essays on the Theory of Art*.
Schusterman, Richard ed. 1989: *Analytic Aesthetics*.

LOÏC J.D. WACQUANT

technocracy The word implies rule or government by administrative managers (after the separation of legal ownership from effective control) who oversee and direct younger bureaucratic line and staff personnel with more recent technical training. At the same time, the job of these managers is highly 'political', whether it is carried out in public or private sector organizations. The term also refers to the shortlived movement in the United States between 1931 and 1933 (see Layton, 1956) based on the attempt to apply the thinking of Thorstein Veblen, particularly his book of essays, *The Engineers and the Price System* (1919). The word was first used by W.H. Smyth, a follower of Veblen, in 1919, after he read some of the essays that were to appear in this book. Smyth defined it as 'the organization of the social order based on principles established by technical experts', echoing the long tradition of French positivist thinking which begins with Saint-Simon and includes François-Charles Fourier, Auguste Comte, Prosper Enfantin and the École Polytechnique in the period between 1815 and 1860.

A major presumption of technocracy, which Smyth's definition only serves to underscore, is that there exists a phenomenon called 'objective' knowledge, that it can be grasped and applied directly to social and economic, as well as technical, problems and that technocrats able to combine such knowledge with organizational and managerial skills are the ones who can best be trusted to realize and maintain this type of social order. (See also RATIONALITY AND REASON.) Organizationally, it ignores the ongoing serious tensions between line and staff, generalist and specialist, which one finds in all established bureaucratic structures, whether in putatively 'capitalist' or 'socialist' societies, or in public-sector or private-sector organizations. Technocracy (and those who endorse its goals and methods) also tends to play down or ignore the consequences of such thinking – and the practice that is alleged to issue from it – for legitimate concerns about the accountability of non-elected to elected officials and the responsibility of elected officials to their electors in representative democracies functioning under the rule of law.

What all too often follows from technocratic presumptions and preferences is the view that political problems are really administrative and managerial in nature, *or that ideally they should be reduced to this* in order to maintain continuity and resist 'destabilizing' tendencies brought about by political parties, campaigns and elections. Technocrats prefer infrequent plebiscitary elections characterized by short campaigns where at least one other 'team' is in place ready to take over the symbolic positions associated with democratic governance in the event that the existing group of politicians is defeated. The social order is comprehended, in the ideal case, as a machine (or 'system') which can operate in various ways, from maximum efficiency at one extreme to gross inefficiency at the other. Furthermore, it is a machine (or system) which, once established on the preferred criteria, can be presumed to require only incremental and piecemeal tinkering to maintain it.

The idea of controlling the discretion of unelected officials is irretrievably compromised with the rise of the view – favoured by business and management training programmes in North America, Western Europe and the British Commonwealth – that there is objective knowledge, that experts can grasp it and that it can be applied directly to social, political and economic problems by the proper blending of technical, managerial and political 'skills'. Though the movement that developed in the United States was initially thought to be a radical one, its true conservative colours quickly manifested themselves – in line with the tradition since Saint-Simon and those who taught him, inspired as they were by Edmund Burke. Technocracy thus has serious consequences not only for representative democracy, and the rule of law that it presupposes, but for the more 'liberal' bias of established bureaucracies in those countries. This is why technocrats prefer conservative parties in power and a conservative agenda, because these latter favour stability, order, efficiency, privatization, deregulation and depoliticization.

See also BUREAUCRACY; MANAGEMENT SCIENCE; SCIENTIFIC-TECHNOLOGICAL REVOLUTION.

Reading
Crozier, Michael 1964: *The Bureaucratic Phenomenon.*
Giddens, Anthony 1973: *The Class Structure of the Advanced Societies.*
Gurvitch, G. 1949: *Industrialisation et technocratie.*
Habermas, Jürgen 1968–9: Technology and science as ideology. In *Toward a Rational Society.*
Hodges, Donald 1980: *The Bureaucratization of Socialism.*
Layton, Edwin 1956: The American engineering profession and the idea of social responsibility. Unpublished Ph.D. dissertation.
Mannheim, Karl 1940: *Man and Society in an Age of Reconstruction.*
Meynaud, Jean 1965: *Technocracy.*
Phillips, Derek 1979: *The Credential Society.*
Thompson, Victor 1961: *Modern Organization.*
Wilensky, Harold 1967: *Organizational Intelligence.*
Wilson, H.T. 1977: *The American Ideology: Science, Technology and Organization as Modes of Rationality in Advanced Industrial Societies.*
Young, Michael 1958: *The Rise of the Meritocracy.*

H.T. WILSON

technological change The experimental alteration of the environment through scientific problem-solving has always been part of human endeavour. The scope, rate and diffusion of technological change has been so dramatic, however, in the twentieth century (particularly in the areas of warfare, civil engineering, transport, communication and medicine) that writers have offered separate theories to account for and assess this particular kind of alteration. A dominant element in these theories is technological determinism. Technological determinism asserts that technological change accounts for changes in culture, politics and economics. A modified version of this theory is technological interactionism, which claims that the relationship between technological and social change is mutual. Thorstein Veblen, for example, argued that technological change is modified and restrained by social beliefs and structure (cultural lag). Where an innovation or invention is introduced to another society, however, it is freed from cultural constraints and alters other institutions and practices (Veblen, 1914, p. 135).

Writers who have accepted either of these theories tend to be divided into two groups in their assessment of the merit of technological change. One position questions the value of these changes from a utilitarian or moral standard. One of the most severe critics of technological change was the German philosopher Martin Heidegger who made a sharp distinction between the nature of ancient and medieval technological change, on the one hand, and modern, on the other. The central characteristic of the latter was the transformation of the entire world into an object of 'standing reserve' for manipulation, in which humans are themselves 'enframed' into a system (Heidegger, 1954). Thus, for Heidegger, the Rhine is transformed under modern technological imperatives from a landscape to a power source. Other writers have also emphasized the autonomous and insulated nature of technological systems (as collections of public and private research laboratories) that ceaselessly create change after change without regard to consequences. Critics thus emphasize the unanticipated effects of technological change, especially in terms of the natural environment, the overlooked harm of, for example, iatrogenic diseases, the psychological and cultural impact of constant rapid change, the use of technological expertise as a source of insulation from democratic evaluation and control. Some argue for the dissolution of technological systems and for measures to arrest technological change (Berry, 1977).

More positive assessments emphasize the rational nature of technological change and its liberating impact. Freed from the constraints of culture and tradition, economic production can be organized more rationally and efficiently, thus alleviating poverty and providing expanded opportunities for leisure and assuring better health. Technological change conceived as progress was an assumption of nineteenth-century thinkers such as Saint-Simon and Marx, and is an axiom of such diverse figures as V. I. Lenin, Frederick Taylor, Le Corbusier and B. F. Skinner in the twentieth century. A somewhat different set of advocates of technological change emphasize the positive aspects of some technological changes, called variously, 'peoples' technology', 'soft technology', or 'intermediate technology'. These writers, including Marshall McLuhan, E. F. Schumacher and Buckminster Fuller, support the introduction and development of technological changes that permit personal and serendipitous use (such as transistor radios and personal computers) and argue that technological change properly directed can fulfill the democratic and utopian visions of Gandhi and Jefferson.

See also INFORMATION TECHNOLOGY AND

THEORY; INVENTION; SCIENTIFIC-TECHNOLOGICAL REVOLUTION.

Reading
Boorstin, Daniel 1978: *The Republic of Technology.*
Ellul, Jacques 1954 (*1965*): *The Technological Society.*
Hughes, Thomas 1989: *American Genesis: A Century of Invention and Technological Enthusiasm.*
Mumford, Lewis 1934 (*1963*): *Technics and Civilization.*
—— 1967: *The Myth of the Machine.*
Teich, Albert H. ed. 1977: *Technology and Man's Future.*
PHILIP ABBOTT

teleology The word comes from the Greek *telos*, meaning purpose. The speculative use of this term, derived from Hegelian and other philosophies of history and imputing a purpose or goal to the whole of human history, has generally lost credence in the course of the twentieth century and has been attacked by such writers as Popper (1957) and Lyotard (1979) (see HISTORICISM). Teleological EXPLANATION of the behaviour of humans and other higher animals in terms of perceived goals has however become more widely accepted. Whereas POSITIVISM and BEHAVIOURISM relied on essentially mechanical explanations in terms of antecedent causes, HERMENEUTICS and RATIONAL CHOICE THEORY and related approaches (Sartre, 1960; Taylor, 1964) have revived the idea that the explanation of human actions must include reference to human intentions and purposes and/or established cultural practices. For REALISM, models of CAUSALITY which focus on the causal powers of entities have also brought explanations of natural events and of human actions into a closer relationship (Bhaskar, 1979).

These developments have weakened the sense of a global opposition between causal or genetic and teleological explanation which pervaded nineteenth- and early twentieth-century philosophy and social thought, especially in central Europe (Adler, 1904; Lukács, 1973). Controversy remains, however, over the apparent reliance of FUNCTIONALISM on a teleological form of explanation which imputes purposes, such as social stability or the development of the productive forces, to supraindividual entities such as social systems or the human species, sometimes invoking dubious biological analogies.

Reading
Taylor, Charles 1964: *The Explanation of Behaviour.*
WILLIAM OUTHWAITE

terrorism *See* POLITICS AND TERRORISM

theatre The modern theatre begins properly in 1889, allowing for some important precursors. The main impetus behind the new theatre was the establishment of the power of the mercantile and manufacturing bourgeoisie, but the directions the theatre took were mainly expressions of opposition to the materialist values of that class. Initially it took two main forms. Beginning with Naturalism and the Théâtre Libre of Antoine in Paris, a reformist movement began to document the evils of capitalism and to demand some form of redress. The theorist of this movement was Emile Zola; its precursor was Henrik Ibsen. Linked to this development was a growing interest in examining the world scientifically, and Naturalism soon extended its range of enquiry beyond the immediacy of the material world, into the sociological and psychological.

In the course of this enquiry, the established dominant form of theatre, the dramatic play, began to be seen as inadequate. Dramatic theatre is based upon here-and-now scenes composed of dialogue in which characters confront one another and are thought to have the power to arrive at some form of resolution of their conflicts or difficulties. The new dramatists encountered certain problems: for Ibsen, the present was found to be conditioned by the past, which intruded into the here-and-now dialogue, while for Strindberg the conflicts were seated in the individual psyche, which could not be dramatized according to traditional methods. The dramatic play had established itself during the rise of the bourgeoisie by representing the values and the struggles of that class on the stage, but once they held the ascendancy the situation changed. Chekhov dramatized the decline of the rural bourgeoisie, while others took up the cause of the working class, though attempts by middle class dramatists to present working-class life were rarely successful, perhaps because they baulked at portraying revolutionary conclusions.

The second line of opposition began by creating an aesthetic theatre which needed no social justification. The Symbolists created imaginary, sensory worlds surrounding hierophantic monodramas. Adolph Appia created fluid forms of staging (for Wagner's operas) which would complement the emotion-arousing qualities of the music, and Gordon Craig put forward the idea of a theatre ruled by one supreme artist and poet: the director.

From these experiments and theories three important approaches to performance began to develop. Craig, with his concept of the *übermarionette*, established an impersonal form of acting, in which a highly trained, athletic actor was able to perform with great expressive skill at the demand and command of the director, whose will and poetic vision determined the nature of the presentation. Isadora Duncan asserted the primacy of the artist/dancer's personal authentic expression, arising from what she called her 'soul-states', which she located in the solar plexus. Stanislavsky began to investigate the psychophysical processes through which the actor works and ended by positing the first scientific study of the actor.

Further important developments to come out of this period were the founding of national theatres as a major instrument of bourgeois cultural hegemony, and the movement towards forming some kind of 'popular' theatre. (See also SOCIOLOGY OF ART.) In France and Germany in particular, at the turn of the century, there were movements to democratize the theatres, which exerted a powerful influence on future developments. In France, under the tutorship of Romain Rolland, a movement developed agitating for government subsidy to establish theatres in the working-class suburbs of Paris, which would ultimately be extended to the rest of France. In various stages, this idea developed into the policy of decentralization of the theatre which has formed the basis of France's postwar policy through the Théâtres Populaires, the Centres Dramatiques and the Maisons de Culture. It is worth noting that the charter of the Arts Council of Great Britain gives its purpose as creating access for the widest possible cross-section of the population. In Germany, the Volksbühne movement began in 1891 to build up a large membership which would enable it to buy performances which would be presented at times and at prices which its largely working-class members would find convenient. From this the movement progressed to financing its own productions and to building and owning its own theatres. This principle of supporting a theatre by block bookings from workers' representative organizations, largely the trade unions, became the state policy of the former socialist states of central and eastern Europe. Throughout Europe this ensured that the theatre was viewed as a social service, worthy of being given state funding – at the expense of being accountable in so far as it promulgated the hegemony of the ruling class or the ideology of the state.

Within the Volksbühne movement questions were raised from the very beginning about the relationship between the theatre and its audience. Should it educate the audience politically through theatre, or culturally through participating in theatre, as an audience? There were two crucial splits. The second of these was occasioned by Erwin Piscator in the mid-1920s. Piscator perceived that the whole movement towards democratization of the theatre was based on the concept of People's Theatre, a set of ideas taken over from the thinking surrounding the French revolution; but by the end of the nineteenth century who the 'people' or 'nation' were was a highly contentious issue. Piscator rejected those tendencies towards reconciling the warring classes and introduced the concept of a committed political theatre, the purpose of which would be to serve the purposes of the most advanced sections of the proletariat. Shortly after World War I, Piscator established the Proletarian Theatre, which toured the workers' halls of Berlin until stopped by the police. In a series of productions for the Volksbühne, for the Staatstheater and two revues for the Communist Party, he developed a repertoire of techniques for ensuring the political significance of any theatrical work. His final outrage drove the Volksbühne to disown him and to state categorically that it had no overt political affiliation or intentions. Piscator went on to define and extend his ideas on the Political Theatre, and was closely followed by Bertolt Brecht.

Piscator himself became more and more seduced by the technical innovations he had introduced but some of these had significant value, particularly his use of film to bring reality on to the stage or to establish the global context within which even the most domestic actions take place. (See also CINEMA.) He proclaimed the death of the dramatic theatre, articulated later by Brecht as arising from the sheer impossibility of finding protagonists whose experience would stand as representative of any large group or class, and the death of the individual playwright because no one individual possessed the necessary range of abilities to understand all the complex factors which influenced the contemporary world. He set up dramaturgical cooperatives, which included economists and political activists as well as writers.

Brecht, who was a member of the cooperative, found a way of involving collaborators but retaining the overall control himself. He followed Piscator in rejecting as moribund the dramatic theatre and in establishing the epic theatre as the only form capable of articulating the twentieth century. Brecht's theatre methods were designed to set the audience in a questioning rather than passive frame of mind and he tried to interpose estrangement devices between the action on the stage and the audience, to block feelings of empathy and arouse critical attitudes. Brecht saw that the two arms of the Modernist movement had grown far apart and conceived his own work as uniting the didactic and entertainment functions of theatre. His theatre was always political but it utilized all the many formal and spectacular devices the art theatres had developed.

From Piscator's work with the Proletarian Theatre and from a parallel movement in the USSR, the 'Blue Blouses', the predominating form of political theatre became *agitational propaganda*, the function of the theatre being to educate the audience in political realities and to rouse them to action. A visit by the Blue Blouses to Germany, on the occasion of the tenth anniversary of the Russian revolution, inspired political movements all over the world to adopt agit-prop as their theatrical style. Ironically, this happened at precisely the time that Stalin disbanded the Blue Blouse movement and established the policy of the Soviet Union as socialist realism, the presentation of typical figures in a typical setting.

The break-up of the Soviet Union and the other socialist states in Europe has largely made redundant any form of political theatre predicated on the principle of contributing to the ending of the capitalist system and its replacement by socialism. However, the techniques of agit-prop and the Blue Blouses have been greatly refined and developed in various parts of the developing world, where the political and general social conditions and needs are different. Theatre has been used to promote literacy, population control, agricultural development and political resistance. In these campaigns theatre has been used by governments to maintain the status quo and by oppositional groups to undermine it. The major development in this field has been through the work of Augusto Boal, drawing on the educational theories of Paolo Freire, and his construct of the Theatre of the Oppressed. Although the Theatre of the Oppressed cannot be reduced to any one single process, there is at the heart of it the idea that oppressed people liberate themselves following or during a process of consciousness raising, through which they are led to objectivize their oppression and exploitation and to work out ways of changing their thinking and acting to create new realities. This kind of theatre requires that even Brecht's work is rejected and the barriers between performer and audience are broken down in a series of steps which place the participant inside the action and in a position to 'rehearse' the possibilities of revolutionary change. Drawing on an affinity of purpose with LIBERATION THEOLOGY, this theatre is often called Liberation Theatre.

The second arm of the Modernist movement, from which Brecht took his ideas of spectacle and entertainment, was never entirely separate from the reformist arm. From Strindberg onwards through Expressionism, the feelings of ANOMIE were not easy to dramatize without recourse to non-realistic forms of staging. Experiments were carried out with Surrealist ideas and out of these emerged the work of Antonin Artaud, rejected by the leading Surrealists but formulating a Theatre of Cruelty which would cut through the restraints of the literary text and the polite refinements and inhibitions of modern society to create an elemental theatre working with images to restore the sense of mystery and the metaphysical dimension which had been lost. Artaud was not alone in his concerns – Craig, Wassily Kandinsky and Alexander Scriabin had preceded him – but he began an involvement with oriental theatre which keeps returning as a source of nourishment for a Western theatre that is in danger of losing its potency.

The application of scientific methods to theatrical techniques continued throughout the twentieth century, particularly in the field of movement and DANCE. The ideas of Frederick Winslow Taylor were a major influence in Meyerhold's concept of Biomechanics and there has been a constant stream of new approaches and methods for the physical training of actors. Rudolf von Laban's work mirrored the concern of Isadora Duncan in seeking to distinguish between authentic and inauthentic impulses to move and dance, and he also established the first scientific categorization of movement in terms of time, space and gravity, as well as inventing the first system for notating movement. Out of the Expressionist movement, Oskar Kokoschka and Kandinsky worked to create a formalist theatre which would complement innovations in the graphic arts. The Bauhaus carried out experiments in these aesthetic principles, and when this work reached the United States in the 1930s and was taken up by John Cage and, later, Merce Cunningham, ideas began to be postulated about theatre forms which would utilize chance, and in which the constituent elements would not cohere but would contrast in random ways. Paradoxically, because Brecht had already established that the image need not illustrate the text or action but could contrast or comment, the way was open to liberate the image in a wide variety of ways. There has been a steady stream of new developments which do not cohere with traditional patterns of dramaturgy but utilize the environment, the individual artist's own body and behaviour patterns, and purely formal montages of images and actions. These become postmodern dance (and recently theatre), performance art, happenings, and a whole series of cross-overs. The work of Robert Wilson is the most complex and, with that of Heiner Müller, the best known.

The most recent concept to arise is that of Third Theatre, which relates companies across the world, stemming originally from the work of the Living Theatre and of Jerzy Grotowski. A Third Theatre company is neither for the status quo, nor does it oppose it, since opposition defines the work of the company as surely as acceptance. Nor are these companies avant-garde experimental companies, although their work is experimental and innovative. They live and work in the world creating within themselves theatre as a way of life. They then look for ways of earning their living, but this is not allowed to determine the nature of their work or to impose restrictions on it. The leading theorist of this movement is Eugenio Barba, of Odin Teatret, who set out the concept of the Floating Islands. If each of these groups is in contact with the others they create their own support system and, like the dispossessed Incas, who lived on reed mats floating on Lake Titicaca, they will eventually create their own overall identity and political reality.

In the 1960s there was a surge of interest in the sociology of theatre. Erving Goffman began to use the language of theatre to describe relations in public and to describe social interaction in terms of dramaturgical strategies. At the same time the theatre itself came under close scrutiny as an institution of society and its processes were subjected to investigation from such angles as COMMUNICATION processes, relationship to ritual and other anthropological considerations. Victor Turner, Richard Schechner and Eugenio Barba have all concerned themselves with theatre anthropology. Schechner has attempted to widen the discipline of theatre studies to performance studies, of which theatrical performance is only a small constituent. Barba has embarked on a study of cross-cultural comparisons and connections in performance techniques. Interest was early aroused by the work of Jean Duvignaud on the sociology of the theatre and then the sociology of the actor. Work has also begun on the psychology of the actor and, recently, the biology. The more traditional performance styles and forms have been investigated from structuralist and poststructuralist approaches to establish theatre SEMIOTICS. Much has been done in this field but in the final analysis it has offered very little which can lead to any advance in the theatre. The approach works best where the performance is based on a solid literary text, which the semiotic approach itself attempts to surpass in order to look at the performance structures of theatre.

It would seem from this, or be arguable, that the long history of theatre seen as a social service now acts against its development. 'New Realism' rejects such a concept and theatre has little else to fall back on. At no time has there been so much interest and activity in studying and analysing theatrical processes, while the established theatre itself seems in danger of disappearing. Against this the emergence of Third Theatre and Theatre in Development companies, who do not equate theatrical activity with subsidy, holds out most hope for the future. There are signs of counter-arguments being formulated for theatre as an art form and not a service, and a growing reaction against didactic or political theatre in favour of a celebratory theatre.

Reading
Barba, Eugenio 1986: *Beyond the Floating Islands.*
Boal, Augusto 1979 (*1988*): *Theatre of the Oppressed.*
Bradley, D. and McCormick, J. 1978: *People's Theatre.*
Brecht, Bertolt 1964 (*1978*): *Brecht on Theatre*, ed. John Willett.
Epsepskamp, C.P. 1988: *Theatre in Search of Social Change.*
Schechner, Richard 1988: *Performance Theory.*

CLIVE BARKER

theology This, including natural theology as practised, say, by Aristotle, may be translated literally as 'discourse about God'. This is a broad description, as St Thomas Aquinas points out in the *Summa*, where he writes, 'theology included in sacra doctrina differs in kind from that theology which is part of philosophy.' This broad sense would also include, today, reflection on the findings of sociology about common or folk RELIGION.

In a narrower sense, theology may be defined as methodical reflection on divine revelation, which can be handed on, used in reasoned discourse and defended. In this form, it is the study of the content of texts which are treated as definitive. In its narrowest sense, and this was the style of the manuals of theology until the middle of this century, theology was a set of tidily unified correlations about divine revelation, fitted together from a harmonizing biblical exegesis and a Denziger-based version of doctrinal history. (H. Denziger's *Enchiridion Symbolorum*, 'manual of the church's doctrinal decisions', symbolizes the neo-scholastic theology which was the key to the structure of traditional Catholic church dogmatics.) In these narrow definitions, theology is an exercise of unpacking the contents of sacred doctrines, and although this is one legitimate meaning, it is not what is commonly indicated by theology today. A broader definition is usually attempted.

Pluralism

A broad definition is used today in order to accommodate that theological pluralism which has become the fashion over the past 20 years. Existentialist philosophy, anthropology and sociology, in turn, have led theologians to acknowledge non-theological factors at work in the definition of orthodoxy. The definition of theology then becomes extended not only to reflection on the propositional elements contained in sacred writings, doctrinal formulations and ecclesial practices, but also to interpretations of self-understanding grasped directly and historically by believers. An older generation of theologian would have claimed two sources of theology: Scripture and tradition. Schillebeeckx (1977), for example, retains the two sources scheme, but says that they are

> on the one hand . . . the whole experiential tradition of the great Jewish-Christian movement; and, on the other . . . today's human experiences shared by both Christians and non-Christians . . . The interpretive experience is an essential part of the concept of revelation.

This experiential approach can end up in the extreme pole of pluralism, at the opposite end, that is, from the narrowest definition already referred to, which is privatized and voluntarist versions of belief. An outstanding example of this genre of theological writing is Hans Küng's recent work, *Theology for the Third Millennium*, in which he states the thesis that 'The first constant, the first pole of a critical ecumenical theology is our present-day world of experience with all its ambivalence, contingency and changeableness (1988, p.166). If this is taken to mean that everything is compatible with Christian theology, then it is difficult to see what intelligible meaning can be attached to theology.

Pluralism and new forms of ecumenism embrace also the theologies of other faiths and world religions such as Hindu religion (based on the revealed scriptures of the Vedic seers) (see also HINDUISM AND HINDU SOCIAL THEORY), BUDDHISM (based on the Buddha's 'wheel of teaching' [the dharma] which takes hold of the 'community' [the sangha]), ISLAM (based on the Qur'an revealed to Muhammad) and the Jewish religion (based on the Torah) (see JUDAISM). Islamic theology affirms the existence and oneness of God, the prophetic mission of Muhammad and the necessity of obeying the basic commandments known as 'the pillars of Islam'. The dogmatic structure erected on these three tenets has scarcely changed since the eighth century. Jewish theology is also based on monotheism, in the form, indeed, of an ethical monotheism connected with the Jewish sense of its historical destiny. It may be described, in one sense, as a theology of law, since the Rabbinic tradition has been preoccupied with subtle and frequently unresolved discussions about Old Testament law and its significance for human life. But such general statements do not do justice to the rich tradition of Jewish theology, which, fundamentally influenced by the holocaust, has begun to develop significant forms of liberation theology.

Theological styles

Pluralism in theology exists also in the acceptable form of different systems of theology, or, in the contemporary idiom, in different styles of theologizing. In *Logic of Theology* (1986) Ritsch has identified two basic types: the first is 'monothematic', in which theology is organized around a single central theme; the second is 'conglomerate', in which a range of appropriate and necessary topics and partial themes are brought together in a coherent theological corpus.

Typical of the first style of theology are Martin Luther (justification by faith alone); liberation theologies (freedom from oppression as a matter of universal religious significance); Küng (ecumenism, which no longer sees in every other theology and church an opponent, but a partner); postmodern theologies (the political problem is central to the theological enterprise); Karl Barth (the sovereignty of God); Karl Rahner (an epistemology in which interpretation of a self-understanding is grasped directly and historically in the act of existence).

The 'conglomerate' style embraces most theology from the *Sentences* of Peter Lombard to the *Summa* of Thomas Aquinas and on to most theological writing, both Catholic and Protestant, from the sixteenth century to the early twentieth, and in the case of Catholic theology, to the middle of the twentieth.

Both styles of theology, however, are subject to the objection that they are closed systems, not easily able to accommodate historical developments, paradigm shifts or prophetic interventions.

Theology as science

Theology may be, and often is, defined as 'the science of faith', if faith is taken to mean methodical reflection along lines appropriate to the subject-matter of any particular discipline. The task of theology is the disciplined exploration of what is contained in divine revelation. This includes the detailed explication of its special subject-matter, which includes the Scriptures and Tradition as well as Christian experience. The total commitment required is compatible with critical reflection. Late twentieth-century theology, then, claims to be scientific in its methodology and to have survived (along with other human sciences) the positivist criticism that it is no more than a compound of moral and evaluative claims that express only opinions and preferences. It would be difficult to imagine a contemporary academic institution excluding theological discourse, as the Royal Society, in the seventeenth century, excluded theology and politics on the grounds that they were not value neutral.

Theology and other sciences

Until the twentieth century, PHILOSOPHY stood alone in mediating human self-understanding to theology. Now there is a large number of anthropologically significant human sciences which are

influencing the theological enterprise. Anthropology itself insists that theological insights, supposedly divorced from human experiences, are conditioned by the culture and structures of thought in which they are apprehended (Pallin, 1990). Sociology has criticized the individualism of classical Western theology. To correct this weakness two influences have been brought to bear: Firstly, German political theology, defined by Metz as a critical corrective to the tendency of contemporary theology to concentrate on the private individual, has encouraged development of the Christian sense of responsibility for public issues; and LIBERATION THEOLOGY has encouraged the recovery of the social meaning of the Scriptures by Latin American Christians who are engaged in the struggle for justice. These sciences are now partners in dialogue with theology, and must be recognized as seminal influences. They have begun already, for example, to indicate ways in which the science of faith is a 'practical science', and have introduced terms such as 'orthopraxis' in order to indicate the partial significance of the act of faith and commitment if defined only in terms of orthodoxy.

Theology of the future, influenced by current developments in philosophy and the social sciences, will surely be modified by postmodern and feminist studies (Milbank, 1990; Rose, 1992).

Reading
Küng, H. 1988: *Theology for the Third Millennium*.
Milbank, J. 1990: *Theology and Social Theory: Beyond Secular Reason*.
Pallin, D.A. 1990: *The Anthropological Character of Theology*.
Ritsch, A. 1986: *Logic of Theory*.
Rose, G. 1992: *The Broken Middle*.
Schillebeeckx, E. 1977: *Interim Report*.

FRANCIS P. MCHUGH

theology, liberation   *See* LIBERATION THEOLOGY

theory   *See* PHILOSOPHY OF SCIENCE

theory, exchange   *See* SOCIAL EXCHANGE THEORY

theory of knowledge   *See* KNOWLEDGE, THEORY OF

Third World   The expression *tiers monde* (Third World) was first used in August 1952 by the French demographer, Alfred Sauvy, in an article in the

Paris newspaper *L'Observateur* entitled 'Trois mondes, une planète'. In a postwar world divided into two 'camps', each headed by one of the two superpowers, the colonies which gained their independence after 1945 seemed to resemble the *tiers état* of pre-revolutionary France, an estate which lacked the privileges of the other two estates, the nobility and the clergy.

In France, the term appealed to both socialists and Gaullists who were looking, in quite different ways, for a 'third way' between Washington and Moscow. The doctrine of 'positive neutralism' – a neutralism which did not simply aspire to keeping out of wars but was committed to national liberation and to 'socialist humanism' – also emerged in other West European countries. By 1949, when Yugoslavia defected from the Soviet bloc, the principle of 'non-alignment' spread to the communist world.

The notion of a Third World took on global significance, however, when it was taken up in the 1950s by a number of major ex-colonial countries – notably Nehru's India, Nasser's Egypt and Sukarno's Indonesia. The Left in Europe saw them as 'proletarian nations' which would take over the role of the proletarian class in the advanced world as the gravedigger of capitalism. But the new states themselves set about a different task: the formation of a 'non-aligned' grouping – not a bloc – of Afro-Asian countries, together with liberation movements in the remaining colonies. The Bandung conference of 1955 marked the arrival of this new grouping on the world stage. As ex-colonies, their first concern was with resistance to any attempt to preserve or reimpose Western political control. Yet their independence was so recent and fragile that even those (many) new regimes which called themselves 'socialist' equally feared falling into the clutches of the communist superpower.

The internationalism of the new states manifested itself in the rejection not only of the political control and the cultural hegemony of the particular colonial power that had governed them, but of colonialism *tout court*. The new states therefore supported struggles in the remaining colonies and against racist regimes, notably South Africa. Pan-Africanists like Nkrumah also hoped to overcome the balkanization of the continent produced by colonial rivalries during the imperialist period (see PAN-AFRICANISM).

By the 1970s, though there had been important revolutionary defections from the control of the capitalist world, notably Vietnam, most of the more radical non-aligned regimes had disappeared: either through 'destabilization', or as victims of internal coups, or rendered impotent through economic weakness. The dominant concern of the (originally) significantly named Organization of African Unity thus became the preservation of the boundaries established during the colonial period, since the new states contained culturally heterogeneous ethnic communities with politically varied pre-colonial constitutions while other ethnic groups were divided by state borders. The danger of border disputes and of internal secession movements, and of the manipulation of these divisions by outside powers, was therefore very real, as the war in Biafra showed. 'Nation-building' – the creation of a new kind of civic identity to counteract what was termed 'tribalism' – therefore became a major project of the rulers of the new states (see also NATIONAL POPULAR REGIME).

The 'non-aligned' organization developed through a succession of conferences, in Cairo, Lusaka, Algiers, Sri Lanka, Havana and elsewhere, as well as in other forums from the United Nations to the 'Tricontinental' movement patronized by Cuba. But increasingly the problems they had to confront were economic rather than political: not just the power of the Western states, or of the increasingly diverse forms of communism, but their common economic interests as predominantly poor, agrarian countries in a world dominated by multinational corporations and financial institutions (See DEVELOPMENT AND UNDERDEVELOPMENT.)

Some successes were achieved: 77 underdeveloped countries won UN backing for the first World Conference on Trade and Development in 1962. From 1974 onwards, too, the joint action of the OPEC group of oil producers to control output and world prices had powerful effects even on the wealthy West.

In a few countries, moreover – including the 'four little tigers' of East Asia (South Korea, Taiwan, Hong Kong and Singapore) – there has been massive foreign investment and consequent industrialization. Some have concluded that the Third World, increasingly, will follow that path. As a whole, however, the underdeveloped countries have not been able to break out of their dependency on the West, and even 'newly industrializing' countries (NICs) like Brazil and Mexico are burdened with massive foreign debt. Black Africa has experienced an actual downturn in production. Frantz Fanon's designation of the Third World as the 'wretched of the earth' therefore still seems valid.

The term has not been without its critics: in the Cold War epoch, the USSR denounced it as an attempt to evade the inevitable choice between capitalism and communism. The notion that the blame for the underdeveloped and 'disinherited' condition of these countries could be laid at the door of the West – that they had been *held back* from developing – did not appeal to many who saw them, rather, as 'young' (sometimes inherently irrational, immature, or even inferior) nations. These were 'developing', however slowly, and would eventually make further progress, or, if they did not, had only their own *internal* short-comings – from 'traditional' social institutions (see TRADITION AND TRADITIONALISM) and cultural heritages to dictatorial regimes – to blame. Some economists and WORLD-SYSTEM theorists have argued that countries can indeed be ranked from the richest to the very poorest, but that there is only one world, with rich and poor countries in it, not a distinctive, separate poor 'world'. And Western charity organizations often unintentionally reinforced the popular notion that famines in tropical countries are the consequence of natural disaster rather than man-made.

Critics within the Third World itself often prefer the term 'non-aligned', since the word 'Third' seems to them a residual category, implying some kind of inferiority to the 'First' and 'Second' worlds. The term has nevertheless passed into general use.

Reading
Fanon, Frantz 1961 (*1983*): *The Wretched of the Earth*.
Singham, A.W. and Hune, Shirley 1986: *Non-Alignment in an Age of Alignments*.
Worsley, Peter 1964: *The Third World*.
—— 1984: *The Three Worlds*.

PETER WORSLEY

totalitarianism As a taxonomic term within the social sciences, totalitarianism has enjoyed a considerable vogue as a way of characterizing a basic feature of modern single-party regimes under personal dictators or autocratic oligarchies. The aspect it throws into relief is that, in marked contrast to *ancien régime* states, such regimes deliberately seek to manufacture CONSENSUS in favour of a small ruling elite by creating organizations of mass regimentation, by monopolizing all means of cultural production (especially the mass media), and by deploying various mechanisms of SOCIAL CONTROL. These include PROPAGANDA, ritual politics to enforce an elaborate cult of the leader and the nation (see Kertzer, 1988), and various techniques of COERCION ranging from legal restrictions on basic freedoms to systematic terror.

The avowed aim of such a state is to channel all social, political, economic and creative energies towards the realization of the utopia identified by official dogma, though the very means employed in order to achieve this goal inevitably create in practice a dystopia. Stalinist Russia, Nazi Germany and, to a lesser extent, Fascist Italy have often been treated as paradigmatic of totalitarianism in this narrower sense (for example, Friedrich and Brzezinski, 1956; Arendt, 1958), and new case studies in its permutations and in the bureaucratized barbarities and human atrocities to which it tends to give rise have been supplied by Pol Pot's Cambodia, Ceauşescu's Romania and Saddam Hussein's Iraq.

As an 'ideal type' even this specialized use of the term 'totalitarianism' has naturally been the subject of controversy, and some experts have questioned its usefulness (see Menze, 1981), particularly in view of the way the Cold War reduced it to little more than a boo-word for those societies held to be 'closed' rather than 'open' (see Popper, 1945), and hence denied membership of the 'free world'. Once the term is shorn of narrow anti-communist connotations, totalitarianism might be read into any sociopolitical system if its policies and institutions have had the combined effect of comprehensively crushing what those of the Enlightenment tradition regard as fundamental human freedoms. Indeed a case could be made for seeing a totalitarian thrust in the many regimes which down through the ages have oppressed their subjects (such as Imperial China) or ruthlessly subjugated indigenous cultures (such as imperialist Spain), as well as in the pervasive collusion of modern liberal (capitalist) democracies with colonization, exploitation and the extensive inculcation of patriarchal or capitalist norms which result in a pervasive ALIENATION of their citizens (see, for example, Marcuse, 1964).

Despite its liability to become a highly value-laden term, 'totalitarian' still retains considerable heuristic value for the investigation of the structural-functional aspects of the many modern personal, military and party dictatorships throughout the world at pains to create an illusion of the dynamism, efficiency and popularity of their leadership among the people (see DICTATORSHIP). There are, however, several caveats to be borne in mind whenever the term is used as a tool of academic analysis. First, radical ideological and structural differences can exist between two societies described as totalitarian (such as Hitler's Germany and Stalin's Russia), so that like is rarely being compared with like. In particular, the degree to which such regimes systematically resort to coercion, terror and mass killing in order to suppress dissidence can vary considerably. Secondly, it should not be forgotten that the totalitarian dream of the comprehensive centralization of power and control over all aspects of society is a chimera, no matter how impressive its outward facade. Any apparently totalitarian regime proves on closer inspection to be polycratic, corrupt and inefficient. In particular, its efforts allegedly to mobilize and energize the masses lead to their extensive *depoliticization* and demoralization, while many of those installed in the inner sanctum of real power will be opportunists and careerists rather than genuine ideologues. This is why pluralism, individualism and creativity quickly flourish wherever the state apparatus of indoctrination and repression is eventually dismantled. In short, the gap between the claims made by a totalitarian regime and the realities over which it presides is total, little else.

Gregor (1969) has demonstrated in the case of the Fascist regime (which boasted of being the first *stato totalitario*) how considerable ideological sophistication can be mustered in the doctrinal underpinning of a would-be totalitarian state by its official apologists and self-appointed theoreticians. The hallmark of such a state in its public or exoteric aspect, however, is its axiomatic denial of genuine dialogue, and hence of all authentic social thought. Perhaps the most penetrating expositions of the characteristic euphemisms and double-think through which it seeks to legitimate itself ideologically, and of the convoluted thoughts and emotions it inspires in those it seeks to subjugate or indoctrinate, are to be found, not in the analyses of social scientists, but in fiction: novels such as Aldous Huxley's *Brave New World*, Arthur Koestler's *Darkness at Noon*, George Orwell's *1984*, Albert Camus's *The Plague*, A. Zinoviev's *Yawning Heights*, and Terry Gilliam's film *Brazil*.

Reading
Popper, K. 1945 (*1966*): *The Open Society and its Enemies*, 2 vols, 5th edn.
Shapiro, L. 1972: *Totalitarianism*.
Talmon, J.L. 1952: *The Rise of Totalitarian Democracy*.
ROGER GRIFFIN

trade unions Collective organizations of workers known as 'trade societies' or 'unions' have existed in Britain since the late eighteenth century. Sidney and Beatrice Webb, in a classic definition (1920, p. 1), declared that 'a trade union, as we understand the term, is a continuous association of wage-earners for the purpose of maintaining or improving the conditions of their working lives.'

Economic orthodoxy, with its paradigm of individual transactions, has found trade unionism incomprehensible (and often improper). Sociology has had difficulty in conceptualizing unions' combination of formal organization with more informal and spontaneous collectivity. The most extensive attempts to apply social analysis to trade unionism have been developed by partisans, and in particular within the Marxist tradition. A central concern has been to what extent, and under what conditions, trade unions advance (or, conversely, inhibit) the cause of proletarian revolution. The works of Marx and Engels provide no systematic or consistent theory of unions, and twentieth-century Marxists have elaborated many conflicting perspectives.

One approach derives from Lenin's pamphlet *What Is To Be Done?* (1902). Partly influenced by his reading of the Webbs' work, Lenin argued that the 'economic struggle' waged by trade unions could never develop spontaneously into a comprehensive political movement; for this, 'trade union consciousness' required the direction of a revolutionary party. The proposition that unions can be effective agencies of resistance to capitalist social relations within the sphere of employment, but can contribute to more radical social transformation only under the leadership of the party, has become central to communist orthodoxy.

Another familiar (and sometimes complementary) argument holds that trade unions as formal institutions develop inherently conservative characteristics, displaying what Roberto Michels (1911) termed an 'iron law of oligarchy'. In different variants of this theme, leaders and officials develop vested interests in conflict with those of the 'rank and file'; become enmeshed in bargaining arrangements with employers and hence committed to the defence of 'industrial legality' (Gramsci, 1910–20); or resist membership militancy through excessive concern for the organizational stability of the union.

Various strategies have been suggested to overcome this tendency. Syndicalists called on unions to eschew agreements with employers and pursue instead a revolutionary general strike (see Ridley, 1970); before 1914, the possibilities of the mass strike were also viewed optimistically by more orthodox Marxists such as Rosa Luxemburg (1906). Others attempted to reconstruct trade unions as comprehensive industrial bodies, able to take over the running of industry; the most notable instance was the Industrial Workers of the World (or 'Wobblies'), formed in the USA in 1905 under the influence of the theories of De Leon (see Dubofsky, 1969). During the 1914–18 period the formation in most belligerent countries of workplace organization, (relatively) independent of formal union structure and able to contest the control of production, provided another alternative model – analysed most sensitively by Gramsci, and developed by others such as Pannekoek as the basis for a theory of 'council communism' (Smart, 1978). After the formation of the Communist International, an important element in left-wing strategy was the creation of oppositional 'rank-and-file movements' within official trade unions. More recently, this tactic has been embraced by various Trotskyist groups.

Since the Soviet revolution, the role of unions in socialist society has provoked argument among Marxists. In the famous 'trade union debate' of 1920–1, Trotsky argued that they should become formally subordinated to the state, while the Workers' Opposition insisted that they should remain an independent force within the economic sphere. Lenin's view won the day: that while formally independent they should follow the leadership of the party, as 'transmission belts from the Communist Party to the masses'. Under Stalin, ironically, Trotsky's model of state control was effectively implemented (see Deutscher, 1950), and after 1945 was extended to the new communist regimes in Eastern Europe. Much later, pressures for greater trade union autonomy emerged. The collapse of communism in the Eastern bloc was preceded in most countries by the assertion of independence by the former official unions, and in many cases by the rise of opposition movements –

most notably, Solidarność in Poland. Today the 'transmission belt' model has been abandoned even in those countries where communist regimes remain.

In the industrialized West, unions have often sought to escape subordination to political parties. In much of continental Europe, mass trade unionism was the product of the rise of social democracy around the turn of the century; but union leaders soon insisted on developing their own strategic priorities. (In southern Europe, where union–party links have been of great importance in the postwar era, similar tendencies have been apparent in recent years.) In the USA, most unions have traditionally eschewed the political links common in Europe, a position aggressively defended in the late nineteenth century by the president of the American Federation of Labor, Samuel Gompers, with his philosophy of 'pure-and-simple unionism'. This conception later obtained intellectual support from the writer Selig Perlman (1928), who argued that trade unions would naturally confine their activities to job-related matters unless seduced by the intervention of intellectuals. Similar arguments have more recently been elaborated by American writers (Lester, 1958; Ross and Hartman, 1960; Kerr et al., 1960), who have all insisted that 'mature' trade unions typically abandon radical political objectives and concentrate on collective bargaining.

A third view of the relationship between unions and politics has been offered by 'corporatism' theorists (see Goldthorpe, 1984). Modern usage of this notion alludes to fascist (and, in particular, Italian and Spanish) systems of state-directed organization embracing both employers and employees within a rhetoric of functional unity. In modern Western societies, it is argued, the state is increasingly a central actor in economic and industrial relations; and this has encouraged the development of tripartite concertation, often integrating unions institutionally in the machinery of national economic planning and management. For some writers, 'neocorporatism' serves to subordinate unions to the requirements of a capitalist state, turning them into agencies for disciplining their members in return for nominal and organizational rewards. Others however identify a system of 'political exchange' whereby unions achieve real material benefits for their members by moderating economic militancy in return for influence over macroeconomic policy; postwar Austria and Sweden are often cited as examples. The logic of both interpretations is that simple 'business unionism', as the American model is often termed, is no longer viable – at least in many national contexts.

Yet another view of trade unionism is as a social movement. Often this conception has derived from Catholic social thought, which altered at the turn of the century from anti-unionism derived from anti-socialism to a more positive view of unions as means of furthering social cohesion and harmony. Anti-communism subsequently provided a powerful motive for Catholic intervention in trade unionism, at times inspiring the formation of separate 'Christian' unions. In some Third World countries, however, 'liberation theology' has encouraged support for radical populist unionism, mobilizing against multinational capital and repressive political regimes. This may be seen as reflecting a situational logic: where the state is powerful and 'civil society' relatively undeveloped, trade unions are one of the few organizations capable of coordinating independent social action on a national scale. At the same time, unions which are unable to achieve stable collective bargaining relationships or to build up substantial formal membership are likely to seek to mobilize and represent a larger constituency than the latter alone.

It is clear that the social meaning of trade unionism is a focus of contention within and between unions themselves; and their role is equally controversial for governments and for movements of political opposition. Possibly the end of the Cold War, and the internationalization of capital and of employment practices, will lead to a greater homogeneity of trade union characteristics.

See also SYNDICALISM.

Reading
Banks, J.A. 1974: *Trade Unionism.*
Clegg, Hugh 1976: *Trade Unions under Collective Bargaining.*
Crouch, Colin 1982: *Trade Unions.*
Flanders, Allan 1952: *Trade Unions.*
Hyman, Richard 1972: *Marxism and the Sociology of Trade Unionism.*
—— 1989: *The Political Economy of Industrial Relations.*
McCarthy, W.E.J. 1985: *Trade Unions*, 2nd edn.
Martin, Ross 1989: *Trade Unionism.*
Mills, C. Wright 1948: *The New Men of Power.*
Munck, Ronaldo 1988: *The New International Labour Studies.*
Sturmthal, Adolf 1972: *Comparative Labor Movements.*
Webb, Sidney and Webb, Beatrice 1897: *Industrial Democracy.*

RICHARD HYMAN

tradition and traditionalism Holding a special place among the customs, conventions, folkways and styles which are the building blocks of human cultures, tradition is commonly reserved for customs which have considerable depth in the past and an aura of the sacred. The word tradition comes from the Latin verb, *tradere* which meant to deliver, transmit, hand down through time. Although the verb could refer to the transmission of trivial things, it gradually became reserved for the very important, for 'deposits' from the past which held an unusual value to the present and, presumably, the future.

Traditions, by long usage, belong to the most important spheres of human life such as KINSHIP, religion, polity, and the upper levels of culture such as literature and art. We speak of traditional Christianity in Europe and of monarchy, patriarchalism, constitutionalism, and the art of the old masters as traditional. For lesser things we are more likely to use 'customs' or 'folkways'.

It is a mistake to think of traditions as inherently static and tending always towards the quiescent. Migrations, wars and revolutions have behind them frequently in HISTORY the desires of groups to defend, protect or even to disseminate cherished traditions. Revolutions and major reform movements spring not only from the pragmatic sense of current injustice but from the historical sense of old traditions being violated. To be able to argue that current practices represent a falling away from honoured traditions in government and law is to add a considerable depth to the position one is taking. As the history of Marxism suggests, left partisans are as quick as those on the right to speak of the 'real', the 'true' Marx in doctrinal controversies, and although they may not use the word 'tradition' very often the substance is there for all to see. Much the same is true of religion. The history of Christianity since the Reformation is in large measure the history of sects and schisms. Almost invariably the authors and prophets of new sects insist that however radical the schism may seem, it is based on a desire to return to 'that old time religion' or, more elegantly put, to the 'pure tradition of Jesus Christ'.

It is difficult to separate the recent history of the idea of tradition from the intellectual currents which were stirred up in Western Europe by those who called themselves, during and after the French revolution, Traditionalists. I refer especially to Louis Gabriel de Bonald and Joseph de Maistre.

Use of 'conservative' as a political term does not commence until the 1820s in both France and England. But traditionalism as a political philosophy, and as a label, appears on the scene by the 1790s. It was Edmund Burke, more than any other single figure, who was responsible for this. Interestingly, he seems not to have used either 'tradition' or 'traditionalism' in his *Reflections on the Revolution in France*, but he did use, boldly, the word 'prejudices', and his argument for 'prejudice, with the reason involved' is one of the most eloquent briefs for tradition and traditionalism ever written.

What Burke and all the traditionalists of the early nineteenth century were attacking was the French revolution and its Enlightenment-spawned ideas of reason, individualism, freedom and equality, enshrined for all Europe to see in the legislation that emerged from successive revolutionary governments. In promulgating these ideas, the revolution was almost necessarily obliged to assault the institutions of the Old Regime: monarchy, aristocracy, church, guild, village community, and so on.

What the revolution assaulted, the self-declared traditionalists made objects of veneration. These were essentially medieval values and structures; it is no accident that medievalism and traditionalism underwent a simultaneous upsurge in the nineteenth century. We see this in the arts and the social sciences alike. In the former field are such figures as Augustus Pugin, William Morris and John Ruskin; in the social sciences Friedrich Karl von Savigny and Hegel in Germany and Auguste Comte and Pierre Le Play in France. Some of them, though in different ways, were lavish in their praise of the Middle Ages and vigorous in the espousal of such traditional institutions as the patriarchal family, the village community, the guild, and a system of social classes. They were equally condemnatory of those forces in the modern world such as industrialism and technology, and also, in some cases, mass democracy and egalitarianism, which appeared to be destroying the foundations of the traditional. It is fair to say that the contrast between Traditional and Modern, as we find it from the early nineteenth century down to the present moment in Western writing, is but a variant of the analogous themes of *Gemeinschaft* and *Gesellschaft*, status and contract, and the types of solidarity Emile Durkheim featured in his *Division of Labour in Society* (1893). Max Weber's distinction between Traditional and Rational is also pertinent.

Finally it must be stressed that traditionalism, CONSERVATISM, and the political right are very far from being the same; at least since the early nineteenth century when all three words acquired their present connotations. Traditionalists by definition give loyalty to the old and hallowed. This, however, does not necessarily make conservatives of them, given the prevailing character of conservatism in contemporary Western politics, nor does traditionalism predictably fall on the right in politics. Thus the traditionalist's reverence for kinship, religion, social class and the sacred is by no means necessarily harmonious with the contemporary conservative's preference for a high degree of individualism, a free market, libertarianism and unrestricted private property and profit. As to relationship to the political right, one has only to think of some of the deeply, fanatically traditionalist groups in the modern world whose absolute loyalty to one or more traditions pushes them at times closer to the revolutionary left than to anything properly denotable as either right or conservative. The Irish Republican Army (IRA) and the Basques are perhaps sufficient illustration, but at the present moment one may think first of the Middle East and certain highly traditionalist Islamic insurgents.

See also CULTURE.

Reading
Kuhn, Thomas S. 1962 (*1970*): *The Structure of Scientific Revolutions*, 2nd edn.
Lerner, David 1958: *The Passing of Traditional Society*.
Lippman, Walter 1929: *A Preface to Morals*.
Lowes, John Livingston, 1922: *Convention and Revolt in Poetry*.
Nisbet, Robert 1986: *Conservatism*.
Radin, Max 1936: Tradition. In *Encyclopedia of the Social Sciences*, vol. 15, pp. 62–7.
Shils, Edward 1981: *Tradition*.

ROBERT NISBET

Trotskyism Loosely referring to a broad current of thought, as well as a small organized movement, within international socialism, the term derives from the name of Leon Trotsky (1879–1940) and the historical influence of his ideas. In its earliest meaning – before 1917 – it stood for no more than a particular, unorthodox view of the character of the coming Russian revolution. But from the mid-1920s Trotskyism, as the principal Marxist opposition to and critique of Stalin's regime in Russia and the Stalinized communist movement internationally, came to embrace a wider set of theses, seeking to defend the values of classical Marxism against what it saw as their misappropriation. The label has covered some diversity of theoretical conception and political practice.

The primary thread, intellectually, has been the theory of PERMANENT REVOLUTION. In the first instance an anticipation of the possibility that backward Russia might set out on the path of socialist revolution before the advanced capitalist countries, the theory emphasized also – and did so the more insistently once the Bolshevik revolution had found itself without early sequel elsewhere – the necessity of complementary revolutions in the West if the Russian effort itself was not to come to grief. It was an emphasis opposed to Stalin's project of a nationally self-sufficient 'socialism in one country', as being a delusory ambition.

An analysis of the type of society that had in fact emerged in the Soviet Union with the political victory of Stalin, formed a companion argument. No longer capitalist, since the major means of production were now owned by the state, nor was the country, according to Trotsky, yet socialist either. It was a transitional society, in which the governing bureaucracy had usurped the political rule of the working class, presiding over as well as benefiting from large and unjustifiable inequalities. Although not a dominant economic class in the Marxist sense, having no direct property in productive resources, this bureaucracy was a privileged stratum, and would have to be overthrown by a political revolution if Russia was eventually to accomplish its transition to socialism – assisted by socialist transformations in the West. Failing this, the bureaucracy threatened to become a vehicle for the restoration of capitalism in Russia.

Trotsky himself, fierce critic though he was of it, did not regard the regime of the Soviet bureaucracy as a new form of class or capitalist rule. This has been the mainstream Trotskyist viewpoint for 50 years since his death: that, authoritarian, 'degenerated' and indeed often criminal as the regime has been, it preserved in some form a key achievement of the October revolution, namely, the overturning of capitalist property. Other currents originating within the Trotskyist tradition have argued, to the contrary, that the Soviet ruling group was indeed a new type of class – state-capitalist or bureaucratic – effectively owning the means of production through its control of the state. The Soviet Union, on this view, was in no sense intermediate between capitalism and socialism.

Owing to its quasi-foundational theoretical perspective – of permanent revolution – the Trotskyist tradition has been strongly internationalist in outlook; an important locus of it being the Fourth International, founded in 1938. The mainstream tradition has defended, too, an uncompromisingly revolutionary concept of socialist strategy. To some Trotskyists the idea of a 'transitional programme', attempting to build a bridge from immediate, limited demands to more far-reaching revolutionary goals, has been central. The Trotskyist movement has seen itself, finally, as being in the line of LENINISM. This has been associated, in the worst cases, with a mentality of 'party-building', hairsplitting, sometimes fantasy-mongering sectarianism. But in the best cases, it has drawn on the historical record of Trotsky's unique and changing – now critical, now persuaded, never worshipful – relationship to the person and politics of Lenin, to sponsor the synthesis of a socialist political theory at once revolutionary *and* committed to democracy and pluralism. Beyond the world of Trotskyist organizations as such, Trotskyism has had a diffuse creative influence on Marxist intellectual debate and scholarship.

Reading
Deutscher, I. 1959: *The Prophet Unarmed. Trotsky: 1921–1929.*
——— 1963: *The Prophet Outcast. Trotsky: 1929–1940.*
Frank, P. 1979: *The Fourth International: The Long March of the Trotskyists.*
Geras, N. 1986: *Literature of Revolution.*
Mandel, E. 1979: *Revolutionary Marxism Today.*
Trotsky, L. 1937 (*1972*): *The Revolution Betrayed.*
——— 1938 (*1973*): *The Transitional Program for Socialist Revolution.*

NORMAN GERAS

trust and cooperation   'Two or more agents can be said *to cooperate* when they engage in a joint venture for the outcome of which the actions of each are necessary' (Williams, 1988, p. 5). Broadly defined, cooperation is therefore relevant for most human undertakings, from play to marriage, from market transactions to international relations, from industrial production to education. Even competition, rather than being an alternative to cooperation, often rests on cooperative arrangements.

Cooperation requires that agents – such as individuals, firms and governments – agree on a set of rules, a 'contract', which is then to be observed in the course of their joint activity (Binmore and

Dasgupta, 1986, p. 3). Agreements and rules, however, need not be the result of explicit communication or even intention. They can develop in the course of interaction itself from tradition, prior successful experience, trial and error or evolutionary processes (Axelrod, 1984; Sugden, 1986). In this sense, *cooperative behaviour* can emerge also among non-human species, in which in fact it is often found – in contrast with the traditional and now disproved view that 'competition for survival' would represent the central feature of the animal world (Hinde, 1982; Bateson, 1986).

Cooperation poses problems of particular interest for the social sciences whenever agents cannot monitor each other's actions effortlessly. Both its social significance and the conceptual sophistication required for its understanding are dramatically enhanced 'when a necessary action by at least one of the parties involved is not under the immediate control of the other party. ... Under this definition, a situation in which two agents cooperate necessarily involves at least one of them *depending on* the other' (Williams, 1988, p. 5). Hence, cooperation becomes at the same time fragile and the object of hazardous decision-making, for the dependent party in particular. When monitoring is difficult, the choice of entering a cooperative venture – which is generally sensitive to costs – becomes particularly susceptible to the risk related to the potential defection of others. Here cooperation brings us close to the notion of *trust*, which represents a salient but little studied ingredient of social interaction.

The object of *trust* may refer to the technical ability of certain individuals on whom at times our well-being depends (such as doctors or pilots). Or it may concern the reliability and effectiveness of groups (say, the Gurkhas), and even of abstract entities (an example would be the transport system) (Luhmann, 1979, 1988; Barber, 1983). However, it is trust in the willingness of other agents to fulfil their 'contractual' obligations that is crucial for cooperation. In this sense trust (or symmetrically distrust) can be described as a particular level of the subjective probability with which an agent assesses whether one or more other agents (A), with whom cooperation is envisaged, will also cooperate (or not) ('Can we trust trust?', in Gambetta, 1988, p. 217). When we say we trust A (or that A is trustworthy) we implicitly mean that the probability that A will perform an action that is beneficial (or at least not detrimental) to us is high enough for

us to engage in cooperation with A. Correspondingly, when we say that we do not trust A we imply that that probability is below the crucial threshold, low enough, that is, for us to avoid cooperation.

Trust represents a non-trivial problem when at least four conditions obtain.

1 Trust in A must have a bearing on *our own* action when that action must be chosen either *before* we can monitor A's relevant action or independently of our capacity of ever being able to monitor it (Dasgupta, 1988, p. 51).
2 A must be free, free especially to disappoint our expectations (trust has been said to represent 'a device for coping with the freedom of others', Luhmann, 1979; Dunn, 1984). But trust is not related to the freedom of others only.
3 We, too, must be free to refrain from cooperation in case we do not trust, as without alternative we would at best hope or rely, but not trust.
4 Finally, if we could achieve perfect information about other agents, trust would not be a problem. Thus trust can also be said to represent a tentative and intrinsically fragile response to our ignorance, a way of coping with 'the limits of our foresight' (Shklar 1985, p. 151).

An important tradition in Western thought – comprising Machiavelli, Hume and Smith, and still common nowadays, especially within economics – equates trust to a resource which would be not only scarce, as are all other resources, but, like love, altruism and solidarity, impossible to produce at will. As a consequence trust ought to be spent with parsimony and we could not sensibly bank on it to bring cooperation about (Elster and Moene, 1988). Albert Hirschman (1984) and Dasgupta (1988), however, have challenged that view and shown that trust is not a resource like others that depletes by being used, rather it depletes by *not* being used. Also, several historical examples plausibly suggest that trust can be intentionally 'produced' (see Velez-Ibanez, 1983) and, certainly, intentionally destroyed (see Pagden, 1988).

Trust and cooperation interact in a variety of subtle ways. For instance, it is not merely relevant to decide whether to trust A, but it may be equally relevant whether A trusts us. Cooperation can fail as a result of A refraining from acting cooperatively, simply because A does not trust *us* to cooperate.

Besides, as GAME THEORY shows, cooperation can fail even if the other agents do not trust the fact that we trust them: A can refrain from acting cooperatively because A believes that we do not trust A to cooperate, and that as a result *we* will not cooperate. To achieve cooperation trust must be *mutual*, and agents must know it is.

Although unconditional distrust makes cooperation impossible among free agents (Gambetta, 1988, pp. 224–9), cooperation does not necessarily depend on high levels of trust. In fact, successful cooperation can come about independently of trust, and positively influence the level of trust itself (Axelrod, 1984). When considering whether to cooperate, there are other factors taken into consideration, which include the amount of loss in case cooperation fails, the prospect of future interactions, A's interests, and A's possibility of inflicting fatal blows.

See also CONSENSUS.

Reading

Akerlof, G. 1970: The market for 'lemons': qualitative uncertainty and the market mechanism. *Quarterly Journal of Economics* 84, 488–500.

Axelrod, R. 1984: *The Evolution of Cooperation*.

Barber, B. 1983: *The Logic and Limits of Trust*.

Gambetta, D. ed. 1988: *Trust: Making and Breaking Cooperative Relations*.

Hirschman, A.O. 1984: Against parsimony: three easy ways of complicating some categories of economic discourse. *American Economic Review Proceedings* 74, 88–96.

Luhmann, N.: *Trust and Power*. Chichester: Wyley, 1979.

DIEGO GAMBETTA

truth   This seems at once the simplest and the most difficult of concepts. Saying 'true' to a proposition is to give one's assent to it – this is its primary function, from which 'redundancy' and 'performative' theories of truth derive their power. But one is thereby committed to a claim *about* the world – roughly to the effect that this is how things are – from which correspondence theories of truth since the time of Aristotle have drawn their currency. This claim carries the normative force of 'trust me – act on it' from which pragmatic theories gain their hold (see PRAGMATISM). At the same time this claim, if challenged, needs to be *grounded*, a requirement that seems to point in the direction of coherence theories. So a truth judgement will typically carry or imply a fourfold dimensionality, possessing expressively-veracious, descriptive, evidential and imperatival-fiduciary aspects. If its basic world-expressive meaning is simple (its descriptive 'this is how things are in the world' aspect), it is equally easy to see that truth talk satisfies a transcendental-axiological *need*, acting as a steering mechanism for language users to find their way about the world.

But 'truth' is also the most difficult of concepts: there is hardly an extant theory without some snare but in which it is equally hard not to find some truth or plausibility. These have ramifications for theories of meaning, reference, perception, causality, agency, experiment, and communication (and thus for philosophical sociology and ONTOLOGY generally). A basic distinction is between theories of *meaning* and *criteria* for truth. Prima facie one would expect the criteria for truth claims to be as varied as the contexts in which they are made.

The most important historical theories of truth in the twentieth century have been the correspondence, coherence, pragmatic, redundancy, performative, consensus and Hegelian theories of truth. Marxist theories have been spread along this spectrum – with classical Marxism committed to a deep correspondence theory, dialectical materialism to a simple reflection theory and Western Marxism typically seeing truth as the practical expression of a subject rather than a theoretically adequate representation of an object, whether this has been in coherentist form (as in György Lukács), pragmatist (as in Karl Korsch) or consensualist (as in Antonio Gramsci) (see Bhaskar, 1991).

Correspondence theories had their heyday during the mid-century supremacy of LOGICAL POSITIVISM, although they were also supported by some critics of logical positivism such as J.L. Austin. The most influential correspondence theories have been the picture theory of the early Wittgenstein, the semantic theory of A. Tarski, and Karl Popper's theory of science as revealing increasing verisimilitude or truth-likeness. For critics of correspondence theories the basic objection has always been that there seems no 'Archimedean' standpoint from which a comparison of the corresponding items can be made.

Coherence theories, in vogue early in the century under the residual impact of absolute idealism but recently defended with vigour by N. Rescher and some others, seem most plausible as an account of the criterion rather than the meaning of truth. Hegelian theories may be regarded as a special case of coherence theories in which it is the conformity of an object to its notion (ultimately the totality or whole) rather than vice versa that defines truth. But, whether in Hegelian dialectical or more standardly Anglo-Saxon declensions, coherence theories seem to presuppose something like a correspondence-theoretic account of 'correctness'.

The two most influential species of pragmatism derive ultimately from the American tradition of C.S. Peirce, William James and John Dewey and from Nietzschean perspectivism respectively. The former has been recently popularized by Richard Rorty, for whom the only workable concept of truth is warranted assertability (and here pragmatism dovetails with constructivist and intuitionist theories of mathematics). This is of course open to the objection that a proposition may be warrantedly assertable yet false. For the Nietzschean tradition, which informs contemporary poststructuralism, truth is 'a mobile army of metaphors', ultimately an arbitrary expression of the will-to-power, which must be thought, as at once both necessary and impossible, 'under erasure'. It is difficult to see this position, whether in its Derridean or Foucauldian guise, as anything other than self-cancelling.

The other theories must be dealt with more briefly. The redundancy theory, initially formulated by F.P. Ramsey, seems either to smuggle in truth by the back door or to deny the axiological necessity of the truth predicate. Performative theories of the sort advocated by P.F. Strawson, R.M. Hare and John Searle seem more satisfactory in this respect, but they in turn underplay the extent to which the use of the truth predicate needs to be grounded, a fact recently stressed by Kripke. Consensus theories, though capable of ideal typical formulations, seem open to the obvious objection that 20 million Frenchmen *can* be wrong!

Bhaskar, developing his critical realism, has recently sketched a truth-tetrapolity and an associated dialectic of truth, in which it is seen as a many-layered concept. The first moment or component of the tetrapolity sees truth as action guiding and social, as normative-fiduciary. The second component sees truth as adequating (warrantedly assertable) and, in the transitive dimension of discourse, as relative. The third component

sees truth as expressive-referential, as an epistemic-ontic dual and truth claims as absolute (saying how things are in the world). The fourth component sees truth as alethic, as genuinely ontological (and accordingly objective), as, in the intransitive dimension, the reasons for the things and phenomena of the world.

Here we are concerned with the truth (nature, purpose or fulfilment) of things (including people), not simply of words. And in the dialectic of science which critical realism describes, we move from *subjective certainty* on the part of a group of scientists about some proposition (or theory) to acceptance by the scientific community of the *intersubjective facthood* of the proposition concerned. The community now seeks to unearth the reason, typically at a deeper level of structure or in a wider totality, for the phenomenon described by that proposition. When it has done so, we reach the level of *objective* or alethic *truth*, where truth now stands for the uncovering or revealing of the reason for the phenomenon. In social life a wider or deeper form of knowledge can often criticize, *ceteris paribus*, a less developed form as the broad tradition of critical theory from Marx to Habermas amply demonstrates.

Critical realism's commitment to moral realism opens up new possibilities in truth theory which cannot be explored here, save to say that Bhaskar has recently argued, in a line paralleling an argument of Habermas, that every expressively veracious statement ultimately implies a commitment to the project of universal human emancipation. This, it can equally be argued, is, *qua* freedom and well-being, a condition for any subjective or intersubjective truth.

Reading
Bhaskar, Roy 1992: *Dialectic*.
Pitcher, G. 1964: *Truth*.
Popper, K. 1972: *Objective Knowledge*.
Ramsey, F.P. 1931: *The Foundations of Mathematics*.
Rescher, N. 1973: *The Coherence Theory of Truth*.
Rorty, R. 1980: *Philosophy and the Mirror of Nature*.
Tarski, A. 1956: *Logic, Semantics and Mathematics*.

ROY BHASKAR

U

uncertainty *See* DECISION THEORY

unconscious The notion of the unconscious has a prolonged history, involving names of thinkers such as G. W. Leibniz, Arthur Schopenhauer, Friedrich Nietzsche and Karl von Hartmann. It really, however, springs into prominence with the work of Sigmund Freud (1856–1939). He is generally hailed, if not as the absolute discoverer of the notion, then at any rate as the man who placed it at the centre of a therapeutic technique, and of a theory which was original and striking, and which very rapidly became the basis of a new vision of human beings (see PSYCHOANALYSIS). The Freudian notion of the unconscious distinguishes it from the merely subconscious, which contains mental contents not present to consciousness. The unconscious has a content which systematically resists being brought up into consciousness. This sustained repression of the content of the unconscious is said to play an important part in the internal organization of the psyche, and in particular in the aetiology of much mental illness. The model popularized by Freud is that the mind 'represses' certain mental contents into the unconscious, that some of the contents so repressed engender mental disturbances and that a cure or alleviation can be brought about by bringing these contents out into the open. It is clearly part of the Freudian notion of the unconscious that its contents are accumulated from the earliest beginnings of life of an individual; in some versions proposed by members of the wider movement, this accumulation even precedes birth. The arguments Freud proposed in *Totem and Taboo* also seem to imply that some of the contents are transmitted from generation to generation, so that contents acquired in one generation are taken over by subsequent ones. Freud has been criticized for this implicitly 'Lamarckian' view of heredity, as applied to the unconscious, as not compatible with modern genetics.

Leaving aside the Freudian doctrine which gave the concept its prominence, and starting from the meaning inherent in the term, one could distinguish a number of different kinds of 'unconscious':

1 Any *process* taking place within the human person but not accessible to consciousness. Most psychological processes fall in this category.
2 *Principles* governing practices which only become accessible to consciousness as a result of serious, possibly arduous research. For instance, most human beings speak without awareness of the grammatical or other rules governing their speech.
3 A collective unconscious, such as was proposed by C. G. Jung (1875–1961), resembling Freud's and historically influenced by Freud's ideas, but differing from it in being shared by an entire community or race. This being so, its contents must of course have been assembled in a manner different from the individual accumulation of a Freudian unconscious (except of course the 'Lamarckian' elements).
4 A different kind of collective unconscious, repressed neither individually nor racially or communally, but by a political unit: the rules of *Newspeak* as described by George Orwell (1903–1950) in *1984* are meant to make certain ideas or affirmations simply unsayable in a given language.

The Freudian unconscious, which probably constitutes the most frequently used meaning of the term, differs from these in that the contents of the unconscious are perfectly accessible in principle and are not proscribed by either the language or by political authority. They are thus *individually* repressed, in response to the individual's particular situations, often with pathogenic consequences. One possible criticism of the Freudian conception of the unconscious is that it is too closely modelled on the familiar model of the conscious mind (whose genesis and functioning seem to be taken as unproblematical): Freudian psychology merely adds a wilder, hidden partner accompanying and dominating it, characteristically manifesting its effects in dreams, 'slips' of behaviour and neurotic symptoms.

It is also important to stress that the Freudian notion of the unconscious plays a dominant part in the overall Freudian system of ideas, therapy and organization of the psychoanalytical guild. This role goes far beyond merely adding one further important item to the inventory of our psychic equipment. Implicit in the notion and in the role ascribed to it, the unconscious constitutes a permanent barrier to sound judgement: unless its secrets are penetrated by the unique technique prescribed by Freudian theory, cognitive claims made by a given individual are suspect and presumably unsound. This being so, the notion of the unconscious implicitly devalues cognitive claims made by human beings not cleared by the *rite de passage* of psychoanalysis, in the manner approved by the guild of its practitioners. So, indirectly but inescapably, the notion, as it occurs within this system, ranks both human beings and their views: it constitutes an implicit social and heuristic programme. It not only invalidates any theory which purports to criticize its criteria, it also invalidates all else. For as far as the unconscious is said to interfere with the evidence concerning its own existence and its own practices, only the unique technique can counteract its wiles, is in a position to decode and concretely assess the evidence. In this way, Freudian theory of the unconscious guarantees its own truth. The theory proposes a world such that, within it, only the theory itself can really pronounce on truth and falsehood. In this way, the Freudian theory of the unconscious is open to the suspicion of being largely circular.

Reading
MacIntyre, A.C. 1958: *The Unconscious.*
                                                    ERNEST GELLNER

underdevelopment *See* DEVELOPMENT AND UNDERDEVELOPMENT

understanding *See* VERSTEHEN

unemployment Unemployment denotes the existence within a society, geographic area or social group of significant numbers of adults seeking paid work, and the prevalence of such a condition. It has been a chronic feature of modern societies, which are based on paid employment. Except for the 30-year period after World War II, these societies have normally not provided enough paid work for the adult population. Unemployment has been the cause of frequent social and political conflict, as well as considerable social and psychological distress. Social and political controversy about the causes and effects of, and remedies for, unemployment was especially intense in the 1920s and 1930s, and also in the 1970s and 1980s, both periods of high unemployment. Over recent decades, attention has shifted to consider the whole future of paid work.

Unemployment was not a problem in hunting and gathering societies; nor was it admitted as a problem in Soviet-type regimes where its existence was not recognized officially. In tribal societies, the performance of subsistence activities involved relatively little time, no special status or payment, and was not regarded as a separate sphere of life. Soviet-type states also did not recognize a distinctive area of civil society, an 'economy', in which workers are employed separate from the state. Hence, they did not acknowledge the existence of unemployment although various forms of 'hidden unemployment' (see below) were widespread. Only with the emergence of 'employment' societies based on paid WORK – organized on a large scale on the basis of the LABOUR MARKET and geared to agricultural, manufacturing and service production – did unemployment assume the social, economic and political significance it has today (see INDUSTRIAL SOCIETY). Under pressures from rapidly growing manufacturing, new and stricter forms of job specialization and factory discipline, accelerating urbanization, compulsory schooling of children and the exclusion of women from the labour market, the ability of individuals to subsist by moving, often on a seasonal basis, between the formal labour market and the informal sector comprising non-market institutions (such as the household) rapidly declined. In consequence, by the last decades of the late nineteenth century, finding and retaining regular paid work – and its converse, unemployment – had become a central aspect of most people's lives and a necessary condition for maintaining household incomes.

The effects of being unemployed are often traumatic, deeply personal, and not confined to loss of income and consumer spending power. They are also highly variable by personality, gender, age, class, type of previous occupation, previous life history and degree of unemployment within one's immediate locality and/or family. Nevertheless, a number of studies (see Pilgrim Trust, 1938; Jahoda et al., 1932; Kelvin and Jarrett, 1985) have pointed to the general features of severe psychological, social and physical distress experienced by people who become unemployed. Psychological effects identified as being associated with unemployment include resignation, negative self-esteem, despair, shame, apathy, depression, hopelessness, a sense of futility, loss of purpose, passivity, lethargy and indifference. Social effects include poverty, loss of status, loss of time discipline and daily routine, social isolation, disruption of family life including divorce, changes in the sexual division of labour, and various forms of anti-social behaviour including theft and vandalism. Physical effects include various forms of illness, insomnia, stress and anxiety sometimes resulting in attempted suicide, intermittent and short-term drunkenness, intra-family violence and child abuse.

The dominant public philosophy of the nineteenth century, prevailing indeed until the 1940s, was that unemployment was unavoidable, primarily short-term, and typically resulted from the personal inadequacies of the unemployed – either their lack of effort and initiative or (after Malthus) their tendency to produce large families. This view was reflected in classical and neoclassical economic thinking: that capitalist economies had a 'natural' tendency towards full employment because, according to Say's Law, supply creates its own demand, that is, creating output will automatically generate demand. As unemployment rose, producing an oversupply of 'idle' labour, wages would fall, allowing more workers to be employed.

Marx, however, explicitly contested the idea that unemployment in capitalist societies was a temporary phenomenon. In *Capital* he argued that it was a basic structural problem tied to the processes of capital accumulation and capitalist exploitation of labour. In a capitalist society subject to recurrent and worsening crises there was no automatic tendency assuring full employment equilibrium, as classical and neoclassical economists claimed. Capitalist economies need to maintain an 'industrial reserve army of labour' which keeps the labour force under permanent pressure. When economic demand expands, the demand for labour increases, thereby reducing the reserve army and inflating the price of labour. When wages rise, both the rate of profit from the accumulation of capital and the rate of accumulation itself fall, reducing aggregate demand, contracting economic activity and increasing the reserve army. The continuing existence of a reserve army thus ensures that wages, even when they are rising sharply, do not threaten profits. Marx distinguished three elements in the reserve army of labour: *floating* industrial workers who move from job to job; a *latent* pool of workers in agricultural areas; and a *stagnant* population of casual workers who are close to paupers. Recent Marxist writers (such as Braverman, 1974) have shown that this traditional reserve army has been increasingly supplemented over recent decades by women and immigrant workers joining the labour market on a temporary basis (as with the *Gastarbeiter*, the 'guest workers', in Germany).

With recurrent economic recessions after the 1870s, and under pressure from the emergent TRADE UNIONS, unemployment soon became a major public issue. By the late nineteenth century, a growing body of reformist social and political opinion was calling for state guarantees of full employment while explicitly rejecting both orthodox and Marxist interpretations of the problem. The proposed solutions varied considerably. Many advocated protectionism or naval and military conscription; others, public guarantees of the right to work, direct job creation by the state and progressive taxation combined with counter-cyclical public works. But no general alternative theory of unemployment was available until the 1930s and 1940s.

Prompted by the mass unemployment of the 1920s and 1930s, J. M. Keynes developed the concepts of aggregate economic demand and demand deficiency (see KEYNESIANISM), and his theory of unemployment was skilfully synthesized into a social democratic programme for a full employment welfare state by William Beveridge in *Full Employment in a Free Society* (1944). In this influential report, Beveridge advocated government guarantees of full employment of labour and capital through WELFARE STATE regulation of the labour market as part of a much broader social and political programme for creating a society which guaranteed justice and freedom to all. Beveridge's case for a full employment welfare state effectively established the parameters for public discussion of unemployment in capitalist societies for the next 30 years.

The creation of full employment welfare states in many capitalist countries coincided with a period after World War II of sustained economic growth, full (male) employment, rising money wages and low inflation. When it seemed necessary, governments in these countries – sometimes within the framework of indicative economic planning and extensive state ownership, as in France – regulated their own spending and taxation to ensure a consistently high level of economic demand and employment. The conclusion was drawn by most commentators and policy-makers that, since governments using Keynesian demand management techniques were able to keep unemployment low and maintain prosperity, these policies must, therefore, ensure these favourable conditions. A number of writers have argued, with the benefit of hindsight, that postwar full employment depended on a conjuncture of many other, more important economic, social and political factors: free trade policies in international commerce and finance; price stability; and a reservoir of growth and technological development potential which more successful economies could exploit; as well as Keynesian policies (see, for example, Matthews, 1968).

Full employment was also the official policy of Soviet-type states as part of socialist command economy strategies designed to achieve rapid industrialization and establish the basis for a socialist society. Typically, these strategies – abandoned by many states in the early 1990s – deliberatively sacrificed greater economic efficiency, did not recognize the existence of unemployment or a labour market, and allocated excess numbers of workers to (state-run) projects and industries, thus concealing various forms of 'hidden' unemployment.

As mass unemployment returned to most of western Europe and North America in the 1970s, Beveridge's social democratic vision came under sustained attack from the New Right whose foremost thinker on the causes of unemployment is the political economist, Milton Friedman (see CHICAGO ECONOMICS). Developing a line of thought traceable to Herbert Spencer and others writing in the last quarter of the nineteenth century, Friedman insists that reliance on the bureaucratic state to guarantee the welfare of individuals has become an end in itself, thereby contradicting the original goal of maximizing individual liberty and equality of opportunity. Full employment cannot be achieved through welfare state means because the type of state planning and regulation recommended by Beveridge and Keynes distorts market mechanisms for determining wages, prices, investment and the distribution of paid work. Specifically, Friedman argues that any monetary or fiscal policies which try to reduce the rate of unemployment below what he calls the 'natural' rate will ultimately accelerate the rate of inflation. Rather, governments should move decisively to establish and maintain strict control over the money supply (in order to control inflation); they should pursue a free market employment strategy aimed at reducing 'structural rigidities' within the economy and in international trade, drastically reducing state intervention in the economy and curtailing the size and cost of the bureaucratic welfare state. In these ways, free competition will ensure a high and sustained level of employment. (See Friedman, 1977; Friedman and Friedman, 1962 and 1980.)

Free market approaches to unemployment had a substantial influence on government policies in the 1980s, especially in Britain and the United States, but like the full employment welfare state they encountered many problems in reducing the high levels of unemployment. Important economic factors accounting for these difficulties were DE-INDUSTRIALIZATION and the new international division of labour which increased 'core' or 'structural' unemployment (as distinct from 'cyclical' or Keynesian unemployment); and demographic trends which increased the number of workers, particularly women and immigrants, demanding jobs.

The high levels of unemployment in the 1970s and 1980s led many writers to question the viability of returning to full employment, and the whole future of paid work. According to André Gorz in his *Farewell to the Working Class* (1980) and *Paths to Paradise* (1984), the last decades of the twentieth century are witnessing the emergence of permanent mass unemployment societies. As more and more paid work is being replaced by microelectronic and telecommunications systems in 'the robot revolution', goods and services can be produced with less investment, fewer raw materials and less labour. It is likely, therefore, that these societies will experience 'jobless growth', that is, economic growth may occur but it will not be associated with equivalent expansions of employment. These developments will not only generate mass unemployment, Gorz concludes, they will also alter the socioeconomic class structure of employment societies. Under pressure from accelerating TECHNOLOGICAL CHANGE, workers will become divided into three substrata: a privileged aristocracy of 'tenured workers', heavily unionized, with full-time jobs; and two substrata forming a 'non-class of non-workers', comprising the permanently unemployed, condemned to poverty and idleness, and a growing number of 'temporarily employed' workers in low-skilled jobs with no job security and no definite class identity (see WORKING CLASS). The only desirable way to avoid these sharp social divisions and permanent mass unemployment is to separate having a job from receiving an income; and to develop a democratic, post-employment society in which socially necessary work is reduced to a minimum and distributed equitably in order 'to do more things by ourselves in our free time' (Gorz, 1984).

Reading

Bottomore, T. 1990: *The Socialist Economy: Theory and Practice.*

Harris, J. 1982: *Unemployment and Politics: A Study in English Social Policy, 1886–1914.*

Hawkins, K. 1984: *Unemployment.*

Jahoda, M. 1982: *Employment and Unemployment: A Social-Psychological Analysis.*

Keane, J. and Owens, J. 1986: *After Full Employment.*

Kumar, K. 1984: Unemployment as a problem in the development of industrial societies: the English experience. *Sociological Review* 32, 185–233.

Moggridge, D.E. 1976: *Keynes.*

Pahl, R.E. 1984: *Divisions of Labour.*

Stewart, M. 1967: *Keynes and After.*

Warr, P. 1987: *Work, Unemployment and Mental Health.*

Winch, D. 1969: *Economics and Policy: A Historical Study.*

JOHN E. OWENS

union *See* TRADE UNION

urbanism Generally used as a synonym for urbanization, this term refers in particular to the sociocultural effects of an increasing part of the population living in cities, especially the large metropolises. It is also used to indicate the specific features of urban life as against those characterizing rural life. In the United States, the same term is often used as a synonym for town planning (like the French word *urbanisme*).

Urbanization in industrialized countries
Urbanization has been one of the most important phenomena in the industrial age not only because it

has involved the displacement of millions of individuals, but also because it has meant radical qualitative changes in modes and problems of social life. In technical language, urbanization is the effect of two distinct phenomena: movement to towns, that is migration from rural to urban areas, and higher rates of natural demographic increase among the urban than the rural population. Whereas in industrialized countries urbanization has almost exclusively been set in motion by migration to towns, in underdeveloped countries, above all in Africa and Asia, the gap in demographic trends also plays a role.

In industrialized countries, a first substantial wave of urbanization and urban growth took place in the nineteenth century (A. Weber, 1899; Mumford, 1966). In the United Kingdom, the urban population rose from 24 per cent of the total in 1800 to 77 per cent by 1900. Manchester was a village with less than 10,000 inhabitants at the start of the eighteenth century; in 1801 there were just over 70,000 and in 1851 more than 300,000. London was already a metropolis in 1900, with 5 million inhabitants and a widely heterogeneous population in terms of ethnic and national origin. However, also in Germany, France and the United States urbanization and the growth of the big cities in the nineteenth century were staggering. For example, Berlin's population rose from more than 200,000 at the start of the century to 1.5 million in 1890; that of Paris from just over 500,000 in 1800 to 2.5 million by the end of the century. None the less, it is only in the present century that urbanism has become a worldwide experience and attracted the growing attention of social scientists. In industrialized countries, three-quarters of the population now live in towns with more than 100,000 inhabitants or in the suburban areas of large multi-million metropolises, while it has been calculated that by the end of the century, the majority of the world's population will be living in urban areas (Hauser and Schnore, 1965; Davis, 1967).

Migration to towns first involved the rural population in the surrounding regions, and then, with the growth of modern transport and communications systems, took on national and international proportions. Concomitantly, the increase in the size of big cities has radically altered the qualitative problems of social life (see also SUBURB) compared to preindustrial situations based on relatively homogeneous and compact, stable communities.

Urbanism and the quality of social life

The socioecological school of CHICAGO SOCIOLOGY (Park et al., 1925) formulated an interpretation based on the American experience. It not only underlined the difference between the urban and the rural way of living, but also within the first highlighted the distinction between, on the one hand, densely populated central districts characterized by population mobility, social heterogeneity and the relative deterioration in the living conditions of low-income strata and, on the other, the more homogeneous and stable suburban settlements, a privilege of higher income strata. The interpretation of the Chicago school was developed further by Wirth, who concentrated his attention on environmental factors as the fundamental matrix for the differences between the quality of urban and rural life and for the differences existing in various kinds of cities.

> We may expect the outstanding features of the urban social scene to vary in accordance with size, density and differences in the functional type of city . . . For sociological purposes a city may be defined as a relatively large, dense and permanent settlement of socially heterogeneous individuals. (Wirth, 1938, pp. 7–8).

The fundamental features of urban social life are identified as anonymity, impersonality and superficiality and are put down to the nature of the urban environment rather than social characteristics.

The emergence of irrefutable empirical evidence has stimulated a vigorous reexamination of the Chicago school's interpretation. The experience of European cities and the development of forms of working-class suburbanization also in American cities throws doubt on the socioecological mapping of the Chicago school. Furthermore, attention is concentrated on sociological variables as against the environmental ones identified by Wirth. For example, Gans maintains that 'under conditions of transience and heterogeneity, people interact only in terms of the segmental roles necessary for obtaining local services. Their social relationships thus display anonymity, impersonality and superficiality' (1968, p. 103). Given that residential instability is not exclusively a feature typical of the city or of some cities, and that it is distributed unequally in various urban areas, the differences in ways of life and social behaviour are interpreted by utilizing classical social variables, such as social classes, life-cycles, family and employment struc-

tures and so on. Starting with these most recent interpretations, formulated by the new urban sociology (Saunders, 1981; Lebas, 1982; Mingione, 1986), urbanism is seen to be reflected in profound social changes in which, however, the environment acts merely as an indispensable backdrop to the change in social relations and life strategies. The crucial problem in this transformation is the progressive weakening and adaptation of reciprocal contexts and resources in conjunction with the expansion of the market economy and the concentration of increasingly larger sections of the population in urban areas, and the concomitant contradictory and uneven growth in monetary resources and associative contexts among classes and interest groups. These factors are giving rise to new important outbreaks of social conflict, inequality and social areas that are penalized and marginalized by the new ways of distributing social resources and organizing the representation of political interests. The persistence of the 'housing question' or of areas of poverty and marginalization, the emergence of growing ecological problems, the increasing difficulties in controlling, running and adapting socially complex systems of services and transportation that are more and more expensive and extend over wider and wider stretches of territory are nothing other than aspects of this transformation which are more manifest in contemporary cities than other aspects, but which cannot be put down mainly or solely to environmental differences.

Urbanism and industrial development

One of the widely debated basic questions of urbanism in industrialized countries is to what extent this phenomenon is a practically exclusive, inevitable and progressive effect of industrial development. The assumption behind 'industrialism' is that industrial development brings about continually rising economies of scale through progressive concentration in big cities. The reason for this is that the latter attract economic resources and labour to foster the growth of industrial production and, in turn, the increase in the city's population and economic activity acts as a basis for attracting new resources and promoting even higher levels of growth and concentration. This assumption is now the target of a whole host of criticisms. It has been noted that in many cases the features of urbanism depend both on historical conditions and factors existing prior to industrial development, as is the case in most cities in continental Europe, and on elements largely independent of industrial concentration and the growth of employment in manufacturing – the case in capital cities. Next, it is clear that there is a whole series of technical, social and economic limits to the idea of a progressive interlinking between INDUSTRIALIZATION and the growth of large cities. These limits, which vary considerably in different contexts and ages, are the cost and time needed to construct the transport network, the difficulty of settling in already over-populated cities, urban congestion and environmental problems.

For all these reasons, industrial development may be considered as the most important source for the diffusion of urbanism, but under variable and discontinuous conditions and in conjunction with other factors. Among these, it is important to consider welfare policies, above all those relating to housing and transport but also the greater or lesser concentration of services in general and the variability in time and space of specific socioeconomic mixes; then there is the persistence of small and medium-sized firms as against the large industrial and financial concentrations, the diversification of the urban economy as against the presence of highly specialized single industries, the impact of labour-saving strategies and economic decentralization as against economies of scale, as well as the possible role of critical environmental conditions such as pollution, traffic, congestion, the high cost of housing and of living in general.

By adopting more sophisticated approaches than that of 'industrialism', it is possible to explain both the features that urbanism has been taking on in the last few decades and the experience of countries under 'real socialism'. In the first case, the idea of counterurbanization (Berry, 1976; Perry et al., 1986) has been put forward since, in the last two decades, the population of the central metropolitan areas has been either diminishing or increasing more slowly than in the small and medium-sized towns and in the countryside. This phenomenon is believed to be the result of industrial restructuring, the decline in the system of large manufacturing industry and the new phase of tertiarization, in which self-employed workers and small firms with up-to-date technology, but also potentially freed from the necessity to be located in large urban areas, are taking on a growing importance (Castells, 1989). In reality, the decline in the importance and attraction of the big metropolitan areas has gone no further than a drop in manufacturing employment

and the decentralization of some industries to smaller towns and industrializing countries. In contrast, the physiognomy of the global cities (Sassen, 1991), nerve centres for the worldwide control of political and economic-financial activities, is becoming the predominant pattern. Where this applies, land in the city centres continually rises in value as it is the focal point for competition between the various uses claimed by administrative localization, the advanced tertiary sector and residential gentrification, the setting up of advanced economic and supervisory activities and the presence of both high-income and informal or low-income work opportunities. In this sense, de-urbanization is the effect of middle- or low-income strata being driven out of the metropolitan centres to the periphery and other less expensive areas and of the increasing difficulty they find in surviving and resisting these forces in the central metropolitan areas. This is counterbalanced, however, by the fact that the big cities are maintaining their importance and extending their influence over an ever wider area.

As for the countries of 'real socialism', there was talk of the under-urbanization syndrome (Konrád and Szelényi, 1977) triggered by redistributional policies that favoured investment for industrial expansion over costly housing and urban infrastructure programmes. In this way, a growing part of the population employed in the new industries and in the urban tertiary sector were unable to find housing and services in the big cities and were forced to commute between their workplace and their abode in villages or small towns, which could be at some distance, put their names down on long waiting lists for insufficient public housing or find other unsatisfactory solutions that increasingly reflected social inequalities (Szelenyi, 1983).

Urbanization and urbanism in underdeveloped countries

In the twentieth century, urbanization and urban gigantism have irresistibly assailed almost all the underdeveloped countries, where today vast and still uncontrollably growing metropolitan areas are located (Breese, 1969; Abu-Lughod and Hay, 1977; Gilbert and Gugler, 1982). In these countries, in addition to the unstoppable migration to the cities of huge masses expelled from the countryside by extensive plantation farming, international competition and the increasing pressure of agricultural rationalization, there is the effect of high urban birth rates and conditions of hygiene and general health in the cities, which, though much lower than the average levels in developed countries, are higher than in the countryside and reflected in marked rises in life chances and life expectancy.

Urbanism in underdeveloped countries is characterized by two very salient phenomena. The first consists of an accentuated and uncheckable polarization between a limited number of middle and high income strata, who enjoy conditions of life and wealth similar to those of the well-off strata in industrialized countries and the services provided by a population available for very low-paid work, and an enormous and heterogeneous population with extremely low monetary income. The second is made up of the survival strategies of this latter group, for the most part living in miserable conditions, huts and shanty dwellings, on illegally occupied land and working in what is called the informal sector: a mix of service, handicraft and street trade activities, construction labouring and homeworking, and other legal or illegal activities (Hart, 1973; Gerry, 1987; Mingione, 1991). Their urban lifestyle also brings into the big cities of the Third World many elements of rural subsistence strategies, from domestic animal rearing to the importance of kinship, ethnic and community networks and of a solidarity between friends and neighbours that is indispensable for surviving where individual income is extremely low.

Reading
Abu-Lughod, J.L. and Hay, R. eds 1977: *Third World Urbanization*.
Ball, M., Harloe, M. and Maartens, H. 1988: *Housing and Social Change in Europe and the USA*.
Berry, B.J.L. ed. 1976: *Urbanisation and Counterurbanisation*.
Bookchin, Murray 1987: *The Rise of Urbanization and the Decline of Citizenship*.
Breese, Gerald ed. 1969: *The City in Newly Developing Countries*.
Castells, Manuel 1989: *The Informational City*.
Davis, K. 1967: The urbanization of the human population. In *Cities*.
Gans, H. 1968: Urbanism and suburbanism as ways of life. In *Readings in Urban Sociology*, ed. R. Pahl.
Gilbert, Alan and Gugler, Josef 1982: *Cities, Poverty and Development*.
Hauser, Philip M. and Schnore, Leo F. eds 1965: *The Study of Urbanization*.
Mingione, Enzo 1986: Urban sociology. In *The Social Reproduction of Organization and Culture*, ed. Ulf Himmelstrand.
—— 1991: *Fragmented Societies*.
Mumford, L. 1966: *The City in History*.
Park, R.C., Burgess, E.W. and McKenzie, R.T. 1925: *The City*.
Perry, R., Dean, K. and Brown, B. 1986: *Counterurbanisation*.
Sassen, Saskia 1991: *The Global City*.
Saunders, Peter 1981: *Social Theory and the Urban Question*.
Szelényi, Ivan 1983: *Urban Inequalities under State Socialism*.
Weber, Alfred 1899: *The Growth of Cities in the Nineteenth Century: A Study in Statistics*.
Wirth, L. 1938: Urbanism as a way of life. *American Journal of Sociology* 44, 1–24.

ENZO MINGIONE

utilitarianism   The tradition in moral, political and social theory that assesses the rightness of acts, choices, decisions and policies by their consequences with regard to human (and possibly animal) welfare has been a particularly influential one. Long associated with the names of Jeremy Bentham and John Stuart Mill, it still has prominent adherents among philosophers, economists and social scientists and occupies a central place in moral, political and social theorizing. But perhaps the greatest testament to the impact of utilitarianism is to be found in the extraordinary number of critics who have tried, and continue to try, and in all kinds of ways, to refute or otherwise dispose of it.

The classical version of utilitarianism, as found in Bentham and Mill, was a form of act-utilitarianism, according to which an act is right if it is productive of best consequences, that is, consequences with regard to human welfare that are at least as good as those of any alternative. While critics often still focus on this version of utilitarianism, other versions have been distinguished from it, such as rule-utilitarianism, utilitarian generalization, motive utilitarianism and cooperative utilitarianism. How far some of these are actually distinct from act-utilitarianism and how far all of them are free of difficulties remain a matter of controversy.

In fact, 'utilitarianism' is the name of a cluster of theories that are variations on a theme, three components of which can be distinguished.

Consequence component
According to the consequence component, rightness is tied in some way to the production of good consequences. The view that consequences alone make acts right or wrong is called consequentialism; it is the consequence component of act-

utilitarianism and may in that context be treated as the view that an act is right if it has best consequences. Consequentialism has been much criticized by those who favour different accounts of what makes right acts right. For example, some argue that consequentialism betokens a corrupt mind in that it cannot proscribe certain acts (for example, lying) independently of their consequences. If consequences make acts right or wrong, then even the most reprehensible of acts could turn out, in certain circumstances, to be right. Others argue that a concern to produce best consequences on each occasion may fail to produce best consequences overall and so may be self-defeating. Still others argue that an impersonal account of rightness, such as best consequences, may not be compatible with pursuit of one's projects, commitments and relationships, and so to some extent may sever one from one's integrity. More generally, impersonal accounts of rightness are accused of failing to take seriously the separateness of persons, that is, of failing to treat people as autonomous individuals, with their own individuality, projects and worth. How far this accusation succeeds – it is, for instance, strongly resisted by R.M. Hare – is disputed, but it has spurred the recent development of schemes of individual moral rights for the protection of persons.

Value component

According to the value component, the goodness or badness of consequences is to be assessed by some standard of intrinsic goodness, the presence of which good in the world is to be maximized. This good in the case of act-utilitarianism has been human welfare; exactly what human welfare is to be taken to consist in, however, has proved a contentious affair. For example, the early utilitarians were hedonists; later ones, such as G.E. Moore, held that other things besides pleasure and/or happiness were good in themselves.

A recent trend has been to move away from standards of goodness that make reference to mental states, and in the direction of desire- or preference-satisfaction views of human welfare. A problem here has been to isolate those desires we are to focus upon. Reflection on difficulties to do with actual or future desires has forced theorists in the direction of informed ones, or those desires we would have if we were fully informed, detached, free from the pressures of the moment, and so on. The assumption appears to be that, under appro-

priate conditions, informed desires become actual, while those of our present desires that fail to pass muster as informed are given up (or at least are not rightly acted upon). Even without introducing problems to do with weakness of will, the details of this exchange of desires, in terms of individual moral psychology, remain a bit murky.

Critics of utilitarian value theory have been legion, and it certainly remains an area of immense controversy, not only as to the nature of those things we are to take as having intrinsic value but also even as to the possibility of there being impersonal or agent-neutral VALUES. Values, it is increasingly argued, are subjective, in the sense of being agent relative; they are the values of agents. Yet utilitarianism requires that desires be aggregated and weighed and balanced in terms of some agent-neutral principle to do, for example, with the general welfare, even as it remains unclear why any particular agent has reason to value pursuit of the general welfare. If one is made better off, one may acquire such a reason; but what if one is required to make deep and systematic sacrifices to maximize general welfare?

Range component

According to the range component, it is consequences of acts as affecting everyone that are to be taken into account in determining rightness. Unless the consequences of an act can be cut off, the class of all those affected by the act, as consequences extend into the future, seems constantly to expand, with possible effect upon rightness. But the major problem the range component has posed for utilitarians has been that it demands for the success of utilitarianism that we be able to make interpersonal comparisons of pleasures and pains or desire satisfactions. We will only be able to maximize desire satisfaction across all those affected by the act if we can compare the effect of the act upon the desire sets of each of those involved and judge the extent and strength of that effect and compare the different results. The early utilitarians thought we could sum pleasures and pains across different persons, but this view is no longer taken seriously. As for desire or preference satisfaction, many economists and social scientists write as if interpersonal comparisons were unproblematic; detailed examination of their theories and of their arguments in support of the specific measuring rod that permits comparisons of desire satisfaction in different persons, however, will be insisted on by critics.

Indirect utilitarianisms

Finally, a recent innovation has been the development of indirect utilitarianisms. For instance, R.M. Hare has developed a two-level account of moral thinking, which is rule-utilitarian at the level of practice but act-utilitarian at the level of theory (or the level of rule or institutional design). Act-utilitarian thinking at the level of theory will select those guides at the level of practice the general acceptance of which will give us the best chance to produce best consequences. In this way, Hare argues that his two-level view enables him to avoid many of the problems that have been held by critics to beset act-utilitarianism at the level of practice. Other two-level theorists, it should be noted, see themselves as developing a plausible form of utilitarianism, not mounting a further case for act-utilitarianism, to whose fate they are indifferent.

See also ETHICS; SOCIAL WELFARE.

Reading

Bentham, J. 1793 (1948): An Introduction to the Principles of Morals and Legislation, ed. J. Harrison.
Brandt, R.B. 1979: A Theory of the Good and the Right.
Hampshire, S. ed. 1978: Public and Private Morality.
Hare, R.M. 1981: Moral Thinking.
Mill, J.S. 1863 (1957): Utilitarianism.
Moore, G.E. 1903 (1959): Principia Ethica.
Regan, D.H. 1980: Utilitarianism and Co-operation.
Scheffler, S. 1982: The Rejection of Consequentialism.
Sen, A. and Williams, B. eds 1972: Utilitarianism and Beyond.
Smart, J.J.C. and Williams, B. eds 1973: Utilitarianism: For and Against.

R.G. FREY

utopia   The word describes an ideal community free from conflict which incorporates a clear set of values and allows the complete satisfaction of human needs. Utopias normally involve a systematic portrayal of life in the imagined society, or sometimes their depiction in a novel. In the present century the pace of social, political and technological change, and the political divisions between capitalism and socialism, have led to new themes in utopian thought in which the proponents of utopia have sometimes been confronted by anti-utopias designed to discredit their schemes for social betterment.

The term utopia, from the Greek for 'not-place', was invented by Sir Thomas More (1516). However, many forms of thought have a utopian element. Depictions of a 'golden age' go back to the Greeks, though, unlike utopias, these are located in the past. The Christian notion of the millennium also has a utopian aspect while numerous political theorists have outlined ideal constitutions. Indeed thought containing utopian elements is far more common than the coherent depiction of utopia itself.

The systematic analysis of utopia as a mode of thought began with the publication of a translation of *Ideology and Utopia* (Mannheim, 1929). Karl Mannheim made a distinction between ideological thought which depicted an idealized version of current reality, and utopian thought which sought a new kind of society. However, the term 'utopia' is generally now used to cover both these meanings.

Utopian thought appears to flourish during times of social insecurity and the breakdown of established authority. Utopias often reflect the boundaries of possibility established by an existing society, including its productive capacity, its conception of the extent of the malleability of human nature and the relative emphasis given to the PUBLIC SPHERE as against the private. Utopias also reflect the social location of the stratum whose ideal is being represented. Thus the utopia of the authorities is generally one of order while that of the people is often the land of plenty and pleasure.

Twentieth-century utopian thought has built on the idea of progress which the nineteenth century incorporated into utopia along with science. The most characteristic form of utopia in the twentieth century has been the idea of socialism, though liberalism has also had a utopian dimension. Despite their protestations to the contrary, the thought of Marx and Engels is deeply utopian (Ollman, 1977). The socialist utopian tradition was developed in the twentieth century in a Fabian vein in several books by H. G. Wells, who also helped to establish science fiction as an important element in modern utopian thought (Hillegas, 1967). Another important aspect in twentieth-century utopian thought can be found in the area of architecture and planning, though this itself may hark back to the Christian ideal of the heavenly city (Fishman, 1977).

Anti-utopia

In the twentieth century, anti-utopians such as George Orwell have had considerable influence. They have depicted societies in ways which mirror utopian thought by reflecting back an abhorrent image of the effects of utopian experiments undertaken at a societal level. They project a nightmare in which established ruling groups have lost control and been replaced by barbaric agents of a new order. In part, anti-utopias are a response to the threat of socialism and to the flawed socialist experiments of the present century. Anti-utopianism has also drawn on viewpoints emphasizing the biological roots of behaviour, such as Freudianism which stresses the role of instinctual factors in behaviour. SOCIOBIOLOGY is a more recent current of a similar kind.

Utopia today

Broad models of sociological, political and economic functioning frequently contain utopian elements since they portray the comprehensive implementation of fundamental principles. Examples include the fully integrated functionalist model of the social system, various models of democracy such as that developed by the pluralist school, and the model of the fully self-regulating market developed in neoclassical economics (see FUNCTIONALISM; PLURALISM; MARKET).

The postwar period in the West gave rise to a new surge of utopian thought. The long boom and the pace of technological advance lay behind a new version of the 'scientific' utopia in the form of POSTINDUSTRIAL SOCIETY (Kumar, 1978). These utopias anticipate an imminent transformation of society due to scientific advance and, increasingly, the development of INFORMATION TECHNOLOGY AND THEORY. The discipline of FUTUROLOGY also has a utopian dimension.

The developing Western cultural crisis of the 1960s and 1970s also gave rise to a resurgence of utopian elements in thought. Utopian experiments such as the 'commune' movement of the 1960s were one response (see COUNTERCULTURE). Another which is still developing is the 'ecotopia': a society where man and nature could at last live in harmony (see ECOLOGY). This continues the tradition of the utopia based on scientific knowledge although now in the form of 'alternative' or 'utopian' technology. A utopian dimension is also present within FEMINISM (Kumar, 1981), linked to the belief that 'the personal is political' and a concern with the 'prefigurative'. This describes the idea that elements of a better society can be established here and now to form a model for relationships and institutions in the future.

It has been suggested that utopia is now within our grasp. It can take the form of a purely interior solution to the tensions of society involving the use of psychotropic drugs, as depicted by Aldous Huxley in his later work. The question of utopia can even be dissolved, as it is in the work of Nozick (1974), who suggests that the utopia of the libertarian right has already arrived. In this utopia there is no single prescribed community or way of life: utopia simply consists of a society where everyone has the right to establish whatever form of community he or she chooses.

Reading

Bauman, Z. 1976: *Socialism: The Active Utopia*.
Dickson, D. 1974: *Alternative Technology*.
Fishman, R. 1977: *Urban Utopias in the Twentieth Century*.
Hillegas, M.R. 1967: *The Future as Nightmare: H.G. Wells and the Anti-Utopians*.
Kumar, K. 1978: *Prophecy and Progress*.
—— 1981: Primitivism in feminist utopias. *Alternative Futures (USA)* 4, 61–7.
—— 1987: *Utopia and Anti-Utopia in Modern Times*.
Mannheim, K. 1929 (*1960*): *Ideology and Utopia*.
More, Thomas 1516 (*1965*): *Utopia*.
Nozick, R. 1974: *Anarchy, State and Utopia*.
Ollman, B. 1977: Marx's vision of communism: a reconstruction. *Critique* 8, 4–41.

TOM BURDEN

V

value   In the eighteenth and early nineteenth centuries, economic theory distinguished value-in-exchange from value-in-use, and attempted to use the former in order to explain exchange ratios, or relative prices, of commodities in the MARKET. That commodities all did have value-in-exchange was ascribed to the value-creating substance common to them all, which was the labour directly involved in their production; that commodities typically had different values-in-exchange was explained by the relative ease or difficulty of their production. This labour theory of value thus said that all value-in-exchange could be ascribed to labour, whether directly employed in production or indirectly employed in producing the raw materials and the tools of production with which labour works. The theory reached its apogee in the work of David Ricardo in the years after 1815 (see Ricardo, 1817).

But the theory proved unsatisfactory as a logical theory of relative price because it implied that if prices were determined by labour values, different commodities would earn different rates of profit, and if the forces of competition equalized the rate of profit, prices could not be explained by labour values. After Ricardo, economic theory fragmented into different theories of value according to how this difficulty was recognized and resolved.

The approach which came to predominate in economic theory was one (called NEOCLASSICAL ECONOMICS) which denied any meaning to the distinction between value and price, and sought the explanation of price ratios in terms of the quantity of one good an individual would be prepared to sacrifice in order to gain a unit of another good. Instead of an emphasis on differing production conditions, the theory presumed optimizing individuals, constrained by their initial endowments, and the trades they were prepared to make. The theory was thus demand driven, a 'subjectivist' theory of value (price). With the addition of production, price is then determined by the interaction of demand for outputs and supply of inputs, derived from the decisions of utility maximizing agents constrained by endowments and income, and the supply of outputs and demand for inputs, derived from the decisions of profit maximizing agents constrained by technology and initial resources.

This methodology was largely established in the 1870s; in the 1930s and the 1940s John R. Hicks (1939) and particularly P. A. Samuelson (1947) showed how different branches of the theory had a common underlying mathematical structure; and in the 1950s work by a number of mathematical economists, culminating in a celebrated book by Gérard Debreu (1959) succeeded in formalizing many of the general equilibrium intuitions of Adam Smith's 'invisible hand'. The price which equates demand and supply is called the 'equilibrium' price. The questions then asked concern the identification of the circumstances under which an equilibrium price exists in each and every market simultaneously, whether such a set of equilibrium prices is unique, and whether it is stable in the sense of being restored if disturbed. The focus is thus on optimizing individuals making quantity decisions on the basis of parametric prices and the interaction of those decisions to determine equilibrium prices. Current research includes the investigation of both aggregative and disaggregative models in which prices are not parametric, market participants have access to different amounts of relevant information, and trades occur at prices which are not equilibrium prices.

A quite different approach was taken by Karl Marx in the 1850s and 1860s. He maintained the distinction between value and price, but reformulated the labour theory of value such that it comprised two propositions: first, that abstract labour is the source of all value; and second, that value takes an independent form of existence as a sum of MONEY. How a content produces its form of appearance is then an immediate issue. Marx took a dialectical approach, in which the development of the concepts of his analysis posits contradictions which are overcome only to be reposited, in a manner which he considered reflected the contradictions of a class-divided world. Price is then the form of appearance in exchange of value created in production (Marx, 1898); how this is actually worked out both by Marx and by subsequent writers in the same tradition is a matter of considerable controversy.

Neither theory of value is compatible with the other. Neoclassical value theory starts with atomistic individuals optimizing, sees no difference between value and price, and focuses on equilibrium situations. Marxian value theory starts with classes, distinguishes value from price, and reflects a contradictory world in which class antagonism is continually being produced and reproduced.

See also VALUES.

Reading
Arrow, K.J. and Hahn, F.H. 1971: *General Competitive Analysis*
Fine, B. 1989: *Marx's Capital*, 3rd edn.
Foley, D.K. 1986: *Understanding Capital*.
Koopmans, T.C. 1957: *Three Essays on the State of Economic Science*.
Marglin, S.A. 1984: *Growth, Distribution, and Prices*.
Rowthorn, R. 1974: Neo-Classicism, neo-Ricardianism and Marxism. *New Left Review* 86, 63–87.
Rubin, I.I. 1928 (*1973*): *Essays on Marx's Theory of Value*.
Sweezy, P.M. ed. 1949: *Karl Marx and the Close of his System, by Eugen von Böhm-Bawerk* [1896] *and Böhm-Bawerk's Criticism of Marx, by Rudolf Hilferding* [1904].

SIMON MOHUN

values In the sense of moral principles and other objects of concern, values form a focus of discussion at three main levels in social theory. First, they appear as an object of investigation, as in recent discussions of value change from materialist to postmaterialist values among the populations of advanced capitalist societies. Second, they are a central category for some theoretical perspectives in sociology, notably structural-functionalism. Third, social theory takes up the philosophical problem of the relation between factual and evaluative statements in methodological reflections which raise fundamental issues of the relationship between systematic social theory and normative orientations and commitments of various sorts.

The systematic study of values as objects depends on a sense of diversity animated both by sociological and especially anthropological research and by the philosophical deconstruction of their alleged universality. In late nineteenth-century Europe, Nietzsche was of course the central figure in this development, but other thinkers, in particular R.H. Lotze (1817–1881) were also central to the emergence of an account of the subjectivity of values which developed in parallel with subjectivist accounts of economic VALUE.

Emile Durkheim remains the paradigmatic exemplar of the scientific study of values as 'moral facts'; what he called the *conscience collective* connotes both consciousness and conscience, and this double meaning indicates the centrality which he assigned to values in social integration. Largely through the influence of Talcott Parsons's *Structure of Social Action* (1937), as well as that of Malinowski's concept of a social *charter*, the idea that social integration is secured primarily by a shared value system became a commonplace of North American functionalism. Parsons slipped smoothly from the 'normative orientation of action' in the trivial sense that actors have to choose between alternative ends, and a conception in which, for social order to be secured (the 'Hobbesian problem') actions must largely be oriented to a common system of normative values. One could of course conceive of social integration as taking place in a more automatic way without reference to value consensus, as David Lockwood's classic article (1964) demonstrated, and what Lockwood called social integration as distinct from the more mechanical process of 'system integration' might be seen as involving argumentation and the *formation* of consensus (Jürgen Habermas) rather than wholesale acceptance of a readymade value system.

In practice, however, FUNCTIONALISM stood and fell on the postulate of value consensus as the central integrating mechanism. Its substantial fall began with the demonstration of subcultural variation in values in the sociology of deviance and youth, and was completed by the rise in the 1960s of subcultures into movements of radical political opposition and the cultivation of alternative lifestyles. Forced to concede the diversity of values, structural-functionalism went on the retreat for some time; its revival, first in (West) Germany and now increasingly in the USA, is in terms of more sophisticated cognitivist and system models. Meanwhile official Marxist-Leninist social theory in the state socialist societies welcomed the theme of a common value system while of course rejecting both functionalist theory and its 'idealist' stress on the primacy of values.

This theoretical context formed the background for the many sociological and social-psychological studies of value systems, whose focus on subjective data was well suited to the tools of survey research. But in both sociology and political science, generalities about value systems on the one hand and the detailed registration of particular opinions on the other left something of a gap where one might have hoped for a genuine sociology of ethical or political orientations. Part of the appeal of Michel Foucault's work was perhaps that he began to fill this gap with his studies of punishment and sexuality; and Pierre Bourdieu, coming from an anthropological tradition which had always been more sensitive to these issues, has also made an important contribution by reviving the notion of the 'habitus', a semi-obligatory way of acting or behaving.

One aspect of the empirical study of values which deserves special mention is the thesis developed by R.F. Inglehart that modern advanced societies, and young members of those societies in particular, are becoming more attracted to postmaterialist values such as free expression and quality of life at the expense of the more traditional 'bread-and-butter' issues of economic growth, full employment and material progress. Though this thesis has been much disputed in its details, it seems to point to a difference in political values between old and new left movements, between middle-class and working-class socialists and between socialists and green supporters. More ambitiously, Ulrich Beck and others have suggested that the distributional conflicts characteristic of industrial societies and summed up in the systemic conflict between workers and capital are tending to be displaced by the complex and shifting product of individual interest and shared (environmental) danger.

As for the methodological role of values in social thought and social science, the twentieth century has seen a continuation of positions staked out by the end of the nineteenth. One can roughly distinguish a Comtean-positivist tradition (see POSITIVISM) carried on by Durkheim, in which objective science can tell us what is normal or pathological in our societies and how their directing organs should remedy any defects; a Weberian tradition which upholds in theory and aspires to in its scientific practice the sharp separation between factual and evaluative statements (while recognizing the role of values in orienting scientific inquiry);

and a Marxist stress on the unity of analysis and prescription in critique.

The original positivist position has always suffered from the difficulty of making its diagnoses plausible; in practice, technocratic social interventions have more often been justified by a simplified version of fact–value separation which simply sees value judgements as extraneous to science and treats values as facts to be recorded and explained, in an uncomplicated calculation of the benefits of alternative policy outcomes.

Max Weber's position was a good deal more complicated. He accepted Heinrich Rickert's notion that what characterizes the phenomena of the 'cultural' as opposed to the 'natural' sciences is their relation to our values rather than to a set of general laws. Although he modified the Rickertian inheritance a good deal in the course of his career, and changed his view of sociology in the process, Weber retained a distinction between merely classificatory concepts or uses of concepts, and ideal-typical ones. The ideal type was not ideal in any evaluative sense, but represented an accentuation of phenomena in reality in relation to a specific (and value-determined) angle of the interest in those phenomena. Despite (or because of) all this, Weber argued, it was still possible to distinguish between scientific statements and expressions of value which have no place in science. Science cannot tell us what we ought to want, but only (perhaps) what we do want and how we might get it, at what cost. Whether the cost is worth paying is again a matter for our own decision. To believe otherwise is not just to contaminate one's science with values, but, more importantly, to abdicate one's moral responsibility to choose between the alternative gods and demons, the alternative value systems, with which human beings are confronted in the modern world. And we should be making these choices: value-freedom does not mean moral indifference.

Weber's position, in a suitably simplified form, has been perhaps the dominant orthodoxy of twentieth-century social science – though it is of course easier to proclaim the value-freedom of science than to implement it in practice, as theories of IDEOLOGY make clear. Even the most committed social scientists, such as the Austro-Marxist, Max Adler, have accepted the need to separate facts and values (see AUSTRO-MARXISM). On the whole, however, Marxists (leaving aside those who unquestioningly accepted a principle of partisanship) have been attracted by the notion of a unity of science and (proposals for) transformative practice embodied in Marx's notion of criticism or critique. *Capital*, for example, was at one and the same time a scientific work of political economy, a critique of political economy as a whole, and a critique of the economy and society of capitalism which entailed *ceteris paribus* the search for a better system.

The critical theory of the FRANKFURT SCHOOL has carried forward this line of argument, stressing, as Marx did, the embeddedness of scientific activity in the general sphere of human practice and the impossibility as well as the undesirability of artificially cutting it off from this context in what Habermas called a 'positivistically bisected rationalism'. The more specifically cognitive line of argument has been developed recently by Roy Edgley and Roy Bhaskar, suggesting that one can move from showing the falsity of a set of beliefs about society to a critique of the social circumstances which sustain these false beliefs.

As the century draws to a close, discussion of values seems subject to three counteracting influences. On the one hand, the possibility of achieving a rigid separation of factual and evaluative statements, especially in social thought, seems less promising than it did in those parts of the world strongly influenced by logical positivism and its aftermath. On the other hand, both Marxism and other sources of political conviction and commitment seem to be in eclipse, and a currently fashionable postmodern relativism treats the discussion of values as somewhat un-chic. Given the magnitude of the crises confronting humanity in the late twentieth century, however, the latter seems likely to be a temporary phenomenon. More promisingly, there is a third tendency towards the GLOBALIZATION of values; scarcely any government in the contemporary world dares not to pay lip-service at least to democracy, the rule of law, and the preservation of human rights. The erosion of the state socialist dictatorships by values which were perhaps 'modern' more clearly than they were democratic, capitalist, or anything else, are a sign of this globalizing tendency. So, admittedly, is the anti-modern fundamentalism in many parts of the world, but this may also prove to be a relatively short-term phenomenon. The abandonment of the hopes of grounding universal values does not preclude a more modest attempt to encourage the generalization of those which seem valid.

See also ETHICS; MORALITY; NORM.

Reading

Beck, Ulrich 1992: *Risk Society*.
Bhaskar, Roy 1986: *Scientific Realism and Human Emancipation*.
Inglehart, R.F. 1977: *The Silent Revolution: Changing Values and Political Styles among the Western Mass Publics*.
Oakes, Guy 1988: *Weber and Rickert: Concept Formation in the Cultural Sciences*.
Ossowska, Maria 1971: *Social Determinants of Moral Ideas*.
Rose, Gillian 1981: *Hegel Contra Sociology*, ch. 1.
Weber, Max 1904 (*1949*): *The Methodology of the Social Sciences*.

WILLIAM OUTHWAITE

verstehen The German word for 'understanding' has come to be used in a more limited sense to refer to the understanding of texts and other human accomplishments such as actions and social and cultural phenomena, where understanding these phenomena is often seen as being in some way like the understanding of a written text. Originally used in the nineteenth century to denote the imaginative penetration of religious and other historical texts (see HISTORICISM), the term was used by the philosopher of history Johann Gustav Droysen (1838–1908) in his attack on the positivist view that history should aim to discover laws like those of the natural sciences (see NATURALISM). We can understand mind (*Geist*) in a different way from nature; we have what Droysen called 'an immediate and subjectively certain understanding of human affairs', but this must be made more precise and 'objective' by the methods of historical research. These ideas were developed further by the philosopher Wilhelm Dilthey (1833–1911) in his attempt to establish the philosophical foundations of the human sciences or *Geisteswissenschaften*. Dilthey's work displays a shift of emphasis from the understanding of subjectively intended meaning of the writer or actor to a more structural approach in which meaning is more the product of a larger system, such as a natural language or set of cultural conventions, and this distinction between subjectively intended and 'objective' meaning has tended to dominate subsequent discussion.

The central figures in verstehende sociology are Georg Simmel and Max Weber. Simmel first systematically addressed these issues in his *Problems of the Philosophy of History* (1892). Weber (1903–6) commended Simmel for distinguishing clearly between the objective understanding of the meaning of an expression and the subjective understanding or interpretation of the motives of the person who uttered it. In Simmel's example, a soldier who receives a verbally ambiguous order may formulate a hypothesis about the motives of the person who issued the order. The latter process, Weber insists, is a form of causal knowledge. Explanations in the social sciences must aim for both meaningful and causal adequacy. In the case of Weber's well-known account of the Protestant ethic and the spirit of capitalism (1904–5), the explanation of the religious origins of Protestant economic innovation in early modern Europe must make sense in terms of what we know about human motivation, and there must be some demonstration that these ideas did in fact influence the conduct of Protestant entrepreneurs and workers. Weber's sociology tends to emphasize subjectively intended meaning, or an IDEAL TYPE of such an intention, arguing that objective or correct meanings are the concern of other disciplines such as philosophy, philology or law. His category of 'direct' or 'immediate' understanding (*aktuelles Verstehen*), however, is close to what has usually been understood as objective meaning.

Alfred Schutz inaugurated what has come to be known as 'phenomenological sociology' with the book translated as *The Phenomenology of the Social World* (1932). Schutz stressed the 'everyday' and 'commonsense' dimension of understanding and the construction of ideal types, and ETHNOMETHODOLOGY continues in this direction, which in turn has been increasingly assimilated into more mainstream social theory, in the work of Anthony Giddens and others.

In a largely separate line of development, rationalists have argued that 'rational action is its own explanation' (Hollis, 1977, p. 21) (see RATIONALITY AND REASON). Whereas HERMENEUTICS stresses the imaginative reconstruction of what Wittgenstein called 'forms of life' (see Winch, 1958 and 1964), rational action theorists in economics, psychology and even sociology and anthropology tend to operate with a universalistic account of human motivation, and to pay relatively little attention to actors' 'self-understandings' – their own sense of what they are doing and why.

In the last decade of the twentieth century, the original oppositions, which Max Weber tried to overcome, between verstehen and explanation (*Erklären*) or between causal and teleological EXPLANATION, have largely passed into the background, like the related oppositions between structuralist and individualist theories or materialist and idealist ones. Critical Theory (see FRANKFURT SCHOOL) is just one way in which social theorists have attempted a synthesis of these oppositions. The more salient opposition is that between individualistic rational action theory, in economics and the other social sciences, and approaches which combine structuralist and culturalist principles in a continuation of the verstehen tradition.

Reading

Apel, Karl-Otto 1979 (*1984*): *Understanding and Explanation: A Transcendental-Pragmatic Perspective.*
Dallmayr, Fred and McCarthy, Thomas eds 1977: *Understanding and Social Inquiry.*
Hollis, Martin 1977: *Models of Man.*
Müller-Doohm, Stefan ed. 1992: *Verstehen und Methoden.*
Outhwaite, William 1975 (*1986*): *Understanding Social Life,* 2nd edn.
Winch, Peter 1958: *The Idea of a Social Science and its Relation to Philosophy.*
—— 1964: Understanding a primitive society. *American Philosophical Quarterly* 1.4, 307–24.
Wright, G.H. von 1971: *Explanation and Understanding.*

WILLIAM OUTHWAITE

Vienna circle   A group of philosophers and scientists in the 1920s and early 1930s who played a crucial role in the formation of the philosophical movement known as logical positivism or logical empiricism. It continued a tradition of empiricist thought in Vienna whose leading representative was the philosopher-scientist Ernst Mach, who in 1895, was appointed to the newly founded chair in the philosophy of the inductive sciences at the University of Vienna and vigorously championed a radically anti-metaphysical positivism. In 1922 Moritz Schlick, again a philosopher-scientist, was appointed to that chair, and it was from a seminar led by Schlick that in 1923 the Vienna circle emerged.

Besides Schlick, the most important members of the circle in terms of its philosophical development were Rudolf Carnap and the economist Otto Neurath. Carnap, like Schlick, was trained both in philosophy and in physics but he was also thoroughly acquainted with the modern developments in logic. He moved to Vienna in 1926 and became *Dozent* (instructor) in philosophy at the university; he quickly became a leading figure in the circle's discussions and was to establish himself as the most prominent expositor of the ideas of logical positivism. Ludwig Wittgenstein, although not himself a member of the Vienna circle, influenced it profoundly through his *Tractatus Logico-philosophicus* (1921) which was intensely discussed in the circle; indeed, Wittgenstein was considered by the Viennese positivists as one of the three most outstanding pioneers of their own 'scientific world-conception', the other two being Albert Einstein and Bertrand Russell.

In the late 1920s the Vienna circle came before the public as a new movement with a comprehensive scientific and educational purpose. It was especially Neurath, both an active socialist and an able organizer, who insisted that the group should act in a party-like manner to promote the enlightenment brought by the scientific world-conception and thereby to serve the development of society. To this end the Ernst Mach Society was founded. The following year, in 1929, there appeared in Vienna the manifesto *Wissenschaftliche Weltauffassung: Der Wiener Kreis* ('The scientific conception of the world: the Vienna circle', Carnap et al., 1929), in which the rigorous elimination of metaphysics from the realm of rational thought and the establishment of unified science (*Einheitswissenschaft*) by way of logical reduction of science to terms of immediate experience were announced as the new movement's basic objectives. In the same year the circle organized, together with the Society for Empirical Philosophy (a Berlin group of similar outlook around Hans Reichenbach), a congress held in Prague. Further congresses followed, and cooperation with other groups and individuals pursuing related aims was established. Thus it was mainly due to the activities of the Vienna circle that in the 1930s an international community of scientific philosophy came into being. In 1930 the journal *Erkenntnis* began to appear as the principal organ of the movement. The circle also published various series of monographs, such as *Schriften zur wissenschaftlichen Weltauffassung* (Writings on the Scientific World-conception) and *Einheitswissenschaft* (Unity of Science).

The Viennese positivists' attack on metaphysics, for which they became notorious, was based on modern mathematical logic as developed, in particular, in Russell's and A.N. Whitehead's *Principia Mathematica* (1910–11), and on the principle of verifiability stating that the meaning of a factual proposition lies in the method of its experiential verification, which they derived from Wittgenstein. Modern logic had shown to their satisfaction that mathematics is part of logic, and the propositions of logic they interpreted, again following Wittgenstein, as empty tautologies perfectly compatible with the central empiricist tenet that all genuine (that is, factual) knowledge derives from experience: thus all sound propositions are either tautologies or else empirical statements. On the other hand, metaphysical assertions such as 'God exists' or 'There are absolute values,' being neither tautological nor empirical but claiming to convey factual information independently of experience, are really meaningless pseudo-propositions (although they may have emotive significance); indeed, metaphysical utterances may be still more radically unsound as they may violate even the rules of logical grammar, a point emphasized in particular by Carnap ever since his *The Logical Structure of the World* and *Pseudo-problems in Philosophy* (both in Carnap, 1928).

This critique, however, was not confined to traditional metaphysics (including, in the circle's view, Kantian apriorism) but was also applied to the traditional theory of knowledge which discussed such topics as the reality of the external world, i.e. the question of whether subjective idealism or realism is true. In his *General Theory of Knowledge* (1918), Schlick rejected traditional metaphysics, but by elaborately defending realism still moved within the bounds of the traditional theory of knowledge. In Carnap's 1928 works, however, the idealism–realism issue is exposed as just another pseudo-problem in philosophy, which view was then taken by Schlick (1932) too.

The rejection of metaphysics, which came to be stated most thoroughly by Carnap (1932 (*1959*)), was to be complemented and reinforced by exhibiting the unity of science. Neurath, particularly, who had strong Marxist leanings, was radically opposed to the division of the sciences, common in the German academic world, into natural and cultural sciences (*Geistes-* or *Kulturwissenschaften*), as a breeding-place of metaphysics. Carnap's *The Logical Structure of the World* was the first systematic effort within the Vienna circle to give content to the unity of science thesis by attempting to show how all scientific concepts can be reduced to, or constructed from, one's own stream of experience. This, then, was on the whole the picture the Vienna circle in the late 1920s presented to the outside world: all empirical statements, as the only meaningful factual statements, were to be reconstructed as statements whose terms referred to immediate experience without thereby implying the metaphysical claim that only such experiences are real, and correspondingly, they were assumed to be conclusively verifiable (or falsifiable) by primitive statements expressing immediate experiences, which statements were on this ground taken to provide an incorrigible rock-bottom of knowledge.

Soon, however, considerable doctrinal changes and developments took place, as the picture outlined gave rise to a number of serious problems. First of all, the verifiability principle threatened to put science on the same level as metaphysics, since the natural laws cannot be conclusively verified. Schlick (1931) therefore proposed to view them not as statements but only as rules which allow us to infer verifiable singular statements. But this move to save the verifiability principle was not successful, for as Carnap (1932 (1934)) pointed out, the singular statements of science are just as unverifiable by experiences as general laws are. So verifiability as the criterion for a statement's having empirical content was subsequently replaced by the weaker notion of confirmability; indeed, already in 1932 Carnap spoke of verification in the sense of only weak verification, that is, of confirmation (Carnap, 1932 (1987)).

Another difficulty concerned the nature of the propositions of scientific philosophy. Wittgenstein in the Tractatus had admitted that his own statements about the structure of the world and of how language relates to the world, although being 'elucidations' aiding our understanding, are not really meaningful propositions asserting anything. Whereas Schlick (1930) accepted Wittgenstein's conclusion that philosophy does not yield any truths but is only the activity of clarifying propositions, Neurath (1932a) protested that unified science is in no need of a metaphysics of elucidations. Carnap tackled the problem by drawing the distinction between the material and the formal (syntactical) mode of speech (Carnap, 1932 (1934)). Philosophy, he explained in his The Logical Syntax of Language (1934), is logical investigation of the syntactical structure of language(s). Thus, to raise the ontological claims that the numbers are a fundamental category of entities, or that they are certain classes, is to express in the misleading

material mode pregnant with metaphysical nonsense what amounts in the correct formal mode to making the syntactical statements that in one language number-words are primitives and that in another language they are construed as certain class-words. Philosophical disputes of the kind indicated (category disputes) reduce therefore to proposing different languages, and since there is no theoretical issue involved in such proposals they should be treated, Carnap suggested, in the conventionalistic spirit of what he called the principle of tolerance.

Furthermore, Neurath was from the outset critical of the conception of science as being, ultimately, about essentially private experiences. He persistently argued that the only form of language fitting the intersubjectivity of science is the intersubjective physicalistic language: therefore, physicalism was to be the proper frame for unified science which would encompass the social sciences in the form of a 'social behaviourism'. Neurath added that the verifiers (or confirmers) of science, which he called protocol statements, must also be part of the physicalistic language if they are to be of any significance for intersubjective science. Consistent with this he denied that the protocol statements are incorrigible, and together with the idea of an absolute foundation of knowledge he rejected as meaningless the notion of comparing a statement with reality, statements being according to him comparable only with other statements; in this he converged with Carnap's evolving syntactical approach. This radical physicalism (as set forth in Neurath, 1932a and 1932b) greatly impressed Carnap who accepted, with modifications, its principal theses and abandoned the view of the protocol statements as being incorrigible immediate-experience statements. Of course, the acceptance of physicalism was for him not a matter of assertion but only of preference for a certain language form, and in the same vein he argued that the question of the proper form of the protocol statements is to be settled by convention (Carnap, 1932 (1987)).

The Neurath-Carnap account of knowledge alarmed Schlick, who saw in it a threat to the very essence of EMPIRICISM; indeed, the claim that statements can be compared only with statements seemed to reactivate the coherence theory of truth which he believed would force us to consider any consistently fabricated tale to be true. Hence Schlick insisted on upholding a link between language and reality, which he saw was provided for by simultaneous reports of immediate experiences having the form of 'Here now blue': it is in these observation statements or 'affirmations' (*Konstatierungen*) that language and reality touch. Because of their immediacy the affirmations cannot be subjected to doubt, but for the same reason they are not, as protocol statements are, a basis on which scientific hypotheses can be erected. Thus they do not come at the beginning of knowledge, as Schlick put it, but rather at its end in that they complete our acts of confirmation and thereby prevent our fabric of knowledge from collapsing into mere coherentism (Schlick, 1934).

Thus within the Vienna circle (never really quite as monolithic as suggested, for instance, by the 1929 manifesto) deep-seated differences had matured: the 'conservative' absolutism defended by Schlick clashed head-on with the 'radical' Carnap – Neurath line of thought. Schlick's reaction to the latter provoked a series of articles in *Erkenntnis* and in the newly founded British journal *Analysis*. But while this debate on the foundation of knowledge was going on, the Vienna circle was already disintegrating as a group. In 1931 Herbert Feigl, a student of Schlick and a member of the circle from its beginning, had gone to the United States where he was to become a distinguished representative of logical empiricism. In 1934 the mathematician Hans Hahn, also a founding member, died. Carnap, who in 1931 had moved to Prague, went in 1935 to the United States. Moreover, the political climate grew hostile to the aspirations of the circle. In 1934 the so-called clerico-fascist regime in Austria, in the course of suppressing the Social Democratic Party, dissolved the Ernst Mach Society as a cooperating club of freethinkers, and Neurath emigrated to Holland. In 1936 Schlick was murdered by a demented student, which the government press presented as a fate not wholly undeserved by a positivist. Finally, the Nazi occupation of Austria in 1938 forced the majority of the remaining members into exile; Neurath fled in 1940 to England.

The Vienna circle had ceased to exist, but its philosophical heritage and its former members who carried on their work in the Anglo-Saxon world remained to exert a profound influence on the further development of Logical Empiricism and of scientific philosophy in general.

See also POSITIVISM; PHILOSOPHY OF SCIENCE; THEORY OF KNOWLEDGE.

Reading

Ayer, A.J. ed. 1959: *Logical Positivism*.
Carnap, R. 1934 (*1937*): *The Logical Syntax of Language*, trans. A. Smeaton.
—— 1963: Intellectual autobiography. In *The Philosophy of Rudolf Carnap*, ed. P.A. Schilpp.
—— 1928 (*1967*): *The Logical Structure of the World* and *Pseudo-problems in Philosophy*, trans. R.A. George.
Carnap, Rudolf, Hahn, H. and Neurath, O. 1929 (*1973*): Wissenschaftliche Weltauffassung: Der Wiener Kreis [The scientific conception of the world: the Vienna circle]. In O. Neurath, *Empiricism and Sociology*, ed. M. Neurath and R.S. Cohen.
Haller, R. 1988: *Questions on Wittgenstein*.
Hanfling, O. 1981: *Logical Positivism*.
—— ed. 1981: *Essential Readings in Logical Positivism*.
Joergensen, J. 1951 (*1970*): The development of logical empiricism. In *Foundations of the Unity of Science*, vol. 2, ed. O. Neurath, R. Carnap and C. Morris, new edn.
Schlick, M. 1918 (*1974*): *General Theory of Knowledge*, trans. A.E. Blumberg, introd. A.E. Blumberg and H. Feigl.
—— 1925–36 (*1979*): *Philosophical Papers*, vol. 2: *1925–1936*, ed. H.L. Mulder and B.F.B. van der Velde-Schlick.
Uebel, T.E. ed. 1991: *Rediscovering the Forgotten Vienna Circle*.

WERNER SAUER

violence There is no agreed, or non-controversial, definition of violence. The term is far too potent for that to be possible. Nevertheless, a commonsense understanding of the term is, roughly, that violence categorizes any physical assault on human beings carried out with the intention of causing them harm, pain or suffering. Similar assaults on other living beings are often also regarded as acts of violence. And it is common to speak also of violence against a certain category of things, namely private property.

The commonsense conception is by no means unproblematic. Consider, first, the question of intention. The stress on intention is important, since surgery and dentistry can both cause pain, and may involve the loss of bodily parts; but the sole proper purpose of these inflictions is the well-being of the patient. Torture, on the other hand, *is* a form of violence, since the suffering which is deliberately inflicted is at best for the benefit of someone or something other than the victim. But it would be wrong to make intention crucial to the definition; while vehicle drivers rarely intend to kill or maim, a traffic accident might well be described as an act, or at least an incident, of violence, especially if caused by culpable negligence or irresponsibility. More centrally, those responsible for both the planting and the dropping of bombs are apt to claim that their intention, or purpose, is only to destroy property, usually military targets of some kind. But since it is often unavoidable that people also are killed and wounded by these attacks, it would be implausible to suggest that these were *not* acts of violence against human beings, simply because their proclaimed purpose or intention was to attack things. If human suffering is an inevitable concomitant and consequence of these attacks, then those responsible are knowingly responsible for acts of violence.

Secondly, some commentators would argue that the definition or description offered above is crucially inadequate, since it is only illegal or unauthorized assaults on people which ought to be described as acts of violence. Such assaults, when carried out by, say, police in the course of their normal and necessary duties, or in the course of a recognized war, are properly described as acts of force, not violence. Thus the Oxford English Dictionary defines violence as the 'unlawful use of force'.

But the question of the legitimacy, moral or legal, of an action is something different from the nature of the act itself. Justified violence – and everyone except the total pacifist accepts that violence can sometimes be the lesser of two evils – is still violence. There is in any case no agreement as to which states or other organizations enjoy the legitimacy which is supposed to convert violence into the less harsh-sounding force.

Only, perhaps, in the case of property is legitimacy or legality a necessary element in the definition of violence. If I decide to destroy my own greenhouse, that would not be called an act of violence. But if others destroy it, against my will and without my permission, that might well be described as an act of violence against property. On the other hand, if, in a fit of rage, I hack to pieces a valuable painting that I own, people might well describe that as an act of violence, despite my legal right to destroy my own property.

A third problem is raised by the notion of 'physical assault'. It is well known that some of the most sophisticated forms of modern torture, which produce a complete disorientation of the senses and can cause lasting damage to the mind and brain, do not involve any direct physical assault on the victims. Somewhat similarly, aerial bombing involves no direct assault by individuals upon others. There is something odd about describing the act of pressing a button which releases a bomb or a missile as an act of violence.

But what these difficulties point to is simply the extent to which modern violence is mechanized and industrialized, while our typical ways of imagining violence or thinking about it are constructed in terms of direct confrontations between individuals or small groups. Such confrontations do, of course, take place, but they account for only a minute proportion of the deaths and injuries caused by deliberate attacks on human beings – the majority of which are carried out by states rather than by independent or illegal organizations or aggressive individuals.

Consequently, the search for the roots of violence in individual psychology is largely misconceived, except perhaps in the case of the murderer who acts on his or her own. The physical distance between those who inflict the death, pain and suffering, and those who are their victims, means that what organized large-scale killing and cruelty generally require is not cadres of sadists and thugs but persons trained in habits of obedience to established authority, who do not feel themselves to be responsible for their own actions. This guilt-free conformity is a mentality which can extend nearly to the top of the responsible organizations, as the Eichmann trial, among other cases, revealed.

If violence does not necessarily involve a direct, confrontational physical assault by some persons on others, then the distinction between violence and other coercive ways of inflicting injury, pain and death is blurred. A policy which either deliberately or knowingly leads to the deaths of people from starvation or disease might well be called a violent policy. This is one reason why slogans such as 'poverty is violence' or 'exploitation is violence' are not mere hyperbole. They raise the question of whether we can plausibly distinguish between ways of inflicting suffering and injury that are conventionally called violent, and those that are not.

They also raise the question of the evaluation of violence. Conventionally, violence is regarded as one of the worst of evils, if not *the* worst. Since, by definition, it involves the infliction of harm or suffering, it must always be an evil. But if equal or worse harm or suffering can be deliberately or knowingly inflicted by other means, usually regarded as non-violent, why should violence be regarded as so much worse than these other evils?

See also Coercion.

Reading

Ackroyd, Carol, Margolis, Karen, Rosenhead, Jonathan and Shallice, Tim 1977: *The Technology of Political Control*.

Arblaster, Anthony 1975: What is violence? In *Socialist Register 1975*, ed. Ralph Miliband and John Saville.

Arendt, Hannah 1970: *On Violence*.

—— 1977: *Eichmann in Jerusalem*.

Honderich, Ted 1980: *Violence for Equality*.

Milgram, Stanley 1974: *Obedience to Authority*.

Moore, Barrington Jr 1972: *Reflections on the Causes of Human Misery*.

Sorel, Georges 1906 (*1972*): *Reflections on Violence*.

Trotsky, Leon, Dewey, John, and Novack, George 1973: *Their Morals and Ours*.

ANTHONY ARBLASTER

W

---

war   The violent clash of organized social units that is war can be approached from several different perspectives. Anatol Rapoport (1968, p. 14) identifies three: the political, the cataclysmic and the eschatological. The first, exemplified by Clausewitz, and still current in the twentieth century, especially among strategists, treats war as a mode of COERCION, 'an act of violence intended to compel our opponent to fulful our will'. In an eschatological perspective, by contrast, war itself (including violent revolution) becomes the unfolding of some grand design: the weakening and overthrow of capitalism (for Marxists); the inauguration of the thousand-year domination of the world by the Third Reich (for the Nazis); or, later in the century, the revival of the Jehad, or Islamic Holy War, particularly as prompted by Iran's Ayatollah Khomeini. Adherents of such 'grand designs' tend to be undeterred by costs, often holding it to be a privilege to die for the cause and thus become part of one of the turning points of history.

The century's most distinctive philosophy of war has been the cataclysmic. Since World War I, in which nine million men were killed in battle, war has widely been seen as an affliction of human society, analogous to road accidents or epidemics. In this perspective, the task is to understand its causes so as to abolish it, or at least reduce its incidence and severity. For many exponents of this view the model was science, and its two pioneers were Lewis Fry Richardson (1960a and 1960b) and Quincy Wright (1942). Richardson's investigations of war, published in book form only posthumously, made extensive use of mathematics. One of his aims was to map the incidence of war objectively. He saw no firm basis for distinguishing between war and civil war, rebellion, mutiny, riot, or even murder, regarding them all as, essentially, 'deadly quarrels', which he graded by magnitude according to whether their death toll came geometrically closest to 1, 10, 100, 1,000, 10,000, 100,000, 1,000,000 or 10,000,000. Confining himself to those of magni-

tude 4 and above (317 or more deaths), he listed 289 such quarrels between 1820 and 1949.

Wright's contribution was to see modern war in perspective as a phenomenon, relating it to animal warfare, warfare among preliterate societies and historic warfare as manifest in literate civilizations up to the Renaissance. He also chronicled its fluctuations, in frequency and intensity. Overall, he emphasized the lag, globally and continentally, between the effects of technological progress and the adjustments, political, social and psychological, the human race makes to them.

World War II, and the rapidity with which it was followed by the confrontation of nuclear-armed alliances known as the Cold War, prompted much research inspired by the cataclysmic philosophy, for which the *Journal of Conflict Resolution*, launched in 1957, became a prominent focus. Waltz (1959) usefully classified all such efforts according to which of three images of international relations they presupposed, that is, whether they located the roots of war in 'the nature and behaviour of man' (p. 17); 'the internal organization of states' (p. 81); or 'the anarchic character of the states system' (p. 160). Since any set of states or other actors could, for analytical purposes, be regarded as a 'system', this third image could be extended to include all influences for war emanating from outside the warring pair; and a fourth image, the dyadic, might be discerned in accounts of war which emphasized the characteristics and patterns of interactions exhibited by the warring pair itself (the 'dyad'), *as a pair*.

First-image explanations of war tend to come from psychologists, psychiatrists, ethologists or, in more pessimistic vein, theologians. It has been seen as a reflection of individuals' need for, or proneness to, AGGRESSION; as a manifestation of territoriality; as a consequence of their ethnocentric attitudes and distorted perceptions (Klineberg, 1957); or of their unquestioning obedience to authority (Milgram, 1974). Of these, only the last contributes directly to explaining war, and the commission of atrocities under orders, in war and peace; and even it does not explain decisions to go to war, or to give such orders, should they be given. The others rest on the assumption that less aggressive and less psychologically immature populations tend to produce less war-prone governments, or at least control their governments' warlike propensities more effectively, than those more aggressive and immature. Granted the minor and often far from straightforward role foreign policy tends to play in national elections, the truth of this assumption may be doubted. Moreover, as Waltz shows, the insights of first-image explanations are not easily applied. Making a country's population, or a substantial segment of it, less aggressive or chauvinistic commonly requires governmental action, and thus takes the analysis into the realms of politics; unilateral psychological disarmament, he argues, is analogous to PACIFISM and could be as hazardous in its effects. Though Waltz here ignores the extent to which even societies whose governments would wish to keep them closed may still be open to transnational influence, this does not wholly invalidate his objection.

The personalities of individual leaders often seem to be influential in the genesis of war, as Hitler's no doubt was in that of World War II; but without analysing the political and social forces which afford such personalities the scope and the support they need to gain power it is hardly possible to guard against the emergence of equally disturbed leaders in the future. Clearly, there is a link between war and human nature, but it is tenuous, and only part of the story.

Second-image thinkers differ radically among themselves as to which types of state are more war-prone than others. Marxists attributed war, and indeed the very division of the world into states, to the essentially competitive nature of capitalism; both would disappear once the Revolution had succeeded. When Marxist revolutions, instead of merging, produced separate and sometimes mutually antagonistic regimes in different states, this claim became untenable.

Historical evidence emphatically supports an alternative second-image view, that liberal democratic states are less war-prone than dictatorships, at least in their relationships with one another. Doyle (1983) notes that there has not been a single instance of war between any two liberal states, though the use of force by the USA, albeit indirectly, to depose Chile's democratically elected Marxist government of Allende in 1973 comes close to constituting one. Liberal states, however, have certainly used force to create and retain empires or quasi-colonial domination, to resist revolutionary change, and to impose their will on their neighbours, amply justifying Doyle's qualification that despite its striking success in creating a zone of peace, liberalism 'has been equally striking as a failure in guiding foreign policy outside the liberal world' (p. 323).

War-proneness can also be seen as a consequence of features of a state's decision-making system, and particularly of that part of it concerned with foreign policy. Karl Deutsch's cybernetic approach is the outstanding example of this (see INTERNATIONAL RELATIONS). Others have claimed that, under conditions of economic depression or domestic political challenges, governments need, and search for, external enemies to sustain their power. Though much statistical investigation failed to corroborate the implied link between the internal and external conflict, Patrick James (1988) showed that if a state had recently experienced increases in domestic conflict, and then became involved in a crisis with a weaker state, it was more likely to go to war with it than one with no such recent experience of conflict at home.

The third image, as Waltz originally saw it, concentrated on the fact of international anarchy – the absence of government and enforceable law between states – as a permissive cause of war. As Claude (1962) showed, this is too simple a view. The existence of a government has not given Ethiopia, Lebanon or Sudan peace; nor has the absence of a common government put relations between Canada and the USA, or those between Norway and Sweden, under perpetual threat of war.

Subsequent 'third-image' explanations of war have been more subtle, aiming to delineate features of international systems affecting the incidence of war, often as part of a wider exploration of the properties of such systems. David Singer's massive 'Correlates of War' project at the University of Michigan (Ann Arbor) enabled hypotheses about the effects on war of such systemic features as polarization, the degree of concentration of power and the extent to which the states making up a system are aggregated into alliances to be rigorously tested against data for all wars falling within their definition between 1816 and 1965. E. H. Carr (1939) offered another plausible (though less rigorously tested) third-image explanation of war, contending that the international economic system of laissez-faire and multilateralism of the 1920s, by accentuating the weakness of the economically weaker, helped to spawn the bellicose nationalism of the 1930s then about to erupt into World War II.

The main types of 'fourth-image' explanations of war are aptly summarized in the title of another work of Rapoport's, *Fights, Games and Debates* (1960). In a 'fight', A's action to defend itself against B is seen by B as threatening, and vice versa. Richardson showed that this process can, on certain assumptions, explode into a runaway arms race, in which the first party, finding itself incapable of increasing its defences 'adequately', is likely to choose war before the ratio of forces turns irrevocably against it. 'Fight-like' escalation can also occur in a dispute where both parties come to have 'too much invested to quit' (see Teger, 1980).

To analyse war in terms of a 'game' implies that it is seen as a coldblooded option, chosen when advantageous. Though often, and sometimes fallaciously, used in the service of the political philosophy of war or military coercion, GAME THEORY can contribute to the understanding of war by helping to show why, in a given situation, it looks advantageous to one or both parties.

'Debates', that is, situations in which the parties differ strongly about what the world is like or what ought to be done, and where there are no agreed procedures for resolution or conflict management, can easily lead to war; the selectivity of perception involved in all learning tends to be reinforced, often mutually, by the 'blindness of involvement'.

Aspects of the first, second and fourth images can be incorporated in a formula suggested by Rosen (1970), who, in the spirit of game theory, characterized war as an instrument of decision; a party faced with a choice of having to yield on an issue or going to war over it will choose the latter if Ct times p exceeds C, where Ct is the party's 'cost-tolerance' for the issue in question, in other words how much it would be prepared to lose or suffer in order to get its way, p is a fraction representing its subjective probability of winning a war, were one to occur, and C the costs it would, in the event of war, actually expect to incur. Thus for 'rational' parties, the subjective values of p will be compatible (adding up

to 1) and the estimates of C realistic. War will be more likely if the issue is of high value for both sides and inherently unamenable to compromise (such as the regime to be installed in a third state, important to them both), the costs of war relatively light, or the outcome uncertain (a certain loser, if rational, would yield without a fight). Rosen's formula can then be linked to the first and second images, by supposing that given popular attitudes or moods, or a given internal political structure, may dispose one or both sides to overconfidence (overestimating p), overvaluation of a peripheral objective (unusually high Ct) or an unusual disregard of the costs of war, for instance when it is seen as paying political dividends domestically. What Rosen's model would not allow for is war by accident or by misinterpretation of an opponent's intentions.

The introduction of nuclear weapons and other means of wholesale destruction into war and war preparations has largely killed the glorification of all-out war among advanced states. It has not eliminated, indeed it has greatly enhanced the two possibilities omitted in Rosen's model; and now war, almost universally repudiated as a tool of policy, has taken more surreptitious forms, such as war by proxy or outside assistance to guerrilla movements (see GUERRILLA). Ironically, whereas in early twentieth-century explanations of war national sovereignty was often seen as the culprit, in the nuclear age much contemporary war is seen to flow from the weakness of states rather than from their strengths.

Reading
Aron, Raymond 1962 (*1966*): *Peace and War.*
Blainey, G. 1971: *The Causes of War.*
Doyle, M.W. 1983: Kant, liberal legacies, and foreign affairs. *Philosophy and Public Affairs* 12, 205–34, 323–52.
James, P. 1988: *Crisis and War.*
Ogley, R.C. 1991: *Conflict Under the Microscope.*
Rapoport, A. 1960: *Fights, Games and Debates.*
Rosen, S. 1970: A model of war and alliance. In *Alliance in International Politics*, ed. J.R. Friedman, C. Bladen and S. Rosen.
Singer, J.D. 1981: Accounting for international war: the state of the discipline. *Journal of Peace Research* 18, 1–18.
Singer, J.D. and Small, M. 1972: *The Wages of War.*
Waltz, K.N. 1959: *Man, the State and War.*
Wright, Q. 1942: *A Study of War.*

RODERICK C. OGLEY

war, guerrilla   *See* GUERRILLA

wealth In modern social thought, the economic concept of wealth – any PROPERTY that has a marketable value or an exchangeable value – has normally been treated as an important and fundamental dimension of social or economic inequality, and has often been discussed or employed by left-wing critics of capitalism or the existing social order. For Marxists, private concentrations of wealth-holding have been part and parcel of the process of bourgeois class control of the means of production, distribution and exchange, and Marxists have generally viewed the question of wealth-holding in the context of the class ownership of productive capital, downplaying other forms of wealth-holding. Non-marxist radicals like R. H. Tawney (1880–1962) and Anthony Crosland (1918–77) have placed greater stress on the role of wealth-holding, especially significant concentrations of inherited wealth, in maintaining political and social inequality in modern capitalist societies. A third stream represented by social scientists like Thorstein Veblen (1857–1929), Joseph Schumpeter (1882–1950) and C. Wright Mills (1916–62) have examined the social category of wealthy persons, particulary those with substantial inherited wealth. Veblen was the first to highlight the vulgar display of 'conspicuous consumption' among the wealthy; Schumpeter examined the allegedly deleterious effects of inherited wealth on entrepreneurial ability among the scions of 'self-made men'; Mills formulated the concept of the 'power elite' to encompass the overlap in personnel between big business, the government, the military, and other elements he discerned in post-1945 America.

Economists and others working from a neoclassical or Keynesian framework have increasingly examined questions of the concentration and distribution of income and wealth from aspects of relevance to social theory. In the 1950s Simon Kuznets put forward the theory – apparently verified by later researchers like Lee Soltow, Jeffrey Williamson and Peter Lindert – that the concentration of income (and, by implication, of wealth) in private hands becomes more unequal during and just after the period of a nation's industrialization, and then becomes increasingly equalized (in contrast to classical Marxist theory). For Britain, empirical research has revealed that the maximum maldistribution of incomes came in the period between about 1870 and 1914, and that income has become progressively less unequally distributed since World War I. The degree of concentration of wealth-holding (as measured by probate records) has followed that of incomes in becoming more equal, after, apparently, the time-lag of a generation. Whether this has occurred because of 'natural' economic processes – the creation of an affluent mass consumer society – or specifically because of redistributionist taxation measures and trade union activities remains unclear.

Social historians have also increasingly examined the rich as a social category as well as the evolution of wealth-holding in modern societies, chiefly by means of probate and other taxation records which allow the identity and wealth level of deceased persons to be learned. The debate on the 'rise of the gentry' in early modern England carried on by R. H. Tawney, Lawrence Stone, J. H. Hexter, Hugh Trevor-Roper and others has examined the economic fortunes of the aristocracy and gentry of Britain from 1500 to 1700 in detail. A comprehensive examination of the probate records of wealthy persons in Britain since 1800, undertaken by W. D. Rubinstein, has shown that far more wealth was earned in finance and commerce, especially in the City of London, than in manufacturing in Britain's industrial heartland; this has led to a debate on the implications of 'capitalism divided' by geography in Britain. Other studies of the English middle classes employing similar sources, by Leonore Davidoff, Catherine Hall and Robert Morris, have appeared, in addition to an ever-growing literature on the wealthy in the United States, France, Germany and elsewhere.

Reading
Daumard, Adeline 1973: *Les Fortunes françaises au XIXe siècle.*
Davidoff, Leonore and Hall, Catherine 1986: *Family Fortunes.*
Lundberg, Ferdinand 1968: *The Rich and the Super-Rich.*
Mills, C. Wright 1956: *The Power Elite.*
Pessen, Edward 1973: *Riches, Class and Power before the Civil War.*
—— ed. 1974: *Three Centuries of Social Mobility in America.*
Rubinstein, W.D. 1986: *Wealth and Inequality in Britain.*
—— ed. 1980: *Wealth and the Wealthy in the Modern World.*
Schumpeter, Joseph 1942 (*1987*): *Capitalism, Socialism, and Democracy.*
Stone, Lawrence and Stone, Jeanne Fawtier 1984: *An Open Elite? England 1540–1880.*
Veblen, Thorstein 1899 (*1953*): *The Theory of the Leisure Class.*

W.D. RUBINSTEIN

welfare economics In choosing between alternative policy options, value judgements are inescapable; welfare economics is the analysis of value judgements in the context of economic decision-making.

In managing an economy, choices have to be made all the time. It is natural to try to ensure that these choices spring from the same consistent set of judgements about VALUES or criteria of SOCIAL WELFARE. Through most of this century, the welfare criterion which economics adhered to was the one associated with the name of Vilfredo Pareto (Pareto, 1897). A *Pareto improvement* for a society is a change which leaves everyone at least as well off as before and one or more persons actually better off. A *Pareto optimal* state is one from which no further Pareto improvements are possible.

One advantage of the Pareto criterion is that it does not depend on interpersonal comparisons. No judgement by this criterion depends on whether the gain of person a is greater or less than the gain of person b. This advantage is, however, earned at the cost of widespread reticence. A policy measure that gives a destitute 100 dollars and leaves a millionaire poorer by one dollar is not something that can be recommended or rejected on Paretian grounds (assuming that the millionaire does perceive the one dollar loss, no matter how minutely).

Not suprisingly, a large part of welfare economics has been concerned with developing more sophisticated approaches for ranking social states. A seminal work towards this was a paper published by Abram Bergson (1938) and further developed by Paul Samuelson (1947). The Bergson-Samuelson approach requires that a society's social welfare be a function of the level of utility enjoyed by each individual in it. Depending on our normative inclinations, we could insist that the function satisfies certain properties. For instance, we could require it to be Pareto *inclusive*. That is, if someone's utility rises and no-one's falls, the level of social welfare must register a rise. One could be more demanding and require that social welfare be the sum of every individual's utility level. This would be equivalent to utilitarianism, espoused in the eighteenth century by Jeremy Bentham.

An intermediate line, developed by John Hicks, Nicholas Kaldor and others, describes a change as an improvement if the beneficiaries from the change can compensate the losers and still retain some positive benefits. This rule has been widely used for real national income comparisons and

cost–benefit analysis but its conceptual basis has come under serious attack. If the beneficiaries, it has been argued, do not actually compensate the losers, then how does it help to know that they *can* do so? And, if they do actually compensate, the Pareto criterion itself will describe the change as desirable; why do we need another rule?

In more recent times welfare economics has received a big boost from the discovery of a theorem of gigantic proportions – Kenneth Arrow's (1951) general impossibility theorem (see SOCIAL CHOICE). Instead of fixing a particular social welfare function, Arrow wrote down some extremely reasonable looking axioms which we would want a social welfare function to satisfy. The general impossibility theorem asserts that these axioms cannot be satisfied together.

A large literature emerged to 'solve' the problem. But even as this literature trundled on, other impossibility theorems, such as Amartya Sen's (1970) influential liberty paradox, kept emerging. More importantly, post-Arrovian welfare economics became a corridor for the meeting of economics and moral philosophy. Questions of individual rights and freedoms could now be taken up in economics. The work of Amartya Sen, for instance, was straddling the formal framework used by welfare economists and the conceptual one of moral philosophers such as John Rawls and Robert Nozick. Welfare economics has also enriched down-to-earth activities such as cost–benefit analysis, poverty and inequality measurement, and public policy making.

Reading
Atkinson, A.B. 1983: *Social Justice and Public Policy*.
Graaf, J. de V. 1957: *Theoretical Welfare Economics*.
Nozick, R. 1974: *Anarchy, State and Utopia*.
Rawls, J. 1971: *A Theory of Justice*.
Sen, A. 1982: *Choice, Welfare and Measurement*.

KAUSHIK BASU

welfare, social *See* SOCIAL WELFARE

welfare state Originating in Britain and often loosely used, the term became widely current both in journalistic and academic circles after World War II. It purported to describe a state which, in contrast to the 'night watchman state' of the nineteenth century, concerned primarily with the protection of property, or the 'power state' of the twentieth century, concerned primarily during

World War II with total victory, would use the apparatus of government to devise, implement and finance policies designed to promote the collective social interests of its members. It would destroy what William Beveridge, who did not like the term, called the five giant evils of want, disease, ignorance, squalor and idleness. The state would in future intervene deliberately to limit or to modify the consequences of the free operation of market forces in circumstances where individuals and families were confronted with social contingencies deemed to be largely beyond their control, notably unemployment, sickness and old age. It would be more, however, than what had come to be called before World War II 'a social service state', for in relation to an agreed range of social services, particularly those concerned with health and education, it would offer comprehensively to all citizens the best services that were available without distinction of status or class. Through taxation there would therefore be a redistributive aspect to it.

The origins of the welfare state have been traced back to the creation of state-provided 'social services' in the aftermath of nineteenth-century industrialization, with particular emphasis being placed on Bismarckian Germany and on early twentieth-century Britain. There were obviously many different, even contrasting, strands in the story, including conservative paternalism, 'new liberalism', Fabian and some other brands of socialism and, not least, feminism. Yet it was when citizens were mobilized during World War II and there was a close association between warfare and welfare that social services ceased to be considered as a form of poor relief. There was a large measure of potential consensus also – then and after the war – that the change was for the good, so that by 1949 a British Conservative Party manifesto, *The Right Road for Britain*, stated that the services constituted 'a co-operative system of mutual aid and self-help provided by the whole nation and designed to give all the basic minimum of security, of housing, of opportunity, of employment and of living standards below which our duty to one another forbids us to permit any one to fall'.

The academic case for the welfare state was put most trenchantly by the sociologist T. H. Marshall, who argued that whereas social service policies had hitherto been thought of as remedial policies to deal bit by bit with the basement of society not with its upper floors, it had now begun to remodel the whole building. The welfare state was the culmination of a long process which had begun with the affirmation of civil rights, had led through to a struggle for political rights, and had ended with the identification and establishment of social rights. Marshall believed that in explaining the rise of the welfare state it was more important to focus on the extension of the ideal of CITIZENSHIP than on the increase in the scope of state power.

This was a British perspective, and the term 'welfare state' neither commanded consensus in all other countries, notably the United States, nor always carried with it agreeable historical resonances, notably in Germany, with its long history of *sozialpolitik*. The term could always be used pejoratively as well as favourably as could the separate words within it – 'welfare' and 'state'. Yet the concept came to be thought of as universal outside communist countries even in regions that had not undergone large-scale industrialization. While the 'complete welfare state' did not exist, Piet Thoenes, a Dutch sociologist, wrote in 1962, 'elements of it' could be found in 'a more isolated form' in present-day France, Italy, West Germany and the United States. A slightly fuller list would have included Sweden and New Zealand.

During World War II an International Labour Conference at Philadelphia had noted the 'deep desire' of people everywhere 'to free themselves from fear of want' and had claimed that after the war the relevance of the phrase 'international society' would be judged 'in terms of human benefit and welfare'; and six years later in 1950 the International Labour Office recorded that there had by then been 'a movement everywhere' to create 'a new organisation for social security, which can be described only as a public service for the citizens at large'.

Already by the end of the 1950s, however, there was ample evidence of the problems associated with welfare state economics and politics and of the beginnings of academic critiques of the concept itself both from left and right. In 1951, for example, the British Labour government placed ceilings on welfare spending and introduced charges on the cost of false teeth and spectacles; and in a collection of essays published in 1958 Richard Titmuss, who had made a detailed study of shifts in British social policy during World War II, claimed that postwar policies, which had not reached a point of finality, had benefited the middle classes more than any other section of the community.

During the next ten years the critique both of the concept and of the practice was sharpened as management issues were spotlighted and as the economic basis of comprehensive welfare expenditures was threatened. Threat changed into reaction during the 1970s as inflation drove up expenditures and efforts were made to cut public spending. The result was the so-called 'crisis of the welfare state'. It was a crisis of values as well as of finance or management. In the words of a British Green Paper on Social Security (1988), 'State provision has an important role in supporting and sustaining the individual; but it should not discourage self-reliance or stand in the way of individual provision or responsibility.'

See also SOCIAL PLANNING.

Reading

Beveridge, W. 1943: *The Pillars of Security*.
Birch, R.C. 1974: *The Shaping of the Welfare State*.
Clarke, J., Cochrane, A. and Smart, C. eds 1987: *Ideologies of Welfare: From Dreams to Disillusion*.
Jallade, J.P. ed. 1988: *The Crisis of Redistribution in European Welfare States*.
Marshall, T.H. 1950 (*1992*): *Citizenship and Social Class*.
Mishra, R. 1984: *The Welfare State in Crisis: Social Thought and Action*.
Mommsen, W.J. ed. 1981: *The Emergence of the Welfare State in Britain and Germany*.
Thoenes P. 1962 (*1966*): *The Elite in the Welfare State*.
Titmuss, R.M. 1958: *Essays on the Welfare State*.

ASA BRIGGS

Weltanschauung In German the word refers literally to an intuitive 'view' or 'outlook' (*Anschauung*) on the 'world' (*Welt*), hence to 'world-views' or the underlying value or cultural principles which define the philosophy of life or conception of the world of a particular society or group. Popularly in English the concept has been used to refer to any general belief system (Christian, liberal, pagan and so on). Though world-views so identified are most typically non-rational in origin and linked to the shared experiences of a group, the term has also been employed to refer to generalized scientific perspectives (for example, Darwinian or Marxist). In social scientific contexts use of the concept has been influenced since the 1920s by the SOCIOLOGY OF KNOWLEDGE, which attempts to explain the origins of world-views in relation to the social locations and interests of actors. In its original, late nineteenth-century German context, however, the notion of a 'theory of world-views' (*Weltanschauungslehre*) was identified

with a theory of the 'human sciences' which rejected the reduction of cultural phenomena to their social causes. Today the term *Weltanschauung* remains useful as a loose designation for general conceptions of the world, but no longer plays a significant part in technical discussions in philosophy or the sociology of culture; nevertheless, the problematic to which it refers touches on many of the key issues of contemporary cultural theory.

Weltanschauung theory is associated with the late nineteenth-century tradition of HISTORICISM, especially Wilhelm Dilthey's theory of the human sciences (*Geisteswissenschaften*) (see Dilthey, 1931, pp. 133–54). Based on an essentially empathetic conception of interpretation or VERSTEHEN (which influenced sociology through Max Weber and psychiatry through the work of Karl Jaspers), Dilthey's hermeneutic theory (see HERMENEUTICS) of cultural totalities stressed the non-rational origins of world-views in deeper aesthetic and religious impulses in 'life', and thus opposed any reductive, materialist explanation of their social genesis. He also tried unsuccessfully to overcome the relativistic implications (see RELATIVISM) of the plurality of competing world-views.

From the turn of the century the rise of sociology in Germany challenged Dilthey's approach to the human sciences by suggesting that world-views could not be interpreted independently of their social origins. In the 1920s, Karl Mannheim (1952) redefined the debate in methodological terms by proposing a hermeneutic sociology of knowledge which criticized the theory of world-views from the perspective of a general conception of IDEOLOGY which avoided the dogmatism of orthodox Marxism but remained relativistic in its implications. In France in the 1950s, Lucien Goldmann (1956) developed a sociology of literature in which 'world-visions' (*visions du monde*) were analysed from the perspective of their homologous relation to class structures.

Most recently, Jürgen Habermas (1968) has traced the failure of Dilthey's approach to an objectivistic hermeneutics rooted in an untenable, irrational vitalism. Habermas's own version of critical theory (see FRANKFURT SCHOOL) represents the most ambitious attempt to resolve the historicist problem of relativism. His argument, influenced by developmental psychology and structuralism, is based in part on an analysis of the evolution of what has been translated as 'world-views' (1976, pp. 95–129), though in the original

German reference is made to 'world-pictures' (*Weltbilder*), apparently to avoid any association with Dilthey's approach.

Reading
Hekman, S.J. 1986: *Hermeneutics and the Sociology of Knowledge*.
Jay, M. 1984: *Marxism and Totality*.
Makkreel, R.A. 1975: *Dilthey: Philosopher of the Human Studies*.
Mannheim, K. 1929 (*1960*): *Ideology and Utopia*.
Outhwaite, W. 1975 (*1986*): *Understanding Social Life: The Method Called Verstehen*, 2nd edn.
Rickman, H.P. 1988: *Dilthey Today: A Critical Appraisal of the Contemporary Relevance of his Work*.
Simonds, A.P. 1978: *Karl Mannheim's Sociology of Knowledge*.

RAYMOND A. MORROW

Western Marxism   This form of Marxist theory is generally thought to encompass such diverse authors as Georg Lukács, Ernst Bloch, Karl Korsch, Antonio Gramsci, members of the FRANKFURT SCHOOL, French thinkers from Jean-Paul Sartre in his later work to Louis Althusser and the earlier part of the still evolving work of Jürgen Habermas. As such it spans a body of theorizing begun around 1920 and ending around 1970. It never meant simply Marxism in the West, or Marxism from the West opposing Marxist orthodoxy in the USSR. Neither a Trotskyist theorist such as Ernest Mandel nor the well-known dissenter Rudolf Bahro are 'Western Marxists' in the philosophical sense. On the other hand, many neo-Marxist enterprises affirmed since the 1960s, such as the revisionist history of Perry Anderson (1976), the Sraffian (that is, neo-Ricardian) left economics of the Cambridge school and the 'analytical Marxism' of Jon Elster and John Roemer should be included under the rubric of Western Marxism.

What, then, is the *differentia specifica* of Western Marxism? The best way to approach the matter is to look at the historical context of its ideas. It was first and foremost a repudiation of the Marxism of the Second (Socialist) International. Marxist theory after the death of Marx had taken an increasingly determinist stance. From the 1890s the doctrine arose that objective economic laws were the driving force of history and that consciousness was but a reflection of physical and social reality. In the 1920s these notions were still upheld by such influential theorists as Karl Kautsky and Nikolai Bukharin, as indeed they were, in some contexts, by Lenin

himself. But they were passionately challenged by young Leninists in the West: Lukács, Bloch, Korsch and Gramsci. The latter went so far as to hail the communist rise to power in 1917 as 'a revolution against *Capital*', by which he meant that it had been a triumph of history against historical determinism.

Gramsci's phrase evinced the main motivation of Western Marxism's revolts against the Second International: impatient radicalism, lit by the 'light of October' and dictated by messianic hopes of human (and not just social) redemption through revolution. Politically speaking the founders of Western Marxism – the above mentioned quartet – marched from various forms of far leftism, such as anarcho-syndicalism or council communism, into Leninist discipline, the eventual position of both Lukács and Gramsci, however diversely defined. Leninist politics was dropped only much later, in the postwar Frankfurt school and its chief heir and reformer, Habermas.

Originally, Western Marxism was political Leninism without the crude determinist materialism of Leninist-Stalinist philosophy. It soon unfolded a humanist epistemology, insisting on the contrast (alien to Marx, Engels, Kautsky and Lenin alike) between *critique* and (social) science. It no longer conceived Marxist analysis as a critique of bourgeois economics but as an *alternative* to the scientific standpoint – proud of its full-blown *dialectic*. Both Kautsky and Bukharin had tacitly reshaped Marxism as a naturalist historical sociology more attached to evolutionism than to dialectics, and hence closer to Ernst Haeckel than to Hegel. But the initiators of Western Marxism were all neo-idealists, as steeped in Fichte and, above all, Hegel as the Austro-Marxists (see AUSTRO-MARXISM) had been in Kant, and their philosophical cast of mind was strongly reminiscent of the left Hegelianism of the 1830s and 1840s.

The rediscovery of idealist sources went along with borrowings from bourgeois culture, and while the young Lukács owed much to Georg Simmel, Wilhelm Dilthey and Max Weber, Gramsci was influenced by Benedetto Croce and the Italian elite theorists, and the Frankfurt school thinkers blended the theme of alienation with Nietzschean elements, Freudian perspectives and modernist motifs. As for French Marxism, the shadow of Heidegger loomed large in its background. This eclecticism worked in an idealist spirit, and more often than not was applied to the analysis of cultural rather than politico-economic problems (though Gramsci specialized in *political* culture). So much so, that the greater part of Western Marxism may be said to be a *Marxism of the superstructure* (see BASE AND SUPERSTRUCTURE). Lukács, Walter Benjamin, Theodor Adorno and Sartre are among the outstanding literary critics and aestheticians of our age. The conjunction of cultural subject matter and humanist epistemology brings Western Marxism close to the hermeneutic tradition as a neo-idealist search for meanings rather than causes, and most of it is intentionally interpretive rather than explanatory.

A last general aspect of Western Marxism (remarkably absent, though, from Korsch, Gramsci or Althusser) was the *animus against modern civilization*. The young Lukács, Bloch and most notably the Frankfurt school injected into Marxism a strong dose of *Kulturkritik*, a principled, doctrinaire and wholesale refusal of the culture of MODERNITY. They were deeply uneasy about industrialism, indifferent to liberal democracy, and quite hostile to science and technology. Such an ideological syndrome was by no means prevalent in prior departures, however bold, from classical Marxism, as in the *fin-de-siècle* revisionism of Eduard Bernstein, or somewhat later in the thought of Georges Sorel or the seminal researches of the Austro-Marxists. Now Marx himself – like Hegel – was a great admirer of modernity, so that Western Marxism in this respect represents a huge reversal of historical outlook within the Marxist camp. The logic of history thesis, like materialism, went by the board.

Western Marxism was born in book form with the essays collected by Lukács in *History and Class Consciousness* (as a justification of Lenin's revolution) and in Korsch's *Marxism and Philosophy*, both published in 1923. The conceptual hero of both books is a social subject, the revolutionary consciousness of the proletariat. Objectification simply mirrors the subject's acts: thus while reification (bad objectification) reflects the bad subject, that is, capitalism and bourgeois culture, the revolutionary paradise will ensue once the proletariat attains a grasp of totality. The 'point of view of totality' is to Lukács the very essence of Marxism, far more important than 'economic themes'. The sense of totality is a conscious PRAXIS, and totality as praxis is self-activated – it is a historical subject, a source of global historical meaning. And the root meaning of the present is revolutionary because alienated labour directly perceives reification, that is, dehumanization, as the soul of capitalism.

In fact the proletariat may or may not exhibit totality-consciousness; but if it does not, no matter, for Lukács thought there was a 'collective will destined to bring real freedom into being' – the Communist Party. Lukács's earlier work had shown an ethical mystique as a way out of decadence, and in embracing Marxism he preserved a messianic moralism. Max Weber, who befriended him in Heidelberg, described him as a quintessential case of the 'ethic of conviction', far removed from responsible realism. Revolution became almost severed from material concerns while communism was made to embody a lofty idea of culture as the realm of meaningful life. As the older Lukács himself acknowledged, the whole work was suffused with 'romantic anti-capitalism'.

The romance between Marxism and *Kulturkritik* went on among Lukács's heirs, the Frankfurt philosophers Max Horkheimer and Theodor Adorno. Their joint book, *Dialectic of Enlightenment* (1947) was the second gospel of Western Marxism. Horkheimer's programme was 'social philosophy': an empirically minded theorizing, yet different from 'positivist' social science in its Lukácsian commitment to 'grasping the whole'. But the Frankfurt thinkers relinquished Lukács's utopianism as well as his metaphysics of the subject and with it the myth of the revolutionary proletariat. In the 1940s they studied anti-Semitism in connection with fascism and the 'authoritarian personality', and after the war they eschewed class analysis, concentrating on a sweeping indictment of modern culture as a 'betrayal of reason'. Instrumental reason (science) was accused of exchanging emancipation for repression in the instinctual, Freudian sense, and the role of 'critical theory' became a kind of pessimistic resistance against mass culture as well as against both capitalism and socialism. Subsequently, these two regimes would be equated as repressive 'one-dimensional' forms of society by Herbert Marcuse. In the hands of Adorno, dialectics became the epitome of an arcane Marxism, in his *Negative Dialectics*, 1966). A strange 'Marxism without the proletariat' emerged, devoid of class struggle and historical optimism. Horkheimer's end was a return to Schopenhauer and to religion.

However, Western Marxist radicalism was not dead. Already the gifted essayist Walter Benjamin had combined or alternated a radical politics with an irrationalist epistemology and the utmost historical pessimism, undisguised in his 'Theses on the philosophy of history' (1939–40, in Benjamin, 1955). In the 1960s, while Jean-Paul Sartre attempted a fusion of existentialism with Marxism, Marcuse began to flirt with student rebelliousness and countercultural movements. The Frankfurt school exiles had turned Western Marxism into one more romanticism of despair; Sartre and Marcuse were determined to rekindle it as a romanticism of revolt.

The next wave, of structuralist Marxism (see STRUCTURALISM) led by Louis Althusser, reacted sharply against the primacy of consciousness in Lukács and Sartre but ended by producing a highly scholastic fundamentalism around the ideal of history as science. Two neo-Marxist developments – the Anglo-French debate on modes of production and the Anglo-German one on the nature of the capitalist state – started as derivations from Althusserian categories. Politically speaking, while Sartre and Marcuse were 'gauchistes', the Althusserians were often Maoists and Althusser himself was one of the last Marxists to renounce the dictatorship of the proletariat.

Gramsci was very different, and his *Prison Notebooks*, written from 1929 to 1935, contain superb if necessarily sketchy pieces of political sociology, subtly analysing the interplay between political change and class structure. Gramsci's remarks on class hegemony and class blocs, on kinds of revolution and modernization, and on the role of intellectuals, are refreshingly free of the crude economic determinism of vulgar Marxism without falling into the arid theoreticism of much Western Marxism. While sharing their distaste for determinism and historicism, he was unlike the German thinkers in being quite free of their *Kulturkritik* pathos; and though a Leninist, he tried earnestly to move communism in a non-sectarian, proto-democratic direction by blending socialism and popular culture. His positions were to inspire Eurocommunism half a century after his death following his imprisonment by the fascist regime.

Both a democratic spirit and the supersession of *Kulturkritik* also distinguish the copious writings of the leading thinker in the second generation of the Frankfurt school, Jürgen Habermas. The gist of his reconstruction of critical theory is an attempt to secure knowledge as emancipation through communicative ethics: 'The paradigm is no longer observation but dialogue.' Critical theory undergoes a 'linguistic turn' similar to the later Wittgenstein or the hermeneutics of Gadamer. But unlike these authors Habermas is no relativist – in fact, he is nowadays the main challenger of the arch-relativist, sceptical thought of poststructuralist thinkers such as Michel Foucault, Jacques Derrida and J.F. Lyotard. In his recent work (1981), Western Marxism, having abandoned the last vestiges of class struggle, dissolves into an encyclopaedic neo-evolutionism centred on the macrohistory of 'communicative action'.

Reading
Anderson, Perry 1976: *Considerations on Western Marxism.*
Geuss, Raymond 1981: *The Idea of a Critical Theory: Habermas and the Frankfurt School.*
Held, David 1980: *Introduction to Critical Theory: Horkheimer to Habermas.*
Jacoby, Russell 1981: *Dialectic of Defeat: Contours of Western Marxism.*
Jay, Martin 1973: *The Dialectical Imagination: A History of the Frankfurt School and the Institute of Social Research, 1923–1950.*
Merquior, J.G. 1986: *Western Marxism.*

J.G. MERQUIOR

women's movement Evoking a collectivity of women who mobilize to protest or to pursue shared goals, the description is often used coterminously with feminist movement, but women's movements pre-date and may be distinct from FEMINISM. They are social movements which display a heterogeneity of goals, and associational or organizational forms (see also SOCIAL MOVEMENT).

Women's movements have emerged in all regions of the world and are mentioned in most periods of documented history. The Qur'an refers to an uprising of women in South Arabia who, according to scholars, were protesting against Mohammed's ban on women trading. The history of colonial Latin America and Africa contains instances of female slave revolts and of peasant women rebelling against the laws or practices of the imperial state or mobilizing to defend their economic interests. In eighteenth-century Europe, women formed their own associations, some of which participated in the French revolution. Later, in the revolutionary turmoil of the 1840s, women's movements developed and a women's rights newspaper, *Les Voix des Femmes* (Women's Voices), was founded. Although there were comparatively few of these early movements, and they remained isolated and sporadic, their incidence, size and momentum grew in the nineteenth and twentieth centuries as civil society developed and as the constraints inhibiting women from entering social and political life weakened.

It was in the nineteenth century that women in many regions of the world began to organize against inequalities based on sex and to demand legal reforms aimed at removing patriarchal controls over women in the family and in society at large. Some of these initiatives were by independent individuals or groups, some were worked out in association with broader movements for social change, some with political parties. Ideas of women's emancipation were attractive in particular to those inspired by the ideas of the Enlightenment. Liberal, socialist and modernizing nationalist movements were important forces supporting legal and social changes in the position of women and drew many women activists into their ranks. For all their ideological differences, they shared a broad commitment to building a modern society in which the traditional structures of patriarchal society and state forms associated with the oppression of women would be replaced by a more rational, just and egalitarian form of civil administration.

Although feminist ideas and writings can be found in earlier centuries, it was also in the nineteenth century that feminism first emerged as an influential ideological and political force. The term feminist was used by women's rights campaigners not only in the USA and Europe, but also in countries such as Japan, Turkey, Russia, Argentina, the Philippines and India. Although diverse in its goals and strategies and therefore open to a variety of interpretations, feminism in different regional and cultural contexts was associated with a commitment to ending sexual inequality and emancipating women from oppression. The early feminist movements, like the Philippine Feminist Association founded in 1905 or Seito (Blue Stocking) established in Japan in 1911, campaigned for the vote and access to education, while they opposed discrimination based on sex and sought to improve the legal situation of women. These women's associations pursued their aims from a variety of different vantage points. Some, like the Persian Women's Society of 1911, confronted entrenched religious laws and attitudes; others worked within the context of liberal states for greater legal equality and the vote; and still others linked their struggle for equality with socialist revolution. In the less developed regions of the

world such as Turkey, India, China and Egypt, feminist associations saw their interests represented within the project of a modernizing nationalism, while others remained independent from political parties, committed to a more radical interpretation of women's liberation, one which went beyond equal rights to embrace questions of sexuality and interpersonal relations.

The history of feminism falls into two broad periods. The 'first wave', as it is sometimes called, is that of the period 1860 to 1920. It is represented above all by equal rights and reform movements, the largest and most successful of which were those of the United States and Britain. The first North American women's rights convention was held on the 19–20 July 1848 in Seneca Falls and is sometimes taken as the founding moment of Western feminism. In Britain, first-wave feminism achieved its most significant mobilization in the early twentieth century with the struggles to achieve female suffrage, eventually won in 1918.

The second period of feminism's greatest organizational strength began in the late 1960s. It grew out of the climate of student radicalism in Europe, and in the USA was part of the civil rights movement. Second-wave feminism built on the insights of earlier theorists such as Simone de Beauvoir and generated a greater diversity of theoretical approaches, goals and strategies than its predecessors. The feminist movements of this period are conventionally divided into two main currents; one, typified as a reform movement, was concerned chiefly with obtaining equal rights and removing discrimination against women; the other, characterized as the women's liberation tendency, was concerned with achieving a more radical programme of social change, and contained radical and revolutionary currents. While the former current, typical of the dominant trend in the United States, was associated with a greater integration and influence on the political system and the achievement of a substantial range of legal reforms, the latter, more characteristic of the European movements, was more critical of reformist measures, and advocated local self-help initiatives within an anti-elitist and decentralized associational form. Both varieties, however, shared a common perspective on some issues and certain goals, and in both cases the campaign for free abortion on demand became as important a mobilizing issue as suffrage had been to first-wave feminists.

Second-wave feminism was one of the most

important social movements of the postwar period and was capable of mobilizing large numbers of women. By 1985, the reformist National Organization of Women (NOW) in the USA had a membership of a quarter of a million, while in Britain, Italy and France, demonstrations of women campaigning on specific issues could reach three-quarters of a million. Beyond the Anglo Saxon world, feminists also began to organize from the early 1970s onwards; feminist groups emerged in Yugoslavia, Mexico, Peru, India and even in the USSR. Some of these initiatives developed into significant social movements in the 1980s.

It is only comparatively recently, following the advent of 'second-wave feminism', that women's movements have begun to receive scholarly attention. Analysts of political phenomena such as urban social movements, revolutions and popular uprisings tended to focus their attention on class dynamics and largely ignored conflict along gender and ethnic lines. As a result they rarely acknowledged the presence of women in these movements or considered the specific characteristics imparted by their participation and by women's own independent organizational efforts. Feminist historians and social scientists were committed to redressing this absence in order to recover what, in Sheila Rowbotham's phrase, had been 'hidden from history'.

The growing interest in women's movements has generated studies of the various types of female collective action which have occurred and this has revealed the breadth of political activity engaged in by women. This has ranged from spontaneous protest movements of various kinds, to feminist equal rights campaigns, and in the 1980s to conservative or fundamentalist mobilizations of women in the USA and in the Islamic world. Such a variety of mobilizations has demonstrated that women have not only been significant political actors, but have also mobilized collectively in pursuit of a wide variety of goals: sometimes the priority was to achieve greater sexual equality; at other times it was to support broader political objectives; and at still other times it was to support legal changes which, on religious grounds, called for a redefinition and, sometimes, as in the case of anti-abortionist movements, a restriction of their previous rights.

This work of discovery has led to a reappraisal of women's political participation and has helped to undermine the commonly held view that women are not political actors and that their proper sphere of influence is within the natural domain of the private sphere. While feminist scholars have acknowledged the masculinization of political space and the historical exclusion of women from it, they have also pointed out that feminism has expanded the meaning of politics itself to include resistance and confrontation over power relations both within the private realm and in society at large. In general, the analysis of women's movements has prompted some writers to propose that they represent above all informal challenges to mainstream politics. Like other 'new social movements', the challenge presented by women's movements is also to orthodox conceptions of the proper content and domain of politics, encapsulated in the feminist slogan, 'the personal is political'.

The variety and character of women's movements have posed a number of as yet unresolved analytic issues. The first concerns the need to differentiate between the various degrees of social (collective) action such that *movement* signifies a qualitative and quantitative advance over forms of solidarity or association that may be small in scale, dispersed and relatively powerless. These latter forms which might arise on the basis of a self-conscious 'women's culture' include networks, clubs, and literary circles. While these may mark the beginning of a movement or form a part of it, they are analytically distinct from it with regard to numerical strength, organizational power and social impact.

A second issue has been that of whether feminism can or should generate goals which can have a universal application. Virginia Woolf wrote: 'As a woman I have no country.' As a woman I have no need of a country'. Robin Morgan's slogan of the 1970s, 'Sisterhood is Global', was criticized by black and Third World feminists for assuming that women of all classes and from all regions necessarily shared common interests and bonds of solidarity. They argued for a more differentiated view of women's interests as being shaped by factors such as class and ethnicity, in ways which could lead to relations of domination and subordination between women. It followed that feminism's goals would be subject to some variation, and different movements formulated their priorities accordingly. While such a recognition need not deny that some basis for collective action and common goals could be worked out, it meant that solidarity among women was not given by the fact of gender alone.

Although the diversity of feminist struggles

within a given country or region of the world makes simple generalizations misleading, certain differences have marked out Western from most other varieties of feminism, including its greater commitment to individual self-realization, within which issues of sexuality, language and culture have been foregrounded. By contrast, many feminists from the post-colonial regions of the world have formulated their goals within an overall strategy which prioritizes work among the poor, national independence and economic and social change.

A third, related issue has revolved around the goals that women's, as opposed to avowedly feminist, movements have tended to pursue. Historically and cross-culturally, a recurrent form of women's movement has arisen on the basis of women's roles in the family. These movements typically involve struggles over basic needs provision or over CITIZENSHIP rights. Such movements have two main characteristics. They are closely identified with particular social constructions of femininity and motherhood and are linked to these identities in important ways. The women who participate in these movements or actions often see their political involvement as a natural extension of their roles in the family and as based on primordial, intrinsically feminine sentiments. Second, as a function of this, the participants in these forms of struggle tend to formulate the goals of their actions in largely altruistic terms rather than as ones designed to advance their own self-interests as women. In most cases their interests are closely identified with the household, the welfare of its members and its conditions of existence in the community. Examples of such 'role-based' movements are the mobilizations of women in the shanty towns of Latin America to demand basic amenities, and the 'motherist' movements which have emerged typically but not exclusively in regions where motherhood has a special social status conferred through religion and culture. 'Motherist' movements such as the Madres de la Plaza de Mayo in Argentina, or pro-peace initiatives such as the 'Women in Black' which have appeared in a number of countries including Israel, are essentially protest movements against state violence and members tend to be drawn from the female relatives (typically mothers and grandmothers) of the victims of repression or war. Such protest movements have usually appeared in contexts where state repression or violence has crushed other forms of organized opposition.

These forms of female mobilization, previously considered the antithesis of self-conscious feminism, have undergone some reappraisal in the 1980s. The pluralization of views over how to characterize women's interests was accompanied by a questioning of models of women's liberation aimed at eliminating differences between women's and men's social roles. Instead of women adapting to men's roles, some feminists argued for a reassessment and revaluation of femininity and of women's traditional roles within the family. One consequence was the strengthening of the conviction among some currents of feminism that women were endowed with special attributes (either through nature or through 'socialization'), and that these were linked to mothering, an activity which predisposed women to nurturing and explained their political concerns with issues such as peace, social life and democracy. One of the clearest indications of the trend was the Mother's Manifesto issued by a section of the West German Green Party in 1987, which claimed recognition of the political importance of mothering and included such demands as a revision of urban design, pay and pensions for home carers, flexible employment, increased leisure time and the facilitation of political activity for mothers.

Although it is sometimes argued that role-based movements of this kind are the quintessential examples of *women's* politics, there is a recourse to NATURALISM in their characterization of women as more ethical than men, more prone to compromise, more democratic and more peace loving. This approach has been criticized for idealizing and essentializing gender attributes; it usually also excludes consideration of the social construction of these attributes and of other forms of female political participation which do not conform to, or flatly contradict, the behavioural model.

Reading
Jayawardena, Kumari 1986: *Feminism and Nationalism in the Third World.*
Rowbotham, Sheila 1972: *Women, Resistance and Revolution.*

MAXINE MOLYNEUX

work The concept is ambiguous and contested, connoting different activities in different societies and historical contexts. In its broadest sense, work is purposeful human endeavour, and involves the transformation of nature through the expenditure of mental and physical capacities. Such an interpretation is at odds, however, with the more limited meaning and experience of work in present-day capitalist societies. For millions of people work is synonymous with *paid* employment, and many activities which would qualify as work on the broader definition are described and experienced as non-work leisure pursuits.

Private DOMESTIC LABOUR is a prime example. Although essential to the survival, health and perpetuation of the human population, domestic labour (cooking, cleaning, childcare, and so on) has low social status, is overwhelmingly undertaken by women and remains unpaid. That the same activities may be performed as paid work for hotel and catering firms, for example, underscores the point that the boundary between paid and unpaid work (or work and so-called LEISURE) is extremely fuzzy. How is it determined?

Within the social sciences there are a number of competing explanations. Economics – at least the dominant neoclassical paradigm – holds that the relative values assigned to different productive and service activities, and hence the rewards and status which accrue to their providers, are governed by the interplay of supply and demand forces in the marketplace. The fact that many women specialize in unpaid, private domestic labour is held to be a rational response to the prevailing structure of relative rewards. Domestic labour yields a relatively high level of satisfaction for its consumers (the family) but commands a low wage if provided as a service through the market. Hence women and men choose to specialize in different activities, so as to maximize household income (satisfaction), with men opting for relatively higher paid jobs and women electing to specialize in domestic duties.

Space precludes a detailed critique of this approach, but it is clear that the argument is tautological: in particular a pre-existing gendered DIVISION OF LABOUR is assumed and then used to 'explain' the resulting division of labour between men and women (and paid work and unpaid labour) in terms of prevailing relative prices. Why different kinds of labour attract different rates of remuneration is not explained, nor crucially are the origins of the wage labour system.

The approach in industrial sociology is quite different. Definitions of work are held to be historically specific and reflective of the dominant values, assumptions and power relationships in society. Paid employment thus occupies a special position within the division of labour under capitalism because of the specific nature and structure of production relations under this system. A defining characteristic of capitalism is that work is undertaken not in order to satisfy the immediate needs of the direct producers and their families, but rather to produce commodities for exchange in the market.

The Marxist analysis, which has had a profound influence on the study of work and workplace relations, develops this basic insight. Work, according to the Marxist perspective, is subordinated to the purpose of reproducing and expanding the material and political dominance of the capitalist class. The mass of the population is separated from the means of production and subsistence and hence is compelled to enter into wage labour in order to survive. Through the wage labour system workers are subject to systematic exploitation: wages are advanced for human capacities and not some determinate quantity of performed labour. Within the production process they are encouraged and cajoled to work for a certain length of time and to a certain level of intensity, so as to ensure that the value they contribute exceeds the value of their wages. The difference, surplus value, forms the basis of the capitalist's profit.

While not all sociologists would accept the Marxist view that capitalism is an exploitative system which degrades the experience of work, as well as the lives of workers, most would accept Wright Mills's view that work may 'be a mere source of livelihood, or the most significant part of one's inner life; it may be experienced as expiation, or as an exuberant expression of self; as bounden duty or as the development of man's universal nature' (Mills, 1951, p. 215). Crucially, what matter are the social relationships governing the performance and experience of work.

Most recently debate and controversy have centred on the question of whether, under new technological and economic imperatives, work organization and work relationships are being fundamentally transformed. Some (see Piore and Sabel, 1984) claim that new forms of democratic work patterns are supplanting the authoritarian, hierarchical systems which governed the development of the mass production system in capitalist and socialist countries alike. The pessimistic scenarios of the 1970s, which followed the publication of Braverman's highly influential Marxist account of the dehumanizing tendencies of the capitalist labour process (Braverman, 1974), have thus given way in some quarters to a more optimistic account of the potentially liberating aspects of new, flexible work organizations. Workers, it is said, are being re-empowered in the workplace as employers have sought to harness their creative capacities in their quest for greater production flexibility and efficiency.

Assessments of the available evidence – which as yet remains rather piecemeal and fragmented – are divided. The new optimists have yet to demonstrate their case, but it is undoubtedly true that as the twenty-first century approaches, patterns of production organization and structures of workplace control are becoming more diverse.

See also SCIENTIFIC-TECHNOLOGICAL REVOLUTION; WORKING CLASS.

Reading
Braverman, H. 1974: *Labor and Monopoly Capital.*
Handy, C.B. 1984: *The Future of Work: A Guide to Changing Society.*
Piore, M. and Sabel, C. 1984: *The Second Industrial Divide.*

PETER NOLAN

workers' council This institution within the context of INDUSTRIAL DEMOCRACY may also be described as a works council, factory council, company council (*comité d'entreprise*) or a soviet. Following Gottschalch (1968, p. 32) we may differentiate between three types of councils: (1) as fighting organizations; (2) as forms of interest representation; (3) as directing organs of the political community. Workers' councils were conceived and practised in all three of these forms.

Local and city councils have existed for a long time as the expression of citizens' movements to run the affairs of a local community or city. In the nineteenth century workers started to organize themselves in guilds, unions, clubs and other forms of association. Workers' councils in the modern sense were first conceived in the context of ANARCHO-SYNDICALISM in the late nineteenth century. They were opposed to centralized socialist parties, unions and other workers' organizations.

Soviets have probably become the most famous council form in the twentieth century. Already in the revolution of 1905 in Russia the workers', peasants' and soldiers' councils played a prominent role (Anweiler, 1958). Lenin in his early writings was a protagonist of this form of social organization,

and 'All power to the soviets!' was the slogan of the first (February) revolution in 1917. Anna Pankratova (1923) described the precise structure and functioning of workers' councils up to 1923, but her book was banned from publication in any state socialist country until recently.

The conflict between 'democractic centralism' (and the dictatorship of the proletariat exercised through the communist party's monopoly of power) and basic democratic self-determination in the form of soviets came to a showdown in the Kronstadt revolt in 1921. Trotsky – later a defender of workers' control – crushed the uprising by military force. This was the beginning of Stalinist rule and the annihilation of all opposition in the Soviet Union from which the region has still not recovered (Ferro, 1980).

Council democracy
The concept of council democracy has developed mainly outside the Soviet Union and in opposition to the practices there. Rosa Luxemburg criticized very harshly and very early the degeneration of the Soviet system, and supported the workers' and soldiers' councils which were formed in the German November revolution of 1918. These councils brought down the Kaiser and led to the first German republic (Oertzen, 1963), but in 1920, as a historic compromise, a works council law which reduced the power of the workers' councils was voted in Berlin (Crusius, 1978). Social democrats and unions were almost as fearful of these basic democratic organizations as were the conservatives.

In 1918–19 there was also a Hungarian Council Republic which lasted for six months, and in 1919 a shortlived Munich Council Republic. Workers' councils also played a prominent role in the Spanish Council Republic between 1936 and 1939.

The most prominent thinker of the group of council communists which constituted itself in the Weimar Republic was Anton Pannekoek. For him a workers' council did not mean a specific, precisely conceived form of organization, which has to be elaborated in more detail, but the principle of control by the workers themselves over the enterprise and production (Pannekoek, 1950). Karl Korsch – another council communist – wrote a handbook on labour law (1922) to help works councillors to put workers' control into practice.

Factory councils, as a specific form of workers' councils, became known primarily in Italy, through the writings of Antonio Gramsci (1910–20, 1921–6) who described them as they were organized from 1919 to 1921, mainly in Turin. According to Gramsci, writing in 1920, factory councils are the expression of producer democracy:

in every factory, in every workshop an organ on a representative base is formed . . . which realizes the power of the proletariat, fights against the capitalist order or exercises the control over production and educates the whole working masses for the revolutionary struggle and for the setting up of the workers' state. (Cited by Széll, 1988, p. 37).

Kibbutzim in Israel may be regarded as a specific form of workers' council, and although their mandate is much wider since they encompass all spheres of social and economic life, their basis is the production community which is organized in a direct democratic way (Rosner, 1976).

Works councils are today the most widespread form of workers' control in the enterprise, and were institutionalized in a number of countries after World War II. They have been made mandatory in nine West European countries: Austria, Belgium, France, Western Germany, Greece, Luxemburg, the Netherlands, Portugal and Spain. In some of the cases the works councils consist only of workers' representatives, in the others they include management representatives as well (Müller-Jentsch, 1990). (See also PARTICIPATION; SELF-MANAGEMENT). The German model has become the best-known. It might seem that this institution is specific to Western Europe, but it is to be found today also in Burundi, Pakistan, Tanzania and Zambia, while similar institutions exist under other names in Bangladesh, Brazil, Denmark, Gabon, Iraq, Mauritania, Mauritius, Mexico, the Philippines, Sri Lanka, Switzerland, Tunisia and Zaïre (International Labour Office, 1981, pp. 205–24; Monat and Sarfati, 1986, pp. 190–208). Naturally it is difficult to compare institutions in countries where the economic, cultural and political conditions are completely different. What can the role of a works council be in a society where unemployment is up to 50 per cent and the informal economy involves 90 per cent? Nevertheless, works councils may be regarded as a weaker form or a prototype of workers' control.

With the breakdown of state socialism, the profound ecological, social, cultural and political crises of capitalist societies, and the resurgence of regionalist and local organizations, a new debate on the democratic organization of production and reproduction seems to be historically necessary. In this context the ideals of workers' control through workers' councils might provide an answer to the crises in East and West, North and South. The problem for the democratization of society is still almost the same as at the beginning of the century: who decides what is produced, how, where, and for whom? The democratic restructuring in the Soviet Union (*perestroika*) was linked with the introduction of shopfloor councils and *glasnost*, and the effects were felt throughout the world. In many of the former state socialist countries workers' councils were created spontaneously. On the other side of the former Iron Curtain (Sturmthal, 1964) citizens' movements and students, women and the unemployed often organized themselves in councils. But womens' movements and the greens as new social movements are normally not much concerned with economic issues. Perhaps for them – as well as for conservative thought – we already live in a postindustrial society where work no longer plays a central role in life. However, for the future of DEMOCRACY it seems important to find some equilibrium between spontaneity and organization (Mattick, 1975), and workers' councils have made an important contribution in this direction.

See also TRADE UNIONS.

Reading
Bouvier, Pierre 1980: *Travail et expression ouvrière: pouvoirs et contraintes des comités d'entreprise.*
Garson, G. David ed. 1977: *Worker Self-management in Industry: The West European Experience.*
Jain, Hem Chand and Giles, Anthony 1985: Workers' participation in Western Europe: implications for North America. *Relations Industrielles* 40.4, 747–74.
Jenkins, David 1973: *Job Power.*
Mandel, Ernest 1970 (*1973*): *Workers' Control, Workers' Councils and Self-Management.*
Széll, György 1988: *Participation, Worker's Control and Self-Management.*
Williams, Gwyn A. 1975: *Proletarian order: Antonio Gramsci, Factory Councils and the Origins of Italian Communism, 1911–1921.*

GYÖRGY SZÉLL

working class A social group comprising workers in mines, factories, transport and related occupations, brought together in rapidly growing industrial towns by the development of capitalist production in the nineteenth century, which became an increasingly important political force as the source of trade unions, cooperatives and political parties inspired by socialist ideas (see SOCIAL-ISM). By the beginning of the twentieth century, working-class parties had established themselves throughout Europe – where some of them, notably in Germany and Austria, were already very large – and also, on a lesser scale, in North America. From that time until the present day, the internal politics of the European countries, and at a later stage politics in other societies, has been dominated by the conflict between working-class parties and those parties which defend the existing economic system and social hierarchy; that is, between parties of the 'left' and the 'right'.

In the course of this century, however, the conditions of existence and the politics of the working class have undergone many changes. Already by the 1890s the extension of the suffrage in Western Europe, achieved largely by working-class pressure, had made possible the emergence of parliamentary socialist parties and the introduction of social reforms which gradually improved the living conditions of workers, while the increasing productivity of modern industry raised the general standard of living, and at the same time tended to increase the numbers of the middle class, engaged in clerical, technical and professional occupations. Workers' parties thus became more deeply involved in detailed issues of social reform, and strong disagreements arose concerning 'reformist' versus 'revolutionary' politics (see REFORMISM; REVISIONISM). In Eastern Europe, and especially in Russia, where the working-class movement confronted an autocratic regime, and that moreover in a predominantly peasant country, more immediately revolutionary politics prevailed; and this division between two kinds of political orientation culminated, after the Russian Revolution, in a formal division between communist (Bolshevik) parties and socialist parties. In contrast with Europe, the working-class movement in the USA, after the first decade of the century when socialism appeared to be a growing force, never succeeded in establishing an independent and distinctive workers' party of national importance, in the face of various countervailing influences, among which those most frequently discussed were the relatively high standard of living, a democratic style of life, the opportunities for geographical and social mobility, and large-scale immigration (Sombart, 1906; Laslett and Lipset, 1974).

The opposition between class-based parties reached a peak in the economic depression of the 1930s, though complicated by communist/socialist antagonisms, and notwithstanding many defeats during that period working-class parties reemerged after 1945 stronger than they had ever been in terms of membership and electoral support. In the following decades, however, economic and social changes profoundly modified the situation of the working class. Its numbers declined relative to the MIDDLE CLASS; its economic situation improved substantially as a result of sustained economic growth at an exceptionally high rate, full employment and more adequate social services in the new 'welfare states'; and the ideological/political expression of class antagonisms was gradually moderated. Some of the European parties ceased to describe themselves as class parties, or to emphasize very strongly their socialist aims, concentrating instead on their commitment to extending social welfare provision and reducing, by various means, the inequalities of wealth and income.

One important factor in this situation was the critical response by most working-class parties to the political dictatorship in the Soviet Union, extended after the war to other countries of Eastern Europe, and the establishment of what were described as societies of 'real socialism'. Through the 1950s and 1960s the suppression of popular uprisings against these regimes produced crises and growing dissident movements internally, and an increasingly rapid decline of communist parties in other countries, culminating in the massive transformation of the East European societies at the end of the 1980s and the virtual disappearance of communism as a major ideological or political orientation in the working class.

In the advanced industrial countries the working class, as it was traditionally conceived, is no longer what Marx described as the 'immense majority' but constitutes at most 50 per cent of the population, and some social scientists have argued that these countries are becoming, or have to a large extent already become, 'middle class' societies, in which new social and political interests and movements emerge – concerned with questions of gender, race and the environment – that increasingly overshadow earlier divisions and conflicts. Against this view, however, it is claimed that there still exists in the capitalist countries a distinctive class structure (now reappearing in some East European countries), that the working class remains a large and important element in this structure, and that class divisions and class conflicts, however greatly modified in their expression, continue to have a preponderant influence on social doctrines and political action.

See also CLASS.

Reading
Bottomore, Tom 1965 (*1991*): *Classes in Modern Society*, new edn.
Goldthorpe, John H. et al. 1969: *The Affluent Worker in the Class Structure*.
Mallet, Serge 1975: *The New Working Class*.
Mann, Michael 1973: *Consciousness and Action among the Western Working Class*.
Thompson, E.P. 1963: *The Making of the English Working Class*.

TOM BOTTOMORE

world-system   This is a relatively new concept. No doubt the phrase has been used from time to time in the past in diverse loose senses. But its current usage, hyphenated to indicate that it is a 'concept', should be traced to the invention of the term *économie-monde* by Fernand Braudel. Braudel himself says he took it from the particular use made by Fritz Rörig in 1933 of the word *Weltwirtschaft*, but it is certainly primarily via Braudel that the concept became known.

The French language (and other Romance languages) permits a distinction in linguistic forms which is impossible in German and difficult in English. Economists have long talked of a world economy, a term they have tended to use synonymously with international economy. It refers primarily to the structure of trade and financial flows between sovereign states, flows that are reflected at the state level by certain standard indicators such as the terms of trade or the balance of payments. In this usage, the word international refers to the flows between nations (that is, sovereign states), and the term 'world' refers to the fact that what economists are analysing flows over the entire globe.

In French the standard translation of 'world economy' is *économie mondiale*. Braudel however invented a different term for what he wished to describe. He used *économie-monde*. By that term, he wished to indicate first that he was referring not to *the* world, but to *a* world; and secondly, that he was not referring to the economic relations *among* constituted political units inside that world, but to the economic processes *within* that world in its entirety.

It was I who attempted to establish this distinction in English translation between *économie mon-*

diale and *économie-monde* by the use of the hyphen. Since 'world economy' was already in use as the equivalent of *économie mondiale*, I used 'world-economy' (with the hyphen) to be the equivalent of *économie-monde*. A world-economy was defined initially as the entity within whose boundaries there was a single overarching division of labour but which in fact included a number of separate state structures.

It became clear on reflection that historically there had existed other large entities which could be said to have had a single division of labour but which did not contain within their boundaries separate state structures. Such seemed to be the case of the ancient empires, say of Rome or of China. By linguistic parallelism with 'world-economy' the term 'world-empire' was coined to denote this latter instance, the two both being taken to be varieties of an entity called a 'world-system'.

Since the early 1970s when this preliminary conceptual exercise was completed, a good deal of empirical and theoretical work on world-systems has been undertaken. Most of this work has been related to the study of one particular world-system, the 'modern world-system', otherwise known as the 'capitalist world-economy'. However, in addition, a number of archaeologists have tried to utilize the concept of a world-system to analyse the various premodern situations with which archaeologists have been largely concerned, suggesting that their reconstructions from the data should lead to the observation of larger spatial zones than previously was done, and that these larger zones were in fact 'world-systems'. Recently, there has in addition been the beginning of interest in the comparative study of different kinds of world-systems.

Every concept, especially when it is new, is an exercise in polemics. It is important to underline what alternative concepts the concept of world-system was directed against. There were three major elements involved in the polemic. The first concerned the unit of analysis. To argue that the modern world should be thought of as a world-system or a capitalist world-economy is to argue that the meaningful primary unit of social constraint and social decision-making is this world-system rather than the nation-state units which have been traditionally used as units of analysis.

From this first premise, the second followed naturally. The units that 'develop' over time were considered *not* to be the so-called nation-states but rather the world-system as a singular world-system. This was an argument against 'developmentalism' or MODERNIZATION theory which assumed the existence of parallel nation-states, each pursuing parallel efforts at linear development, albeit with unequal success to date. Modernization theory furthermore tended to be a theory of eventual homogenization; analysis from a world-systems perspective tended to emphasize the polarization of the world-systemic structure over time.

The third element in the polemic then involved the mode of analysis, or the stance on traditional epistemological questions. Analyses using the nation-state as a unit of analysis, and theorizing from a developmentalist perspective, tended to be nomothetic, searching for appropriate lawlike statements which could explain the processes observed. The epistemology of a 'world-systems perspective' was based on the view that world-systems are 'historical systems'. Historical systems are simultaneously systemic, with structures determining ongoing, largely cyclical processes, and historical, that is, they develop over time and have beginnings and eventually ends. This has led world-systems analysis to two major epistemological conclusions. One has been a stance rejecting both nomothetic and idiographic methodologies in favour of an analysis of the particular sets of general rules governing particular types of world-systems. The second has been a sympathy for the theorizing within the sciences that rejects Newtonian linear dynamics in favour of a model of non-linear processes which eventually bifurcate.

The concept of 'world-system' is a controversial one in twentieth-century thought. It tends to go against the views of the mainstream, defined both quantitatively and socially. Of course, denuded of its polemical baggage, this concept could easily be included within almost any standard theorizing about social behaviour, but thus denuded it would be vitiated and would scarcely add any insights of significance.

See also GLOBALIZATION; INTERNATIONAL DIVISION OF LABOUR; INTERNATIONAL RELATIONS.

Reading
Braudel, Fernand 1981–4: *Civilization and Capitalism*, 3 vols.
Wallerstein, Immanuel 1974–89: *The Modern World-System*, 3 vols.
—— 1991: *Unthinking Social Science*.

IMMANUEL WALLERSTEIN

Y

youth culture Considered distinct from the dominant culture, youth culture refers to the unique symbols, beliefs and behaviour of young people in society. The term has two usages. First, it represents the values and norms of the youth population in general in society; and second, it includes the ideals and practices of specific youthful subgroups, such as subcultural or countercultural groups (see COUNTERCULTURE). Discussions and studies of youth culture have resulted in somewhat separate literatures dealing with the teenage years (early and mid-adolescence) and with the stage of youth (late adolescence and early adulthood). At issue is the extent to which young people's attitudes and behaviour deviate from societal norms (adult or youth) and the relative support given by youth to particular types of peer-related activities.

Historical trends such as modernization, industrialization, urbanization, the rise of the middle class and the extension of public education have fostered the age-based segregation and stratification of youth, which in turn have promoted the development of youth culture (Parsons, 1964). The formation of youth cultures was given impetus in nineteenth-century Europe with the glorification and romanticization of young people by philosophers, writers, artists and the 'youthful freedom fighters' active during the Age of Revolution (Gillis, 1974). Youth cultures continued to form throughout modern history – sometimes separate from and sometimes in tandem with youth movements for political change (see YOUTH MOVEMENT). In the latter half of the twentieth century, technological advances, rapid communications and commercialization facilitated the spread of youth-related activities on a worldwide scale.

The wider youth culture – sometimes referred to as the 'generalized', 'mass' or 'pop' youth culture – does not represent a marked break with adult society but revolves around the adoption of certain fads, fashions, leisure pursuits and lifestyles by large numbers of young people (Douglas, 1970). For example, the 1920s ('roaring '20s', 'jazz age') and the 1960s ('age of Aquarius', 'Postmaterialism') were extraordinary periods when young people created their own styles of dress, language, music, artistic expression, sexual practices and communities. In any era, however, not all young people support the larger youth culture. Important considerations for identifying a youth culture include the extent to which young people endorse and express a shared set of values and norms.

An antagonistic orientation towards adult society is reflected in the deviant subcultures or countercultures of relatively small numbers of young people (Brake, 1985). Subcultures accept certain features of the dominant value system but also express sentiments and beliefs unique to their own group, whereas a counterculture is a subculture that challenges the dominant culture and society. One way to distinguish between the two forms of youth culture is to note that subcultural groups withdraw from conventional society, while countercultural groups are more rejecting and confrontational. Examples of subcultural groups include avant-garde artists and writers, juvenile delinquents, gangs, bohemians and autonomous youth centres ('free space' communities). Countercultural youth may be largely expressive (cults, hippies, Skinheads, punks), or they may participate in rebellious political activity such as radical ideological-utopian groups and aggressive political dissidents (see also NEW LEFT; NEW RIGHT). Social class is a significant factor differentiating subcultural groups in society. For example, certain youth subcultures appeal largely to lower-class and working-class youngsters (hooligans, punks, rockers), whereas other subcultures and countercultures attract middle-class youth (bohemianism, hippies, Yippies).

Understanding youth culture (whether mass, subcultural or countercultural) involves both sociohistorical and psychological considerations. From a sociohistorical perspective, structural-functional, generational conflict and symbolic interactionist theories have been employed to account for the rise of youth cultures. Taken together, these theories suggest that youth cultures are likely to form when the size of the youth cohort is relatively large; when societies are undergoing rapid change, are pluralistic and have problems integrating their young people into mainstream institutions (due to factors such as unemployment, broken homes, high mobility, alienation, segregation, class and status conflicts); and when members of the younger generation have grown up under different conditions from their elders and express dissatisfaction with conventional society by creating their own values and lifestyles.

From a psychological perspective, explanations of youth cultures have been based on psychodynamic, developmental, cognitive, personality, behaviourist and social psychological theories. The contentions are that those young persons who support some form of youth culture may be motivated by the life-cycle needs of youth (identity formation, self-determination, psychosocial experimentation, peer affiliation and bonding); personality traits (the desire to break the bounds of conventionality, engage in high risk-taking behaviour, weak control of impulses, personal conflicts); and because they decide there is more to gain than lose by involving themselves in some form of peer-related activity and therefore join reference groups supporting their values and goals.

The conclusions reached in studying youth cultures may be influenced partially by the research procedures employed. For example, cross-cultural surveys of young people indicate that most youngsters are supportive of their society's values, whereas observational and interview studies of specific youth groups are likely to suggest the existence of dissatisfaction coupled with highly active and intense demands for societal change by young people (Braungart and Braungart, 1986; Dornbusch, 1989). Empirical investigations of youth culture may benefit from a multiple research strategy: employing quantitative *and* qualitative methodologies; including historical, societal, group and individual levels of analyses; and using comparative designs (cross-cultural, historical, intergroup and intragroup).

While some social scientists have interpreted the formation of youth cultures as indicating a 'failure of adult socialization', others have argued that the various forms of youth culture signify young people's discontent with the status quo and their desire to create a better (or at least different) world

for their generation. Whatever the interpretation, there is general agreement that youth cultures represent a force for change and are influenced by, as well as having a significant impact on, modern society.

Reading

Bernard J. ed. 1961: Teen-age culture. *Annals of the American Academy of Political and Social Science* 338, entire issue.
Frith, S. 1984: *The Sociology of Youth.*
Mannheim, K. 1952: The problem of generations. In *Essays on the Sociology of Knowledge*, ed. P. Kecskemeti, pp. 276–322.
Smith, D.M. 1985: Perceived peer and parental influences on youths' social world. *Youth and Society* 17, 131–56.
Yinger, J.M. 1982: *Countercultures.*

RICHARD G. BRAUNGART AND
MARGARET M. BRAUNGART

youth movement   Involving the organized and conscious attempt of young people (between late adolescence and early adulthood) to bring about or resist social and political change, a youth movement may appear when traditional institutions fail to meet the needs of an age group in society, and when a critical number of young people become aware of their common plight and feel something can be done to alleviate their problems. The perceived discrepancy between the individual needs or aspirations of the younger generation and the existing social, cultural and political conditions lies at the root of youth unrest (see SOCIAL MOVEMENT).

Youth movements are not merely random forms of collective behaviour but are direct responses to historical events and forces. Youthful political activity is most likely to occur in countries undergoing rapid transformation, where for a variety of reasons, the particular mix of circumstances tests the ability of a political system to perform necessary functions and services. Societies that experience institutional instability along with weakened legitimacy and effectiveness provide the ideal environments for protest behaviour. In addition to political protests, youth movements may take other forms, including student movements, cultural (literary, artistic, music) movements, religious and ethnic-based movements, environmental movements, peace/anti-war movements and countercultural movements (see STUDENT MOVEMENT; YOUTH CULTURE; PEACE MOVEMENT; COUNTERCULTURE).

While the problem of youthful rebelliousness

and acting out against adult society can be traced to antiquity, organized youth movements – as consciously mobilized forces for change – are a relatively recent phenomenon of modern history that originated with the drive for nationalism. Since the early nineteenth century, there have been five distinguishable periods of extraordinary youth movement activity: Young Europe (1815 to 1848, 1860 to 1890); Post-Victorian (1890 to 1910); Great Depression (1930 to 1940); 1960s Generation (1960 to 1970); and 1980s Generation (1980 to 1990). What began as an unprecedented eruption of youth movements nearly two centuries ago had by the 1960s become global in scope (Braungart and Braungart, 1990b; Esler, 1971).

Youth movements are generational struggles that include both intergenerational and intragenerational forms of conflict. Intergenerational conflict involves two dynamic processes. First, young people denounce adult institutions for their weakness and failures. Next, based on their ability to mobilize, youth authorize their own generation to bring about the desired change. The existence of intergenerational conflict as a destabilizing force in society enhances the likelihood of intragenerational conflict, which occurs when generation units within the same generation compete for power and control (Mannheim, 1952). These competing generation units may be spontaneous (initiated by young people themselves) or sponsored by adult organizations. Generation units represent the spectrum of political orientations ranging from left-wing to right-wing and from moderate to radical groups (see also NEW LEFT; NEW RIGHT).

Explanations of youth movements have come from different scholarly disciplines. Social psychological explanations focus on the developmental characteristics of young people that promote age-based conflict and discrepant political orientations, the specific family backgrounds and personality traits of youthful political activists and the attitudes and behaviour of youth movement participants. A fundamental reason why young people are so receptive to forming and joining youth movements involves the life-cycle tendencies of late adolescence and early adulthood, particularly the advances in cognitive thinking, a fresh social and political awareness, the search for identity, a desire for self-determination and independence, and the need for belief–behaviour consistency (Erikson, 1968; Keniston, 1971).

Sociological explanations of youth movements emphasize the importance of political socialization (especially family, peers, school and media), the shared experiences of a cohort of youth growing up together in a rapidly changing society, and the societal conditions and opportunity structures that facilitate the formation of youth movements (Heberle, 1951; Jenkins, 1987). Similarly, historical explanations focus on the unique, eruptive nature of youth movements and identify some of their cyclical features. Social scientists and historians alike have noted that youth movements tend to appear when a relatively large youth cohort feels they share a common set of values and experiences that makes them an exceptional generation, and when they face certain historical discontinuities and have the opportunity to mobilize (Esler, 1971; Moller, 1968). A rich interactive framework for studying and comparing youth movements involves the consideration of life-cycle, cohort and historical-period effects and the ways in which these forces combine (Braungart and Braungart, 1989).

Empirical investigations of youth movements and their participants gained worldwide attention during the 1960s and have continued ever since. Some of the principal findings are that young people's life-course development – the direction of their political views and whether they are radical or more moderate – is strongly influenced by family political socialization experiences. Moreover, the generational values, social bonds and political orientations expressed during their youthful activist years are likely to carry over into adulthood rather than change or fade with time (Braungart and Braungart, 1990a; Whalen and Flacks, 1989).

The study of youth movements benefits from an interdisciplinary, interactive approach that attempts to discover how life-course, cohort and period effects combine to produce youth movement activity. Analysis may be undertaken at a number of levels: historical, international, national, local, group and individual. Both quantitative and qualitative methodologies are appropriate, and comparative strategies are recommended. Research investigations indicate that youth movements arise partially because of the inability of political regimes and adult society to resolve old problems and adapt to new conditions. The historical significance and global spread of youth movements are testimony to the persistence of young people as a critical and renovative force in modern history.

Reading

Altbach, P.G. ed. 1989: *Student Political Activism: An International Reference Handbook.*

Braungart, R.G. and Braungart, M.M. 1986: Life-course and generational politics. *Annual Review of Sociology* 12, 205–31.

—— 1989: Generational conflict and intergroup relations as the foundation for political generations. In *Advances in Group Processes*, vol. 6, eds E. J. Lawler and B. Markovsky, pp. 179–203.

Eisenstadt, S.N. 1956: *From Generation to Generation.*

Feuer, L.S. 1969: *The Conflict of Generations.*

Lipset, S.M. and Altbach, P.G. eds 1969: *Students in Revolt.*

RICHARD G. BRAUNGART AND
MARGARET M. BRAUNGART

BIOGRAPHICAL APPENDIX

Adorno, Theodor Wiesengrund (*b.* 1903, Frankfurt am Main; *d.* 1969, Visp, Switzerland) German philosopher and musicologist. Educated in Frankfurt and Vienna. Adorno was a member of the Frankfurt Institute for Social Research (the source of the FRANKFURT SCHOOL of critical theory) which he joined in 1931. He studied composition and piano in Vienna with Alban Berg and was a strong supporter of Schönberg. Adorno left Germany in 1934, staying first in England and then joining the Institute in exile in the USA. Returning to Frankfurt in 1950, Adorno became director of the Institute in 1958. His works include *Dialectic of Enlightenment* (1947, with Max Horkheimer), *Philosophy of Modern Music* (1949), *The Authoritarian Personality* (1950), *Negative Dialectics* (1966) and contributions to *The Positivist Dispute in German Sociology* (1969).

Althusser, Louis (*b.* 1918, Birmandreis, Algeria; *d.* 1990, Yvelines, near Paris) French communist and philosopher, he was educated at the Ecole Normale Supérieure in Paris. Influenced by French rationalism and structuralism, he identified a radical break between Marx's early and later writings, and favouring the latter argued for Marxism as a science, emphasizing its anti-humanism. His works *For Marx* (1965) and (with Etienne Balibar) *Reading 'Capital'* (1970) gained him a wide, but often critical, audience.

Arendt, Hannah (*b.* 1906, Hanover; *d.* 1975, New York) German/American philosopher. Educated at the universities of Königsberg, Marburg, Freiburg and Heidelberg, she completed her Ph.D. under Jaspers. In 1933 she fled to Paris and then in 1941 to the USA, where she worked in publishing until 1963, and was prominent in Jewish organizations, e.g. Research Director of the Conference on Jewish Relations, New York (1944–6). In 1963 she became a Professor of the Committee on Social Thought, and from 1967 until her death was a Professor of the Graduate Faculty, New School of Social Research. Major publications include *The Origins of Totalitarianism* (1958), *The Human Condition* (1958), *On Revolution* (1965) and *On Violence* (1970).

Bakhtin, Mikhail Mikailovitch (*b.* 1895, Orel, south of Moscow; *d.* 1975, Moscow) Russian philosopher and literary theorist. Educated at the universities of Odessa (Philological Faculty) and St Petersburg, Bakhtin worked for thirty years in Kazakhstan, Saransk and Moscow in relative obscurity. In 1957 he became head of the Department of Russian and Foreign Literature at the University of Moscow, until his retirement in 1961. He published a number of books under the names of his friends: *The Formal Method in Literary Scholarship* (1928) was attributed to P.N. Medvedev and *Marxism and the Philosophy of Language* (1929) to V.N. Vološinov. This has been a source of controversy, but it is generally believed that Bakhtin was the author of these works. In 1929 he published *Problems of Dostoyevsky's Poetics* and in 1966, *Rabelais and His World*. His work has influenced Julia Kristeva and the *Tel Quel* group.

Barthes, Roland Gérard (*b.* 1915, Cherbourg; *d.* 1980, Paris) French writer/critic. Educated at the Sorbonne, Barthes held a number of posts in Hungary before starting his career in France where he held posts at the Ecole Pratique des Hautes Etudes, Paris as Director of Studies and Professor of the Sociology of Signs, Symbols and Collective Representations (1962–76) and at the Collège de France, Paris as Professor of Literary Semiology. In 1953 he helped to establish the review *Théâtre populaire*, and in the same year published *Writing Degree Zero* which, along with *Mythologies* (1957), established him as a post-Saussurean theorist. His other works include *The Pleasure of the Text* (1973) and the autobiographical *Roland Barthes by Roland Barthes* (1975). See SEMIOTICS.

Beauvoir, Simone de (*b.* 1908, Paris; *d.* 1986, Paris) French philosopher/novelist. Educated at the Ecole Normale Supérieure, she taught philosophy in lycées at Marseilles, Rouen and Paris. A leading figure in EXISTENTIALISM and FEMINISM, de Beauvoir was a life-long associate of Sartre, whom she met in 1929 and with whom she founded and edited *Les Temps Modernes* (1944). She was critical of Sartre's over-emphasis on the freedom of the subject in the face of social norms. In *The Second Sex* (1949) de Beauvoir developed these ideas with reference to the subordination of women. Apart from her philosophical works she wrote several novels and three volumes of autobiography and a memoir of Sartre.

Benjamin, Walter (*b.* 1892, Berlin; *d.* 1940, Port Bou, France) A literary theorist and critic, educated at Freiburg, Berlin, Munich and Berne, Benjamin was denied an academic post when his thesis was rejected at Frankfurt in 1925, although it was published in 1928 as *The Origin of German Tragic Drama*. An associate of Lukács, Adorno, Brecht and Bloch, Benjamin turned to Marxism (see FRANKFURT SCHOOL). In 1933 he emigrated to Paris where he studied Baudelaire, and when France was defeated and partly occupied in 1940 Benjamin fled south, but was stopped on the Franco-Spanish border where, faced with the prospect of being handed over to the Nazis, he took his own life. Some of his later writings were collected in *Illuminations* (1961).

Bergson, Henri Louis (*b.* 1859, Paris; *d.* 1941, Paris) French philosopher. Educated at the Ecole Normale Supérieure (1877–81). From 1881–97 he taught in lycées and wrote *Time and Free Will: An Essay on the Immediate Data of Consciousness* (1889), a work which embodied his crucial distinction between time as continuous duration in everyday life, and time as represented by science – mechanical and discrete. In 1897 he taught at the Ecole Normale Supérieure and subsequently at the Collège de France (1900–14). Between 1912 and 1918 Bergson went on diplomatic missions to America and Spain and in 1928 won the Nobel Prize for Literature. Major works include *Creative Evolution* (1907) in which he rejected mechanical, deterministic accounts and *The Two Sources of Morality and Religion* (1932).

Bernstein, Eduard (*b.* 1850, Berlin; *d.* 1932, Berlin) German politician and political theorist. He joined the German Social Democratic Workers' Party (*Eisenachers*) in 1871 – editing the party organ, *Der Sozialdemokrat* (1881–90) – and became a Marxist, but in exile in London (1880–1901) he was also influenced by the Fabians as well as becoming a close friend of Engels. Based on articles in *Die Neue Zeit* (1896–8) his major revisionist work *Die Voraussetzungen des Sozialismus* was published in 1899 (see REVISIONISM). Essentially he favoured a gradualist approach to secure economic and social rights, and eventually political power for the working class, rather than 'waiting for the revolution'.

Bloch, Ernst (*b.* 1885, Ludwigshaven; *d.* 1977, Tübingen) German philosopher. Educated at Munich and Würzburg, Bloch was influenced by Marxism, German idealism and Christian and Jewish theology. While in Switzerland he composed his first book, *Spirit of Utopia* (1918), which saw art, poetry and music as embodying a human potential of fulfilment. As a free-lance writer in Berlin in the 1920s he became friendly with Brecht, Weill, Benjamin and Lukács, and joined the Communist Party. In 1933 he left Germany and settled in the USA in 1938. Returning to East Germany in 1949 he held the Chair in Philosophy at the University of Leipzig, but fell into disfavour with the authorities and moved to West Germany as Professor of Philosophy in Tübingen.

Brecht, Bertolt (*b.* 1898, Augsburg; *d.* 1956, East Berlin) German dramatist and poet. Brecht studied medicine at Munich University and worked for a time in a medical hospital in Augsburg. A vehement opponent of World War I, Brecht came under the influence of Marxism and the political THEATRE of Piscator. His plays reflected this influence and were later blacklisted by the Nazis. In 1933 he fled to Switzerland and eventually to the USA where he was subpoenaed by the House Committee on Un-American Activities during the McCarthy witch hunt. In 1949 he returned to East Berlin where he founded the Berliner Ensemble. Brecht's works include *Baal* (1918), *Man Equals Man* (1926), *Threepenny Opera* (1928) and *Mother Courage* (1939).

Bukharin, Nikolai Ivanovich (*b.* 1888, Moscow; *d.* 1938, Moscow) Russian revolutionary and Marxist theorist. Bukharin joined the Russian Social Democratic Party in 1906 and led the Bolsheviks in Moscow in 1908. Arrested and sent into internal exile, he escaped in 1911 to Vienna, where he attended Böhm-Bawerk's lectures, became acquainted with the Austro-Marxists and wrote a critique of Austrian marginalism (*Economic Theory of the Leisure Class* 1914) and a study of imperialism (*Imperialism and World Economy* 1917–18). He returned to Moscow in 1917 and was elected to the Central Committee of the Bolsheviks, also becoming editor of *Pravda*. After 1922 Bukharin, in contrast to Preobrazhensky, advocated concessions to the peasants, and the balancing of economic growth in the agricultural and industrial sectors. In 1928 he opposed Stalin over collectivization and was removed from his posts at *Pravda* and in the Politbureau. He edited *Izvestia* (1934–7), but was expelled from the Communist Party in 1937, tried for treason and executed in 1938.

Carnap, Rudolf (*b.* 1891, Rhine-Westphalia; *d.* 1970, California) German/American philosopher. Educated at Freiburg and Jena in physics and mathematics. Invited to Vienna by Schlick in 1926 he became a leading figure in the VIENNA CIRCLE of logical positivism. In *The Logical Structure of the World* (1928) he argued that scientific concepts could be constructed out of a small number of basic concepts all of which were directly related to sense experience. In 1930 he founded, with Reichenbach, *Erkenntnis*, the official journal of logical positivism. As Professor of Natural Philosophy at the German University of Prague from 1931 he published *The Logical Syntax of Language* (1934). In 1935 he emigrated to the USA, teaching at the University of Chicago from 1936, and subsequently at the Institute for Advanced Study, Princeton (1952–4) and UCLA (1954–61).

Chomsky, Avram Noam (*b.* 1928, Philadelphia) American linguist, philosopher and political activist. Educated at the University of Pennsylvania, Chomsky has taught at the Massachusetts Institute of Technology since 1955. He has written extensively on LINGUISTICS, formulating a new conception of grammatical structure as innate rather than learned, and on social theory, where he has been a trenchant critic of American foreign policy (e.g. *American Power and the New Mandarins* 1969). He makes clear that these two domains of his work should be treated separately.

Croce, Benedetto (*b.* 1866, Percasseroli; *d.* 1952, Naples) Italian idealist philosopher. Croce was an independent scholar who did not hold any academic post, but he was Italian Minister of Education from 1920–1 and again after World War II. Strongly influenced by Hegel, he developed a philosophy of the spirit containing four types of experience: cognitive experience of the particular and of the universal (the domain of aesthetics and logic respectively); and practical experience of the particular and the universal (the domain of economics and ethics respectively). History is the description of the activity of spirit in these domains; philosophy is an account of the methodology of history and is inseparable from history. Croce also wrote on the work of a number of other thinkers, including Hegel, Marx and Vico.

Derrida, Jacques (*b.* 1930, El Biar, Algiers) French philosopher/literary theorist. Educated at the Ecole Normale Supérieure, Paris and Harvard, Derrida taught at the Sorbonne (1960–4) and has been at the Ecole Normale Supérieure since 1965. In 1962 he won the Prix Cavaillès for his translation of Husserl's *Origin of Geometry* for which he wrote a long introduction. His study of Husserl was part of his critique of Western metaphysics which he developed in *Speech and Phenomena* (1967), *Writing and Difference* (1967) and *Of Grammatology* (1976). Derrida's critique is of the philosophy of *presence*, dominant in Western philosophy since Plato, to which he opposes a textual strategy known as DECONSTRUCTION.

Dewey, John (*b.* 1859, Vermont; *d.* 1952, New York) American pragmatist philosopher. Educated at Vermont and Johns Hopkins universities, Dewey taught at Michigan (1884–94), Chicago (1894–1904) and Columbia (1904–29). He knew George Herbert Mead and helped to establish the 'Chicago School' (see CHICAGO SOCIOLOGY). Central to Dewey's PRAGMATISM was that philosophy should concern itself with everyday problems and reasoning, and should be critical of the everyday world, not merely a contemplative activity. Later, he applied his philosophy to moral problems which, he argued, could be judged in a matter-of-fact way according to how efficacious moral maxims were in solving human problems.

Dilthey, Wilhelm (*b.* 1833, Hesse; *d.* 1911, South Tyrol, Austria) German hermeneutic philosopher. Educated in Heidelberg and Berlin, Dilthey taught at Basle (1866), Kiel (1868) and Breslau (1871) and became Professor of History and Philosophy at Berlin (1882). Dilthey is best known for his radical separation of natural and social scientific analysis, the former dealing with events that can be subsumed under laws, whereas the latter deals with phenomena that are only understandable in terms of the intentions or meanings of agents (*Introduction to the Sciences of Spirit* 1883). This anti-naturalistic position was originally manifested as social scientific psychologism, a position from which Dilthey later diverged.

Durkheim, Emile (*b.* 1858, Epinal; *d.* 1917, Paris) French sociologist. Educated at the Ecole Normale Supérieure, he taught at the University of Bordeaux until 1902, when he was appointed to a chair at the Sorbonne. His major publications were concerned with sociological methods, the forms of social solidarity and the social functions of religion. After the foundation of the influential journal, *Année sociologique* (1898), Durkheim became particularly interested in the study of archaic societies, and of primitive religion and social organization. The dominant theme in all his work was that society has a reality over and above the individuals comprising it, the latter being constrained by transcendent 'social facts' in the form of common beliefs and sentiments. Durkheim was one of the founding fathers of modern sociology, and in particular of the functionalist theory.

Einstein, Albert (*b.* 1879, Ulm; *d.* 1955, Princeton) German natural philosopher and theoretical physicist. Studied mathematics and physics at the Swiss Federal Polytechnic in Zürich. Influenced by Hume and Mach, Einstein made fundamental contributions to theoretical physics, particularly in his theory of relativity (1916). His work came to challenge the belief in empiricism which dominated the philosophy of physics in the early part of this century. In his later years he was active in movements to limit the development and spread of nuclear weapons.

Elias, Norbert (*b.* 1897, Breslau; *d.* 1990, Amsterdam) German sociologist. Educated in medicine, philosophy and psychology at the universities of Breslau and Heidelberg, after which he worked with Karl Mannheim in Frankfurt. Elias fled from Nazi Germany in 1933, going first to France and then to Britain where he was Lecturer in Sociology at the University of Leicester (1945–62) and later held posts at the University of Ghana

(1962–4) and at the Zentrum für Interdisziplinäre Forschung in Bielefeld. He developed an approach which he called 'figurational sociology' that examines the emergence of social configurations as the unintended consequences of social interaction, outlined in *What Is Sociology?* (1970). His best-known work is *The Civilising Process* (2 vols., 1939), analysing the effects of state-formation in Europe on individual lifestyles, personality and moralities.

Engels, Friedrich (*b.* 1820, Barmen; *d.* 1895, London) German social philosopher and businessman. Engels was, with Marx, one of the founders of modern communism. Convinced that the working class emerging from the industrial revolution would be the instrument of revolutionary transformation, his *Condition of the Working Class in England* (1845) attracted wide attention. With Marx he published numerous works, including the *Communist Manifesto* (1848), and after Marx's death he continued work on *Capital* from Marx's drafts, publishing the second and third volumes in 1885 and 1894. While he played down his own role, his work on political economy and the development of class consciousness were significant contributions to Marxism, and before 1914, it was he, more than Marx, who was chiefly responsible for the diffusion of Marxist ideas.

Fanon, Frantz (*b.* 1925, Martinique; *d.* 1962, Washington DC) French psychiatrist and social philosopher. Educated in medicine and psychiatry at the University of Lyons, Fanon went to Algeria in the 1950s where he headed the Psychiatric Department at Blida-Joinville Hospital (1953–6), and became sympathetic to the Algerian rebels, supporting their armed struggle. *Black Skin, White Masks* (1952), is an account of the psychological degradation of both indigenous Algerians and the French colonists resulting from colonial rule. In 1960 he was appointed Ambassador to Ghana by the Algerian Provisional Government but had to go to the USSR and then Washington for leukemia treatment. Fanon advocated revolution throughout the Third World in his *The Wretched of the Earth* (1961).

Foucault, Michel (*b.* 1926, Poitiers; *d.* 1984, Paris) French philosopher and historian of ideas. Studied at the Ecole Normale Supérieure from 1946, and later held academic posts in various European institutions, culminating in his election to the Collège de France in 1969. He offered new insights into a range of disciplines, such as psychology, psychiatry, medicine and philosophy, and his many publications reflect the broad scope of his research. He was particularly concerned with how various 'power-knowledge' discourses – such as medicine, psychiatry, penology and sexuality – operate upon the individual.

Freud, Sigmund (*b.* 1856, Freiberg; *d.* 1939, London) Austrian psychologist and founder of psychoanalysis. Educated in medicine at Vienna, specializing in neurology (1874–9), and from 1885–6 studied under Jean Charcot in Paris. Worked in the Vienna General Hospital 1882–5, became a lecturer in the University in 1885 and established a private practice the following year. In 1902 he founded the Vienna Psychoanalytic Society and in 1910 the International Association of Psychoanalysis. He also founded the two journals: *Zeitschrift für Psychoanalyse und Imago* and *Jahrbuch der Psychoanalyse*. In 1938 he came to Britain as a refugee from Nazism. His writings are collected as the *Standard Edition of the Complete Works of Sigmund Freud* (ed. J. Strachey, 24 vols., 1953–74).

Fromm, Erich (*b.* 1900, Frankfurt; *d.* 1980, Locarno) German/American psychologist. Educated in the 1920s at the universities of Heidelberg and Munich and at the Institute of the German Psychoanalytic Society. Lectured in psychoanalysis at the Institute for Social Research (Frankfurt 1929–32) where he worked with other members of the FRANKFURT SCHOOL, and set out to establish a relation between psychoanalysis and Marxism. Continued his association with the Institute in exile at Columbia University (1934–8). Subsequently Professor of Psychoanalysis at the National Autonomous University of Mexico from 1951, and in his later years devoted much of his time to the study of aggression (*The Anatomy of Human Destructiveness* 1973), as well as supporting the peace movement and the dissident democratic socialists of Eastern Europe.

Gadamer, Hans-Georg (*b.* 1900, Marburg) German hermeneutic philosopher. Educated in Munich and Marburg, a friend and pupil of Heidegger, Gadamer was a Professor of Philosophy at Marburg (1937–9), Leipzig (1939–47), Frankfurt (1947–9) and Heidelberg (1949–68) after which he retired. His main work is *Truth and Method* (1960) in which he outlines his approach to hermeneutics as an active, creative, not a merely passive process, which is mediated by the cultural tradition of the interpreter. See HERMENEUTICS.

Gandhi, Mahatma [Mohandas Karamchand] (*b.* 1869, Porbandar; *d.* 1948, Delhi) Indian nationalist and spiritual leader. Educated in India and Britain, he qualified as a barrister in London. From 1920 he dominated the Indian National Congress turning it into a mass movement. Famous for his advocacy of 'non-violent resistance', Gandhi led Indian nationalists in a series of confrontations with the British Raj, espousing the force of truth and non-violence in the struggle against evil. See HINDUISM AND HINDU SOCIAL THEORY.

Gramsci, Antonio (*b.* 1891, Ales, Sardinia; *d.* 1937, Rome) Marxist political activist and theorist. In 1911 Gramsci won a scholarship to the University of Turin and became involved with the Italian Socialist Party (PSI), but abandoned his studies without graduating and devoted himself to helping to publish the socialist papers *Avanti!* and *Il Grido del Popolo* (The People's Cry). In May 1919 he helped launch a weekly paper, *L'Ordine Nuovo* (The New Order), was its editor in 1919–20 and also the central organizer of the Turin factory councils. One of the founding members of the Italian Communist Party (PCI) he became its leader in 1924. Arrested in 1926, he was sentenced to imprisonment in 1928, and spent the next nine years in prison, where he began to write his *Prison Notebooks*, on themes ranging from art and culture to political strategy, which have profoundly influenced later Marxist thought. See HEGEMONY.

Habermas, Jürgen (*b.* 1929, Düsseldorf) German social philosopher and sociologist educated at Göttingen and Frankfurt, he has taught at Heidelberg and Frankfurt and was Director of the Max Planck Institute, Starnberg (1971–82). Habermas has developed a critique of the technocratic consciousness which encroaches on the 'life-world' in late capitalist societies. His critical theory aims to engender a consciousness of the two-fold nature of rationality, as instrumental and communicative (*The Theory of Communicative Action* 1981). More recently he has been a trenchant critic of postmodernism (*The Philosophical Discourse of Modernity* 1985). See FRANKFURT SCHOOL.

Hayek, Friedrich August von (*b.* 1899, Vienna; *d.* 1992) Austrian economist. Educated at Vienna University, Hayek was the first director of the Austrian Institute for Economic Research (1927–31). From 1931–50 he was Professor of Economic Science at the London School of Economics. During this period he developed AUSTRIAN ECONOMICS in several books (e.g. *Prices and Production* 1931). Hayek's post-war works tended to diverge into political philosophy, law and epistemology. His analysis of the nature of knowledge in society (in *Individualism and Economic Order* 1949) forms a crucial element in his critique of central planning. He also developed a critique of POSITIVISM (*The Counter-Revolution of Science* 1952) and made important contributions to liberal political philosophy (*Law, Legislation and Liberty* 1973–9).

Heidegger, Martin (*b.* 1889, Messkirch; *d.* 1976, Messkirch) German philosopher. Educated at Freiburg (under Husserl) and taught at Marburg (1923–8) before becoming Rector of Freiburg where he declared allegiance to Hitler. He was removed from teaching after World War II by the occupying forces but continued to exert a great influence over philosophy. His magnum opus is *Being and Time* (1927) which set an agenda for his life's work to follow, examining human being – *Dasein* – in its temporal character. Although he is associated with, and influenced, EXISTENTIALISM he did not see himself in those terms.

Hilferding, Rudolf (*b.* 1877, Vienna; *d.* 1941, Paris) Marxist economist. Studied medicine in Vienna and practised as a doctor until 1906, but devoted most of his time to the study of political economy. He became known for his frequent contributions on economic subjects to *Die Neue Zeit*, and for his rejoinder (published in 1904) to Böhm-Bawerk's critique of Marx's economic theory. In 1920, after becoming a Prussian citizen, he was appointed to the Reich Economic Council, was a member of the Reichstag from 1924 to 1933, and Minister of Finance in two governments (1923 and 1928/9). After the Nazi seizure of power he went into exile, but in 1941 committed suicide while in the hands of the Gestapo. He is best known for his work *Finance Capital* (1910) in which he analysed the latest developments in capitalism, and

particularly the role of the banks, imperialism and the danger of war. See AUSTRO-MARXISM.

Husserl, Edmund Gustav Albrecht (*b.* 1859, Prossnitz, Austrian Moravia; *d.* 1938, Freiburg) German philosopher, founder of PHENOMENOLOGY. Educated in mathematics at Leipzig, Vienna and Berlin, Husserl tried to establish the foundations of mathematics and logic, and then of the sciences, by attempting to identify the fundamental structures of consciousness. Phenomenology (a science of appearances) holds in abeyance questions about the existential status of the objects of consciousness in order to intuit essences as constituted by the transcendental ego (*Logical Investigations* 1900–1). Husserl taught at Halle, Göttingen and Freiburg (where Heidegger was his pupil and succeeded him). Husserl's Jewish heritage (which he had rejected in favour of Protestantism) resulted in his persecution by the Nazis.

James, William (*b.* 1842, New York; *d.* 1910, New Hampshire) American psychologist and philosopher. Educated at Harvard (in medicine) where he subsequently became Professor of Philosophy and Psychology, James was the brother of novelist Henry James. He began to publish on psychology but also wrote on religion (*The Varieties of Religious Experience* 1902). He was one of the founders of PRAGMATISM, arguing that ideas are instruments which must have 'cash value' in terms of their consequences if they are to be considered worthy of anything at all, and his work influenced George Herbert Mead.

Jaspers, Karl Theodor (*b.* 1883, Oldenburg; *d.* 1969, Basle) German/Swiss philosopher. Educated in law at Heidelberg and Munich, and in medicine (in which he received a doctorate) at Berlin, Jaspers's early work was in psychology (*Psychology of World Views* 1919). He was an existentialist philosopher, and Professor of Philosophy at Heidelberg. He was banned from lecturing by Hitler and stripped of his professorship in 1937. Crucial to his philosophy is the distinction between *Dasein* and *Existenz*.

Jung, Carl Gustav (*b.* 1865, Kesswil; *d.* 1961, Lucerne) Swiss psychiatrist. Educated at Basle (1895–1900) and worked at Burghölzli Psychiatric Clinic, Zurich (1900–9). Lectured at the University of Zurich (1905–13) and started his private practice in 1909. Professor of Psychology at the Federal

Polytechnical University of Zurich (1933–41) and Professor of Medical Psychology from 1944. Jung worked with Freud, whose *The Interpretation of Dreams* (1900) had much in common with Jung's work, but after 1913 Jung became increasingly critical of Freud, believing that the latter focused too strongly on sexual repression and trauma in his explanatory schema. Jung's writings have been published as *The Collected Works of C.G. Jung* (ed. H. Read, 19 vols., 1953–79). See PSYCHOANALYSIS.

Keynes, John Maynard Lord (*b.* 1883, Cambridge; *d.* 1946, Tilton, Sussex) English economist. Educated at Eton and King's College, Cambridge, Keynes remained at Cambridge after graduating, to study economics under Alfred Marshall. After a brief spell in the Civil Service he returned to Cambridge to lecture in economics, and became editor of the *Economic Journal* in 1911. During World War I he worked at the Treasury and was its principle representative at Versailles. In World War II Keynes was responsible for negotiating with the USA on Lend-Lease and he took part in the Bretton Woods agreement which established the International Monetary Fund. Keynes is best known for his writings in economics, particularly *The General Theory of Employment, Interest and Money* (1936); see KEYNESIANISM.

Kristeva, Julia (*b.* 1941, Bulgaria) Literary and cultural theorist, linguist and psychoanalyst. Influenced by Russian FORMALISM (especially the work of Bakhtin), but also by Marxism and psychoanalysis, Kristeva emigrated to France in 1966 and now teaches at the University of Paris VII. In *The Revolution in Poetic Language* (1974) she developed a theory of the 'semiotic' – the realm of the pre-linguistic child – which becomes enveloped and repressed by the language and rationality imposed in later life. Since then she has been engaged in a psychoanalytically-inspired feminism.

Kropotkin, Peter Alekseevich (*b.* 1842, Moscow; *d.* 1921, Moscow) Anarchist theorist. Educated at the elite Corps of Pages in St Petersburg, he abandoned a scientific career in 1871 to devote himself to revolutionary activity. Imprisoned in 1874, he escaped in 1876 to the West where he remained in exile until 1917 when he returned to Russia. Kropotkin constructed a 'scientific' theory of society: mutual aid, not Darwinian competition, was the fundamental law of evolution in nature and

society. In several books, he criticized the centralized state for its large-scale production, division of labour and coercive powers, believing it would be swept away by a revolution. He favoured a society of small communities based on voluntary co-operation which would enable the development of the individual's capacities. See ANARCHISM.

Kuhn, Thomas Samuel (*b.* 1922, Cincinatti) American philosopher and historian of science. Educated at Harvard as a physicist, Kuhn turned to the history of science to write a widely cited and controversial book, *The Structure of Scientific Revolutions* (1962), in which he contrasted the historical development of science with the commonplace view of science as a purely rational enterprise. Scientific practice, he argued, is usually governed by a paradigm, a world-view sanctioned by the scientific community, but as anomalies accumulate this 'normal science' may be overthrown by a 'revolution' in which the reigning paradigm is replaced by a new one. This thesis engendered much debate after its publication and later developments of Kuhn's work have often led in relativistic directions. See SOCIOLOGY OF SCIENCE.

Lenin, Vladimir Ilyich [Vladimir Ilyich Ulyanov] (*b.* 1870, Simbirsk; *d.* 1924, Gorki) Russian revolutionary statesman and political theorist. Studied briefly at Kazan University and then devoted himself entirely to revolutionary activities. On the outbreak of the Russian Revolution he returned from exile and led the second (Bolshevik) phase of the revolution, becoming chairman of the Council of People's Commissars. In works such as *What Is To Be Done?* (1902) and *State and Revolution* (1917) he outlined the nature of the socialist state and gave a different emphasis to Marx's theory of revolution by stressing the centrality of class struggle led by a tightly organized Party, and in *Imperialism: the Highest Stage of Capitalism* (1916), he elaborated a theory of imperialism as the final stage of capitalism. Through the Communist International which he inspired, his views spread throughout the world. He was the most influential political leader and theorist of Marxism in the early twentieth century, but the appeal of LENINISM waned later in the century.

Lévi-Strauss, Claude (*b.* 1908, Brussels) French anthropologist. Studied at the Faculty of

Law in Paris and the Sorbonne. Influenced by the approaches of Saussure, Trubetzkoy, Jakobson and Mauss, he developed what became known as 'structural anthropology', his major publications including: *The Elementary Structures of Kinship* (1949), *The Savage Mind* (1962), *Mythologiques* (1964–72). His work also had a considerable impact on other social sciences and on some forms of Marxist thought. See ANTHROPOLOGY, STRUCTURALISM.

Lorenz, Konrad Zacharius (*b.* 1903, Vienna) Austrian ethologist. The founder of modern ethology, he was educated at Columbia University and Vienna (where he studied medicine). He taught at Vienna (1937–40) and Königsberg (1940–2), established a comparative ethology department at the Max Planck Institute, Bulden, and directed the Department of Animal Sociology, Institute of Comparative Ethology, Austrian Academy of Science (1973). Among his major works are *On Aggression* (1966) and *The Foundations of Ethology* (1978).

Lukács, György [Georg] (*b.* 1885, Budapest; *d.* 1971, Budapest) Philosopher and literary critic. Studied at the University of Budapest, where he obtained his doctorate in 1906. He also studied privately with Heinrich Rickert in Heidelberg (1912–15). Author of many books and essays, his best-known theoretical work (and also one of his earliest) was *History and Class Consciousness* (1923) in which he developed his theory of class consciousness and reassessed the significance of Hegel for Marxism, and elaborated a theory of alienation and reification well before Marx's early manuscripts on the subject were published. A leader of the Hungarian communist movement, he was politically active in the Hungarian Commune of 1919 and again in the shortlived government established after the revolt of 1956.

Luxemburg, Rosa (*b.* 1871, Zamość, Poland; *d.* 1919, Berlin) Polish revolutionary socialist. Studied mathematics, natural sciences and political economy at Zurich University, then helped to create the Social Democratic Party of Poland, and subsequently moved to Germany. Luxemburg upheld the cause of revolution and outlined her opposition to REFORMISM in her *Social Reform or Revolution* (1899). In her *Mass Strike, the Political Party and the Trade Unions* (1906) she proposed the mass strike, not the organized vanguard favoured by

Lenin, as the most important instrument of the proletarian revolution. And in her major theoretical work, *The Accumulation of Capital* (1913), she identified IMPERIALISM as a competitive struggle between capitalist nations that will lead to the collapse of the capitalist system. With Karl Liebknecht she founded the Spartakist League, and both were brutally murdered by right-wing officers in 1919, after the suppression of an abortive rising in Berlin.

Malinowski, Bronislaw (*b.* 1884, Cracow; *d.* 1942, New Haven, Connecticut) Social anthropologist. Trained and began his career in England. Malinowski contributed to the transformation of nineteenth-century ANTHROPOLOGY into a modern science based upon fieldwork and to the establishment of a British school of social anthropology. The author of numerous works such as *Magic, Science and Religion* (1925, *1948*), he undertook extensive studies of small-scale non-literate societies and was one of the originators of a functionalist approach to the study of culture. See FUNCTIONALISM.

Mannheim, Karl (*b.* 1893, Budapest; *d.* 1947, London) Hungarian sociologist. Educated at the universities of Berlin, Budapest, Paris and Freiburg, he was associated with Lukács in the Hungarian Commune of 1919, was then obliged to flee to Germany in 1919 and again from Germany to England in 1933. He taught at Heidelberg, Frankfurt, the London School of Economics and the Institute of Education (University of London). Mannheim founded what came to be called the SOCIOLOGY OF KNOWLEDGE, which set out to show the social roots of knowledge (*Ideology and Utopia* 1929, and *Essays on the Sociology of Knowledge* 1952), and he was primarily concerned with the possibility of transcending the partial standpoints of various social and political factions in order to produce some degree of consensus through the work of 'socially unattached' intellectuals.

Mao Zedong [Mao Tse-tung] (*b.* 1893, Shaoshan; *d.* 1976, Peking) Chinese revolutionary and statesman. Mao Zedong was the leader of the Chinese Revolution of 1949 and the architect of the new communist China. He placed great faith in the revolutionary potential and creative capacity of the peasantry and the masses generally, but there is much debate over the nature and originality of his theoretical contributions to Marxism. His opposition to bureaucracy inspired the 'Cultural Revolution' of 1966–76, which caused a decade of chaos and political upheaval in China. See MAOISM.

Marcuse, Herbert (*b*. 1898, Berlin; *d*. 1979, Munich) Social and political theorist. Studied philosophy at Berlin and Freiburg, and joined the Frankfurt Institute of Social Research in 1933, subsequently becoming a key figure in the FRANKFURT SCHOOL. He was a prominent spokesman of the NEW LEFT in the 1960s and early 1970s and critic of the nature of contemporary society (*One-Dimensional Man* 1964). His social theory drew upon a number of sources, in particular the early Marx, Hegel, Heidegger and Freud, and its eclectic nature is reflected in his writings (e.g. *Reason and Revolution* (1941) on Hegel; *Eros and Civilisation* (1955) on Freud).

Marshall, Alfred (*b*. 1842, London; *d*. 1924, Cambridge) English economist. Educated at Merchant Taylor's School and St John's College, Cambridge where he graduated in mathematics. In 1868 Marshall lectured in moral science at Cambridge during which time he initiated his study of economics. He returned to Cambridge (after teaching at Bristol) as Professor of Political Economy in 1885 and established himself as the dominant force in British economics with the publication of *Principles of Economics* (1890). Marshall was instrumental in establishing a new Tripos in Economics and Politics at Cambridge in 1903, having partially to finance it himself. See ECONOMICS; MARGINALIST ECONOMICS.

Marx, Karl Heinrich (*b*. 1818, Trier; *d*. 1883, London) German social philosopher and revolutionary. Educated at the universities of Bonn and Berlin, Marx developed a materialist conception of history (*German Ideology*, written with Engels, 1845–6) and envisaged a global revolution as the culmination of the conflict between the capitalists and the proletariat, to be followed by the construction of a classless, communist society. The *Communist Manifesto* (written with Engels, 1848) was one of the most influential political tracts of all time, and the three volumes of *Capital* (1867, 1885, 1894) gave a profound analysis of the capitalist process of production. Politically active, Marx was a key figure in establishing the International Working Men's Association in 1864, eventually becoming its leader. He is the most important figure in the

history of socialist thought and his ideas have profoundly changed social life and the social sciences in the twentieth century. See MARXISM.

Mauss, Marcel (*b*. 1872, Epinal in Lorraine; *d*. 1950, Paris) French sociologist and anthropologist. Studied philosophy at Bordeaux and the history of religion at the Ecole Pratique des Hautes Etudes. Throughout his career he was heavily involved in collaborative work with Durkheim – the notion of 'total social facts' is attributed to Mauss – and others, and he played a major part in editing the journal *Année sociologique*. His theoretical contributions derive mainly from his application and refinement of Durkheimian sociology (see ANTHROPOLOGY; DURKHEIM SCHOOL), and his studies such as *The Gift* (1925) greatly influenced later French anthropologists, among them Lévi-Strauss.

Mead, George Herbert (*b*. 1863, Massachusetts; *d*. 1931, Chicago) American philosopher and sociologist. Educated at Oberlin College, Harvard (where he studied under William James), Leipzig and Berlin, Mead spent most of his working life at Chicago University (from 1894) where he was instrumental in forming the 'Chicago School' of PRAGMATISM, which had a large impact on the development of SYMBOLIC INTERACTIONISM. Mead argued that the development of the self was a process that occurred only in social interaction (*Mind, Self and Society*, 1934).

Mead, Margaret (*b*. 1901, Philadelphia; *d*. 1978, New York) American anthropologist and cultural commentator. Studied at Barnard College, New York and Columbia University. Throughout her career her anthropological studies were very much oriented towards challenging accepted conventions, particularly in terms of GENDER roles, and in the nature-nurture debate she distinctly favoured the latter (*Male and Female* 1949). In addition to her anthropological work, she also commented upon disarmament, feminism and youth culture. See ANTHROPOLOGY.

Merleau-Ponty, Maurice (*b*. 1908, Rochefort sur-Mer; *d*. 1961, Paris) French existentialist philosopher. Educated at the Ecole Normale Supérieure, he taught in several lycées and subsequently at Lyons (1945–8), the Sorbonne (1949–52) and the Collège de France (1952–61). He founded and co-edited, with Sartre and de Beauvoir, the review *Les*

Temps Modernes (1944). Influenced by Husserl, Merleau-Ponty nevertheless tried to affirm the existence of a world which transcends consciousness but is only accessible through perception (*Phenomenology of Perception* 1945). He was sympathetic to, but critical of, Marxism, and in *Adventures of the Dialectic* (1955) he criticized the 'vulgar' Marxism pervading the communist movement, and disavowed the ideas of historical determinism. He was also critical of Sartre's views on the ultimate autonomy of the subject. See EXISTENTIALISM; PHENOMENOLOGY.

Pareto, Vilfredo Federico Damaso (*b.* 1848, Paris; *d.* 1923, Geneva) Italian economist/sociologist. Educated at the Polytechnical Institute of Turin and Turin University where he studied mathematical sciences. Pareto worked in the engineering industry for 20 years and only turned to a career in economics in the 1890s. In 1893 he was appointed Professor of Political Economy at the University of Lausanne. His *Cours d'économie politique* (1897) and *Manual of Political Economy* (1906) abounded in the mechanistic metaphors of natural science, and in these very abstract texts *Homo oeconomicus* made his first appearance. Pareto then turned his attention increasingly to sociology, arguing that 'in general men act in a nonlogical way', so that the ideal world of *Homo oeconomicus* was uninformative in describing the real world. In his *The Mind and Society* (1916–19) he elaborated the category of nonlogical action and also an influential theory of elites.

Parsons, Talcott (*b.* 1902, Colorado Springs; *d.* 1979, Munich) American sociologist. Studied at Amherst College, the London School of Economics and Heidelberg. The common theme of his major works (*The Structure of Social Action* 1937, *The Social System* 1951) is his belief in a functionalist theory, according to which social life is regulated by common norms and values. This was a dominant theoretical perspective in American sociology during the 1940s and 1950s, and Parsons was the dominant sociologist of this period.

Piaget, Jean (*b.* 1896, Neuchâtel; *d.* 1980, Geneva) Swiss psychologist, biologist and philosopher. Trained as a biologist, Piaget was concerned throughout his career with the origins and conditions of knowledge. He studied psychology in Zurich (1918) and the Sorbonne (1919). His best-known work is on the developmental psychology of children's intelligence in books such as *The Early Growth of Logic in the Child* (1959, with Bärbel Inhelder) and *The Psychology of the Child* (1966), and he has had a massive influence on cognitive developmental psychology since the early 1960s. But he also wrote more generally on epistemology and STRUCTURALISM.

Popper, Sir Karl Raimund (*b.* 1902, Vienna) Philosopher of science. Educated in Vienna in mathematics, physics and philosophy, he had contact with, but was not a member of, the VIENNA CIRCLE. In his first book, *The Logic of Scientific Discovery* (1934), Popper claimed to solve Hume's problem of induction by replacing the Vienna circle's criterion for scientificity (the verification principle) with his famous falsification principle. After the war Popper moved to England and taught at the London School of Economics. He turned his attention to the study of social and political philosophy, developing a critique of enemies of the OPEN SOCIETY (in particular Plato, Hegel and Marx) and of HISTORICISM, which he defined as the belief that there are discoverable laws of history (*The Open Society and Its Enemies* 1945, *The Poverty of Historicism* 1957).

Poulantzas, Nicos (*b.* 1936, Athens; *d.* 1979, Paris) Greek social and political theorist. Educated at an experimental school attached to Athens University and then at an Institut Français, Poulantzas went on to study law at Athens University where he became involved with the Greek Communist Party. After compulsory military service, he went to Germany to study but quickly moved to France, where he subsequently taught at the Sorbonne and the University of Vincennes. His first book (*Political Power and Social Classes* 1968) revealed Althusserian leanings, arguing that the state was so structured that irrespective of its personnel it would act in the interest of the bourgeoisie. Later works include *Classes in Contemporary Capitalism* (1974) and *State, Power, Socialism* (1978).

Radcliffe-Brown, Alfred Reginald (*b.* 1881, Birmingham; *d.* 1955, London) British anthropologist, educated at Trinity College, Cambridge, where he was the first student of the anthropologist W.H.R. Rivers, Radcliffe-Brown came under the influence of Durkheim and developed a functionalist approach to anthropology (see FUNCTIONA-LISM). He was a Fellow of Trinity College, Cambridge (1908–14), and subsequently taught at the universities of London (1909–10), Cape Town (1921–5), Sydney (1925–31), Chicago (1931–7) and Oxford (1937–46). His major works include *The Andaman Islanders* (1922, *1948*), *Structure and Function in Primitive Society* (1952) and *A Natural Science of Society* (1957).

Rawls, John Boardley (*b.* 1921, Baltimore) American moral philosopher. Educated at Princeton, Rawls has held posts at Princeton (1950–2), Cornell (1953–62) and Harvard (since 1962). He is the author of *A Theory of Justice* (1971), a Kantian inspired (and hence anti-utilitarian) outline of a contemporary moral philosophy in the contractarian tradition, and probably the best-known moral philosophical work since World War II.

Russell, Bertrand Arthur William (*b.* 1872, Gwent; *d.* 1970, Gwynedd) British philosopher. Educated at Trinity College, Cambridge, where he took the Mathematical and Moral Tripos. Taught at Trinity (1895–1916) where his pupils included Wittgenstein, but was removed from his post by Trinity Council for opposing British entry into World War I. Joined the No-Conscription Fellowship in 1915 and was fined and imprisoned. Went to the USA after the war but was barred from teaching in New York for his over-liberal ideas on sex, education and war. Russell was active in the anti-war movement after World War II; he was President of the Campaign for Nuclear Disarmament (1958–60), founded the Bertrand Russell Peace Foundation (1963) and co-organized the International War Crimes Tribunal (1966) in which Sartre, amongst others, took part. His major philosophical work was concerned with logic and epistemology (*Principia Mathematica*, with A.N. Whitehead, 1910–13; *Human Knowledge*, 1948), but he also wrote much on social and political issues. See PHILOSOPHY.

Sartre, Jean-Paul (*b.* 1905, Paris; *d.* 1980, Paris) Philosopher, novelist, playwright. Educated at the Ecole Normale Supérieure and Freiburg. Sartre largely shunned the life of a conventional academic although he taught for several years in various lycées. Influenced by Husserl and Heidegger, Sartre expounded his EXISTENTIALISM in *Being and Nothingness* (1943). He served in the French army

in the war, was captured at Padoux in 1940 but escaped in 1941, and after the war devoted himself to writing, founded (with de Beauvoir and Merleau-Ponty) *Les Temps Modernes*, and turned towards Marxism, which he saw as being compatible with his existentialist philosophy (*Critique of Dialectical Reason* 1960). But he was always highly critical of the French Communist Party, from which he made a complete break after 1968. His left-wing existentialist philosophy profoundly shaped French culture for a decade after the war.

Saussure, Ferdinand de (*b.* 1857, Geneva; *d.* 1913, near Geneva) The founder of modern linguistics. Studied Indo-European languages at the universities of Leipzig and Berlin. His *Course in General Linguistics* (1916) is generally regarded as the most significant work of linguistics written this century. Saussure's influence was also evident in the STRUCTURALISM of the 1960s, which was essentially an attempt to apply his linguistic theory to objects and activities other than language itself. See LINGUISTICS; SEMIOTICS.

Scheler, Max (*b.* 1874, Munich; *d.* 1928, Frankfurt) German philosopher and sociologist. Studied medicine and philosophy at the universities of Berlin, Munich and Jena. Although not an 'orthodox' phenomenologist, much of his philosophy was in line with the work of Franz Brentano and Edmund Husserl (see PHENOMENOLOGY) and he actually went beyond Husserl, who criticized him for doing so. His phenomenological period lasted until 1920; during 1920–4 he was interested in religious philosophy following his conversion to Catholicism, and this was succeeded by a 'metaphysical period' (1924–8) characterized by Vitalism and Pantheism. His main contributions to social thought lie in the domain of social psychology and the SOCIOLOGY OF KNOWLEDGE.

Schumacher, Ernst Fritz (*b.* 1911, Bonn; *d.* 1977, Switzerland) German economist. Educated at Oxford where he was one of the first German Rhodes Scholars after World War I. He spent most of the 1930s in England and the USA. In 1943 he advocated an international payments system similar to that of Keynes which became a central part of the Bretton Woods system. He was advisor to the British Control Commission in Germany (1946–50) and to British Coal (1950–70), regarding nuclear power as too environmentally unfriendly to use. In 1955 he visited Burma, where he was converted to Buddhism and wrote *Small is Beautiful* (1973) deriding Western living standards for having been attained at the expense of a debased culture. See ENVIRONMENTALISM.

Schumpeter, Joseph Alois (*b*. 1883, Triesch, Moravia; *d*. 1950, Connecticut) Austrian economist. Educated at Vienna University and began teaching at the University of Graz in 1911. He was Austrian Minister of Finance in 1919–20 before resuming teaching at Bonn (1925–32) and Harvard (1932–50). Schumpeter developed a sympathetic interest in Marxism to which he was first exposed as a student in Vienna in debates between Austrian economists (Böhm-Bawerk and von Mises) and the Austro-Marxists (Hilferding and Bauer). He is best known for his *Theory of Economic Development* (1911), for his studies of economic cycles, making use of Kondratiev's conception of 'long waves', *Business Cycles* (1939), and for his analysis of the probable decline of capitalism in *Capitalism, Socialism and Democracy* (1942). See AUSTRO-MARXISM.

Schutz, Alfred (*b*. 1899, Vienna; *d*. 1959, New York) Austrian sociologist. Educated at the University of Vienna in law and social sciences where he was a pupil of von Mises. He moved to New York in 1939 where he joined the New School of Social Research but also took a position as a banker to alleviate financial hardship. Schutz used Husserlian concepts to augment Weber's analysis of social action, and investigated the constitution of the 'lifeworld' and intersubjectivity in work that strongly influenced ethnomethodology. His main analytical framework is set out in *The Phenomenology of the Social World* (1932).

Simmel, Georg (*b*. 1858, Berlin; *d*. 1918, Strasbourg) German philosopher and sociologist. Studied history, psychology, anthropology and philosophy at the University of Berlin. Simmel employed the methodology of a variety of disciplines to study cultural phenomena such as religion, the money economy, the rise of morality and the self-preservation of groups. Probably his best-known application of this approach is in his book *The Philosophy of Money* (1907) where he studied the impact of the money economy on human social relations.

Sorel, Georges Eugène (*b*. 1847, Cherbourg; *d*. 1922, Boulogne-sur-Seine, Paris) French social philosopher. He trained in Paris at the Ecole Polytechnique where he excelled in mathematics and qualified as an engineer. He pursued this profession until 1892 when he resigned to concentrate on the study of social and political affairs. Although often associated with Mosca and Pareto, Sorel is more widely known as an innovator in Marxist theory and the methodology of the social sciences; rejecting the universalistic claims of positivist conceptions of science, he favoured an intellectual and methodological pluralism. From 1896 he began a reinterpretation of Marxism, identifying the central tenets of Marxism as 'myths' – notably that of the general strike – capable of inspiring the working class to action outside the framework of parliamentary democracy (*Reflections on Violence*, 1906).

Spencer, Herbert (*b*. 1820, Derby; *d*. 1903, Brighton) British philosopher and sociologist. Spencer never attended secondary school or university. He began his career as a railway engineer before turning to writing and the study of philosophy, publishing his first book, *Social Statistics*, in 1851. Spencer was an evolutionist before Darwin and it was he who coined the phrase 'survival of the fittest'. He sought to trace the principles of evolution in all branches of knowledge in his multi-volume work *A System of Synthetic Philosophy*, of which volume 3, *The Principles of Sociology* (1896), was his most influential. In his book *The Man Versus the State* (1873) he defended a *laissez-faire* position, attacking all forms of state interference as impinging upon individual freedom. He is perhaps best known for his optimistic belief in human progress through evolution. See EVOLUTIONARY PROCESSES IN SOCIETY.

Teilhard de Chardin, Pierre (*b*. 1881, Sarcenat, France; *d*. 1955, New York) French theologian and palaeontologist. Educated as a Jesuit in France and England (1893–1911) he was ordained as a Jesuit priest. From 1912–22 he studied geology at the Institut Catholique (where he subsequently taught, 1920–3), and palaeontology at the Museum of Natural History. From 1923–46 he was assigned to a Jesuit Collège des Hautes Etudes in China. His interests were in both theology and science, but his scientific writings were banned from publication in his lifetime by his Jesuit superiors. In *The Pheno-*

menon of Man (1955) he argued that having gone through a divergent phase in which cultures of great variety emerged, human evolution will enter a convergent phase in which disparate cultures will come together in unanimity.

Tönnies, Ferdinand (*b.* 1855, Eiderstedt, Schleswig-Holstein; *d.* 1936, Kiel, Schleswig-Holstein) German social theorist and philosopher. Studied a number of disciplines at several universities, taking his doctorate in Classical Philology at Tübingen in 1877. He taught at the University of Kiel from 1881 to 1933, when he was removed by the Nazis. His principal work, *Gemeinschaft und Gesellschaft* (1887), is one of the classics of sociology, and he is best known indeed for introducing the terms *Gemeinschaft* (COMMUNITY) – a social form characterized by personal relationships, an intense emotional spirit, constituted by co-operation, custom and religion and found in the family, village and small-town community; and *Gesellschaft* (society) – a large scale organization, such as the city, state or nation, based on impersonal relations, particular interests, law and public opinion.

Toynbee, Arnold Joseph (*b.* 1889, London; *d.* 1975, London) English historian. Educated at Balliol College, Oxford (1907–11) and the British Archaeological School, Athens (1911–12), Toynbee taught at Balliol (1912–15), was Professor of Byzantine and Modern Greek Language, Literature and History at the University of London from 1919, and also Director of Studies, Royal Institute of International Affairs, London (1925–55). He is best known for *A Study of History* (vols. I–III, 1934; vols. IV–VI, 1939; vols. VII–X, 1954; vols. XI–XII, 1961), which examined 21 civilizations that he saw as manifesting similar patterns of growth and decay.

Trotsky, Leon [Lev Bronstein] (*b.* 1879, Yanovka, Ukraine; *d.* 1940, Coyoacan, Mexico) Russian communist revolutionary and military leader. In 1917 Trotsky joined the Bolsheviks, becoming one of the principal organizers of the successful October Revolution. In the first Soviet government he was Commissar for Foreign Affairs and negotiated the Peace of Brest-Litovsk (1918) by which Russia withdrew from World War I. As Commissar for War (1918–24) he formed the Red Army and his direction of the Russian Civil War

saved the Bolshevik revolution. He was expelled from the party in 1927 and exiled. Shortly after founding the Fourth International (1937) to oppose Stalinism, he was murdered in Mexico. He was an internationalist, dedicated to world revolution, and opposed Stalin's 'Socialism in one country'. His main contribution to Marxist thought was the theory of 'uneven and combined development', and the derived doctrine of 'permanent revolution'. See TROTSKYISM.

Veblen, Thorstein (*b.* 1857, Manitowas County, Wisconsin; *d.* 1929, Menlo Park, California) American institutional economist and radical social thinker. Educated at Johns Hopkins and Yale universities, Veblen became an iconoclastic figure in economics, criticizing neoclassical orthodoxy for neglecting broader social and cultural issues germane to economics. In books such as *The Theory of the Leisure Class* (1899) and *The Theory of Business Enterprise* (1904), partly influenced by his wide reading of socialist and Marxist literature, he introduced concepts such as 'conspicuous consumption' and 'ostentatious waste', which became widely familiar. He taught at several universities but his eccentric lifestyle, his originality and his account of American universities in *The Higher Learning in America* (1918) alienated him from the academic mainstream.

von Mises, Ludwig Edler (*b.* 1881, Lemberg, Austria-Hungary; *d.* 1973, New York) Austrian economist. Educated at Vienna University where he participated in Böhm-Bawerk's seminar group, he was an economist at the Vienna Chamber of Commerce (1909–34), a professor at the University and an advisor to the Austrian government. He made theoretical contributions to monetary theory (*The Theory of Money and Credit* 1912) and initiated the SOCIALIST CALCULATION debate by arguing that no government could calculate sufficiently well to plan an economy (*Collectivist Economic Planning*, ed. Hayek, 1935). In *Human Action* (1949) he provided a classic outline of Austrian subjectivism in economics. See AUSTRIAN ECONOMICS.

Weber, Max (*b.* 1864, Erfurt; *d.* 1920, Munich) German sociologist/economist. Educated at Heidelberg, Strasbourg, Göttingen and Berlin where he studied law, economics, history and philosophy, Weber held chairs in Political Economy at Freiburg and Heidelberg but retired from teaching in 1898 after a nervous breakdown. He was largely responsible for establishing sociology as an academic discipline in Germany, and from 1904 edited a major social science journal, the *Archiv für Sozialwissenschaft und Sozialpolitik*. He wrote on a great range of issues, taking as his central themes the development of capitalism and the RATIONALIZATION of the social world; notably in such works as *The Protestant Ethic and the Spirit of Capitalism* (1904–5), *General Economic History* (1923), *Economy and Society* (1921). He also contributed substantially to methodological debates concerning 'interpretation' (*Verstehen*) and causal explanation, values and objectivity (*The Methodology of the Social Sciences* 1904).

Webb, Beatrice [née Potter]   (*b.* 1858, Gloucester; *d.* 1943, Passfield Corner, Hampshire) Social reformer and historian. Educated at home by governesses. Personally investigated social and industrial conditions; contributed to Charles Booth's *Life and Labour of the People in London* (1892–7). Published *The Co-operative Movement in Great Britain* (1891).

Webb, Sidney James, Baron Passfield   (*b.* 1859, London; *d.* 1947, Passfield Corner, Hampshire) Social reformer and historian. Educated in Switzerland and Mecklenburg-Schwerin, at the Birkbeck Institute and the City of London College. Joined the Fabian Society in 1885 and wrote a number of Fabian tracts; *Facts for Socialists* (1887), *Facts for Londoners* (1889), and made a significant contribution to *Fabian Essays in Socialism* (1889). Elected member of the London County Council for Deptford (1892–1910). Founder of the London School of Economics. Author of many books with Beatrice Webb, 'the firm of Webb' as she called it, and with her a leading figure in the socialist movement. Their joint works include *The History of Trade Unionism* (1894, *1920*); *Industrial Democracy* (1897) and *Soviet Communism: A New Civilisation?* (1935).

Wittgenstein, Ludwig Josef Johann   (*b.* 1889, Vienna; *d.* 1951, Cambridge) Studied at Berlin-Charlottenburg, Manchester and Trinity College, Cambridge (where he was taught by Bertrand Russell). Taken prisoner in Italy in World War I, he sent Russell a draft of the *Tractatus Logico-Philosophicus* (1921). After the war he forsook academic philosophy and became a school teacher in Austria, but kept in touch with developments in philosophy through the VIENNA CIRCLE. In 1929 he returned to Cambridge, and in 1939 succeeded G. E. Moore as professor of philosophy. During World War II he worked at Guy's Hospital and was a medical technician in Newcastle. His changing philosophical views during the 1930s and 1940s were largely conveyed in seminars and discussions, and manuscripts and notes of this period were published after his death (e.g. *Philosophical Investigations*, 1953). Wittgenstein was the principal source of the LINGUISTIC PHILOSOPHY which flourished in Britain in the first postwar decades.

BIBLIOGRAPHY

Note: The convention 1910 (*1987*) indicates a work first published in 1910 but most readily accessible in a translation or edition of 1987, to which the publication details refer.

Abbott, Andrew 1988: *The System of Profession: an Essay on the Division of Expert Labor*. Chicago: University of Chicago Press.

Abbott, Philip 1987: *Seeking New Inventions: the Idea of Community in America*. Nashville: University of Tennessee Press.

Abdel-Malek, Anouar 1981: *Civilization and Social Theory*. London: Macmillan.

Abercrombie, N. and Urry, J. 1983: *Capital, Labour and the Middle Classes*. London: Allen & Unwin.

Abercrombie, N. et al. eds 1984: *The Penguin Dictionary of Sociology*. London: Allen Lane.

Abercrombie, N. et al. 1980: *The Dominant Ideology Thesis*. London: Allen & Unwin.

Abrahamsson, B. 1972: *Military Professionalization and Political Power*. Beverly Hills, CA: Sage.

Abrams, P. 1968: *The Origins of British Sociology*. Chicago: University of Chicago Press.

Abrams, P. 1982: *Historical Sociology*. County of Somerset: Open Books.

Abu-Lughod, J. L. and Hay, R. eds 1977: *Third World Urbanization*. Chicago: Maaroufa.

Ackerknecht, E. 1967: *Medicine at the Paris Hospital 1774–1848*. Baltimore: Johns Hopkins University Press.

Ackerman, B. A. 1980: *Social Justice in the Liberal State*. New Haven, CT: Yale University Press.

Ackroyd, Carol et al. 1977: *The Technology of Political Control*. Harmondsworth: Penguin.

Adam, G. and Reynaud, J.-D. 1978: *Conflits du travail et changement social*. Paris: PUF.

Adam, Heribert 1971: *Modernizing Racial Domination*. Berkeley: University of California Press.

Adams, J. 1951: *The American Revolution: Sources and Documents*. 2nd edn, Oxford: Oxford University Press.

Adizes, Ichak 1971: *Industrial Democracy Yugoslav Style: the Effect of Decentralization on Organizational Behaviour*. New York: Free Press.

Adler, F. et al. eds 1986: *Automation and Industrial Workers: a Fifteen Nation Study*, Vol. 2. Oxford: Pergamon.

Adler, Max 1904: *Kausalität und Teleologie im Streite um die Wissenschaft*. Vienna: Wiener Volksbuchhandlung Ignaz Brand.

Adler, Max 1922: *Die Staatsauffassung des Marxismus: ein Beitrag zur Unterscheidung von soziologischer und juristischer Methode*. Vienna: Wiener Volksbuchhandlung.

Adler, Max 1925: *Kant und der Marxismus*. Berlin: E. Laub'sche.

Adler, Max 1930 (*1964*): *Soziologie des Marxismus*. Vienna: Europa.

Adler, Max 1933: Wandlung des Arbeiterklasse? Trans. in *Austro-Marxism*, ed. Tom Bottomore and Patrick Goode. Oxford: Clarendon.

Adorno, Theodor W. 1963: *Quasi una fantasia*. Frankfurt am Main: Suhrkamp.

Adorno, Theodor W. 1966 (*1973*): *Negative Dialectics*. London: Routledge & Kegan Paul.

Adorno, Theodor W. 1967: *Prisms*. London: Spearman.

Adorno, Theodor W. 1973: *Gesammelte Schriften*. Frankfurt am Main: Suhrkamp.

Adorno, Theodor W. 1976: *Introduction to the Sociology of Music*. New York: Seabury.

Adorno, Theodor W. 1984: *Aesthetics Theory*. London: Routledge & Kegan Paul.

Adorno, Theodor W. et al. 1950: *The Authoritarian Personality*. New York: Harper & Row.

Adorno, Theodor W. et al. 1969 (*1976*): *The Positivist Dispute in German Sociology*. London: Heinemann.

Agarwal, B. ed. 1988: *Structures of Patriarchy*. London: Zed.

Aglietta, M. 1976 (*1979*): *A Theory of Capitalist Regulation: the US Experience*. London: Verso.

Aglietta, M. 1982: World capitalism in the eighties. *New Left Review* 136, 5–42.

Aglietta, M. and Orlean, A. 1982: *La violence de la monnaie*. Paris: PUF.

Aigner, D. and Zellner, A., eds 1988: *Causality*. *Journal of Econometrics* 39.1-2.

Aitchison, J. 1981: *Language Change: Progress or Decay*. London: Fontana.

Ajala, A. 1973: *Pan-Africanism: Evolution, Progress and Prospects*. New York: St Martin's.

Ajami, Fuad, 1981: *The Arab Predicament: Arab Political Thought and Practice since 1967*. Cambridge: Cambridge University Press.

Akerlof, G. 1970: The market for 'lemons': qualitative uncertainty and the market mechanism. *Quarterly Journal of Economics* 84, 488-500.

Akin, William 1977: *Technocracy and the American Dream*. Berkeley: University of California Press.

Albanese, L. et al. 1973: *I consigli di fabbrica*. Rome: Riuniti.

Albertoni, Ettore A. 1987: *Mosca and the Theory of Elitism*. Oxford: Blackwell.

Albrow, M. and King, E. eds 1990: *Globalization, Knowledge and Society*. London: Sage.

Alchian, Armen A. 1950 (*1977*): Uncertainty, evolution and economic theory. In *Economic Forces at Work*. Indianapolis: Liberty.

Alexander, J. C. 1982: *Theoretical Logic in Sociology*, vol. 1: *Positivism, Presuppositions, and Current Controversies*. Berkeley: University of California Press.

Alexander, J. C. ed. 1988: *Durkheimian Sociology: Cultural Studies*. Cambridge: Cambridge University Press.

Alique, Ferdinand 1965: *The Philosophy of Surrealism*. Ann Arbor: University of Michigan Press.

Allen, J. 1987: *Natural Language Understanding*. Menlo Park, CA: Benjamin/Cummins.

Allport, G. W. 1935: Attitudes. In *A Handbook of Social Psychology*, ed. C. Murchison. Worcester, MA: Clark University Press.

Allport, G. W. 1937: *Personality: a Psychological Interpretation*. New York: Holt, Rinehart & Winston.

Allport, G. W. 1961: *Patterns and Growth in Personality*. New York: Holt, Rinehart & Winston.

Allport, G. W. 1968: The open system in personality theory. In *Modern System Research for Behavioural Science*, ed. W. Buckley. Chicago.

Allport, G. W. 1976: Prejudice and the individual. In *The Black American Reference Book*, ed. M. M. Smythe. Englewood Cliffs, NJ: Prentice-Hall.

Almond, G. A. 1956: Comparative political systems. *Journal of Politics* 18, 391-409.

Almond, G. A. and Powell, G. B. 1976: *Comparative Politics*. Boston: Little, Brown.

Almond, G. A. and Verba, S. 1963: *The Civic Culture*. Princeton, NJ: Princeton University Press.

Almond, G. A. and Coleman, James S. eds 1960: *The Politics of Developing Areas*. Princeton, NJ: Princeton University Press.

Altbach, P. G. ed. 1989: *Student Political Activism: an International Reference Handbook*. Westport, CT: Greenwood Press.

Altheide, D. L. and Johnson, J. M. 1980: *Bureaucratic Propaganda*. Boston: Allyn & Bacon.

Althusser, Louis 1965 (1969): *For Marx*. London: Allen & Unwin; New York: Pantheon.

Althusser, Louis 1971: Ideology and ideological state apparatuses. In *Lenin and Philosophy and Other Essays*. London: New Left.

Althusser, Louis and Balibar, E. 1970: *Reading 'Capital'*. London: New Left; New York: Pantheon.

American Center for the Quality of Working Life 1978: *Industrial Democracy in Europe: a 1977 Survey*. Washington, DC: German Marshall Fund.

Amin, Samir 1970 (*1974*): *Accumulation on a World Scale*. New York: Monthly Review Press.

Anderson, Benedict 1983: *Imagined Communities: Reflections on the Origin and Spread of Nationalism*. London: Verso.

Anderson, J. R. 1980: *Cognitive Psychology and its Implications*. San Francisco: W. H. Freeman.

Anderson, P. 1964: Origins of the present crisis. *New Left Review* 23.

Anderson, P. 1976: *Considerations on Western Marxism*. London: New Left Books.

Anderson, P. 1976-7: The antinomies of Antonio Gramsci. *New Left Review* 100.

Anderson, S. R. 1985: *Phonology in the Twentieth Century*. Chicago: University of Chicago Press.

Andrew, J. D. 1976: *The Major Film Theories*. New York: Oxford University Press.

Angell, N. 1908 (*1971*): *The Great Illusion*. New York: Garland.

Annerstedt, J. and Jamieson, A. 1988: *From Research Policy to Social Intelligence: Essays for Stevan Dedijer*. London: Macmillan.

Anscombe, G. E. M. 1958: Modern moral philosophy. *Philosophy* 33, 1-19.

Anscombe, G. E. M. 1971: *Causality and Determination*. Cambridge: Cambridge University Press.

Antal, Frederic 1948: *Florentine Painting and its Social Background: the Bourgeois Republic before Cosimo de' Medici's Advent to Power: XIV and Early XV Centuries*. London: Routledge & Kegan Paul.

Anthias, F. and Yuval-Davis, N. 1983: Contextualising feminism: gender, ethnic and class divisions. *Feminist Review* 15.

Antonius, G. 1965 (*1969*): *The Arab Awakening*. New York/Beirut.

Antonovsky, A. 1987: *Unraveling the Mystery of Health*. San Francisco: Jossey-Bass.

Anweiler, Oskar 1958 (*1974*): *The Soviets: the Russian Workers', Peasants' and Soldiers' Councils*. New York: Pantheon.

Apel, K.-O. 1973 (*1980*): *Toward a Transformation of Philosophy*. London: Routledge & Kegan Paul.

Apel, K.-O. 1979 (*1984*): *Understanding and Explanation: a Transcendental-Pragmatic Perspective*. Abridged edn, Cambridge, MA: MIT Press.

Appadurai, Arjun ed. 1986: *The Social Life of Things: Commodities in Cultural Perspective*. Cambridge: Cambridge University Press.

Apter, D. E. 1965: *The Politics of Modernization*. Chicago: University of Chicago Press.

Apter, D. E. 1968: Nkrumah, charisma, and the coup. *Daedalus* 97, 757–92.

Apter, D. E. and Joll, J. eds 1971: *Anarchism Today*. London: Macmillan.

Arato, A. 1974: The neo-idealist defence of subjectivity. *Telos* 21, 108–61.

Arato, A. and Gebhardt, E. eds 1978: *The Essential Frankfurt School Reader*. Oxford: Blackwell.

Arato, Andrew and Cohen, Jean 1992: *Civil Society and Democratic Theory*. Cambridge, MA: MIT Press.

Arblaster, Anthony 1975: What is violence? In *The Socialist Register 1975*, ed. Ralph Miliband and John Saville. London: Merlin.

Archibuggi, D. 1989: Peace and democracy: why such an unhappy marriage? In *Studies in the History of European Peace Ideas*, ed. Vilho Harle. Tampere: Peace Research Institute.

Arendt, Hannah 1958 (*1966*): *The Origins of Totalitarianism*. London: Allen & Unwin.

Arendt, Hannah 1960: What is Authority? In *Between Past and Future: Eight Exercises in Political Thought*. New York: Viking.

Arendt, Hannah 1965: *On Revolution*. New York: Viking.

Arendt, Hannah 1970: *On Violence*. London: Allen Lane; New York: Harcourt, Brace.

Arendt, Hannah 1977: *Eichmann in Jerusalem*. Harmondsworth: Penguin.

Argyle, M. 1975: *Bodily Communication*. London: Methuen.

Ariès, Philippe 1960 (*1962*): *Centuries of Childhood: a Social History of Family Life*. New York: Knopf.

Arkoun, M. 1984: *Pour une critique de la raison islamique*. Paris: Maisonneuve.

Armentano, D. T. 1982: *Antitrust and Monopoly*. New York: Wiley.

Armstrong, D. 1968: *A Materialist Theory of Mind*. London: Routledge & Kegan Paul.

Armstrong, D. 1983: *The Political Anatomy of the Body: Medical Knowledge in Britain in the Twentieth Century*. Cambridge: Cambridge University Press.

Armstrong, John 1982: *Nations before Nationalism*. Chapel Hill: University of North Carolina Press.

Armstrong, Nancy 1987: *Desire and Domestic Fiction*. New York and Oxford: Oxford University Press.

Arney, W. R. and Bergen, B. J. 1984: *Medicine and the Management of Living: Taming the Last Great Beast*. Chicago: University of Chicago Press.

Arnold, Thurman W. 1935: *The Symbols of Government*. New Haven, CT: Yale University Press.

Aron, Raymond 1950 (*1988*): Social structure and the ruling class. In *Power, Modernity and Sociology*. Aldershot: Edward Elgar.

Aron, Raymond 1962 (*1966*); *Peace and War*. London: Weidenfeld & Nicolson.

Aron, Raymond 1964: *La lutte de classes*. Paris: Gallimard.

Aron, Raymond 1965 (*1968*): *Democracy and Totalitarianism*. London: Weidenfeld & Nicolson.

Aron, Raymond 1965, 1968: *Main Currents in Sociological Thought*, 2 vols. London: Weidenfeld & Nicolson.

Aron, Raymond 1967: *The Industrial Society: Three Essays on Ideology and Development*. London: Weidenfeld & Nicolson.

Aronson, N. 1984: *Relativism and the Rhetoric of Subsistence*. Evanston, IL: Northwestern University.

Arrighi, G. 1983: *The Geometry of Imperialism*. 2nd edn, London: Verso.

Arrow, K. 1951 (*1963*): *Social Choice and Indi-*

vidual Values, revised edn. New Haven, CT: Yale University Press.

Arrow, K. J. and Hahn, F. H. 1971: *General Competitive Analysis*. San Francisco: Holden Day; Edinburgh: Oliver & Boyd.

Asch, S. E. 1952: *Social Psychology*. New York: Prentice-Hall.

Ash, M. G. and Woodward, W. R. eds 1987: *Psychology in Twentieth-Century Thought and Society*. Cambridge: Cambridge University Press.

Ash, T. G. 1989: Refolution [*sic*]. In *The Uses of Adversity*. Cambridge: Granta.

Ashmore, M. 1989: *The Reflexive Thesis: Wrighting the Sociology of Scientific Knowledge*. Chicago and London: University of Chicago Press.

Atkinson, A. 1989: *Poverty and Social Security*. London: Wheatsheaf.

Atkinson, A. B. 1983: *The Economics of Inequality*. 2nd edn, Oxford: Clarendon.

Atkinson, A. B. 1983: *Social Justice and Public Policy*. Brighton: Wheatsheaf; Cambridge, MA: MIT Press.

Atkinson, J. M. 1978: *Discovering Suicide: Studies in the Social Organization of Sudden Death*. London: Macmillan.

Atkinson, J. M. and Drew, P. 1979: *Order in Court: the Organisation of Verbal Interaction in Judicial Settings*. London: Macmillan.

Atkinson, J. M. and Heritage, J. C. eds 1984: *Structures of Social Action: Studies in Conversation Analysis*. Cambridge: Cambridge University Press.

Atkinson, M. 1984: *Our Masters' Voices*. London: Methuen.

Atkinson, R. M. 1992: *Children's Syntax*. Oxford: Blackwell.

Attfield, C. L. F. et al. 1985: *Rational Expectations in Macroeconomics*. Oxford: Blackwell.

Aumann, R. J. and Hart, S. eds 1992: Handbook of Game Theory with Economic Applications. Amsterdam: North-Holland.

Austin, J. L. 1962: *Sense and Sensibilia: How to Do Things with Words*. Cambridge, MA: Harvard University Press.

Austin, John 1885 (*1955*): *The Province of Jurisprudence Determined and the Uses of the Study of Jurisprudence*. London: Weidenfeld & Nicolson.

Austin, John 1961 (*1970*): A plea for excuses. In *Philosophical Papers*. Oxford: Oxford University Press.

Avineri, Shlomo 1968: *The Social and Political Thought of Karl Marx*. Cambridge: Cambridge University Press.

Axelos, Kostas 1976: *Alienation, Praxis and Techne in the Thought of Karl Marx*. London: University of Texas Press.

Axelrod, R. 1984: *The Evolution of Cooperation*. New York: Basic Books.

Ayer, A. J. 1936 (*1946*): *Language, Truth and Logic*. 2nd edn, London: Victor Gollancz.

Ayer, A. J. ed. 1959: *Logical Positivism*. Glencoe, IL: Free Press.

Bacchi, Carol Lee 1990: *Same Difference: Feminism and Sexual Difference*. Sydney: Allen & Unwin.

Bacharach, M. O. L. and Hurley, S. L. eds 1991: *Foundations of Decision Theory: Issues and Advances*. Oxford: Blackwell.

Bachelard, Gaston 1934 (1984): *The New Scientific Spirit*. Boston: Beacon Press.

Bachrach, P. and Baratz, M. S. 1962: The two faces of power. *American Political Science Review* 56, 947–52.

Bachrach, P. and Baratz, M. S. 1970: *Power and Poverty: Theory and Practice*. New York: Oxford University Press.

Bachrach, P. 1967: *The Theory of Democratic Elitism*. Boston: Little, Brown.

Backhaus, H.-G. 1969 (*1980*): On the dialectics of the value-form. *Thesis XI* 1, 94–120.

Backstrom, P. 1974: *Christian Socialism and Co-operation in Victorian England*. London: Croom Helm.

Baechler, J. 1979: *Suicides*. Oxford: Blackwell.

Baehr, P. 1987: Accounting for Caesarism. *Economy and Society* 16, 341–56.

Baehr, P. 1988: Max Weber as a critic of Bismarck. *European Journal of Sociology* 29, 149–64.

Baehr, P. 1989: Weber and Weimar: the 'Reich President' proposals. *Politics* 9, 20–5.

Baehr, P. 1990: The 'masses' in Weber's political sociology. *Economy and Society* 19, 242–65.

Bagehot, W. 1867 (*1963*): *The English Constitution*. London: Collins.

Bahro, R. 1982: *Socialism and Survival*. London: Heretic.

Bahro, R. 1984: *From Red to Green*. London: Verso.

Bailey, A. M. and Llobera, J. R. 1974–5: The Asiatic mode of production. *Critique of Anthropology* 2, 95–103; 4–5, 165–76.

Bailey, A. M. and Llobera, J. R. 1979: Karl Wittfogel and the Asiatic mode of production: a reappraisal. *Sociological Review* 27, 541–59.

Bailey, Peter 1978: *Leisure and Class in Victorian England.* London: Routledge & Kegan Paul.

Bailyn, L. 1989: Toward the perfect workplace? *Communications of the ACM* [Association of Computer Manufacturers] 32.4.

Baker, J. 1987: *Arguing for Equality.* London: Verso.

Baker, J. R. 1942: *The Scientific Life.* London: Allen & Unwin.

Bakhtin, M. 1934–5 (*1981*): *The Dialogic Imagination: Four Essays,* ed. M. Holquist. Austin: University of Texas Press.

Balandier, Georges 1974: *Anthropo-logiques.* Paris: Presses Universitaires de France.

Baldwin, Peter 1990: Social interpretations of Nazism. In *Journal of Contemporary History* 25, 5–37.

Baldwin, Thomas 1986: Sartre, *Existentialism and Humanism.* In *Philosophers Ancient and Modern,* ed. G. Vesey. Cambridge: Cambridge University Press.

Bales, R. F. 1950: *Interaction Process Analysis: a Method for the Study of Small Groups.* Cambridge, MA: Addison-Wesley.

Bales, R. F. 1953: The equilibrium problem in small groups. In *Working Papers in the Theory of Action,* ed. T. Parsons. Glencoe, IL: Free Press.

Bales, R. F. 1968: Interaction process analysis. In *International Encyclopedia of the Social Sciences,* vol. 7, ed. D. L. Sills. New York: Macmillan and Free Press.

Bales, R. F. and Cohen, S. P. 1979: *SYMLOG: a System for the Multiple Level Observation of Groups.* New York: Free Press.

Balibar, René 1974: *Les Français fictifs: le rapport des styles litteraires au Français National.* Paris: Hachette.

Ball, M. et al. 1988: *Housing and Social Change in Europe and the USA.* London and New York: Routledge.

Ball, Stephen J. ed. 1990: *Foucault and Education.* London: Routledge.

Balogh, T. 1965: *Planning for Progress: a Strategy for Labour.* London: Fabian Society.

Banaji, J. 1977: Modes of production in a materialist conception of history. *Capital and Class* 2.

Bandon, M. 1965: *Roles: an Introduction to the Study of Social Behavior.* London: Basic Books.

Bandura, A. 1973: *Aggression: a Social Learning Analysis.* Englewood Cliffs, NJ, Prentice-Hall.

Banks, J. A. 1974: *Trade Unionism.* London: Collier-Macmillan.

Bann, S. and Boult, J. E. eds 1973: *Russian Formalism.* Edinburgh: Scottish Academic Press.

Banton, M. 1970: The concept of racism. In *Race and Racialism,* ed. S. Zubaida. London: Tavistock.

Banton, M. 1983: *Racial and Ethnic Competition.* Cambridge: Cambridge University Press.

Banton, M. 1987: *Racial Theories.* Cambridge: Cambridge University Press.

Baran, Paul 1957 (*1973*): *The Political Economy of Growth.* Harmondsworth: Penguin.

Baran, Paul and Sweezy, Paul 1966: *Monopoly Capitalism.* New York: Monthly Review Press.

Barba, Eugenio 1986: *Beyond the Floating Islands.* New York: PAJ Publications.

Barber, B. 1983: *The Logic and Limits of Trust.* New Brunswick, NJ: Rutgers University Press.

Barber, Benjamin R. 1984: *Strong Democracy: Participatory Politics for a New Age.* Berkeley: University of California Press.

Barber, Bernard 1963: Some problems in the sociology of the professions. *Daedalus,* fall, 669–88.

Barber, Bernard 1968: Social stratification. In *International Encyclopedia of the Social Sciences,* ed. D. L. Sills. New York: Macmillan.

Barbour, S. and Stevenson, P. 1990: *Variation in German.* Cambridge: Cambridge University Press.

Barker, E. 1947: *Social Contract.* London: Oxford University Press.

Barkun, M. 1974: *Disaster and the Millennium.* New Haven, CT: Yale University Press.

Barnard, A. and Good, A. 1984: *Research Practices in the Study of Kinship.* London and Orlando, FL: Academic Press.

Barnard, Chester 1938: *Functions of the Executive.* Cambridge, MA: Harvard University Press.

Barraclough, G. 1964: *An Introduction to Contemporary History.* London: Watts.

Barrett, Cyril ed. 1965: *Collected Papers on Aesthetics.* Oxford: Blackwell.

Barrett, Cyril 1989: The concept of leisure: idea and ideal. In *The Philosophy of Leisure,* ed. Cyril Barrett and Tom Winnifrith. London: Macmillan.

Barrett, M. 1980 (*1988*): *Women's Oppression Today:* the Marxist/Feminist Encounter. 2nd edn, London: Verso.

Barrett, M. 1991: *The Politics of Truth*. Cambridge: Polity.

Barrett, M. 1992: Words and things: materialism and method in contemporary feminist analysis. In *Destabilizing Theory: Contemporary Feminist Debates*, ed. M. Barrett and A. Phillips. Cambridge: Polity.

Barron, Iann and Curnow, Ray 1979: *The Future with Microelectronics*. London: Frances Pinter.

Barry, B. 1965: *Political Argument*. London: Routledge & Kegan Paul.

Barry, B. 1989: *A Treatise on Social Justice*, vol. 1: *Theories of Justice*. Berkeley: University of California Press; London: Harvester Wheatsheaf.

Barry, B. and Hardin, R. eds 1982: *Rational Man and Irrational Society*. Beverly Hills and London: Sage.

Barry, Brian 1970: *Sociologists, Economists and Democracy*. London: Collier-Macmillan.

Barry, Norman P. 1980 (*1986*): *On Classical Liberalism and Libertarianism*. London: Macmillan.

Barry, Norman P. 1981: *An Introduction to Modern Political Theory*. London: Macmillan.

Barry, Norman P. 1991: *Welfare*. London: Tavistock.

Barth, Frederick 1969: *Ethnic Groups and Boundaries*. London: Allen & Unwin.

Barthes, Roland 1957 (*1973*): *Mythologies*. St Albans: Granada.

Barthes, Roland 1964 (*1967*): *Elements of Semiology*. New York: Hill & Wang.

Barthes, Roland 1967 (1983): The Fashion System. New York: Hill & Wang.

Barthes, Roland 1970 (*1975*): *S/Z*. London: Cape.

Bartholomew, D. J. 1988: Social statistics. In *Encyclopaedia of Statistical Sciences*, vol. 8, ed. S. Kotz et al. Wiley-Interscience.

Bartra, R. et al. 1976: *Modos de producción en América Latina*. Lima: Delva.

Basham, A. L. 1954: *The Wonder that was India*. London: Collins.

Bateson, P. P. G. 1986: Sociobiology and human politics. In *Science and Beyond*, ed. S. Rose and L. Appignanesi. Oxford: Blackwell.

Bateson, P. P. G. and Klopfer, P. H. eds 1989: *Perspectives in Ethology*, Vol. 8: *Whither Ethology?* New York: Plenum.

Bauer, Otto 1907 (*1924*): *Die Nationalitätenfrage und die Sozialdemokratie*. 2nd edn, Vienna: Wiener Volksbuchhandlung.

Bauer, Otto 1923 (*1925, 1970*): The Austrian Revolution. Abridged Eng. edn, New York: Burt Franklin.

Bauer, Otto 1927 (*1978*): What is Austro-Marxism? In *Austro-Marxism*, ed. Tom Bottomore and Patrick Goode. Oxford: Clarendon Press.

Bauer, Otto 1936: *Zwischen zwei Weltkriegen?* Bratislava: Eugen Prager.

Bauman, Z. 1976: *Socialism: the Active Utopia*. London: Allen & Unwin.

Bauman, Z. 1978: *Hermeneutics and Social Science*. London: Hutchinson.

Baumeister, R. F. 1986: *Identity: Cultural Change and the Struggle for Self*. Oxford: Oxford University Press.

Baumol, W. J. 1968: Entrepreneurship in economic theory. *American Economic Review* 58.

Baxandall, Michael 1980: *Limewood Sculptors of Renaissance Germany*. New Haven, CT: Yale University Press.

Baylis, John et al. 1987: *Contemporary Strategy*, 2 vols. London: Croom Helm.

Beardon, C. 1989: *Artificial Intelligence Terminology*. Chichester: Ellis Horwood.

Beardsley, Monroe 1958: *Aesthetics: Problems in the Philosophy of Criticism*. New York: Harcourt, Brace.

Beaufre, André 1972: *La guerre révolutionnaire: les forces nouvelles de la guerre*. Paris: Fayard.

Beaugrands, R. de and Dressler, W. 1981: *Introduction to Textlinguistics*. London: Longman.

Beauvoir, Simone de 1949 (*1962*): *The Second Sex*. London: New English Library.

Bebbington, P. and McGuffin, P. 1988: *Schizophrenia: the Major Issues*. London: Heinemann.

Beck, Ulrich, 1986 (*1992*): *Risk Society*. London: Sage.

Becker, C. L. 1932: *The Heavenly City of the Eighteenth-Century Philosophers*. New Haven, CT: Yale University Press.

Becker, H. 1963: *Outsiders: Studies in the Sociology of Deviance*. New York: Free Press; London: Macmillan.

Becker, H. ed. 1964: *The Other Side*. New York: Free Press.

Becker, Howard S. 1982: *Art Worlds*. Berkeley and London: University of California Press.

Beckerman, W. 1974: *In Defence of Economic Growth*. London: Jonathan Cape.

Beckford, J. A. 1975: *The Trumpet of Prophecy: a Sociological Study of Jehovah's Witnesses*. Oxford: Blackwell.

Beckford, J. A. 1985: *Cult Controversies: the Socie-*

tal Response to the New Religious Movements. London: Tavistock.

Beckford, J. A. 1989: *Religion and Advanced Industrial Societies*. London: Unwin-Hyman.

Beechey, V. 1977: Some notes on female wage labour in capitalist production. *Capital and Class* 3, 45–66.

Beechey, V. 1987: *Unequal Work*. London: Verso.

Beeghley, L. 1989: *The Structure of Social Stratification in the United States*. New York: Allyn & Bacon.

Beer, S. 1956: Pressure groups and parties in Britain. *American Political Science Review* 50, 1–23.

Beer, S. M. 1948: *A History of British Socialism*. London: Allen & Unwin.

Beetham, David 1981: Michels and his critics. *European Journal of Sociology* 22.1, 81–99.

Beetham, David 1987: Reformism and the 'bourgeoisification' of the labour movement. In *Socialism and the Intelligentsia*, ed. Carl Levy. London: Routledge.

Begg, D. K. H. 1982: *The Rational Expectations Revolution in Macroeconomics*. Oxford: Philip Allan.

Bell, Colin and Newby, Howard 1971: *Community Studies*. London: Allen & Unwin.

Bell, D. 1961: *The End of Ideology*. New York: Collier Books.

Bell, D. 1974: *The Coming of Post-Industrial Society: a Venture in Social Forecasting*. New York: Basic Books; London: Heinemann.

Bell, Daniel, ed. 1963: *The Radical Right*. New York: Doubleday.

Bell, Daniel 1968: Socialism. In *International Encyclopedia of the Social Sciences*, ed. David L. Sills, vols. 13–14. New York: Macmillan and Free Press.

Bell, Daniel 1976 (*1979*): *The Cultural Contradictions of Capitalism*. 2nd edn, London: Heinemann.

Bell, Daniel 1979: The social framework of the information society. In *The Computer Age: a Twenty-Year View*, ed. Michael L. Dertouzos and Joel Moses. Cambridge, MA: MIT Press.

Bell, Quentin 1972: *Virginia Woolf: a Biography*, 2 vols. London: Hogarth Press.

Bellah, R. N. 1964: Religious evolution. *American Sociological Review* 29.

Bellah, R. N. 1967: Civil religion in America. *Daedalus* 96.

Bellah, R. N. 1970: *Beyond Belief: Essays on Religion in a Post-Traditional World*. New York: Harper & Row.

Bellah, R. N. 1970: Christianity and symbolic realism. *Journal for the Scientific Study of Religion* 9, 89–96.

Bellah, R. N. 1989: Christian faithfulness in a pluralist world. In *Postmodern Theology*, ed. F. B. Burnham. New York: Harper & Row.

Bellah, R. N. et al. 1985: *Habits of the Heart: Individualism and Commitment in American Life*. Berkeley: University of California Press.

Bendix, R. 1966: *Max Weber: an Intellectual Portrait*. London: Methuen.

Bendix, R. 1971: Charismatic leadership. In *Scholarship and Partisanship: Essays on Max Weber*, ed. R. Bendix and G. Roth. Berkeley: University of California Press.

Bendix, Reinhard and Lipset, Seymour M. eds 1966: *Class, Status, and Power*. New York: Free Press.

Benedict, R. 1983: *Race and Racism*. London: Routledge.

Benhabib, S. 1986: *Critique, Norm and Utopia*. New York: Columbia University Press.

Benhabib, S. and Dallmayr, F., eds 1990: *The Communicative Ethics Controversy*. Cambridge, MA: MIT Press.

Beniger, James R. 1986: *The Control Revolution: Technological and Economic Origins of the Information Society*. Cambridge, MA: Harvard University Press.

Benjamin, Walter 1974: Über den Begriff der Geschichte. In *Gesammelte Schriften*, vol. 1. Frankfurt am Main: Suhrkamp.

Benn, S. I. 1988: *A Theory of Freedom*. Cambridge: Cambridge University Press.

Bennett, Tony 1979: *Formalism and Marxism*. London: Methuen.

Bennington, Geoffrey and Derrida, Jacques 1991: *Jacques Derrida*. Chicago: University of Chicago Press.

Bensman, J. and Givant, M. 1975: Charisma and modernity: the use and abuse of a concept. *Social Research* 42, 570–614.

Benston, Kimberly W. 1984: I yam what I am: the topos of un(naming) in Afro-American literature. In *Black Literature and Literary Theory*, ed. Henry Gates. New York and London: Methuen.

Benthall, J. ed. 1973: *The Limits of Human Nature*. London: Allen & Unwin.

Bentham, Jeremy 1776 (*1988*): *A Fragment on*

Government. Cambridge: Cambridge University Press.

Bentham, Jeremy *c.*1780–2 (*1970*): *Of Laws in General.* London: Athlone.

Bentham, Jeremy 1793 (*1948*): *An Introduction to the Principles of Morals and Legislation*, ed. J. Harrison. Oxford: Blackwell.

Bentley, A. F. 1908 (*1967*): The Process of Government. Cambridge, MA: Harvard University Press.

Benyon, J. and Bourne, C. eds 1986: *The Police: Powers, Procedures and Proprieties.* Oxford: Pergamon.

Benz, Wolfgang ed. 1989: *Rechtsextremismus in der Bundesrepublik.* Frankfurt am Main: Fischer.

Berger, P. L. 1961: *The Noise of Solemn Assemblies.* Garden City, NY: Doubleday.

Berger, P. L. 1963: Charisma and religious innovation: the social location of Israelite prophecy. *American Sociological Review* 28, 940–50.

Berger, P. L. 1966: *Invitation to Sociology: a Humanistic Perspective.* Harmondsworth: Penguin.

Berger, P. L. 1967: *The Sacred Canopy: Elements of a Sociological Theory of Religion.* Garden City, NY: Doubleday.

Berger, P. L. 1973: *The Homeless Mind.* Harmondsworth: Penguin.

Berger, P. L. 1974: Some second thoughts on substantive versus functional definitions of religion. *Journal for the Scientific Study of Religion* 13, 125–33.

Berger, P. L. and Luckmann, Thomas 1961: *The Social Construction of Reality: a Treatise in the Sociology of Knowledge.* New York: Doubleday; London: Allen Lane.

Berger, S. D. ed. 1981: *Organizing Interests in Western Europe: Pluralism, Corporatism and the Transformation of Politics.* Cambridge: Cambridge University Press.

Berghe, P. L. van den 1981: *The Ethnic Phenomenon.* New York and Oxford: Elsevier.

Bergmann, Uwe et al. 1968: *Rebellion der Studenten oder die neue Opposition.* Reinbek: Rowohlt.

Bergonzi, Bernard 1990: *Exploding English.* Oxford: Clarendon Press.

Bergson, A. 1938: A reformulation of certain aspects of welfare economics. *Quarterly Journal of Economics* 52, 310–34.

Bergson, A. 1966: Socialist economics. In *Essays in Normative Economics.* Cambridge, MA: Harvard University Press.

Bergson, A. 1967: Market socialism revisited. *Journal of Political Economy* 75, 655–73.

Bergson, Henri 1932 (*1935*): *The Two Sources of Morality and Religion.* London: Macmillan.

Berkes, N. 1964: *The Development of Secularism in Turkey.* Montreal: McGill University Press.

Berkowitz, L. 1962: *Aggression: a Social Psychological Analysis.* New York: McGraw Hill.

Berle, A. A. and Means, G. C. 1932: *The Modern Cooperative and Private Property.* New York: Macmillan.

Berlin, I. 1939 (*1968*): *Karl Marx: his Life and Environment.* New York: Oxford University Press.

Berlin, I. 1958 (*1969*): Two concepts of liberty. In *Four Essays on Liberty.* Oxford: Oxford University Press.

Berlin, I. 1964: Does political theory still exist?. In *Philosophy, Politics and Society*, Series II, ed. P. Laslett and W. G. Runciman. Oxford: Blackwell.

Berlin, I. 1978: Equality. In *Concepts and Categories.* London: Hogarth Press.

Berliner, J. 1976: *The Innovation Decision.* Cambridge, MA: MIT Press.

Berman, Marshall 1983: *All that is Solid Melts into Air: the Experience of Modernity.* London: Verso.

Bermant, Chaim and Weitzman, Michael 1979: *Ebla.* London: Weidenfeld & Nicolson.

Bernal, J. D. 1939: *The Social Function of Science.* London: Routledge & Kegan Paul.

Bernal, Martin 1987: *Black Athena: the Afro-Asiatic Roots of Classical Civilization.* London: Free Association Books.

Bernard, C. 1865 (*1961*): *An Introduction to the Study of Experimental Medicine.* New York: Collier.

Bernard, J. ed. 1961: Teen-age culture. *Annals of the American Academy of Political and Social Science* 338.

Bernard, J. 1972: *The Future of Marriage.* New York: World.

Bernoulli, D. 1738 (*1954*): Exposition of a new theory on the measurement of risk. *Econometrica* 22, 23–36.

Bernstein, Eduard 1899 (*1961*): *Evolutionary Socialism.* New York: Schocken.

Bernstein, M. A. 1987: *The Great Depression: Delayed Recovery and Economic Change in America, 1929–1939.* Cambridge: Cambridge University Press.

Bernstein, R. 1983: *Beyond Objectivism and Relativism*. Oxford: Blackwell.

Berry, B. J. L. ed. 1976: *Urbanization and Counterurbanization*. London: Arnold.

Berry, C. J. 1986: *Human Nature*. London: Macmillan.

Berry, Wendell 1977: *The Unsettling of America*. San Francisco: Sierra.

Bertalanffy, L. 1968: *General System Theory: Foundations, Developments, Applications*. New York: Brazillier.

Berthelot, J. M. ed. 1985: Les sociologies et le corps. *Current Sociology* 33.2.

Besnard, P. ed. 1983: *The Sociological Domain: the Durkheimians and the Founding of French Sociology*. Cambridge: Cambridge University Press.

Besnard, P. 1987: *L'anomie: ses usages et ses fonctions dans la discipline sociologique depuis Durkheim*. Paris: Presses Universitaires de France.

Bestor, A. E. 1948: The evolution of the socialist vocabulary. *Journal of the History of Ideas* 9.

Beteille, A. 1966: *Caste, Class and Power: Changing Patterns of Stratification in a Tanjore Village*. Cambridge: Cambridge University Press.

Bettelheim, C. 1978: *Class Struggles in the USSR*. New York: Monthly Review Press.

Betti, E. 1955: *Teoria generale della interpretazione*, trans into German as *Allgemeine Auslegungslehre als Methodik der Geisteswissenschaften*. Tübingen: J. C. B. Mohr.

Betts, Raymond F. 1985: *Uncertain Dimensions: Western Overseas Empires in the Twentieth Century*. Oxford: Oxford University Press.

Beveridge, W. H. 1942: *Social Insurance and Allied Services*. London: HMSO (Cmnd 6404).

Beveridge, W. H. 1943: *The Pillars of Security*. London: Allen & Unwin.

Beveridge, W. H. 1944: *Full Employment in a Free Society*. London: Allen & Unwin.

Bhaskar, Roy 1975 (*1978*): *A Realist Theory of Science*. 2nd edn, Hemel Hempstead: Harvester Press.

Bhaskar, Roy 1979 (*1989*): *The Possibility of Naturalism*. 2nd edn, Hemel Hempstead: Harvester-Wheatsheaf.

Bhaskar, Roy 1986: *Scientific Realism and Human Emancipation*. London: Verso.

Bhaskar, Roy 1991: Truth. In *A Dictionary of Marxist Thought*, ed. Tom Bottomore. Oxford: Blackwell.

Bhaskar, Roy 1992: *Dialectic*. London: Verso.

Bhatt, G. S. 1968: Brahmo Samaj, Arya Samaj, and the church-sect typology. *Review of Religious Research* 10, 23–32.

Bickerton, D. 1981: *Roots of Language*. Ann Arbor, MI: Karoma.

Biddle, B. S. 1979: *Role Theory: Expectations, Identities and Bahavior*. New York: Academic Press.

Biderman, A. D. 1971: Towards redefining the military. *Teachers College Record* 73, 47–58.

Bietak, Manfred 1979: Urban archaeology and the 'town' problem. In *Egyptology and the Social Sciences*, ed. Kent R. Weeks. Cairo: American University in Cairo Press.

Billig, M. G. 1978: *Fascists: a Social Psychological View of the National Front*. London: Academic Press.

Binford, L. R. 1983: *In Pursuit of the Past*. London: Thames & Hudson.

Binkley, Timothy 1977: Piece: contra aesthetics. *Journal of Aesthetics and Art Criticism*, 265–77.

Binmore, K. 1990: *Essays on the Foundations of Game Theory*. Oxford: Blackwell.

Binmore, K. and Dasgupta, P. eds 1986: *Economic organizations as Games*. Oxford: Blackwell.

Binmore, K. and Dasgupta, P. 1987: *Economics of Bargaining*. Oxford: Blackwell.

Birch, A. H. 1964: *Representative and Responsible Government: an Essay on the British Constitution*. London: Allen & Unwin.

Birch, R. C. 1974: *The Shaping of the Welfare State*. London: Longman.

Birnbaum, P. 1976: Power divorced from its sources: a critique of the exchange theory of power. In *Power and Political Theory: Some European Perspectives*, ed. B. Barry. London: Wiley.

Bishop, Jeff and Hoggett, Paul 1986: *Organizing around Enthusiasms: Patterns of Mutual Aid in Leisure*. London: Comedia.

Black, D. 1958: *The Theory of Committees and Elections*. Cambridge: Cambridge University Press.

Blackaby, F. ed. 1979: *De-industrialisation*. London: Heinemann.

Blackbourn, Davis and Eley, Geoff 1984: *The Peculiarities of German History*. Oxford: Oxford University Press.

Blainey, G. 1971: *The Causes of War*. London: Macmillan.

Blalock Jr, H. M. 1967: *Toward a Theory of Minority-Group Relations*. New York: Wiley.

Blalock Jr, H. M. 1982: *Race and Ethnic Relations*. Englewood Cliffs, NJ: Prentice-Hall.

Blanchard, O. J. and Fischer, F. 1989: *Lectures on Macroeconomics*. Cambridge, MA, and London: MIT Press.

Blau, P. M. 1964: *Exchange and Power in Social Life*. New York: Wiley.

Blau, P. M. 1987: Microprocess and macrostructure. In *Social Exchange Theory*, ed. K. S. Cook. Newbury Park: Sage.

Blaug, M. 1962 (*1985*): *Economic Theory in Retrospect*. 4th edn, Cambridge: Cambridge University Press.

Blaug, M. 1986: *Economic History and the History of Economics*. London.

Blauner, Robert 1964: *Alienation and Freedom*. London: University of Chicago Press.

Bleicher, J. 1980: *Contemporary Hermeneutics*. London: Routledge & Kegan Paul.

Bleicher, J. 1982: *The Hermeneutic Imagination*. London: Routledge & Kegan Paul.

Bloch, Ernst 1985: *Essays on the Philosophy of Music*. Cambridge: Cambridge University Press.

Bloch, Ernst et al. 1977: *Aesthetics and Politics*. London: New Left Books.

Bloch, Marc 1940 (*1961*): *Feudal Society: Social Classes and Political Organization*. London: Routledge & Kegan Paul; Chicago: University of Chicago Press.

Bloch, Marc 1954: *The Historian's Craft*. Manchester: Manchester University Press.

Bloch, Marc 1974: The rise of dependent cultivation and seignorial institutions. In *Cambridge Economic History of Europe*, vol. 1. Cambridge: Cambridge University Press.

Bloch, Maurice ed. 1975: *Marxist Analyses and Social Anthropology*. London: Malaby.

Bloch, Maurice 1985: *Marxism and Anthropology*. Oxford: Oxford University Press.

Block, Walter 1976: *Defending the Undefendable*. New York: Fleet.

Blondel, J. 1981: *The Discipline of Politics*. London: Butterworths.

Bloomfield, L. 1933: *Language*. New York: Holt, Rinehart & Winston.

Bloor, David 1976: *Knowledge and Social Imagery*. London: Routledge & Kegan Paul.

Bluché, F. 1980: *Le Bonapartisme*. Paris: Nouvelles Editions Latines.

Blum, F. M. 1978: *Pseudoscience and Mental Ability*. New York: Monthly Review Press.

Blumer, H. 1937: Social Psychology. In *Man and Society*, ed. E. P. Schmidt. New York: Prentice-Hall.

Blumer, H. 1939 (*1951*): Collective behavior. In *Principles of Sociology*, ed. Alfred McClung Lee. New York: Barnes & Noble.

Blumer, H. 1969: *Symbolic Interactionism: Perspective and Method*. Englewood Cliffs, NJ: Prentice-Hall.

Blumer, Martin 1984: *The Chicago School of Sociology: Institutionalization, Diversity, and the Rise of Sociological Research*. Chicago: University of Chicago Press.

Boal, Augusto 1979 (*1988*): *Theatre of the Oppressed*. London: Pluto.

Boas, Franz, 1911 (*1963*): *The Mind of Primitive Man*. New York: Collier.

Boaz, Franziska, ed. 1972: *The Function of Dance in Human Society*. New York: Dance Horizons.

Bobbio, N. 1989: *Democracy and Dictatorship: the Nature and Limits of State Power*. Cambridge: Polity.

Bock, G. et al. eds 1990: *Machiavelli and Republicanism*. Cambridge: Cambridge University Press.

Bocock, R. 1986: *Hegemony*. London: Tavistock.

Boden, D. forthcoming: *The Business of Talk*. Cambridge: Polity.

Boden, D. and Zimmerman, D. H. 1991: *Talk and Social Structure*. Cambridge: Polity.

Boden, M. A. 1986: *Artificial Intelligence and Natural Man*. 2nd edn, Brighton: Harvester/Basic.

Boff, L. 1985: *Church, Charism and Power*. London: SCM Press.

Boff, L. and Boff, C. 1987: *Introducing Liberation Theology*. Tunbridge Wells: Burns & Oates.

Bohannan, P. and Middleton, J. eds 1968: *Kinship and Social Organization*. Garden City, NY: Natural History Press.

Böhmer, J. F. 1868: *Leben, Briefe und kleinere Schriften*, 3 vols. Vol. 1, ed. J. J. Janssen. Freiburg: Herder.

Bokor, A. 1984: Deprivation: dimensions and indices. In *Stratification and Inequality*, ed. R. Andor and T. Kolosi. Budapest: Institute for Social Sciences.

Boland, L. A. 1985: *The Foundations of Economic Method*. London: Allen & Unwin.

Bondurant, J. V. ed. 1971: *Conflict: Violence and Non-Violence*. Chicago: Aldine Atherton.

Bonino, J. 1983: *Towards a Christian Political Ethics*. London: SCM Press; Minneapolis: Augsburg Fortress.

Bonner, A. 1961: *British Co-operation*. Manchester: Co-operative Union.

Bookchin, M. 1982: *The Ecology of Freedom*. Palo Alto, CA: Cheshire.

Bookchin, Murray 1987: *The Rise of Urbanization and the Decline of Citizenship*. San Francisco: Sierra Club Books.

Boole, G. 1854 (*1954*): *An Investigation of the Laws of Thought*. New York: Dover.

Boorstin, Daniel 1978: *The Republic of Technology*. New York: Harper & Row.

Booth, C. 1892-7 (*1902-3*): *Life and Labour of the People of London*, 17 vols. London: Macmillan.

Booth, T. A. ed. 1979: *Planning for Welfare*. Oxford: Blackwell and Martin Robertson.

Bordwell, D. et al. 1985: *The Classical Hollywood Cinema*. London: Routledge & Kegan Paul.

Bosanquet, B. 1951: *The Philosophical Theory of the State*. London: Macmillan.

Bose, C. 1979: Technology and changes in the division of labour in the American home. *Women's Studies International Quarterly* 2, 295–304.

Boserup, Ester 1965: *The Conditions of Agricultural Growth*. Chicago: Aldine.

Boswell, J. 1990: *Community and the Economy: a Theory of Public Co-operation*. London: Routledge.

Bosworth, W. 1962: *Catholicism and Crisis in Modern France: French Catholic Groups at the Threshold of the Fifth Republic*. Princeton, NJ: Princeton University Press.

Bottomley, K. and Pease, K. 1986: *Crime and Punishment: Interpreting the Data*. Milton Keynes: Open University Press.

Bottomore, Tom 1964 (*1993*): *Elites and Society*. 2nd edn, London: Routledge.

Bottomore, Tom 1965 (*1991*): *Classes in Modern Society*. London: Routledge.

Bottomore, Tom 1979 (*1992*): *Political Sociology*. London: Pluto Press.

Bottomore, Tom 1981: Introduction to Rudolf Hilferding, *Finance Capital*. London: Routledge & Kegan Paul.

Bottomore, Tom ed. 1983 (*1991*): *A Dictionary of Marxist Thought*. Oxford: Blackwell.

Bottomore, Tom 1984: *The Frankfurt School*. Chichester: Ellis Horwood.

Bottomore, Tom 1985: *Theories of Modern Capitalism*. London: Routledge.

Bottomore, Tom ed. 1988: *Interpretations of Marx*. Oxford: Blackwell.

Bottomore, Tom 1989: Austro-Marxist conceptions of the transition from capitalism to socialism. *International Journal of Comparative Sociology* 30, 1–2.

Bottomore, Tom 1990: *The Socialist Economy: Theory and Practice*. Hemel Hempstead: Harvester Wheatsheaf.

Bottomore, Tom and Brym, Robert J. eds 1989: *The Capitalist Class: an International Study*. Hemel Hempstead: Harvester Wheatsheaf.

Bottomore, Tom and Goode, Patrick eds 1978: *Austro-Marxism*. Oxford: Clarendon Press.

Bottomore, Tom and Nisbet, Robert eds 1978: *A History of Sociological Analysis*. New York: Basic Books.

Bottoms, A. E. and Light, R. 1987: *Problems of Long-Term Imprisonment*. Aldershot: Gower.

Boudon, Raymond 1973: *Mathematical Structures of Social Mobility*. Amsterdam: Elsevier.

Boudon, Raymond 1979: Generating models as a research strategy. In *Qualitative and Quantitative Social Research*, ed. R. Merton et al. London: Macmillan.

Boudon, Raymond 1986: *Theories of Social Change*. Cambridge: Polity.

Boudon, Raymond and Bourricaud, François 1989: *A Critical Dictionary of Sociology*. London: Routledge & Kegan Paul.

Bouglé, C. 1908 (*1971*): *Essays on the Caste System*. Cambridge: Cambridge University Press.

Boulding, K. 1962: *Conflict and Defense*. New York: Harper & Row.

Bourdet, Yvon 1970: *La Délivrance de Prométhée: pour une théorie politique de l'autogestion*. Paris: Anthropos.

Bourdieu, Pierre 1970 (*1990*): *The Love of Art*. Cambridge: Polity.

Bourdieu, Pierre 1977: The economics of linguistic exchanges. Social Sciences Information, 16. 6.

Bourdieu, Pierre 1979 (1984): *Distinction: a Social Critique of the Judgement of Taste*. London: Routledge & Kegan Paul; Cambridge, MA: Harvard University Press.

Bourdieu, Pierre 1980: *Questions de sociologie*. Paris: Minuit.

Bourdieu, Pierre 1987: The historical genesis of a pure aesthetics. *Journal of Aesthetics and Art Criticism*, special issue on Analytic Aesthetics, 201–10.

Bourdieu, Pierre 1987: What makes a social class? On the theoretical and practical existence of groups. *Berkeley Journal of Sociology* 32, 1–17.

Bourdieu, Pierre 1991: *Language and Symbolic Power*. Cambridge: Polity.

Bourdieu, Pierre and Passerson, J. C. 1970 (*1977*): *Reproduction in Education, Society and Culture*. London: Sage.

Bourdieu, Pierre et al. 1973 (*1991*): *The Craft of Sociology: Epistemological Preliminaries*. Berlin and New York: De Gruyter.

Bournis, R. and Giles, H. 1976: The Language of cooperation in Wales. *Language Sciences* 42, 13–16.

Bouvier, Pierre 1980: *Travail et expression ouvrière: pouvoirs et contraintes des comités d'entreprise*. Paris: Galilée.

Bowen, Barbara E. 1982: Untroubled voice: call and response in Cane. Black American Literary Forum 16, 1.

Bowker, J. 1973: *The Sense of God*. Oxford: Clarendon Press.

Bowler, P. J. 1987: *Theories of Human Evolution: a Century of Debate*. Oxford: Blackwell.

Bowles, S. and Edwards, R. 1985: *Understanding Capitalism: Competition, Command and Change in the US Economy*. New York: Harper & Row.

Bowles, Samuel and Gintis, Herbert 1976: *Schooling in Capitalist America*. London: Routledge.

Bowley, A. L. and Bennett-Hurst, A. 1915: *Livelihood and Poverty*. London: Bell.

Box, S. 1981: *Deviance, Reality and Society*. New York: Holt, Rinehart & Winston.

Boyd, Robert and Richerson, Peter J. 1985: *Culture and the Evolutionary Process*. Chicago: University of Chicago Press.

Boyer, R. 1979: Wage formation in historical perspective: the French experience. *Cambridge Journal of Economics* 3.2, 99–118.

Bracher, K. D. 1971: *The German Dictatorship: the Origins, Structure and Effects of National Socialism*. London: Weidenfeld & Nicolson.

Brada, J. C. and Estrin, S. eds 1990: Advances in Indicative Planning. *Journal of Comparative Economics* 14.4, special issue.

Bradbury, Malcolm and McFarlane, James eds 1976: *Modernism 1890–1930*. Harmondsworth: Penguin.

Bradley, D. and McCormick, J. 1978: *People's Theatre*. London: Croom Helm.

Brady, R. 1933: *The Rationalization Movement in German Industry*. Berkeley: University of California Press.

Brain, P. ed. 1986: *Alcohol and Aggression*. London: Tavistock.

Brake, M. 1985: *Comparative Youth Culture*. London: Routledge & Kegan Paul.

Bramwell, A.: *Ecology in the 20th Century: a History*. New Haven, CT, and London: Yale University Press.

Brandt, R. B. 1979: *A Theory of the Good and the Right*. Oxford: Clarendon Press.

Brandt, W. 1980: *North–South: a Programme for Survival*. London: Pan.

Brantlinger, P. 1983: *Bread and Circuses: Theories of Mass Culture as Social Decay*. Ithaca, NY: Cornell University Press.

Braudel, F. 1980: *On History*. London: Weidenfeld & Nicolson.

Braudel, Fernand 1949 (*1973*): *The Mediterranean and the Mediterranean World in the Age of Philip II*. New York: Harper & Row.

Braudel, Fernand 1958 (*1972*): History and the social sciences: *the longue durée*. In *Economy and Society in Early Modern Europe*, ed. Peter Burke. New York: Harper & Row; London: Routledge & Kegal Paul.

Braudel, Fernand 1967, 1979, 1981–4: *Civilization and Capitalism, 15th–18th Century*, 3 vols. New York: Harper & Row.

Braungart M. M. and Braungart R. G. 1990: The life-course development of left- and right-wing youth activist leaders from the 1960s. *Political Psychology* 11, 243–82.

Braungart, R. G. and Braungart, M. M. 1986: Life-course and generational politics. *Annual Review of Sociology* 12, 205–31.

Braungart, R. G. and Braungart, M. M. 1986: Youth problems and politics in the 1980s: some multinational comparisons. *International Sociology* 1, 359–80.

Braungart, R. G. and Braungart, M. M. 1989: Generational conflict and intergroup relations as the foundation for political generations. In *Advances in Group Processes*, vol. 6, ed. E. J. Lawler and B. Markovsky. Greenwich, CT: JAI Press.

Braungart, R. G. and Braungart, M. M. 1989: Political generations. In *Research in Political Sociology*, vol. 4. Greenwich, CT: JAI Press.

Braungart, R. G. and Braungart, M. M. 1990: Youth movements in the 1980s: a global perspective. *International Sociology* 5, 157–81.

Braunthal, J. 1961, 1963 (*1966, 1967*): *History of the International 1864–1914*, 2 vols. New York: Praeger.

Braverman, H. 1974: *Labor and Monopoly Capital: the Degradation of Work in the Twentieth Century*. New York: Monthly Review Press.

Bray, M. 1985: Rational expectations, information and asset pricing. *Oxford Economic Papers* 37, 161–95.

Braybrooke, D. 1987: *Meeting Needs*. Princeton: Princeton University Press.

Brecht, Bertolt 1938 (1977): Against Georg Lukács. In *Aesthetics and Politics*, ed. Ernst Bloch et al. London: New Left Books.

Brecht, Bertolt 1964 (1978): *Brecht on Theatre*, ed., John Willett. New York: Hill & Wang.

Breese, Gerald, ed. 1969: *The City in Newly Developing Countries*. Englewood Cliffs, NJ: Prentice-Hall.

Breger, P. and Luckmann, T. 1966: *The Social Construction of Reality: an Essay in the Sociology of Knowledge*. Garden City, NY: Doubleday.

Breiger, Ronald L. 1981: The social class structure of occupational mobility. *American Journal of Sociology* 87, 578–611.

Breitenbach, Hans et al. 1990: *Features of a Viable Socialism*. Hemel Hempstead: Harvester-Wheatsheaf.

Brenan, G. 1950: *The Spanish Labyrinth*. 2nd edn, Cambridge: Cambridge University Press.

Brenner, Robert 1977: The origins of capitalist development: a critique of neo-Smithian Marxism. *New Left Review* 104. July–Aug.

Breuilly, J. 1982: *Nationalism and the State*. Manchester: Manchester University Press.

Briffault, R. and Malinowski, B. 1957: *Marriage: Past and Present*. Boston: Porter Sargent.

Briggs, Asa 1966: History and society. In *A Guide to the Social Sciences*, ed. Norman MacKenzie. London: Weidenfeld & Nicolson.

Brink, D. 1989: *Moral Realism and the Foundations of Ethics*. Cambridge: Cambridge University Press.

Brinson, Peter 1983: Scholastic tasks of a sociology of dance. *Dance Research Journal* 1, 100–7; 2, 59–68.

Brock, P. 1968: *Pacifism in the United States*. Princeton, NJ: Princeton University Press.

Bronfenbrenner, M. ed. 1969: *Is the Business Cycle Obsolete?* New York and London: Wiley-Interscience.

Broszat, Martin 1981: *The Hitler State:* the Foundation and Development of the Internal Structure of the Third Reich. New York: Longman.

Brown, G. et al. 1982: Aggression, suicide and serotonin: relationships to CSF amine metabolites. *American Journal of Psychiatry* 139, 741–6.

Brown, Geoff 1977: *Sabotage*. Nottingham: Spokesman.

Brown, R. 1986: *Social Psychology*. 2nd edn, New York: Free Press; London: Collier-Macmillan.

Brownmiller, Susan 1976: *Against our Will: Men, Women and Rape*. Harmondsworth: Penguin.

Brozen, Y. 1982: *Concentration, Mergers and Public Policy*. New York: Macmillan.

Brubaker, R. 1984: *The Limits of Rationality: an Essay on the Social and Moral Thought of Max Weber*. London: Allen & Unwin.

Brubaker, W. Rogers ed. 1989: *Immigration and the Politics of Citizenship in Europe and North America*. Lanham, NY, and London: University Press of America.

Brubaker, W. Rogers 1992: *Citizenship and Nationhood in France and Germany*. Cambridge, MA: Harvard University Press.

Bruce, S. 1986: *'God Save Ulster!' The Religion and Politics of Paisleyism*. Oxford: Clarendon Press.

Bruce, S. 1990: *Pray TV: the Sociology of Televangelism*. London: Routledge & Kegan Paul.

Bruegmann, W. G. 1981: Target is industrial democracy: thirty years of co-determination in the Federal Republic of Germany. *Sozial-Report* 10, 1–23.

Brunner, K. ed. 1981: *The Great Depression Revisited*. Boston: Martinus Nijhoff.

Brunt, P. A. and Moore, J. M. eds 1967: *Res Gestae Divi Augusti*. Oxford: Oxford University Press.

Brus, W. 1961 (*1972*): *The Market in a Socialist Economy*. London: Routledge & Kegan Paul.

Brus, Wlodzimierz and Laski, Kazimierz 1989: *From Marx to the Market: Socialism in Search of an Economic System*. Oxford: Clarendon Press.

Bryant, C. G. A. 1985: *Positivism in Social Theory and Research*. London: Macmillan.

Bryant, C. G. A. and Jary, D. 1990: *Anthony Giddens*. London: Routledge & Kegan Paul.

Brym, Robert J. 1980: *Intellectuals and Politics*. London: Allen & Unwin.

Buchanan, A. E. 1982: *Marx and Justice*. London: Methuen.

Buchanan, J. M. 1975: *The Limits of Liberty: Between Anarchy and Leviathan*. Chicago: University of Chicago Press.

Buchanan, J. M. 1979: *What Should Economists Do?* Indianapolis: Liberty Press.

Buchanan, J. M. 1982: Order defined in the process of its emergence. *Literature of Liberty* 5, 5.

Buchanan, J. M. 1986: *Liberty, Market and the State.* Brighton: Wheatsheaf.

Buchanan, J. M. and Tullock, G. 1962: *The Calculus of Consent.* Ann Arbor: University of Michigan Press.

Buchanan, J. M. and Wagner, R. 1977: *Democracy in Deficit: the Political Legacy of Lord Keynes.* New York: Academic Press.

Buci-Glucksmann, C. 1982: Hegemony and consent. In *Approaches to Gramsci*, ed. A. S. Sassoon. London: Writers and Readers Publishing Cooperative.

Buckley, W. 1967: *Sociology and Modern Systems Theory.* Englewood Cliffs, NJ: Prentice-Hall.

Buck-Morss, S. 1977: *The Origin of Negative Dialectics: Theodor W. Adorno, Walter Benjamin and the Frankfurt Institute.* New York: Free Press.

Bukharin, N. 1917–18 (*1972*): *Imperialism and World Economy.* London: Merlin; New York: Monthly Review Press (1973).

Bukharin, N. 1921 (1925): *Historical Materialism: a System of Sociology.* New York: International Publishers.

Bukharin, N. 1982: *Selected Writings on the State and the Transition to Socialism*, ed. R. Day. New York: M. E. Sharpe.

Bulka, Reuven P. 1983: *Dimensions of Orthodox Judaism.* New York.

Bull, H. 1969: International theory: the case for a classical approach. In *Contending Approaches to International Politics*, ed. K. Knoor and J. N. Rosenau. Princeton, NJ: Princeton University Press.

Bull, H. 1977: *The Anarchical Society.* London: Macmillan.

Bull, Hedley and Watson, Adam eds 1984: *The Expansion of International Society.* Oxford: Clarendon Press.

Bullock, 1977: *Report of a Committee of Inquiry on Industrial Democracy.* London: HMSO, Cmd. 6706.

Bullough, Edward 1957: *Aesthetics.* Palo Alto, CA: Stanford University Press.

Bulmer, M. ed. 1985: *Essays on the History of British Sociological Research.* Cambridge: Cambridge University Press.

Bulmer, R. 1967: Why is the cassowary not a bird? *Man*, NS, 2.

Burckhardt, J. 1860 (*1955*): *The Civilisation of the Renaissance in Italy.* London: Phaidon.

Bürger, Peter 1984: *Theory of the Avant-Garde.* Manchester: Manchester University Press.

Burgess, R. L. and Bushell, D. Jr 1969: *Behavioral Sociology: the Experimental Analysis of Social Process.* New York: Columbia University Press.

Burke, E. 1790 (*1968*): *Reflections on the Revolution in France.* Harmondsworth: Penguin.

Burke, Peter 1980: *Sociology and History.* London: Allen & Unwin.

Burke, Peter 1990: *The French Historical Revolution.* Cambridge: Polity.

Burke, Peter 1992: *History and Social Theory.* Cambridge: Polity.

Burkitt, Ian 1991: *Social Selves: Theories of the Social Formation of Personality.* London: Sage.

Burnham, J. 1941: *The Managerial Revolution.* New York: John Day.

Burnier, Michel 1980: *FIAT: conseils ouvriers et syndicats.* Paris: Éditions Ouvrières.

Burns, A. F. and Mitchell, W. C. 1946: *Measuring Business Cycles.* New York: National Bureau of Economic Research.

Burns, J. 1979: *Leadership.* New York: Harper & Row.

Burns, T. and Stalker, G. M. 1961: *The Management of Innovation.* London: Tavistock.

Burrell, Gibson and Morgan, Gareth 1979: *Sociological Paradigms and Organizational Analysis.* London: Heinemann.

Burridge, K. 1969: *New Heaven, New Earth.* Oxford: Blackwell.

Burrow, J. 1966: *Evolution and Society: a Study in Victorian Social Theory.* Cambridge.

Bury, J. B. 1923: *The Idea of Progress.* London: Macmillan.

Bury, M. R. 1986: Social constructionism and the development of medical sociology. *Sociology of Health and Illness* 8, 137–69.

Bush, Michael 1983: *Noble Privilege.* Manchester: Manchester University Press.

Bush, Michael 1988: *Rich Noble, Poor Noble.* Manchester: Manchester University Press.

Butler, Christopher 1980: *After the Wake: the Contemporary Avant-Garde.* Oxford: Clarendon Press.

Button, G. and Lee, J. R. E. eds 1987: *Talk and*

Social Organisation. Clevedon: Multilingual Matters.

Caillois, Roger 1962: *Esthétique généralisée*. Paris: NRF.

Cairns, John 1984: Blackstone: an English institutist. *Oxford Journal of Legal Studies* 4, 318.

Callinicos, A. 1983: *Marxism and Philosophy*. Oxford: Clarendon Press.

Calvert, P. 1982: *The Concept of Class*. London: Hutchinson.

Calvin, M. 1969: *Chemical Evolution: Molecular Evolution towards the Origin of Living Systems on the Earth*. New York: Oxford University Press.

Cameron, D. 1985: *Feminism and Linguistic Theory*. London: Macmillan.

Campbell, A. 1982: Female aggression. In *Aggression and Violence*, ed. P. Marsh and A. Campbell. Oxford: Blackwell.

Campbell, Colin 1987: *The Romantic Ethic and the Spirit of Modern Consumerism*. Oxford: Blackwell.

Campbell, C. 1971: *Towards a Sociology of Irreligion*. London: Macmillan.

Campbell, T. D. 1988: *Justice*. London: Macmillan.

Camus, Albert 1951 (*1956*): *The Rebel*. New York: Vintage.

Cannadine, D. 1983: Context, performance and meaning of ritual: the British monarchy and the invention of tradition, c. 1820–1977. In *The Invention of Tradition*, ed. E. Hobsbawm and T. Ranger. Cambridge: Cambridge University Press.

Cannadine, D. 1984: The past and the present in the English industrial revolution, 1880–1980. *Past and Present* 103, 131–72.

Canovan, M. C. 1981: *Populism*. London: Junction Books.

Caporale, R. and Grumelli, A. eds 1971: *The Culture of Unbelief*. Berkeley: University of California Press.

Capra, F. and Spretnak, C. 1984: *Green Politics*. London: Hutchinson.

Cardinal, Roger and Short, Robert Stuart 1970: *Surrealism: Permanent Revelation*. London: Studio Vista.

Cardoso, F. H. and Faletto, E. 1969 (*1979*): *Dependency and Development in Latin America*. Los Angeles: University of California Press.

Carlyle, T. 1904 (*1966*): *On Heroes, Hero-Worship and the Heroic in History*, ed. C. Niemeyer. Lincoln: University of Nebraska Press.

Carnap, R. 1928 (*1967*): *The Logical Structure of the World and Pseudo-problems in Philosophy*. Berkeley: University of California Press; London: Routledge & Kegan Paul.

Carnap, R. 1932 (*1987*): On protocol sentences. *Nous* 21, 457–70.

Carnap, R. 1932 (*1959*): The elimination of metaphysics through logical analysis of language. In *Logical Positivism*, ed. A. J. Ayer. Glencoe, IL, Free Press.

Carnap, R. 1932 (*1934*): *The Unity of Science*. London: Kegan Paul.

Carnap, R. 1934 (*1937*): *The Logical Syntax of Language*. London: Kegan Paul; New York: Harcourt.

Carnap, R. 1936: Testability and meaning. In *Readings in the Philosophy of Science*, ed. H. Feigl and M. Brodbeck. New York: Appleton-Century-Crofts.

Carnap, R. 1950: *The Logical Foundations of Probability*. Chicago: University of Chicago Press.

Carnap, R. 1956: Methodological character of theoretical concepts. In *Minnesota Studies in the Philosophy of Science*, ed. H. Feigl and M. Scriven. Minneapolis: University of Minnesota Press.

Carnap, R. 1963: Intellectual autobiography. In *The Philosophy of Rudolf Carnap*, ed. P. A. Schilpp. La Salle, IL, Open Court; London: Cambridge University Press.

Carnap. R. et al. 1929 (*1973*): The scientific conception of the world: the Vienna circle. In *Empiricism and Sociology*, ed. M. Neurath and R. S. Cohen. Dordrecht: Reidel.

Carnoy, Martin and Shearer, Derek 1980: *Economic Democracy: the Challenge of the 1980s*. White Plains, NY: Sharpe.

Carr, E. H. 1939 (*1964*): *Twenty Years' Crisis*. London: Macmillan; New York: Harper Torchbook.

Carr, E. H. 1952: *The Bolshevik Revolution, 1917–23*, vol. 2. Harmondsworth: Penguin.

Carr, E. H. 1958: Stalin. In *Socialism in One Country, 1924–1926*, vol. 1. London: Macmillan.

Carr, E. H. 1961: *What is History?*. Harmondsworth: Penguin.

Carr, E. H. 1966: *The Bolshevik Revolution 1917–1923*, 3 vols. Harmondsworth: Penguin.

Carr-Saunders, A. M. and Wilson, P. A. 1933 (*1964*): *The Professions*. London: Frank Cass.

Carrithers, S. et al. 1985: *The Category of the Person: Anthropology, Philosophy, History*. Cambridge: Cambridge University Press.

Carson, R. 1972: *Silent Spring*. Harmondsworth: Penguin.

Carter, April 1992: *Peace Movements: International Protest and World Politics since 1945*.

Carter, B. 1985: *Capitalism, Class Conflict and the New Middle Class*. London: Routledge & Kegan Paul.

Cashdan, Asher and Jordan, Martin 1987: *Studies in Communication*. Oxford: Blackwell.

Cassirer, E. 1944: *An Essay on Man*. New Haven, CT: Yale University Press.

Cassirer, E. 1951: *The Philosophy of the Enlightenment*. Princeton, NJ: Princeton University Press.

Cassirer, Ernst 1923: *Substance and Function and Einstein's Theory of Relativity*. Chicago: Open Court.

Castells, Manuel 1989: *The Informational City*. Oxford: Blackwell.

Castles, F. C. ed. 1982: *The Impact of Parties*. London and Los Angeles: Sage:

Castles, Stephen and Kosack, G. 1973: *Immigrant Workers and Class Structure in Western Europe*. London: Oxford University Press.

Castles, S. et al. 1984: *Here for Good: Western Europe's New Ethnic Minorities*. London: Pluto Press.

Caute, David 1988: *Sixty-Eight: the Year of the Barricades*. London: Hamish Hamilton.

Cavan, R. 1965: *Suicide*. New York: Russell & Russell.

Cave, J. and Hare, P. 1981: *Alternative Approaches to Economic Planning*. London: Macmillan.

Cawson, A. ed. 1985: *Organized Interests and the State: Studies in Meso-Corporatism*. London: Sage.

Cawson, A. 1986: *Corporatism and Political Theory*. Oxford: Blackwell.

Cawson, A. and Saunders, P. 1983: Corporatism, competitive politics and class struggle. In *Capital and Politics*. London: Routledge & Kegan Paul.

Ceadel, M. 1987: *Thinking about Peace and War*. Oxford: Oxford University Press.

Centers, R. 1949: *The Psychology of Social Classes*. Princeton, NJ: Princeton University Press.

Ch'en, J. 1970: *Mao Papers*. London: Oxford University Press.

Chadwick-Jones, J. K. 1976: *Social Exchange Theory: its Structure and Influence in Social Psychology*. New York: Academic Press.

Chaliand, Gérard 1979 (*1984*): *Stratégies de la guérilla*. Paris: Gallimard.

Chalk. F. and Jonassohn, K. 1990: *The History and Sociology of Genocide*. New Haven, CT: Yale University Press.

Chalmers, Alan F. 1982: *What is Science? An Assessment of the Status and Nature of Science and its Methods*. St Lucia: University of Queensland Press.

Chambliss, W. and Mankoff, M. 1976: *Whose Law? What Order?* New York: Wiley.

Champfleury [J.-F.-F. Husson] 1869: *Histoire de l'imagerie populaire*. Paris.

Chandler, A. D. 1977: *The Visible Hand*. Cambridge, MA: Harvard University Press.

Chandler, R. W. 1981: *War of Ideas: the US Propaganda Campaign in Vietnam*. Boulder, CO: Westview.

Charny, I. W. ed. 1988: *Genocide: a Critical Bibliographic Review*. New York: Facts on File.

Chayanov, A. V. 1987: *The Theory of Peasant Economy*. Madison: Wisconsin University Press.

Chayanov, A. V. 1991: *The Theory of Peasant Cooperatives*. London.

Chazel, F. 1985: Les ruptures révolutionnaires. In *Traité de science politique*, ed. J. Leca and M. Grawitz. Paris: Presses Universitaires de France.

Chenery, H. B. et al. 1986: *Industrialization and Growth: a Comparative Study*. New York: Oxford University Press.

Cherlin, Andrew 1982: *Marriage, Divorce, Remarriage*. Cambridge, MA: Harvard University Press.

Chessyne, R. 1989: Softly, softly. *New Statesman and Society*, 24 November, 20–1.

Chevalier, L. 1973: *Labouring Classes and Dangerous Classes*. London: Routledge & Kegan Paul.

Childs, H. L. 1965: *Public Opinion: Nature, Formation, and Role*. Princeton, NJ: Van Nostrand.

Chodorow, Nancy 1978: *The Reproduction of Mothering: Psychoanalysis and the Sociology of Gender*. Berkeley: University of California Press.

Chomsky, N. 1957: *Syntactic Structures*. The Hague: Mouton.

Chomsky, N. 1959: Review of B. F. Skinner's *Verbal Behaviour. Language* 35, 26–58.

Chomsky, N. 1965: *Aspects of the Theory of Syntax*. Cambridge, MA: MIT Press.

Chomsky, N. 1966: *Cartesian Linguistics: a Chapter in the History of Rationalist Thought*. New York.

Chomsky, N. 1980: *Rules and Representations*. Oxford: Blackwell.

Chomsky, N. 1981: *Lectures on Government and Binding*. Dordrecht: Foris.

Chomsky, N. 1986: *Barriers*. Cambridge, MA: MIT Press.

Chomsky, N. 1986: *Knowledge of Language: its Nature, Origin and Use*. New York: Praeger.

Chomsky, N. and Halle, M. 1968: *The Sound Pattern of English*. New York: Harper & Row.

Choukas, M. 1965: *Propaganda Comes of Age*. Washington, DC: Public Affairs Press.

Chow, N. W. S. 1982: *Poverty in an Affluent City: a Report of a Survey of Low Income Families in Hong Kong*. Hong Kong: Chinese University of Hong Kong.

Christie, N. 1982: *Limits to Pain*. Oxford: Martin Robertson.

Churchland, P. 1979: *Scientific Realism and the Plasticity of Mind*. Cambridge: Cambridge University Press.

Cicero 1958: *Pro Sestio and In Vatinium*. London: Heinemann.

Cicourel, A. V. 1968: *The Social Organization of Juvenile Justice*. New York: Wiley.

Cixous, Hélène 1975 (*1976*): The laugh of the medusa. *Signs* 1, 875–99.

Cixous, Hélène 1976 (*1981*): Castration or decapitation. *Signs* 7. 1, 41–55.

Clark, A. 1989: *Microcognition: Philosophy, Cognitive Science, and Parallel Distributed Processing*. Cambridge, MA: Bradford/MIT Press.

Clark, Colin 1968: *Population Growth and Land Use*. London: Macmillan.

Clark, J. et al. eds 1990: *Anthony Giddens: Consensus and Controversy*. London and New York: Falmer Press.

Clark, T. J. 1973: *The Absolute Bourgeois: Artists and Politics in France 1848–1851*. London: Thames & Hudson.

Clarke, J. et al. eds 1987: *Ideologies of Welfare: From Dreams to Disillusion*. London: Hutchinson.

Clarke, John and Critcher, Chas 1985: *The Devil Makes Work: Leisure in Capitalist Britain*. London: Macmillan.

Clarke, M. 1981: *Fallen Idols*. London: Junction Books.

Clarke, P. 1978: *Liberals and Social Democrats*. Cambridge.

Clarke, Simon 1980: Althusserian Marxism. In *One Dimensional Marxism: Althusser and the Politics of Culture*, ed. Simon Clarke et al. London: Alison & Busby.

Clarke, Simon 1982 (*1991*): *Marx, Marginalism and Modern Sociology*. London: Macmillan; Atlantic Highlands, NJ: Humanities.

Clarke, Simon 1988: *Keynesianism, Monetarism and the Crisis of the State*. Aldershot: Edward Elgar.

Claude, I. L. 1956 (*1964*): *Swords into Plowshares*. 3rd edn, New York: Random House.

Claude, I. L. 1962: *Power in International Relations*. New York: Random House.

Clausewitz, Carl Von 1832 (*1976*): *On War*. Princeton, NJ: Princeton University Press.

Clecak, P. 1983: *America's Quest for the Ideal Self: Dissent and Fulfillment in the 60's and 70's*. New York: Oxford University Press.

Clegg, Hugh 1976: *Trade Unions under Collective Bargaining*. Oxford: Blackwell.

Clegg, Stewart 1980: *Organization, Class and Control*. London: Routledge & Kegan Paul.

Clegg, Stewart 1990: *Organization Theory and Class Analysis*. Berlin: De Gruyter.

Cleland, J. and Wilson, C. 1987: Demand theories of the fertility transition: an iconoclastic view. *Population Studies* 41, 5–30.

Clinard, M. 1963: *Sociology of Deviant Behaviour*. New York: Holt.

Clogg, C. C. 1992: The impact of sociological methodology on statistical methodology. *Statistical Science* 7.

Clyne, M. 1984: *Language and Society in the German-speaking Countries*. Cambridge: Cambridge University Press.

Coale, A. J. 1972: *The Growth and Structure of Human Populations*. Princeton, NJ: Princeton University Press.

Coates, J. 1986: *Women, Men and Language*. London: Longman.

Coates, J. F. and Jarrat, J. eds 1992: *The Future: Trends into the Twenty-First Century*. Special issue of *Annals of the American Academy of Political and Social Science* 552, July.

Coates, Ken and Topham, Tony 1975: *Industrial Democracy in Great Britain*, 3 vols. Nottingham: Spokesman.

Cobban, A. 1939: *Dictatorship: its History and Theory*. London: Jonathan Cape.

Cochetti, Stefano 1985: *Mythos und 'Dialektik der Aufklärung'*. Königstein: Athenäum.

Cochrane, A. L. 1972: *Effectiveness and Efficiency*. London: Nuffield Provincial Hospitals Trust.

Cockburn, C. 1983: *Brothers*. London: Pluto Press.

Coffield, F. et al. 1980: *A Cycle of Deprivation?*. London: Heinemann.

Cohen, A. 1966: *Deviance and Control*. London: Prentice Hall.

Cohen, A. 1974: *Two-Dimensional Man*. Berkeley: University of California Press.

Cohen, Anthony 1985: *The Symbolic Construction of Community*. London: Routledge.

Cohen, G. A. 1978: *Karl Marx's Theory of History: a Defence*. Oxford: Clarendon Press; Princeton, NJ: Princeton University Press.

Cohen, Ira J. 1989: *Structuration Theory: Anthony Giddens and the Constitution of Social Life*. London: Macmillan; New York: St Martin's Press.

Cohen, L. J. 1986: *The Claims of Reason*. Oxford: Oxford University Press.

Cohen, S. ed. 1971: *Images of Deviance*. Harmondsworth: Penguin.

Cohen, S. 1985: *Visions of Social Control*. Cambridge: Polity.

Cohen, S. and Scull, A., eds 1983 (*1985*): *Social Control and the State*. Oxford: Blackwell.

Cohen, Stephen S. and Zysman, John: *Manufacturing Matters: the Myth of the Post-Industrial Economy*. New York: Basic Books.

Cohen, Ted and Guyer, Paul eds 1982: *Essays in Kant's Aesthetics*. Chicago: University of Chicago Press.

Cohn, Norman 1970: *The Pursuit of the Millennium*. Rev edn, New York: Oxford University Press.

Cole, G. D. H. 1913: *The World of Labour*. London: Bell.

Cole, G. D. H. 1917 (*1972*): *Self Government in Industry*. London: Hutchinson.

Cole, G. D. H. 1920: *Guild Socialism Re-stated*. London: Leonard Parsons.

Cole, G. D. H. 1945: *A Century of Co-operation*. Manchester: Co-operative Union.

Cole, G. D. H. 1953–60: *A History of Social Thought*, 5 vols. London: Macmillan.

Cole, L. C. 1958 (*1971*): The ecosphere. In *Man and the Ecosphere*, ed. P. R. Ehrlich et al. San Francisco: Freeman.

Coleman, D. C. 1987: *History and the Economic Past: an Account of the Rise and Decline of Economic History in Britain*. Oxford.

Colletti, L. 1972: *From Rousseau to Lenin*. London:

New Left Books; New York: Monthly Review Press.

Colletti, L. 1975: Marxism and the dialectic. *New Left Review* 93.

Collingwood, R. G. 1938: *The Principles of Art*. Oxford: Clarendon Press.

Collingwood, R. G. 1940: *An Essay on Metaphysics*. Oxford: Clarendon Press.

Collingwood, R. G. 1946: *The Idea of History*. Oxford: Oxford University Press.

Collini, S. et al. 1983: *That Noble Science of Politics: a Study in Nineteenth-Century Intellectual History*. Cambridge.

Collini, Stefan 1979: *Liberalism and Sociology: L. T. Hobhouse and Political Argument in England 1880–1914*. Cambridge: Cambridge University Press.

Collins, H. 1982: *Marxism and Law*. Oxford: Clarendon Press.

Collins, R. 1988: *Theoretical Sociology*. San Diego: Harcourt Brace Jovanovich.

Collins, Randall 1975: *Conflict Sociology: Toward an Explanatory Science*. New York: Academic Press.

Compton, B. 1952: *Mao's China: Party Reform Documents, 1942–1944*. Seattle: University of Washington Press.

Comte, Auguste 1830–42 (*1970*): *Introduction to Positive Philosophy*. Indianapolis: Bobbs-Merrill.

Comte, Auguste 1830–42 (*1896*): *The Positive Philosophy of Auguste Comte*. London: Bell.

Comte, Auguste 1974: *The Essential Comte*, ed. Stanislav Andreski. London: Croom Helm.

Cone, J. 1969: *Black Theology and Black Power*. New York: Seabury.

Conger, J. A. 1989: *The Charismatic Leader: Beyond the Mystique of Exceptional Leadership*. San Francisco: Jossey-Bass.

Conger, J. A. and Kanungo, R. N. eds 1988: *Charismatic Leadership: the Elusive Factor in Organisational Effectiveness*. San Francisco: Jossey-Bass.

Congregation for the Doctrine of the Faith 1984: *Instruction of Certain Aspects of the Theology of Liberation*. Rome: Vatican Press.

Connolly, W. E. 1983: *The Terms of Political Discourse*. Oxford: Martin Robertson.

Connolly, William, ed. 1984: *Legitimacy and the State*. Oxford: Blackwell.

Connor, Steven 1989: *Postmodernist Culture: an*

Introduction to Theories of the Contemporary. Oxford: Blackwell.

Conquest, R. 1971: *The Great Terror: Stalin's Purge of the Thirties.* Harmondsworth: Penguin.

Converse, J. M. 1987: *Survey Research in the United States: Roots and Emergence, 1890–1960.* Berkeley: University of California Press.

Cook, K. S. ed. 1987: *Social Exchange Theory.* Newbury Park: Sage.

Cooley, C. H. 1909 (*1962*): *Social Organization.* New York: Schocken.

Cooper, David E. 1990: *Existentialism: a Reconstruction.* Oxford: Blackwell.

Coplestone, F. 1963: *A History of Philosophy*, 9 vols. Vol. 1: *Fichte to Nietzsche.* London: Burns & Oates.

Corbin, Alain 1982 (*1986*): *The Foul and the Fragrant.* Cambridge, MA: Harvard University Press.

Cornforth, M. 1980: *Communism and Philosophy: Contemporary Dogmas and Revisions of Marxism.* London: Lawrence & Wishart.

Coser, Lewis A. 1956: *The Functions of Social Conflict.* New York: Free Press.

Coser, Lewis A. 1965: *Men of Ideas: a Sociologist's View.* New York: Free Press.

Coser, Lewis A. 1967: *Continuities in the Study of Social Conflict.* New York: Free Press.

Coser, Lewis A. 1988: The Functions of Dissent. In *A Handful of Thistles: Collected Papers in Moral Conviction.* New Brunswick, NJ: Transaction Books.

Cosgrove, D. 1985: *Social Formation and Symbolic Landscape.* Totowa, NJ: Barnes & Noble.

Cotgrove, S. 1982: *Catastrophe or Cornucopia: the Environment, Politics and the Future.* Chichester: Wiley.

Coulthard, M. and Montgomery, M. eds 1979: *Studies in Discourse Analysis.* London: Routledge & Kegan Paul.

Court, W. H. B. 1970: *Scarcity and Choice in History.* London.

Cousin, Bernard 1980: Longue durée et temps court: l'impact de la révolution française sur l'ex-voto peint. *Annales historiques de la Révolution française* 240, 280–93.

Cowen, Tyler 1982: Say's law and Keynesian economics. In *Supply-Side Economics: a Critical Appraisal*, ed. Richard H. Fink. Frederick, MD: University Publications of America.

Cragg, K. 1965: *Islamic Surveys: Counsels in Contemporary Islam.* Edinburgh: Edinburgh University Press.

Cranston, M. 1953: *Freedom: a New Analysis.* London: Longmans, Green.

Crawford, R. 1977: You are dangerous to your health: the ideology and politics of victim blaming. *International Journal of Health Services* 7, 665–80.

Crenshaw, M. ed. 1983: *Terrorism, Legitimacy and Power.* Middletown, CT: Wesleyan University Press.

Crick, B. 1959: *The American Science of Politics.* London: Routledge & Kegan Paul.

Crick, B. R. 1992: *In Defence of Politics.* 3rd edn, London: Weidenfeld & Nicolson.

Croce, Benedetto 1922: *Aesthetics as Science of Expression and General Linguistic*, trans. D. Ainslie. London: Macmillan.

Croix, G. de Ste 1981: *The Class Struggle in the Ancient Greek World.* London: Duckworth.

Crone, Patricia 1989: *Pre-Industrial Societies.* Oxford: Blackwell.

Cross, Gary 1986: The political economy of leisure in retrospect: Britain, France and the origins of the eight-hour day. *Leisure Studies* 5.

Cross, W. R.: *The Burned-over District: the Social and Intellectual History of Enthusiastic Religion in Western New York State 1800–1850.* Ithaca, NY: Cornell University Press.

Crossman, R. H. S. 1963: Introduction to W. Bagehot, *The English Constitution.* London: Fontana.

Crouch, Colin 1982: *Trade Unions.* London: Fontana.

Crozier, Michael 1964: *The Bureaucratic Phenomenon.* Chicago: University of Chicago Press.

Crusius, Reinhard ed. 1978: *Die Betriebsräte in der Weimarer Republik: von der Selbstverwaltung zur Mitbestimmung*, 2 vols. Berlin: Olle & Wolter.

Crystal, D. 1985: *A Dictionary of Linguistics and Phonetics.* Oxford: Blackwell.

Culler, J. 1976 (*1986*): *Saussure.* London: Fontana.

Culler, J. 1982: *On Deconstruction: Theory and Criticism after Structuralism.* Ithaca: Cornell University Press.

Cumont, Franz 1911 (*1956*): *The Oriental Religions in Roman Paganism.* New York: Dover.

Curle, A. 1971: *Making Peace.* London: Tavistock.

Curran, James and Seaton, Jean 1988: *Power without Responsibility.* 3rd edn, London: Routledge.

Curtis, D. 1973: *Dartmoor to Cambridge*. London: Hodder & Stoughton.

Curtis, Michael ed. 1986: *Antisemitism in the Contemporary World*. London: Westview Press.

Dahl, R. A. 1948: Marxism and free parties. *Journal of Politics*.

Dahl, R. A. 1956 (*1966*): *A Preface to Democratic Theory*. New Haven, CT: Yale University Press.

Dahl, R. A. 1958: A critique of the ruling elite model. *American Political Science Review* 52.

Dahl, R. A. 1961: *Who Governs? Democracy and Power in an American City*. New Haven, CT, and London: Yale University Press.

Dahl, R. A. 1963: *Modern Political Analysis*. Englewood Cliffs, NJ: Prentice-Hall.

Dahl, R. A. ed. 1973: *Regimes and Oppositions*. New Haven, CT: Yale University Press.

Dahl, R. A. 1982: *Dilemmas of Liberal Democracies*. New Haven, CT: Yale University Press.

Dahl, R. A. 1985: *A Preface to Economic Democracy*. Cambridge: Polity; New Haven, CT: Yale University Press.

Dahl, R. A. 1989: *Democracy and its Critics*. New Haven, CT, and London: Yale University Press.

Dahrendorf, R. 1957 (*1959*): *Class and Class Conflict in Industrial Society*. Stanford, CA: Stanford University Press.

Dahrendorf, R. et al. 1977: *Scientific-Technological Revolution: Social Aspects*. London: Sage.

Dallmayr, F. and McCarthy, T. eds 1977: *Understanding and Social Inquiry*. Notre Dame, IN: University of Notre Dame Press.

Daly, Mary 1978: *Gyn/Ecology: the Metaethics of Radical Feminism*. London: Women's Press.

Daniel, G. and Renfrew, A. C. 1988: *The Idea of Prehistory*. Edinburgh: Edinburgh University Press.

Danziger, K. 1976: *Interpersonal Communication*. New York: Pergamon.

Darwin, Charles 1859 (*1959*): *On the Origin of Species by Means of Natural Selection*, ed. Morse Peckham. Philadelphia: University of Philadelphia Press.

Darwin, Charles 1871 (*1874*): *The Descent of Man*. 2nd edn, London: John Murray.

Dasgupta, P. 1988: Trust as a commodity. In *Trust: Making and Breaking Cooperative Relations*, ed. D. Gambetta. Oxford: Blackwell.

Daumard, Adeline 1973: *Les fortunes françaises au XIXe siècle*. Paris: Mouton.

Davidoff, Leonore and Hall, Catherine 1986: *Family Fortunes: Men and Women of the English Middle Class, 1780–1850*. London: Hutchinson.

Davidoff, R. 1979: The separation of home from work. In *Fit Work for Women*, ed. S. Burnham. London: Croom Helm.

Davidson, Basil 1955: *The African Awakening*. London: Jonathan Cape.

Davidson, D. 1974 (*1984*): On the very idea of a conceptual scheme. In *Inquiries into Truth and Interpretation*. Oxford: Clarendon Press.

Davidson, D. 1980: *Essays on Actions and Events*. Oxford: Oxford University Press.

Davidson, Donald 1977: Handeln. In *Analytische Handlungstheorie*, vol. 1, ed. Georg Meggle. Frankfurt am Main.

Davies, R. W. 1989: *Soviet History in the Gorbachev Revolution*. London: Macmillan.

Davies, S. et al. 1988: *Economics of Industrial Organisation*. Harlow: Longman.

Davis, K. 1945: The world demographic transition. *Annals of the American Academy of Political and Social Science* 273, 1–11.

Davis, K. 1967: The urbanization of the human population. In *Cities*. Harmondsworth: Penguin.

Davis, Kingsley 1949: *Human Society*. New York: Macmillan.

Davis, Kingsley 1953: Reply [to 'Some principles of stratification: a critical analysis' by Melvyn M. Tumin]. *American Sociological Review* 18, 394–7.

Davis, Kingsley and Blake, Judith 1956: Social structure and fertility: an analytic framework. *Economic Development and Cultural Change* 4, 211–35.

Davis, Kingsley and Moore, Wilbert E. 1945: Some principles of stratification. *American Sociological Review* 10, 242–9.

Davis, M. ed. 1965: *The Undecidable*. New York: Raven Press.

Dawe, Alan 1978: Theories of social action. In *A History of Sociological Analysis*, ed. Tom Bottomore and Robert Nisbet. New York: Basic Books.

Dawkins, R. 1976: *The Selfish Gene*. Oxford: Oxford University Press.

Dawkins, R. 1986 (*1988*): *The Blind Watchmaker*. Harmondsworth: Penguin.

Day, M. H. 1975: *Mao Zedong 1917–1925: Documents*. Stockholm.

Day, R. D. 1976: The theory of long waves:

Kondratiev, Trotsky, Mandel. *New Left Review* 99, 67–82.

Debreu, G. 1959: *Theory of Value: an Axiomatic Analysis of Economic Equilibrium*. New Haven, CT: John Wiley.

Deely, J. 1990: *Basics of Semiotics*. Bloomington: Indiana University Press.

Della Porta, D. and Pasquino, G. 1983: *Terrorismo e violenza politica*. Bologna: Il Mulino.

Della Volpe, G. 1950 (*1980*): *Logic as a Positive Science*. London: New Left Books.

Delphy, C. 1984: *Close to Home: a Materialist Analysis of Women's Oppression*. London: Hutchinson.

de Man, Paul 1979 (*1983*): *Blindness and Insight: Essays in the Rhetoric of Contemporary Criticism*. London: Methuen.

Demeny, P. 1972: Early fertility decline in Austria-Hungary: a lesson in demographic transition. In *Population and Social Change*, ed D. V. Glass and R. Revelle. London: Edward Arnold.

Demerath, N. J. and Peterson, R. A., eds 1967: *System, Change and Conflict*. New York: Free Press.

Demsetz, H. 1982: Barriers to entry. *American Economic Review* 72, 47–57.

Derber, Milton 1970: *The American Idea of Industrial Democracy: 1865–1965*. Urbana: University of Illinois Press.

Derrida, Jacques 1967 (*1976*): *Of Grammatology*. Baltimore: Johns Hopkins University Press.

Derrida, Jacques 1967 (*1978*): *Writing and Difference*. London: Routledge; Chicago: University of Chicago Press.

Derrida, Jacques 1972 (*1981*): *Positions*. London: Athlone.

Desai, M. 1986: On defining the poverty threshold. In *Excluding the Poor*. London: Child Poverty Action Group.

Desai, M. and Shah, A. 1988: An econometric approach to the measurement of poverty. *Oxford Economic Papers* 40, 505–22.

Desroche, H. 1964: *Co-opération et développement: mouvements co-opératifs et stratégie du développement*. Paris: Presses Universitaires de France.

Dessoir, Max 1906 (*1970*): *Aesthetics and Theory of Art*. Detroit: Wayne State University Press.

Deutsch, K. W. 1963: *The Nerves of Government*. New York: Free Press.

Deutsch, K. W. 1966: *Nationalism and Social Communication*. 2nd edn, Cambridge, MA: MIT Press.

Deutsch, K. W. and Singer, J. D. 1964: Multipolar systems and international stability. *World Politics* 16, 390–406.

Deutsch, K. W. et al. 1957: *Political Community and the North Atlantic Area*. Princeton, NJ: Princeton University Press.

Deutscher, I. 1950: *Soviet Trade Unions*. London: RIIA.

Deutscher, I. 1954: *The Prophet Armed: Trotsky, 1879–1921*. London: Oxford University Press.

Deutscher, I. 1959: *The Prophet Unarmed: Trotsky, 1921–1929*. London: Oxford University Press.

Deutscher, I. 1963: *The Prophet Outcast: Trotsky, 1929–1940*. London: Oxford University Press.

Devine, P. 1988: *Democracy and Economic Planning*. Cambridge: Polity.

Devos, T. 1981: *US Multinationals and Worker Participation in Management: the American Experience in the European Community*. London: Aldwych.

de Vroey, M. 1984: A regulation approach interpretation of contemporary crisis. *Capital & Class* 23, 45–66.

Dewey, J. 1938: *Logic: the Theory of Inquiry*. New York: Holt.

Dewey, John 1917 (*1976*): The need for a recovery of philosophy. In *John Dewey: Middle Works, 1898–1924*, vol. 10. Carbondale: Southern Illinois Press.

Dewey, John 1927 (*1981*): The Public and its Problems. In *John Dewey: Later Works, 1925–1953*, vol. 2. Carbondale: Southern Illinois Press.

Dewey, John 1966: *Selected Educational Writings*, ed. F. W. Garforth. London: Heinemann.

Dharmasiri, Gunapala 1989: *Fundamentals of Buddhist Ethics*. Antioch, CA: Golden Leaves.

DHSS 1980: *Inequalities in Health: the Black Report*. London: Department of Health and Social Security.

Di Tella, Torcuato S. 1989: *Latin American Politics: a Theoretical Approach*. Austin: Texas University Press.

Diakonoff, Igor M. 1974: *Structure of Society and State in Early Dynastic Sumer*. Los Angeles: Undena Press.

Diani, Marco 1992: *The Immaterial Society: Design, Culture and Technology in the Postmodern World*. Englewood Cliffs, NJ: Prentice-Hall.

Dickie, George 1962: Is psychology relevant to aesthetics? *Philosophical Review* 71, 285–302.

Dickie, George 1971: *Aesthetics: an Introduction.* New York: Bobbs-Merrill.

Dickson, D. 1974: *Alternative Technology.* Glasgow: Fontana/Collins.

Dickson, D. 1984: *The New Politics of Science.* New York: Panther.

Diffey, T. J. 1984: The sociological challenge to aesthetics. *British Journal of Aesthetics* 24, 168–71.

Dilthey, W. 1927 (*1958*): *Gesammelte Schriften*, 18 vols. Vol. 7, *Der Aufbau der geschichtlichen Welt in den Geisteswissenschaften.* Leipzig and Berlin: B. G. Teubner.

Dilthey, W. 1931 (*1976*): *Dilthey: Selected Writings*, ed. H. P. Rickman. Cambridge: Cambridge University Press.

Dirlik, A. 1989: *The Origins of Chinese Communism.* New York: Oxford University Press.

Dittmar, N. 1976: *Sociolinguistics.* London: Arnold.

Dix, R. 1983: Varieties of revolution. *Comparative Politics* 15, 281–93.

Djilas, M. 1957: *The New Class: an Analysis of the Communist System.* London: Unwin; New York: Praeger.

Dobb, M. 1946: *Studies in the Development of Capitalism.* London: Routledge.

Dobb, M. H. 1939 (*1955*): A note on saving and investment in a socialist economy. In *On Economic Theory and Socialism.* London: Routledge & Kegan Paul.

Dobbelaere, K. 1981: Secularization: a multidimensional concept. *Current Sociology* 29.2.

Döbert, R. and Nunner-Winkler, G. 1978: Performanzbestimmende Aspekte moralischen Bewusstseins. In *Sozialisation und Moral*, ed. G. Portele. Weinheim.

Dobzhansky, T. 1962: *Mankind Evolving: the Evolution of the Human Species.* New Haven, CT: Yale University Press.

Doeringer, P. and Piore, M. 1971: *Internal Labor Markets and Manpower Analysis.* Heath Publishers.

Dolan, J. P. 1978: *Catholic Revivalism: the American Experience 1830–1900.* Notre Dame, IN: University of Notre Dame Press.

Domar, E. 1946: Capital expansion, rate of growth, and employment. *Econometrica* 14, 137–47.

Donagan, A. 1966: The Popper-Hempel theory reconsidered. In *Philosophical Analysis in History.* New York: Harper & Row.

Donajgrodzki, A. P. ed. 1977: *Social Control in Nineteenth-Century Britain.* London: Croom Helm.

Donzelot, Jacques 1977 (*1980*): *The Policing of Families.* London: Hutchinson.

Donzelot, Jacques 1984: *L'invention du social.* Paris: Fayard.

Dornbusch, S. 1989: The sociology of adolescence. *Annual Review of Sociology* 15, 233–89.

Dosi, G. et al. 1988: *Technical Change and Economic Theory.* London: Pinter.

Dos Santos, Theotonio 1970: The structure of dependence. *American Economic Review* 60.

Douglas, J. 1967 (*1970*): *The Social Meanings of Suicide.* Princeton, NJ: Princeton University Press.

Douglas, J. and Scott R. 1972: *Theoretical Perspectives on Deviance.*

Douglas, J. D. 1970: *Youth in Turmoil.* Washington, DC: US Government Printing Office.

Douglas, M. 1970: *Natural Symbols: Explorations in Cosmology.* New York: Pantheon.

Dowding, K. M. 1991: *Rational Choice and Political Power.* Aldershot: Edward Elgar.

Dower, N. 1983: *World Poverty.* York: Ebor Press.

Downes, D. and Rock, P. 1979: *Deviant Interpretations.* Oxford: Martin Robertson.

Downes, D. and Rock, P. 1988: *Understanding Deviance.* Oxford: Oxford University Press.

Downes, W. 1984: *Language and Society.* London: Fontana.

Downs, A. 1957: *An Economic Theory of Democracy.* New York: Harper & Row.

Doyle, Brian 1989: *English and Englishness.* London and New York: Routledge.

Doyle, M. W. 1983: Kant, liberal legacies, and foreign affairs. *Philosophy and Public Affairs* 12, 205–34; 323–52.

Drake, Duran et al. 1920 (*1941*): *Essays in Critical Realism.* New York: P. Smith.

Draper, H. *Karl Marx's Theory of Revolution*, 2 vols. Vol. 1, *State and Bureaucracy.* New York: Monthly Review Press.

Drever, J. 1964: *A Dictionary of Psychology.* Rev. edn, Harmondsworth: Penguin.

Drew, P. and Heritage, J. eds 1991: *Talk at Work.* Cambridge: Cambridge University Press.

Drewnowski, J. and Scott, W. 1966: *The Level of Living Index: Report No. 4.* Geneva: Research Institute of Social Development.

Drèze, J. and Sen, A. 1989: *Hunger and Public Action.* Oxford: Clarendon Press.

Driver, Godfrey Rolles and Miles, John C. eds

1952–5: *The Babylonian Laws*. Oxford: Clarendon Press.

Dror, Y. 1983: Terrorism as a challenge to governments. In *Terrorism, Legitimacy and Power*, ed. M. Crenshaw. Middletown, CT: Wesleyan University Press.

Drucker, Peter F. 1979: The first technological revolution and its lessons. In *Technology and Change*, ed. John G. Burke and Marshall C. Eakin. San Francisco: Boyd & Fraser.

Dubiel, Helmut 1978 (*1985*); *Theory and Politics: Studies in the Development of Critical Theory*. Cambridge, MA: MIT Press.

Dubofsky, Melvyn 1969: *We Shall Be All: a History of the IWW*. Chicago: Quadrangle.

Du Bois, W. E. B. 1965: *The World and Africa: an Inquiry into the Part which Africa has Played in World History*. New York: International.

Dubos, R. 1961: *Mirage of Health*. New York: Andor.

Dubos, R. 1968: *So Human an Animal*. New York: Scribner's.

Duby, Georges 1974: *The Early Growth of the European Economy: Warriors and Peasants from the Seventh to the Twelfth Century*. Ithaca, NY: Cornell University Press.

Duchac, R. 1974: *La Sociologie des migrations aux États Unis*. Paris: La Haye, Mouton.

Duhem, Pierre 1906 (*1954*): The Aim and Structure of Scientific Theory. Princeton, NJ: Princeton University Press.

Duijn, J. J. van 1983: *The Long Wave in Economic Life*. London.

Dumont, L. 1970: *Homo Hierarchicus*. London: Weidenfeld & Nicolson.

Dumont, L. 1971: *Introduction à deux théories d'anthropologie sociale*. Paris and The Hague: Mouton.

Dumont, L. 1975: *Dravidien et Kariera: l'alliance de mariage dans l'Inde du Sud et en Australie*. Paris and The Hague: Mouton.

Dumont, L. and Pocock, D. eds 1957–69: *Contributions to Indian Sociology*, 9 vols. Paris and The Hague: Mouton.

Dumoulin, Heinrich ed. 1976: *Buddhism in the Modern World*. New York: Collier.

Duncan, S. and Fiske, W. 1977: *Face-to-Face Interaction*. Hillsdale: Erlbaum.

Dunhill, C. ed. 1989: *The Boys in Blue: Women's Challenge to the Police*. London: Virago.

Dunlop, John and Whyte, William F. 1950: Framework for the analysis of industrial relations: two views. *Industrial and Labor Relations Review* 3, 383–401.

Dunlop, John T. 1950: *Wage Determination under Trade Unions*. New York: Augustus M. Kelley.

Dunlop, John T. 1958: *Industrial Relations Systems*. New York: Henry Holt.

Dunn, J. 1979: *Western Political Theory in the Face of the Future*. Cambridge: Cambridge University Press.

Dunn, J. 1984: The concept of trust in the politics of John Locke. In *Philosophy in History*, ed. R. Rorty et al. Cambridge: Cambridge University Press.

Dunn, John 1984: *The Politics of Socialism*. Cambridge: Cambridge University Press.

Durand, G. 1969: *Les Structures anthropologiques de l'imaginaire*. Paris: Bordas.

Durand, G. 1979: *Figures mythiques et visages de l'oeuvre*. Paris: Berg.

Durkheim, Emile 1893 (*1984*): *The Division of Labor in Society*. London: Macmillan; New York: Free Press.

Durkheim, Emile 1895 (*1982*): *The Rules of the Sociological Method*. London: Macmillan; New York: Free Press.

Durkheim, Emile 1897 (*1963*): *Suicide: a Sociological Study*. New York: Free Press; London: Routledge & Kegan Paul.

Durkheim, Emile 1900 (*1973*): Sociology in France in the nineteenth century. In *Emile Durkheim on Morality and Society: Selected Writings*, ed. R. N. Bellah. Chicago: University of Chicago Press.

Durkheim, Emile 1925: *L'éducation morale*. Paris: Alcan.

Durkheim, Emile 1928 (*1962*): *Socialism*. New York: Collier.

Durkheim, Emile 1912 (*1976*): *The Elementary Forms of the Religious Life: a Study in Religious Sociology*. New York: Free Press; London: Allen & Unwin.

Durkheim, Emile 1950 (*1957*): *Professional Ethics and Civic Morals*. London: Routledge & Kegan Paul.

Durkheim, Emile 1960: *Emile Durkheim 1858–1917: a Collection of Essays, with Translations and a Bibliography*, ed. K. Wolf. Columbus: Ohio State University Press.

Durkheim, Emile and Mauss, M. 1903 (*1963*): *Primitive Classification*, ed. R. Needham. London: Cohen & West; Chicago: University of Chicago Press.

Duster, T. 1970: *The Legislation of Morality*. New York: Free Press.

Duverger, M. 1955: *Political Parties*. London: Methuen.

Duvignaud, J. 1967 (*1972*): *The Sociology of Art*. London: Paladin.

Duvignaud, J. 1975: *La planète des jeunes*. Paris.

Dworkin, Andrea 1981: *Pornography: Men Possessing Women*. London: Women's Press.

Dworkin, R. 1978: *Taking Rights Seriously*. Rev. edn, London: Duckworth.

Dworkin, R. 1981a: Equality of welfare. *Philosophy and Public Affairs* 10, 185–246.

Dworkin, R. 1981b: Equality of resources. *Philosophy and Public Affairs* 10, 283–345.

Eagleton, Terry 1983: *Literary Theory: an Introduction*. Oxford: Blackwell.

Easton, D. 1953: *The Political System*. New York: Knopf.

Eatwell, John et al. 1989: *The Invisible Hand*. New York: Norton.

Eckstein, S. 1982: The impact of revolution on social welfare in Latin America. *Theory and Society* 11, 33–94.

Eco, U. 1976 (*1984*): *A Theory of Semiotics*. London: Macmillan.

Eco, U. 1983 (*1986*): *Faith in Fakes*. London: Secker.

Edelman, M. 1971: *Politics as Symbolic Action*. Chicago: Markham.

Eder, K. 1985: *Geschichte als Lernprozess?* Frankfurt am Main: Suhrkamp.

Edmonds, M. 1988: *Armed Services and Society*. Leicester: Leicester University Press.

Edwards, C. 1985: *The Fragmented World*. London: Routledge.

Edwards, Jay 1984: Structural analysis of the Afro-American trickster tale. In *Black Literature and Literary Theory*, ed. Henry Gates. New York and London: Methuen.

Edwards, R. 1979: *Contested terrain: the Transformation of the Workplace in the Twentieth Century*. New York: Basic Books; London: Heinemann.

Edwards, R. C. et al. 1978: *The Capitalist System*. 2nd edn, Englewood Cliffs, NJ: Prentice-Hall.

Ehrenreich, B. and Ehrenreich, J. 1979: The professional-managerial class. In *Between Labour and Capital*, ed. P. Walker. New York: Monthly Review Press.

Ehrlich, H. J. 1973: *The Social Psychology of Prejudice*. New York: Wiley.

Eibl-Eibesfeldt, I. 1971: *Love and Hate*. New York: Holt, Rinehart & Winston.

Eichner, A. S. ed. 1979: *A Guide to Post-Keynesian Economics*. New York: M. E. Sharpe; London: Macmillan.

Eisenstadt, S. N. 1955: *The Absorption of Immigrants*. Glencoe, IL: Free Press.

Eisenstadt, S. N. 1956: *From Generation to Generation*. New York: Free Press.

Eisenstadt, S. N. 1961: *Essays on Sociological Aspects of Political and Economic Development*. The Hague: Mouton.

Eisenstein, Elizabeth L. 1983: *The Printing Revolution in Early Modern Europe*. Cambridge: Cambridge University Press.

Eisenstein, H. 1984: *Contemporary Feminist Thought*. London: Unwin.

Ekeh, P. P. 1974: *Social Exchange Theory: the Two Traditions*. Cambridge, MA: Harvard University Press.

Ekins, P. and Mex-Neef, M. eds 1992: *Real-life Economics*. London: Routledge.

Eldridge, J. E. T. ed. 1972: *Max Weber*. London: Nelson.

Eley, G. 1984: The British model and the German road: rethinking the course of German history before 1914. In *The Peculiarities of German History*, ed. D. Blackbourn and G. Eley. Oxford: Oxford University Press.

Eliade, M. 1958: *Patterns in Comparative Religion*. New York: Sheed & Ward.

Eliade, M. 1968: *Myths, Dreams and Mysteries*. London: Collins.

Elias, Norbert 1939 (*1978–82*): The Civilizing Process, 2 vols. Oxford: Blackwell; New York: Pantheon.

Elias, Norbert 1970: *What is Sociology?* London: Hutchinson.

Elias, Norbert 1974: Towards a theory of communities. In *The Sociology of Community*, ed. Colin Bell and Howard Newby. London: Cass.

Elias, Norbert 1991: *The Society of Individuals*, ed. Michael Schroter. Oxford: Blackwell.

Elias, Norbert and Dunning, Eric 1986: *Quest for Excitement*. Oxford: Blackwell.

Eliot, T. S. 1939: *The Idea of a Christian Society*. London: Faber.

Eliot, T. S. 1948: *Notes Towards the Definition of Culture*. London: Faber.

Ellis, H. 1912: *The Task of Social Hygiene*. Boston and New York: Houghton Mifflin.

Ellis, John 1975: *A Short History of Guerrilla Warfare*. London: Ian Allen.

Ellis, M. H. 1987: *Towards a Jewish Theology of Liberation*. New York: Orbis.

Ellis, W. D. ed. 1938: *A Sourcebook of Gestalt Psychology*. London: Routledge & Kegan Paul.

Elliston, Frederick and McCormick, Peter eds 1977: *Husserl: Expositions and Appraisals*. Notre Dame, IN, and London: University of Notre Dame Press.

Ellman, M. 1979: *Socialist Planning*. Cambridge: Cambridge University Press.

Ellul, Jacques 1954 (*1965*): *The Technological Society*, trans. John Wilkinson. New York: Knopf.

Ellul, Jacques 1965: *Propaganda: the Formation of Men's Attitudes*. New York: Knopf.

Elmer, M. C. 1917: *Technique of Social Surveys*. Los Angeles: Miller.

Elshtain, J. 1981: *Public Man, Private Woman*. Princeton, NJ: Princeton University Press.

Elson, D. 1988: Socialization of the Market. *New Left Review* 172, 3–44.

Elson, D. ed. 1991: *Male Bias in the Development Process*. Manchester: Manchester University Press.

Elster, J. 1978: *Logic and Society*. Chichester: Wiley.

Elster, J. 1983: *Sour Grapes: Studies in the Subversion of Rationality*. Cambridge: Cambridge University Press.

Elster, J. 1985: *Making Sense of Marx*. Cambridge: Cambridge University Press.

Elster, J. ed. 1986: *Rational Choice*. Oxford: Blackwell.

Elster, J. 1989: *The Cement of Society*. Cambridge: Cambridge University Press.

Elster, J. 1989: *Nuts and Bolts for the Social Sciences*. Cambridge: Cambridge University Press.

Elster, J. and Moene, K. eds 1988: *Alternatives to Capitalism*. Cambridge: Cambridge University Press.

Elton, William ed. 1954: *Aesthetics and Language*. Oxford: Blackwell.

Emerson, R. M. 1962: Power-dependency relations. *American Sociological Review* 27, 31–41.

Emery, F. E. and Thorsrud, Einar 1969: *Form and Content in Industrial Democracy: Some Experiences from Norway and Other European Countries*. London: Tavistock; Assem: Van Gorcum.

Emery, F. E. and Trist, E. L.: Socio-technical systems. In *Management Science, Models and Techniques*, vol. 2, ed. C. W. Churchman and M. Verhulst. Oxford: Pergamon.

Encyclopedia Judaica, 1971. Jerusalem.

Endler, N. S. and Magnusson, D., eds 1976: *Interactional Psychology and Personality*. Washington, DC: Hemisphere.

Engelberger, J. F. 1980: *Robotics in Practice*. London: Kogan Page.

Engels, Friedrich 1847 (*1914*): Principles of Communism. First pubd in *Vorwärts*, Berlin: Eduard Bernstein.

Engels, Friedrich 1871 (*1968*): Introduction to Karl Marx, '*The civil war in France*'. In *Marx and Engels: Selected Works in One Volume*. London: Lawrence & Wishart.

Engels, Friedrich 1884 (*1972*): *The Origin of the Family, Private Property and the State*, ed. E. Leacock. London: Lawrence & Wishart.

Engels, Friedrich 1888: *Ludwig Feuerbach and the End of Classical German Philosophy*.

Engels, Friedrich 1888 (*1967*): Note added to Eng. edn of the *Communist Manifesto*. New York: Vintage.

Engels, Friedrich 1894 (*1934*): Engels to Starkenburg. In K. Marx and F. Engels, *Correspondence 1846–1895*. London: Martin Lawrence.

Entwistle, Harold 1979: *Antonio Gramsci: Conservative Schooling for Radical Politics*. London: Routledge.

Enzenberger, H. M. 1988: A critique of political ecology. In *Dreamers of the Absolute*. London: Hutchinson/Radius.

Epsepskamp, C. P. 1988: *Performance Theory*. New York: Routledge.

Erikson, E. 1958: *Young Man Luther*. New York: Norton.

Erikson, E. 1969: *Gandhi's Truth*. New York: Norton.

Erikson, E. H. 1968: *Identity: Youth and Crisis*. London: Faber & Faber; New York: Norton.

Erikson, Kai T. 1966: *Wayward Puritans: a Study in the Sociology of Deviance*. New York: Wiley.

Esler, A. 1971: *Bombs, Beards, and Barricades: 150 Years of Youth in Revolt*. New York: Stein & Day.

Esping-Anderson, G. 1985: *Politics Against the Market*. Princeton, NJ: Princeton University Press.

Esposito, J. L. ed. 1980: *Islam and Development:*

Religion and Sociopolitical Change. Syracuse, NY: Syracuse University Press.

Etherington, Norman 1984: *Theories of Imperialism: War, Conquest and Capital*. London: Croom Helm.

Etzioni, Amitai 1961: *A Comparative Analysis of Complex Organizations: On Power, Involvement, and their Correlates*. New York: Free Press.

Etzioni, Amitai 1961: *Complex Organizations: a Sociological Reader*. New York: Holt, Rinehart & Winston.

Evans, B. and Waites, B. 1981: *IQ and Mental Testing: an Unnatural Science and its Social History*. London: Macmillan.

Evans-Pritchard, E. E. 1951: *Kinship and Marriage among the Nuer*. Oxford: Clarendon Press.

Evers, A. and Wintersberger, H. 1988: *Shifts in the Welfare Mix*. Vienna: European Centre for Social Welfare Training and Research.

Ewald, François 1986: *L'état providence*. Paris: Grasset.

Eysenck, H. J. 1947: *Dimensions of Personality*. London: Routledge & Kegan Paul.

Eysenck, H. J. 1982: *Personality, Genetics and Behaviour*. New York: Springer.

Fackenheim, Emil 1987: *What is Judaism? An Interpretation for the Present Age*. New York: Summit Books.

Fanon, Frantz 1961 (*1983*): *The Wretched of the Earth*. Harmondsworth: Penguin.

Faris, Robert, E. L. 1967: *Chicago Sociology: 1920–1932*. Chicago: University of Chicago Press.

Fasold, R. 1984: *The Sociolinguistics of Society*. Oxford: Blackwell.

Fasold, R. 1990: *The Sociolinguistics of Language*. Oxford: Blackwell.

Fayol, H. 1916 (*1949*): *General and Industrial Management*. London: Pitman.

Feagin, J. R. 1970 (*1989*): *Racial and Ethnic Relations*. 3rd edn, Englewood Cliffs, NJ: Prentice-Hall.

Fearon, P. 1987: *War, Prosperity and Depression: the US Economy 1917–45*. Oxford: Philip Allan.

Featherstone, M. ed. 1990: *Global Culture: Nationalism, Globalization and Modernity*. London: Sage.

Febvre, Lucien 1950: Un livre qui grandit: la Méditerranée et le monde méditerranéen à l'époque de Philippe II. *Revue historique* 203.2, 224.

Febvre, Lucien 1953: Avant-propos. In *Combats pour l'histoire*. Paris: SEVPEN.

Federer, W. T. 1991: *Statistics and Society*. 2nd edn, New York: Marcel Dekker.

Fehér, F. et al. 1983: *Dictatorship over Needs: an Analysis of Soviet Societies*. Oxford: Blackwell.

Feigenbaum, E. A. and Feldman, J. eds 1963: *Computers and Thought*. New York: McGraw Hill.

Fein, H. 1979: *Accounting for Genocide*. New York: Free Press.

Fein, H. 1990: Genocide: a sociological perspective. *Current Sociology* 38, 1.

Fellner, W. *Competition Among the Few*. New York: Kelley.

Femia, J. V. 1979: Elites, participation, and the democratic creed. *Political Studies* 27, 1–20.

Femia, J. V. 1981: *Gramsci's Political Thought: Hegemony, Consciousness and the Revolutionary Process*. Oxford: Oxford University Press.

Fenn, R. K. 1978: *Toward a Theory of Secularization*. Storrs, CT: Society for the Scientific Study of Religion.

Fenn, R. K. 1981: *Liturgies and Trials*. Oxford: Blackwell.

Ferge, Zsuzsa 1979: *A Society in the Making*. Harmondsworth: Penguin.

Ferge, Zsuzsa and Miller, S. M., eds 1987: *The Dynamics of Deprivation: a Cross-National Study*. London: Gower Press.

Ferguson, C. 1959: Diglossia. *Word* 15, 325–40.

Ferkiss, Victor 1977: *Futurology*. London: Sage.

Ferro, Marc 1980: *Des soviets au communisme bureaucratique: les mécanismes d'une subversion*. Paris: Gallimard/Julliard.

Festinger, L. 1957: *A Theory of Cognitive Dissonance*. Stanford, CA: Stanford University Press.

Fetscher, I. and Rohrmoser, G. 1981: *Ideologien und Strategien: Analysen zum Terrorismus*, vol. 1. Opladen: Westdeutscher Verlag.

Feuer, Lewis S. 1969: *The Conflict of Generations: the Character and Significance of Student Movements*. New York: Basic Books.

Feyerabend, Paul K. 1971: *Against Method*. London: New Left Books.

Fiedler, F. A. 1964: Contingency model of leadership. In *Advances in Experimental Social Psychology*, ed. L. Berkowitz. New York: Academic Press.

Fiedler, F. E. 1967: *A Theory of Leadership Effectiveness*. New York: McGraw-Hill.

Fieldhouse, D. K. 1966: *The Colonial Empires: a Comparative Survey from the Eighteenth Century*. London: Weidenfeld & Nicolson.

Figgis, J. N. 1913: *Churches in the Modern State*. London: Longmans.

Fine, B. 1989: *Marx's Capital*. 3rd edn, London: Macmillan.

Fine, B. and Harris, L. 1979: *Rereading Capital*. London: Macmillan.

Finer, S. E. 1958: *Anonymous Empire*. London: Pall Mall.

Finer, S. E. 1962: *The Man on Horseback: the Role of the Military in Politics*. Lonson: Pall Mall Press.

Finnegan, Ruth 1989: *The Hidden Musicians: Music-making in an English Town*. Cambridge: Cambridge University Press.

Firestone, Shulamith 1970 (*1979*): *The Dialectic of Sex*. New York: Bantam.

Fischler, M. A. and Firscheim, O. eds 1987: *Readings in Computer Vision: Issues, Problems, Principles and Paradigms*. Los Altos, CA: Kaufman.

Fischoff, E. 1944: The Protestant ethic and the spirit of capitalism: the history of a controversy. *Social Research* 11, 61–77.

Fish, Stanley 1980: *Is There a Text in this Class? The Authority of Interpretive Communities*. Cambridge, MA: Harvard University Press.

Fisher, F. et al. 1983: *Folded, Spindled and Mutilated: Economic Analysis and US vs. IBM*. Cambridge, MA: MIT Press.

Fisher, H. A. L. 1928: *Bonapartism: Six Lectures*. London: Oxford University Press.

Fishman, J. 1965 (*1972*): The relationship between micro- and macro-sociolinguistics in the study of who speaks what language to whom and when. In *Sociolinguistics*, ed. J. B. Pride and J. Holmes. Harmondsworth: Penguin.

Fishman, J. 1967: Bilingualism with or without diglossia: diglossia with or without bilingualism. *Journal of Social Issues* 32, 29–38.

Fishman, J. ed. 1968: *Advances in the Sociology of Language*, vol. 1. The Hague: Mouton.

Fishman, R. 1977: *Urban Utopias in the Twentieth Century*. New York: Basic Books.

Flacks, Richard 1967: The liberated generation: an exploration of the roots of student protest. *Journal of Social Issues* 23, 52–75.

Flanders, Allan 1952: *Trade Unions*. London: Hutchinson.

Flanders, N. A. 1969: *Analyzing Teacher Behavior*. Reading. MA: Addison-Wesley.

Flew, A. 1981: *The Politics of Procrustes*. London: Temple Smith.

Florence, P. S. 1951: *Ownership, Control and Success of Large Companies*. London: Sweet & Maxwell.

Foley, D. K. 1986: *Understanding Capital*. Cambridge, MA, and London: Harvard University Press.

Foot, P. 1978: *Virtues and Vices*. Oxford: Blackwell.

Forbes, I. and Smith, S., eds 1983: *Politics and Human Nature*. London: Pinter.

Fondazione Istituto Gramsci 1990: *Bibliografia gramsciana*.

Forester, Tom ed. 1985: *The Information Technology Revolution*. Oxford: Blackwell.

Forester, Tom 1987: *High-Tech Society: the Story of the IT Revolution*. Oxford: Blackwell.

Forester, Tom ed. 1989: *Computers in the Human Context: Information Technology, Productivity and People*. Oxford: Blackwell.

Forester, Tom and Morrison, Perry 1990: *Computer Ethics: Cautionary Tales and Ethical Dilemmas in Computing*. Oxford: Blackwell.

Forslin, J. et al. eds 1979: *Automation and Industrial Workers: a Fifteen Nation Study*, Vol. 1. Oxford: Pergamon.

Forster, E. M. 1947: *Howards End*. London: Arnold.

Forsyth, M. 1989: *Federalism and Nationalism*. Leicester: Leicester University Press.

Fortes, M. 1949: *The Web of Kinship among the Tallensi*. Oxford: Oxford University Press.

Foucault, Michel 1963 (*1976*): *The Birth of the Clinic*. London: Tavistock.

Foucault, Michel 1966 (*1973*): *The Order of Things*. London: Tavistock.

Foucault, Michel 1969 (*1974*): *The Archaeology of Knowledge*. London: Tavistock.

Foucault, Michel 1969 (*1979*): What is an author? *Screen* 20. 1.

Foucault, Michel 1975 (*1977*): *Discipline and Punish*. London: Allen Lane.

Foucault, Michel 1976 (*1981*): *The History of Sexuality*, vol. 1, *An Introduction*. Harmondsworth: Penguin.

Foucault, Michel 1976: *Power/Knowledge: Selected Interviews and Other Writings 1972–77*, ed. C. Gordon. New York: Random House.

Foucault, Michel 1986: *The Foucault Reader*, ed. Paul Rabinow. Harmondsworth: Penguin.

Fournier, J. and Questiaux, N. 1979: *Le pouvoir du social*. Paris: Presses Universitaires de France.

Fowles, J. ed. 1978: *Handbook of Futures Research*. Dorsey, IL: Greenwood Press.

Fox, B. ed. 1980: *Hidden in the Household: Women's Domestic Labour under Capitalism*. Toronto: Women's Press.

Fox, J. ed. 1989: *Health Inequalities in European Countries*. Aldershot: Gower and European Science Foundation.

Fox, R. 1967: *Kinship and Marriage: an Anthropological Perspective*. Harmondsworth: Penguin.

Fox, Robin, 1968: *Encounter with Anthropology*. Harcourt, Brace Jovanovich.

Fox-Piven, F. and Cloward, R. A. 1988: *Why Americans Don't Vote*. New York: Pantheon.

Fraenkel, Ernst 1941: *The Dual State*. New York.

Francastel, Pierre 1965: Oeuvres II, *La Réalité figurative, éléments structurels de sociologie de l'art*. Paris: Denoël/Gonthier.

Francis, E. K. 1976: *Interethnic Relations: an Essay in Sociological Theory*. New York: Elsevier.

Frank, A. G. 1969 (*1971*): *Capitalism and Underdevelopment in Latin America: Historical Studies of Chile and Brazil*. Harmondsworth: Penguin.

Frank, A. G. 1969: *Latin America: Underdevelopment or Revolution*. New York: Monthly Review Press.

Frank, A. G. 1972: Sociology of development and underdevelopment of sociology. In *Dependence and Underdevelopment*, ed. J. D. Cockcroft et al. New York: Anchor.

Frank, P. 1961: *Modern Science and its Philosophy*. New edn, New York: Collier.

Frank, P. 1979: *The Fourth International: the Long March of the Trotskyists*. London: Ink Links.

Franklin, M. N. 1985: *The Decline of Class Voting in Britain*. Oxford: Clarendon Press.

Fraser, Ronald 1988: *1968: a Student Generation in Revolt*. New York: Pantheon.

Freedman, Lawrence 1989: *The Evolution of Nuclear Strategy*. 2nd edn, London: Macmillan.

Freedman, R. 1982: Fertility decline. In *International Encyclopaedia of Population*, ed. J. A. Ross. New York: Free Press.

Freeman, C. ed. 1984: *Long Waves in the World Economy*. London: Frances Pinter.

Freeman, C. 1987: *Technology Policy and Economic Performance: Lessons from Japan*. London: Frances Pinter.

Freeman, J. and Sebba, L. eds 1989: *International Review of Victimology*, vol. 1. London: Academic.

Frege, G. 1879 (*1971*): Begriffsschrift: eine der arithmetischen nachgebildete Formelsprache des reinen Denkens. In *From Frege to Gödel: a Source Book in Mathematical Logic*, ed. J. Van Heijenoort. 2nd edn, Cambridge, MA: Harvard University Press.

Freidson, Eliot 1970: *Profession of Medicine: a Study in the Sociology of Applied Knowledge*. New York: Dodd, Mead.

Freire, P. 1970: *Pedagogy of the Oppressed*. New York: Herder & Herder.

French, P. A. et al. eds 1988: *Ethical Theory: Character and Virtue*. Notre Dame, IN: University of Notre Dame Press.

Freud, S. 1905 (*1949*): *Three Essays on the Theory of Sexuality*. London: Imago.

Freud, S. 1915–17 (*1922*): *Introductory Lectures on Psycho-Analysis*. London: Allen & Unwin.

Freud, S. 1917 (*1957*): *Mourning and Melancholia*. London: Hogarth Press.

Freud, S. 1920 (*1961*): Beyond the pleasure principle. In *Standard Edition of the Complete Psychological Works of Sigmund Freud*, vol. 18, ed. J. Strachey. London: Hogarth Press; New York: Norton.

Freud, S. 1921 (*1959*): *Group Psychology and the Analysis of the Ego*. New York: Norton.

Freud, S. 1923 (*1961*): The ego and the id. In *Standard Edition of the Complete Psychological Works of Sigmund Freud*, vol. 19, ed. J. Strachey. London: Hogarth Press; New York: Norton.

Freud, S. 1927 (*1964*): *The Future of an Illusion*. Garden City, NY: Anchor.

Freud, S. 1930 (*1063*): Civilization and its discontents. In *Standard Edition of the Complete Psychological Works of Sigmund Freud*, vol. 21, ed. J. Strachey. London: Hogarth Press; New York: Norton.

Freud, S. 1933 (*1964*): New introductory lectures on psycho-analysis. In *Standard Edition of the Complete Psychological Works of Sigmund Freud*, vol. 22, ed. J. Strachey. London: Hogarth Press; New York: Norton.

Freund, J. 1984: *La décadence*. Paris.

Friedland, W. H. 1964: For a sociological concept of charisma. *Social Forces* 43, 18–26.

Friedman, David 1989: *The Machinery of Freedom*. 3rd edn, La Salle, IL: Open Court.

Friedman, M. 1953: *Essays in Positive Economics*. Chicago: University of Chicago Press.

Friedman, M. 1968: *The role of monetary policy*. *American Economic Review* 58, 1–17.

Friedman, M. 1977: *From Galbraith to Economic Freedom*. London: Institute of Economic Affairs.

Friedman, M. 1977: *Inflation and Unemployment: the New Dimension of Politics*. London: Institute of Economic Affairs.

Friedman, M. and Friedman, R. 1962: *Capitalism and Freedom*. Chicago: University of Chicago Press.

Friedman, M. and Friedman, R. 1980: *Free to Choose*. London: Secker & Warburg.

Friedman, M. and Schwartz, A. 1963: *A Monetary History of the United States, 1867–1960*. Princeton, NJ: Princeton University Press.

Friedmann, G. 1955 (*1961*): *The Anatomy of Work*. London: Heinemann.

Friedmann, Georges and Naville, Pierre 1961–2: *Traité de sociologie du travail*, 2 vols. Paris: A. Colin.

Friedrich, C. 1958: *Authority*. Cambridge, MA: Harvard University Press.

Friedrich, C. J. and Brzezinski, Z. K. 1956: *Totalitarianism, Dictatorship and Autocracy*. Cambridge, MA: Harvard University Press.

Frisby, David 1988: *Fragments of Modernity*. Cambridge: Polity.

Frith, S. 1978: *The Sociology of Rock*. London: Constable.

Frith, S. 1984: *The Sociology of Youth*. County of Lancashire: Causeway Books.

Fromm, Erich 1973: *The Anatomy of Human Destructiveness*. New York: Holt.

Früchtl, J. 1986: *Mimesis-Konstellation eines Leitbegriffs bei Adorno*. Würzburg: Königshausen & Neumann.

Fry, Roger 1920: *Vision and Design*. London: Chatto & Windus.

Frydman, R. and Phelps, E. S. 1983: *Individual Forecasting and Aggregate Outcomes*. Cambridge: Cambridge University Press.

Fuller, Steve 1988: *Social Epistemology*. Bloomington: Indiana University Press.

Furlough, E. 1991: *The Politics of Consumption: the Consumer Co-operative Movement in France, 1834–1930*. Ithaca: Cornell University Press.

Furlough, E. and Strikwerda, C., eds forthcoming: *Consumer Co-operation in Europe and America*. Ithaca: Cornell University Press.

Furnivall, J. S. 1939: *Netherlands India: a Study of Plural Economy*. Cambridge: Cambridge University Press.

Furnivall, J. S. 1948: *Colonial Policy and Practice*. London.

Furtado, Celso 1964: *Development and Underdevelopment*; Berkeley: University of California Press.

Fusfeld, Daniel R. 1990: *The Age of the Economist*. 6th edn, Glenview, IL, and London: Scott Foresman.

Futoran, G. C. et al. 1989: TEMPO: a time-based system for analysis of group interaction process. *Basic and Applied Social Psychology* 10, 211–32.

Gadamer, Hans-Georg 1960 (*1975*): *Truth and Method*. London: Sheed & Ward; New York: Seabury.

Gagnon, J. H. and Simon, W. 1973: *Sexual Conduct: the Social Sources of Human Sexuality*. Chicago: Aldine.

Galbraith, J. K. 1977: *The Affluent Society*. 3rd rev. edn, London: Andre Deutsch.

Galbraith, J. K. 1967: *The New Industrial State*. London: Hamish Hamilton; Boston: Houghton Mifflin.

Galeski, B. 1972: *Basic Concepts of Rural Sociology*. Manchester: Manchester University Press.

Gallie, W. B. 1978: *Philosophers of War and Peace*. Cambridge: Cambridge University Press.

Galton, F. 1883 (*1907*); *Inquiries into Human Faculty and its Development*. New York: Dutton.

Gambetta, D. ed. 1988: *Trust: Making and Breaking Cooperative Relations*. Oxford: Blackwell.

Gamble, A. 1981: *An Introduction to Modern Social and Political Thought*. London: Macmillan.

Gamboni, Dario 1983: Méprises et mépris: elements pour une étude de l'iconoclasme contemporain. *Actes de la recherche en sciences sociales* 49, 2–28.

Gandhi, Mohandas Karamchand (Mahatma) 1951 (*1971*): *Selected Writings of Mahatma Gandhi*, ed. R. Duncan. London: Collins.

Gane, M. 1984: Institutional socialism and the sociological critique of communism. *Economy and Society* 13.3.

Gans, H. J. 1968a: *People and Plans*. New York: Basic Books.

Gans, H. J. 1968b: Regional and urban planning. In *International Encyclopedia of the Social Sciences*. vol. 12. New York: Macmillan and Free Press.

Gans, H. 1968: Urbanism and suburbanism as

ways of life. In *Readings in Urban Sociology*, ed. R. Pahl. Oxford: Pergamon.

Gans, Herbert 1974: *Popular Culture and High Culture: an Analysis and Evaluation of Taste*. New York: Basic Books.

Ganssmann, H. 1988: Money: a symbolically generalized medium of communication? *Economy and Society* 17.3, 285–316.

Gardenförs, P. and Sahlin, N.-E. eds 1988: *Decision, Probability and Utility*. Cambridge: Cambridge University Press.

Gardner, H. 1985: *The Mind's New Science*. New York: Basic Books.

Garfinkel, H. 1967: *Studies in Ethnomethodology*. Englewood Cliffs, NJ: Prentice-Hall.

Garland, D. 1990: *Punishment and Modern Society*. Oxford: Oxford University Press.

Garson, G. David ed. 1977: *Worker Self-Management in Industry: the West European Experience*. New York and London: Praeger.

Gasché, Rodolphe 1986: *The Tain of the Mirror: Deconstruction and the Philosophy of Reflection*. Cambridge, MA: Harvard University Press.

Gates, Henry ed. 1984: *Black Literature and Literary Theory*. New York and London: Methuen.

Gauthier, D. 1977: The social contract as ideology. *Philosophy and Public Affairs* 6, 13–164.

Gauthier, D. 1986: *Morals by Agreement*. Oxford: Clarendon Press.

Gay, P. 1967, 1969: *The Enlightenment: an Interpretation*, 2 vols. New York: Knopf.

Gay, Peter 1952: *The Dilemma of Democractic Socialism*. New York: Columbia University Press.

Gazdar, G. and Mellish, C. 1989: *Natural Language Processing in Prolog: an Introduction to Computational Linguistics*. Reading, MA: Addison-Wesley.

Geary, Dick 1981: *European Labour Protest*. London: Methuen.

Geen, R. G. and Donnerstein, E. I. eds 1983: *Aggression: Theoretical and Empirical Reviews*, vol. 2: *Issues in Research*. New York: Academic Press.

Geer, J. H. and O'Donohue, W. T. eds 1987: *Theories of Human Sexuality*. New York and London: Plenum Press.

Geertz, C. 1972: *The Interpretation of Cultures*. New York: Basic Books.

Geertz, Clifford 1963: *Old Societies and New States: the Quest for Modernity in Asia and Africa*. Glencoe, IL: Free Press.

Geertz, G. 1980: *Negara: the Theatre State in Nineteenth-Century Bali*. Princeton, NJ: Princeton University Press.

Geiger, T. 1949: *Die Klassengesellschaft im Schmelztiegel*. Cologne: Kipeuheur & Wisch.

Geiss, I. 1974: *The Pan-African Movement: a History of Pan-Africanism in America, Europe and Africa*, trans. A. Keep. New York: Africana.

Gelder, M. et al. 1986: *Oxford Textbook of Psychiatry*. Oxford: Oxford University Press.

Gellner, E. 1959: *Words and Things*. London: Gollancz.

Gellner, Ernest 1973: *Cause and Meaning in the Social Sciences*. London: Routledge & Kegan Paul.

Gellner, E. 1974: *Legitimation of Belief*. Cambridge: Cambridge University Press.

Gellner, E. 1979: *Spectacles and Predicaments*. Cambridge: Cambridge University Press.

Gellner, E. 1983: *Nations and Nationalism*. Oxford: Blackwell.

Gellner, E. 1985: *The Psychoanalytic Movement or The Cunning of Unreason*. London: Paladin.

Gellner, E. 1991: Civil society in historical context. *International Social Science Journal* 43, 495–510.

Gelzer, M. 1969: *Caesar: Politician and Statesman*, trans. P. Needham. Oxford: Blackwell.

Genette, Gérard 1982: *Narrative Discourse*. Oxford: Blackwell.

George, V. 1988: *Wealth, Poverty and Starvation*. London: Wheatsheaf.

George, V. and Wilding, P. 1976: *Ideology and Social Welfare*. London: Routledge & Kegan Paul.

George, V. and Wilding, P. 1984: *The Impact of Social Policy*. London: Routledge & Kegan Paul.

Geras, N. 1971: Essence and appearance: aspects of fetishism in Marx's *Capital*. *New Left Review* 65, 69–86.

Geras, N. 1976: *The Legacy of Rosa Luxemburg*. London: New Left Books.

Geras, N. 1985: The controversy about Marx and justice. *New Left Review* 150.

Geras, N. 1986: *Literature of Revolution*. London: Verso.

Gergen, J. G. et al. eds 1980: *Social Exchange: Advances in Theory and Research*. London: Plenum Press.

Gergen, K. J. 1973: Social psychology as history.

Journal of Personality and Social Psychology 26, 309–20.

Germani, G. 1965: *Politica y sociedad en una epoca de transición*. Buenos Aires: Paidos.

Germani, Gino 1978: *Authoritarianism, Fascism, and National Populism*. New Brunswick, NJ: Transaction Books.

Germany, Federal Republic of 1972: *German Works Councils Act 1972*. Chicago: Commerce Clearing House.

Gerry, C. 1987: Developing economies and the informal sector in historical perspective. In *The Informal Economy: the Annals of the American Academy of Political and Social Science*, vol. 493. London and Beverly Hills, CA: Sage.

Gerschenkron, A. 1962: Economic backwardness in historical perspective. In *The Progress of Under-developed Areas*, ed. B. F. Hoselitz. Chicago: University of Chicago Press.

Gershuny, J. 1978: *After Industrial Society*. London: Macmillan.

Gershuny, J. 1983: *Social Innovation and the Division of Labour*. Oxford: Oxford University Press.

Gerstel, Naomi and Gross, Harriet eds 1987: *Families and Work*. Philadelphia: Temple University Press.

Gerth, H. and Mills, C. W. *Character and Social Structure*. London: Routledge & Kegan Paul.

Geuss, Raymond 1981: *The Idea of a Critical Theory: Habermas and the Frankfurt School*. Cambridge: Cambridge University Press.

Gewirth, A. 1984: Are there any absolute rights? In *Theories of Rights*, ed. J. Waldron. Oxford: Oxford University Press.

Ghai, D. et al. 1979: *Planning for Basic Needs in Kenya*. Geneva: International Labour Office.

Ghai, D. P. et al. 1977: *The Basic Needs Approach to Development: Some Issues Regarding Concepts and Methodology*. Geneva: International Labour Office.

Ghodse, H. and Maxwell, G. eds 1990: *Substance Abuse and Dependence: an Introduction for the Caring Professions*. London: Macmillan.

Gibb, C. 1951: The principles and traits of leadership. *Journal of Abnormal and Social Psychology* 42, 267–84.

Gibb, C. 1968: Leadership: psychological aspects. In *International Encyclopedia of the Social Sciences*, vol. 9. pubn details?

Gibbs, J. and Martin, W. 1964: *Status Integration and Suicide: a Sociological Study*. Eugene: University of Oregon Press.

Gibbs, J. P. 1965: Norms: the problem of definition and classification. *American Journal of Sociology* 70, 586–94.

Giddens, A. 1971: *Capitalism and Modern Social Theory*. Cambridge: Cambridge University Press.

Giddens, A. 1973: *The Class Structure of the Advanced Societies*. London: Hutchinson.

Giddens, A. ed. 1974: *Positivism and Sociology*. London: Heinemann.

Giddens, A. 1976: *New Rules of Sociological Method: a Positive Critique of Interpretive Sociologies*. London: Hutchinson; New York: Basic Books.

Giddens, A. 1977: Functionalism: après la lutte. In *Studies in Social and Political Theory*. London: Hutchinson.

Giddens, A. 1977: *Studies in Social and Political Theory*. London: Hutchinson; New York: Basic Books.

Giddens, A. 1978: Positivism and its critics. In *A History of Sociological Analysis*, ed. Tom Bottomore and Robert Nisbet. New York: Basic Books.

Giddens, A. 1979: *Central Problems in Social Theory: Structure and Contradiction in Social Analysis*. London: Macmillan; Berkeley: University of California Press.

Giddens, A. 1981: *A Contemporary Critique of Historical Materialism*. Vol. 1, *Power, Property, and the State*. London: Macmillan; Berkeley: University of California Press.

Giddens, A. 1984: *The Constitution of Society: an Outline of the Theory of Structuration*. Cambridge: Polity; Berkeley: University of California Press.

Giddens, A. 1985: *The Nation-state and Violence: Volume Two of a Contemporary Critique of Historical Materialism*. Cambridge: Polity; Berkeley: University of California Press.

Giddens, A. 1987: *Social Theory and Modern Sociology*. Cambridge: Polity; Stanford, CA: Stanford University Press.

Giddens, A. 1990: *The Consequences of Modernity*. Cambridge: Polity; Stanford, CA: Stanford University Press.

Giddens, A. and Mackenzie, G. eds 1982: *Social Class and the Division of Labour*. Cambridge: Cambridge University Press.

Gierke, O. von 1900: *Introduction* to F. W. Maitland, *Political Theories of the Middle Ages*. Cambridge: Cambridge University Press.

Gierke, O. von 1957: *Natural Law and the Theory of Society: 1500–1800*. Boston: Beacon.

Giglioli, P. P. ed. 1972: *Language and Social Context*. Harmondsworth: Penguin.

Gilb, C. L. 1966: *Hidden Hierarchies: the Professions and Government*. New York: Harper & Row.

Gilbert, Alan and Gugler, Josef 1981: *Cities, Poverty and Development*. Oxford: Oxford University Press.

Gilbert, M. 1989: *On Social Facts*. London: Routledge.

Gilbert, M. 1990: Rationality, coordination, and convention. *Synthese* 84, 1–21.

Gilbert, Sandra M. and Gubar, Susan 1979: *The Madwoman in the Attic*. New Haven, CT, and London: Yale University Press.

Giles, H. and Bournis, R. 1976: Methodological issues in dialect perception: some social psychological perspectives. *Anthropological Linguistics* 187, 294–304.

Gilligan, C. 1982: *In a Different Voice*. Cambridge, MA: Harvard University Press.

Gillis, J. R. 1974: *Youth and History*. New York: Academic Press.

Gilpin, R. 1891: *War and Change in World Politics*. Cambridge and New York: Cambridge University Press.

Giner, S. 1976: *Mass Society*. London: Martin Robertson.

Gitlin, Todd 1987: *The Sixties: Years of Hope, Days of Rage*. New York: Bantam.

Giuberg, Achsch 1986: *The Map of Time: Seventeenth Century English Literature and Ideas of Patterns in History*. Urbana: University of Illinois Press.

Glaser, B. and Strauss, A. 1967: *The Discovery of Grounded Theory: Strategies for Qualitative Research*. New York: Sociology Press.

Glasner, P. E. 1977: *The Sociology of Secularization: a Critique of a Concept*. London: Routledge & Kegan Paul.

Glass, D. V. 1954: *Social Mobility in Britain*. London: Routledge & Kegan Paul.

Glass, D. V. 1956: Some aspects of the development of demography. *Journal of the Royal Society of Arts* 104, 854–68.

Glass, Ruth 1955 (*1989*): Urban sociology in Great Britain. In *Clichés of Urban Doom*. Oxford: Blackwell.

Glatzer, N. N. ed. 1968: *Martin Buber: Humanism*. London.

Gleason, P. 1983: Identifying identity: a semantic history. *Journal of American History* 69, 910–31.

Glock, C. Y. 1971: The study of unbelief: perspectives and research. In *The Culture of Unbelief*, ed. R. Caporale and A. Grumelli. Berkeley: University of California Press.

Glock, C. Y. and Hammond, P. E. eds 1973: *Beyond the Classics? Essays in the Scientific Study of Religion*. New York: Harper & Row.

Glover, J. 1990: *Utilitarianism and its Critics*. New York: Macmillan.

Glover, J. et al. 1989: *Fertility and the Family: the Glover Report on Reproductive Technologies to the European Commission*. London: Fourth Estate.

Gluckman, M. 1965: *The Ideas in Barotse Jurisprudence*.

Gluckman, Max 1956: *Custom and Conflict in Africa*. Oxford: Blackwell.

Glyptis, Sue 1989: *Leisure and Unemployment*. Milton Keynes: Open University Press.

Godelier, Maurice 1966 (*1972*): *Rationality and Irrationality in Economics*. London: New Left Books.

Godelier, Maurice 1972: Structure and contradiction in *Capital*. In *Ideology in Social Science*, ed. Robin Blackburn. London: Fontana.

Godelier, Maurice 1973 (*1977*): *Perspectives in Marxist Anthropology*. Cambridge: Cambridge University Press.

Godwin, W. 1793 (*1963*): *Enquiry Concerning Political Justice*. Harmondsworth: Penguin.

Goffman, E. 1959: *The Presentation of Self in Everyday Life*. Garden City, NY: Doubleday.

Goffman, E. 1961: *Asylums: Essays on the Social Situation of Mental Patients and Other Inmates*. Garden City, NY: Anchor.

Goffman, E. 1967: *Interaction Ritual: Essays in Face to Face Behavior*. Chicago: Aldine.

Goffman, E. 1968: *Asylums*. Harmondsworth: Penguin.

Goffman, E. 1974: *Frame Analysis*. New York: Harper & Row.

Goitein, Sholomo D. 1967–83: *A Mediterranean Society: the Jewish Communities of the Arab World as Portrayed in the Documents of the Cairo Geniza*, 4 vols. Berkeley: University of California Press.

Goldberg, D. and Huxley, P. 1992: *Common*

Mental Disorders: a Biosocial Model. London: Tavistock/Routledge.

Golding, Peter 1974: *The Mass Media.* Harlow: Longman.

Goldmann, Lucien 1964: *The Hidden God.* London: Routledge & Kegan Paul.

Goldmann, Lucien 1967: Sociology of literature: status and problems of method. *International Social Science Journal* 19. 4.

Goldmann, Lucien 1970: *Marxism et sciences humaines.* Paris: Gallimard.

Goldschmidt, W. 1959: *Man's Way: a Preface to the Understanding of Human Society.* New York: Holt, Rinehart & Winston.

Goldsmith, M. and Mackay, A. 1964: *The Science of Science.* London: Souvenir Press.

Goldstone, J. A. 1990: *State Breakdown: Revolution and Rebellion in the Early Modern World 1640–1848.* Berkeley: University of California Press.

Goldstone, J. A. et al. eds 1990: *Revolutions of the Late 20th Century.* Boulder, CO: Westview Press.

Goldthorpe, J. 1980 (*1987*): *Social Mobility and Class Structure in Modern Britain.* 2nd edn, Oxford: Clarendon Press.

Goldthorpe, J. ed. 1984: *Order and Conflict in Contemporary Capitalism: Studies in the Political Economy of Western European Nations.* Oxford: Oxford University Press.

Goldthorpe, J. et al. 1969: *The Affluent Worker in the Class Structure.* Cambridge: Cambridge University Press.

Gollwitzer, H. 1987: The Caesarism of Napoleon III as seen by public opinion in Germany, trans. G. C. Wells. *Economy and Society* 16, 357–404.

Gombrich, E. H. 1963: *Meditations on a Hobby Horse and other Essays on the Theory of Art.* London: Phaidon.

Gomulka, S. 1986: *Growth, Innovation and Reform in Eastern Europe.* Madison: University of Wisconsin Press.

Gomulka, S. and Rostowski, J. 1988: An international comparison of material intensity. *Journal of Comparative Economics* December.

Good, A. 1981: Prescription, preference and practice: marriage patterns among the Kondaiyankottai Maravar of South India. *Man*, NS 16, 108–29.

Goode, W. J. 1960: A theory of role strain. *American Sociological Review* 25, 483–96.

Goodenough, W. 1956: Componential analysis and the study of meaning. *Language* 32, 195–216.

Goodin, Robert F. 1992: *Green Political Theory.* Cambridge: Polity.

Goodman, N. 1955 (*1973*): *Fact, Fiction and Forecast.* 3rd edn, New York: Bobbs Merrill.

Goodman, Nelson 1947: A query on confirmation. *Journal of Philosophy* 83.

Goodpaster, K. 1978: On being morally considerable. *Journal of Philosophy* 75.

Goodrich, Peter 1986: *Reading the Law.* Oxford: Blackwell.

Goodrich, Peter 1990: *Languages of Law: from Logics of Memory to Nomadic Masks.* London: Weidenfeld & Nicolson.

Goodwin, B. 1987: *Using Political Ideas.* Chichester: Wiley.

Goodwin, C. 1981: *Conversational Organisation: Interaction between Speakers and Hearers.* New York: Academic Press.

Goody, J. R. ed. 1971: *Kinship: Selected Readings.* Harmondsworth: Penguin.

Goody, J. R. ed. 1973: *The Character of Kinship.* Cambridge and New York: Cambridge University Press.

Gopal, S. 1965: *British Policy in India 1858–1905.* Cambridge: Cambridge University Press.

Gorbachev, M. 1988: *Using the Potential of Co-operatives for Furthering Perestroika.* Moscow: Novosti Press.

Gordon, D. 1945: *Business Leadership in Large Corporations.* Washington, DC: Brookings Institution.

Gordon, R. J. ed 1986: *The American Business Cycle.* Chicago: University of Chicago Press.

Gordon, R. J. 1986: *Introduction: continuity and change in theory, behavior and methodology.* In *The American Business Cycle.* Chicago: University of Chicago Press.

Gorer, G. et al. 1966: *Psychoanalysis Observed.* London: Constable.

Gorz, A. ed. 1973 (*1976*): *The Division of Labour: the Labour Process and Class Struggle in Modern Capitalism.* Hassocks: Harvester.

Gorz, A. 1980: *Ecology as Politics.* London: Pluto.

Gorz, A. 1980 (*1982*): *Farewell to the Working Class,* trans. M. Sonenscher. London: Pluto Press.

Gorz, A. 1984: *Paths to Paradise.* London: Pluto.

Gostin, L. ed. 1988: *Civil Liberties in Conflict.* London: Routledge.

Gottschalch, Wilfried ed. 1968: *Parlamentarismus und Rätedemokratie*. Berlin: Wagenbach.

Gould, C. C. 1980: *Rethinking Democracy, Freedom and Social Cooperation in Politics, Economy, and Society*. Cambridge: Cambridge University Press.

Gould, S. J. 1980: *Ever Since Darwin*. Harmondsworth: Penguin.

Gould, S. J. 1983: *The Panda's Thumb*. Harmondsworth: Penguin.

Gouldner, A. 1950: *Studies in Leadership: Leadership and Democratic Action*. New York: Harper & Row.

Gouldner, A. 1954: *Patterns of Industrial Bureaucracy*. Glencoe, IL: Free Press.

Gouldner, A. 1959: Organizational analysis. In *Sociology Today*, ed. Robert Merton et al. New York: Basic Books.

Gouldner, A. 1960: The norm of reciprocity: a preliminary statement. *American Sociological Review* 25, 161–79.

Gouldner, A. 1962: Introduction. In Émile Durkheim, *Socialism*, New York: Collier-Macmillan.

Gouldner, A. 1964: Anti-minotaur: the myth of value-free sociology. In *The New Sociology*, ed. I. Horowitz. New York: Oxford University Press.

Gouldner, A. 1979: *The Future of Intellectuals and the Rise of the New Class*. New York: Seabury Press.

Gouldner, A. 1980: Civil society in capitalism and socialism. In *The Two Marxisms*. London: Macmillan.

Graaf, J. de V. 1957: *Theoretical Welfare Economics*. Cambridge: Cambridge University Press.

Graburn, N. ed. 1971: *Readings in Kinship and Social Structure*. New York: Harper & Row.

Graham, L. R. 1987: *Science, Philosophy, and Human Behavior in the Soviet Union*. New York: Columbia University Press.

Gramsci, A. 1910–20 (*1977*): *Selections from Political Writings*, vol. 1: *1910–1920*. London: Lawrence & Wishart; New York: International Publishers.

Gramsci, A. 1921–6 (*1978*): *Selections from Political Writings*, vol. 2: *1921–1926*. London: Lawrence & Wishart.

Gramsci, A. 1929–35 (*1971*): *Selections from the Prison Notebooks*, ed. Q. Hoare and G. Nowell Smith. London: Lawrence & Wishart; New York: International.

Gramsci, A. 1985: *Selections from Cultured Writings*. London: Lawrence & Wishart.

Granet, M. 1975: *The Religion of the Chinese People*, trans. M. Freedman. Oxford: Blackwell.

Granovetter, M. and Tilly, C. 1988: Inequality and labor process. In *Handbook of Sociology*, ed. N. Smelser. London and New Delhi: Sage.

Grant, W., ed. 1985: *The Political Economy of Corporatism*. London: Macmillan.

Graumann, C. F. ed. 1972: *Handbuch der Psychologie*, vol. 7. Gottingen: Verlag für Psychologie.

Graunt, John 1662 (*1939*): *Natural and Political Observations Made upon the Bills of Mortality*. Baltimore: Johns Hopkins University Press.

Gravelle, H. and Rees, R. 1981: *Microeconomics*. London and New York: Longman.

Gray, Alexander 1946: *The Socialist Tradition*. London, New York and Toronto: Longman, Green.

Gray, John 1989: *Liberalism*. London: Routledge.

Grebing, Helga 1986: *Der 'deutsche Sonderweg' in Europa 1806–1945*. Stuttgart: Kohlhammer.

Green, F. and Sutcliffe, B. 1987: *The Profit System*. Harmondsworth: Penguin.

Green, R. W. ed. 1959: *Protestantism and Capitalism: the Weber Thesis and its Critics*. Boston: Heath.

Green, T. H. 1941: *Lectures on the Principles of Political Obligation*. London: Longmans, Green.

Greenwood, E. 1957: Attributes of a profession. *Social Work* 3, 44–55.

Greer, Germaine 1970: *The Female Eunuch*. London.

Greffe, X. 1975: *La politique du social*. Paris: Presses Universitaires de France.

Gregor, A. J. 1969: *The Ideology of Fascism: the Rationale of Totalitarianism*. New York: Free Press.

Gregory, D. and Urry, J. eds 1985: *Social Relations and Spatial Structures*. London: Macmillan.

Gregory, D. and Walford, R. eds 1989: *Horizons in Human Geography*. London: Macmillan.

Gregory, P. R. and Stuart, R. C. 1986: *Soviet Economic Structure and Performance*. 3rd edn, New York: Harper & Row.

Grice, H. P. 1975: Logic and conversation. In *Syntax and Semantics*, vol. 3: *Speech Acts*, ed. P. Cole and J. Morgan. New York: Academic Press.

Groh, D. 1972: Cäsarismus, Napoleonismus, Bonapartismus, Führer, Chef, Imperialismus. In *Geschichtliche Grundbegriffe*, 7 vols. Vol. 1, ed. O. Brunner et al. Stuttgart: Ernst Klett.

Groves, E. R. 1928: *The Marriage Crisis*. New York: Longmans.

Gubrum, Jaber F. and Holstein, James A. 1990: *What is Family?*. Mount View, CA: Mayfield.

Guérin, D. 1970: *Anarchism*. New York: Monthly Review Press.

Guile, Bruce R. ed. 1985: *Information Technologies and Social Transformation*. Washington, DC: National Academy Press.

Guillemard, Anne-Marie 1982: Old age, retirement and the social class structure: toward an analysis of the structural dynamics of the later stage of life. In *Ageing and the Life Course*, ed. T. Hareven. New York: Guilford Press.

Guillemard, Anne-Marie, ed. 1983: *Old Age and the Welfare State*. London: Sage.

Guillemard, Anne-Marie 1986a: *Le Déclin du social: formation et crise des politiques de la vieillesse*. Paris: Presses Universitaires de France.

Guillemard, Anne-Marie 1986b: State, society and old-age policy in France from 1945 to the current crisis. *Social Science and Medicine* 23, 1319–26.

Gumperz, J. 1982: *Discourse Strategies*. Cambridge: Cambridge University Press.

Gumperz, J. and Hymes, D. eds 1972 (*1986*): *Directions in Sociolinguistics*. Oxford: Blackwell.

Gupta, Pártha Sarathi 1975: *Imperialism and the British Labour Movement 1914–1964*. London: Macmillan.

Gurney, P. J. 1989: *The Making of Co-operative Culture in England, 1870–1918*. DPhil dissertation, University of Sussex.

Gurr, T. and Scarritt, J. 1989: Minorities at risk: a global survey. *Human Rights Quarterly* 11, 375–405.

Gurr, T. R. 1970: *Why Men Rebel*. Princeton, NJ: Princeton University Press.

Gurvitch, G. 1949: *Industrialisation et technocratie*. Paris: Collin.

Gurvitch, G. 1955: *Déterminismes sociaux et liberté humaine*. Paris: Presses Universitaires.

Gurvitch, G. ed. 1958 (*1962*): *Traité de sociologie*. Paris: Presses Universitaires de France.

Gutmann, A. 1980: *Liberal Equality*. Cambridge: Cambridge University Press.

Guttierez, G. 1973: *A Theology of Liberation: History, Politics and Salvation*. New York: Orbis.

Guttsman, W. L. 1981: *The German Social Democratic Party, 1875–1933*. London: Allen & Unwin.

Guyau, M. 1911: *Les problèmes de Lesthétique contemporaine*. Paris: Alcan.

Haakonssen, Knud, ed. 1988: *Traditions of Liberalism*. Sydney: Centre for Independent Studies.

Haberler, G. 1937 (*1958*): *Prosperity and Depression*. London: Allen & Unwin.

Habermas, Jürgen 1962 (*1989*): *The Structural Transformation of the Public Sphere*. Cambridge: Polity.

Habermas, Jürgen 1967 (*1989*): *On the Logic of the Social Sciences*. London: Heinemann; Cambridge, MA: MIT Press.

Habermas, Jürgen 1968 (*1971*): *Knowledge and Human Interests*. Boston: Beacon Press.

Habermas, Jürgen 1968–9 (*1970*): *Toward a Rational Society*. Boston: Beacon Press.

Habermas, Jürgen 1969 (*1970*): *Protestbewegung und Hochschulreform*. Frankfurt am Main: Suhrkamp; part trans. in *Toward a Rational Society*. Boston: Beacon Press.

Habermas, Jürgen 1971 (1976): *Theory and Practice*. Boston: Beacon Press.

Habermas, Jürgen 1971: Vorbereitende Bemerkungen zu einer Theorie der kommunikativen Kompetenz. In *Theorie der Gesellschaft oder Sozialtechnologie*, ed. J. Habermas and N. Luhmann. Frankfurt am Main: Suhrkamp.

Habermas, Jürgen 1973 (*1976*): *Legitimation Crisis*. London: Heinemann; Boston: Beacon Press.

Habermas, Jürgen 1976 (*1979*): *Communication and the Evolution of Society*. Boston: Beacon Press.

Habermas, Jürgen 1981 (*1984, 1989*): *The Theory of Communicative Action*, 2 vols. Boston: Beacon Press; Cambridge: Polity.

Habermas, Jürgen 1983 (*1990*): *Moral Consciousness and Communicative Action*. Cambridge: Polity Press.

Habermas, Jürgen 1984: *Autonomy and Solidarity*, ed. P. Dews. London: Verso.

Habermas, Jürgen 1985 (*1988*): *The Philosophical Discourse of Modernity*. Cambridge: Polity; Cambridge, MA: MIT Press.

Habermas, Jürgen 1988: *Nachmetaphysisches Denken*. Frankfurt am Main: Suhrkamp.

Habermas, Jürgen 1989: *Philosophical-Political Profiles*. Cambridge: Polity.

Hacker, F. 1976: *Crusaders, Criminals, Crazies: Terror and Terrorism in our Time*. New York: N. W. Horton.

Hackett, Sir John 1983: *The Profession of Arms*. London: Sidgwick & Jackson.

Hagopian, M. N. 1975: *The Phenomenon of Revolution*. New York: Dodd, Mead.

Hahn, F. 1973: *On the Notion of Equilibrium in Economics*. Cambridge and New York: Cambridge University Press.

Hahn, F. 1980: *Money and Inflation*. Oxford: Blackwell

Hahn, F. 1981: General equilibrium theory. In *The Crisis in Economic Theory*, ed. Daniel Bell and Irving Kristol. New York: Basic Books.

Hahn, F. 1984: *Equilibrium and Macroeconomics*. Oxford: Blackwell.

Haight, R. 1985: *An Alternative Vision: an Interpretation of Liberation Theology*. Mahwah, NJ: Paulist Press.

Hailsham, Lord: *Elective Dictatorship*. London: BBC.

Haim, S. 1962 (*1974*): *Arab Nationalism: an Anthology*. Berkeley: University of California Press.

Halbwachs, M. 1933: *Les causes du suicide*. Paris: Alcan.

Halbwachs, M. 1938 (*1958*): *The Psychology of Social Classes*. London: Heinemann.

Halbwachs, M. 1980: *The Collective Memory*. New York: Harper & Row.

Halebsky, S. 1976: *Mass Society and Political Conflict*. Cambridge: Cambridge University Press.

Haley, P. 1980: Rudolph Sohm on charisma. *Journal of Religion* 60, 185–97.

Halfpenny, P. 1982: *Positivism and Sociology: Explaining Social Life*. London: Allen & Unwin.

Hall, A. D. and Fagen, R. E. 1968: Definition of systems. In *Modern System Research for the Behavioral Scientist*, ed. W. Buckley. Chicago.

Hall, C. et al. 1985: *Introduction to Theories of Personality*. New York: Wiley.

Hall, J. and Ikenberry, J. 1989: *The State*. Milton Keynes: Open University.

Hall, P. 1981: *Great Planning Disasters*. Harmondsworth: Penguin.

Hall, S. 1983: The 'little Caesars' of social democracy. In *The Politics of Thatcherism*, ed. S. Hall and M. Jacques. London: Lawrence & Wishart.

Hall, S. and Jacques, M. eds 1991: *The Changing Face of Politics in the 1990s*. London: Lawrence & Wishart.

Haller, M. 1963: *Eugenics: Hereditarian Attitudes in American Thought*. New Brunswick, NJ: Rutgers University Press.

Haller, R. 1986: *Fragen zu Wittgenstein und Aufsätze zur österreichischen Philosophie*. Amsterdam: Rodopi.

Haller, R. 1988: *Questions on Wittgenstein*. London: Routledge; Lincoln: University of Nebraska Press.

Halliday, F. 1983: *The Making of the Second Cold War*. London: Verso.

Halliday, M. A. K. 1978: *Language as Social Semiotic*. London: Arnold.

Halliday, M. A. K. 1985: *An Introduction to Functional Grammar*. London: Arnold.

Halliday, M. A. K. ed 1987: *New Developments in Systemic Linguistics*. London: Pinter. ' 413

Halliday, M. A. K. and Hasan, R. 1976: *Cohesion in English*. London: Longman.

Halsey, A. H. et al. 1980: *Origins and Destinations: Family, Class and Education in Modern Britain*. Oxford: Oxford University Press.

Haltiwanger, J. and Waldman, M. 1985: Rational expectations and the limits of rationality. *American Economic Review* 75, 326–40.

Hamilton, A. and Madison, J. 1787–88 (*1937*): *The Federalist Papers*. New York: Modern Library.

Hamlin, A. 1986: *Ethics, Economics and the State*. Brighton: Wheatsheaf.

Hammer, K. and Hartmann, P. C. 1977: *Der Bonapartismus: historisches Phänomen und politischer Mythos*. Munich: Artemis.

Hammond, Michael et al. 1991: *Phenomenology*. Oxford: Blackwell.

Hampshire, S. ed. 1978: *Public and Private Morality*. Cambridge: Cambridge University Press.

Hampson, N. 1968: *The Enlightenment*. Harmondsworth: Penguin.

Handel, W. 1979: Normative expectations and the emergence of meaning as solutions to problems: convergence of structural and interactionist views. *American Journal of Sociology* 84, 855–81.

Handlin, Oscar 1951: *The Uprooted*. Boston: Little, Brown.

Handy, C. B. 1984: *The Future of Work: a Guide to Changing Society*. Oxford: Blackwell.

Hanfling, O. ed. 1981: *Essential Readings in Logical Positivism*. Oxford: Blackwell.

Hanmer, J. and Saunders, S. 1984: *Well-Founded Fear: a Community Study of Violence to Women*. London: Hutchinson.

Hanmer, J. et al. eds 1989: *Women, Policing and Male Violence: International Perspectives*. London and New York: Routledge.

Hansen, M. 1991: *Babel and Babylon: Spectatorship in American Silent Film*. Cambridge, MA: Harvard University Press.

Hanson, N. R. 1958: *Patterns of Discovery*. Cambridge: Cambridge University Press.

Harcourt, G. C. 1982: Post-Keynesianism: quite

wrong and/or nothing new?. *Thames Papers in Political Economy*, summer.

Hardach, Gerd and Karras, Dieter 1978: *A Short Hostory of Socialist Economic Thought*. London: Edward Arnold.

Hardin, R. 1982: *Collective Action*. Baltimore: Johns Hopkins University Press.

Harding, N. 1977, 1981: *Lenin's Political Thought*. London: Macmillan.

Harding, Sandra 1984: *The Science Question in Feminism*. Ithaca, NY: Cornell University Press.

Harding, Sandra and Hintinkka, Merrill eds 1983: *Discovering Reality: Feminist Perspectives on Epistemology, Methodology, and Philosophy of Science*. Dordrecht: Reidel.: Peace Politics in Twentieth Century Britain, 264

Hare, A. R. 1976: *Handbook of Small Group Research*. 2nd edn, New York: Free Press.

Hare, R. M. 1981: *Moral Thinking*. Oxford: Clarendon Press.

Harff, B. and Gurr, T. 1990: Victims of the state: genocides, politicides and group repression since 1945. *International Review of Victimology* 1, 1–19.

Hargreaves Heap, S. P. 1989: *Rationality in Economics*. Oxford: Blackwell.

Harré, R. 1970: *The Principles of Scientific Thinking*. London: Macmillan; Chicago: University of Chicago Press.

Harré, R. 1981: *Great Scientific Experiments: Twenty Experiments that Changed our View of the World*. Oxford: Oxford University Press.

Harré, R. and Madden, E. H. 1975: *Causal Powers: a Theory of Natural Necessity*. Oxford: Blackwell.

Harré, R. and Secord, P. F. 1972: *The Explanation of Social Behaviour*. Oxford: Blackwell.

Harrell, Jean 1972: Aesthetics as philosophy. *Personalist* 53, 115–26.

Harries-Jenkins, G. 1977: *The Army in Victorian Society*. London: Routledge & Kegan Paul.

Harries-Jenkins, G. and Moskos, C. C. 1981: Armed forces and society. *Current Sociology* 29, 1–170.

Harrington, M. 1989: *The Next Left: the History of the Future*. New York: Henry Holt.

Harris, J. 1982: *Unemployment and Politics: a Study in English Social Policy, 1886–1914*. Oxford: Oxford University Press.

Harris, M. 1968: *The Rise of Anthropological Theory: a History of Theories of Culture*. New York: Thomas Crowell.

Harris, Nigel 1986: *The End of the Third World: Newly Industrializing Countries and the Decline of an Ideology*. Harmondsworth: Penguin.

Harrison, G. A. et al. 1988: *Human Biology: an Introduction to Human Evolution, Variation, Growth and Adaptability*. Oxford: Oxford University Press.

Harriss, J. ed. 1982: *Rural Development*. London: Hutchinson.

Harrod, R. F.1939: An essay in dynamic theory. *Economic Journal* 49, 14–33.

Harrod, R. F. 1951: *The Life of John Maynard Keynes*. London: Macmillan.

Harrop, M. and Miller, W. L. 1987: *Elections and Voters*. London: Macmillan.

Harsanyi, J. C. 1955: Cardinal welfare, individualistic ethics and interpersonal comparisons of welfare. *Journal of Political Economy* 63, 309–21.

Hart, H. L. A. 1955: Are there any natural rights? *Philosophical Review* 64, 175–91.

Hart, H. L. A. 1961: *The Concept of Law*. Oxford: Clarendon Press.

Hart, K. 1973: Informal income opportunities and urban employment in Ghana. *Journal of Modern African Studies* 11, 61–89.

Harte, N. ed. 1971: *The Study of Economic History: Collected Inaugural Lectures, 1893–1970*. London.

Hartmann, E. von 1931: *The Philosophy of the Unconscious*. London: Kegan Paul, Trench, Trubner.

Hartmann, H. 1979: Capitalism, patriarchy and job segregation by sex. In *Capitalist Patriarchy*. New York: Monthly Review Press.

Hartmann, Heidi 1981: The unhappy marriage of Marxism and feminism: towards a more progressive union. In *Women and Revolution*, ed. Lydia Sargent. London: Pluto Press.

Harvey, D. 1982: *The Limits to Capital*. Chicago: University of Chicago Press.

Harvey, D. 1985: *Consciousness and the Urban Experience*. Baltimore: Johns Hopkins University Press.

Harvey, D. 1989: *The Condition of Postmodernity: an Enquiry into the Origins of Cultural Change*. Oxford: Blackwell.

Hasbach, W. 1895: Zur Geschichte des Methodestreites in der politischen Ökonomie. *Jahbuch für Gesetzgebung, Verwaltung und Volkswirtschaft*, NF Jg.19, 465–90, 751–808.

Hasselman, E. 1989: Japan's consumer movement. *Review of International Co-operation* 82, 1.

Hatzfeld, H. 1971: *Du paupérisme à la sécurité sociale*. Paris: Armand Colin.

Haug, M. R. 1973: Deprofessionalization: an alternative hypothesis for the future. *Sociological Review Monograph* 20, 195–211.

Hauser, Arnold 1954: *The Philosophy of Art History*. London: Routledge & Kegan Paul.

Hauser, Philip M. and Schnore, Leo F. eds 1965: *The Study of Urbanization*. New York: Wiley.

Havel, Václav et al. 1987: *Václav Havel or Living in Truth*, ed. J. Vadislav. London: Faber.

Hawkins, K. 1984: *Unemployment*. Harmondsworth: Penguin.

Hawthorn, G. 1987: *Enlightenment and Despair: a History of Social Theory*. 2nd edn, Cambridge.

Hayek, F. A. ed. 1935: *Collectivist Economic Planning: Critical Studies on the Possibilities of Socialism*. London: Routledge.

Hayek, F. A. 1940 (*1948*): The competitive solution. In *Individualism and Economic Order*. Chicago: University of Chicago Press.

Hayek, F. A. 1940: Socialist calculation: the competitive solution. *Economics*, new series 7, 125–49.

Hayek, F. A. 1944 (*1962*): *The Road to Serfdom*. 2nd edn, London: Routledge & Kegan Paul.

Hayek, F. A. 1945: The use of knowledge in society. *American Economic Review* 35, 519–30.

Hayek, F. A. 1948 (*1980*): *Individualism and Economic Order*. Chicago: University of Chicago Press.

Hayek, F. A. 1948: The meaning of competition. In *Individualism and Economic Order*. Chicago: University of Chicago Press.

Hayek, F. A. 1960: *The Constitution of Liberty*. London: Routledge & Kegan Paul.

Hayek, F. A. 1967: The non sequitur of the 'dependence effect'. In *Studies in Philosophy, Politics and Economics*. London: Routledge & Kegan Paul.

Hayek, F. A. 1973–9 (*1982*): *Law, Legislation and Liberty*. Vol. 1: *Rules and Order* (1973); vol. 2: *The Mirage of Social Justice* (1976); vol. 3: *The Political Order of a Free People* (1979). Collected in a single vol. with revised preface. London: Routledge & Kegan Paul.

Hayek, F. A. 1978: Competition as a discovery procedure. In *New Studies in Philosophy, Politics, Economics and the History of Ideas*. Chicago: University of Chicago Press.

Hayek, F. A. 1983: *Knowledge, Evolution and Society*. London: Adam Smith Institute.

Hazard, P. 1935 (*1953*): *The European Mind*. London: Hollis & Carter.

Hazard, P. 1946 (*1954*): *European Thought in the Eighteenth Century*. London: Hollis & Carter.

Heal, G. M. 1973: *The Theory of Economic Planning*. Amsterdam: North Holland.

Hearnshaw, L. S. 1987: *The Shaping of Modern Psychology*. London: Routledge & Kegan Paul.

Heath, A. 1976: *Rational Choice and Social Exchange: a Critique of Exchange Theory*. Cambridge: Cambridge University Press.

Heath, A. 1981: *Social Mobility*. London: Fontana.

Heath, C. 1986: *Body Movement and Speech in Medical Interaction*. Cambridge: Cambridge University Press.

Hebb, D. O. 1949: *The Organization of Behaviour*. New York: Wiley.

Heberle, R. 1951: *Social Movements*. New York: Appleton-Century-Crofts.

Hechter, Michael 1975: *Internal Colonialism*. London: Routledge.

Hedborg, Anna and Meidner, Rudolf 1986: *The Concept of the Swedish Model*. Stockholm: LO.

Hegedüs, A. 1976: *Socialism and Bureaucracy*. London: Allison & Busby; New York: St Martin's Press..

Heidegger, Martin 1927 (*1949, 1962*): *Being and Time*, trans. J. MacQuarrie and E. Robinson. London: SCM Press.

Heidegger, Martin 1977: *The Question Concerning Technology and Other Essays*, trans. William Lovitt. New York: Garland.

Heider, F. 1958: *The Psychology of Interpersonal Relations*. New York: Wiley.

Heiss, J. 1981: Social roles. In *Social Psychology: Sociological Perspectives*, ed. M. Rosenberg and R. H. Turner. New York: Basic Books.

Hekman, S. J. 1986: *Hermeneutics and the Sociology of Knowledge*. Cambridge: Polity; Notre Dame, IN: Notre Dame University Press.

Hekman, S. J. 1990: *Gender and Knowledge*. Cambridge: Polity.

Held, D. 1980: *Introduction to Critical Theory: Horkheimer to Habermas*. Berkeley: University of California Press; London: Hutchinson.

Held, D. 1987: *Models of Democracy*. Cambridge: Polity.

Held, D. and Thompson, J. eds 1990: *Social Theory of Modern Societies: Anthony Giddens and his*

Critics. Cambridge: Cambridge University Press.

Heller, A. 1970 (*1984*): *Everyday Life*. London: Routledge & Kegan Paul.

Heller, A. 1976: *The Theory of Need in Marx*. London: Allison & Busby.

Hempel, C. G. 1958: The theoretician's dilemma. In *Minnesota Studies in the Philosophy of Science*, vol. 2, ed. H. Feigl et al. Minneapolis: University of Minnesota Press.

Hempel, C. G. 1965: *Aspects of scientific explanation*. In *Aspects of Scientific Explanation*. New York: Free Press.

Hempel, C. G. and Oppenheim, P. 1948: Studies in the logic of explanation. *Philosophy of Science* 15, 135–75.

Hendry, D. F. 1987: Econometrics methodology: a personal perspective. In *Advances in Econometrics Fifth World Congress*, vol. 2, ed. T. F. Bewley. Cambridge: Cambridge University Press.

Henle, M. 1986: *1879 and All That: Essays in the Theory and History of Psychology*. New York: Columbia University Press.

Hennis, W. 1988: *Max Weber: Essays in Reconstruction*, trans. K. Tribe. London: Allen & Unwin.

Henry, A. and Short, J. 1954: *Suicide and Homicide*. Glencoe, IL: Free Press.

Herberg, W. 1955: *Protestant–Catholic–Jew: an Essay in American Religious Sociology*. New York: Doubleday.

Herbst, K. and Paykel, E. 1989: *Depression: an Integrative Approach*. London: Heinemann.

Heritage, J. 1984: *Garfinkel and Ethnomethodology*. Cambridge: Polity.

Heritage, J. 1989: Current developments in conversation analysis. In *Interdisciplinary Approaches to Interpersonal Communication*, ed. D. Roger and P. Bull. Clevedon: Multilingual Matters.

Héritier-Augé, F. 1981: *L'exercice de la parenté*. Paris: Gallimard.

Héritier-Augé, F. 1985: La cuisse de Jupiter: réflexions sur les nouveaux modes de procréation. *L'Homme* 94, 5–22.

Herman, E. O. 1981: *Corporate Control, Corporate Power*. Cambridge: Cambridge University Press.

Hermeren, Göran 1983: *Aspects of Aesthetics*. Lund: CWK Gleerup.

Herodotus 1972: *The Histories*, ed. Aubrey de Sélincourt, rev. with notes by A. R. Burn. Harmondsworth: Penguin.

Hertz, Heinrich 1894: *Die Prinzipien der Mechanik*. Leipzig: J. A. Barth.

Hertz, R. 1907 (*1960*): Contribution à une étude sur la représentation collective de la mort. In *Death and the Right Hand*, trans. R. Needham and C. Needham. London: Cohen & West.

Hertz, R. 1909 (*1960*): La préeminence de la main droite. In *Death and the Right Hand*, trans. R. Needham and C. Needham. London: Cohen & West.

Herz, J. H. 1959: *International Politics in the Atomic Age*. New York: Columbia University Press.

Herzlich, C. 1973: *Health and Illness: a Social Psychological Analysis*. London: Academic Press.

Hession, C. H. 1972: *John Kenneth Galbraith and his Critics*. New York: New American Library.

Hewstone, M. and Brown, R. 1986: *Contact and Conflict in Intergroup Encounters*. Oxford: Blackwell.

Hexter, J. H. 1961: *Reappraisals in History*. London: Longmans.

Hexter, J. H. 1971: *The History Primer*. New York: Basic Books.

Hey, J. and Winch, D. eds 1990: *A Century of Economics*. Oxford: Blackwell.

Hicks, J. R. 1931: *Value and Capital: an Inquiry into Some Fundamental Principles of Economic Theory*. Oxford: Clarendon Press.

Hicks, J. R. 1937: Mr Keynes and the 'classics': a suggested interpretation. *Econometrica* 5.

Hicks, J. R. 1939: The foundations of welfare economics. *Economic Journal* 49.

Hicks, J. R. 1939: *Value and Capital: an Inquiry into some Fundamental Principles of Economic Theory*. 2nd edn, Oxford: Oxford University Press.

Hicks, J. R. 1946: *Value and Capital*. 2nd edn, Oxford: Oxford University Press.

Hilferding, Rudolf 1904 (*1949*): *Bohm Bawerk's Criticism of Marx*. New York: Augustus M. Kelley.

Hilferding, Rudolf 1910 (*1985*): *Finance Capital: a Study of the Latest Phase of Capitalist Development*, trans. Morris Watnick and Sam Gordon, ed. Tom Bottomore. London and Boston: Routledge & Kegan Paul.

Hilferding, Rudolf 1927 (*1978*): Die Aufgaben der Sozialdemokratie in der Republik. trans, but no Eng. title given In Austro-Marxism, ed. Tom

Bottomore and Patrick Goode. Oxford: Clarendon Press.

Hilferding, Rudolf 1941 (*1954*): *Das historische Problem*. First pubd in *Zeitschrift für Politik* 1.

Hill, Christopher 1975: *The World Turned Upside Down: Radical Ideas During the English Revolution*. Harmondsworth: Penguin.

Hillegas, M. R. 1967: *The Future as Nightmare: H. G. Wells and the Anti-Utopians*. New York: Oxford University Press.

Hilsberg, W. 1988: *The German Greens*. London and New York: Verso.

Himes, Joseph S. 1980: *Conflict and Conflict Management*. Athens: University of Georgia Press.

Himmelfarb, G. 1984: *The Idea of Poverty: England in the Early Industrial Age*. London: Faber & Faber.

Himmelstrand, U. 1981a: Introduction to *Spontaneity and Planning in Social Development*. Beverly Hills, CA: Sage.

Himmelstrand, U. 1981b: Spontaneity and planning in mixed economies and under self-managing labour. In *Spontaneity and Planning in Social Development*. Beverly Hills, CA: Sage.

Himmelweit, S. and Mohun, S. 1977: Domestic labour and capital. *Cambridge Journal of Economics* 1.

Hinde, R. A. 1982: *Ethology: its Nature and Relations with Other Sciences*. Oxford: Oxford University Press.

Hindess, B. 1971: *The Decline of Working Class Politics*. London: Merlin.

Hindess, B. and Hirst, P. 1975: *Pre-Capitalist Modes of Production*. London: Routledge & Kegan Paul.

Hindess, B. 1988: *Choice, Rationality, and Social Theory*. London: Unwin Hyman.

Hinsley, F. H. 1963: *Power and the Pursuit of Peace*. Cambridge: Cambridge University Press.

Hinton, G. E. and Anderson, J. A. 1981: *Parallel Models of Associative Memory*. Hillsdale, NJ: Lawrence Erlbaum.

Hinton, J. 1989: *Protests and Visions*. London: Hutchinson.

Hintze, O. 1975: The origins of the modern ministerial system: a comparative study. In *The Historical Essays of Otto Hintze*, ed. F. Gilbert. New York: Oxford University Press.

Hirsch, M. and Keller, Evelyn Fox eds 1990: *Conflicts in Feminism*.

Hirschman, A. O. 1977: *The Passions and the Interests*. Princeton, NJ: Princeton University Press.

Hirschman, A. O. 1984: Against parsimony: three easy ways of complicating some categories of economic discourse. *American Economic Review Proceedings* 74, 88–96.

Hirst, P. 1989: *After Thatcher*. London: Collins.

Hobbes, T. 1651 (*1968*): *Leviathan*. Harmondsworth: Penguin.

Hobhouse, L. T. 1911: *Liberalism*. London: Williams & Norgate.

Hobhouse, L. T. 1913: The historical evolution of property, in fact and in idea. In *Property: its Duties and Rights*, ed. Charles Gore. London: Macmillan.

Hobsbawm, E. J. 1959: *Primitive Rebels*. Manchester: Manchester University Press.

Hobsbawm, E. J. 1964: Introduction to K. Marx, *Pre-Capitalist Economic Formations*, ed. E. J. Hobsbawm. London: Lawrence & Wishart.

Hobsbawm, E. J. 1977: Civilians versus military in twentieth-century politics. In *Revolutionaries*. London: Quartet.

Hobsbawm, E. J. 1987: *The Age of Empire 1875–1914*. London: Weidenfeld & Nicolson.

Hobsbawm, E. J. 1990: *Nations and Nationalism since 1780: Programme, Myth, Reality*. Cambridge: Cambridge University Press.

Hobson, J. A. 1902 (*1968*): *Imperialism: a Study*. London: Allen & Unwin.

Hobson, J. A. 1909: *The Crisis of Liberalism: New Issues of Democracy*. London: P. S. King & Son.

Hodder, I. 1990: *Reading the Past*. Cambridge: Cambridge University Press.

Hodge, B. and Kress, G. 1988: *Social Semiotics*. Cambridge: Polity.

Hodges, Donald 1980: *The Bureaucratization of Socialism*. Amherst: University of Massachusetts Press.

Hodgkin, Thomas 1981: *Vietnam: the Revolutionary Path*. London: Macmillan.

Hodgson, D. 1988: Orthodoxy and revisionism in American demography. *Population and Development Review* 14, 541–69.

Hodgson, Derek 1984: *The Profits of Crime and their Recovery*. London: Heinemann.

Hodgson, Marshall G. S. 1974: *The Venture of Islam*. Chicago and London: University of Chicago Press.

Hoffer, E. 1963: *The Ordeal of Change*. New York: Harper & Row.

Hofstadter, Richard 1945 (*1955*): *Social Darwinism in American Thought, 1860–1915*. Philadelphia: University of Pennsylvania Press.

Hofstadter, Richard 1963: *Anti-intellectualism in American Life*. New York: Alfred A. Knopf.

Hofstede, G. 1980: *Culture's Consequences*. London: Sage.

Hoggart, Richard 1957: *The Uses of Literacy*. London: Chatto & Windus.

Hoggart, Richard 1970: *La culture du pauvre*. Paris.

Holbrook, D. 1987: *Evolution and the Humanities*. Aldershot: Gower.

Holden, B. 1974: *The Nature of Democracy*. London: Nelson.

Holden, B. 1988: *Understanding Liberal Democracy*. Oxford: Philip Allan.

Holland, H. 1984: *The Chemical Evolution of the Atmosphere and Oceans*. Princeton, NJ: Princeton University Press.

Holland, Stuart 1976: *Capital Versus the Regions*. London: Macmillan.

Hollander, E. 1958: Conformity, status and idiosyncrasy credit. *Psychology Review* 65, 117–27.

Hollis, M. 1977: *Models of Man*. Cambridge: Cambridge University Press.

Hollis, M. 1987: *The Ruse of Reason*. Cambridge: Cambridge University Press.

Hollis, M. and Lukes, S. eds 1982: *Rationality and Relativism*. Oxford: Blackwell.

Holquist, M. 1990: *Dialogism*. London: Methuen.

Holt, E. B. 1912: *The New Realism: Cooperative Studies in Philosophy*. New York: Macmillan.

Holton, R. J. 1976: *British Syndicalism 1900–1914*. London: Pluto.

Holton, R. J. 1986: *Cities, Capitalism and Civilization*. London: Allen & Unwin.

Holyoake, G. J. 1896: *The Origin and Nature of Secularism*. London.

Homans, G. C. 1948: *The Human Group*. New York: Harcourt Brace.

Homans, G. C. 1961 (*1974*): *Social Behavior: its Elementary Forms*. Rev. edn, New York: Harcourt, Brace, Jovanovich.

Homans, G. C. and Schneider, D. M. 1955: *Marriage, Authority, and Final Causes: a Study of Unilateral Cross-Cousin Marriage*. New York: Free Press.

Honderich, Ted 1980: *Violence for Equality*. Harmondsworth: Penguin.

Honneth, Axel 1985: *Critique of Power: Stages of Reflection of a Critical Theory of Society*, trans. Ken Baynes. Cambridge, MA: MIT Press.

Honneth, Axel 1987: Critical Theory. In *Social Theory Today*, ed. A. Giddens and J. Turner. Cambridge: Polity.

Honneth, Axel and Joas, Hans eds 1991: *Communicative Action*. Cambridge: Polity.

Honneth, Axel and Wellmer, Albrecht eds 1986: *Die Frankfurter Schule und die Folgen*. Berlin and New York: De Gruyter.

Honore, A. 1970: *Social justice*. In *Essays in Legal Philosophy*, ed. R. S. Summers. Oxford: Blackwell.

Hoogvelt, A. M. M. 1976: *The Sociology of Developing Societies*. London: Macmillan.

Hoogvelt, A. M. M. 1982: *The Third World in Global Development*. London: Macmillan.

Hook, S. 1943: *The Hero in History: a Study in Limitation and Possibility*. Boston: Beacon Press.

Hooks, B. 1984: *Feminist Theory: from Margin to Center*. Boston: South End Press.

Horkheimer, Max 1932: Geschichte und Psychologie. *Zeitschrift für Sozialforschung* 1.

Horkheimer, Max 1941a: The end of reason. *Zeitschrift für Sozialforschung* 9, 366–88.

Horkheimer, Max 1941b: Art and mass culture. *Zeitschrift für Sozialforschung* 9, 290–304.

Horkheimer, Max 1947: *The Eclipse of Reason*. New York: Oxford University Press.

Horkheimer, Max 1968: *Kritische Theorie*, ed. Alfred Schmidt, 2 vols. Frankfurt am Main: Fischer.

Horkheimer, Max 1972: Die gegenwärtige Lage der Sozialphilosophie und die Aufgaben eines Instituts für Sozialforschung. In *Sozialphilosophische Studien*, ed. Werner Brede. Frankfurt am Main: Fischer.

Horkheimer, Max 1974: *Notizen 1950 bis 1969 und Dämmerung*. Frankfurt am Main: Fischer.

Horkheimer, Max 1985: *Gesammelte Schriften*, ed. Alfred Schmidt and Gunzelin Schmid Noerr. Frankfurt am Main: Fischer.

Horkheimer, Max and Adorno, Theodor W. 1947 (*1972, 1979*): *The Dialectic of Enlightenment*, trans. John Cummings. London: Verso.

Horne, John et al., eds 1987: *Sport, Leisure and Social Relations*. London: Routledge & Kegan Paul.

Horton, J. 1964: The dehumanization of alienation and anomie: a problem in the ideology of sociology. *British Journal of Sociology* 15, 283–300.

Horvat, B. et al. 1975: *Self-Governing Socialism*, 2

vols. New York: International Arts and Sciences Press.

Hoselitz, B. F. 1965: *Sociological Aspects of Economic Growth*. New York: Free Press.

Houndshell, David A. 1975: Elisha Grey and the telephone: on the disadvantage of being an expert. *Technology and Culture* 16.

Hourani, A. H. 1962 (*1983*): *Arabic Thought in the Liberal Age, 1798–1939*. Cambridge: Cambridge University Press.

Hourani, A. H. 1991: *A History of the Arab Peoples*. London and Cambridge, MA: Faber & Faber.

Howard, Dick 1977: *The Marxian Legacy*. London: Macmillan.

Howey, R. S. 1960: *The Rise of the Marginal Utility School 1870–1889*. Lawrence: University of Kansas Press.

Hoy, D. C. 1982: *The Critical Circle: Literature, History and Philosophical Hermeneutics*. Berkeley: University of California Press.

Hroch, M. 1985: *Social Preconditions of National Revival in Europe: a Comparative Analysis of the Social Composition of Patriotic Groups among the Smaller European Nations*, trans. Ben Fowkes. Cambridge: Cambridge University Press.

Huaco, George A. 1966: The functionalist theory of stratification: two decades of controversy. *Inquiry* 9, 215–40.

Hubert, H. and Mauss, M. 1899 (*1964*): *Sacrifice: its Nature and Function*, trans. W. D. Hall. London: Cohen & West.

Hudson, R. A. 1980: *Sociolinguistics*. Cambridge: Cambridge University Press.

Huebner, J. W. 1981: *Worker Participation: a Comparative Study Between the Systems of the Netherlands, the Federal Republic of Germany and the United States*. Leiden: University of Leiden.

Huff, D. 1954 (*1973*): *How to Lie with Statistics*. Harmondworth: Penguin.

Hughes, D. 1977: Everyday and medical knowledge in categorising patients. In *Health Care and Health Knowledge*, ed. R. Dingwall et al. London: Croom Helm.

Hughes, E. 1971: *The Sociological Eye: Selected Papers*. Chicago: University of Chicago Press.

Hughes, Thomas A. 1989: *American Genesis: a Century of Invention and Technological Enthusiasm*. New York: Viking.

Hull, Clark L. 1943: *Principles of Behaviour*. New York.

Hülsberg, W. 1988: *The German Greens*. London and New York: Verso.

Hume, D. 1748 (*1975*): *An Enquiry Concerning Human Understanding*, ed. L. A. Selby Bigge. Oxford: Clarendon Press.

Hume, D. 1752 (*1955*): Essays. In *Writings on Economics*. London and New York: Nelson; New York: Books for Libraries (1972).

Hunnicutt, Benjamin Kline 1988: *Work Without End: Abandoning Shorter Hours for the Right to Work*. Philadelphia: Temple University Press.

Hunt, Alan 1977: *The Sociological Movement in Law*. London: Macmillan.

Hunter, F. 1953: *Community Power Structure*. Chapel Hill: University of North Carolina Press.

Hunter, J. 1983: *American Evangelicalism and the Quandary of Modernity*. New Brunswick, NJ: Rutgers University Press.

Huntington, S. P. 1957: *The Soldier and the State: the Theory and Politics of Civil-Military Relations*. Cambridge, MA: Harvard University Press.

Huntington, S. P. 1968: *Political Order in Changing Societies*. New Haven, CT: Yale University Press.

Husband, C. ed. 1982: *'Race' in Britain: Continuity and Change*. London: Hutchinson.

Husserl, Edmund 1900 (*1970*): *Logical Investigations*, trans. J. N. Findlay. London: Routledge & Kegan Paul.

Husserl, Edmund 1931 (*1962*): *Ideas*, trans. W. R. Boyce Gibson. New York: Collier.

Husserl, Edmund 1931 (*1977*): *Cartesian Meditations*, trans. Dorion Cairns. The Hague: Martinus Nijhoff.

Husserl, Edmund 1938 (*1970*): *The Crisis of European Sciences and Transcendental Phenomenology*, trans. David Carr. Evanston, IL: Northwestern University Press.

Hutcheon, Linda 1988: *A Poetics of Postmodernism*. London: Routledge.

Hutchinson, G. E. 1965: *The Ecological Theater and the Evolutionary Play*. New Haven, CT: Yale University Press.

Hutchinson, T. W. 1953: *A Review of Economic Doctrines 1870–1929*. Oxford: Clarendon Press.

Hutchison, T. W. 1981: Carl Menger on philosophy and method. In *The Politics and Philosophy of Economics*. Oxford: Blackwell.

Huxley, J. S. 1974: *Evolution: the Modern Synthesis*. 3rd edn, London: Allen & Unwin.

Hyman, H. and Singer, E. eds 1968: *Readings in Reference Group Behavior*. New York: Free Press.

Hyman, R. 1972: *Marxism and the Sociology of Trade Unionism*. London: Pluto.

Hyman, R. 1983: André Gorz and his disappearing proletariat. In *The Socialist Register 1983*, ed. R. Miliband and J. Saville. London: Merlin.

Hyman, R. 1989: *The Political Economy of Industrial Relations*. London: Macmillan.

Hyman, R. and Price, R. eds 1983: *The New Working Class? White Collar Workers and their Organizations: a Reader*. London: Macmillan.

Hyman, R. and Streeck, W. eds 1988: *New Technology and Industrial Relations*. Oxford: Blackwell.

Hymes, D. 1974 (*1977*): *Foundations in Sociolinguistics*. London: Tavistock.

Ibn Khaldun 1377 (*1967*): *The Muqaddimah: an Introduction to History*, trans. F. Rosenthal. Princeton, NJ: Princeton University Press.

IDE 1981: *Industrial Democracy in Europe*. Oxford University Press. New York: Pantheon.

Iga, M. 1986: *The Thorn in the Chrysanthemum*. Berkeley: University of California Press.

Ignatieff, M. 1984: *Needs of Strangers*. London: Chatto & Windus.

Illich, Ivan 1971: *Deschooling Society*. London: Calder & Boyars.

Illich, Ivan 1975: *Medical Nemesis: the Expropriation of Health*. New York: Pantheon.

Illich, Ivan 1978: *Toward a History of Needs*. New York: Pantheon.

Ingarden, Roman 1985: *Selected Papers in Aesthetics*. Washington, DC: Catholic University of America Press.

Inglehart, R. F. 1977: *The Silent Revolution: Changing Values and Political Styles among the Western Mass Publics*.

Innis, Harold A. 1950: Empire and Communications. London: Oxford University Press.

Innis, Harold A. 1951: *The Bias of Communication*. Toronto: University of Toronto Press.

Institute of Jewish Affairs 1988: *Christian Jewish Relations* 21.1: London: Institute of Jewish Affairs.

Institute of Social Studies and Indian Institute of Management 1981: *Industrial Democracy and Development: Building on Experience*. The Hague: IISS.

International Handbook of Participation in Organizations, 1989–92, 4 vols. Oxford: Oxford University Press.

International Labour Office 1976: *Employment Growth and Basic Needs: a One-World Problem*. Geneva: International Labour Office.

International Labour Office 1977: *Meeting Basic Needs: Strategies for Eradicating Mass Poverty and Unemployment*. Geneva: International Labour Office.

International Labour Office 1981: *Workers' Participation in Decisions within Undertakings*. Geneva: International Labour Office.

Industrial Democracy in Europe International Research Group 1981: *Industrial Democracy in Europe*. Oxford: Oxford University Press.

Ionescu, Ghita and Gellner, Ernest eds 1969: *Populism: its Meaning and National Characteristics*. New York: Macmillan.

Irele, Abiola 1981: *The African Experience in Literature and Ideology*. London: Heinemann.

Irigaray, Luce 1974 (*1985*): *Speculum of the Other Woman*, trans. G. C. Gill. Ithaca, NY: Cornell University Press.

Irigaray, Luce 1985: *This Sex Which is Not One*. Ithaca: Cornell University Press.

Irvine, J. et al. eds 1979: *Demystifying Social Statistics*. London: Pluto.

Iser, Wolfgang 1978: *The Implied Reader*. London and Henley: Routledge.

Israel, J. and Tajfel, H. 1972: *The Context of Social Psychology*. London and New York: Academic Press.

Jäckel, Eberhard: *Hitler's Weltanschauung*. Middletown, CT: Wesleyan University Press.

Jackson, J. Hampden 1957: *Marx, Proudhon and European Socialism*. London: English Universities Press.

Jacobs, Paul and Landau, Saul eds 1966: *The New Radicals: a Report with Documents*. New York: Random House.

Jacobsen, Thorkild 1976: *The Treasures of Darkness: a History of Mesopotamian Religion*. New Haven, CT: Yale University Press.

Jacoby, Russell 1981: *Dialectic of Defeat*. Cambridge: Cambridge University Press.

Jaffe, J. and Feldstein, S. 1970: *Rhythms of Dialogue*. New York: Academic Press.

Jaggar, A. 1983: *Feminist Politics and Human Nature*. Brighton: Harvester.

Jaggar, A. and Rothenberg, P. S. eds 1978 (*1984*): *Feminist Framework*. 2nd edn, New York: McGraw Hill.

Jaguaribe, Helio 1973: *Political Development: a*

General Theory and a Latin American Case Study. New York: Harper & Row.

Jahoda, M. 1982: *Employment and Unemployment: a Social-Psychological Analysis*. London: Cambridge University Press.

Jahoda, M. et al. 1972: *Marienthal: the Sociography of an Unemployed Community*. London: Tavistock.

Jain, Hem Chand and Giles, Anthony 1985: Workers' participation in Western Europe: implications for North America. *Relations industrielles* 40, 747–74.

Jallade, J. P. ed. 1988: *The Crisis of Redistribution in European Welfare States*. Stoke-on-Trent: Trentham Brooks.

James, P. 1988: *Crisis and War*. Kingston and Montreal: McGill & Queen's University Press.

James, William 1878 (*1978*): The sentiment of rationality. *Works of William James: Essays in Philosophy*. Cambridge, MA: Harvard University Press.

James, William 1892 (*1961*): *Psychology: the Briefer Course*. New York: Harper & Row.

James, William 1908 (*1975*): Pragmatism. *Works of William James: Essays in Philosophy*. Cambridge, MA: Harvard University Press.

Jameson, Frederic 1972: *The Prison-House of Language*. Princeton, NJ: Princeton University Press.

Jameson, Fredric 1991: *Postmodernism, or, The Cultural Logic of Late Capitalism*. London: Verso.

Janda, K. 1980: *Political Parties: a Cross-National Survey*. New York: Free Press.

Janowitz, M. 1960 (*1971*): *The Professional Soldier*. Rev. edn, New York: Free Press.

Janowitz, M. 1975: *Military Conflict: Essays in the Institutional Analysis of War and Peace*. Beverly Hills, CA: Sage.

Janowitz, M. 1977: *Military Institutions and Coercion in the Developing Nations*. Chicago: University of Chicago Press.

Janowitz, M. ed. 1981: *Civil–Military Relations: Regional Perspectives*. Beverly Hills, CA: Sage.

Jaques, E. 1976: *A General Theory of Bureaucracy*. London: Heinemann.

Jardine, Alice 1985: *Gynesis: Configurations of Women and Modernity*. Ithaca, NY: Cornell University Press.

Jaspers, Karl 1969–71: *Philosophy*, 3 vols, trans E. B. Ashton.Chicago: University of Chicago Press.

Jay, Martin 1973: *The Dialectical Imagination: a History of the Frankfurt School and the Institute of Social Research 1923–50*. London: Heinemann.

Jay, Martin 1984: *Marxism and Totality*. Berkeley and Los Angeles: University of California Press.

Jayawardena, Kumari 1986: *Feminism and Nationalism in the Third World*. London: Zed Books.

Jean, Marcel 1970: *The History of Surrealist Painting*. London: Weidenfeld & Nicolson.

Jeffrey, R. C. 1965 (*1983*): *The Logic of Decision*. 2nd edn, Chicago: University of Chicago Press.

Jellinek, E. M. 1960: *The Disease Concept of Alcoholism*. New Haven, CT: Hillhouse Press.

Jencks, Christopher and Riesman, David 1968: *The Academic Revolution*. New York: Doubleday.

Jenkins, David 1973: *Job Power*. Harmondsworth: Penguin.

Jenkins, J. C. 1987: Interpreting the stormy 1960s: three theories in search of a political age. In *Research in Political Sociology*, vol. 3, ed. R. G. Braungart and M. M. Braungart. Greenwich, CT: JAI Press.

Jensen, M. C. and Meckling, W. 1976: Theory of the firm: managerial behaviour, agency costs and ownership structure. *Journal of Financial Economics* 3, 304–60.

Joas, H. 1985: *G. H. Mead: a Contemporary Reexamination of his Thought*. Cambridge: Polity.

Joas, H. 1993: *Pragmatism and Social Theory*. Chicago: University of Chicago Press.

Jobert, Bruno 1981: *Le social en plan*. Paris: Éditions Ouvrières.

Joergensen, J. 1970: The development of logical empiricism. In *Foundations of the Unity of Science*, vol. 2, ed. O. Neurath et al. New edn, Chicago and London: University of Chicago Press.

Johansen, L. 1978: *Lectures on Macroeconomic Planning*, 2 vols. Amsterdam: North Holland.

Johnson, Norman 1987: *The Welfare State in Transition*. Brighton: Wheatsheaf.

Johnson, Terry 1972: *Professions and Power*. London: Macmillan.

Johnson, Terry 1984: Professionalism: occupation or ideology? in *Education for the Professions: Quis Custodiet . . . ?*, ed. Sinclair Goodlad. Guildford: Society for Research into Higher Education & NFER-Nelson.

Johnson-Laird, P. N. 1983: *Mental Models*. Cambridge: Cambridge University Press.

Johnson-Laird, P. N. 1988: *The Computer and the Mind*. London: Fontana.

Johnstone, J. K. 1954: *The Bloomsbury Group*. London: Secker & Warburg.

Joll, James 1964: *The Anarchists*. London: Eyre & Spottiswoode.

Jolowicz, H. F. 1967: *Historical Introduction to the Study of Roman Law*. Cambridge: Cambridge University Press.

Jones, B. 1894: *Co-operative Production*. Oxford: Oxford University Press.

Jones, E. E. and Gerard, H. B. 1967: *Foundations of Social Psychology*. New York: Wiley.

Jones, Ernest 1963: *The Life and Work of Sigmund Freud*, ed. Lionel Trilling and Steven Marcus. London: Hogarth Press.

Jones, G. 1980: *Social Darwinism and English Thought*. Brighton: Harvester.

Jones, R. K. 1984: *Ideological Groups: Similarities of Structure and Organization*. Aldershot: Gower.

Jones, Richard Foster 1961 (*1982*): *Ancients and Moderns: A Study in the Rise of the Scientific Movement in Seventeenth Century England*. New York: Doubleday.

Jones, Stephen G. 1986: *Workers at Play: a Social and Economic History of Leisure 1918–1939*. London: Routledge & Kegan Paul.

Jordan, A. G. and Richardson, J. J. 1987: *British Politics and the Policy Process*. London: Unwin Hyman.

Jouvenel, Bertrand de 1948: *On Power*. New York.

Jouvenel, Bertrand de 1957: *Sovereignty: an Inquiry into the Political Good*, trans. J. F. Huntington. Chicago: University of Chicago Press.

Jowett, G. S. and O'Donnell, V. 1986: *Propaganda and Persuasion*. Beverly Hills, CA: Sage.

Judt, T. 1986: *Marxism and the French Left*. New York: Oxford University Press.

Juergensmeyer, M. 1982: *Religion as Social Vision*. Berkeley: University of California Press.

Jumar, Krishan 1987: *Utopia and Anti-Utopia in Modern Times*. Oxford: Blackwell.

Jung, C. J. ed. 1964: *Man and his Symbols*. London: Aldus.

Justice 1980: *Breaking the Rules*. London: Justice. (British section of the International Commission of Jurists).

Kadish, A. 1989: *Historians, Economists and Economic History*. London.

Kahn, A. J. 1969: *Theory and Practice of Social Planning*. New York: Russel Sage Foundation.

Kahneman, D. and Tversky, A. 1979: Prospect theory: an analysis of decision under risk. *Econometrica* 47, 263–91.

Kahneman, D. et al. eds 1982: *Judgment under Uncertainty, Heuristics and Biases*. Cambridge: Cambridge University Press.

Kairys, David ed. 1982: *The Politics of Law*. New York: Pantheon.

Kaldor, N. 1939: Welfare comparisons of economics and interpersonal comparisons of utility. *Economic Journal* 49.

Kaldor, N. 1955–6: Alternative theories of distribution. *Review of Economic Studies* 23, 94–100.

Kalecki, M. 1971: *Selected Essays on the Dynamics of the Capitalist Economy*. Cambridge: Cambridge University Press.

Kamenka, Eugene, ed. 1983: *The Portable Karl Marx*. New York: Viking Penguin.

Kamenka, Eugene and Tay, Alice Erh-Soon 1980: Socialism, anarchism and law. In *Law and Society: the Crisis in Legal Ideals*, ed. E. Kamenka et al. London: Edward Arnold; New York: St Martins.

Kamminga, H. 1990: Understanding chaos. *New Left Review* 181.

Kanigel, R. 1986: *Apprentice to Genius: the Making of a Scientific Dynasty*. New York: Macmillan.

Kant, I. 1790 (*1952*): *Critique of Judgement*, trans. J. C. Meredith. Oxford: Oxford University Press.

Kant, I. *1977*: *Kant's Political Writings*, ed. H. Reiss. Cambridge: Cambridge University Press.

Kantorowicz, Ernst 1957: *The King's Two Bodies*. Princeton, NJ: Princeton University Press.

Kaplan, M. A. 1957: *System and Process in International Politics*. New York: Wiley.

Kardelj, Edvard 1978: *Developmental Trends in the Political System of Socialist Self-Management*. 2nd edn, Belgrade: Komunist.

Katz, Jacob 1980: *From Prejudice to Destruction: Antisemitism 1700–1933*. Cambridge, MA: Harvard University Press.

Katz, Ruth, 1973: The egalitarian waltz. *Comparative Studies in Society and History* 15, 3.

Katzenstein, P. 1985: *Small States in World Markets*. Ithaca, NY: Cornell University Press.

Kau, M. and Leung, J. eds 1986: *The Writings of Mao Zedong*, vol. 1. New York: M. E. Sharpe.

Kautsky, K. 1899 (*1987*): *The Agrarian Question*. Madison: Wisconsin University Press.

Kautsky, K. 1902: *The Social Revolution*. Chicago: Charles H. Kerr.

Kautsky, K. 1913–14: Der Imperialismus. *Neue Zeit* 32.2, 908–22.

Kavanagh, D. 1972: *Political Culture*. London: Macmillan.

Kay, C. 1989: *Latin American Theories of Development and Underdevelopment*. London: Routledge.

Keane, J. 1984: *Public Life and Late Capitalism*. Cambridge: Cambridge University Press.

Keane, J. 1988: Dictatorship and the decline of parliament: Carl Schmitt's theory of political sovereignty. In *Democracy and Civil Society*. London: Verso.

Keane, J. ed. 1988: *Civil Society and the State: New European Perspectives*. London: Verso.

Keane, J. and Owens, J. 1986: *After Full Employment*. London: Hutchinson.

Keat, R. and Urry, J. 1981: *Social Theory as Science*. London: Routledge & Kegan Paul.

Kedouri, Elie 1960: *Nationalism*. London: Hutchinson.

Kelley, D. 1972: *Why Conservative Churches are Growing*. New York: Harper & Row.

Kelley, H. H. 1967: Attribution theory in social psychology. In *Nebraska Symposium on Motivation*, vol. 15, ed. D. Levine. Lincoln: University of Nebraska Press.

Kelly, L. 1988: *Surviving Sexual Violence*. Cambridge: Polity.

Kelly, Michael 1982: *Modern French Marxism*. Oxford: Blackwell.

Kelsen, Hans 1976: *Pure Theory of Law*. Berkeley: University of California Press.

Kelvin, P. and Jarrett, J. 1985: *Unemployment: its Social Psychological Effects*. Cambridge: Cambridge University Press.

Kemp, Barry J. 1983: Old kingdom, new kingdom and second intermediate period c.2686–1552 BC. In *Ancient Egypt: a Social History*, ed. Brian J. Trigger and Barry Kemp. Cambridge: Cambridge University Press.

Kemp, Tom 1978: *Historical Patterns of Industrialization*. London: Longman.

Keniston, K. 1971: *Youth and Dissent*. New York: Harcourt, Brace Jovanovich.

Keniston, Kenneth 1965: *The Uncommitted Alienated Youth in American Society*. New York: Harcourt, Brace & World.

Kennan, George F. 1968: *Democracy and the Student Left*. Boston: Little, Brown.

Kennick, W. E. 1958: Does traditional aesthetics rest on mistake? *Mind* 47, 317–34.

Kenrick, D. T. and Funder, D. C. 1988: Profiting from controversy: lessons from the person-situation debate. *American Psychologist* 43, 23–34.

Keohane, R. O. and Nye, J. S. 1977: *Power and Interdependence*. Boston: Little, Brown.

Kerlinger, F. N. 1973: *Foundations of Behavioral Research*. 2nd edn, New York: Holt, Rinehart & Winston.

Kermode, Frank 1971: *Modern Essays*. London: Collins Fontana.

Kern, Horst and Schumann, Michael 1984 (*1989*): *The End of the Division of Labour?* London.

Kerr, Clark and Fischer, Lloyd H. 1957: Plant sociology: the elite and the aborigines. In *Common Frontiers of the Social Sciences*, ed. Mira Komarovsky. New York: Free Press.

Kerr, Clark et al. 1960 (*1973*): *Industrialism and Industrial Man: the Problems of Labor and Management in Economic Growth*. Harmondsworth: Penguin.

Kershaw, Ian 1989: *The Nazi Dictatorship*. 2nd edn, London: Edward Arnold.

Kershaw, Ian 1991: *Hitler*. London: Longman.

Kertzer, D. I. 1988: *Ritual Politics and Power*. New Haven, CT: Yale University Press.

Kesselring, T. 1978: *Entwicklung und Widerspruch*. Frankfurt am Main: Suhrkamp.

Kesselring, T. 1984: *Die Produktivität der Antinomie*. Frankfurt am Main: Suhrkamp.

Kevles, D. J. 1985: *In the Name of Eugenics: Genetics and the Use of Human Heredity*. New York: Knopf.

Key, E. 1911 (*1949*): *Love and Marriage*, trans. G. Chater. New York and London: Free Press.

Key, V. O. Jr 1961: *Public Opinion and American Democracy*. New York: Alfred A. Knopf.

Keyes, Charles F. 1989: Buddhist politics and their revolutionary origins in Thailand. *International Political Science Review* 10, 121–42.

Keynes, J. M. 1930: *Treatise on Money*, 2 vols. London: Macmillan; New York: St Martin's Press.

Keynes, J. M. 1936 (*1964, 1973*): *The General Theory of Employment, Interest and Money*. London: Macmillan.

Keynes, J. M. 1949: *Two Memoirs*. London: Hart-Davis.

Kiernan, V. G. 1982: *From Conquest to Collapse: European Empires from 1815 to 1960*. Glasgow: Collins; New York: Pantheon.

Kiessling, B. 1988: *Kritik der giddensschen Sozialtheorie: ein Beitrag zur theoretisch-methodischen Grundlegung der Sozialwissenschaften*. Frankfurt am Main: Peter Lang.

Killingback, N. 1988: Limits to mutuality: economic and political attacks on co-operation during the 1920s and 1930s. In *New Views of Co-operation*, ed. S. Yeo. London: Routledge & Kegan Paul.

Kilminster, Richard 1979: *Praxis and Method: a Sociological Dialogue with Lukács, Gramsci and the Early Frankfurt School*. London: Routledge & Kegan Paul.

Kilminster, Richard 1982: Theory and practice in Marx and Marxism. In *Marx and Marxisms*, ed. G. H. R. Parkinson. Cambridge: Cambridge University Press.

Kilminster, Richard 1989: The limits of transcendental sociology. *Theory, Culture and Society* 6, 655–63.

Kimber, R. and Richardson, J. J., ed. 1974: *Pressure Groups in Britain*. London: Dent.

Kin, I. 1985: *Einfuerung in die Sexuologie*. Berlin: VEB Deutscher Verlag der Wissenschaften.

Kindratieff, N. 1926: *Die langen Wellen der Konjunktur*. Archiv für Sozialwissenschaft und sozialpolitik 56, 573–609.

King, A. 1990: *Global Cities: Post-imperialism and the Internationalization of London*. London: Routledge.

King, Ambrose Yeo-Chi 1991: Kuan-hsi and network building: a sociological interpretation. In *The Living Tree: the Changing Meaning of Being Chinese Today*, special issue of *Daedalus* 120, 63–84.

King, Charles D. and Vall, Mark van de 1978: *Models of Industrial Democracy: Consultation, Co-Determination and Workers' Management*. The Hague: Mouton.

King, D. 1987: *The New Right: Politics, Markets and Citizenship*. London: Macmillan.

King, David A. 1978: Islamic mathematics and astronomy. *Journal for the History of Astronomy* 9, 212–28.

King, David A. 1980: The exact sciences in medieval Islam: some remarks on the present state of research. *Middle East Studies Association of North America, Bulletin* 14, 10–26.

King, P. 1982: *Federalism and Federation*. London and Canberra: Croom Helm.

King's College Sociobiology Group eds 1982: *Current Problems of Sociobiology*. Cambridge: Cambridge University Press.

Kinsey, A. C. et al. 1948: *Sexual Behavior in the Human Male*. Philadelphia: W. B. Saunders.

Kirby, Michael 1969: *The Art of Time: Essays on the Avant-Garde*. New York: Dutton.

Kirchheimer, Otto 1976: *Von der Weimarer Republik zum Faschismus: die Auflösung der demokratischen Rechtsordnung*, ed. W. Luthardt. Frankfurt am Main: Suhrkamp.

Kirchhoff, G. R. 1874 (1877): *Vorlesung über mathematische Physik, Mechanik*, 2 vols. Leipzig: B. G. Tuebner.

Kirk, Russell ed. 1982: *The Portable Conservative Reader*. Harmondsworth and New York: Viking Penguin.

Kirk, Russell 1986: *The Conservative Mind*. 7th edn, Washington, DC: Regnery.

Kirzner, I. 1973: *Competition and Entrepreneurship*. Chicago: University of Chicago Press.

Kirzner, I. 1979: *Perception, Opportunity and Profit*. Chicago: University of Chicago Press.

Kirzner, I. 1985: *Discovery and the Capitalist Process*. Chicago: University of Chicago Press.

Kitay, E. and Meyers, D. eds 1987: *Women and Moral Theory*. Totowa, NJ: Rowman & Littlefield.

Kitchen, M. 1974: August Thalheimer's theory of fascism. *Journal of the History of Ideas* 34, 67–78.

Kitchen, M. 1976: *Fascism*. London: Macmillan.

Klein, L. and Goldberger, A. 1955: *An Econometric Model of the United States*. Amsterdam: North Holland.

Klein, R. and O'Higgins, M. 1985: *The Future of Welfare*. Oxford: Blackwell.

Klineberg, O. 1957: *The Human Dimension in International Relations*. New York: Holt, Rinehart and Winston.

Klineberg, O. 1968: Prejudice: the concept. In *International Encyclopedia of the Social Sciences*, vol. 12, ed. D. Sills. New York: Macmillan & Free Press.

Klingender, Francis D. 1968: *Art and the Industiral Revolution*, ed. and rev. Arthur Elton. London: Evelyn, Adams & Mackay.

Kluckhon, Clyde 1944: *Navaho Witchcraft*. Cambridge, MA: Peabody Museum.

Knapp, G. F. 1905 (*1924*): *The State Theory of Money*, abridged edn. London: Macmillan; New York: Kelley.

Kneale, W. and Kneale, M. 1962: *The Development of Logic*. Oxford: Clarendon Press.

Knei-Paz, B. 1978: *The Social and Political Thought of Leon Trotsky*. Oxford: Oxford University Press.

Knight, F. H. 1921: *Risk, Uncertainty and Profit*. New York: Houghton Mifflin.

Knight, F. H. 1935: *The Ethics of Competition*. London: Allen & Unwin.

Knorr, K. and Rosenau, J. N. eds 1969: *Contending Approaches to International Politics*. Princeton, NJ: Princeton University Press.

Knorr-Cetina, K. D. 1981: *The Manufacture of Knowledge: an Essay on the Constructivist and Contextual Nature of Science*. Oxford: Pergamon Press.

Kocka, Jurgen 1986: Problems of working-class formation in Germany: the early years, 1800–1875. In *Working Class Formation*, ed. Ira Katznelson and Aristide R. Zolberg. Princeton, NJ: Princeton University Press.

Koebner, R. and Schmidt, H. D. 1965: *Imperialism: the Story and Significance of a Political Word, 1840–1960*. Cambridge: Cambridge University Press.

Koffka, K. 1935: *Principles of Gestalt Psychology*. New York: Harcourt, Brace.

Kohler, W. 1925: *The Mentality of Apes*. London: Kegan Paul, Trench & Trubner.

Kohler, W. 1947: *Gestalt Psychology*. New York: Liverlight.

Kohler, W. 1967: *The Task of Gestalt Psychology*. Princeton, NJ: Princeton University Press.

Kohli, Rein et al. 1991: *Time for Retirement: Comparative Studies of Early Exit from the Labour Force*. New York: Cambridge University Press.

Kohn, Hans 1962: *The Age of Nationalism*. New York: Harper & Row.

Kohn, Hans 1967: *The Idea of Nationalism*. New York: Collier.

Kohn, M. L. 1969: *Class and Conformity*. Homewood, IL: Dorsey Press.

Kohn, M. L. et al. 1990: Position in the class structure and psychological functioning: a comparative analysis of the United States, Japan, and Poland. *American Journal of Sociology* 95.

Kojève, A. 1947 (*1980*): *Introduction to the Reading of Hegel*. Ithaca: Cornell University Press.

Kolakowski, L. 1966 (*1972*): *Positivist Philosophy: From Hume to the Vienna Circle*. Harmondsworth: Penguin.

Kolakowski, L. 1971: Karl Marx and the classical definition of truth. In *Marxism and Beyond*. London: Paladin.

Kolakowski, L. 1978: *Main Currents of Marxism*, 3 vols. Oxford and New York: Oxford University Press.

Kolakowski, L. and Hampshire, S. eds 1974: *The Socialist Idea: a Reappraisal*. London: Weidenfeld & Nicolson.

Kolodko, G. W. and McMahon, W. W. 1988: Stagflation and shortageflation: a comparative approach. *Kyklos* 40.2.

Kon, I. 1985: *Einführung in die Sexologie*. Berlin: VEB Deutscher Verlag der Wissenschaften.

Kondratieff, N. 1935: The long waves in economic life. *Review of Economic Statistics* 17, 105–15.

Konrád, G. and Szélenyi, I. 1977: Social conflicts of underurbanization. In *Captive Cities*, ed. M. Harloe. New York: Wiley.

Koopmans, T. C. 1947 (*1965*): Measurement without theory. In *Readings in Business Cycles*, ed. R. A. Gordon and L. Klein. Homewood, IL: Richard D. Irwin.

Koopmans, T. C. 1957: *Three Essays on the State of Economic Science*. New York and London: McGraw-Hill.

Koot, G. M. 1980: English historical economics and the emergence of economic history in England. *History of Political Economy* 12, 174–205.

Koot, G. M. 1987: *English Historical Economics, 1870–1926: the Rise of Economic History and Neomercantilism*. Cambridge.

Korn, M. et al. 1990: Serotonin and suicide: a functional/dimensional viewpoint. In *Current Concepts of Suicide*, ed. D. Lester. Philadelphia: Charles Press.

Kornai, J. 1980: *Economics of Shortage*. Amsterdam: North Holland.

Kornhauser, W. 1959: *The Politics of Mass Society*. Glencoe, IL: Free Press.

Korsch, Karl 1922 (*1968*): *Arbeitsrecht für Betriebsräte*. Frankfurt am Main: EVA.

Korsch, Karl 1923 (*1970*): *Marxism and Philosophy*. London: New Left Books.

Korsch, Karl 1938 (*1967*): *Karl Marx*. London: Chapman & Hall; revd German edn, Frankfurt: Europäische Verlaganstalt.

Korthals, Michael 1985: Die kritische Gesellschaftstheorie des frühen Horkheimer. *Zeitschrift für Soziologie* 14, 315

Kosellek, R. 1973 (*1987*): *Critique and Crisis*, Leamington Spa: Berg.

Kosellek, R. 1976: Krise. In *Historisches Wörterbuch der Philosophie*, vol. 4. Darmstadt: Wissenschaftliche Buchgesellschaft.

Kotz, S. et al. eds 1988: *Encyclopaedia of Statistical Sciences*, 9 vols. Wiley-Interscience.

Kowalski, R. 1979: *Logic for Problem Solving*. Amsterdam: North Holland.

Kracauer, Siegfried 1937 (*1938*): *Orpheus in Paris: Offenbach and the Paris of his Time*. New York: Knopf.

Kracke, W. 1978: *Force and Persuasion: Leadership in an Amazonian Tribe*. Chicago: University of Chicago Press.

Krader, L. 1975: *The Asiatic Mode of Production*. Assen: Van Gorcum.

Kraft, V. 1953: *The Vienna Circle: the Origin of Neo-Positivism*, trans. A. Pap. New York: Philosophical Library.

Kramer, Samuel Noah 1963: *The Sumerians*. Chicago: University of Chicago Press.

Krampen, M. 1981: Phytosemiotics. *Semiotica* 36. 3/4, 187–209.

Kranzberg, Melvin 1985: The information age: evolution or revolution? In *Information Technologies and Social Transformation*, ed. Bruce R. Guile. Washington, DC: National Academy Press.

Krauch, H. 1970: *Prioritäten für die Forschungspolitik*. Munich: Carl Hanser.

Krause, C. G. 1990: *Theory of Industrial Economics*. Oxford: Blackwell.

Krebs, J. R. and Davis, N. B. 1981 *An Introduction to Behavioural Ecology*. Oxford: Blackwell.

Kriesberg, Louis 1982: *Social Conflicts*. 2nd edn, Englewood Cliffs, NJ: Prentice-Hall.

Kristeva, Julia 1986: *The Kristeva Reader*, ed. Toril Moi. Oxford: Blackwell.

Kroeber, A. L. 1909: Classificatory systems of relationship. *Journal of the Royal Anthropological Institute* 39, 77–84.

Krüger, H.-P. et al. 1988: Stability and variability in interactive behavior as measured by methods of 'Speech Chronemics'. *International Journal of Small Group Research* 4, 95–121.

Krupp, Sherman 1961: *Pattern in Organization Analysis*. New York: Holt, Rinehart & Winston.

Kuhn, Thomas S. 1962 (*1970*): *The Structure of Scientific Revolutions*. 2nd edn, Chicago: University of Chicago Press.

Kuipers, S. K. and Lanjouw, G. J. eds 1980: *Prospects of Economic Growth*. Amsterdam.

Kumar, K. 1976: Industrialism and post-industrialism: reflections on a putative transition. *Sociological Review* 24.3, 439–78: the Sociology of Industrial and Post-industrial Society.

Kumar, K. 1978: *Prophecy and Progress*. Harmondsworth: Penguin.

Kumar, K. 1981: Primitivism in feminist utopias. *Alternative Futures (USA)* 4, 61–7.

Kumar, K. 1984: Unemployment as a problem in the development of industrial societies: the English experience. *Sociological Review* 32, 185–233.

Kumar, K. 1987: *Utopia and Anti-Utopia in Modern Times*. Oxford: Blackwell.

Kumar, K. 1988: *The Rise of Modern Society*. Oxford: Blackwell.

Küng, Hans 1988: *Theology for the Third Millenium*. London: Anchor Books.

Kuper, A. 1982: *Anthropology and Anthropologists*. London: Routledge & Kegan Paul.

Kuper, L. and Smith, M. G. 1969: *Pluralism in Africa*. Berkeley: University of California Press.

Kuper, Leo 1981: *Genocide: its Political Use in the Twentieth Century*. New Haven, CT: Yale University Press.

Kurtz, Lester R. 1984: *Evaluating Chicago Sociology: a Guide to the Literature, with an Annotated Bibliography*. Chicago: University of Chicago Press.

Kushnirsky, F. I. 1982: *Soviet Economic Planning, 1965–80*. Boulder, CO, and London: Westview Press.

Kuznets, Simon 1966: *Modern Economic Growth: Rate, Structure, and Spread*. New Haven, CT: Yale University Press.

Kymlicka, W. 1990: *Contemporary Political Philosophy*. Oxford: Clarendon.

Labedz, L. ed. 1962: *Revisionism*. London: Allen & Unwin.

Labica, G. 1980: *Marxism and the Status of Philosophy*. Brighton: Harvester Press.

La Boétie, Emile de 1975: *Discourse on Voluntary Servitude*.

Labov, W. 1966: *The Social Stratification*. Washington, DC: Center for Applied Linguistics.

Labov, W. 1970 (*1972*): The study of language in its

social context. In *Sociolinguistics*, ed. J. B. Pride and J. Holmes. Harmondsworth: Penguin.

Labov, W. and Fanshel, D. 1977: *Therapeutic Discourse: Psychotherapy as Conversation*. New York: Academic Press.

Lacan, Jacques 1982: *Feminine Sexuality: Jacques Lacan and the École Freudienne*, ed. Juliet Mitchell and Jacqueline Rose. London: Macmillan.

Lacey, Colin 1970: *Hightown Grammar*. Manchester: Manchester University Press.

Lachmann, Ludwig M. 1986: *The Market as an Economic Process*. Oxford and New York: Blackwell.

Laclau, Ernesto 1977: *Politics and Ideology in Marxist Theory: Capitalism, Fascism and Populism*. London: Verso.

Laclau, Ernesto 1977: *Politics and Ideology in Marxist Theory*. London: New Left Books.

Ladurie, E. Le Roy 1980: Peasants. In *The Cambridge Modern History*, vol. 13. Cambridge: Cambridge University Press.

Laidlaw, A. F. 1981: *Co-operation in the Year 2000*. Ottawa: Co-operative Union of Canada.

Lakoff, S. A. 1966: *Knowledge and Power: Essays on Science and Government*. New York: Free Press.

Lal, Deepak 1983 (*1985*): *The Poverty of 'Development Economics'*. Cambridge, MA: Harvard University Press.

Lalive d'Epinay, C. 1969: *Haven of the Masses*. London: Lutterworth.

Lamain, Jorge 1979: *The Concept of Ideology*. London: Hutchinson.

Lamain, Jorge 1989: *Theories of Development*. Cambridge: Polity.

La Nauze, J. A. 1953: The conception of Jevons; utility theory. *Econometrica* 20.

Landes, D. 1986: What do bosses really do? *Journal of Economic History* 46, 585–623.

Landes, David S. 1969: *The Unbound Prometheus: Technological Change and Industrial Development in Western Europe from 1750 to the Present*. London: Cambridge University Press.

Landgrebe, Ludwig 1966: *Major Problems in Contemporary European Philosophy, from Dilthey to Heidegger*. New York: Frederick Ungar.

Landis, P. A. 1956: *Social Control: Social Organisation and Disorganisation in Process*. Chicago: University of Chicago Press.

Lane, C. 1981: *The Rites of Rulers*. Cambridge: Cambridge University Press.

Lane, D. 1984: *Foundations for a Social Theology*. Dublin: Gill & Macmillan.

Lane, Robert 1966: *The decline of politics and ideology in a knowledgeable society*. American Sociological Review 31.5, 647–62.

Lang, Berel 1968: The form of aesthetics. *Journal of Aesthetics and Art Criticism* 27, 35–47.

Lange, O. 1936–7 (*1964*): On the economic theory of socialism. In *On the Economic Theory of Socialism*, ed. B. E. Lippincott. New York: McGraw-Hill.

Lange, Oskar and Taylor, F. M. 1938: *On the Economic Theory of Socialism*. Minneapolis: University of Minnesota Press.

Lannoy, R. 1971: *The Speaking Tree: a Study of Indian Culture and Society*. Oxford: Oxford University Press.

Lanternari, V. 1963: *The Religions of the Oppressed: a Study of Modern Messianic Cults*, trans. L. Sergio. New York: Knopf.

Lapalombara, J. 1964: *Interest Groups in Italian Politics*. Princeton, NJ: Princeton University Press.

Laqueur, W. 1977: *Terrorism*. London: Weidenfeld & Nicolson.

Laqueur, W. 1977: *Guerrillas: a Historical and Critical Study*. London: Weidenfeld & Nicolson.

Larrain, J. 1979: *The Concept of Ideology*. London: Hutchinson.

Larrain, J. 1989: *Theories of Development*. Cambridge: Polity.

Larsen, Stein et al. eds 1980: *Who Were the Fascists?* Bergen: Universitetsforlaget.

Larson, Magali Sarfatti 1977: *The Rise of Professionalism: a Sociological Analysis*. London: University of California Press.

Lasch, S. and Urry, J. 1984: The new Marxism of collective action: a critical analysis. *Sociology* 18, 33–50.

Laski, H. J. 1921: The problem of administrative areas. In *The Foundations of Sovereignty and Other Essays*. London: Allen & Unwin.

Laski, H. J. 1948: Authority as federal. In *A Grammar of Politics*. 5th edn, London: Allen & Unwin.

Lasky, M. J. 1976: *Utopia and Revolution*. Chicago: University of Chicago Press.

Laslett, John H. M. and Lipset, Seymour M. eds 1974: *Failure of a Dream? Essays in the History of American Socialism*. Rev. edn, Berkeley: University of California Press.

Laslett, Peter 1976: Societal development and ageing. In *Handbook of Ageing and the Social Sciences*, ed. R. Binstock and E. Shanas. New York: Van Nostrand Reinhold.

Lasswell, H. D. 1930: *Psychopathology and Politics*. Chicago: University of Chicago Press.

Lasswell, H. D. 1941: The garrison state. *American Journal of Sociology* 46, 455–68.

Laszlo, E. 1987: *Evolution: the Grand Synthesis*. Boston and London: New Science Library.

Latham, E. 1952: *The Group Basis of Politics*. Ithaca, NY: Cornell University Press.

Latour, B. 1987: *Science in Action*. Milton Keynes: Open University Press.

Latour, Bruno and Woolgar, Steve 1979: *Laboratory Life*. Beverly Hills, CA: SAGE.

Lauck, W. Jeff 1926: *Political and Industrial Democracy 1776–1926*. New York: Funk & Wagnalls.

Lavoie, D. 1985: *Rivalry and Central Planning: the Socialist Calculation Debate Reconsidered*. Cambridge: Cambridge University Press.

Lavoie, D. 1986: The market as a procedure for discovery and conveyance of inarticulate knowledge. *Comparative Economic Studies* 28, 1–19.

Laycock, G. and Heal, K. eds 1986: *Situational Crime Prevention*. London: HMSO.

Layton, Edwin 1956: The American engineering profession and the idea of social responsibility. Unpublished PhD dissertation, Dept of History, University of California at Los Angeles.

Lazarsfield, P. F. 1961: Notes on the history of quantification in sociology: trends, sources and problems. *Isis* 52, 277–333.

Lazarsfeld, P. F. and Morris, Rosenberg 1955: *The Language of Social Research*. Glencoe, IL: Free Press.

Leach, E. R. 1961: *Rethinking Anthropology*. London: Athlone.

Leach, E. R. 1968: Social structure: the history of the concept. In *International Encyclopedia of the Social Sciences*, ed. D. L. Sills, vol. 14. New York: Macmillan.

Leach, E. R. 1970: *Lévi-Strauss*. London: Fontana/Collins.

Leach, E. R. 1982: *Social Anthropology*. London: Fontana.

Leach, E. R. and Aycock, Alan 1983: *Structural Interpretations of Biblical Myth*. Cambridge: Cambridge University Press.

Leacock, E. ed. 1970: *The Culture of Poverty: Review and Critique*. New York: Simon & Schuster.

Leamer, E. E. 1987: Econometric metaphors. In *Advances in Econometrics Fifth World Congress*, vol. 2, ed. T. F. Bewley. Cambridge: Cambridge University Press.

Lebas, Elizabeth: Urban and regional sociology in advanced industrial societies: a decade of Marxist and critical perspectives. *Current Sociology* 30, 1–271.

Lebedoff, David 1983: *The New Elite: the Death of Democracy*. Chicago: Contemporary Books.

Le Bon, G. 1952: *The Crowd: a Study of the Popular Mind*. London: Ernest Benn.

Lebowitz, M. 1988: Analytical Marxism. *Science and Society* 52.2.

Lefebvre, H. 1968: *La Vie quotidienne dans le monde moderne*. Paris: Gallimard.

Legendre, Pierre 1983: *L'empire de la vérité*. Paris: Fayard.

Legendre, Pierre 1988: *Le Désir politique de Dieu: étude sur les montages de l'état et du droit*. Paris: Fayard.

Le Grand, J. 1982: *The Strategy of Equality: Redistribution and the Social Services*. London: Allen & Unwin.

Legum, C. 1976: *Pan-Africanism: a Short Political Guide*. Westport, CT: Greenwood Press.

Lehergott, S. 1984: *The Americans: an Economic Record*. New York: Norton.

Leibfried, S. 1982: Existenzminimum und Fürsorge-Richtsatze in der Weimarer Republik. *Jahrbuch der Sozialarbeit* 4.

Leibfried, S. and Tennstedt, F. eds 1985: *Regulating Poverty and the Splitting of the German Welfare State*. Frankfurt am Main: Suhrkamp.

Leijonhufvud, A. 1968: *On Keynesian Economics and the Economics of Keynes* Oxford: Oxford University Press.

Leiss, William 1976: *The Limits to Satisfaction: an Essay on the Problem of Needs and Commodities*. Toronto: University of Toronto Press.

Lemaine, G. et al. 1982: *Noopolis: les laboratoires de recherche fondamental: de l'atelier à l'usine*. Paris: Centre Nationale de la Recherche Scientifique.

Lemert, E. 1951: *Social Pathology*. New York: McGraw-Hill.

Lemkin, R. 1944: *Axis Rule in Occupied Europe*. Washington, DC: Carnegie Endowment for International Peace.

Lemon, L. T. and Reis, M. J. eds 1965: *Russian*

Formalist Criticism: Four Essays. Lincoln: University of Nebraska Press.

Lenin, V. I. 1902 (*1961*): What is to be done? In *Collected Works*, vol. 5. Moscow: Progress.

Lenin, V. I. 1908 (*1970*): *Materialism and Empirio-Criticism.* Moscow: Progress.

Lenin, V. I. 1916 (*1948, 1964*): *Imperialism: the Highest Stage of Capitalism.* Moscow: Progress.

Lenin, V. I. 1917 (*1969*): *State and Revolution.* In *Collected Works*, vol. 25. London: Lawrence & Wishart.

Lenin, V. I. *1960–70: Collected Works.* Moscow: Foreign Languages Publishing House.

Lenin, V. I. *1964a:* The beginning of Bonapartism. In *Collected Works*, vol. 25. Moscow: Progress Publishers.

Lenin, V. I. *1964b:* They do not see the wood for the trees. In *Collected Works*, vol. 25. Moscow: Progress Publishers.

Lenin, V. I. *1967: The proletarian revolution and the renegade Kautsky.* In *Selected Works*, 3 vols. Vol. 3. Moscow: Progress.

Lenski, G. 1966: *Power and Privilege: a Theory of Stratification.* New York: McGraw-Hill.

Lenski, G. and Lenski, J. 1987: *Human Societies: an Introduction to Macrosociology.* 5th edn, New York: McGraw-Hill.

Lentricchia, Frank 1978: *After the New Criticism.* London: Athlone Press.

Lepage, Henri 1982: *Tomorrow, Capitalism: the Economics of Economic Freedom,* trans. Sheilagh Ogilvie. La Salle, IL, and London: Open Court.

Leppert, R. and McClary, S., eds 1987: *Music and Society: the Politics of Composition, Performance and Reception.* Cambridge: Cambridge University Press.

Lequin, Y. 1977: *Les ouvriers de la région lyonnaise, 1848–1914.* Lyon: PUL.

Lerner, D. 1958: *The Passing of Traditional Society.* New York: Free Press.

Lerner, David 1958: *The Passing of Traditional Society.* Glencoe, IL: Free Press?.

Le Roy Ladurie, E. 1973 (*1979*): *The Territory of the Historian.* Brighton: Harvester.

Leser, Norbert 1966: Austro-Marxism: a reappraisal. *Journal of Contemporary History*, 1, 2.

Leser, Norbert 1968 (*1985*): *Zwischen Reformismus und Bolchewismus: der Austromarxismus als Theorie und Praxis.* 2nd abridged edn, Vienna: Europa Verlag.

Lessnoff, M. 1986: *Social Contract.* London: Macmillan.

Lester, D. ed. 1990: *Current Concepts of Suicide.* Philadelphia: Charles Press.

Lester, Richard A. 1958: *As Unions Mature.* Princeton, NJ: Princeton University Press.

Letwin, W. ed. 1983: *Against Equality.* London: Macmillan.

Levenson, Joseph R. 1958–65: *Confucian China and its Modern Fate,* 3 vols. Berkeley: University of California Press.

Levin, Nora 1978: *Jewish Socialist Movements 1871–1917.* London.

Levine, D. N. 1985: Rationality and freedom, inveterate multivocals. In *The Flight from Ambiguity: Essays in Social and Cultural Theory.* Chicago: University of Chicago Press.

Levine, Lawrence W. 1988: *Highbrow/Lowbrow: the Emergence of Cultural Hierarchy in America.* Cambridge, MA: Harvard University Press.

LeVine, R. A. and Campbell, D. T. 1972: *Ethnocentrism: Theories of Conflict, Ethnic Attitudes and Group Behavior.* New York: Wiley.

Levinson, D. J. et al. 1978: *The Seasons of a Man's Life.* New York: Knopf.

Levinson, Ronald B. 1953: *In Defense of Plato.* Cambridge, MA: Harvard University Press.

Levinson, S. C. 1983: *Pragmatics.* Cambridge: Cambridge University Press.

Lévi-Strauss, C. 1949 (*1969*): *The Elementary Structures of Kinship,* trans. J. H. Bell et al., ed. R. Needham. 2nd edn, Boston: Beacon Press; London: Eyre & Spottiswoode.

Lévi-Strauss, C. 1958 (*1963*): *Structural Anthropology.* New York: Basic Books.

Lévi-Strauss, C. 1962 (*1966*): *The Savage Mind.* London: Weidenfeld & Nicolson.

Levi-Strauss, C. 1964–72: *Mythologiques,* 3 vols. Paris.

Lévi-Strauss, C. 1966: The future of kinship studies. *Proceedings of the Royal Anthropological Institute for 1965.*

Lewin, K. et al. 1939: Patterns of aggressive behavior in experimentally created 'social climates'. *Journal of Social Psychology* 10, 271–99.

Lewin, M. 1973: *Lenin's Last Struggle.* London: Wildwood House.

Lewin, M. 1985: *The Making of the Soviet System: Essays in the Social History of Interwar Russia.* London: Methuen.

Lewis, D. 1969: *Convention.* Cambridge, MA: Harvard University Press.

Lewis, D. K. 1983: Radical interpretation. *Synthese* 23, 331–44.

Lewis, G. Cornewall 1832 (*1898*): *Remarks on the Use and Abuse of Some Political Terms*. Oxford: Clarendon Press.

Lewis, O. 1961: *The Children of Sanchez: Autobiography of a Mexican Family*. New York: Random House.

Lewis, O. 1967: *La Vida*. New York: Panther.

Lewis, Paul ed. 1992: *Democracy and Civil Society in Eastern Europe*. London: Macmillan.

Lewis, W. 1954: Economic development with unlimited supplies of labour. *Manchester School of Economic and Social Studies* 22, 139–91.

Lewontin, R. C. 1968: The concept of evolution. In *International Encyclopedia of the Social Sciences*, ed. D. L. Sills, vol. 5. New York: Macmillan and Free Press.

Lichtenstein, H. 1977: *The Dilemma of Human Identity*. New York: Jason Aronson.

Lichtheim, George 1961: *Marxism: an Historical and Critical Study*. London: Routledge & Kegan Paul; New York: Praeger.

Lichtheim, George 1969: *The Origins of Socialism*. New York: Praeger.

Lichtheim, George 1970: *A Short History of Socialism*. London: Weidenfeld & Nicolson; New York: Praeger.

Liddell Hart, B. H. 1967: *Strategy: the Indirect Approach*. London: Faber & Faber.

Lieberman, E. J. 1964: Threat and assurance in the conduct of conflict. In *International Conflict and Behavioural Science*, ed. R. Fisher. New York: Basic Books.

Liebman, M. 1973 (*1975*): *Leninism under Lenin*. London: Jonathan Cape.

Lindbeck, A. 1977: *The Political Economy of the New Left: an Outsider's View*. 2nd edn, New York: Harper & Row.

Lindblom, C. E. 1959: The science of muddling through. *Public Administration Review* 19, 79–88.

Lindblom, C. E. 1977: *Politics and Markets*. New York: Basic Books.

Lindholm, C. 1990: *Charisma*. Oxford: Blackwell.

Ling, T. 1980: *Buddhist Revival in India*. New York: St Martin's Press.

Linklater, A. 1982: *Men and Citizens in the Theory of International Relations*. London: Macmillan.

Linton, R. 1936: *The Study of Man*. New York: Appleton-Century-Crofts.

Linz, Juan and Stepan, Alfred eds 1978: *The Breakdown of Democratic Regimes*. Baltimore: Johns Hopkins University Press.

Lipietz, A. 1986: Behind the crisis: the exhaustion of a regime of accumulation: a 'regulation school' perspective on some French empirical works. *Review of Radical Political Economics* 18.1–2, 13–32.

Lipietz, A. 1987: *Mirages and Miracles: the Crises of Global Fordism*. London: Verso.

Lipietz, A. 1992: *Choosing Audacy: an Alternative for the XXIst Century*. Cambridge: Polity.

Lippmann, Walter 1922: *Public Opinion*. London: Allen & Unwin.

Lippman, Walter 1929: *A Preface to Morals*. New York.

Lipset, S. M. 1960: *Political Man: the Social Bases of Politics*. Garden City, NY: Doubleday.

Lipset, S. M. ed. 1986: *Unions in Transition: Entering the Second Century*. San Francisco: ICS Press.

Lipset, S. M. 1990: No third way: a comparative perspective on the left. *National Interest* 20.

Lipset, S. M. and Altbach, P. G. eds 1969: *Students in Revolt*. Boston: Houghton Mifflin.

Lipset, S. M. and Wolin, Sheldon S. eds 1965: *The Berkeley Student Revolt*. New York: Anchor.

Lipset, S. M. and Zetterberg, H. 1966: A theory of social mobility. In *Class, Status and Power*, ed. R. Bendix and S. M. Lipset. New York: Free Press.

List, F. 1841 (*1904*): *The National System of Political Economy*. London: Longman.

Lister, R. 1990: *The Exclusive Society: Citizenship and the Poor*. London: Child Poverty Action Group.

Lister, R. 1991: Concepts of Poverty. *Social Studies Review* 6, 192–5.

Little, R. W. ed. 1971: *Handbook of Military Institutions*. Beverly Hills, CA: Sage.

Littlechild, Stephen ed. 1990: *Austrian Economics*, 3. vols. Aldershot: Edward Elgar; Brookfield, VT: Gower.

Littler, C. and Salaman, G. 1984: *Class at Work: the Design, Allocation and Control of Jobs*. London: Batsford.

Litwak, Eugene 1965: Extended family relations in an industrial society. In *Social Structure and the Family: Generational Relations*, ed. E. Shanas and G. Strieb. Princeton, NJ: Princeton University Press.

Lively, J. 1976: The limits of exchange theory. In *Power and Political Theory: Some European Perspectives*, ed. B. Barry. London: Wiley.

Livergood, Norman 1967: *Activity in Marx's Philosophy*. The Hague: Martinus Nijhoff.

Llewellyn, K. and Hoebel, E. 1941: *The Cheyenne Way*.

Lloyd, Alan B. 1983: The late period, 664–323 BC. In *Ancient Egypt: a Social History*, ed. B. J. Trigger and B. Kemp. Cambridge: Cambridge University Press.

Lloyd, P. 1979: *Slums of Hope?* Harmondsworth: Penguin.

Lobkowicz, Nicholas 1967: *Theory and Practice: History of a Concept from Aristotle to Marx*. Notre Dame, IN: University of Notre Dame Press.

Locke, John 1690: *An Essay Concerning Human Understanding*. London: Bassett.

Locke, John 1690 (*1960*): *Two Treatises of Government*, ed. Peter Laslett. Cambridge: Cambridge University Press.

Locke, John *1812*: *Works*, Vol. 5. London: W. Otridge & Son.

Lockwood, D. 1958: *The Blackcoated Worker: a Study in Class Consciousness*. London: Allen & Unwin.

Lockwood, D. 1964: Social integration and system integration. In *Explorations in Social Change*, ed. Z. Zollschau and W. Hirsch. London: Routledge & Kegan Paul.

Lodge, David, ed. 1988: *Modern Criticism and Theory: a Reader*. London and New York: Longman.

Lofland, J. 1969: *Deviance and Identity*.

Lo Piparo, F. 1979: *Lingua intellettuali egemonia in Gramsci*. Rome and Bari: Laterza.

Lorenz, K. 1966: *On Aggression*, trans. M. Latzke. London: Methuen.

Lotka, A. 1939: *Théorie analytique des associations biologiques*. Paris: Hermann.

Lovell, Terry 1987: *Consuming Fiction*. London: Verso.

Lovibond, Sabina 1983: *Realism and Imagination in Ethics*. Oxford: Blackwell.

Low, S. 1904: *The Governance of England*. London: T. Fisher Unwin.

Löw-Beer, Martin 1990: *Selbsttäuschung*. Freiburg.

Lowe, P. D. and Rudig, W. 1986: Political ecology and the social sciences: the state of the art. *British Journal of Political Science* 16, 513–50.

Lowes, John Livingston 1922: *Convention and Revolt in Poetry*. New York.

Lowie, R. H. 1950: *Social Organization*. London: Routledge & Kegan Paul.

Löwith, K. 1932 (*1982*): *Max Weber and Karl Marx*. London and Boston: Allen & Unwin.

Lowy, M. 1981: *The Politics of Combined and Uneven Development*. London: Verso.

Lozovsky, S. 1925: *Lenin i professional'noe dvizhenie*. Moscow.

Lucas, R. E. 1981: *Studies in Business Cycle Theory*. Oxford: Blackwell.

Lucas, R. E. Jr 1977: Understanding business cycles. In *Stabilization of the Domestic and International Economy*, ed. K. Brunner and A. H. Meltzer. New York and Oxford: North-Holland, Carnegie-Rochester Conference Series on Public Policy, vol. 5.

Luce, R. D. and Raiffa, H. 1957: *Games and Decisions: Introduction and Critical Survey*. New York: Wiley.

Luckman, T. 1967: *The Invisible Religion: the Problem of Religion in Modern Society*. New York: Macmillan.

Luckmann, T. ed. 1978: *Phenomenology and Sociology*. Harmondsworth: Penguin.

Luckmann, T. 1983: *Lifeworld and Social Realities*. London: Heinemann.

Ludmerer, K. M. 1972: *Genetics and American Society: a Historical Appraisal*. Baltimore: Johns Hopkins University Press.

Luhmann, N. 1969 (*1975*): *Legitimation durch Verfahren*. 2nd edn, Neuwied: Luchterhand.

Luhmann, N. 1970–90: *Soziologische Aufklärung*, vols. 1–5. Opladen: Westdeutscher Verlag.

Luhmann, N. 1972: Einfache Sozialsysteme. *Zeitschrift für Soziologie* 1, 51.

Luhmann, N. 1976: Die Legeshierarchie und die Trennung von Staat und Gesellschaft. In *Staat und Gesellschaft*, ed. E. Böckenförde. Darmstadt: Wissenschaftliches Buchgesellschaft.

Luhmann, N. 1977: *Die Funktion der Religion*. Frankfurt am Main: Suhrkamp.

Luhmann, N. 1979: *Trust and Power*. Chichester: Wiley.

Luhmann, N. 1981: *Gesellschaftsstruktur und Semantik*. Frankfurt am Main.

Luhmann, N. 1982: Systems theory, evolution theory, and communication theory. In *The*

Differentiation of Society. New York: Columbia University Press.

Luhmann, N. 1983: Das sind Preise: ein sociologisch-systemtheoretischer Klärungsversuch. *Soziale Welt* 34.2, 153–70.

Luhmann, N. 1984: Die Wirtschaft der Gesellschaft als autopoietisches System. *Zeitschrift für Soziologie* 13.4, 308–27.

Luhmann, N. 1988: *Erkenntnis als Konstruktion.* Bern.

Luhmann, N. 1988: Familiarity, confidence and trust: problems and alternatives. In *Trust: Making and Breaking Cooperative Relations,* ed. D. Gambetta. Oxford: Blackwell.

Luk, M. 1990: *The Origins of Chinese Bolshevism.* Hong Kong: Oxford University Press.

Lukács, György 1910 (*1974*): *The Soul and the Forms.* London: Merlin; Cambridge, MA: MIT Press.

Lukács, György 1923 (*1971*): *History and Class Consciousness.* London: Merlin Press.

Lukács, György *1970*: *Writer and Critic and Other Essays,* ed. A. Kahn. London: Merlin.

Lukes, S. 1967: Alienation and anomie. In *Philosophy, Politics and Society,* ed. P. Laslett and W. G. Runciman. Oxford: Blackwell.

Lukes, S. 1973: *Émile Durkheim.* London: Allen Lane.

Lukes, S. 1973: *Individualism.* Oxford: Blackwell.

Lukes, S. 1974: *Power: a Radical View.* London: Macmillan.

Lukes, S. 1974: Socialism and equality. In *The Socialist Idea,* ed. L. Kolakowski and S. Hampshire. London: Weidenfeld & Nicolson.

Lukes, S. 1978: Power and authority. In *A History of Sociological Analysis,* ed. Tom Bottomore and Robert Nisbet. New York: Basic Books.

Lukes, S. 1985: *Marxism and Morality.* Oxford: Oxford University Press.

Lundberg, Ferdinand 1968: *The Rich and the Super-Rich.* New York: Bantam.

Luttgens, A. and Perelman, S. 1988: *Comparing Measures of Poverty and Relative Deprivation: an Example for Belgium.* Mannheim: University of Mannheim.

Luttwak, E. 1969: *Coup d'État: a Practical Handbook.* New York: Knopf.

Luxemburg, R. 1899 (*1937*): *Reform or Revolution.* New York: Three Arrows.

Luxemburg, R. 1906 (*1925*): The Mass Strike, the Political Party and Trade Unions. Detroit: Marxian Educational Society.

Luxemburg, R. 1913 (*1951*): *The Accumulation of Capital.* London: Routledge & Kegan Paul.

Luxemburg, R. *1970*: Organizational questions of Russian social democracy. In *Rosa Luxemburg Speaks,* ed. M. A. Waters. New York: Pathfinder.

Luxemburg, R. *1970*: The Russian revolution. In *Rosa Luxemburg Speaks,* ed. M. A. Waters. New York: Pathfinder.

Luxemburg, Rosa *1970*: *Rosa Luxemburg Speaks.* New York: Pathfinder.

Lycan, W. 1990: *Mind and Cognition: a Reader.* Oxford: Blackwell.

Lynch, M. 1985: *Art and Artifact in Laboratory Science.* London: Routledge.

Lyon, Bruce 1972: *The Origins of the Middle Ages: Pirenne's Challenge to Gibbon.* New York: Norton.

Lyon, David 1988: *The Information Society: Issues and Illusions.* Cambridge: Polity.

Lyons, J. 1977: *Semantics,* 2 vols. Cambridge: Cambridge University Press.

Lyotard, J.-F. 1979 (*1984*): *The Postmodern Condition.* Minneapolis: University of Minnesota Press.

Maasdorp, G. and Humphreys, A. S. V. eds 1975: *From Shanty Town to Township: an Economic Study of African Poverty and Rehousing in a South African City.* Cape Town: Juta.

Mabbott, J. D. 1948 (*1958*): *The State and the Citizen.* London: Grey Arrow.

McBriar, A. M. 1966: *Fabian Socialism and English Politics 1884–1914.* Cambridge: Cambridge University Press.

McCarthy, J. 1963: A basis for a mathematical theory of computation. In *Computer Programming and Formal Systems,* ed. P. Braffort and D. Hirschberg. Amsterdam: North Holland.

McCarthy, W. E. J. 1985: *Trade Unions.* 2nd edn, Harmondsworth: Penguin.

McCawley, J. D. 1981: *Everything that Linguists Have Always Wanted to Know about Logic.* Chicago: University of Chicago Press.

McClelland, D. 1961: *The Achieving Society.* Princeton, NJ: Van Nostrand.

McCorduck, P. 1979: *Machines Who Think.* San Francisco: W. H. Freeman.

MacCorquodale, K. and Meehl, P. E. 1948: On a distinction between hypothetical constructs and intervening variable. *Psychological Review* 85, 95–107.

McCracken, Grant: *Culture and Consumption: New*

Approaches to the Symbolic Character of Consumer Goods and Activities. Bloomington: Indiana University Press.

MacDonald, M. 1947–8: Natural rights. *Proceedings of the Aristotelian Society*, 35–55.

Mach, Ernst 1886 (*1959*): *The Analysis of Sensations, and the Relation of the Physical to the Psychical.* New York: Dover.

Mach, Ernst 1894: *Popular Scientific Lectures.* Chicago.

Machajski, J. W. 1904 (*1937*): Fragments (on the expropriation of the capitalist class). In *Making of Society: an Outline of Sociology*, ed. V. F. Calverton. New York: Random House.

Macherey, Pierre 1966 (*1978*): *A Theory of Literary Production.* London and Boston: Routledge.

Machiavelli, N. 1513 (*1965*): *The Prince, Selections from the Discourses and Other Writings*, ed. J. Plamenatz. London: Fontana.

Machiavelli, N. 1970: *The Discourses.* Harmondsworth: Penguin.

McIntosh, M. 1978: The state and the oppression of women. In *Feminism and Materialism*, ed. A. Kuhn and A. M. Wolpe. London: Routledge.

McIntosh, Susan 1981: Leisure studies and women. In *Leisure and Social Control*, ed. Alan Tomlinson. Eastbourne: Leisure Studies Association.

MacIntyre, A. 1981 (*1985*): *After Virtue.* 2nd edn, London: Duckworth.

MacIntyre, A. 1988: *Whose Justice? Which Rationality?* London: Duckworth.

MacIntyre, A. C. 1958: *The Unconscious.* London: Routledge & Kegan Paul.

Mack, J. and Lansley, S. 1984: *Poor Britain.* London: Allen & Unwin.

McKendrick, Neil et al. 1982: *The Birth of a Consumer Society: the Commercialization of Eighteenth-Century England.* London: Europa.

McKenzie, N. and McKenzie, J. 1977: *The First Fabians.* London: Weidenfeld & Nicolson.

Mackenzie, W. J. M. 1955: Pressure groups in British Government. *British Journal of Sociology* 6, 133–48.

McKeown, T. 1976 (*1979*): *The Role of Medicine.* Oxford: Blackwell.

Mackie, J. L. 1965: Causes and conditions. *American Philosophical Quarterly* 2, 245–64.

Mackie, J. L. 1974: *The Cement of the Universe.* Oxford: Oxford University Press.

Mackie, J. L. 1977: *Ethics.* Harmondsworth: Penguin.

McLellan, David 1980: *The Thought of Karl Marx.* 2nd edn, London: Macmillan.

McLellan, David ed. 1983: *Marx: the First Hundred Years.* London: Fontana.

McLennan, J. F. 1865 (*1970*): *Primitive Marriage: an Inquiry into the Origin of the Form of Capture in Marriage Ceremonies*, ed. P. Rivière. Chicago: University of Chicago Press.

McLoughlin, W. 1959: *Modern Revivalism.* New York: Ronald Press.

McLoughlin, W. 1978: *Revivals, Awakenings and Reform.* Chicago: University of Chicago Press.

McLuhan, M. 1962: *The Gutenberg Galaxy.* London: Routledge.

McLuhan, M. 1964: *Understanding Media.* London: Routledge & Kegan Paul.

McNaulty, P. 1967: A note on the history of perfect competition. *Journal of Political Economy* 75, 395–9.

McNaulty, P. 1968: Economic theory and the meaning of competition. *Quarterly Journal of Economics* 82, 639–56.

McNees, S. K. 1988: How accurate are macroeconomic forecasts? *New England Economic Review* July–August, 15–36.

Macpherson, C. B. 1962: *The Political Theory of Possessive Individualism.* Oxford: Oxford University Press.

Macpherson, C. B. 1966: *The Real World of Democracy.* Oxford: Clarendon Press.

Macpherson, C. B. 1977: *The Life and Times of Liberal Democracy.* Oxford: Oxford University Press.

McQuail, Denis 1987: *Mass Communication Theory.* London: Sage.

McReynolds, P. and DeVoge, S. 1978: Use of improvisational techniques in assessment. In *Advances in Psychological Assessment*, vol. 4, ed. P. McReynolds. San Francisco: Jossey-Bass.

McWilliams, W. C. 1973: *The Idea of Fraternity in America.* Berkeley: University of California Press.

Maddison, A. 1982: *Phases of Capitalist Development.* Oxford: Oxford University Press.

Maddison, A. 1991: *Dynamic Forces in Capitalist Development.* Oxford: Oxford University Press.

Maddock, K. 1973: *The Australian Aborigines: a Portrait of their Society.* London: Allen Lane.

Madge, C. 1968: Introduction to *International*

Encyclopedia of the Social Sciences, vol.12. New York: Macmillan and Free Press.

Maffesoli, M. 1976: *Logique de la domination*. Paris: Presses Universitaires de France.

Maffesoli, M. 1979: *La Conquête du Présent: pour une sociologie de la vie quotidienne*. Paris: Presses Universitaires de France.

Maffesoli, M. 1982 (*1985*): *L'Ombre de Dionysus*. 2nd edn, Paris: Méridiéns.

Maffesoli, M. 1985: *La Connaissance ordinaire, précis de sociologie compréhensive*. Paris: Méridiéns.

Maffesoli, M. 1989: The sociology of everyday life. *Current Sociology* 37.1.

Magee, Bryan 1971: *Modern British Philosophy*. London: Secker & Warburg.

Magee, Bryan 1973: *Popper*. London: Fontana.

Magee, Bryan 1983: *The Philosophy of Schopenhauer*. Oxford: Clarendon Press.

Magnus, Philip 1958 (*1968*): *Kitchener: Portrait of an Imperialist*. Harmondsworth: Penguin.

Magraw, R. 1983: *France 1815–1914: the Bourgeois Century*. London: Fontana.

Mahar, J. M. ed. 1972: *The Untouchables in Contemporary India*. Tucson: University of Arizona Press.

Maier, C. 1988: *In Search of Stability*. Cambridge and New York: Cambridge University Press.

Mailer, Norman 1968: *Miami and the Siege of Chicago*. New York: Donald I. Fine.

Maine, Henry 1861: *Ancient Society*. London: Everyman.

Makkreel, R. A. 1975: *Dilthey: Philosopher of the Human Studies*. Princeton, NJ: Princeton University Press.

Malcolm, Janet 1982: *Psychoanalysis: the Impossible Profession*. London: Picador.

Malinowski, B. 1922: *Argonauts of the Western Pacific*. London: Routledge & Kegan Paul.

Malinowski, B. 1925 (*1948*): *Magic, Science and Religion and Other Essays*. Glencoe, IL: Free Press.

Malinowski, B. 1932: *Crime and Custom in Savage Society*. London: Paul Trench, Trubner.

Malinowski, B. 1944: The functional theory. In *A Scientific Theory of Culture and Other Essays*. Chapel Hill: University of North Carolina Press.

Malinvaud, E. 1967: Decentralised procedures for planning. In *Activity Analysis in the Theory of Growth and Planning*, ed. E. Malinvaud and M. O. L. Bacharach. London: Macmillan.

Mallet, Serge 1975: *The New Working Class*. Nottingham: Spokesman.

Malloy, J. ed. 1977: *Authoritarianism and Corporatism in Latin America*. Pittsburgh: Pittsburgh University Press.

Maloney, J. 1976: Marshall, Cunningham and the emerging economics profession. *Economic History Review* 29, 440–51.

Malthus, Thomas 1798 (*1970*): *An Essay on the Principle of Population*. Harmondsworth: Penguin.

Mandel, E. 1970 (*1973*): *Workers' Control, Workers' Councils and Self-Management*, 3 vols. London.

Mandel, E. 1975: *Late Capitalism*. London: New Left Books.

Mandel, E. 1977: The Leninist theory of organization. In *Revolution and Class Struggle: a Reader in Marxist Politics*, ed. R. Blackburn. Glasgow: Fontana.

Mandel, E. 1979: *Revolutionary Marxism Today*. London: New Left Books.

Mandel, E. 1980: *Long Waves of Capitalist Development: the Marxist Interpretation*. Cambridge: Cambridge University Press.

Mandel, E. 1986: In defence of socialist planning. *New Left Review* 159, 5–38.

Mandel, E. 1988: The myth of market socialism. *New Left Review* 169, 108–21.

Manicas, Peter 1987: *A History and Philosophy of the Social Sciences*. Oxford: Blackwell.

Mann, M. 1973: *Consciousness and Action among the Western Working Class*. London: Macmillan.

Mann, M. 1986: *Sources of Social Power*, vol. 1, *A History of Power from the Beginning to AD 1760*. Cambridge: Cambridge University Press.

Mann, M. 1988: Ruling class strategies and citizenship. *Sociology* 21, 339–54.

Mann, M. 1988: *States, War and Capitalism*. Oxford: Blackwell.

Mannheim, K. 1929 (*1936, 1960*): *Ideology and Utopia: an Introduction to the Sociology of Knowledge*. London: Routledge.

Mannheim, K. 1940: *Man and Society in an Age of Reconstruction*. London: Routledge & Kegan Paul.

Mannheim, K. 1952: The problem of generations. In *Essays on the Sociology of Knowledge*, ed. P. Kecskemeti. London: Routledge & Kegan Paul.

Mannheim, K. 1956: *Essays on the Sociology of Culture*. London: Routledge & Kegan Paul.

Manove, M. 1971: A model of Soviet-type economic planning. *American Economic Review*, June.

Mansfield, Peter 1971: *The British in Egypt*. London: Weidenfeld & Nicolson.

Mao Zedong 1986: *The Writings of Mao Zedong*, vol. 1, ed. M. Kau and J. Leung. New York: M. E. Sharpe.

Maravall, J. M. 1979: The limits of reformism: parliamentary socialism and the Marxist theory of the state. *British Journal of Sociology* 30, 267–90.

March, J. G. 1976: The technology of foolishness. In *Ambiguity and Choice in Organizations*, ed. J. G. March and J. P. Olsen. Bergen: Universitetsforlaget.

March, James and Simon, Herbert 1958: *Organizations*. New York: John Wiley.

Marcuse, Herbert 1937: Philosophie und kritische Theorie. *Zeitschrift für Sozialforschung* 6, 632–47.

Marcuse, Herbert 1941 (*1955*): *Reason and Revolution: Hegel and the Rise of Social Theory*. New York: Oxford University Press.

Marcuse, Herbert 1955: *Eros and Civilization: a Philosophical Inquiry into Freud*. Boston: Beacon Press.

Marcuse, Herbert 1964: *One-Dimensional Man: the Ideology of Industrial Society*. London: Routledge & Kegan Paul; Boston: Beacon Press.

Marcuse, Herbert 1969: *An Essay on Liberation*. Boston: Beacon Press.

Marcuse, Herbert 1978: *Schriften*. Frankfurt am Main: Suhrkamp.

Marglin, S. A. 1974–5: What do bosses do? The origins and function of hierarchy in capitalist production. *Review of Radical Political Economics* 6.2, 60–112; 7.1, 20–37.

Marglin, S. A. 1984: *Growth, Distribution, and Prices*. Cambridge, MA, and London: Harvard University Press.

Margolis, Joseph 1980: *Art and Philosophy: Conceptual Issues in Aesthetics*. Atlantic Highlands, NJ: Humanities Press.

Margolis, Joseph, ed. 1987: *Philosophy Looks at the Arts*. Philadelphia: Temple University Press.

Maris, R. 1969: *Social Forces in Urban Suicide*. State of Illinois: Dorsey Press.

Marković, Mihailo 1974: *From Affluence to Praxis: Philosophy and Social Criticism*. Ann Arbor: University of Michigan Press.

Marković, Mihailo and Cohen, Robert S. 1975: *Yugoslavia: the Rise and Fall of Socialist Humanism*. Nottingham: Spokesman.

Marks, Elaine and Courtivron, Isabelle de eds 1980: *New French Feminisms*. Brighton: Harvester.

Marlatt, A. and Gordon, J. 1985: *Relapse Prevention*. New York: Guilford Press.

Marmot, M. G. et al. 1984: Inequalities in death: specific explanations of a general pattern? *Lancet* I, 1003–6.

Marr, D. 1982: *Vision*. Oxford: Freeman.

Marris, P. 1982: *Community Planning and Conceptions of Change*. London: Routledge & Kegan Paul.

Marsh, C. 1982: *The Survey Method: the Contribution of Surveys to Sociological Explanation*. London: Allen & Unwin.

Marsh, D. ed. 1983: *Pressure Politics: Interest Groups in Britain*. London: Junction Books.

Marsh, P. 1978: *Aggro: the Illusion of Violence*. London: Dent.

Marsh, P. 1982: Rhetorics of violence. In *Aggression and Violence*, ed. P. Marsh and A. Campbell. Oxford: Blackwell.

Marshall, A. 1890 (*1920*): *Principles of Economics*. 8th edn, London: Macmillan.

Marshall, G. 1982: *In Search of the Spirit of Capitalism: an Essay on Max Weber's Protestant Ethic Thesis*. London: Hutchinson.

Marshall, G. et al. 1988: *Social Class in Modern Britain*. London: Unwin Hyman.

Marshall, T. H. 1938: *Class Conflict and Stratification*. London: The Play House.

Marshall, T. H. 1950 (*1992*): *Citizenship and Social Class*. London: Pluto Press.

Marshall, T. H. 1965: *Class, Citizenship and Social Development*. Golden City, NY: Anchor.

Marshall, T. H. 1967: *Social Policy in the Twentieth Century*. 2nd edn, London: Hutchinson.

Marshall, T. H. 1970 (*1985*): *Social Policy*. London: Hutchinson.

Marshall, T. H. 1981: *The Right to Welfare and Other Essays*. London: Heinemann.

Martin, B. M. et al. 1986: *Intellectual Suppression: Australian Case Histories, Analysis and Responses*. Sydney and London: Angus & Robertson.

Martin, Bernice 1981: *A Sociology of Contemporary Cultural Change*. Oxford: Blackwell.

Martin, C. J. and McQueen, D. V. 1989: *Readings for a New Public Health*. Edinburgh: Edinburgh University Press.

Martin, David. A. 1969: *The Religious and the Secular: Studies in Secularization*. London: Routledge & Kegan Paul.

Martin, David. A. 1978: *A General Theory of Secularization*. Oxford: Blackwell.

Martin, K. 1937: *The Magic of Monarchy*. London: Nelson.

Martin, K. 1962: *The Crown and the Establishment*. London: Hutchinson.

Martin, P. and Bateson, P. 1986: *Measuring Behaviour*. Cambridge: Cambridge University Press.

Martin, R. and Rowthorn, R. eds 1986: *The Geography of De-industrialisation*. London: Macmillan.

Martin, Ross 1989: *Trade Unionism.* Oxford: Clarendon Press.

Marx, K. 1843 (*1975*): Contribution to the critique of Hegel's philosphy of law: introduction. In K. Marx and F. Engels, *Collected Works*, vol. 3. London: Lawrence & Wishart.

Marx, K. 1844 (*1967*): *Economic and Philosophical (Paris) Manuscripts*. Moscow: Progress.

Marx, K. 1845 (*1967*): Theses on Feuerbach. In *Karl Marx: Selected Writings in Sociology and Social Philosophy*, ed. Tom Bottomore and Maximilien Rubel. Harmondsworth: Penguin.

Marx, K. 1847: *The Poverty of Philosophy*. Paris: A. Franck.

Marx, K. 1850 (*1973*): The class struggles in France, 1848–50. In *Surveys from Exile*. Harmondsworth: Penguin.

Marx, K. 1852 (*1973*) The eighteenth brumaire of Louis Bonaparte. In *Surveys from Exile*. Harmondsworth: Penguin.

Marx, K. 1857–8 (*1973*): *Grundrisse*. Harmondsworth: Penguin.

Marx, K. 1859 (*1971*): *A Contribution to the Critique of Political Economy*. London: Lawrence & Wishart.

Marx, K. 1861–79 (*1905–10*): *Theories of Surplus Value*, ed. Karl Kautsky. Stuttgart: J. H. W. Dietz Nacht.

Marx, K. 1867 (*1976*): *Capital*, vol. 1. Harmondsworth: Penguin.

Marx, K. 1871 (*1968*): The civil war in France. In *Marx and Engels: Selected Works in One Volume*. London: Lawrence & Wishart.

Marx, K. 1885 (*1933*): *Capital*, vol. 2, *The Process of Circulation of Capital*, ed. F. Engels. Chicago: Charles H. Kerr.

Marx, K. 1894 (*1972*): *Capital*, vol. 3, *The Process of Capitalist Production as a Whole*. London: Lawrence & Wishart.

Marx, K. 1898 (*1950*): Wages, price and profit. In K. Marx and F. Engels, *Selected Works in Two Volumes*. London: Lawrence & Wishart.

Marx, K. 1975: *Early Writings*. Harmondsworth: Penguin.

Marx, K. 1964: *Pre-capitalist Economic Formations*, ed. E. J. Hobsbawm. London: Lawrence & Wishart.

Marx, K. and Engels, F. 1845–6 (*1970*): *The German Ideology*. London: Lawrence & Wishart.

Marx, K. and Engels, F. 1848 (*1967*): *The Communist Manifesto*. Harmondsworth: Penguin.

Marx, K. and Engels, F. 1850 (*1975*): Address of the Central Authority to the League, March 1850. In *Collected Works*, vol. 10. London: Lawrence & Wishart.

Marx, K. and Engels, F. 1969: *Selected Works in Three Volumes*. Moscow: Progress.

Marx, K. and Engels F. 1975: *Marx–Engels Selected Correspondence*. Moscow: Progress.

Maslow, A. H. 1968: *Toward a Psychology of Being*. New York: Van Nostrand.

Maslow, A. H. 1987: *Motivation and Personality*. 3rd edn, New York: Harper & Row.

Mason, E. S. 1939: Price and production policies of large-scale enterprise. *American Economic Review (Papers and Proceedings)* 29, 61–74.

Massey, D. 1984: *Spatial Divisions of Labour: Social Structures and the Geography of Production*. London: Methuen.

Massing, Paul W. 1967: *Rehearsal for Destruction*. New York: Howard Fertig.

Masters, W. H. et al. 1982: *Masters and Johnson on Sex and Human Loving*. Boston and Toronto: Little, Brown.

Masuda, Yoneji 1980 (*1981*): *The Information Society as Post-Industrial Society*. Bethesda, MD: World Future Society.

Matejka, L. and Pomorska, K., eds 1971: *Readings in Russian Poetics*. Cambridge, MA: MIT Press.

Mathieson, Margaret 1975: *The Preachers of Culture*. London: Allen & Unwin.

Matthews, Fred. H. 1977: *Quest for an American Sociology: Robert E. Park and the Chicago School*. Montreal and London: McGill–Queens University Press.

Matthews, R. C. O. 1968: Why has Britain had full employment since the war? *Economic Journal* 88, 555–69.

Matthiae, Paolo 1980: *Elba: an Empire Rediscovered*. London: Hodder & Stoughton.

Mattick, Paul 1975: *Spontaneität und Organisation*. Frankfurt am Main: Suhrkamp.

Maturana, U. 1982: *Erkennen*. Braunschweig.

Matza, D. 1966: The disreputable poor. In *Class, Status and Power*, ed. R. Bendix and S. M. Lipset. London: Routledge & Kegan Paul.

Matza, D. 1969: *Becoming Deviant*. Englewood Cliffs, NJ: Prentice-Hall.

Mauss, M. 1925 (*1954*): *The Gift*. London: Cohen & West.

Mauss, M. 1935 (*1973*): Les techniques du corps. Trans. in *Economy and Society* 2.1, 70–88.

Mauss, M. and Beuchat, H. 1906 (*1979*): *Seasonal Variations of the Eskimo: a Study in Social Morphology*. London: Routledge & Kegan Paul.

Mauss, M. and Hubert, H. 1904 (*1972*): *A General Theory of Magic*. London: Routledge & Kegan Paul.

Mayer, Arno J. 1988: *Why Did the Heavens Not Darken?* New York: Pantheon.

Mayer, Kurt B. and Buckley, Walter 1970: *Class and Society*. New York: Random House.

Mayer, R. H. 1972: *Social Planning and Social Change*. Englewood Cliffs, NJ: Prentice-Hall.

Mayer, T. ed. 1978: *The Structure of Monetarism*. New York: Norton.

Mayhew, H. 1851–62: *London Labour and the London Poor*. London.

Mayhew, P. et al. 1989: *The 1988 British Crime Survey*. London: HMSO.

Maynard Smith, J. 1958 (*1975*): *The Theory of Evolution*. 3rd edn, Harmondsworth: Penguin.

Maynard Smith, J. 1984: *Evolution and the Theory of Games*. Cambridge: Cambridge University Press.

Mayo, Elton: 1933 (*1946*): *The Human Problems of an Industrial Civilization*. 2nd edn, Cambridge, MA: Harvard University Press.

Mayo, Elton 1945: *The Social Problems of an Industrial Civilization*. Cambridge, MA: Harvard University Press.

Mayr, E. 1982: *The Growth of Biological Thought*. Cambridge, MA: Harvard University Press.

Mazrui, A. A. 1977: *Africa's International Relations: the Diplomacy of Dependency and Change*. London: Heinemann.

Mead, G. H. 1918: The psychology of punitive justice. *American Journal of Sociology* 23, 577–602.

Mead, G. H. 1934 (*1962*): *Mind, Self and Society*, ed. Charles W. Morris. Chicago: University of Chicago Press.

Mead, G. H. *1964*: *Selected Writings*, ed. A. J. Reck. Indianapolis: Bobbs-Merrill.

Meadows, D. H. et al. 1972: *Limits to Growth: a Report for the Club of Rome's Project on the Predicament of Mankind*. New York: Universe Books; London: Earth Island.

Medvedev, R. 1981: The dictatorship of the proletariat. In *Leninism and Western Socialism*. London: Verso.

Medvedev, Z. A. 1969: *The Rise and Fall of T. D. Lysenko*. New York: Columbia University Press.

Meidner, Rudolf 1978: *Employee Investment Funds: an Approach to Collective Capital Formation*. London: Allen & Unwin.

Meier, C. 1983 (*1990*): *The Greek Discovery of Politics*. Cambridge, MA: Harvard University Press.

Meillassoux, C. 1981: *Maidens, Meal and Money*. Cambridge: Cambridge University Press.

Meinecke, Friedrich 1946 (*1972*): *Historicism: the Rise of a New Historical Outlook*. London: Routledge & Kegan Paul.

Meisner, M. 1977: *Mao's China*. New York: Free Press.

Meisner, M. 1982: *Marxism, Maoism and Utopianism*. Madison: University of Wisconsin Press.

Meisner, M. 1986: *Mao's China and After*. New York: Free Press.

Meja, Volker and Stehr, Nico eds 1990: *Knowledge and Politics: the Sociology of Knowledge Dispute*. London: Routledge.

Melden, A. I. 1959: *Rights and Right Conduct*. Oxford: Blackwell.

Melden, A. I. 1961: *Free Action*. London: Routledge & Kegan Paul.

Melden, A. I. 1977: *Rights and Persons*. Oxford: Blackwell.

Mellor, D. H. ed. 1990: *Ways of Communicating*. Cambridge: Cambridge University Press.

Melnyk, G. 1985: *The Search for Community: From Utopia to a Co-operative Society*. Montreal: Black Rose Books.

Menger, C. 1883 (*1985*): *Investigations in the Method of the Social Sciences with Special Reference to Economics*. New York: New York University Press.

Menninger, K. 1938: *Man Against Himself*. New York: Harcourt, Brace.

Menze, E. A. ed. 1981: *Totalitarianism Reconsidered*. London: Kennikat Press.

Merchant, C. 1980: *The Death of Nature, Women, Ecology and the Scientific Revolution*. New York: Harper & Row.

Merleau-Ponty, Maurice 1945 (*1962*): *Phenomenology of Perception*. London: Routledge & Kegan Paul.

Merleau-Ponty, Maurice 1955 (*1973*): *Adventures of the Dialectic*. Evanston, IL: Northwestern University Press.

Merquior, J. G. 1975: *The Politics of Obedience: the Discourse of Voluntary Servitude*. Montreal: Black Rose Books.

Merquior, J. G. 1986: *Western Marxism*. London: Paladin.

Merquior, J. G. 1980: *Rousseau and Weber: a Study in the Theory of Legitimacy*. London: Routledge & Kegan Paul.

Merrington, J. and Marazzi, C. 1977: Notes on money, crisis and the state. *CSE Conference Papers*. London.

Merton, R. K. 1938: Social structure and anomie. *American Sociological Review* 8, 672–82.

Merton, R. K. 1949 (*1968*): *Social Theory and Social Structure*. Rev. edn, New York: Free Press.

Merton, R. K. 1957: Role-set: problems in sociological theory. *British Journal of Sociology* 8, 106–20.

Merton, R. K. 1961 (*1976*): Introduction. In *Contemporary Social Problems*, ed. R. K. Merton and R. A. Nisbet. New York: Harcourt, Brace Jovanovich.

Merton. R. K. 1973: *The Sociology of Science: Theoretical and Empirical Investigations*. Chicago and London: University of Chicago Press.

Merton, Robert K. and Nisbet, Robert eds 1961 (*1976*): *Contemporary Social Problems*. 4th edn, New York: Harcourt, Brace Jovanovich.

Mertz, J. T. 1914: *History of European Thought in the Nineteenth Century*, 4 vols. Vol. 4, *On Society*. London.

Mészáros, István 1970: *Marx's Theory of Alienation*. London: Merlin Press.

Metz, J.-B. 1968: The church's social function in the light of political theology. *Concilium* 6.4, 3.

Metz, J.-B. 1969: *Theology of the World*. New York: Herder & Herder.

Meyer, A. G. 1962: *Leninism*. New York: Praeger.

Meyer, Michael A. 1988: *Response to Modernity: a History of the Reform Movement in Judaism*. Oxford.

Meyers, William R. 1981: *The Evaluation Enterprise*. San Francisco: Jossey-Bass.

Meynaud, Jean 1965: *Technocracy*. London: Faber & Faber.

Meyrowitz, Joshua 1985: *No Sense of Place*. New York: Oxford University Press.

Michels, Roberto 1911 (*1949, 1962*): *Political Parties: a Sociological Study of the Oligarchical Tendencies of Modern Democracy*. New York: Free Press.

Michie, D. 1974: *On Machine Intelligence*. Edinburgh: Edinburgh University Press.

Midgley, M. 1978: *Beast and Man*. Brighton: Harvester.

Mies, Maria 1986: *Patriarchy and Accumulation on a World Scale: Women in the International Division of Labour*. London: Zed Books.

Milbank, J. 1990: *Theology and Social Theory: Beyond Secular Reason*. Oxford: Blackwell.

Miles, I. 1985: *Social Indicators for Human Development*. London: Frances Pinter.

Miles, Ian et al. 1988: *IT Horizons: the Long-Term Social Implications of New Information Technology*. Aldershot: Edward Elgar.

Miles, R. 1982: *Racism and Migrant Labour: a Critical Text*. London: Routledge.

Miles, R. 1989: *Racism*. London: Routledge.

Milgram, Stanley 1974: *Obedience to Authority*. London: Tavistock.

Miliband, R. 1969: *The State in Capitalist Society*. London: Weidenfeld & Nicolson.

Miliband, R. 1983: *Class Power and State Power*. London: Verso.

Miliband, R. 1989: *Divided Societies: Class Struggle in Contemporary Capitalism*. Oxford: Clarendon Press.

Mill, James 1972: *The History of British India*. London and New Delhi: Associated Publishing House.

Mill, John Stuart 1859 (*1991*): *On Liberty and Other Essays*. Oxford: World's Classics.

Mill, John Stuart 1863 (*1957*): *Utilitarianism*. Indianapolis: Bobbs-Merrill.

Miller, D. 1984: *Anarchism*. London: Dent.

Miller, D. 1990: Equality. In *Philosophy and Politics*, ed. G. M. K. Hunt. Cambridge: Cambridge University Press.

Miller, D. and Siedentop, L. eds 1983: *The Nature of Political Theory*. Oxford: Clarendon Press.

Miller, Daniel, 1987: *Material Culture and Mass Consumption*. Oxford: Blackwell.

Miller, David 1976: *Social Justice*. Oxford: Clarendon.

Miller, G. A. 1981: *Language and Speech*. Oxford: Freeman.

Miller, James 1987: *Democracy is in the Streets: from Port Huron to the Siege of Chicago*. New York: Simon & Schuster.

Miller, Michael B. 1981: *The Bon Marché: Bourgeois Culture and the Department Store 1869–1920*. Princeton, NJ: Princeton University Press.

Miller, S. M. and Riessman, F. 1968: *Social Class and Social Policy*. New York: Basic Books.

Millerson, G. 1964: *The Qualifying Associations: a Study in Professionalization*. London: Routledge & Kegan Paul.

Millett, Kate 1970: *Sexual Politics*. London: Sphere.

Mills, C. W. 1948: *The New Men of Power*. New York: Harcourt, Brace.

Mills, C. W. 1951: *White Collar*. New York: Oxford University Press.

Mills, C. W. 1956: *The Power Elite*. New York and Oxford: Oxford University Press.

Mills, C. W. 1959: *The Sociological Imagination*. New York: Oxford University Press.

Milne, A. J. M. 1968: *Freedom and Rights*. London: Allen & Unwin.

Milton, John 1925: Areopagitica. In *Milton's Prose: a Selection*. Oxford: Oxford University Press.

Milton, John 1981: The origins and development of the concept 'law of nature'. *European Journal of Sociology* 23.

Mingione, Enzo 1986: Urban sociology. In *The Social Reproduction of Organization and Culture*, ed. Ulf Himmelstrand. London: Sage.

Mingione, Enzo 1991: *Fragmented Societies*. Oxford: Blackwell.

Minois, Georges 1987 (*1989*): *History of Old Age: From Antiquity to the Renaissance*. Cambridge: Polity.

Minsky, H. 1975: *John Maynard Keynes*. New York: Columbia University Press.

Minsky, M. 1967: *Computation: Finite and Infinite Machines*. Englewood Cliffs, NJ: Prentice-Hall.

Mintz, B. and Schwartz, M. 1985: *The Power Structure of American Business*. Chicago: University of Chicago Press.

Mishan, E. 1967: *The Costs of Economic Growth*. London: Staples Press.

Mishra, R. 1981: *Society and Social Policy*. 2nd edn, London: Macmillan.

Mishra, R. 1984: *The Welfare State in Crisis: Social Thought and Action*. Brighton: Wheatsheaf.

Mitchell, A. 1977: Bonapartism as a model for Bismarckian politics. *Journal of Modern History* 49, 181–99.

Mitchell, C. R. 1981: *Peacemaking and the Consultant's Role*. Farnborough and New York: Gower.

Mitchell, J. 1974 (*1984*): *Women's Estates*. Harmondsworth: Penguin.

Mitchell, J. 1974 (*1984*): *Women: the Longest Revolution*. Harmondsworth: Penguin.

Mitchell, J. 1975: *Psychoanalysis and Feminism*. Harmondsworth: Penguin.

Mitchell, W. 1973: The hydraulic hypothesis: a reappraisal. *Current Anthropology* 14, 532–4.

Mitrany, D. 1946: *A Working Peace System*. London: Chatham House.

Mitterauer, Michael and Sieder, Reinhard 1982: *The European Family*. Chicago: University of Chicago Press.

Moe, T. M. 1980: *The Organization of Interests: Incentives and the Internal Dynamics of Political Interest Groups*. Chicago: University of Chicago Press.

Moers, Ellen 1978: *Literary Women*. London: Women's Press.

Moggridge, D. E. 1976: *Keynes*. Glasgow: Fontana.

Moi, Toril 1985: *Sexual/Textual Politics*. London and New York: Methuen.

Moi, Toril, ed. 1987: *French Feminist Thought: a Reader*. Oxford: Blackwell.

Moles, Robert 1987: *Definition and Rule in Legal Theory*. Oxford: Blackwell.

Moll, Peter 1991: *From Scarcity to Sustainability: Futures Studies and the Environment*. Frankfurt am Main and New York: Peter Lang.

Mollat, M. 1978: *Les Pauvres au moyen Age*. Paris: Hachette.

Moller, H. 1968: Youth as a force in the modern world. *Comparative Studies in Society and History* 10, 237–60.

Molyneux, M. 1979: Beyond the domestic labour debate. *New Left Review* 116, 3–38.

Momigliano, A. 1956: Per un riesame della storia dell'idea di Cesarismo. In *Cesare nel bimillenario della morte*, ed. Radio Italiana. Turin: Radio Italiana.

Momigliano, A. 1962: J. Burckhardt e la parola 'Cesarismo'. *Rivista storica italiana* 74, 369–71.

Mommsen, T. 1901: *The History of Rome*, 5 vols. London: Everyman.

Mommsen, Wolfgang J. 1974: *The Age of Bureaucracy: Perspectives on the Political Sociology of Max Weber*. Oxford: Blackwell.

Mommsen, Wolfgang J. 1977: Max Weber as critic of Marxism. *Canadian Journal of Sociology* 2, 373–98.

Mommsen, Wolfgang J. ed. 1981: *The Emergence of the Welfare State in Britain and Germany*. London: Croom Helm.

Mommsen, Wolfgang J. 1981: Max Weber and Roberto Michels: an asymmetrical partnership. *European Journal of Sociology* 22.1, 100–16.

Mommsen, Wolfgang J. and Osterhammel, Jürgen eds 1986: *Imperialism and After: Continuities and Discontinuities*. London: Allen & Unwin.

Monat, Jacques and Sarfate, Hedva 1986: *Workers' Participation: a Voice in Decisions, 1981–85*. Geneva: ILO.

Money, J. and Musaph, H. eds 1977: *Handbook of Sexology*. New York: Elsevier North-Holland.

Montagu, Ashley 1972: *Statement on Race*. Oxford: Oxford University Press.

Montague, R. 1974: *Formal Philosophy*. New Haven, CT: Yale University Press.

Montesquieu, C. 1749 (*1962*): *The Spirit of the Laws*. 2 vols., London: Hafner.

Moore, Barrington Jr 1967: *Social Origins of Dictatorship and Democracy*. Harmondsworth: Penguin.

Moore, Barrington Jr 1972: *Reflections of the Causes of Human Misery*. London: Allen Lane.

Moore, G. E. 1903a: The refutation of Idealism. *Mind* 12.

Moore, G. E. 1903b (*1959*): *Principia Ethica*. Cambridge: Cambridge University Press.

Moore, G. E. 1925 (*1959*): A defence of common sense. In *Philosophical Papers*. London: Allen & Unwin.

Moore, G. H. 1983: *Business Cycles, Inflation and Forecasting*. 2nd edn, Cambridge, MA: Ballinger.

Moore, S. 1980: *Marx on the Choice between Socialism and Communism*. Cambridge, MA: Harvard University Press.

Moore, S. F. and Myerhoff, B. G., eds 1977: *Secular Ritual*. Assen: Van Gorcum.

Moore, W. E. 1963: But some are more equal than others. *American Sociological Review* 28, 13–28.

Moore, W. E. 1963: *Social Change*. Englewood Cliffs, NJ: Prentice-Hall.

Morawski, Stefan 1973: *O przedmiocie i metodzie estetyki*. Warsaw: Ksigzka i Wiedze.

Morawski, Stefan 1987: Czy zmierzch estetyki? In *Zmierzch estetyki: rzekomy czy autentyczny?* Warsaw: Czytelnik.

More, Thomas 1516 (*1965*): *Utopia*. Harmondsworth: Penguin.

Moreno, J. L. 1934 (*1953*): *Who Shall Survive?* Beacon, NY: Beacon House.

Morgan, G. 1986: *Images of Organization*. London: Sage.

Morgan, L. H. 1871: *Systems of Consanguinity and Affinity of the Human Family*. Washington, DC: Smithsonian Institution.

Morgan, L. H. 1877 (*1963*): *Ancient Society: Researches in the Lines of Human Progress from Savagery through Barbarism to Civilization*, ed. E. B. Leacock. Cleveland and New York: World.

Morgan, Robin 1984: *Sisterhood is Global: the International Women's Movement Anthology*. New York: Anchor.

Morgan, R. and Smith, D. J. eds 1989: *Coming to Terms with Policing*. London and New York: Routledge.

Morgenthau, H. J. 1951 (*1952*): *American Foreign Policy*. London: Methuen.

Morgenthau, H. J. 1968: *Politics among Nations*. New York: Knopf.

Morin, Edgar et al. 1968: *Mai 68: la brèche*. Paris: Fayard.

Morison, Samuel Eliot et al. 1970: *Dissent in Three American Wars*. Cambridge, MA: Harvard University Press.

Morris, A. 1987: *Women, Crime and Criminal Justice*. Oxford: Blackwell.

Morris, C. 1971: *Writings on the General Theory of Signs*. The Hague: Mouton.

Morriss, P. 1987: *Power: a Philosophical Analysis*. Manchester: Manchester University Press.

Morson, G. and Emerson, C. 1990: *Mikhail Bakhtin: Creation of a Prosaics*. Stanford, CA: Stanford University Press.

Mosca, G. 1896 (*1939*): *The Ruling Class*, ed. Arthur Livingston. New York: McGraw-Hill.

Moseley, K. P. and Wallerstein, I. 1978: Precapitalist social structures. *Annual Review of Sociology* 4, 259–90.

Moser, C. A. and Kalton, G. 1971: *Survey Methods in Social Investigation*. London: Heinemann.

Mosetič, Gerald 1987: *Die Gesellschaftstheorie des*

Austromarxismus. Darmstadt: Wissenschaftlische Buchgesellschaft.

Moskos, C. C. 1976: The Military. *Annual Review of Sociology* 2, 55–77.

Moskos, C. C. 1988: Institutional and occupational trends in armed forces. In *The Military: More than Just a Job*, ed. C. C. Moskos and F. R. Wood. Washington, DC: Pergamon-Brassey's.

Mosse, George L. 1964: *The Crisis of German Ideology*. New York: Grosset & Dunlop.

Mosse, George L. 1971: Caesarism, circuses and monuments. *Journal of Contemporary History* 6, 167–82.

Mosse, George L. 1975: *The Nationalization of the Masses*. New York: Howard Fertig.

Mosse, George L. 1978: *Toward the Final Solution: a History of European Racism*. London: Dent.

Mouffe, C. 1979: Hegemony and ideology in Gramsci. In *Gramsci and Marxist Theory*. London: Routledge & Kegan Paul.

Moulin, Raymonde 1967: *Le Marché de la peinture en France*. Paris: Minuit.

Mouzelis, N. P. 1986: *Politics in the Semi-Periphery: Early Parliamentarism and Late Industrialisation in the Balkans and Latin America*. London: Macmillan.

Mowery, D. C. and Rosenberg, N. 1989: *Technology and the Pursuit of Economic Growth*. Cambridge: Cambridge University Press.

Mukerji, Chandra 1983: *From Graven Images: Patterns of Modern Materialism*. New York: Columbia University Press.

Mulhern, Francis 1979: *The Moment of 'Scrutiny'*. London: Verso.

Mulkay, M. 1979: *Science and the Sociology of Knowledge*. London: Allen & Unwin.

Mulkay, M. 1985: *The Word and the World: Explorations in the Form of Sociological Analysis*. London: Allen & Unwin.

Müller-Doohm, Stefan ed. 1992: *Verstehen und Methoden*. Frankfurt am Main: Suhrkamp.

Müller-Jentsch, Walther 1990: Works council. In *Concise Encyclopedia of Participation and Co-Management*, ed. György Szell. Berlin and New York: de Gruyter.

Mumford, Lewis 1934 (*1963*): *Technics and Civilization*. New York: Harcourt, Brace, World.

Mumford, Lewis 1966: *The City in History*. Harmondsworth: Penguin.

Mumford, Lewis 1967: *The Myth of the Machine*. New York: Harcourt, Brace, Jovanovich.

Munck, Ronaldo 1988: *The New International Labour Studies*. London: Zed.

Munro, Thomas 1956: *Towards Science in Aesthetics*. New York: Liberal Art Press.

Murdock, G. P. 1949: *Social Structure*. New York and London: Macmillan

Murdock, George 1967: *Ethnographic Atlas*. Pittsburgh: University of Pittsburgh Press.

Murmis, Miguel and Portantiero, Juan Carlos 1971: *Estudios sobre los orígenes del peronismo*. Buenos Aires: Siglo Veintiunto.

Murray, H. A. 1959: Preparations for the scaffolding of a comprehensive system. In *Psychology: a Study of a Science*, ed. S. Koch. New York: McGraw-Hill.

Muth, J. F. 1961: Rational expectations and the theory of price movements. *Econometrica* 29, 315–35.

Myers, L. H. 1935 (*1984*): *The Root and the Flower*. London: Secker & Warburg.

Myrdal, G. 1944 (*1962*): *An American Dilemma*. New York: Harper & Brothers.

Myrdal, G. 1953: *The Political Element in the Development of Economic Theory*. London: Routledge & Kegan Paul.

Nadeau, Maurice 1968: *The History of Surrealism*. London: Jonathan Cape.

Naess, A. 1973: The shallow and the deep, long-range ecology movement: a summary. *Inquiry* 16.

Naess, A. 1989: *Ecology, Community and Lifestyle*, ed. D. Rothenburg. Cambridge: Cambridge University Press.

Nairn, T. 1988: *The Enchanted Glass: Britain and its Monarchy*. London: Radius.

Namier, L. 1958: The first mountebank dictator. In *Vanished Supremacies*. London: Hamish Hamilton.

Naphtali, Fritz 1928 (*1977*): *Wirtschaftsdemokratie*. 4th edn, Frankfurt am Main: EVA.

Nash, J. 1951: Non-cooperative games. *Annals of Mathematics* 54, 286–95.

Natanson, Maurice, ed. 1970: *Phenomenology and Social Reality: Essays in Memory of Alfred Schutz*. The Hague: Martinus Nijhoff.

Nattiez, J. J. 1990: *Music and Discourse: Toward a Semiology of Music*, trans. C. Sabbate. Princeton, NJ: Princeton University Press.

Navarro, Vincente 1976: *Medicine under Capitalism*. London: Croom Helm.

Needham, R. 1962: *Structure and Sentiment: a Test*

Case in Social Anthropology. Chicago and London: University of Chicago Press.

Needham, R. 1973: Prescription. *Oceania* 42, 166–81.

Needham, R. ed. 1971: *Rethinking Kinship and Marriage.* London: Tavistock.

Needham, R. 1986: Alliance. *Oceania* 56, 165–80.

Negri, A. 1972: *Crisi dello stato-piano.* Florence: Clusf.

Negri, A. 1979 (*1984*): *Marx Beyond Marx,* trans. A. Negri. State of Massachusetts: Bergin & Gervey.

Neisser, U. 1976: *Cognition and Reality.* San Francisco: Freeman.

Nelkin, Dorothy and Pollak, Michael 1981: *The Atom Besieged.* Cambridge, MA: MIT Press.

Nell, E. J. ed. 1980: *Growth, Profits and Property: Essays in the Revival of Political Economy.* Cambridge: Cambridge University Press.

Nelson, R. R. 1987: *Understanding Technical Change as an Evolutionary Process.* Amsterdam: North Holland.

Nelson, Richard R. and Winter, Sidney G. 1981: *An Evolutionary Theory of Economic Change.* Cambridge, MA: Harvard University Press.

Nesbitt, E. M. 1991: '*My Dad's Hindu, My Mum's Side are Sikhs': Issues in Religious Identity.* Charlbury: National Foundation for Arts Education.

Nettl, B. 1983: *The Study of Ethnomusicology.* Urbana: University of Illinois Press.

Neumann, Franz 1942 (*1944*): *Behemoth.* New York: Oxford University Press.

Neumann, Franz 1957: Notes on the theory of dictatorship. In *The Democratic and the Authoritarian State,* ed. H. Marcuse. New York: Free Press.

Neumann, Franz 1978: *Wirtschaft, Staat, Demokratie: Aufsätze 1930–1954,* ed. Alfons Söllner. Frankfurt am Main: Suhrkamp.

Neurath, O. 1932a (*1959*): Sociology and physicalism. In *Logical Positivism,* ed. A. J. Ayer. Glencoe, IL: Free Press.

Neurath, O. 1932b (*1959*): Protocol sentences. In *Logical Positivism,* ed. A. J. Ayer. Glencoe, IL: Free Press.

Neuringer, C. 1976: Current developments in the study of suicidal thinking. In *Suicidology: Contemporary Developments,* ed. E. Schneidman. London: Grune & Stratton.

Newell, A. and Simon, H. 1972: *Human Problem Solving.* New York: Prentice-Hall.

Newell, A. and Simon, H. 1976 (*1981*): Computer science as an empirical enquiry. In *Mind Design,* ed. J. Haugeland. Cambridge, MA: MIT Press.

Newfield, Jack 1967: *A Prophetic Minority.* New York: New American Library.

Newman, G. 1976: *Comparative Deviance.* Elsevier.

Newman, K. S. 1983: *Law and Economic Organization: a Comparative Study of Preindustrial Societies.* Cambridge: Cambridge University Press.

Newmeyer, F. J. ed. 1988: *Linguistics: the Cambridge Survey,* 4 vols. Cambridge: Cambridge University Press.

Newton, J. 1988: *Preventing Mental Illness.* London: Routledge & Kegan Paul.

Nicholls, D. 1975: *The Pluralist State.* London: Macmillan.

Nichols, T. ed. 1980: *Capital and Labour: Studies in the Capitalist Labour Process.* London: Fontana.

Niebuhr, H. R. 1929 (*1957*): *The Social Sources of Denominationalism.* Cleveland: World.

Nielsen, K. and Patten, S. eds 1981: Marx and Morality. *Canadian Journal of Philosophy,* Supp. vol. 7.

Nielsen, K. and Pedersen, O. K. 1988: The negotiated economy: ideal and history. *Scandinavian Political Studies* 2, 79–101.

Nietzsche, F. 1873 (1954): On truth and lie in an extra-moral sense. In *The Portable Nietzsche,* ed. W. Kaufman. New York: Viking.

Nietzsche, F. 1901 (*1964*): *The Will to Power.* New York: Russell & Russell.

Nisbet, Robert 1953: *The Quest for Community.* New York: Oxford University Press.

Nisbet, Robert 1966: *The Sociological Tradition.* New York: Basic Books; London: Heinemann (1967).

Nisbet, Robert 1969: *Social Change and History.* New York: Oxford University Press.

Nisbet, Robert 1974: *The Sociology of Emile Durkheim.* New York: Oxford University Press.

Nisbet, Robert 1975: *The Twilight of Authority.* New York: Oxford University Press.

Nisbet, Robert 1976: *Sociology as an Art Form.* New York: Oxford University Press.

Nisbet, Robert 1980: *History of the Idea of Progress.* New York: Basic Books.

Nisbet, Robert 1986: *Conservatism.* London and Minneapolis.

Nisbet, Robert 1986: Developmentalism: a critical analysis. In *The Making of Modern Society*. Brighton: Wheatsheaf.

Nisbett, R. and Ross, L. 1980: *Human Inference*. Englewood Cliffs, NJ: Prentice-Hall.

Nissel, M. 1987: *People Count: a History of the General Register Office*. London: HMSO.

Nkrumah, K. 1963: *Africa Must Unite*. New York: Praeger.

Noakes, Jeremy and Pridham, G. eds 1983–8: *Nazism 1919–1945: a Documentary Reader*, 3 vols. (vol. 4 forthcoming).

Nochlin, Linda 1989: *Women, Art, and Power and Other Essays*. London: Thames & Hudson.

Noiriel, G. 1988: *Le Creuset français*. Paris: Seuil.

Nora, Simon and Minc, Alain 1978 (*1980*): *The Computerization of Society*. Cambridge, MA: MIT Press.

Nordlinger, E. 1967: *The Working-Class Tories: Authority, Deference, and Stable Democracy*. London: MacGibbon and Kee.

Norman, D. A. ed. 1981: *Perspectives on Cognitive Science*. State of New Jersey: Erlbaum.

North, C. C. 1926: *Social Differentiation*. Chapel Hill: University of North Carolina Press.

Notestein, F. W. 1945: Population: the Long-view. In *Food for the World*, ed. T. W. Schultz. Chicago: University of Chicago Press.

Nove, A. 1964: *Was Stalin Really Necessary?* London: Allen & Unwin.

Nove, A. 1977: *The Soviet Economic System*. London: Allen & Unwin.

Nove, A. 1983: *The Economics of Feasible Socialism*. London: Allen & Unwin.

Nove, A. 1987: Markets and socialism. *New Left Review* 161, 98–104.

Nove, A. and Nuti, D. M. eds 1972: *Socialist Economics*. Harmondsworth: Penguin.

Novikov, I. D. 1983: *Evolution of the Universe*. Cambridge: Cambridge University Press.

Nowak, L. 1983: *Property and Power: Towards a Non-Marxian Historical Materialism*. Dordrecht: Reidel.

Nozick, R. 1969: Newcomb's problem and two principles of choice. In *Essays in Honor of Carl Hempel*, ed. N. Rescher. Dordrecht: Reidel.

Nozick, R. 1974: *Anarchy, State, and Utopia*. New York: Basic Books; Oxford: Blackwell.

Nwodo, Christopher 1984: Philosophy of Art versus Aesthetics. *British Journal of Aesthetics* 24, 195–205.

Nyerere, J. 1968: *Freedom and Socialism*. Dar es Salaam: Oxford University Press.

Oakes, Guy, 1988: *Weber and Rickert: Concept Formation in the Cultural Sciences*. Cambridge, MA, and London: MIT Press.

Oakeshott, Michael 1962 (*1974*): *Rationalism in Politics and Other Essays*. 2nd edn, London: Methuen.

Oakeshott, Michael 1975: *Hobbes on Civil Association*. Oxford: Blackwell.

Oakeshott, Michael 1975 (*1991*): *On Human Conduct*. Oxford: Clarendon Press.

Oakley, A. 1974: *The Sociology of Housework*. Oxford: Martin Robertson.

Oakley, A. 1985: *Subject Woman*. Harmondsworth: Penguin.

Oberschall, A. ed. 1972: *The Establishment of Empirical Sociology: Studies in Continuity, Discontinuity and Institutionalisation*. New York: Harper & Row.

Oberschall, Anthony 1973: *Social Conflict and Social Movements*. Englewood Cliffs, NJ: Prentice-Hall.

O'Connor, J. 1973: *The Fiscal Crisis of the State*. New York: St Martin's Press.

O'Donnell, Guillermo 1973: *Modernization and Bureaucratic Authoritarianism: Studies in South American Politics*. Berkeley: University of California Press.

O'Donnell, Guillermo et al. eds 1986: *Transitions from Authoritarian Rule: Prospects for Democracy*. Baltimore: Johns Hopkins University Press.

O'Driscoll, Gerald P. Jr and Rizzo, Mario J. 1985: *The Economics of Time and Ignorance*. Oxford: Blackwell.

OECD 1963: *The Measurement of Scientific and Technical Activities*. Paris: OECD.

OECD 1963: *Report of Inter-Ministerial Meeting on Sciences*. Paris: OECD.

OECD 1963: *Science, Economic Growth and Government Policy*. Paris: OECD.

OECD 1988: *The Future of Social Protection*. Paris: OECD.

Oertzen, Peter V. 1963 (*1976*): *Betriebsräte in der Novemberrevolution*. 2nd edn, Berlin: Dietz.

Offe, C. 1976: *Industry and Inequality*. New York: St Martin's Press.

Offe, C. 1984: *Contradictions of the Welfare State*, ed. John Keane. Cambridge, MA: MIT Press.

Offe, C. 1985: *Disorganized Capitalism*, ed. John Keane. Cambridge, MA: MIT Press.

Offe, C. and Wiesenthal, H. 1980: Two logics of collective action: theoretical notes on social class and organizational form. *Political Power and Social Theory* 1, 67–115.

Ogburn, William Fielding 1930: Three obstacles to the development of a scientific sociology. *Social Forces* 8.3, 347–50.

Ogley, R. C. 1991: *Conflict under the Microscope*. Aldershot: Avebury.

O'Hear, Anthony 1980: *Karl Popper*. London: Routledge & Kegan Paul.

Okamoto, Hermann 1981: *Collective Bargaining and Industrial Democracy in Western Europe, North America and Japan*. Tokyo: Hosei University Press.

Okun, A. 1980: Rational-expectations-with-misperceptions as a theory of the business cycle. *Journal of Money, Credit and Banking* 12, 817–25.

Ollman, B. 1977: Marx's vision of communism: a reconstruction. *Critique* 8, 4–41.

Olsen, Greg 1992: *The Struggle for Economic Democracy in Sweden*. Aldershot: Avebury.

Olson, M, 1965: *The Logic of Collective Action*. Cambridge, MA: Harvard University Press.

Olsson, G. 1980: *Birds in Egg, Eggs in Bird*. London: Pion.

Ó Maoláin, C. 1987: *The Radical Right*. Harlow: Longman.

Omran, A. 1971: The epidemiologic transition: a theory of the epidemiology of population change. *Milbank Memorial Fund Quarterly* 49, 509–38.

O'Neill, J. ed. 1973: *Modes of Individualism and Collectivism*. London: Heinemann.

O'Neill, William L. 1971: *Coming Apart: an Informal History of America in the 1960s*. Chicago: Quadrangle.

Oppenheim, Adolf L. 1969: Mesopotamia: land of many cities. In *Middle Eastern Cities: a Symposium on Ancient, Islamic and Contemporary Middle Eastern Urbanism*. Berkeley: University of California Press.

Orford, J. 1985: *Excessive Appetites: a Psychological View of Addiction*. Chichester: Wiley.

O'Riordan, T. 1981: *Environmentalism*. 2nd edn, London: Pion.

Orru, M. 1987: *Anomie: History and Meanings*. Boston: Allen & Unwin.

Ortega y Gasset, José 1941: *History as a System*. New York: Norton.

Ortega y Gasset, José 1972: *The Dehumanization of Art, and Other Writings on Art, Culture and Literature*. Princeton, NJ: Princeton University Press.

Osborn, F. 1951: Preface to *Eugenics*. New York: Harper.

Osborne, Harold ed. 1968: *Aesthetics in the Modern World*. New York: Weybright & Talley.

Osborne, Harold 1970: *Aesthetics and Art Theory: an Historical Introduction*. New York: Dutton.

Osborne, Harold ed. 1972: *Aesthetics*. Oxford: Oxford University Press.

O'Shea, T. and Eisenstadt, M. eds 1984: *Artificial Intelligence*. New York: Harper & Row.

Ossowska, Maria 1971: *Social Determinants of Moral Ideas*. London: Routledge & Kegan Paul.

Ossowski, S. 1957 (*1963*): *Class Structure in the Social Consciousness*. New York: Free Press; London: Routledge & Kegan Paul.

Ossowski, S. 1978: *The Foundations of Aesthetics*. Dordrecht: Reidel; Warsaw: PWN.

Ostergaard, G. 1982: *Nonviolent Revolution in India*. New Delhi: Gandhi Peace Foundation.

Ostrogorski, M. 1902: *Democracy and the Organisation of Political Parties*. Vol. 1. London: Macmillan.

O'Sullivan, N. 1983: *Fascism*. London: Dent.

O'Sullivan, N. ed. 1986: *Terrorism, Ideology and Revolution*. Brighton: Wheatsheaf.

O'Toole, R. 1977: *The Precipitous Path: Studies in Political Sects*. Toronto: PMA.

Otto, R. 1917 (*1950*): *The Holy*. Harmondsworth: Penguin.

Outhwaite, William 1975 (*1986*): *Understanding Social Life: the Method Called Verstehen*. 2nd edn, Lewes: Jean Stroud.

Outhwaite, William 1987a: *New Philosophies of Social Science: Realism, Hermeneutics, and Critical Theory*. London: Macmillan; New York: St Martin's Press.

Outhwaite, William 1987b: Laws and explanations in sociology. In *Classic Disputes in Sociology*, ed. R. J. Anderson et al. London: Allen & Unwin.

Owen, H. and Schultze, C. L. eds 1976: *Setting National Priorities*. Washington, CD: Brookings Institution.

Owen, Robert 1812–16 (*1963*): *A New View of Society and Other Writings*, ed. and introd. G. D. H. Cole. London.

Ozga, John and Lawn, M. 1981: *Teachers, Professionalism and Class*. Barcombe: Falmer Press.

Padmore, G. 1972: *Pan-Africanism or Communism*. Garden City, NY: Doubleday.

Pagden, A. 1988: The destruction of trust and its economic consequences in the case of eighteenth-century Naples. In *Trust: Making and Breaking Cooperative Relations*, ed. D. Gambetta. Oxford: Blackwell.

Pahl, R. E. 1984: *Divisions of Labour*. Oxford: Blackwell.

Paige, G. 1977: *The Scientific Study of Leadership*. New York: Free Press.

Paige, J. 1975: *Agrarian Revolution*. New York: Free Press.

Paine, T. 1791–2 (*1937*): *Rights of Man*. London: Watts.

Pallin, D. A. 1990: *The Anthropological Character of Theology*. Cambridge: Cambridge University Press.

Panitch, L. 1976: *Social Democracy and Industrial Militancy*. Cambridge: Cambridge University Press.

Panitch, L. 1980: Recent theorizations of corporatism. *British Journal of Sociology* 31.

Pankratowa, Anna 1923 (*1976*): *Fabrikäte in Rußland: der Kampf um die sozialistische Fabrik*. Frankfurt am Main: Fischer.

Pannekoek, Anton 1950: *Workers' Councils*. Melbourne.

Pannenberg, W. 1976: *Theology and the Philosophy of Science*. London: Darton, Longman & Todd.

Parekh, B. 1982: *Contemporary Political Thinkers*. Oxford: Martin Robertson.

Paret, Peter ed. 1986: *Makers of Modern Strategy: from Machiavelli to the Nuclear Age*. Princeton, NJ: Princeton University Press.

Pareto, V. 1897: *Cours d'économie politique*. Lausanne: Rouge.

Pareto, V. 1916–19 (*1963*): *The Mind and Society: a Treatise on General Sociology*. New York: Dover.

Paris, C. ed. 1982: *Critical Readings in Planning Theory*. Oxford: Pergamon Press.

Park, R. C. et al. 1925: *The City*. Chicago: University of Chicago Press.

Park, R. E. 1967: *On Social Control and Collective Behavior: Selected Papers*. Chicago: University of Chicago Press.

Park, Robert E. 1928: Human migration and the marginal man. *American Journal of Sociology* 33, 881–93.

Park, Robert E. and Burgess, R. W. 1929: *Introduction to the Science of Sociology*. Chicago: University of Chicago Press.

Parker, Stanley 1976: *The Sociology of Leisure*. London: Allen & Unwin.

Parkin, Frank 1979: *Marxism and Class Theory: a Bourgeois Critique*. New York: Columbia University Press; London: Tavistock.

Parkin, S. 1989: *Green Parties: an International Guide*. London: Heretic.

Parsons, T. 1937: *The Structure of Social Action*. New York: McGraw-Hill.

Parsons, T. 1949: The professions and social structure. In *Essays in Sociological Theory Pure and Applied*. Glencoe, IL: Free Press.

Parsons, T. 1951: *The Social System*. Glencoe, IL: Free Press; London: Routledge & Kegan Paul.

Parsons, T. 1958: The pattern of religious organizations in the United States. *Daedalus* 87.

Parsons, T. 1964: *Social Structure and Personality*. New York: Free Press.

Parsons, T. 1966: *Societies: Evolutionary and Comparative Perspectives*. Englewood Cliffs, NJ: Prentice-Hall.

Parsons, T. 1967: On the concept of political power. In *Sociological Theory and Modern Society*. New York: Free Press; London: Collier-Macmillan.

Parsons, T. 1967: Pattern variables revisited: a response to Robert Dublin. In *Sociological Theory and Modern Society*. New York: Free Press.

Parsons, T. 1968: Social Interaction. In *International Encyclopedia of the Social Sciences*, vol. 7, ed. D. L. Sills. New York: Macmillan and Free Press.

Parsons, T. 1969: *Politics and Social Structure*. New York: Free Press.

Parsons, T. 1971: *The System of Modern Societies*. Englewood Cliffs, NJ: Prentice-Hall.

Parsons, T. and Shils, E. 1951 (*1962*): Values, motives and systems of action. In *Toward a General Theory of Action*. New York: Harper & Row.

Parsons, T. and Bales, R. 1955: *Family Socialization and Interaction Patterns*. Glencoe, IL: Free Press.

Partee, B. H. et al. 1990: *Mathematical Methods in Linguistics*. Dordrecht: Kluwer.

Pasinetti, L. 1961–2: Rate of profit and income distribution in relation to the rate of economic growth. *Review of Economic Studies* 29, 267–79.

Paskins, B. 1978: Obligation and the understanding of international relations. In *The Reason of States*, ed. M. Donelan. London: Allen & Unwin.

Passmore, J. 1974: *Man's Responsibility for Nature*. London: Duckworth.

Passmore, John 1957 (*1968*): *A Hundred Years of Philosophy*. Harmondsworth: Penguin.

Pateman, Carole 1970: *Participation and Democratic Theory*. Cambridge: Cambridge University Press.

Pateman, Carole 1988: *The Sexual Contract*. Cambridge: Polity.

Pateman, T. 1987: *Language in Mind and Language in Society*. Oxford: Oxford University Press.

Pateman, T. 1989: Bakhtin/Vološinov: pragmatics in semiotics. *Journal of Literary Semantics* 18.3, 203–16.

Patinkin, D. 1981: *Essays on and in the Chicago Tradition*. Durham, NC: Duke University Press.

Patnaik, P. ed. 1986: *Lenin and Imperialism*. Hyderabad: Orient Longman.

Patnaik, U. ed. 1990: *Agrarian Regulations and Accumulation*. Delhi: Oxford University Press.

Pavlov, Ivan 1927: *Conditioned Reflexes*. London.

Pavlov, Ivan 1932 (*1958*): *Experimental Psychology and Other Essays*. Moscow: Foreign Language Press; London: Peter Owen; New York: Philosophical Library.

Pawson, Ray 1989: *A Measure for Measures*. London: Routledge & Kegan Paul.

Payne, G. 1987: *Employment and Opportunity*. London: Macmillan.

Payne, G. 1987: *Mobility and Change in Modern Society*. London: Macmillan.

Payne, G. 1989: Social mobility. *British Journal of Sociology* 40, 471–92.

Payne, G. 1991: Competing views of contemporary social mobility and social divisions. In *Class and Consumption*, ed. R. Burrows and C. Marsh. London: Macmillan.

Payne, G. and Abbott, P. 1991: *The Social Mobility of Women*. London: Falmer Press.

Payne, Stanley 1970: *The Spanish Revolution*. London: Weidenfeld & Nicolson.

Pearce, D. W. and Turner, R. K. 1990: *The Economics of Natural Resources and the Environment*. London: Harvester-Wheatsheaf.

Pearce, F. 1989: *The Radical Durkheim*. London: Unwin Hyman.

Pearson, E. S. ed. 1978: *The History of Statistics in the 17th and 18th Centuries*. London and High Wycombe: Charles Griffin.

Pearson, Karl 1892: *Grammar of Science*. London: Walter Scott.

Peel, J. D. Y. 1971: *Herbert Spencer*. London: Heinemann.

Peet, R. and Thrift, N. eds 1989: *New Models in Geography: the Political-Economy Perspective*, 2 vols. London: Unwin Hyman.

Peirce, C. S. 1877 (*1931*): The fixation of belief. In *Collected Papers of Charles Sanders Peirce*, vol. 1. Cambridge, MA: Harvard University Press.

Peirce, C. S. 1878 (*1931*): How to make our ideas clear. In *Collected Papers of Charles Sanders Peirce*, vol. 1. Cambridge, MA: Harvard University Press.

Peirce, C. S. *1931–58*: *Collected Papers*. Cambridge, MA: Harvard University Press.

Pelinka, A. 1983: *Social Democratic Parties in Europe*. New York: Praeger.

Pellicani, Luciano 1988: Weber and the myth of Calvinism. *Telos* 75, 57–85.

Penley, C. ed. 1988: *Feminism and Film Theory*. London: BFI; New York: Routledge.

Pennock, J. R. 1979: *Democratic Political Theory*. Princeton, NJ: Princeton University Press.

Pennock, J. R. and Chapman, J. W. eds 1972: *Coercion*. Chicago: Aldine Atherton.

Pennock, J. R. and Chapman, J. W. eds 1978: *Anarchism*. New York: New York University Press.

Pepper, D. 1986: *The Roots of Modern Environmentalism*. London and New York: Routledge.

Perelman, Chaim 1976: *Logique juridique, nouvelle rhétorique*. Paris: Dalloz.

Perez-Diaz, V. M. 1978: *State, Bureaucracy and Civil Society: a Critical Discussion of the Political Theory of Karl Marx*. London: Macmillan

Perlman, Selig 1928: *The Theory of the Labor Movement*. New York: Macmillan.

Perrow, Charles 1967: A framework for the comparative analysis of organizations. *American Sociological Review* 32, 194–208.

Perrow, Charles 1972: *Complex Organizations*. New York: McGraw Hill.

Perry, R. et al. 1986: *Counterurbanisation*. Norwick: Geo Books.

Pesaran, M. H. 1987: *The Limits to Rational Expectations*. Oxford: Blackwell.

Pessen, Edward 1973: *Riches, Class and Power before the Civil War*. New York: D. H. Heath.

Pessen, Edward ed. 1974: *Three Centuries of Social Mobility in America*. Lexington, MA: D. H. Heath.

Pestman, Pieter W. 1983: Some aspects of Egyptian law in Graeco-Roman Egypt. In *Egypt and the Hellenistic World*, ed. E. van't Dack et al. Leuven: Lovanii.

Peters, R. 1967: Authority. In *Political Philosophy*, ed. A. Quinton. Oxford: Oxford University Press.

Peters, R. S. 1958: *The Concept of Motivation*. London: Routledge & Kegan Paul.

Pettigrew, T. F. 1971: *Racially Separate or Together?* New York: McGraw-Hill.

Pettigrew, T. F. 1976: Prejudice and the situation. In *The Black American Reference Book*, ed. M. M. Smythe. Englewood Cliffs, NJ: Prentice-Hall.

Petty, R. E. and Cacioppo, J. T. 1981: *Attitudes and Persuasion*. Dubuque, IA: W. C. Brown.

Peukert, Detlev 1982 (*1987*): *Inside Nazi Germany*. Harmondsworth: Penguin.

Phan, P. C. 1984: *Social Thought: Message of the Fathers of the Church*. Collegeville, MN: Liturgical Press.

Phelps Brown, H. 1988: *Egalitarianism and the Generation of Inequality*. Oxford: Clarendon.

Philips, D. C. 1987: *Philosophy, Science, and Social Inquiry*. Oxford: Pergamon.

Phillips, Anne ed. 1987: *Women and Equality*. Oxford: Blackwell.

Phillips, D. and Carstensen, L. 1988: The effect of suicide on various demographic groups. *Suicide and Life Threatening Behaviour* 18, 100–14.

Phillips, Derek 1979: *The Credential Society*. New York: Academic Press.

Phizacklea, A. ed. 1983: *One Way Ticket: Migration and Female Labour*. London: Routledge & Kegan Paul.

Piaget, J. 1968 (*1970*): *Structuralism*. New York: Basic Books.

Piaget, J. and Inhelder, B. 1955 (*1958*): *The Growth of Logical Thinking from Childhood to Adolescence*. London: Routledge & Kegan Paul.

Piatelli-Palmarini, M. ed. 1980: *Language and Learning: the Debate between Jean Piaget and Noam Chomsky*. London: Routledge & Kegan Paul.

Pickens, D. K. 1968: *Eugenics and the Progressives*. Nashville: Vanderbilt University Press.

Pike, Chris, ed. 1979: *The Futurists, the Formalists and the Marxist Critique*. Ink Links.

Pilgrim Trust 1938: *Men Without Work*. Cambridge: Cambridge University Press.

Pillay, P. N. 1973: *A Poverty Datum Line Study among Africans in Durban*. University of Nepal.

Pimlott, B. ed. 1984: *Fabian Essays in Socialist Thought*. London: Heinemann.

Pinker, R. 1971: *Social Theory and Social Policy*. London: Heinemann.

Piore, M. and Sabel, C. 1984: *The Second Industrial Divide: Possibilities for Prosperity*. New York: Basic Books.

Pirenne, Henri 1925: *Medieval Cities*. Princeton, NJ: Princeton University Press.

Pirsig, R. 1974: *Zen and the Art of Motorcycle Maintenance: an Inquiry into Values*. London: Bodley Head.

Pitcher, G. 1964: *Truth*. Englewood Cliffs, NJ: Prentice-Hall.

Pitkin, H. L. 1967: *The Concept of Representation*. Berkeley: University of California Press; Cambridge: Cambridge University Press.

Pitkin, Hanna 1972: *Wittgenstein and Justice*. Berkeley: University of California Press.

Pius XI 1933: *Casti Connubii*. Vatican.

Pivčević, Edo 1970: *Husserl and Phenomenology*. London: Hutchinson.

Piven, F. F. and Cloward, R. A. 1971: *Regulating the Poor*. New York: Vintage Books.

Pizzorno, A. 1974–8: *Lotte operaie e sindicato in Italia, 1968–1978*. Bologna: Il Mulino.

Plamenatz, J. 1954: *German Marxism and Russian Communism*. London, New York and Toronto: Longmans, Green & Co.

Plant, R. 1991: *Modern Political Thought*. Oxford: Blackwell.

Plato 1961: Timaeus, Critias, Phaedrus, Philebus, Laws. In *Collected Dialogues*, ed. Edith Hamilton and Huntington Cairns. Princeton, NJ: Bollingen.

Platt, J. R. ed. 1965: *New Views of the Nature of Man*. Chicago: University of Chicago Press.

Plekhanov, G. V. 1895 (*1975*): The Development of the Monist View of History. In *Selected Philosophical Works in Five Volumes* (1961–81), vol. 1. Moscow: Progress; London: Lawrence & Wishart.

Plummer, K. 1979: Misunderstanding labelling perspectives. In *Deviant Interpretations*, ed. D. Downes and P. Rock. Oxford: Martin Robertson.

Plutarch *1928*: Isis and Osiris. In Moralia, bk 5, trans. F. C. Babbitt. London: Heinemann.

Pocock, J. G. A. 1975: *The Machiavellian Moment: Florentine Political Thought and the Atlantic Republican Tradition*. Princeton, NJ: Princeton University Press.

Poggi, G. 1978: *The Development of the Modern State*. London: Hutchinson.

Poggi, G. 1983: *Calvinism and the Capitalist Spirit*. London: Macmillan.

Poggioli, Renato 1968: *The Theory of the Avant-Garde*. Cambridge, MA: Harvard University Press.

Poincaré, Henri 1902 (*1952*): *Science and Hypothesis*. New York: Dover.

Polanyi, K. 1944: *The Great Transformation: the Political and Economic Origin of our Time*. Boston: Beacon Press.

Polanyi, M. 1967: *The Tacit Dimension*. London: Routledge & Kegan Paul.

Poliakov, Leon 1965–85: *History of Antisemitism*, 4 vols. Oxford: Oxford University Press.

Pollak, Michael 1979: Paul Lazarsfeld, fondateur d'une multinationale scientifique. *Actes de la recherche en sciences sociales* 25, 45–59.

Pollard, Sidney 1981: *Peaceful Conquest: the Industrialization of Europe, 1760–1960*. Oxford: Oxford University Press.

Pollner, M. 1987: *Mundane Reason: Reality in Everyday and Sociological Discourse*. Cambridge: Cambridge University Press.

Pollock, Griselda 1988: *Vision and Difference: Femininity, Feminism and the Histories of Art*. London: Routledge.

Pollock, Griselda 1992: Painting, feminism, history. In *Destabilizing Theory: Contemporary Feminist Debates*, ed. M. Barrett and A. Phillips. Cambridge: Polity.

Polsby, N. W. 1963 (*1980*): *Community Power and Political Theory*. 2nd edn, New Haven, CT: Yale University Press.

Pomeroy, W. J. 1970: *American Neo-Colonialism: its Emergence in the Philippines and Asia*. New York: International Publishers.

Pool, Ithiel de Sola ed. 1977: *The Social Impact of the Telephone*. Cambridge, MA: MIT Press.

Poole, J. B. and Andrews, K. 1972: *The Government of Science in Britain*. London: Weidenfeld & Nicolson.

Poole, Michael 1978: *Workers' Participation in Industry*. London: Sage.

Poponoe, D. 1988: *Disturbing the Nest: Family Change and Decline in Modern Societies*. New York: Aldine de Gruyter.

Popper, Karl 1934 (*1959*): *Logic of Scientific Discovery*. London: Hutchinson.

Popper, Karl 1945 (*1966*): *The Open Society and its Enemies*, 2 vols. 5th edn, London: Routledge & Kegan Paul.

Popper, Karl 1957: *The Poverty of Historicism*. London: Routledge & Kegan Paul.

Popper, Karl 1972: *Objective Knowledge*. Oxford: Clarendon Press.

Popper, Karl 1976: *Unended Quest*. London: Fontana.

Porritt, J. 1984: *Seeing Green*. Oxford: Blackwell.

Posner, M. 1989: *Foundations of Cognitive Science*. Cambridge, MA: Bradford/MIT Press.

Post, K. and Wright, P. 1989: *Socialism and Underdevelopment*. London: Routledge.

Poster, Mark 1990: *The Mode of Information*. Cambridge: Polity.

Potter, J. and Wetherell, M. 1987: *Discourse and Social Psychology*. London: Sage.

Poulantzas, N. 1974: *Classes in Contemporary Capitalism*. London: Verso.

Poulantzas, N. 1974: *Fascism and Dictatorship*. London: New Left Books.

Poulantzas, N. 1976: *The Crisis of the Dictatorships*. London: New Left Books.

Powis, J. 1984: *Aristocracy*. Oxford: Blackwell.

Pratt, V. 1987: *Thinking Machines*. Oxford: Blackwell.

Pred, A. 1990: *Making Histories and Producing Human Geographies: the Local Transformation of Practice, Power Relations and Consciousness*. Boulder, CO: Westview.

Preobrazhensky, E. 1926 (*1965*): *The New Economics*. Oxford: Oxford University Press.

Pressat, R. 1985: *The Dictionary of Demography*, ed. C. Wilson. Oxford and New York: Blackwell.

Presthus, Robert 1962 (*1978*): *The Organizational Society*. Rev. edn, New York: St Martin's Press.

Price, D. de Solla 1963: *Little Science, Big Science*. New York: Yale University Press.

Pride, J. B. and Holmes, J. eds 1972: *Sociolinguistics*. Harmondsworth: Penguin.

Pridham, Geoffrey 1988: The Social Democratic Party in Britain: protest or new political tendency? In *When Parties Fail*, ed. Kay Lawson and Peter H. Merkl. Princeton, NJ: Princeton University Press.

Prinz, Michael and Zitelmann, Rainer eds 1991:

Nationalsozialismus und Modernisierung. Darmstadt: Wissenschaftliche Buchgemeinschaft.

Prior, A. N. 1962: *Formal Logic*. Oxford: Oxford University Press.

Pronovost, Giles 1989: The sociology of time. *Current Sociology* 37.

Proudhon, P.-J. 1840: *What is Property?* London: Reeves.

Proudhon, P.-J. 1865: *Du principe de l'art et de sa destination sociale*. Paris.

Prychitko, David 1990: The welfare state: what is left? *Critical Review* 4.

Pugh, D. S. 1966: Modern organization theory: a psychological and sociological study. *Psychological Bulletin* 66.

Pugh, D. S. 1990: Introduction. In *Organization Theory: Selected Readings*. 3rd edn, Harmondsworth: Penguin.

Pugh, D. S. and Hickson, D. J. 1976: *Organization Structure in its Context*. Farnborough: Gower Press.

Pugh, D. S. and Hickson, D. J. 1989: *Writers on Organizations*. 4th edn, Harmondsworth: Penguin.

Putnam, H. 1962: It ain't necessarily so. *Journal of Philosophy* 59, 658–71.

Putnam, H. 1976: The mental life of some machines. In *The Philosophy of Mind*, ed. J. Glover. Oxford: Oxford University Press.

Putnam, H. 1978: *Meaning and the Moral Sciences*. London: Routledge & Kegan Paul.

Pye, L. and Verba, S. eds 1965: *Political Culture and Political Development*. Princeton, NJ: Princeton University Press.

Qualter, T. H. 1962: *Propaganda and Psychological Warfare*. New York: Random House.

Qualter, T. H. 1985: *Opinion Control in the Democracies*. London: Macmillan.

Quine, W. V. O. 1951 (*1963*): Two dogmas of empiricism. In *From a Logical Point of View*. New York: Harper & Row.

Quine, W. V. O. 1952 (*1963*): *From a Logical Point of View*. New York: Harper & Row.

Quine, W. V. O. 1960: *Word and Object*. Cambridge, MA: MIT Press.

Quinney, R. 1979: *Criminology: Analysis and Critique of Crime in America*. Boston: Little Brown.

Quinton, A. ed. 1967: *Political Philosophy*. Oxford: Oxford University Press.

Rabinowicz, H. 1970: *The World of Hasidism*. London.

Radcliffe-Brown, A. R. 1922 (*1948*): *The Andaman Islanders*. New York: Free Press.

Radcliffe-Brown, A. R. 1952 (*1965*): *Structure and Function in Primitive Society*. New York: Free Press.

Radhakrishnan, S. 1927: *The Hindu View of Life*. London: Allen & Unwin.

Radin, Max 1936: Tradition. In *Encyclopedia of the Social Sciences*, vol. 15. New York: Macmillan and Free Press.

Radzinowicz, Leon and Hood, R. G. 1986: *The Emergence of Penal Policy*. London: Stevens.

Rains, P. 1971: *Becoming an Unwed Mother*. Chicago: Aldine.

Ramsey, F. P. 1926 (*1988*): Truth and probability. In *Decision, Probability and Utility*, ed. P. Gardenförs and N.-E. Sahlin. Cambridge: Cambridge University Press.

Ramsey, F. P. 1931: *The Foundations of Mathematics*. London: Routledge & Kegan Paul.

Rancière, Jacques 1983: *Le philosophe et ses pauvres*. Paris: Fayard.

Rand, Ayn 1957: *Atlas Shrugged*. New York: Random House.

Randall, V. ed. 1988: *Political Parties in the Third World*. London and Los Angeles: Sage.

Raphael, Max 1968: *The Demands of Art: Towards an Empirical Theory of Art*. London: Routledge & Kegan Paul.

Rapoport, A. 1960: *Fights, Games and Debates*. Ann Arbor: University of Michigan Press.

Rapoport, A. ed. 1968: *Clausewitz: On War*. Harmondsworth: Penguin.

Rapp, Rayna 1978: Family and class in contemporary America: notes toward an understanding of ideology. *Science and Society* 42, 278–300.

Rasmusen, E. 1989: *Games and Information*. Oxford: Blackwell.

Rattansi, A. 1982: *Marx and the Division of Labour*. London: Macmillan.

Ravetz, J. 1971: *Scientific Knowledge and its Social Problems*. Oxford: Oxford University Press.

Rawls, John 1971: *A Theory of Justice*. Cambridge, MA: Harvard University Press; Oxford: Oxford University Press.

Ray, L. J. 1987: The Protestant ethic debate. In *Classic Disputes in Sociology*, ed. R. J. Anderson et al. London: Allen & Unwin.

Raz, J. 1975: *Practical Reason and Norms*. London: Hutchinson.

Raz, J. 1986: *The Morality of Freedom*. Oxford: Clarendon Press.

Reckless, W. 1940: *Criminal Behaviour*. New York and London: McGraw-Hill.

Reder, M. W. 1987: Chicago School. In *The New Palgrave Dictionary of Economics*, vol. 1, ed. J. Eatwell et al. London: Macmillan.

Redfield, R. 1947: The Folk Society. *American Journal of Sociology* 52.

Redfield, R. 1955: *The Little Community*. Chicago: University of Chicago Press.

Reedy, W. Jay 1986: Art for society's sake: Louis de Bonald's sociology of aesthetic and theocratic ideology. *Proceedings of the American Philosophical Society* 130. 1, 101–129.

Regan, D. H. 1980: *Utilitarianism and Co-operation*. Oxford: Clarendon Press.

Reichenbach, H. 1951: *The Rise of Scientific Philosophy*. Berkeley and Los Angeles: University of California Press.

Reid, G. C. 1987: *Theories of Industrial Organization*. Oxford: Blackwell.

Reid, G. C. and Jacobsen, L. R. 1988: *The Small Entrepreneurial Firm*. Aberdeen: Aberdeen University Press.

Rein, M. 1968: Welfare Planning. In *International Encyclopedia of the Social Sciences*, vol. 12. New York: Macmillan and Free Press.

Rein, M. 1970: Problems in the definition and measurement of poverty. In *The Concept of Poverty*, ed. P. Townsend. London: Heinemann.

Rein, M. 1979: *Social Policy*. New York: Random House.

Reiner, R. 1985: *The Politics of the Police*. Brighton: Harvester.

Reiss, I. L. 1986: *Journey into Sexuality: an Exploratory Voyage*. Englewood Cliffs, NJ: Prentice-Hall.

Rémond, R. 1966: *The Right Wing in France: from 1815 to De Gaulle*. Philadelphia: University of Pennsylvania Press.

Renan, Ernest 1945: Qu'est-ce qu'une nation? In *Ernest Renan et l'Allemagne: textes recueillis et commentés par Emile Bure*. New York.

Renner, Karl 1899: *Staat und Nation*. Vienna: Josef Dietl.

Renner, Karl 1902: *Der Kampf der Österreichischen Nationen um den Staat*. Leipzig and Vienna: Franz Deuticke.

Renner, Karl 1904 (*1949*): *The Institutions of Private Law and their Social Functions*, ed. Otto Kahn-Freund. London: Routledge & Kegan Paul.

Renner, Karl 1916: Probleme des Marxismus. *Der Kampf* 9.

Renner, Karl 1953: *Wandlungen der modernen Gesellschaft: zwei Abhandlungen über die Probleme der Nachkriegszeit*. Vienna: Wiener Volksbuchhandlung.

Rescher, N. 1973: *The Coherence Theory of Truth*. Oxford: Oxford University Press.

Research Policy 1987: 16.2-4, special issue in honour of Yvann Fabian.

Resolutions and Selected Speeches from the Sixth Pan-African Congress 1976. Dar es Salaam: Tanzania Publishing House.

Reves, E. 1945: *The Anatomy of Peace*. New York: Harper & Bros.

Review 1.3–4, 1978. New York: Fernand Brandel Centre, Binghamton University.

Rex, J. 1961: *Key Problems of Sociological Theory*. London: Routledge & Kegan Paul.

Rex, J. 1983: *Race Relations in Sociological Theory*. London: Routledge & Kegan Paul.

Rex, J. 1986: *Race and Ethnicity*. Milton Keynes: Open University Press.

Rey, P.-P. 1976: *Les alliances de classes*. Paris: François Maspéro.

Reznick, M. 1987: *Choices: an Introduction to Decision Theory*. Minneapolis: University of Minnesota Press.

Ricardo, D. 1817 (*1951*): *Principles of Political Economy*. Cambridge: Cambridge University Press.

Rich, Adrienne 1980: Compulsory heterosexuality and lesbian existence. *Signs* 5, 631–60.

Richards, V. 1983: *Lessons of the Spanish Revolution*. 3rd edn, London: Freedom Press.

Richardson, L. F. 1960a: *Arms and Insecurity*. Pittsburgh: Boxwood Press; Chicago: Quadrangle.

Richardson, L. F. 1960b: *Statistics of Deadly Quarrels*. Pittsburgh: Boxwood Press; Chicago: Quadrangle.

Richter, M. 1981: Modernity and its distinctive threats to liberty: Montesquieu and Tocqueville on new forms of illegitimate domination. In *Alexis de Tocqueville: zur Politik in der Demokratie*, ed. M. Hereth and J. Hoffken. Baden-Baden: Nomos.

Richter, M. 1982: Toward a concept of political illegitimacy: Bonapartist dictatorship and democratic legitimacy. *Political Theory* 10, 185–214.

Richter, M. 1988: Tocqueville, Napoleon and Bonapartism. In *Reconsidering Tocqueville's Democracy in America*, ed. A. S. Eisenstadt. New Brunswick, NJ: Rutgers University Press.

Rickert, H. 1989 (*1962*): *Science and History: a Critique of Positivist Epistemology*. New York: Van Nostrand.

Rickert, Heinrich 1902 (*1986*): *The Limits of Concept Formation in Natural Science*. Abridged edn, Cambridge: Cambridge University Press.

Rickman, H. P. 1988: *Dilthey Today: a Critical Appraisal of the Contemporary Relevance of his Work*. New York: Greenwood Press.

Ricoeur, P. 1974: *The Conflict of Interpretations: Essays in Hermeneutics*. Evanston, IL: Northwestern University Press.

Ridley, F. F. 1970: *Revolutionary Syndicalism in France*. Cambridge: Cambridge University Press.

Riedel, M. 1975: Bürger, Staatsbürger, Bürgertum. In *Geschichtliche Grundbegriffe*, vol. 1. Stuttgart: Klett Cotta.

Riedel, M. 1984: 'State' and 'civil society': linguistic context and historical origin. In *Between Tradition and Revolution: the Hegelian Transformation of Political Philosophy*. Cambridge: Cambridge University Press.

Rieff, P. 1966: *The Triumph of the Therapeutic*. London: Chatto & Windus.

Riencourt, A. de 1958: *The Coming Caesars*. London: Jonathan Cape.

Riesman, David 1964: *Abundance for What? and Other Essays*. London: Chatto & Windus.

Riesman, David 1980: *Galbraith and Market Capitalism*. London: Macmillan.

Riesman, David et al. 1950 (*1966*): *The Lonely Crowd: a Study in the Changing American Character*. New York: Doubleday Anchor.

Rigby, T. H. ed. 1966: *Stalin*. Englewood Cliffs, NJ: Prentice-Hall.

Riker, W. H. 1982: *Liberalism against Populism*. San Francisco: W. H. Freeman.

Riley, Denise 1988: *Am I That Name? Feminism and the Category of 'Woman' in History*. London: Macmillan.

Rimlinger, G. V. 1971: *Welfare Policy and Industrialization in Europe, America and Russia*. New York: Wiley.

Ritsch, A. 1986: *Logic of Theory*. London.

Ritter, A. 1980: *Anarchism*. Cambridge: Cambridge University Press.

Rizzi, B. 1985: *The Bureaucratization of the World*. London: Tavistock.

Roach, J. and Thomaneck, J. eds 1985: *Police and Public Order in Europe*. Beckenham: Croom Helm.

Robert, P. 1966: *Dictionnaire alphabétique et analogique de la langue française*. Paris: Robert.

Roberts, A. ed. 1967: *The Strategy of Civilian Defence*. London: Faber & Faber.

Roberts, David 1979: *The Syndicalist Tradition and Italian Fascism*. Manchester: Manchester University Press.

Roberts, Kenneth 1981: *Leisure*. 2nd edn, London: Longman.

Roberts, Paul Craig and Stephenson, Matthew A. 1971: *Marx's Theory of Exchange, Alienation, and Crisis*. Stanford, CA: Hoover Institution Press.

Robertson, R. 1970: *The Sociological Interpretation of Religion*. Oxford: Blackwell.

Robertson, R. 1985: The sacred in the world-system. In *The Sacred in a Secular Age*, ed. P. E. Hammond. Berkeley: University of California Press.

Robertson, R. 1990: Mapping the global condition: globalization as the central concept. In *Global Culture: Nationalism, Globalization and Modernity*, ed. M. Featherstone. London: Sage.

Robins, R. H. 1979: *A Short History of Linguistics*. London: Longman.

Robinson, J. 1956: *The Accumulation of Capital*. London: Macmillan.

Robinson, J. 1961: Prelude to a critique of economic theory. *Oxford Economic Papers* 13.

Rocker, R. 1989: *Anarcho-Syndicalism*. London: Pluto Press.

Roemer, J. 1982: *A General Theory of Exploitation and Class*. Cambridge: Cambridge University Press.

Roemer, J. ed. 1986: *Analytical Marxism*. Cambridge: Cambridge University Press.

Roemer, J. 1988: *Free to Lose: an Introduction to Marxist Economic Philosophy*. London: Radius.

Roethlisberger, F. J. and Dickson, W. J. 1939 (*1961*): *Management and the Workers: an Account of a Research Program Conducted by the Western Electric Company, Hawthorne Works, Chicago*. Cambridge, MA: Harvard University Press.

Roff, W. R. ed. 1987: *Islam and the Political Economy of Meaning: Comparative Studies of*

Muslim Discourse. Berkeley and Los Angeles: University of California Press.

Rojek, Chris 1985: *Capitalism and Leisure Theory*. London: Tavistock.

Rojek, Chris ed. 1989: *Leisure for Leisure: Critical Essays*. London: Macmillan.

Rojek, Chris 1990: Baudrillard and leisure. *Leisure Studies* 9. 1.

Romaine, S. ed. 1982: *Sociolinguistic Variation in Speech Communities*. London: Arnold.

Romieu, M. A. 1850: *L'Ère des Césars*. Paris: Ledoyen.

Rorty, R. 1980: *Philosophy and the Mirror of Nature*. Oxford: Blackwell; Princeton, NJ: Princeton University Press.

Rorty, R. et al. eds 1984: *Philosophy in History*. Cambridge: Cambridge University Press.

Rose, A. M. 1967: *The Power Structure*. New York: Oxford University Press.

Rose, A. M. 1970: Distance of migration and socioeconomic status of migrants. In *Readings in the Sociology of Migration*, ed. C. J. Jansen. Oxford: Pergamon Press.

Rose, G. 1978: *The Melancholy Science: an Introduction to the Thought of Theodor W. Adorno*. London: Macmillan.

Rose, G. 1981: *Hegel Contra Sociology*. London: Athlone Press.

Rose, G. 1992: *The Broken Middle*. Oxford: Blackwell.

Rose, Margaret A. 1991: *The Post-modern and the Post-industrial: a Critical Analysis*. Cambridge: Cambridge University Press.

Rose, N. 1989: *Governance of the Soul*. London: Routledge.

Rose, N. 1990: *Governing the Soul: the Shaping of the Private Self*. London: Routledge.

Rose, Steven et al. 1984: *Not in our Genes*. Harmondsworth: Penguin.

Rosen, Michael 1982: *Hegel's Dialectic and its Criticism*. Cambridge: Cambridge University Press.

Rosen, P. ed. 1986: *Narrative, Apparatus, Ideology*. New York: Columbia University Press.

Rosen, S. 1970: A model of war and alliance. In *Alliance in International Politics*, ed. J. R. Friedman et al. Boston: Allyn & Bacon.

Rosenbaum, W. A. 1975: *Political Culture*. London: Thomas Nelson.

Rosenberg, N. and Frischtak, C. R. 1984: Technological innovation and long waves. *Cambridge Journal of Economics* 8, 7–24.

Rosner, M. 1976: *The Kibbutz as a Way of Life*. State of California: Institute for Cooperative Communities.

Ross, Arthur M. and Hartman, Paul T. 1960: *Changing Patterns of Industrial Conflict*. New York: Wiley.

Ross, E. A. 1929: *Social Control: a Survey of the Foundations of Order*. London: Macmillan.

Ross, G. et al. 1987: *The Mitterand Experiment*. New York: Oxford University Press.

Ross, J. A. ed 1982: *International Encyclopaedia of Population*. New York: Free Press.

Ross, W. D. 1939: *Foundations of Ethics*. Oxford: Clarendon Press.

Rossi, P. et al. eds 1983: *Handbook of Survey Research*. New York: Academic Press.

Rossi, Paolo 1968: *Francis Bacon: from Magic to Science*. Chicago: University of Chicago Press.

Rossiter, C. L. 1948: *Constitutional Dictatorship: Crisis Government in the Modern Democracies*. Princeton, NJ: Princeton University Press.

Rostow, E. V. 1962: *Planning for Freedom*. New Haven, CT: Yale University Press.

Rostow, W. W. 1960 (*1985*): *The Stages of Economic Growth: a Non-communist Manifesto*. Cambridge: Cambridge University Press.

Rostow, W. W. 1978: *The World Economy: History and Prospect*. Austin and London: University of Texas Press.

Roszak, Theodore 1969: *The Making of a Counter-Culture*. New York: Anchor.

Roszak, Theodore 1986: *The Cult of Information*. New York: Pantheon.

Rotenstreich, Nathan 1965: *Basic Problems of Marx's Philosophy*. New York: Bobbs-Merrill.

Roth, G. 1979: Charisma and the counterculture. In *Max Weber's Vision of History: Ethics and Methods*, ed. G. Roth and W. Schluchter. Berkeley: University of California Press.

Rothbard, Murray N. 1970: Professor Galbraith and the sin of affluence. In *Man, Economy and State*, vol. 2. Los Angeles: Nash.

Rothbard, Murray N. 1972: *America's Great Depression*. Los Angeles: Nash.

Rothbard, Murray N. 1973 (*1978*): *For a New Liberty: the Libertarian Manifesto*. Rev. edn, New York: Collier.

Rothblatt, B. ed. 1968: *Changing Perspectives on Man*. Chicago: University of Chicago Press.

Rothman, Stanley and Lichter, S. Robert 1982: *Roots of Radicalism: Jews, Christians and the New Left*. New York: Oxford University Press.

Rousseau, J.-J. 1762 (*1973*): *The Social Contract and Discourses*. London: Dent.

Rousseau, Mark O. and Zariski, Raphael 1987: *Regionalism and Regional Devolution in Comparative Perspective*. London: Praeger.

Routh, G. 1975: *The Origin of Economic Ideas*. London: Macmillan.

Routley, R. and Routley, V. 1979: Against the inevitability of human chauvinism. In *Ethics and Problems of the 21st Century*, ed. K. Goodpaster and K. Sayre. Notre Dame, IN: University of Notre Dame Press.

Rowbotham, Sheila 1972: *Women, Resistance and Revolution*. Harmondsworth: Penguin; New York: Pantheon.

Rowbotham, Sheila 1975: *Hidden from History*. London: Pluto.

Rowntree, B. S. 1901: *Poverty: a Study of Town Life*. London: Macmillan.

Rowntree, B. S. 1918 (*1937*): *The Human Needs of Labour*. London: Longmans.

Rowntree, B. S. 1941: *Poverty and Progress: a Second Survey of York*. London: Longmans.

Rowthorn, R. 1974: Neo-classicism, neo-Ricardianism and Marxism. *New Left Review* 86, 63–87.

Royal College of Psychiatrists 1986: *Alcohol: our Favourite Drug*. London and New York: Tavistock.

Royal College of Psychiatrists 1987: *Drug Scenes*. London: Royal College of Psychiatrists.

Rozman, Gilbert ed. 1991: *The East Asian Region: Confucian Heritage and its Modern Adaptation*. Princeton, NJ: Princeton University Press.

Rubel, M. 1960: *Karl Marx devant le Bonapartisme*. Paris: Mouton.

Rubin, I. I. 1928 (*1973*): *Essays on Marx's Theory of Value*. Detroit: Black and Red; Montreal: Black Rose Books.

Rubinstein, W. D. ed. 1980: *Wealth and the Wealthy in the Modern World*. London: Croom Helm.

Rubinstein, W. D. 1986: *Wealth and Inequality in Britain*. London: Faber.

Rueschemeyer, D. 1986: *Power and the Division of Labour*. Cambridge: Polity.

Rule, J. B. 1978: *Insight and Social Betterment*. New York: Oxford University Press.

Rumelhart, D. E. et al. 1986: *Parallel Distributed Processing: Explorations in the Microstructure of Cognition*, 2 vols. Cambridge, MA: Bradford/MIT Press.

Runciman, W. G. 1966 (*1972*): *Relative Deprivation and Social Justice*. Harmondsworth: Penguin.

Runciman, W. G. 1969: *Social Science and Political Theory*. Cambridge: Cambridge University Press.

Runciman, W. G. 1974: Towards a theory of social stratification. In *The Social Analysis of Class Structure*, ed. Frank Parkin. London: Tavistock.

Runciman, W. G. 1989: *A Treatise on Social Theory*, vol. 2: *Substantive Social Theory*. Cambridge: Cambridge University Press.

Rusche, G. and Kirchheimer, O. 1968: *Punishment and Social Structure*. New York: Russell & Russell.

Ruse, M. 1973: *The Philosophy of Biology*. London: Hutchinson.

Ruse, M. 1985: *Sociobiology*. 2nd edn, Dordrecht: Reidel.

Russell, Bertrand 1914a: Logic as the essence of philosophy. In *Our Knowledge of the External World*. London: Allen & Unwin.

Russell, Bertrand 1914b (*1957*): Relation of sense-data to physics. In *Mysticism and Logic*. New York: Doubleday.

Russell, Bertrand 1917 (*1929*): *Mysticism and Logic*. 2nd edn, London: Allen & Unwin.

Russell, Bertrand 1918 (*1971*): The philosophy of logical atomism. In *Logic and Knowledge*, ed. R. C. Marsh. New York: Capricorn.

Russell, Bertrand 1938 (*1975*): *Power: a New Social Analysis*. London: Allen & Unwin.

Russell, Bertrand and Whitehead, A. N. 1910–11: *Principia Mathematica*, 3 vols. Cambridge: Cambridge University Press.

Rust, Frances 1969: *Dance in Society*. London: Routledge & Kegan Paul.

Rutter, M. and Giller, H. 1983: *Juvenile Delinquency*. Harmondsworth: Penguin.

Rutter, M. and Madge, N. 1976: *Cycles of Disadvantage*. London: Heinemann.

Ryan, A. ed. 1979: *The Idea of Freedom*. Oxford: Oxford University Press.

Ryan, A. 1984: *The Political Theory of Property*. Oxford: Blackwell.

Ryder, N. B. 1968: Cohort analysis. In *International Encyclopaedia of the Social Sciences*, ed. D. E. Sills. New York: Macmillan & Free Press.

Ryle, Gilbert 1949 (*1963*): *The Concept of Mind*. London: Hutchinson.

Ryle, M. 1988: *Ecology and Socialism*. London: Hutchinson/Radius.

Sachedina, A. A. 1980: *Islamic Messianism: the Idea of the Mahdi in Twelver Shi'ism*. Albany, NY: State University of New York Press.

Sacks, H. et al. 1974: A simplest systematics for the organisation of turn-taking in conversations. *Language* 50. 4, 696–735.

Sacks, Harvey 1992: *Lectures on Conversation*, 2 vols, ed. G. Jefferson. Oxford: Blackwell.

Sadurski, W. 1985: *Giving Desert its Due: Social Justice and Legal Theory*. Dordrecht: Reidel.

Sahlins, M. D. 1965: On the sociology of primitive exchange. In *The Relevance of Models for Social Anthropology*, ed. Association of Social Anthropologists of the Commonwealth. London: Tavistock.

Sahlins, M. D. and Service, E. R. eds 1960: *Evolution and Culture*. Ann Arbor: University of Michigan Press.

Said, E. 1978: *Orientalism*. London: Routledge & Kegan Paul.

Said, E. 1983: *The World, the Text, and the Critic*. Cambridge, MA: Harvard University Press.

Said, K. A. M. et al. eds 1990: *Modelling the Mind*. Oxford: Oxford University Press.

Sainsbury, P. 1955: *Suicide in London*. London: Chapman & Hall.

Saint-Simon, H. de 1953: *Selected Writings*, ed. F. M. H. Markham. Oxford: Blackwell.

Saint-Simon, H. de 1964: *Social Organization, The Science of Man, and Other Writings*. New York: Harper.

Samuel, Geoffrey 1990: Science, law and history. *Northern Ireland Legal Quarterly* 41, 1.

Samuelson, P. A. 1947: *Foundations of Economic Analysis*. Cambridge, MA: Harvard University Press.

Samuelson, P. A. 1976: *Economics*. 10th edn, New York and London: McGraw-Hill

Sandel, M. 1982: *Liberalism and the Limits of Justice*. New York and Cambridge: Cambridge University Press.

Sapelli, G. ed. 1981: *Il movimento co-operativo in Italia*. Turin: Einaudi.

Sapir, E. 1929: The status of linguistics as a science. *Language* 5.

Sargent, T. J. 1987: *Macroeconomic Theory*. 2nd edn, Orlando and London: Academic Press.

Sarkar, Sunit, 1989: *Modern India 1885–1947*. London: Macmillan.

Sarkissian, Sam S. ed. 1975: *Revolutionary Guerrilla Warfare*. Chicago: Precedent.

Sartori, G. 1969: From the sociology of politics to political sociology. *Government and Opposition* 4, 195–214.

Sartori, G. 1976: *Parties and Party Systems*. Cambridge: Cambridge University Press.

Sartori, G. 1987: *The Theory of Democracy Revisited*. Chatham, NJ: Chatham House.

Sartre, Jean-Paul 1936–7 (*1957*): *The Transcendence of the Ego*. New York: Noonday Press.

Sartre, Jean-Paul 1938 (*1965*): *Nausea*. Harmondsworth: Penguin.

Sartre, Jean-Paul 1943 (*1956*): *Being and Nothingness: an Essay on Phenomenological Ontology*. London: Methuen.

Sartre, Jean-Paul 1946 (*1973*): *Existentialism and Humanism*. London: Methuen.

Sartre, Jean-Paul 1947: *Huis clos*. New York: Knopf.

Sartre, Jean-Paul 1947 (*1965*): *Situations*. New York: Braziller.

Sartre, Jean-Paul 1948 (*1950*): *What is Literature?* London: Methuen.

Sartre, Jean-Paul 1960 (*1976*): *Critique of Dialectical Reason*. London: New Left Books.

Sartre, Jean-Paul 1983: *Cahiers pour une morale*. Paris: Gallimard.

Sassen, Saskia 1991: *The Global City*. Princeton, NJ: Princeton University Press.

Sassoon, A. S. 1980 (*1987*): *Gramsci's Politics*. 2nd edn, London: Hutchinson.

Saunders, P. 1981: *Social Theory and the Urban Question*. London: Hutchinson.

Saunders, P. 1990: *Social Class and Stratification*. London: Routledge.

Saussure, F. de 1916 (*1983*): *Course in General Linguistics*. London: Duckworth.

Savage, L. J. 1954: *The Foundations of Statistics*. New York: Wiley.

Say, Jean Baptiste 1803 (*1971*): *A Treatise on Political Economy*. New York: Augustus M. Kelley.

Sayer, A. 1984 (*1992*): *Method and Social Science*. 2nd edn, London: Hutchinson.

Scanlan, J. P. 1985: *Marxism in the USSR: a Critical Study of Current Soviet Thought*. Ithaca, NY: Cornell University Press.

Scanlon, T. M. 1982: Contractualism and utilitarianism. In *Utilitarianism and Beyond*, ed. A. Sen and B. Williams. Cambridge: Cambridge University Press.

Scarre, C. ed. 1988: *Past Worlds: the Times Atlas of World Archaeology*. London: Times Books.

Schaar, John 1969: Legitimacy in the modern state. In *Power and Community*, ed. P. Green and S. Levinson. New York: Random House.

Schaffer, M. E. 1989: The credible-commitment problem in the center-enterprise relationship. *Journal of Comparative Economics* 13.3.

Schechner, Richard 1988: *Performance Theory*. New York: Routledge.

Scheff, T. J. 1966: *Being Mentally Ill: a Sociological Theory*. Chicago: Aldine.

Scheffler, H. W. and Lounsbury, F. G. 1971: *A Study in Structural Semantics: the Siriono Kinship System*. Englewood Cliffs, NJ: Prentice-Hall.

Scheffler, S. 1982: *The Rejection of Consequentialism*. Oxford: Clarendon Press.

Scheler, Max 1926 (*1980*): *Problems of a Sociology of Knowledge*. London: Routledge & Kegan Paul.

Schelling, T. 1971: Some questions on civilian defence. In *Conflict: Violence and Non-Violence*, ed. J. V. Bondurant. Chicago: Aldine Atherton.

Schelling, T. C. 1960: *The Strategy of Conflict*. Cambridge, MA: Harvard University Press.

Schenkein, J. ed. 1978: *Studies in the Organisation of Conversational Interaction*. New York: Academic Press.

Scherer, F. M. and Ross, D. 1990: *Industrial Market Structure and Economic Performance*. 3rd edn, Dallas: Houghton Mifflin.

Schillebeeckx, E. 1977: *Interim Report*. Freiburg.

Schilpp, Paul Arthur ed. 1974: *The Philosophy of Karl Popper*, 2 vols. La Salle, IL: Open Court.

Schlatter, Richard 1951: *Private Property: the History of an Idea*. London: Allen & Unwin.

Schlick, M. 1918 (*1974*): *General Theory of Knowledge*, introduction A. E. Blumberg and H. Feigl. Vienna and New York: Springer.

Schlick, M. 1930 (*1979*): The turning-point in philosophy. In *Philosophical Papers*, vol. 2, (*1925–1936*), ed. H. L. Mulder and B. F. B. van de Velde-Schlick. Dordrecht: Reidel.

Schlick, M. 1931 (*1979*): Causality in contemporary physics. In *Philosophical Papers*, vol. 2, (*1925–1936*), ed. H. L. Mulder and B. F. B. van de Velde-Schlick. Dordrecht: Reidel.

Schlick, M. 1932 (*1979*): Positivism and realism. In *Philosophical Papers*, vol. 2, (*1925–1936*), ed. H. L. Mulder and B. F. B. van de Velde-Schlick. Dordrecht: Reidel.

Schlick, M. 1934 (*1979*): On the foundation of knowledge. In *Philosophical Papers*, vol. 2, (*1925–1936*), ed. H. L. Mulder and B. F. B. van de Velde-Schlick. Dordrecht: Reidel.

Schluchter, W. 1981: *The Rise of Western Rationalism: Max Weber's Developmental History*. Berkeley: University of California Press.

Schmalensee, R. and Willig, R. eds 1989: *Handbook of Industrial Organization*. Amsterdam: Elsevier.

Schmid, Michael and Wuketits, Franz, eds 1987: *Evolutionary Theory in Social Science*. Dordrecht: Reidel.

Schmidt, Alfred 1974: *Zur Idee der kritischen Theorie: Elemente der Philosophie Max Horkheimers*. Munich: Hanser.

Schmidt, Alfred 1976: *Die kritische Theorie als Geschichtsphilosophie*. Munich: Hanser.

Schmidt, Alfred and Altwicker, Norbert eds 1986: *Max Horkheimer heute: Werk und Wirkung*. Frankfurt am Main: Fischer.

Schmidt, S. J. ed. 1987: *Der Diskurs des radikalen Konstruktivismus*. Frankfurt am Main: Suhrkamp.

Schmitt, C. 1928: *Die Diktatur*. Munich and Leipzig: Duncker & Humblot.

Schmitter, P. C. 1974: Still the century of corporatism? *Review of Politics* 36, 85–131.

Schmitter, P. C. and Lehmbruch, G. eds 1979: *Trends Toward Corporatist Intermediation*. Beverly Hills and London: Sage.

Schmoller, G. 1883: Zur Methodologie der Staats- und Sozial-Wissenschaften. In *Jahrbuch für Gesetzgebung, Verwaltung und Volkswirtschaft*, NF Jg.7, 975–94.

Schneider, D. M. 1984: *A Critique of the Study of Kinship*. Ann Arbor: University of Michigan Press.

Schoenbaum, David 1966: *Hitler's Social Revolution*. London: Weidenfeld & Nicolson.

Scholem, Gershom G. 1961 (*1973*): *Major Trends in Jewish Mysticism*. Rev. edn, New York: Schocken.

Schram, S. 1967: *Mao Tse-tung*. Harmondsworth: Penguin.

Schram, S. 1967: Mao Tse-tung as a charismatic leader. *Asian Survey* 7, 383–4.

Schram, S. 1969: *The Political Thought of Mao Tse-tung*. Rev. edn, New York: Praeger.

Schram, S. ed. 1974: *Mao Tse-tung Unrehearsed.* Harmondsworth: Penguin.

Schram, S. 1989: *The Thought of Mao Tse-tung.* Cambridge: Cambridge University Press.

Schram, S. G. and Turbett, J. P. 1983: Civil disorder and the welfare explosion: a two-step process. *American Sociological Review* 48, 408–14.

Schumpeter, J. A. 1911 (*1961*): *The Theory of Economic Development.* New York: Oxford University Press.

Schumpeter, J. A. 1919 (*1951*): The sociology of imperialisms. In *Imperialism and Social Classes,* ed. Paul Sweezy. New York: Augustus M. Kelley.

Schumpeter, J. A. 1939: *Business Cycles: a Theoretical, Historical and Statistical Analysis of the Capitalist Process.* New York: McGraw-Hill.

Schumpeter, J. A. 1942 (*1987*): *Capitalism, Socialism and Democracy.* 6th edn, London: Allen & Unwin.

Schumpeter, J. A. 1946 (*1951*): Capitalism. In *Essays on Economic Topics.* Port Washington, NY: Kennikat Press.

Schumpeter, J. A. 1954: *A History of Economic Analysis.* New York: Oxford University Press.

Schur, E. 1971: *Labelling Deviant Behaviour.* London: Harper & Row.

Schusterman, Richard ed. 1989: *Analytic Aesthetics.* Oxford: Blackwell.

Schutz, Alfred 1932 (*1972*): *The Phenomenology of the Social World.* London: Heinemann.

Schutz, Alfred 1940 (*1968*): Phenomenology and the social sciences. In *Philosophical Essays in Memory of Edmund Husserl,* ed. Marvin Farber. London: Greenwood Press.

Schutz, Alfred *1962–6: Collected Papers,* 3 vols. The Hague: Martinus Nijhoff.

Schutz, Alfred and Luckmann, Thomas 1974: *The Structures of the Lifeworld.* London: Heinemann.

Schwartz, B. 1979: *Chinese Communism and the Rise of Mao.* Rev. edn, Cambridge, MA: Harvard University Press.

Schwarz, B. 1985: Conservatism and 'caesarism', 1903–22. In *Crises in the British State 1880–1930,* ed. M. Langen and B. Schwarz. London: Hutchinson.

Schwartz, B. M. ed. 1967: *Caste in Overseas Indian Communities.* San Francisco: Chandler.

Schweitzer, A. 1984: *The Age of Charisma.* Chicago: Nelson-Hall.

Schwendinger, H. and Schwendinger, J. 1975: Defenders of order or guardians of human rights. In *Critical Criminology,* ed. I. Taylor et al. London: Routledge & Kegan Paul.

Scott, A. J. and Storper, M. eds 1986: *Production, Work, Territory: the Geographical Anatomy of Industrial Capitalism.* Boston: Allen & Unwin.

Scott, Alan, 1990: *Ideology and the New Social Movements.* London: Unwin Hyman.

Scott, Allen J. 1988: *Metropolis: from the Division of Labor to Urban Form.* Berkeley, Los Angeles and London: University of California Press.

Scott, J. 1986: *The Weapons of the Weak.* New Haven, CT: Yale University Press.

Scott, Joan W. 1990: Deconstructing equality-versus-difference: or, the uses of poststructuralist theory for feminism. In *Conflicts in Feminism,* ed. Marianne Hirsch and Evelyn Fox Keller. London: Routledge.

Scott, John 1982: *The Upper Classes: Property and Privilege in Britain.* London: Macmillan.

Scott, John 1985: *Corporations, Classes, and Capitalism.* 2nd edn, London: Hutchinson.

Scott, John 1986: *Capitalist Property and Financial Power.* Brighton: Wheatsheaf.

Scott, R. 1969: *The Making of Blind Men.* New York: Russell Sage Foundation.

Scott, William G. 1967: *Organization Theory.* Homewood, IL: Dorsey Press.

Scriven, M. 1962: Explanation, prediction and laws. In *Minnesota Studies in the Philosophy of Science,* vol. 3, ed. H. Feigl and G. Maxwell. Minneapolis: University of Minnesota Press.

Scriven, Michael 1958: A study of radical behaviourism. In *Minnesota Studies in the Philosophy of Science,* ed. H. Feigl and M. Scriven. Minneapolis: University of Minnesota Press.

Scruton, Roger 1980 (*1984*): *The Meaning of Conservatism.* 2nd edn, London: Macmillan.

Scruton, Roger ed. 1988: *Conservative Thinkers.* London: Claridge Press.

Scruton, Roger ed. 1988: *Conservative Thoughts: Essays from the Salisbury Review.* London: Claridge Press.

Seal, Anil 1968: *The Emergence of Indian Nationalism.* Cambridge: Cambridge University Press.

Searle, G. R. 1976: *Eugenics and Politics in Britain 1900–1914.* Leyden: Noordhoff.

Sebeok, T. A. 1976: *Contributions to the Doctrine of Signs.* Bloomington: Indiana University Press.

Seccombe, W. 1974: The housewife and her labour under capitalism. *New Left Review* 83, 3–24.

Seddon, David ed. 1978: *Relations of Production: Marxist Approaches to Economic Anthropology*. London: Frank Carr.

Segundo, J.-L. 1973: *The Community Called Church*. New York: Orbis.

Seldon, Raman 1989: *Practising Theory and Reading Literature: an Introduction*. New York and London: Harvester Wheatsheaf.

Sellin, T. 1938: *Culture, Conflict and Crime*. London: Social Science Research Council.

Sen, A. 1970 (*1979*): *Collective Choice and Social Welfare*. Amsterdam: North Holland.

Sen, A. 1970: *Growth Economics*. Harmondsworth: Penguin.

Sen, A. 1973: *On Economic Inequality*. Oxford: Clarendon.

Sen, A. 1977: Social choice theory: a re-examination. *Econometrica* 45, 58–89.

Sen, A. 1981: *Poverty and Famines: an Essay in Entitlement and Deprivation*. Oxford: Clarendon Press.

Sen, A. 1982: *Choice, Welfare and Measurement*. Oxford: Blackwell.

Sen, A. 1983: Poor relatively speaking. *Oxford Economic Papers* 35, 153–69.

Sen, A. 1985: A reply. *Oxford Economic Papers* 37, 669–76.

Sen, A. 1986: Social choice theory. In *Handbook of Mathematical Economics*, vol. 3, ed. K. J. Arrow and M. Intriligator. Amsterdam: North-Holland.

Sen, A. 1987: *On Ethics and Economics*. Oxford: Blackwell.

Sen, A. 1987: Social choice. In *The New Palgrave: a Dictionary of Economics*, vol. 4, ed. John Eatwell et al. London: Macmillan.

Sen, A. and Williams, B. eds 1972: *Utilitarianism and Beyond*. Cambridge: Cambridge University Press.

Sennett, Richard 1978: *The Fall of Public Man*. New York: Vintage.

Service, E. 1975: *The Origins of the State and Civilization*. New York: Norton.

Seton-Watson, Hugh 1977: *Nations and States*. London: Methuen.

Shanin, T. ed. 1987: *Peasants and Peasant Societies*. 2nd edn, Oxford: Blackwell.

Shanin, T. 1990: *Defining Peasants*. Oxford: Blackwell.

Shapiro, Kenneth Joel 1985: *Bodily Reflective Modes: a Phenomenological Method for Psychology*. Durham, NC: Duke University Press.

Shapiro, L. 1972: *Totalitarianism*. London: Macmillan.

Shapiro, S. et al. 1987: *Encyclopaedia of Artificial Intelligence*. New York: Wiley.

Shariati, A. 1980: *On the Sociology of Islam*. Berkeley, CA: Mizan Press.

Sharma, G. K. 1989: The Indian co-operative movement: present situation and future prospects. *Review of International Co-operation* 82, 2.

Sharp, G. 1971: The technique of non-violent action. In *Conflict: Violence and Non-Violence*, ed. J. V. Bondurant. Chicago: Aldine Atherton.

Sharp, G. 1973: *The Politics of Non-Violent Action*. Boston: Porter Sargent.

Sharpe, E. J. 1975: *Comparative Religion: a History*. London: Duckworth.

Sharpe, J. 1988: The history of crime in England. In *A History of British Criminology*, ed. P. Rock. Oxford: Oxford University Press.

Sharpe, J. A. 1990: *Judicial Punishment in England*. London: Faber & Faber.

Sharpe, Myron E. 1973: *John Kenneth Galbraith and the Lower Economics*. White Plains, NY: International Arts and Sciences Press.

Sharples, M. et al. 1989: *Computers and Thought*. Cambridge, MA: MIT Press.

Shaw, G. B. ed. 1889 (*1931, 1962*): *Fabian Essays in Socialism*. London: Allen & Unwin.

Shaw, M. and Miles, I. 1979: The social roots of statistical knowledge. In *Demystifying Social Statistics*, ed. J. Irvine et al. London: Pluto.

Sheehy, G. 1976: *Passages: Predictable Crises of Adult Life*. New York: E. P. Dutton/Bantam.

Sheffrin, S. M. 1983: *Rational Expectations*. Cambridge: Cambridge University Press.

Sheldon, W. H. and Stevens, S. S. 1942: *The Varieties of Temperament: a Psychology of Constitutional Differences*. New York: Harper.

Shepherdson, J. C. 1983: Calculus of reasoning. In *Intelligent Systems*, ed. J. E. Hayes and D. Michie. Chichester: Ellis Horwood.

Sherratt, A. G. ed. 1980: *The Cambridge Encyclopedia of Archaeology*. Cambridge: Cambridge University Press.

Shils, Edward 1965: Charisma, order and status. *American Sociological Review* 30, 199–213.

Shils, Edward 1972: *The Intellectuals and the Powers and Other Essays*. Chicago: University of Chicago Press.

Shils, Edward 1975: '*Consensus*' *in Center and*

Periphery: Essays in Macrosociology. Chicago: University of Chicago Press.

Shils, Edward 1981: *Tradition*. London: Faber.

Shils, Edward and Young, M. 1953: The meaning of the coronation. *Sociological Review* 1, 63–81.

Shklar, J. N. 1985: *Ordinary Vices*. Cambridge, MA: Harvard University Press.

Shorter, E. and Tilly, C. 1974: *Strikes in France*. Cambridge: Cambridge University Press.

Shortliffe, E. 1976: *Computer-based Medical Consultations*. New York: Elsevier.

Shotter, J. 1975: *Images of Man in Psychological Research*. London: Methuen.

Showalter, Elaine 1978: *A Literature of their Own*. London: Virago.

Showalter, Elaine, ed. 1986: *The New Feminist Criticism: Essays on Women, Literature and Theory*. London: Virago.

Shryock, H. S. and Siegal, J. S. 1976: *The Methods and Materials of Demography*, ed. E. G. Stockwell. London and New York: Academic Press.

Shubik, M. 1988: *A Game Theoretic Approach to Political Economy*. Cambridge, MA: MIT Press.

Shusterman, Richard, ed. 1989: *Analytic Aesthetics*. Oxford: Blackwell.

Sian, G. 1985: *Accounting for Aggression*. London: Allen & Unwin.

Siltanen, Janet and Stanworth, Michelle 1984: *Women and the Public Sphere*. London: Hutchinson.

Silverman, David 1970: *The Theory of Organizations*. London: Heinemann.

Silvers, Anita 1988: Letting the sun shine in: has analytic aesthetics made aesthetics clear? *Journal of Aesthetics and Art Criticism* 46, 137–49.

Simiand, F. 1907: *Le Salaire des ouvriers des mines de charbon en France*. Paris: Société Nouvelle de Librairie et d'Edition.

Simiand, F. 1932: *Le Salaire, l'évolution et la monnaie*. Paris: Alcan.

Simmel, Georg 1890: *Über soziale Differenzierung: soziologische und psychologische Untersuchungen*. Leipzig: Duncker & Humblot.

Simmel, Georg 1892: *Die Probleme der Geschichtsphilosophie*. Leipzig: Duncker & Humblot.

Simmel, Georg 1902: The number of members as determining the sociological form of the group. *American Journal of Sociology* 8.

Simmel, Georg 1903 (*1957*): The metropolis and mental life. In *Cities and Society*, ed. P. K. Hatt and A. J. Reiss. Glencoe, IL: Free Press.

Simmel, Georg 1907 (*1978*): *The Philosophy of Money*. London and Boston: Routledge & Kegan Paul.

Simmel, Georg 1908 (*1955*): *Conflict and the Web of Group Affiliations*. New York: Free Press; London: Collier-Macmillan.

Simmel, Georg 1908 (*1959*): The problem of sociology, and How is society possible? In *Georg Simmel 1858–1918*, ed. Kurt H. Wolff. Columbus: Ohio State University Press.

Simmel, Georg 1959: *Georg Simmel 1858–1918: a Collection of Essays with Translations and a Bibliography*, ed. K. H. Wolff. Columbus: Ohio University Press.

Simon, A. and Boyer, E. G. eds 1974: *Mirrors for Behavior III: an Anthology of Observation Instruments*. Wyncote, PA: Communication Materials Center.

Simon, H. A. 1947 (*1957*): *Administrative Behaviour*. 2nd edn, New York: Free Press & Macmillan.

Simon, H. A. 1957: *Models of Man*. New York: Wiley.

Simon, H. A. 1970: *The Sciences of the Artificial*. Cambridge, MA: MIT Press.

Simon, H. A. 1983: *Reason in Human Affairs*. Oxford: Blackwell.

Simon, H. A. 1986: Rationality in psychology and economics. *Journal of Business* 59, S209–25.

Simon, Walter M. 1963: *European Positivism in the Nineteenth Century*. Ithaca: Cornell University Press.

Simonds, A. P. 1978: *Karl Mannheim's Sociology of Knowledge*. Oxford: Clarendon Press.

Simons, H. C. 1948: *Economic Policy for a Free Society*. Chicago: University of Chicago Press.

Simpson, G. G. 1949: *The Meaning of Evolution: a Study of the History of Life and of its Significance for Man*. New Haven, CT: Yale University Press.

Simpson, G. S. and Yinger, J. M. 1953 (*1985*): *Racial and Cultural Minorities*. 5th edn, New York: Harper & Row.

Simpson, R. L. 1959: Vertical and horizontal communication in formal organizations. *Administrative Science Quarterly* 4.

Sims, C. A. 1987: Making economics credible. In *Advances in Econometrics Fifth World Congress*, vol. 2, ed. T. F. Bewley. Cambridge: Cambridge University Press.

Sinclair, R. K. 1988: *Democracy and Participation in Athens*. Cambridge: Cambridge University Press.

Singer, J. D. 1981: Accounting for international war: the state of the discipline. *Journal of Peace Research* 18, 1–18.

Singer, J. D. and Small, M. 1972: *The Wages of War*. New York: Wiley.

Singer, P. 1977: *Animal Liberation*. St Albans: Paladin.

Singer, P. ed. 1986: *Applied Ethics*. Oxford: Oxford University Press.

Singh, A. 1977: UK industry and the world economy: a case of de-industrialisation? *Cambridge Journal of Economics* 1.2, 113–16.

Singham, A. W. and Hune, Shirley 1986: *Non-Alignment in an Age of Alignments*. London: Zed Press.

Sitney, P. A. 1974: *Visionary Film: the American Avant-Garde Film*. New York: Oxford University Press.

Skillen, A. 1977: *Ruling Illusions*. Hassocks: Harvester Press.

Skinner, B. F. 1938: *The Behaviour of Organisms*. New York: Appleton Century.

Skinner, B. F. 1953: *Science and Human Behaviour*. New York: Macmillan.

Skinner, B. F. 1959: *Verbal Behaviour*. London: Methuen.

Skinner, B. F. 1971: *Beyond Freedom and Dignity*. Harmondsworth: Penguin.

Skinner, Q. ed. 1985: *The Return of Grand Theory in the Human Sciences*. Cambridge: Cambridge University Press.

Sklair, L. 1991: *Sociology of the Global System*. Hemel Hempstead: Harvester Wheatsheaf.

Skocpol, T. 1979: *States and Social Revolutions*. Cambridge and New York: Cambridge University Press.

Slater, Philip and Bennis, Warren G. 1964: Democracy is inevitable. *Harvard Business Review* 42, 51–9.

Slattery, M. 1986: *Official Statistics*. London: Tavistock.

Smart, David A. 1978: *Pannekoek and Gorter's Marxism*. London: Pluto Press.

Smart, J. J. C. and Williams, B. eds 1973: *Utilitarianism: For and Against*. Cambridge: Cambridge University Press.

Smart, N. 1973: *The Science of Religion and the Sociology of Knowledge*. Princeton, NJ: Princeton University Press.

Smelser, N. J. 1964: Toward a theory of modernization. In *Social Change*, ed. A. Etzioni and E. Etzioni. New York: Basic Books.

Smelser, N. J. 1988: Social structure. In *Handbook of Sociology*. Newbury Park, CA: Sage.

Smith, Adam 1776 (*1976*): *An Inquiry into the Nature and Causes of the Wealth of Nations*, ed. R. H. Campbell et al. Oxford and New York: Oxford University Press.

Smith, A. D. 1971 (*1983*): *Theories of Nationalism*. 2nd edn, London: Duckworth.

Smith, A. D. 1973: *The Concept of Social Change*. London: Routledge & Kegan Paul.

Smith, A. D. 1979: *Nationalist Movements in the 20th Century*. London: Macmillan.

Smith, A. D. 1991: *National Identity*. Harmondsworth: Penguin.

Smith, D. E. 1971: *Religion, Politics and Social Change in the Third World*. New York: Free Press.

Smith, D. M. 1985: Perceived peer and parental influences on youths' social world. *Youth and Society* 17, 131–56.

Smith, John E. 1978: *Purpose and Thought: the Meaning of Pragmatism*. New Haven, CT: Yale University Press.

Smith, Michael Garfield 1963: *The Plural Society in the British West Indies*. Berkeley: University of California Press.

Smith, Michael Garfield 1974: *Corporations and Society*. London: Duckworth.

Smith, W. C. 1957: *Islam in Modern History*. Princeton, NJ: Princeton University Press.

Smolensky, P. 1988: On the proper treatment of connectionism. *Behavioural and Brain Sciences* 11, 1–74.

Snipp, C. Matthew 1985: Occupational mobility and social class: insights from men's career mobility. *American Sociological Review* 50, 475–93.

Snow, E. 1968: *Red Star over China*. Rev. edn, New York: Grove Press.

Snyder, B. G. 1971: *The Hidden Curriculum*. New York: Knopf.

Sobrino, J. 1978: *Spirituality of Liberation*. New York: Orbis.

Sohn-Rethel, A. 1978: *Intellectual and Manual Labour*. London: Macmillan.

Soja, Edward W. 1989: *Postmodern Geographies: the Reassertion of Space in Critical Social Theory*. London and New York: Verso.

Söllner, Alfons 1979: *Geschichte und Herrschaft: Studien zur materialistischen Sozialwissenschaft 1929–1942*. Frankfurt am Main: Suhrkamp.

Solow, R. 1956: A contribution to the theory of economic growth. *Quarterly Journal of Economics* 70, 65–94.

Sombart, W. 1906 (*1976*): *Why is there no Socialism in the United States?* London: Macmillan.

Sombart, W. 1913 (*1967*): *The Quintessence of Capitalism*, trans. M. Epstein. New York: Howard Fertig.

Sontag, S. 1979: *Illness as Metaphor*. London: Allen Lane.

Soper, Kate 1981: *On Human Needs: Open and Closed Theories in a Marxist Perspective*. Brighton: Harvester.

Sorel, Georges, 1906 (*1972*): *Reflections on Violence*. New York and London: Macmillan.

Sorokin, P. A. 1927: *Social Mobility*. New York: Harper.

Sorokin, P. A. 1937–41: *Social and Cultural Dynamics*, 4 vols. Englewood Cliffs, NJ: Bedminster Press.

Sorokin, P. A. et al. eds 1965: *Systematic Source Book in Rural Sociology*. Russell & Russell.

Sosa, E. ed. 1975: *Causation and Conditionals*. Oxford: Oxford University Press.

Sparshott, Francis 1963: *The Structure of Aesthetics*. Toronto: University of Toronto Press.

Spearman, C. E. 1927: *The Abilities of Man*. London: Macmillan.

Spector, M. and Kitsuse, J. I. 1987: *Constructing Social Problems*. New York: Aldine de Gruyter.

Spence, Kenneth 1956: *Behaviour Theory and Conditioning*. New Haven, CT: Yale University Press.

Spencer, F. ed. 1982: *A History of American Physical Anthropology*. New York: Academic Press.

Spencer, H. R. 1963: Coup d'état. In *Encyclopedia of the Social Sciences*, ed. Edwin R. A. Seligman and Alvin Johnson, vols 3–4. New York: Macmillan.

Spencer, Herbert 1858 (*1966*): Prospectus of a system of philosophy issued by Herbert Spencer in 1858. In *Herbert Spencer's Sociology: a Study in the History of Social Theory*, ed. J. Rumney. New York: Atherton.

Spencer, Herbert 1876–96 (*1925–9*): *The Principles of Sociology*, 3 vols. New York: Appleton.

Spencer, Herbert 1879–92 (*1978*): *The Principles of Ethics*. Indianapolis: Liberty Classics.

Spencer, Jane 1986: *The Rise of the Woman Novelist*. Oxford: Blackwell.

Spencer, M. E. 1973: What is charisma? *British Journal of Sociology* 24, 341–54.

Spencer, Paul, ed. 1985: *Society and the Dance*. Cambridge: Cambridge University Press.

Spender, D. 1983: *Women of Ideas*. London: Ark.

Spengler, O. 1918–22 (*1926–8*); *The Decline of the West*, 2 vols. New York: Knopf.

Sperber, D. and Wilson, D. 1986: *Relevance*. Oxford: Blackwell.

Spero, Shubert 1983: *Morality, Halakha and the Jewish Tradition*. New York.

Spiegel-Rösing, I. and Price, D. de Solla 1977: *Science, Technology and Society: a Cross-Disciplinary Perspective*. London: Sage.

Spiegelberg, Herbert 1982: *The Phenomenological Movement*, 2 vols. 3rd edn, The Hague: Martinus Nijhoff.

Spiro, M. 1966: Religion: problems of definition and explanation. In *Anthropological Approaches to the Study of Religion*, ed. M. Banton. London: Tavistock.

Spitz, E. 1984: *Majority Rule*. Chatham, NJ: Chatham House.

Spivak, Gayatri Chakravorty 1988: *In Other Worlds: Essays in Cultural Politics*. New York and London: Routledge.

Sprent, P. 1988: *Taking Risks: the Science of Uncertainty*. Harmondsworth: Penguin.

Sprent, P. 1988: *Understanding Data*. Harmondsworth: Penguin.

Sprigge, T. L. S. 1984: *Theories of Existence*. Harmondsworth: Penguin.

Springborg, P. 1981: *The Problem of Human Needs and the Critique of Civilization*. London: Allen & Unwin.

Sprinzak, E. 1972: Weber's thesis as an historical explanation. *History and Theory* 11, 294–320.

Sraffa, P. 1960: *Production of Commodities by Means of Commodities*. London: Cambridge University Press.

Srinivas, M. N. 1962: *Caste in Modern India*. Bombay: Asia Publishing House.

Srinivas, M. N. 1967: *Social Change in Modern India*. Berkeley: University of California Press.

Stacey, M. 1981: The division of labour revisited or overcoming the two Adams. In *Practice and Progress: British Sociology 1950–1980*, ed. P. Abrams et al. London: Allen & Unwin.

Stack, Carol 1974: *All our Kin*. New York: Harper & Row.

Stalin, Joseph V. 1940: *Dialectical and Historical*

Materialism. London: Lawrence & Wishart; New York: International.

Stalin, Joseph V. 1952–5: *Works*, vols. 1–13. London: Lawrence & Wishart.

Stalin, Joseph V. *1972: The Essential Stalin: Major Theoretical Writings*, ed. B. Franklin. Garden City, NY: Anchor.

Staniszkis, J. 1981: *The Self-Limiting Revolution*. Cambridge: Cambridge University Press.

Stanworth, M. 1983: *Gender and Schooling*. London: Hutchinson.

Stanworth, M. ed. 1986: *Reproductive Technologies*. Cambridge: Polity.

Starr, J. 1979: *Continuing the Revolution*. Princeton, NJ: Princeton University Press.

Starr, P. 1982: *The Social Transformation of American Medicine*. New York: Basic Books.

Staub, E. 1989: *The Roots of Evil*. Cambridge: Cambridge University Press.

Stavenhagen, Rodolfo 1968: Seven fallacies about Latin America. In *Latin America: Reform or Revolution*, ed. J. Petras and M. Zeitlin. Greenwich, CT: Fawcett.

Stearns, Peter 1971: *Revolutionary Syndicalism and French Labour*. New Brunswick, NJ: Rutgers University Press.

Stedman Jones, G. 1973: Engels and the end of classic German philosophy. *New Left Review* 79.

Stedman Jones, G. 1983 (*1985*): Class expression versus social control? A critique of recent trends in the social history of 'leisure'. In *Social Control and the State*, ed. S. Cohen and A. Scull. Oxford: Blackwell.

Steedman, Carolyn 1982: *The Tidy House*. London: Virago.

Stehr, Nico and Meja, Volker eds 1984: *Society and Knowledge: Contemporary Perspectives in the Sociology of Knowledge*. New Brunswick, NJ, and London: Transaction.

Stein, H. 1969: *The Fiscal Revolution in America*. Chicago: University of Chicago Press.

Stein, H. 1988: *Presidential Economics: the Making of Economic Policy from Roosevelt to Reagan and Beyond*. Washington, DC: American Enterprise Institute for Public Policy Research.

Stein, M. R. et al. eds 1960: *Identity and Anxiety: Survival of the Person in Mass Society*. Glencoe, IL: Free Press.

Stengel, E. 1973: *Suicide and Attempted Suicide*. Harmondsworth: Penguin.

Stengel, E. and Cook, N. 1958: *Attempted Suicide*. Oxford: Oxford University Press.

Stepelevich, Lawrence S. ed. 1983: *The Young Hegelians: an Anthology*. Cambridge: Cambridge University Press.

Stephenson, Carl 1969: *Medieval Feudalism*. Ithaca, NY: Cornell University Press.

Stevenson, L. 1974: *Seven Theories of Human Nature*. Oxford: Clarendon Press.

Steward, J. 1977: *Evolution and Ecology*. Urbana, IL: Urbana University Press.

Stewart, M. 1967: *Keynes and After*. Harmondsworth: Penguin.

Stich, S. 1985: Is man a rational animal? Notes on the epistemology of rationality. *Synthese* 64, 115–35.

Stigler, G. J. 1941: *Production and Distribution Theories: the Formative Period*. New York: Macmillan.

Stigler, G. J. 1965: *Essays in the History of Economics*. Chicago: University of Chicago Press.

Stigler, G. J. 1968: *The Organization of Industry*. Chicago: University of Chicago Press.

Stigler, G. J. 1988: *Memories of an Unregulated Economist*. New York: Basic Books.

Stigler, George J. and Becker, Gary S. 1977: De gustibus non est disputandum. *American Economic Review* 67, 76–90.

Stigler, S. M. 1986: *The History of Statistics: the Measurement of Uncertainty Before 1900*. Cambridge, MA: Harvard University Press.

Stillings, N. A. et al. 1987: *Cognitive Science: an Introduction*. Cambridge, MA: Bradford/MIT Press.

Stinchcombe, Arthur L. 1968: *Constructing Social Theories*. New York: Harcourt, Brace, and World.

Stirner, M. 1845 (*1912*): *The Ego and his Own*, trans. S. T. Byington. London: Fifield.

Stocking, G. W. 1968: *Race, Culture and Evolution*. London: Collier-Macmillan.

Stokes, C. 1962: A theory of slums. *Land Economics* 8.3.

Stolnitz, Jerome 1960: *Aesthetics and Philosophy of Art Criticism*. Boston: Houghton Mifflin.

Stone, K. 1974: The origins of job structures in the steel industry. *Review of Radical Political Economics* 6.2, 113–73.

Stone, Lawrence 1977: *The Family, Sex and Marriage*. New York: Harper & Row.

Stone, Lawrence and Stone, Jeanne Fawtier 1984: *An Open Elite? England 1540–1880*. Oxford: Clarendon.

Storper, M. and Walker, R. 1989: *The Capitalist Imperative: Territory, Technology and Industrial Growth*. Oxford: Blackwell.

Stouffer, S. A. et al. 1949: *The American Soldier: Adjustments during Army Life*. Princeton, NJ: Princeton University Press.

Stouffer, S. A. et al. *The American Soldier*. Princeton, NJ: Princeton University Press.

Strachey, G. Lytton 1948: *Eminent Victorians*. London: Chatto & Windus.

Strachey, J. 1935: *The Nature of Capitalist Crisis*. London: Gollancz.

Strachey, Ray 1928 (*1978*): *The Cause*. London: Virago.

Strauss, A. 1969: *Mirrors and Masks: the Search for Identity*. State of California: Sociology Press.

Strauss, A. 1978: *Negotiations: Varieties, Contexts, Processes, and Social Order*. San Francisco: Jossey-Bass.

Strauss, L. 1949: *Natural Right and History*. Chicago: University of Chicago Press.

Strayer, Joseph R. 1971: The two levels of feudalism. In *Medieval Statecraft and the Perspectives of History*. Princeton, NJ: Princeton University Press.

Streeck, W. and Schmitter, P. C., eds 1985: *Private Interest Government: Beyond Market and State*. London: Sage.

Stryker, S. 1980: *Symbolic Interactionism*. Menlo Park, CA: Benjamin-Cummings.

Sturmthal, Adolf 1964: *Workers' Councils: a Study of Workplace Democratization on Both Sides of the Iron Curtain*. Cambridge, MA: Harvard University Press.

Sturmthal, Adolf 1972: *Comparative Labor Movements*. Belmont: Wadsworth.

Sugden, R. 1981: *The Political Economy of Public Choice*. Oxford: Martin Robertson.

Sugden, R. 1986: *The Economics of Rights, Cooperation and Welfare*. Oxford: Blackwell.

Suh Kwang-sun, D. 1983: A biographical sketch of an Asian theology. In *Minjung Theology: People as the Subjects of History*, ed. Commission on Theological Concerns of the Christian Conference of Asia. New York: Orbis.

Sulloway, Frank J. 1980: *Freud: Biologist of the Mind*. London: Fontana.

Supicic, I. 1987: *Music in Society: a Guide to the Sociology of Music*. Stuyvesant, NY: Pendragon Press.

Süssmilch, Johann 1761–2: *Die göttliche Ordnung in der Veränderungen des menschlichen Geschlechts aus der Geburt, dem Tode, und der Fortpflanzung desselben Erwiesen*. 2nd edn, Berlin.

Sutcliffe, B. 1972: Conclusion. In *Studies in the Theory of Imperialism*, ed. R. Owen and B. Sutcliffe. London: Longman.

Sutherland, E. and Cressey, D. 1974: *Principles of Criminology*. Philadelphia: J. B. Lippincott.

Sutherland, E. H. 1937: *The Professional Thief*. Chicago: Phoenix Press.

Sutherland, John 1978: *Fiction and the Fiction Industry*. London: Athlone Press.

Svalastoga, Kaare 1965: *Social Differentiation*. New York: David McKay.

Swan, T. 1956: Economic growth and capital accumulation. *Economic Record* 32.

Swearer, Donald K. 1981: *Buddhism and Society in Southeast Asia*. Chambersburg, PA: Anima Books.

Sweezy, P. M. ed. 1949: *Karl Marx and the Close of his System, by Eugen von Böhm-Bawerk* [1896], *and Böhm-Bawerk's Criticism of Marx, by Rudolf Hilferding* [1904]. New York: Augustus M. Kelley.

Swingewood, A. 1977: *The Myth of Mass Culture*. London: Macmillan.

Szelényi, Ivan 1983: *Urban Inequalities under State Socialism*. Oxford: Oxford University Press.

Szell, György 1988: *Participation, Workers Control and Self-Management*. London: Sage.

Szell, György ed. 1992: *Concise Encyclopedia of Participation and Co-management*. Berlin and New York: de Gruyter.

Szent-Gyorgyi, A. 1971: Looking back. *Perspectives in Biology and Medicine* 15, 1–5.

Sztompka, P. 1981: The dialectics of spontaneity and planning in sociological theory. In *Spontaneity and Planning in Social Development*, ed. U. Himmelstrand. Beverly Hills, CA: Sage.

Taine, Hyppolite 1853: *La Fontaine and his Fables*. Paris.

Tajfel, H. ed. 1978: *Differentiation between Social Groups*. London: Academic Press.

Tajfel, H. 1981: *Human Groups and Social Categories*. Cambridge: Cambridge University Press.

Talmon, J. L. 1952: *The Rise of Totalitarian Democracy*. Boston: Beacon Press.

Tannenbaum, F. 1938: *Crime and the Community*. New York: Columbia University Press.

Tarde, G. 1903 (*1962*): *The Laws of Imitation*. Gloucester: Peter Smith.

Tarski, A. 1930 (*1982*): The concept of truth in

formalized language. In *Logic, Semantics and Metamathematics*, ed. J. Woodger. Indianapolis: Hackett.

Tatarkiewicz, W. 1970–4: *History of Aesthetics*, 3 vols. Warsaw: PWN; The Hague: Mouton.

Tatarkiewicz, W. 1980: *A History of Six Ideas: an Essay in Aesthetics*. Warsaw: PWN; The Hague: M. Nijhoff.

Tawney, R. H. 1931: *Equality*. London: Allen & Unwin.

Tawney, R. H. *1975*: *Religion and the Rise of Capitalism*. Harmondsworth: Penguin.

Tax, S. ed. 1960: *Evolution After Darwin: the University of Chicago Centennial*, vols. 1 and 2. Chicago: University of Chicago Press.

Tax, S. and Callender, C. eds 1960: *Evolution after Darwin: the University of Chicago Centennial*, vol. 3. Chicago: University of Chicago Press.

Taylor, B. 1983: *Eve and the New Jerusalem*. London: Virago.

Taylor, C. 1964: *The Explanation of Behaviour*. London: Routledge & Kegan Paul.

Taylor, C. 1975: *Hegel*. Cambridge: Cambridge University Press.

Taylor, C. 1977: Interpretation and the sciences of man. In *Understanding and Social Inquiry*, ed. Fred Dallmayr and Thomas McCarthy. Notre Dame: University of Indiana Press.

Taylor, C. 1985: Atomism. In *Philosophical Papers*, vol. 2. Cambridge: Cambridge University Press.

Taylor, C. 1989: *Sources of the Self*. Cambridge, MA: Harvard University Press.

Taylor, F. W. 1947 (*1964*): *Scientific Management*. New York: Harper & Row.

Taylor, L. R. 1949: *Party Politics in the Age of Caesar*. Berkeley: University of California Press.

Taylor, M. 1982: *Community, Anarchy and Liberty*. Cambridge: Cambridge University Press.

Taylor, M. 1987: *The Possibility of Cooperation*. Cambridge: Cambridge University Press.

Taylor, S. 1982: *Durkheim and the Study of Suicide*. London: Macmillan.

Teger, A. I. 1980: *Too Much Invested to Quit*. New York: Pergamon.

Teich, Albert H. ed. 1977: *Technology and Man's Future*. New York: St Martin's Press.

Teilhard de Chardin, Pierre 1955 (*1959*): *The Phenomenon of Man*. London: Collins.

Telser, L. G. 1972: *Competition, Collusion and Game Theory*. Chicago: Aldine-Atherton.

Ten, C. L. 1988: *Crime, Guilt and Punishment*. Oxford: Oxford University Press.

Tench, D. 1981: *Towards a Middle System of Law*.

Thayer, Horace S. 1981: *Meaning and Action: a Critical History of Pragmatism*. 2nd edn, Indianapolis: Hackett.

Therborn, G. 1980: *What Does the Ruling Class Do When it Rules? State Apparatuses and State Power under Feudalism, Capitalism and Socialism*. London: Verso.

Thibaut, J. W. and Kelley, H. H. 1959: *The Social Psychology of Groups*. New York: Wiley.

Thody, P. 1989: *French Caesarism: from Napoleon I to Charles de Gaulle*. London: Macmillan.

Thoenes, P. 1962 (*1966*): *The Elite in the Welfare State*. London: Faber & Faber.

Thomas, H. and Logan, C. 1982: *Mondragon: an Economic Analysis*. London: Allen & Unwin.

Thomas, W. I. and Znaniecki, F. 1918 (*1974*): *The Polish Peasant in Europe and America*, 2 vols. New York: Octagon.

Thomason, Burke C. 1982: *Making Sense of Reification: Alfred Schutz and Constructionist Theory*. London: Macmillan.

Thompson, E. P. 1963: *The Making of the English Working Class*. London: Gollancz.

Thompson, E. P. 1967: Time, work discipline and industrial capitalism. *Past and Present* 38.

Thompson, E. P. 1991: *Customs in Common*. London: Merlin.

Thompson, F. M. L. 1981: Social control in Victorian Britain. *Economic History Review*, 2nd series, 34. 2.

Thompson, James 1967: *Organizations in Action*. New York: McGraw-Hill.

Thompson, John B. 1984: *Studies in the Theory of Ideology*. Cambridge: Polity.

Thompson, John B. 1990: *Ideology and Modern Culture*. Cambridge: Polity.

Thompson, P. 1983: *The Nature of Work: an Introduction to Debates on the Labour Process*. London: Macmillan.

Thompson, V. B. 1969: *Africa and Unity: the Evolution of Pan-Africanism*. London: Longmans.

Thompson, Victor 1961: *Modern Organization*. New York: Alfred Knopf.

Thorne, Barrie and Yalom, Marilyn eds 1982: *Rethinking the Family*. New York: Longman.

Thornton, A. P. 1978: *Imperialism in the Twentieth Century*. London: Macmillan.

Thrift, N. 1983: On the determination of social action in space and time. *Society and Space* 1, 23–57.

Tibi, B. 1981: *Arab Nationalism: a Critical Enquiry*. London: Macmillan.

Tickner, Lisa 1988: Feminism, art history and sexual difference. *Genders* 3.

Tilly, C. ed. 1975: *The Formation of National States in Western Europe*. Princeton, NJ: Princeton University Press.

Tilly, C. 1978: *From Mobilization to Revolution*. Reading, MA: Addison-Wesley.

Timpanaro, S. 1976: *On Materialism*. London: New Left Books.

Tinbergen, J. 1939: *Statistical Testing of Business Cycle Theories*, 2 vols. Geneva: League of Nations.

Tinbergen, N. 1963: On aims and methods of ethology. *Zeitschrift für Tierpsychologie* 20.

Tingsten, Herbert 1973: *The Swedish Social Democrats*. Towota, NJ: Bedminster Press.

Tirole, J. 1988: *Theory of Industrial Organization*. Cambridge, MA: MIT Press.

Titmuss, R. M. 1958: *Essays on the Welfare State*. London: Allen & Unwin.

Titmuss, R. M. 1968: *Commitment to Welfare*. London: Allen & Unwin.

Tocqueville, A. de 1835–40 (*1966*): *Democracy in America*. New York: Harper.

Tocqueville, A. de 1854 (*1955*): *The Old Regime and the French Revolution*. New York: Doubleday.

Todorov, Tzvetan 1973: *The Fantastic*. Ithaca, NY: Cornell University Press.

Toffler, Alvin 1980: *The Third Wave*. London: Collins.

Tolman, E. C. 1958: *Behaviour and Psychological Man*. Berkeley: University of California Press.

Tomlinson, Alan ed. 1990: *Consumption, Identity and Style: Marketing, Meanings and the Packaging of Pleasure*. London: Routledge.

Tomlinson, Alan 1991: Leisure as consumer culture. In *Ideology, Leisure Policy and Practice*, ed. David Botterill and Alan Tomlinson. Eastbourne: Leisure Studies Association.

Tomlinson, G. 1984: The web of culture: a context for musicology. *19th-Century Music* 7, 350–62.

Tönnies, Ferdinand 1887 (*1955*): *Community and Association*. London: Routledge & Kegan Paul; East Lancing, MI: University Press.

Tönnies, Ferdinand 1917: *Der englische Staat und der deutsche Staat*. Berlin: Karl Curtius.

Tonry, M. and Morris, N. 1979: *Crime and Justice*. Chicago: University of Chicago Press.

Toulmin, Stephen 1972: *Human Understanding: the Collective Use and Evolution of Concepts*. Princeton, NJ: Princeton University Press.

Touraine, Alain 1965: *La Conscience ouvrière*. Paris: Seuil.

Touraine, Alain 1965: *Sociologie de l'action*. Paris: Seuil.

Touraine, Alain 1968 (*1971*): *The May Movement*. New York: Random House.

Touraine, Alain 1968 (*1971*): *The Post-industrial Society*. New York: Random House.

Touraine, Alain 1972 (*1974*): *The Academic System in American Society*. New York: McGraw Hill.

Touraine, Alain 1973 (*1977*): *The Self-production of Society*. Chicago: University of Chicago Press.

Touraine, Alain 1981: *The Voice and the Eye*. New York: Cambridge University Press.

Touraine, Alain 1984: *Le Retour de l'acteur*. Paris: Fayard.

Touraine, Alain 1988: *La Parole et le sang*. Paris: Odile Jacob.

Touraine, Alain 1993: *Towards a New Economic Order*. Cambridge: Polity.

Touraine, Alain et al. 1982: *Solidarité, analyse d'un mouvement social: Pologne 1980–81*. Paris: Fayard.

Touraine, Alain et al. 1987: *The Workers' Movement*. Cambridge: Cambridge University Press.

Townsend, P. 1975: *Sociology and Social Policy*. London: Allen Lane.

Townsend, P. 1979: *Poverty in the United Kingdom*. London: Allen Lane

Townsend, P. 1985: A sociological approach to the measurement of poverty: a rejoinder to Professor Amartya Sen. *Oxford Economic Papers* 37, 659–68.

Townsend, P. 1987: Deprivation. *Journal of Social Policy* 16, 125–46.

Townsend, P. 1992: *The International Analysis of Poverty*. London and New York: Simon & Schuster.

Toye, J. 1987: *Dilemmas of Development: Reflections on the Counter-revolution in Development Theory and Policy*. Oxford: Blackwell.

Toynbee, Arnold 1934–61: *A Study of History*, 12. vols. Oxford and New York: Oxford University Press.

Trice, H. M. and Beyer, J. M. 1986: Charisma and its routinisation in two social movement organisations. *Research in Organisational Behaviour* 8, 113–64.

Trigg, R. 1982: *The Shaping of Man*. Oxford: Blackwell.

Trigger, Brian J. 1983: The rise of Egyptian civilization. In *Ancient Egypt: a Social History*, ed. B. J. Trigger and B. Kemp. Cambridge: Cambridge University Press.

Trimberger, E. K. 1978: *Revolution from Above*. New Brunswick, NJ: Transaction Books.

Trivers, R. 1985: *Social Evolution*. Menlo Park, CA: Benjamin/Cummins.

Troeltsch, E. 1911 (*1931, 1981*): *The Social Teaching of the Christian Churches*. Chicago: University of Chicago Press.

Troeltsch, E. 1912 (*1955*): *Protestantism and Progress: an Historical Study of the Relation of Protestantism to the Modern World*. London: Pitman's.

Troeltsch, E. 1922: Der Historismus und seine Probleme. In *Gesammelte Schriften*, vol. 3. Tübingen: J. C. B. Mohr

Trotsky, L. 1906, 1930 (*1962*): *The Permanent Revolution and Results and Prospects*. London: New Park.

Trotsky, L. 1922 (*1972*): *1905*. London: Allen Lane.

Trotsky, L. 1932 (*1977*): *History of the Russian Revolution*. Ann Arbor: University of Michigan Press; London: Pluto.

Trotsky, L. 1932 (*1975*): *The Struggle Against Fascism in Germany*. Harmondsworth: Penguin.

Trotsky, L. 1937 (*1972*): *The Revolution Betrayed*. 5th edn, New York: Pathfinder.

Trotsky, L. 1938 (*1973*): *The Transitional Program for Socialist Revolution*. New York: Pathfinder.

Trotsky, L. et al. 1973: *Their Morals and Ours*. New York: Pathfinder.

Trubetzkoy, N. S. 1939 (*1969*): *Principles of Phonology*. Berkeley: University of California Press.

Trudgill, P. 1974: *Sociolinguistics*. Harmondsworth: Penguin.

Trudgill, P. 1975: *Accent, Dialect and the School*. London: Edward Arnold.

Trudgill, P. ed. 1978: *Sociolinguistic Patterns in British English*. London: Arnold.

Truman, D. B. 1951: *The Governmental Process*. New York: Alfred Knopf.

Tucker, R. C. 1968: The theory of charismatic leadership. *Daedalus* 97, 731–56.

Tucker, R. C. 1973: Culture, political culture, and communist society. *Political Science Quarterly* 88, 173–190.

Tucker, R. C. 1973: *Stalin as Revolutionary, 1879–1929: a Study of Personality and History*. New York: Norton.

Tucker, R. C. 1981: *Politics as Leadership*. Columbia: University of Missouri Press.

Tucker, R. C. 1991: *Stalin in Power: the Revolution from Above, 1928–1941*. London: W. W. Norton.

Tudor, H. 1972: *Political Myth*. London: Pall Mall.

Tudor, H. and Tudor, J. M. eds 1988: *Marxism and Social Democracy: the Revisionist Debate 1896–1898*. Cambridge: Cambridge University Press.

Tugendhat, E. 1979: *Self-consciousness and self-determination*. Cambridge, MA: MIT Press.

Tullock, G. 1965: *The Politics of Bureaucracy*. Washington, DC: Public Affairs Press.

Tully, James ed. 1988: *Meaning and Context: Quentin Skinner and his Critics*. Cambridge: Polity.

Tuma, E. H. 1971: *Economic History and the Social Sciences: Problems of Methodology*. Berkeley: University of California Press.

Turing, A. M. 1954: Can a machine think? In *The World of Mathematics*, vol. 3, ed. J. R. Newman. New York: Simon & Schuster.

Turnbull, C. 1971: *The Mountain People*. London: Jonathan Cape.

Turner, Bryan S. 1974: *Weber and Islam: a Critical Study*. London: Routledge & Kegan Paul.

Turner, Bryan S. 1978: *Marx and the End of Orientalism*. London: Allen & Unwin.

Turner, Bryan S. 1984: Orientalism and the problem of civil society. In *Orientalism, Islam and Islamists*, ed. Asaf Hussain et al. Brattleboro, VT: Amana Press.

Turner, Bryan S. 1986: *Citizenship and Capitalism: the Debate over Reformism*. London: Allen & Unwin.

Turner, J. F. C. 1967: Barriers and channels for housing development in modernizing countries. *Journal of the American Institute of Planners* 32, 167–81.

Turner, J. H. 1986: *The Body and Society*. Oxford: Blackwell.

Turner, J. H. 1988: *A Theory of Social Interaction*. Stanford, CA: Stanford University Press.

Turner, J. H. 1991: *The Structure of Sociological Theory*. 5th edn, Belmont, CA: Wadsworth.

Turner, R. 1984: *Logics for Artificial Intelligence*. Chichester: Ellis Horwood.

Turner, R. H. 1962: Role taking: process versus conformity. In *Human Behavior and Social Processes*, ed. A. Rose. Boston: Houghton Mifflin.

Turner, R. H. 1968: Role: sociological aspects. In

International Encyclopedia of the Social Sciences, ed. David L. Sills. New York: Macmillan.

Turner, R. H. 1974: Rule learning and role learning: what an interactive theory of roles adds to the theory of social norms. *International Journal of Critical Sociology* 1, 52–73.

Turner, R. H. 1979: Strategy for developing an integrated role theory. *Humboldt Journal of Social Relations* 7, 114–22.

Turner, R. H. and Colomy, P. 1987: Role differentiation: orienting principles. *Advances in Group Processes* 7, 40–69.

Turner, R. H. and Killian, M. 1957: *Collective Behavior*. Englewood Cliffs, NJ: Prentice-Hall.

Turner, Victor 1968: Myth and symbol. In *International Encyclopaedia of the Social Sciences*, ed. David L. Sills, vols. 9–10. London and Chicago: Macmillan and Free Press.

Tuveson, Ernest Lee 1964: *Millennium and Utopia: a Study in the Background of the Idea of Progress*. New York: Harper & Row.

Tuveson, Ernest Lee 1968: *Redeemer Nation: the Idea of America's Millennial Role*. Chicago: University of Chicago Press.

Tu Wei-ming 1984: *Confucian Ethics Today: the Singapore Challenge*. Singapore: Federal.

Tu Wei-ming 1985: *Confucian Thought: Selfhood as Creative Transformation*. Albany: State University of New York Press.

Tu Wei-ming 1991: The search for roots in industrial East Asia: the case of the Confucian revival. In *Fundamentalisms Observed*, ed. Martin E. Marty and R. Scott Appleby. Chicago: University of Chicago Press.

Twining, William 1986: *Legal Theory and Common Law*. Oxford: Blackwell.

Udy, S. H. 1968: Social structure: social structural analysis. In *International Encyclopedia of the Social Sciences*, ed. D. L. Sills, Vol. 14. New York: Macmillan.

Uebel, T. E. ed. 1991: *Rediscovering the Forgotten Vienna Circle*. Austrian Studies on Otto Neurath and the Vienna Circle. Dordrecht: Kluwer.

Ullman-Margalit, E. 1977: *The Emergence of Norms*. Oxford: Oxford University Press.

UNESCO 1978: *Study in Depth on the Concept of Basic Human Needs in Relation to Various Ways of Life and its Possible Implications for the Action of the Organisations*. Paris: UNESCO.

UNESCO 1984: Industrial democracy: participation, labour relations and motivation. *International Social Science Journal* 36, 196–402.

UNESCO 1986: *Participate in Development*. Paris: UNESCO.

United States Department of Health, Education and Welfare 1976: *The Measure of Poverty: a Report to Congress as Mandated by the Education Amendments of 1974*. Washington, DC: Government Printer.

Uno, K. 1980: *Principles of Political Economy: Theory of a Purely Capitalist Economy*. Brighton: Harvester.

Urbach, E. E. 1975: *The Sages: their Concepts and Beliefs*, 2 vols. Jerusalem.

Urry, John 1990: *The Tourist Gaze: Leisure and Travel in Contemporary Societies*. London: Sage.

Useem, M. 1984: *The Inner Circle*. New York: Oxford University Press.

Utitz, Emil 1914–20: *Grundlegung der allgemeinen Kunstwissenschaft*, 2 vols. Stuttgart.

Uzawa, H. 1961: On a two sector model of economic growth. *Review of Economic Studies* 29.

Van den Berghe, Pierre Louis 1978: *Race and Racism: a Comparative Perspective*. New York: Wiley.

Van der Leeuw, G. 1938: *Religion in Essence and Manifestation*. London: Allen & Unwin.

Van Doorn, J. A. 1975: *The Soldier and Social Change*. Beverly Hills, CA: Sage.

Van Duijn, J. J. 1983: *The Long Wave in Economic Life*. London: Allen & Unwin.

Van Heijenoort, J. 1967 (*1985*): Logic as calculus and logic as language. *Synthse* 17, 324–30 (1967). Also in *Selected Essays*, Naples: Bibliopolis (1985).

Van Heijenoort, J. ed. 1967 (*1971*): *From Frege to Gödel: a Source Book on Mathematical Logic*. 2nd edn, Cambridge, MA: Harvard University Press.

Van Parijs, P. 1981: *Evolutionary Explanation in the Social Sciences*. London: Tavistock.

Veblen, Thorstein 1899 (*1953*): *The Theory of the Leisure Class: an Economic Study of Institutions*. Rev. edn, New York: New American Library.

Veblen, Thorstein 1904: *The Theory of Business Enterprise*. New York: Scribner.

Veblen, Thorstein 1914: *The Instinct of Workmanship and the State of the Industrial Arts*. New York: Viking.

Veblen, Thorstein 1918 (*1957*): *The Higher Learning in America*. New York: Sagsmore Press.

Veblen, Thorstein 1919: *The Engineers and the Price System*. Boston: Huebsch.

Veeser, H. A. ed. 1989: *The New Historicism*. London: Routledge.

Velez-Ibanez, G. 1983: *Bonds of Mutual Trust*. New Brunswick, NJ: Rutgers University Press.

Venturi, Lionello 1936: *History of Art Criticism*. New York: Dutton.

Venturi, Robert et al. 1977: *Learning from Las Vegas*. Rev. edn, Cambridge, MA: MIT Press.

Vile, M. J. C. 1967: *Constitutionalism and the Separation of Powers*. Oxford: Clarendon Press.

Vincent, David 1981: *Bread, Knowledge and Freedom: a Study of Nineteenth-Century Working-Class Autobiography*. London: Methuen.

Viner, J. 1978: *Religious Thought and Economic Society*. Durham, NC: Duke University Press.

Voegelin, E. 1952: *The New Science of Politics*. Chicago and London: University of Chicago Press.

Vološinov, V. N. 1926 (*1983*): Discourse in life and discourse in poetry. In *Bakhtin School Papers: Russian Poetics in Translation*, vol. 10, ed. Ann Shukman. Oxford.

Vološinov, V. N. 1929 (*1973*): *Marxism and the Philosophy of Language*. New York: Seminar Press.

Von Mises, Ludwig 1912 (*1934*): *The Theory of Money and Credit*. London: Jonathan Cape.

Von Mises, Ludwig 1920 (*1972*): Economic calculation in the socialist commonwealth. In *Socialist Economics*, ed. A. Nove and D. M. Nuti. Harmondsworth: Penguin.

Von Mises, Ludwig 1922 (*1936*): *Socialism: an Economic and Sociological Analysis*. London: Jonathan Cape.

Von Mises, Ludwig 1949 (*1966*): *Human Action: a Treatise on Economics*. 3rd edn, Chicago: Contemporary Books.

Von Neumann, J. and Morgenstern, O. 1944: *The Theory of Games and Economic Behavior*. Princeton, NJ: Princeton University Press.

Vozlensky, Michail 1985: *Nomenklatura: the Ruling Class of USSR*. London: Overseas Publishing House.

Waardenburg, J. ed. 1973–4: *Classical Approaches to the Study of Religion: Aims, Methods and Theories of Research*, 2 vols. The Hague: Mouton.

Wach, J. 1958: *The Comparative Study of Religions*. New York: Columbia University Press.

Wachterhauser, B. R. 1986: *Hermeneutics and Modern Philosophy*. New York: State University of New York Press.

Wagner, Richard 1849: *The Art-work of the Future*.

Waismann, F. 1967: *Ludwig Wittgenstein and the Vienna Circle*, ed. B. F. MacGuinness. Oxford: Blackwell.

Walby, S. 1986: *Patriarchy at Work*. Cambridge: Polity.

Walby, S. 1990: *Theorizing Patriarchy*. Oxford: Blackwell.

Waldo, Dwight 1961: Organization theory: an elephantine problem. *Public Administration Review* 21. 4, 216–27.

Waldo, Dwight 1963: *Theory of Organization: Status and Problems*. Paper given at the Annual Meeting of the American Political Science Association, New York.

Waldron, J. ed. 1984: *Theories of Rights*. Oxford: Oxford University Press.

Walker, A. 1984: *Social Planning: a Strategy for Socialist Welfare*. Oxford: Blackwell and Martin Robertson.

Walker, N. 1977: *Behaviour and Misbehaviour*. Oxford: Blackwell.

Walker, N. 1980: *Punishment, Danger and Stigma*. Oxford: Blackwell.

Walker, N. 1988: *Crime and Criminology*. Oxford: Oxford University Press.

Walker, Richard 1981: A theory of suburbanization. In *Urbanization and Urban Planning in Capitalist Society*, ed. M. J. Dear and A. G. Scott. London and New York: Methuen.

Wallerstein, Immanuel 1974: *The Modern World System: Capitalist Agriculture and the Origins of European World Economy in the Sixteenth Century*. New York: Academic Press.

Wallerstein, Immanuel 1974, 1980, 1989: *The Modern World-System*, 3 vols. New York and San Diego: Academic Press.

Wallerstein, Immanuel 1979: *The Capitalist World Economy*. Cambridge: Cambridge University Press.

Wallerstein, Immanuel 1991: Beyond *Annales*? *Radical History Review* 49, 7–15.

Wallerstein, Immanuel 1991: *Unthinking Social Science*. Cambridge: Polity Press.

Wallis, R. ed. 1975: *Sectarianism*. London: Peter Owen.

Wallis, R. 1976: *The Road to Total Freedom: a Sociological Analysis of Scientology*. London: Heinemann.

Wallis, R. 1982: Charisma, commitment and control in a new religious movement. In *Millennia-*

lism and Charisma. Belfast: Queen's University Press.

Wallis, Wilson D. 1943: *Messiahs: their Role in Civilization*. Washington, DC: American Council on Public Affairs.

Walton, J. 1984: *Reluctant Rebels*. New York: Columbia University Press.

Waltz, K. 1959: *Man, the State and War*. New York: Columbia University Press.

Waltz, K. N. 1979: *Theory of International Politics*. Reading, MA: Addison-Wesley.

Walzer, M. 1983: *Spheres of Justice*. Oxford: Martin Robertson.

Ward, C. 1982: *Anarchy in Action*. London: Freedom Press.

Warde, Alan 1990: Introduction to the sociology of consumption. *Sociology* 24. 1.

Warner, W. L. 1936: American class and caste. *American Journal of Sociology* 42, 234.

Warner, W. L. 1959: *The Living and the Dead: a Study of the Symbolic Life of Americans*. New Haven, CT: Yale University Press.

Warnke, G. 1987: *Gadamer: Hermeneutics, Tradition and Reason*. Cambridge: Polity.

Warnock, Mary 1970: *Existentialism*. Oxford: Oxford University Press.

Warr, P. 1987: *Work, Unemployment and Mental Health*. Oxford: Clarendon Press.

Warren, B. 1980: *Imperialism: Pioneer of Capitalism*. London: New Left Review.

Wartofsky, M. W. 1979: *Models: Representation and the Scientific Understanding*. Dordrecht, Boston and London: Reidel.

Wartofsky, M. W. 1988: The liveliness of aesthetics. *Journal of Aesthetics and Art Criticism* 46, 211–18.

Wason, P. 1968: Reasoning about a rule. *Quarterly Journal of Experimental Psychology* 20, 273–81.

Waterhouse, E. S. 1920: Secularism. In *Encyclopaedia of Religion and Ethics*, ed. J. Hastings, vol. 2. Edinburgh: T. & T. Clark.

Waterman, A. S. ed. 1985: *The Psychology of Individualism*. London: Praeger.

Waterston, A. 1965: *Development Planning: Lessons of Experience*. Baltimore: Johns Hopkins University Press.

Watkins, W. H. 1970: *The International Co-operative Alliance, 1895–1970*. Manchester: Co-operative Union.

Watson, Alan 1981: *The Civil Law Tradition*. Cambridge, MA: Harvard University Press.

Watson, J. B. 1924: *Behaviourism*. Chicago: University of Chicago Press.

Watt, W. M. 1988: *Islamic Fundamentalism and Modernity*. London: Routledge.

Watts, M. J. 1985: *Silent Violence: Food, Famine and Peasantry in Northern Nigeria*. Berkeley: University of California Press.

Watzlawick, P. et al. 1967: *Pragmatics of Human Communication: a Study of Interactional Patterns, Pathologies and Paradoxes*. New York: Norton.

Waxman, C. I. 1977: *The Stigma of Poverty*. New York: Pergamon.

Weale, A. 1979: *Equality and Social Policy*. London: Routledge & Kegan Paul.

Webb, Beatrice 1891: *The Co-operative Movement in Great Britain*. London: Sonnenschein.

Webb, C. ed. 1904 (*1907*): *Industrial Co-operation: the Story of a Peaceful Revolution*. 3rd edn, Manchester: Co-operative Union.

Webb, C. 1927: *The Woman with the Basket*. Manchester: Co-operative Union.

Webb, Sidney 1935 (*1937*): *Soviet Communism: a New Civilisation?* London: Gollancz.

Webb, Sidney and Webb, Beatrice 1894 (*1920*): *The History of Trade Unionism, 1666–1920*. 2nd edn, London: Longmans.

Webb, Sidney and Webb, Beatrice 1897: *Industrial Democracy*, 2 vols. London, New York and Bombay: Longmans, Green.

Webb, Sidney and Webb, Beatrice 1920: *A Constitution for the Socialist Commonwealth of Great Britain*. London: the authors.

Webber, Carolyn and Wildavsky, Aaron 1986: Finance in the private governments of medieval Europe. In *A History of Taxation and Expenditure in the Western World*. New York: Simon & Schuster.

Weber, Alfred 1899: *The Growth of Cities in the Nineteenth Century: a Study in Statistics*. New York: Cornell University Press.

Weber, Max 1903–6 (*1975*): *Roscher and Knies*. New York: Free Press.

Weber, Max 1904 (*1949*): *The Methodology of the Social Sciences*. Glencoe, IL: Free Press.

Weber, Max 1904 (*1949*): 'Objectivity' in social science and social policy. In *The Methodology of the Social Sciences*. Glencoe, IL: Free Press.

Weber, Max 1904–5 (*1930, 1974*): *The Protestant Ethic and the Spirit of Capitalism*. London: Allen & Unwin.

Weber, Max 1906 (*1985*): Churches and sects in North America. *Sociological Theory* 3, 7–13.

Weber, Max 1910 (*1968, 1978*): Antikritisches Schlusswort zum 'Geist des Kapitalismus'. In *Max Weber, Die protestantische Ethik II: Kritiken und Antikritiken*, ed. J. Winckelmann. Munich: Siebenstern (1968). Part trans.: Anticritical last word on 'the spirit of capitalism'. *American Journal of Sociology* 83, 1105–31 (1978).

Weber, Max 1918 (*1967*): Parliament and government in a reconstructed Germany. In *Economy and Society*. New York: Bedminster Press.

Weber, Max 1918 (*1970*): Socialism. In *Max Weber: the Interpretation of Social Reality*, ed. J. E. T. Eldridge. London: Michael Joseph.

Weber, Max 1920 (*1970*): Politics as a vocation. In *From Max Weber: Essays in Sociology*, ed. H. Gerth and C. W. Mills. London: Routledge & Kegan Paul.

Weber, Max 1920 (*1946, 1970*): *From Max Weber: Essays in Sociology*. New York: Oxford University Press (1946); London: Routledge & Kegan Paul (1970).

Weber, Max 1921–2 (*1967, 1978*): *Economy and Society: an Outline of Interpretive Sociology*. 3-vol. edn, New York: Bedminster Press (1967); 2-vol. and 3-vol. edns, Berkeley: University of California Press (1978).

Weber, Max 1922 (*1947*): *The Theory of Social and Economic Organization*. New York: Oxford University Press.

Weber, Max 1923 (*1961, 1981*): *General Economic History*, ed. I. J. Cohen. New York: Collier (1961); New Brunswick, NJ: Transaction (1981).

Weber, Max *1946*: Bureaucracy. In *From Max Weber: Essays in Sociology*. New York: Oxford University Press.

Weber, Max *1946*: Class, status, and party. In *From Max Weber: Essays in Sociology*, ed. H. H. Gerth and C. W. Mills. New York: Oxford University Press.

Weber, Max *1951*: *The Religion of China*. Glencoe, IL: Free Press.

Weber, Max *1958*: *The Rational and Social Foundations of Music*. Carbondale, IL: Southern Illinois University Press.

Weber, Max *1965*: *Essai sur la théorie de la science*. Paris.

Weber, Max *1968*: *On Charisma and Institution Building*, a selection ed. S. N. Eisenstadt. Chicago: University of Chicago Press.

Webster, Charles 1975: *The Great Instauration*. London: Duckworth.

Weedon, C. 1987: *Feminist Practice and Poststructuralist Theory*. Oxford: Blackwell.

Weeks, J. 1985: *Sexuality and its Discontents*. London and New York: Routledge & Kegan Paul.

Weffort, Francisco 1978: *O populismo na política brasileira*. Rio de Janeiro: Paz e Terra.

Wehler, H.-U. 1970: Bismarck's imperialism 1862–1890. *Past and Present* 48, 119-55.

Wehler, H.-U. 1972: *Bismarck und der Imperialismus*. Cologne: Kiepenheuer & Witsch.

Wehler, H.-U. 1985: *The German Empire 1871–1918*. Leamington Spa: Berg.

Weick, Karl E. 1979: *The Social Psychology of Organizing*. 2nd edn, New York: Random House.

Weick, Karl E. 1985: Systematic observational methods. In *Handbook of Social Psychology*, vol. 1, *Theory and Method*, ed. G. Lindzey and E. Aronson. 3rd edn, New York: Random House.

Weinberg, Meyer 1986: *Because They Were Jews: a History of Antisemitism*. New York: Greenwood Press.

Weinstein, James 1967: *The Decline of Socialism in America 1912–1925*. New York: Monthly Review Press.

Weintraub, Sidney, ed. 1977: *Modern Economic Thought*. Philadelphia: University of Pennsylvania Press.

Weitz, Morris 1956: The role of theory in aesthetics. *Journal of Aesthetics and Art Criticism* 15, 27–35.

Weitz, Morris ed. 1959: *Problems in Aesthetics*. New York: Macmillan.

Weizenbaum, Joseph 1976: *Computer Power and Human Reason*. San Francisco: W. H. Freeman.

Welch, Holmes 1968: *The Buddhist Revival in China*. Cambridge, MA: Harvard University Press.

Wellmer, Albrecht 1969 (*1974*): *Critical Theory of Society*. New York: Seabury.

Wellmer, Albrecht 1979: G. H. V. Wright über 'Erklären' und 'Verstehen'. *Philosophische Rundschau* 1. 2, 3.

Wenke, R. 1989: *Pattern of the Past*. New York: Oxford University Press.

Wenzel, Bernice M. 1968: Taste and smell. In *International Encyclopedia of the Social Sciences*, ed. David L. Sills. New York: Macmillan and Free Press.

Werckmeister, Otto 1971: *Ende der Ästhetik*. Frankfurt am Main: Reihe Fisher.

Wesołowski, W. 1966 (*1979*): *Classes, Strata and Power*. London: Routledge & Kegan Paul.

Westen, D. 1985: *Self and Society*. Cambridge: Cambridge University Press.

Westergaard, J. and Resler, H. 1975: *Class in a Capitalist Society*. Harmondsworth: Penguin.

Westergard-Thorpe, W. 1978: Towards a syndicalist international: the 1913 London Congress. *International Review of Social History* 23.

Westermarck, E. 1906: *The Origin and Development of the Moral Ideas*. London: Macmillan.

Westermarck, E. 1936: *The Future of Marriage in Western Civilisation*. New York: Macmillan.

Westley, F. 1983: *The Complex Forms of the New Religious Life*. Chico, CA: Scholars Press.

Westwood, S. and Bhachu, P. eds 1988: *Enterprising Women: Ethnicity, Economy and Gender Relations*. Routledge & Kegan Paul.

Whalen, J. and Flacks, R. 1989: *Beyond the Barricades: the Sixties Generation Grows Up*. Philadelphia: Temple University Press.

White, Harrison C. 1981: Where do markets come from? *American Journal of Sociology* 87, 517–47.

White, Lynn T. 1963: The act of invention: causes, contexts, continuities and consequences. In *The Technological Order*, ed. Carl F. Stoner. Detroit: Wayne State University Press.

White, Morton 1957: *Social Thought in America: the Revolt against Formalism*. Boston: Beacon Press.

White, S. 1979: *Political Culture and Soviet Politics*. London: Macmillan.

Whitehead, A. N. 1925: *Science and the Modern World*. New York: Macmillan.

Whiting, J. W. and Child, I. L. 1953: *Child Training and Personality: a Cross-Cultural Study*. New Haven, CT: Yale University Press.

Whyte, L. L. 1962: *The Unconscious before Freud*. London: Tavistock.

Whyte, W. F. 1943 (*1965*): *Street Corner Society: the Social Structure of an Italian Slum*. Chicago: University of Chicago Press.

Whyte, W. F. 1951: Observational field-work methods. In *Research Methods in Social Relations: with Special Reference to Prejudice*, ed. M. Johada. New York: Dryden Press.

Whyte, W. H. 1960: *The Organisation Man*. London.

Wicksteed, P. H. 1933: *The Common Sense of Political Economy and Selected Papers and Reviews on Economic Theory*, ed. Lionel Robbins. London: Routledge.

Wieder, D. L. 1974: *Language and Social Reality*. The Hague: Mouton.

Wiegert, A. J. et al. 1986: *Identity and Society*. Cambridge: Cambridge University Press.

Wiese, Leopold von 1933: *System der Soziologie als Lehre von den sozialen Prozessen und den sozialen Gebilden der Menschen (Beziehungslehre)*. Munich: Duncker & Humblot.

Wieviorka, M. 1988: *Sociétés et terrorisme*. Paris: Fayard.

Wieviorka, M. and Wolton, D. 1987: *Terrorisme à la une*. Paris: Gallimard.

Wiggerhaus, Rolf 1986: *Die Frankfurter Schule: Geschichte, theoretische Entwicklung, politische Bedeutung*. Munich: Hanser.

Wight, M. 1979: *Power Politics*. Harmondsworth: Penguin.

Wilensky, H. L. and Lebeaux, C. N. 1965: *Industrial Society and Social Welfare*. New York: Free Press.

Wilensky, H. L. 1967: *Organizational Intelligence*. New York: Basic Books.

Wiles, P. 1980: *Economic Institutions Compared*. Oxford: Blackwell.

Williams, B. 1985: *Ethics and the Limits of Philosophy*. London: Collins.

Williams, B. A. O. 1988: Formal structures and social reality. In *Trust: Making and Breaking Cooperative Relations*, ed. D. Gambetta. Oxford: Blackwell.

Williams, G. A. 1975: *Proletarian Order: Antonio Gramsci, Factory Councils and the Origins of Italian Communism, 1911–1921*. London: Pluto.

Williams, G. A. 1989: *Artisans and Sans-Culottes: Popular Movements in France and Britain during the French Revolution*. 2nd edn, London: Libris.

Williams, R. M. Jr 1964: Prejudice and society. In *The Black American Reference Book*, ed. M. M. Smythe. Englewood Cliffs, NJ: Prentice-Hall.

Williams, R. M. Jr 1964: *Strangers Next Door*. Englewood Cliffs, NJ: Prentice-Hall.

Williams, R. M. Jr 1968: The concept of norms. In *International Encyclopedia of the Social Sciences*, ed. D. L. Sills, vol. 16. New York: Macmillan and Free Press.

Williams, R. M. Jr 1977: *Mutual Accommodation: Ethnic Conflict and Cooperation*. Minneapolis: University of Minnesota Press.

Williams, Raymond 1976 (*1983*): *Keywords: a*

Vocabulary of Culture and Society. London: Fontana/Flamingo.

Williams, Raymond 1977: *Marxism and Literature*. Oxford and New York: Oxford University Press.

Williams, Raymond 1983: *Writing and Society*. London: Verso.

Williams, Raymond 1989: *The Politics of Modernism: Against the New Conformists*. London: Verso.

Williams, Rosalind H. 1982: *Dream Worlds: Mass Consumption in Late Nineteenth Century France*. Berkeley: University of California Press.

Williamson, O. E. 1975: *Markets and Hierarchies: Analysis and Anti-Trust Implications*. Glencoe, IL: Free Press.

Williamson, O. E. 1980: The organization of work. *Journal of Economic Behaviour and Organization* 1, 5–38.

Williamson, O. E. 1985: *The Economic Institutions of Capitalism*. New York: Free Press.

Williamson, P. 1989: *Corporatism in Perspective*. London: Sage.

Willis, Paul 1977: *Learning to Labour*. Farnborough: Saxon House.

Willis, Paul et al. 1990: *Common Culture: Symbolic Work at Play in the Common Cultures of the Young*. Milton Keynes: Open University Press.

Willner, A. R. 1984: *The Spellbinders: Charismatic Political Leadership*. New Haven, CT: Yale University Press.

Wilson, B. R. 1961: *Sects and Society*. London: Heinemann.

Wilson, B. R. 1966: *Religion in Secular Society: a Sociological Comment*. London: Watts.

Wilson, B. R. ed. 1967: *Patterns of Sectarianism*. London: Heinemann.

Wilson, B. R. ed. 1970: *Rationality*. Oxford: Blackwell.

Wilson, B. R. 1970: *Religious Sects*. London: Weidenfeld & Nicolson.

Wilson, B. R. 1976: *Contemporary Transformations of Religion*. London: Oxford University Press.

Wilson, B. R. 1982: *Religion in Sociological Perspective*. Oxford: Oxford University Press.

Wilson, E. O. 1975: *Sociobiology: the New Synthesis*. Cambridge, MA: Harvard University Press.

Wilson, E. O. 1978: *On Human Nature*. Cambridge, MA: Harvard University Press.

Wilson, E. O. and Lumsden, C. J. 1981: *Genes, Mind and Culture*. Cambridge, MA: Harvard University Press.

Wilson, G. K. 1981: *Interest Groups in the United States*. Oxford: Clarendon Press.

Wilson, H. T. 1971: The dismal science of organization reconsidered. *Canadian Public Administration* 14.1, 82–99.

Wilson, H. T. 1973: Rationality and decision in administrative science. *Canadian Journal of Political Science* 6.3, 271–94.

Wilson, H. T. 1977: *The American Ideology: Science, Technology and Organization as Modes of Rationality in Advanced Industrial Societies*. London: Routledge.

Wilson, J. Q. and Herrnstein, R. J. 1985: *Crime and Human Nature*. New York: Simon & Schuster.

Wilson, Michael 1982: *Das Institut für Sozialforschung und seine Faschismusanalysen*. Frankfurt am Main and New York: Campus.

Wilson, W. 1980: *The Declining Significance of Race: Blacks and Changing American Institutions*. 2nd edn, Chicago: University of Chicago Press.

Wilson, W. 1987: *The Truly Disadvantaged*. Chicago: University of Chicago Press.

Wiman, R. 1987: *From the Welfare State to a Welfare Society*. Helsinki: National Board of Social Welfare.

Wimbush, Erica and Talbot, Margaret eds 1988: *Relative Freedoms: Women and Leisure*. Milton Keynes: Open University Press.

Winch, D. 1969: *Economics and Policy: a Historical Study*. London: Hodder & Stoughton.

Winch, Peter 1958 (1976): *The Idea of a Social Science and its Relation to Philosophy*. London: Routledge & Kegan Paul.

Winch, Peter 1964: Understanding a primitive society. *American Philosophical Quarterly* 1.4, 307–24.

Winch, Peter 1967: Authority. In *Political Philosophy*, ed. A. Quinton. Oxford: Oxford University Press.

Winckelmann, J. ed. 1968: *Max Weber, Die protestantische Ethik II: Kritiken und Antikritiken*. Munich: Siebenstern.

Wind, Edgar 1958: *Pagan Mysteries in the Renaissance*. London: Faber.

Winner, Langdon 1989: Mythinformation in the high-tech era. In *Computers in the Human Context: Information Technology, Productivity and People*, ed. Tom Forester. Oxford: Blackwell.

Winograd, T. 1972: *Understanding Natural Language*. Edinburgh: Edinburgh University Press.

Winograd, T. 1983: *Language as a Cognitive Process*. Reading, MA: Academic press.

Winograd, T. and Flores, F. 1986: *Understanding Computers and Cognition*. Norwood, NJ: Ablex.

Winzeler, R. 1976: Ecology, culture, social organization and state formation in Southeast Asia. *Current Anthropology* 17, 623–40.

Wippermann, W. 1983: *Die Bonapartismustheorie von Marx und Engels*. Stuttgart: Klett-Cotta.

Wirth, L. 1938: Urbanism as a way of life. *American Journal of Sociology* 44, 1–24.

Wistrich, Robert 1991: *Anti-semitism: the Longest Hatred*. London: Methuen.

Wittfogel, K. 1957: *Oriental Despotism: a Comparative Study of Total Power*. New Haven, CT: Yale University Press.

Wittgenstein, Ludwig 1921 (*1972*): *Tractatus Logico-Philosophicus*. London: Routledge & Kegan Paul.

Wittgenstein, Ludwig 1953 (*1967*): *Philosophical Investigations*. Oxford: Blackwell.

Wittgenstein, Ludwig n.d.: *Lectures and Conversations on Aesthetics, Psychology and Religious Belief*. Berkeley: University of California Press.

Wittkower, Rudolf and Wittkower, Margot 1963: *Born under Saturn: the Character and Conduct of Artists: a Documentary History from Antiquity to the French Revolution*. London: Weidenfeld & Nicolson.

Wolf, E. R. 1966: *Peasants*. Englewood Cliffs, NJ: Prentice-Hall.

Wolf, E. R. 1971: *Peasant Wars of the Twentieth Century*. London: Faber & Faber.

Wolf, Leonard ed. 1968: *Voices from the Love Generation*. Boston: Little, Brown.

Wolfe, Tom 1976: The 'me' decade and the third great awakening. *New York*, 23 August, 26–40.

Wolfe, Tom 1968: *The Purple Decade: a Reader*. New York: Berkeley.

Wolfe, Tom 1975: *The Painted Word*. New York: Farrar, Straus & Giroux.

Wolff, J. 1975: *Hermeneutic Philosophy and the Sociology of Art*. London: Routledge & Kegan Paul.

Wolff, Janet 1981: *The Social Production of Art*. London: Macmillan.

Wolff, Janet 1983: *Aesthetics and the Sociology of Art*. London: Allen & Unwin.

Wolff, Kurt H. 1978: Phenomenology and sociology. In *A History of Sociological Analysis*, ed. Tom Bottomore and Robert Nisbet. New York: Basic Books.

Wolff, R. P. 1970 (*1976*): *In Defense of Anarchism*. 2nd edn, New York: Harper & Row.

Wolfgang, M. E. 1958: *Patterns in Criminal Homicide*. Philadelphia: Pennsylvania University Press.

Wolfgang, M. E. and Weiner, N. A. 1982: *Criminal Violence*. Beverly Hills: Sage.

Wolinetz, S. ed. 1988: *Parties and Party Systems in Liberal Democracies*. London: Routledge & Kegan Paul.

Wollstonecraft, Mary 1792 (*1989*): *A Vindication of the Rights of Woman*. In *A Wollstonecraft Anthology*, ed. Janet Todd. Cambridge: Polity.

Wolpe, H. ed. 1980: *The Articulation of Modes of Production*. London: Routledge.

Womack, B. 1982: *The Foundations of Mao Tse-tung's Political Thought*. Honolulu: University Press of Hawaii.

Woodcock, G. 1963 (*1986*): *Anarchism*. 2nd edn, Harmondsworth: Penguin.

Woods, R. 1979: *Population Analysis in Geography*. London: Longman.

Woodworth, Warner et al. eds 1985: *Industrial Democracy: Strategies for Community Revitalization*. London and Beverly Hills, CA: Sage.

Woolf, L. S. 1916 (*1971*): *International Government*. New York: Garland.

Woolf, S. 1986: *The Poor in Western Europe in the Eighteenth and Nineteenth Centuries*. London and New York: Methuen.

Woolf, Virginia 1927 (*1977*): *To the Lighthouse*. London: Grafton.

Woolf, Virginia 1938: *Three Guineas*. London: Hogarth Press.

Woolf, Virginia *1966*: *Collected Essays*, 4 vols. London: Hogarth Press.

Woolgar, S. ed. 1988: *Knowledge and Reflexivity: New Frontiers in the Sociology of Knowledge*. London and Beverly Hills, CA: Sage.

Wootton, Barbara 1959: *Social Science and Social Pathology*. London: Allen & Unwin.

World Health Organization 1948: The constitution of Health Organization. *Official Records* [WHO] 2, 100.

World Health Organization 1981: Nomenclature and classification of drug- and alcohol-related problems. *Bulletin of the World Health Organisation* 59, 225–42.

Worsley, Peter 1957 (*1970*): *The Trumpet Shall Sound: a Study of 'Cargo' Cults in Melanesia*. London: McGibbon & Kee.

Worsley, Peter 1964: *The Third World*. London:

Weidenfeld & Nicolson; Chicago: University of Chicago Press.

Worsley, Peter 1984: *The Three Worlds*. London: Weidenfeld & Nicolson; Chicago: University of Chicago Press.

Wright, E. O. 1978: *Class, Crisis and the State*. London: New Left Books.

Wright, E. O. 1985: *Classes*. London: Verso.

Wright, G. H. von 1971: *Explanation and Understanding*. London: Routledge & Kegan Paul.

Wright, Q. 1942: *A Study of War*. Chicago: University of Chicago Press.

Wrigley, A. M. 1988: *Continuity, Chance and Change: the Character of the Industrial Revolution in England*. Cambridge: Cambridge University Press.

Wrong, D. 1977: The oversocialized conception of man in modern sociology. In *Skeptical Sociology*. London: Heinemann.

Wrong, Dennis H. 1959: The functional theory of stratification: some neglected considerations. *American Sociological Review* 24, 772–82.

Wylie, R. 1980: *The Emergence of Maoism*. Stanford, CA: Stanford University Press; Honolulu: University Press of Hawaii.

Yavetz, Z. 1983: *Julius Caesar and his Public Image*. London: Thames & Hudson.

Yeo, S. 1987: Notes on three socialisms – collectivism, statism and associationism – mainly in late-nineteenth- and early-twentieth-century Britain. In *Socialism and the Intelligentsia 1880–1914*, ed. C. Levy. London: Routledge & Kegan Paul.

Yinger, J. M. 1957: *Religion, Society, and the Individual*. New York: Macmillan.

Yinger, J. M. 1970: *The Scientific Study of Religion*. New York: Macmillan.

Yinger, J. M. 1982: *Countercultures: the Promise and Peril of a World Turned Upside Down*. New York: Free Press.

Yolton, John W. et al. eds 1991: *Blackwell Companion to the Enlightenment*. Oxford: Blackwell.

Young, Michael 1958: *The Rise of the Meritocracy*. Harmondsworth: Penguin.

Zald, Mayer N. and McCarthy, John D. eds 1979: *The Dynamics of Social Movements*. Cambridge, MA: Winthrop.

Zarnowitz, V. 1985: Recent work on business cycles in historical perspective: a review of theories and evidence. *Journal of Economic Literature* 23, 523–80.

Zaslavskaya, T. I. 1981: Spontaneity versus planning in social development. In *Spontaneity and Planning in Social Development*, ed. U. Himmelstrand. Beverly Hills, CA: Sage.

Zeidenberg, M. 1989: *Neural Network Models of Artificial Intelligence and Cognition*. Chichester: Ellis Horwood.

Zeitlin, M. R. 1989: *The Large Corporation and Contemporary Classes*. Cambridge: Polity.

Zeldin, T. 1958: *The Political System of Napoleon III*. London: St Martin's Press.

Zeldin, T. 1979: *France 1848–1945: Politics and Anger*. Oxford: Oxford University Press.

Zellner, A. 1983: Statistical theory and econometrics. In *Handbook of Econometrics*, vol. 1, ed. Z. Griliches and M. D. Intriligator. Amsterdam: North Holland.

Zetterberg, Hans L. 1954: *On Theory and Verification in Sociology*. Totowa, NJ: Bedminster Press.

Zimmerman, Bonnie 1985: What never has been: an overview of lesbian feminist criticism. In *Making a Difference: Feminist Literary Criticism*, ed. Gayle Greene and Coppelia Kahn. London and New York: Methuen.

Zitelman, Rainer 1987 (*1990*): *Hitler: Selbstverständnis eines Revolutionärs*. Darmstadt: Wissenschaftliche Buchgesellschaft.

Znaniecki, Florian 1940: *The Social Role of the Man of Knowledge*. New York: Columbia University Press.

Zubaida, S. 1970: *Race and Racialism*. London: Tavistock.

Zubaida, S. 1988: *Islam: the People and the State*. London.

INDEX

Note: Page references in **bold** type indicate major treatment of a topic or individual. Where names of contributors to the *Dictionary* are indexed, the references are to citations in articles other than their own.